California Master Gardener Handbook

Dennis R. Pittenger

Editor

University of California
Agriculture and Natural Resources
Publication 3382

The *California Master Gardener Handbook* has been made possible with a grant from the Elvenia J. Slosson Foundation.

For information about ordering this publication, contact

University of California
Agriculture and Natural Resources
Communication Services
6701 San Pablo Avenue, 2nd Floor
Oakland, California 94608-1239

Telephone (510) 642-2431
1-800-994-8849
FAX (510) 643-5470
Visit ANR Communication Services online at http://anrcatalog.ucdavis.edu

Publication 3382

 This publication has been anonymously peer reviewed for technical accuracy by University of California scientists and other qualified professionals. This review process was managed by the ANR Associate Editor for Environmental Horticulture.

ISBN 1-879906-54-6
Library of Congress Control Number: 2001089734

Printed in the United States of America.

Fifth printing, 2009

We gratefully acknowledge permission to reprint tables A.1, A.2, A.3, A.4, and A.5 from the National Academy Press, Washington, D.C., copyright 1989, 1998, and 2001. The illustration of berries on p. 431 is adapted from the cover of the Cayuga Lake Nursery Catalog, spring 1885 (Union Springs, NY).

Illustrations by ANR CS staff except: David Kidd, figs. 7.5, 7.12 (granary weevil), 7.13, 7.14 (fly), 7.15, 7.17, 7.22–25, 8.3, 8.8–8.10, 8.14–15, 8.17, 8.20–24, 8.26; table 8.5.

To simplify information, trade names of products have been used. No endorsement of named or illustrated products is intended, nor is criticism implied of similar products that are not mentioned or illustrated.

 Printed on recycled paper.

7m-rep-11/09-SB/WFS/CR

Contents

Preface and Acknowledgments

The California Master Gardener Program is a volunteer program by which the University of California Cooperative Extension (UCCE) extends research-based information in home horticulture and pest management, verified by UC experts, to the citizens of our state. I have been affiliated with the program since 1981 and have personally observed the commitment of volunteer certified volunteer Master Gardeners to disseminate the information they have learned in the training program. The Master Gardener program represents an effective partnership between the University and motivated citizens interested in sharing scientifically accurate information about home horticulture and pest management.

The *California Master Gardener Handbook* was conceived and developed to provide a statewide resource manual for Master Gardeners. It is intended as a reference tool for use during and after completion of the formal Master Gardener training program and is the first compilation of horticultural training and reference materials designed primarily for Master Gardeners statewide. The contents reflect the diversity and depth of knowledge and information in horticulture and related disciplines that UCCE possesses. Because the Master Gardener training program does not require participants to have any formal training in horticulture, entomology, or any other plant-related science, handbook chapters were developed assuming no prior knowledge on the part of the reader. Previously, Master Gardeners in each county were given a unique medley of study materials and UC publications that were often developed for other audiences.

The publication of the *California Master Gardener Handbook* represents the culmination of planning and teamwork among numerous UC colleagues who deserve recognition for their commitment to the project.

Authors

The following colleagues developed chapters for the first *California Master Gardener Handbook*, an arduous undertaking that deserves acknowledgment.

MARY LU ARPAIA, Extension Subtropical Horticulturalist, Botany and Plant Sciences Department, UC Riverside and Kearney Agricultural Center

L. W. BARCLAY, Former Staff Research Associate, Entomology Department, UC Berkeley

ALLISON M. BEALE, Former Environmental Toxicology and Water Quality Farm Advisor, Sacramento County, UCCE

BERTHOLD O. BERGH, Specialist Emeritus, Botany and Plant Sciences Department, UC Riverside

LAWRENCE CLEMENT, County Director and Farm Advisor, Solano and Yolo Counties, UCCE

BEN FABER, Soils and Water Farm Advisor, Ventura and Santa Barbara Counties, UCCE

DELBERT S. FARNHAM, County Director and Farm Advisor Emeritus, Amador County, UCCE

NANCY GARRISON, Horticultural Advisor, Santa Clara County, UCCE

RALPH C. GAY, Farm Advisor and 4-H Youth Development Advisor (retired), Yolo County, UCCE

PAMELA M. GEISEL, Landscape and Turf Management Farm Advisor, Fresno County, UCCE

DEBORAH D. GIRAUD, Plant Science Farm Advisor, Humboldt and Del Norte Counties, UCCE

M. Ali Harivandi, Turfgrass, Soil, and Water Farm Advisor, Alameda, Santa Clara and Contra Costa Counties, UCCE

Janet Hartin, Environmental Horticulture Farm Advisor, San Bernardino County, UCCE

Nancy C. Hinkle, Former Extension Veterinary Entomologist, Entomology Department, UC Riverside

Donald R. Hodel, Environmental Horticulture Farm Advisor, Los Angeles County, UCCE

John F. Karlik, Environmental Horticulture Farm Advisor, Kern County, UCCE

John Klotz, Extension Urban Entomologist, Entomology Department, UC Riverside

Carlton S. Koehler, Extension Entomologist Emeritus, Entomology and Parasitology Department, UC Berkeley

Demetrios G. Kontaxis, Farm Advisor Emeritus, Contra Costa County, UCCE

Vincent Lazaneo, Environmental Horticulture and Urban Pest Management Farm Advisor, San Diego County, UCCE

Carol Lovatt, Professor, Plant Physiology, Botany, and Plant Sciences Department, UC Riverside

Richard H. Molinar, Farm Advisor, Fresno County, UCCE

Julie Newman, Environmental Horticulture Farm Advisor, Ventura and Santa Barbara Counties, UCCE

Deborah Silva, Freelance Technical Editor and Writer

Paul M. Vossen, Tree Fruits and Nuts Farm Advisor, Sonoma and Marin Counties, UCCE

Collaborators

In addition to chapter authors, the following colleagues provided background information, guidance, or technical review during the development of chapters in the handbook.

Don Appleton, County Director Emeritus, Tuolumne County, UCCE

Barbara Bania, Master Gardener, El Dorado County, UCCE

Andrew C. Chang, Professor, Soil and Environmental Sciences Department, UC Riverside

Richard Cowles, Former Extension Entomologist Emeritus, Entomology Department, UC Riverside

David M. Crohn, Assistant Professor and Extension Biological Systems Engineer, Soil and Environmental Sciences Department, UC Riverside

Dave Cudney, Extension Weed Scientist, Botany and Plant Sciences Department, UC Riverside

El Dorado County UCCE Master Gardeners

Jim Downer, Environmental Horticulture Farm Advisor, Ventura County, UCCE

Mary Louise Flint, Director, IPM Education and Publications, Statewide IPM Project and IPM Specialist, Entomology Department, UC Davis

Yvonne Freeman, Former Urban Agriculture/Adult Education Coordinator and Coordinator, Backyard Composter Program, Los Angeles County, UCCE

Victor Gibeault, Extension Environmental Horticulturist, Botany and Plant Sciences Department, UC Riverside

Sue Giordano, Food and Nutrition Education Coordinator, Los Angeles County, UCCE

Gary Hickman, County Director/Horticulture Farm Advisor, Mariposa County, UCCE

Jodie S. Holt, Professor, Botany and Plant Sciences Department, UC Riverside

Milton McGiffen, Extension Vegetable Specialist, Botany and Plant Sciences Department, UC Riverside

Glenn McGourty, Plant Science Farm Advisor, Mendocino County, UCCE

Jewell Meyer, Extension Irrigation and Soils Specialist Emeritus, Soil and Environmental Sciences Department, UC Riverside

Pat O'Connor-Marer, Pesticide Training Coordinator, Statewide Integrated Pest Management Project, UC Davis

Jennifer Otten, Communications Specialist, Food and Nutrition Board, Institute of Medicine, National Academy of Sciences

Albert Paulus, Extension Plant Pathologist, Plant Pathology Department, UC Riverside

Mikeal L. Roose, Professor of Genetics, Botany and Plant Sciences Department, UC Riverside

Sandra Schlicker, Senior Staff Officer, Food and Nutrition Board, Institute of Medicine, National Academy of Sciences

Ursula Schuch, Former Extension Nursery Crops Specialist, Botany and Plant Sciences Department, UC Riverside

Rainer Scora, Professor Emeritus, Botany and Plant Sciences Department, UC Riverside

Ron Tyler, Farm Advisor Emeritus, Santa Cruz and Monterey Counties, UCCE

Richard Whitkus, Former Assistant Professor, Botany and Plant Sciences Department, UC Riverside

Timothy E. Williams, Staff Research Associate, Botany and Plant Sciences Department, UC Riverside

Melanie Zavala, Farm Worker Pesticide Training Coordinator, Statewide Integrated Pest Management Project, UC Davis

Peer Reviewers

In 1995, UCCE instituted a new peer review process in which editors were appointed in specific disciplines to ensure uniform quality standards and to oversee publication of peer-reviewed manuscripts. The *California Master Gardener Handbook* is one of the first comprehensive statewide publications to have undergone the scrutiny of this new policy and procedure. The following people have reviewed final manuscript drafts of the handbook, under the coordination of Pamela M. Geisel, ANR Associate Editor, Environmental Horticulture: Harry Andris, Donald Appleton, Mary Lu Arpaia, Gary Bender, Mary Bianchi, Pam Bone, David Burger, Andrew Chang, Pete Christensen, Laurence Costello, Richard Cowles, David Crohn, David W. Cudney, A. James Downer, Roger Duncan, Clyde Elmore, Richard Evans, Mary Louise Flint, Mark Francis, Carol Frate, Yvonne Freeman, Victor A. Gibeault, Sue Giordano, Deborah Giraud, Marcella Grebus, M. Ali Harivandi, Janet Hartin, Gary Hickman, Donald Hodel, Scott Johnson, John Karlik, Anne King, Carlton Koehler, Steve Koike, Vernard Lewis, Patricia Lindsey, Mark Mahady, Milton E. McGiffen, Glenn McGourty, Jewell Meyer, Richard Molinar, Maxwell Norton, Albert Paulus, Ed Perry, John Radewald, Karen Robb, Michael Rust, Nick Sakovich, Rainer Scora, Larry Schwankl, Ronald Tyler, Garth Veerkamp, Paul Vossen, and Richard Whitkus.

Special Acknowledgment

I especially thank Deborah Silva for her dedicated service as Technical Editor of this book. In addition to her authorship role in 6 chapters and Appendix A, she assisted in assimilating and organizing materials for several other chapters and edited draft manuscripts of all chapters. Her previous experience in the Master Gardener program and technical knowledge were tremendous assets in producing a book of this scope.

I hope that the *California Master Gardener Handbook* proves to be a valuable, practical resource for those who choose to serve their fellow citizens and the UCCE as certified Master Gardeners. I also hope that the handbook will be of use to other serious amateur horticulturists and professionals seeking a general horticultural reference book.

Dennis R. Pittenger
Editor
Area Environmental Horticulture Advisor
UCCE Central Coast & South Region /
UCCE Los Angeles County / Botany and
Plant Sciences Department, UC Riverside

California
Master Gardener
Handbook

1

Overview of the California Master Gardener Program

THE UNIVERSITY OF CALIFORNIA has trained and certified more than 7,000 Master Gardeners since 1980, when the first pilot projects began in Riverside and Sacramento counties. Today, about 1,800 certified volunteer Master Gardeners actively serve in 36 counties throughout the state. Certified Master Gardeners staff booths at county fairs and local farmers' markets, host plant clinics at community centers, appear on public-access television, conduct workshops at garden clubs and elementary schools, develop community gardens, write advice columns in local newspapers, coordinate speakers' bureaus, and operate hotlines at county offices, answering thousands of telephone requests for information by the gardening public. Some are also involved in conducting applied research projects addressing local gardening problems.

The California Master Gardener program is one of many throughout the United States and Canada. Since 1972, when the first Master Gardener program started in Washington state, the program has spread to more than 45 states and four Canadian provinces and claims 45,000 volunteers, who share and disseminate the information they have learned in exchange for Master Gardener training by local university experts.

Overview of the California Master Gardener Program

Mission of the California Master Gardener Program

The purpose of the University of California Master Gardener program is to extend to the public research-based information verified by UC experts about home horticulture and pest management. In exchange for the training and materials received from the UC, Master Gardeners perform volunteer services in a myriad of venues.

The Master Gardener program is an example of an effective partnership between the University and motivated citizens. Because Certified Master Gardeners represent UC Cooperative Extension (UCCE), they broaden UCCE's clientele base and sphere of influence via about 146,700 public contacts annually. In 2000 alone, Master Gardeners donated more than 16,000 hours of service to the public and the University; since inception of the program, over 1.4 million hours of service have been donated.

Master Gardener Program Administration

The Master Gardener program is administered locally by participating county offices of UCCE, the principal outreach and public service arm of the University's Division of Agriculture and Natural Resources. UCCE serves Californians with county offices located throughout the state, from Alturas to San Diego. These offices are local problem-solving centers. County-based advisors and campus-based specialists work as a CE team to bring UC's research-based information to Californians living on the farm and in the urban environment. CE sponsors the Master Gardener training program, 4-H Youth Development program, Master Food Preserver program, programs to help small-scale growers develop marketing strategies, and workshops and symposia too numerous to cite.

The Master Gardener Training Program in California

The University takes the Master Gardener training program and the certification process very seriously. Each county has the privilege of tailoring the Master Gardener training program to local needs, while providing more than 30 hours (typically 50) of classroom instruction in such topics as

- horticulture
- plant diseases
- insect pests
- weed science
- plant propagation
- vegetables
- soils, fertilizers, and irrigation
- controlling garden pests safely
- integrated pest management
- fruit and landscape trees
- lawns
- diagnosing plant problems

Classes, which typically meet 1 day per week for 2 to 4 hours, are designed to include lecture, demonstration, practical field experience, and questions. The entire training program may last 15 or more weeks. Instructors in the program include UCCE farm advisors and specialists; professors, who are faculty on the UC campuses and members of the University's Agricultural Experiment Station; and other experts from industry and local colleges or universities.

People from all walks of life are attracted to the Master Gardener training program: business and professional people, educators, retired citizens, homemakers, and students. Adults of all ages, ethnicities, and backgrounds, with varying degrees of prior experience in home horticulture and pest management participate in the program.

After completing the training program and passing the written examination, the new Master Gardener graduate is required to volunteer a minimum number of service hours (usually 50) within 1 year to the UC Cooperative Extension county office where the training was received. To remain certified, additional continuing education hours (usually 6 to 12) are required annually. Certified Master Gardener volunteers receive technical support and follow-up training, as needed, from UCCE farm advisors and specialists. Volunteer activities of certified Master Gardeners are overseen and structured by the 36 county offices statewide that currently participate in the training program (figure 1.1).

The Master Gardener training program and the volunteer activities of its certified graduates, in conjunction with numerous other UCCE programs, enable UCCE to fulfill its responsibility to the citizens of our state.

Master Gardeners and The Many Philosophies of Home Gardening

Gardeners today are faced with a multitude of choices in gardening products and philosophies. The Master Gardener training program provides scientifically based information approved by University of California experts so that Master Gardeners and the people they assist can make informed choices. When Master Gardeners make recommendations, they are expected to disseminate scientifically defensible information approved by the University of California.

University of California Master Gardeners work with gardeners who have many different philosophies. Even though Master Gardeners respect individual beliefs, they do not provide information, especially a pest or disease control recommendation, that does not have a scientific basis. For pest and disease control advice, Master Gardeners use only University of California publications and recommendations that have been reviewed for accuracy by the Statewide Pesticide Coordinator.

For a more in-depth discussion of gardening philosophies and approaches, please see the discussion of "The Many Approaches to Home Gardening" in chapter 3, "Soil and Fertilizer Management."

The *California Master Gardener Handbook*

The *California Master Gardener Handbook* is designed as a reference tool for use during and after completion of the formal Master Gardener training program. This handbook is the first compilation of horticultural training and reference materials designed primarily for Master Gardeners statewide. It was developed assuming no prior knowledge of the topics on the part of the reader and from the perspective that UCCE Master Gardeners will become problem solvers. Chapters were developed as stand-alone units providing in-depth information, and they reflect the unique writing style of their authors. Thus, there is some repetition of key concepts and there are some noticeable differences in form among the chapters. The handbook contains detailed information and important facts not found in other texts written for this audience.

Chapters 2 through 10 include important background information on disciplines related to the general culture and management of horticultural crops. Chapters 11 through 19 address the specific culture and management of numerous horticultural crops important in California. Chapters 20 through 22 provide information on landscape design and developing problem-solving skills. Nutritional composition data is provided for many of the edible crops covered in the handbook. Appendix A contains background information on how the nutritional data was derived and how to interpret it. Useful conversions for many units of measure encountered in the handbook or in caring for crops are found in Appendix B.

As representatives of the University of California, it is important that Master Gardeners provide clients with information that has been verified by UC experts. Therefore, the bibliographies of most chapters contain references to other useful UC publications that are to be used as primary resources. Additional information on UC publications can be found at the UC Agriculture and Natural Resources Communications Services website, http://anrcatalog.ucdavis.edu/, and up-to-date pest-related information can be found at the UC Statewide Integrated Pest Management Project website http://www.ipm.ucdavis.edu/. Because of its attributes, the *California Master Gardener* *Handbook* will be a valuable general reference to serious amateur horticulturists, retail nursery professionals, and many other professional horticulturists.

Figure 1.1

Distribution of the California Master Gardener program. Shading indicates counties with active Master Gardener training programs. UC Cooperative Extension is organized into three regions statewide: (1) North Coast and Mountain, (2) Central Valley, and (3) Central Coast and South Region.

2

Introduction to Horticulture

Dennis R. Pittenger

LEARNING OBJECTIVES

- Learn principal characteristics of green plants, their structure, and common horticultural terminology.

- Understand general vegetative and reproductive growth processes of plants and the factors that influence them.

- Learn classic applications of fundamental horticultural knowledge.

Introduction to Horticulture

Horticulture is usually described as both an art and a science. Understanding fundamental principles of plant physiology and basic botany combined with skill and intuition in employing these scientific principles ensures the maximum use and enjoyment of plants.

Botany is the study of plants and all facets of their structure and physiology. Horticulture is an applied science because it uses basic scientific principles, largely from botany, to develop practical technologies. The present classification of agricultural crops into the specialties of horticulture and agronomy can be traced back to the medieval period, when land was divided into large districts called manors. Extensive field plantings of grains and forages were possible under the manor system, giving rise to the discipline of agronomy.

Horticulture originates from the medieval practice of growing intensively managed kitchen gardens that provided fruits, vegetables, herbs, and ornamental plant materials for the lord's manor. The English word *horticulture* is derived from the Latin words *hortus*

[garden] and *colere* [to cultivate]. Today, horticulture embraces the intensive culture of fruits, vegetables, ornamentals, herbs, and other high-value, often perishable, specialty crops. In contrast, agronomy includes crops such as corn, wheat, rice, alfalfa, and other grains and forages that are usually grown on a large scale with less intensive management.

The size, productivity, or other quantitative characters of a given plant are determined by the interaction of its genetic potential (traits) with the environment. The range of expression for any trait is set by the plant's genetic blueprint, whereas the specific expression within the range depends on the environment. For example, a given tomato variety may be genetically able to produce up to 25 pounds (11.3 kg) of fruit, but can produce only 10 pounds (4.5kg) when inadequately watered. Horticulturists employ scientific methods to investigate and understand plant responses to various environmental conditions and then develop and employ technologies to manipulate the environment to yield predictable plant responses. Such intensive management is often required to produce horticultural commodities. Intensive management is economically feasible because the produce grown commands premium prices or has high intrinsic value to consumers and home gardeners.

What Plants Are

Plants are living organisms without consciousness or mobility. Green plants are essentially living factories that produce their own food and serve directly or indirectly as the source of food and support for nearly all other living organisms. Like animals, they are composed of microscopic cells, three-dimensional blocklike structural units. Unlike animals, however, green plants produce their own food via photosynthesis, regenerate certain lost organs and tissues, and possess rigid cell walls made mostly of cellulose.

All essential life processes occur within cells or groups of cells. A simplified plant cell is shown in figure 2.1. The content of cells, known as *cytoplasm*, is composed of 85 to 90 percent water (by weight), 1 to 3 percent

Figure 2.1

Simplified plant cell showing the nucleus, chloroplasts (plastids that contain chlorophyll), cytoplasm, and vacuole. Plant cells are bounded by a membrane and cell wall. Most of the cell volume is occupied by the vacuole in this plant cell.

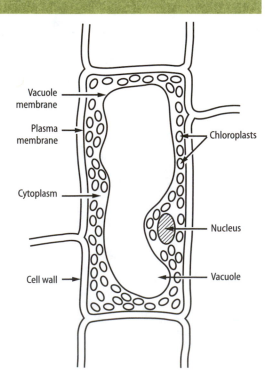

Vacuole membrane

Plasma membrane

Cytoplasm

Cell wall

Chloroplasts

Nucleus

Vacuole

minerals dissolved in the cell sap, and 10 to 15 percent assorted organic compounds and substances. Water serves as the solvent in sap that transports dissolved minerals from the soil and sugars from the leaves to all cells in the plant. It also serves as an essential component in many plant processes, maintains cell turgor (rigidity), and indirectly regulates growth. Thus, water typically constitutes 85 percent or more of the weight of a plant. *Pectin* serves as a cementing agent between cells. Immediately inside the cell wall lies a selectively permeable membrane that serves to help regulate inflow and outflow of materials and compounds. Within the cell, most of the liquid substances (cell sap) are found in the *vacuole*, a large cavity. Important solid structures in cells are the nucleus and plastids. The control center of the cell, the *nucleus*, contains the genetic code information (DNA) that controls the physiological functions of cells and the overall features of the whole plant (the information is identical from cell to cell). *Plastids* are specialized bodies within plant cells; plastids containing the green pigment chlorophyll (*chloroplasts*) are the most significant because they conduct photosynthesis.

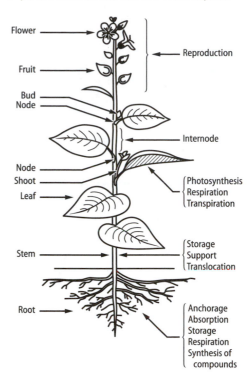

Figure 2.2

Important structures and functions of a seed plant.

Plant Structure

Although plant cells are independent units, the sophisticated organization and specialization of cells make up the whole plant and carry out essential life processes (fig. 2.2). Masses of similar kinds of cells form tissues, and groups of tissues may form organs. Many horticultural crops are prized for their production of unique adaptations of certain tissues or organs (fig. 2.3).

Meristems

Meristems are plant tissues in which cells divide to reproduce, grow, and develop new tissue. The most common meristems are *apical* (terminal) and *lateral*. Found in shoot tips, root tips, and buds, apical meristems are responsible for the increase in the length of these plant parts. The increase in stem and root diameter or thickness is due to the growth of a lateral meristem called the *cambium* (figs. 2.4, 2.6). In many grasses, the meristem responsible for shoot growth is found near the base of the plant. For example, mowing turfgrass at the proper height does

not injure or remove the growing point of the plants.

Meristematic areas, which are normally just a few cells deep, may produce shoots (vegetative growth) or flowers (reproductive growth), depending on when and where the meristem is active. All active meristems receive priority for the food materials and minerals available within the plant. For this reason, they are often referred to as *sinks*.

Roots

The primary functions of roots are to take up water and soluble mineral nutrients from the soil, produce essential compounds, store excess food materials, and anchor the plant (see fig. 2.2). Roots require water and oxygen from the soil and food materials produced in the shoots in order to function and grow properly. Examples of horticultural crops grown for their edible roots include carrots and sweet potatoes.

Structurally, roots may be woody or nonwoody. Cambial (meristematic) tissue in roots causes them to increase in diameter over time, particularly in perennial and woody plants.

Figure 2.3

Modified structures of selected horticultural plants. (A) Tuberous root (sweet potato; modified root). (B) Tuber (Irish/white potato; modified stem). (C) Corm (gladiolus; modified stem). (D) Rhizome (bermudagrass; modified stem). (E) Runner or stolon (strawberry; modified stem). (F) Bulb (onion: modified stem and leaves).

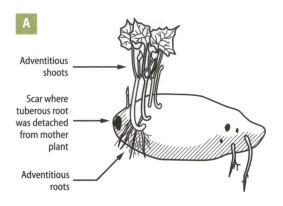

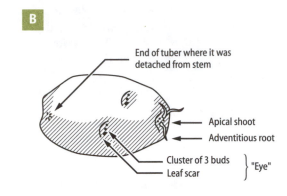

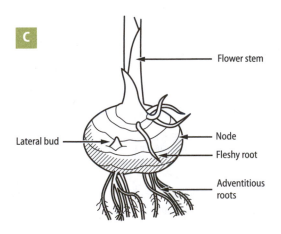

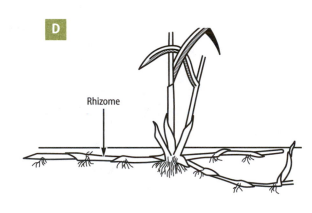

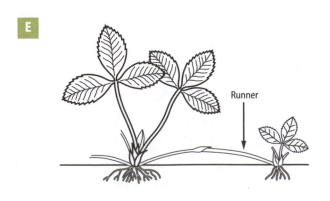

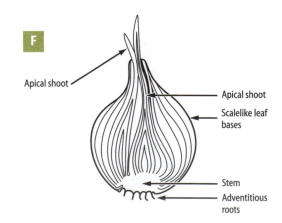

Figure 2.4

Apical meristems of shoots and roots. The shoot apical meristem (left) and root apical meristem (right) are involved in the formation of new cells via cell division and in plant growth via cell enlargement. Note that the root apical meristem is not at the very tip of the root but instead is protected by the root cap.

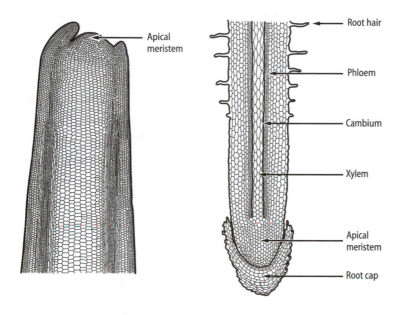

Figure 2.5

Structures of a woody twig (stem) with opposite bud and leaf arrangement. Annual growth is measured by the distance between terminal bud scale scars and the current terminal bud.

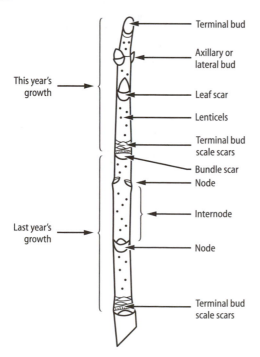

Most of the water and nutrient uptake occurs in the fine nonwoody roots of plants.

The root tip is the meristematic area responsible for increasing root length. Frequently, root hairs are present just behind the root tip. These hairs serve to increase the surface area of the root system and allow it to take up water and minerals more efficiently. Particularly in woody plants, a large main root, the taproot, develops with a small number of smaller structural or fibrous roots growing from it, whereas other plants form only a dense network of fine, fibrous roots. Plants grown from cuttings and those grown in containers seldom develop a taproot system. Taproots diminish in size as the plant matures.

Some plant parts, such as leaves and stems, have the capacity to regenerate roots after being removed from the plant. Roots arising from some plant part other than roots are known as *adventitious* roots (see fig. 2.3).

Stems and Shoots

Stems and shoots are often the most prominent aboveground portion of a plant (see fig. 2.2). *Shoot* refers to tissue made up of developing stems and leaves (leafy shoots) or stems and flowers (flowering shoots). Shoots support the food-producing foliage, store food materials, and contain tissues that conduct water and photosynthetically produced food materials throughout the plant. Unique features of stems are that they contain buds and nodes. *Nodes* are enlarged portions of a stem from which leaves or buds grow, and the portion of stem between two nodes is an *internode* (fig. 2.5).

The *phloem* is tissue that conducts photosynthetically produced food and other compounds from the leaves to other plant parts. Materials can move up or down in the phloem. Water and dissolved mineral nutrients from the soil are conducted from the roots upward to all the aboveground parts via the *xylem*. Together, phloem and xylem are known as *vascular tissue* and usually form a continuous multibranched system from every root tip to every shoot and leaf tip (fig. 2.6).

The cambium is responsible for the increased diameter growth of stems and roots and is usually associated with the vascular tissue. In typical woody stems, the xylem and phloem occur as concentric zones separated by the cambium, which is a few cells wide. Plants in the grass family, however, have xylem

Figure 2.6

Vascular tissues are continuous from the root tips to the shoot tips. They are organized differently in monocots and dicots.

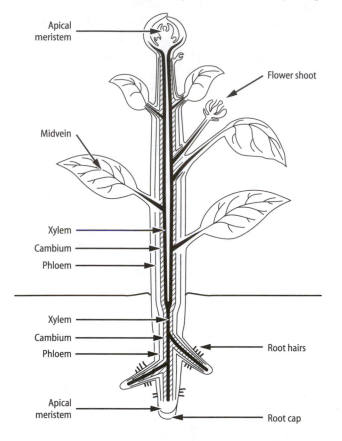

Apical meristem
Flower shoot
Midvein
Xylem
Cambium
Phloem
Xylem
Cambium
Phloem
Root hairs
Apical meristem
Root cap

VASCULAR SYSTEM OF A MONOCOTYLEDONOUS STEM

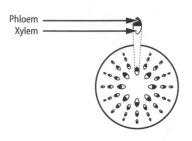

Phloem
Xylem

VASCULAR SYSTEM OF A DICOTYLEDONOUS STEM

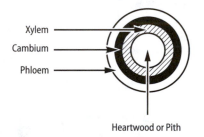

Xylem
Cambium
Phloem
Heartwood or Pith

Figure 2.7

Cross-section of a hardwood dicot tree trunk. Vascular tissues, phloem and xylem, are concentrically arranged. The functional phloem is a narrow layer of cells immediately underneath the bark. Cambial tissue separates the phloem from the xlyem. Sapwood is the active portion of the xylem; heartwood is the inactive xylem that makes up most of the wood in large stems and trees.

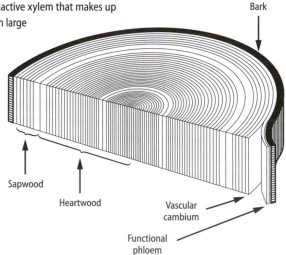

Bark
Sapwood
Heartwood
Vascular cambium
Functional phloem

and phloem occurring together in numerous vascular bundles scattered throughout the stem. Cambial tissue is present in each bundle. The two types of xylem in woody plants are active xylem, or *sapwood*, and inactive xylem, or *heartwood* (fig. 2.7). Although the sapwood is usually not very thick, the heartwood is the "wood" that makes up the trunk and the center portion of large tree limbs. Inactive xylem cannot transport water and minerals, but it does provide structural integrity and a food storage area for the plant. The inactivity of the heartwood explains why "hollow" trees can often remain alive: the active xylem, cambium, and phloem exist in the very outer perimeter of the trunk.

Nonwoody (*herbaceous*) plants and stems have a thin outer protective tissue, or *epidermis*. In herbaceous plants, the water-filled cells provide adequate strength to support the plant, much like the stiffening of a garden hose under pressure. Because this mechanism is insufficient to support larger plants, a stiffening process called *secondary*

Figure 2.8

Common arrangements
of buds and resulting
shoots around a stem.

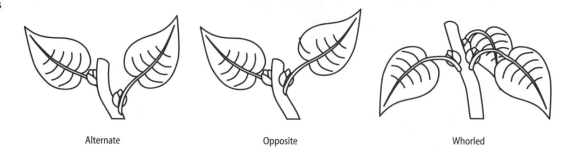

Alternate   Opposite   Whorled

Figure 2.9

Simple leaf. The parts of a
simple leaf are shown in
relation to typical stem
and bud structures.

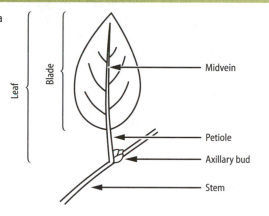

Leaf

Blade

Midvein

Petiole

Axillary bud

Stem

growth occurs, giving rise to woody plants. Woody stems, such as those in trees and shrubs, may develop a thick or tough protective exterior tissue, or *bark* (see fig. 2.7). In woody plants, specialized tissues (*fibers*) begin to form as the stem elongates, and the stem becomes more or less rigid a short distance below the apical meristem. Because the stem cannot elongate in growth below the apical meristem, it is limited to increases in diameter. Thus, the length of the nodes (the distance between leaves and branches) remains constant for the life of the plant.

Stems may be greatly modified from the classic form, and many horticultural crops are grown for their unique stems. Aboveground stem modifications consist of crowns, runners, stolons, and spurs; belowground modifications are bulbs, corms, tubers, and rhizomes (see fig. 2.3).

Buds

Buds are meristematic structures along the stem that are composed of compressed, immature leafy shoots, flowers, or both. They may be dormant for a portion of the year or for many years before they become active.

Buds are named according to position (see fig. 2.5). Those found at the tips of shoots are *terminal* or *apical* buds, and those found along the sides of stems are *lateral* buds. Lateral buds that occur in the area where the leaf attaches to the stem (the leaf *axil*) are *axillary* buds.

The arrangement of buds and resulting shoots around a stem occurs in a particular pattern for each plant species. These patterns, along with bud appearance, are particularly useful when identifying a plant. The most common arrangement patterns are alternate, opposite, and whorled. In the *alternate* arrangement, singular buds occur in one plane but alternate from one side to the other in a zigzag fashion. Buds in an *opposite* arrangement occur in pairs with one bud on each side of a plane simultaneously. A *whorled* arrangement occurs when three or more buds occur in different planes at one point on a stem or when single buds occur in three or more planes along a stem (fig. 2.8).

There are some specialized buds in horticultural crops (see fig. 2.3). For example, the "eyes" of Irish potato tubers are actually leaf scars or nodes in which three buds occur. The center buds normally break dormancy and produce new leafy shoots. Brussels sprouts are large vegetative lateral buds occurring on the main stem of the plant.

Leaves

Leaves provide the surface area needed for the plant to collect sunlight and conduct photosynthesis, which produces food for the plant. A simple leaf and its components are shown in figure 2.9. Note the distinct blade and petiole. A bud is present and can be seen at the point where the petiole attaches to the stem. Horticultural plants possess leaves that vary greatly in appearance, structure, and function. Blades

Figure 2.10

Compound leaves are composed of multiple petiole and blade segments referred to as *leaflets*. Note the absence of any buds where leaflets attach to the petiole.

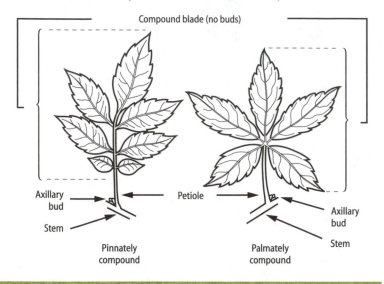

Compound blade (no buds)

Axillary bud

Stem

Petiole

Axillary bud

Stem

Pinnately compound

Palmately compound

Figure 2.11

Leaf venation patterns.

Parallel

Pinnate

Palmate

Figure 2.12

Internal structure of a leaf in cross-section.

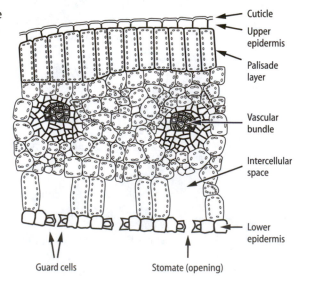

Cuticle

Upper epidermis

Palisade layer

Vascular bundle

Intercellular space

Lower epidermis

Guard cells

Stomate (opening)

vary widely and may be simple (if not divided) or compound (if divided into smaller segments, or *leaflets*; see fig. 2.10). In compound leaves, buds are not present where the leaflet attaches to the petiole. Compound leaves may be *palmate*, if they are handlike in form, or *pinnate*, if the segments are arranged like a feather. The margins of leaf blades also vary in pattern among species. The area on the stem or shoot that is above where a leaf attaches is the *axil*.

Leaf veins are the continuation and termination of xylem and phloem from the roots and stems. The *midvein* (or midrib) is the most prominent. Three patterns of venation (palmate, pinnate, and parallel) commonly occur in plants (fig. 2.11).

Leaves have a thin protective layer of cells, or *epidermis*, on their upper and lower surfaces (fig. 2.12). Some species have a wax or varnishlike coating (cuticle) that provides additional protection and reduces water loss. The epidermis and cuticle thicken as the leaf matures. The thickness of the epidermis and cuticle depends on the amount of light the leaf receives. A plant in a shady location has a thinner cuticle and epidermis than the same plant in full sun.

Immediately under the upper epidermis are densely packed cells that contain *chlorophyll*, the green pigment necessary in photosynthesis. Inside the lower epidermis are widely spaced cells that also have chlorophyll. The open spaces between these cells permit free movement of water vapor, carbon dioxide, and oxygen in and out of the leaves through tiny openings, or *stomata* (see fig. 2.12). Pairs of specialized cells (guard cells) control the opening and closing of each stomate. Guard cells respond to light so that stomata are normally open in daylight and closed in the dark. The number and size of stomata vary widely among species. Among tree species, for example, the number varies from approximately 100 stomata per square millimeter to 600 stomata per square millimeter of leaf surface. Stomata are usually found in higher numbers on the lower leaf surface.

Flowers

Flowers contain the male or female (or both) sexual structures of plants and are, therefore, the organs where sexual reproduction occurs. Depending on the species, flowers may contain both male and female structures (*perfect* or *complete*) or have only male or only female structures (*imperfect* or *incomplete*) (fig. 2.13). The principal male structure is the *stamen*, and the principal female structure is the *pistil*. Incomplete flowers that have only male structures are *staminate*, whereas those that have only female structures are *pistillate*. Plants with both staminate and pistillate flowers (e.g., corn, squash, pumpkins, melons, begonias, oaks, some maples, some ashes, and birches), are *monoecious*. Species in which staminate and pistillate flowers occur on separate individuals (e.g., asparagus, date palm, kiwifruit, holly, poplars, spinach, and willow) are *dioecious*.

Within the stamen, the *anther* holds the *pollen grains*, and in the pistil, the *ovary* contains the *ovules*. When pollination and fertilization occur (see "Reproductive Development" in this chapter), the ovary and sometimes the receptacle swell to form a fruit and one or more ovules develop into seeds. *Petals* are normally the most conspicuous part of a flower, although some plants (poinsettia, *Anthurium*, sunflower, broccoli) are known and grown for their other flower parts. *Sepals* are the small, green, leaflike structures found at the base of flowers (see fig. 2.13) and are the "caps" on tomatoes and strawberries. The *receptacle* is the plant part where the floral structures are attached, and in some species, such as apple, it becomes integrated into the fruit as it develops.

Seeds

In most species, the seed is the product of sexual reproduction. The seed is important because it contains an embryonic plant in a dormant state of development along with food reserves to sustain it through germination (fig. 2.14). The food reserves may be carbohydrates, fats, oils, or proteins. A protective covering, the seed coat, is also found on most seeds.

Fruits

Botanically speaking, a fruit is the plant part that contains the mature, swollen ovary and seed, such as an orange, apple, or tomato (fig. 2.15). In some species, other flower parts may be included as part of the fruit (e.g., the receptacle in apples). Numerous horticultural plants are grown specifically for their delicious or aesthetic fruit. Some fruits are commonly (and erroneously) called vegetables because they are consumed as vegetables at meals and because nutritionists speak of them as vegetables. Botanically speaking, however, squashes, (zucchini, pumpkin, acorn, etc.), green beans, cucumbers, tomatoes, and eggplant are fruits, as are apples, pears, plums, strawberries, oranges, and lemons.

Fruits, similar to meristems, are referred to as *sinks* since they also receive priority for food materials within the plants.

Figure 2.13

Complete, male, and female flowers. (A) Generic complete (perfect) flower in vertical section. (B) Male squash flower. (C) Female squash flower.

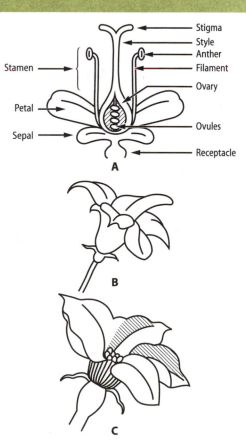

Figure 2.14

Typical seed structures illustrated in a garden bean seed.

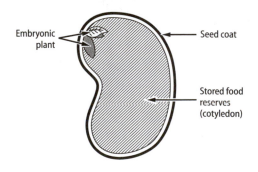

Figure 2.15

Simple fruits.

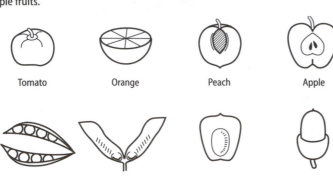

Tomato · Orange · Peach · Apple

Pea pod · Maple samara · Corn kernel · Oak acorn

Classification of Plants

In order to study and fully understand plants, it is necessary to record and communicate information about them in a structured, orderly fashion. Grouping and classifying plants according to their use or readily observed characteristics provides methods for achieving this. Although various terms are employed in systems that classify and characterize plants, the most common classification systems are growth habit, structure or form, leaf retention, climatic adaptation, use, and scientific or botanical classification.

Growth Habit

Plants can usually be classed as annuals, perennials, or biennials. Annuals complete a life cycle from seed to flowering to reseeding in 1 year or one growing season and then die. Perennials continue growing for several years. A perennial may go through repeated annual flowering and seed-producing cycles before it dies, or it may grow for several years before it performs a single seed-production cycle and then dies. Agave species are classic examples of the latter, whereas common woody landscape plants are examples of the former. Horticulturists often use the term perennial to describe the diverse assortment of ornamental plants that are nonwoody but continue to live from year to year. The aboveground parts of perennials such as daffodils, yarrow, and foxglove die back and regrow each year.

Biennials require 2 years or two growing seasons to complete their life cycle. Plants grow leaves and shoots the first year, then flower the second year. These plants typically require a cold dormant period after the first year in order to develop flowers the second year. Cabbage is a good example of a biennial plant.

It is important to note that a crop may be an annual under certain environmental conditions and a perennial under other conditions. Tomatoes, for example, are usually considered annual plants, but they may live more than one season in areas where freezing temperatures are infrequent.

Structure or Form

The basic structure, size, and form of plants can be used to group or classify them in very broad terms. Plants that have hard, fibrous stems are *woody*, whereas those that do not are *herbaceous*. Tender-stemmed species in general are sometimes called *herbs*.

When woody plants are grouped according to their form, the terms *vine*, *shrub*, and *tree* are often used. Vines trail along the ground unless offered some type of support. Short, upright-growing plants with several main stems are considered to be shrubs, and tall ones with a single or a few main stems are usually considered to be trees. Trees may be further defined according to the general shape that their canopies naturally develop. A number of terms are used to describe them (fig. 2.16).

Leaf Retention

Perennial plant species generally fall into one of two categories: deciduous or evergreen. *Deciduous* plants lose all their leaves for some period of time in the fall and winter months. *Evergreen* plants do not lose all their leaves, although they do cast off old leaves on a periodic basis. At any one time, however, an evergreen plant always has green leaves. Evergreens are further divided into broadleaf (e.g., azalea, some magnolias) and needle-leaved (e.g, pine, redwood).

Climatic Adaptation

Perennial plants are classified according to the minimum temperatures they normally tolerate. *Tropical* plants are injured severely or killed when temperatures remain near freezing (32°F, or 0°C). *Subtropical* plants tolerate short exposures to temperatures at or slightly below freezing and usually tolerate overnight temperatures around freezing. In contrast, *temperate* plants are well adapted to prolonged subfreezing temperatures that occur in cold winter climates and can endure temperatures considerably below freezing.

Most annual vegetables, flowers, and turf-grasses are classified in a similar fashion. Those that tolerate some amount of short-term freezing are known as *cool-season* or *hardy* crops, whereas those that are killed or injured by freezing temperatures are *warm-season* or *tender* crops. Cool-season crops grow best and produce highest-quality produce during seasons that feature average daytime temperatures of 55° to 75°F (13° to 24°C), and warm-season crops grow and develop best when average daytime temperatures are 65° to 95°F (18° to 35°C).

Use

Plants are often categorized by their use or the part of the plant consumed. When a plant is cultivated primarily for its aesthetic beauty or environmental enhancement qualities, it is considered an ornamental. Horticultural plants grown principally for some edible organ(s) are called fruits, nuts, herbs, or vegetables. Although, botanically, a fruit is the plant structure that contains the seed, from a use standpoint, a fruit is any plant part consumed for its dessert qualities; parts consumed during the main portion of a meal are considered herbs or vegetables. For example, tomatoes contain seed and are technically fruits, but they are consumed in salads and other main course dishes (and rarely in desserts) and are therefore considered vegetables.

Botanical or Scientific Classification

The most precise and least confusing method of classifying or categorizing plants is the internationally recognized botanical or scientific binomial classification system, which provides specific, positive identification for thousands of plants worldwide. Use of this system eliminates the confusion arising from multiple common names for the same plant. The common name of a given plant can vary from one locality or country to another, but its scientific name is consistent from one location to another over time.

The scientific binomial name of a plant consists of two parts—the genus followed by the *specific epithet,* sometimes incorrectly called the species—that are taken from Latin or Greek. Together, the two words are referred to as a "species." For example, *Rubus idaeus* is the scientific name of the species red raspberry. Latin is the primary language used for these terms because it was the scholarly language in use when the scientific classification system was developed. Scientific names are italicized or underlined. Genus names are nouns and are always capitalized, whereas the specific epithets are usually adjectives and are always lowercase.

The scientific system is based on the principle that plants can be grouped according to similarities in morphological structures that are a result of their common ancestral history. As an analogy, the generic name of a plant is somewhat like the last name of a person. Thus, the last name Smith is analogous to the genus *Quercus* (oak).

All plants within a genus are closely related and possess similar morphological characteristics. Similarities of flowers and fruits are the most widely used criteria in classification. Species within a genus vary according to slight

Figure 2.16

Forms and shapes of trees.

Oval   Vase   Irregular

Broad & Spreading   Weeping   Pyramidal

Columnar   Fan   Fastigate (upright)

differences in these common morphological characters. The genetic makeup of individual plants in a species is very similar, so individuals may be identical in appearance. Plants in the same species and often those in the same genus can be grafted to one another. Moreover, plants in a species, and among species within a genus, are often sexually compatible. There are a number of exceptions to this general rule among horticultural commodities, however.

A great deal of confusion surrounds the term *variety* because it is used in two different ways. In scientific classification, a variety is a subclassification of a species in which plants growing in the wild developed and possess some minor but important morphological trait that is readily heritable. However, *variety* can also refer to a subclassification of a species that was developed and retains desirable characteristics only through human propagation and cultivation; but this is properly termed a *cultivar* (cultivated variety). For example, the three botanical varieties of the pea plant are:

Pisum sativum var. *sativum*: common English pea

Pisum sativum var. *arvense*: field pea

Pisum sativum var. *saccharatum*: sugar pea

Each botanical variety of the pea has some unique morphological characteristic that developed naturally. When pea seeds are sold, however, only cultivated variety or cultivar names are used, as in Progress #9 or Little Marvel, to identify the variety of pea.

In another example, the tomato is scientifically known *as Lycopersicon esculentum*, but there are a number of tomato cultivars that are not botanical varieties, based on their unique fruit or plant characteristics (i.e., Celebrity, Big Boy). Many other examples come from fruit, vegetable, and ornamental species.

The convention for writing a species and its cultivar is demonstrated as follows: *Liquidambar styraciflua* 'Palo Alto' or *Liquidambar styraciflua* cv. Palo Alto, which is the Palo Alto cultivar of the sweet gum tree species. It has unique, consistent fall color and growth habit and is maintained through budding or grafting.

The term *clone* is related to variety and cultivar. A clone is a group of genetically identical plants originating from a single individual and reproduced by vegetative means such as cuttings, grafts, etc. A clone is a specific type of cultivar, but a cultivar is not necessarily a clone, because cultivars may be propagated by sexual (seed) or asexual means.

A basic understanding of the plant classification system is helpful, as it enables horticulturists to identify or predict problems and similarities among related plants. Historically, plants have been classified in the kingdom Plantae, whereas the other kingdom, Animalia, comprised animals. Today, plants have been divided among four kingdoms, one of which contains most of the horticulturally important species. Of the 12 divisions within this kingdom (Plantae), 8 include plants with vascular systems (xylem and phloem), roots, stems, and leaves. Most of the horticulturally important plants belong to two divisions of seed-bearing plants: the cone-bearing plants, or *conifers* (Coniferphyta), including pines, firs, and spruces; and the true flowering plants, or *angiosperms* (Anthrophyta) comprising most of the plants familiar to gardeners. Flowering plants are called angiosperms because their seeds are typically enclosed in a dry or fleshy fruit that develops from the ovary within the flower. Ferns, cycads, and ginkgos belong to other divisions. Conifers, cycads, and ginkgos are often called *gymnosperms* because their seeds lie exposed at the base of scales, usually in a cone.

Flowering plants, the most diverse group, are subdivided into two classes: monocotyledons (grasses, palms, lilies, orchids) and dicotyledons, which comprise all other flowering plants. The terms *monocotyledon* (monocot) and *dicotyledon* (dicot) mean "one seed leaf" and "two seed leaves," respectively. Thus, the first shoots that arise from monocot seeds have a single leaf, whereas those from dicot seeds have a pair of leaves.

Monocots and dicots differ in other morphological features. Monocots are characterized by one seed leaf, flower parts in threes or multiples of three, vascular tissues arranged in bundles, and usually parallel leaf veins. Dicots are characterized by two seed leaves, flower parts in fours or fives or multiples of these, vascular tissues arranged in concentric zones, and a netted pattern of leaf veins. In addition, monocots and dicots differ in certain physiological processes (fig. 2.17).

At the family level of classification, a number of structural and cultural similarities among plants often becomes evident. For example, a well-known family of monocots are the grasses (Gramineae), and a well-known family of dicots includes roses, apples, pears, and firethorn (Rosaceae). (Family names, unlike the genus and specific epithet, are never italicized.) Although these two families are very different, the individuals within them have many similar structural features, cultural requirements, and pest problems.

The scientific system of plant classification can be a very useful tool to horticulturists for identifying unknown plants and developing or understanding the cultural practices and problems associated with a given plant.

Plant Growth

Plant growth is an irreversible increase in plant size caused by an increase in cell number and/or size, which results in the development of new or expanded plant tissues, organs, or other structures. The process of growth is controlled by the integration of a plant's genetic potential and the surrounding environmental conditions. Plant growth requires a source of water, carbohydrates, chemical energy, and mineral nutrients. In green plants, the essential physiological processes responsible for producing and using these items are carried out in individual cells, multicellular tissues, and organs.

Photosynthesis

Photosynthesis is the process by which green plants produce their own carbohydrates, or nutrients, and obtain a source of chemical energy. Plant cells, in the presence of chlorophyll and light, convert carbon dioxide (CO_2) and water (H_2O) to carbohydrates (simple sugars), thereby transforming light energy into stored chemical energy. Energy is stored in the chemical bonds of the carbohydrate molecules ($C_6H_{12}O_6$) that are synthesized in the process. A by-product of this reaction is the evolution of free oxygen (O_2) (fig. 2.18). The chemical equation that describes photosynthesis is

$$6\,CO_2 + 6\,H_2O \xrightarrow[\text{chlorophyll}]{\text{light}} C_6H_{12}O_6 + 6\,O_2$$

In order for photosynthesis to occur, the stomata must be open to allow carbon dioxide to enter the leaf, adequate light must be striking the leaf, and water must be available to the plant. Plant species vary somewhat in the light levels needed for optimal photosynthesis. In addition, certain mineral elements must be present in adequate concentration for photosynthesis to occur efficiently. Information provided in chapter 3, "Soil and Fertilizer Management," clarifies the importance of minerals in photosynthesis, as components of chlorophyll molecules, and as catalysts of the process.

Figure 2.17

Differences between monocots and dicots.

MONOCOT

Vascular tissues scattered in stem

DICOT

Vascular tissues in a circular pattern or joined into a ring

Flower parts in 3s or multiples

Flower parts in 4s or 5s or multiples

Leaf venation parallel

Leaf venation branched

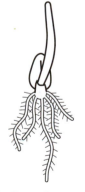

Seedlings with one seed leaf

Seedlings with two seed leaves

The chemically rich carbohydrates formed in photosynthesis are first metabolized and then combined with certain essential mineral elements (e.g., nitrogen, sulfur, magnesium, phosphorus) to synthesize more complex compounds needed to produce new cells (growth); or converted to more complex carbohydrates (sugars and starch) or fats and stored in fruits, seeds, stems, or roots; or biologically combusted to release the chemical energy needed for cells to function.

Respiration

Respiration is the process in which chemical energy is obtained from the controlled biological breakdown of carbohydrates. Superficially, it is the reverse process of photosynthesis. Respiration is accomplished in cells through a complicated series of reactions regulated by enzymes. Complex carbohydrates are broken down into simple carbohydrates, carbon dioxide, and water. The energy released is used in many other cell processes and functions. In plants, respiration normally uses oxygen along with carbohydrates (see fig. 2.18). The chemical equation that describes respiration is

$$C_6H_{12}O_6 + 6\,O_2 \xrightarrow{\text{enzymes}} 6\,CO_2 + 6\,H_2O + \text{Energy}$$

The relative rate of respiration depends largely on temperature and the availability of oxygen and carbohydrates. It nearly doubles for every 18°F (10°C) rise in temperature between 40°F (4°C) and 96°F (36°C) (fig. 2.19). At any given temperature, plant tissues also vary in their respiration rates, with the highest rates occurring in rapidly growing tissues and the lowest in dormant ones. Respiration occurs at all times in living material, including plant parts removed from the plant during harvest. For recommended storage conditions (temperature, length of time, preservation methods) of produce, see table 14.2. These recommendations are based on scientific knowledge of postharvest respiration and pathology.

Cycling of Photosynthesis and Respiration

Photosynthesis and respiration form a cycle by which plants acquire the basic building blocks and the energy needed for growth and development. The photosynthetic portion of the cycle requires light, which typically peaks during midday and ceases at night and at nearly dark periods of the day. Meanwhile, the respiration portion occurs 24 hours a day at variable rates, depending largely on temperature. In order for a plant to grow and develop normally, photosynthesis must occur at a rate that greatly exceeds the respiration rate so that there are enough stored energy and carbohydrates available to support nighttime

---

Figure 2.18

Schematic representation of photosynthesis and respiration. In photosynthesis, which occurs in green leaves, light energy is converted to chemical energy and oxygen (O$_2$) is liberated. Carbon dioxide (CO$_2$) from the air and water (H$_2$O) taken up by the plant's roots combine in the presence of light and chlorophyll (which reflects the color green) and other co-factors to synthesize sugars (carbohydrates, such as glucose [C$_6$H$_{12}$O$_6$]), and oxygen as a by-product. The sugars synthesized in photosynthesis are translocated throughout the plant and are often converted to starch in storage organs such as fruits or tubers. Respiration occurs in all plant cells above and below the soil line. Carbohydrates such as glucose react with oxygen in the presence of enzymes to release chemical energy and carbon dioxide as a by-product. The energy released serves as fuel for plant growth and developmental processes.

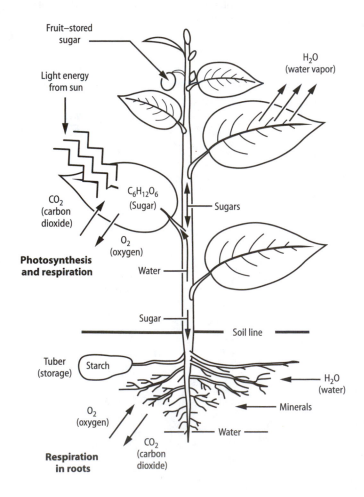

respiration and other growth and development processes (fig. 2.19).

An adverse imbalance between photosynthesis and respiration can occur for various reasons. If water becomes limited during the plant's growing season because of drought or damage to the root system while the temperature remains seasonal, respiration could easily exceed photosynthetic production and cause a decline in vigor. When this daily cycle is unbalanced for a prolonged period, plant growth and development will stop unless the plant has sufficient stored food reserves (e.g., complex carbohydrates, starches, fats, oils) that can be used. Without such reserves, a plant will typically become severely stressed and enter premature dormancy or die. The use of stored food reserves may reduce the vigor of a plant and its ability to develop high-quality flowers, fruit, seed, or storage organs such as tubers.

Water and Nutrient Uptake

Plant growth and development depend on the availability of water and several essential mineral nutrients (see chapter 3, "Soil and Fertilizer Management"). These mineral nutrients are needed in various processes, including photosynthesis and respiration, and are combined with carbohydrates to form important compounds.

Plants obtain all of their water and most of their mineral nutrients from the soil. Most of the water and mineral uptake occurs in roots along the very small fibrous portions of a plant's root system through a combination of chemical and physical processes. Some of these processes require root cells to expend chemical energy. Most of the soil water, however, moves into the plant passively by diffusion or movement along a force gradient. Soil water is largely pulled from the soil up through the plant and out of the stomata by means of this force gradient. Some of the plant-essential nutrients are dissolved in the soil water and are transported to the root surface during this process. Nutrients also move to the root surface by diffusing along a concentration gradient or by physically intercepting growing root tips. Once nutrients are near the root surface, their uptake by the roots often involves the expenditure of chemical energy.

Transpiration

Transpiration, the evaporative loss of water vapor from plant leaves through the stomata, is closely related to the translocation of water and dissolved minerals from the roots through the xylem. Water moves along a force gradient from relatively high in the soil and root area to relatively low in the air and leaf area. A continuous, flowing column of water is maintained in the xylem as long as the stomata are open and water is available in the soil. The transpiration process depends on the unique properties of water, which allow a long column of water to be pulled up like a thread from the roots to the top of the plant. A coast redwood, for example, has a column more than 300 feet (90 m) long (see also "How Water Moves Through Plants" in chapter 4, "Water Management").

The rate of transpiration depends on environmental factors (temperature, relative humidity, wind, etc.) that affect the evaporation rate and the degree of stomatal opening, as well as the amount of available soil water. Transpiration ceases at night in most plant species adapted to temperate climates because their stomata are closed. Transpiration helps to cool plants on hot days and serves to transport minerals from the soil and organic compounds produced in the roots to plant cells.

In succulents and some other plants native to hot, tropical climates, stomata are open at

Figure 2.19

Relationship of respiration, photosynthesis, and plant growth to temperature.

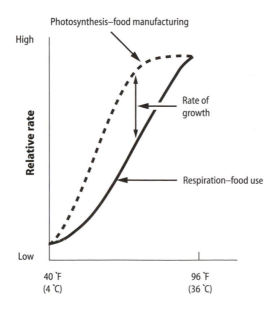

night and closed during the day (the opposite of the temperate pattern), allowing carbon dioxide used in photosynthesis to accumulate in leaves at night and reducing water loss via transpiration during the day.

Translocation

Translocation is the movement of water, mineral nutrients, food (carbohydrates), and other dissolved compounds from one part of the plant to another. It can occur from cell to cell in the space between cells, but it takes place largely in the xylem and phloem tissues. By this process, water and essential mineral nutrients are distributed from the roots to other tissues, and carbohydrates produced in the leaves are moved to meristematic areas (shoot and root tips, cambium, buds), storage organs (fruits, seeds, stems, and roots), and other tissues in need. Certain externally applied substances (e.g., systemic pesticides) may enter some plant parts and be moved to others by this process.

Plant Development

Like growth, plant development is an integrated expression of a plant's genetic potential and its environment. Although horticultural plants vary widely in their specific growth and development patterns, they are all basically annuals, biennials, or perennials that go through vegetative and reproductive phases of a growth cycle. Vegetative growth involves the development and increase in root, stem, or leaf tissues, whereas reproductive growth involves the development and increase of flower, fruit, and seed tissue. A generalized growth and development cycle starts with seed germination and proceeds through juvenility, maturity, flowering, and fruiting. Once the fruit matures, the cycle is essentially completed. For annual plants, the development of fruit is followed by the final phase of growth, which is senescence and death. For perennials, the vegetative and reproductive phases of a growth cycle may be repeated each year, or each phase may continue for more than a year.

Internal Regulation of Plant Growth and Development

Although growth and development are indirectly controlled by the availability of light, water, carbohydrates, chemical energy, and mineral nutrients, hormones provide direct internal regulation of these processes. *Plant hormones* are substances that are produced in one plant part or organ and are translocated to another part where they have a pronounced effect. Plant hormones (sometimes called *phytohormones*) are effective in relatively small quantities and provide control or regulation of most plant processes. The five major groups of plant hormones—gibberellins, auxins, cytokinins, ethylene, and abscisic acid—and their major effects on growth and development are listed in table 2.1. The production of hormones often occurs in meristematic tissue or new-growth regions and is sometimes triggered by specific environmental conditions. Plant age and species also dictate the type and amount of hormone that is produced. Depending on the amount present, the hormone's effect may be dramatically different. For example, at low concentrations, auxins promote root formation, but at higher concentrations, auxins can kill broadleaf weeds (see table 2.1).

Dormancy

Plant growth is not always continuous. Shoots, buds (leaf and flower), and other vegetative parts of a plant that are alive but not actively growing are said to be dormant. Seeds that are alive and viable and yet do not germinate under favorable conditions are also dormant. Dormancy is a mechanism by which plants survive unfavorable environmental conditions and seeds delay germination until they are in a favorable environment. In order to survive such periods, a plant or seed must contain sufficient stored food reserves (carbohydrates) to support ongoing low-level respiration.

Seed dormancy may be physical, physiological, or a combination of the two, depending on the plant species. Physical dormancy is most frequently caused by a hard, impervious seed coat that prevents water or oxygen from entering the seeds. Several treatments can be applied to seeds that are physically dormant (see chapter 5, "Plant Propagation"). Physiological dormancy may be caused by special internal processes, certain plant hormones, or other inhibitory compounds that are present in the seed or fruit. Sometimes physiological dormancy is caused by the presence of an immature embryo in the seed, and the seed must first go through an after-ripening process before an embryo can develop fully. More commonly, the hormone abscisic acid or some other inhibitory compound is present in the seed, and a specific set or series of environmental conditions (i.e., cold, heat, rainfall, etc.) must occur to either remove the substances or trigger physiological processes that overcome them.

Dormancy of plants is usually triggered by the onset of unfavorable environmental conditions, such as the shorter days and colder weather of autumn and winter or inadequate soil moisture that may severely stress plants during summer droughts. Once sufficient hours of cold temperatures (i.e., hours below 45°F [7 °C]) have accumulated and warmer weather returns, winter-dormant plants resume growth. Similarly, plants that are dormant because of drought stress may resume growth once sufficient soil moisture is restored.

Because of *apical dominance*, many lateral buds remain dormant and lateral shoots show reduced vigor under favorable growth conditions until the terminal bud or shoot is removed. Removing terminal growth removes the source of auxin production that has been suppressing the lateral growth (see table 2.1).

Vegetative Development

For annual and biennial plants as well as some perennial plants, the vegetative growth phase begins with seed germination or the breaking of leaf buds and ends with the initiation of flower development. In woody perennials, vegetative and reproductive phases often exist concurrently. Seeds and buds are usually dormant until specific environmental conditions are present or a series of environmental conditions and physiological processes occurs. Seeds and buds are alive and respiring. Seeds depend on internal stored food reserves to survive, whereas buds have access to food compounds produced or stored by the plant.

Seed Germination

Annual plants and most biennial plants begin their growth and development cycles at seed

Table 2.1

FIVE GROUPS OF PLANT HORMONES AND THEIR EFFECTS

Hormone group	Effects
auxins	regulate cell enlargement
	suppress lateral bud development, creating apical dominance of main buds and shoots
	direct shoot growth toward a light source
	direct horizontal growth upward
	suppress fruit- or leaf-drop mechanisms
	promote formation of adventitious roots from stems or leaves
	low concentration: promote root formation
	high concentration: kill broadleaf weeds
	promote fruit set and development or fruit abortion, depending on the plant species
gibberellins	regulate cell division and stem elongation
	promote flowering in some plant species
	activate enzymes in germinating seeds
cytokinins	stimulate cell division, frequently in conjunction with auxins and gibberellins, to regulate processes listed under each of those
ethylene	accelerates fruit ripening
	induces flowering in some species
	hastens senescence and abscission of leaves and fruits
	interacts with auxins in certain processes often produced by plants or plant parts that have been injured
abscisic acid	regulates and promotes dormancy in shoots and seeds
	responsible for abscission (dropping-off) of leaves on deciduous plants and closing of stomata on leaves of plants under severe stress

germination. Many perennial plants also begin their first growth cycle this way. Seeds capable of germination are said to be *viable*. They contain a living embryo that is respiring at a low level.

Germination starts when a seed first takes in water and ends when the seedling is self-sustaining. Before germination can occur, a seed must be surrounded by suitable environmental conditions. The environmental factors affecting seed germination are water, oxygen, temperature, and light. All species require a continuous supply of oxygen and water for germination, but they vary considerably in their specific temperature and light requirements. Usually a species only needs the temperature to remain within a certain range, rather than at a specific degree, in order to germinate. Germination rates under optimal environmental conditions vary among species, but the relative rate of germination for a species is determined largely by how closely the surrounding environmental conditions match the optimal ones. For a detailed discussion of seed germination, see "How to Store Seeds" in chapter 14, "Home Vegetable Gardening," and "Sexual Propagation" in chapter 5, "Plant Propagation."

Juvenility

A plant is considered juvenile from the time it is a seedling until it is mature and capable of initiating flowers. Juvenility is the portion of the vegetative growth phase marked by relatively vigorous, uninterrupted growth (except for normal seasonal dormancy). In annual species, juvenility may last for a few weeks to a few months. In some perennial plants like fruit trees, juvenility may last for a few years. A small number of plants, such as bamboo and agave, remain juvenile for 10 years or more.

Some species exhibit distinctly different morphological features during juvenility and maturity. Juvenile pears may have thorns, whereas mature ones do not; leaves of *Hedera* species are clearly lobed on juvenile plants and smooth on mature ones; the opposite occurs in *Philodendron* species. Juvenile *Hedera* stems are trailing and require support to grow upright, whereas mature stems freely grow upright with no support.

As a general rule, juvenile plants or plant parts more readily initiate adventitious roots than mature plants or plant parts do. Juvenile plant parts are also more readily grafted than older sections of the plant.

Maturity

Maturity is reached when the plant is fully developed and is capable of initiating flowers. Certain morphological and physiological changes may occur in mature plants. During the mature phase of vegetative growth, bulbs, tubers, fleshy roots, and runners are produced by horticultural crops with the genetic potential to do so (see fig. 2.3).

Although a plant is capable of developing flowers and other specialized organs when it reaches maturity, it may not do so. The environmental conditions at maturity usually control whether the plant will flower.

Reproductive Development

Flower, fruit, or seed production is the goal for growing many horticultural plants. Understanding reproductive physiology and how reproductive development may be manipulated is therefore very important to horticulturists and home gardeners.

Flower Induction

In flowering plants, the reproductive growth phase begins when certain vegetative meristems (actively growing shoot tips or buds) are induced to produce reproductive organs (flowers), and it ends with the formation of fruit or the senescence of the plant. Once a meristem is induced to flower, it follows a process of initiating cells that form new tissues of a flower or a flower cluster known as an *inflorescence*. The process is normally irreversible after it is initiated. In other words, the meristem will no longer initiate the vegetative cells of shoots it initiated previously. The length of time needed to induce a meristem to become reproductive and the length of time needed for induced meristems to produce flowers vary among species from a few weeks to several months. These time frames may also vary slightly within a species, depending on temperature or other factors. The number of meristems on a plant that are induced to flower may also vary widely from plant to plant.

The time of year when flower induction occurs and the length of time from induction to flowering for a given species are important for home gardeners to know. Many perennial plants initiate cells of flower tissue within meristems months before flowers develop. Flower buds of spring-flowering woody plants, for example, are usually initiated the previous summer. Pruning such species during winter months will thus reduce the number of flowers they produce in the spring. Annual plants, however, may reach maturity and flower within several weeks of seed germination.

Flower and Fruit Development

Some plant species are self-induced to flower and are not greatly influenced by environmental factors. In many other species, a number of factors, aside from a plant's genetic potential, control flower induction and development. The primary factors are day length (the photoperiod, or the number of daylight hours), light intensity, temperature, soil moisture content, and the internal nutritional status of the plant. Many of these factors also influence the development of fruits from flowers.

Once a flower is developed and opens fully, a number of events must take place for a fruit to develop. As noted earlier, the ovary of the flower, and sometimes other flower parts, mature to form a fruit. For normal fruit development, the flower's stigma must receive viable pollen, which in turn must germinate and fertilize the ovule(s) (see fig. 2.13). Fertilization is not assured even when pollination takes place. Each ovule must be fertilized by a separate pollen grain. Several physiological processes are initiated upon pollination that result in *fruit set*, or the inhibition of flower or fruit drop. Fertilization does not always occur even though pollination and fruit set take place.

Pollination and fertilization are complex processes that require precise environmental conditions to proceed normally. After ovules in the flower are fertilized, the size of the developing fruit increases rapidly. The raw materials and energy needed for this growth are supplied by the plant's photosynthetic activity. The nutritional status of the plant and moisture availability greatly affect fruit size and quality. There must be a sufficient number of leaves to produce the photosynthetic products needed to support developing fruits and to meet the other basic needs of the plant. For example, it has been calculated that a minimum of 40 illuminated leaves are needed to support the growth of one apple on a mature tree. Adequate soil moisture must be available for the same reason, or fruit may be small and poorly developed, or they may drop prematurely.

It is possible, though less common, for fruit development to continue without fertilization. No seed develop in this situation, which results in seedless fruit. A few crops normally develop fruit without ovule fertilization, including bananas, navel oranges, some grapes, pineapple, persimmon, and some cucumbers. Sometimes fruit set even though only a portion of the ovules are fertilized, which results in small or misshapen fruit, as is common in some tomato cultivars.

Only a fraction of the flowers normally produce mature fruit in most tree fruit crops. A significant number of set fruit drop from tree fruit crops just after the petals fall or about 4 to 6 weeks later in what is known as a June drop. Even when fertilization appears to have been completed, plants may drop some or all of their immature fruit. Incomplete or faulty fertilization, internal nutrition imbalances, water stress, or temperature extremes may cause fruit drop. However, fruit drop during the early stages of development may be normal and may serve to adjust the fruit load to a level that the plant can adequately support.

Flowers may be self-pollinated or cross-pollinated. Most plants are cross-pollinated. In self-pollination, pollen from a plant usually pollinates a flower of that same plant. This is common in beans, eggplant, peas, peppers, and tomatoes. In cross-pollination, pollen from one plant normally pollinates flowers of another plant of the same species. Wind and insect (particularly bee) activity are usually important in cross-pollination. Species that normally cross-pollinate have more genetic variation among plants and have a greater chance of adapting to long-term changes in the environment. A number of physical and physiological plant characteristics ensure that cross-pollination occurs. Self-incompatibility of many temperate tree fruit varieties is a good example. Entire varieties of these crops are often self-incompatible so that two or more varieties must be interplanted to allow cross-pollination between varieties (see chapter 17, "Temperate Tree Fruit and Nut Crops").

Although the term *hybrid* is defined as the progeny of any two parents, it is used in most of the horticultural trade to describe the progeny or cultivar that comes from genetically diverse parents of the same species in which cross-pollination is controlled or manipulated.

Fruit Quality and Ripening

As fruit matures, sugars and aromatic compounds that contribute to flavor begin to accumulate. During this final development phase, the ripening fruit typically change color and may soften. Fruit of some species may be picked from the plant when they are physiologically mature but not fully ripened, and they will develop good eating quality (e.g., tomatoes, bananas, pears, avocados, apples, etc.). Fruit of other crops must be allowed to fully ripen on the plant in order to reach good eating quality (e.g., grapes, citrus, strawberries, etc.). Adequate soil moisture, bright sunny days, and, for many fruit crops, cool nights, are necessary during the ripening stages to ensure that fruit is sweet and has good flavor and color. Environmental conditions that maximize photosynthetic sugar production and minimize its loss through respiration result in high-quality fruit.

Two widely held notions are that planting cantaloupes or muskmelons near cucumbers will result in poorly flavored melons, and that planting a yellow-fruited apple tree near a red-fruited one will result in poorly colored fruit. Neither of these beliefs is true. First, cross-pollination between two plant species, as would be necessary for cantaloupes and cucumbers, very rarely occurs and does not occur between these two species. Second, when cross-pollination does occur, as it can between yellow- and red-fruited apple cultivars, only the resulting seed would be affected. Fruit develops from the ovary and sometimes other parts of the flower, which develop from tissue of the mother plant. Thus, pollen cannot affect melon flavor or apple fruit color. Poor flavor in melons and poor color in apples most often occurs when plants are diseased, fruits are harvested too immature, or cloudy, cool weather persists during the final ripening period.

How Plants Function

Environmental conditions and plant nutrition can dramatically influence plant growth and development. These factors can greatly influence when a plant switches from the vegetative growth phase to the reproductive growth phase. Light, temperature, soil moisture con-

tent, and nitrogen nutrition are the principal factors that affect plant development. It is important to note that two or more environmental factors often interact in very complex ways to impact the growth and development of a given plant. The regulatory mechanisms in plants that are influenced by environmental conditions are not fully understood, because they involve a series of biochemical processes and interactions with plant hormones, whose effects depend on their concentration. At a low concentration, a hormone may induce a particular response, and at higher concentration it may inhibit that same response.

As discussed previously, the degree to which flowering or other developmental processes are induced by environmental conditions varies among plant species. These processes are largely self-induced in some plants and are not significantly influenced by environmental factors. For many horticultural plants, a great deal of effort focuses on controlling or manipulating environmental or nutritional factors that promote the development of desirable plants or plant parts. For other plants, their entire growth cycle may be carefully scheduled so they reach maturity in the season that naturally provides the environmental conditions that promote flowering or other desirable growth and development phases.

Plant Responses to Day Length

Some horticultural crops initiate flowers, form specialized vegetative organs, or initiate dormancy in response to a specific length of daylight in a 24-hour period (known as a *photoperiod*). Such plants are called photoperiodic. Plant leaves are the sensors or receptors of critical photoperiods, and the stimulus is transported by some unknown biochemical or hormonal mechanism to meristems. A number of successive days (often 60 or more) in which the critical photoperiod occurs is needed before the specific organ initiation occurs. Once a particular plant response is induced, altering the photoperiod does not interfere with the growth response that was initiated.

Short-day plants are induced to flower or develop other special organs in response to a succession of days that have a light period less than 12 hours long. Conversely, *long-day* plants are sensitive to photoperiods that are 12 hours or longer (usually 14 hours or more). Many plants are called *day-neutral* because their flowering or other developmental processes are not affected by specific day lengths (see table 2.2).

The natural leaf-drop and color-change responses of deciduous plants in the fall are largely short-day responses. As day length shortens during late summer and fall, deciduous plants are induced to stop chlorophyll production in their leaves and develop a zone of special cells at the base of the leaf petioles that allows the leaves to separate from the plant. The consequences are a loss of green color that unmasks other leaf pigments and the eventual dropping of leaves.

Knowledge of photoperiodic responses has been used widely in the commercial chrysanthemum industry. Although chrysanthemums are short-day plants, they are now available in flower year-round. Growers use artificial lighting to maintain long days during the months when the natural photoperiod is less than 12 hours until the plants reach the desired height. When lighting is stopped, the plants receive natural short-day conditions and are induced to flower. When natural photoperiods are too long for mums to initiate flowers, growers cover plants of the desired size with black cloth about 5:00 P.M. This practice artificially shortens the days and induces the plants to flower.

The important processes of photosynthesis and transpiration are affected by day length. Theoretically, total photosynthetic production and the amount of water transpired is lower on short days than long days if everything else is held constant. Photosynthesis uses light directly, but transpiration depends on light to trigger the opening of stomata, which in turn enables transpiration to occur.

Specific vegetative growth responses that are controlled by photoperiod in some species include seed germination, tuber formation, bulb formation, shoot dormancy, leaf abscission, and runner and stolon development.

Plant Responses to Light Intensity

The intensity or brightness of light influences a number of processes and qualitative characteristics of horticultural plants. A widely used unit of light intensity is the foot-candle. Full sun measures about 10,000 foot-candles; bright, naturally lighted interiors are typically 400 to 1,000 foot-candles, whereas poorly lighted interiors are as low as 30 foot-candles. Plants have an optimal range of light intensity in which they grow and develop best. If light conditions are consistently beyond either end of the optimal range, the plant will not grow normally and may eventually die. Horticulturists strive to place plants where they will receive near-optimal light intensity, or they manipulate the light by supplementing it or by providing shade to produce near-optimal levels.

Light intensity may affect plants at any developmental stage, depending on the species. For a few species, seed germination is inhibited by the presence of light, whereas in a few others, it is required for germination. As light intensity increases, air and leaf temperatures often increase, stomata open fully, and the relative rate of transpiration may increase. For many fruit, vegetable, and ornamental crops, high light intensity is necessary for development of maximum color and for the best sugar and flavor in edible crops. Leaves of plants that are in full sun all day are often relatively smaller in area and slightly thicker than those on the same plant that are shaded all day.

Shoot bending in response to light is very common. The mechanism is believed to be

Table 2.2

LONG-DAY, SHORT-DAY, AND DAY-NEUTRAL PLANTS

Category	Common name	Scientific name
long-day	bentgrass	*Agrostis palustris*
	coneflower	*Rudbeckia bicolor*
	dill	*Anethum graveolens*
	fuchsia	*Fuchsia hybrida*
	ryegrass, perennial	*Lolium perenne*
	sedum	*Sedum spectabile*
	spinach	*Spinacia oleracea*
short-day	chrysanthemum	*Chrysanthemum morifolium*
	cosmos	*Cosmos sulphureus*
	kalanchoe	*Kalanchoe blossfeldiana*
	poinsettia	*Euphorbia pulcherrima*
	strawberry (June-bearing)	*Fragaria* × *ananassa*
	violet	*Viola papilionacea (V. cucullata)*
day-neutral	bluegrass, annual	*Poa annua*
	Cape jasmine	*Gardenia jasminoides*
	corn (maize)	*Zea mays*
	cucumber	*Cucumis sativus*
	fruit and nut trees	
	grapes	*Vitis* spp.
	strawberry (everbearing)	*Fragaria* × *ananassa*
	tomato	*Lycopersicum esculentum*
	Viburnum spp.	

linked to larger auxin concentrations on the shaded side of the stem. Light apparently stimulates either a transfer of auxin to the shaded portion of a stem or a breakdown of auxin on the lighted portion of the stem. In either case, the auxin concentration is higher on the shaded stem portion where it stimulates growth, causing the stem to bend toward the light source.

At relatively low light intensities or in shaded conditions, shoots of plant species that are not adapted to shade become elongated and thin. This stretching of shoots causes them to be weak, less vigorous, and spindly and results in a plant that is of very low quality. Plants of such species may die if more intense light is not provided.

Many plants adjust to a change in light intensity if the change is gradual. Abrupt changes in light intensity may harm foliage. In most plant species, reducing light intensity abruptly causes leaf drop, whereas an abrupt increase in light intensity causes leaf yellowing or sunburning.

Plant Responses to Light Quality

Light quality is an expression of the color of the light source. Sunlight has equal amounts of all colors and appears white. Most artificial light sources do not have a balance of all colors and impart some color other than white. Because photosynthesis is most efficiently conducted with red and blue light, reddish-blue fluorescent light bulbs have been designed specifically for growing plants under artificial lighting. Recent research, however, has demonstrated that cool-white fluorescent lamps are actually the most effective for growing foliage plants without natural light.

The color of light can affect seed germination in a few plants. Blue and red light stimulate or inhibit germination, depending on the species. Under natural full-sun conditions, there is enough red and blue light present to cause these effects.

Plant Responses to Temperature

Many plant growth phases and physiological processes are controlled or affected by temperature. The effects of temperature on a sensitive species usually depend on the length of time that a critically high or low temperature is maintained. Plant metabolic processes gradually shut down in many species as tem-

peratures exceed 96°F (36°C) or drop below 40°F (4°C).

The respiration rate in plants and other organisms greatly depends on temperature. Within the range of 40° to 96°F (4° to 35°C), the respiration rate doubles for every 18°F (10°C) increase in temperature (fig. 2.19). Growth rates of healthy plants also increase as temperature increases within a species' critical temperature range. Harvested crops (vegetables, fruits, cut flowers, etc.) remain alive and continue to respire stored carbohydrates after they are removed from a plant. Holding these products at low, near-freezing temperatures until they are used can greatly extend their shelf life quality because respiration is significantly reduced. Some crops of tropical origin (e.g., tomatoes and bananas) may be injured or lose quality if storage temperatures are too cool, however. For optimal temperatures in vegetable crops, refer to table 14.2.

Transpiration in many species also increases as temperature increases, provided there is adequate soil moisture. The stomata of some species close during hot daylight hours even though the sun remains bright. This reaction halts transpiration and provides a drought-avoidance mechanism for such species.

Seed germination in some species is controlled by temperature. Many temperate species produce seed that require several weeks of exposure to cold (45°F [7°C] or less), moist soil in order to break dormancy and germinate, a process called *stratification*. Seed of a few species, like lettuce, express a high temperature dormancy if they are exposed to soil temperatures that are too warm, usually above 85°F (30°C).

Dormancy of buds and shoots of deciduous plants is generally controlled by temperature. Although photoperiod triggers the onset of dormancy in these plants, a certain amount of cold exposure is necessary to break their dormancy. These chilling requirements vary widely among species and are important characteristics to know for most varieties of temperate tree fruit crops. Buds and shoots of these species remain dormant until a critical number of hours (typically 200 to 800) of cold temperature (usually below 45°F [7°C]) accumulates. The occurrence of warm temperatures between episodes of cold, such as day-night fluctuations, before the chilling requirement is met does not offset previous cold hours (see "Dormancy and Winter Chill" in chapter 17, "Temperate Tree Fruit and Nut Crops").

In some plants, an exposure to cold temperatures for a sufficient period (usually 41°F [5°C] or less for 6 to 12 weeks) is required before they will initiate flowers. This phenomenon, known as *vernalization*, is usually the mechanism that controls flowering in biennial plants. Active shoot meristems are the receptor for this stimulus. Vernalization can be reversed if plants are subsequently exposed to high temperatures. Onion growers can use this knowledge commercially. Onion sets are commonly harvested and then stored for several weeks at near-freezing temperatures to reduce respiration and retard spoilage. They are vernalized during this time and will flower quickly after spring planting from storage. Thus, onion sets from cold storage must be exposed to temperatures above 80°F (27 °C) for 2 to 3 weeks before planting to devernalize them and facilitate bulb formation. Sometimes the terms *vernalization* and *chilling requirement* are used synonomously when discussing crop culture.

The development of flowers and fruit is often affected by temperature. Extremes in temperature can reduce or inhibit pollination and fruit set in crops. Color development, particularly red pigments in flowers and fruits, can be inhibited by high temperatures during the maturation period. Color intensity is typically enhanced by the occurrence of clear, bright, moderately warm days and cool nights.

Interactions of Photoperiod and Temperature

Temperature can interact with light to modify plant responses to a given photoperiod. Poinsettias initiate flowers in 65 days when grown in short-days at 70°F (21°C) but require 85 days if the temperature is 60°F (16°C). June-bearing strawberry cultivars initiate flowers under short-day conditions and runners under long-day conditions unless temperatures remain below 67°F (20°C). At temperatures below 67°F (20°C) these cultivars initiate flowers under any day-length conditions. In similar fashion, flowering in Christmas cactus is a short-day response, but plants will flower at any day length if temperatures are below 65°F (18°C).

Plant Responses to Soil Moisture Conditions

All plant growth and development processes are adversely affected when soil moisture is inadequate or when a plant's root or vascular system becomes impaired and cannot supply adequate amounts of water to plant tissues. Photosynthesis, transpiration, and nutrient uptake are among the processes first affected by insufficient water. The tissue in drought-stressed plants is usually less succulent; leafy vegetable crops thus become tough when water is limiting. A reduction in the rate of growth in shoots and roots, poor fruit set, and poorly developed flowers, fruits, or storage organs follows closely afterward. Without adequate moisture in the soil, seeds will not germinate.

In general, plants suffering from drought will be stunted and light green or grayish-green in color, and leaves and shoots may wilt. Additional information regarding soil moisture, drought, and growing plants in the home garden is found in chapter 3, "Soil and Fertilizer Management," and in chapter 4, "Water Management."

Plant Responses to Carbon Dioxide and Oxygen Concentrations

Carbon dioxide is an essential component in the process of photosynthesis, and oxygen is essential to all plant tissues so that they can carry on respiration. Air surrounding plants, including indoor air, normally supplies adequate amounts of these two gases to the shoots of plants. However, the soil surrounding plant roots does not always contain enough air to provide adequate amounts of oxygen to plant roots. When soils are severely compacted, water-logged, or are artificially deepened more than a few inches over a plant's root system, oxygen may be insufficient for root respiration. Roots die if these conditions occur for an extended period.

Germinating seeds also require oxygen because they are respiring. Thus, the soil or propagation media in which they are placed must be well aerated.

The fact that respiration requires the presence of oxygen is exploited to extend the shelf life of many horticultural commodities that are held in commercial storage. Remember that plant tissues and organs continue to respire even though they are removed from the plant. By removing the oxygen from the air in storage rooms or containers, the respiration rate of these commodities is stopped, and the product will remain fresh for a long time, so long as temperatures are kept cool to minimize spoilage and moisture is maintained to prevent dehydration.

Relationship of Nitrogen Nutrition to Plant Growth and Development

Abundant levels of available nitrogen stimulate growth of new root and shoot tissue and may lead to increased disease problems and reduced fruit quality. The presence of new vegetative growth usually inhibits initiation of flowers. If nitrogen levels in the plant subside as the new vegetative growth matures, plants often have an abundance of carbohydrates produced by the new growth. At this point, flower initiation readily occurs while growth and photosynthetic production of carbohydrates is maintained to support flower and fruit development. If a combination of relatively low nitrogen and low photosynthesis occurs, growth and flowering are both usually reduced. Thus, a relative balance of nitrogen and carbohydrates is essential in the plant for it to flower readily.

Plant Responses to Stress

Stress can be defined as any combination of nonoptimal growing conditions for a given plant. Stress includes extremes in temperature, insufficient light or water, inadequate nutrients, poor soil aeration, or any combination of these factors. Under conditions of stress, a plant will have a shorter juvenile growth phase, low vigor, and weak, tough vegetative growth. A stressed plant may enter dormancy prematurely or remain in extended dormancy. Premature defoliation and abnormal color may occur under severe stress. In general, the quality of vegetable, fruit, and ornamental crops is reduced if severe or prolonged stress occurs.

Reproductive development is also affected by stress. Early flower initiation along with heavy flowering and fruit set often occur in plants under moderate to severe stress. However, the size and overall quality of flowers and fruit of stressed plants are often greatly reduced. Seed produced from stressed plants may be small or have low viability.

A short period of mild stress is often imposed on bedding plants and other plants just before they are transplanted into the landscape or garden. Withholding water and nitrogen fertilizer along with gradual exposure to full sun are known as *hardening* or *hardening-off* plants. These practices reduce plant growth slightly and toughen them somewhat so that they can readily adjust and survive the transplant operation.

Bibliography

Bienz, D. R. 1980. The why and how of home horticulture. San Francisco: Freeman.

Hartmann, H. T., and W. J. Flocker. 1981. Plant science. Englewood Cliffs, N.J.: Prentice-Hall.

Janick, J. 1979. Horticultural science. 2nd ed. San Francisco: Freeman.

Kader, A. A., ed. 2002. Postharvest technology of horticultural crops. 3rd ed. Oakland: University of California Division of Agriculture and Natural Resources Publication 3311.

Kozlowski, T. T., and S. G. Pallardy. 1997. Physiology of woody plants. San Diego: Academic Press.

Leopold, A. C., and P. E. Kriedemann. 1975. Plant growth and development. 2nd ed. New York: McGraw-Hill.

Schumann, D. N. 1980. Living with plants. Eureka, CA: Mad River Press.

University of California Riverside, Department of Botany and Plant Sciences. 1995. Botany 130/Introductory botany lab manual. Riverside: University of California.

3

Soil and Fertilizer Management

Ben Faber, Lawrence Clement,
Deborah D. Giraud, and Deborah Silva

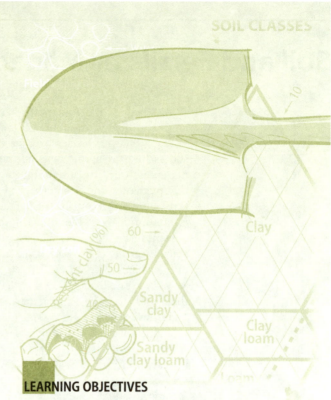

LEARNING OBJECTIVES

- Learn the four components of soil. Understand the basic principles of soil formation, soil function, and soil profiles.

- Learn about the physical properties of soil and their effects on plant growth. Know the difference between soil texture and soil structure. Understand the basic properties of soil minerals, organic matter, cation exchange, and carbon-to-nitrogen ratio.

- Develop an understanding of the basic concepts of soil water and its availability to plants in different soil types.

- Learn the basic concepts of soil fertility and pH. Learn the 17 essential elements needed by plants and their sources. Learn about essential nutrient function, deficiency, and toxicity symptoms.

- Be able to define what a fertilizer is. Learn about fertilizer analysis, sources, formulations, and application methods. Understand the differences and similarities between organic and inorganic fertilizers and amendments.

- Learn which nutrients are most often needed in fertilizers in California. Learn the basics of composting and rapid backyard composting.

- Learn when and how to amend landscape soils, how to prevent compaction and structure breakdown, how to rejuvenate good structure, and how to manage lead contamination.

Soil and Fertilizer Management

There is an old adage that has been printed in a number of University of California leaflets over the years: The successful gardener fertilizes adequately, but not excessively; irrigates thoroughly and not too frequently; and promotes good soil structure by mixing in organic matter and by minimum tillage of the soil when the moisture content is medium wet. This sage advice sums up many of the take-home messages of this chapter.

Webster's Collegiate Dictionary defines soil as the upper layer of earth that may be plowed and in which plants grow. Depending on the location, soil can be a few inches to more than 100 feet deep, overlying the rocks known as the earth's crust. Soil is an important component of the environment; it is a complex, dynamic, natural material in which physical, chemical, and biological reactions are constantly occurring. Soil is created over thousands of years, primarily from disintegrated and decomposed rocks and organic matter. Different kinds of soils form in different locations because soils retain some of the chemical and physical characteristics of the parent rocks from which they derive. For example, in California the volcanic cinders in Tehama County give rise to a soil quite different from the solid granite rock in Riverside County.

The principal components of soil are minerals, organic matter, air, and water. Soil minerals are derived from decomposed rocks. Soil organic matter consists of plant and animal residues in various stages of decomposition, living soil organisms (earthworms, fungi, bacteria), and the substances they synthesize. Together, organic matter, minerals, air, and water provide nutrients, moisture, and anchorage for plants. In different kinds of soils, these four components are present in varying amounts that can render the soil fertile and hospitable or deficient as a medium for plant growth.

Soil minerals and organic matter make up the solid part of the soil, and air and water occupy the pore spaces between the solid particles. Soils drenched by excessive irrigation or rainfall are waterlogged and have very little air (oxygen) in their pore spaces. During periods of drought, the percentage of air in soil pores is high and the percentage of water is too low. A "western" soil with an ideal moisture content for plant growth is about equally divided between solid materials and pore space on a volume basis, with the pore space equally divided between water-filled and air-filled pores (fig. 3.1). Most California soils are mineral soils because they have an organic matter content that is less than 10 percent (often less than 5%) by weight of the solid phase.

Soil Formation

The development of soils from "parent" rocks can take thousands of years, requiring physical and chemical weathering of rocks into unconsolidated, loose rock particles and biological activity among plants and animals in the surrounding environment. The gradual transformation of rock into soil is called soil formation, which is a dynamic, continuous process.

Five essential, natural factors influence the soil formation process:

- climate: temperature and rainfall

- organisms: microscopic and macroscopic plants, animals, bacteria, fungi

- relief: topography of land surfaces (affects runoff and drainage)

Figure 3.1

Four principal components of a soil with ideal moisture content for plant growth. The pore space is 25% water and 25% air; the solid phase is 45% minerals and 5% organic matter in a representative mineral soil.

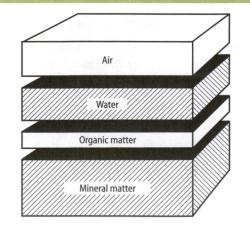

Air

Water

Organic matter

Mineral matter

- parent material: rocks from which the soil formed

- time: period when parent materials are subjected to these processes

Interactions among these five factors were termed the CLORPT equation by the late Hans Jenny of UC Berkeley. Changes in climate, particularly temperature, can lead to cracking, chipping, swelling, and shrinking of the original parent materials. These physical changes break the rocks into smaller pieces, exposing a larger total surface area to the environment. The chemical action of water, oxygen, carbon dioxide, and various acids can reduce the sizes of rock fragments and change their chemistry (mineral composition). The metabolism of living microorganisms and the organic compounds associated with decaying plant and animal life contribute organic matter to the weathered rock material, and a true soil begins to form. Two definitions of soil given in a standard college textbook are "the collection of natural bodies occupying parts of the earth's surface that support plants and that have properties due to the integrated effect of climate and living matter acting upon parent material, as conditioned by relief, over periods of time," and "a dynamic natural body on the surface of the earth in which plants grow, composed of mineral and organic materials and living forms" (Brady and Weil 1999, p. 855).

The properties of individual soils are closely related to the properties of the parent materials, the rocks from which they originate. Parent material determines the amount and kinds of nutrients naturally present to support plant growth, the soil's natural texture, and many other physical and chemical properties of the soil.

The natural soil formation process occurs over geologic time, over hundreds and thousands of years. Nonetheless, we can observe the effects of man-made factors such as irrigation management and the addition of amendments and fertilizers on the soil's chemical and physical properties.

Soil Profile

A vertical section through a typical soil reveals its profile, as shown in figure 3.2. As soils age, the profile is differentiated into distinct layers, or horizons, which are distinguished with letters. Mineral soils have three general horizons. The uppermost horizon, commonly called the

Figure 3.2

A typical soil profile showing the three general soil horizons. *Source:* After California Fertilizer Association 1998, p. 4.

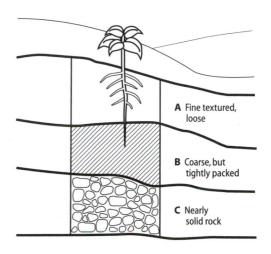

surface soil or topsoil, is the A horizon, the layer from which crop plants obtain water and nutrients. This soil layer may vary in thickness from several inches to several feet and is the layer most influenced by climate and most enriched by the accumulation of organic matter. The zone of greatest biological activity, this layer contains more microorganisms and is typically darker than underlying horizons. The A horizon is also known as the zone of leaching because in climates with high rainfall or excessive irrigation, plant nutrients leach downward from the A horizon into the soil profile. Where rainfall is low, the A horizon can contain an excessive amount of salts.

Underlying the surface soil and immediately below the A horizon is the subsoil, or the B horizon (see fig. 3.2). Although fewer roots and microorganisms are found in the B horizon, it commonly accumulates many materials leached and transported from the surface soil. Clay particles, oxides of iron and aluminum, calcium carbonate, calcium sulfate, and other salts from the A horizon are deposited in the B horizon, resulting in the formation of a soil layer that is more compact than the topsoil. In young soils, where clay has had insufficient time to accumulate, no B horizon is present. As soils age, increasing amounts of clay and other salts migrate and accumulate until the B horizon forms. It is usually lighter in color than the A horizon.

The layer of loose soil beneath the A or B horizons, which is largely unaffected by clay accumulation or organic matter, is the C horizon. Little or no biological activity occurs there. When a soil develops "in place," the C horizon is similar in chemical composition to the original parent materials from which the overlying A and B horizons formed. The C horizon is much less affected than the A or B horizons by physical, chemical, or biological agents. Soil materials that form the C horizon in their original position, by weathering of bedrock, are *sedentary* or *residual*, whereas soil materials that have been moved to a new location by natural forces are said to have been *transported*. When water is the transporting agent, the surface soil is classified as *alluvial* (stream-deposited), *marine* (sea-deposited), or *lacustrine* (lake-deposited). Wind-deposited surface soils are *aeolian*, and surface materials transported by glaciers are *glacial*.

The A, B, and C horizons together with the unconsolidated rock fragments on top of the bedrock are known as the *regolith*. Soils that form in a hilly or mountainous terrain usually have a consolidated rock layer below the three soil horizons, termed the R horizon. If the depth to consolidated rock is deeper than 6 to 7 feet (1.8 to 2.1m), the soil is usually considered lacking an R horizon.

The soil around houses and condominium and apartment complexes has often been disturbed by construction processes and may not show the neat soil profile and distinct horizons shown in figure 3.2. The surface soil may not even be from the site. The best locations to see soil horizons and the results of the natural soil formation process are at road cuts or where excavation is occurring.

Soil profiles and individual horizons may vary from a fraction of an inch to many feet deep. A typical natural soil profile will extend to a depth of about 3 to 6 feet (0.9 to 1.8m). Soil profiles in many western states such as California are less developed than soils in more humid climates along the East Coast because less water percolates through western soils. As a result, many western surface soils contain more calcium, potash (potassium), phosphate, and other nutrient elements than do eastern soils because less of the nutrients has leached through the profile.

Physical and Chemical Properties of Soil

A soil's physical and chemical properties affect plant growth and soil management. Some important physical and chemical properties of soil are mineral content, texture, cation exchange capacity, bulk density, structure, porosity, organic matter content, carbon-to-nitrogen ratio, color, depth, fertility, and pH.

Soil Minerals

Soils consist of particles with many sizes and shapes. Very coarse particles, such as gravel and stones, are inert or detrimental to plant cultivation. Soil mineral particles active in supporting plant growth are divided into three categories by size: sand, silt, and clay. Sand grains can be seen with the naked eye. Silt

Table 3.1

SIZES AND SURFACE AREA OF SOIL MINERAL PARTICLES

Soil type	Particle diameter (mm) USDA system	Particle diameter (mm) International Soil Science Society system	Surface area per gram (sq cm)
very coarse sand	2.0–1.0	—	11
coarse sand	1.0–0.5	2.0–0.2	23
medium sand	0.5–0.25	—	45
fine sand	0.25–0.10	0.20–0.02	91
very fine sand	0.10–0.05	—	227
silt	0.05–0.002	0.02–0.002	454
clay	below 0.002	below 0.002	8,000,000

Source: Adapted from Foth 1978, p. 26.

particles can be seen with magnification (a 10× hand lens). Clay particles cannot be seen without an electron microscope. Both the U.S. Department of Agriculture (USDA) and the International Soil Science Society have established standards for the size limits of sand, silt, and clay particles (table 3.1). The two systems do not agree completely, but the key points for Master Gardeners are

- The largest sand particles (2.0 mm diameter, or 0.08 inches) are 1,000 times larger than the largest clay particles (less than 0.002 mm in diameter).

- The smallest sand particle is 10 to 25 times larger than the largest clay particle, depending on the classification system.

- Silt particles are intermediate in size.

- Clay has thousands of times more surface area per gram than silt and almost a million times more surface area per gram than very coarse sand.

Table 3.1 illustrates that, for a fixed amount of soil, the total surface area increases as particle size decreases. Because many physical and chemical reactions in soil occur at the surfaces of mineral particles, clay minerals, on the basis of size alone, would be expected to have the greatest effect on soil mineral dynamics.

Soil mineral particles contain elements important to plant nutrition, such as potassium, calcium, sodium, iron, and magnesium, that are bound up within their crystalline structures. Sand and silt are composed mainly of primary minerals such as quartz, feldspar, mica, hornblende, and augite. The clay fraction contains secondary minerals (e.g., kaolinite, montmorillonite, and illite) that form as the primary minerals weather. As the primary minerals weather into secondary minerals, the elements that were bound within their crystalline structures are released, and the important plant nutrient elements become available for absorption by plant roots.

Soil Texture

Soil texture—the relative proportions of sand, silt, and clay mineral particles in a given soil—is one of the most important physical properties affecting plant growth because it determines tilth (fitness as a medium for growing plants) as well as nutrient and water-holding capacities. A sandy, coarse-textured soil is often called a *light* soil, whereas a clay or fine-textured soil is referred to as a *heavy* soil. The terms reflect the relative ease of working the two soil types. Twelve basic soil textural classes are recognized, based on the USDA classification system in table 3.1. Figure 3.3 shows the names of the textural classes and the percentages of sand, silt, and clay associated with them.

Soil texture, as determined by its subjective "feel" to the experienced gardener, is a good indicator of the soil's physical properties and behavior. The hands-on, experiential "feel" method shown in figure 3.4 can be used to deduce the majority of the basic soil textural classes identified in figure 3.3, which are based on precise particle size distribution data. With experience, the texture of a soil can be felt and determined simply by rubbing moist soil between thumb and forefinger and noticing its characteristics: how it ribbons or is pushed out into a thin strip, how it hangs together, and how sticky, smooth, or gritty it is.

The feel method of examining a moist soil yields an approximate measure of the particle-

Figure 3.3

Soil textural classes. The chart shows the percentages of sand, silt, and clay in the 12 basic soil textural classes, according to the USDA. Although organic matter may have a significant effect on a soil's physical properties, it is not considered in defining the soil's textural class. Each class is represented by an area in the textural triangle diagram. Thus, two soils may have the same texture but different particle size distributions. *Source:* After Wildman and Gowans 1978, p. 3.

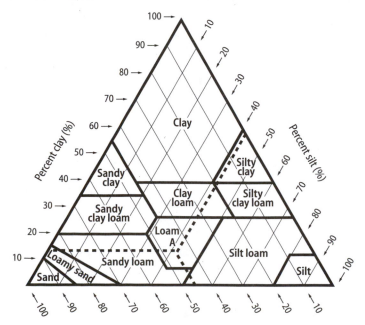

Figure 3.4

Determining soil texture by the feel method.

A

(A) Loamy sand, a coarse-textured soil. A cast will form when moist soil is squeezed in the hand. The cast cannot be handled without breaking; no ribbon can be formed.

(B) Loam, a medium-textured soil. A short ribbon can be formed with moist soil. The ribbon will split readily and will break away when about 1/2 inch long. A moist cast of a loam soil will bear some handling.

B

C

(C) Clay loam, a medium-textured soil. A ribbon can be formed easily in moist soil. This ribbon is moderately strong, but will break away when it is 3/4 inch long. A moist cast of a clay loam soil will bear moderate handling.

(D) Clay, a fine-textured soil. A strong ribbon can be formed in moist soil. The ribbon often will be more than 1 inch long. A moist cast will bear considerable handling.

D

Source: After Wildman and Gowans 1978, p. 4.

size distribution that can be measured precisely in the laboratory. Coarse and fine sand particles have a marked to moderate gritty feel and do not form cohesive balls. Silt feels smooth when dry and silky (slippery) when wet. Clay soils are sticky and plastic (able to be molded) when wet and hard and compact when dry. Organic matter makes a soil feel smoother, as if it has a higher silt content.

The 12 soil textural classes can be grouped into 3 general texture categories: coarse texture (sandy soils), medium texture (loamy soils), and fine texture (clay soils):

- coarse (sandy soils): sand, loamy sand

- medium (loamy soils—moderately coarse, medium, moderately fine): sandy loam, loam, silt loam, silt, clay loam, sandy clay loam, silty clay loam

- fine (clay soils): clay, sandy clay, silty clay

Effect of Soil Texture on Plant Growth. With regard to plant growth, a textural class description of the soil reveals critical information about expected soil-plant interactions. The coarser the soil texture, the faster the soil warms up in the spring. A sandy soil, the coarsest of the mineral particles that actively support plant growth, may give the gardener a few days advantage in planting date because of better soil temperature conditions for germination and early seedling growth.

Water-holding and nutrient-storage capacities are determined largely by the distribution of particle sizes in the soil. Soils with finer texture (higher percentages of silt and clay) hold more water and nutrients than coarser-textured soils (higher percentages of sand). Sandy soils have rapid water infiltration and good aeration but low water-holding and nutrient-storage capacities. Water may move too rapidly through a soil comprised almost entirely of sand, with little water retention for plant use. If a soil contains an inadequate amount of sand, however, the soil's pores may be too small to support good drainage. Silt, with particles of intermediate size, has twice as much surface area per gram than very fine sand. Compared to sand, silt weathers faster because of its increased surface exposure, and it has smaller pore spaces between particles. Thus, silty soils have a slower water infiltration rate but a higher water-holding capacity than sandy soils. Clay soils retain more water, have slower air and water movement, and hold more mineral nutrients than sandy soils. Soils composed chiefly of very fine clay particles have very limited movement of water and air because the individual pores are so small. Because water and air move more slowly in the pores of finer-textured soils, these types can be more difficult to manage because their pore sizes can be too small for suitable water percolation and aeration.

Loam, sandy loam, and silt loam, which contain about 5 to 10 percent organic matter, are said to be the best soils for home garden cultivation because they provide a mixture of sand, silt, and clay that retains sufficient water but also permits infiltration and percolation.

In the mineral soils typical throughout the state, retention of plant nutrients is correlated with the amount and kind of clay in the soil. Clay, the smallest-sized mineral fraction, exhibits some unusual properties that would be unexpected if it were merely composed of smaller particles of the same minerals that make up sand and silt. Clay is composed largely of secondary minerals, which are the weathering products of the primary minerals-quartz, feldspar, mica, hornblende, and augite-of which sand and silt are largely composed.

Clay minerals are charged particles. They have net negative charges on their surfaces that naturally attract positively charged ions (cations), such as calcium (Ca^{2+}), magnesium (Mg^{2+}), potassium (K^+), ammonium (NH_4^+), aluminum (Al^{3+}), hydrogen (H^+), iron (Fe^{3+}), and sodium (Na^+), among others. Many of these cations are essential elements in plant nutrition. The attraction of ions or molecules to the surfaces of a solid, such as soil particles, is called *adsorption*. The adsorption of plant nutrient cations onto the surfaces of clay minerals balances the negative charges on their surfaces (fig. 3.5). Note that adsorption is different from *absorption*, which refers to the active or passive movement of ions or water into plant roots.

Cation Exchange Capacity. There is a constant exchange of plant nutrients between clay minerals and the soil solution and between the soil solution and crop plants. Because clay minerals are so active in these nutrient exchanges, they are major determiners of the chemical and physical properties of a given soil, and they largely determine how well plants will grow in that soil. Cations replace one another on the surfaces of clay minerals because of their relative affinities for the surfaces of the soil particles and because the soil maintains chemical equilibrium between the ions adsorbed onto soil surfaces and those located in the soil solution. Climate, relative humidity, and drainage can also affect how strongly particular ions are adsorbed. When cation exchange occurs, the cation released from the clay mineral into the soil solution becomes available for absorbtion by plant roots (see fig. 3.5).

The cation exchange capacity measures the amount of cations that can be adsorbed or held by a soil. It is measured in units of milliequivalents per 100 grams of soil. Mineral soils with a higher cation exchange capacity are usually more fertile than those with a lower exchange capacity because the former more effectively resist the loss of plant nutrient cations through the leaching process.

The amount and kind of clay in soils are critical factors in plant growth because of the clay's capacity to adsorb cations is important in plant nutrition. The types of clays that predominate in California have a higher exchange capacity than those typically found, for example, in the southeastern United States. Clay particles repel negatively charged plant nutrient ions, such as nitrate (NO_3^-) and sulfate (SO_4^{2-}). These important plant nutrients are available for plant use when they are dissolved in the water held in soil pores (the soil solution).

Clay minerals have a very high affinity for water. The negative charges on the clay minerals attract the positive charges on the hydrogen ions (H^+) in water (H_2O). Montmorillonite clay, a type found commonly in California, swells greatly when wetted and shrinks when dry, leaving wide cracks. An intermediate amount of clay in a soil (loamy texture) improves its capacity to hold water and plant nutrient ions because of the negative

Figure 3.5

Schematic showing the exchange of cations between a negatively charged clay particle and the soil solution. Cations in the soil solution are available to be absorbed by plant roots. Cations are attracted to and held by negatively charged soil particles, while negatively charged ions (anions) are repelled and move with soil water. *Source:* After California Fertilizer Association 1998, p. 12.

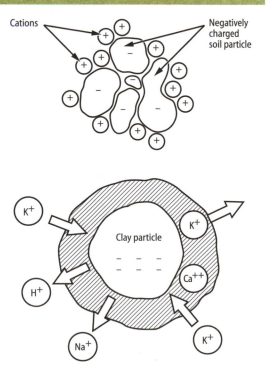

charges on clay minerals' surfaces and the large surface area associated with clay particles. A soil of clay particles has almost 100,000 times more surface area than a soil of fine sand grains of the same weight. This is an important concept for understanding chemical reactions in soil because most of the plant-available nutrients and water are adsorbed onto the surfaces of soil particles. As soil particles become smaller and smaller (from gravel to sand to silt to clay), the soil has more surfaces available for chemical reactions to occur.

Bulk Density

A pound of cement and a pound of feathers both have the same weight, but the volume of each material needed to obtain that pound is vastly different. These characteristics are the basis of bulk density, which measures the weight per volume of a substance. A piece of solid rock has a bulk density of approximately 2.65 grams per cubic centimeter; that is, for every cubic centimeter of volume, a piece of solid rock weighs approximately 2.65 grams.

When solid rock is crushed, some of the volume will include air with the rock; as rock materials are crushed more and more finely, the air occupying a given volume increases, and the bulk density decreases. Bulk density provides a means of evaluating the amount of air or pore space in a given soil. Undisturbed sandy soils generally have a bulk density of about 1.6 grams per cubic centimeter, lower than that of solid rock. Clay soils, which contain particles that are much smaller than sandy soils, have a bulk density of approximately 1.2 grams per cubic centimeter. Usually, as particle size decreases, bulk density decreases and total porosity increases because fine-textured soils usually develop better structure (see "Soil Structure," below). Although bulk density is related to the amount of pore space in a soil, bulk density does not indicate whether pores are large or small.

Soil Structure

Except for sand grains, soil particles typically do not exist as single particles but rather coalesce into groups of particles known as *aggregates* or *peds*. *Soil structure* refers to the way in which aggregates are arranged. Plant growth is strongly influenced by soil structure because it affects moisture availability to plants (water movement), fertility, aeration, porosity, heat transfer, bulk density, and mechanical impedance of root growth. Plants require air, water, and nutrients from the soil, and the air-water relationship depends largely on soil structure. A soil with good structure will have good water infiltration, drainage, aeration, and overall tilth.

A soil aggregate is a clump of soil particles held together in a unit so that it functions as a single large particle. Soil aggregates are naturally occurring structures that may vary from a fraction of an inch to several inches in diameter. Aggregates have characteristic shapes and sizes. Although for all practical purposes soil texture cannot be changed, soil structure can change within a single growing season, especially in the A horizon, because of weather and soil management practices. The structure of the subsoil horizons is less subject to change.

Soil structure development (aggregation) is enhanced as clay and organic matter (humus, plant and microbial exudates, and earthworm activity) increase because they act as *binding* agents. Soil particles also aggregate because of physical forces such as tilling operations, plant root growth, and climatic cycles of wetting, drying, freezing, and thawing. Climate influences soil structure, affecting rainfall, temperature, and the types of plants that will grow, which in turn affect the soil's organic matter content. Calcium salts contribute to aggregation, whereas sodium salts tend to disperse (deflocculate) soil particles, destroying the underlying structure.

Aggregation is very weak to nonexistent in sandy soils, which have very little organic matter and clay. The structure of sandy soils is called *single-grained.* Sandy soils drain well but do not retain much moisture, requiring more frequent irrigation and fertilization for plant roots to thrive.

Table 3.2 describes the most common aggregate shapes: granular (crumbly), platy (flat), blocky (cubical), prismatic (columnar), and massive. A granular structure (rounded, crumbly aggregates) provides an ideal environment for plant roots and is particularly helpful for establishing plants from seeds or transplants. The larger pores between the granular aggregates are continuous, and roots may penetrate them with ease. Water drains readily through a granular soil structure, yet moisture is held back sufficiently in the aggregates to supply root needs. Clay can promote porous, rounded granules in medium-textured soils, such as loams. Granular structure is also com-

Table 3.2

PRIMARY TYPES OF SOIL AGGREGATES

Aggregate type[*]	Shape	Description	Common location in soil
single grain		usually individual sand grains not held together by organic matter or clay	sandy or loamy textured soils
granular		porous granules held together by organic matter and some clay	A horizons
platy		aggregates that have a thin vertical dimension with respect to the lateral dimension	compacted layers
blocky		roughly equidimensional peds; usually higher in clay than other structural aggregates	B horizons with clay; common in subsoils in humid regions
prismatic		structural aggregates that have a much greater vertical than lateral dimension	B horizons; common in subsoils in arid regions
massive		no definite structure or shape; usually hard	C horizons and compacted, transported materials

Source: Adapted from Balge 1993.
Note: [*]The size of aggregates can be coarse (large), medium, or fine (small); the degree of expression can be strong, moderate, or weak. The type, size, and definition of aggregates found in a particular soil varies with the soil texture, composition, depth, management, and mode of formation.

mon in surface soils in which the organic matter content is high and can occur in some clay soils near the surface.

When the particles are arranged around a vertical axis bounded by relatively flat vertical surfaces, the structure is prismatic (prismlike, or columnar). Prismatic or blocky structures most often occur as a result of shrinking and cracking of clay loam and clay soil layers when they dry. The large cracks that are visible at the surface of dry clay soils may extend to 3 feet (0.9 m) or more in depth. The elongated chunks of soil between these vertical cracks are called prisms. The lower portions of the prisms often have horizontal cracks intersecting the vertical ones so that a more or less equidimensional blocky structure results. Prismatic or blocky aggregates may vary

considerably in size but are always coarser than those of granular structure. The aggregates swell when wet and fit together so tightly that water drains through them rather slowly. Plant roots may follow cracks downward but do not usually penetrate to the centers of prismatic or blocky aggregates. Thus, the roots may not have access to a significant portion of the water and nutrients in these soils.

Platy structure refers to the occurrence of thin layers of soil stacked on top of one another (an arrangement around a horizontal plane), which can occur when silty soil materials are deposited in thin layers by stream overflow. The discontinuities caused by this minute layering may interrupt the movement of water, air, and roots into the soil. Artificial platy structure may be caused by repeated compression of soils in farm roadways. (Clods are soil aggregates that are created artificially by tillage or digging.)

Many medium-textured soils in California do not have well-defined structural aggregates because their organic matter content is much lower than that of, for example, most midwestern soils. If particles are bound together in the whole soil mass, soils are said to have a *massive* structure. These soils may still provide a favorable root environment if they are open and porous, but if they are dense and compact, root growth will be restricted by slow water penetration, limited aeration, and increased soil strength.

Soil management practices are important factors in preserving or ruining soil structure. Soil structure takes years to form but can be broken down rapidly through mismanagement, improper tillage, or intensive cultivation. Working or walking on soil when it is wet leads to compaction and loss of structure. Soil needs to be somewhat moist to work, but wetting a soil and immediately working it ruins its structure. A soil should be allowed to drain for at least 1 to 2 days after watering before working it. The length of time depends on soil texture: the more clay, the longer the time required.

A soil profile may have a single type of aggregation, but typically each horizon has a characteristic structural pattern (see table 3.2) determined largely by the degree of soil weathering, which is a function of the five primary factors that govern the soil formation process (CLORPT equation; see "Soil Formation" above).

Soil Porosity

When soil solids (minerals and organic matter) are packed together tightly, tiny voids (pore spaces) still exist between the solids. The pore space is the conveyor of oxygen, water, and dissolved mineral nutrients and the provider of space in which roots grow. Soil air occupies the pores not occupied by water, which are typically the larger pores (macropores) (fig. 3.6), from which water drains by the force of gravity. In moist soil conducive to plant growth, the pore space is occupied about equally by air and water (see fig. 3.1). Small pores (micropores) are responsible primarily for water storage. Plant roots grow through the same channels as soil air and water; thus, soil with good pore structure has a balance of macropores and micropores that ensures adequate aeration and water movement.

Oxygen is a constituent of soil air that is essential for root respiration, other root functions, and the metabolism of soil organisms. Air-filled pores provide a pathway for the intake of oxygen and the release of carbon dioxide. Soil aeration is the two-way process of oxygen intake by plant roots and carbon dioxide escape. When soil is overwatered, all of the pore spaces fill with water. Because oxygen is not readily available in waterlogged soil, plant roots cannot respire efficiently; they become oxygen-starved and cannot make efficient use of available nutrients. Suffocating roots contributes to poor growth. Seeds sown in waterlogged soil may fail to germinate because oxygen is inadequate for respiration.

Nitrogen also cannot be released in waterlogged soil. Nitrogen that would normally be available to plants is converted to forms that plant roots cannot absorb when the supply of oxygen is inadequate in root-zone pores. Keeping soil pores filled with a mixture of air and water is very important for plant growth. Other chemical properties and reactions important to plants may be adversely affected when soil oxygen levels are severely limited.

Soil Color

Soil color can be determined easily and is one of the most useful characteristics in soil classification and identification. Color is a function

---

Figure 3.6

Soil texture and structure influence the total porosity and pore configuration. Total porosity increases with decreasing particle size, but pore size decreases as mineral particle size decreases. Thus, a sandy soil (higher bulk density, lower porosity) will drain better than a clay soil (higher porosity, lower bulk density) because the clay soil has much smaller pores than the sandy soil. The smaller pores are less able to transmit water and gases. Both total porosity and pore arrangement determine water movement in soil and soil oxygen availability.

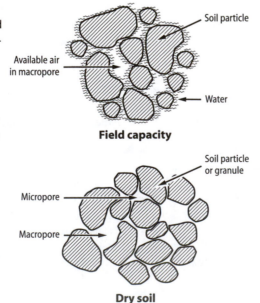

Field capacity

Dry soil

of the amount of organic matter, the original parent material, the degree and kind of weathering of the soil, the amount and type of salts present in the surface layer, and the aeration of the soil. Although soil color does not have a direct influence on soil productivity, it often can provide information about the chemical makeup or drainage status of the soil. Organic matter tends to darken soil color, which influences soil temperature. Dark soil is warmer than light-colored soil, but it is not necessarily more fertile. A few generalizations can be made about soils of different colors.

Gray and brown soils form the largest group of California soils. They are moderately low in organic matter but include some of the state's most productive and fertile alluvial soils, the soils that form from periodic flooding by streams and the accompanying deposition of soil materials. Nearly all soils on the floors of the Central Valley and the coastal valleys of California are alluvial, as opposed to residual soils that form in place from the underlying rocks in upland areas. The gray soils on the eastern side of the Central Valley formed from granitic alluvium and are coarse- to medium-textured. The brown soils on the western side of the Central Valley formed from sedimentary alluvium and are medium- to fine-textured.

Black soils are relatively high in organic matter, but the amount can vary from less than 5 percent (mineral soils) to more than 50 percent (peats and mucks). In the Central Valley, black soils that have formed under poorly drained conditions are either peaty or clayey in texture, but with good management practices they can be highly productive for field and vegetable crops. In upland and coastal areas, black soils with strong granular structure have formed under native grassland, on fine-textured parent materials, and in cool climates.

The color of older soils is generally red or yellow, which indicates that the soils are losing nutrients. Red soils are generally old soils that have undergone intensive weathering. Often, their subsoils have restrictive claypans (a noticeable increase in clay) or hardpans (dense rocklike layers) that act as barriers to root and water penetration. Water may accumulate above these layers, and roots may be injured because of poor aeration. Red soils are often deficient in nitrogen, phosphorus, zinc, and sulfur. Iron oxides usually contribute yellow and red colors to these soils. During periods of poor aeration caused by poor drainage, these soils can have a rust-colored, mottled appearance.

White or light-gray soils are usually sandy or calcareous (containing lime). Sandy soils may exhibit this color if they have water-holding problems and nutrient deficiencies. In calcareous soils of this color, iron deficiency may be a problem for orchard crops. In arid or poorly drained environments, white-colored salts, such as calcium carbonate, calcium sulfate, or sodium carbonate, can accumulate at the surface. Sodium salts cause organic matter to oxidize, turning it black, and they also cause aggregates to disperse.

Blue or blue-gray layers are usually found in poorly aerated subsoils where organic matter is decomposing anaerobically (without air). These soils can have a sewerlike odor because they contain gases and dissolved matter toxic to plant roots. Extensive aeration can restore these soils to a condition suitable for plant growth.

Soil Depth

The deeper the soil, the greater the total water and nutrient storage capacity available to plants. *Soil depth* refers to the vertical distance from the soil surface to a layer that stops the downward growth of plant roots. The barrier that stops downward root growth and water penetration may be rock, gravel, a claypan, a hardpan, or a partially cemented layer of soil. Soil depth is referred to as

- very shallow, less than 10 inches (25 cm)
- shallow, from 10 to 20 inches (25 to 50 cm)
- moderately deep, from 20 to 36 inches (50 to 90 cm)
- deep, from 36 to 60 inches (90 to 1.5 m)
- very deep, deeper than 60 inches (1.5 m)

Soil Organic Matter

The organic fraction of the soil is the solid phase that originates from living organisms, unlike the mineral fraction, which originates from nonliving rocks. Soil organic matter consisting primarily of carbon (50 to 55%) and nitrogen (7 to 8%), is a reservoir of plant nutrient elements. It includes living organisms (fungi, bacteria, earthworms) and organic matter derived from plant and animal residues in various stages of decomposition. Soil bacteria

Figure 3.7

Decomposition of soil organic matter releases nutrients, particularly nitrogen, phosphorus, and sulfur, which are taken up by plant roots. Humus improves soil fertility and water retention and infiltration rates. *Source:* After Chaney, Drinkwater, and Pettygrove 1992, p. 4.

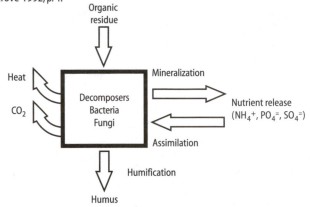

and fungi that use plant and animal residues in the soil as their source of food and nutrition constantly decompose soil organic matter. When soil organic matter derived from plant and animal residues becomes resistant to further decomposition, it is called *humus* (fig. 3.7).

In California the organic matter content of the soil varies according to climate and soil type. Organic matter comprises less than 1 percent in the well-drained soils of warm, dry regions; 1 to 10 percent in the mineral soils of the cool, moist regions; and 5 to more than 50 percent in poorly drained valley soils originating in swamps. Frequent tillage and crop removal tend to reduce the natural organic matter content of a soil.

Humus. Even though the mineral soils of the West Coast contain only small amounts of organic matter, the chemical and physical properties of these soils are mainly functions of humus and clay minerals. Like clay minerals, soil humus has negative charges on its surfaces and attracts water and plant nutrient cations, such as ammonium (NH_4^+), calcium, (Ca^{2+}), magnesium (Mg^{2+}), hydrogen (H^+), and potassium (K^+), etc. Humus increases a soil's cation exchange capacity and improves soil fertility because the adsorbed cations remain available in the root zone for absorption by plants. There is a constant exchange of nutrients between soil solids (clay minerals and humus) and the soil solution and between the soil solution and crop plants (see fig. 3.5). Humus also aids in the formation of granular

aggregates, thereby improving soil structure (see table 3.2). Humus tends to be brown or very dark brown, and soils rich in organic matter tend to take on this darker hue. The predominant components of humus are humic and fulvic acids.

Earthworms, Saprophytes, and Other Beneficial Soil Organisms. Earthworms and saprophytic soil organisms contribute to soil fertility. Most of these creatures live near the soil surface in the root zone of crop plants. A gram of soil may contain as many as 4 billion bacteria, 1 million fungi, 20 million actinomycetes, and 300,000 algae. Some of these soil organisms are visible to the naked eye, whereas others are microscopic. Although most are beneficial to crop plants, a few destructive plant pathogens use garden crops as their food source. These disease-causing soil microorganisms are described in chapter 6, "Plant Pathology."

Earthworms are segmented worms that are part of the beneficial soil macrofaunae visible to the naked eye. As earthworms feed on plant residues and move about, they stir and aerate the soil by leaving holes in it, improving soil structure. After they feed and digest decaying organic plant residues, the excreta and casts of earthworms are very high in plant-available nutrients, such as phosphates (PO_4^{3-}, HPO_4^{2-}), potassium (K^+), nitrate nitrogen (NO_3^-), and exchangeable calcium (Ca^{2+}) and magnesium (Mg^{2+}).

Soil saprophytes are beneficial soil microorganisms (bacteria and fungi) that are known as decomposers and recyclers because they feed on decaying plant residues left in the soil after harvest, decompose them, and recycle them into beneficial products such as humus. Saprophytes also release plant nutrient elements in simple mineral forms—formerly bound up in complex organic molecules in soil organic matter—that then become available for uptake by plants. Recycling nutrient elements and synthesizing humus are two important functions of these microbes.

Beneficial saprophytic soil bacteria and fungi have important roles in the improvement of soil fertility and structure and the recycling of organic waste (see fig. 3.7). As they feed on dead and decaying plant residues from the previous crop, soil saprophytes use enzymes to break down the residues and metabolize them into mineral forms of nitrogen (NH_4^+), sulfur (SO_4^{2-}), and phosphorus (PO_4^{3-}) that the current crop can use and absorb through its roots. Because plant roots cannot absorb nutrients in complex organic forms, the saprophytic soil organisms perform an invaluable recycling function when they decompose plant residues left in the soil into simpler mineral forms needed by plants. In this way, soil organic matter can serve as a slow-release fertilizer that provides a steady supply of inorganic nitrogen, phosphorus, and sulfur to garden plants.

As they feed on organic residues, saprophytes churn the soil and excrete gummy substances that bind and stabilize aggregates, improving soil structure. Soil organic matter promotes a crumblike granular soil structure. Improved aggregation is coupled with better pore structure, which is a more even distribution of large and small pores that improves water-holding capacity, water infiltration rate, and aeration. Saprophytic bacteria and fungi also release carbon dioxide (CO_2) into the soil atmosphere. (see fig. 3.7). Carbon dioxide can move directly from the soil atmosphere to the air or it can combine with water (H_2O) to form carbonic acid (H_2CO_3). Together with other acids, H_2CO_3 facilitates weathering of soil minerals, which increases nutrient availability to plants by releasing ions previously bound within the structure of the soil minerals.

Not all beneficial soil bacteria and fungi are saprophytes. Instead of feeding on decaying organic matter, other groups of beneficial fungi and bacteria form associations with plant roots. Some groups of soil bacteria and fungi can *fix* atmospheric nitrogen (N_2), which means that they can convert N_2 into ammonia (NH_3) or ammonium ions (NH_4^+). Crop plants cannot use N_2, but they can absorb NH_4^+. For example, *Rhizobia* spp. bacteria that live in association with the roots of legume plants inhabit nodules in the roots and make nitrogen available to the legume plants by fixing N_2. Other species of beneficial bacteria convert NH_4^+ into nitrites (NO_2^-) and nitrates (NO_3^-), which plants can also absorb.

Mycorrhizae. More than 75 percent of all terrestrial plants, including the crops in your garden, form associations between their roots and soil fungi. These root-fungal associations are called mycorrhizae and are beneficial to both the crop plant and the fungus. The plant roots provide carbon-containing compounds that serve as a food source for the fungi, and the fungi improve the plant roots' absorption of phosphorus and sometimes other plant nutrients. Mycorrhizae are also common in conifers and other woody plants.

Many beneficial soil microorganisms (bacteria, fungi, actinomycetes) that are associated with plant roots synthesize plant hormones (auxins, gibberellins, cytokinins, ethylene, and abscisic acid) and have positive effects on plant growth and development. Rhizobacteria, such as *Rhizobia* spp., and mycorrhizal fungi synthesize and release plant hormones that are absorbed by plant roots. The study of microbially derived plant hormones and their regulatory effects on plant growth and development are active areas of research in soil science.

Effect of Organic Matter on Soil Fertility: The Carbon-to-Nitrogen Ratio

Because organic matter is known to improve soil fertility, it is often added to garden soils in large amounts. Nevertheless, adding organic matter to garden soil may not improve soil fertility immediately. The cyclical relationship between the activities of decomposers (saprophytic fungi and bacteria) in the soil and the availability of nitrate nitrogen (NO_3^-) to plants is illustrated in figure 3.8. The ratio of carbon to nitrogen (C:N) is the amount of carbon versus the amount of nitrogen present in soil organic matter. In most productive soils, this ratio is fairly constant, varying from about 10:1 to 12:1, which means that the carbon level is about 10 to 12 times the nitrogen level.

Figure 3.8

The cyclical relationship between activities of decomposers and nitrate-nitrogen levels in soils when organic residues with a high carbon to nitrogen ratio are incorporated into the soil.

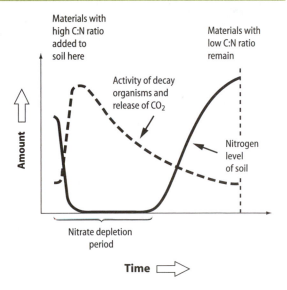

Materials with high C:N ratio added to soil here

Materials with low C:N ratio remain

Activity of decay organisms and release of CO_2

Nitrogen level of soil

Amount

Nitrate depletion period

Time

Garden plants and soil microorganisms need carbon and nitrogen to grow. The level of carbon in the soil, even though it exceeds the level of nitrogen, is an important limiting factor in controlling microbial populations. What happens when undecomposed organic matter, such as leaf litter, bark, straw (C:N = 80:1), or sawdust (C:N = 500:1) (table 3.3) is added to the soil or when the plant residues from the previous crop are left to decay in the soil? The decomposers in the soil receive a bonanza food supply that is carbon-rich, with a C:N greater than 10:1 to 12:1. When undecomposed organic residues with a high C:N—such as leaf litter, straw, or sawdust—are added to the soil, the populations and activities of decomposers increase first, and nitrogen becomes a limiting factor. The decomposers multiply and feed on the decaying organic matter that was added, incorporating the nitrogen in the organic material into their own body tissues as well as robbing the soil of inorganic nitrogen, so that the levels of nitrogen in the soil available to plants are reduced, as shown in figure 3.8. The microbes compete directly with the garden plants for inorganic nitrogen (NH_4^+) and (NO_3^-).

Therefore, it is best to add an inorganic nitrogen fertilizer to the soil when undecomposed organic residues that have a high C:N are incorporated just before planting or during plant growth. The length of the NO_3^- depression period depends on the types of organic residues added to the soil. As the process of humus formation nears completion and many of the decomposers die and their activities decrease, the NO_3^- levels in the soil increase (see fig. 3.8) because another group of bacteria, the nitrifiers, feed on the decaying bodies of the decomposers and convert the organic nitrogen in their dead body tissues into NO_3^-, an inorganic form that garden plants can use. In time, the soil should become more fertile and more productive because nitrogen availability to plants increases. Soil structure may improve because of the synthesis of humus.

When organic matter with a high C:N is applied to the soil surface as a mulch (which means that it is not incorporated into the soil), nitrogen deficiency as shown in figure 3.8 is not usually a problem. Organic mulches can also reduce weeds and retain soil moisture.

What happens when organic residues with a low C:N (less than 25:1) are incorporated into the soil? They decompose rapidly; nitro-

Table 3.3

CARBON-TO-NITROGEN (C:N) RATIO OF GREEN AND BROWN COMPOSTING INGREDIENTS

Ingredient	C:N
GREENS	
alfalfa hay	12:1
food wastes	15:1
grass clippings	19:1
rotted manures	20:1
fruit wastes	35:1
BROWNS	
cornstalks	60:1
leaves	60:1
straw	80:1
sawdust	500:1
wood	700:1

gen levels will not be limiting; and the decomposition process will release nitrogen from organic matter in mineral (inorganic) forms (both NH_4^+ and NO_3^-) that garden plants can absorb. A NO_3^- depression period does not occur.

Backyard composting, which is explained later in this chapter, lowers the C:N of undecomposed organic matter residues, such as tree leaves, grass clippings, and other plant wastes from the garden. Composting consists of storing the organic residues in a pile and maintaining levels of moisture, aeration, and temperature favorable for decomposition. As the organic residues decompose, much of the carbon, hydrogen, and oxygen are released as water (H_2O) and carbon dioxide (CO_2), but important plant nutrients, such as nitrogen, are conserved. The loss of carbon and conservation of nitrogen in the compost pile results in a narrowing of C:N. The decomposed organic matter that derives from composting can be incorporated into the soil without the nitrogen depletion problems shown in figure 3.8, or it can be used as an organic mulch on the soil surface.

The length of time it takes for fresh organic matter to become compost depends on the composition and condition of the materials in the pile and the management practices of the gardener, as explained in the next section. The general rule of thumb is that the pile needs to be warm, aerated, and moist and comprise nearly equal proportions of chopped green, fresh material (grass clippings, kitchen scraps) and dry, brown materials (straw, paper, dry leaves) (see table 3.3). The end products of decomposition for all plant materials are H_2O, CO_2, and minerals important to plant nutrition and soil fertility.

Rapid Backyard Composting

Composting is a process in which organic substances are reduced from large volumes of rapidly decomposable materials to small volumes of materials that continue to decompose slowly. In this process, the ratio of carbon to other elements is brought into balance, avoiding temporary immobilization of nutrients. One of the many benefits of adding compost to the soil is that the nutrients in compost are released slowly to the soil and are then available for use by plants. Decomposition occurs in soil if undecomposed organic materials are added to it, but, in the breakdown process, nutrients may be unavailable for plants, and certain phytotoxic compounds may be generated. Nutrient deficiencies and poor growth may result, especially if large amounts of undecomposed materials are added.

The traditional method of composting was to pile organic materials and let them stand for about a year, at which time the materials would be ready for use. The main advantage of this method is that little working time or effort is required from the composter. Disadvantages are that space is used for an entire year; some nutrients might leach out because of exposure to rainfall; disease-producing organisms, some weeds, weed seeds, and insects are not controlled; and odors may develop.

A new "backyard" method addresses some problems associated with traditional composting. Backyard compost can be made, on the average, in 4 to 6 weeks with this new process. With extra effort, the backyard composting process can take as little as 14 days. For gardeners interested in converting organic materials that are usually wasted into a valuable soil amendment, composting is worthwhile. Several factors and concepts are essential to success in rapid backyard

composting. All are important; there is no significance to the order of presentation here.

Material will compost best if pieces are ½ to 1½ inches (12 to 37 mm) in size. Soft, succulent tissues need not be chopped into very small pieces because they decompose rapidly. Harder or more woody tissues need to be divided into smaller pieces to decompose rapidly. Woody material should be put through a chopper or shredder. Most grinders chop herbaceous materials too finely for good composting. Chopping material with a sharp shovel is effective. When plants are pruned, the material can be cut into small pieces with the pruning shears. It takes a little effort but the results (and the exercise!) are worthwhile. Other alternatives for cutting materials into small pieces include running them through a lawn mower or placing them in a trash can and using a weed whacker or string-line weed trimmer.

For the composting process to work most effectively, the material to be composted should have a C:N of 30:1. This cannot be measured easily, but experience has shown that mixing equal volumes of green plant material with equal volumes of naturally brown plant material will give a C:N of about 30:1 (see table 3.3). All composting ingredients generally fall under one of two categories, *browns* or *greens*. Browns are dry materials such as wood chips, dried leaves, dried grass, straw, and prunings. Greens are fresh, moist materials such as grass cuttings and food scraps (avoid meats, fats, and grease), weeds, and manures (see comments about weeds at the end of this section). Contrary to popular opinion, eucalyptus and oleander can go into a compost pile; decomposition will detoxify them. Greens may be easier to find in fall and early spring. Paper bags, cardboard egg cartons, cereal boxes, and paper can be used for browns, but they must be finely chopped or shredded. Cartons should be washed before adding to the compost pile. Milk cartons can be composted. Newspapers can be used if shredded and thoroughly mixed with plant tissues to prevent matting, which excludes the oxygen necessary for rapid decomposition. Some greens, such as grass clippings, also may mat if dry materials are not used to separate them.

An optimal compost pile is about 3 to 4 feet (0.9 to 1.2 m) square. Larger piles tend to hold moisture better and decompose faster.

Equal amounts of browns and greens should be placed in a heap or bin, and food scraps should always be covered with other composting materials. The pile should be soaked with water to create uniform dampness—damp as a wrung-out sponge—and covered with a tarp or other material to retain moisture and to prevent oversoaking from rain.

Heat accelerates composting and is supplied by the respiration of microorganisms as they break down the organic materials. To conserve heat, a minimum volume of material is essential: a pile at least 36 × 36 × 36 inches (90 × 90 × 90 cm) is recommended. If each measurement is less than 32 inches (80 cm), the rapid process will not occur. Because heat retention is better in bins than in open piles, bins promote rapid composting. In addition, bins are neater. High temperatures favor the microorganisms that are the most rapid decomposers. These microorganisms function at about 160°F (71°C), and a good pile will maintain itself initially at about that temperature. A good compost pile starts at a high temperature that gradually tapers off. In

the Los Angeles County Cooperative Extension Backyard Composter Program, piles typically reach temperatures of 135° to 150°F (58° to 66°C). The higher temperatures are common for the first week and can even extend into the second week, but after that, temperatures drop to about 130°F (55°C) and lower. By the sixth week, temperatures are typically about 90°F. A composting thermometer (about 20 inches [50 cm] long) can be helpful for measuring temperature inside the pile. Thermometers can be purchased from gardening catalogs or local nurseries and home centers. Insects do not usually survive the composting process. Some may be attracted to the pile, but if they lay their eggs in the compost, its heat will destroy them.

Turn the compost to prevent overheating. If the compost gets much warmer than 160°F (72°C), the microorganisms will be killed, the pile will cool, and the whole process will have to start from the beginning. Turning the pile also aerates it, which is necessary to keep the most active decomposers functioning.

Turn the pile so that material on the outside is moved to the center, allowing all the material to reach optimal temperature at various times. Because of heat loss around the margins, only the central portion of the pile is at the optimal temperature. It is desirable to have two bins so the material can be turned from one into another. Bins that can be moved section by section and bins with removable slats in the front make the turning process easier (fig. 3.9). Bins with covers retain heat better than those without them. Once the decomposition process starts, the pile becomes smaller and, because the bin is no longer full, some heat is lost at the top. Heat loss can be prevented by placing a piece of polyethylene plastic directly on the top of the turned compost and tucking it in around the edges.

Longer intervals between turning lengthen the time to compost completion. Turning the pile every 3 to 10 days results in finished compost in 4 to 6 weeks. If the pile is turned every other day, composting may take about 3 weeks. If the pile is turned every day, composting may take as little as 2 weeks.

Monitoring the moisture content of the pile is essential because piles will dry out because of the high temperatures they attain. Composting works best if the moisture content of materials is about 50 percent. This is not easy to measure, but it has been estimated to be

Figure 3.9

Home-built compost box designed by the Backyard Composter Program, Los Angeles County Common Ground Garden Program, UC Cooperative Extension.

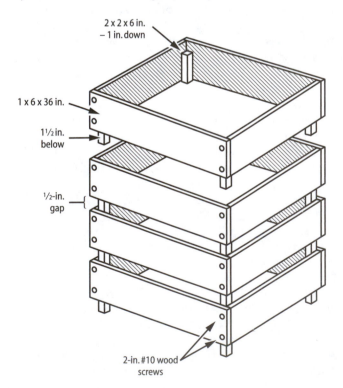

2 x 2 x 6 in. – 1 in. down

1 x 6 x 36 in.

1½ in. below

½-in. gap

2-in. #10 wood screws

about the moisture content of a wrung-out sponge. Too much moisture makes a soggy mass, and decomposition will be slow and smelly. If the organic material is too dry, decomposition will be very slow or will not occur at all. When turning the pile, moisten each layer of compost using a spray nozzle for uniform coverage.

If greens and browns are mixed properly, only water needs to be added to a compost pile. Nothing else needs to be added to promote decomposition. The microorganisms active in the decomposition process are ubiquitous, and their populations grow rapidly in any compost pile.

Once a pile is started, add only water. Do not add new materials, because the organic materials need time to break down and added material must start the process anew, lengthening decomposition time for the whole pile. Excess materials should be kept as dry as possible during storage until a new pile is started. Moist materials will start to decompose and will not be effective in the next compost pile.

If constructed correctly, a pile will heat to high temperatures within 24 to 48 hours. If it does not, the pile is too wet or too dry or there is not enough green material (or nitrogen) present. If the pile is too wet, the material should be spread out to dry. If it is too dry, add moisture. If neither of these is the problem, then the nitrogen is low (high C:N), which can be corrected by adding more greens or nitrogen (N) fertilizer. If necessary, add nitrogen fertilizer at the rate of ½ percent of the volume of the composting material. For example, a compost pile weighing about 20 pounds (9 kg) per cubic foot requires 1 pound (0.454 kg) N every 10 cubic feet of material, the equivalent of 5 pounds (2.27 kg) ammonium sulfate (21% N) or 3 pounds (1.35 kg) ammonium nitrate (33% N). It is essential to place the organic material in layers together with the fertilizer.

If the C:N is less than 30:1, the organic matter decomposes very rapidly but nitrogen is given off as ammonia. The odor of ammonia in or around a composting pile indicates that valuable nitrogen is being lost in the air. Adding sawdust to the pile counteracts the nitrogen loss because sawdust is very high in carbon and low in nitrogen (high C:N). If sawdust is difficult to obtain, shredded leaves or paper should achieve the same objective.

Rapid decomposition can be detected by a relatively pleasant odor, by the heat produced (visible as water vapor given off during the turning of the pile), by a reduction of volume, and by the change in color of the materials to dark brown.

As composting nears completion, the temperature drops and, finally, little or no heat is produced. Within 6 weeks, temperatures typically drop off to 90°F (32°C). Although the compost is then ready to use, the compost should remain in the pile to cure for up to 2 weeks. If, in the preparation of the compost, the material was not chopped in small pieces, screening the material through 1-inch (2.5-cm) mesh chicken wire will hold back larger pieces, which can be added to the next pile where they eventually will decompose.

The following materials should NOT be added to a compost pile.

- Soil. Soil adds nothing but weight to a compost pile and will discourage the turning of the pile that is necessary for the rapid composting process.

- Ashes from a stove or fireplace. Because most soils in California have a basic pH and wood ashes are basic, they should not be added to a compost pile or to the soil. Wood ashes do not decompose.

- Meat, fat, or cooked fruits and vegetables. Raw fruits and vegetables, peelings, and egg shells are perfect for the compost pile, but many cooked foods, meat, and fat should not be added.

- Manure from meat-eating animals as well as human waste. Manure from carnivorous animals such as dogs, cats, lions, tigers, etc., could contain disease-producing organisms that might infect humans. Because the rapid composting process may not kill these organisms, such manures should not be used. Manures from herbivorous animals such as rabbits, goats, cattle, horses, elephants, or fowl can be used, but such manures are not essential for making compost. You can make compost without adding any manure to the pile.

- Certain seed-bearing weeds. Most weeds and weed seeds are killed by the high temperatures of the pile, but not all. Some weeds, such as oxalis bulbs, seeds of burr clover, some amaranthus seeds, and seeds of cheeseweed, are not killed. Exclude seed-bearing weeds from the pile to reduce the potential spread of weeds.

■ Plant materials that look diseased. Performed correctly, rapid composting kills most, but not all, plant disease–producing organisms; it does not inactivate heat-resistant viruses such as tobacco mosaic virus. Examine greens for evidence of viral diseases and exclude them from the pile.

Table 3.4 mentions some possible causes and solutions to common composting problems.

Soil Water

Soil water occupies the pore space not occupied by soil air (see fig. 3.1). Soil water is the solvent in which plant mineral nutrients are dissolved to form the soil solution, and it serves to transport these nutrients to plant roots where they are taken up to meet plants' nutritional needs for growth and development. Many other minerals and compounds are dissolved in the soil solution.

How water acts in soil—how it moves and how it is held—is a complex subject that requires an understanding of physics and chemistry. Only the most basic concepts are introduced here. Suppose you add a cup of water to your favorite house plant or vegetable in the garden. The water enters the pore spaces between the soil particles. Does it just move downward? Do the plant roots absorb the whole cup of water over the next few days? Is all the water available to plant roots? The answer is that not all the water contained in soils is available to plants. The forces of attraction between water molecules are known as *cohesion* (mainly the result of hydrogen bonding), and the forces of attraction between soil particles and water molecules are known as *adhesion*. Soil water is said to be adsorbed

Table 3.4

TROUBLESHOOTING COMPOSTING PROBLEMS

Problem	Possible causes	Solution
rotten odor	not enough air; excess moisture (anaerobic conditions)	turn pile; add dry, porous materials such as dry leaves, sawdust, wood chips, or straw
	compaction	turn pile or make it smaller
ammonia odor	excess greens (nitrogen)	add browns (carbon), such as dry leaves, wood chips, or straw
low pile temperature	pile too small	enlarge pile or insulate sides
	insufficient moisture	add water while turning pile or cover top
	poor aeration	turn pile
	lack of greens (nitrogen)	mix in greens, such as grass clippings, manure, or food scraps
	cold weather	increase pile size or insulate pile with an extra layer of material such as straw
high pile temperature (>140°F, 60°C)	pile too large	reduce pile size
	insufficient ventilation	turn pile
pests (insects, rats, raccoons)	presence of meat scraps or fatty food waste	remove meat and fatty foods from pile; cover with a layer of soil, leaves, or sawdust; use an animal-proof compost bin; turn pile to increase temperature
pile is damp and warm only in the middle	pile too small	make pile bigger

onto the soil particle surfaces. The water closest to a soil particle is held very tightly by the forces of adhesion, preventing the water from being available to plants. Adhesion is greatest at the soil-water interface and decreases with distance from soil particles. Both cohesion and adhesion give rise to capillary forces that hold soil water against the force of gravity and are largely responsible for upward and lateral movements of soil water.

The roots of crop plants must "pull" water away from other water molecules—they must compete with the forces of cohesion—to supply plant needs for water. The total pore volume (porosity) of a soil and the size of a soil's pores play important roles in the availability of water to plants because they determine how much water the soil will hold (the water-holding capacity) and how tenaciously the water is held. The forces of cohesion and adhesion are much stronger in finer-textured soils, such as clay, because of their smaller individual pore sizes, smaller particle size, larger total pore volume, and the negative charges on clay minerals, which strongly attract the positive charges on the hydrogen ions (H^+) in water. Conversely, coarse-textured soils, such as sands, have larger mineral particles, larger pores, smaller total pore volumes, lesser amounts of clay, and lesser forces of cohesion and adhesion. Their water-holding capacity is much less than that of a clay soil.

Plants are able to pull water from soil primarily because there is a continuous stream of water molecules flowing from the root tip to leaf via the transpiration process, as discussed at the beginning of chapter 2, "Introduction to Horticulture." For every water molecule that exits the leaf, one is pulled into the root from the soil by capillary forces in the plant's vascular system. Because plant roots must exert force to extract soil water, scientists measure soil water not only in terms of total quantity (soil moisture content) but also in terms of forces, which are measured in units of pressure or tension called *atmospheres* or *bars*.

Water Availability

As a result of rain or irrigation, water surrounds the soil particles as films of water. With continued irrigation, the water films surrounding each soil particle thicken. The water closest to the soil particles is held very tightly by forces of adhesion and is not available to

plants. When the soil is irrigated adequately, the water farthest away from each soil particle is held loosely. The downward force of gravity acts to pull away the loosely held water beyond the root zone. The soil is said to be *saturated* when all of the pores are filled with water, and the *soil moisture tension* (SMT) is 0 bars. *Gravitational water* is the water that drains freely from the soil because of the downward force of gravity. The water that remains in the root zone does so because the forces of cohesion and adhesion are stronger than the downward pull of gravity.

Field capacity (FC) is the maximum amount of water that a soil can hold against the downward force of gravity when excess water has been applied to the soil. According to textbooks, a soil at FC holds water at a tension of ⅓ bar. The FC can also be measured in terms of the moisture content of the soil. The texture of the soil, its structure, and organic matter content influence the amount of water held at FC and the amount of plant-available water in a given soil. Sandy soils hold less water at FC than clay soils, for example. Soil texture is the property most responsible for water availability at FC. The amount of water held at FC can be changed slightly with the addition of organic amendments and improved soil management practices. The *permanent wilting percentage* (PWP) is the percentage of water in the soil when plants wilt permanently and the soil cannot supply water at a rate sufficient to maintain plants. At PWP, soil water is held at 15 bars. According to textbooks, plant-available water is soil water held between ⅓ bar (FC) and 15 bars (PWP). In practice, plant-available water is held at a tension of ¹⁄₁₀ bar in coarse-textured soils, and more than 90 percent of plant-available water is extracted from a soil when SMT reaches 1 bar. The majority of soil water is held at an SMT of ⅓ to 1 bar for medium- and fine-textured soils. Figure 3.10 depicts plant-available water as a function of soil texture, and table 3.5 provides average plant-available water data for five soil textural classes, paralleling figure 3.10.

Table 3.5 shows that FC increases as clay content increases. At FC (an SMT of ⅓ bar), clay holds the greatest amount of water followed by clay loam, silt loam, loam, and fine sand. At FC, sands can vary from 5 to 10 percent water, but a clay loam can vary from 25 to 35 percent water (g H_2O/100 g soil). But along with the increased moisture content at

Figure 3.10

Plant-available water as a function of soil texture.

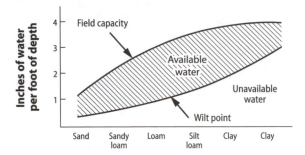

absorb it quickly enough to maintain optimal growth and health. Most plants grow best at SMT of ⅓ to ½ bar. If the soil is at FC or wetter for long periods, insufficient oxygen is available in soil pores for efficient respiration and other vital plant functions. As SMT exceeds ½ bar, however, it becomes more and more difficult for plant roots to extract enough water to support maximum growth. It is generally acceptable for SMT to be significantly less than ⅓ bar for a day or two after irrigation or rainfall and for SMT to reach or slightly exceed ½ bar just before irrigation or rainfall. A device known as a tensiometer is sometimes used in commercial horticulture operations to measure SMT so that irrigation needs can be accurately monitored.

However, a tensiometer is not necessary to measure SMT in the garden. Dig a hole at the location and depth to be tested. If the soil sample does not form a ball when it is compressed, the soil is too dry, and SMT is most likely greater than 1 bar. If the soil sample forms a ball that crumbles easily when thumb pressure is applied, the SMT is probably adequate if the soil is from an appropriate depth in the root zone. If the ball glistens and will not disintegrate and crumble under thumb pressure, the soil is too wet and the SMT is probably less than FC, which means that very few pore spaces are filled with air. The plant roots may be waterlogged and starved for oxygen. This technique for interpreting soil moisture is discussed in detail in chapter 4, "Water Management."

FC, a greater amount of water is held at the PWP. At the PWP, clay soil holds more water unavailable to plants than does the clay loam (14.7 versus 10.2 g H_2O/100 g soil). Figure 3.10 and table 3.5 illustrate that a clay loam soil actually has more plant-available water than a clay soil. In other words, fine-textured soils have the maximum total water-holding capacity, but medium-textured soils have the maximum plant-available water.

Adding organic matter to sandy soils increases the amount of plant-available water by encouraging aggregation and reducing the volume of some of the large pores so that they can hold water against the downward force of gravity. Addition of organic matter to fine-textured soils also encourages aggregation and increases the plant-available water by increasing the number of pores that are large enough to permit water extraction by plant roots but still small enough to hold the water against the force of gravity.

For gardening purposes, enough water should be available so that plant roots can

Water Balance

Scientists use specific terms to describe water inputs, movement, and losses from soil. Water inputs include natural rainfall (precipitation)

Table 3.5

SOIL MOISTURE CHARACTERISTICS OF FIVE SOIL TEXTURES. VALUES ARE PERCENT WATER EXPRESSED AS GRAMS OF WATER PER 100 GRAMS OF SOIL.

Soil texture	Permanent wilting percentage (PWP)	Field capacity (FC)	Plant-available water (FC minus PWP)
fine sand	1.7	6.8	5.1
loam	6.8	18.1	11.3
silt loam	7.9	19.8	11.9
clay loam	10.2	26.5	16.3
clay	14.7	28.6	13.9

and irrigation. Water losses include transpiration, evaporation, runoff, and leaching. *Irrigation* is the artificial application of water to soil, usually applied when rainfall is insufficient for crop growth. Not all of the rainfall or irrigation water penetrates the soil. Some water is lost as vapor (gas) and as a liquid. *Transpiration* is water vapor lost at leaf surfaces through stomates, and *evaporation* is water vapor lost at the soil surface. The two vapor losses can be combined in the term *evapotranspiration*. The home gardener has little control over transpiration but can reduce evaporation losses by applying, at the soil surface, mulches (straw, peat, gravel, wood chips, or opaque plastic sheeting) that act as physical barriers to evaporation. When water evaporates, the salts that were dissolved in it remain in the soil. The hot, dry climate in many areas of California favors water evaporation and subsequent salt accumulation in the root zone. Overwatering or excess rainfall can result in liquid water loss (rather than vapor) because of runoff and leaching. *Runoff*, which is water lost as it flows along the soil surface, can lead to soil erosion because the water carries small soil particles with it. *Leaching* is the loss of water, dissolved plant nutrients, and salts that move downward in the soil profile beyond the root zone. When water moves into the soil, it is called *infiltration*, whereas movement of water through the soil is called *percolation*, which is often accompanied by leaching.

Soil Fertility and Plant Nutrition

A fertile soil contains nutrient elements in amounts favorable for optimal growth of crop plants and in a chemical form that crop roots can absorb (a plant-available form, usually inorganic). Plant nutrition is a plant's need for and use of 17 chemical elements for growth and development. Plant nutrition and fertilization are two distinct concepts that should not be confused. Fertilization is the application of plant nutrient elements to the environment around a plant to meet its nutritional needs. Fertilizers and fertilization are discussed later in this chapter.

Essential Plant Nutrients
Today 17 nutrient elements are known to be essential for plant growth and development

(table 3.6). Of the 17 essential nutrients, 3 are taken from the air and water, and the other 14 are absorbed from the soil by plant roots. As the source of the majority of necessary plant nutrients, soil solids are critical to plant health. All 17 elements are equally essential for plant growth and development, but the 14 derived from the soil are divided into three categories based on the relative amounts required: primary nutrients, secondary nutrients, and micronutrients (see table 3.6). The primary and secondary nutrients (also referred to as macronutrients) are measured on a percent (parts per 100) dry-weight tissue basis. Most of the micronutrients are measured on a parts per million (ppm) dry-weight basis. For example, a typical analysis of a dried leaf from a healthy tomato plant might yield 3 percent nitrogen, 1 percent potassium, 100 ppm iron, and 100 ppm boron. The number of essential plant nutrients may increase in the future as scientists discover new information about the mineral nutrition of plants. For example, the micronutrient nickel is required in such small concentrations (50 to 100 parts per billion [ppb]) that it was not identified as an essential plant nutrient until 1987. The list of chemical forms of the nutrients commonly absorbed by plants given in table 3.6 will probably be updated. Plants cannot absorb the essential nutrient elements from the soil in complex organic (carbon-containing) forms or in complex inorganic combinations.

Essential nutrients are usually absorbed with soil water, which can be passively or actively taken up by plant roots. Passive diffusion of water occurs when the salt concentration inside the roots and surrounding cortical tissue is higher than the salt concentration in the soil solution. Essential nutrients dissolved in the soil solution can be carried along with this passive flow of water. Active absorption of water and nutrients can occur when roots expend energy from respiration (see chapter 2, "Introduction to Horticulture").

Hunger Signs in Plants
Since Greek and Roman times, the appearance of plants has been used to help identify their health status. Plants speak through distress signals. The message may be that there is simply too little or too much water, or the sign may tell of a disease caused by a microorganism, such as a fungus, virus, or bacterium. Plants may show symptoms of attack by nematodes, insects, or rodents, or injuries

from frost or lightning. The distress signals may also be linked to the nutritional status of a plant. Learning to recognize the general signs and symptoms of nutrient deficiency, toxicity, or imbalance can alert horticulturists and Master Gardeners to take appropriate steps to correct the problem.

Table 3.7 provides a brief overview of basic information about 17 essential nutrient elements. Soil fertilization techniques (discussed in this chapter) allow gardeners some control over the supply of soil nutrients to plants.

Although plants require much higher concentrations of primary and secondary nutrients (parts per 100 or percent) than micronutrients (parts per million or billion), all 17 essential elements need to be present for a healthy plant. An excess, deficiency, or even an imbalance of these elements leads to individual symptoms that can be generalized in most plants (see table 3.7). The most common nutritional problems in California are related to deficiencies of nitrogen, phosphorus, potassium, zinc, and iron and toxicity symptoms caused by excesses in boron, chlorine, and sodium. Symptoms are listed in table 3.7. Because most nutritional disorders of plants are difficult to diagnose from visual symptoms alone, tissue and soil analysis are often needed as well. In some instances, plants do not show symptoms of nutritional deficiencies until severe stress has occurred.

Table 3.6

ESSENTIAL PLANT NUTRIENTS

Element	Chemical symbol by crop plants	Chemical forms absorbed	Source
carbon	C	CO_2	air
hydrogen	H	H_2O	water
oxygen	O	O_2, H_2O	air, water
PRIMARY NUTRIENTS			
nitrogen	N	NO_3^-, NH_4^+	soil solids[*]
potassium	K	K^+	soil solids
phosphorus	P	$H_2PO_4^-, HPO_4^{2-}, PO_4^{3-}$	soil solids
SECONDARY NUTRIENTS			
calcium	Ca	Ca^{2+}	soil solids
magnesium	Mg	Mg^{2+}	soil solids
sulfur	S	SO_4^{2-}	soil solids
MICRONUTRIENTS[†]			
boron	B	BO_3^{3-}	soil solids
chlorine	Cl	Cl^-	soil solids
copper	Cu	Cu^+, Cu^{2+}	soil solids
iron	Fe	Fe^{3+}	soil solids
manganese	Mn	Mn^{2+}	soil solids
molybdenum	Mo	MoO_4^{2-}	soil solids
nickel	Ni	Ni^{2+}	soil solids
zinc	Zn	Zn^{2+}	soil solids

Notes:

[*]Some microorganisms that live in association with legume plant roots (*Rhizobia*, for example) can fix atmospheric nitrogen (N_2), converting it to inorganic forms, including ammonium ions (NH_4^+), which crop plants can absorb. In this case, it can be said that some plants obtain their essential nitrogen from the air in symbiotic relationship with soil microorganisms.

[†]The term *micronutrient* has been restricted to mean those elements known to be essential for the growth of higher plants that are needed in minute or trace quantities (ppm or ppb). Although the term *trace elements* is often used interchangeably with micronutrients, it has been used rather loosely in the scientific literature to describe elements with no known physiological function that may be toxic to plants and animals. Unfortunately, the terms *micronutrients, trace elements, microelements, heavy metals, trace metals,* and *trace inorganics* are used interchangeably. To avoid confusion, it is best to use the term *micronutrients* to refer to mineral elements that are essential for plant growth in trace quantities.

Table 3.7

CHARACTERISTICS OF ESSENTIAL PLANT NUTRIENTS SUPPLIED BY SOIL SOLIDS

Nutrient	Function and comments	Absorption and movement in soil	Symptoms of deficiency	Symptoms of excess
nitrogen (N)	A constituent of amino acids, proteins, enzymes, and chlorophyll; important in photosynthesis, metabolism, protoplasm reactions; a component of nucleic acids, the backbone of DNA; important for many growth and developmental processes.	Taken up by plants primarily as NO_3^- (nitrate), since it is mobile and moves with soil water to plant roots where absorption occurs. Plant roots can also absorb NH_4^+ (ammonium), but it is often bound to soil particle surfaces and cannot move as easily to the roots. Nitrogen in fertilizers is converted to NO_3^- by soil microorganisms. The nitrogen cycle and reactions in soil involving nitrogen are complex. Nitrogen leaches easily from the root zone. Deficiency symptoms begin in older tissue because nitrogen is mobile within plants and moves from older to younger tissue when in short supply. Several species of soil microbes fix atmospheric nitrogen (N_2), making it available to plants having a symbiotic relationship with them.	Slow growth, stunting, and yellow-green color (chlorosis); more pronounced in older tissue; "firing" of tips and margins (turning brown and dying); premature death.	Excessive vegetative growth, dark green color, excessive transpiration, reduced yield; delayed maturity; few fruits.
phosphorus (P)	Constituent of proteins, phospholipids, enzyme systems, and nucleic acids. Important for energy systems (ATP); stimulates early growth and root formation; promotes seed formation. Important in photosynthesis.	Depending on soil pH, phosphorus is absorbed by plants as $H_2PO_4^-$, or PO_4^{2-}, or PO_4^{3-}. Soil phosphorus is often tied up chemically in relatively insoluble compounds. Phosphorus fertilizer uptake is more efficient in the presence of nitrogen. Synergistic effect is seen in banded fertilizer applications.	Slow growth, stunting, and purplish color (anthocyanins) on foliage or dark green color; dying leaf tips; marginal interveinal chlorosis; delayed maturity; poor fruit or seed development.	Excess can interfere with micronutrient absorption; may mimic Zn deficiency.
potassium (K)	Affects membrane permeability and H^+ relationships, stomate opening/closing, internal water relations, cell division, starch and protein synthesis, and sugar translocation; increases size and quality of fruits and vegetables; increases disease resistance.	Taken up by plants as K^+. Unlike nitrogen and phosphorus, it is not synthesized into compounds in plants but instead stays as a simple ion in plant cells and tissues. Potassium is abundant in soils, but much of it is tied up in soil minerals and unavailable to plants.	Slow growth; leaf tip and marginal burn and necrosis (starts on more mature leaves); weak stalks (plants lodge); small fruit and shriveled seeds.	Light green foliage; tendency for Ca^{2+} and Mg^{2+} deficiency symptoms to appear.

Table 3.7 cont.

Nutrient	Function and comments	Absorption and movement in soil	Symptoms of deficiency	Symptoms of excess
calcium (Ca)	Regulates membrane permeability and cell integrity, cell acidity; promotes cell elongation; essential component of plant cell walls and membranes; believed to counteract the toxic effects of oxalic acid.	Absorbed by plants as Ca^{2+}. It has limited mobility in plants so young tissues show deficiency symptoms first. Often applied as a foliar spray on celery, apples, pears, and cherries. Excess calcium leads to high pH.	Reduced terminal growth of shoots (buds) and roots, resulting in plant death; blossom end rot of tomatoes, peppers, melons; pits on apples, pears; tip burn of young leaves in lettuce, cabbage.	Excess Ca^{2+} interferes with micronutrient availability.
magnesium (Mg)	Constituent of chlorophyll molecule; required cofactor in many enzymatic reactions; aids mobility and efficiency of phosphorus.	Absorbed by plants as Mg^{2+}. It is essential for photosynthesis because it is a constituent of the chlorophyll molecule. Most commonly used in fertilization of celery and citrus. Very mobile within plants and can easily translocate from older to younger tissue under deficiency conditions.	Marginal necrosis and interveinal chlorosis, beginning in older leaves; leaves curl upward along margins; marginal yellowing with green "Christmas tree" area along midribs of leaves.	Excess Mg^{2+} interferes with uptake of Ca^{2+}.
iron (Fe)	Essential for chlorophyll synthesis, stability; catalyst in respiration, photosynthesis, nitrogen fixation; important in cell division.	Taken up by plants as Fe^{3+}. Iron deficiency is common in western soils and can be due to high pH, poor aeration, high Mn concentrations, and lime. Turf, certain trees, and ornamentals are especially susceptible to iron deficiency.	Interveinal chlorosis of young leaves; (veins remain green); twig dieback; reduced growth and death in severe cases.	Mimics P, Mn deficiency.
manganese (Mn)	Important enzyme catalyst in many metabolic reactions; catalyst with Fe in chlorophyll synthesis; role in chloroplast structure; promotes pigment and vitamin C synthesis.	Taken up by plants as Mn^{2+}. Excess Mn induces Fe deficiency. Commercial citrus usually requires foliar sprays of Mn with Zn. Other tree crops may show deficiencies.	Interveinal, marginal chlorosis of young leaves, but no sharp distinction between veins and interveinal areas as with Fe.	Mimics Fe deficiency; loss of foliage color, bronzing of leaf margins, necrotic areas.
zinc (Zn)	Important component of enzymes, including ones involved in zinc synthesis of plant hormones (auxins) that regulate growth and development; role in chlorophyll synthesis.	Taken up by plants as Zn^{2+}. It is the micronutrient most often deficient in the West. Citrus, other tree fruits, nuts, grapes, beans, onions, tomatoes, corn, rice, and cotton generally require zinc fertilization. Terminal growth areas are affected first.	Interveinal chlorosis on young leaves; decrease in stem length; rosetting of terminal leaves, reduced fruit bud formation; twig dieback after first year.	not known

Nutrient	Function and comments	Absorption and movement in soil	Symptoms of deficiency	Symptoms of excess
boron (B)	Role in differentiation of meristem cells; regulates carbohydrate (sugar) metabolism; formation of pectins, tissue lignification; facilitates Ca movement.	Taken up by plants as BO_3^{2-}. Intensive cropping has caused deficiencies to become more common. Like calcium, boron is not remobilized in plants once it is assimilated. Plants require a continuous supply at growing points. Deficiency symptoms are noted first in youngest tissues of plant.	Death of terminal growth (meristems); "witches'-broom"; thickened, curled, wilted, chlorotic leaves; soft, necrotic spots on fruits, tubers; reduced flowering; cell differentiation errors.	Rare except in inland deserts with high boron-contaminated water; marginal necrosis on grape leaves.
copper (Cu)	Cofactor in enzymatic reactions important in carbohydrate and protein metabolism; role in chlorophyll and vitamin A synthesis.	Taken up by plants as Cu^+ or Cu^{2+}. Fertilization is rarely needed in California. An exception may be tree crops and some plants growing on sandy or organic soils. Do not fertilize unless need has been established because copper can be highly toxic.	Stunted growth; dieback of terminal shoots in trees; poor pigmentation (carotenes) wilting, death of leaf tips; gum pockets, scabby rind on citrus.	Reduced growth; necrosis.
chlorine (Cl)	Required for photosynthesis; influences cell membrane permeability; prevents desiccation.	not known	Very rare; wilting, followed by chlorosis; branching of lateral roots; leaf bronzing.	Poor growth; marginal leaf necrosis.
molybdenum (Mo)	Required for nitrogen use. Needed for conversion of NO_3 into amino acids and for N_2 fixation; role in plant hormones.	Taken up by plants as the molybdate ion (MoO_4^{2-}). Deficiency symptoms are similar to nitrogen deficiency since molybdenum has a key role in nitrogen use by plants.	Stunting, reduced yield; lack of vigor, chlorosis; marginal scorching, cupping, rolling of leaves (whiptail of cauliflower).	not known
nickel (Ni)	Important enzyme component; important in nitrogen metabolism, especially during seed germination.	not known	Leaf tip necrosis.	Induces Fe and Zn deficiency; chlorosis symptoms.

Some excellent publications (with photographs) that will aid in identifying the hunger signs of plants can be obtained at nurseries and libraries. If a nutrient problem must be diagnosed, a commercial laboratory can perform a diagnostic test using the specimen tissue for around $50.00 per sample. If a cheaper diagnosis is desired, sweet corn can be planted as a bioindicator. Corn expresses deficiency symptoms very clearly and unambiguously if an essential nutrient is lacking.

Nutrient deficiencies and toxicities can sometimes be corrected by the addition of appropriate inorganic fertilizers, manures, and amendments and by soil and water management. For example, yellowing of leaves (chlorosis) can be a symptom of both overwatering and underwatering, as well as a symptom of nitrogen or sulfur deficiency. Iron chlorosis is associated with waterlogged conditions, and until irrigation is corrected, iron chlorosis will persist no matter how much iron chelate is applied to the soil. Appropriate water management is very important, especially if water is of poor quality (high in salts, chloride, sodium, or boron). When a plant transpires water through its leaves, any salts that were in the water are left behind. These salts can accumulate and cause toxicities if rainfall is inadequate or if the amount of irrigation water applied is insufficient to leach these salts below the root zone. In plants grown on well-managed soils, the deficiency and toxicity symptoms described in table 3.7 may never appear.

What appears to be a deficiency symptom, such as yellowish leaves, may sometimes be a normal occurrence for a plant. Subtropicals, such as lemon and avocado, often have yellowish leaves in the cooler parts of the year and then naturally green up when the weather gets warmer. It pays to know your plants before taking corrective action that may not be necessary.

Soil pH

The pH of a garden soil—its relative acidity or alkalinity—is important information because it influences numerous chemical reactions that occur in the soil, including the availability of the 17 nutrient elements essential for plant growth and development. The soil pH is a function of the hydrogen ion (H^+) concentration in the soil. The pH scale consists of 14

divisions from 1 to 14, with the value of 7 being neutral, 1 being most acidic, and 14 being most alkaline or basic. Like the scale for measuring earthquakes, the pH scale is logarithmic, not linear. A pH of 5.0 is 10 times more acidic than a pH of 6.0 and 100 times more acidic than a pH of 7.0. A pH of 7 means that alkalinity and acidity are equally balanced in the soil. Soils in California typically range from pH 5 to 8.5.

Most crops do best when the pH is slightly acidic to neutral (pH of 5.5 to 7.5) because mineral nutrients essential for plant growth that are derived from the soil are in chemical forms that plant roots can absorb in this pH range. At lower and higher pH, some nutrients form precipitates that are insoluble in water, which means that the nutrients will not dissolve in the soil solution and cannot be absorbed by plant roots. Even if the plant nutrients are present, they are unavailable to crop plants at extreme pH (less than 5 and greater than 9). Many plants exhibit deficiency symptoms unless soil pH is maintained near 6 to 8, but some plants prefer a more acid soil (e.g. azaleas, rhododendrons, and blueberries).

Soil pH is critical to plant growth not only because it affects the availability of essential nutrients (fig. 3.11) but also because it affects the solubility of detrimental or toxic mineral elements. For example, moderately to very acid soils (pH too low) may contain inadequate levels of plant-available nitrogen, phosphorus, potassium, sulfur, calcium, magnesium, and molybdenum, but they may also contain toxic levels of aluminum and manganese. Very alkaline soils (pH too high) are deficient in plant-available nitrogen, phosphorus, iron, and manganese but also may contain excessive concentrations of soluble salts or sodium, both of which are detrimental or toxic to plant growth.

The topsoil can lose calcium, magnesium, and potassium via leaching or removal by growing crops. With the loss of these particular cations, the soil can become more acidic. When the pH of a soil is too low, it can be adjusted upward by additions of lime (calcium carbonate, calcium hydroxide, calcium oxide, or dolomite, among others) or wood ashes. When the soil's pH is too high, it can be adjusted with additions of sulfur. The materials need to be incorporated into the rooting area (root zone) of the soil, and the process can take some time. Soil pH can increase

Figure 3.11

The effect of pH on plant nutrient availability

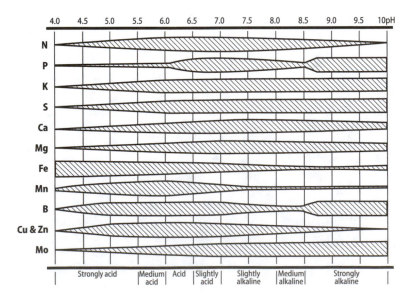

rather quickly after lime has been added to the soil, but it may take several months for sulfur to lower soil pH. Acidifying the soil usually takes longer because the conversion of sulfur to acid is mediated by soil microorganisms and depends on temperature and moisture.

A saline soil is a soil that has excessive soluble salts and (usually) a high pH in the root zone inhibiting plant growth. Saline soils can develop in the arid climates of California because evaporation of water vapor from the soil surface occurs more often than leaching, leaving the salts behind in the root zone. Saline soils typically develop surface incrustations of whitish-looking materials (salts) that are brought to the surface as water vapor evaporates. When the soil has a high concentration of soluble salts, pH is typically high and water tends to move from plant cells into the soil, causing crops to become dehydrated and wilt. Many ornamental plants are very susceptible to salinity. Saline soils should be irrigated with water beyond the amount required by the plants in order to wash away the excess salts from the root zone. The extra water is called the *leaching component* or *leaching fraction*. Organic and synthetic mulches on the soil surface can reduce evaporation, which also reduces the accumulation of salts in the root zone.

Other western soils, known as sodic soils, have pH readings that are too high (pH greater than 8.5) because of sodium (Na^+) accumulation alone without the presence of excessive concentrations of other salts. High concentrations of Na^+ are toxic to plants. Some soils are both sodic and saline. Gypsum (calcium sulfate) and sulfur are used to reclaim sodic soils. A common misconception is that gypsum lowers soil pH, but its major effect is to improve water infiltration of sodic soils or high-sodium irrigation water. Large amounts of water must be added to gypsum-treated sodic soils to leach away sodium displaced by gypsum. If excessive sodium is not present, adding gypsum will not improve water infiltration.

Fertilization of Garden Soils

Garden soils are rarely fertile enough to supply all of the nutrients required for the best growth of plants. It is equally rare, however, for a soil to be deficient in several of the mineral nutrients that plants need. Because California soils contain most of the elements known to be essential to plants, it is necessary to add only the ones that are deficient in a particular soil. In general, gardeners have a tendency either to underfertilize or overfertilize. Too little fertilization results in poor plant growth and appearance. Too much fertilization, regardless of the source, is unnecessarily expensive and may cause plant injury.

Types of Fertilizers

Commercially available inorganic fertilizers vary in the plant nutrients they contain. Table 3.8 provides an analysis of the primary nutrient content of common inorganic fertilizers. *Complete* inorganic fertilizers are mixes containing the three primary nutrients: nitrogen, phosphorus, and potassium. *Incomplete* fertilizers may contain a single nutrient material, such as ammonium nitrate, or double nutrient compounds, such as ammonium phosphate. The term *complete* should not be interpreted to mean that the fertilizer supplies all the nutrients a plant needs, nor should it be interpreted to mean that the primary nutrients are the only ones supplied in the fertilizer. In fact, the fertilizer may have constituents other than those listed on the label, but if their proportions cannot be guaranteed consistently, they are not listed.

By law, the guaranteed content of the fertilizer, expressed as a percentage of each plant nutrient supplied, must be stated on the bag. Under this labeling method, the first number shown is the percentage of nitrogen (N); the second is the percentage of phosphorus (P), expressed as P_2O_5 (phosphoric acid); and the third is the percentage of potassium (K), expressed as K_2O (potash) (see fig. 3.12). A 100-pound (45.4-kg) bag of a 12-12-12 grade fertilizer contains 12 pounds (5.45 kg) each of N, P_2O_5, and K_2O. The other 64 pounds in the bag is filler, which facilitates even spreading of fertilizer. (See the notes in table 3.8 about fertilizer grade and correcting for the elemental content of P and K.) If a secondary nutrient or micronutrient has been added to the fertilizer, then it must be listed on the bag with its guaranteed percentage. Sample calculations for applying fertilizer are given in figure 3.13.

Inorganic fertilizers are characteristically fast-acting and relatively low in cost per pound of actual nutrient. Some inorganic fertilizers,

Table 3.8

ANALYSIS* OF INORGANIC AND SYNTHETIC FERTILIZERS

Fertilizer	Formula	Nitrogen (N %)	Available phosphorus (P_2O_5 %)[†]	Potassium (K_2O %)[‡]
urea	$CO(NH_2)_2$	45	0	0
ammonium nitrate	NH_4NO_3	33.5	0	0
ammonium sulfate	$(NH_4)_2SO_4$	21	0	0
calcium nitrate	$Ca(NO_3)_2$	16	0	0
sodium nitrate	$NaNO_3$	16	0	0
ammonium phosphate	$NH_4H_2PO_4$ (mostly)	11	48	0
diammonium phosphate	$(NH_4)_2HPO_4$	18	46	0
superphosphate	$Ca_2H_2(PO_4)_2$	0	20	0
basic slag[§]	Ca, Mg, Al silicates	0	8	0
rock phosphate	$3Ca_3(PO_4)_2CaF_2$	0	5	0
muriate of potash	KCl	0	0	60
potassium sulfate	K_2SO_4	0	0	50
potassium nitrate	KNO_3	13	0	44
12-12-12	—	12	12	12
8-16-6	—	8	16	16
5-10-5	—	5	10	5
slow-release fertilizers	varies	varies	varies	varies

Source: Adapted from California Fertilizer Association 1990, pp. 127–129.

Notes:

*Sometimes the terms *analysis* and *grade* are used interchangeably. The term *grade* should be applied only to the three primary nutrients, N, P, and K. The fertilizer grade is expressed as the guaranteed percentage of nitrogen, phosphoric acid, and potash. For example, a 12-12-12 grade would contain 12% nitrogen, 12% available phosphate, and 12% potash. The ratio is the relative proportion of each of the primary nutrients. A 12-12-12 grade is a 1:1:1 ratio. A zero in a grade or ratio means that the particular nutrient is not present in that fertilizer.

[†]Phosphoric acid (P_2O_5) actually contains 43% phosphorus. The percentages given for the oxide can be converted to percentages of the element by multiplication: $P = P_2O_5 \times 0.43$.

[‡]Potash (K_2O) actually contains 83% potassium. The percentages given for the oxide can be converted to percentages of the element by multiplication: $K = K_2O \times 0.83$.

[§]Basic slag is a by-product of the steel manufacturing process that contains lime, phosphates, and small amounts of other plant nutrients, such as sulfur, manganese, and iron. Basic slags may contain from 10 to 17% phosphate (P_2O_5), 35 to 50% calcium oxide (CaO), and 2 to 10% magnesium oxide (MgO). The available phosphate content of most American slag ranges from 8 to 10%.

such as ammonium fertilizers, can acidify the soil (lower the pH) with long-term use. Because inorganic fertilizers are salts, key disadvantages are their potential to leach and burn crops if mismanaged. Slow-release nitrogen fertilizers are available at much higher cost, and their release rates are governed by environmental factors such as soil moisture content and temperature. Slow-release inorganic nitrogen is sometimes called water-insoluble nitrogen (WIN).

Manures are composed primarily of animal excrement, plant remains, or mixtures of both. When used correctly, manures can be a good organic garden fertilizer. They supply garden plants with many essential nutrients and can help improve soil structure. Until they decompose, manures supply plant nutrients in their carbon-containing, organic form. The general belief that plant or animal manures are better sources of plant nutrients than inorganic forms is not correct. For both sources to be beneficial to plants, their nutrients must be changed into chemical forms that plants can absorb and use, as shown in table 3.6. Because manures may contain undesirable weed seeds and relatively high amounts of salts, they should be used cautiously where weeds or salts could create problems. Apply manure by mixing it into the soil at least one month before preparing the soil for planting. Advance application allows time for partial rotting or decomposition of the manure and leaching of excess mineral salts from the root zone before planting.

Manures can vary greatly in nutrient content. Table 3.9 provides an average analysis of the primary nutrient content of common organic fertilizers without accounting for losses from leaching or decomposition. It is difficult to guarantee the analysis because it varies from season to season and according to the length of time the fertilizers have been exposed to decomposition. Manures are typically more complete than most inorganic fertilizers, because they contain many of the essential nutrients required for plant growth and development. Dry chicken manure is the most concentrated animal manure with respect to primary nutrients, and it can serve as the only garden fertilizer applied. Dairy manure is much less concentrated and usually has less nitrogen readily available to plants. Dairy manure may require additional commercial nitrogen fertilizer. Steer manure from animals fattened on concentrated feeds is richer in nutrients than dairy manure. If it has been handled to prevent nitrogen losses, it can usually be the sole source of nitrogen.

The recommended rates of manure application for fertilizing vegetables are given in chapter 14 under the heading "Fertilizers." If dairy or steer manure is used annually, decrease the amount applied each year. Use 70 percent the second year, 60 percent the third year, and 50 percent every year thereafter. Because two of the breakdown products of organic matter are ammonium ions (NH_4^+)

and carbon dioxide (CO_2)—or carbonic acid (H_2CO_3) when it is dissolved in water—repeated additions of various organic materials tend to lower the pH of soil over time.

The principal limitations of organic fertilizers are their bulk, availability, odor, potential salt and weed seed hazards, and expense per pound of nutrient. Organic concentrates—such as bonemeal, cottonseed, and fish emulsion—also contain a variety of nutrients, but their cost per pound of nutrients is high relative to inorganic fertilizers. The value of manures and organic concentrates does not lie solely in their nutritional value, however. Organic materials also have beneficial effects on the soil's physical properties, in which case they are classified as soil amendments. Organic amendments can decrease soil bulk density, improve water infiltration and nutrient-holding capacities, and often add small amounts of micronutrients.

When applying either organic fertilizers (manures) or inorganic fertilizers, use good judgment, based on local experience, to supply the necessary plant nutrients in the amounts needed. Many successful gardeners use a combination of inorganic and organic fertilizers. Regardless of which fertilizers you apply, use them efficiently to reduce cost, prevent plant injury, and to prevent unwanted changes in the environment, such as leaching of nitrogen.

Fertilizer or Amendment: Which One Is It?

Whether a material is considered a soil amendment or a fertilizer is usually determined by its effect on plant growth. Fertilizers affect plant growth directly by improving the supply of available nutrients in the soil. Amendments, on the other hand, influence plant growth indirectly by improving the soil's physical condition (e.g., soil tilth, water infiltration). The distinction between these two concepts is clear when you compare materials such as ammonium nitrate (a fertilizer) and gypsum (an amendment). It is more difficult to distinguish between amendments and fertilizers when evaluating natural or organic products. Animal manure, for example, easily falls into either category, depending on your reasons for applying it. Manure can be a source of readily available nutrients, but it can also supply significant quantities of organic matter, which improves soil aeration and water retention.

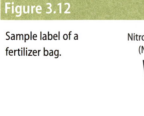

Figure 3.12

Sample label of a fertilizer bag.

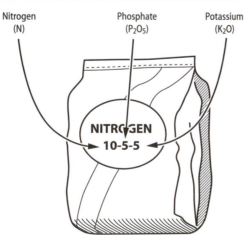

Nitrogen (N)

Phosphate (P_2O_5)

Potassium (K_2O)

NITROGEN
10-5-5

Figure 3.13

SAMPLE CALCULATIONS FOR APPLYING FERTILIZER

Problem 1: You have decided that 20 flower and shrub beds 10 x 10 feet each are to be fertilized at the rate of 2 lb nitrogen (N) per 1,000 sq ft with a 10-12-12 fertilizer that costs $15 for 100 lb.

How many pounds of fertilizer will be needed? How much will it cost?

Solution:
Find the total area to be fertilized.

> 10 x 10 feet per bed x 20 beds = 2,000 sq ft

Find the amount of fertilizer required (Note: the 10 lb N below is the amount of N in 100 lb of 10-12-12 fertilizer):

> (2 lb N ÷ 1,000 sq ft) x (100 lb fertilizer ÷ 10 lb N) x 2,000 sq ft = 40 lb fertilizer

Find the cost of the fertilizer required:

> 40 lb fertilizer x ($15 ÷ 100 lb fertilizer) = $6.00

Problem 2: How much 20-10-5 fertilizer would it take to apply 2 lb of phosphorus (P) per 1,000 sq ft to a 20 x 10 foot garden?

Solution:
Find the area to be fertilized:

> 20 x 10 feet = 200 sq ft

The fertilizer grade lists the phosphoric acid (P_2O_5) percentage (note that P_2O_5 is 43% P) ; we must find the amount of elemental P:

> (2 lb P ÷ 1,000 sq ft) x (100 lb fertilizer ÷ 10 lb P_2O_5) x (1 lb P_2O_5 ÷ 0.43 lb P) x 200 sq ft = 9.3 lb fertilizer

9.3 lb = 9 lb 4.8 oz. You can round to 9 lb or 9 lb + 1/2 cup (4 oz) + 1 tbsp (0.5 oz) + 2 tsp (0.33 oz) to be more precise. Be scant on the 2 tsp, or you will have applied 0.03 lb in excess (see the conversion tables at the end of this book).

Problem 3: How much ammonium sulfate would it take to apply 1 lb nitrogen (N) per 1,000 sq ft to a lawn that is 5,000 sq ft?

Solution:
The area to be fertilized = 5,000 sq ft
Ammonium sulfate is 21-0-0, containing 21% N:

> (1 lb N ÷ 1,000 sq ft) x (100 lb fertilizer ÷ 21 lb N) x 5,000 sq ft to be fertilized = 23.81 lb ammonium sulfate

You can round up to an application of 24 lb.

Problem 4: How much of a 20-4-10 liquid fertilizer would have to be applied to a 2,000-sq ft lawn to obtain a fertilization rate of 2 lb nitrogen (N) per 1,000 sq ft?

Solution:
Calculating the amount of liquid fertilizer to use is more difficult because the analysis is expressed as a percentage but the amount of fertilizer in the container is expressed on a volume basis.

First, determine the weight of a given volume of fertilizer and then calculate the weight of N, P, and K in that volume of fertilizer. One gallon of water weighs 8 lb. Assume we know that 1 gallon of this fertilizer weighs 11.5 lb.

> (2 lb N ÷ 1,000 sq ft) x (1 lb fertilizer ÷ 0.20 lb N) x (1 gal fertilizer ÷ 11.5 lb fertilizer) x 2,000 sq ft = 1.74 gal fertilizer

1.74 gal = 1 gal + 2.96 qt, or approximately 1 gal + 3 qt (see conversion tables in appendix B).

California state fertilizing materials law eliminates some of the confusion by defining specific quality standards and characteristics for the production and sale of these materials. Legal definitions of fertilizing materials can be found in *Fertilizing Materials Laws and Regulations* (California Department of Food and Agriculture 1992). Important legal definitions from that source include:

- *Packaged soil amendment.* Any substance distributed for the purpose of promoting plant growth or improving the quality of

crops by conditioning soil solely through physical means. This category includes all of the following: hay; straw; peat moss; leaf mold; sand; wood products; any product or mixture of products intended for use as a potting medium, planting mix, or soilless growing media; manures sold without guarantees for plant nutrients; or any other substance or product that is intended for use solely because of its physical properties.

- *Natural organic fertilizer.* Materials derived from either plant or animal products containing one or more nutrients other than carbon, hydrogen, and oxygen, which are essential for plant growth; which may be subjected to biological degradation processes under normal conditions of aging, rainfall, sun-curing, air drying, composting, rotting, enzymatic or anaerobic/aerobic bacterial action, or any combination of these; which shall not be mixed with synthetic materials or changed in any physical or chemical manner from their initial state except by physical manipulations such as drying, cooking, chopping, grinding, shredding, or pelleting.

- *Commercial fertilizer.* Any substance that contains 5 percent or more of nitrogen (N), available phosphoric acid (P_2O_5), or soluble potash (K_2O), singly or collectively, which is distributed in this state for promoting or stimulating plant growth. Commercial fertilizer includes both agricultural and "specialty" fertilizers.

- *Specialty fertilizer.* Any packaged commercial fertilizer labeled for home gardens, lawns, shrubbery, flowers, and other similar noncommercial uses. These products may contain less than 5 percent nitrogen, available phosphoric acid, or soluble potash, singly or collectively, detectable by chemical methods.

Table 3.9

ANALYSIS* OF ORGANIC FERTILIZERS

Fertilizer	Nitrogen[†] (N %)	Phosphorus[‡] (P_2O_5 %)	Potassium[§] (K_2O %)
BULKY ORGANIC MATERIALS			
chicken manure (dry)	2.00–4.50	4.60–6.00	1.20–2.40
steer manure (dry)	1.00–2.50	0.90–1.60	2.40–3.60
dairy manure (dry)	0.60–2.10	0.70–1.10	2.40–3.60
peanut hulls	1.50	0.12	0.78
sheep manure (fresh)	1.05	0.40	1.00
poultry manure (fresh)	1.00	0.85	0.45
horse manure (fresh)	0.65	0.25	0.50
grain straw	0.60	0.20	1.10
seaweed (kelp)	0.60	0.09	1.30
cattle manure (fresh)	0.55	0.15	0.45
sawdust and wood shavings	0.20	0.10	0.20
ORGANIC CONCENTRATES			
dried blood	13.0	1.5	2.5
hoof and horn meal	12.0	2.0	0
fish meal	10.0	6.0	0
soybean meal	7.0	1.2	1.5
fish scrap	5.0	3.0	0
bone meal	4.0	23.0	0
cocoa shell meal	2.5	1.5	2.5
wood ashes[//]	0	2.0	6.0

Notes:
*Analysis reported is an average for primary nutrients without accounting for losses caused by leaching or decomposition; 1 cubic foot of air-dry manure weighs about 25 pounds.

[†]Analysis based on dry weight except for fresh manures, which contain about 65% to 85% water.

[‡]Analysis based on dry weight except for fresh manures, which contain about 65% to 85% water. Phosphoric acid (P_2O_5) actually contains 43% phosphorus. The percentages given for the oxide can be converted to percentages of the element by multiplication: $P = P_2O_5 \times 0.43$.

[§]Analysis based on dry weight except for fresh manures, which contain about 65% to 85% water. Potash (K_2O) actually contains 83% potassium. The percentages given for the oxide can be converted to percentages of the element by multiplication: $K = K_2O \times 0.83$.

[//]Burning eliminates organic matter and forms inorganic compounds.

Nutrients Most Commonly Needed in Fertilizers

Because nitrogen is naturally low in almost all California soils, additional amounts are needed to ensure optimal plant growth. Nitrogen may be the only supplement necessary, however. The most prominent plant symptom of nitrogen deficiency is chlorosis (yellowing) of older leaves.

Phosphorus may be low in some highly weathered California soils, which are often reddish and have hardpan or claypan layers in the subsoil. Other soils may be low in available phosphorus because of long-term cropping or because of alkalinity, which makes soil phosphorus unavailable. Soil analysis can help to diagnose phosphorus deficiency; plant symptoms include stunting and purplish casts on leaves. Phosphorus is relatively immobile in soil.

Potassium is not needed in most gardens because California soils naturally contain this element. If there is any question, soil analysis can help to diagnose a potassium deficiency. Deficiency symptoms include scorching (firing or necrosis) along leaf margins of older leaves, slow growth, weak stems, and poorly developed root systems.

Iron deficiency is common when acid-loving plants are grown in alkaline soils. Symptoms include interveinal (between the veins) chlorosis in younger leaves. Iron deficiency can be corrected by acidifying the soil or using iron fertilizers (iron chelate or iron sulfate) according to package directions.

Zinc deficiency may occur in gardens where the surface soil has been removed during building and leveling operations. Soil analysis may help to diagnose a deficiency. Plant symptoms may include interveinal chlorosis in younger leaves, the growth of small leaves, and rosette formation (leaves clustered in a circular pattern near branch tips). Fertilizers containing zinc, such as zinc sulfate, zinc ammonium nitrate, or zinc chelate, can correct the problem.

Sulfur deficiencies are not widespread in California, but they may occur in areas with high rainfall (leaching) or with irrigation water containing little or no sulfur. Soil tests for sulfur deficiency may be difficult to interpret.

Commercial Fertilizer Application Methods, Rates, and Timing

Fertilizer application methods, rates, and timing should be matched to the nutritional needs of particular plants and to the nutrient deficiencies of the soil. The most effective strategy varies according to the specifics of the gardening situation. Fertilizers may be applied to the soil surface, below the soil surface (subsurface application), to the plant foliage (foliar application), through the irrigation system (chemigation), on mixed with certain pesticides. More than one application method may be appropriate during the growing season because plants may require multiple applications at different stages of growth and development. According to the *Western Fertilizer Handbook, Horticultural Edition* (California Fertilizer Association 1990), the following points should be considered when choosing the appropriate method of fertilizer application:

- rooting characteristics of the species being planted
- plant's demand for various nutrients at different stages of growth
- physical and chemical characteristics of the soil
- physical and chemical characteristics of the fertilizer materials being applied
- moisture availability
- type of irrigation system, if irrigation is the sole or major water source

Broadcasting. The broadcast method of applying fertilizer, which is effective for large lawn areas or garden plots, consists of uniformly distributing dry or liquid fertilizer materials onto the soil surface. Many home gardeners use a drop spreader or spinning-type spreader to facilitate uniform application of dry fertilizer. Before preparing the seedbeds for planting vegetables, annuals, or turfgrass, fertilizer may be broadcast and promptly worked into the soil to prevent nitrogen losses through ammonia volatilization. Broadcasting is an effective means of applying nitrogen and potassium to existing large gardens and turf areas but is not effective for applying phosphorus, which is immobile and must be incorporated into the soil to ensure uptake by roots.

All fertilizers that can be broadcast on the soil surface can be injected in a subsurface application. Injection requires special equipment, but it can be an excellent method of putting immobile nutrients into the root zone to allow for more efficient uptake by plant roots or to conserve nutrients that are lost when they are applied to the soil surface.

Band Placement. Band placement is a subsurface application method in which narrow bands of fertilizer are placed several inches to the side and/or below seeds or established plants. The plants, soil type, and fertilizer determine whether bands are placed to the side and below the seed or only directly below the seed. Fertilizer placed too close to seeds or transplants may damage roots or inhibit seed germination.

In vegetable gardens, an alternative to broadcasting is band placement at seeding time, as described in chapter 14, "Home Vegetable Gardening." Band applications of a phosphate-containing fertilizer at planting time may be more effective than broadcasting because phosphorus has limited mobility in the soil. With a band application, the phosphorus will be closer to the plant roots for uptake. Ammonium phosphate (16-20-0 or 11-48-0) or several of the complete fertilizers, such as 5-10-5, 8-16-16, or 12-12-12 are acceptable materials. Dig a shallow trench 2 to 4 inches (5 to 10 cm) to one side of the row and 2 to 4 inches (5 to 10 cm) below where the seed is to be placed. Place 1 to 2 pounds (0.45 to 0.9 kg) of fertilizer per 100 feet (30 m) of row in the bottom of the trench and cover it with soil. When using furrow irrigation, place the fertilizer band between the seed or plant row and the irrigation furrow. If sprinkler irrigation is used, band the fertilizer on either side of the row.

Sidedressing. A method appropriate at critical growth stages, sidedressing is the application of dry fertilizer beside actively growing plants to replace nutrients that have been leached or used up in the growth process. For example, after vegetable plants are well established and 3 to 4 inches (7.5 to 10 cm) tall, sidedressing with nitrogen is very effective at rates similar to those for banding fertilizer. The trench should be at least 4 inches (10 cm) from the side and below the plant row to prevent burning the roots. Subsequent irrigations will move the nitrogen into the root zone. Do not sidedress with large amounts of nitrogen after the vegetable plants have begun to mature because the fertilizer will encourage vegetative growth at the expense of fruiting and of storage organ production.

Foliar Applications. Applying fertilizer to plant leaves can correct micronutrient deficiencies. Spray the foliage using equipment like that used for pesticide application. Because plant response can be affected by droplet size and other technicalities, this method is not recommended for general fertilizer application. Attempting to supply macronutrients such as nitrogen in sufficient quantities with this method is very expensive and inefficient because only very small amounts of nutrient elements can enter a plant through leaf tissue. However, it is feasible to supply adequate amounts of certain formulations of micronutrients by this method. To fertilize vines and fruit and nut trees, certain nutrients can be applied to the foliage in combination with pesticide sprays during the latter part of the dormant season. Check labels for specific instructions regarding legal requirements and usage.

To fertilize newly planted trees, shrubs, vines, and ground covers, refer to the nitrogen fertilization recommendations (rate, frequency, and timing) in table 13.5.

Management of the Soil's Physical Properties

Optimal plant growth derives equally from favorable physical and chemical (soil fertility) environments. Depending on the intensity of management and the resources available, gardeners can employ many methods to improve the soil's physical characteristics. Garden soil in good physical condition (good tilth) can hold and provide adequate quantities of nutrients, water, and air to plant roots. It will also drain well when large quantities of water are applied and will be easy to work without becoming sticky when wet and crusted when dry. Poor tilth can be improved by organic matter amendments (compost, manure, sawdust, leaves, lawn clippings, or peat moss), which improve aeration and moisture conditions principally by improving structure (aggregation), porosity, and bulk density. Although such amendments may be impractical to use on large areas because of the expense, volume, or unavailability of material, recommended rates of application to garden areas for several organic materials are shown in table 3.10. Additional nitrogen may be needed when an organic material with a wide carbon-to-nitrogen ratio is used. (See related discussion under "Amending Landscape Soils: When and How.")

A permanent buildup of large amounts of organic matter in the soil is impossible because organic matter decomposes quickly. However, occasional addition of organic matter, either as plant residues or manures, ensures a continuous supply of energy for soil

Table 3.10

ORGANIC AMENDMENTS FOR IMPROVING GARDEN SOIL TILTH

Organic amendment	Amount to add per 100 sq ft	Synthetic nitrogen to be added in weight of amendment per 100 lb *
leaves	75 lb (3–4 bu)	0.50–1.0 lb
straw	60 lb (1 bale)	0.50–1.0 lb
hay, legume	60 lb (1 bale)	none
hay, grass	60 lb (1 bale)	0.25–0.50 lb
corncobs (ground)	50 lb (2 bu)	1.0–1.5 lb
sawdust	50 lb (2 bu)	1.25–1.5 lb
wood chips	50 lb (2 bu)	1.25–1.5 lb
compost	10–20 cu ft	none
peat moss	6–10 cu ft	none
lawn clippings	4 bu	none

Note: *1 lb nitrogen = 10 lb of 10-10-10 fertilizer or 3 lb of ammonium nitrate (33.5-0-0).

microorganisms. As the soil microbes decompose the organic matter, they convert it into inorganic nutrients that can be used by growing plants, and they also help to maintain good soil structure. Soil structure is improved through the process of decomposition, the release of compounds into the soil environment that cement small soil particles together.

Maintaining or improving soil structure is one of the most important phases of soil management in the garden. Cultivate or till your soil only when it has a medium moisture content and the soil crumbles easily. Working soil when it is too dry creates large clods or powdery dust, whereas working overly wet soil creates puddling or packing.

Compaction

Compaction can develop in almost all soils, although some soils seem more susceptible than others. Forces holding soil particles together in aggregates may not be strong enough to resist the crushing effect of heavy tillage equipment and excess traffic or the shearing effect that results from working the soil when its moisture content is too high. In the resulting compact soil mass, large pores have collapsed because the granular structure has been crushed. In the absence of large pores, water penetration becomes very slow. The small pores that are still present may fill slowly with water after irrigation, but they will drain even more slowly because water is held strongly by clay mineral surfaces. Thus, water movement to lower depths is very slow in compacted soils, and little or no air space is left. Feeder roots of most crops will die if deprived of air for only a few hours.

The more dense layers resulting from man-made soil compaction usually show up within the first foot of the surface. Compression by tillage equipment may cause some compaction as deep as 2 feet (60 cm) below the soil surface. Regardless of soil permeability beneath the compact layer, water cannot percolate or infiltrate faster than the limiting rate set by the restricted pore space in the compacted layer.

Compaction confounds the native bulk density of a soil. When pressure (foot traffic, a fallen tree, cultivating equipment) is placed on soil, especially wet soil, the pore space is compressed and the volume is reduced, increasing the bulk density. Although sandy soils have a higher bulk density than clay soils, the coarse-textured sandy soils are more resistant to compaction than the finer-textured clay soils because a compacted sandy soil of the same moisture content as a clay soil may only increase its bulk density to 1.8 grams per cubic centimeter whereas the clay soil's bulk density may increase to 2.0 grams per cubic centimeter. A surface soil will often have a higher bulk density than the subsurface soil because it has been compacted. Especially in hilly areas, a compacted surface leads to lower water-holding capacity and infiltration rate, which can lead to more rainfall runoff and erosion. One reason for cultivating is to reduce the bulk density of soil to make plant root penetration and water infiltration easier.

Preventing Soil Structure Breakdown

Although breakdown of structure within the upper foot of surface soil may be inevitable where land is intensively cultivated or where it has been disturbed during grading and construction, an understanding of soil texture and structure enables the gardener to apply soil cultural practices with a minimum of structural breakdown. Structural breakdown is easier to prevent than to cure, and the following recommendations will help prevent it.

■ Cultivate and plow soil at an intermediate moisture content—not too wet, not too dry.

- Avoid recompaction of freshly loosened or plowed soil. The less tillage and traffic after loosening the better.

- Reduce traffic, designate traffic areas, and keep trips over the soil to a minimum, especially when it is very wet.

Tillage stirs the soil and is useful for mixing in manures, fertilizers, composts, clippings, or other crop residues. It also temporarily loosens the soil and helps control weeds that compete with crops for moisture and plant nutrients. Frequent stirring or cultivation does not improve the soil, however, because soil loosened by cultivation usually returns to its original condition after one or two irrigations. It is usually unnecessary to spade or turn the soil more than once a season, even though rains or irrigations have beaten it down.

Till garden soil only for some useful purpose, such as turning under organic matter, controlling weeds, making irrigation furrows, or loosening a small amount of soil for planting seed. Some gardeners maintain the beds and irrigation furrows for several years and till only a narrow strip on top of the beds to plant seeds. To avoid packing garden soil, provide paths for walking and other traffic.

Rejuvenating Good Soil Structure

When compaction is severe, good soil structure can be rejuvenated. The following factors favor the formation of granular structure.

- Bacterial decomposition of plant residues produces gums that help to bond soil particles together.

- Planting fibrous-rooted cover crops (grasses) promotes pushing soil particles together, which yields aggregates with continuous pore spaces between them.

- Cycles of wetting and drying cause swelling and shrinking of soils, resulting in improved aggregation.

Amending Landscape Soils: When and How

Amending landscape soils is frequently considered essential to establishing new plantings and rejuvenating existing ones even though research findings indicate such practices are not beneficial, except in extreme situations.

Proper soil management is necessary to ensure survival of newly transplanted material and to maintain mature plants, but no amount of soil amendment will overcome poor initial design or improper horticultural management.

Sometimes the soil to be landscaped has been amended or modified to construct building foundations or roadways or to create new physical environments, such as hills or lakes. Unfortunately, such soil alterations are performed to engineering standards, not horticultural standards. The discrepancy in the two standards often presents considerable problems in establishing and maintaining woody landscape plant materials. In some circumstances, soil amendment may be appropriate.

In mature landscapes, detrimental changes in soil chemical or physical properties can occur with use and management of the area. Soil compaction is one of the most common and potentially harmful changes that occurs as a result of foot and vehicle traffic. Overfertilization can create high soluble-salt levels. As plants grow and develop more extensive root systems, they also may encounter subsoil conditions that limit plant growth because of original construction or parent material.

When should landscape soils be amended? First, not all sites require soil amendment, and most do not. No research data support the wholesale amendment of planting holes to guarantee plant survival. The cost-benefit ratio must be considered before any site is amended, which means that the site must be studied and analyzed scientifically. New sites should be examined with probes, augers, and shovels to check for layered soils or subsurface compaction zones. Original grading specifications should also be reviewed and considered when subsurface changes that could cause soil structure problems are suspected. The soil should be examined for extremes in soil texture, such as high clay or high sand content. A soil test of pH, soluble salts, and any suspected pesticide or other phytotoxic compounds should also be obtained. In mature sites, poor plant vigor may be caused by one of the soil disorders listed above, but thorough investigations of the soil are needed to confirm the diagnosis.

If the on-site investigations indicate that soil amendment would be beneficial (compaction zones, layered soils, excessive clayey or sandy texture, high salts, or other problems), proper procedures must be followed to modify the area effectively. The first rule is that the amendment must be completed to a depth that will solve the problem. Surface applications of organic material will have no effect on a subsurface plow plan layer, for example. Keep in mind that the active roots of most trees and shrubs are no deeper than about 24 to 30 inches (60 to 75 cm) even in optimal soil conditions. Thus, subsurface problems normally need to be modified if they affect this zone. A barrier to drainage at a 36-inch (90-cm) depth will still be problematic because it impedes the removal of water in the active root zone.

Common Chemical Problems in Landscape Soil

Most plants grow best in a pH range of 5.5 to 7.5. Soils may be made less acidic (more alkaline) by raising the pH with additions of lime (calcium carbonate). They may be made more acidic (less alkaline) by lowering the pH with additions of elemental sulfur or aluminum sulfate. For example, in Southern California, most soil pH problems result from pH levels that are too high. Applications of elemental sulfur at 2 to 4 pounds per 100 square feet (0.9 to 1.8 kg per 30 sq m) can reduce pH about 1 point when mixed at a depth of 6 to 8 inches (15 to 20 cm). Beneficial results may not be seen for several months after application. In existing landscapes, apply sulfur in monthly increments of a few ounces per 100 square feet (a few grams per 30 sq m) and follow each with an irrigation.

Gypsum (calcium sulfate) has no effect on pH but can be used to add calcium or sulfur to soils. It is also useful on high-sodium soils that have poor water infiltration. Spreading a total of about 20 pounds per 100 square feet (9 kg per 30 sq m) may be effective on new sites. Several months may be required before effects are noticeable. Apply small increments of gypsum to existing landscapes over several months. Irrigate heavily and repeatedly after any gypsum application (see related discussion under "Soil pH").

Soluble salts can reduce plant growth significantly at low to moderate levels (electrical conductivity [EC] of 2.0 to 3.0 mhos). Levels of two to four times this amount are usually necessary before easily diagnosed foliar symptoms (leaf burn or scorch, leaf drop) are expressed. Salts may be reduced by continuous leaching of the soil profile with successive irrigations. Be careful to irrigate fertilizers thoroughly into soil and do not overfertilize the area. Keep high-salt soils evenly moist to minimize damage to plants.

Physical Problems in Landscape Soil

Additions of physical amendments (sand or organic materials) are designed to dilute existing soil particles to benefit soil structure. The material selected should be the same or larger in grain size than the bulk of the existing soil. The following guidelines are suggested to amend the physical properties of landscape soils.

Sand can be effective if enough is added so that it is at least 45 percent of the soil volume to the depth requiring amendment. This usually means that sand is too expensive as an amendment. Using sand in small volumes usually only compounds the original problem.

Organic materials are very effective when landscape soil is amended at least 30 percent by volume (see table 3.11). Organic materials are typically much less expensive than sand and have many benefits besides diluting soil particles, but their effects are not permanent because they decompose after an extended period of time. Coarse materials last longer. Organic material should be composted or nitrogen-stabilized before use. Nitrogen fertilizer should be incorporated with the organic material at a rate of 1 to 3 pounds nitrogen per 1,000 square feet (0.45 to 1.36 kg per 300 sq m) of area amended. Research

Table 3.11

VOLUME OF ORGANIC SOIL AMENDMENTS TO ADD BASED ON TREATMENT DEPTH

| % Amendment | Volume of soil amendment (cu yd/1,000 sq ft) at depth of amended soil | | |
	3 in	6 in	9 in
30	2.78	5.56	8.33
35	3.24	6.49	9.72
40	3.70	7.41	11.13
45	4.16	8.34	12.52
50	4.63	9.26	13.88

Source: Adapted from California Fertilizer Association 1990, p. 222.

studies have demonstrated that composted eucalyptus trimmings are generally safe to use as amendments.

New landscape sites do not need to be amended in their entirety. Individual planting holes can be amended if they are enlarged to about three times the size of the transplants' root systems. This should be done only if site analysis uncovers an amendable soil problem similar to those discussed earlier. Compacted zones can often be treated more effectively without adding amendments. Physically breaking them up at planting is usually satisfactory. Keep in mind that plant roots will eventually outgrow the planting hole anyway.

Established landscapes can be amended for chemical problems as outlined earlier. Physical amendments are limited. It is not practical to try to dilute soils around mature plants by adding organic materials. Compaction and similar problems can be best remedied with turf aerators, power augers, or water jets that create numerous holes around and in landscape plantings. These techniques are not well proven through research, but limited observations indicate that they may be effective.

Managing Lead Contamination of Urban Garden Soils

In urban areas, home gardeners can grow crops that are subject to lead contamination. Lead can build up in soil because of land application of sewage sludges, fallout from airborne lead particles, and accumulated paint scrapings from demolished buildings that were covered with lead-based paints. Under normal soil conditions, lead is rather inert because it is readily bound to oxides, clays, and organic matter. Soils that are phosphate deficient or that have a low pH contain more soluble lead for plant uptake, however. Soilborne lead adheres to plant roots, and when taken up by plants, accumulates primarily in root tissue and secondarily in leaf tissue. Fruits of most crops contain little lead.

Airborne lead is largely a byproduct of motor vehicle emissions, and it is virtually ubiquitous, resulting in deposits of lead on plant foliage and urban soil surfaces. Fortunately, there is little evidence that airborne lead enters leaves or is translocated through plants.

The following cultural practices are recommended for gardeners who wish to reduce potential lead pollution in their crops.

- Locate plantings as far away from streets and roads as is practical, at least 75 feet (22.9 m) if possible.

- Maintain soil pH near 7.0 and keep phosphate levels up.

- Add as much organic material (composts, manure) as possible.

- Wash all produce thoroughly; discard older, outer leaves of leafy vegetables; peel all root crops grown under contaminated conditions.

- Avoid growing leafy crops (lettuce, spinach, beet tops, collards, cabbage) near streets or in highly contaminated soils. Fruiting crops, such as tomato, pepper, squash, and melons, can be grown in these situations, however.

- When high concentrations of soilborne lead are known or suspected, reduce or eliminate possible uptake of lead by removing and replacing topsoil, establishing high raised beds, or growing crops in containers.

Various Approaches to Home Gardening

Described below are some of the gardening approaches and philosophies that are popular today. They center on various methods of managing and improving soil health. Some of these techniques have parallels in commercial farming practices. For details on how UCCE Master Gardeners work with various gardening philosophies, please see chapter 1, "Overview."

Gardening Philosophies

The following philosophies of gardening have national and international clubs where members can get additional information.

Organic Gardening. In the 1940s, Sir Albert Howard, a British agronomist, first popularized organic gardening and farming. He worked in rural India, where farmers had to recycle natural nutrients from waste products because they could not afford to buy off-farm inputs. Sir Albert was disturbed by the newly emerging petroleum-based fertilizer products because he thought the natural cycles of building soil health were being ignored. He taught farmers to return wastes to the soil, avoid petrochemicals in combating insects, and avoid synthetic fertilizers. J. I. Rodale continued Sir Albert's work through the Rodale Institute, which today is a major publisher of organic gardening information.

In commercial agriculture, *organic* has a legal definition. Farmers must comply with regulations to sell their products as organic. In each county, the agricultural commissioner's office registers organic growers and provides lists of allowable materials. Organic gardeners use only naturally derived materials and no synthetic substances. Because soil health is stressed, organic growers compost and add organic matter to the soil to improve tilth and to keep plants fit to fight pests and disease. To combat pests, botanical insecticides, soaps, and other largely nontoxic controls are used, whereas cultural controls, such as cultivation and mulching, are used to fight weeds. Resistant varieties, pheromone confusion, and beneficial insects are newer technologies employed by organic gardeners.

Biodynamic Gardening. Biodynamic or French intensive gardening was developed from the writings of Austrian philosopher Rudolph Steiner. Soil fertility is maximized through environmentally balanced gardening. Raised beds, double digging, and compost additions are used. Double digging prepares the soil two spades or about 24 inches (60 cm) deep. Organic materials are dug into the lowest level and then the top 12 inches (30 cm) are prepared. A loose, well-draining soil is created in the beds.

Biodynamic gardening uses two basic preparations or preps that are sold as soil enhancers. The first preparation is made by filling cows' horns with manure and burying them at certain times in winter according to the moon's cycles. The resulting compound is composted organic matter that is dissolved in water and applied to the soil. This prep is said to contain life forces that make the soil very fertile and conducive to plant growth. The other preparation, a white powder made in summer by mixing flowers together, is used as a pest and disease control and is believed to be an anti–life force substance.

Recycling Kitchen Organic Waste

Some consumers have success with adding fresh kitchen garbage, including fruit and vegetable wastes, to the compost pile. Other consumers have reported that their kitchen wastes tend to turn slimy and degrade slowly and that animals attracted to the pile scatter the waste around the yard and burrow into the piles. One recycling alternative to composting kitchen organic waste is burying the waste in the garden soil to a depth of 2 to 3 feet (60 to 90 cm) with a posthole digger. Another option is vermiculture.

Vermiculture. The practice of raising redworms in boxes and feeding them kitchen wastes is known as vermiculture. Because worms eat their own weight each day, a pound of worms eat a pound of food every day. Native to Egypt, redworms are often known as manure worms. It may be necessary to purchase worms to get the box started. Many gardeners are interested in vermiculture for its recycling attributes and for the worm castings that provide a high-quality soil amendment with some fertilizer effects.

Vermiculture requires a box that has a hinged lid (about 4 ft [120 cm] long by 2 ft [60 cm] wide) and ¾-inch (1.9-cm) holes drilled on all sides. The box should be covered with screen and placed on a stand so that air can circulate under and around it. Bedding for the worms can be well-shredded newspaper or any loose organic matter. The worms need to be kept moist in a cool, shady place, and should be fed daily or every few days with kitchen wastes. After the worms have turned all the bedding and food into rich castings, the castings should be pushed to one side of the box and fresh bedding and food added to the empty side. In a few days to a week, the worms will have moved into the new area to feed, and the castings can be used in the garden. A screen with large openings can also be used to divide the box into two compartments.

Bibliography

Balge, R. J. 1993. Soils, nutrition and fertilizers. In D. D. Sharp, ed., Maryland Master Gardener handbook. College Park: University of Maryland Cooperative Extension.

Brady, N. C., and R. R. Weil. 1999. The nature and properties of soils. Upper Saddle River, NJ: Prentice Hall.

California Department of Food and Agriculture. 1992. Fertilizer materials laws and regulations. Sacramento: CDFA Division of Feed, Fertilizer, and Livestock Drugs.

California Fertilizer Association. 1990. Western fertilizer handbook: Horticulture edition. Danville, IL: Interstate Publishers.

California Fertilizer Association. 1998. Western fertilizer handbook: Second horticulture edition. Danville, IL: Interstate Publishers.

Chaney, D. E., L. E. Drinkwater, and G. S. Pettygrove. 1992. Organic fertilizers and soil amendments. Oakland: University of California Division of Agriculture and Natural Resources Publication 21505.

Foth, H. D. 1978. Fundamentals of soil science. New York: Wiley.

Hartin, J. S., ed. 1991. Dry wit: Making the most of a dry situation. Oakland: University of California Division of Agriculture and Natural Resources Special Tabloid.

Raabe, R. D. 1981. The rapid composting method. Oakland: University of California Division of Agriculture and Natural Resources Publication 21251.

U. S. Department of Agriculture. 1972. Yearbook of agriculture: Landscape for living. Washington, D.C.: U.S. Government Printing Office.

Wildman, W. E., and K. D. Gowans. 1978. Soil physical environment and how it affects plant growth. Oakland: University of California Division of Agriculture and Natural Resources Publication 2280.

4

Water Management

Janet Hartin and Ben Faber

LEARNING OBJECTIVES

- Develop an understanding of basic concepts of water management and plant water availability in different soil types.

- Understand basic principles of irrigation and water management. Learn four methods of scheduling irrigation when needed and learn to use an appropriate amount of water at each irrigation. Learn the basics about irrigation systems.

- Learn how to conserve water in home orchards and landscapes.

- Learn how to manage drought in California landscapes.

- Become familiar with the basic concept of evapotranspiration (ET).

Water Management

Along with minerals, light, oxygen, and carbon dioxide, plants require water. In fact, about 90 percent of a plant is water. Water is necessary for chemical reactions in cells and is also used in photosynthesis, which is the process of converting light energy into chemical energy. Water also keeps cells rigid so that plants do not wilt.

Understanding the water cycle of plants is useful for developing efficient watering schedules and for recognizing and correcting signs of water stress.

How Water Moves through Plants

Water and minerals enter land plants through the roots in the xylem, which is part of the vascular-conducting tissue of the plant. Water uptake is driven by the loss of water vapor through stomata, the tiny pores on the undersides of leaves. This water loss is referred to as *transpiration*. The amount of water lost through transpiration is enormous, and all or most of it must be replaced if the plant is to remain active and healthy. As water transpires from a leaf, the water potential of the leaf subsequently drops, and more water moves into the leaf. This water potential gradient, which moves water from areas of high water potential to areas of low water potential, continues to the roots (fig. 4.1).

But how does water taken up by roots move upward, sometimes 50 to 100 feet (15 to 30 m) or more, to eventually reach leaves of tall trees? The answer lies in the remarkable properties of water molecules themselves. In addition to the hydrogen bonds within a single water molecule, strong hydrogen bonds hold oxygen atoms from neighboring water molecules tightly together, producing great tensile strength. Water molecules carried in xylem vessels that are linked to one another form a long, narrow, continuous strand of water that extends downward to the root tips. As a water molecule moves into the leaf cell, it pulls the next molecule with it. The energy required for this movement of water through the plant is supplied by the sun, not by the plant.

How Water Moves through Soil

Movement of water into the soil is called *infiltration*. When the application rate of the irrigation system is greater than the infiltration

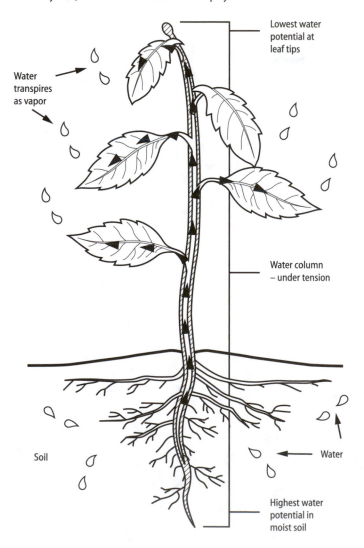

Lowest water potential at leaf tips

Water transpires as vapor

Water column – under tension

Soil

Water

Highest water potential in moist soil

rate of the soil, runoff will occur, potentially wasting large amounts of water. Conversely, when water is applied for a long period to a sandy soil that drains freely, water can be lost below the root zone, a process called *deep percolation*. Sandy soils hold less water than clay soils and need to be watered more often; clay soils hold more water and take in water much more slowly than sandy soils and do not need to be watered as often. Table 4.1 indicates the amount of water available for plant use by four types (textures) of soil. Figure 4.2 depicts the relative water penetration of an equal amount of water in three soil types. (See also "Soil Water" in chapter 3, "Soil and Fertilizer Management".)

How Deep To Water

How deeply to water depends largely on how deeply the plants will potentially root. Although plants vary widely in their rooting depth depending on species, soil texture, soil structure, and watering practices, they tend to fall into three general classifications, as indicated below. Applying water to these depths at each irrigation is recommended to meet moisture requirements of mature plants. Younger plants and plants growing in compacted or shallow soil are not as deeply rooted and do not need to be watered as deeply.

- Leafy vegetables and annual bedding plants: 6 inches to 1 foot (15 to 30 cm)

- Small shrubs, cool-season turfgrass, corn, tomatoes: 1 to 2 feet (30 to 60 cm)

- Large shrubs, trees, warm-season turfgrass: 1.5 to 5 feet (45 to 150 cm)

How Much Water Do Plants Require?

A large amount of water applied to plants is lost through transpiration. All or most of this water must be replaced to enable the plant to continue to grow and develop normally. In addition to the water lost through transpiration, more water, which also needs to be replaced, is lost through evaporation from the soil. The combination of water lost from transpiration and evaporation is referred to as *evapotranspiration* (ET). ET rates are determined by environmental factors, including temperature, relative humidity, solar radiation, and wind speed. ET rates vary among plant species because of differences in water requirements and the ability of different plants to adapt physiologically or to avoid water deficiencies through various mechanisms, such as by producing deep root systems able to mine additional water.

Evapotranspiration

To avoid overwatering or underwatering, it is important to know how much water your

Table 4.1

SOIL WATER CHARACTERISTICS FOR TYPICAL SOIL TEXTURE CLASSES

Soil texture	Plant-available water per foot of soil depth (inches)	Gallons of water per cubic foot of soil
sand	0.5–1.0	0.33–0.66
sandy loam	1.0–1.5	0.66–1.00
clay loam	1.5–2.0	1.00–1.33
clay	1.5–2.5	1.00–1.66

Note: Values reported are approximate. An inch of water is the amount that would cover the surface 1 inch deep; 1 gallon = 11/2 inches covering 1 square foot.

Figure 4.2

Penetration of equal amounts of water in furrows consisting of three soil types. For the three textures depicted, clay holds the greatest amount of available water per foot of depth, and sand holds the least amount of water per foot of depth. *Source:* After Pittenger 1992, p. 20.

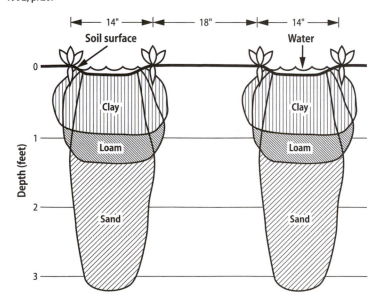

Table 4.2

AVERAGE DAILY EVAPOTRANSPIRATION (ET) RATES BY LOCATION IN CALIFORNIA (INCHES PER DAY)

Location (see fig. 4.3)	Jan	Feb	Mar	Apr	May	Jun	Jul	Aug	Sep	Oct	Nov	Dec
Zone 1. North Coast	0.02	0.04	0.06	0.08	0.11	0.12	0.11	0.11	0.09	0.06	0.04	0.02
Zone 2. North Coast Interior Valleys	0.03	0.04	0.08	0.11	0.16	0.20	0.23	0.20	0.15	0.09	0.04	0.02
Zone 3. Northeastern Mountain Valleys	0.02	0.04	0.07	0.12	0.16	0.19	0.26	0.23	0.16	0.09	0.03	0.02
Zone 4. Sacramento Valley	0.04	0.06	0.10	0.15	0.19	0.24	0.26	0.22	0.17	0.11	0.06	0.03
Zone 5. San Joaquin Valley	0.03	0.06	0.10	0.15	0.21	0.25	0.25	0.21	0.16	0.11	0.05	0.02
Zone 6. Central Coast Interior Valleys	0.05	0.08	0.11	0.14	0.18	0.21	0.22	0.19	0.16	0.12	0.08	0.05
Zone 7. Sierra (Tahoe Basin)	—	—	—	0.10	0.13	0.16	0.20	0.17	0.13	0.09	—	—
Zone 8. Central Coast	0.06	0.08	0.10	0.13	0.15	0.16	0.17	0.16	0.13	0.10	0.07	0.05
Zone 9. Southern Coast	0.06	0.09	0.10	0.13	0.14	0.17	0.18	0.18	0.15	0.11	0.09	0.07
Zone 10. Southern Inland Valleys	0.06	0.09	0.11	0.14	0.16	0.20	0.22	0.22	0.17	0.12	0.08	0.06
Zone 11. Southern Deserts	0.09	0.13	0.19	0.25	0.33	0.38	0.37	0.31	0.28	0.20	0.12	0.06

Source: Harris and Coppick 1977, p. 2.
Note: Each of the 11 locations listed is considered a climate zone within the state.

Table 4.3

AVERAGE SEASONAL EVAPOTRANSPIRATION (ET) RATES BY LOCATION IN CALIFORNIA (INCHES)

Location (see fig. 4.3)	Nov–Mar	Apr–Oct	Annual
Zone 1. North Coast	5.3	20.8	26.1
Zone 2. North Coast Interior Valleys	6.3	34.9	41.2
Zone 3. Northeastern Mountain Valleys	5.1	37.1	42.2
Zone 4. Sacramento Valley	8.5	40.7	49.2
Zone 5. San Joaquin Valley	7.9	40.7	49.0
Zone 6. Central Coast Interior Valleys	10.8	37.5	48.3
Zone 7. Sierra (Tahoe Basin)	—	30.0	—
Zone 8. Central Coast	10.7	30.6	41.3
Zone 9. Southern Coast	12.1	32.3	44.4
Zone 10. Southern Inland Valleys	11.5	37.9	49.4
Zone 11. Southern Deserts	17.7	65.1	82.2

Source: Harris and Coppick 1977, p. 2.
Note: Each of the 11 locations listed is considered a climate zone within the state.

landscape and garden plantings lose through ET. Average daily reference ET rates for the 11 climate zones in the state are given in table 4.2. The lawn watering guide (see tables 4.4 and 4.5) was based on these ET rates with necessary conversions already implemented. Table 4.3 lists average seasonal reference ET rates for the 11 zones.

The numbers in table 4.2 reflect the average daily water use by 4-inch- (10-cm)-tall cool-season turfgrass when soil water is unlimited.

It is the reference ET rate used by scientists to compare water use among plant species. This water usage reflects the amount of water that many large-scale continuous plantings use if soil moisture is plentiful and if the soil surface is at least 80 percent covered or shaded by plant foliage. You can use the ET rates listed in tables 4.2 and 4.3 to estimate the actual daily and seasonal amounts of soil moisture being used by your plants. In estimating the ET rate for landscape and garden plantings, consider the following three factors.

The figures in table 4.2 and 4.3 are historical averages. The actual water loss ranges up or down somewhat, possibly 10 to 25 percent, during unusually hot or windy days or unusually cool, cloudy days.

Larger plants may use more water than turfgrass, depending on their shape and exposure to the sun. Solid or almost solid plantings of shrubs or trees may use 10 or 20 percent more water than indicated in table 4.2. A large solitary shrub or tree, because of its greater exposure to the sun and wind, may use two or three times as much water as a comparable area of turf. The larger root system compensates for the additional water use.

Many garden plants and turf species can be maintained on considerably less water than the amount listed for ET rates. Most woody landscape plants need about half as much. Although certain drought-resistant plants use significantly less water, many plants considered drought-resistant are really "water-spenders" and have daily average ET rates similar to those listed in table 4.2 when water is not limiting.

Effective Lawn Watering

In order to use ET information, the lawn watering guide (tables 4.4 and 4.5) lists the number of minutes to water a lawn each week for every month of the year, based on whether the lawn is a warm-season or cool-season turfgrass species and based on how much water the sprinkler system puts out each hour. Using the lawn watering guide requires three steps.

1. **Determine the type of lawn.**

   - Warm-season (bermudagrass, zoysiagrass, St. Augustinegrass)

   - Cool-season (tall fescue, Kentucky bluegrass, perennial ryegrass)

2. **Determine the output of the sprinklers.**

   - Set six or more straight-sided cans of the same type (tuna or cat food work well) on the lawn between the sprinkler heads. Run the sprinklers for 20 minutes and measure the water in each can with a ruler. Determine the average depth in inches of water in each can. Multiply by 3 to determine the sprinkler output in inches per hour.

   - If more than a 15 to 20 percent difference exists among the depths of water in individual cans, some significant problems with the irrigation system probably need to be corrected to improve the evenness (uniformity) of the water application. Table 4.6 lists some common problems with sprinkler irrigation systems and some suggested remedies.

3. **Determine how long to water the lawn each week.**

   - Locate the appropriate lawn watering zone in figure 4.3. Tables 4.4 and 4.5 list the total number of minutes to water each week based on the location (see fig. 4.3), the lawn type (step 1, above), and the information obtained from the sprinkler output (step 2, above).

   - Additional minutes (more water) may be needed if the sprinkler system does not apply water uniformly as determined in step 2 above.

Knowing when and how long to water is just as important as knowing how much water to apply. Applying too much water at one time can result in substantial water loss from runoff or deep percolation. To determine how long to water, turn on the irrigation system at the same time of day it is normally operated (preferably early morning) and measure the amount of time it takes for runoff to just begin. Divide this number into the weekly number of minutes obtained from the lawn watering guide to determine how many times to water. Two examples of using the lawn watering guide, based on lawn type, location,

Figure 4.3

Map of Northern and Central California (left) and Southern California (right), dividing the state into 11 lawn watering (climate) zones: Zone 1, North Coast; Zone 2, North Coast Interior Valleys; Zone 3, Northeastern Mountain Valleys; Zone 4, Sacramento Valley; Zone 5, San Joaquin Valley; Zone 6, Central Coast Interior Valleys; Zone 7, Sierra; Zone 8, Central Coast; Zone 9, Southern Coast; Zone 10, Southern Inland Valleys; and Zone 11, Southern Deserts. *Source*: After Hartin 1991, pp. 2–3.

Table 4.4

LAWN WATERING GUIDE FOR NORTHERN AND CENTRAL CALIFORNIA (MINUTES TO WATER EACH WEEK) (FOR LOCATION OF ZONES, SEE FIG. 4.3)

ZONE 1. NORTH COAST
Warm-season turf—not recommended
Cool-season turf

Month	Hourly sprinkler output (inches)			
	0.5	1.0	1.5	2.0
Jan.	15	7	5	4
Feb	36	18	12	9
Mar	55	27	18	14
Apr	67	34	22	17
May	88	44	29	22
Jun	97	48	32	24
Jul	95	47	32	24
Aug	90	45	30	23
Sep	76	38	25	19
Oct	48	24	16	12
Nov	32	16	11	8
Dec	21	11	7	5

ZONE 2. NORTH COAST INTERIOR VALLEYS
Warm-season turf

Month	0.5	1.0	1.5	2.0
Jan	19	9	6	5
Feb	32	16	11	8
Mar	50	25	17	13
Apr	69	35	23	17
May	101	50	34	25
Jun	126	63	42	32
Jul	132	66	44	33
Aug	120	60	40	30
Sep	95	47	32	24
Oct	57	28	19	14
Nov	25	13	8	6
Dec	13	6	4	3

ZONE 2. NORTH COAST INTERIOR VALLEYS
Cool-season turf

Month	0.5	1.0	1.5	2.0
Jan	25	13	8	6
Feb	42	21	14	11
Mar	67	34	22	17
Apr	92	46	31	23
May	134	67	45	34
un	168	84	56	42
Jul	176	88	59	44
Aug	160	80	53	40
Sep	126	63	42	32
Oct	76	38	25	19
Nov	34	17	11	8
Dec	17	8	6	4

ZONE 3. NORTHEASTERN MOUNTAIN VALLEYS
Warm-season turf—not recommended
Cool-season turf

Month	0.5	1.0	1.5	2.0
Jan	17	8	6	4
Feb	34	17	11	8
Mar	59	29	20	15
Apr	101	50	34	25
May	134	67	45	34
Jun	168	84	56	42
Jul	210	105	70	53
Aug	176	88	59	44
Sep	126	63	42	32
Oct	76	38	25	19
Nov	25	13	9	6
Dec	17	9	6	4

ZONE 4. SACRAMENTO VALLEY
Warm-season turf

Month	0.5	1.0	1.5	2.0
Jan	19	9	6	5
Feb	44	22	15	11
Mar	69	35	23	17
Apr	101	50	34	25
May	126	63	42	32
Jun	158	79	53	39
Jul	164	82	55	41
Aug	145	72	48	36
Sep	113	57	38	28
Oct	82	41	27	20
Nov	38	19	13	9
Dec	19	9	6	5

ZONE 4. SACRAMENTO VALLEY
Cool-season turf

Month	0.5	1.0	1.5	2.0
Jan	25	13	8	6
Feb	59	29	20	15
Mar	92	46	31	23
Apr	134	67	45	34
May	168	84	56	42
Jun	210	105	70	53
Jul	218	109	73	55
Aug	193	97	67	78
Sep	151	76	50	38
Oct	109	55	36	27
Nov	50	25	17	13
Dec	25	13	8	6

Source: Hartin 1991, p. 2.
Note: If runoff or brown spots occur with weekly watering, divide the weekly total by 2, 3, or 4 to water two, three, or four times a week for fewer minutes. Desert areas especially need several shorter waterings. Watering should be suspended during any period when rainfall equals or exceeds the ET rates found in Tables 4.2 and 4.3. Values assume assume a sprinkler uniformity of 80%.

ZONE 5. SAN JOAQUIN VALLEY
Warm-season turf

Month	Hourly sprinkler output (inches)			
	0.5	1.0	1.5	2.0
Jan	19	9	6	5
Feb	38	19	13	9
Mar	69	35	23	17
Apr	101	50	34	25
May	132	66	44	33
Jun	164	82	55	41
Jul	170	85	57	43
Aug	145	72	48	36
Sep	113	57	38	28
Oct	69	35	23	17
Nov	32	16	11	8
Dec	13	6	4	3

ZONE 5. SAN JOAQUIN VALLEY
Cool-season turf

Month	Hourly sprinkler output (inches)			
	0.5	1.0	1.5	2.0
Jan	25	13	8	6
Feb	50	25	17	13
Mar	92	46	31	23
Apr	134	67	45	34
May	176	88	59	44
Jun	218	109	73	55
Jul	227	113	76	57
Aug	193	97	64	48
Sep	151	76	50	38
Oct	92	46	31	23
Nov	42	21	14	11
Dec	17	8	6	4

ZONE 6. CENTRAL COAST INTERIOR VALLEYS
Warm-season turf

Month	Hourly sprinkler output (inches)			
	0.5	1.0	1.5	2.0
Jan	32	16	11	8
Feb	44	22	15	11
Mar	69	35	23	17
Apr	95	47	32	24
May	113	57	38	28
Jun	113	57	38	28
Jul	132	66	44	33
Aug	126	63	42	32
Sep	107	54	36	27
Oct	76	38	25	19
Nov	44	22	15	11
Dec	32	16	11	8

ZONE 6. CENTRAL COAST INTERIOR VALLEYS
Cool-season turf

Month	Hourly sprinkler output (inches)			
	0.5	1.0	1.5	2.0
Jan	42	21	14	11
Feb	59	29	20	15
Mar	92	46	30	23
Apr	126	63	42	32
May	151	76	50	38
Jun	151	76	50	38
Jul	176	88	59	44
Aug	168	84	56	42
Sep	126	71	48	36
Oct	143	71	48	36
Nov	59	29	20	15
Dec	42	21	14	11

ZONE 7. SIERRA
Warm-season turf—not recommended
Cool-season turf

Month	Hourly sprinkler output (inches)			
	0.5	1.0	1.5	2.0
Jan	31	15	10	8
Feb	43	22	14	11
Mar	79	39	26	20
Apr	124	62	41	31
May	164	82	55	41
Jun	207	103	69	52
Jul	231	115	77	58
Aug	198	99	66	50
Sep	141	70	47	35
Oct	96	48	32	24
Nov	40	20	13	10
Dec	20	10	7	5

ZONE 8. CENTRAL COAST
Warm-season turf

Month	Hourly sprinkler output (inches)			
	0.5	1.0	1.5	2.0
Jan	38	19	13	9
Feb	50	25	17	13
Mar	63	32	21	16
Apr	88	44	29	22
May	101	50	34	25
Jun	113	57	38	28
Jul	95	47	32	24
Aug	113	57	38	28
Sep	95	47	32	24
Oct	69	35	23	17
Nov	50	25	19	13
Dec	38	19	13	9

ZONE 8. CENTRAL COAST
Cool-season turf

Month	Hourly sprinkler output (inches)			
	0.5	1.0	1.5	2.0
Jan	50	25	17	13
Feb	67	34	22	17
Mar	84	42	28	21
Apr	118	59	39	29
May	134	67	45	34
Jun	151	76	50	38
Jul	126	63	42	32
Aug	151	76	50	38
Sep	126	63	42	32
Oct	92	46	31	23
Nov	67	34	22	17
Dec	50	25	17	13

Table 4.5

LAWN WATERING GUIDE FOR SOUTHERN CALIFORNIA (MINUTES TO WATER EACH WEEK) (FOR LOCATION OF ZONES, SEE FIG. 4.3)

ZONE 9. SOUTHERN COAST
Warm-season turf

Month	Hourly sprinkler output (inches)			
	0.5	1.0	1.5	2.0
Jan	44	22	15	11
Feb	57	28	19	14
Mar	63	32	21	16
Apr	76	38	25	19
May	88	44	29	22
Jun	95	47	32	24
Jul	107	54	36	27
Aug	95	47	32	24
Sep	82	41	27	20
Oct	69	35	23	17
Nov	50	25	17	13
Dec	38	19	13	9

ZONE 9. SOUTHERN COAST
Cool-season turf

Month	Hourly sprinkler output (inches)			
	0.5	1.0	1.5	2.0
Jan	59	29	20	15
Feb	76	38	25	19
Mar	84	42	28	21
Apr	101	50	34	25
May	118	59	39	29
Jun	126	63	42	32
Jul	143	71	48	36
Aug	126	63	42	32
Sep	109	55	36	27
Oct	92	46	31	23
Nov	67	34	22	17
Dec	50	25	17	13

ZONE 10. SOUTHERN INLAND VALLEYS
Warm-season turf

Month	Hourly sprinkler output (inches)			
	0.5	1.0	1.5	2.0
Jan	42	21	14	10
Feb	57	28	19	14
Mar	80	40	27	20
Apr	96	48	32	24
May	119	60	40	29
Jun	144	72	48	36
Jul	165	83	55	41
Aug	455	77	52	39
Sep	124	62	41	31
Oct	88	44	29	22
Nov	54	27	16	14
Dec	42	21	14	10

ZONE 10. SOUTHERN INLAND VALLEYS
Cool-season turf

Month	Hourly sprinkler output (inches)			
	0.5	1.0	1.5	2.0
Jan	56	28	19	14
Feb	75	38	25	19
Mar	106	53	35	27
Apr	128	64	43	32
May	159	80	53	40
Jun	193	96	64	48
Jul	221	110	74	55
Aug	207	103	69	52
Sep	165	82	55	42
Oct	117	59	39	29
Nov	73	36	24	18
Dec	55	28	19	14

ZONE 11. SOUTHERN DESERTS
Warm-season turf

Month	Hourly sprinkler output (inches)			
	0.5	1.0	1.5	2.0
Jan	54	27	18	14
Feb	75	38	25	19
Mar	121	61	40	30
Apr	165	83	55	41
May	211	106	70	53
Jun	243	121	81	61
Jul	251	126	84	63
Aug	218	109	73	54
Sep	180	90	60	45
Oct	121	61	40	30
Nov	69	35	23	17
Dec	43	22	14	11

ZONE 11. SOUTHERN DESERTS
Cool-season turf

Month	Hourly sprinkler output (inches)			
	0.5	1.0	1.5	2.0
Jan	65	32	22	17
Feb	90	46	30	23
Mar	145	73	48	36
Apr	198	100	66	49
May	253	127	84	64
Jun	292	145	97	73
Jul	301	151	101	76
Aug	262	131	88	65
Sep	216	108	72	54
Oct	145	73	48	36
Nov	83	42	28	20
Dec	52	26	17	13

Source: Hartin 1991, p. 3.

Note: If runoff or brown spots occur with weekly watering, divide the weekly total by 2, 3, or 4 to water two, three or four times a week for fewer minutes. Desert areas especially need several shorter waterings. Watering should be suspended during any period when rainfall equals or exceeds the ET rates found in Tables 4.2 and 4.3. Values assume assume a sprinkler uniformity of 80%.

season, sprinkler output, and length of time until runoff begins, are shown below.

Example 1. In Claremont (Zone 10), a bermudagrass lawn (warm-season turf) has an irrigation system with a sprinkler output of 1.0 inch/hour, and runoff occurs after 15 minutes. During May, the lawn should be watered for 15 minutes four times per week (15 min × 4 times/week = 60 min/week).

Example 2. In Santa Clara (Zone 6), the irrigation system of a tall fescue lawn (cool-season turf) has a sprinkler output of 1.5 inches/hour, and runoff occurs after 10 minutes. During March, the lawn should be watered for 10 minutes three times per week (10 min × 3 times/week = 30 min).

Save Water with Regular Sprinkler Maintenance

A sprinkler system that needs repair could be wasting 20 to 30 percent of the water applied to the lawn. Even a properly designed system needs regular upkeep to water effectively. A common problem of lawn sprinklers is lack of uniformity. Brown spots often result from uneven watering (see fig. 4.4). Water is wasted if the whole lawn is overwatered to compensate for a few dry areas caused by poor coverage. A better approach is to troubleshoot and find out why coverage is uneven. A few simple repairs and adjustments can save water, money, and frustration. If a lawn shows signs of uneven watering, check for common problems and make needed changes (see table 4.6).

Ways to Save Water in Lawns. Making necessary repairs to the sprinkler system and scheduling waterings according to the lawn watering guide (see tables 4.4 and 4.5) can reduce the amount of water used on a lawn. Other measures can save water while maintaining a healthy lawn in drought or plenty.

- Water early in the morning to reduce evaporation.

- Water the lawn separately from trees, shrubs, and ground covers, if possible.

- Remove thatch in spring if it is more than ½ inch (12.5 mm) thick. Thatch should not be removed in the heat of the summer.

- Control weeds, which compete for water, light, and nutrients.

- Fertilize moderately, applying the low end of recommended rates.

- Aerate as necessary to prevent soil compaction. Proper aeration requires removal of plugs (local rental businesses often rent aerators). Aeration allows water to move more freely into the soil. Clay soils in particular may need regular aeration.

- Mow the lawn at the correct height (see chapter 12, "Lawns," for recommended mowing heights of turfgrasses).

Watering the Lawn and Surrounding Plants with a Hose-End Sprinkler

Many Californians do not have automatic watering systems but use hose-end sprinklers to water their yards. Some methods for reducing water waste and retaining an attractive landscape without converting to an expensive automated system are listed below.

- Check for leaks between the faucet and host. A new rubber washer is inexpensive and easy to install.

- Place the sprinkler in a central location with lawn all around it, instead of watering sidewalks, the driveway, or the house.

Table 4.6

COMMON SPRINKLER PROBLEMS AND THEIR SOLUTIONS

Problem	Solution
broken sprinkler	replace with a sprinkler that applies water at the same rate
unmatched sprinklers	replace with sprinklers that apply water at a common rate
sunken sprinkler risers	raise the sprinklers or replace
crooked sprinklers	straighten to an upright position
turfgrass growing around sprinklers	mow or chemically remove grass
sand or debris plugging sprinklers	flush out sprinklers to remove sprinklers debris; replace sprinklers as necessary

- When watering lawn areas with tree blockage, move the sprinkler to several locations to prevent dry areas. (Keep tree trunks dry!)

- Water until the first signs of runoff occur. It may be necessary to cycle waterings or reduce the volume applied to get the water into the soil.

- Check the depth of watering. Lawns and flower beds should be watered to about 1 foot (30 cm); shrubs to 1 or 2 feet (30 to 60 cm); and trees to 2 or 3 feet (60 to 90 cm).

- Refer to the lawn watering guide for the total number of minutes to water each week. To keep sprinkler output consistent during each watering, keep a record of how many turns of the faucet gave the preferred volume. Use an inexpensive household timer to track the total watering time.

- Water in the early morning, and avoid watering during windy periods.

- Water trees and shrubs with a conventional hose on low volume to allow water to soak in slowly and deeply, or use a soaker hose or deep-root irrigator.

When To Water Landscape and Garden Plants

Expensive and sometimes inaccurate equipment or tests are generally not necessary to determine when to water landscape and garden plants. The simple, useful methods described below can help establish a watering schedule.

Plant Symptoms
Close observation of landscape plants is an obvious method of determining when to water. Most plants show common moisture stress symptoms when they are too dry. Symptoms include

- wilting or folded leaves

- dull or gray-green foliage

- leaf drop

- new leaves smaller than normal

These symptoms, which first appear during the hottest part of the day, indicate that the plant should be watered immediately. Some plants are severely stressed by the time symptoms become evident, however.

The Feel Test
The "feel" test is a quick, easy way to help determine the water-holding capacity of garden soil (see "Soil Texture" in chapter 3, "Soil and Fertilizer Management," for feel test to determine soil texture). Although it may seem somewhat difficult or awkward at first, familiarity with using this method in different soil textures makes the task easier. To conduct a feel test for soil moisture content, dig down 6 to 8 inches (15 to 20 cm) in the garden with a trowel or shovel and place a handful of soil in the palm of the hand. Table 4.7 presents guidelines for interpreting the results of the feel test. A general rule of thumb is to water home plantings when 50 percent soil moisture depletion has occurred, or when about half of the water held in the soil at field capacity has been depleted (also see "Soil Water" in chapter 3).

Example 1. A sandy loam soil that forms a loose ball that is just starting to fall apart but does not ooze water still retains 50 to 75 percent of the total amount of water it originally held when watered to maximum capacity. This soil is not quite ready to be watered again (see table 4.7).

Example 2. A crumbly clay loam soil that barely holds together holds less than 50 percent of the total water it originally held at field capacity. At this stage, the soil is ready to be watered again, and some plants may even be showing symptoms of drought (see table 4.7).

Portable Soil Moisture Meters
Small, portable, and relatively inexpensive soil moisture meters may be useful for determining when to water home plantings. Once gardeners get the knack for knowing what color and feel soils have that are still holding about 50 percent of their maximum water supply, they can judge the moisture content of soil fairly accurately without the meters.

Using A Water Budget
A water budget is like balancing a bank account. The soil holds water just as the bank account holds money. Irrigation and rainfall represent deposits and daily ET rates represent withdrawals. The amount of plant-available

water that various soils can hold is calculated by multiplying the values in Table 4.1 by the estimated rooting depth (in feet) of the plants grown. By subtracting the daily ET rates from the soil water content value, the days until the soil dries out can be closely estimated. Irrigation should be scheduled on or before the day all the plant-available water is gone. As noted earlier, many landscape plants can be maintained at ET rates as low as 50 percent of those found in table 4.3. Applying a lower ET rate in the water budget calculations will schedule irrigation less frequently. Adjust the ET rate or use one of the other above methods to fine-tune the water budget so that landscape plants maintain the appearance and growth desired. (See related discussion under "How to Manage Drought in California Landscapes," below.)

General Principles for Watering Garden and Landscape Plants and Fruit Trees

Water deeply and infrequently. Although their genetic potential leads plants to vary in their ability to root deeply, watering deeply enough to wet the entire root zone and a little beyond encourages many plants to root deeper than they would with shallow watering. Watering too often and too shallowly also encourages excessive soil evaporation and may result in salt buildup and provide optimal conditions for certain diseases.

Table 4.7

PRACTICAL HAND-FEEL TEST TO INTERPRET SOIL MOISTURE

Available moisture	Sand (gritty when moist, like beach sand)	Sandy loam (gritty when moist, dirties fingers, contains silt and clay)	Clay loam (sticky, plastic when moist)	Clay (very sticky when moist; behaves like modeling clay)
close to 0%: little or no moisture available	dry, loose, single-grained; flows through fingers	dry, loose, flows through fingers	dry clods that break down into powder	hard, baked cracked surface; hard clods difficult to break
50% or less: approaching time to irrigate	still appears dry, will not form ball with pressure	still appears dry, will not form a ball	a little crumbly but will hold together under pressure	somewhat pliable, will ball under pressure
50% to 75%: enough moisture available	same as comments for 50% or less	tends to ball under pressure but seldom will hold together	forms a ball; a little plastic; might slick with pressure	forms a ball; will ribbon out between thumb and forefinger
75% to field capacity: plenty of moisture available	sticks together slightly; may form a very weak ball under pressure	forms weak ball, breaks easily, will not become slick	forms a ball, very pliable, becomes slick if high in clay	easily ribbons out between fingers; feels slick
at field capacity: soil will not hold any more water after draining	upon squeezing, no free water appears but moisture is left on hand	same as sand	same as sand	same as sand
above field capacity: unless water drains out, soil will be waterlogged	free water appears when soil is bounced on hand	free water will be released when kneading	can squeeze out free water	puddles and free water form on surface

Source: Harris and Coppick 1977, p. 4.

Apply water uniformly. Evenly applied water wastes less water and improves plant health. A sprinkler system that applies water only half as evenly as a neighbor's system requires the application of twice as much water (see fig. 4.4). Over the course of a hot summer, this practice can lead to higher water bills as well as a significant amount of wasted water. Regularly conduct can tests and correct hardware problems (see fig. 4.4). Drip systems are a great way of watering gardens and individual plants, but they need to be checked regularly for clogging.

Turn off an automatic watering system during rainy weather. If you plan to be on vacation for an extended period during the rainy season, you should familiarize a neighbor with the controller so that they can turn off the system if needed.

Watering Systems for Garden and Landscape Plants and Fruit Trees

Drip, furrow, and sprinkler systems are all useful for watering home plantings. Although no single system is perfect for every situation, some general principles can aid in system selection. Correctly installing and maintaining any watering system is important for the long-term success of the system and the health and development of plantings.

Automated Sprinkler Systems. To use automatic sprinklers efficiently, determine the rate at which the sprinklers apply water (see point 2 under "Effective Lawn Watering" in this chapter.) Place several empty cans under the sprinkler spray at various spots. Keep track of the length of time the sprinklers are on and then measure the depth of the water in the cans when the watering is completed. Average the various depths to determine how much water is being applied to the garden at each irrigation. For most soils, sprinkling until 2 to 3 inches (5 to 7.5 cm) has accumulated in the cans will give sufficient irrigation for mature shrubs and trees. The objective for landscape trees and shrubs is to wet the soil to a depth of 1 to 3 feet (30 to 90 cm) at each irrigation to promote a deep root system. Several hours of short cycles of irrigation may be required to minimize runoff. Using sprinklers to irrigate ground covers and vegetable gardens may take less time to wet the root zone, depending on the type of plant. Refer to the list of approximate rooting depths earlier in this chapter under "How Deep to Water."

Furrow Irrigation. Unlike sprinklers, furrow irrigation does not wet foliage, thereby reducing the incidence of some plant diseases. Irrigating with this method is most practical in fruit and vegetable plantings. For furrow irrigation of vegetables, use raised beds (see chapter 14, "Home Vegetable Gardening").

Drip Irrigation. Drip watering is the frequent, slow application of water to soil through emitters. Emitters are built in or attached to small plastic water delivery lines that carry water to each plant. A drip system has three parts: a control head, which includes a control and filter; a transmission system of plastic pipes or hose; and the emitters. Drip irrigation can reduce water application and usage because of controlled water distribution and lower evaporation losses. This type of irrigation works well for vegetable gardens, ornamental and fruit trees, shrubs, vines, and outdoor container plants.

In addition, drip irrigation can offer several advantages to home gardeners. Water is placed more accurately and efficiently in the root zone; water is applied at a slow rate that reduces water loss from runoff; dry soil between plants permits work in the garden during irrigation; and management functions are reduced. Disadvantages include the cost of equipment and installation, and problems with plugging of tiny drip orifices, which require routine checking.

Figure 4.4

Sprinkler placement for overlapping coverage. For sprinkler irrigation, place the sprinklers so the spray of each overlaps with that of each nearby sprinkler. Otherwise, the soil at the outer edges of the sprinkler spray range does not receive adequate water to produce maximum plant growth. *Source:* After Pittenger 1992, p. 21.

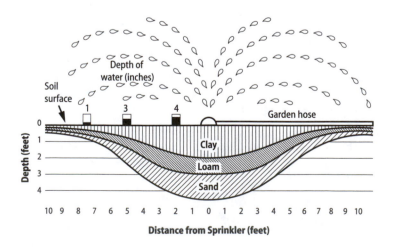

Correct operation is important to obtain the advantages of drip irrigation. Drip wets a smaller area than sprinkling or flooding and therefore must be performed more frequently. Although water should be applied daily or on alternate days during the watering season, it is still important to allow the soil to dry some between waterings. The amount of water needed for daily applications can usually be supplied by operating the system for about 15 minutes in the spring and a few hours in the summer. The key to success is to water deep enough at each irrigation to supply adequate water to the root zone. (Refer to the preferred rooting depths of various plant types under "How Deep to Water" above and in table 4.7.) Using a soil auger or a hand trowel to determine how deep the water is penetrating is recommended.

Are drip systems really the most efficient? Drip or other microsprinkler systems are no better than their management. Overirrigation is easily possible with drip systems. On hilly, uneven terrain, a drip system may be the best choice, but if the emitters are clogged by algae, sand, or debris, then the system is not doing its job. In fact, the most efficient irrigation method for trees or shrubs may be to create a small basin around the plant. A second berm of earth is built several inches away from the trunk to protect it and crown roots from becoming waterlogged. The basin rapidly fills with water up to 2 inches (5 cm) deep.

How To Manage Drought in California Landscapes

Water shortages have happened in the past in California and can very well happen again in the future. Gardeners should follow these suggestions if it is unlikely that there will be enough water available for all their landscape plants.

In the spring, make a water budget for the coming season (see "Using A Water Budget," above). First, estimate the inches of water that will be available to plants during the growing season by adding the amount already stored in the soil and the amount of expected irrigation water. To estimate the amount of moisture in the soil available to plants at the start of the growing season, determine the water-storage

capacity of the soil available for plant uptake. The soil reservoir is the water storage capacity of the soil where the plant roots are growing. The storage capacity depends largely on the soil texture, as documented in table 4.1, but also on the soil depth that will be penetrated by plant roots during the growing season. When the soil contains normal moisture, the top 3 or 4 feet (90 to 120 cm) can be considered the soil reservoir for most trees and shrubs. In dry periods, deep-rooted plants draw water from farther down, but shallow-rooted plants, such as most grasses, have a shallower soil reservoir. If a hardpan, bedrock, or some other restricting layer is close to the soil surface, the soil reservoir will be limited accordingly.

After determining the storage capacity of the soil reservoir, use the feel test to estimate how full the reservoir is. Second, determine the expected inches of ET loss during the growing season in your California climate zone (see table 4.3). Finally, estimate the minimum water requirements of the plants. (The ET rates given in this chapter are close to maximum. Many plants can be maintained and survive on less.) For shallow-rooted landscape plants that must be saved, almost all of the potential ET loss must be replaced. Deeper-rooted woody plants in deep soil should survive on half to a fourth of ET.

If the amount of expected available water is less than the minimum amount required, decide how many square feet of landscape will be irrigated during the coming season and how many square feet will have to go without water. If necessary, make a priority list of which plants to save. Consider the following points:

- Most established drought-resistant plants on soil at least 4 feet (1.2 m) deep should be able to survive in fairly good condition with no irrigation if they start the growing season with a soil reservoir full of water. For trees and shrubs, fill up the soil reservoir at the start of the season, if possible, even if little water remains for later irrigation.

- To survive, most woody plants need irrigation once or twice during the growing season in addition to a full soil reservoir early in the season. After initially filling up the soil reservoir, divide the remainder of the available water into two equal amounts and apply them after the plants show symptoms of moisture stress. If water is in extremely short supply, plants may be damaged but survive with only one irrigation.

- Wait until symptoms of water stress develop before irrigating. Stressing each shrub, tree, or plant bed close to its limit can save as much water as possible while keeping the plants alive.

- Check soil moisture under nonirrigated trees and shrubs. Those that have not normally been irrigated or those which were benefiting from nearby irrigation may have been surviving primarily on winter rainfall. After an unusually dry winter or two, their soil moisture supply could be almost depleted. If so, they may need irrigation to survive.

- Consider severe pruning of overgrown shrubs, hedges, and vines that will grow back. This can cut water use and revitalize the plants. Most shrubs will look better if the branches are thinned out or cut back to laterals rather than to stubs. This is particularly true of conifers, most of which do not sprout from old wood.

- To reduce water requirements of container-grown plants, move them to a shaded area.

- Sprays to reduce transpiration (anti-transpirants) may increase the chances that a plant will survive critically dry periods, although research on their benefits is not conclusive. Because these products are not recommended for all plants and situations, they should be used only on specimen plants and other high-value plants. There are two types of antitranspirants: reflecting materials (whitewash or white, water-based paint) that reflect sunlight and thereby reduce transpiration; and emulsions, such as wax emulsions that can plug pores on leaves. Reflecting materials are more effective when sprayed on upper leaf surfaces. Emulsions must be sprayed on the lower surface of each leaf where most or all of the pores (stomates) are located. An antitranspirant may reduce transpiration for a few days to several weeks, depending on the material, how well it is applied, environmental conditions, and the amount of new growth after spraying.

Most people tend to overwater rather than underwater. Keeping the watering system in good repair by fixing broken sprinklers and straightening crooked ones can reduce water waste more than anything else.

It is not necessary to add drought-resistant landscaping or remove all the lawn. Many nonnative plants do well on about the same amount of water as natives. Choose plants that are adapted to the climate you live in. How and when to water (watering only when plants need the moisture) are the more critical issues in water conservation. Use the lawn watering guide (see fig. 4.3; tables 4.4 and 4.5) and follow University of California Division of Agriculture and Natural Resources recommendations to reduce water use by 20 to 50 percent or more.

Knowing when to apply water to the landscape plants is as important as knowing how much water to put on. Although lawns prefer more frequent waterings, trees and shrubs prefer deeper, less frequent waterings. Soil texture also determines when to water. Because clay soils hold more water than sandier ones, they do not need to be watered as often.

How To Check Household Water Usage

Homeowners can use the water meter to help detect slow plumbing leaks that can add up to significant water waste over time. To check for leaks, turn off all water-using appliances and faucets in the home. Find the water meter (usually in a concrete box near the street), and write down an initial reading. Wait 1 hour and record the meter reading again. If this number is different from the first reading, there is a leak. Now is the time to troubleshoot further; call a plumber if necessary.

Homeowners can also check weekly household water usage. Most families use 25 to 50 percent of their total household water for landscape irrigation. Record the meter reading at the beginning and at the end of the week at the same time of day. Most meters record in cubic feet. Use the following example to convert a meter reading to gallons of water used per week or day.

Example. Assume the first reading was 15,500 cubic feet and the second was 15,250 cubic feet. Subtract the first reading from the second to determine the cubic feet of water used. In this example, the household used 250 cubic feet in one week

(15,500–15,250 = 250). To convert cubic feet to gallons, multiply cubic feet by 7.5 (the number of gallons of water in 1 cubic foot). In the example: 7.5 gal/cu ft × 250 cu ft = 1,875 gal used. Divide the number of gallons by 7 days. In the example, the average daily household water use is 1875 ÷ 7 = 268 gal/day.

Keeping Plants Alive under Severe Water Restrictions

When water is not adequate to apply the optimal amount to landscape plants, most plants can survive on less, at least for one season. The key to survival is applying the water at the right time. Do not apply water to sandy soils too quickly because the water can move below the root zone rapidly. Clay soils take up water more slowly and hold more water than sandier soils. For information on keeping fruit and nut trees alive during severe water shortages, see the section below, "Conserving Water in Home Orchards."

Lawns can also survive major water restrictions. Warm-season lawns such as bermudagrass will go dormant when water is inadequate. Cool-season lawns such as tall fescue require more water than warm-season turfgrasses. All lawns need water year-round to continue to grow. The lawn watering guide in figure 4.3 and tables 4.4 and 4.5 indicate weekly water requirements for optimal growth of warm-season and cool-season turfgrasses. Both types can survive on reductions of about 40 percent, as long as sprinkler systems apply water uniformly to all areas of the lawn, although the lawn will probably look unsightly for the rest of the season.

Many ground covers will survive on about half the amount of water received under optimal conditions. They should be watered about every 3 to 6 weeks from April through September. Some ground covers will lose leaves and may die back temporarily.

Replacing the Landscape To Save Water

It is not necessary to replace a traditional landscape with an alternative one to save water. In fact, putting in a new landscape might take more water. Since most people tend to overwater rather than underwater landscapes, conserving water has more to do with keeping the sprinkler system in good working order and properly watering plants to apply only what they need.

Cementing over the soil can actually increase the water demand of surrounding plants because of "heat islands" created by the concrete. Cooling costs inside the house can also increase if shade-producing plants are removed.

Not all native plants take less water than introduced species. Plants should be chosen based on climate. There are many native and nonnative plants to choose from that are adapted to your area. Ask for specific suggestions from a local nursery or landscape professional or refer to a reliable garden book.

New plantings need steady watering to establish themselves. After one or two seasons, watering can be somewhat reduced. Replanting the landscape takes lots of time and effort and can require more water than the current landscape.

Mulches Can Save Water

Mulches are materials put on top of the soil around trees and shrubs to reduce water evaporation, prevent weed problems, and buffer soil temperatures. Soil amendments, on the other hand, are products mixed into a soil to improve soil tilth (see chapter 3).

What types of materials make good mulch? Backyard compost and decomposed lawn clippings are often recycled into mulch, but many commercially available products include decorative bark, gravel, compost, redwood sawdust, peat moss, and composted sewage sludge mixtures. Yard waste used as mulch must be well decomposed. Otherwise, nitrogen fertilizer may have to be added to plantings, because undecomposed material can rob nitrogen from the soil. Fresh lawn clippings may contain herbicides harmful to trees and shrubs.

Because mulches work by preventing sunlight from reaching the soil, dark products are preferred. Add 2 to 6 inches (5 to 15 cm) of mulch (depending on the material) for an effective barrier, or use a black plastic underlay.

Mulches should be applied in late spring when soils are warm. When used around trees, they should begin a few inches from the trunk and spread outward toward the drip line. Never apply mulch next to the trunks of trees because crown rot and other problems can result. In the case of shrubs, mulches should cover the soil surrounding the planting to reduce soil evaporation. Mulches added between plants throughout the bed can also save water in flower bed plantings.

Remember to water through the mulch layer into the soil. Because they apply water directly into the root zone, drip systems work well with mulched plantings, but common garden hoses can also be used.

How To Save Water and Keep Trees Healthy

Besides their beauty, trees provide shade, cooling, privacy, and oxygen. Even when water is in short supply, tree care should be a high priority. Some ways to keep landscape trees healthy and reduce water waste include the following.

Water trees separately from surrounding plants. Trees prefer fewer, deeper waterings than do lawns. A garden hose, minisprinkler or microsprinkler, deep-root irrigator, or drip emitters all work well.

- Water trees to a depth of 2 to 3 feet (60 to 90 cm) to help promote a deep root system. To check how deep the water is going, push a metal rod, soil probe, or straightened coat hanger into the soil a day or so after watering. It will move easily through moist soil but will become hard to push as the soil becomes drier deeper down.

- Keep turfgrass and other plants at least 1 foot (30 cm) from tree trunks to promote faster tree growth and reduce competition for water. This also helps prevent tree damage from string weed trimmers (weed whips) and lawn mowers.

- Apply mulch around trees, keeping it a few inches away from tree trunks. Mulch reduces water evaporation from soil, buffers soil temperatures, and reduces weeds. Water through the mulch and into the root area.

- Control weeds around trees. Weeds compete for water and nutrients and can harbor insects and disease-causing organisms.

- Avoid soil compaction around trees. Compaction restricts water movement into the soil and decreases the amount of oxygen available for plant growth. Construction activities should be kept several feet from tree trunks.

- Do not routinely fertilize landscape trees. Too much fertilizer (especially nitrogen) causes new growth flushes, requiring additional water. Many trees can live well for several years without fertilization.

- Severe pruning of trees to conserve water should be attempted only in extreme drought conditions. To reduce water requirements of a tree significantly, it must be cut back enough to reduce its size markedly. Otherwise, previously shaded leaves are exposed to the sun, increasing the transpiration rate. If it is done improperly, severe pruning may lead to sunburn or other injury or cause structural weakness in the tree. Remove dead and diseased wood, dangerous branches, and suckers growing from the base of the tree. Pruning stimulates shoot growth, which increases the need for water; therefore, do not prune trees heavily in the early spring.

Watering Plants on Slopes

Turfgrass and ground covers are often planted on slopes to control erosion, but efficient watering on slopes is difficult. The main challenge is to apply sufficient water to the upper plantings and still prevent excess runoff below. Although completely avoiding runoff is almost impossible, it can be reduced by cycling water in several short intervals. Apply water for 5 to 10 minutes every hour, and repeat the cycle to let the water soak into the soil before running off.

The Lawn Watering Guide (table 4.5) provides the total number of minutes for watering turfgrass each week. Most ground covers take about the same amount of water as warm-season turfgrass. To determine how many watering cycles are necessary, divide the weekly minutes required for turfgrass by the length of each cycle. Determine whether the sprinklers are applying water faster than the soil can absorb it. Slopes with clay soil are especially prone to runoff because water can easily be applied more quickly than the soil can take it up. On slopes, sprinkler outputs of over $\frac{1}{2}$ inch (1.2 cm) per hour often lead to excessive runoff. Drip irrigation of slope plantings of shrubs and many ground covers places water around each plant's root zone and decreases runoff. The newer micro- and minisprinklers are excellent for this purpose, and they put out water at a slower rate than conventional lawn sprinklers.

A Few Common Questions and Answers about Drought

Q. **If water use becomes more restricted, how should I prioritize to save my landscape plants?**

A. Remove plants in crowded beds or low-priority plants competing for soil moisture with other plants. When water is limited, most people choose to water fruit trees and landscape trees. Although lawns, groundcovers, bedding plants, and shrubs can be reestablished over a relatively short time, mature trees take years to develop and are less easily replaced. One or two deep, thorough waterings in spring and early summer can be enough to keep trees alive when water is in short supply. Under-watered fruit trees probably will not produce any fruit, but will survive.

Q. **Should I use polymers?**

A. Polymers increase the amount of water a soil can hold, but plants still need the same amount of water. Field research studies with polymers so far are few and inconclusive. Early results suggest that, although most polymers can extend the time between waterings, some are not effective when fertilizers and salts are present in the soil. Add enough polymers to effectively amend the soil and mix them evenly into the soil.

Q. **Can dishwater and clothes wash water (gray water) be used on plants?**

A. Because the use of gray water for landscape watering is still restricted in most counties of California, check with the county health department before using it. Gray water should not be used on edible plants or house plants. Outdoors, gray water does not harm most ornamental plants unless the water contains added borax or chlorine bleaches or comes from home water softeners. To be safe, dilute dishwater or water used to wash clothes with fresh water. Phosphates in soaps and detergents may be beneficial to plants (see "Using Household Wastewater on Plants," below).

Q. **How much water is normally used to water a home landscape?**

A. About 40 to 50 percent of a household's water is used for outdoor activities, such as watering landscapes, washing cars, and filling swimming pools.

Q. **How much water can I save by removing my lawn?**

A. Water savings depends on what type of turfgrass the lawn is and which plants, if any, will replace it. Although turfgrass water requirements vary by species, they are not much different from the water needs of other landscape plants. Warm-season lawns, such as bermudagrass, take about 20 percent less water than cool-season lawns, such as tall fescue.

Q. **Can swimming pool water be used for watering plants?**

A. Water treated with normal swimming pool disinfectants is too salty for landscape plants. It is not practical to clean it up for yard use.

Q. **What plants are drought resistant?**

A. No native or commonly used landscape plant is drought-resistant until it becomes established in the site: all plants require a steady supply of moisture when first planted. Many California native plants used for landscaping originate in the cool, moist climate of the coast or the Sierra Nevada foothills, making them susceptible to drought in some areas of the state and prone to damage during long, dry periods. Once a landscape plant is established and has a deep root system, it requires less water.

Q. **When should trees, shrubs, and other landscape plants be planted in a dry year?**

A. To take advantage of fall and winter rains, prepare the planting site in spring or summer, but hold off planting until fall or winter.

Q. **How often should newly planted trees and shrubs be watered?**

A. Newly planted trees and shrubs need to be kept moist until a network or roots grows into native soil. Newly planted container plants may need watering every day for several weeks during warm weather. Adding a thick layer of mulch reduces water waste and weed problems. Try to delay planting until after the beginning of fall rains.

Q. **How long will it take a lawn to die from lack of water?**

A. If you stop watering your lawn, it will gradually die or become dormant. This may take from 3 to 6 weeks for most lawn grasses, but it takes longer for deep-rooted grasses like bermudagrass. The first signs will be wilting of grass blades and a bluish-gray appearance. Next, leaf blades will yellow and eventually become brown. The lawn will probably not turn from a uniform green to a uniform brown, but will instead look mottled, with green, yellow-green, gray, and brown areas.

Q. If my lawn dies, when should I replant?
A. Replant when there is enough water available to grow a new lawn. The best time to plant lawns is in the fall or spring for cool-season turfgrasses and late spring for warm-season turfgrasses. Summer or winter planting is not recommended for turfgrasses.

Using Household Wastewater on Plants

If California is experiencing a drought crisis and there is no longer fresh water to irrigate outdoor plantings, can gardeners use dishwater, bath water, or laundry water without hurting the plants? Yes, if they use reasonable care.

But, first, a warning: Household wash water, also called gray water, contains food residues and other organic matter that may attract insects and rodents. It also may contain bacteria and viruses that could cause illness. Public health officials have indicated that it may be used for home irrigation, but check with local health and building officials before using gray water.

Effects on Plants
Household wash water is much better for plants than no water at all, but there are possible problems. If the home has no water softener, bath water and rinse water from dishes and laundry are all of good quality for irrigation. Soapy wash water from dishes and laundry might better be saved to flush the toilet but can be used for irrigation.

Although using a water softener makes household wash water higher in sodium than it would be otherwise, it is still usable with some precautions. Over long periods of time—months, at least—sodium may cause soils to become more compact and resistant to water

penetration. To counteract the effects of sodium, work gypsum (up to ¼ lb per square foot, or about 1 kg per square meter) into the soil surface. In addition, watering on only one side of a tree or shrub bed means that a smaller area will be affected by the sodium and the water still can be used effectively by trees and shrubs.

- Soapy wash water from dishes or laundry will help keep plants alive in an emergency, but the following can become a problem.

- Chlorine. Bleaches commonly contain chlorine, which can damage plants, particularly if it touches the foliage. One toxicity symptom is a tendency for new, expanding leaves to appear bleached. When irrigating plants with wash-cycle laundry water, it is safer not to use a bleach in the wash cycle. If that is not practical, use as little bleach as possible and let the water stand overnight before irrigating with it.

- Boron. Many laundry products contain boron compounds (sometimes known as borax). Some have fairly high levels that can be toxic to plants. Plant damage from excess boron first shows up as burning of leaf edges. Boron content is not shown on container labels, but the trade name may provide clues. A product name that sounds somewhat like boron or borax probably indicates a significant amount of boron. When using wash water for irrigation, avoid adding packaged softeners because these products probably contain boron or metaphosphates, or both. Sodium in the metaphosphates tends to seal up the soil; accumulations of boron may be toxic to plants.

The phosphates in ordinary detergents will not hurt plants and usually act as plant fertilizer. Phosphates can overfertilize lakes and streams, but they are generally not a problem in the soil.

Applying Gray Water
Listed below are some rules for irrigating with "used" water that reduce the chances of plant damage.

- Mix wash-cycle laundry water with rinse-cycle water before using it on plants. Mixing cuts the concentration of harmful chemicals, probably enough to avoid plant damage.

- Watch closely for signs of plant damage. If certain plants show symptoms first, they are probably more sensitive to damage; if possible, irrigate them with better-quality water. Avoid using wash water on very salt-sensitive plants such as azaleas and strawberries.

- Do not use wash water for potted plants. With their restricted root zones, potted plants are much more subject to damage. Save cold water from the shower (before the water warms up) for potted plants or other special uses.

- Do not pour water directly onto the base of tree trunks or shrubs. This may cause crown rot. The feeder roots that take up water are located well away from the base of the tree.

- Apply enough water to give the plants a good drink. Merely wetting the surface of the ground around deeper-rooted plants gives little benefit.

Conserving Water in Home Orchards

Full-sized fruit and nut trees require large quantities of water to maintain themselves, increase the size of their fruit, and grow new shoots and flower buds to bear succeeding crops. On an average summer day, a bearing tree may transpire from 40 to 60 gallons (150 to 230 l) of water. On a very hot day, a large tree may use more than 100 gallons (380 l) if that much water is available in the soil.

The amount of water used by orchard trees changes with the climate. In cool coastal areas, trees use the equivalent of about 18 inches (45 cm) of rainfall during the spring and summer growing seasons. In the hot Central Valley, fruit and nut trees transpire about 36 inches (90 cm) of water in a season. About two-thirds of that total is used during June, July, and August. Fruit and nut trees require these amounts of rainfall or irrigation water to grow normally and to produce good crops of well-sized fruits or nuts. In a drought, it is possible to keep trees alive and moderately healthy with as much as one-third less water. Size and quality of the crop will be sacrificed, however.

Crucial Periods

To produce good yields, deciduous fruit and nut trees need some available soil moisture continuously from bloom until harvest. After harvest—in August, September, and later in the fall—these trees can survive on a minimum of soil moisture without tree injury or reduction of the following year's crop. Evergreen trees such as citrus need soil moisture during both summer and fall to maintain leaves and fruit size. Normal soil moisture in the spring is also necessary for fruit set in citrus. Grapes need ample soil moisture in April for the beginning of cane growth and during the early summer for cane and leaf growth and fruit set. Withholding water during late summer and fall does not hurt the vines and increases sugar content in the grapes.

Regardless of irrigation schedules, it is very important to start the growing season with moist soil throughout the root zone. In years with fewer than 10 to 12 inches (25 to 30 cm) of winter rainfall, it usually is necessary to irrigate fruit trees 2 to 5 weeks before they bloom to encourage adequate root growth. A second irrigation usually is needed in late May. During June, July, and August, a reasonable schedule requires irrigating sandy soil every 2 or 3 weeks and heavier loams or clay loams every 3 or 4 weeks. If the weather is unusually cool, intervals can be lengthened.

Watering Home Orchards

How can the family orchardist irrigate fruit and nut trees adequately and still conserve water? Often, much water is wasted by surface runoff during irrigation, and weeds, ground covers, and grass may use water that trees need. To conserve water:

- prevent surface runoff while irrigating

- eliminate weeds or other competing plant growth around trees

- irrigate when the soil is fairly dry (see table 4.7)

To prevent runoff and ensure that all the water applied stays in the root zone, make a basin under each tree 4 to 6 inches (10 to 15 cm) deep, with a good ridge of soil at the outer edge. If the water supply is adequate, extend the basin about 3 feet (90 cm) beyond the outer edge of the tree so that the whole root zone will be wetted. If water is restricted, make the basin only to the outer edge. In an extreme water shortage, the basin may be limited to one side of the tree. Use a hose or sprinkler to fill the basin. If the land is not level, several small basins or even furrows can be used. To help maintain water pressure and even out the demand on a water distribution system, irrigate trees at night or at other off-peak periods.

The amount of water to apply in a single irrigation depends on the soil's capacity to store water (see chapter 3). In the top 6 feet (1.8 m), sandy soils generally hold 4 to 6 inches (10 to 15 cm) of water, and loams and clay loams hold from 6 to 12 inches (15 to 30 cm), depending on how fine-textured they are (see table 4.1). Because the roots of most fruit and nut trees are in the upper 6 feet (1.8 cm), do not apply more than these amounts. Additional applied water will be wasted if it goes below the root zone.

Refer to chapters 17, 18, and 19 for additional tree fruit and nut crop information.

Fruit Thinning

It is usually desirable to thin fruit when they are small so that those remaining will be of good size at harvest (see chapter 17, "Temperate Tree Fruit and Nut Crops"). If water is limited, thinning is essential. The easiest way to thin the tree is to cut about one-fourth or one-third of the limbs out of the tree. This pruning is usually completed in winter, but in an emergency it can be done in spring or early summer.

When the young fruit are ½ to ¾ inch (1.2 to 1.9 cm) in diameter (usually in May), individual fruit can be pulled off the tree by hand or knocked off with a padded pole to prevent injury to the bark on the limbs. The less water available, the fewer fruit should be left on the tree after thinning. Normally, with good water supply, peaches and nectarines are left 8 inches (20 cm) apart. Plums and apricots are left 4 to 5 inches (10 to 12.5 cm) apart, and apples and pears are thinned so that one or two fruit remain per cluster. If water is expected to be in short supply, remove even more fruit, possibly spacing them about twice as far apart as normal. Thinning usually removes more fruit than is left on the tree, so do not be concerned about the number of small fruit left on the ground.

What to Do in a Real Emergency

When the water supply is extremely limited, fruit and nut trees have a better chance of survival if they are irrigated early in the season rather than late. Under these conditions, many deciduous trees can survive on only one to two good irrigations, although they will not size fruit and may produce only a limited number of flower buds for the next year. If the trees run out of water, they adopt a semidormant condition for the rest of the summer. When this happens, trees usually drop their leaves, exposing large limbs to the sun. To minimize sunburn, which can be very damaging to trees, paint the upper side of the limbs with white water-based paint that reflects the heat.

Of all common fruit and nut trees, almonds, figs, and olives are the most tolerant of drought. Apples, apricots, cherries, pears, prunes, and walnuts are moderately tolerant, and nectarines, peaches, and citrus are least tolerant.

What Other Water Conservation Measures Can Home Fruit Growers Use?

Mulches on the soil can prevent weed growth and minimize surface evaporation. Grass clippings, shredded bark, and dark plastic sheets can be used as mulches.

Heavy pruning and crop removal in June can sometimes reduce water loss slightly, but if done too early, it causes extra shoot growth, which increases water use.

To guarantee that the soil is dry and to prevent wasting water, wait until a light wilt shows in the leaves in the afternoon before irrigating. This procedure can result in small-sized fruit unless the trees have been very heavily thinned.

Bibliography

Harris, R. W., and R. H. Coppick. 1977. Saving water in landscape irrigation. Oakland: University of California Division of Agriculture and Natural Resources Publication 2976.

Hartin, J. S., ed. 1991. Dry wit: Making the best of a dry situation. Riverside: UC Cooperative Extension special tabloid.

Pittenger, D. R. 1992. Home vegetable gardening. Oakland: University of California Division of Agriculture and Natural Resources Publication 21444.

U.S. Department of Agriculture, Soil Conservation Service. 1964. National engineering handbook. Washington, D.C.: U.S. Government Printing Office.

5

Plant Propagation

Pamela M. Geisel

LEARNING OBJECTIVES

- Understand basic principles of sexual and asexual plant propagation.

- Learn how to germinate seeds.

- Know how to propagate a plant asexually from a stem, leaf, or root cutting.

- Learn the basics of grafting, budding, and home tissue culture techniques.

Plant Propagation

Plant propagation is the process of increasing the numbers of a given species. There are two types of propagation: sexual and asexual. Sexual propagation in higher plants, which is also known as sexual reproduction, involves the floral parts of the plant. The *egg* (the female gamete contained in the ovary of the flower) and the *sperm* (the male gamete contained in the pollen) unite in a process that can mirror sexual reproduction in human beings by drawing from the gene pool of two parents (flowers) to create a new individual. Unlike sexual propagation in humans, however, the process in plants may involve only one parent, because some flowers contain both male and female sex organs and can self-reproduce. Asexual propagation uses the vegetative or nonfloral parts of the plant (stems, leaves, or roots) to generate a new plant. Propagation by asexual methods occurs very readily in higher plants. Genetically, the asexually propagated new individual plant is identical to its parent stem, leaf, or root and could be called a clone of its parent. Typically, greater genetic diversity exists in plants propagated by sexual methods. The discussion of plant progation that follows is adapted from materials presented in Frey 1993.

Both sexual and asexual propagation have advantages. Sexual propagation may be less expensive and quicker than other methods; it may be the only way to obtain new varieties and maintain hybrid vigor. In certain species, it is the only practical method of propagation, and it can reduce the transmission of certain diseases. The primary advantage of asexual propagation is that it perpetuates favorable characteristics of the parent plant as closely as possible. In some species, it may also be easier and faster, and it may be the only way to reproduce some cultivars.

Sexual Propagation

Sexual propagation involves the union of the sperm, contained in the pollen grains, with the egg, located in the female plant parts (the ovary and ovules), which together produce a zygote that later divides into many cells to form the embryo of the seed. Seeds, which are the products of sexual propagation in plants, comprise three parts: the outer seed coat that protects the seed; the endosperm, a food reserve tissue; and the embryo, which is actually a developing young plant in a relatively dormant state. When a seed is mature and placed in a favorable environment, it will germinate (begin active growth) and develop into a seedling and later a mature plant.

Obtaining and Storing Quality Seeds

High-quality plants begin with high-quality seeds purchased from a reliable dealer. Select varieties adapted to your area that provide the size, color, and growth habit desired. Many new vegetable and flower varieties are hybrids, which are more expensive than open-pollinated (nonhybrid) types, but hybrid plants usually have more vigor, more uniformity, and better productivity than nonhybrids and sometimes possess resistance to specific diseases or other unique characteristics.

Although some seed keep for several years if stored properly, it is advisable to purchase only enough for the current year's use. Even high-quality seed may contain minute amounts of noncrop seed, but they will almost always be void of noxious weed seed. Printing on the seed packet must note the year for which the seed were packaged, the germination percentage expected, and any chemical seed treatments. If seeds are obtained well in advance of the actual sowing date, or if they are stored as surplus, keep them in a cool, dry place. Laminated foil packets help ensure dry storage. Paper packets are best kept in tightly closed jars or other closed containers and maintained around 40°F (4°C) in low humidity. The average refrigerator provides ideal conditions for seed storage.

Some gardeners save seeds from their own gardens. Such seed is, however, the result of random, open pollination by insects or other natural agents (birds, butterflies) and may not produce plants identical to the parents, whereas purchased hybrid varieties are guaranteed to have the desirable traits of the specific, selected parent plants from which they were bred.

Seed Germination

Most seed companies take great care in handling seeds properly. Usually, about 80 percent or more of the seeds sown will germinate if optimal conditions for the species are provided. From the seeds that germinate, expect about 75 percent to produce vigorous and sturdy seedlings. Seed germination begins when environmental conditions are satisfactory and when certain internal requirements have been met. A seed must have a mature embryo, contain an endosperm large enough to nurture the embryo, and have sufficient hormones, such as gibberellins and auxins, to initiate the germination process.

The percentage of seeds that germinate may be tested at home using a rolled-towel test. Lay moistened paper toweling on a flat surface and place rows of seeds on the toweling, starting along one side. As rows are completed, loosely roll up the toweling with the seeds inside. Place the rolled toweling and seeds under optimal temperature, moisture, and light conditions to induce germination. Check the rolls every few days for up to 10 days. Then, count the germinated seeds and calculate the germination percentage. For small amounts of seed, test a minimum of 20 seeds. If a large amount of seed is available, test 100 seed.

Environmental Factors Affecting Germination

Four environmental factors affect seed germination: water, oxygen, light, and temperature. Optimal levels of light and temperature vary among species, but all seeds require continuous water and oxygen for germination to occur.

Water. Germination begins with the seed absorbing or imbibing water. The amount of available water in the germination medium greatly affects water uptake. An adequate, continuous supply of water is important to ensure germination. Once the germination process has begun, a dry period will cause an embryo to die.

Oxygen. Respiration takes place in all viable seeds. The respiration rate of seeds is low, but some oxygen is required. Because the respiration rate increases during germination, the medium in which the seeds are placed should be loose and well aerated. If the oxygen supply during germination is limited or reduced, germination can be severely retarded or inhibited.

Light. Light stimulates germination in some species and inhibits it in others. In some species, light may have little or no effect. Examples of plants that require light to assist seed germination are ageratum, begonia, browallia, impatiens, lettuce, and petunia. Conversely, calendula, centaurea, pansy, annual phlox, verbena, and vinca are examples of plants whose seed germinate best in the dark. Other plants' light requirements are not specific at all. Seed catalogs and seed packets often list germination or cultural tips for individual species. Table 5.1 lists light requirements for germination. When sowing light-requiring seeds, leave them on the soil surface. If they are covered at all, cover them lightly with fine peat moss or fine vermiculite. If applied very thinly, these two materials permit some light to reach the seeds. Fluorescent lights that are suspended 6 to 12 inches (15 to 30 cm) above the seeds and kept in operation 16 hours a day can provide supplemental light in low-light situations (e.g., indoors).

Temperature. Favorable temperatures in the germination medium are also important and affect not only the germination percentage but also the rate of germination (table 5.2). Some seeds germinate over a wide range of temperatures, whereas others require a narrow range. Many seeds have minimum, maximum, and optimal temperatures at which they germinate. For example, tomato seed has a minimum germination temperature of 50°F (10°C), a maximum temperature of 95°F (35°C), and an optimal germination temperature of about 80°F (27°C). When germination temperatures are listed, they are usually the optimal temperatures, unless otherwise specified. Generally, 65°F to 75°F (18° to 24°C) is best for most plants, which means that germination flats may have to be placed in special warming chambers or on radiators, heating cables, or heating mats to maintain optimal temperature. The importance of maintaining proper temperature to achieve maximum germination percentages cannot be overemphasized (for specific information, see table 5.2).

Breaking Dormancy

For germination to occur, seeds must be physically and physiologically ready to break dormancy. One of the functions of dormancy is to prevent a seed from germinating before it is surrounded by a favorable environment.

Even when the environment is ideal, dormancy is difficult to break in some trees and shrubs. Various special treatments may be required for the seed to break dormancy and stimulate germination.

Table 5.1

TEMPERATURE AND LIGHTING REQUIREMENTS FOR SEED GERMINATION OF SELECTED ANNUAL FLOWERING PLANTS

Scientific name	Common name	Optimal soil temperature °F	°C	Light required*	Days to germinate†
Ageratum spp.	golden ageratum	70	21	D	5
Ageratum houstonianum (A. mexicanum)	regular ageratum varieties	70	21	L	5
Alcea rosea	hollyhock (annual)	60	16	DL	10
Antirrhinum majus	snapdragon	65	18	L	10
Begonia semperflorens	begonia (fibrous-rooted)	70	21	L	15
Browallia spp.	amethyst flower, browallia	70	21	L	15
Calendula officinalis	calendula, pot marigold	70	21	D	10
Callistephus chinensis	annual aster, China aster	70	21	DL	8
Catharanthus roseus (Vinca rosea)	periwinkle	70	21	D	15
Celosia argentea	cockscomb, celosia	70	21	DL	10
Centaurea cyanus	cornflower, bachelor's button	65	18	D	10
Centaurea gymnocarpa	dusty miller	65	18	D	10
Coleus blumei (C. hybridus)	coleus	65	18	L	10
Cosmos bipinnatus	cosmos	70	21	DL	5
Dahlia pinnata	dahlia (from seed)	70	21	DL	5
Dianthus chinensis, Dianthus spp.	annual carnation, annual pinks, dianthus, sweet william	70	21	DL	5–20
Gaillardia pulchella	gaillardia (annual)	70	21	DL	20
Impatiens wallerana (I. sultanii)	impatiens	70	21	L	15
Lathyrus odoratus	sweet pea	55	13	D	15
Lobelia erinus	lobelia	70	21	DL	20
Lobularia maritima	sweet alyssum, alyssum	70	21	DL	5
Nicotiana alata (affinis)	nicotiana, flowering tobacco	70	21	L	20
Nierembergia caerulea	dwarf cupflower, nierembergia	70	21	DL	15
Petunia hybrida	petunia	70	21	L	10
Phlox drummondii	annual phlox	65	18	D	10
Portulaca grandiflora	moss rose, portulaca	70	21	D	20
Rudbeckia hirta	rudbeckia, gloriosa daisy, black-eyed Susan, coneflower	70	21	DL	10
Salvia splendens	scarlet sage	70	21	L	15
Tagetes spp.	marigold (dwarf types and tall types)	70	21	DL	5
Valeriana officinalis	heliotrope	70	21	DL	25
Verbena hybrida (V. hortensis)	garden verbena	65	18	D	20
Viola tricolor, Viola hybrids	pansy, Johnny-jump-up	65	18	D	10
Zinnia elegans	zinnia	70	21	DL	5

Notes:
*D = seeds germinate best in darkness; DL = no light requirement; L = seeds germinate best in light.
†Usual number of days required for uniform germination at optimal temperature. This information was adapted by the Ohio State University Cooperative Extension Service from USDA research results released by H. M. Cathey.

Seed Scarification. Seed scarification involves breaking, scratching, or softening the seed coat so that water can enter and begin the germination process. There are several methods of scarifying seed. In acid scarification, seed are put in a dry, glass container and covered with concentrated sulfuric acid at about twice the volume of seed. (This technique is not recommended for amateur horticulturists because concentrated sulfuric acid is extremely dangerous.) The seed are gently stirred and allowed to soak from 10 minutes to several hours, depending on the hardness of the seed coat. When the seed coat has become thin, the seed can be removed, washed under cold water for 10 minutes, and then planted. A second method is mechanical scarification. Seed are filed with a metal file, nicked with a knife, rubbed with sandpaper, or cracked with a hammer to weaken the seed coat. In hot-water scarification seeds are placed in hot water (170° to 212°F [77° to 100°C]), where they soak for 12 to 24 hours as the water cools. The seed are then planted. A fourth method is warm, moist scarification, in which seed are stored in nonsterile, warm, damp containers, where the seed coat is broken down by decay over several months.

Seed Stratification. Seed of some fall-ripening temperate zone trees and shrubs will not germinate naturally unless chilled underground as they overwinter. Some examples include tulip tree, golden rain tree, oaks, sweet gum, and pyracantha. Simulating the environmental requirements for moist chilling may be accomplished artificially by a special treatment called seed stratification.

To stratify seed, put sand or vermiculite in a clay pot to about 1 inch (2.5 cm) from the top. Place the seed on top of the medium and cover with ½ inch (1.2 cm) of sand or vermiculite. Wet the medium thoroughly and allow excess water to drain through the hole in the pot. Place the pot containing the moist medium and the seed in a plastic bag and tie the bag using a twist tie or rubber band. Place the bag in a refrigerator where the temperature is kept at 35°F to 45°F (2° to 7°C). Periodically check to ensure that the medium is moist but not saturated. Additional water will probably not be necessary. After 10 to 12 weeks, remove the bag from the refrigerator. Take the pot out and set it in a warm place in the house. Water often enough to keep the medium moist. The seedlings should soon emerge. When the young seedlings have developed their first true leaves, transplant them into individual pots until it is time to set them outside.

Another successful germination procedure for seeds of woody plants uses sphagnum moss, fine-textured vermiculite, or sand. Wet the medium thoroughly, then allow the excess water to drain. You may need to squeeze excess water from wet moss by hand. Mix seed with the moist media and place in a plastic bag. Use a twist tie or rubber band to secure the top and put the bag in a refrigerator kept at 35°F to 45°F (2° to 7°C). Check periodi-

Table 5.2

SOIL TEMPERATURE CONDITIONS FOR VEGETABLE SEED GERMINATION

Vegetable	Minimum °F	Minimum °C	Optimal range °F	Optimal range °C	Maximum °F	Maximum °C
asparagus	50	10	75–85	24–30	95	35
bean, green	60	16	75–85	24–30	95	35
bean, Lima	60	16	75–85	24–30	85	30
beet	40	4	65–85	18–30	95	35
broccoli	40	4	60–85	16–30	95	35
cabbage	40	4	60–85	16–30	95	35
carrot	40	4	65–85	18–30	95	35
cauliflower	40	4	65–85	18–30	95	35
celery	40	4	*		*	
chard, Swiss	40	4	65–85	18–30	95	35
corn	50	10	65–95	18–35	105	41
cucumber	60	16	65–95	18–35	105	41
eggplant	60	16	75–85	24–30	95	35
lettuce	32	0	60–75	16–24	85	30
muskmelon (canteloupe)	60	16	75–85	24–30	105	41
okra	60	16	85–95	33–35	105	41
onion	32	0	65–85	18–30	95	35
parsley	40	4	65–85	18–30	95	35
parsnip	32	0	65–75	18–24	85	30
pea	40	4	65–75	18–24	85	30
pepper	60	16	65–75	18–24	95	35
pumpkin	60	16	85–95	30–35	105	41
radish	40	4	65–85	18–30	95	35
spinach	32	0	65–75	18–24	75	24
squash	60	16	85–95	30–35	105	41
tomato	50	10	65–85	18–30	95	35
turnip	40	4	60–95	16–35	105	41
watermelon	60	16	75–95	24–35	105	41

Source: Adapted from Harrington and Minges 1954.
Note: *Celery requires diffuse light and a night temperature from 10° to 15°F (18° to 27°C) lower than the day temperature for good germination. Optimal conditions are 85°F (30°C) day, 70°F (21°C) night with diffuse light and high moisture.

cally to ensure that the medium is moist. After 10 to 12 weeks, remove the bag from the refrigerator and plant the seed in pots or flats to germinate and grow. Handle seeds carefully: often the small roots and shoots are emerging at the end of the stratification period, and care must be taken not to break them off.

Starting Plants from Seed

Germinating Media. Many materials can be used to start seed, ranging from straight vermiculite to mixtures of soilless artificial media to the various amended soil mixes. With experience, you can determine what works best under local conditions. Always keep in mind the ideal characteristics of a germinating medium: fine and uniform in texture, yet well aerated and loose; free of insects, disease organisms, and weed seed; low in total soluble salts; and able to hold moisture yet also drain well. One mixture that possesses these characteristics is a combination of one-third sterilized sand, one-third vermiculite or perlite, and one-third peat moss. Do not use garden soil by itself to start seedlings as it is too heavy, not sterile, does not drain well, and shrinks from the sides of containers if allowed to dry out.

It is very important to use sterile media and containers. To sterilize a small quantity of soil mixture in an oven, place slightly moistened soil in a covered, heat-resistant container or pan and then place the container in an oven set at about 250°F (121°C). Use a candy or meat thermometer to ensure that the mix reaches a temperature of 180°F (82°C) for at least 30 minutes. Avoid overheating as this can damage the soil. The process may produce an unpleasant odor. This treatment should kill damping-off fungi and prevent many other plant diseases, eliminate potential insect pests, and kill many weed seeds. Containers and implements should be washed to remove any debris, then rinsed in a solution of 1 part chlorine bleach to 9 parts water. Avoid recontamination of the medium and tools.

An artificial soilless mix may also provide the desired qualities of a good germination medium. The basic ingredients of lightweight mix are sphagnum peat moss and vermiculite, both of which are generally free of weed seeds and insects.

Ready-made "peat-lite" mixes or similar products are commercially available. To make them at home, combine 4 quarts (3.8 l) of shredded sphagnum peat moss, 4 quarts

(3.8 l) of a fine-grade vermiculite, 1 tablespoon (15 ml) of superphosphate, and 2 tablespoons (30 ml) of ground limestone. Another combination is 50 percent vermiculite or perlite and 50 percent milled sphagnum peat moss with fertilizer. Mix thoroughly. Because these mixes have little fertility, seedlings must be watered with a diluted fertilizer solution soon after they emerge.

Containers for Sowing Seed. Wooden or plastic flats and trays can be purchased or made from scrap lumber. A convenient size is about 12 to 18 inches (30 to 45 cm) long and 12 inches (30 cm) wide with a depth of about 2 inches (5 cm). Leave cracks of about ⅛ inch (3 mm) between the boards in the bottom or drill a series of holes to ensure drainage. Flower pots of clay or plastic can be used. As long as drainage is adequate, recycled household items—such as cottage cheese containers, the bottoms of milk cartons or bleach containers, and pie pans—can be used for starting seed. Containers should be washed thoroughly, then soaked and rinsed in a solution of 1 part chlorine bleach to 9 parts water. This procedure prevents most seedling diseases from occurring.

Numerous types of pots and strips made of compressed peat can also be used to start seed. Plant bands and plastic cell packs are available as well. Each cell or minipot holds a single plant, which reduces the risk of root injury when transplanting. Peat pellets, peat- or fiber-based blocks, and expanded plastic foam cubes can also be used for seeding. Here, the growing medium itself forms the container unit. When soaked in water, compressed peat pellets expand to form compact individual pots. They make good use of space and maintain their integrity better than peat pots. If you wish to avoid transplanting seedlings, compressed peat pellets can be set directly out in the garden, and seeds may be sown directly in them. Cell packs, which are strips of connected individual pots, are also available in plastic and are frequently used by commercial bedding-plant growers because they withstand frequent handling. If using recycled cell packs, wash them in a 1 to 9 bleach-to-water solution to sterilize.

Seeding Procedures. Time the sowing of seeds for transplants so that plants may safely be moved out doors after germination. The sowing period may range from 4 to 18 weeks before transplanting, depending on the speed of germination, the rate of growth, and the cultural conditions provided. A common mistake is to sow seeds too early and then attempt to hold the seedlings back under poor light or improper temperature ranges, which usually results in tall, weak, and spindly plants that do not perform well in the garden.

After selecting a container, fill it to ¾ inch (19 mm) from the top with the moistened medium you have chosen. For very small seeds, at least the top ¼ inch (6 mm) should be a fine, screened mix or a layer of vermiculite. Firm the medium at the corners and edges using your fingers or a block of wood to provide a uniform, flat surface. For medium to large seed, make furrows about 1 to 2 inches (2.5 to 5 cm) apart and ⅛ to ¼ inch (3 to 6 mm) deep across the surface of the container using a narrow board or pot label. Sowing in rows gives good light and air movement and helps prevent the spread of damping-off fungus should it appear. Seedlings in rows are easier to label and to handle at transplanting time than those that have been sown in a broadcast manner. Sow the seed thinly and uniformly in the rows by gently tapping the seed packet as it is moved along the row. If they require darkness for germination, use a flour sifter to cover the seed with an even layer of dry vermiculite.

A suitable planting depth is usually about two to four times the diameter of the seed. Follow printed recommendations on the package. Do not plant seeds too deeply. Extremely fine seed, such as petunia, begonia, and snapdragon, are not covered but are lightly pressed into the medium or watered in with a fine mist spray. If these seeds are broadcast, strive for a uniform stand by sowing half the seed in one direction, then sowing the other way with the remainder.

Large seeds are frequently sown into a small container or cell pack, which eliminates the need for early transplanting. Usually, two or three seed are sown per unit and later thinned to allow the strongest seedling to grow. Peach seed should be removed from the hard pit first. Care must be taken when cracking the pits, as any injury to the seed itself can provide entry for disease organisms.

Seed Tape. Most garden stores and seed catalogs offer indoor and outdoor seed tapes. Seed tape has precisely spaced seed enclosed in an organic, water-soluble material. When planted, the tape dissolves and the seed germinate normally. Although they are expensive, seed tapes are especially convenient for tiny, hard-to-handle seed. Seed tapes allow uniform emergence of seedlings, eliminate overcrowding, and permit sowing in perfectly straight rows. The tapes can be cut at any point for multiple-row plantings, and thinning is rarely necessary.

Pregerminating Seed. Another method of starting seed is pregermination, which involves sprouting seed before they are planted in pots or in the garden. Lay seed between the folds of cotton cloth on a layer of vermiculite or similar material in a pan. Keep them moist in a warm place. This technique reduces the time to germination, as the temperature and moisture are easy to control, and it guarantees a high percentage of germination because no seeds will be lost to environmental factors. When roots begin to show, place the seeds in containers or plant them directly in the garden. While transplanting seedlings, be careful not to break off tender roots or to allow the seedlings to dry out. Continued attention to watering is critical.

When planting seed in a container that will be set out in the garden later, place one pregerminated seed in a 2- to 3-inch (5- to 7.5-cm) container. Plant the seed at only half the recommended depth. Gently press a little soil over the sprouted seed and then add to the soil surface about ¼ inch (6 mm) of milled sphagnum or sand, which will keep the surface uniformly moist but allow shoots to push through easily. Keep the pots in a warm place and care for them just as for any other newly transplanted seedlings.

A convenient way to plant small, delicate, pregerminated seed is to suspend them in a gel. Make a gel by blending cornstarch with boiling water until the mixture is thick enough for the seed to stay suspended. Cool thoroughly before use and then place the gel with seedlings in a plastic bag with a hole in it. Squeeze the gel through the hole along a premarked garden row. Because spacing of seed is determined by the number of seed in the gel, add more gel if the spacing is too dense, and add more seed if spacing is too wide. The gel keeps the germinating seed moist until they establish themselves in the garden soil.

Watering during Germination. After seeds have been sown, moisten the planting mix thoroughly. Use a fine mist spray or place the containers in a pan or tray that has about

1 inch (2.5 cm) of warm water in the bottom. Avoid splashing or excessive flooding, which might displace the seeds. When the planting mix is saturated, set the container aside to drain. The soil should be moist but not wet.

Ideally, seed flats should remain sufficiently moist during the germination period so that adding water is unnecessary. One way to maintain moisture is to slip the whole flat or pot into a clear plastic bag or cover it with clear plastic wrap after the initial watering. The plastic should be at least 1 to 1½ inches (2.5 to 3.7 cm) from the soil. Keep the container out of direct sunlight to prevent high temperatures from harming the seeds. Many home gardeners cover their flats with panes of glass instead of using plastic. Be sure to remove the cover as soon as the first seedlings appear. Light watering of the surface can then be practiced if care and good judgment are used.

Lack of uniformity, overwatering, and drying out are problems related to hand-watering. Excellent germination and moisture uniformity can be obtained with a low-pressure misting system. Four seconds of mist every 6 minutes, or 10 seconds every 15 minutes, during the daytime in spring seems to be satisfactory. Bottom heat is an asset with a mist system. Subirrigation, or watering from below, may work well to keep the flats moist. If the flats or pots sit in water constantly, however, the soil may absorb too much water and the seeds may rot because they lack oxygen or have disease problems.

Temperature and Light Requirements of Seedlings. After germination, move the flats to a bright, airy, cooler location that is kept at 55° to 60°F (13° to 16°C) at night and 65° to 70°F (18° to 21°C) during the day. Place them in a window facing south, if possible. If a large, bright window is not available, place the seedlings under fluorescent lights. Use two 40-watt, cool-white fluorescent tubes or special plant-growth lamps. Position the plants 6 inches (15 cm) from the tubes and keep the lights on about 16 hours each day. As the seedlings grow, the lights should be raised accordingly to prevent soft, leggy growth and minimize disease troubles. Some crops, of course, may germinate or grow best at a different constant temperature and must be handled separately from the bulk of the plants. Keep the soil evenly moist and do not allow seedlings to wilt. Regular fertilization with half-strength soluble plant fertilizer solution is recommended.

Transplanting and Handling

If the plants have not been seeded in individualized containers, they must be transplanted to give them proper growing space. One of the most common mistakes is leaving seedlings in the seed flat too long. The ideal time to transplant young seedlings is when they are small and there is little danger from setback, which is usually when the first true leaves develop above or between the cotyledon leaves (the cotyledons or seed leaves are the first leaves the seedling produces).

Seedling growing mixes and containers can be purchased or prepared similarly to those for seed germination. The medium should contain more plant nutrients than a germination mix, however. Some commercial soilless mixes have fertilizer already added. Use a soluble house plant fertilizer at the dilution recommended by the manufacturer about every 2 weeks after the seedlings are established. Young seedlings are easily damaged by too much fertilizer, especially if they are under moisture stress.

To transplant, carefully dig and lift small plants with a knife or wooden plant label. Handle small seedlings by their leaves, not their delicate stems. Gently ease them apart in small groups, so that it is easier to separate individual plants. Avoid tearing roots in the process. In the medium into which the seedling will be planted, make a hole the same depth at which the seedling was growing in the seed flat. Small plants or slow growers should be placed 1 inch (2.5 cm) apart, and rapid-growing, large seedlings should be placed about 2 inches (5 cm) apart. After planting, firm the soil and water the transplants gently. Keep newly transplanted seedlings in the shade for a few days or place them under fluorescent lights. Keep them away from sun and direct heat sources. Continue watering and fertilizing using the same procedures as for the seed flats.

Most plants transplant well and can be started indoors. The few plants that are difficult to transplant are generally seeded directly outdoors or sown directly into individual containers indoors; examples include zinnias, melons, squash, carrots, and potatoes.

A wide variety of containers is available for transplanting seedlings. Containers should be economical and durable and make good use of space. The type of container to use depends on the plant and on individual growing conditions. Cell packs, which provide space for several plants, are generally made of plastic, pressed paper, or fiber. Standard pots may be used, but they waste a great deal of space and may not dry out rapidly enough for the seedling to have sufficient oxygen for proper development. Pots made of pressed peat can be purchased in varying sizes. Individual pots or strips of connected pots fit closely together, are inexpensive, and can be planted directly in the garden. When setting out plants grown in peat pots, care should be used to cover the pot completely. If the top edge of the peat pot extends above the soil level, it may act as a wick and draw water away from the soil in the pot. To avoid this problem, tear off the top lip of the pot and plant flush with the soil level.

Hardening Plants

Hardening is the process of slowing plant growth to withstand changes in environmental conditions that occur when transplants are transferred from a greenhouse or home to the garden. A severe check in growth may occur if plants produced in a controlled environment are planted outdoors without a transition, or hardening, period. Hardening is critical with early crops, when adverse climatic conditions can be expected

Hardening can be accomplished by gradually lowering temperatures and relative humidity and reducing water, causing an accumulation of carbohydrates and a thickening of cell walls. A change from a soft, succulent type of growth to a firmer, harder type of growth is desired. The hardening process should be started at least 2 weeks before planting in the garden. If possible, plants should be moved to a 45° to 50°F (7° to 10° C) temperature indoors or outdoors in a shady location. A cold frame is excellent for this purpose. When put outdoors, plants should be shaded and then gradually moved into sunlight, increasing the length of exposure each day. Reduce the frequency of watering to slow growth, but do not allow plants to wilt. Tender seedlings should not be placed outdoors on windy days or when temperatures are below 45°F (7°C). Even cold-hardy plants will be hurt if exposed to very cold or freezing temperatures before they are hardened. After proper hardening, however, they can be planted outdoors and light frosts will not damage them.

Propagation of Ferns by Spores

Some gardeners desire to raise ferns from spores, even though ferns are more easily propagated by asexual methods. Reproduction via spores, which are located on the undersides of fronds, involves sexual propagation but no seeds, because ferns do not produce seeds. To propagate small quantities of ferns, first sterilize a brick by baking at 250°F (121°C) for 30 minutes. Place the sterilized brick in a pan and add water to cover the brick. When the brick is wet throughout, squeeze a thin layer of equal amounts of moist soil and peat onto the top of the brick. Pack a second layer about 1 inch (2.5 cm) thick on top of the first. Sprinkle spores on top. Cover with plastic (not touching the spores) and put in a warm place in indirect light. It may take up to a month or more for the spores to germinate. Keep moist at all times. A prothallus (one generation of the fern) will develop first from each spore, forming a light green mat. Mist lightly once a week to maintain high surface moisture; the sperm must be able to swim to the archegonia (female parts). After about 3 weeks, fertilization should have occurred. Pull the mat apart with tweezers in ¼-inch (0.6-cm) squares and space them ½ inch (1.2 cm) apart in a flat containing a 2-inch (5-cm) layer of sand, ¼ inch (0.6 cm) of charcoal, and about 2 inches (5 cm) of soil and peat mix. Cover with plastic and keep moist. When fern fronds appear and become crowded, transplant to small pots. Gradually reduce the humidity until they can survive in the open. Light exposure may be increased at this time.

Asexual Propagation

Asexual propagation is the best way to produce cultivars that closely resemble the parent. Clones are groups of plants identical to one parent; therefore, they can only be propagated asexually. The Bradford pear and the Peace rose are two examples of clones that have been asexually propagated for many years. The principal methods of asexual propagation are cuttings, layering, division, budding, and grafting. Cuttings involve rooting a severed vegetative piece of the parent plant; layering involves rooting a part of the parent and then severing it; division involves separating a multicrowned plant into separate plants; and budding and grafting join two plant parts from different varieties or species.

Cuttings

A cutting is a vegetative plant part severed from the parent plant that is induced to regenerate itself, forming a new plant. Many woody and herbaceous plants are propagated by cuttings from stems, leaves, roots, or specialized vegetative structures. Cuttings should be made from vigorous plants that are free of diseases and insect pests and have known identities, including varietal names. Cuttings are classified by the plant part from which they were obtained. Stem cuttings are the most widely used and most important type of cutting. Leaf and root cuttings are used less frequently but may be the primary propagation method for some species.

Take cuttings with a sharp knife or razor blade to reduce injury to the parent plant. Dip the cutting tool in rubbing alcohol or a solution of 1 part bleach to 9 parts water to prevent transmitting diseases from infected plant parts to healthy ones. Remove flowers and flower buds from stem cuttings so that their energy and stored carbohydrates are used for adventitious root and shoot formation rather than fruit and seed production. A rooting hormone may be used to hasten rooting, to increase the number of roots, or to obtain uniform rooting, except on soft fleshy stems. To prevent disease contamination of the entire supply of rooting hormone, put some of it in a separate container for dipping cuttings.

Insert cuttings into a rooting medium, such as a mixture of coarse sand, vermiculite, soil, and water or a mixture of peat, vermiculite, and perlite. For optimal rooting in the shortest time, choose a sterile rooting medium that is low in fertility, drains well enough to provide oxygen, and retains enough moisture to prevent water stress. Moisten the medium before inserting cuttings, and keep it evenly moist while cuttings are rooting and forming new shoots. Place stem and leaf cuttings in bright, indirect light. Keep root cuttings dark and moist until new shoots appear. Success with cuttings may be variable because of the nitrogen status of the plant, dormancy, and perhaps even the phase of the moon. For example, hardwood cuttings of forsythia taken in January root significantly better than those taken in December or November. Keep notes to document your successes and to allow for repeated success. Small-scale propagation units suitable for the home gardener's cuttings are described later in this chapter.

Softwood Stem Tip Cuttings. Cuttings prepared from soft, succulent new spring growth of deciduous or evergreen species are classified as softwood cuttings. Detach a 2- to 6-inch (5- to 15-cm) piece of stem, including the terminal bud. Make the cut just below a node. Remove lower leaves that would touch or be below the rooting medium, and dip the stem in rooting hormone. Insert the cutting into the rooting medium deeply enough to support itself. At least one node must be below the surface. Softwood stem tip cuttings generally work best if you gather cutting material early in the day and use lateral shoots that still have some flexibility but are mature enough so that they would break if bent sharply. Avoid weak, thin, interior stems as well as vigorous, very thick, woody ones, because both will root poorly. The stem tissue that works best can be bruised easily by a nail and will support leaf growth with a gradation in leaf sizes, from small, undeveloped end

Figure 5.1

Stem-tip cuttings for propagating ground covers. Using a sharp knife, clippers, or scissors, take a 4- to 6-inch (10- to 15-cm) cutting from the tip growth. Remove foliage from the lower 2 inches (5 cm) of stem to reduce water loss. Dip in rooting hormone (optional). Insert cuttings into flats or small pots of moist rooting medium. Keep cuttings enclosed in plastic bags to increase humidity around the rootless plants. Use popsicle sticks, half straws, or other props to hold the plastic off the leaves. Store cuttings in bright but indirect light until roots form. After the cuttings begin to root, gradually open the plastic to let in drier air, and move the flat or pots to brighter light. When the cuttings are well-rooted, transplant them to the garden. *Source:* Adapted from Roth 1991.

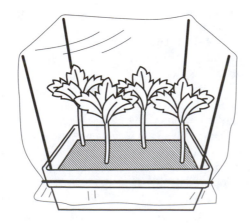

leaves to mostly older leaves of full size. The timing of softwood cuttings depends on the growth characteristics of the species. Softwood cuttings tend to wilt; keep them moist and cool at all times. Typical softwood stem tip cuttings tend to root in 2 to 5 weeks. A number of ornamentals (pyracantha, oleander, and veronica) and ground covers (periwinkle, English ivy, lamium) can be propagated using this technique, as shown in figure 5.1.

Cuttings from Canelike Stems. Cut cane-like stems, such as those from dracaena, dieffenbachia, and croton, into sections containing one or two nodes. Dust the ends with fungicide or activated charcoal and allow them to dry for several hours. Lay the stem cuttings horizontally, as shown in figure 5.2, with about half of the cutting below the rooting medium surface, eye facing upward. Cane cuttings are usually potted when roots and new shoots appear.

Semi-hardwood Stem Cuttings. Broadleaf evergreen species, such as photinia, osmanthus, euonymus, holly, pittosporum, magnolia, and camellia, are propagated best as semi-hardwood cuttings from mid-July to early September. The plants are ready for cutting when the growth flush is completed, the wood is firm, and leaves have matured. Use cuttings from 3 to 6 inches (7.5 to 15 cm) long with the basal half of the leaves removed. Remove any soft growth at the terminus. Dip the stem end into a rooting hormone before sticking them into the flat. Rooting the cuttings will take from 4 to 6 weeks. Rooting media such as a 1 to 1 mixture of perlite and peat moss or perlite and vermiculite give good results. Commercially, the cuttings are placed under a

misting system during the rooting process. Bottom heating cables speed up the process.

Hardwood Stem Cuttings. From October through late winter, during the dormant season, hardwood cuttings can be taken from deciduous plants that have lost their leaves. Collect wood from last season's growth and cut the stems from 6 to 20 inches (15 to 21 cm) long. Treat the basal end with a rooting hormone and bundle the cuttings together. Place the cuttings in a plastic bag or in moist sawdust or peat moss and keep them in a dark, cool location. Placing bottom heating cables under the bundles may facilitate the rooting process. Once rooting occurs, cuttings can be planted outdoors.

Hardwood cuttings of deciduous species are one of the least expensive, easiest methods of vegetative propagation. The cuttings are easy to prepare, are not perishable, and do not require special equipment during rooting. Wood of moderate size and vigor provides the best stock material for propagation. Central and basal stem cuttings are the best because they contain ample supplies of stored foods to nourish the developing adventitious roots and shoots until the new plants can sustain themselves. Tip portions of the shoot usually have lower amounts of stored food and should not be used for hardwood cuttings. The diameter of the cuttings may range from 1/4 inch (0.6 cm) to 2 inches (5 cm), depending on the species. Three different types of cuttings can be prepared, as shown in figure 5.3: *straight cut*, which does not include any older wood; *heel*, which includes a small piece of older wood; and *mallet*, which includes a short section of stem from older wood. The straight cut is the most common and usually gives satisfactory results.

Leaf Cuttings. Leaf cuttings (fig. 5.4) are used almost exclusively for a few indoor plants. Leaves of most plants produce a few roots but will not produce a plant; instead, they will just decay. In plants that can regenerate from leaves, such as sansevieria, *Begonia rex*, peperomia, African violet, and jade plant, the leaf blade or the leaf blade plus the petiole are used to start the new plant. Adventitious roots and an adventitious shoot will form at the base of the leaf. The original leaf does not become a part of the new plant.

African violets can be propagated from leaf cuttings consisting of an entire leaf (the leaf blade plus petiole), the leaf blade only, or a

Figure 5.2

Cutting from a cane-like stem.

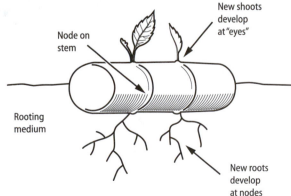

Node on stem

New shoots develop at "eyes"

Rooting medium

New roots develop at nodes

Figure 5.3

Types of hardwood stem cuttings. Tip, straight, heel, and mallet hardwood stem cuttings. *Source:* Adapted from Bienz 1980, p. 349.

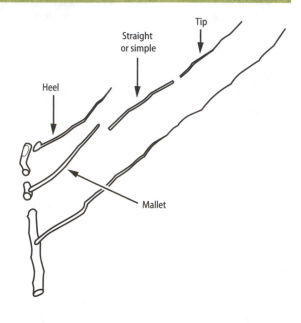

Figure 5.4

Leaf cutting examples. Adventitious roots and shoots develop at the base of leaf or at the point of slit.

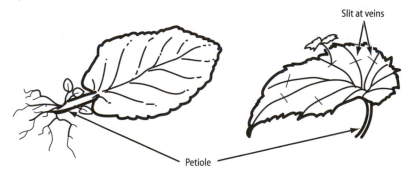

portion of the leaf blade. The new plant(s) form at the base of the petiole or at the midrib of the leaf blade. Insert leaf cuttings vertically into the rooting medium. Leaf cuttings should be rooted under the high-humidity conditions used for softwood stem cuttings. Root-promoting hormones are often helpful. The original leaf may be removed when the new plant has its own roots.

In plants that have leaves with split veins, such as *Begonia rex*, detach a mature leaf from the stock plant. Slit its large veins on the lower leaf surface. Lay the leaf cutting flat, lower side down (where the wounds are), on the rooting medium. Under humid conditions, new plants will form where the veins were cut. If the leaf

tends to curl up, hold it in place by covering the margins with the rooting medium. The old leaf blade will disintegrate.

Leaf sections can be used for asexual propagation in some plants, such as snake plant (*Sansevieria*) and fibrous-rooted begonias. Cut fibrous-rooted begonia leaves into wedges with at least one vein. Lay leaves flat on the rooting medium. A new plant will arise at the cut vein. Cut snake plant leaves into sections 2 to 4 inches (5 to 10 cm) long. Make the lower cut slanted and the upper cut straight so you can distinguish top from bottom. Insert the basal end of the snake plant leaf section vertically into the rooting medium, covering about three-fourths of its height. Roots will form fairly soon. In time, a new plant will appear at the base of the leaf section, and the original cutting will disintegrate. These and other succulent cuttings will rot if kept too moist.

Root Cuttings. Root cuttings are usually taken from 2- to 3-year-old plants during their dormant season, before new growth starts and while they still have a large carbohydrate supply. Avoid taking root cuttings when the parent plant is actively producing new shoots. Root cuttings of some species produce new adventitious shoots, which then form their own root systems, whereas root cuttings of other plants develop root systems before producing new shoots. When using root cuttings for propagation, it is important to maintain the correct polarity, or the cutting will be planted upside down. To propagate plants with large roots, make a straight top cut of the root section nearer the crown of the plant. Make a slanted cut 2 to 6 inches (5 to 15 cm) below the first cut at the distal (bottom) end. After storing the root cutting for about 3 weeks in moist sawdust, peat moss, or sand at 40°F (4°C), remove from storage. Insert the root cutting vertically into the rooting medium so that the proximal end (the top end, with the straight cut) is approximately level with the surface of the rooting medium. When root cuttings are used to propagate some plants with variegated foliage, such as aralias and pelargoniums, the new plants will lose the variegated form. Plants that can be propagated by root cuttings include the lesser flowering quince, California poppies, and phlox.

To propagate plants with small, delicate roots, take 1- to 2-inch (2.5- to 5-cm) sections of the roots and insert the cuttings horizontally into flats about ½ inch (1.2 cm) below the medium surface. After watering the cuttings, place a polyethylene cover or pane of glass over the flat to prevent the cuttings from drying. Set the flats in the shade. This method is usually done indoors or in a hotbed.

Small-Scale Units for Propagating Cuttings. Small-scale units for propagating cuttings may be made from inexpensive materials commonly found around the home. The units described below are easy to use and care for, do not require constant attention, and can be located in the kitchen, on a porch, or outdoors in a shady location. As shown in figure 5.5, an aquarium can make an ideal unit for home propagation of cuttings. Put 3 to 4 inches (7.5 to 10 cm) of rooting medium into the aquarium, moisten the medium, and the unit is ready for placing cuttings. Cover the aquarium with glass or plastic to maintain high humidity, to prevent the cuttings from wilting, and to hasten rooting. Instead of putting the rooting medium on top of the pea gravel you may place small pots or plastic trays containing the rooting medium on the gravel layer.

As shown in figure 5.5, large plastic pots of 6 to 8 inches (15 to 20 cm) in diameter can also be converted into excellent propagation units. Seal the drainage hole with putty and fill the pot with rooting medium. Put a 2-inch (5-cm) clay pot in the center of each large pot. Plug up the drainage hole of the small pot and add water. The water will pass slowly through the porous sides of the clay pot into the rooting medium, keeping it uniformly moist. At the same time, evaporation from the surface will maintain a suitable relative humidity inside the propagation unit. If all of the water is used up before rooting occurs, fill the pot again. Place a plastic bag over the cuttings and tie the open end against the pot. Use stakes or wire hoops to keep the plastic from collapsing on the cuttings.

For easy-to-root plants, such as coleus and chrysanthemums, plastic bags alone can be used to root cuttings. Tie a ball of moist sphagnum moss around the base of the cuttings, put them in the plastic bag, and close the opening.

Small wooden boxes, like the one in figure 5.5, may be converted into propagation units for cuttings. The box should be approximately 12 inches (30 cm) deep, with the top sloped from one side to the other. Seal any cracks or holes. Place a 1 inch (2.5 cm) layer of pea gravel on the bottom, and put 4 inches (10 cm) of rooting medium on top of the pea gravel. Moisten the medium, insert the cuttings, and cover the top with plastic.

The location of the propagation units determines the relative success of rooting the cuttings. Maintain a temperature of 65° to 75°F (18° to 24°C). The units must remain in heated locations during the winter, but when it is warm enough, they can stay outdoors in a shady location. Control the intensity of light on the cuttings. Do not place the units in full sunlight because the temperature inside the sealed unit will become too hot and damage the cuttings. Indoors, place the units in a north-facing window or under fluorescent lights that are on for 12 to 16 hours a day. Fluorescent aquarium lights may be used with the aquarium. Although each unit is designed to prevent moisture loss and is therefore expected to retain adequate moisture, moisture levels should be monitored and water added as needed.

After the cuttings have rooted, they should be hardened by gradual exposure to normal

Figure 5.5

Small-scale units for propagation of cuttings at home. *Source:* Adapted from Furuta 1976, p. 1.

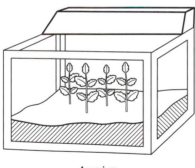

Aquarium

Large flower pot

Plastic bag

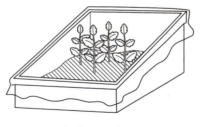

Small wooden box

growing conditions. Gradually remove the plastic coverings over a period of several days. Removing the coverings too suddenly results in wilting, injury, or death of the plants.

Tables 5.3 and 5.4 list methods of propagation for common perennials, house plants, and other garden plants.

Table 5.3

METHODS OF PROPAGATION FOR COMMON PERENNIALS

| Plant | | | | Optimal temperature | | Germination | Cold period | | | | | |
Scientific name	Common name	Type*	Method of propagation†	°F	°C	time (days)	Required‡	°F	°C	Length (days)	Response to light§	Comments
Achillea spp.	yarrow	HP	D, S	68	20	10						Divide every 2 to 4 yr.
Achimenes spp.	various	b	C, D, S	70	21							Divide rhizomes after bloom. Use softwood cuttings in spring, leaf cuttings in summer.
Aconitum spp.	monkshood	HP	S				Y	40	4	42		Poisonous. Do not transplant.
Allium spp.	ornamental onion	b	D, S	68	20	10						Plant bulbets.
Aloe spp.	aloe	ss	C, D, S	72	22	25						Plant offshoots, soft cuttings.
Althaea rosea (*Alcea rosea*)	hollyhock	B	S	68	20	18						
Alyssum spp.	alyssum	HP	C, D, S	77	25	25	Y	50	10	5	L	Divide or use softwood cuttings in spring.
Amaryllis spp. (*Hippeastrum*)	amaryllis	Tb	S									Seed yields flowering bulb in 2 to 4 yr.
Anchusa spp.	bugloss, Cape forget-me-not	HA/B	C, D, S	77	25	25						Seed produces poor-quality plant. Divide or take root cuttings in spring and fall.
Anthemis spp.	chamomile, golden marguerite	HP	D, S	68	20	21						Divide clumps or start seed in spring.
Aquilegia spp.	columbine	HP	S	77	25	27	Y	41	5	25	L	Use commercial seed. Replace every 3 yr.
Arabis spp.	rock cress	HP	D, S	68	20	25						Divide in spring or fall. Softwood cuttings after bloom.
Aster spp.	aster	HP	D, S	68	20	21						Divide and discard old clump.
Aubrieta spp.	various	HP	C, D, S	55	13	21						Dividing is difficult. Use softwood cuttings after blooming.
Begonia spp.	begonia	TP	C, D, S	68	20	28					L (fibrous-rooted)	Cut rhizomes into sections. Take cuttings in spring and summer. Divide tuberous begonia types.
Bellis perennis	English daisy	HP	D, S	68	20	14					L	Sow seed in spring or summer. Mulch in fall. Divide every year.
Browallia spp.	amethyst flower, bush violet	TP	C, S	68	20	21					L	Softwood cuttings in fall or spring.
cactus (various genera)	cactus	TP	S	68	20	Slow						
Campanula spp.	bellflower, Canterbury bell	HP / HB	C, D, S / C, D, S	70 / 77	21 / 25	21 / 21						Divide clumps in early spring. Sow in late spring or early summer.
Canna spp.	various	TP	D, S	68	20	28						Divide rhizomes in fall. Soak seeds to hasten germination.

| Plant | | | | Optimal temperature | | Germination | Cold period | | | | | |
| Scientific name | Common name | Type* | Method of propagation† | °F | °C | time (days) | Required‡ | Temperature | | Length (days) | Response to light§ | Comments |
								°F	°C			
Centaurea spp.	dusty miller, cornflower	TP	C, D, S	77	25	25					D	Softwood and leaf cuttings in summer. Divide every 2 to 4 yr. Sow seeds in spring or summer.
Cerastium tomentosum	snow-in-summer	HP	C, D, S	68	20	28					L	Softwood cuttings in summer after flowering. Divide in fall.
Cheiranthus spp.	wallflower	hhP	C, S	54	12	21					L	Take stem cuttings in early summer. Sow seeds in early summer.
Chrysanthemum spp.	chrysanthemum, daisy, marguerite	HP	C, D, S	68	20	28						Take stem cuttings in late spring. Divide clumps every 3 to 4 yr.
Coleus hybridus (*C. blumei*)	coleus	TP	C, S	77	25	21					L	Take cuttings anytime.
Convallaria majalis	lily of the valley	HP	D									Seedlings take several years to flower. Divide pips early spring. Mulch in fall.
Crocus vernus	crocus	HP	D									Seedlings take several years to flower. Separate corms in fall.
Cyclamen spp.	cyclamen	TP	D, S	68	20	27					D	Seedlings take several years to flower.
Dahlia spp.	dahlia	TP	D, S	77	25	21						Propagate cultivars asexually. Store clumps over winter at 50°F (10°C).
Delphinium spp.	delphinium	HP	C, D, S	54	12	28						Divide in spring or fall. Sow seed in spring. Softwood cuttings in spring.
Dianthus spp.	carnation, garden pinks	HP	C, S	68	20	21						Softwood cuttings in early summer. Sow seed in early spring/summer. Do not mulch.
Dicentra spp.	bleeding heart	HP	C, D, S				Y	41	5	42		Softwood cuttings in spring after flowering. Divide in spring or fall and every 4 yr. Sow seeds in fall.
Doronicum spp.	leopard's bane	HP	D, S	68	20	21						Divide in spring or fall and every 3 yr. Sow seed in spring.
Echinops exaltatus	globe thistle	HP	C, D, S	77	25	28						Take root cuttings in early spring, softwood cuttings in fall. Divide in spring.
Freesia spp.	freesia	TP	D, S	68	20							Propagate from small corms developing on old corms. Dig and store in fall. Soak seed 24 hr before planting.
Geum spp.	geum, avens	HP	D, S	77	25	28						Divide spring or fall.
Helleborus spp.	hellebore, Christmas rose	HP	S	75	24	45	Y	40	4	42		Do not divide. Best to grow from seed sown in fall.
Heuchera spp.	coral bells, alum root	HP	C, D, S	77	25	21					L	Take leaf cuttings in fall. Needs fungicidal treatment. Divide in spring or fall. Use commercial seed.
Iberis spp.	candytuft	HA and P	C, D, S	77	25	14					L	Take softwood cuttings in summer. Divide in fall. Sow seed in spring.
Impatiens spp.	impatiens	hhA or TP	C, S	68	20	28					L	Start cuttings indoors in spring.
Iresine spp. (*Achyranthes* ssp.)	bloodleaf	TP	C, S									Start cuttings indoors in winter/spring. Dig and store.
Kniphofia uvaria	red-hot poker, torch lily	hhP	D, S	77	25	28						Divide or sow seed in spring. Best if left undisturbed.
Lantana spp.	lantana	TP	D, S	77	25	21						Divide in spring.

Table 5.3 cont.

Plant		Type*	Method of propagation†	Optimal temperature		Germination time (days)	Cold period				Response to light§	Comments
Scientific name	Common name			°F	°C		Required‡	Temperature °F	°C	Length (days)		
Lavandula officinalis	lavender	hhP	C, D, S	70	21	21						Disturb plantings only for propagation. Take softwood cuttings in summer after bloom. Plant seed in winter.
Liatris spp.	gayfeather, blazing star	HP	D, S	77	25	28						Divide in spring. Sow seed in spring.
Linum spp.	flax	P	C, S	54	12	28						Cuttings from nonflowering stems in summer. Do not divide. Sow seed in spring or summer.
Lobelia spp.	lobelia	TP	S	77	25	21					L	Plant seed in early spring. Divide in spring or fall.
Lobularia maritima	sweet alyssum	P	S	68	20	14					L	Sow seed spring through summer.
Lunaria annua (*L. biennis*)	money plant, honesty	B	S	68	20	21						Sow seed in summer or spring.
Nepeta spp.	catnip, catmint	HP	C, D	68	20	21						Take softwood cuttings in summer. Divide in spring and discard old clumps.
Nierembergia spp.	cup flower	TP	C, D, S	77	25	21						Take softwood cuttings in summer. Divide in spring, then leave undisturbed.
Oenothera spp.	evening primrose	HP or B	D, S	77	25	21						Divide in fall.
Papaver spp.	poppy	HP	C, S	54	12	14						Use root cuttings of dormant plants. Sow most seed in late summer.
Pentstemon spp.	various	hhP	C, D, S	77	25	21						Take stem cuttings in spring. Divide in spring.
Petunia spp.	petunia hybrids	TP	C	68	20	14					L	Softwood cuttings late summer or fall.
Physalis spp.	Chinese lantern, ground cherry	HP or TP	C, D, S	70	21	28					L	Root cuttings in fall. Divide in spring or fall. Sow seed in spring.
Polemonium spp.	Jacob's ladder	HP	C, D, S	77	25	28						Use cuttings or division in spring or summer.
Primula spp.	primrose	HP	D, S	68	20	42					L	Take cuttings in spring. Divide after flowering.
Ranunculus spp.	buttercup, ranunculus	TP	D, S	68	20	28						Soak tubers in water for 4 hr before planting. Divide in spring or fall. Sow seed in spring.
Sedum spp.	stonecrop	ss	C, D, S	85	30	varies						Take cuttings in summer. Disturb only to divide.
Senecio spp.	dusty miller, cineraria, various	TP	C, D, S	68	20	21						Depending on species, take cuttings or divide in spring, sow seed in spring or late summer.

| Plant | | | | Optimal temperature | | Germination | Cold period | | | | | |
Scientific name	Common name	Type*	Method of propagation†	°F	°C	time (days)	Required‡	Temperature °F	°C	Length (days)	Response to light§	Comments
Stokesia laevis	Stokes aster	HP	C, D, S	77	25	42						Take root cuttings and divide in spring. Sow seed in spring.
Thymus spp.	thyme	HP	C, D	70	21	14					L	Take softwood cuttings in summer. Divide in spring.
Tropaeolum spp.	nasturtium	TP	C, S	68	20	14						Use softwood cuttings only.
Verbena spp.	verbena, vervain	TP	C, S	77	25	28					D	Take softwood cuttings in summer.
Veronica spp.	speedwell	HP	C, D, S	70	21	14						Take softwood cuttings in spring or summer. Divide in spring or fall.
Vinca major *V. minor*	periwinkle, myrtle	TP	C, D, S	68	20	21						Propagate by softwood cuttings or division in summer.
Viola spp.	violet	HP	C, D, S	70	21	21					D	Take cuttings from named varieties. Sow seed in late summer.
Yucca spp.	yucca	TP	C, D	68	20	slow						Take root cuttings or divide offshoots in spring.

Notes:
*A = annual; B = biennial; H = hardy; P = perennial; b = bulb; t = tender; hh = half hardy; ss = succulent.
†C = softwood or leaf cuttings; D = division; S = seed.
‡Y = cold period required for germination. Data given for only those species that require cold to germinate.
§L = seed germinates best in light; D = seed germinates best in dark. Data given for only those species that require light or darkness to germinate.

Figure 5.6

Special layering manipulations used to stimulate rooting. *Source:* Adapted from Hartmann and Kester 1990, p. 410.

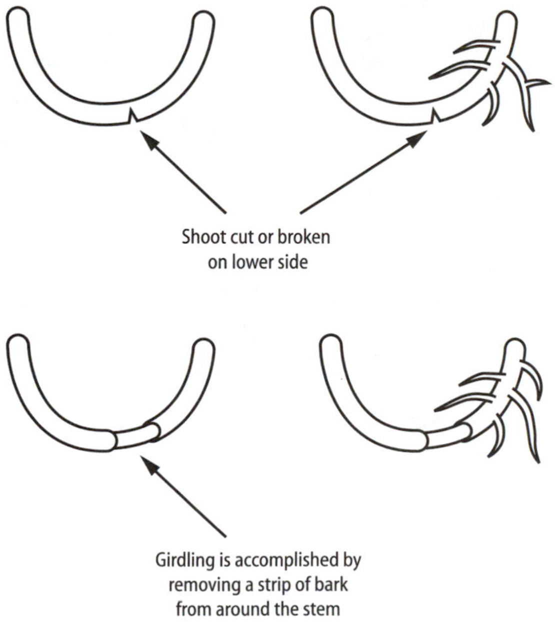

Shoot cut or broken on lower side

Girdling is accomplished by removing a strip of bark from around the stem

Layering

Layering is an asexual propagation method in which adventitous roots are caused to form on a stem that is still attached to the parent plant. Later, the rooted or layered stem is severed to form a new individual plant that grows on its own roots. This method of vegetative propagation promotes a high success rate because it prevents the water stress and carbohydrate shortage that sometimes plague cuttings. Because the stem being layered is still attached, the parent plant continuously supplies water, minerals, and carbohydrates, often making this method more successful than propagation by cuttings. Some plants, such as black raspberries, trailing blackberries, gooseberries, and currants, layer themselves naturally, but sometimes plant propagators and home gardeners assist the process through artificial methods. For the home gardener, layering requires less skill, effort, and equipment than is necessary with cuttings.

Various manipulations of the stem, including girdling, can stimulate adventitious root formation during the layering process, as shown in figure 5.6. Each manipulation of the

Table 5.4

METHODS OF ASEXUAL PROPAGATION FOR SELECTED HOUSE PLANTS AND OTHER COMMON GARDEN PLANTS

Plant						
Scientific name	Common name	Tip or stem cutting	Leaf cutting	Division	Air layer	Other
Abutilon spp.	flowering maple	■				seed
Acacia spp.	wattle	■		■		seed
Acalypha hispida	chenille plant	■				
Acalypha wilkesiana	copper-leaf	■				
Achimenes spp.	various	■		■		seed
Adiantum cuneatum	maidenhair fern			■		spores
Aechmea spp.	air plant, bromeliad	■		■		seed
Aeschynanthus spp.	lipstick plant	■				seed
Agave americana	century plant			■		seed
Aglaonema modestum (*A. commutatum, A. simplex*)	Chinese evergreen	■		■	■	
Albizia julibrissin	silk tree			■		seed
Aloe spp.	unguentine plant			■		
Anthurium andraeanum, A. scherzerianum	tall flower			■	■	seed
Aphelandra squarrosa	zebra plant	■	■	■	■	seed
Araucaria excelsa	Norfolk Island pine	■				seed
Asparagus asparagoides	baby smilax	■		■		seed
Asparagus spp.	asparagus fern			■		seed
Aspidistra elatior	cast iron plant			■		
Asplenium spp.	birdsnest fern			■		spores
Aucuba japonica	golddust plant	■		■		
Azalea spp.	azalea	■				
Begonia spp.	begonia					
fibrous		■				seed
rhizomatous		■		■		seed
rex		■	■	■		seed
tuberous				■		seed
Beloperone guttata	shrimp plant	■				
Bougainvillea spp.	bougainvillea	■	■			
Browallia spp.	bush violet	■				seed
Cactus (various genera)	cactus	■				seed
Caladium spp.	elephant ears			■		bulbs
Calceolaria herbeohybrida	pocketbook plant	■				seed
Callisia spp.	inch plant	■			■	
Callistemon citrinus	bottlebrush plant	■				
Camellia spp.	camellia					seed
Campanula isophylla	bellflower	■				seed
Capsicum annuum	Christmas pepper					seed
Carissa macrocarpa	Natal plum	■				
Ceropegia woodii	rosary vine	■		■		
Chamaedorea elegans	neanthe bella palm					seed
Chlorophytum spp.	spider plant			■		
Chrysanthemum spp.	chrysanthemum	■		■		seed
Cissus antarctica	kangaroo vine	■	■			
Cissus rhombifolia	grape ivy	■				
Citrus spp.	dwarf citrus varieties	■			■	seed
Clerodendrum thomsoniae	bleeding heart vine	■		■		seed

Scientific name	Common name	Tip or stem cutting	Leaf cutting	Division	Air layer	Other
Clivia spp.	Kaffir lily					bulbs
Codiaeum variegatum	croton	■		■	■	bulbs
Coleus spp.	coleus	■				seed
Columnea microphylla	goldfish plant	■				seed
Cordyline terminalis	Hawaiian ti plant	■		■		
Crassula spp.	jade plant, various	■	■	■		seed
Crossandra infundibuliformis	firecracker flower	■				seed
Cyclamen spp.	cyclamen			■		seed
Cymbalaria muralis	Kenilworth ivy	■				seed
Cyphomandra betacea	tree tomato					seed
Cyrtomium falcatum	fishtail fern					spores
Davallia fejeensis	rabbit's foot fern			■		spores
Dianthus caryophyllus	carnation	■				seed
Dieffenbachia spp.	dumbcane	■		■	■	seed
Dizygotheca elegantissima	false aralia	■				seed
Dracaena spp.	various	■		■	■	seed
Dracocephalum virginianum	obedient plant			■		seed
Echeveria spp.	various					seed
Epiphyllum spp.	orchid cactus		■			
Episcia spp.	flame violet		■	■		seed
Eucharis grandiflora	Amazon lily					bulbs
Euphorbia pulcherrima	poinsettia	■				seed
Euphorbia splendens	crown of thorns	■				seed
Fatshedera lizei	botanical wonder	■	■			
Ficus elastica	rubber plant	■			■	seed
Ficus lyrata	fiddleleaf fig	■			■	seed
Ficus microphylla	little leaf fig	■				seed
Ficus pumila	creeping fig	■		■	■	seed
Ficus religiosa	rusty fig	■				seed
Fittonia spp.	mosaic plant	■			■	
Fuchsia spp.	fuchsia	■				seed
Grevillea robusta	Australian silk tree	■				seed
Gynura sarmentosa	velvet plant	■				
Hedera helix	English ivy	■		■		
Helxine soleiroli	baby tears	■		■		
Hemigraphis colorata	red ivy	■			■	
Hibiscus rosa-sinensis	Chinese hibiscus	■				seed
Hippeastrum spp. (*Amaryllis*)	amaryllis			■		bulbs
Hoya carnosa	wax plant	■	■			
Hypoestes sanguinolenta	polka-dot plant	■				seed
Impatiens sultanii	various	■				seed
Iresine spp.	bloodleaf, achyranthes	■	■			
Ixora coccinea	flame-of-the-woods	■				
Jabobinia carnea	various	■				
Jasminum gracile	graceful jasmine	■	■			
Justicia spp.	water willow	■				seed
Kalanchoe blossfeldiana, K. tornentosa	kalanchoe, panda plant	■	■			seed
Kohleria amabilis	tree gloxinia	■				seed
Lantana camara	yellow sage	■				seed
Lunaria annua	money plant			■		seed

Table 5.4 cont.

METHODS OF ASEXUAL PROPAGATION FOR SELECTED HOUSE PLANTS AND OTHER COMMON GARDEN PLANTS

| Plant | | | | | | |
Scientific name	Common name	Tip or stem cutting	Leaf cutting	Division	Air layer	Other
Maranta leuconeura	prayer plant	■		■		
Mesembrianthemum spp.	fig marigold					seed
Mimosa pudica	sensitive plant					seed
Monstera spp.	various	■			■	seed
Musa coccinea	dwarf banana			■		seed
Nautilocalyx forgetii	various	■				
Nerium oleander	oleander	■				
Oxalis acetosella	wood sorrel					bulbs
Pandanus veitchi	screw pine			■		seed
Passiflora caerulea	passion flower	■	■			seed
Pentas lanceolata	Egyptian star cluster	■				seed
Peperomia spp.	various	■	■	■		seed
Philodendron spp.	philodendron	■	■	■	■	seed
Phoenix roebelenii	pygmy date palm					seed
Physalis spp.	lantern plant			■		seed
Pilea cadierei	aluminum plant	■		■		seed
Pilea involucrata	friendship plant	■		■		seed
Pilea microphylla	artillery plant	■		■		seed
Pilea nummulariilfolia	creeping charlie	■		■	■	seed
Piper ornatum	ornamental pepper	■				seed
Pittosporum spp.	Australian laurel	■				seed
Platycerium spp.	staghorn fern			■		spores
Plecantranthus australis	Swedish ivy	■		■		
Plumbago capensis	leadwort	■		■		seed
Podocarpus spp.	various	■				seed
Polypodium spp.	polypody fern					spores
Polyscias spp.	various	■				
Portulacaria afra	elephant bush	■		■		
Primula spp.	primose			■		seed
Pteris ensiformis	table fern			■		spores
Rheo discolor	Moses-in-the-cradle			■		seed
Rhoicissus capensis	Cape grape	■				
Saintpaulia spp.	African violet		■	■		seed
Sanchezia nobilis	sanchezia	■	■			
Sansevieria trifasciata (*S. zeylanica*)	snake plant, mother-in-law's tongue		■	■		
Saxifraga stolonifera	strawberry begonia			■		seed
Schefflera actinophylla	umbrella plant	■			■	seed
Schizanthus spp.	fringe flower					seed
Schlumbergera truncata	Christmas cactus	■				
Scindapsus aureus	pothos, devil's ivy	■	■		■	seed
Sedum morganianum	burro's tail	■				
Senecio articulatus	candle plant	■				
Senecio cineraria candissimus	dusty miller			■		seed
Senecio cruentus	string of pearls	■				seed
Setcreasea purpurea	purple heart	■				seed
Sinningia speciosa	gloxinia		■			seed/bulbs

Plant		Tip or stem cutting	Leaf cutting	Division	Air layer	Other
Scientific name	Common name					
Spathiphyllum clevelandii	white anthurium			■		
Stephanotis floribunda	Madagascar jasmine	■				
Strelitzia spp.	bird of paradise			■		seed
Streptocarpus hybridis	Cape primrose		■			seed
Streptocarpus saxorum	Cape primrose	■		■		seed
Syngonium spp.	arrowhead plant	■	■		■	
Tolmiea menziesii	piggyback plant		■			
Trevesia palmata	snowflake plant	■			■	
Tripogandra spp.	bridal veil	■				
Veltheimia viridifolia	unicorn root					bulbs
Vriesia spp.	king of the bromeliads			■		
Zebrina spp.	wandering jew	■		■		
Zephyranthes spp.	zephyr lily					bulbs

stem causes interruption in the downward translocation of carbohydrates, growth hormones, and other nutrients from leaves and growing shoot tips so that these materials accumulate near the point of stem manipula-

tion. Rooting occurs in this general area even though the stem is still attached to the parent plant. Light is typically withheld from the stem area where root formation is desired. The rooting medium should provide good aeration and a constant supply of moisture. Rooting hormones, applied as a powder, in lanolin, or in a water-soluble form, may facilitate rooting during layering.

Tip Layering. In tip layering, rooting takes place near the shoot tip of the current year's growth when the shoot tip begins to grow downward into the soil. Later, the stem bends and recurves to grow upward. Roots form at the bend and the recurved tip becomes a new plant. Remove the tip layer and plant it in the early spring or late fall. This natural method of reproduction is typical of black and purple raspberries and trailing blackberries.

Simple Layering. Simple layering begins with bending the stem to the ground and covering part of it with soil or rooting medium, leaving the last 6 to 12 inches (15 to 30 cm) exposed, as shown in figure 5.7. Next, bend the stem tip into a vertical position and stake it in place. The sharp bend often induces rooting, but wounding the lower side of the branch or loosening the bark by twisting the stem may help. Examples of plants for which this method is effective are rhododendron, honeysuckle, wisteria, grape, and dieffenbachia. Simple layering is usually performed on 1-year-old shoots.

Compound (Serpentine) Layering. Compound layering is essentially the same as simple layering except that the stem is alter-

Figure 5.7

Simple layering. Shoots are bent over to the ground in early spring or fall. The tip may simply be buried. In some species a second bend is made in the shoot, which is buried and held in place while the tip is staked upright. Rooted layers are removed from the parent plant. *Source:* Adapted from Hartmann and Kester 1990, p. 413.

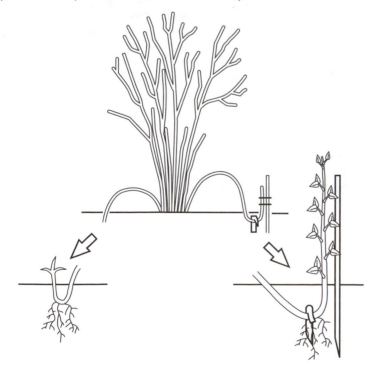

nately covered and exposed along its length. Compound layering works well for plants with flexible stems. Wound the lower side of the stem sections to be covered. The exposed portions of the stem should have at least one bud to develop a new shoot. After rooting occurs on the covered portions, the branch is cut in sections made up of new shoots and roots. Several new plants can grow from a single branch. Examples of plants for which this method is effective are heart-leaf philodendron, pothos, wisteria, and clematis.

Air Layering. Air layering is used to propagate some indoor plants with thick stems or to rejuvenate them when they become leggy. Girdle or slit the stem vertically just below a node about 6 to 12 inches (15 to 30 cm) from the stem tip. Pry the slit open with a toothpick

and remove a strip of bark about ½ to 1 inch (1.2 to 2.5 cm) wide. Surround the wound with wet, unmilled sphagnum moss and insert some moss into the cut. Wrap clear plastic around the sphagnum moss and tie it in place at both ends, as shown in figure 5.8. Polyethylene film is durable, highly permeable to respiratory gases (oxygen and carbon dioxide), and permits little transmission of water vapor. When roots pervade the moss and the stem is not growing too actively, cut the plant off below the root ball. Examples of plants for which this method is effective are dumbcane, rubber tree, and *Ficus* species. Air layering works best using wood from branches about 1 year old that have numerous active leaves that tend to speed up root formation at the site of treatment.

Mound (Stool) Layering. Cut the plant back to 1 inch (2.5 cm) above the ground in the dormant season. Mound soil over the emerging shoots in the spring to enhance their rooting. When roots develop, the buried shoots can be cut from the base of the parent plant. Examples of plants for which this method is effective are gooseberries and apple rootstocks.

Asexual Propagation of Specialized Stems and Roots

Some plants have special vegetative structures whose primary function is food storage and whose secondary function is vegetative (asexual) propagation by natural forms of layering.

Stolons, Rhizomes, and Runners. Stolons and rhizomes are horizontally growing, often fleshy stems that can root and then produce new shoots where they touch the soil or rooting medium. *Stolons* are horizontal stems that grow above the soil surface, and *rhizomes* are horizontal stems that grow below it. Dogwood, bermudagrass, and mint can layer naturally (asexually propagate) via stolons. Rhizome structures are found in a number of ornamentals and economically important plants, such as sugar cane, bamboo, banana, ginger, turfgrasses, iris, and lily of the valley. Such plants are propagated when the rhizomes are cut into sections, with each rhizome piece having one lateral bud or *eye*. A *runner* is a slender, specialized stem that originates in a leaf axil. The runner grows along the ground, forming new plants at its nodes, or it can grow downward from a hanging basket, producing a new plant at its tip. Plants that produce these structures

Air layering. (A) Completely remove a strip of bark at least ¹⁄₂ inch (1.2 cm) wide from the internode of the stem. (B) Cover the girdled section with a ball of moist sphagnum moss. (C) Wrap polyethylene film around the sphagnum moss and tie it at each end.

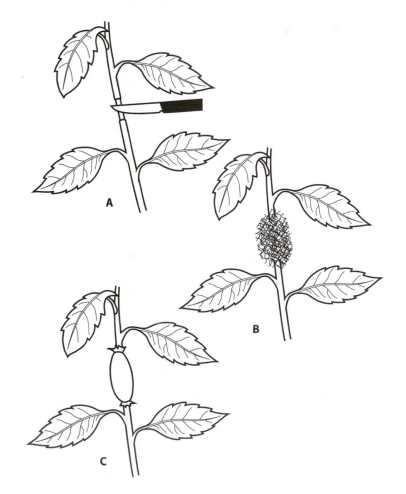

and naturally layer in this way are propagated by severing the new plants from the parent plants. Plantlets at the tips of runners may be rooted while still attached to the parent, or detached and placed in a rooting medium. Examples of plants that produce runners are strawberries and spider plant. In many strawberry cultivars, runner formation is linked to day length and temperature.

Offsets. Plants with rosetted stems often reproduce by forming new shoots at their base or in leaf axils known as offsets or offshoots. Sever the new shoots from the parent plant after they have developed their own root systems. Unrooted offsets of some species may be removed and placed in a rooting medium. Some of these must be cut off, but others may be lifted off the parent stem. Examples of plants for which this type of natural layering occurs are date palm, pineapple, haworthia, bromeliads, and many cacti.

Bulbs. Bulbs are specialized underground stems with a rather complex anatomy that can produce new bulbs asexually via a natural form of layering and can also reproduce sexually, giving rise to flowers and (sometimes) seed. Also, new bulbs can form asexually beside the originally planted parent bulb. Separate these bulb clumps every 3 to 5 years to encourage large blooms and to increase bulb population. Dig up the clump after the leaves have withered. Gently pull the bulbs apart and replant them immediately so their roots can begin to develop. Small new bulbs may not flower for 2 or 3 years, but large ones should bloom the first year. Examples of plants for which this natural method of layering occurs are tulip, narcissus (daffodil), hyacinth, Cape belladonna, and various lilies.

Corms. A *corm* is the swollen base of a stem axis enclosed by dry, scalelike leaves. Unlike a bulb, which consists of predominantly leaf scales, a corm is a solid stem structure with distinct nodes and internodes. A large new corm can form on top of the old corm, and tiny cormels can form around the large corm. After the leaves wither, dig up the corms and allow them to dry in indirect light for 2 or 3 weeks. Remove the cormels and then gently separate the new corm from the old corm. Dust all new corms with a fungicide and store them in a cool place until planting time. Crocus and gladiolus reproduce naturally via corms.

Tuberous Stems and Roots. Tuberous stems and roots are thickened underground fleshy structures that contain stored food and may produce new shoots, roots, and plants by asexual propagation. True tubers, the term used to describe tuberous stems, have the same anatomy as a stem. The eyes, which are arranged spirally, are nodes, each having one or more axillary buds. The basal end of the tuber is attached to a stolon on the parent plant. Tubers may be kept whole or cut into sections with one or more buds or eyes for planting. Tuber pieces are planted 3 to 4 inches (7.5 to 10 cm) deep and allowed to develop new roots and shoots. Examples of plants that reproduce via true tubers are white potatoes, Jerusalem artichoke, and caladium. Tuberous begonias, cyclamen, and gloxinia reproduce via tuberous structures that resemble stems.

Unlike true tubers, tuberous roots have the internal and external structures of roots. They lack nodes and internodes, and buds are present only on the stem end. Polarity is the reverse of that of the true tuber. Tuberous roots are kept whole and usually placed 2 inches (5 cm) deep in moist, warm sand to promote root and shoot development. Examples of plants that reproduce via tuberous roots are sweet potatoes and dahlia.

Separation and Division

Procedures for vegatively propagating bulbs and corms are called *separation* because the bulblets and cormels detach naturally. When the propagator must cut the plant part into sections for propagation, as with rhizomes, tubers, and tuberous roots, the process is called *division*. Plants with more than one rooted crown may be separated and the crowns planted separately. If the stems are not joined, gently pull the plants apart. If the crowns are united by horizontal stems, such as rhizomes, cut the stems and roots with a sharp knife to minimize injury. Divisions of some outdoor plants should be dusted with a fungicide before they are replanted (see tables 5.3 and 5.4).

Grafting. *Grafting* and *budding* are methods of asexual plant propagation that join plant parts so that they will grow as one plant. These techniques are used to propagate cultivars that do not reproduce well by cuttings, layering, division, or other asexual methods, or whose own root systems are inadequate. Many species of fruit and nut trees and woody plants are propagated by grafting and budding. New cultivars can be added to existing varieties. The *scion*, the portion of the cultivar that is to be propagated, is a piece of shoot with dormant buds that will produce the stem and branches. The *rootstock*, or stock, provides the new plant's root system and sometimes the lower part of the stem. All methods of joining plants are types of grafting, but when the scion is simply a piece of bark (and sometimes wood) containing a single bud, the propagation operation is called *budding*.

Grafting and budding are preferred to planting seeds of a named variety of fruit tree because more than 99 percent of all seedling trees bear fruit inferior to that produced by the parent trees. The fruit of seedlings is the same species, but it is unlike that of the parent tree in flavor, color, date of ripening, and many other characteristics. To obtain a true-to-type fruit tree that is a clone of the parent tree, it is necessary to graft or bud onto the desired rootstock. When seedling trees or limbs are larger than 1 inch (2.5 cm) in diameter, grafting is preferable because it is difficult to bud large-diameter wood.

Table 5.5

GRAFTING COMPATIBILITIES OF COMMON DECIDUOUS FRUIT TREES

Rootstock	Scion[a]								
	Almond	Apple	Apricot	Cherry	Peach and nectarine	Pear	Plum (European and Japanese)[b]	Quince	English walnut
almond	S	I	U	I	P[c]	I	P	I	I
apple	I	S	I	I	I	U	I	U	I
apricot	U	I	S	I	P[d]	I	P[e]	I	I
cherry									
Mazzard	I	I	I	S	I	I	I	I	I
Mahaleb or Stockton Morello	I	I	I	P	I	I	I	I	I
peach	S	I	P	I	S	I	P	I	I
pear	I	U	I	I	I	S	I	U	I
plum									
Myrobalan	U	I	P	I	U	I	S	I	I
Marianna 2624	P[f]	U	S	I	U	I	S	I	I
quince	I	U	I	I	I	P[g]	I	S	I
walnut (Northern California black or Paradox)	I	I	I	I	I	I	I	I	S

Notes:

[a] I = incompatible combination for grafting; the grafts either do not grow or growth is quite weak and short lived; P = partly satisfactory for grafting (most cultivars grow and fruit normally on this rootstock, although some cultivars and some trees do not make satisfactory or permanent graft unions; S = satisfactory for grafting; U = unsatisfactory for grafting, although grafts may grow for a time.

[b] In general, many European and Japanese plums may be grafted on most European plums. Although many Japanese cultivars do well on other Japanese cultivars, European cultivars are not successful on Japanese stocks. Peaches, almonds, and apricots may sometimes be grafted on Japanese and European plums with reasonable success, but, as a rule, the grafts fail to grow or do not grow satisfactorily.

[c] Peach trees are short-lived and become dwarfed on almond rootstock, but those that are successful make normal trees.

[d] Many individual peach trees fail to grow well on apricot rootstock, but those that are successful make normal trees.

[e] Some Japanese plum cultivars are compatible with some apricot seedlings. In contrast, most European plums are not compatible with apricot rootstocks.

[f] Some almond cultivars, such as Nonpareil, do not make a satisfactory union with Marianna 2624, so an interstock of Havens 2B plum must be used to work such cultivars on this stock. Other cultivars, such as Ne Plus Ultra and Mission, make reasonably satisfactory unions with Marianna 2624.

[g] Some pear cultivars, such as Bartlett, do not make good unions with quince, although other cultivars, such as Old Home and Hardy, do. Therefore, such cultivars as Bartlett are double worked, using one of the compatible cultivars.

Certain trees selected for their desirable fruits or ornamental qualities may have root systems that are less desirable. Other varieties of the same species may have desirable root systems that resist soilborne pests, fungus, and viral pathogens (e.g., *Fusarium*, *Verticillium*, *Tristeza*, *Armillaria*) and may withstand unfavorable soil conditions (drought, high salinity) more effectively than their cousins that have the better fruit and ornamental appearance. When the better scions are grafted onto the better rootstocks, a more vigorous variety of higher commerical value can be developed. In citrus species, some rootstocks yield higher quality, better-sized fruit in the scion cultivar than others. If desired, the selection of size-controlling rootstocks can cause the composite, grafted tree to become partially dwarfed. For more information, see chapter 17, "Temperate Tree Fruit and Nut Crops."

Budding and grafting have additional practical advantages. For example, to extend the fruit-bearing season of a peach tree, a gardener can bud or graft another variety of peach onto it. To save space, a pollinating variety could be added to a particular fruit tree by grafting.

Figure 5.9

Whip and tongue graft. (A) Diagonally cut stock. (B) Cut tongue in stock. (C) Diagonally cut scion with tongue. (D) Fit whip graft together. (E) Wrap whip graft and apply grafting paste. *Source:* Adapted from Beutel and Hartmann 1990, p. 5.

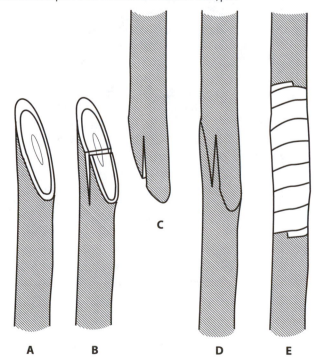

Table 5.5 lists grafting compatibilities of common deciduous fruit trees. Locating bud or graft wood of the desired variety can be difficult unless you have neighbors or friends who can help or you are willing to purchase a budded tree from a nursery. In general, nurseries, government agencies, colleges, and universities do not sell or give away small quantities of bud or graft (scion) wood of fruit and nut tree varieties. Ideally, scions are hardened first-year or second-year wood ⅜ to ¾ inch (9 to 19 mm) in diameter with three or four mature leaf buds (no fruiting buds and no terminal bud). Scions should be stripped of their leaves before grafting. Depending on the technique used, scion wood can be taken from a tree and used promptly, or it can be taken during a dormant period, wrapped in wet paper, sealed, and stored in a refrigerator for later use.

The *cambium*, a layer of meristematic cells located between the wood (xylem) and bark (phloem) of a stem, is a critical layer of cells in the grafting process. New bark cells and new wood cells will originate in the cambium after successful grafting. The four conditions of successful grafting are

1. The cambial layers of the scion and rootstock must come into intimate contact under favorable environmental conditions (both temperature and relative humidity).

2. The scion and rootstock must be compatible for cambial cells to establish the new vascular tissue connection between them.

3. Both the scion and stock must be at the proper physiological stage (usually the scion buds are dormant).

4. The graft union must be kept moist until the wound has healed. For the graft union to be successful, new vascular tissue—both xylem (water-conducting tissue) and phloem (sugar-conducting tissue)—must develop to permit the passage of nutrients and water between the stock and scion.

The cells in the cambial area produce callous tissue, which heals the scion (the new top) to the stock.

Whip and Tongue Grafting. Whip grafting (fig 5.9) is often used for small material ¼ to ½ inch (6 to 12 mm) in diameter. The scion and rootstock are usually of the same diameter, but the scion may be narrower than the stock. The technique results in a strong graft that heals quickly and provides excellent cambial contact. Make one 2½-inch-long (6.5-cm-long) sloping cut at the top of the rootstock and a matching cut at the base of the

Figure 5.10

Cleft grafting. (Left) Scions inserted in place. (Center) Part of the stock has been removed to show how the cambium of the scion is brought into contact with the cambium of the stock. You can place the scions at a slight outward slant to make sure the cambiums touch in at least one place. (Right) Completed graft covered with wax. *Source:* Adapted from Beutel and Hartmann 1990, p 7.

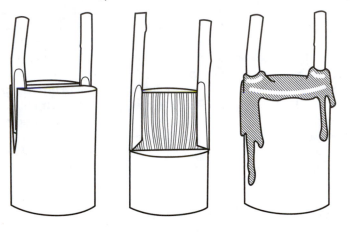

Figure 5.11

Bark grafting. Scion prepared for grafting: (A) Side of scion that is placed against the wood of the stock. (B) Side view of scion. (C) Side of scion opposite to that shown in (A). (Right) Scions inserted and nailed into stock; graft is now ready to wax. Cover all exposed cut surfaces, including the tops of the scions, with grafting asphaltum compound. *Source:* Adapted from Beutel and Hartmann 1990, p. 7.

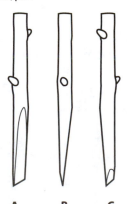

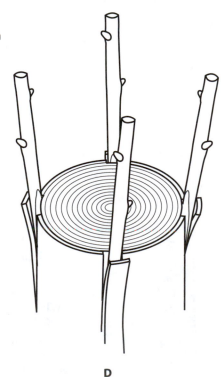

A   B   C   D

scion. On the cut surface, slice downward into the stock and up into the scion so the pieces (tongues) will interlock. Fit the pieces together, then tie and wax the union or wrap with plastic tie tape, as shown. The best season for whip grafting in California is January through March. Collect the scion wood (also known as the graft wood) in January and use it immediately, or store it wrapped in moist paper and a plastic bag in the refrigerator for use in February or March. About a month after grafting, the buds on the scion will start to grow. At that time, use a sharp knife to cut through the material tying the graft union. If necessary, use a stake to support the new top.

Cleft Grafting. Cleft grafting (fig. 5.10) is often used in topworking trees to change the cultivar or top growth of a shoot or a young tree (usually a seedling). It is especially successful if done in late winter or early spring when the buds of the rootstock are swelling but not actively growing. Collect scion wood ⅜ to ⅝ inch (9 to 15 mm) in diameter. Cut the limb or small tree trunk to be reworked (the rootstock) perpendicular to its length. Make a 2-inch (5-cm) vertical cut through the center of the previous cut, being careful not to tear the bark, and keep this cut wedged apart. Prepare two scion pieces 3 to 4 inches (7.5 to 10 cm) long. Cut the lower end of each scion piece into a wedge. Insert the scions at the outer edges of the cut in the stock. Tilt the top of the scion slightly outward and the bottom slightly inward so that the cambial layers of the scion and stock touch. Remove the wedge and cover all cut surfaces with grafting wax.

Bark Grafting. Unlike most grafting methods, bark grafting (fig. 5.11) can be used on large limbs. The technique works well with persimmon, apple, and pear trees and does not require special equipment or training. The technique depends on separating the bark readily from the wood; therefore, it can be done only in the spring after the rootstock has started active growth. Collect scion wood ⅜ to ½ inch (9 to 12 mm) in diameter in January when the plant is dormant, and store the wood wrapped in moist paper in a plastic bag in the refrigerator. Saw off the limb or trunk of the rootstock at a right angle to itself. In the spring when the bark is easy to separate from the wood ("slipping"), make a ½-inch (1.2-cm) diagonal cut on one side of the scion, and a 1- to 1½-inch (2.5- to 3.7-cm) diagonal cut on the other side. Leave two buds above the longer cut. Cut through the bark of the stock a little wider than the scion and remove the top third of the bark from this cut. Insert the scion with the longer cut against the wood and nail the graft in place with flat-headed wire nails. Cover all wounds with grafting compound.

Graft Care. Grafting will be successful if proper care is maintained for the following year or two. If a binding material, such as strong cord or nursery tape, is used on the graft, it must be cut shortly after growth starts to prevent girdling and subsequent dying of the graft. Rubber budding strips are superior to other materials in that they expand with growth and usually do not need to be cut because they deteriorate and break after a short time. Inspect grafts after a 2- to 3-week period to see if the wax has cracked. Rewax the exposed areas, if necessary. After this period, the graft union will probably be strong enough so that more waxing is not necessary. For the first year, one or two limbs of the old variety that were not selected for grafting should be maintained as nurse limbs. The total leaf surface of the old variety should be reduced gradually as that of the new one increases. Completely removing all the limbs of the old variety at the time of grafting increases the shock to the tree and causes excessive suckering. The scions may grow too fast, making them susceptible to wind dam-

age. By the end of 1 or 2 years, the new variety will have taken over.

Budding

Budding, or bud grafting, is the union of a bud and a small piece of bark from the scion with a rootstock. The nursery industry uses this technique for propagating roses and fruit trees sold to home gardeners and orchardists. Budding involves the same physiological processes as grafting, but it is faster and forms a stronger union than grafting. It is especially useful when scion material is limited. Commonly used budding techniques depend on the bark's slipping, a condition in which bark separates easily from wood. Slipping occurs from spring to fall when the plant is growing, cambial cells are dividing actively, and newly formed tissues can be torn as bark lifts from the wood.

In California, the season for budding is April through August. To bud trees from June through August, select bud wood from the current season's growth that is 2 to 10 months old and can easily be cut. Use wood that is ¼ to ⅜ inches (6 to 9 mm) in diameter, and cut off the leaves. Good bud wood is firm and has narrow, pointed leaf buds, not flower buds. If you are planning to bud in April, collect wood from dormant trees in January. Wrap the dormant wood in moist (not wet) paper and place it in a plastic bag in a refrigerator set at 32° to 35°F (0° to 2°C) until needed.

For trees budded from April through June, use the techniques described below and cut off the top of the stock just above the bud, forcing the bud to grow. To bud trees in August, however, do not cut off the top of the seedling until the following spring because the bud should remain dormant. In March, cut August-budded trees above the inserted bud to force growth of the bud. About a month after budding an actively growing tree, cut the ties around the bud, beginning on the side opposite the bud, so that they do not girdle or choke the growth of the tree. Remove sucker shoots that grow on the rootstock after budding. Use stakes to support the new, growing shoot, if necessary. Some plants bud in spring, others in the fall. To force the bud to develop the following spring, cut the stock off 3 to 4 inches (7.5 to 10 cm) above the bud. The new shoot may be tied to the resulting stub to prevent wind damage. After the shoot has made a strong union with the stock, cut the stub off close to the budded area.

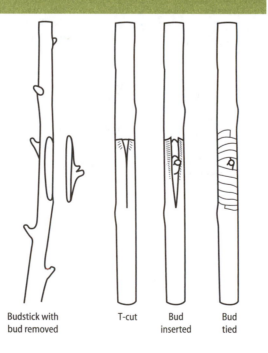

Figure 5.12

T-budding. Make a T-shaped cut in the stock. Cut the bud from the stock. Insert bud in the stock. Wrap bud. *Source: Adapted from Beutel and Hartmann 1990, p. 4.*

Budstick with bud removed | T-cut | Bud inserted | Bud tied

T-Budding. The budding technique most commonly used by nurserymen in propagating roses, fruit trees, and ornamental shrubs is called *T-budding* because of the T-like appearance of the cut in the stock. Its use is limited to actively growing stocks that are ¼ to 1 inch (0.6 to 2.5 cm) in diameter and have fairly thin bark that separates easily from the wood. Figure 5.12 illustrates steps in making a T-bud.

Patch Budding. In patch budding, a rectangular patch of bark is removed completely from the stock and replaced with a patch of bark of the same size containing a bud of the cultivar to be propagated. For thick-barked trees, especially walnut and pecan, the patch bud often outperforms the T-bud or chip bud. Trees should be patch-budded while they are actively growing in late summer or early fall so that their bark slips easily. Remove a rectangular piece of bark from the scion. If the rootstock's bark is thicker than that of the scion, pare it down to meet the thinner bark so that when the union is wrapped, the patch will be firmly held in place.

Chip Budding. Chip budding can be done when the bark is not slipping. Slice downward into the rootstock at a 45° angle through one-fourth of the wood. Make a second cut upward from the first cut, about 1 inch (2.5 cm) long. Remove a bud and attending chip of bark and wood from the scion shape so that it fits the rootstock wound. Fit the bud chip to the stock and wrap the union.

Plant Tissue Culture for the Home Gardener

Although technical procedures for aseptic (sterile) culture of plant cells, tissues, and organs are as diverse as the plant materials on which they are practiced, a simplified general procedure can be followed in the home. The necessary supplies can be obtained at the local grocery store. The procedures outlined below can be used for plants that are easy to propagate (African violets, coleus, chrysanthemums) or those that are difficult (orchids, ferns, weeping figs). Although the propagation techniques are simple and straightforward, the media can easily become contaminated by bacteria, and this method may not always work at home.

Medium Preparation. To prepare 2 pints (about 1 l) of growth medium for plant tissue culture, mix the following ingredients in a 1-quart (about 1-l) home canning jar:

- ⅛ cup (30 ml) sugar

- 1 teaspoon (5 ml) all-purpose soluble fertilizer mixture (check the label to make sure it has all of the major and minor elements, especially ammonium nitrate; if the latter is lacking, add ⅓ teaspoon (1.6 ml) of a 35–0–0 soluble fertilizer).

- 1 tablet (100 mg) of inositol (myo-inositol), which can be obtained at most health food stores

- one-quarter of a pulverized vitamin tablet containing 1 to 2 mg thiamine

- 4 tablespoons (60 ml) coconut milk (cytokinin source) drained from a fresh coconut (the remainder can be frozen and used later)

- 0.002 ounce (¹⁄₄₀₀ teaspoon, or about 0.013 ml) of a commercial rooting compound that has 0.1 active ingredient IBA (indolebutyric acid, a type of auxin)

Add distilled or deionized water to fill the jar. If purified water is not available, substitute water that has been boiled for several minutes. Shake the mixture and make sure all materials have dissolved.

Baby food jars or other heat-resistant glass receptacles with lids can be used as individual culture jars. To support the plant material, add cotton or paper until the jar is half full. Pour medium into each culture bottle so that the support material is just above the solution.

When all bottles contain the medium and have their lids screwed on loosely, they are ready to be sterilized. Place the jars in a pressure cooker and sterilize them under pressure for 30 minutes, or place them in an oven at 320°F (161°C) for 4 hours. After removing the bottles from the sterilizer, place them in a clean area and allow the medium to cool. If the bottles will not be used for several days, wrap groups of culture bottles in foil before sterilizing and then sterilize the whole package. Then the bottles can be removed and cooled without removing the foil cover. Sterilized water, tweezers, and razor blades, which will be needed later, can be prepared in the same manner.

Plant Disinfection and Culture. Once the growth medium is sterilized and cooled, plant material can be prepared for culture. Various plant parts can be cultured, but small, actively growing portions usually produce the most vigorous plantlets. For example, ferns are most readily propagated by using only ½ inch (1.2 cm) of the tip of a rhizome. For other plants, ½ to 1 inch (1.2 to 2.5 cm) of the shoot tip is sufficient. Remove leaves attached to the tip and discard. Because plants usually harbor bacterial and fungal spores, they must be cleaned (disinfected) before placement on the sterile medium. Otherwise, bacteria and fungi may grow faster than the plantlets and dominate the culture. Place the plant part into a solution of 1 part bleach to 9 parts water for 8 to 10 minutes. Submerge all plant tissue in the bleach solution. After this time, rinse off excess bleach by dropping the plant part into sterile water. Remember, once the plant material has been in the bleach, it has been disinfected and should be touched only with sterile tweezers.

After rinsing, remove any bleach-damaged tissue with a sterile razor blade. Then remove the cap of a culture bottle containing sterile medium, place the plant part onto the support material in the bottle (making sure that it is not completely submerged in the medium), and recap quickly. These procedures, known as the *transferring process* (transferring the plants into the culture jars), should be done as quickly as possible in a clean environment. Scrub hands and counter tops with soap and water just before beginning to disinfect plant material. Rubbing alcohol or a diluted bleach solution can be used to wipe down the work surface.

After all plants have been cultured, place them in a warm, well-lit (no direct sunlight) environment to encourage growth. If contamination of the medium has occurred, it will be obvious within 3 to 4 days. Remove and wash contaminated culture bottles as quickly as possible to prevent the spread of disease to uncontaminated cultures.

When plantlets have grown to sufficient size, transplant them into soil. Handle them as gently as possible because the plants will be leaving the warm, humid environment of the culture jar for the cool, dry soil. After transplanting, water the plants thoroughly and place them in a clear plastic bag for several days. Gradually remove the bag to acclimate the plants to their new environment. Start with 1 hour per day, and gradually increase time out of the bag over a 2-week period until the plants are strong enough to dispense with the bag altogether.

Bibliography

Bailey, L. H., and E. Z. Bailey. 1976. Hortus third. New York: Macmillan.

Bienz, D. R. 1980. The why and how of home horticulture. San Francisco: Freeman.

Beutel, J., and H. Hartmann. 1995. Budding and grafting fruit trees in the home garden. Oakland: University of California Division of Agriculture and Natural Resources Leaflet 2990.

Brenzel, K. N., ed. 2001. Sunset western garden book. Menlo Park: Sunset Publishing.

Cathey, H. M. 1991. Temperature and lighting requirements for germination of selected annual flowering plants. Washington, D.C.: USDA.

Dirr, M. A., and C. W. Heuser Jr. 1987. The reference manual of woody plant propagation: From seed to tissue culture. Athens, GA: Varsity Press.

Furuta, T. 1976. Small scale propagation units. Oakland: University of California Division of Agriculture and Natural Resources Leaflet 2565.

Frey, D. 1993. Plant propagation. In D. D. Sharp, ed., Maryland and Delaware Master Gardener handbook. College Park: University of Maryland Cooperative Extension.

Harrington, J. F., and P. A. Minges. 1954. Vegetable seed germination. Oakland: University of California Division of Agriculture and Natural Resources, unnumbered leaflet.

Hartmann, H. T., and D. E. Kester. 1990. Plant propagation: Principles and practices. 5th ed. Englewood Cliffs, NJ: Prentice Hall.

Johnson, H. 1982. Vegetable crops: Planting and harvesting periods for Calfiornia. Oakland: University of California Division of Agriculture and Natural Resources Publication 2282.

LeRoy, T. R. 1989. Plant propagation. In D. F. Welsh, ed., The Texas Master Gardener Handbook. College Station: Texas A&M University Agricultural Extension Service.

Lorenz, O. A., and D. N. Maynard, 1980. Knott's handbook for vegetable growers. 2nd ed. New York: Wiley.

Macdonald, B. 1990. Practical woody plant propagation for nursery growers. Portland, OR: Timber Press.

Michigan master gardener syllabus. 1974. East Lansing: Michigan State University Cooperative Extension.

Relf, D. 1994. Virginia master gardener handbook. Blacksburg: Virginia Polytechnic Institute and Virginia State University.

Roth, S. A. 1991. The weekend garden guide: Work-saving ways to a beautiful backyard. Emmaus, PA: Rodale Press.

6

Plant Pathology

Deborah Silva and Demetrios G. Kontaxis

LEARNING OBJECTIVES

- Develop a general understanding of basic plant disease concepts and principles. Become acquainted with the terminology professionals use to describe and discuss plant diseases and their control.

- Learn the major types of pathogens (parasitic agents) and environmental factors (nonparasitic agents) that cause diseases in plants.

- Develop a general understanding of how plant pathogens may or may not cause disease when they interact with the surrounding environment and their hosts.

- Learn examples of common plant diseases.

- Develop an understanding of how to distinguish disease symptoms from other plant injuries.

- Learn the basic strategies for controlling plant diseases.

  This chapter is intended to be used in conjunction with *Pests of the Garden and Small Farm* (Flint 1998); *Pests of Landscape Trees and Shrubs* (Dreistadt 1994); and the *UC Guide to Solving Garden and Landscape Problems* CD-ROM (2000).

Plant Pathology

What Is Plant Pathology?

Plant pathology, or phytopathology, is the study of plant diseases. A plant pathologist is a "plant doctor," who has the knowledge to recognize disease symptoms, diagnose their cause(s), and recommend strategies to prevent and manage disease outbreaks. (The term *phytopathology* derives from the Greek *phyton*, meaning plant, *pathos*, meaning disease, and *logos*, meaning study.) Plant pathologists study diseases caused by fungi, bacteria, viruses, viroids, phytoplasmas (formerly known as mycoplasmalike organisms), spiroplasmas, nematodes, parasitic plants, and protozoa, all of which are collectively called *plant pathogens*. Of course, not all fungi, bacteria, and nematodes are pathogens; most species are actually beneficial to plant growth, but those that cause disease are known as pathogens.

Crop plants under pathogen attack are known as *host plants*. Host plants may or may not be susceptible to getting a disease, depending on their inherent genetic resistance, overall health, and the surrounding environmental conditions, which include temperature, moisture, sunlight, and soil status. Because

environmental conditions must be favorable for disease to occur, plant pathologists must study the interactions among the pathogen, the environment, and specific host plants to evaluate preventive measures, alleviate damage, and develop effective control strategies.

Plant pathologists also study abiotic plant disorders caused by environmental factors in the absence of pathogens, such as air pollution, drought, nutrient deficiencies, mineral toxicities, freezing temperatures, pesticide toxicities, lack or excess of light, or improper cultural practices. Plant damage caused by insects or animals is usually not included in the study of plant pathology, although insects can serve as vectors (carriers) that transmit certain pathogens to plants. When insect carriers are an important factor in the development of a particular disease, the combined expertise of plant pathologists and entomologists can contribute to effective control strategies.

Plant pathology is a practical science born of necessity for man's survival. Among the earliest written records of plant diseases are those found in the Bible's Old Testament, describing blights and mildews (see 1 Kings 8:37). The Greek philosopher Theophrastus (374–288 B.C.) wrote his observations and speculations about diseases of trees, cereals, and legumes. The Romans revered the rust god, Robigo, whom they appeased to protect grain crops from rust diseases. Every spring, before rusts could take hold, the Romans celebrated Robigalia by sacrificing red dogs and sheep to pacify Robigo and protect the harvest.

For nearly 2,000 years, little progress was made in the science of plant pathology. Not until the compound microscope was invented in the middle of the seventeenth century were significant advances made in understanding the causes of plant disease and in managing them. Many pathogens of economic importance are microscopic in size and cannot be seen and studied without the aid of a compound microscope. Figure 6.1 is a schematic diagram depicting the shapes and sizes of several plant pathogens in relationship to the size of a generic plant cell. Some pathogens cannot be visualized without the aid of a phase-contrast or electron microscope. Since the

Figure 6.1

Shapes and sizes of certain plant pathogens in relationship to a plant cell. *Source:* After Agrios 1997, p. 6.

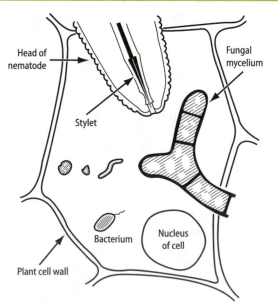

Head of nematode

Fungal mycelium

Stylet

Bacterium

Nucleus of cell

Plant cell wall

invention of these viewing aids, the roles of fungi, bacteria, viruses, and other microorganisms in the development of plant disease have been studied and elucidated.

Despite significant advances in plant pathology and other biological sciences, huge crop losses are still experienced throughout the world, showing that much is yet to be learned about plant diseases and their control. An estimated $9 billion in crops—roughly about 10 to 12 percent of the crop before harvest—is lost annually to plant disease in the United States alone. Such preharvest losses from disease in the field must be combined with postharvest losses from pathogens that attack food in storage to arrive at a rough total of the significant effect of plant disease on the food supply. The total annual food losses bring into sharp focus the reality that plant pathology has yet to overcome many microbial pathogens and environmental stresses. When the effects of plant disease are coupled with food losses from insect pests and weeds, an even more striking picture emerges. Preharvest and postharvest losses caused by the three major pests of crops—diseases, insects, and weeds—are estimated at 40 percent of the total crop in the United States and 48 percent worldwide, despite all of the advances in pest control techniques.

In their mildest forms, plant diseases can be a localized, manageable problem confined to one person's garden. Although a disease epidemic is commonly thought of as a widespread, severe outbreak that occurs over a large area within a relatively short time, technically speaking, an epidemic is any increase in the frequency of disease. An epidemic can occur on a very small scale or it can have profound, far-reaching effects. If a disease epidemic involves an important food crop, it can result in famine and death to millions of people. If a disease epidemic involves an important nonfood crop, it can devastate the economy of an industry. For example, in 1845 and 1846, a microscopic plant pathogenic fungus, *Phytophthora infestans*, destroyed the potato crop in Ireland and caused a severe disease outbreak known as the Late Blight of Potato Epidemic, which resulted in the death of nearly a third of Ireland's population and led to the emigration of millions of people to the United States. By 1940, about 35 years after its introduction into New York City, *Endothia parasitica*, the fungus that causes

chestnut blight disease, destroyed nearly all American chestnut trees in the eastern United States and devastated the hardwood timber industry. Nearly two million people starved to death in the Bengal famine of 1943 because of the *Helminthosporium* fungus that causes the disease known as brown spot of rice. The citrus *Tristeza* virus almost destroyed the citrus industry in California in the 1940s because the sour orange rootstock on which the sweet orange scions were grafted at the time was susceptible to the disease. Scientists at the University of California identified the disease, determined how it was transmitted, and conducted research to test for and develop a tristeza-resistant rootstock (Troyer citrange). Today, Troyer citrange is one of the rootstocks of choice in the California citrus industry because of its resistance to the *Tristeza* (quick decline) virus. Coffee rust, the most destructive coffee disease, caused by the fungus *Hemileia vastatrix*, destroyed all coffee trees in Southeast Asia in the late 1800s. In Great Britain, coffee rust was an important factor in tea replacing coffee as that nation's refreshment of choice. Coffee rust appeared for the first time in the Western Hemisphere in 1970 and continues to spread steadily into the world's important coffee-producing countries in South America. Today, disease-resistant varieties of coffee trees minimize losses.

Plant pathogens introduced into an area via modern global transportation would be expected to cause more damaging epidemics than local pathogens. Crops previously unexposed to the foreign pathogen would not have been pressured to select for genes resistant to the pathogen and would be more vulnerable to attack by the invader. Recognizing this danger, Congress passed quarantine laws in 1912 to restrict the entry of foreign plants, plant products, soil, and other materials into the United States to protect the nation's agriculture, gardens, and forests. Today, the Agricultural Plant Health Inspection Service (APHIS) has quarantine inspectors stationed at entry points into the United States and at certain interstate points to prevent the introduction of foreign plant pathogens into new areas. Other countries also impose quarantines.

Advances in genetic engineering of viruses, bacteria, and fungi and their application to management of crops and landscape plants are expected to usher in a new era of controlling diseases. Plant pathologists are currently studying the genes that enable pathogens to be virulent in order to identify, isolate, modify, inhibit, and neutralize them. Scientists are also studying the genes that enable certain host plants to resist attack by certain pathogens. Plant pathologists are in the process of developing techniques to transfer pathogen-inhibition genes and disease-resistance genes to crop plants to protect them from pathogen attack. Diagnostic test kits based on genetic engineering principles are under development to detect and diagnose diseases caused by particular pathogens. Others are already on the market. It is difficult to predict how and when biotechnology techniques will significantly reduce annual crop losses from plant disease, but many plant pathologists are very hopeful that these new technologies will be as important as the compound microscope in advancing the science of plant pathology.

What Is Plant Disease?

Not all plant pathologists agree about the precise definition of plant disease. In the current scientific literature, two points of view predominate. The first view is that only pathogens (fungi, bacteria, viruses, etc.) can cause plant disease, whereas nonliving environmental stresses (smog, nutrient deficiencies, mineral toxicities, etc.) cause abiotic plant disorders or damage, not disease, even though many symptoms they induce on host plants are similar to those caused by pathogens. A more inclusive definition of disease encompasses pathogens and environmental stresses as causes of disease. Plant pathologists subscribing to the second definition identify the diseases caused by pathogens as infectious diseases and the diseases caused by environmental factors as noninfectious diseases. Because noninfectious diseases occur in the absence of pathogens, they cannot be transmitted from diseased to healthy plants. Environmental factors can increase the incidence of pathogen-mediated disease by rendering plants more susceptible to pathogen attack.

Examples of the two different perspectives on plant disease are evident in textbooks and in University of California Integrated Pest Management manuals. One of the standard university-level textbooks, *Plant Pathology* (Agrios 1997), defines plant disease as follows:

Disease…can be defined as the series of invisible and visible responses of plant cells and tissues to a pathogenic microorganism or environmental factor that result in adverse changes in the form, function, or integrity of the plant and may lead to partial impairment or death of the plant or its parts. (p. 4)

Infectious diseases are those that result from infection of a plant by a pathogen. In such diseases, the pathogen can grow and multiply rapidly on diseased plants, it can spread from diseased to healthy plants and, it can cause additional plants to become diseased. (p. 43)

The common characteristic of noninfectious diseases of plants is that they are caused by the lack or excess of something that supports life [soil moisture, mineral nutrients, light, air pollutants, extremes in temperature]. Noninfectious diseases occur in the absence of pathogens, and cannot, therefore, be transmitted from diseased to healthy plants. Noninfectious diseases…may cause damage in the field, in storage, or at the market…. Symptoms may range from light to severe, and affected plants may even die. (p. 215)

Disease. Any malfunctioning of host cells and tissues that results from continuous irritation by a pathogenic agent or environmental factor and leads to development of symptoms. (p. 609)

Integrated Pest Management for Citrus (Kobbe and Dreistadt 1991), published by the University of California, concurs with the Agrios text:

A number of microorganisms and environmental stresses can cause disease in citrus. Microorganisms, including fungi, bacteria, and viruses, produce biotic or infectious diseases. Abiotic diseases, such as genetic disorders, nutrient deficiencies, or adverse soil and weather conditions, may create conditions favoring the development of biotic diseases or produce disease symptoms of their own. (p. 110)

However, an equally important and well-respected UC publication, *Pests of Landscape Trees and Shrubs* (Dreistadt 1994), has two separate chapters entitled "Diseases" and "Abiotic Disorders," which suggest a different approach. The "Abiotic Disorders" chapter opens with the following paragraph:

> Abiotic (nonliving or noninfectious) disorders are diseases induced by adverse environmental conditions, often the result of human activity. These causes include nutrient deficiencies or excesses, salt, cold, heat, herbicides or other pesticides, air pollution, or too little or too much water. Activities that compact soils, change soil grade, or injure trunks or roots also cause abiotic disorders. In addition to directly damaging plants, abiotic disorders can predispose trees and shrubs to attack by insects and pathogens. (p. 215)

These issues are discussed to point out that not all scientists, including UC scientists, agree on the precise definition of plant disease. Some practicing plant pathologists would object strongly to using the term *noninfectious disease* for abiotic disorders and damage. In other words, they restrict the definition of disease to pathogen-mediated symptoms, using the terms *plant damage* or *abiotic disorder* exclusively when describing environmental stresses and their symptoms. Other plant pathologists would accept the definition of disease in the Agrios text quoted above. Regardless of their positions on this debatable issue, pathologists do concur on the adverse symptoms expressed in host plants.

The discussion in this chapter is based on the more inclusive definition of plant disease, as stated in the Agrios text. A distinction is made between infectious diseases caused by pathogens and noninfectious diseases caused by environmental stresses. Abiotic disorders and damage are described as symptoms of noninfectious disease in this chapter.

Basic Concepts and Principles of Infectious Plant Disease

How and When Infectious Disease Develops: The Disease Cycle

Infectious diseases are dynamic, biological processes caused by the continuous interaction of a pathogen with a host under environmental conditions that favor disease development. Plant diseases disrupt normal, healthy plant growth. For an infectious disease to develop, a series of events called the *disease cycle* must occur: inoculation; penetration; establishment of infection (which includes invasion of host plant tissues, growth, and reproduction of the pathogen); dissemination of the pathogen; and survival of the pathogen (overwintering or oversummering in the absence of the host).

Inoculation. The first event in the disease cycle is inoculation, which occurs when the pathogen comes in contact with a susceptible host. Pathogens capable of causing infection that come into contact with host plants are known as *inoculum*. One unit of pathogen inoculum is called a *propagule*. Wind currents, irrigation or rain water, and insects can carry the inocula of many pathogens to host plants. An inoculum may consist of a single wind-borne fungus spore, or it may consist of millions of bacteria carried in a droplet of irrigation water. Successful inoculation requires favorable environmental conditions, such as relative humidity and temperatures favorable to the inoculum interacting with a susceptible host. If temperatures are too hot or cold and relative humidity is too low, the inoculum can desiccate and die before infection ever has a chance to occur.

Penetration. After inoculation, penetration of the host tissue can occur. Some pathogens can directly penetrate into cells: they produce enzymes that soften the cell walls of the host and use mechanical force to pierce through and gain entry into the host under attack. Many fungi, nematodes, and parasitic plants attack their hosts by direct penetration. Other pathogens enter passively through wounds, stomata (the pores on leaves through which plants respire), or other natural openings. Because fungi, bacteria, and some viruses can enter plants through wounds, it is important to prune plants carefully and at the appropriate times of year, when penetration by pathogen inoculum and disease development are not favored.

Infection. Infection is the process by which an inoculum establishes continuous contact with susceptible cells or tissues of the host plant and sets up a parasitic relationship, procuring its food (nutrients) from the host. Penetration may or may not lead to infection or disease, depending on environmental conditions and the host's susceptibility or resistance to the pathogen. When infection occurs, pathogens grow and multiply on or within host plant tissues, invading other tissues of the host's body, reproducing there, and feeding on the host. Many pathogens release enzymes, toxins, and growth regulators inside the host plant, which lead to disorganized, unhealthy growth in susceptible host plants and ever-increasing populations of the pathogen feeding inside the host. Successful infection may lead to disease symptoms, such as wilting, leaf curling, the appearance of discolored, malformed, or dying (necrotic) areas on the host plant; fruit drop; or stunted growth. Other infections are latent, and symptoms do not occur immediately. The interval between inoculation and the appearance of disease symptoms is known as the incubation period, which may last from a few days to years, depending on the particular host-pathogen combination and surrounding environmental conditions.

During the infection stage of the disease cycle, pathogens invade host plant tissues, either intercellularly (between cells) or intracellularly (within the cell). Infection may be localized, involving a single cell or small area of the host plant, or it may be systemic, involving susceptible cells and tissues and spreading throughout the plant. Many pathogens (bacteria, viruses, viroids, nematodes, protozoa) reproduce within the host plant during the infection stage. Their populations increase rapidly and they are said to colonize the host.

Dissemination. Infectious diseases do not spread from plant to plant; pathogens do. Pathogen dissemination may occur via a number of agents, including wind, rain, irrigation water, insects, mites and other vectors, infested debris, infested equipment, animals, and humans (fig. 6.2) through their use of contaminated pruning shears, importation of infested plants, worldwide travels, disregard of quarantines, and transport of infested soil. Pathogens can survive in perennial plants and in infected plant parts, such as roots, bulbs, stems, and bud scales. Because annual hosts die at the end of the growing season, pathogens overwinter or oversummer in insect vectors, seeds, infested crop debris, weeds, soil, and fruit mummies, where they form resting structures until the next growing season, when susceptible annual hosts can be attacked again.

Figure 6.3 shows an example of key processes in the disease cycle of anthracnose diseases caused by several species of fungi. Inoculation, infection, common host symptoms associated with infection, pathogen dissemination, and overwintering are depicted. Many fungal diseases have similar disease cycles. The pathogen's disease cycle is distinct from its life cycle, which refers to the growth of the pathogen from one generation to the next, from its juvenile to adult stages. A particular disease cycle may correspond closely to the life cycle of a particular pathogen, but the disease cycle refers to both the symptoms in

Figure 6.2

Common methods of disseminating plant pathogenic fungi and bacteria. *Source:* After Agrios 1997, p. 57.

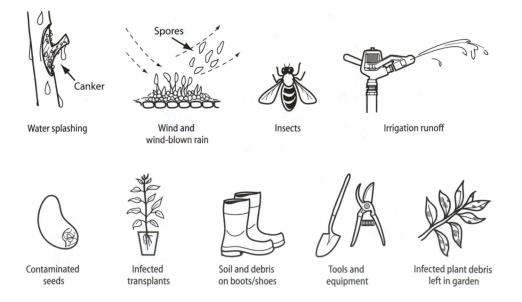

Water splashing — Canker

Wind and wind-blown rain — Spores

Insects

Irrigation runoff

Contaminated seeds

Infected transplants

Soil and debris on boots/shoes

Tools and equipment

Infected plant debris left in garden

Figure 6.3

Disease cycle of anthracnose diseases. *Source:* *Anthracnose*, UC IPM Pest Note 7420, p.2.

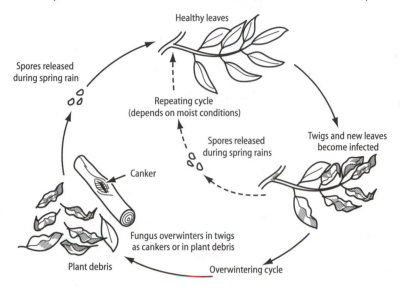

the host plant and its interactions with the pathogen and may include a period of time within a growing season or extend from one growing season to the next. If more than one disease cycle occurs per growing season of the crop, the amount of inoculum multiplies many times.

The Infectious Disease Triangle

To summarize infectious disease principles, plant pathologists use a disease triangle (fig. 6.4), which graphically depicts the compatible interactions of three essential components required for the development of an infectious disease: a pathogen in contact with the host, a susceptible host plant, and an environment favorable to the pathogen. An infectious disease will not occur if one of these components is missing.

- *Host.* Important host-related factors are overall plant health, developmental stage, and the plant's degree of susceptibility, tolerance, or genetic resistance to the pathogen. Some host plants may defend themselves against pathogen attack via structural features that act as physical barriers to pathogen entry and via biochemical reactions that produce substances toxic to pathogens. Both types of weapons (structural features and biochemical reactions) may be preexisting (predate the attack of a particular pathogen) or may be induced by pathogen attack.

- *Pathogen.* Factors affecting the pathogen's virulence (its ability to cause disease) include the size of its population, the degree to which it can contact the host, and the intensity with which it can parasitize the host plant.

- *Environment.* Weather and soil conditions, especially temperature and moisture, are essential factors affecting the environmental component of the disease triangle. In general, most infectious diseases develop best when temperatures are warm and relative humidity is high. If weather conditions are too hot, too cold, or too dry, pathogens may be unable to mount an attack; a host plant susceptible under normal environmental conditions may be able to resist the pathogen under extreme environmental conditions.

The significance of the disease triangle as a visual representation of important theoretical plant disease concepts is summarized in Agrios (1997, p. 45):

Each side of the triangle represents one of the three components. The length of each side is proportional to the sum total of the characteristics of each component that favor disease. For example, if the plants are resistant, the wrong age, or widely spaced, the host side—and the amount of disease—would be small or zero: whereas, if the plants are susceptible, at a susceptible stage of growth, or densely planted, the host side would be long and the potential amount of disease could be great. Similarly, the more virulent, abundant, and active the pathogen, the longer the pathogen side would be and the greater the potential amount of disease. Also, the more favorable

Figure 6.4

The plant disease triangle.

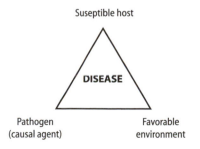

the environmental conditions that help the pathogen, (e.g., temperature, moisture, and wind) or that reduce host resistance, the longer the environment side would be and the greater the potential amount of disease. If the three components of the disease triangle could be quantified, the area of the triangle would represent the amount of disease in a plant or in a plant population. If any of the three components is zero, there can be no disease.

A proper understanding of the disease triangle concept makes it possible to devise effective control programs. Some disease management programs focus on excluding or removing the pathogen. This is the objective of quarantine programs that seek to prevent introduction of a pathogen from one area to another. Seed treatments attempt to avoid the transport and introduction of a pathogen living on or in plant seeds. Other management programs focus on planting resistant or pathogen-tolerant hosts.

A third alternative for controlling diseases, control of the environment, may be achieved more completely in the greenhouse than under field or backyard conditions. Even under backyard conditions, the principle can be applied by manipulating planting dates, selecting short- or long-season varieties, and selecting planting sites with favorable drainage capacities. Because pathogens have the ability to adapt to varying environmental conditions and selection pressures, they may not be controlled as effectively by a single control approach as by a combination of control measures. The most effective disease control programs weaken more than one link in the disease triangle.

Because infectious disease epidemics develop as a result of the timely combination of the elements that give rise to plant disease, plant pathologists often graphically illustrate epidemics with a disease pyramid, or disease tetrahedron, in which the disease triangle serves as the base, and time is the height of the pyramid (a perpendicular line arising from the center of the triangle base); humans may be associated with the pyramid. Time is a critical factor in the development of epidemics. Humans can interact with and influence each of the four primary epidemic components (host plant, pathogen, environment, length of interaction time) and can increase or decrease the magnitude of an epidemic. In addition,

humans can be profoundly affected by epidemics when they cause famine or devastate the economy of a nonfood crop.

Causes of Infectious Plant Disease

Pathogens

A large number of organisms function as plant pathogens, causing infectious plant diseases. The majority are microscopic, and the most common groups are fungi, bacteria, and viruses. Also important are nematodes, parasitic seed plants, spiroplasmas, and phytoplasmas (formerly known as mycoplasmalike organisms). Visible pathogen structures on the surface of the host, such as a fungal mycelium (a mass of hyphae that make up the body of a fungus), masses of spores, or nematodes with a spearlike stylet are called *signs* of disease. Pathogen signs are distinct from disease *symptoms* of the host plant, which are the external appearance of the host plant and the internal alterations in host metabolism and physiology caused by the pathogen. Pathogens can interfere with photosynthesis by attacking leaves, defoliating plants, and reducing photosynthetic surface area; they can attack roots and interfere with water absorption before any aboveground symptoms appear; they can infect and plug up the vascular tissues (xylem, phloem, or both) and interfere with water transport or translocation of photosynthates (sugars) throughout the plant body; and they can increase the respiration rate in infected plant cells, alter the permeability of cell membranes, and alter the synthesis of proteins, including enzymes, and metabolism of genetic materials (DNA/RNA) in infected host plants.

Just as other organisms are divided into species, so are plant pathogens; however, the hierarchical terminology in recent usage has become complex and is not particularly uniform. It would not be surprising if the terminology were to change in the future so that there would be more uniformity across pathogen types. Certain individuals of a fungus species that attack only certain host crops (wheat or oats, etc.) are known as *varieties* or *special forms* (*forma specialis*, or f. sp.). Many species of pathogenic bacteria consist of strains that differ only in the host plant species they infect and are known as *pathovars*. Within each special form or variety of pathogenic fungus, some individuals, known as a *race*, attack only certain varieties of the host plant. In viruses, pathologists usually refer to strains rather than races. Variants of a fungus race can evolve when they develop the capability of infecting host varieties that they could not infect previously. Asexual progeny of a variant are known as a *biotype*. Each race can consist of several biotypes.

Fungi

Fungi are the single most important cause of plant disease. Of the 100,000 known species of fungi, more than 10,000 can cause diseases in plants. All plants are attacked by some types of disease-causing fungi, and each of the plant pathogenic fungi can attack one or more kinds of host plants. Many have a very wide host range. Fungi damage susceptible plants by producing toxins and enzymes that disrupt normal plant growth and physiology. About 100 species of fungi cause diseases in man and animals. Thus, not all fungi are harmful to plants, man, and animals.

The majority of fungus species are saprophytes that feed on dead organic matter and are beneficial to the soil environment. Some saprophytes are beneficial because they use toxic chemicals as a source of food and, as a by-product of their metabolism, degrade the toxics to simpler chemicals that are nontoxic to man. Other saprophytes are beneficial because they feed on decaying plant residues left in the soil after harvest, decompose them, and recycle them into beneficial products, such as humus (soil organic matter that resists further decomposition and improves soil structure and fertility), and they release plant nutrient elements in simple mineral forms that then become available for uptake by plants. (See the discussion about soil organic matter in chapter 3, "Soil and Fertilizer Management.") Other beneficial fungi live in association with plant roots (e.g., mycorrhizae) and may synthesize plant growth-regulating hormones beneficial to growth, yield, and resistance to pathogens. See *Phytohormones in Soils* (Frankenberger and Arshad 1995) for a technical and comprehensive discussion of microbially derived plant growth regulators.

Pathogenic fungi usually grow on or through diseased plant tissue as fine, thread-like structures called *hyphae* that form a network known as a mycelium, the fungus body. Fungi are microscopic, but when many

hyphae aggregate to form a mycelium, the fungus can become macroscopic, visible to the naked eye. Fungi usually reproduce and multiply by means of spores, specialized reproductive bodies analogous to seeds. Fungal spores are usually produced at or near the surfaces of host tissues, ensuring prompt, efficient pathogen dissemination. Fungal spores can be spread by wind, irrigation or rainwater, insects, tools, birds, movement of soil, or anything that the spores contact. When spores land on a susceptible host plant and environmental conditions are favorable, they germinate to produce new fungal mycelia. Often, the mycelia include haustoria, specialized structures fungi use to pierce and penetrate host tissue directly and to absorb host nutrients for their own growth. Fungi can also attack their hosts through wounds and natural openings, such as stomata. Fungi can overwinter or oversummer as sclerotia (compact masses of hyphae), rhizomorphs (rootlike masses of hyphae), or spores.

Some common disease symptoms caused by pathogenic fungi are listed in table 6.1. Some of these symptoms—smuts, molds, sooty molds, and powdery mildews—are caused only by pathogenic fungi. These kinds of symptoms and the signs associated with them are critical to identifying and diagnosing the pathogenic fungi that cause the disease; however, other symptoms listed in table 6.1— galls, cankers, leaf spots, leaf curls, scabs, blights, soft rots, and root rots—are typical of both pathogenic fungi and bacteria. When disease symptoms are not specific, identification of the offending pathogen is more difficult and requires additional analysis. A hand lens, which can magnify characteristic fungal structures (signs), may aid in a cursory identification process in the field. To confirm identification and diagnosis, fungi often must be analyzed in plant pathology labs by staff trained in sterile techniques for isolating pathogens from diseased host tissue. Special nutrient media are used for growing the pathogen in culture, and the pathogen's biochemistry and anatomy (spores, spore-bearing structures) are studied to facilitate accurate identification and to recommend control measures.

In California, the fungus *Phytophthora cinnamomi* causes root rot of avocados, azaleas, oaks, and many other trees, shrubs, and ornamental plants. Two of its relatives,

Table 6.1

COMMON DISEASE SYMPTOMS ASSOCIATED WITH PLANT PATHOGENIC FUNGI

Disease or symptom	Description
anthracnose	Necrotic and sunken, ulcerlike lesion on the stem, leaf, fruit, or flower of the host plant; often called leaf, shoot, bud, or twig blight; infects trees (ash, elm, oak, sycamore) and shrubs throughout the U.S.
basal stem rot	Disintegration of the lower part of the stem.
blight	General and extremely rapid browning of leaves, branches, twigs, and flower organs, resulting in their death.
canker	Localized wounds or necrotic lesions, often sunken beneath the surface of a stem or branch of a woody plant.
damping-off	Rapid death and collapse of seedlings in the seedbed or field; found worldwide in tropical and temperate climates in forest soils, valleys, greenhouses, and backyards.
decline	Plants growing poorly; small, brittle, yellowish or red leaves; defoliation and dieback.
dieback	Extensive necrosis of twigs beginning at their tips and advancing toward their bases.
downy mildew	Yellow to brown spots on upper leaf surfaces; fuzzy spore growth, primarily on lower leaf surfaces, especially after rain or heavy fog; requires high relative humidity and cool weather; primarily a problem on a few vegetable crops in California.
dry rot	Maceration and disintegration of fruit, roots, bulbs, tubers, and fleshy leaves.
galls	Enlarged tumorous overgrowths on host plant.
leaf curls	Distortion, thickening, and curling of leaves.
leaf spots	Localized lesions on host leaves consisting of dead, collapsed cells.
powdery mildew	Chlorotic (yellowed) or necrotic areas on leaves, stems, and fruit; infected leaves, stems, and fruit are usually covered with whitish-colored mycelia, and spore-containing fungus structures, which look powdery (an exception is powdery mildew on tomatoes, eggplants, and peppers, which produces yellow patches on leaves often without powdery mycelia). Disease affects many vegetables and fruit trees, but is more serious on grapes and fruit trees than on vegetables; does not require high relative humidity (unlike downy mildew) and can establish and thrive under the warm, dry conditions of the California summer
mold	Profuse, wooly fungus growth on host tissue (signs).
root rot	Disintegration or decay of part or all of the host root system.
rust	Numerous, small, rusty-colored pustules (spore masses) on leaves or stems; rusts have caused famines due to destruction of cereal grains. Also infect birch, cottonwood, fuchsia, hawthorn, pine, juniper, rose, rhododendron.
scab	Localized lesions on host fruit, leaves, tubers, usually slightly raised or sunken and cracked, giving a scabby appearance.
shot hole	Holes on affected leaves; discolored spots on buds, leaves, shoots, and fruit; infects *Prunus* spp. (almond, apricot, plum). First appears as reddish, purplish, or brown spots about 1/10 inch (2.5 mm) in diameter on new buds, leaves, and shoots; spots expand and centers turn brown; centers of spots on leaves often fall out, leaving holes (most holes on leaves are caused by chewing insects but not these spots). More severe after warm, wet winters.
soft rot	Maceration and disintegration of fruit, roots, bulbs, tubers, and fleshy leaves.
sooty mold	Sooty coating on foliage, stems, and fruit, formed by dark fungal mycelia that live in the honeydew secreted by insects, such as aphids, mealybugs, scales, and whiteflies (signs of disease).
smut	Characterized by masses of dark, powdery spores (signs).
wilt	Droopy leaves or shoots due to disturbances of the host's vascular system (food and water-conducting tissues) in roots or stems. Fungi grow primarily in the host's vascular system and plug it up, preventing the flow of water and nutrients to leaves and shoots, which results in secondary wilting symptoms.
witches' brooms	Profuse upward branching of twigs.

Source: Adapted from Agrios 1997, pp. 254–255.
Note: Two UC IPM manuals, *Pests of Landscape Trees and Shrubs* (Dreistadt 1994) and *Pests of the Garden and Small Farm* (Flint 1998), have excellent color photographs of disease symptoms on garden plants, trees, and shrubs commonly affected in California. The information in the text in these two manuals has considerable detail about symptoms, fungus species, biology, and disease management.

P. citrophthora and *P. parasitica*, cause rots on citrus trees. They infect the tree trunk at or near the soil line, causing a gummy sap to ooze from trunk lesions (foot rot or gummosis), or infect the roots (root rot) or fruit, which develop brown spots that become soft (brown rot). All of these diseases are favored by high soil moisture and atmospheric humidity coupled with low temperatures.

Until 1990, plant pathologists considered the various *Phytophthora* species that cause plant disease true fungi; now, they are reclassified for scientific purposes as "fungallike organisms." For practical purposes, when referring to the disease symptoms they cause, the fungallike organisms are treated as fungi. This handbook refers to the various *Phytophthora* species that cause important diseases in California as fungi.

Armillaria mellea causes root rots on a wide variety of herbaceous plants, shrubs, and trees, including almonds, walnuts, apples, citrus, grapes, stone fruits, and strawberries. After a winter rain, *Armillaria* fungi often form clusters of mushrooms at the bases of infected trees. *Fusarium oxysporum* and *Verticillium dahliae* are the primary causes of vascular wilts, which typically start first on the lower parts of the garden plant or orchard tree. Affected leaves become yellow, curl, wilt, turn brown, and die. Both *Verticillium* and *Fusarium* fungi plug up the vascular system. Peeling back the bark on a newly infected branch may reveal dark stains along the vascular tissues. *Penicillium italicum* and *P. digitatum* fungi cause postharvest blue mold and green mold, respectively, of citrus fruits in storage. Typically, the blue-green or olive-green spores are surrounded by a ring of white mycelium. *Rhizopus*, the common bread mold fungus, also causes soft rots of many fleshy fruits, vegetables, flowers, bulbs, corms, and seeds.

A number of *Taphrina* species cause deformed leaves, flowers, and fruits on peaches, plums, and cherries.

Worldwide, *Botrytis*-caused diseases are probably the most common, widely distributed diseases of vegetables, ornamentals, fruits, and field crops. *Botrytis*-caused diseases on a number of commodities are called gray mold. Fungal spores known as conidia are spread by wind.

Powdery mildews, which are caused by a number of fungi, are probably among the most easily recognizable plant diseases. In warm, dry climates typical of California, powdery mildews infect roses, fruit trees, vegetables, weeds, grasses, cereals, and forest trees. Characteristic signs of the fungus are the appearance of spots or patches of a white to grayish powdery growth on young plant tissues or on entire leaves.

Fungi have numerous mechanisms for survival. They can live in host tissue and plant debris, as overwintering spores, or in special protected nesting structures, such as sclerotia or rhizomorphs. Management of fungal diseases, discussed at the end of this chapter, can involve cultural practices, host resistance, and chemicals known as *fungicides* that are designed to kill fungi.

Bacteria and Other Prokaryotic Plant Pathogens

Of the 1,600 species of bacteria identified to date, about 100 cause diseases in plants. The vast majority of bacterial species are beneficial soil saprophytes that decompose organic matter and thereby improve soil fertility and recycle nutrients, making them available to plants in mineral form (see "Soil Organic Matter" in chapter 3). Some bacterial species cause diseases in humans, such as tuberculosis, typhoid fever, and bacterial pneumonia. Each plant pathogenic species may consist of numerous pathovars (abbreviated pv.) differing only in the host plant species they infect.

Bacteria are microscopic, one-celled prokaryotes (single-celled organisms whose genetic material is not organized into a nucleus). Plant pathogenic bacteria are rod-shaped, spherical, spiral, filamentous, or threadlike and have a rigid cell wall. The cell wall may be surrounded by a thin gummy material known as a *slime layer*, or it may be surrounded by a thick gummy material known as a *capsule*. Most plant pathogenic bacteria (but not all) have delicate, threadlike flagella, which project from the cell and enable the bacteria to move. Bacteria enter host plants through wounds or natural openings and use susceptible crop plants for their source of food. Bacteria multiply rapidly, reproducing by fission, in which one bacterium simply divides into two bacteria, which then divide into four bacteria, which divide into eight bacteria. The population can grow rapidly. Under favorable environmental conditions, many bacteria species can divide every 20 minutes. At this doubling rate, one bacterium could have more than a million offspring in less than half a day. The progeny of a single bacterium are known as a *colony*. Under the microscope, the colony may look circular, oval, or have an irregular shape and may be a fraction of a millimeter to several centimeters in diameter. Warm temperatures and high relative humidity (moisture) are required for bacteria to multiply; thus, they are not as serious as fungal pathogens in most areas of California. However, sprinkler irrigation can lead to bacterial problems, even in dry areas.

Bacterial inoculum is commonly spread by splashing water and rain, but it can also be windblown, carried by insects, or moved by humans on contaminated tools and soil (see fig. 6.2). Bacteria can survive for many months in a dormant state (overwinter or oversummer) in host tissues, such as in seeds, storage organs, cankers, and plant debris, or in the intestines of the insects that carry them to their hosts.

Plant pathogenic bacteria cause many types of disease symptoms that are similar to those caused by pathogenic fungi. Common symptoms of bacterial diseases are spots on leaves, stems, blossoms, and fruits; rapidly advancing necroses of these organs, known as blights; soft rots of fruits, roots, and other storage organs; scabs; vascular wilts; galls; and cankers on stems and tree trunks. Refer to the descriptions in table 6.1. Bacteria are associated with wilts when they plug up the water-conducting vascular system of the host; with necrotic blights, characterized by rapidly expanding areas of dead and discolored tissue on stems, leaves, and flowers; with soft rots of fleshy storage organs (potatoes); and with crown galls, overgrowths resembling tumors at the stem bases (crowns) of many plants.

Bacteria that cause some of the more common plant diseases in California are species of *Agrobacterium, Corynebacterium, Erwinia, Pseudomonas, Streptomyces, Xanthomonas*, and *Xylella*. Figure 6.5 gives one example, the disease cycle of *Erwinia amylovora* bacteria that cause fire blight, infecting apple and pear trees in the orchard and ornamental apples and pears in the landscape. Closely related landscape and garden plant species, such as firethorn, loquat, and hawthorn, can also be seriously injured by the disease. Note the complex interactions among bacteria populations, insects, rain, host flowers, twigs, leaves, and overwintering structures in the disease process. The bacteria overwinter in cankers on the tree. Inoculum is carried by wind, rain, and insects. The first symptom is blossom blight, with

---

Figure 6.5

Disease cycle of fire blight of pear and apple caused by *Erwinia amylovora*. *Source: Fire Blight*, UC IPM Pest Note 7414, p. 2.

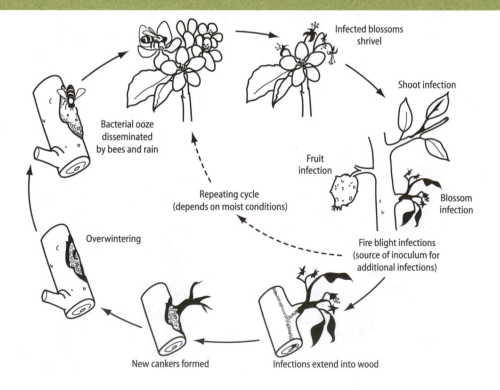

Bacterial ooze disseminated by bees and rain

Infected blossoms shrivel

Shoot infection

Fruit infection

Blossom infection

Repeating cycle (depends on moist conditions)

Fire blight infections (source of inoculum for additional infections)

Overwintering

New cankers formed

Infections extend into wood

flowers appearing water-soaked. They shrivel and turn brown. The bacteria move from the infected flower into the fruit spurs and twigs. The disease intensifies as shoot tips become blighted and turn black, as if scorched by fire. Pathogen movement slows in woody branches. *Erwinia* bacteria form cankers that will initiate the next infection cycle. Mechanisms by which bacteria damage plants include the production of toxins, gums, enzymes, and growth hormones that disrupt healthy plant function.

Phytoplasmas. Phytoplasmas (formerly known as mycoplasmalike organisms [MLOs]) are microscopic prokaryotes that are bacterialike, except that they lack a cell wall and flagella. They are spherical, elongated, or constricted chains smaller than bacteria but larger than viruses. Phytoplasmas that cause plant diseases are similar to mycoplasmas that can cause respiratory and urogenital diseases in humans and animals, hence their former name, mycoplasmalike organisms. In animals, mycoplasmas are also associated with arthritic and nervous disorders. Phytoplasmas were first recognized as plant pathogens in 1967 and were referred to as MLOs then. More than 200 plant diseases, some of which are important diseases of fruit trees, are now known to be caused by phytoplasmas. They are transmitted primarily by insect vectors (mostly leafhoppers, some psyllids) and by grafting. The insect vectors cannot transmit phytoplasmas immediately after feeding on an infected plant because the incubation period varies with temperature and may range from 10 to 45 days. During this period, the phytoplasmas multiply in the insect vectors. When the concentration of phytoplasmas in the salivary glands of the infected insects is high enough, the insects are then capable of injecting the pathogens into susceptible host plants via their mouthparts and retain the capability for the rest of their lives.

Phytoplasmas invade primarily the food-conducting elements of the host's vascular system (phloem tissue) and disrupt its normal function. Phytoplasmas induce disease symptoms that are quite similar to those caused by viruses: yellowing, leaf curling, twisting of stems, and progressive weakening of the host. Common phytoplasma-caused diseases that can occur in California are pear decline, peach yellows, aster yellows (on carrots, onion, celery, spinach, potato, aster, gladiolus, and phlox), elm phloem necrosis, and big bud of

tomato. Plants diseased by phytoplasmas are usually stunted and have reduced yields. Phytoplasmas can overwinter in weeds such as dandelions and wild carrots. Leafhoppers are important insect vectors in the transport of phytoplasmas from infected weeds to healthy plants.

Phytoplasma diseases can be suppressed by heat treatments in growth chambers or by immersing dormant organs in hot water (30° to 50°C) for 10 minutes at the higher temperature and for 3 days at the lower temperature. Although not available to backyard gardeners, antibiotics in the tetracycline group (terramycin, aureomycin) have been documented to suppress phytoplasma diseases; some diseases are sensitive to erythromycin and chloramphenicol, but the symptoms usually reappear if the antibiotic treatment stops. On diseased trees, antibiotics are applied by direct injection into the trunks. Treatments must be reapplied periodically (annually or biannually) to diseased trees to be effective. Most phytoplasmas are completely resistant to penicillin.

Spiroplasmas. Spiroplasmas are helical-shaped prokaryotes very similar to phytoplasmas but distinct from them primarily in that they can be cultured on nutrient media and have a spiral shape. Spiroplasmas cause a number of important diseases in susceptible corn and citrus trees, such as citrus stubborn disease (*Spiroplasma citri*) and corn stunt. Citrus stubborn disease is one of the worst threats to production of sweet oranges and grapefruit in California because diseased trees produce fewer fruit and the fruit are smaller, reducing overall yield. Detection is difficult, and the spread of disease is insidious. The pathogen infects the phloem and can be transmitted by budding, grafting, and leafhoppers. Experimentally, the trunks of diseased trees have been treated with antibiotics such as erythromycin or tetracycline to reduce symptoms, but the antibiotics do not control the disease. Control depends on the use of disease-free scion wood and rootstocks, removal of infected trees, and detection of the pathogen by nucleic acid–based methods (polymerase chain reaction [PCR]) or culturing.

Fastidious vascular bacteria. Fastidious vascular bacteria (formerly known as rickettsialike organisms) are a type of plant pathogenic bacteria first identified in 1972, almost a century after bacteria were identified as pathogens that cause plant disease (1882).

Their relationship to other plant pathogenic bacteria is not well understood at this time. Previously thought to be rickettsialike organisms, they are rod-shaped bacteria transmitted to susceptible plant hosts by insect vectors, such as leafhoppers and psyllids. Some fastidious vascular bacteria infect the phloem of their host plants, causing symptoms such as leaf stunting and clubbing, shoot proliferation, witches' brooms, and greening on floral parts. Others infect the xylem, causing symptoms such as marginal leaf necrosis, internal discoloration, and an important xylem-limited disease known as Pierce's disease in grapes and leaf scorch in oleander. Vectors can acquire and transmit some of these bacteria in less than 2 hours. Experimentally, some plants infected with fastidious vascular bacteria respond to injections of antibiotics in the tetracycline group, but injections must be repeated annually.

Viruses

Viruses differ from other plant pathogens in that they are not made up of cells, do not divide to increase their population, and can be seen only with the aid of an electron microscope. Viruses consist of a DNA or RNA core (a core of genetic material comprised of nucleic acid) surrounded by a protein coat known as a *capsid* (a protective sheathing of amino acids) and are known as DNA viruses or RNA viruses, respectively. The nucleic acid of the majority of viruses that infect plants is RNA, but at least 25 plant pathogenic viruses have been shown to contain DNA. Individual virus particles are known as *virions*. Viruses do not produce any specialized reproductive structures such as spores or seeds. Instead, they reproduce and multiply by inducing the host plant to manufacture more virus particles. Once inside the host plant, viruses take charge, disrupting normal plant function. Viral DNA or RNA orders the DNA (genetic material) of the host plant to manufacture virus RNA or DNA, which the virus needs to make more virus particles, and the host plant begins to show symptoms of disease as a result of abnormal plant metabolism and physiology induced by the virus infection. For example, viruses can cause a decrease in photosynthesis, a decrease in the level of carbohydrates in host tissues, a decrease in nitrogen, and a decrease in the concentration of plant hormones as well as the synthesis of viral nucleic acids (viral

RNA or DNA). Plant pathogenic viruses are not known to contain any enzymes, toxins, or other substances involved in the pathogenicity of other types of fungal and bacterial inoculum, but some viruses can lyse (decompose or destroy) host plant cells. Viruses take up space in host plant cells and wreak havoc on the normal order of plant metabolism and physiology.

About one-fourth of the more than 2,000 known viruses attack and cause diseases in plants. In addition to viruses that attack plants, some viruses attack humans and animals and cause diseases such as influenza (flu), polio, smallpox, rabies, and warts. Other viruses attack fungi, bacteria, and phytoplasmas.

The vast majority of virus infections in plants are systemic, occurring throughout the host plant as the virus moves from cell to cell, but symptoms may be localized, as with necrotic lesions that develop only at the point of virus entry into the plant. Once a plant is infected by a systemic virus, it will usually remain infected its entire life (chronic infection). Symptoms commonly associated with systemic viral diseases are mosaics (light green, yellow, or white areas intermingled with the normal green color of the foliage, or whitish areas intermingled with the normal color of flowers or fruit); ring spots (chlorotic or necrotic rings or patterns on leaves, stems, or fruit); and overall stunting and reduced growth rate. Depending on symptom severity, mosaic-type symptoms may be described as mottling, streaking, veinclearing, or veinbanding. Mosaics, mottles, and ring spots are not associated exclusively with viruses; they are also associated with nutrient deficiencies or toxicities. Other symptoms associated with viruses are leaf curling, leaf rolling, yellows, tumors, stem pitting, or malformation of plant parts. Virus-infected flowers may fail to open properly. Infected fruit may be small and poorly shaped, and yield will be reduced.

Most plant pathogenic viruses have a wide host range, and more than one virus may infect a plant simultaneously. Viruses can enter plant cells through wounds or can be injected by vectors, such as plant-feeding insects, mites, fungi, and nematodes when they feed. When a vector contains a virus and is capable of transmitting it to a host, the vector is said to be *viruliferous*. The most common means of virus transmission from infected to healthy plants in the same generation is by insect vectors, primarily aphids, whiteflies, and leafhoppers (Homoptera), which have piercing and sucking mouthparts. Other insect groups can transmit viruses to plants, but none are as important as aphids, whiteflies, and leafhoppers. Aphids are the most important vectors of plant viruses, which they carry on their stylets (stylet-borne, or nonpersistent, viruses) or accumulate in their guts and transmit to host plants via their mouthparts when they feed (circulative, or persistent, viruses). Aphids transmit the majority of stylet-borne viruses, which they can acquire after feeding on a diseased plant for 30 seconds or less and can transmit to a healthy plant after feeding on it for a few seconds. After acquiring a stylet-borne virus, aphids may remain viruliferous for a few minutes to several hours. Although aphids cannot transmit circulative viruses immediately after feeding on a virus-infected host, once they do become viruliferous, which can take several hours, they are capable of transmitting the virus for several days. Aphids can spread virus pathogens relatively long distances when they are carried by prevailing winds.

Leafhopper-transmitted viruses are circulative and typically cause disturbances in the phloem, disrupting the transport of photosynthates in the host plant. After acquisition feeding on an infected host, leafhoppers may take up to 2 weeks to become viruliferous, but then they can remain viruliferous for the rest of their lives. Whitefly-transmitted viruses are either circulative or semipersistently transmitted. They are particularly problematic in semiarid and tropical areas of the world.

The most important means of virus transmission from one generation to the next is via infected vegetative propagation materials, because almost all fruit trees and many ornamental trees and shrubs are propagated by budding, grafting, or cuttings and because many field crops and florist's crops are propagated by tubers, corms, or cuttings. Viruses can also be transmitted via infected pollen grains, infected ovules, and infected seeds. Viruses are also spread to healthy plants by virus-infected fungi, mites, nematodes, parasitic seed plants (dodder), natural root grafts, and cultural practices, including infested equipment. Viruses can survive in weeds, insects, and diseased plant material.

In addition to typical plant viruses, satellite viruses can be associated with viruses and affect their ability to multiply and cause disease. *Viroids* are "naked" (they lack a protein coat), single-stranded, circular RNAs that can cause plant disease by themselves. Virusoids are viroidlike and can be present inside typical RNA viruses; together they infect the plant host. Satellite RNAs may be found in the virus particles of certain viruses, but they may be related to the RNA of the virus or the host plant. Generally, they reduce the effects of viral infection and may represent a protective response by the host to fight virus infection.

Nematodes

Plant parasitic nematodes are microscopic, unsegmented roundworms invisible to the naked eye that usually dwell in the soil and feed on plant roots; however, some species do feed on aboveground plant parts, such as stems, buds, leaves, or bulbs. Nematodes should not be confused with segmented earthworms, which are beneficial to soil structure and fertility, as discussed in the "Soil Organic Matter" section of chapter 3. Many diseases once thought to be caused by fungi, viruses, or soil deficiencies are now recognized as the work of nematodes. Plant pathologists and nematologists study nematode-induced diseases. Some common plant pathogenic nematode groups are root-knot nematodes (*Meloidogyne* spp.), citrus nematode (*Tylenchulus semipenetrans*), cyst nematodes (*Heterodera* spp. and *Globodera* spp.), root lesion nematodes (*Pratylenchus* spp.), and stem and bulb nematodes (*Ditylenchus* spp.). Tumorlike overgrowths on roots are characteristic symptoms of root-knot nematodes.

Nematodes enter host plants via direct penetration, using repeated thrusts of their sharp mouthpieces, known as stylets, which act like hypodermic needles to puncture and pierce through the roots of their hosts. Then the pathogenic nematodes secrete a salivalike substance that contains enzymes, which digest the nutrients of the plant root tissue. Next, they suck up the host plant's nutrients for their own food. When nematodes use the host root's nutrients for their own growth, the roots are weakened. Typically, nematodes do not kill their hosts, but, by causing wounds in the root system and reducing their vigor, they predispose the host's roots to diseases. Bacterial, viral, and fungal pathogens can invade these nematode-weakened, infected, and mechanically wounded roots, compounding the direct damage caused by the nematodes themselves. Nematodes can transmit viruses to healthy plants via their stylets for up to several months after they have fed on a virus-infected host. Some nematodes function as endoparasites (they enter the host's roots and feed from within the root tissue); others function as ectoparasites (they do not enter the roots, but feed on the host's cells near the root surfaces).

Nematodes induce a variety of disease symptoms, such as root galls, root knots, root lesions, excessive root branching, injured root tips, and general stunting, yellowing, and distortions of whole plants. Nematode infestation impairs root uptake of water and minerals from the soil. As a result, plants wilt, become yellowed, and develop symptoms indicative of root problems similar to those associated with drought injury and mineral deficiencies.

When plant pathogenic nematodes form complexes with plant pathogenic fungi in the soil (*Fusarium*, *Verticillium*, *Pythium*, *Rhizoctonia* and *Phytophthora*), susceptible plants are damaged more than would be predicted from each pathogen alone. In these cases, the nematodes do not transmit the fungus, but plants already infected by the nematodes have much worse symptoms from the fungal infection. Varieties normally resistant to the fungi can become susceptible after infection by nematodes. One example is potato early dying disease, caused by *Verticillium dahliae* and *Pratylenchus penetrans*. Fewer such nematode-bacterial disease complexes are known. Nematodes can also serve as vectors of certain viral diseases.

Warm, moist soil conditions favor the nematode life cycle, which may be completed in 3 to 4 weeks (egg to egg) under optimal environmental conditions. Females lay eggs that hatch to young larvae shaped like the mother nematodes. The larvae undergo four larval stages before they become adults. Populations may build rapidly, but, unlike other pests, initial nematode infestation does not spread rapidly. Nematodes normally move only a foot or more during the growing season, traveling through a series of undulating wormlike body movements around soil particles and plant roots. Nematode populations are typically localized to a relatively small area of a garden or field. Nematodes can survive (overwinter and oversummer) for a year or more in soil as eggs or cysts in the absence of a susceptible host. Plant pathogenic nematodes can be disseminated from one place to another on infested plant parts and cultural implements, contaminated soil, animals, or even dust.

Parasitic Seed Plants

Higher plants that depend on other plants for their food are known as parasitic seed plants. Of the more than 2,500 species known, few cause important diseases on agricultural crops or forest trees, but some of these parasites—dodder, mistletoe, witchweed, and broomrape—are pathogenic to crop plants, and plant pathologists do study them. Parasitic seed plants produce flowers and seed just like the plants they parasitize, but they depend on their hosts for water and mineral nutrients. Parasitic seed plants enter their hosts via direct penetration; they pierce the plant surface by mechanical force and use their haustoria to steal water and nutrients from the host for themselves. Parasitized plants or plant parts (e.g., tree branches) lose vigor and eventually die. Parasitic plants attack perennial and annual plants and spread via their seed.

Dwarf Mistletoes of Conifers. The dwarf mistletoes (*Arceuthobium* spp.) are a very serious pathogen of Western conifers, such as pines, firs, spruce, and hemlock. Infected branches develop swellings and cankers. Dwarf mistletoes can produce shoots, inconspicuous leaves, flowers, and fruit that become turgid at maturity. The fruit release their seed forcibly, sometimes up to a distance of 50 feet (15 m). The seed are covered with a sticky substance, which enables them to adhere to whatever they contact. Dwarf mistletoes are controlled by physically removing the pathogens.

Leafy Mistletoes. Leafy mistletoes (*Phoradendron* spp.) produce nearly oval, large leaves and may infect woody perennials, such as apple, citrus, cherry, black walnut, ash, alder, birch, oak, and maple. European mistletoe (*Viscum album*) is present in Sonoma County and can infect primarily alder, apple, black locust, cottonwood, and maple trees. Leafy mistletoes produce sticky seed disseminated mainly by birds that eat the seed. If seed drop on a susceptible tree, they may germinate. An otherwise healthy tree can tolerate a few mistletoes, but individual branches may die. Pruning infested branches promptly can suppress leafy mistletoes. Planting species that appear to be resistant is another control strategy. Chinese pistache, crape myrtle, eucalyptus, ginkgo, golden rain tree, liquidambar, persimmon, sycamore, and conifers are rarely infested.

Dodder. Dodder (*Cuscuta* sp.) A slender, twining plant, dodder produces a dense, tangled mat of yellow or orange strands that entwine and spread over host plants such as tomatoes, alfalfa, cantaloupe, flax, onion, and sugarbeet. Dodder seed overwinters in the soil, where it germinates and enters the host tissue. Control of *Cuscuta* can be difficult. Recommended control measures include the use of dodder-free seed and selected herbicides.

Broomrape. Broomrape (*Orobanche ramosa*) is a parasite of tomato in California. Clubs of whitish-yellow to blue stems arise from the ground at the base of the host plant. The seed germinates only in the presence of a susceptible host. It can overwinter and survive in the soil for more than 10 years. Broomrape seed germinate only when roots of certain plants grow near them. Soil fumigation can control this parasitic plant.

Basic Concepts and Principles of Noninfectious Plant Disease

Environmental Factors that Cause Noninfectious Plant Disease

The common trait of noninfectious diseases is that they are caused by a lack of, excess of, or extremes in an important environmental component that supports plant growth and development. Nutritional deficiencies, mineral excesses, air pollution, lack of or excessive moisture, extremes in temperature, excessive wind, and extremes in light duration and quality can cause noninfectious disease in plants. Because these diseases occur in the absence of pathogens, they cannot be transmitted from diseased to healthy plants. Plant diseases that result from unfavorable environmental factors are not contagious or pathogenic; however, symptoms caused by noninfectious agents can be as serious as those associated with pathogen-induced infectious diseases and may mimic symptoms associated with viruses, phytoplasmas, and root pathogens.

Most of the disorders in home gardens and landscapes are due to disease caused by noninfectious, environmental agents. Plants killed or damaged by noninfectious diseases can be overrun by secondary, infectious organisms, compounding the difficulty of diagnosing the causal agent. Some plants heavily fertilized with nitrogen are more susceptible to pathogen attack. The disease triangle (see fig. 6.4) shows that prevailing environmental factors—temperature, moisture, light, soil nutrient status, and soil pH—can affect the development of pathogen-mediated, infectious plant diseases. After a pathogen comes in contact with a susceptible host, prevailing environmental conditions or stresses can increase or reduce host susceptibility or pathogen virulence and thus may even determine whether an infectious disease will occur. In addition, microclimates (the environment of an individual plant or portion of a plant) may vary, making only some plants susceptible; for example, wet patches in a garden cause patchy disease distribution.

Lack of Moisture or Excessive Moisture. Moisture imbalance in the soil (a lack of soil moisture or excessive soil moisture) is the single most important environmental factor in noninfectious diseases. Moisture may take the form of rain, dew, irrigation water on plant surfaces or around roots, or relative humidity in the air. Overly moist, saturated soils caused by poor drainage, flooding, or overirrigation can suffocate roots and enhance several root diseases because of a lack of oxygen. Many fungal root pathogens also thrive in overly wet soils. Plants wilt, leaves are chlorotic, and plants may even die. Drought, on the other hand, can also cause disease symptoms, such as chlorosis, plant wilting, stunting, yield reduction, desiccation, increased salt concentration, and death. Plants weakened by drought are more susceptible to infection by certain pathogens.

Low relative humidity (lack of moisture in the atmosphere) by itself seldom causes damage, but when it is accompanied by high temperatures and high wind velocity, plants may show symptoms of excessive water loss from leaves. Fruit may shrivel and plants may wilt, if only temporarily. House plants are often subjected to relative humidities of 15 to 25 percent, which can be injurious since this is equivalent to growing under dry, desert-like conditions.

The most important effect of moisture on infectious disease development seems to be its influence on the germination of fungal spores and their penetration into the host. Some important soil pathogenic fungallike organisms (*Pythium* [damping off] and *Phytophthora* spp.) that attack underground parts of plants (roots, tubers, young seedlings) cause their most severe symptoms in soils near saturation. Moisture is also required by many foliar fungal and bacterial pathogens and by nematode pathogens. Unlike most fungi, powdery mildews prefer lower relative humidities and are common in dry areas.

Extremes in Temperature. At different stages of their growth and development, plants will differ in their ability to withstand extremes in temperature. In general, though, extremely low temperatures cause far greater damage to crops than do extremely high temperatures. Temperatures below freezing can kill buds of fruit trees and damage the fruit and succulent twigs of most trees. Low winter temperatures may kill young roots of trees and herbaceous plants or cause bark splitting and canker development. The degree of chilling and frost injuries depends on the duration of the cold temperatures and the degree of temperature drop. (For techniques for protecting trees from frost injury, see chapters 17, "Temperate Tree Fruit and Nut Crops"; 18, "Citrus"; and 19, "Avocados.") Low temperatures can also adversely affect house plants.

High soil temperatures can damage succulent seedlings and lead to the formation of cankers at the crowns of older plants. High air temperatures in conjunction with drought or excessive sunlight may cause bud drop, wilting, leaf scorch, leaf tip burn, and sunscald injuries, particularly on the sun-exposed sides of fleshy fruits and vegetables, such as peppers, apples, tomatoes, onion bulbs, and potato tubers. On hot, sunny days, the temperature of tissues beneath the skin on the sun-exposed sides of fruits and vegetables may be much higher than the temperature of the tissues on the shaded side and also of the prevailing air. Fruits and vegetables may become discolored, develop a water-soaked appearance, blister, and desiccate beneath the skin,

leading to sunken areas on the fruit surface. Fleshy-leaved house plants placed near windows with a southern exposure may develop symptoms of sunscald in the spring or summer if the sun on hot days is allowed to heat the leaves to an excessive temperature.

Extremes in temperature also influence the development or progression of infectious plant disease. The most rapid development of infectious disease (the shortest time required for the completion of a disease cycle) occurs when the temperature is optimal for pathogen development but above or below the optimum for host development. The shorter the disease cycle, the greater the number of new infections that can occur during the growing season.

Wind. Wind is a critical factor in the spread of propagules of pathogens that cause infectious disease. Insect vectors that transmit plant pathogens are often carried long distances by wind currents. In contrast, wind may also deter infectious diseases by drying out plant surfaces before penetration can occur.

Light Intensity and Duration. Inadequate light can slow formation of chlorophyll and lead to leaves becoming pale green and plants becoming leggy or etiolated (spindly growth with long internodes). High light intensities combined with high temperatures can lead to sunscald and other noninfectious disease symptoms, as noted previously. In house plant culture, improper lighting (usually inadequate light) can be a significant problem. Insufficient or excess light stress can increase plant susceptibility to infection in the presence of a pathogen.

Nutritional Deficiencies and Mineral Excesses. In addition to carbon, oxygen, and hydrogen, primary nutrients (nitrogen, phosphorus, potassium), secondary nutrients (magnesium, calcium, sulfur), and micronutrients (iron, copper, manganese, zinc, chlorine, molybdenum, nickel, and boron), are needed for normal plant growth and development. Mineral excesses and deficiencies have profound effects on plant development, inducing plant disorders and diseases and causing symptoms on leaves, stems, roots, flowers, fruits, and seeds. (For a comprehensive discussion about essential plant nutrients and symptoms associated with deficiencies and excesses, see chapter 3.)

Lower-than-adequate amounts of most essential elements usually result in a reduction in growth and yield. Deficiency symptoms, such as yellowing, leaf marginal necrosis (death), leaf scorch, interveinal yellowing (chlorosis), discoloration, distortion, and stunting are common. Many plant diseases occur annually because of reduced amounts or reduced availability of one or more essential elements in the soil. Low levels of nitrogen in the soil may cause plants to be stunted and chlorotic. An excessive amount of lime in the soil increases soil alkalinity (pH), which binds iron, rendering it unavailable to plants and leading to iron deficiency, known as lime-induced iron chlorosis.

Soils also can contain excessive amounts of essential elements that can cause injury, increase plants' disease susceptibility, or cause toxicity symptoms in plants. Excessive sodium induces calcium deficiency, causes alkali injury, and results in symptoms that may range from chlorosis, stunting, leaf burn, and wilting to death of seedlings and young plants. Excessive boron in irrigation water can kill certain vegetables and trees.

Air Pollution. Common air pollutants in California are ozone, PAN (peroxacetyl nitrate), nitrogen oxides associated with automobile exhaust, sulfur dioxide, suspended particles (particulate matter), and fluorides (table 6.2). The primary components of smog are ozone (O_3) and PAN. Ozone is formed in the presence of sunlight when oxygen (O_2) reacts with nitrogen oxides that derive from incompletely combusted hydrocarbons from automobile exhaust. The O_3 further reacts with nitric oxide (NO) and unburned hydro-

Table 6.2

AIR POLLUTION INJURY TO PLANTS

Pollutant	Source	Some susceptible plants	Disease symptoms	Comments
ozone (O_3)	automobile exhaust	expanding leaves of all plants, particularly beans, citrus, petunia, pine, corn, grapes, alfalfa	stippling, mottling, chlorosis on leaves, primarily on upper leaf surfaces; spots are small to large bleached white to tan, brown, or black; premature defoliation and stunting may occur in citrus, grapes	most destructive air pollutant to plants; major smog component; enters via stomata
peroxyacetyl nitrates (PAN)	automobile exhaust	many kinds of plants: spinach, petunia, tomato, lettuce	causes "silver leaf," bleached white to bronze spots on lower leaf surfaces that may spread throughout leaf and resemble ozone injury	can be severe in metro areas with smog and inversion layers
sulfur dioxide (SO_2)	automobile exhaust, factories	many kinds of plants: violet, conifers, pea, cotton, bean	general chlorosis (low concentration); bleaching of interveinal leaf tissues at higher concentrations	toxic at 0.3–0.5 ppm; may form acid rain if combines with moisture
nitrogen dioxide (NO_2)	combustion	many kinds of plants: beans, tomato	bleaching and bronzing similar to SO_2; may also suppress growth	toxic at 2–3 ppm
particulate matter (PM) (dusts)	dust from factories	all plants	forms dust layer on plant surfaces; plants become chlorotic, grow poorly	measured as PM-10 (particles <10 microns); Riverside and San Bernardino Counties have worst PM-10 levels in U.S.
hydrogen fluoride (HF)	oil refineries	many kinds of plants: corn, peach, tulip	leaf margins of dicots and leaf tips of monocots turn brown and die	toxic at 0.1–0.2 ppb

Source: Adapted from Agrios 1997, p. 235.

carbon radicals to yield PAN and additional ozone, which contributes to buildup of the O_3 concentration. Smog has a number of negative effects on human beings (scratchy throats, burning eyes, reduced visibility, respiratory problems), but it can also induce disease symptoms in plants.

Ozone causes more plant damage than any other air pollutant. The disease symptoms caused by air pollutants—chlorosis, leaf necrosis, white spots or bleached areas on leaves, defoliation, silvery bands or bronzing on lower leaf surfaces—are difficult to distinguish from disease symptoms caused by certain nutrient (fertilizer) deficiencies, pathogens, or insects. Making a correct diagnosis often requires a well-trained specialist. When plants are exposed to mixtures of air pollutants and a range of pathogens (fungi, bacteria, viruses), insect pests, and adverse environmental factors all at once, diagnosis becomes more difficult.

A plant's stage of development influences its response to air pollutants. Some plants are sensitive when young and insensitive at maturity. Certain varieties of common garden plants (tomato, onion, corn) are more sensitive to air pollution than others (beans, citrus, grapes). Many air pollutants enter plants through stomata, the tiny pores concentrated primarily on the lower surface of leaves. When air pollutants penetrate the leaves of a susceptible plant via the stomata, they can decrease the rate of plant metabolism and can damage the chlorophyll molecules responsible for the green color of leaves. Destruction of chlorophyll causes leaves to become chlorotic (yellowed). Pollutants may weaken plants and predispose them to infectious diseases or insect infestation.

Air pollutants produce their negative effects in minute quantities measured in parts per million (ppm) or parts per billion (ppb), as noted in table 6.2. The median toxic dose refers to the amount of pollutant that results in 50 percent of the plants showing injury and damage. Both the concentration of the pollutant in ppm or ppb and the exposure time determine the dose. Federal and state guidelines have established air-quality standards to protect human beings and vegetation from injurious doses of air pollutants.

Identifying and Diagnosing Diseases

Identifying and diagnosing plant problems are essential for developing effective control strategies, which are discussed briefly in this chapter and in chapter 10 ("Controlling Garden Pests Safely"), while diagnosing problems is discussed in more detail in chapter 22 ("Diagnosing Plant Problems"). When disease occurs, the causal agent must be identified first, and then effective management strategies can be implemented. Diagnosis of the causal agent is not an easy task, because many disease symptoms associated with pathogens and environmental factors are similar to symptoms associated with insect pests. Also, most plant pathogens are microscopic. When pathogens are detected on the surfaces of a host plant or inside the vascular tissues of a host plant, particularly at the margins of diseased tissue, or when they are detected on or in roots, the pathogens are probably the cause of the disease symptoms. When fungi and bacteria are detected, it is important to determine that pathogenic, rather than saprophytic, species have been detected before pronouncing the fungi or bacteria as the causal agent of disease. Detection and identification require careful observation, an 8× to 10× magnification hand lens, a notebook for keeping records, small vials and plastic bags for collecting samples to identify, and, depending on the pathogen's size, professional examination under a compound, phase-contrast, or electron microscope, and lab tests. Plant pathologists are designing more sophisticated nutrient media for growing pathogens in pure culture in the laboratory to aid in identification and diagnosis. Plant pathologists are also developing and refining diagnostic tests using serological and molecular techniques (such as DNA fingerprinting).

The following list indicates the primary information needed to diagnose disease problems. The list is not comprehensive. Additional detailed questions are usually necessary for each specific situation (for a broader perspective, see chapter 22). Unfortunately, by the time disease symptoms occur, it may be too late to eradicate the problem during the current growing season, but the kinds of information below will be useful for preventing and managing disease in subsequent growing seasons.

- Types of disease symptoms present: damping-off, root galls, internal discoloration, wilt, blight, shot holes, yellowing, leaf curling, defoliation, mosaic, leaf spots, stunting, etc.

- Host plant, including species, variety, and source of stock; its developmental stage; and the common disease problems in the area (e.g., cucurbits and powdery mildew; pears and fireblight).

- Time of the year.

- Pattern of symptoms (in rows, scattered).

- Cultural practices (irrigation method, pruning methods, raised beds).

- Environmental conditions: air quality, fertilization or pesticide practices, prevailing temperatures, rainfall, soil quality, light.

- Pathogen signs, especially the presence of resting or fruiting spores.

- Laboratory tests: isolation, identification, verification of pathogenicity.

In general, it is much more difficult to diagnose the causes of disease symptoms than it is to diagnose the causes of symptoms associated with insect pests because disease symptoms tend to be more variable. Some pathogen-caused disease symptoms mimic those caused by abiotic stresses, and many pathogens are microscopic in size. When comparing symptoms in the backyard with the color photographs and descriptions in the University of California Integrated Pest Management manuals referenced in this chapter or other resource books, examine several affected plants at several stages of ill health. Look for plants with different stages of disease symptoms because the information will help determine the progression of disease. Do not rely on a single symptom for diagnosis, and examine as many parts of the diseased plant as possible. Pull plants up to check roots, because many aboveground symptoms are caused by pathogens and stresses that attack roots.

Principles of Plant Disease Management

The disease development process must be understood to devise effective management strategies. Many effective disease-control measures are primarily preventative and need to begin *before* symptoms are observed, ideally before pathogen penetration has taken place. Almost all control techniques focus on protecting plants from becoming diseased rather than on curing them once disease has occurred. By the time disease symptoms are expressed, the pathogen (with few exceptions) is already inside the host plant in a relatively safe environment, and it may be too late to reverse the damage. In some cases, after disease symptoms occur, no effective management strategy exists other than removal of the diseased plants. Correct diagnosis of the current problem will allow for planning a control strategy to prevent the disease during the next growing season, and measures can be taken to make the garden inhospitable to pathogens, which will help limit the need for pesticide applications.

Five basic principles of plant disease control are

- pathogen exclusion

- pathogen eradication or reduction of pathogen inoculum

- plant protection

- use of resistant plant varieties

- integrated management

The majority of regulatory control measures focus on pathogen exclusion from certain host plants or a geographic area. Biological control measures focus on improving the resistance of host plant varieties or on techniques that favor microorganisms antagonistic to the pathogen. Chemical and physical control measures focus on protecting host plants from pathogen inoculum and on minimizing an infection in progress. The majority of cultural control measures focus on pathogen reduction and eradication and on techniques to protect plants from contact with pathogen inoculum.

Familiarity with crops, their diseases, and the insect vectors associated with them is useful in planning control programs. Some diseases occur every season; others occur sporadically. Some can be easily controlled using proper methods; others are more challenging. Except for fruit and landscape trees, the loss of one or a few plants is considered unimportant; control measures focus on saving the population rather than a few individuals. Knowing the proper control method to use at the proper time requires integrating the strategies described below. Usually, success in controlling plant disease occurs when a combination of management methods is used.

Pathogen Exclusion

Exclusion strategies attempt to prevent the importation and spread of pathogens into an area. Government-regulated quarantines, inspections, and voluntary or compulsory eradication of certain host plants are common exclusion techniques. As a nation, we attempt to exclude certain pathogens by establishing quarantines and by stationing plant inspectors at various points of entry into the country, as discussed in the introduction to the chapter. The Plant Quarantine Act of 1912 prohibits or restricts entry into or passage through the United States of plants, plant materials, soil, and other materials from foreign countries that carry or are likely to carry plant pathogens not known to be established here. The U.S. Agricultural Plant Health Inspection Service (APHIS) has quarantine inspectors stationed at entry points into the United States and at certain interstate points to prevent the introduction of foreign plant pathogens into new areas. Quarantine inspectors from the United States also travel abroad to inspect the flower fields in Holland for diseases because flower bulbs are imported annually. In California, intrastate transport of citrus budwood and trees is regulated to keep pathogens out of certain areas. Intrastate transport of citrus fruits is regulated during outbreaks of the Mediterranean fruit fly.

Backyard gardeners can practice pathogen exclusion by purchasing certified disease-free seed and vegetative propagating materials and by inspecting planting stock from the nursery carefully for signs and symptoms before transporting them into the yard. Buying the highest quality seed and planting stock available from a reputable supplier can prevent diseases from being transmitted in nursery stock, transplants, and seeds.

Pathogen Eradication or Reduction of Pathogen Inoculum

Once a pathogen is present in the environment, one principle of effective disease control is to keep the population density of the pathogen at very low, nondamaging levels. In such situations, effective control may not mean complete eradication of the pathogen. In other cases, pathogen eradication is the goal, and infected host plants must be destroyed. Twice this century, when citrus canker became a problem in Florida, millions of diseased orchard and nursery trees were destroyed, and the disease was brought under control. Not all such programs are as successful. Attempts by coffee-producing countries in South America to eradicate coffee rust have been frustrated by the continual spread of the pathogen. Backyard gardeners can significantly reduce pathogen inoculum using practical cultural techniques such as those described below.

Careful Sanitation. Keep garden tools clean to avoid spreading contaminated soil or pathogens from infected plants. When working with diseased plants, sterilize equipment with household bleach diluted 1 to 9 with water. Use this weak bleach solution to sterilize pruning shears when removing diseased limbs from trees and other diseased tissue. Wash treated tools before storing them, because bleach is corrosive. If you suspect soil pathogens, clean off your shoes, too. Tires of vehicles and carts can transport pathogen-infested soil and should also be sanitized. Wash your hands thoroughly after handling diseased plants.

Roguing and Pruning. Remove diseased plants and plant parts promptly as soon as you observe them. Bag them and discard them. Prune and destroy diseased foliage from trees and shrubs to prevent spread to adjacent healthy tissues.

Crop Rotation. Planting a crop that is not a host for a particular pathogen for a period of 3 to 4 years can eliminate the pathogen from the soil. If this type of formal rotation is not feasible, backyard gardeners should at least avoid planting exactly the same crop or crops from the same family year after year in the same part of the garden to prevent inoculum buildup. It is unwise to plant the same crops or even closely related crops (such as the potato family or the cucurbit family) in the same garden location every year.

Elimination of Weeds and Other Alternate Hosts. Weeds can serve as alternate hosts for a number of disease-causing fungi and viruses. Control weeds in the garden and in adjacent areas.

Techniques that Disfavor Insect Vectors. Reflective mulches of aluminum or whitish-gray polyethylene sheets along the edges of crops susceptible to virus diseases vectored by aphids seem to provide some protection by repelling aphids and reducing the inoculum load.

Soil Solarization. In the warmer areas of California, a number of soil pathogens can be killed or their populations reduced significantly by covering moist soil with clear plastic (1 to 2 mils thick) for 2 months (4 to 6 weeks) in midsummer. The soil will heat up to temperatures that are lethal to many pathogenic fungi, nematodes, weeds, weed seeds, and other pest organisms.

Plant Protection

Crop protection involves practical disease avoidance techniques and the use of pesticides, organic and synthetic chemicals that kill or control pests. Pesticides that kill or control fungi are known as *fungicides*; those that kill or control bacteria are known as *bactericides*; and those that kill or control nematodes are known as *nematicides*. No viricides have been developed to date. The use of pesticides as a plant protection strategy is discussed at length in chapter 10. According to *Pests of the Garden and Small Farm*, "The diligent backyard gardener who is willing to sacrifice a few plants to disease should be able to get by with very little use of pesticides for the control of pathogens if he or she follows a careful cultural management program" (Flint 1998, p.139). Flint does note two exceptions: peach leaf curl on peaches and nectarines and powdery mildew on grapes.

Backyard gardeners can protect plants and avoid diseases by using a number of practical techniques.

- Plant at a time of year that does not favor the pathogen.

- Choose a particular geographic area or planting site in a local area that provides adequate sunlight and good drainage. Powdery mildew and molds are more serious problems in shady areas; and root diseases, particularly those caused by

pathogenic nematodes and *Pythium* (damping-off) fungi, are more of a problem in soils with poor drainage.

- Choose plants that have a history of success in the particular microclimate and use resistant varieties when available.

- Provide adequate plant spacing. Crowding favors damping-off fungi and Botrytis gray mold on vegetables. Make conditions unfavorable for pathogens.

- Use adequate fertilization and irrigation to promote plant health. Do not overwater, as excess water favors root pathogens. Water early in the day so foliage can dry out quickly, because many fungal and bacterial pathogens need high relative humidity to begin attacking host tissue. Maintain an even water supply during the growing season.

- Group plants according to their water and sunlight requirements. Do not plant a crop that needs frequent light watering next to one that needs infrequent deep watering.

- Handle plants and plant parts carefully during harvest and storage.

- Avoid injuries and wounds when handling, harvesting, or caring for plants. Such practices allow a plant's natural protective mechanisms to remain intact.

- Use disease-free planting stock, sanitary cultural practices, and crop rotation, as appropriate.

Use of Resistant Plant Varieties

Disease-resistant host varieties provide the best, most reliable, and most economical method of controlling diseases caused by certain viruses, fungi, and nematodes. A number of crop plant varieties on the market today are resistant to fungi-causing rusts, smuts, powdery mildews, vascular wilts, certain viruses, pathogenic bacteria, and nematodes. A number of rootstocks for fruit and nut trees resist attack by common pathogens. Some resistant crop varieties inhibit pathogen attack because of their synthesis of toxic or repellent compounds; others resist pathogens through physical factors, such as thick cuticles; and still others are tolerant, which means that they resist pathogens and disease by suffering little or no damage after pathogen attack. Proper culture of a crop can enhance host resistance and/or tolerance and prolong the lifetime of a resistant and/or tolerant variety after its release.

Resistance is not the same as immunity. *Immunity* means that the crop would not be attacked by the pathogen even under the most favorable conditions; *resistance* means that the crop can endure attack by a particular pathogen. Check with the nursery or seed supplier to see if resistant varieties are available and which one(s) are best suited to local conditions and needs. Keep in mind that improper culture of a resistant variety may negate resistance traits.

Integrated Management

The University of California encourages gardeners to manage disease-causing pathogens and other pests using an integrated pest management (IPM) strategy (see chapter 10, "Controlling Garden Pests Safely"). A central concept in IPM is that of integrating several control methods, such as resistant varieties, cultural practices, biological controls, and the least-toxic pesticides for long-term management of pests. An IPM approach encourages methods that provide long-term prevention or suppression of pest problems with minimum impact on human health, the environment, and nontarget organisms.

The principal components of an IPM program are:

- pest identification (pathogen, insect, weed)

- methods for detecting, monitoring, and predicting pest outbreaks

- knowledge of the biology of the pest and its ecological interactions with hosts, natural enemies, and competitors

- ecologically sound methods of preventing or controlling pests

When possible and practical, take action to prevent disease problems before they occur by choosing resistant varieties, providing optimal conditions for plant growth, and taking preventive action against pathogens known to be a problem in the area. Purchase seed and vegetative propagating material from reputable suppliers, and when appropriate, purchase certified, disease-free seed, scions, rootstocks, and vegetative propagules. Once the home garden and home landscape are planted, inspect plants (vegetables, shrubs, and landscape and fruit trees) at least once a week (twice a week at the peak of the growing season or more often if it appears that a problem may be brewing) for disease symptoms, pathogen signs, and other evidence of pest infestation. Rogue out diseased plants.

When you do find diseased plants, try to identify the causal agent or at least rule out certain possibilities, using the information and principles learned in this chapter. When checking trees, check a few leaves on each side of the tree as well as the trunk. Examine fruit on the tree and those that have fallen to the ground. Cut fruit open and inspect. If plants appear wilted, pull up a few and observe the roots to check for signs of nematodes, vascular pathogens, or root-infesting insects. If a pathogen or insect does not seem to be associated with the symptoms, try to determine whether one of the abiotic noninfectious disease factors highlighted in this chapter may be the cause. As part of this process, evaluate fertilization and irrigation regimes, soil quality, drainage, and the prevailing weather. Keep notes of your observations, the date, time of day, stage of crop development, any intervention that you took, and the results.

Pest control strategies will most likely fail when the pest is not identified properly, since the control action will probably not be effective against the offending organism that was misidentified at the outset. Some problems may require professional diagnosis. The county agricultural commissioner's office and the UC Cooperative Extension farm advisor for the county may be able to help identify a pest problem or direct you to professional diagnostic services. See chapter 22 for more information on diagnosing plant problems.

A fundamental concept of IPM is that a certain amount of disease (or pest damage) can be tolerated. Broad-spectrum pesticides are used only as a last resort when careful monitoring and preestablished guidelines indicate that they are needed. An IPM program can be carried out in most garden situations with almost no use of pesticides, which are more toxic than fungicidal and insecticidal soaps, horticultural oils, or microbials. Backyard gardeners must be willing to sacrifice a few vegetable plants, for example, and tolerate a little cosmetic damage so that the use of pesticides can be minimized. Backyard produce does not need to meet industry or grocers' standards.

Applying General Disease Management Principles to Control of Infectious Disease

Chapter 10, "Controlling Garden Pests Safely," provides a comprehensive discussion of the principles and practices of managing diseases, insects, and weeds. *Pests of the Garden and Small Farm* (Flint 1998) and *Pests of Landscape Trees and Shrubs* (Dreistadt 1994) recommend very practical control measures for dealing with infectious diseases, as well as for dealing with insect pests, weeds, and abiotic agents. Both publications have color photographs of disease symptoms, pathogen signs, insect pests, and weeds. This discussion briefly applies only the general principles of managing infectious disease.

Management of Diseases Caused by Fungi

A number of effective organic and synthetic fungicides are available for managing plant pathogenic fungi. Most fungicides are applied on the foliage as sprays or dusts to control or prevent diseases on the aboveground parts of susceptible hosts. Because many fungicides are protectants, which protect host plants from infection by a pathogen, they must be applied before a pathogen infects the plant. Fungicides should be reapplied throughout the growing season to protect newly developed foliage that was not covered during previous applications and to replace chemical that has degraded while on the plant. The timing of fungicide application is critical for success. It is usually too late to spray once disease symptoms are noticed. Diagnosing this season will enable management plans to be developed for control the next season, but the severity of some fungus diseases will fluctuate with the prevailing weather conditions, which may be different during the next growing cycle. Determine whether a foliar fungicide or a soil fungicide would be more effective in the particular disease situation in question. Apply the fungicide properly, cover the plant thoroughly, and use rates recommended on the label, following all label directions and precautions. For detailed information about pesticide labeling, applica-

tion techniques, and safety precautions, see chapter 10.

Plant breeders have developed a number of resistant varieties of crop plants that have the genetic makeup to resist major classes of fungal pathogens, such as powdery mildew and vascular wilts, under typical, prevailing environmental conditions. Try to select and plant resistant varieties in your backyard. Use pathogen-free seed or propagating stock.

Practical cultural practices, such as destruction of plant parts or debris harboring the pathogen and use of clean tools and containers, will lessen the inoculum load. Fungal disease risk can be further reduced with proper soil drainage and aeration, appropriate irrigation practices, and other cultural practices that minimize plant stress. Crop rotation can help control diseases caused by some fungi, but not for those having a wide host range or those that can survive for long periods as resting structures in the soil.

Management of Diseases Caused by Bacteria

Effective strategies for controlling bacterial diseases rely on a combination of management techniques: planting resistant host varieties, when available; practicing sanitation by removing infected debris and using clean tools; employing cultural practices that do not favor bacteria, such as avoiding sprinkler irrigation, planting in well-drained areas, and not crowding plants; and using certified disease-free seed. At the nursery, rejecting roses or fruit trees with suspicious bumps may limit bacterial pathogen spread.

Management of Diseases Caused by Viruses

Viruses can be difficult to manage; thus, it is most effective to keep viruses out of an area via quarantine, inspection, and certification programs, such as those for citrus in California. For information about the certified disease-free citrus budwood program at the University of California, see chapter 18, "Citrus."

No chemical viricides have been developed for controlling virus diseases in the field, so practices that exclude or remove virus pathogens are commonly followed to limit virus spread, including the use of virus-free propagating materials, disposing of infected plants, controlling insects and other vectors to the extent possible, and using disinfested, clean tools. Plant breeders have developed some varieties of crop plants resistant to certain viruses.

Some viruses will invade apical meristems, but other viruses do not invade the growing points of stems or roots of infected plants. If the apices of roots and stems remain virus-free, scientists who specialize in tissue culture techniques can use the virus-free apical meristems to culture virus-free clones of specific plants in the laboratory, even though the majority of the tissues of the specific plant in question are infected by the virus.

Management of Diseases Caused by Nematodes

Management of nematodes is achieved through cultural practices, such as sanitation and crop rotation to nonhost plants, planting resistant varieties, soil sterilization with heat, and soil fumigation with nematicides, chemicals designed to kill or control nematodes. Backyard gardeners cannot control nematode diseases with chemicals because no nematicides are registered for use by homeowners. In the garden, interplanting with marigolds is said to provide some measure of control because they are toxic to nematodes, but the scientific evidence for interplanting is questionable. Asparagus plants produce a chemical toxic to many nematode species.

Bibliography

Agrios, G. N. 1997. Plant pathology. 4th ed. New York: Academic Press.

Ali, A. D., and C. L. Elmore. 1989. Turfgrass pests. Oakland: University of California Division of Agriculture and Natural Resources Publication 4053.

Dreistadt, S. H. 1994. Pests of landscape trees and shrubs: An integrated pest management guide. Oakland: University of California Division of Agriculture and Natural Resources Publication 3359.

———. 2001. Integrated pest management for floriculture and nurseries. Oakland: University of California Division of Agriculture and Natural Resources Publication 3402.

Flaherty, D. L., ed. 1992. Grape pest management. 2nd ed. Oakland: University of California Division of Agriculture and Natural Resources Publication 3343.

Flint, M. L. 1992. Integrated pest management for cole crops and lettuce. Oakland: University of California Division of Agriculture and Natural Resources Publication 3307.

———. 1993. Integrated pest management for walnuts. 2nd ed. Oakland: University of California Division of Agriculture and Natural Resources Publication 3270.

———. 1998. Pests of the garden and small farm: A grower's guide to using less pesticide. 2nd ed. Oakland: University of California Division of Agriculture and Natural Resources Publication 3332.

Flint, M. L., and S. H. Dreistadt. 1998. Natural enemies handbook: The illustrated guide to biological pest control. Oakland: University of California Division of Agriculture and Natural Resources Publication 3386.

Frankenberger, W. T., Jr., and M. Arshad 1995. Phytohormones in soils: Microbial production and function. New York: Marcel Dekker.

Fry, W. E. 1982. Principles of plant disease management. New York: Academic Press.

Kobbe, B., and S. H. Dreistadt. 1991. Integrated pest management for citrus. 2nd ed. Oakland: University of California Division of Agriculture and Natural Resources Publication 3303.

Ohlendorf, B. L. P. 1996. Integrated pest management for cotton. 2nd ed. Oakland: University of California Division of Agriculture and Natural Resources Publication 3305.

―――. 1999. Integrated pest management for apples and pears. 2nd ed. Oakland: University of California Division of Agriculture and Natural Resources Publication 3340.

Rice, R. E., W. J. Bentley, and R. H. Beede. 1988. Insect and mite pests of pistachios in California. Oakland: University of California Division of Agriculture and Natural Resources Publication 21452.

Strand, L. L. 1992. Integrated pest management for potatoes. Oakland: University of California Division of Agriculture and Natural Resources Publication 3316.

―――. 1994. Integrated pest management for strawberries. Oakland: University of California Division of Agriculture and Natural Resources Publication 3351.

―――. 1998. Integrated pest management for tomatoes. 4th ed. Oakland: University of California Division of Agriculture and Natural Resources Publication 3274.

―――. 1999. Integrated pest management for stone fruits. Oakland: University of California Division of Agriculture and Natural Resources Publication 3389.

―――. 2002. Integrated pest management for almonds. 3rd ed. Oakland: University of California Division of Agriculture and Natural Resources Publication 3308.

UC guide to solving garden and landscape problems (CD-ROM). 2000. Oakland: University of California Division of Agriculture and Natural Resources Publication 3400.

UC IPM pest management guidelines. For many agricultural crops; updated regularly. Oakland: University of California Division of Agriculture and Natural Resources Publication 3339.

UC IPM pest management guidelines for turfgrass. Updated regularly. Oakland: University of California Division of Agriculture and Natural Resources Publication 3365-T.

UC IPM pest note series. B. L. P. Ohlendorf, ed. University of California Division of Agriculture and Natural Resources, Statewide Integrated Pest Management Program. Updated regularly. Available through UC Cooperative Extension county offices; also available on the World Wide Web at http://www.ipm.ucdavis.edu

7

Entomology

Richard H. Molinar, Carlton S. Koehler,
and L. W. Barclay

LEARNING OBJECTIVES

- Understand basic insect and mite pests in the home garden in California.

- Learn about basic insect structure (anatomy), life cycles, and distribution.

- Become familiar with the major groups of insects in the home garden.

- Learn basic information about diagnosing plant problems caused by insects and mites

- Learn about methods and rules for controlling insect pests and basic concepts of integrated pest management (IPM).

This chapter is intended to be used in conjunction with *Pests of the Garden and Small Farm* (Flint 1998) and *Pests of Landscape Trees and Shrubs* (Dreistadt 1994). Additional insect pest management and diagnosis information appears in chapters 8, 10, and 22 of this book.

Entomology

Insects occupy virtually all habitats on earth except the open ocean. Insects live in or on animals, plants, soil, the dry wood of structures and furniture, streams, lakes, ocean shores, and stored grain and other foods.

Insects are the most abundant animals on this planet. About one million different kinds, or species, of insects are known to exist, and the final count may be far greater. The total number of species may never be determined for certain, because scientists who classify insects are continually combining several species into one or separating insects previously considered a single species into two or more species.

By no means should all insects be considered destructive. The vast majority are neutral or have a beneficial affect. Bees and many other insects serve as pollinators in many crops. Killing bees with the indiscriminate use of insecticides reduces honey production and also reduces fruit set in crops that are pollinated by bees. Other beneficial insects prey on or parasitize pest insects, using them as a source of food and keeping pest populations under control.

Worldwide, only about 10,000 species of insects (about 1 percent of known species) are pests. Pest insects cause serious economic damage by destroying food crops in the field and in storage. It is estimated that one-sixth of the world's food crops are consumed by insect pests. They also carry viral, bacterial, and fungal diseases, which they transmit to crop plants, livestock, and humans.

Insects and Insect Relatives

Insects belong to the group of animals known as Arthropods ("jointed legs"), which includes crabs, lobsters, spiders, and ticks. The scientists who study insects are known as entomologists. To be classified as an insect, the adult form must have all the features listed below (see fig. 7.1).

Three distinct body regions. Insects have a distinct head, thorax, and abdomen. Their exterior skeleton, known as an exoskeleton, provides support but differs from the internal skeleton of mammals. The thorax is divided into three segments. Insects breathe through pores on their abdomens known as *spiracles*. Many insecticides enter the insect pest's body through the spiracles.

Jointed legs (3 pairs). An insect's six legs are attached to the thorax (1 pair per thorax segment) and can be specialized for jumping, grasping, or walking.

Antennae (1 pair). The antennae, attached to the head, are sensory organs. The antennae can be short, long, smooth, serrated, and feathery.

Wings (0, 1, or 2 pairs). Some insects are sessile, meaning that they do not fly; others fly. The wings are attached to the thorax and vary from very ornamental and colorful to clear. The vein pattern on the wings of insects is an important identifying marker.

Unlike humans, insects are cold-blooded; the ambient temperature of the environment in which they live determines their body temperature. The majority of insects are most active during warmer months and during the warmer part of the day.

A number of other arthropods that are not insects are commonly called insects by mistake. These insect relatives include pillbugs (crustaceans), centipedes (chilopods), millipedes (diplopods), snails and slugs (molluscs), and spiders, ticks, and mites (arachnids). Arachnids are characterized by two main body

Figure 7.1

Sketch of an insect showing body parts. *Source:* After Barker et al. 1991, p. 1.

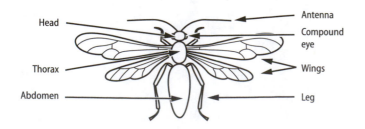

Figure 7.2

Spider mite.

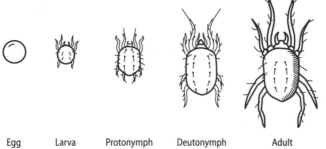

Egg   Larva   Protonymph   Deutonymph   Adult

Figure 7.3

Black widow spider.

Figure 7.4

House spider.

regions—a cephalothorax and an abdomen—and eight legs, no antennae, and no wings. Mites have bodies that appear to be all one part with little or no segmentation. The following section gives a brief overview of common insect relatives in the home and garden.

Common Insect Relatives in the Home and Garden

Arachnids: Mites, Spiders, Ticks

Arachnids have no antennae; no wings; two body regions, the cephalothorax and abdomen). Adults have four pairs of jointed legs, whereas adult insect have six legs.

Mites (fig. 7.2) are smaller than a period on this page, and a good hand lens is necessary see most of them. They are common pests of many fruit and nut trees, vegetable crops, ornamentals, and house plants. They feed on plants by inserting their piercing mouthparts into the host and sucking up the liquid cell contents. Plants exhibit yellowish stippling at the feeding site, general decline, leaf drop, and distortion of leaves, fruit, or blossoms. Two families cause the majority of mite damage in California. The tetranychid family includes webspinning spider mites, red mites, and brown mites. The webspinning spider mites are the most common mite pests and are among the most ubiquitous of all pests in the garden (Flint 1998) according to The University of California book *Pests of the Garden and Small Farm: A Grower's Guide to Using Less Pesticide*. Examples are the two-spotted spider mite, strawberry spider mite, and Pacific spider mite. Webspinning spider mites live in colonies, primarily on lower leaf surfaces. In

favorable environmental conditions (hot, dusty), it takes 1 week to complete a generation. Because a number of predatory mites and various insects are natural enemies of webspinning spider mites, application of some insecticides, which kill pest and beneficial insects, may lead to increased mite infestation. In the garden, regular, forceful spraying of plants with water, with good coverage on the undersides of leaves, will often reduce spider mite infestation to a manageable level.

The eriophyid mite family includes the rust, bud, and blister mites, which have four legs rather than the eight characteristic of other arachnids.

Spiders are larger than mites and the two body regions are more distinct. Most spiders are beneficial predators that feed on insects and other small animals by paralyzing their prey with venom. Many spiders do not form webs; instead they lie in wait for their prey. In some species, the female kills and eats the male after mating. Two species of spiders that are not beneficial predators are the black widow spider (fig. 7.3) and the desert recluse spider, which are both poisonous. The black widow spider lives in damp, dark places and spins a messy web. It is shiny black, with a reddish or orange hourglass marking on the underside of the abdomen. Desert recluse spiders are found primarily in the southeastern portion of the state. The house spider (fig. 7.4) is frequently found indoors where it makes cobwebs in corners of rooms. It is non-venomous.

Figure 7.5

Centipede.

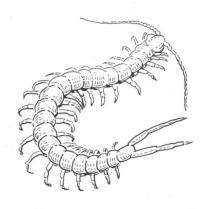

Figure 7.6

Pillbug.

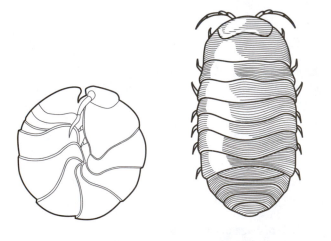

Figure 7.7

Millipede.

Chilopods: Centipedes

Centipedes (fig. 7.5) are wormlike insect predators that resemble millipedes, but their bodies are more flattened. They have one pair of legs on most body segments and longer antennae. Centipedes are common in soil, debris, under bark, and in rotting wood. In a few instances, larger ones can bite humans with their poison jaws, an injury similar to a bee sting.

Crustaceans: Sowbugs and Pillbugs (Isopods)

Sowbugs are soil-dwelling, oval-shaped crustaceans related to crayfish. They breathe through gills and have a hard, outer, multisegmented shell. Sowbugs that roll up into a ball when disturbed are called pillbugs (fig. 7.6). Sowbugs have seven pairs of legs and are active at night. They feed on decaying plant material and are therefore important in decomposing organic matter in the garden. Occasionally, they feed on seedlings, new roots, leaves, fruits (strawberries), or vegetables (squashes) lying directly on the soil. Sowbugs are blamed for causing more problems than they do because they are frequently associated with decaying plant material that was initially damaged by other pests, such as snails or slugs. Sowbugs are favored by sprinkler irrigation and organic mulch. Black plastic mulches discourage sowbugs because they get too hot. Limiting the moist, organic decaying matter in the garden will reduce the sowbug population.

Diplopods: Millipedes

Millipedes (fig. 7.7) are wormlike, have a visible head, one pair of short antennae, and an elongate, rounded body. They have two pairs of legs on most body segments. They are often found in soil and feed on fungi and decaying organic matter.

Molluscs: Snails and Slugs

The brown garden snail (*Helix aspersa*) (fig. 7.8) and the gray garden slug (*Agriolimax reticulatus*) (fig. 7.9) are among the most bothersome pests in California gardens. Slugs lack the snail's external spiral shell. Both pests are most active at night and on foggy or cloudy days. They move by sliding along mucus or slime trails secreted by a single foot. Both feed on decaying organic matter, seedlings, and low-growing leafy vegetables

Figure 7.8

Brown garden snail.

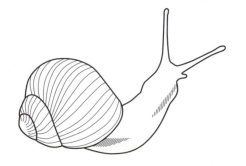

Figure 7.9

Gray garden slug.

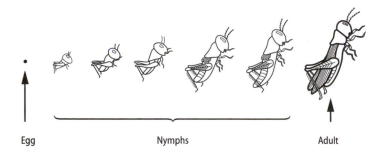

Figure 7.10

Gradual metamorphosis. Insects in this group change gradually. There are three stages of growth, each looking more like an adult. *Source:* After Barker et al. 1991, p. 12.

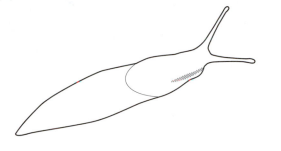

Egg   Nymphs   Adult

Figure 7.11

Complete metamorphosis. All insects in this group go through four stages of growth. None of the young looks like the adult. There is a great change in shape when the adult emerges from the pupal stage. *Source:* After Barker et al. 1991, p. 12.

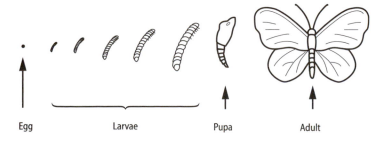

Egg   Larvae   Pupa   Adult

and ripening fruits, such as lettuce, strawberries, and tomatoes. Three tools for managing snail and slug pests are eliminating their daytime hiding places, handpicking them frequently, and trapping them under boards and flower pots positioned throughout the garden. Crushing them or using sprays of a 1:1 solution of household ammonia and water on the collected snails and slugs will kill them.

Insect Growth and Development

Every insect begins life as an egg; however, the eggs of some destructive insects, such as many aphid species, hatch within the body of the female parent, and immatures are born as living, young insects. Insect eggs are often tiny and difficult to spot, but they are often a good indicator of future outbreaks. Examples of some of the more distinctive egg shapes are shown in Flint (1998).

Insects grow by shedding their outer skin (exoskeleton), which is quite rigid. The skin-shedding process, called *molting*, results in an increase in size and slight to significant modifications in appearance. Immature insects may molt as many as six times. The change in form and appearance from juvenile to adult insect is known as *metamorphosis*.

In some insect species, metamorphosis is gradual and relatively indistinct (fig. 7.10). For example, young grasshoppers, crickets, termites, and true bugs look like small versions of their adult counterparts. The immature stages of these insects are known as *nymphs*. Except for size and the lack of fully formed wings, the nymphs and adults look very much alike.

In other insect species, metamorphosis is marked by four distinct stages, known as *complete metamorphosis* (fig. 7.11): egg, larva (a feeding, destructive stage), pupa (an inactive stage), and adult (reproductive stage). Bees, ants, wasps, flies, beetles, butterflies, moths, and mosquitoes exhibit complete metamorphosis.

The eggs of insects that exhibit complete metamorphosis hatch into larvae that are quite different in appearance from the adult forms. The larval stages of insects that undergo complete metamorphosis typically have different feeding habits from the adult stages. For example, the larvae of butterflies, moths, and flies may cause damage to crop plants, but the adults consume only nectar or do not feed at all. On the other hand, some beetle species, such as cucumber beetles or flea beetles, cause damage as adults but do little harm to crop plants during their larval stages.

The pupal stage follows the larval stage in insects with complete metamorphosis. Molting occurs as insects grow during the larval nymphal stage. Depending on the insect species, pupae may be found inside cocoons, in earthen cells in the ground, or exposed in or on the ground, vegetation, or other places. The adult stage follows the pupal stage. Once the adult form appears, no further molting or increase in size occurs. If an insect has functional wings, it clearly has reached the adult stage.

Mating in adult insects is followed by egg laying by the female and the death of the adults. The females of some insects, such as many aphids and scales, can reproduce in the absence of males, a process known as *parthenogenesis*. The males of certain insect species are, in fact, unknown or extremely rare.

The life cycle of development from the egg to the production of an egg by the subsequent adult stage is called a *generation*. Many insect species have only one generation each year, while others have several; the 17-year cicada, however, requires many years to complete a single generation. During a calendar year, a generation need not begin with the egg stage. Many species spend the winter (overwinter) as larvae or pupae; the subsequent adults mate and produce eggs in the spring or summer. In any given area, an insect species normally overwinters in the same stage each year.

Insect Feeding

Insect pests have two basic feeding patterns, chewing and sucking, and each is associated with specialized mouthparts. The larvae of many pest insects have chewing mouthparts. Insect pests that feed by chewing are equipped with strong jaws for that purpose, and their mandibles resemble teeth used for chewing. These larvae and adult insects literally eat their way through the plant, leaving a trail of distinct holes and tunnels in leaves, twigs, fruits, and stems. Chewing damage may be done inside stems and branches (borers), inside leaves (leafminers), or openly on leaves (defoliators and skeletonizers) or other plant parts.

Pests that do not have chewing mouthparts have sucking mouthparts. Leafhoppers, aphids, true bugs, scale insects, thrips, and whiteflies, among others, pierce plants with a probelike device, known as a *stylet*, through which plant sap is sucked up. The plant's cells are deprived of the products of photosynthesis. Sucking insects cause injury symptoms that include curling, stunting, brown mottling, and deformed plant parts (because the parts are starved for photosynthates), and they can cause overgrowths such as galls. Some piercing insects inject toxic saliva into the plant as they feed, giving rise to discoloration of the foliage or dieback of woody plant parts. Insects such as aphids and leafhoppers are vectors of microbial plant pathogens, particularly viruses. If these pest insects have previously fed on diseased plant tissue, they transmit the disease to their next host plant when their saliva mixes with plant sap.

Pests with sucking mouthparts seldom cause loss of plant tissue surface. In some cases, however, the piercing of leaves or flowers may result in holes or irregularities in the margins of plant tissue because of abnormal growth of the plant following insect attack. In contrast, pests with chewing mouthparts cause visible loss of plant tissue. Distinguishing the damage as being caused by a chewing or a sucking insect is a first step in identifying a pest.

Larvae and adults of the same species often have different types of mouthparts and feed on different foods. Caterpillars (larvae with chewing mouthparts) usually feed on leaves or other vegetation, resulting in a noticeable loss of plant tissue. By contrast, adult moths or butterflies feed on fluids such as nectar because they have a sucking tube that forms siphoning mouthparts.

Insect Classification and Identification

All insects known to science are grouped into about 30 categories called *orders*. Each order contains dozens, hundreds, or even thousands of species. The similarities among particular species allows scientists to group them. Not all insect orders contain species associated with garden plants. Listed below are examples of some insect orders.

- Coleoptera: beetles, weevils
- Dermaptera: earwigs
- Diptera: flies, mosquitoes, gnats, midges
- Hemiptera: true bugs
- Homoptera: leafhoppers, aphids, scales, whiteflies
- Hymenoptera: bees, wasps, ants, etc.
- Isoptera: termites
- Lepidoptera: butterflies, moths
- Neuroptera: lacewings, antlions, etc.
- Odonata: damselflies, dragonflies
- Orthoptera: grasshoppers, crickets, cockroaches
- Psocoptera: booklice, barklice
- Siphonaptera: fleas
- Thysanura: silverfish, firebrats
- Thysanoptera: thrips

Entomologists use anatomical features (body parts) examined under a microscope to identify, distinguish, and classify insects. Written keys are available to determine the identity of a particular insect. The most important plant-feeding pest insects in the garden are found in the orders Coleoptera, Hemiptera, Homoptera, and Lepidoptera.

The association of insects with plants does not automatically mean that the insects are destructive. Insects in the orders listed below are often found on plants and many are *beneficials*, functioning as parasites or predators of plant-feeding pest insects, pollinators, or scavengers of dead vegetation or the products left behind by other insects on plants.

- Coleoptera: beetles, weevils
- Diptera: flies, mosquitoes, gnats, midges
- Hymenoptera: bees, wasps, ants, etc.
- Neuroptera: lacewings, antlions, etc.
- Psocoptera: booklice, barklice

Insect orders are subdivided into smaller groups known as families, genera, and species. Two examples are listed below.

Codling moth (common name)
Order: Lepidoptera
Family: Olethreutidae
Genus: *Cydia*
Species: *pomonella*

Oystershell scale (common name)
Order: Homoptera
Family: Diaspididae
Genus: *Lepidosaphes*
Species: *ulmi*

The majority of pest insect species, and many others that are not pests, have common names. As noted above, the common name of *Laspeyresia pomonella* is codling moth, and that of *Lepidosaphes ulmi* is oystershell scale. Common names are also often given at higher levels of classification, such as the family and order. The order Lepidoptera refers to the butterflies and moths, and the order Homoptera, family Diaspididae, refers to armored scales.

Identifying a given insect to the species level is often difficult, and in some cases, may not be necessary for the home gardener as long as the gardener is careful to distinguish pest insects from nonpests. For example, to be able to offer good advice for controlling most aphids does not require that the exact aphid species in question be determined. The same could be said about most soft scales, mealybugs, spider mites, and many other common garden pests as long as the plant host has been identified.

When attempting to identify a plant-feeding "insect," it is of great importance to know the identity of the plant on which the insect was found. Although some insect pests are general feeders, that is, they feed only on a variety of different plants, many are quite host-specific. The juniper twig girdler, for example, attacks only juniper. It is never found on pine, cypress, oak, camellia, or any other plant. The tomato hornworm occurs only on tomatoes, and the California oakworm, for all practical purposes, only on oak. Examples of specific and general pests that may occur on different garden plants are described in detail and shown in color photographs at various stages of development in Flint (1998) and Dresitadt (1994). Master Gardeners should refer to these two resources to narrow the possibilities in the insect identification process.

Knowing the identity of the host plant and pest is of critical importance when offering advice on chemical pest control, especially when the plant is a vegetable, fruit, or other food-bearing plant. The reason for this is discussed later in this chapter under "Insect Control by Chemicals."

Common Insects in the Home and Garden

Coleoptera: Beetles and Weevils

- Metamorphosis: Complete

- Mouthparts: Chewing

- Attributes: Larvae (grubs, wireworms, borers) have head capsules. Adults have two pairs of wings. Horny, leathery front wings meet in a straight line down back and cover membranous hind wings underneath, used for flying. Usually noticeable antennae. Weevils are beetles with snouts.

Beetles are very common (about 40% of all insect species), but only a few are garden pests. Many species, such as lady beetles (ladybugs) (fig. 7.12), are beneficial predators of pests, such as aphids and mites. Flea beetles, wireworms (click beetle larvae), cucumber beetles (fig. 7.12), vegetable weevils, and green fruit beetles are common pests in California home vegetable gardens. Boring beetles attack trunks and branches of fruit and nut trees. Granary weevils (fig. 7.12) attack stored products. Adult pest beetles may feed on the same crops as their larvae, unlike other pest groups, such as caterpillars (larvae of butterflies and moths) and maggots (larvae of flies), whose adults do little damage.

Dermaptera: Earwigs

- Metamorphosis: Gradual

- Mouthparts: Chewing

- Attributes: Elongate, flattened insects with strong, movable forceps on rear end. Adults and nymphs resemble each other, but wings are small or absent on nymphs. Two pairs of modified wings—front pair thickened, leathery, short, meet in a straight line down the back, and cover the membranous hind wings. Antennae are threadlike, about half of the body length.

Earwigs (fig. 7.13) can be pests or beneficials in the home garden. They are effective predators of aphids in apple orchards, but they are pests in the vegetable garden. Earwigs feed on plant shoots, seedlings, and a variety of dead and living organisms. Earwigs can be trapped in rolled up newspaper or tuna cans filled with vegetable oil, fish oil, or bacon fat. They are nocturnal and hide during the day in leaf litter and mulch or under bark.

Diptera: Flies, Mosquitoes, Gnats, Midges

- Metamorphosis: Complete

- Mouthparts: Larvae, chewing or mouth hooks; adults, piercing or sponging

- Attributes: Larvae of flies (maggots) are legless, white, worm-like, lack head capsule. Adults are soft-bodied, have compound eyes, one pair of membranous wings, and are hairy. Mosquito larvae have head capsules.

Adult houseflies (fig. 7.14) can infest homes, poultry houses, or livestock barns. Maggots (larvae) of houseflies are found in manure and decaying matter. Important garden and agricultural pests include the cabbage maggot, which infests roots; seedcorn maggot, which damages seeds and germinating seedlings of many vegetables; and onion maggot, which attacks bulbs of onions, leeks, and

Figure 7.12

Lady beetle (left), Spotted cucumber beetle (center), and granary weevil (right).

Figure 7.13

Earwig.

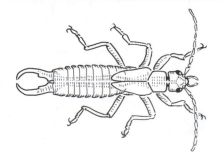

Figure 7.14

Housefly (left) and mosquito (right).

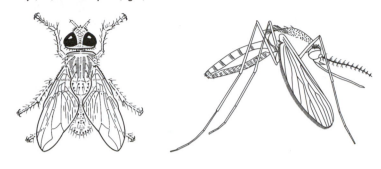

Figure 7.15

Stink bug (left) and harlequin bug (right).

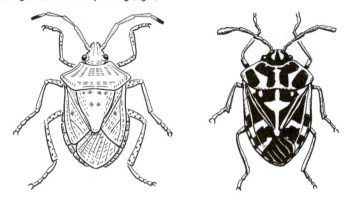

garlic. It is almost impossible to distinguish these three species of maggots in the field. Adults resemble the common, gray housefly. Diptera are active year-round and produce several generations per year. Other important fly pests are the carrot rust fly, walnut husk fly, apple maggot, fruit flies, and leafminers. The Mediterranean fruit fly (*Ceratitis capitata*) is a serious pest of citrus. Syrphid fly larvae are important predators of aphids.

Adult mosquitoes (fig. 7.14) are slender, frail flies. Mosquito larvae typically live in water. The adult female mosquito uses her mouthparts to pierce the skin of humans and livestock and then sucks their blood, transmitting diseases, such as malaria, to humans in the process.

Hemiptera: True Bugs

- Metamorphosis: Gradual

- Mouthparts: Piercing-sucking

- Attributes: Nymphs are smaller versions of adults. They look alike, except nymphs

lack wings until about half-grown. Adults have two pairs of wings. When wings are folded, their tips overlap to form a well-defined X on the back of the bug body. Some also have an inverted triangle behind their heads. The inverted triangle and X-formation facilitate recognition. Eggs are cylindrical, barrel, or keg-shaped. One to several generations occur per year.

Adults and nymphs can cause damage and many are important plant-feeding pests of many fruits and vegetables. Examples are stink bugs (fig. 7.15), lygus bugs, squash bugs, and harlequin bugs (fig. 7.15). Stink bugs, such as the harlequin bug, are shield-shaped with a large inverted triangle on their backs. Nymphs of lygus bugs can be confused with aphids, but they move faster than aphids and have red-tipped antennae. Squash bugs feed on vines and fruit of cucurbit crops. Control them by handpicking adults and brown egg masses from leaves. True bug pests suck out contents of plant cells, damaging and distorting their hosts. Species that inject toxins while feeding cause yellow spots on leaves and ripening fruit. Symptoms may not appear until long after the bugs have left, making diagnosis difficult.

Some true bugs are predators of pests and function as important beneficials in the garden: assassin bugs, damsel bugs, minute pirate bugs, and certain stink bugs.

Homoptera: Aphids, Scales, Leafhoppers, Cicadas, Whiteflies, Mealybugs

- Metamorphosis: Gradual

- Mouthparts: Sucking

- Attributes: Small, soft-bodied insects, except for cicadas. Winged and unwinged forms. Many are carriers of plant pathogens. Many aphid species have two cornicles (tubelike projections) protruding from the rear end.

Aphids (fig. 7.16) come in many sizes, shapes, and colors (green, black, yellow, brown, red) and attack numerous vegetables, legumes, stone-fruit crops, apples, and ornamentals. Dozens of species are in California. Curled, distorted leaves, and sticky honeydew exudates on leaves are strong signs of aphid infestation. Aphids have numerous generations per year in California climate. Some species

Figure 7.16

Aphid (left) and San Jose scale (right).

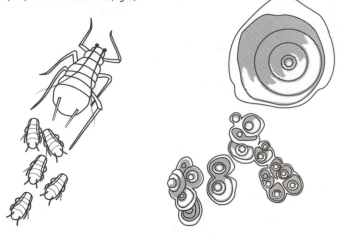

Figure 7.17

Honey bee (left) and common ant (right).

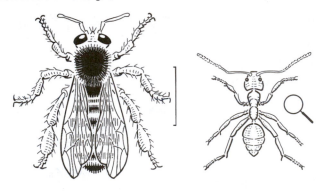

Scale insects (fig. 7.16) are serious pests of fruit and nut trees and grapevines. Scales are usually quite small, round or football-shaped, and armored (California red scale, walnut scale) or soft-bodied (cottony cushion scale). Like aphids, soft scales excrete honeydew, which attracts ants and causes sooty mold fungus. Adult female scales and many immature forms are sessile. Some scales are controlled with natural enemies and oil sprays.

Mealybugs are considered a type of scale. They are oval, segmented, and covered with wax. They are common pests of houseplants and greenhouse plants.

Whiteflies are tiny sapsuckers found in vegetables, ornamentals, and citrus trees. When these pests are disturbed on their hosts, clouds of winged adult whiteflies fly into the air. They excrete honeydew like aphids. Leaves of infested plants may turn yellow, get sticky, and have black sooty mold. In the Imperial Valley, the silverleaf whitefly transmits several viruses that devastate vegetable crops. Whiteflies have complete metamorphosis. They are attacked by a number of natural enemy predators and parasites. Insecticidal soap applied to undersides of leaves can help control whiteflies.

Hymenoptera: Bees, Wasps, Ants, Sawflies

- Metamorphosis: Complete

- Mouthparts: Chewing

- Attributes: Legless larvae (wasps, bees, ants) are legless or have legs on thorax and abdomen. Stinger is used for offense and defense. Only females can sting. Adults have two pairs of membranous wings and soft or slightly hardened bodies. Ants have narrow waists.

The order Hymenoptera is large. Many of its members are important beneficials—pollinators, such as honey bees (fig. 7.17), leafcutter bees, alkali bees; parasites, such as tiny, stingerless wasps that are natural enemies or biological control agents of many pest insects; and predators, such as yellowjacket wasps—whose sting is painful and dangerous to susceptible people. As a group, ants (fig. 7.17) are important natural enemies of many insect pests, but some species, such as the Argentine ant, can be a problem because they feed on honeydew excreted by some pest insects (aphids, soft scales, mealybugs, white-

mate and reproduce sexually, producing eggs in fall or winter, but most pest aphids in California reproduce asexually, with adult females giving birth to live offspring without mating or laying eggs. Some aphids transmit viral diseases as they feed on young leaves and stems. Low to moderate populations of aphids can be tolerated in most home gardens. Aphids can be controlled by hosing them off with jets of water, by soap solution sprays, and by naturally occurring predators (lady beetles, lacewing larvae) and parasitic wasps.

Leafhoppers feed on undersides of leaves and transmit viruses and other diseases. Beans, cucurbits, potatoes, eggplants, grapes, and apples are hosts. Low to moderate populations of leafhoppers can be tolerated in most home gardens.

flies) and thus protect these pests from their natural enemies. Sawfly larvae can be important pests of garden plants, shrubs, and trees.

Isoptera: Termites

- Metamorphosis: Gradual

- Mouthparts: Chewing

- Attributes: Small, soft-bodied insects that resemble ants. Antennae are straighter and waists are thicker than those of ants. Various stages are winged or wingless.

Termite (fig. 7.18) colonies occur in the ground or in wood. Two major groups in California are the drywood and subterranean termites. Both feed on wood and wood products. Protozoa in their guts eat the cellulose in the wood. Subterranean termites build their nests in soil and normally require continuous contact with soil to get moisture for survival. When wood is in contact with soil, termites can burrow from the soil directly into the wood. If a barrier, such as a concrete slab, exists between the soil and wood, subterranean termites build earthen tubes to bridge the barrier. Subterranean termite infestations can destroy the structural integrity of a building.

Many species of drywood termites damage buildings, furniture, utility poles, fences, and piled lumber. Unlike subterranean termites, they do not require contact with soil. As their name implies, they attack dry wood and carry out their work completely inside the wood. Attics are common areas of drywood termite infestation. Often, the only evidence of their presence is a few small holes through which they push frass (fecal material and undecomposed wood formed into tiny, football-shaped pellets) out of the galleries.

Termites are organized into a caste system (reproductive caste, supplementary reproduc-

tives [swarmers], soldiers, and workers). Workers are white and usually sterile; they collect food and feed the queen, soldiers, and young. Soldiers are usually sterile with large heads and mandibles; they fend off intruders. Reproductives have four nearly identical wings longer than their bodies.

Lepidoptera: Moths, Butterflies

- Metamorphosis: Complete

- Mouthparts: Larvae, chewing; adults, sucking

- Attributes: Larvae are wormlike, voracious feeders with prolegs on abdomen and thorax. Adults are soft-bodied with two pairs of membranous wings covered with small scales. Adult mouthparts are coiled sucking tubes.

Caterpillar larvae—cutworms, loopers, leafminers, skeletonizers, webworms, borers—cause cosmetic and economic damage to fruits and leaves of numerous crops. Leaf-eating caterpillars (tomato hornworm, armyworms, loopers) chew irregular holes. Many small caterpillars roll leaves to form shelters. Codling moth, corn earworm (tomato fruitworm), and other caterpillars that feed directly on fruit or nuts are more damaging, in general, than leaf-feeders. They blemish fruit surfaces, penetrate fruit, and bore into the core, leaving holes and open wounds for rot-producing bacteria and fungi. Codling moth larvae are the most serious caterpillar pest of apples, pears, and walnuts in California. They also attack stone-fruit crops. For early detection in the vegetable garden, get on your hands and knees, use a hand lens, turn over leaves and inspect fruit. For fruit trees, get on a ladder and inspect into the tree canopy.

Many adult Lepidoptera (fig. 7.19) feed on nectar; unlike larvae, adults are not pests. Some adult butterflies and moths are beneficials (pollinators) essential for healthy fruit set.

Neuroptera: Lacewings, Antlions

- Metamorphosis: Complete

- Mouthparts: Chewing

- Attributes: Adults have two pairs of membranous wings, about the same size, with numerous cross-veins and long antennae. Wings held rooflike over body at rest.

Figure 7.18

Termite.

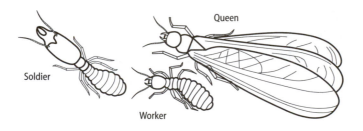

Soldier

Queen

Worker

Figure 7.19

Swallowtail (left), Polyphemus (right).

Figure 7.20

Lacewing.

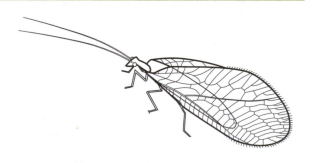

Many species of Neuroptera are predaceous. Lacewing larvae are important predators of aphids and mites, sometimes called aphidlions because of their feeding habit. Eggs of the green lacewing are easy to recognize because they are laid at the end of tall, thread like stalks, usually attached to foliage. Adult lacewings (fig. 7.20) are fragile in appearance with greenish, transparent wings that have a fine network of veins. Wings are longer than bodies. Antlions feed on ants and other insects. Antlion adults resemble damselflies but are softer-bodied and have conspicuous, knobbed antennae.

Odonata: Damselflies, Dragonflies

- Metamorphosis: Gradual

- Mouthparts: Chewing

- Attributes: Very short, bristle like antennae. Large eyes. Two pairs of elongate, membranous, many-veined wings, similar in size, shape. Long, slender abdomen. Many bright colors.

Nymphs of damselflies and dragonflies are aquatic. Adults can fly. All life stages are predaceous, feeding on mosquitoes, midges, and other small insects, helping to keep their populations under control. At rest, damselflies fold their wings over their backs, whereas dragonflies (fig. 7.21) extend their wings horizontally.

Figure 7.21

Dragonfly.

Figure 7.22

Grasshopper (left), cockroach (right).

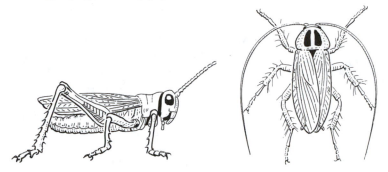

Figure 7.23

Flea.

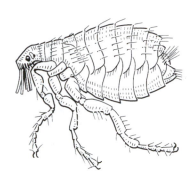

Orthoptera: Grasshoppers, Locusts, Crickets, Mantids, Cockroaches

- Metamorphosis: Gradual

- Mouthparts: Chewing

- Attributes: Moderate to large, hard-bodied adults with two pairs of wings. Front wings are hard, leathery, rooflike over hind wings. Both adults and nymphs cause damage. Nymphs resemble adults, except for being wingless. Insects in this order "sing" by rubbing body parts against one another. Some have rear legs modified for jumping.

Crickets and grasshoppers (fig. 7.22) only occasionally require control in home gardens. Populations of grasshoppers can build up in foothills and rangelands after a wet spring. In early summer, as the grasshoppers migrate to fields and gardens, they defoliate everything in sight. Cockroaches (fig. 7.22) can be serious household pests.

Siphonaptera: Fleas

- Metamorphosis: Complete

- Mouthparts: Sucking

- Attributes: Small (<5 mm), wingless insects that often live as ectoparasites on birds and mammals. Short antennae. Body laterally flattened. Often jumping. Larvae are tiny, whitish, legless, and resemble maggots.

Adult fleas (fig. 7.23) suck blood and feed on the blood of the host. Many fleas are not host-specific. Fleas are important vectors of disease (bubonic plague, endemic typhus).

Figure 7.24

Western flower thrips.

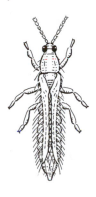

Thysanoptera: Thrips

- Metamorphosis: Gradual

- Mouthparts: Sucking

- Attributes: Adults are minute (<$\frac{1}{20}$ inch [1.2 mm]), slender, soft-bodied. Two pairs of long, narrow, membranous wings fringed with long hairs. Short antennae. Color ranges from yellow to black.

Some species of thrips (fig. 7.24) are beneficial, feeding on mites and other insects, but others feed on plants and scar leaf and fruit surfaces with their rasping-sucking mouthparts. The cosmetic damage they cause to leaves is unattractive, but yields are not reduced.

Insecticide treatments are not usually recommended in home gardens. Thrips attack citrus, raspberries, grapes, and numerous vegetables and may transmit diseases.

Thysanura: Silverfish, Firebrats

- Metamorphosis: Gradual

- Mouthparts: Chewing

- Attributes: Adults have no wings. Bristles on tip of abdomen. Adults about ½ inch (1.2 cm) long. Three tail-like bristly projections or appendages attached at their posterior.

Silverfish and firebrats (fig. 7.25) are household pests that feed on starchy substances, such as glue, book bindings, starched clothing, paste in wallpaper, curtains, linens, silks, paper, and foods that contain starch.

Insect Movement and Spread

The adults of many insects have wings, and flight is a principal means of locomotion and spread into areas previously uninfested. Because moths are frequently night fliers, many species are not often seen as adults. Flying insects locate their host plants by specific odors emanating from these host plants, by chemical messages released by the first few insects reaching the host, or by other means, some of which are poorly understood. They then lay eggs on the plant, giving rise to a larval infestation.

Most adult insects and most larvae stages have legs and can walk from plant to plant or from overwintering and hiding sites to plants. Like some flying insects, certain walking insect pests are most active at night, and it may be necessary to inspect plants by flashlight to determine the cause of disappearing foliage.

Wind or ordinary air currents can transport pests from place to place. For example, newborn scales, called crawlers, are tiny, flattened insects easily blown from one plant to another. Crawlers then settle down on the plant, insert their long, slender mouthparts into the host tissue, and usually remain there for the rest of their lives. Scales in the crawler stage may also be transported on the feet of birds or visiting insects. Spider mites are carried long distances by air currents, which may explain infestations on house plants believed to be pest-free at purchase. Spider mites enter homes through open doors and windows.

Some caterpillars produce silken strands by which they "string down" from vegetation, distributing their numbers on a tree or shrub. If the larvae are general feeders, they may string down to understory vegetation, causing damage to plants other than those on which the eggs were laid.

Purchase of already-infested plants at the nursery or garden center is a very important means of insect movement and spread. It is difficult to inspect plants sufficiently to detect the eggs or tiny larvae of pests. Consider isolating newly purchased house plants and not placing them in a room or home greenhouse with existing plants until it can be determined that they are free from pests.

Insect Outbreaks

Pest insects and their relatives do not occur in the same numbers each year. The reasons why populations may be high one year and low the next are not completely understood. Temperature, rainfall, availability of suitable food, and the presence or relative absence of parasites, predators, and disease-causing agents all have a bearing on the fluctuations of populations. Because insect pests are numerous one year does not mean that their populations will be as great a problem the next year.

Figure 7.25

Silverfish (right) and firebrat (left).

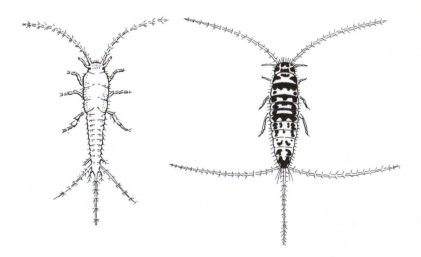

Insect Distribution

Some pest insects are widely distributed throughout the world, causing damage to plants in numerous countries on several continents. Many other insects are more regional in their occurrence. Although jet travel has made it much easier for pests to be introduced into new areas, most insect pests have rather precise climatic and other environmental requirements that limit where they occur, survive, thrive, and spread.

Within California, the climatic differences among coastal, interior valley, and mountainous areas greatly influence the ability of many pests to survive in a given region. For example, the cypress tip miner (*Argyresthia cupressella*) is limited as a pest to regions strongly influenced by coastal fog. It is never found in the Central Valley, the Sierras, or mountainous regions of northern California, even though its host plants grow there. The green fruit beetle (*Cotinis mutabilis*) is a pest in Southern California and the San Joaquin Valley but has caused limited damage to fruit in the San Jose area.

In other cases, the distribution of a pest is limited by the availability of its host plants. Two species of iceplant scales, *Pulvinaria mesembryanthemi* and *Pulvinaria delottoi*, occur widely in central California and are controlled by biological control methods. Yet, because iceplant scales will not tolerate winter temperatures much below freezing, controlling these scale pests is not a necessity in some colder climates.

Diagnosing Plant Problems Caused by Insects and Mites

The diagnosis of plant problems is aided by a knowledge of the distribution of pests. Many good reference publications on pests offer information about where various pests occur in the state (see also chapter 22, "Diagnosing Plant Problems," for further diagnosis concepts and information). Narrowing the possibilities of the cause of plant problems is a cornerstone of problem diagnosis.

Determining the basic causes of poor plant performance is difficult because Master Gardeners and other diagnosticians must often analyze with incomplete evidence. The diagnostic process entails the gathering of bits of evidence from the specimen submitted and from the person submitting the specimen, organizing the evidence, then drawing on past experience, published references on the subject, and other resources to reach a conclusion. Unfortunately, it is often not possible to visit the site where the specimen was taken. In most cases, the site would yield additional information that could facilitate diagnosis. Poor plant performance is attributable to a wide variety of causes, some of which act alone and others of which act collectively. A partial list of causes of poor plant performance includes:

- insects and their relatives

- plant disease

- improper cultural practices or conditions, including:
    water excess or deficiency
    poor drainage
    deficient or excess light
    physical or chemical injury
    poor adaptation to growing site
    temperature too high or low
    excess or deficient fertilizer nutrients

Several factors may work collectively to cause poor plant performance: for example, drought-stressed pine trees (an improper cultural condition) are often selected for attack by bark beetles. Because this chapter deals with insects and other arthropod pests, several important causes of poor plant performance are not addressed here. Master Gardeners, however, must keep all options in mind to conclude a diagnosis successfully.

A single pest may cause more than one symptom. Aphids, for example, often cause twisted or cupped leaves and yellowed foliage, and they also produce honeydew, which may lead to sooty mold that blackens plant parts, depending on the species of aphid and host. Greenhouse thrips cause bleaching of foliage and always leave behind spots of varnishlike excrement. Approaching diagnosis of insect-related plant problems first through signs and symptoms is preferable to searching the sample for the pest that may or may not be present. Knowing the kinds of symptoms that various pests produce narrows the possibilities of causal agent. Refer to the diagnostic tables in *Pests of the Garden and Small Farm* (Flint 1998) and *Pests of Landscape Trees and Shrubs* (Dreistadt 1994) for comprehensive information. Both publications are excellent resources that Master Gardeners should consult routinely for diagnosing and managing plant pest problems. See also the following section for brief comments on the subject, and see chapter 22, "Diagnosing Plant Problems," for a broader perspective on diagnosis.

Tips for Master Gardeners Diagnosing Insect Problems

- Most of the problems brought to your attention will be attributable to factors other than insects or mites.

- The cause of poor plant performance may not be evident on the plant sample given to you for diagnosis. For example, wilted leaves may be caused by a pest attacking roots. The presence of insects or mites does not always mean that they are the real cause of the problem.

- If the entire plant is dead, the chances are great that insects or mites were not the cause of death. Insects and mites seldom kill their host plants, but there are a few exceptions.

- Most insects and mites show specificity in their choice of host plants. Some are general feeders, but the majority are not. Knowing the name of the affected plant is therefore extremely helpful and frequently essential in determining the identity of the pest, because much of the reference literature is organized by the host plant that is being attacked.

- By the time many people notice a pest problem and seek advice, it is often too late in that particular growing season to take corrective action. In some cases, a pest insect may be gone, and only the damage remains.

- People tend to magnify the actual size of an insect when they are describing it. In general, do not make recommendations based on the client's verbal description. It is important to see the damage and the insect itself to avoid incorrect identification. Use a hand lens, when needed. Incorrect identification leads to ineffective control measures,

unnecessary expense, and potential damage to beneficial insects.

- Do not be afraid to say that you do not know the answer. When in doubt, do not make a diagnosis.

- Master Gardeners represent the University of California. Make a diagnosis or give advice based on information that has been verified by UC experts. Consult UC resources listed at the end of this chapter.

- Insects and mites must feed to survive and reproduce. Evidence of their feeding will nearly always remain on the plant even after the insect or mite is gone.

Principles of Integrated Pest Management

The University of California encourages gardeners to manage insects and other pests using an integrated pest management (IPM) strategy (see chapter 10, "Controlling Garden Pests Safely"). A central concept in IPM is that of integrating several control methods, such as resistant varieties, cultural practices, biological controls, and the least-toxic pesticides, for long-term management of pests. An IPM approach encourages methods that provide long-term prevention or suppression of pest problems with minimum impact on human health, the environment, and nontarget organisms.

The principal components of an IPM program are

- pest identification (pathogen, insect, weed)

- methods for detecting, monitoring, and predicting pest outbreaks

- knowledge of the biology of the pest and its ecological interactions with hosts, natural enemies, and competitors

- ecologically sound methods of preventing or controlling pests

When possible and practical, take action to prevent insect problems before they occur by choosing resistant varieties, providing optimal conditions for plant growth, and taking preventive action against insects known to be a problem in the area. Purchase insect-free plant material from reputable suppliers. Once the home garden and landscape are planted, inspect shrubs and landscape trees occasionally and vegetables and fruit trees at least once a week (twice a week at the peak of the growing season or more often if it appears that a problem may be brewing) for possible insect pests or signs an infestation.

When you do find insects, try to identify them, or at least rule out the possibility that they are pests, using the information and principles learned in this chapter. When checking trees, check a few leaves on each side of the tree as well as the trunk. Examine fruit on plants and any that have fallen to the ground. If plants appear wilted, observe the roots to check for signs of pathogens or root-infesting insects. If an insect or pathogen does not seem to be associated with the symptoms, try to determine whether one of the abiotic non-infectious disease factors highlighted in chapter 6 may be the cause. As part of this process, evaluate fertilization and irrigation regimes, soil quality, drainage, and the prevailing weather. Keep notes of your observations, the date, time of day, stage of crop development, any intervention that you took, and the results.

Pest control strategies will most likely fail when the pest is not identified properly, since the control action will probably not be effective against the offending organism that was misidentified at the outset. Some problems may require professional diagnosis. The county agricultural commissioner's office and the UC Cooperative Extension farm advisor for the county may be able to help identify a pest problem or direct you to professional diagnostic services. See chapter 22 for more information on diagnosing plant problems.

A fundamental concept of IPM is that a certain amount of insect damage can be tolerated. Broad-spectrum pesticides are used only as a last resort when careful monitoring and preestablished guidelines indicate that they are needed. IPM programs can be carried out in most gardens with almost no use of pesticides that are more toxic than soaps, horticultural oils, or microbials. Backyard gardeners must be willing to sacrifice a few vegetable plants, for example, and tolerate a little cosmetic damage so that the use of pesticides can be minimized. Backyard produce does not need to meet industry or grocers' standards.

IPM is a knowledge-based decision making system, and an essential element of it is a well-trained and informed decision maker. Refer to *Pests of the Garden and Small Farm* (Flint 1998), *Pests of Landscape Trees and Shrubs* (Dreistadt 1994), and the *UC IPM Pest Note Series* for general overviews of designing pest management programs and IPM programs for specific pest problems.

Major Methods of Controlling Insect Pests

Five major methods are used to control insect pests. This section briefly presents these main control strategies. For more detailed information, see Flint (1998) and chapter 10, "Controlling Garden Pests Safely."

Legislative Control. Federal, state, and county quarantines are sometimes established in an attempt to prevent the movement of certain goods and commodities that are likely to harbor pests not known to occur at their destination. Quarantines have been established in California to prevent the entry or further spread of pests such as Japanese beetle, Mediterranean fruit fly, and Dutch elm disease. Maintenance of inspection stations at the borders of California is another form of legislative control. The Master Gardener is not directly involved in this type of control but can cooperate in these efforts by submitting specimens of suspect insects to the local county agricultural commissioner for confirmation of identification.

Physical or Mechanical Control. Examples of physical methods to control insect pests include placing cardboard or tar paper collars around young tomato, cabbage, or other transplants to exclude cutworms; handpicking tomato hornworm larvae from plants; and screening windows to prevent the entry of flies and mosquitoes. Physical control methods may be preventive or curative.

Cultural Control. Examples of cultural pest insect control include planting a pest-resistant variety or species of vegetable, fruit, or ornamental; rotating from year to year the location of tomatoes, eggplant, and other vegetables susceptible to Verticillium wilt; and maintaining a cover crop of turf in the home orchard to discourage a spider mite buildup occasioned by dust.

Biological Control. Biological control entails the use, preservation, conservation, and augmentation of parasites, predators, and disease-causing microorganisms (pathogens) to bring about the control of insect pests. Some biological control agents can be purchased for release and use in the garden. The pest insect pathogen *Bacillus thuringiensis* (Bt), a bacterium sold commercially as Dipel, Thuricide, or under many other brand names, is quite specific in its action against certain caterpillar pests and causes minimal harm to other forms of insect life in other orders. Avoiding the use of certain insecticides, or avoiding the use of them at times or in ways that interfere the least with biological control agents already present, represent biological control practices known as *preservation* or *conservation*. (For more information about Bt, see chapter 10.)

UC entomologists travel worldwide in search of biological controls (natural enemies) for some of the more aggressive pest insects that cause economic damage to California agriculture. In recent years, UC entomologists have imported tiny, stingerless wasps that parasitize certain aphids. The adult wasps deposit their eggs inside the pest aphids. After the wasp eggs hatch, the wasp larvae feed on the aphids until the aphids die and look like mummies. The wasp larvae then pupate, cut exit holes, and emerge from the dead aphid as adult wasps.

Although the control of pests by predators and parasites can be very effective, results can vary depending on factors such as weather, pest populations, and the predator or parasite species selected. Lady beetles will sometimes disperse and fly to other sites, invariably helping with pest predation but not at the intended site. Research is ongoing at UC Davis to address this problem.

Chemical Control. Chemicals for insect and mite pest control include insecticidal soaps, horticultural oils, various inorganic materials, botanical compounds, microbial insecticides, and synthetic organic materials. Technically, all of these chemicals are insecticides, though their toxicity to pests and to humans and other animals varies greatly. Some chemicals are used in advance of a pest infestation as preventive treatments; however, most are used after the infestation begins. Botanical insecticides are a type of organic insecticide derived from plant sources and are sold in chemicals containing rotenone, sabadilla, and pyrethrum. Their main advantages are short residual activity, less impact on nontarget

organisms, and in many cases they can be applied up to the day of harvest. For additional information about pesticides and their relative effectiveness and safety, refer to *Pests of the Garden and Small Farm* (Flint 1998), *Pests of Landscape Trees and Shrubs* (Dreistadt 1994), and chapter 10.

Basic Rules for Successful Pest Insect Control

Three basic rules for successful pest insect control are discussed briefly below. For additional information, refer to chapter 10 in this book and the references listed at the end of this chapter.

Identify the Problem. People vary greatly in what they perceive to be a problem. Some gardeners will tolerate aphids on roses; others who grow roses to be shown may wish to take action at the first sign of aphids or even before. In many cases, problems are brought to a Master Gardener when it is already too late to take effective action that year. It does little good to control mature caterpillars that have already done their damage. Many homeowners called UC Cooperative Extension after their oak trees had already been defoliated by the California oakworm (*Phyrganidia californica*) wanting some recommendation to control the pest. The last pest generation was already pupating, and nothing could really be done; killing mature or pupating caterpillars so the problem will be less severe the next year is faulty reasoning. Solving the problem entails much more than just identifying the insect pest in question.

Select a Proper Management Strategy. Select a proper management strategy and apply it properly at the most vulnerable time in the life cycle of the insect. For example, the only vulnerable point in the life cycle of the juniper twig girdler is a brief period when the adult moths are active (March to May in Southern California; June to mid-July in the Bay Area). During the rest of the year, the insect is tunneling beneath the bark and cannot be controlled by any known means.

The choice of control measures is often quite broad and should be guided by safety to the environment and to all people involved. The best choice will often be a combination of appropriate methods. People vary greatly in the kind of control they wish to apply, particularly when insecticides may be involved. When several alternatives exist, offer all that are reasonable and approved by the University of California. *Then, let the individual make the choice.*

Evaluate the Results. Evaluate pest-control results from the point of view of avoiding the problem in the future or improving control in the future. Cabbage planted in the spring may need almost constant attention to keep it free from damaging numbers of the imported cabbageworm *Pieris rapae*. Fuchsia is a favored host of the greenhouse whitefly (*Trialeurodes vaporariorum*). Consider planting an ornamental that has fewer plant protection needs.

Insect Control by Chemicals

Because of the toxic nature of pesticides, it is important to devote special attention to their proper use. For further information on pesticide labeling, types of pesticides, modes of action, application methods, formulations, additives, legal requirements, prevention of pesticide poisoning, protective equipment and clothing, application equipment, calibration of sprayers and spray patterns, storage and disposal, and environmental concerns, see chapter 10.

Pesticides must be used in strict accordance with label instructions, which means that the ornamental or food crop must be listed on the label or referred to under a general heading (e.g., trees, shrubs, lawns, and other ornamentals). Products with identical ingredients are offered for sale by different manufacturers, but formulations, pests, and sites listed on their labels may vary. The user is responsible for locating a product with for the desired application.

When food crops are involved, it is extremely important to comply with the *preharvest interval* indicated on the label. This interval is the minimum number of days that must elapse between application of a pesticide and harvest of the crop. For some insecticide products on some food crops, the preharvest interval is zero days, which means that the material can lawfully be applied the same day as harvest, but most gardeners would have no need to spray and harvest the same day. Nonetheless, because home gardening is labor-intensive, exposure to the pesticide could occur. Pesticides with a brief preharvest interval are, however, useful for crops such as strawberries and tomatoes, which are harvested over a long period but which may require treatment with a pesticide between pickings.

The maximum amount of a pesticide residue allowed by law to remain on a raw food crop at harvest is called its *tolerance*. Tolerance is a legal term and does not refer to the amount of pesticide the human body can tolerate from a medical standpoint. Normally the tolerance for a given pesticide is a tiny fraction (usually $1/100$) of the amount of that pesticide calculated to cause the first sign of harm in humans, as determined from tests on laboratory animals. Other factors used to establish the tolerance for a pesticide include the following:

- the quantity of a particular crop an individual is likely to consume regularly, assuming that the crop was always treated with pesticides

- the quantity of other foods a person is likely to consume to which pesticides have also been applied

- the rate of breakdown of the pesticide deposit on the crop as a result of agents such as sunlight, wind, rain, crop growth, etc.

- the rate of elimination of the pesticide from the human body

Tolerances must be approved by federal and state regulatory agencies before a pesticide can be offered for sale. Applying a pesticide according to the label directions with regard to the crop, dosage, and preharvest interval is the only way to ensure that the tolerance will not be exceeded. A person not willing or able to read and follow label instructions should be advised not to use pesticides.

Master Gardeners encounter people who prefer not to use pesticides under any circumstances. Some prefer to handpick pests, grow other crops, use a biological control, or spray insecticides such as insecticidal soaps, oils, or microbials that present little or no health risk. When effective alternatives to synthetic pesticides are available, they should be mentioned along with the chemical control to allow the individual to make the choice.

Pesticides for the home gardener are available in several different forms (formulations). Selected formulation types are listed below with very brief comments. These formulations, additional formulations, and pesticide additives are discussed in more detail in chapter 10.

- *Liquid concentrates* in small portions (usually given in teaspoons or tablespoons) must be mixed with a given amount of water and then applied with a sprayer. The liquids are true solutions.

- *Wettable powders* are dry formulations that, like liquid concentrates, are intended to be mixed with water (diluted) and applied with a sprayer. Particles are suspended and require some agitation.

- *Dusts* are dry formulations intended for application with no further dilution. A duster is used for applying them, but some home and garden dusts can be shaken out or "puffed" through the container in which they were purchased.

- *Granules* have the consistency of sand and require no dilution. Most are intended to be applied dry to the soil or to established turfgrass.

- *Baits* are in pellet form; others have a flake-like consistency. Baits are usually scattered on the ground. Care should be taken, as pets may be attracted to some baits.

- *Aerosols* are contained in a pressurized can and are released when a button on top of the can is pressed. They are most useful when only a few patio or house plants require treatment. Holding the nozzle too close to the plant may result in foliage injury.

Most insecticides are applied using a sprayer. The most useful unit is the hand-compression, or backpack, sprayer with a capacity of 1 to 3 gallons (3.8 to 11.4 l). The hose-end sprayer unit is useful for large jobs, but it does not produce as uniform a spray: the droplets are larger and may tend to run off the foliage more easily, making it more wasteful; it is harder to spray the undersides of some leaves of smaller plants; and it's range is limited by the length of garden hose available.

The sprayer used for applying herbicides should never be used for applying insecticides and fungicides because some herbicides are extremely difficult to clean from a sprayer tank and hose. Insecticides and fungicides can be safely applied with the same sprayer and are sometimes mixed together. Check the label of each product to determine whether the two products can be mixed together safely.

Details about controlling pests and using pesticides safely can be found in chapter 10, in *Pests of Landscape Trees and Shrubs* (Dreistradt 1994), and in *The Safe and Effective Use of Pesticides* (O'Connor-Marer 2000).

Bibliography

Ali, A. D., and C. L. Elmore. 1989. Turfgrass pests. Oakland: University of California Division of Agriculture and Natural Resources Publication 4053.

Barker, P. C., W. R. Bowen, V. E. Burton, C. S. Davis, A. S. Deal, L. D. McGraw, W. G. Schneeflock, W. R. Schrader, and J. E. Swift. 1991. A study of insects: 4-H entomology project. Oakland: University of California Division of Agriculture and Natural Resources Publication 2949.

Borror, D. O., and R. E. White. 1970. A field guide to the insects of America north of Mexico. Boston: Houghton Mifflin.

Dreistadt, S. H. 1994. Pests of landscape trees and shrubs: An integrated pest management guide. Oakland: University of California Division of Agriculture and Natural Resources Publication 3359.

———. 2001. Integrated pest management for floriculture and nurseries. Oakland: University of California Division of Agriculture and Natural Resources Publication 3402.

Essig, E. O. 1958. Insects and mites of western North America. New York: Macmillan.

Flaherty, D. L., ed. 1992. Grape pest management. 2nd ed. Oakland: University of California Division of Agriculture and Natural Resources Publication 3343.

Flint, M. L. 1992. Integrated pest management for cole crops and lettuce. Oakland: University of California Division of Agriculture and Natural Resources Publication 3307.

———. 1993. Integrated pest management for walnuts. 2nd ed. Oakland: University of California Division of Agriculture and Natural Resources Publication 3270.

———. 1998. Pests of the garden and small farm: A grower's guide to using less pesticide. 2nd ed. Oakland: University of California Division of Agriculture and Natural Resources Publication 3332.

Flint, M. L., and S. H. Dreistadt. 1998. Natural enemies handbook: The illustrated guide to biological pest control. Oakland: University of California Division of Agriculture and Natural Resources Publication 3386.

Furniss, R. L., and V. M. Carolin. 1977. Western forest insects. USDA Forest Service Misc. Publ. 1339.

Johnson, W. T., and H. H. Lyon. 1988. Insects that feed on trees and shrubs. 2d ed. Ithaca, NY: Cornell University Press.

O'Connor-Marer, P. J. 1991. Residential, industrial and institutional pest control. Oakland: University of California Division of Agriculture and Natural Resources Publication 3334.

———. 2000. The safe and effective use of pesticides. 2nd ed. Oakland: University of California Division of Agriculture and Natural Resources Publication 3324.

Ohlendorf, B. L. P. 1996. Integrated pest management for citrus. 2nd ed. Oakland: University of California Division of Agriculture and Natural Resources Publication 3303.

———. 1999. Integrated pest management for apples and pears. 2nd ed. Oakland: University of California Division of Agriculture and Natural Resources Publication 3340.

Olkowski, W., S. Daar, and H. Olkowski. 1991. Common sense pest control. Newton, CT: Taunton Press.

Powell, J. A., and C. L. Hogue. 1979. California insects. Berkeley: University of California Press.

Rice, R. E., W. J. Bentley, and R. H. Beede. 1988. Insect and mite pests of pistachios in California. Oakland: University of California Division of Agriculture and Natural Resources Publication 21452.

Smith, M. D., ed. 1989. Ortho problem solver. San Ramon, CA: Ortho Information Services.

Strand, L. L. 1992. Integrated pest management for potatoes. Oakland: University of California Division of Agriculture and Natural Resources Publication 3316.

———. 1994. Integrated pest management for strawberries. Oakland: University of California Division of Agriculture and Natural Resources Publication 3351.

———. 1998. Integrated pest management for tomatoes. 4th ed. Oakland: University of California Division of Agriculture and Natural Resources Publication 3274.

Strand, L. L. 1999. Integrated pest management for stone fruits. Oakland: University of California Division of Agriculture and Natural Resources Publication 3389.

———. 2002. Integrated pest management for almonds. 3rd ed. Oakland: University of California Division of Agriculture and Natural Resources Publication 3308.

UC guide to solving garden and landscape problems (CD-ROM). 2000. Oakland: University of California Division of Agriculture and Natural Resources Publication 3400.

UC IPM pest management guidelines. For many agricultural crops; updated regularly. Oakland: University of California Division of Agriculture and Natural Resources Publication 3339.

UC IPM pest management guidelines for turfgrass. Updated regularly. Oakland: University of California Division of Agriculture and Natural Resources Publication 3365-T

UC IPM pest note series. B. L. P. Ohlendorf, ed. University of California Division of Agriculture and Natural Resources, Statewide Integrated Pest Management Program. Updated regularly. Available through UC Cooperative Extension county offices; also available on the World Wide Web at http://www.ipm.ucdavis.edu

8

Household and Structural Pests

Nancy C. Hinkle, John Klotz, Deborah Silva, and Vincent Lazaneo

LEARNING OBJECTIVES

- Become familiar with common household and structural pests in California.

- Learn some basic information about the anatomy, characteristics, and life cycles of common household and structural pests.

- Become familiar with the damage caused by household and structural pests. Learn about basic prevention and control strategies.

This chapter is intended to be used in conjunction with chapters 7, "Entomology," and 10, "Controlling Garden Pests Safely," in this handbook and with the *UC IPM Pest Notes*, a series of up-to-date answer sheets on common household and home and garden pests published by the UC Division of Agriculture and Natural Resources Integrated Pest Management (IPM) Education and Publications, UC Statewide IPM Project, UC Davis. The *Pest Notes* are available through the local UC Cooperative Extension county office and are also on the World Wide Web at http://www.ipm.ucdavis.edu.

Household and Structural Pests

The most common household and structural pests in California include

- cockroaches

- bees and wasps

- other stinging and biting arthropods (spiders, mosquitoes, ticks, lice, black flies)

- ants

- wood-destroyers (termites, wood-decay fungi, wood-boring beetles, carpenter ants and bees, wood wasps)

- pests that attack pets (fleas, certain ticks and mosquitoes that serve as disease vectors)

- pests of the pantry and stored products (carpet beetles, flour moths, mealworms, clothes moths, silverfish)

- houseplant pests

- general nuisance pests (earwigs, sowbugs and pillbugs, crickets, house flies, fruit flies, dust mites, molds, and grass pollen)

Two household insect pests—ants and fleas—generate the largest number of inquiries to UC Cooperative Extension every year. At the end of the chapter is a special section on how to respond to people with delusory parasitosis, an emotional condition in which people believe that mites or insects are present on or in their skin.

Table 8.1 provides a list of common noninsect arthropod pests in the household that are discussed in this chapter. Table 8.2 provides a list of the household and structural insect pests described in this chapter, organized by the insect orders to which they belong. Also listed are their types of metamorphosis, mouthparts, and a few distinguishing attributes. Although wood-decay fungi, molds, and grass pollen are not pests like the other household pests (they are plant pathogens and plant sperm, respectively), they have been included in this chapter because of their structural significance (wood-decay fungi) and medical significance (molds and grass pollen) to many households in California.

Cockroaches

Cockroaches (fig. 8.1) are some of the most noxious nocturnal insects in the household. They run fast, feed at night, hide in cracks during the day, scurry for cover when lights are turned on, and can have an unpleasant odor. Their populations in the household are often higher than assumed because they hide during the day. Cockroaches eat most foods consumed by people and pets, and they also

Table 8.1

COMMON NONINSECT ARTHROPOD PESTS OF THE HOUSEHOLD

Class	Attributes
Arachnids spiders ticks mites pseudoscorpions scorpions	two body regions (cephalothorax, abdomen); no wings, no antennae; adult has 8 legs (adult insect has 6 legs); not wormlike
Chilopods house centipede	wormlike insect predators; resemble millipedes, but their bodies are more flattened; one pair of legs per body segment; longer antennae; poison jaws paralyze prey
Crustaceans sowbugs and pillbugs (isopods) amphipods	soil-dwelling, small crustaceans related to crayfish; breathe through gills; hard, outer, multisegmented shell; 7 pairs of legs

Table 8.2

COMMON HOUSEHOLD INSECT PESTS

Order	Metamorphosis	Mouthparts	Attributes
Anoplura human lice	simple	sucking	Minute (<⅙ inch, or 4 mm) wingless insects. Immature stages resemble adults. Two species (crab/pubic lice and head/body lice) are ectoparasites of man. Suck blood of host; irritating bites.

Coleoptera
carpet beetles
wood-boring beetles
bean and pea weevil
rice weevil
pantry and stored products
    beetles (drugstore and
    cigarette beetles, saw-
    toothed grain beetles,
    confused flour beetles, etc.)
	complete	chewing	Larvae (grubs, wireworms, borers) have head capsule. Adults have two pairs of wings. Horny, leathery front wings meet in a straight line down back and cover membranous hind wings underneath, used for flying. Usually noticeable antennae. Weevils are beetles with snouts.

Dermaptera earwigs	gradual	chewing	Elongate, flattened insects with strong, movable forceps on rear end. Adults and nymphs resemble each other, but wings are small or absent on nymphs. Two pairs of modified wings: front pair thickened, leathery, short, meet in a straight line down the back and covering the membranous hind wings. Antennae are threadlike, about half of the body length.
Diptera house flies fruit flies mosquitoes fungus gnats black flies	complete	larvae: chewing adults: piercing or sponging	Larvae of flies (maggots) are legless, white, wormlike, lack head capsule. Adults are soft-bodied, have one pair of membranous wings, are hairy. Compound eyes. Mosquito larvae have a head capsule.
Hemiptera bedbugs	gradual	piercing- sucking	Small, flat, oval, reddish brown with vestigial wings. Exposed antennae.
Homoptera aphids, scales, mealybugs, and whiteflies on house plants	gradual	sucking	Small, soft-bodied; winged and unwinged forms.
Hymenoptera household ants carpenter ants wood wasps, horntails carpenter bees honey bees (European and Africanized) bumblebees yellowjackets paper wasps mud daubers	complete	chewing	Legless larvae (wasps, bees, ants) or with legs on thorax and abdomen. Stinger may be used for offense and defense. Adults have two pairs of membranous wings and soft or slightly hardened bodies. Ants have narrow waists. Many species, but not all, are social insects with castes.
Isoptera termites	gradual	chewing	Small, soft-bodied. Resemble ants, but antennae are straighter and waists thicker than those of ants. Winged or wingless. Castes. Social insects.
Lepidoptera clothes moths Mediterranean flour moth Indianmeal moth stinging hair caterpillars	complete	larvae: chewing adults: sucking	Larvae are wormlike, voracious feeders with prolegs on abdomen and thorax. Adults are soft-bodied with two pairs of membranous wings covered with small scales.

Table 8.2 cont.

COMMON HOUSEHOLD INSECT PESTS

Order	Metamorphosis	Mouthparts	Attributes
Orthoptera cockroaches crickets	gradual	chewing	Hard-bodied adults with two pairs of wings. Front wings hard, leathery, rooflike over hind wings. Adults, nymphs cause damage; nymphs look like adults, but wingless, smaller. Some species chirp by rubbing body parts against one another. Some have rear legs modified for jumping.
Psocoptera booklice	simple	chewing	Small to minute (<5 mm or $\frac{1}{5}$ inch), insects with 0 to 4 wings, long, slender antennae that often live in buildings or debris. Feed primarily on dry organic matter, molds, fungi. Wingless forms called booklice; winged forms are barklice. Booklice may damage books by feeding on starchy materials in bindings.
Siphonaptera fleas	complete	sucking	Small (<5 mm or $\frac{1}{5}$ inch), wingless insects that often live as ecto-parasites on birds and mammals. Short antennae. Body laterally flattened. Often jumping. Larvae are tiny, whitish, legless, resemble maggots.
Thysanoptera thrips on house plants	gradual	sucking	Minute adults (<1.5 mm or $\frac{1}{20}$ inch), slender, soft-bodied. Two pairs of long, narrow, membranous wings fringed with long hairs. Short antennae. Sucking mouthparts are asymmetrical, a conical beak at base of head.
Thysanura silverfish firebrats	gradual	chewing	No wings. Bristles on tip of abdomen. Adults about $\frac{1}{2}$ inch. Three taillike projections or appendages at posterior.

eat waste products. Species common in California urban centers are the

- reddish-brown American cockroach (*Periplaneta americana*), which is about 1¾ to 2 inches (4.4 to 5 cm) long and is also known as the "sewer roach"

- brown-banded cockroach (*Supella longipalpa*), which is much smaller, about ½ to ⁹⁄₁₆ inch (12 to 14.5 mm) long, with two pale bands at the base and tip of the wings in the adult

- German cockroach (*Blattella germanica*), which is about ½ to ⁹⁄₁₆ inch (12 to 13 mm) long and light brown with two black lengthwise stripes

- Oriental cockroach (*Blatta orientalis*), which is black, about 1 to 1¼ inches (2.5 to 3.1 cm) long, and also known as the water-bug or black beetle (males have wings, females have rudimentary wings)

- smokybrown cockroach (*Periplaneta fuliginosa*), which is about 1 to 1½ inches (2.5 to 3.7 cm) long and dark brown to black (smokybrown cockroaches are not shown in fig 8.1).

Most of these cockroach species have a flattened, oval shape, spiny legs, and long, filamentous antennae. They develop from an egg to an adult in about 2 to 20 months, depending on the species; the adult life span is about 3 to 15 months. Female cockroaches deposit 12 or more eggs in a bean-shaped, leathery egg case in out-of-the-way places, or they carry the eggs until they are ready to hatch. Cockroach eggs hatch in about a month. Adult males have wings. Immature cockroaches (nymphs) resemble adults, but they are smaller and have undeveloped wings. Immature roaches inhabit the same locales as their parents.

Some cockroaches live outdoors in wood piles, compost, mulch, and debris, and in other materials where moisture is available. They enter households at night to forage for food. The American cockroach, the largest of the domestic roaches, prefers sewers and basements; indoors, it often lives around furnaces, heating ducts, bathtubs, and clothes hampers. Adult American cockroaches are hardy, surviving outdoor freezing temperatures and at least 2 to 3 months without food and a month without water. They are common in sewers in the Central Valley and desert regions of California.

Figure 8.1

Common house-occurring cockroaches in California (actual size).

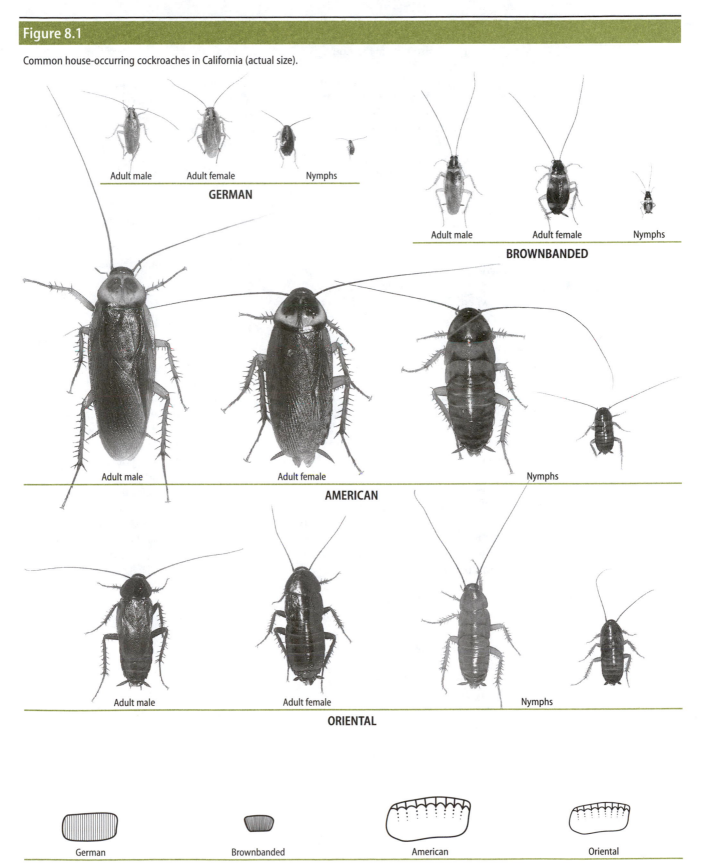

GERMAN
Adult male   Adult female   Nymphs

BROWNBANDED
Adult male   Adult female   Nymphs

AMERICAN
Adult male   Adult female   Nymphs

ORIENTAL
Adult male   Adult female   Nymphs

EGG CAPSULES
German   Brownbanded   American   Oriental

Smokybrown cockroaches live primarily outdoors, but they also invade the home, preferring fireplaces and the attic. They are a subtropical species that likes high temperatures and humidity. Females attach egg cases to cracks, depressions, or corners of bricks, concrete, or wood. Egg cases are often located near window casements and draperies.

The German cockroach (Croton bug) and the brownbanded cockroach dwell almost exclusively indoors. Brownbanded cockroaches will infest any room in the house, hiding in furniture, behind wall decorations, and in closets, and will even feed on starchy, nonfood materials such as wallpaper paste. German cockroaches prefer moist, warm areas and are commonly found in the bathroom and kitchen, where they can infest small electrical appliances on countertops. The German cockroach is often brought into the household with groceries, laundry, or cardboard cartons and can also migrate from nearby infested dwellings, particularly multiunit structures. German cockroaches are the most common roaches found in households, restaurants, supermarkets, hospitals, and other buildings where food is prepared, stored, and served. German cockroaches produce more eggs (30 to 40 per egg case) and have more generations per year than other common household roaches. The female carries her egg case until it is ready to hatch. At room temperature, two females may produce, on average, four to five egg cases in their lifetime, which may last more than 200 days. Just a few individuals can spawn an annoying infestation. During the day, German cockroaches hide around baseboard moldings, in cracks around cabinets, in closets or pantries, and in and under stoves, refrigerators, and dishwashers. If deprived of food and water, adult German cockroaches and brown-banded cockroaches will die within about 2 weeks.

Waterbugs (Oriental cockroaches) prefer dark, damp habitats and are often found indoors in basements and outdoors in water meter boxes. They are more sluggish and considered filthier than the other domestic roaches. They invade households through cracks, sewer and drain pipes, cracked foundations, and doors. They hide under refrigerators, washing machines, and sinks and feed on garbage.

Controlling Cockroaches

Sanitation. Thorough cleaning and proper sanitation inside and outside the home are effective in minimizing cockroach infestations. Neglected housekeeping chores are a major contributing factor to roach outbreaks. Below is a list of measures that discourage roach infestations.

- Unwashed dishes and kitchen utensils and uncovered food should not be left out overnight.

- Do not leave leftover pet food in the feeding dish overnight.

- Clean up spilled food and liquids.

- Clean areas beneath cabinets, pantry shelves, sinks, stove, and refrigerator.

- Seal cracks in foundations and openings around plumbing fixtures and furnace flues.

- Eliminate entry points and hiding spaces. Caulk around air conditioning units, windows, doors, pipes, and other openings into the home to discourage cockroach entry. Thorough caulking or other methods of sealing small gaps will help eliminate hiding spaces and access points. Adult German cockroaches can hide in a crack $1/16$ inch (1.6 mm) wide. They can hide in—or gain access to the house through—cracks and crevices in floors, walls, and ceilings, around plumbing and electrical fixtures, around door and window frames, along baseboards and molding.

- Remove and crush any egg cases you find.

- Keep yard debris and firewood away from the home or garage to minimize opportunities for roach infestation.

- Rinse cans and bottles before putting them in the trash or recycling.

- Store garbage in tightly covered containers. Put containers on clean racks.

- Eliminate cockroach shelters by reducing clutter.

Traps. A number of commercial cockroach traps are available. Although they are very useful for indicating the presence of cockroaches and where they are most active, they are not the most effective control measure. Once inside the trap, cockroaches cannot escape. They are not poisoned, but starve to death.

Traps should be placed along edges and in out-of-the-way corners of cabinets and cupboards, as shown in figure 8.2. Information obtained from trap catches should be used to direct the placement of baits, sprays, and dusts.

To build a cockroach trap, dust the inside of a jar with talcum powder or smear a thin layer of petroleum jelly to a width of about 2 inches (5 cm) around the inside lip of a pint jar. The jelly forms a barrier that prevents roaches from escaping the jar. Place the jar upright, with bait inside, where the roaches are located (see fig. 8.2). Apples and potatoes are effective bait for American and brown-banded cockroaches; German cockroaches prefer banana peels. Change the bait often because roaches prefer fresh food. Destroy the trapped roaches by dropping them into hot, soapy water. Homemade traps will not eradicate cockroaches, but their population numbers may be reduced to acceptable levels.

Inorganic Insecticides (Dusts and Powders). Inorganic insecticides such as boric acid powder and silica aerogel dust are relatively inexpensive, low in toxicity to people and pets, effective long after the initial application in controlling roach infestations in the home, and efficacious in roach hiding places that cannot be sealed off (see fig. 8.2). Research shows that properly applied boric acid powder (95 to 99% concetration) is more effective than spray applications of insecticides. Apply the boric acid powder to cockroach hiding places, which can be identified by using a flashlight in a dark room to observe where roaches flee. Use gloves and avoid inhaling the powder during application. Although these chemicals are slow-acting (they can take a week or more to reduce population numbers), roaches have not developed resistance to them.

Boric acid powder acts primarily as a stomach poison, but it can also penetrate the roach's body. Roaches do not recognize boric acid as an insecticide, and, unlike other insecticidal dusts, it does not repel them when used sparingly. Boric acid powder sticks to cockroach legs and antennae and is ingested when roaches clean themselves.

Boric acid powder can be placed in corners of infested cupboards and cabinets; a fine layer can be applied under stoves and refrigerators; and small amounts can be blown into otherwise inaccessible areas (see fig. 8.2). Do not leave thick trails of powder in the open. Use less than half a teaspoon in any one place. Boric acid powder is slippery and should be removed from surfaces where people walk. Do not treat surfaces where food is prepared. Keep boric acid in airtight, labeled containers away from children, pets, and plants. It can burn or kill plants and should not be used outdoors.

Silica aerogel dust absorbs the waterproof layer of wax on the cockroach's body. It is a good repellent to apply in attics, wall voids, and other closed spaces to prevent roaches from entering the home. Apply a thin film of dust to cockroach hiding places. Because silica aerogel loses effectiveness when it becomes wet, it cannot be used in damp areas.

Organic Insecticides. Several organic insecticides are registered for use on cockroaches. Different formulations (sprays, aerosols, baits) are sold at supermarkets, hardware stores, nurseries, and home and garden centers. Before using an insecticide, always read the label and follow directions and safety precautions. Apply sprays for cockroach control in a 2- to 4-inch (5- to 10-cm) wide band along the edges of infested areas (see fig. 8.2). Spray until the surface is wet but the mixture

Figure 8.2

Cockroach control: Where to place traps and use sprays, dusts, and powders.

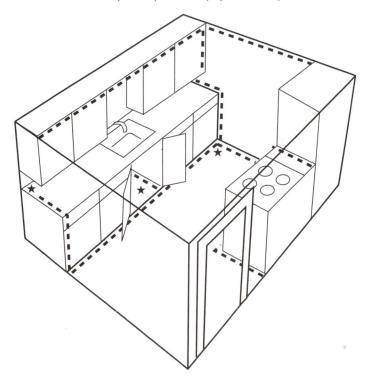

does not run off. Some aerosols are sold with wands for crack and crevice treatment, which is the most effective type of application because it is more target-specific and reduces human exposure to pesticides. Too little spray may not leave a toxic residue, and too much is wasteful and can be hazardous. Before treatment, remove everything from kitchen drawers, cabinets, cupboards, and closets. Do not replace the items until the spray is dry.

Because cockroaches are repelled by most pesticides, they will seek untreated areas. Thus, spray treatments must be thorough. Treating individual apartments can result in cockroaches moving from infested to uninfested apartments nearby, and many reputable pest control firms will not guarantee their work unless entire buildings can be treated. Total-release aerosols can be used in heavily infested areas to rapidly reduce large numbers of cockroaches. Disadvantages of these products include inadequate penetration of cracks and crevices and unnecessary contamination of surfaces not needing treatment.

Toxicant-Laced Bait Stations. In contrast to the more traditional approach of using sprays is the recent resurgence of interest in baits for controlling cockroaches. Baits offer a distinct advantage over sprays: Very little insecticide is required, and the toxicant is contained within a bait station. Consequently, baits are safer for the homeowner. Several over-the-counter cockroach baits are very effective. Like some of the roach traps, commercially available bait stations also lure in cockroaches, but the bait contains a toxicant that poisons cockroaches when they consume it. Most of these toxicants act sufficiently slowly that the poisoned cockroaches can still return to their hiding places before they die. Because cockroaches commonly consume the feces and dead bodies of other cockroaches, the toxicant in the bait is passed on to other cockroaches and kills them also. Some of the newer bait stations contain biological control agents such as fungi or nematodes that prey on cockroaches and contaminate their bodies but are harmless to humans.

Bait should be placed as close as possible to cockroach harborages to maximize the chances of roaches encountering it. Stations should be placed in out-of-the-way corners of cabinets and cupboards, as shown in figure 8.2. Use the information obtained from the roaches caught in sticky traps to determine where to place baits. Baits are most effective when other food is unavailable. Therefore, good sanitation measures are imperative for good control. In fact, sanitation is the single most important factor in successful baiting programs. Poor sanitary habits reduce the effectiveness of control because the baits must compete with other food items.

Frequently Asked Questions about Cockroaches

Q. **Other than being a nuisance, do cockroaches serve any purpose?**

A. Cockroaches have been present on earth for over 300 million years. Of the 3,500 species of cockroaches found worldwide, 60 species exist in the United States. Of those, the German cockroach is the most widely recognized. Cockroaches are able to adapt to most environments, although most live in environments that are warm and usually dark, such as kitchens and bathrooms. In nature, they are scavengers that recycle nutrients, an important link in the food chain.

Q. **What causes the abnormal-looking cockroaches I see around the house?**

A. Most likely these abnormal-looking cockroaches have been exposed to an insect growth regulator (IGR). IGRs are chemical compounds that interfere with the normal growth and reproduction of cockroaches. Unlike some of the more conventional insecticides, which are fast-acting, the effects of IGRs may not occur for a number of days or even weeks after exposure. IGRs are selectively active during one or a few developmental stages in the cockroach life cycle and result in developmental abnormalities that impair the cockroach's ability to survive and reproduce. Sometimes these abnormalities are deformities, of which twisted, curled, or crinkled wings are the most noticeable.

Q. **Do cockroaches carry diseases?**

A. Although cockroaches are commonly viewed as nuisance insects, their impact on human health is a primary concern. In restaurants and health-care facilities, cockroaches can act as carriers of many bacteria that can cause disease. They contaminate food with their excrement and salivary secretions and can transmit bacterial diseases. The most common forms of bacteria transferred by cockroaches are *Salmonella* spp., *Shigella* spp., streptococci, and *Escherichia coli*. By walking across contaminated surfaces and thus acquiring bacteria, the insects are capable of contaminating any other surfaces they touch.

Q. Can cockroaches cause allergies?

A. Unlike many other species of cockroaches, the German cockroach is entirely restricted to indoor environments. They produce numerous allergens, causing discomfort for some people. Allergy to cockroaches is now widely recognized as the second most common allergy among asthmatics. Reactions are due to hypersensitivity to allergens from the cockroach body, cast-off skins, egg shells, and feces. Symptoms usually manifest as allergic rhinitis or bronchial asthma. For asthmatics, acute episodes can be life-threatening.

Q. How are cockroaches killed with bait stations using fungi?

A. Control of cockroaches is difficult. Resistance to some chemical pesticides has occurred. Increasing consumer movement toward environmentally safe products has prompted a new nonchemical approach. One such method is the use of *Metarrhizium* spp., a fungus. The container is similar to the well-known cockroach bait station but contains fungi instead of toxic bait. The cockroach enters an inoculation chamber (because of the dark environment provided) and comes in contact with the fungus. Once the cockroach contacts the fungus, conidia (spores) attach to the cuticle of the insect. The conidia then begin to grow hyphae (growing filaments), which penetrate the cockroach's body cavity and eventually kill it. Hyphae reemerge from the cadaver and begin to produce more conidia, which can then be passed on to other cockroaches coming into contact with the conidia.

Q. Is biological control an option for cockroach management?

A. Generally, biological control is regarded as a safe alternative to traditional chemical pesticides. Because the fungi used are living microorganisms, they produce proteins and other substances that may be potentially allergenic to humans. In fact, a recent study examining reactivity of *Metarrhizium anisopliae* extract to mold-allergic people showed that serum in 4 of 15 patients exhibited high degrees of cross-reactivity. The authors concluded that the fungus could pose health risks when placed in the homes of highly mold-sensitive asthmatics. Although biological control agents are unequivocally beneficial from a health viewpoint in outdoor settings, potential allergenicity to humans may preclude or limit use indoors for such pests as the German cockroach. Further health studies are warranted.

Q. Why are cockroach baits becoming so popular?

A. A large part of the reason has to do with the pressure from regulatory agencies, environmental groups, and consumers for less pesticide use. Some new compounds have great potential as bait toxicants. Some, like hydramethylnon, have already been realized, and others like abamectin and sulfluramid are relatively new. Hydramethylnon ushered in a new era of effective baits. It has had a tremendous success, for example, in over-the-counter sales for cockroach control and is extremely effective in controlling German cockroaches. The bait is enclosed in a childproof tray that allows cockroaches to feed on the bait. Abamectin is one member of a new class of insecticides, the avermectins, natural insecticides originally isolated from a *Streptomyces* soil fungus. It is a neurotoxin, but unlike some of the more commonly used neurotoxins, it is effective at very low concentrations. Another new class of insecticides in baits are the sulfluramids, delayed-action toxicants that interfere with respiration at the cellular level.

Q. Why is placement of cockroach baits so critical for their success?

A. An important consideration for an effective control strategy is bait placement. Roaches are not attracted to baits from great distances; they basically run into them by chance. In the next generation of baits, perhaps volatile odors that can attract roaches from afar will be added. For the present, increasing the number of bait placements increases the chances of exposing the population to a bait, and the closer the bait is to the cockroach harborage, the more effective it is. Always position baits along edges or in corners where the roaches tend to travel.

Bees and Wasps

Bees and wasps (fig. 8.3) are some of the most important stinging insects that people encounter. Some of the more common bees and wasps in California include European honey bees, bumblebees, yellowjackets, paper wasps, and mud daubers. Africanized honey bees, which are close relatives of European honey bees, are a new threat to California.

European Honey Bees

Honey bees (*Apis mellifera*) are important to agricultural production in California as pollinators of fruits, vegetables, flowers, and seed and forage crops (alfalfa, clover) and also as producers of honey and wax. Because up to

Figure 8.3

Common bees and wasps. All insects are shown approximately life size.

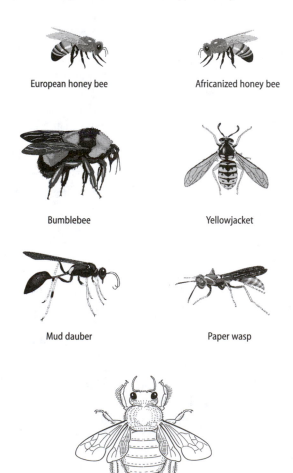

European honey bee

Africanized honey bee

Bumblebee

Yellowjacket

Mud dauber

Paper wasp

Carpenter bee

one-third of our average diet depends on honey bee pollination, hives of European honey bees managed by beekeepers play an important role in our lives. In and around the household, however, honey bees are unwelcome guests because they can sting people and pets. Honey bees collecting water or gathering pollen and nectar from flowers are not aggressive but will sting if provoked or harmed. They defend their hive or nest and will attack and sting anyone in their territory believed to be a threat to the colony. Thus, honey bees are most likely to sting when an established colony is disturbed. To reduce the risk of being stung, it is important to learn about bee behavior and to remove unwanted colonies of bees near the home.

Because honey bees and social wasps (yellowjackets and hornets) look somewhat similar to the casual observer, honey bees are often blamed for misdeeds of wasps; however, the two can be distinguished by their physical form and by their nesting materials. The type of nesting material used by honey bees is different from that of wasps. Honey bees form a wax comb to rear their young and store food. Social wasps form nests of paperlike material. Wasps are more likely to be a problem near the home because, unlike honey bees, which can sting only once, wasps can sting repeatedly, and wasps nest in open areas under eaves of the house, under porches, steps, or benches.

Foraging and Swarming. Bees foraging for food are unlikely to sting people because they are away from home, where it is not necessary to defend the colony. Generally speaking, if left alone, they will not bother people. Reducing sources of food and water—flowers, ripening fruit, soda cans, and water dishes—can discourage bees from foraging in and around the home. Brightly colored clothing and certain perfumes and aftershaves may also attract foraging bees.

Honey bees swarm as part of the process of establishing a new colony, but they are unlikely to sting when swarming because there is nothing to defend. The swarm does not contain stored food or young bees to protect. Once the swarm selects a nesting site, they begin building a comb in which to store food and rear young bees. Within 2 to 4 weeks, the colony of bees will have developed the defensive behavior that the swarm lacks.

A swarm of bees may indicate that a colony is nearby since a swarm tends to gather near the colony it left. Swarms may cluster on a fence, mailbox, or tree branch for several hours to several days while scout bees search for an acceptable nesting site. Swarms may move into voids in walls, attics, or chimneys through openings as small as ¼ inch (6 mm).

Controlling Swarms. It is prudent to contact a licensed beekeeper or professional pest control company to control a swarm of bees. If you decide to tackle them yourself, however, you must wear protective clothing, including a bee veil that protects the face and eyes, does not have holes, and does not touch the skin. Other protective clothing includes a hat and loose-fitting coveralls, leather gloves, and boots. No skin should be exposed. Any potential entry paths to skin, such as pants legs, pants pockets, and shirt sleeves should be closed with tape, zippers, or velcro. Honey bee swarms can be controlled by a wide variety of insecticides labeled for killing them. When a swarm of bees is in an exposed location, mixture of 1 cup of liquid soap or detergent in 1 gallon of water will kill bees by drowning them. If the bees are in a protected area and cannot be completely covered, this method of control should not be used.

Honey Bees in Buildings. Because honey bees prefer to nest in a protected location or cavity, prevent them from entering a building by caulking and sealing cracks in window frames, knotholes in wood siding, and holes in walls where pipes or electric wires enter. If bees are already in a wall, do not block their entrance, because bees trapped in a wall will search for an alternate exit and may find a way to get inside the building.

Honey bees already inside a building should be removed promptly before they begin to build comb in which to rear young bees and store honey. Only when the bees first enter the building can they be killed without opening the wall to remove large quantities of dead bees, wax, and honey. If the colony has been in place for a period of time, the bees are more likely to be defensive. After an established colony is killed, it must be removed to prevent odor problems from decaying bees, stains from melting combs, and the attraction of other insect pests to dead bees, honey, and wax.

Controlling Colonies. Before beginning any control measures of a colony inside a wall a pest control company should determine the location of the colony in relation to the flight entrance and, if possible, determine the number of entrances. The nest may be far enough away from the entrance(s) that insecticides applied at the entrance(s) will not reach the bees. Two techniques for locating a nest are tapping on the wall at night and listening for the area where the buzzing sounds are loudest, and feeling the warmth of the wall, because bees keep the nest center at about 92°F (34°C).

Insecticides labeled for use on bees are the safest, quickest, and most effective materials for killing colonies. It is prudent to contact a professional pest control operator to handle the job, but it is worthwhile for you to have some knowledge, even if you are not the one to do it yourself. Either dust or spray formulations can be used within a wall or other cavity, but dusts generally disperse better. Apply the insecticide at night through the entrance hole if it has been determined that the colony is near the entrance or if the nest cannot be located. A large colony may require more than one treatment. If colonies are treated during the day, bees that return from the field in the evening will need to be sprayed. After the insecticide treatment, the wall will need to be opened to remove dead bees, combs, and honey because dead bees attract other bees. An additional insecticide application will prevent another swarm from entering, and the wall should be sealed. If you do not do the work yourself, you may need to hire a contractor to open the wall, clean out the bees, honey, and wax, and repair the wall.

Africanized Honey Bees

Africanized honey bees (also known as "killer bees") became established in Texas in 1990 and have spread to other southern states. In 1995, they were found in the Coachella Valley in California, and they are expected to migrate throughout the state. Although this bee's killer reputation has been greatly exaggerated, its presence in California will increase chances of people being stung. People can coexist with the Africanized honey bee by learning about this bee and its habits and taking necessary precautions, which can lower the risk of being injured.

Africanized honey bees are closely related to European honey bees used in agriculture for crop pollination and honey production. The two types of bees look the same, and their behavior is similar in many respects, although there are some differences (table 8.3). Neither is likely to sting when gathering nectar and pollen from flowers, but both will sting in defense if provoked. A swarm of bees in flight or briefly at rest seldom bothers people. However, all bees become defensive when they settle and begin to produce wax combs and raise young bees.

Africanized honey bees nest in many locations where they can easily be encountered: empty boxes, cans, buckets or other containers; old tires and infrequently used vehicles; lumber piles; holes and cavities in fences, trees, and the ground; sheds, garages, and other outbuildings; and in spaces under decks and buildings.

General Precautions. Be careful wherever bees may be found. Remove potential nest sites around buildings, but do not disturb a nest or swarm. Contact a pest control company or an emergency response organization. Be alert when participating in all outdoor sports and activities, and listen for buzzing that indicates a nest or swarm of bees. Use care when entering sheds or outbuildings where bees may nest. Examine work areas before using lawn mowers, weed cutters, and other power equipment. Examine areas before tying up or penning pets or livestock. Teach children to be cautious and respectful of all bees. Check with a doctor about carrying bee sting kits and the proper procedures for using them if a member of your family is sensitive to bee stings. Develop a safety plan for your home and yard. Consider organizing a meeting to inform neighbors about Africanized honey bees to help increase neighborhood safety and knowledge.

As a general rule, stay away from all honey bee swarms and colonies. If bees are encountered, get away quickly. Take shelter in a car or building, because water or thick brush do not offer enough protection. While running away, try to protect your face and eyes as much as possible. Do not stand and swat at bees; rapid motions will cause them to sting. Do not attempt to trick the bees by playing dead or hiding because they will continue to attack as long as you are within their territory.

Bee-Proofing Your Home. Remove possible nesting sites around your home and yard. Inspect outside walls and eaves of your home and outbuildings. Seal openings larger than $\frac{1}{8}$ inch (3 mm) in walls and around chimneys and plumbing. Install fine screens ($\frac{1}{8}$-inch [3-mm] hardware cloth) over tops of rain spouts, vents, and openings in water meter and utility boxes. From spring to fall, check once or twice a week for bees entering or leaving the same area of your home or yard.

What to Do If Stung. If you are stung, go quickly to a safe area. The most important response to bee stings is to remove the stinger as rapidly as possible by any means available. Contrary to general wisdom, pinching the stinger will not cause additional venom to be injected into the wound. Because the poison sac attached to the stinger has muscles that continue to pump venom after being detached

Table 8.3

EUROPEAN AND AFRICANIZED HONEY BEES

Similarities

- Look alike (they are the same species and cannot be distinguished in the field).

- Protect their nests and sting in defense, if provoked.

- Sting only once.

- Have the same (chemically identical) venom.

- Pollinate flowers.

- Produce honey and wax.

Differences

- Africanized honey bees are more defensive, less predictable than European honey bees.

- Africanized honey bees will defend a greater area around their nests. Keep all unprotected people and pets at least 400 yards away.

- Africanized honey bees respond faster and sting in greater numbers when provoked, although each bee can sting only once.

- Africanized honey bees will pursue an enemy $\frac{1}{4}$ mile or more.

- Africanized honey bees can sense a threat from people or animals 50 feet or more from the nest; they can sense vibrations from power equipment 100 feet or more from the nest.

- Africanized honey bees swarm frequently to establish new nests.

- Africanized honey bees nest in small cavities and sheltered areas.

- Beekeepers will continue to maintain colonies of European honey bees after Africanized honey bees spread into California.

Source: Africanized Bees in California website, June 22, 2000.

from the bee's body, it is important to remove the stinger from the skin as quickly as possible to minimize the dose of venom. Scrape the stinger out with a fingernail, knife blade, or credit card. Wash the sting area with soap and water, and apply an ice pack for a few minutes to relieve pain and swelling. Seek medical attention if your breathing is troubled, if you are stung numerous times, or if you are allergic to bee stings.

Yellowjackets and Paper Wasps

Yellowjackets (*Vespula* spp.) and paper wasps (*Polistes* spp.) are beneficial insects in that they are predators of house flies and insect pests that damage landscape trees and crops. However, several species scavenge for meat and sweets, seek out garbage cans, and are familiar pests at picnics and backyard barbecues. Because they are beneficial insects, control them only when necessary.

Yellowjackets build two types of nests. One group nests below the soil in burrows (subterranean nest) and inside the walls of houses; and the second group builds aerial nests under the eaves of houses, in sheds, and in trees. Both types make wood-fiber nests that are completely enclosed except for a small entrance at the bottom. Like yellowjackets, paper wasps also build wood-fiber nests, but their nests consists of a naked comb without an enclosing envelope. The nests of paper wasps are most noticeable under the eaves of houses, but they can also be constructed in logs and grass clumps, under rocks, and inside pipes used as clothesline poles.

Yellowjackets and paper wasps have annual colonies that die during winter. Only the inseminated queens overwinter in protected locations under bark, in stumps and hollow logs, and often in attics. They emerge in spring, select a nest site, and build a small paper nest where they lay their eggs. When the eggs hatch, the queen feeds the young larvae for about 18 to 20 days. Then the larvae pupate and develop into infertile females known as workers. After the first 5 to 7 workers emerge from the pupal stage, they take over feeding and rearing the brood. The queen rarely ventures outside the nest again. The colony expands and may consist of up to 5,000 workers and 10,000 to 15,000 cells. By August or September, the colony reaches maximum size. Reproductive cells are built and new males and queens are produced.

They mate, the males die, and inseminated queens seek sheltered locations for overwintering. Abandoned nests decompose rapidly, and the cycle begins again the following spring.

General Control Principles. Yellowjackets and paper wasps do not reuse their nests the following year. Knowing this may help you to determine whether to implement control measures or risk getting stung if the nest is located in a rarely used part of the yard. If you decide to leave the yellowjackets alone, the nest will usually disintegrate during the winter. If the nest is located under the eaves of the house or in the attic, remove it after the yellowjackets are gone because the nest may serve as a home for carpet beetles or other pests.

Wear protective clothing (bee suit, veil, gloves) during these control operations because wasps and yellowjackets will try to defend their colonies and larvae. They usually swarm out and attack in defense of the nest. Cover your head, face, neck, and hands and wear goggles to protect your eyes. Some aerial species can squirt their venom for short distances.

Do not attempt any of the control measures described if you are allergic to bee or wasp stings or are unsure whether you are allergic. Allergy symptoms may be immediate or delayed for several hours and may include swelling, nausea, dizziness, difficulty breathing, or shock. People who are not allergic may experience a minor annoyance or irritation from a sting.

Wasps and yellowjackets are attracted to the sweet scent of decaying fruit in later summer; therefore, do not wear perfume, hair spray, or other scents when you are in areas frequented by wasps and yellowjackets. Avoid brightly colored clothing and other colors typical of flowers, such as bright yellow, light blue, orange, and fluorescent red, which attract yellowjackets and wasps. Teach children not to throw rocks at the nests of wasps and yellowjackets because it agitates them and makes them more likely to sting.

Garbage Cans and Dumpsters. Keep garbage cans covered. Spray the inside of the empty can with insecticides registered for use on wasps, if necessary.

Aerial Nests. Aerial nests can be controlled with aerosol products registered for use on yellowjackets and paper wasps that propel the insecticide up to 20 feet (6 m) with hand or pump sprayers. Apply the insecticide in the coolest part of the evening after the yellowjackets or wasps have returned to the nest. Direct the initial spray stream into the entrance hole of the nest, and then thoroughly wet the nest. Do not remove the nest until all the yellowjackets or wasps are dead, which may take a day or two because some foragers do not return to the nest at night. When they do return, insecticide residues will kill them.

Underground Nests. Aerosol formulations of insecticides effective against aerial nests will also control subterranean nests. Direct the material carefully into the entrance hole after dark. During the day, wear a bee suit to avoid getting stung. After treating the nest, leave the entrance hole unplugged to allow returning foragers to enter the nest and be killed by the insecticide residue.

Nests in Wall Voids. Aerosol formulations that control aerial nests can be used to control nests in wall voids. If dusts are used, plug the entrance hole with steel wool and dust the wool and surrounding area with insecticide. This treatment can be performed during the day because foragers returning in the evening chew at the steel wool coated with insecticide dust and succumb. Wear protective clothing (bee suit, veil, gloves) during the entire operation.

Control at Picnics and Barbecues. A number of commercial traps are available to control yellowjackets and paper wasps outdoors. You can also make your own by hanging fish or liver on a string just above a bucket of water with detergent added. The yellowjackets will try to fly away with pieces of fish or liver that are too heavy for them to carry and they will fall into the soapy water. The detergent acts as a wetting agent to trap the yellowjackets, which drown because they are unable to fly away. However, baiting for yellowjackets is not the most effective control strategy. In areas where yellowjackets are a problem, the best method is to exclude wasps by dining in a screened enclosure.

Yellowjacket and Wasp Stings. If stung by a yellowjacket or wasp, immediately apply a pinch of moistened table salt directly to the sting site and leave it in place for about 30 minutes. The differential in concentrations of salt between the venom and the applied salt tends to draw some of the venom out of the flesh. You can do this in conjunction with administering antihistamine tablets. Other methods include immediate application of a poultice (moist mixture) of a meat tenderizer (an enzyme), which breaks down the components of the sting fluid and reduces pain if the sting is not too deep. A commercial preparation can also be used. Antihistamine tablets and ointments seem to be effective in reducing reactions to stings. People who are allergic to stings should carry emergency kits, such as Epi-Pens or Ana-Kits, that contain syringes with premeasured doses of aqueous epinephrine for injection, and they should also consult their physicians about the merits of desensitization procedures.

Ground-Nesting Bees and Wasps

Ground-nesting bees and wasps, such as bumblebees, mining bees (sweat bees), sand wasps, and leaf-cutting bees, are important pollinators in agricultural production and important predators of harmful pests. But when their nests are located in your yard, garden, flower beds, or playground, you may want to control them to reduce the chances of getting stung.

Sweat bees (halictid bees) commonly gather pollen and nectar from garden flowers, making their nests in cavities in weeds or shrubs or in the ground.

Adult leaf-cutting bees may resemble honey bees in appearance, but unlike the social honey bees, they are solitary and do not form colonies. Female leaf-cutting bees nest in the ground, logs, hollow stems, twigs, and wood siding. They cut oval, dime-sized disks from leaf margins of roses, bougainvillea, ash, and other ornamental shrubs and trees and use them to make thimble-sized cells within their nests. After pollen and nectar are provided, one egg is laid in each cell, and each cell is sealed with pieces of round-cut leaf disks slightly larger than the cell diameter, permitting a tight fit. Typically, leaf-cutting bees are not particularly aggressive in defending their nests and are not a stinging hazard to humans, but they may frighten people who mistake them for honey bees.

Bumblebees are stout-bodied, robust-looking bees with black or gray hairs tinged with yellow, orange or red. Because of their long tongues, they are important pollinators of clover, which is fed to dairy and meat animals. Bumblebees pollinate roses, sunflowers, thistle, nettle, and red clover and other types of clover. Bumblebees have three castes—overwintering queens, males, and workers (undeveloped females). Queens and workers can inflict a painful sting. The three castes range in size from $\frac{1}{3}$ to $\frac{3}{8}$ inch (8 to 9 mm) long, with queens being larger than males, which are larger than workers. Overwintering queens come out of hibernation in May and usually nest in the ground, old stumps, abandoned mattresses, old bales of hay, cornhusks, or old nests of field mice. Nests can be detected by noting the males that often fly around the nest entrance. Workers are territorial and will aggressively pursue an intruder who has invaded their territory and is attempting to escape.

If possible, tolerate ground-nesting bees and wasps because they are valuable pollinators and biological control agents of harmful pests. If the nests are located in areas that increase the likelihood of family members being stung, control is justified. During the day, watch carefully to determine where the nest entrances are located. After dark, treat the tunnels and surrounding areas with insecticide dusts registered for use on ground-nesting bees and wasps. Always read the label and follow directions and safety precautions. Other lawn and garden insecticide sprays can be used, but dusts have the advantage of not soaking into the soil. People allergic to bee stings should contact a licensed professional pest control operator to treat the nest.

Mud Daubers

Mud daubers (*Trypoxylon* spp., *Sceliphron* spp., and *Chalybion* spp.) are solitary wasps that can become a nuisance when they build mud nests on ceilings, walls, and under roof overhangs around the home and other areas where people work and play. These solitary wasps are not aggressive, and controls are rarely needed. Black and yellow mud daubers are black or brown with yellow markings, thread-waisted, and about 1 to 1-$\frac{1}{4}$ inch (2.5 to 3.1 cm) long. They build their nests on the underside of boards, logs, and rocks. Blue mud daubers are metallic blue to blackish with blue wings, thread-waisted, and about $\frac{1}{2}$ to $\frac{3}{4}$ inch (1.2 to 1.9 cm) long.

Solitary wasps such as mud daubers are very different from social wasps (yellowjackets, paper wasps, and hornets) in that they do not have a worker caste and the queens must care for their own young. Queens use their sting to paralyze prey (spiders), not to defend the nests. Males guard the nest while females forage. Mud daubers can be beneficial because they can kill spiders that are dangerous to humans, such as the black widow. Mud daubers are nonaggressive and rarely sting unless touched or caught in clothing.

If you use insecticides to control mud daubers, scrape away the nest with a putty knife or other tool and dispose of it to prevent emergence of developing young and infestations of beetles.

Selected Stinging and Biting Arthropods

Spiders

Spiders (fig. 8.4) are arachnids, with eight legs and two body parts but lack wings and antennae. The tips of their abdomens have silk-spinning glands for spinning webs to entrap prey. Many spiders do not build webs but rather lie in wait for their prey. Young spiders resemble adults, except that they are smaller in size and their coloring may be different. Males are usually smaller than females. Depending on the species, female spiders may produce as many as 3,000 or as few as 3 to 4 eggs per egg sac.

Most spiders produce venom that is poisonous to their prey, which are usually insects and other small arthropods; the venom of these spiders is harmless to humans. Typically, spiders that live indoors are small and not hairy. Outdoor spiders that accidentally invade the home are usually larger ($\frac{1}{2}$ inch [1.2 cm] or more), hairy, distinctly patterned, and able to run, jump, and move rapidly.

House or cobweb spiders (Family Theridiidae) are about $\frac{1}{3}$ inch (8 mm) long and gray to brown with rounded, globular abdomens like those of black widow spiders. House spiders spin webs in dark corners indoors and outdoors, hanging upside down in the center of irregular cobwebs that entrap many insects, particularly flies, which are bitten and sucked dry. Cobweb spiders are cannibalistic. Cellar spiders (Family Pholcidae) have slender legs up to 2 inches (5 cm) long and hang upside down in their webs in dark corners of the house. Cellar spiders characteristically bounce in their webs when disturbed.

Jumping spiders (Family Salticidae) vary in size from very small to over $\frac{1}{2}$ inch (1.2 cm)

Figure 8.4

Examples of harmless spiders: (A) cobweb spider; (B) house spider; (C) cellar or daddy longlegs spider; (D) jumping spider; (E) crab spider; (F) wolf spider; (G) orb or black and yellow garden spider.

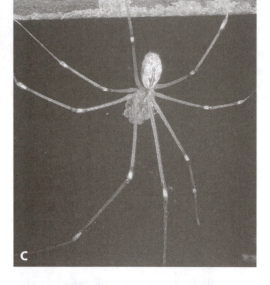

in length and depend on their eyesight and leaping ability to catch prey. They are hairy, stockily built, and can jump several times their length. They normally live outdoors and are active during the day, but they can also be found indoors on walls, windows, screens, and doors.

The crab spider (Family Thomisidae) can walk forward, backward, or sideways, holding its legs in a crablike position. Crab spiders that frequent flowers mimic the colors of the flowers (red, green, yellow, orange, white) and ambush their prey. Those that inhabit trees are usually gray, brown, or black.

Wolf spiders (Family Lycosidae), often confused with tarantulas, can run rapidly after their prey. They are nocturnal and occur primarily outdoors. Except for one genus, wolf spiders do not construct webs.

The orb weaver or black and yellow garden spider (Family Araneidae) constructs a typical wheel-like (orb) web that traps flying insects. This species has poor vision and locates its prey by feeling the vibration and tension of the threads in the web and then wraps the prey in silk. They can bite if handled, but they are not considered dangerous.

The webs of grass spiders (Family Agelenidae) are most conspicuous when morning dew makes their webs glisten in the lawn or shrubs. These spiders, which are about ½ inch (1.2 cm) long, hide in a narrow end of the funnel, and when they feel the vibration of an insect crossing the web, they dash out, bite their prey, and carry it back to eat.

Sanitation is critical for controlling these harmless spider species. Collect and destroy spider webs, egg sacs, and spiders with a strong suction vacuum cleaner, using attachments to reach out-of-the way places, especially ceiling corners. Move furniture and dust thoroughly. Eliminate spider prey—such as flies, ants, and cockroaches—from the house. Control excess humidity by sealing or caulking cracks and crevices around the house foundation, windows, and doors. Insecticides may be used for quick kill and knockdown of spiders. Outdoors, remove woodpiles, trash, and other debris where spiders live and use a high-pressure hose to knock down webs and to destroy egg sacs and spiders.

Black Widow Spiders (Family Theridiidae). Black widow spiders (*Latrodectus hesperus*) are considered the most venomous spiders in the United States (fig. 8.5) Although their venom is highly toxic to humans, the amount injected with a single bite from a spider is minute. Mortality from black widow spider bites occurs in fewer than 1 percent of cases, and most healthy people recover completely in 2 to 5 days. These spiders tend to occur outdoors and are not aggressive unless disturbed or accidentally trapped in clothing or shoes. These spiders are associated with

Figure 8.5

Black widow spider.

dry, undisturbed piles of firewood, old limbs, rock piles, bales of hay, and wooden buildings. Thus, removing these items and other trash from around the house eliminates likely habitats. Do not go barefoot near firewood or handle it without gloves. Sweep outside with a stiff broom to remove webbing. Seal and caulk crevices where spiders can enter the house.

Adult black widow spiders have shiny, jet black, rounded, globular abdomens with two reddish or yellowish triangles on the underside that resemble an hourglass (see fig. 8.5). Adult males are harmless and about half the size of the female. Juveniles of both sexes resemble the male and are also harmless. Young western black widow spiders are predominantly white or yellowish-white and acquire more black color with each molt. This species spins tangled webs of coarse silk in dark places, primarily outdoors, such as garages, sheds, rubble piles, and trash.

Each female produces four to nine egg sacs per summer with 300 to 400 eggs per sac. Growth and development of spiderlings takes about 2 to 4 months, depending on the availability of prey. Females mature about 92 days after emerging from the egg sac and live about another half year. Males mature more quickly after emergence (71 days) but live only one more month.

Female black widow spiders are nocturnal and rarely leave the web. They hang belly upward in the web and trap cockroaches, beetles, and other arthropods. Cold weather and drought are two environmental factors that can drive these spiders into buildings.

Black widow spider bites. The severity of a person's reaction to a black widow spider bite depends on the area of the body bitten, the amount of venom injected, the depth of the bite, the air temperature, and the health status of the person bitten. The bite may feel like a pinprick, or it may not be felt at all. At first, there may be light, localized swelling and two faint red spots surrounded by local redness at the bite site. Pain may become intense in 1 to 3 hours and may continue for 48 hours. Pain usually progresses from the bite site up or down the arm or leg and then settles in the abdomen or back. Abdominal muscles may become rigid and boardlike with severe cramps. Other symptoms may include nausea, vomiting, profuse perspiration, tremors, labored breathing, and feeble pulse, in which case the person needs prompt medical atten-

tion. Serious long-term complications are rare. In most individuals, symptoms will diminish and be gone in several days.

Treatment of black widow spider bites. If you are bitten, try to remain calm. Get medical attention immediately by contacting your physician, hospital, or poison information center. First aid is of limited help. Collect the spider, if possible, for positive identification by an entomologist. Applications of a mild antiseptic, such as iodine or hydrogen peroxide, can prevent infection. People younger than 16 and older than 60, especially those with heart conditions, may require a hospital stay. Physicians can prescribe antivenin compounds or other medications to relieve pain.

Insecticides can be effective against black widow spiders, but be sure to read the label and follow directions and safety precautions. Certain insecticides for black widow control can only be applied by licensed pest control operators.

Violin or Recluse Spiders (Family Sicariidae). Contrary to popular belief, the brown recluse spider (*Loxosceles reclusa*) does not occur in California. Other *Loxosceles* species such as *L. deserta* and *L. laeta*, do occur; however, they are rarely encountered. Recluse spiders prefer seclusion and are not aggressive but will bite when crushed against skin. People usually come in contact with these spiders when they put on clothing or shoes that have not been worn for long periods of time, when they are cleaning out undisturbed storage areas (sheds and garages), or when they sleep in a bed that has been unused and they roll over onto the spider. Bites can be serious in children, the elderly, and people in poor physical condition.

Adult recluse spiders are yellowish-tan to dark brown, about ¼ to ½ inch (6 to 12 mm) long, and have long, delicate grayish to dark brown legs covered with short, dark hairs. They are distinguished by three pairs of eyes arranged in a semicircle and an indistinct violin-shaped dark mark behind the semicircle of eyes, with the neck of the violin pointing toward the bulbous abdomen. Males and females are equally toxic and look alike. Juveniles resemble adults, except that they are smaller; they have venom, but their small mouthparts cannot penetrate the skin.

Recluse spiders are most active at night when foraging for cockroaches and other small insects. During the day, they take shelter indoors in bathrooms, bedrooms, closets, and crevices; behind or under baseboards, furniture, appliances and carpets; in clothing, old shoes, and towels left undisturbed for long periods of time. Outdoors, they can be found in debris, storage sheds, and garages. They are active in temperatures ranging from 45° to 110°F (7° to 43°C).

These spiders spin small, irregular webs. Females lay eggs from May through August in off-white silken sacs about ⅓ inch (8 mm) in diameter. Each female may lay up to 300 eggs in her lifetime (about 40 per egg sac), and she guards the eggs until her death. Spiderlings emerge in about a month. They can survive for long periods without food or water and may live as long as 2 years.

Recluse spider bites. As with black widow spider bites, the severity of a person's reaction to a recluse spider bite is influenced by the amount of venom injected and the health status of the person bitten. Symptoms, which can include a stinging sensation followed by intense pain, may be immediate or delayed. At the bite site, a small white blister usually develops and is surrounded by a large, congested, swollen area. Systemic symptoms may occur in 24 to 36 hours and are characterized by restlessness, fever, chills, nausea, weakness, and joint pain. The spider's venom contains an enzyme that destroys cell membranes in the wound area, which can result in tissue sloughing away, exposing a volcano-shaped lesion within 24 hours. The open wound can range in size from an adult's thumbnail to the span of a hand. It can take 6 to 8 weeks for the ulcerating sore to heal. Full recovery can take several months, and skin grafts and plastic surgery may be necessary.

To prevent bites from these spiders, shake out clothing and shoes before dressing, and inspect bedding and towels before using them. Do not handle firewood without gloves, and do not go barefoot into storage areas. Remove trash, old boxes, lumber piles, old clothing, and other unwanted items. Dust and vacuum thoroughly, especially around windows and room corners, under furniture, and in undisturbed places to eliminate spiders, webs, and egg sacs. Install screens on doors and windows, and seal or caulk cracks and crevices where spiders can enter the house. Wash off the outside of the house, including roof eaves. Certain insecticides can be effective in controlling recluse spiders, but some of them can

only be applied by licensed, certified pest control operators. Read the label and follow directions and safety precautions before using insecticides to control these spiders.

What to do if bitten by a recluse spider. Recluse spider bites are extremely rare, and almost all necrotic lesions attributed to spider bites originate from other causes. In the rare event of a bite, try to remain calm. Get medical attention immediately by contacting your physician, hospital, or Poison Information Center. If possible, collect the spider for positive identification. Apply an antiseptic solution to prevent infection and ice packs to the bite site to relieve local swelling and pain. An effective antivenin is not available; however, your physician can prescribe medications that help.

Tarantulas (Family Theraphosidae). Most tarantulas are nonaggressive and rarely bite. The bites from tarantula species typically found in the United States are not considered dangerous and are similar to a bee sting, feeling like a pin prick and resulting in mild stinging pain and soreness. Tarantulas are covered with hollow, needlelike barbed hairs, especially on their abdomens. Tarantula hairs may cause a skin rash and even anaphylactic shock in allergic people. Anyone considering a tarantula for a pet should be aware of the potential hazard of allergic reaction to their hairs.

Many species of tarantulas, the world's largest spiders, live in the tropical jungles of South America. About 30 species live north of Mexico in the southwestern United States. The largest tropical tarantulas are about 3½ inches (9 cm) with a leg span of 9½ inches (24 cm). The largest tarantulas in the United States are about 2 inches (5 cm) with a leg span of about 6 inches (15 cm). They are nocturnal and hide during the day inside cavities in the ground. Tarantulas may feed on cockroaches, crickets, grasshoppers, and newborn mice. Female tarantulas may live as long as 35 years and molt annually. Males live only 5 to 7 years and do not molt after maturity.

Mosquitoes

Mosquitoes are small, delicate insects capable of spoiling leisure time around the home. They have slender, delicate bodies, narrow wings, and long, thin legs (fig. 8.6). Female mosquitoes have firm mouthparts that are well adapted to piercing skin and sucking blood. Male mosquitoes cannot suck blood and do not bite. Both male and female mosquitoes feed on the nectar of various flowers. Some mosquito species are active at night, whereas others are active during the day. The most common mosquito genera in California are *Aedes, Anopheles,* and *Culex.* The females of different species prefer different hosts. Some infected female mosquitoes are capable of transmitting serious diseases to people, such as malaria, yellow fever, and encephalitis. Other infected mosquitoes transmit heartworm to dogs.

Mosquitoes undergo complete metamorphosis. Their life cycle consists of four stages: egg, larva, pupa, and adult. Eggs are laid in batches of 50 to 200, and one female may lay several batches in her lifetime. Usually, female mosquitoes require a blood meal for eggs to become mature. All mosquito species need water to breed. Contrary to popular opinion, mosquitoes do not breed in the undergrowth of weeds, bushes, or shrubs, although these

locations can serve as excellent refuges for adults. Eggs can hatch in 2 to 3 days, and larvae change into comma-shaped pupae in about a week, which transform into adults in about 2 days.

Control of mosquitoes is both a public issue and an individual concern. Sometimes mosquito infestations in the area cannot be controlled by individual efforts at home but instead must be addressed and organized by the local community. Contact your local health department for information. At home, it is important to find and eliminate mosquito breeding places on your property. Old tires, tin cans, junk automobiles, rain barrels, and certain plants hold enough water to create mosquito breeding opportunities. To keep mosquitoes from being a problem inside the home, make sure that screens are tight-fitting and in good repair.

At home, mosquitoes may be controlled chemically with repellents and sprays. An effective repellent prevents mosquitoes from biting people. When applied properly to the neck, face, arms, legs, ankles, and other exposed skin surfaces, repellents can provide protection from mosquito bites from 2 to 12 hours. Old clothing may also be sprayed with repellent to provide additional protection. Repellents should not be applied to eyes, lips, or other mucous membranes. The most common repellent for mosquitoes is DEET. Note that some repellents have special precautions on the label for use on children.

Oil of citronella is another type of effective mosquito repellent. It is the active ingredient in many candles, torches, and coils that can be burned to produce a smoke that repels mosquitoes outdoors. These repellents are most effective when the wind speed is minimal. Oil of citronella is the active ingredient in Avon's Skin-So-Soft, which is marketed as a mosquito repellent and moisturizer. Insecticide sprays may also be used to control mosquitoes. Follow label directions and all safety precautions stated on the container.

Ticks

Ticks are arachnids (adults have eight legs) that have piercing-sucking mouth parts and feed exclusively on the blood of animals. Many ticks common in California are known as three-host ticks, which means that they require three separate blood meals, generally from different hosts, to complete specific

Figure 8.6

Mosquito, showing the pupal stage and the larvae of *Culex* and *Anopheles* spp.

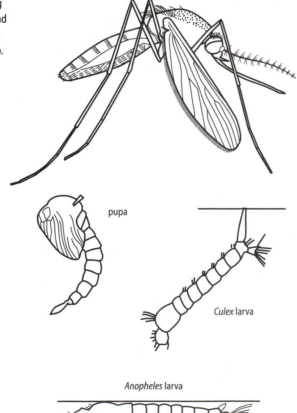

pupa

Culex larva

Anopheles larva

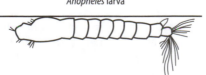

developmental stages. After a tick becomes fully engorged with host blood, which may take several hours to several days, it can more than double in size. The tick leaves the host at the end of each blood meal to molt or lay eggs. Ticks are most active from December to June. They are more abundant in areas with grasses and brush in urban and rural settings where vegetation will support their hosts. Ticks do not fly, jump, or drop from trees. Instead, they climb to the tips of vegetation, typically along animal trails or paths, and wait for a host to brush against them. This behavioral method of finding a host is called "questing."

Tick bites can be dangerous to people because of the effects of the bites themselves and because of microbes that can cause diseases, transmitted to people by infected ticks. Tick bites can cause dermatitis, secondary infections, and a condition known as tick paralysis (a rare complication). Throughout the United States, Rocky Mountain spotted fever is transmitted by the Rocky Mountain wood tick. In California and the western United States, the western black-legged tick (*Ixodes pacificus*) is the vector of Lyme disease (see discussion below). Not all ticks carry disease; however, among those that do, feeding must occur for several hours for transmission to occur. The bites of some ticks may produce paralysis in pets and other animals. For a discussion of several ticks that can attack pets, see the Pests of Pets section in this chapter.

General Control Strategies for Ticks. Control strategies vary with the pest species. A tick can be submitted in alcohol to the local Public Health Department for identification. Because the majority of ticks are encountered outdoors, control means preventing tick bites. Protective clothing should be worn when walking through tick-infested areas to reduce the number of ticks capable of reaching your skin. Inspect your body carefully after returning from an outing, and inspect your children carefully. Tick repellents provide some protection and can be applied to clothing and exposed skin. Follow label directions and avoid exposure to eyes and mouth.

Tick Removal. If a tick does become attached to your skin, remove it carefully and promptly. Removing ticks is difficult because they have barbs along the shaft of the mouth that facilitate anchoring in the host. Prompt removal may prevent any infection or disease transmission. If the tick is firmly attached, grasp it with tweezers or forceps (not your fingers) and pull it slowly and steadily until its head is free of the skin. If possible, have someone else remove the tick from you. If you must touch the tick, use a tissue to protect your hand. Turning the tick over onto its back may facilitate removal. Do not crush the tick, jerk it, or break off its mouthparts. Mouthparts left in the skin can cause infection, so apply antiseptic to the tick bite. Wash hands thoroughly with soap and water after handling ticks. Dispose of ticks in alcohol or by flushing them down the toilet. Use the same precautions and procedures when removing ticks from pets.

Reducing infestations (population numbers) is the preferred method of preventing tick attacks. Clearing brush and mowing grass helps to reduce populations of free-living ticks.

Western Black-Legged Tick and Lyme Disease in California. Lyme disease is transmitted by the bite of a western black-legged tick infected with a spiral-shaped bacterium (a spirochete) that may persist in the human body for several years if not treated properly with antibiotics. This disease was identified for the first time in 1975 in Old Lyme, Connecticut, and first seen in California in 1978. Because symptoms are variable and occur in stages, diagnosis can be difficult.

The western black-legged tick is a three-host tick. It is present in 50 of the 58 counties in California and requires three separate blood meals to complete specific developmental stages. The tick leaves the host at the end of each blood meal to molt or lay eggs, as shown in the life cycle in figure 8.7. Larvae and nymphs feed on small rodents, rabbits, lizards, birds, and some large mammals. Adult black-legged ticks feed on large mammals (dogs, deer, and humans).

Preliminary studies indicate the primary reservoirs of Lyme disease in California are wild rodents. Larvae and nymphs of the black-legged tick acquire spirochetes from the blood of infected mammals as they feed on them. Then, as infected adult ticks undergo metamorphosis, they transmit the spirochetes to other mammals, including dogs and humans, as they feed on them. In California, only a small percentage (<2%) of the ticks tested were infected with the Lyme disease spirochete.

The adult female black-legged tick is about ⅛ inch (3 mm) long, shaped like a teardrop, and red-brown with black legs. Males are smaller and brownish-black. Western black-legged ticks exhibit typical questing behavior. They can be found under leaf litter and duff in woodlands, and along trails or paths, waiting for a host to pass them. They are more common in humid coastal areas and on the western slopes of the Sierra Nevada range.

Early symptoms of Lyme disease include a spreading rash, flulike symptoms, fever, and aches. Complications may involve the heart, nervous system, and severe arthritis. The disease typically has three stages.

Stage 1. The rash, known as erythema migrans (EM) occurs 3 to 30 days after the bite of an infected tick. EM is a red, blotchy, circular, expanding rash that has a ringlike appearance. More than one EM lesion may occur, not necessarily at the tick bite site. EM may be preceded or accompanied by flulike symptoms. In some cases, the rash does not appear and, even if present, is sometimes difficult to see, especially on people with dark skin color.

Stage 2. Long-term complications in the heart (blockage) or nervous system (meningitis, encephalitis, Bell's palsy) may develop weeks or months after initial symptoms. Migratory pain in joints, tendons, muscles, and bones may occur without joint swelling or redness.

Stage 3. Months or years after disease onset, arthritis may appear and reappear intermittently or may become chronic, with erosion of cartilage and bone. Arthritis is the most common long-term symptom of Lyme disease. Large joints, such as the knees, are most often affected.

Early recognition of Lyme disease is important. If you have found a tick attached to your skin or if you were in an area where ticks are known to occur and you have any of the characteristic symptoms of Lyme disease, you should contact your physician immediately. A blood test will help your physician make a diagnosis. Treatment with antibiotics during the early stages of the disease is effective and can prevent complications.

Black-Legged Tick Avoidance: Personal Care.

- Tuck pants into boots or socks, and shirt into pants.

- Wear light-colored clothing so ticks can be seen easily.

- Apply tick repellent on pants, socks, and shoes.

- Avoid sitting on the ground in areas covered with leaf litter or duff.

- Avoid trail margins, brush, and grassy areas when in tick country.

- Check yourself and your children frequently.

- If a tick does become attached to you, remove it by following the instructions under "Tick Removal." If ticks are crushed or squeezed with fingers, exposure to body fluids may lead to transmission of Lyme or other disease agents.

Figure 8.7

Life cycle of the western black-legged tick.

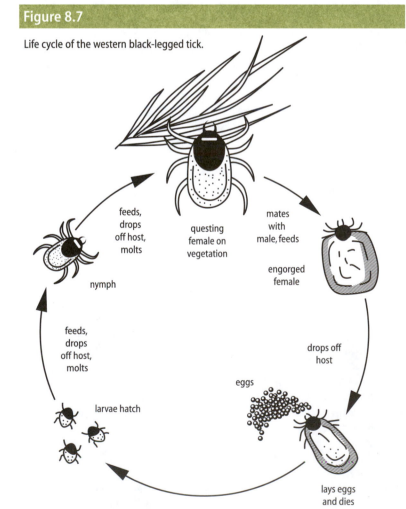

feeds, drops off host, molts

questing female on vegetation

mates with male, feeds

engorged female

nymph

drops off host

feeds, drops off host, molts

eggs

larvae hatch

lays eggs and dies

Figure 8.8

Human lice: body louse (left); crab louse (right).

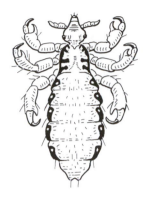 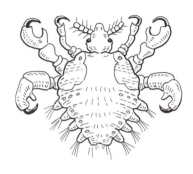

Black-Legged Tick Avoidance: Environmental Care.

■ Mow grass along trails, buildings, and camping areas.

■ Remove brush along trails or other areas of high activity by people.

■ Area application of insecticides is not effective for tick control.

Black Flies

Black flies can be among the most annoying biting pests to campers, fishermen, and residents of foothills. If you notice black flies around your home, call your local health department or mosquito abatement district. These agencies have personnel trained to address the problem. Black flies are usually most active from dusk to nightfall and in the early morning in the early spring and summer months. Black flies are commonly found in streams, creeks, and man-made waterfalls. Eggs are laid in water. When larvae hatch, they attach themselves to rocks and vegetation. Males are primarily flower feeders, whereas females seek blood meals from human beings and animals. If you know you will be in an area infested with black flies, wear loose clothing that is closed at the neck, wrists, and ankles. Wearing repellents may be effective, but only for short periods of time.

Human Lice

Two lice species (fig. 8.8) live and breed on humans: head and body lice (*Pediculus humanus*) and crab or pubic lice (*Phthirus pubis*). Both species feed by sucking host blood. Lice eggs are known as nits. Lousiness is one of the most common communicable conditions in the United States. Human lice are not found on household pets and are not transferred from pets to people.

Head lice attach their nits to hairs on the head (near the ears and at the back of the neck are favorite spots) and may be spread by sharing combs, hair brushes, or hats. Head lice infestations are normally found on children, but they can be spread to adults. Special shampoos are available to control head lice. Although they are not considered disease vectors, head lice are annoying pests.

Body lice are spread from person to person by direct contact, on clothing, or on bedding. Body lice usually occur in crowded conditions and when people do not bathe or change clothes for long periods. Thus, they are associated with poor personal hygiene and poverty. Body lice typically lay their eggs on clothing, often near seams and creases, and feed on the person's body. Body lice are important disease vectors, but not in the United States. They can transmit typhus after they have become infected with the disease. A louse becomes infective after it has bitten a typhus patient; infection of another individual can occur when that individual scratches the infected louse or its feces into the skin. Body lice can be controlled by changing clothes daily and laundering them. When infested clothing is removed from the host for several days all the lice will usually succumb. Pillow cases, sheets, and blankets should be washed in hot, soapy water to kill adult lice and their eggs.

Compared to body louse, the crab louse has a short, broad body and generally has the appearance of a crab. Eggs of the crab louse attach to body hairs, primarily in the pubic region. They are well-adapted for survival where coarse hair grows. The female crab louse produces about 25 eggs that hatch within a week into nymphs that mature into adults in 15 to 20 days. Adults suck blood periodically and inject salivary secretions into wounds, causing pale blue spots. Off the host, crab lice have an even shorter life span (<1 day) than body lice. If you suspect crab lice, you should consult your physician.

Bed Bugs

Bed bugs (*Cimex lectularius*) and their relatives feed primarily at night on the blood of

Figure 8.9

Bed bug.

humans and other warm-blooded animals. These insects (fig. 8.9) bite with their piercing-sucking mouthparts, inject a salivary secretion in the process, and cause small, hard, swollen, white welts that itch and can become inflamed. Blood stains on sheets and dark spots of excreta on sheets and mattresses, bed clothes, and walls are signs of infestation. Bed bugs are not known to transmit diseases with their bites. They can have a sweet, musty odor.

Adults have flattened, oval-shaped bodies about ¼ to ⅝ inch (6 to 16 mm) long and are reddish-brown to mahogany. After a blood meal, their bodies become engorged and dull red. Each female bed bug can lay about 200 eggs (3 to 4 per day over a 2-month period) under favorable conditions, which include an adequate food supply (regular feeding on blood) and temperatures about 70°F (21°C). In one year, bed bugs may have three or more generations. Adult bed bugs are very hardy and can survive without food for several months to a year.

Prevent bed bug infestations by laundering bedding routinely in hot water, vacuuming, and repairing cracks in plaster. In multi-occupant dwellings, bed bugs may spread quickly from one unit to another and require the services of a licensed professional pest control operator.

House Centipedes

The house centipede (*Scutigera coleoptrata*) can be beneficial because it feeds on roaches, clothes moths, spiders, and house flies. A few recorded cases of bites by house centipedes exist, but the pain is not usually severe; however, some species can inflict a painful bite. (The jaws of young centipedes usually are not strong enough to cause more than a slight pinch.) The mature house centipede is 2 to 3 inches (5 to 7.5 cm) long and grayish-tan, with long antennae and 15 or more pairs of long legs (especially the last pair) that extend all along its body. The last pair of hind legs are modified to lasso and hold insect victims until they are paralyzed by venom from the centipede's jaws, which are connected to poison glands.

House centipedes prefer damp, moist basements, cellars, bathrooms, and crawl spaces. They can run and climb walls very quickly. They do not damage the structure of the home, household possessions, or foodstuffs.

Centipedes are controlled by low humidity. Keep old boards, rotting wood, grass clippings, trash, and leaf litter away from the house foundation so that the soil is exposed to drying from sunlight and air circulation. Repair and seal cracks and openings in the foundation wall and around door and window frames. Indoors, seal cracks, crevices, and other hiding places under clothes washers or dryers and in bathrooms, and control the house centipede's food sources (cockroaches, clothes moths, spiders, house flies).

Stinging Hair Caterpillars

The larvae of certain moths (caterpillars) have stinging hairs that can cause symptoms ranging from mild irritation with local reddening, swelling, burning, and itching to severe pain, nausea, and systemic reactions requiring hospital treatment, depending on the sensitivity of the individual in contact with them. The stinging hairs can be hollow and connected to poison glands, in which case the venom flows on contact, or they can be similar to glass fibers (the hairs break off in skin easily). In California, the silverspotted tiger moth (*Halisidota argentata*) has larvae about 1½ inches (3.8 cm) long that are densely covered with tufts of brown or black stinging, poisonous hairs.

Adult moths emerge in July and August and deposit eggs on needles or twigs of conifer trees. The larvae feed in clusters on pines, firs, and other conifers. They spin cocoons of silk and body hairs, attaching to twigs, needles, and tree trunks. They overwinter inside the web and then disperse the following spring.

It is important to teach children not to handle or play with hairy, colorful, fuzzy caterpillars because of their possibly painful stings and because it can be difficult to distinguish between harmless and venomous insect larvae. Do not handpick hairy, fuzzy, or spiny caterpillars unless you are wearing heavy leather gloves. Wear long-sleeved shirts, trousers, and gloves when harvesting sweet corn in later summer to reduce stings from larvae of the Io moth (*Automeris io*).

Treat stings by immediately applying adhesive or transparent tape over the sting site and then pulling it off to remove broken hairs or spines. Washing the area with soap and water may remove irritating venom. An ice pack or baking soda poultice should help reduce pain and swelling. Contact a physician to handle severe reactions.

Pseudoscorpions

Pseudoscorpions can be found occasionally in the home in sinks, bathtubs, between book pages, and in stacks of newspapers. They can also be found outside in mulch and leaf litter and under tree bark. They are small, harmless arachnids ($\frac{1}{16}$ to $\frac{1}{8}$ inch [1.5 to 3 mm]) long with a pair of pincerlike claws. They resemble true scorpions but lack the long tail and stinger. They are considered beneficial because they are predators of clothes moth larvae, carpet beetle larvae, booklice, ants, mites, and small flies. No special control measures are needed for pseudoscorpions. Discourage infestation by removing prey.

Scorpions

Scorpions are arachnid relatives of ticks, mites, and spiders but do not resemble them. Fourteen scorpion species live in California, ranging in size from $\frac{1}{2}$ inch (1.2 cm) to more than 7 inches (18 cm) long. The body is long and slender, with a segmented tail that ends in a bulblike poison gland. They have four pairs of legs and two large pincer-bearing arms in front. Although they have small eyes, scorpions are nearly blind and use the sense of touch to detect and capture their prey, which include insects, spiders, centipedes, other scorpions, and earthworms. Scorpions can be found under stones, the bark of fallen trees, or wood.

When disturbed, scorpions can inflict a painful sting, which may be toxic because some scorpion species inject neurotoxins in their victims, and some people are allergic to their bites. Treat a sting by applying an ice pack to the affected area to reduce pain. If swelling or pain persists or if difficulty in breathing occurs, contact a physician.

Measures for controlling scorpions include sanitation (removing trash, logs, stones, and bricks from around the home), keeping grass mowed, weather-stripping around loose-fitting doors and windows, caulking, and keeping screens in good repair.

Wood-Destroying Pests

The most common wood-destroying pests in California include subterranean, drywood, and dampwood termites, wood-decay fungi, wood-boring beetles, carpenter ants, carpenter bees, and wood wasps (also known as horntails). Nationwide and in California, the damage caused by wood-destroying insects has an important economic effect. Across the United States, the cost of control and repair of damage is estimated at about $5 billion annually; the outlay in California and Hawaii alone exceeds $1 billion a year.

Wood-destroying pests compromise the structural integrity of the home; inspections for these pests should be conducted at intervals of not more than 2 years because of the structural hazard and high cost of repair of advanced infestations or decay problems. Because recognition of structural pest infestations and subsequent damage requires experience and training, in California, the Structural Pest Control Board examines and licenses individuals who make professional structural inspections. The Pest Control Operators of California, Inc., provides information to educate the public about the contents of an inspection report, the Structural Pest Control Act of California, Board regulations, and sample forms that will be filled out during an inspection. The Pest Control Operators of California, Inc., can be contacted in West Sacramento at (530) 372-4363.

A structural pest control inspection is advisable prior to making final payment to a contractor on a newly built structure because the Structural Pest Control Act of California has requirements not addressed by most building codes. The first owner may have to bear the expense of alterations required by the inspection report (removal of cellulose debris, correction of earth-wood contacts, faulty grade levels) at the time of the first resale, unless these matters are addressed before final payment to the contractor responsible for the construction.

Figure 8.10

Termites.

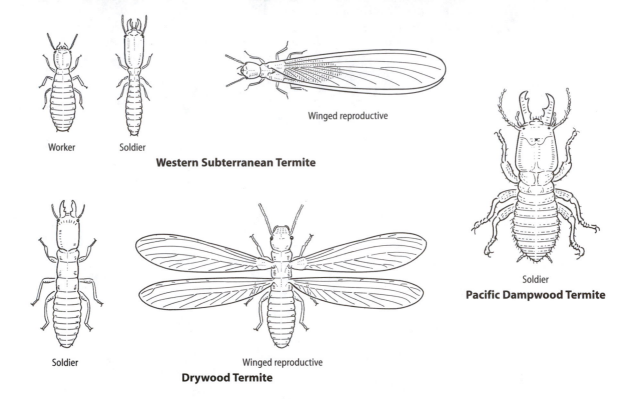

Western Subterranean Termite

Worker Soldier Winged reproductive

Drywood Termite

Soldier Winged reproductive

Pacific Dampwood Termite

Soldier

Termites

Three major groups of termites (fig. 8.10) occur in California—drywood termites (infesting dry wood), subterranean termites (nesting in the soil), and dampwood termites (infesting damp wood). Some of the species occurring in California are listed below.

- Drywood termites
    western drywood termites (*Incisitermes minor*)
    desert drywood termites (*Marginitermes hubbardi*)

- Subterranean termites
    western subterranean termites (*Reticulitermes hesperus*)
    Formosan subterranean termites (*Coptotermes formosanus*)
    desert subterranean termites (*Heterotermes aureus*)
    arid land subterranean termites (*Reticulitermes tibialis*)

- Dampwood termites
    Pacific dampwood termites (*Zootermopsis angusticollis*)
    Nevada dampwood termites (*Zootermopsis nevadensis*)

Termites feed on wood, fiberboard, paper, and other wood products and cause serious damage to wooden structures and posts. Protozoa (one-celled microscopic animals) that live in termites' guts convert the cellulose in wood into simple sugars, permitting termites to derive nourishment from wood and wood products. Termites may also attack stored food, household furniture, and plastics.

Depending on the species, termite nests consist of chambers excavated in wood (drywood and dampwood) or in the soil (subterranean). As social insects, termites live in large, organized colonies (communities), with duties and roles of individuals determined by caste. As with ants, individuals may include reproductives, soldiers, and workers with three growth stages: egg, nymph, and adult. White, wingless, and usually sterile, workers collect food; feed the queen, soldiers, and young; and construct chambers. Because there is no worker caste in drywood termites, immature termites carry out those duties. Subterranean termite workers are about ⅛ inch (3 mm) long. Soldiers are wingless, usually sterile, with large heads and mandibles (jaws), which they use to defend the colony and attack intruders, such as ants. Early in adult life, reproductives (queens and kings) are distinguished by four nearly identical wings, which are longer than their bodies. These wings are lost after the reproductives disperse from their natal colony.

Termites initiate new colonies by sending out winged reproductives from an established colony. They swarm and fly to a new location, drop to the ground, shed their wings, and pair off. If they find a hospitable spot, the pair forms a chamber in which eggs are laid and a new generation develops. Sometimes, winged termite reproductives (queens and kings) are confused with winged forms of ants, which also leave their underground nests in large numbers to establish new colonies and swarm in a similar manner often at the same time of year; the distinguishing physical features are shown in figure 8.11.

Subterranean Termites. Western subterranean termites are the most destructive termites found in California. In the lower desert regions of southeastern California, the desert subterranean termite can also be very destructive. Even though subterranean termites nest in the soil, they can attack structures by building mud tubes that connect their nests in soil to wood in structures (fig. 8.12). Colonies include reproductives, workers, and soldiers.

Reproductive, winged forms are dark brown to brownish black, with brownish gray wings. The wings are about twice the length of the bodies. Reproductives often swarm on warm, sunny days after spring or fall rains.

Subterranean termites build their nests in soil and normally require continuous contact with soil to get sufficient moisture for survival. When wood is in contact with soil, termites can burrow from the soil directly into the wood. However, they can build their nests in aboveground parts of a structure without maintaining soil contact, if there is a continuous supply of water, such as a leaky pipe. If a barrier such as a concrete slab exists between the soil and wood, subterranean termites build earthen mud tubes, sometimes as long as 50 to 60 feet (15 to 18 m), to bridge the barrier. Thus, subterranean termites can infest and destroy the structural integrity of a building even if wood is not in direct contact with the ground. Subterranean termites construct four types of tubes or tunnels (see fig. 8.12). Working tubes are constructed from nests in the soil to wooden structures and may travel up concrete.

Formosan subterranean termites were discovered for the first time in California in the 1990s in La Mesa (near San Diego). The source of the infestation is believed to have been personal belongings imported into the state from an infested area in Hawaii. Although the California climate is much drier than that of many areas where the Formosan subterranean termite is established, properties that are heavily shaded and irrigated can provide a suitable microhabitat for survival and

Figure 8.11

Distinguishing features of termites and ants.

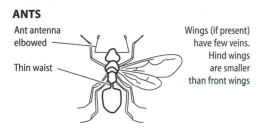

ANTS

Ant antenna elbowed

Thin waist

Wings (if present) have few veins. Hind wings are smaller than front wings

TERMITES

Termite antenna not elbowed

Broad waist

Wings (if present) have many veins. Front and hindwings are same size

Figure 8.12

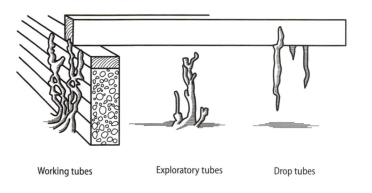

Working tubes   Exploratory tubes   Drop tubes

Mud tubes of subterranean termites. Mud tubes connect the colony in the soil with wood in the structure. Subterranean termites construct three basic types of tubes or tunnels. Working tubes are constructed from nests in the soil to wooden structures and may travel up concrete or stone foundations. Exploratory (and also migratory) tubes arise from the soil but do not connect to wood structures. Drop tubes extend from the wooden structure back to the soil.

Figure 8.13

Comparison of fecal pellets of drywood and damp-wood termites.

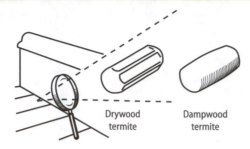

Drywood termite   Dampwood termite

infestation. All that is required is a pair of mated adults transported under conditions favorable for their survival and placement in an appropriate setting on arrival, such as in potted plants, nursery material, or outdoor furniture.

The Formosan subterranean termite is native to China but has spread to Japan, Guam, South Africa, Hawaii, and several southern states. This termite can spread to new areas aboard ship and via infested soil, wooden crates, or other wood products.

Drywood Termites. Many species of drywood termites damage buildings, furniture, utility poles, fences, piled lumber, and shade and orchard trees. Unlike subterranean termites, they do not require contact with soil and build their nests aboveground. As their name implies, they attack and infest dry, undecayed wood. They have a low moisture requirement and can tolerate dry conditions for prolonged periods. Attics are common areas of drywood termite infestation. These termites carry out their work completely inside the wood. Often, the only evidence of their presence is a few small holes through which they push frass (fecal material and undecomposed wood formed into tiny, football-shaped pellets) out of the galleries. Their fecal pellets are distinctive in appearance, as shown in figure 8.13.

Drywood termites are the most common termite in Southern California, but they also occur along the coast, in the Central Valley, and in the southern desert. Winged reproductives of western drywood termites, which are dark brown with smoky black wings and a reddish-brown head, swarm seasonally to buildings on warm, sunny days in the fall. They are noticeably larger than subterranean termites. Winged forms of the desert drywood

termite are pale in color.

Dampwood Termites. Dampwood termites require high amounts of moisture. They can nest in wood buried in the ground, but contact with the ground is not necessary if the infested wood has a high moisture content. The largest termites in California, Pacific dampwood termites (see fig. 8.10) are found most often in cool, humid areas along the coast and are common pests of beach houses. Nevada dampwood termites occur in higher, drier areas of the Sierras and can be pests in mountain cabins and along the northern California coast.

Winged reproductives of both species typically swarm on warm evenings between July and October, but they can be active at other times of year. Like drywood termites, dampwood termites produce distinctive fecal pellets (see fig. 8.13), which are elongated and rounded but lack the longitudinal ridges of drywood termites. Dried dampwood termite pellets resemble those of drywood termites.

Damage Caused by Termites. Termites are the most ruinous wood-destroyers in the United States. Annually at least 1% of the nation's housing units require treatment to control termites. In California, subterranean and drywood termites are responsible for more than 95% of all costs associated with wood-destroying insects. It is impossible to build structures resistant to termite damage, but a number of prevention, detection, and control strategies are effective.

Detecting Termite Infestations. Most termite species swarm in late summer or fall, although subterranean termites may also swarm in spring. Mating of winged reproductives occurs during these flights, and males and females form new colonies. An infestation begins when a mated pair finds a suitable nesting site near or in wood and constructs a small chamber, which they enter and seal. The female begins egg laying, and the king and queen feed the young on predigested food until they are able to feed themselves. Once workers are produced, they feed the king and queen. Soldiers begin to defend the colony. Termites undergo incomplete metamorphosis; nymphs resemble adult termites, except that they are smaller.

Homeowners should be on the lookout for signs of infestation, which include swarming of winged reproductives in fall or spring, mud tubes, fecal pellets, and evidence of tunneling in wood. Termite wings break off shortly after the mating flight; the presence of discarded wings indicates a colony is nearby, even if the actual swarming has not been observed. Because termites are attracted to light, their broken-off wings are often located near doors or windows. Darkening or blistering of wooden members is a typical symptom of termite damage. Galleries of subterranean termites can often be detected by tapping wood every few inches with the handle of a screwdriver. Damaged wood sounds hollow, is usually thin, and can easily be punctured with a knife or screwdriver.

Because subterranean termites build earthen, mud tubes about ¼ to 1 inch (0.6 to 2.5 cm) wide to protect them from low humidity and predation, houses should be inspected at least once a year for evidence of tubes. If the house has a crawl space, inspect the inside and outside of foundations for tubes. In houses with concrete slab floors, cracks in the concrete and places where pipes and utilities go through the slab should be examined. Cracks in concrete foundations and voids in concrete block foundation are also hidden avenues of entry. A common, although often overlooked, area of infestation is the space between a brick veneer wall and the actual wall of a building.

Preventing Termite Infestation. Look for conditions within and around the home that favor termite attack, such as excessive moisture and wood in contact with the soil. Correct these problems, if possible. All substructure wood should be at least 18 inches (45 cm) above the soil beneath the building. Keep attic and foundation areas well ventilated and dry. Use screening over attic vents and seal other openings, such as knotholes and cracks, to discourage the entry of winged, drywood termites. Screening of foundation vents into the substructure may block termite entry, but it also may interfere with adequate ventilation, leading to increases in moisture retention.

Use termite-resistant wood, if possible, and chemically treated (pressure-treated) wood for foundations. Inspect utility and service boxes attached to the building to make sure that they do not provide shelter or a point of entry into the building. Inspect porches, fence posts, poles, and other structural or foundation wood for signs of termites. Remove dead limbs and tree stumps, stored lumber, untreated fence posts, and buried scrap wood near the structure that may attract termites.

Recent research has validated the effectiveness of foundation sand barriers for subterranean termite control. Sand with particle sizes in the range of 10 to 16 mesh is used to replace soil around the foundation of a building and sometimes in the crawl space. Subterranean termites are unable to construct their tunnels through the sand and cannot invade wooden structures resting on the foundation. Stainless steel mesh that is small enough to prevent penetration by termite workers is another means of blocking entry by subterranean termites. This technique is used in some areas but is limited to preconstruction installation.

Some of the best strategies to prevent future termite infestations are accomplished by carefully considered construction plans. Before constructing a new home or office, consult your local UC Cooperative Extension office to obtain literature about preconstruction treatment of structures, foundation walls and piers, and concrete slabs.

General Control Principles. Implementing a termite control program is not for the novice, because it requires an understanding of building construction. In most cases, it is advisable to hire a professional pest control company to implement the program. More than one species of termite can infest a building at the same time, which influences the control approach. Because subterranean and dampwood termites can have nests at or near ground level, control methods for them can be similar, but different tactics are required for drywood termites, which nest above ground level (frequently in attics). Upon request, a professional pest control company will conduct an inspection, verify the presence of termites (or other structural pests), identify them, and determine the extent of the infestation and damage.

Controlling Drywood Termites. Chemical fumigation with insecticides registered for use on drywood termites has been the method of choice for controlling these pests for years. Currently, it is the most efficacious method for controlling drywood termites. The structure to be treated is enclosed in a tent, the fumigant is released inside, and the gas is held long enough for it to penetrate to all parts of the structure. Afterward, the structure is ventilated, and the remaining fumigant is released

Table 8.4

SUBTERRANEAN AND DRYWOOD TERMITE INFESTATIONS AND THEIR CONTROL

Characteristic	Drywood termites	Subterranean termites
location of nest	inside wood	in soil
exterior tunnels, mud tubes	never	often
foraging	inside same wood as nest	often remote from nest
control	destroy colonies	establish barrier between structure and nests
residual effects of treatment	none in fumigation; residuals in localized treatments	several to many years, depending on treatment
fumigation appropriate	yes	no

into the atmosphere. No significant residues are left inside the structure. The procedure does not leave any chemical residual to deter future infestations. Registered fumigants are safe to building residents when applied correctly. Treating the entire structure means that fumigation does not depend on detection of all colonies or infested wood. The disadvantages of the treatment are that the building must be vacated; sensitive materials must be removed during treatment; and it is relatively expensive. Fumigation to control drywood termites is considered a whole-structure treatment and is a common practice in the pest control industry because of its effectiveness. Fumigation of drywood termites is a big business in California. Recently, whole-structure heat treatment has become a viable nonchemical option.

Drywood termite colonies are sometimes small, permitting a localized control approach known as spot treatment. If treatment is prompt and all colonies and all infested areas have been detected, local treatment can be effective. The problem with spot treatment is that termite colonies can be hidden within inaccessible parts of structures and detecting all infested areas can be difficult, if not impossible. Current detection technology lags far behind treatment methods. Thus, claims that all infested wood can be detected and spot-treated may not be true in a particular case.

Controlling Subterranean and Dampwood Termites. Subterranean and dampwood termites cannot be controlled by fumigation, heat treatment, freezing, microwaves, or electrocutor devices because the reproductives and nymphs are concentrated in nests near or below ground level in areas that cannot be reached by these methods. Whenever possible, it is best to destroy shelter tubes of subterranean termites so that their access to the wooden substructure is interrupted and colonies are exposed to attack by natural enemies, such as ants.

Subterranean termite control consists of placing a chemical or physical barrier between soil nests and the wooden parts of the structure, which may be done at the time of construction or as a remedial treatment. The colonies themselves are not treated directly, largely because no one knows how to find them. In contrast, drywood termite colonies are treated directly because they feed within the same piece of wood in which the nest is located. Their colonies and nests are thus restricted to the structure (confined within the wood) and also tend to be smaller than those of subterranean termites. In contrast, subterranean termites make tunnels over the surface of wood, concrete, or soil, which makes detection easier but control more difficult. Termite baits and borates are new and exciting areas of research and development for termite control (see "Frequently Asked Questions about Termites," below). For a comparison chart of control measures for drywood and subterranean termites, see table 8.4.

The accessible nests of small dampwood termite infestations can be destroyed by removing infested wood. Nest areas of subterranean and dampwood termites can be spot-treated with a liquid formulation of a long-lasting insecticide. If colonies are numerous or inaccessible, a pest control professional will apply soil drenches of a long-lasting (3 to 7 years) liquid insecticide directly under the building or injected through the foundation or beneath the concrete slabs. Foundations and structural wood can be protected by injecting insecticides into the soil beneath structures by horizontal or vertical drilling and rodding.

Subterranean and drywood termite control should be carried out by a licensed professional because special hazards are involved with applying insecticides to the soil around and under buildings. Soil-applied insecticides must not leach through the soil profile to contaminate groundwater. The mobility of insecticides in soil is a chemical property influenced by soil type, weather, and application techniques. Applications in the wrong place can cause insecticide contamination of heating ducts, radiant heat pipes, or plumbing used for water or sewage under the treated building. Hire a professional pest control operator who understands these hazards, who will guarantee the work, and who will use the least-toxic but effective insecticide. Confine insecticide use to areas where termites are detected and to inaccessible areas.

Frequently Asked Questions about Termites

Q. How do you tell the difference between termites and ants?

A. Without careful examination, it is difficult to distinguish termites from ants. Worker ants, which are wingless adults, are easily recognized; however, winged reproductive ants that leave nests in warm weather to mate and establish new colonies can be confused with winged termites, which also leave their nests to mate. The three primary physical differences between termites and ants are shown in figure 8.11. Note that the ant's abdomen is constricted, giving it a "thin waistline"; its hind wings are smaller than its front wings; and its antennae are elbowed. In termites, the waistline is thick, antennae are straight, and front and hind wings are about equal in size.

Q. How does one select a good termite control service?

A. If you think termites are attacking your home, do not panic. These insects work slowly, and your house will not be ruined or collapse overnight. Purchase termite control service from a reliable company that has an established place of business. Use the same discernment, precaution, and comparison-shopping techniques in purchasing this service as you would in purchasing other services for your property. Investigate before you make a decision and get estimates from two or three reliable companies. The pest control company should make a complete inspection of the entire house (dwelling, garage, and surrounding property) to determine the extent and origin of the infestation. Proper treatment cannot be recommended without a thorough inspection. A written report should be provided regarding the extent of the infestation and probable origin (aerial or ground). Do not allow a company to pressure you by leading you to believe that you must handle this matter immediately. You have time to get a second or third opinion about the extent of damage and the proposed method of treatment.

Do not automatically purchase service from the lowest bidder. Evaluate the company's credentials by checking references. Request a written statement of the work the termite control specialist proposes to do and obtain precise language (guarantee) backing the company's work. Read the proposed contract. A vague guarantee statement referring to termite control should not be accepted. Determine whether a yearly charge will be levied during the guarantee period or whether this service is included in the initial price of the job. Be a shrewd shopper. A guarantee is not evidence that a company is reliable. It is only as trustworthy as the person or company authorizing it. Many pest control companies are well-established, respected businesses in the community, but fraudulent operators do exist, and nothing prevents them from having flashy contracts and guarantees as part of their sales promotion package. Beware of companies that offer a secret formula or ingredient for termite control or that claim to be endorsed by the University of California.

Q. What about alternatives to fumigation for control of drywood termites? Are these nonchemical techniques effective?

A. UC scientist Vernard Lewis and Michael Haverty of the USDA Forest Service published a scientific evaluation of spot treatments with nonchemical methods of drywood termite control and compared them with fumigation. The nonchemical methods tested were excessive heat or cold, electrocution, and microwaves. Except for the excessive-heat treatment, which can be used on a whole structure, the other nonchemical methods are classified as local or spot treatment methods. The results of the

Lewis and Haverty study were reported in the *Journal of Economic Entomology* in August 1996 (see the bibliography at the end of the chapter).

Electrocution using an Electrogun, a device marketed to kill drywood termites by emitting high-frequency electricity, was generally not an effective treatment, unless the "drill and pin technique" was used, and even then only 90 percent of the termites were killed, not 98 percent or 100 percent as with fumigation. Lewis and Haverty concluded (p. 931): "This control method [electrocution], more than any of the others evaluated in this study, requires precise information as to the extent and location of the drywood termite infestation. Without accurate delimiting of the infestation, efficacy will likely drop to unacceptable levels."

Results of the microwave tests were mixed. Lewis and Haverty wrote (p. 932): "The microwave method of drywood termite control appears to have promise as an effective spot treatment technique. However, we feel more information is needed to determine the correct exposure time to achieve the desired level of control. Studies are needed on penetration of microwave energy into wood for varying wattage levels. Monitoring temperature changes in building materials during treatment could improve efficacy."

Heating the infested wood above the drywood termites' survival threshold or chilling the wood below the minimum survivable temperature and maintaining the lethal temperatures long enough to kill the termites are two alternative control treatments based on sound biological principles. Both methods involve covering the structures to be treated with tarpaulins and insulating pads. The heat treatment requires the use of propane burners and hot air blown inside the structure through ducts. The goal is to achieve a temperature of at least 120°F (49°C) inside infested wood for at least 30 minutes. To achieve this goal, the structure must be heated to 150° to 180°F (66° to 83°C) for several hours. Because hot air rises, it is not always possible to heat the lower parts of the structure to the desired temperature. In the Lewis and Haverty study, the results of the whole-structure heat treatment were "very similar" to the results achieved with fumigant gases, which demonstrated nearly 100% elimination of drywood termites. Mortality results with heat treatment significantly exceeded 90 percent and in some tests exceeded 99 percent.

Spot cold treatment involves pumping liquid nitrogen into and around infested areas, which lowers temperatures to −20°F (−30°C) in infested wood, which is lethal to drywood termites. The cold treatment does not involve release of any gases not already found in the atmosphere, since approximately 80 percent of the earth's atmosphere consists of gaseous nitrogen. In the Lewis and Haverty study, localized treatment with 4.9 pounds per cubic foot (381.8 kg/m³) of liquid nitrogen was efficacious at the 90 percent level. The 0.7 pounds per cubic foot (57.3 kg/m³) liquid nitrogen treatment was not efficacious, and the authors concluded that dosage rates below 2.6 pounds per cubic foot (200 kg/m³) are not likely to achieve the minimal lethal temperature or result in eradication of drywood termites in walls.

Currently, only whole-structure fumigation with registered fumigant gases provides reliable, nearly 100 percent elimination of drywood termite infestations, although the heat-treatment results were notable in the recent UC study. Consumers equally committed to not using fumigant gases and to reducing drywood termite populations might consider an alternative. Treated areas should be reinspected yearly to ensure eradication of drywood termites.

Q. How do termite baits work?

A. The most recent development in urban entomology is using baits for subterranean termite control. The toxicants used in these new baits are either slow-acting stomach poisons or insect growth regulators (IGRs). The baits typically use some type of cellulose food as an attractant. One method uses a bait-and-switch technique in which untreated wood is used to lure the termites and is then replaced with the treated bait, which is distributed throughout the termite colony. Once the termite activity ceases, the bait is removed, and monitoring with the untreated bait is resumed. The idea is simple: if the bait is attractive, these social insects will recruit to it, return to the nest with it, and distribute it to all of their nestmates, eliminating the entire colony. The emphasis in pest control therefore is shifting from a treatment strategy based on applying large volumes of pesticides to make an impervious barrier to a strategy that uses bait toxicants to exploit the social behavior of the termites and reduce pesticide use.

Q. How are liquid borate sprays used in termite control?

A. Liquid borate applications are used to treat wood for remedial or preventative purposes. When applied to wood, they repel or deter termite feeding in areas of high borate concentration and, where concentrations are low, the treated wood is toxic when ingested. Many factors influence the degree of borate penetration into wood, but the most important is moisture content. Drier wood accepts more borate solution; however, wood with a higher moisture content allows deeper penetration. Preferred locations for borate treatments include attics and crawl spaces. Multiple applications with adequate drying time in between are recommended to build borate concentration both at the wood surface and inward by diffusion. Active galleries and access points in wood should be flooded by pressure with a borate solution.

Q. Are some types of wood more resistant than others to infestation by termites?

A. The heartwood of redwood is resistant to termite attack, but much of the redwood sold today is not. The primary building material for homes is Douglas-fir, with some spruce, hemlock, and redwood also used. Because Douglas-fir is frequently used, it is important to note that it does not accept wood treatments very well, including borates.

Wood-Decay Fungi and Dry Rot

All fungi that inhabit wood require moisture to grow, but often the inappropriate term "dry rot" is used to described the structural damage caused by wood-decay fungi. Wood-decay fungi (*Serpula lacrimans, Poria incrassata*) exist almost everywhere in soil. They dissolve wood with enzymes they produce and use the wood decomposition products for food. The combination of wood and water are all the resources that decay fungi require for eventual total destruction of wood. Decay fungi cause a loss of strength in the infested wood before the symptoms of advanced decay are reached.

Two main classes of wood decay caused by these fungi are brown rot and white rot. Wood in the advanced stages of brown rot will be discolored dark brown and may be crumbly, powdery, and dry. The wood will look shrunken. White rots give the wood a bleached appearance and render it soft and spongy. In both cases, there are no tunnels or mines in the wood, which would be typical of termite damage, nor is there any sawdust, which would be evident with carpenter ant infestation. Surface molds, mildew, and stain fungi are often confused with decay fungi because the former grow on the surface of damp wood and discolor the wood, causing it to turn various shades of green, gray, or black. Unlike decay fungi, they do not break down wood fibers or weaken their structure. The presence of surface molds, mildew, and stain fungi indicates that moisture is available and that decay would proceed if wood-rotting fungi were to become established.

Wood that remains damp will decay no matter where it is located in the structure, unless it is naturally decay-resistant heartwood or has been pressure-treated with a preservative. It is therefore important to repair leaks and other sources of moisture contacting wood. Soil in contact with structural wood is the most severe exposure condition for a building because the soil is a relatively continuous source of moisture and a bountiful source of fungal inoculum for infection.

To manage wood-decay fungi, remove the source of moisture and all decayed wood to a point several feet beyond the decay because, in all likelihood, this wood has also lost much of its strength. If possible, replace the wood with decay-resistant heartwood or with preservative-treated (pressure-treated) wood. Dipped, sprayed, or brushed applications of preservative are not very effective because they penetrate only about $\frac{1}{16}$ inch (1.5 mm) below the surface, and any superficial damage will quickly breach the treated zone, making it ineffective. If soil contact cannot be avoided, the wood should be pressure-treated with preservatives to provide a reasonable length of service.

Wood-Boring Beetles

Three families of beetles in California have species of wood borers that damage structural wood, decorative wood, and furniture: powderpost beetles (Lyctidae family, *Lyctus* spp.); false powderpost beetles (Bostrichidae family, *Polycaon* spp.); and beetles of the Anobiidae family, which are known as deathwatch beetles (*Hemicoelus* spp.). Deathwatch beetles are closely related to drugstore and cigarette beetles, pantry and stored product pests discussed later in this chapter.

Powderpost Beetles. Lyctid larvae attack bamboo and large-pored hardwoods, such as oak, hickory, ash, mahogany, and walnut. Adult powderpost beetles, which are reddish to brown, lay their eggs in the pores of the wood, and the emerging larvae, which are "C"-shaped, mine the wood (fig. 8.14). Infestations are most likely to occur in wood paneling, molding, window and door frames, plywood, hardwood floors, bamboo articles, tool handles, antiques, and other furniture.

Powderpost beetle larvae mine the wood interior and reduce it to talcum powder-fine dust, known as frass, which they leave behind after they feed. The frass, which consists of feces and food fragments, can fall out of exit holes into small piles on floors or other surfaces. Powderpost beetles have a life cycle ranging from 3 to 12 months, depending on temperature, humidity, and the nutritional quality of the wood.

Because the physical differences between powderpost beetles and other beetles are not easily recognizable, a suspected powderpost beetle infestation should be confirmed by an entomologist who has had experience with these species. Other adult beetles may emerge from wood after it has been placed in the home, just as adult powderpost beetles emerge, but if the larvae of the other species cannot reinfest dry wood and are only pests of fresh logs that still contain bark, their larvae may not be a problem requiring treatment. Although these other species may not be a threat to wood in the home, an entomologist should confirm the identification.

Powderpost beetles pose a significant threat to a home and should be controlled as soon after detection as possible because they can reduce a piece of wood to powder inside a paper-thin exterior shell of undamaged wood. They can also move to major structural members and other valuables in the home, such as floors, art objects, and musical instruments. Sometimes, the only signs of infestation are the tiny, round exit holes made by emerging adult beetles; only after the adults exit does the powdered frass become visible.

False Powderpost Beetles. False powderpost beetles (fig. 8.15) pack their galleries with frass that has the consistency of coarse powder, which distinguishes them from the powderpost and deathwatch beetles. In buildings, false powderpost beetles infest floors, furniture, hardwood paneling, and other wooden objects. The bamboo borer (*Dinoderus minutus*), a false powderpost beetle (Bostrichidae), can be found in baskets, furniture, and picture frames imported in bamboo material from Asia. Another bostrichid, *Heterobostrychus*

Figure 8.14

Powderpost beetle and larva.

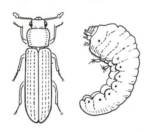

Figure 8.15

False powderpost beetle.

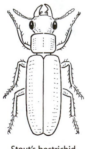

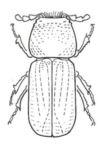

Stout's bostrichid   Leadcable borer

Figure 8.16

Deathwatch beetle and larva.

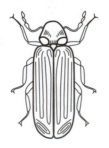

aequalis, is occasionally found in hardwoods imported from Southeast Asia.

Deathwatch Beetles. Anobiid larvae attack Douglas-fir, the species most often used for structural members in California buildings. Deathwatch beetles (fig. 8.16) supposedly got their name in medieval Europe when people who heard their tapping against wood were sitting up with a sick or dying person during the night. Deathwatch beetle adults are reddish to dark brown and lay eggs in crevices or pores in unfinished wood. Two years may be necessary to complete one generation.

These beetles are found primarily in soft woods, including beams, foundation timbers, and some types of furniture. Unlike other species of powderpost beetles, they prefer wood that is more moist, and partially decayed, or old wood. Their "C"-shaped larvae fill their galleries with pelleted frass, not fine powder, distinguishing them from other wood-boring beetles.

Prevention and Control of Wood-Boring Beetles. As with drywood termites, full-structure fumigation with a toxic gas is the control measure of choice for powderpost beetles, unless evidence is convincing that the infestation can be managed by spot treatment. Lyctids commonly enter the home in infested hardwood cabinetry or flooring or in dry, large-pored hardwood firewood. If the infestation is caught early, spot treatment may be efficacious, but if structural members are involved, the entire structure should be tented and fumigated. Fumigation will kill the powderpost beetles, but, because it does not offer residual effect, reinfestation can occur. Most powderpost beetle infestations are present in wood and wood products before you purchase them for use in your home. Prevention and control really need to begin at the lumber mill.

In the home, sanitation is the best strategy for preventing wood-boring beetle attacks. Good air circulation and the elimination of any excess moisture in crawl spaces can reduce the development of an infestation. If the wood is dry (moisture content below 14 percent) and has little food value (starch in cells of sapwood) and a high resin content, larvae of wood-boring beetles will die. To prevent accidental introduction of wood borers into the home, inspect furniture and other objects before purchasing them and bringing them inside. Look for exit holes where adult beetles have emerged.

Small, infested items can be frozen to kill existing beetles and grubs in the wood. Keep the articles in the freezer at or below 0°F (18°C) for 72 hours. Or, they may be heated in an oven at 120° to 140°F (49° to 60°C) for 6 hours. Wood thicker than 2 inches (5 cm), may require longer treatment times.

Destroy infested wood by burning it or taking it to a landfill area, if possible. If removal is not possible, liquid insecticides registered for use on wood-boring beetles may be used.

Carpenter Ants

Carpenter ants (*Camponotus* spp.) are distinguished from household ants and included among the wood-destroyers because of their nesting habits. They can invade buildings and may cause serious structural damage when they bore into wood, hollowing it out to build their nests. Unlike termites, carpenter ants do not actually eat wood, but they excavate galleries in it to rear their young. If main structural beams are hollowed out, unsafe conditions can occur. As carpenter ants expand their nesting facilities, they remove wood and eject it in the form of coarse sawdust. The sawdust they produce is distinctly different from the frass produced by termites. Carpenter ant frass usually contains body parts of dead ants and other insects mixed in with tiny pieces of wood. Carpenter ants also nest in wall voids, hollow doors, cracks, and crevices, furniture, and termite galleries.

Nests constructed indoors may be satellite colonies of a larger outdoor nest located near the house, usually in trees or stacked wood. Several satellite nests may be associated with a single-parent nest that contains the queen, and ants usually maintain a trail between the satellite and parent nest. Peak traffic occurs at night. Outdoors, carpenter ants feed on dead and living insects. They also collect honeydew from aphids and can often be observed tending them. Aphids are small plant-sucking, soft-bodied true bugs that excrete copious quantities of honeydew, rich in sugars. Husbandry of aphids by ants is usually viewed as detrimental to the host plants because the aphid population usually grows under the ants' protection, and aphids damage plant tissue. In contrast, aphid husbandry may be beneficial because the ants kill many phytophagous (plant-eating) insects that destroy the host plants. Indoors, carpenter ants feed on any sweets, juices of ripe fruit, and household food scraps. Sometimes, they enter buildings searching for food.

Most carpenter ants are dark brown or black; others may have reddish coloration along with black so that they appear two-toned. They can be very large, ranging from $^3/_{16}$ to $^5/_8$ inch (5 to 16 mm) long. They are found throughout California, particularly in the foothills and mountains, but they may also invade buildings in urban locations. Infestations can occur in new buildings when land clearing disturbs native colonies. In the wild, carpenter ants nest in soil, beneath rocks, and in living and dead trees and stumps. Carpenter ants do not sting, but they can inflict a painful bite when handled and can emit a noxious secretion (formic acid) when disturbed.

To exclude carpenter ants from buildings, caulk cracks and crevices. Trim tree limbs and shrubs that touch the building to prevent ants from gaining access via landscape plants. Use an inorganic mulch (gravel or stones) around the house perimeter to discourage nesting. Inside the house, store sweet foodstuffs in sealed containers. When colonies are found inside tree stumps, destroy them. Eliminate damp conditions that promote wood decay. Replace decayed or damaged wood, and correct problems that caused the decay, if possible. Physically remove nests and use a vacuum to collect ants. Discourage carpenter ant colonies by unclogging rain gutters, increasing ventilation to damp areas beneath the building and in attics, and storing firewood off the ground and more than 100 yards (90 m) away from the house. Use decorative wood in the landscape near the home with caution, recognizing that it may harbor carpenter ants and that it offers a convenient site for colony establishment.

For effective control, it is important to locate both the parent and satellite colonies by observing ant trails, especially at night. Trails may lead from the house to evergreen trees and shrubs. Inside the house, carpenter ants often travel along the tops of water pipes and electrical wires. These go through floor and wall joists and give ants easy access to all parts of the house. Try to find gallery openings, which are small oval holes. Look for sawdust accumulations near these openings. To locate nests, tap floor joists with a metal rod or hammer and listen for differences in sound; a nest cavity will give a hollow ring. In addition, tapping disturbs the ants, causing them to create

their own tapping and rustling noises, which can be heard. A knife blade will readily penetrate infested wood.

Once the parent and satellite nests are located, chemical treatment can provide good control when applied directly to the colonies, trails, and perimeter of the house (against the foundation and inside the foundation if the house has a crawl space instead of a basement). Desiccant dusts or insecticide formulations may be applied through gallery openings and other holes drilled into galleries. Desiccant dusts are inert dusts combined with absorptive powders (diatomaceous earth or silica gel) that kill insects by removing their protective outer body cover, causing them to desiccate. Although desiccant dusts are low in toxicity to humans, they should not be inhaled because they can seriously irritate lung tissue. Unless they get wet, desiccant dusts do not lose effectiveness over time.

Because these ants frequently follow electrical lines, remove electrical plates and apply insecticide dust through the access into the void between the walls. Unlike sprays, dusts will not cause electrical shorts when applied into the wall void onto electrical wires. Nevertheless, as a safety precaution, turn off the main power switch prior to treatment.

Dust formulations of certain insecticides can be very effective against ants because ants are hairy and the dust adheres to their body surfaces. Certain materials must be applied by a licensed applicator.

Carpenter Bees

Carpenter bees (*Xylocopa* spp.) (fig. 8.17), which are similar in appearance to bumble bees (see fig. 8.3), build their nests in wood and weaken wooden structures but rarely cause severe damage. They help pollinate various crop and landscape plants. Carpenter bees are about 1 inch (2.5 cm) long and are blue-black with a green or purplish metallic sheen. The thorax is covered with bright yellow, orange, or white hairs. Unlike bumble bees, carpenter bees have a shiny, hairless abdomen. Males fly around aggressively, but they lack a stinger. Females rarely sting.

Carpenter bees weaken structural wood as they build nests, and they leave ugly holes and stains on building surfaces. They usually choose unpainted, sound wood for nesting sites, preferring softer woods, such as southern yellow pine, white pine, California redwood, cedar, ash, cypress, Douglas-fir, mimosa, mulberry, and pecan. They avoid harder woods.

Female carpenter bees bore into sound or sometimes decaying wood to make their nests, which consist of tunnels about ½ inch (1.2 cm) in diameter and 6 to 10 inches (15 to 25 cm) deep, partitioned into several chambers (cells), each containing an egg and food, which consists of pollen and regurgitated nectar. Development from egg to adult takes about 3 months, but there is only one generation per year. Adults emerge in spring and mate. Females place food provisions into the tunnels, lay eggs on top of the food mass, and close each cell with wood pulp. Each female may have 6 to 8 sealed brood cells in a linear row in one gallery. Female carpenter bees excavate the galleries at a rate of about 1 inch (2.5 cm) every 6 days. Larvae develop on the food mass, and new adults chew through the cell partitions. Adults overwinter in old tunnels.

Figure 8.17

Carpenter bee.

Figure 8.18

Larva and adult of the Western horntail wasp, a common wood wasp.

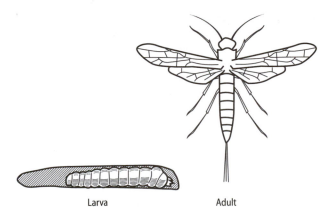

Larva   Adult

Prevention is the primary management strategy. Exterior wood should be hardwoods, which are not normally attacked by carpenter bees. Paint or varnish exposed wood surfaces to reduce weathering and the likelihood of attack. Fill depressions and cracks in wood surfaces so they are less attractive to bees. Fill unoccupied holes with steel wool and caulk to prevent reuse. After bees have emerged, fill the tunnels and paint or varnish the repaired surfaces. Wire screening or metal flashing protects timber ends.

Although preventive measures are usually sufficient, liquid or dust insecticide formulations or desiccant dusts (see "Carpenter Ants," above) may be effective if an infestation is severe. After the brood is killed, repair holes with steel wool and wood filler, and then repaint or varnish the repaired surfaces.

Wood Wasps (Horntails)

Several kinds of wood-boring insects that infest lumber are described as "wood wasps"; they are also known as horntails (fig. 8.18). About a dozen species of large, nonstinging wasps in California (Families Siricidae, Xiphydriidae, Anaxyelidae, and Orussidae) complete their life cycles in recently dead or dying conifer trees and may infest lumber weakened by fire, disease, or attack from other insects.

In buildings constructed with infested lumber, these wasps may eventually emerge as adults in completed buildings up to 2 to 3 years after construction. Emerging adults, which are 1 inch (2.5 cm) long and often black or metallic dark blue, will fly away and leave perfectly round, clean-cut exit holes about ¼ inch (6 mm) in diameter.

Although the flying adults may appear frightening because the female's long ovipositor (egg-laying apparatus) looks like an enormous stinger, these wasps do not sting or bite people, nor are they harmful to buildings. The holes leave cosmetic damage, defacing floors, walls, and interior surfaces, but wood wasps do not reinfest seasoned dry wood, and the larvae rarely create any structural damage. Holes in wood can be filled and refinished.

Life Cycle. Female wood wasps insert their ovipositors nearly ¾ inch (1.9 cm) into wood of weakened or decaying conifer trees and lay one to seven eggs, which hatch in 3 to 4 weeks. Larvae tunnel into wood parallel with the grain, chewing the softer sapwood just under the bark, move into the heartwood, and return to the sapwood to complete feeding. Development into pupae may take 2 to 5 years. After 5 to 6 weeks as a pupa, an adult emerges by chewing a round exit hole through about ¾ inch (1.9 cm) of wood.

Management. Wood wasps can occur anywhere infested lumber is used for construction. In an infested building, the only management strategy is to wait until the life cycle is complete and repair the resulting cosmetic damage after adults emerge from their exit holes. The most effective method of preventing wood wasp activity is the application of heat to lumber. Larvae cannot survive in lumber kiln-dried at temperatures in excess of 150°F (66°C) for 2 hours. Temperatures of 170°F (77°C) are recommended as an additional safety factor. The moisture content of the wood, its thickness, the kiln's efficiency, and the temperature of the wood when introduced into the kiln will determine how long treatment is required before the optimal temperature is reached.

Household Ants

Ants are prevalent pests in buildings, where they can find food and water; they are common inhabitants of households, hospitals, restaurants, offices, and warehouses. Once ants establish a colony in a particular location, they can be difficult to control. Some ant species are considered beneficial because they can feed on termites and fleas and other dead insects, but ants can also be serious problem pests because they contaminate human food in the house; damage lawns, gardens, seedbeds, and orchards by their nesting habits; and destroy plants, fruits, seeds, and nuts by their foraging habits. Ants protect honeydew-producing insect pests such as aphids, whiteflies, soft scales, and mealybugs from their natural enemies, which can lead to increased damage from these pests.

About 200 species of ants exist in California, but fewer than a dozen are important pests (table 8.5). The most common ant that invades households, landscaped areas, and agricultural settings in California is the Argentine ant (*Linepithema humile,* formerly *Iridomyrmex humilis*), a dull brown-colored ant. Argentine ants tend to move rapidly in distinctive trails. Long trails of hundreds of ants may lead from nests to favored food sources, such as syrup, honey, fruit juice, fruits, and sugar and other sweet things to eat. Besides recruitment to food sources, Argentine ants also trail to water in hot, dry weather. Argentine ants reproduce by budding, whereby a large colony with many queens may break up into smaller colonies.

Other common ant pests are the Pharaoh ant (*Monomorium pharaonis*), the odorous house ant (*Tapinoma sessile*), the thief ant (*Solenopsis molesta*), the California harvester ant (*Pogonomyrmex californicus*), the pavement ant (*Tetramorium caespitum*), and the Southern fire ant (*Solenopsis xyloni*). Red imported fire ants (*Solenopsis invicta*) have been introduced into California and are now present in several counties. These invasive ants are infamous for their painful stings as well as their economic impact on urban, agricultural, and wildlife environments.

The odorous house ant ranks second to the Argentine ant as a household pest. Odorous house ants are shiny black to dark brown and produce a strong coconutlike odor when crushed. They also follow distinct trails. Thief ants resemble small Pharaoh ants but have a two-segmented club on their antennae versus the three-segmented club of the Pharaoh ant. They often enter houses to feed on grease, cheese, animal matter, or sweets and can be a serious household pest. Pavement ants are found primarily in the Central Valley. They often invade households and nest in lawns, sidewalks, and orchards, feeding on honeydew, sweets, insects, nuts, and dried or fresh fruit.

Pharaoh ants are thought to be African in origin. Their name originated with Linnaeus and the belief that these ants were one of the original plagues, along with flies and locusts, during the reign of the Egyptian pharaohs. Pharaoh ants are problems in the household because of their preference for sweets (syrup, sugar, honey, cake), grease, meat, and fat. They can also pose a serious health threat in hospitals and veterinary clinics because they are attracted to intravenous units, medical preparations, and open wounds.

Although ants can bite with their pincerlike jaws, most species rarely bite, but a few species sting. The Southern fire ant, which is mainly an outdoor species, has a shiny red head and thorax and black abdomen. It is found from Southern California to the Sacramento Valley in households, landscaped areas, and agricultural settings. One of California's

Table 8.5

COMMON ANTS OF CALIFORNIA

Common name (Scientific name)	Description
Argentine ant (*Linepithema humile*, formerly *Iridomyrmex humilis*) 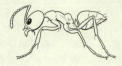	Node erect. Dull brown ants with erect node on waist that produce a slightly musty odor when crushed. Found throughout California. Worker ants move rapidly on distinct trails. One of California's most serious ant pests, invading households, landscaped areas, and agricultural settings seeking honeydew, sweets, and insects. Generally do not bite.
California harvester ant (*Pogonomyrmex californicus*)	Shiny red, hairy ants, 1/5 to 1/4 inch (5.5 to 6 mm), with large heads and mandibles. Found throughout California. Do not run in trails. Nest in large colonies with several openings with chaff and debris piles nearby. Bite or sting quite painfully, quite pugnacious. Harvest seeds and dead insects.
carpenter ant (*Camponotus* spp.)	Large (>6 mm [1/4 inch]), black or black and red ants found throughout California, particularly in the foothills and mountains. Thorax smooth and convex. Nests often associated with wood, but may also be located in the soil. Often found in wooden structures and houses.
pavement ant (*Tetramorium caespitum*)	Workers 1/12 to 1/8 inch (2 to 3 m) long, dull blackish brown. Head and thorax with many parallel furrows. Found in the Central Valley, often invading households. Nests in lawns, under stones, in sidewalks, and in orchards. Feeds on honeydew, sweets, insects, nuts, and dried or fresh fruit.
Pharaoh ant (*Monomorium pharaonis*) 	Workers are 1/25 to 1/16 inch (1 to 1.5 mm) long. Yellowish, shiny with 13-segmented antennae with 3-segmented club. Usually with rear portion of abdomen darker colored than remainder of body. Behavior similar to thief ant.
red imported fire ant (*Solenopsis invicta*)	Workers polymorphic, (3-6 mm) long, almost uniform dark reddish brown; 10-segmented antennae with a two-segmented club. In the late 1990s imported fire ants were found in Kern, Fresno, Orange, Riverside, Los Angeles, and Santa Barbara Counties. Imported fire ants can build large mounds. Worker ants are aggressive and can sting, commonly causing a white pustule to form. If red imported fire ants are suspected, call California Department of Food and Agriculture Pest Hotline at 1-800-491-1899.
Southern fire ant, California fire ant (*Solenopsis xyloni*)	Workers polymorphic, 1/10 to 1/6 inch (2.5 to 4.5 mm) long, with shiny red head and thorax and black abdomen. Entire body covered with golden hairs; 10-segmented antennae with a 2-segmented club. Found from southern California to Sacramento Valley. Active in morning and evening, but will swarm out of nests at midday if disturbed. Nest are flattened, irregular craters usually located in warm, sunny areas but sometimes in wood or masonry. May bite or sting when provoked. One of California's most serious ant pests, feeding on seeds, almonds, young tree bark, honeydew, and other sweet substances. May be found in households, landscaped areas, and agricultural settings.
thief ant (*Solenopsis molesta*) 	Workers extremely small, 1/25 to 1/16 inch (1 to 1.5 mm) long. Yellowish, shiny with 10-segmented antennae with 2-segmented club. Found throughout California in nests of other ants or in their own nest. Often enter houses to feed on grease, cheese, and animal matter or sweets; can be a serious household pest. Also feed on germinating seeds.

Source: Klotz n.d., n.p.

most serious ant pests, feeding on seeds, almonds, young tree bark, honeydew, and other sweets, the Southern fire ant is active in the morning and evening but swarms out of the nest in midday if disturbed. Nests are usually located in warm, sunny areas, but sometimes can be found in wood or masonry. All fire ants are characterized by a two-segmented petiole (the narrow waist between the thorax and the abdomen), ten-segmented antennae with a two-segmented club, and a sting. The red imported fire ant is very similar in appearance to the Southern fire ant, but it differs in that it is almost uniformly dark reddish-brown as opposed to shiny red. Also, Southern fire ant mounds are irregular craters, while red imported fire ant mounds are frequently built up into domes.

Found throughout the state, California harvester ants are shiny, red, hairy, with painful stings. They do not move in trails but nest in large colonies that have several openings with chaff and debris piles nearby. They harvest seeds and dead insects. California is home to several other species of harvester ants that vary in color and are also capable of stinging.

The life cycle of the Argentine ant is depicted in figure 8.19. All ants undergo complete metamorphosis. Larvae are wormlike and immobile and do not resemble adults. Development from egg to adult may take from 6 weeks to 2 months in some species.

Ant Society

Ants are social insects that live in communities (colonies) with duties divided among three different castes of adults (queens, workers, and males). The life span varies, depending on the caste. Queens oversee the reproductive functions of the colony; they mate with males, lay eggs, and sometimes participate in feeding and grooming larvae. Queens are larger than other ants and typically have wings until they mate. Depending on the species, ants may have one or more queens within a nest. Workers are sterile females and make up the bulk of the colony's population. They gather food, care for and feed larvae predigested and regurgitated food, build tunnels, and repair and defend the colony. Males are few in number and do not participate in colony activities. The only role that males seem to have is to mate with queens; they die after mating.

Depending on the species, workers may resemble each other or be variable in size and appearance. Adult workers of the Argentine ant and odorous house ant are about 1/8 inch (3 mm) long and range from light to dark brown. Workers of the Pharaoh and thief ant are smaller, about 1/16 inch (1.5 mm) long, and are monomorphic (one size). Workers of the Southern fire ant have a red head and thorax but a black abdomen; they are polymorphic (many-sized), ranging from 1/10 to 3/16 inch (2.5 to 4.5 mm) long. The red imported fire ant is also polymorphic and is 1/8 to 1/4 inch (3 to 6 mm) long.

Workers locate food by random searching. When a scout finds food that seems promising, she may carry some back to the nest and also leave a scent trail that other workers can follow to the food source. A worker transports water and honeydew to the colony in her crop, which is a specialized storage chamber in her abdomen.

Ants set up new colonies primarily by two methods. In harvester ants, odorous house ants and fire ants, winged reproductives leave the nest on mating flights and establish colonies in new locations. New colonies are established by a single, newly mated queen. She lays her first eggs after weeks or months of confinement under ground. After the eggs hatch, she feeds the white, legless larvae, unaided by workers and using her own salivary secretions, with nutrients from her fat reserves and degenerating wing muscles. The larvae transform into pupae, which transform

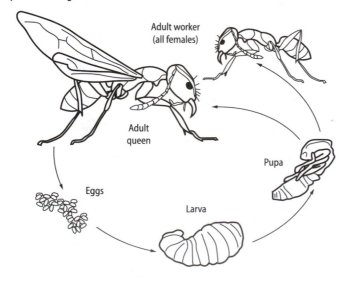

Figure 8.19

Life cycle of the Argentine ant.

Adult worker
(all females)

Adult queen

Pupa

Eggs

Larva

into sterile female adult workers that dig their way out of the nest to collect food for themselves, for the queen (who continues to lay eggs), and for the next larval generation. As the population increases, new chambers and galleries are added to the nest. After a few years, the colony begins to produce winged males and queens that leave the nest to mate and form new colonies.

The second method, budding, which is employed by Pharaoh and Argentine ants and sometimes by red imported fire ants, occurs when one or more queens leave the nest with workers who aid in establishing and caring for the new colony. The life span of a colony may extend over a period of years. Depending on the species, time of year, and food availability, the population of a colony may range from a dozen to thousands of individuals.

Household ants often nest outdoors in soil next to buildings, along sidewalks, and near food sources (plants) that harbor honeydew-producing aphids and soft scales.

Management of Household Ants

Management of household ants requires diligence and the combined use of sanitation, exclusion, and chemical control. The best approach is cleanliness. Focus on excluding ants from buildings, valuable plants, and food and water sources. It is unrealistic to expect to eliminate household ants from the outdoor area around your home.

Inspection. Keep records of where ants have been seen in and around the home. They are often found where food and water are consistently available (near leaky faucets, pet food dishes, and food crumbs). Reduce moisture sources (condensation and leaks) that provide water for ants. For species that follow definite trails, try to follow them to the nest. Because they like to watch ants, children often can be very helpful in monitoring ant movements and tracing their trails. Ants may nest in wall voids, behind baseboards, or under the house. Ant trails may enter through a crack, but the nest may be some distance away: some ant species forage long distances from their nesting site. Outdoors, you can try to locate ant nests by taking note of their excavations. Fire ants build conspicuous nests but other ants may construct nests next to or under the house foundation, under sidewalks, driveways and patios, or in decaying logs or tree trunks.

Exclusion and Sanitation. An effective nonchemical technique for ant control is pest-proofing, or exclusion, that is, finding out where the ants are getting into a structure and then sealing or caulking that area. In their natural habitat, foraging ants prefer to follow preexisting edges and other structural features in the environment to and from their nest. This natural behavior predisposes ants to travel along structural elements that we create in the urban environment such as wires, pipes, and conduits. An effective strategy for keeping out ants is pestproofing at the points of entry of these utility lines into a structure. Caulk cracks and crevices around the foundations of buildings and eliminate cracks and crevices in kitchens and other food preparation and storage areas. Store foods that are attractive to ants (sugar, syrup, honey, and other sweets) in closed containers that have been washed to remove any residue from outer surfaces. Rinse empty soft drink cans and bottles before putting them in the recycling bin. Do not store garbage indoors, and be thorough in cleaning up grease and spills. Inspect potted indoor plants for evidence of infestation. If ants are nesting in the soil, discard the plant, or place the plant in a bucket or plastic trash can outdoors and fill the container with water to the top of the house plant pot to force the ants out of the soil. Wash the container in soapy water. Do not plant trees and shrubs that are highly susceptible to aphid infestation next to buildings.

Baits. Baits capitalize on the social behavior of ants, whereby scout ants recruit nestmates to a newly discovered bait, and the recruits return to a centrally located nest to share the bait with the rest of the colony. Toxic baits (stakes, granules, or bait stations) can be effective in controlling ants because they get poison into the nests when nests are difficult to find or treat directly. Control may take several weeks. When other food sources are not available, workers are attracted to the bait, carry it back to the nest, and give it to other workers, larvae, and reproductive forms, leading to elimination of the entire colony. Because ants will not eat bait if more attractive food sources are nearby, sanitation must precede baiting. Be sure to remove any particles of food or other sweet substances from cracks around sinks, pantries, and other areas.

Bait stations used indoors should be placed so that they are accessible to ant pests but not accessible to small children or pets. The effectiveness of baits varies with the ant species, the bait material, and the availability of alternative food sources.

Outdoors, bait stations should be placed around the foundation and at nest openings, if they can be found. Ant stakes (enclosed bait) may be placed near nests or on ant trails beneath plants. For the most effective and economical control, treat in early spring when ant populations are low.

Insecticides. If necessary, an insecticide labeled for ant control can immediately kill foraging ants while sanitation and exclusion measures are being implemented. However, mopping or cleaning with soapy water may eliminate the need for insecticide because the cleaning treatment removes the ants' scent trail and washes ants away from the area.

When insecticides are used they should be applied along wires, pipes, supports, etc., to optimize efficacy and minimize the amount used. Dust is an excellent formulation for this purpose. Ants readily pick up dusts that are lightly applied to their trailways. Ideally, dusts should be applied during construction when there is easy access to wall voids, but they can also be applied for remedial treatment.

To prevent ants from entering a building, spot applications of insecticide may be sprayed at entry points. Pyrethroids are good insecticides for this purpose because they are generally very repellent. Read and follow label directions precisely. To control outdoor colonies, apply insecticides directly to nests. If buildings are on a raised foundation, treat crawl spaces with a dust formulation.

Plants covered with ants may indicate that the plants are harboring honeydew-producing aphids or soft scales. Banding tree trunks with sticky substances keeps these ants out of trees. Young or sensitive trees can be protected by wrapping the trunk with a collar of duct tape or fabric tree wrap and coating it with the sticky material. Inspect the sticky material once every 2 weeks to make sure that it is not clogged with debris or dead ants that would allow ants to cross.

Frequently Asked Questions about Ants

Q. Do colonies of ants sometimes migrate to new locations?

A. Ants can move an entire colony to a new, more favorable location, if necessary. Ants may enter buildings suddenly to seek food, water, warmth, and shelter from environmental conditions outdoors (flooding, lack of food, or hot, cold, or dry weather,). Pharaoh ants like warmth and make nests inside buildings in wall voids, under flooring, or near hot-water pipes and heating systems.

Q. What are the dietary preferences of ants?

A. Like all living organisms, ants have certain nutritional requirements: carbohydrates, proteins, and fats. In nature, they obtain these essential nutrients from a varied diet of insect prey (proteins and fats), nectar, aphid honeydew, and other plant products (carbohydrates). These nutrients are found in either liquid or solid form. Although ants naturally strive for a balanced diet to optimize the growth of the colony, the amount of each of these three dietary requirements necessary for optimal growth may vary seasonally. For example, "bait switching" is well documented in some species of ants that have satisfied their appetite for one food and then choose another. As structural pests, the ants' opportunity to achieve a balanced diet is limited only by sanitation practices and the baits used to control them. Ideally, sanitation problems can be corrected, so that baits do not have to compete with other food items, thus forcing the ants to feed on whatever bait is provided.

Q. What do ant baits contain?

A. A bait for ants consists of four basic components: an attractant, usually a food that prompts ants to pick up the bait readily; a palatable carrier, which gives the physical structure, or matrix, to the bait; other materials added for reasons of formulation, such as emulsifiers, preservatives, waterproofing, or antimicrobial agents; and a toxicant, which should be nonrepellent and provide delayed action. A delayed-action toxin will allow time for the ants to share their food and spread the poison throughout the colony before it begins to kill them.

Q. **How is trailing behavior in ants important for their control?**

A. Trailing ants can lead you to their nest, where they can then be treated. Trails may also indicate where ants are getting into or onto a structure. A tree limb touching a roof is a good physical trailway for ants to crawl onto a structure. Trimming vegetation away from a structure eliminates this potential problem. Frequently, ants enter a structure by following utility lines. Sealing the points where these lines enter the structure closes these entrance holes. These nonchemical measures can help control or prevent ant infestations.

Q. **Are insecticidal dusts good for treating ant infestations?**

A. Using dusts for ant control has several advantages. Dusts "float" into areas such as voids where sprays cannot effectively penetrate. Active dust particles remain available on surfaces and are not absorbed. In addition, the static electricity of the tiny dust particles makes them stick to vertical surfaces, resulting in good coverage. Dusts provide long residual life, as long as they stay dry. Some inorganics, such as boric acid, may remain effective for the lifetime of a structure. Dusts are easily picked up by ants, partly because of the many hair bristles on an ant's body and also because the electrical charge of the dust particles causes them to stick to the ant. Dusts eliminate the risk of electrical shorting that may occur with liquid sprays. These advantages are realized only if dusts are applied properly. The most commonly made mistake is over-application. Dust should be applied in very light, thin layers because they become repellent—especially to ants—when applied heavily.

Q. **What is a barrier or perimeter treatment for ants?**

A. A barrier spray is a band of insecticide applied around the outside perimeter of a structure to act as a barrier to any ants attempting to cross it. The choice of insecticide and formulation is an important consideration. It is best to choose one with a long residual effect, so that it will persist over as much of the active season as possible. Additionally, the insecticide should be readily picked up by the ants.

Q. **What is meant by integrated pest management of ants?**

A. The objective of any integrated pest management (IPM) system is to protect human health and property from pests in the yard, home, institutions, industry, and community by using techniques that are the least environmentally disruptive but are also effective and economical. Three general methods are available for control of urban ants. *Habitat modification* is habitat destruction or environmental modification, so that conditions are no longer suitable for ants. *Mechanical methods* include the use of traps, screens, barriers and other mechanical devices or construction practices to prevent or exclude ants. *Chemical methods* use baits, contact sprays, and repellents to control ants.

Pests of Pets

The primary pests of pets are fleas, ticks, mites, lice, mosquitoes, and flies. The cost of controlling arthropod pests of dogs and cats combined with prevention and treatment of their associated diseases is estimated at $11 billion per year.

Fleas

Fleas are the most common, annoying, and costly pest of dogs and cats because they bite these animals and their owners. Fleas are second only to ants in the number of inquiries handled by UC Cooperative Extension. Members of the order Siphonaptera, fleas are small (<¼ inch [6 mm]), wingless insects that are obligate ectoparasites of mammals (dogs, cats, and humans) and birds. Four types of fleas that attack companion animals are the cat flea (*Ctenocephalides felis*), the dog flea (*C. canis*), the human flea (*Pulex simulans*), and the sticktight flea of poultry (*Echidnophaga gallinacea*). Cat and dog fleas are almost indistinguishable physically. The human flea can be found on swine and may transfer to dogs. The sticktight flea is usually found on poultry, but can be a pest of dogs and cats that associate with infested chickens, and it is also found on ground squirrels. Sticktight fleas typically attach to the face and ear margins of cats and dogs and between the toes of dogs.

Figure 8.20

Cat flea.

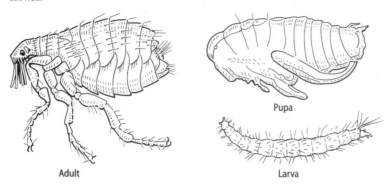

Adult

Pupa

Larva

Cat Flea. The cat flea is the most common ectoparasite of cats and dogs in the United States (fig. 8.20). The dog flea is primarily found in Europe; cat fleas infest both dogs and cats in the United States. Occasionally, other flea species invade the home (as from rats nesting in the attic, for instance), but this is the exception.

Depending on climate, the cat flea can be a year-round or seasonal pest. Because of its lack of host specificity and tendency to feed on humans, the cat flea is a pest of companion animals and their owners. Reactions of humans to flea bites vary from individual to individual, ranging from simple irritation caused by the mechanical injury of the mouthparts piercing the skin, to severe rash, itching, and prolonged allergic response to the flea's salivary secretions.

Biology. Unlike rodent fleas and other nest fleas, adult cat fleas spend their entire lives on the host, feeding, mating, and reproducing. Female fleas lay eggs that sift through the coat of the pet and collect in the environment. Simultaneously, adult flea feces collected in the coat fall into the same environment and serve as food for flea larvae when they hatch from the eggs. Typically, the eggs hatch within 24 to 72 hours of being laid.

Larvae are white, soft-bodied, and about ⅛ inch (3 mm) long. The larvae complete three instars in as little as 10 days under favorable conditions. Cooler temperatures, lack of food, or other unsuitable environmental conditions may increase the larval developmental time to several weeks or months.

The third instar voids its gut approximately 24 hours before initiating cocoon construction.

The white prepupa wanders until it locates an appropriate site for pupation and then begins to spin a cocoon from silk that it produces itself, much as a caterpillar does when it gets ready to pupate and turn into a moth. Under good conditions, within about 4 days, the larva molts and is transformed into the pupa and continues metamorphosis to the adult flea. Frequently, debris from the surroundings is incorporated into the cocoon, adhering to the sticky silk fibers, so that the cocoon may appear as a small dirt clod, carpet fuzz, or lint ball. Careful examination will seldom reveal a flea cocoon, even if a home is heavily infested with fleas, because cocoons are constructed at the base of carpet fibers.

Once the adult flea is formed, it can remain within the cocoon for weeks or months, depending on environmental conditions. This preemerged adult stage is the most variable in the life cycle of the flea, ranging from less than a day to several months (or perhaps a year). The mechanisms are not understood, but it appears that some individuals are programmed to delay emergence. It may be a survival strategy whereby offspring emerge over an extended interval, increasing the odds that some successfully encounter hosts. Mechanical stimuli (such as vacuuming) or increased carbon dioxide concentration, or warmth, or movement have been demonstrated to serve as releasers, causing the adult flea to emerge from the cocoon. Obviously, these stimuli are triggers associated with a mammalian host. If the flea emerges and does not locate a host immediately, it can survive for approximately a week to 10 days or possibly longer under conditions of high humidity and favorable temperatures. If it fails to find a host, it will die of starvation within a couple of weeks.

When an adult flea attaches to a host, it begins to feed and mate and females begin egg-laying within a couple of days. If a flea is dislodged from its host after initiating feeding, its survival time is greatly reduced, unless it can regain a host. On the host, a female flea averages about one egg per hour. The eggs are deposited in the coat of the host, sift through the hair, and fall off. Because a female flea can live for several weeks, her potential production can be more than 1,000 eggs. The actual egg production per female lifetime is usually less than 200 eggs because host grooming is a significant mortality factor for adult fleas. Most fleas are removed by the host within a week, cats are estimated to consume half the fleas on their bodies within a week through grooming.

When adult fleas bite, the cutting blades of their mouthparts, the maxillae, pierce the skin of the host and a salivary secretion is injected to prevent blood clotting. Many people who have been bitten by fleas have called this secretion the most irritating substance known to man. Fleas use a pumping action to create a vacuum and then draw the host's blood into their mouths. As adult fleas feed, they produce feces that consist of partially digested blood, which serve as food for developing flea larvae. Coils of feces are extruded from the anus of the adult as it feeds on the host. The feces dry and sift through the coat of the pet to collect beneath, in the rug, bedding, carpet, or yard. As the pet moves on, both flea feces and eggs are left behind. When larvae hatch from the eggs, they are surrounded by this fecal food source. One important function of vacuuming is to remove this source of food so that larvae starve to death.

Tapeworms and flea allergy dermatitis. Cat fleas are the obligate intermediate hosts of the dog tapeworm (*Dipylidium caninum*), which means that they are the source of transmission of this tapeworm that infects both dogs and cats. In fact, the flea and the tapeworm have evolved a very complex interrelationship. The tapeworm lives in the gut of the cat or dog, but how does it get there? Periodically, portions of the tapeworm break off and migrate down the intestine of the pet animal and crawl out the anus. Once outside, it dries into what is known as a tapeworm proglottid, which looks like a sesame seed. Proglottids collect wherever the pet animal spends a lot of time, such as in bedding. Flea larvae, in their indiscriminate feeding on organic debris in the environment, can encounter and bite into tapeworm proglottids, thereby ingesting the tapeworm eggs inside the proglottids (from 5 to 30 eggs per capsule). The tapeworm eggs hatch inside the flea larvae, and the tapeworm enters into a quiescent state as the flea goes through its subsequent metamorphosis.

Larval tapeworms complete their development in the adult flea. While grooming, a cat or dog can ingest a tapeworm-infected adult flea. When a cat or dog swallows an infected flea, the cat or dog becomes infected with tapeworms. When the infected flea reaches the dog or cat's intestines, the tapeworm emerges and attaches to the intestinal wall. As the tape-

worm matures, terminal segments fill with eggs, break off, and travel down the intestinal tract. The proglottids actively crawl out of the anus and quickly dry to the characteristic egg packets upon exposure to air and are ready to be eaten by flea larvae and begin a new cycle of infection.

This remarkable scenario is the only way the animal can become infected with tapeworms. A cat or dog does not become infected by eating proglottids, because the tapeworm eggs must hatch and go through certain developmental stages within the flea before they can infect a cat or dog. The only way to prevent infestation with the dog tapeworm is to control fleas.

Some animals are highly allergic to the salivary secretions of fleas, resulting in a condition called flea allergy dermatitis. It is more common in dogs than in cats and can be extremely debilitating. In response to a single flea bite, some flea-allergic dogs will scratch and bite themselves until they have open, running sores that can lead to secondary bacterial skin infection. Animals have been euthanized because the owner could not bear to see the suffering. Flea allergy dermatitis (miliary dermatitis, weeping dermatitis) is a severe condition in which hyperallergenicity causes the exaggerated responses to the flea allergen. Your veterinarian can refer you to a veterinary dermatologist who can assist you in attempting to alleviate the severe reaction your pet experiences to fleas. Until an immunotherapy is developed to cope with flea allergy dermatitis, the most successful treatment is prevention—doing everything you can to prevent your pet from being bitten by even a single flea, which means ridding fleas from the animal's environment.

Flea control. Annual expenditures for flea control in the United States, including homeowner markets, veterinary suppliers, and pest control companies, exceed $4.6 billion. In some areas of the country, fleas and the diseases associated with them make up more than half of the caseload of veterinary practices. More money and energy are spent battling fleas than any other problem in veterinary medicine.

Because the adult flea is the pest stage, it is the object of most control efforts. However, adult fleas on the pet animal are not the only problem; fleas in the environment also need to be controlled. Because fleas must have blood from a mammalian host to survive, treating host animals is the most efficient and effective means of suppressing fleas. There are several on-animal products that are effective for flea control. Many contain pyrethrins, which are safe, effective products, but they kill only the fleas on the animal at the time of treatment and do not provide residual control. Other over-the-counter compounds include spot-on permethrin products; notice that the labels caution against use on cats as these products can be lethal. Always read and follow label directions.

Your veterinarian can recommend products that provide several weeks of flea control with a single application. Products prescribed by veterinarians for on-animal flea control are applied in a small volume (a few milliliters) on the back of the animal's neck. The material then distributes over the surface of the body in skin oils. In addition to the spot-on formulation, some products are available as sprays. These adulticides kill all fleas on the animal within a few hours, then provide residual flea suppression for several weeks. While most flea products are not effective against ticks, there are now some that demonstrate a high level of tick control, but they must be applied more frequently than for flea suppression. Ask your veterinarian to recommend a product that suppresses ticks.

To forestall flea infestations, pets can be started on flea developmental inhibitors early in the season to prevent a flea problem from developing. Products containing insect development inhibitors are given orally, as a monthly pill for dogs or a liquid added to a cat's food, or as a 6-month-injectable formulation for cats. Any flea that feeds on the blood of treated animals subsequently is unable to reproduce.

Once the pets have been treated, it will take a while for fleas in the environment to die and numbers to decline. Meanwhile, as they emerge, fleas will hop onto the animal; the host will continue to "harvest" fleas in the environment until they have been killed and no more are emerging.

On-pet control measures. At the same time that the premises are treated, it is necessary to treat the pet. Two types of pills are available for flea control. One contains an insect growth regulator (a chitin synthesis inhibitor) that does not kill fleas but prevents them from reproducing. This product is safe for the pet

and is convenient, because the pill is taken only once a month. A second type of pill contains an organophosphate insecticide. It is a prescription medication available only through your veterinarian. It is not registered for cats. When given orally to a dog, it causes the animal's blood to be lethal to fleas that consume it. After sucking the blood, the flea will die, but because it has already injected its salivary secretions into the dog, flea-allergic dogs will react anyway. It is important not to expose a dog that is taking this medication to any other organophosphates (by attaching an organophosphate-containing flea collar, spraying the home for cockroaches or fleas, or treating the yard, etc.). Exposure to any additional organophosphates could kill the dog.

Outdoor control measures. Outdoor flea control can be the most challenging of the three components of flea control. The primary thing to remember is that fleas will exist where the eggs were laid. Because the eggs are laid on the pet and fall off into the soil, most flea development is going to occur where the pet spends a lot of time. If the pet naps under the porch, then hundreds of flea larvae are developing under there. When they mature into adult fleas and seek a host, they emerge and move toward anything warm and moving. So, they hop on you as you approach the steps. Be sure to treat such areas as under porches and in the crawl spaces beneath the house. These are ideal places for flea development and frequently serve as a source for continual reinfestation. Outdoors, flea larvae are often located in specific microhabitats, such as under shrubs and porches. Keep animals away from treated areas until they have dried completely (this period is a good time to take pets to the kennel to be dipped). Any questions should be directed to the control material supplier or to your local UC Cooperative Extension office.

Boric acid, which is effective against flea larvae, should not be used outdoors because it acts nonselectively as a herbicide and will kill most plants.

Indoor control measures. A wide range of conventional insecticides are registered for flea control as water-diluted sprays, total release aerosols, or hand-held aerosols. Carefully follow label directions when using these products. Many of them are unacceptable to pet owners who are uncomfortable with synthetic insecticides. Some pet owners fear contaminating the pet and its bed with insecticides. In addition to conventional insecticides, some nonchemical alternatives, primarily cleanliness measures, and some very safe insect growth regulators (see "Frequently Asked Questions about Fleas") can be used to combat fleas, even in areas where pets are repeatedly exposed.

For immediate relief, all carpeted surfaces should be steam-cleaned (not chemically treated). The heat of the steam is one of the few interventions that kills all life stages of fleas. Flea breeding indoors can be reduced by establishing one sleeping area for the pet that gets cleaned thoroughly on a routine basis and using bedding material that is laundered weekly or thrown away weekly. If your dog sleeps on a rug, hundreds of flea larvae can develop there. Pet bedding and rugs where the pet rests should be washed in hot water and detergent at least every 7 days to prevent fleas from reaching adulthood, the pestiferous stage.

Vacuum regularly to control fleas. Although flea larvae and pupae are very difficult to remove by vacuuming, flea eggs and feces, the essential food source for developing larvae, can be vacuumed up readily, helping to starve the larvae. Attachments should be used to vacuum cracks, crevices, and upholstered furniture where pets rest. In addition, the action of the vacuum actually stimulates the adults to emerge from their cocoons and to be exposed to insecticide residues. It is difficult to remove the larvae because they coil up like snakes around carpet fibers and cling to them when disturbed by suction from a vacuum cleaner.

Because of flea biology and behavior, several conventional indoor insecticide treatments usually kill the larval stage, a seldom-seen nonpest stage. If control measures are successful against larvae and eggs, fleas never reach the pestiferous, biting adult stage. Furthermore, because adult fleas are protected in their cocoons, which are often constructed at the base of carpet fibers in secluded locations and camouflaged by debris from their surroundings, insecticide sprays seldom reach them. Thus, residual insecticide applications are frequently ineffective against adults. If a flea is immediately successful in finding a host once it leaves the cocoon it experiences minimal exposure to any residual insecticide, since it has minimal contact with the treated surface. Thus, even the most efficacious chemical may not be effective because the flea does not receive sufficient exposure. No matter what insecticide is used, adults may continue to emerge from cocoons.

After completing the cleanliness measures, a pest control operator can treat with boric acid or a borate product (which are effective against larvae and have relatively low toxicity) or a registered adulticide (a compound that kills adult fleas) combined with an IGR. If the premises are treated with an IGR, all the larvae produced from that time on will be killed. Within a couple of weeks, you should notice a striking reduction in the flea population. For a discussion of IGRs, their safety, and how they work to control fleas, see "Frequently Asked Questions about Fleas."

Feeding your pet garlic, brewer's yeast, or B vitamins has not been proven to have any effect against fleas. Pennyroyal, eucalyptus, rosemary, and citronella have not been demonstrated to be effective against fleas and may be irritating or toxic to your pet. Cases have been reported of pennyroyal oil (typically obtained from a health food store) that resulted in acute illness, vomiting, and death in dogs. It is important to avoid the fallacy that "natural" always equates with "better" or "safer." Cats are particularly susceptible to poisoning by crude citrus extracts, as well as the refined d-limonene, with toxicosis resulting in hypersalivation, muscle tremors, ataxia, depression, and hypothermia. When not adequately diluted, flea dips containing d-limonene have produced severe dermatitis, with sloughing of skin. Another botanical ectoparasiticide appearing in the popular press is Melaleuca oil. Melaleuca oil toxicosis is characterized by depression, weakness, uncoordination, and muscle tremors. In addition to being toxic, Melaleuca oil contains a number of sensitizing components producing contact dermatitis in susceptible individuals.

Combing the pet with a flea comb is an effective but time-consuming method for controlling fleas. It is most effective on cats, which do not tolerate baths very well. Fleas removed with a comb should be disposed of by dropping them in soapy water.

Some of the pesticides registered for use on fleas are botanicals known as pyrethrums, which are extracts of dried chrysanthemum flowers. Pyrethrums are known for their rapid knockdown of fleas; however, fleas can recover in time. After treatment with a pyrethrum dust, pets should be bathed to remove the fleas stunned by the pyrethrum and to reduce the risk of accidental ingestion by the pet. Some people prefer dusts to sprays or dips. Dusts are considered safer than sprays or shampoos because there is no solvent to carry the pesticide through the host's skin.

Flea collars are not effective for flea control. Flea traps capture some fleas, but no evidence suggests that they control flea populations. Traps are useful for population monitoring. Ultrasonic pest-repelling devices have been shown to be completely useless.

Frequently Asked Questions about Fleas

Q. What are insect growth regulators?

A. Insect growth regulators (IGRs) are compounds that interfere with arthropod growth or metamorphosis. They are effective at very low concentrations (less than 10 parts per billion) and are nontoxic to mammals. If you can tolerate fleas for the time it takes these compounds to eliminate a flea population, the IGRs are effective by themselves. Expect to wait at least 2 weeks before noticeable flea reductions and 1 to 2 months before complete control.

The two main groups of IGRs used in flea control are *juvenoids*, which mimic the insect's juvenile hormone and prevent the immature flea from becoming an adult, and *chitin synthesis inhibitors* (or insect development inhibitors), which interfere with development of the body wall in fleas. Chitin forms the exoskeleton of all insects, and fleas cannot survive without it. Some juvenoids break down quickly in sunlight and are recommended for indoor use only. Others are photostable and can be used indoors and in outdoor flea breeding areas. Products containing IGRs for on-pet use are available through veterinarians. These products coat the hair of the animal with the IGR so that all eggs laid on the animal are exposed to the IGR as they fall off the animal. Juvenoid IGRs are active against the egg stage, actually killing the embryo within the egg so that it never hatches and the population dies out. IGR products are very effective and need only be used once a month.

IGRs that inhibit chitin synthesis in fleas are marketed as prescription drugs and are available only through veterinarians. One product is formulated as a pill for dogs, as a liquid meant to be applied to cat food, or in a feline-injectable formulation. Because mammals do not have chitin, the IGR has no effect on the dog or cat. When a female flea bites a dog or cat that is taking the IGR, however, the IGR gets into the flea eggs. Any female flea taking a blood meal from a dog or cat on a chitin synthesis inhibitor will get a sufficient dose of the chitin inhibitor to kill her progeny. Prices for a six-month supply are usually under $50. For effective suppression, both cats and dogs in a household should be on the IGR.

The chitin synthesis inhibitor will not make the extremely flea-allergic dog or cat less likely to react to the occasional flea bite. In fact, the IGR relies on the animal being bitten by fleas. The IGR eliminates massive numbers of fleas thriving in all life stages on your premises. Because the IGR alone will not instantly solve a severe flea infestation problem, it is prudent to combine IGR treatment with adult flea-killing products (adulticides). IGRs will help maintain a noninfested house and will produce results in 3 to 6 weeks after being started (roughly one to two flea life cycles) in premises with existing infestations.

Q. How should insect growth regulators (IGRs) be used?

A. Ideally, IGRs should be used before fleas become a problem. They are only effective against the immature stages of fleas, so they should be applied in areas where flea eggs are deposited and larval development occurs.

IGRs should be used before flea season to interrupt development of immature fleas in the home, preventing a few fleas on the pet from resulting in an infestation. By the time the flea population on the animal has reached numbers such that the owner perceives a problem, there are usually tremendous numbers of fleas developing off the host. At this point, immediate control with IGRs is very difficult, if not impossible.

Request that the pest control operator treat carpeted areas of the home with a mixture of a juvenoid IGR with an adulticide (a chemical that kills adult fleas). Be sure to specify that the pest control company include an IGR. To forestall a flea problem the following year, have the pest control operator treat only with an IGR early in the spring before flea development begins. This should prevent subsequent flea development and problems in the home.

Q. Can integrated pest management strategies be used in combating fleas?

A. Yes. Integrated pest management (IPM) has many components. IPM starts with identification of the pest to make sure that the strategy is appropriate. The next step is determination of the proper course of action, based on the pest, the particular situation in which it is found, the tools available, the time frame in which action is required, and the expected results. IPM uses a combination of techniques (cultural, mechanical, and chemical) to reduce flea infestation. Cultural methods may be as simple as keeping the cat indoors all the time. Physical strategies may involve replacing carpet with wood flooring or tile. Mechanical pest control involves such techniques as combing the cat or dog with a flea comb to remove adult fleas from its coat. Sanitation reduces the potential for development of immature fleas in the environment. Steam cleaning kills all the life stages of the flea while simultaneously removing larval food. Use of nonchemical alternatives includes environmental manipulation, which is using altered atmospheres or techniques such as heat, chilling, drying (desiccation with salt), flooding, or other modifications to make the environment inhospitable to fleas.

Q. When we go away on vacation, we board our dogs at the kennel and leave the house closed up for almost 2 weeks. But as soon as we walk in the house we get covered in fleas up to our knees. What's going on?

A. Again, you are removing the fleas' natural hosts (the dogs) by taking the dogs to the kennel. During those 2 weeks, all the fleas that were in the egg and larval stages when you left have matured and pupated and are sitting in their cocoons waiting for the stimulation of a host (such as movement, breath, or warmth) to entice them to emerge and seek a blood meal. Whoever is

first in the house when it is reopened stimulates the fleas to emerge and gets attacked. It is very important to keep eggs and larvae from developing to the pupal stage. So, before leaving for vacation, have your home treated with both an adulticide (an insecticide that kills adult fleas) and a juvenoid insect growth regulator (IGR), which prevents immature fleas from reaching adulthood.

Q. My husband gets eaten up with flea bites while my son and I are never bothered. Why?

A. Some people are more attractive to insects. For a variety of reasons (the chemicals they exhale, their clothing, etc.), some individuals attract blood-feeding insects like mosquitoes and fleas more than other people. In addition, some people can hardly feel the bite of a flea, whereas others experience the bite as a severe irritation. This is an allergic response to the allergens in flea saliva and, depending on the degree of sensitization, the person can experience brief irritation or prolonged itching.

Q. We always have a terrible flea problem in the spring and fall but hardly notice them during the middle of the summer. Where do they go?

A. The explanation involves two almost contradictory statements. Fleas do best in warm conditions, as long as the humidity is high; and flea larvae, which develop outdoors in the soil, can be flooded and drowned by heavy rain. Thus, during the summer, if temperatures are high and relative humidity is low, flea larvae developing outdoors die. In winter, if temperatures and relative humidity are both low, the weather is detrimental to flea development. But in the fall, as temperatures cool off after a hot, dry summer, the survival of flea larvae improves. If spring rains are heavy they can submerge larvae for a sufficient period of time to drown them, but if rains are light, temperatures and relative humidity may be favorable for flea development.

Q. My veterinarian tells me that fleas spend most of their time off the pet. Where are they?

A. Your veterinarian means that fleas spend most of their life cycle some place other than on the pet. Adult fleas live on the dog or cat. The females even lay their eggs on the animal, but the eggs roll off and collect around the host (imagine all these flea eggs rolling off into the animal's bed while it is napping). When the eggs hatch, the larvae (which are about ⅛ inch long [3 mm]) feed on the debris in the environment, particularly the feces of adult fleas, which are partially digested blood. When the larvae are ready to pupate, they form cocoons in protected cracks nearby. As soon as the adult fleas emerge from the cocoons, they start looking for a host, and when they find a dog or cat, they jump on and remain until the fleas die. Although adult fleas can live for several weeks, the usual life span is only a week or two. The egg, larval, and pupal stages together last about a month, twice as long as the pestiferous adult flea stage. Thus, it is true that fleas spend more than half their life cycle off the host (your pets).

Ticks

The general discussion about ticks, their life cycles, common species found in California, general control measures, and the role of the western black-legged tick in Lyme disease is in the section "Selected Stinging and Biting Arthropods" earlier in this chapter. Described here are the ticks that attack pets.

Cats are not exempt from parasitism by ticks, and they can experience tick paralysis, but ticks are less common on cats than on dogs, probably because cats are fastidious in their grooming. One of the common tick species in California is the American dog tick (*Dermacentor variabilis*), the most widespread tick species in the United States and the one most commonly found on pets. Nymphs and adults of the American dog tick feed on dogs or humans, whereas larvae feed almost exclusively on small rodents. A female of this species can lay 4,000 to 6,500 eggs. Adults can live 2 years without feeding.

The brown dog tick (*Rhipicephalus sanguineus*) can infest lawns, dog runs, and areas around homes and kennels. It rarely bites humans. Females lay eggs in cracks and crevices. Larvae, nymphs, and adults can parasitize dogs, and larvae and nymphs can also feed on rodents and rabbits. Both the home and the kennel must be treated when brown dog ticks are found. Brown dog ticks tend to climb above ground level; they are often found

in cracks around windows, doors, moldings, or in furniture. Treat under cages, and around false ceilings and door frames, because the larvae typically crawl upward.

Use the same precautions and procedures when removing ticks from pets as you would when removing them from yourself, as described in the discussion about general tick control strategies in the section "Selected Stinging and Biting Arthropods" earlier in this chapter.

Just as decreasing population numbers is the preferred method of preventing tick attacks on humans, restricting pet activities to areas where tick populations have been reduced will diminish their opportunity to acquire ticks. Area-wide treatment has never been shown to reduce tick numbers. Hand-search your pets for ticks and destroy any that are found to prevent female ticks from establishing their next generation near your home. On-animal tick products are also available, including tick collars. Tick treatments for cats are formulated as shampoos, dusts, or sprays. It is important to protect pets from ticks and the diseases they transmit. Not all flea control products are effective against ticks. Consult your veterinarian for recommendations and follow label directions.

Mosquitoes

Mosquitoes are the intermediate host of *Dirofilaria immitis*, the dog heartworm, a filarial worm that infests dogs but rarely cats or humans. More than 70 species of mosquitoes can transmit the immature stages of this pest (worm larvae), which develop in the mosquitoes after they ingest embryonic forms of the worm parasite, or microfilariae. While the mosquito feeds on your pet, infective worm larvae are transmitted along with the mosquito bite. Dog heartworm is enzootic (constantly present) in the eastern half of the United States and in Hawaii. Dog heartworm occurs less frequently in the western continental United States, but there is an emerging focus of infection in northern California. Adult worms can be as long as 12⅖ inches (31 cm).

When a dog becomes infected, adult worms reach the dog's heart in 3 to 4 months, mate, and produce large numbers of the embryonic form of the parasite (microfilariae), which circulate in the dog's bloodstream; however, they do not mature into adult heartworms in that particular dog. The microfilariae mature into infective larvae in mosquitoes.

Adult worms lodge in the right ventricle of the dog's heart and the pulmonary artery, restricting circulation and resulting in loss of exercise tolerance, chronic cardiac insufficiency, and heart failure. Two common symptoms include a persistent cough aggravated by exercise and more pronounced tiring after exertion. Based on circulating microfilariae, surveys of dogs from various locations in the United States indicate that 0 to 55 percent of dogs are estimated to have heartworm.

The filariae of *D. immitis* may reach maturity in humans, locating in the heart and adjacent vessels. The worm cannot reproduce in humans, but 70 cases of complications from the worm have been reported in the United States. The problem is probably more widespread than suspected in certain areas, such as the southeastern United States, where vector mosquitoes are numerous.

Source reduction is the most effective and preferred method of mosquito control. Treating hosts with insecticides and repellents is minimally effective. Eliminate breeding sites and suppress immature stages to prevent development of the pestiferous blood-sucking adult mosquito stage. Drain standing water and remove structures that hold water to eliminate potential mosquito larvae habitats. Traditional chemicals and IGRs and larvicides, such as *Bacillus thuringiensis israelensis*, may be effective.

A standard method of preventing dog heartworm is prophylactic treatment of dogs, which includes an initial veterinary examination and subsequent examinations throughout the season of potential mosquito activity. To prevent infection, dog heartworm medications are available from veterinarians. Treating an infected dog includes testing for microfilariae, hospitalizing the animal during treatment, and prescribing medications, therapy, and follow-up examinations. Adult heartworms are usually destroyed by a series of injections of an arsenical compound, but dead parasites can occlude (block) pulmonary vessels, resulting in serious complications or mortality. Death can be caused by blockage of the pulmonary artery with emboli (masses of debris) resulting from the drug's effect on the worms.

Insect and Mite Pests of House Plants

Common pests of house plants include aphids, mealybugs, whiteflies, scales, thrips, and mites. For a discussion of these pests and some effective control measures, see chapter 7, "Entomology," and chapter 11, "House Plants."

Fungus gnats (*Sciara* spp. and *Orfelia* spp.) become a nuisance indoors when the adult mosquitolike flies emerge from potted plants or flower boxes. Adults are attracted to lights and may be noticed for the first time near windows. Larvae can injure the roots of bedding plants, African violets, carnations, cyclamens, geraniums, poinsettias, and foliage plants. Symptoms of infestation include sudden wilting, loss of vigor, poor growth, off-colored plants, and foliage loss. These flies are harmless to humans.

Adult fungus gnats are about $\frac{1}{10}$ to $\frac{1}{8}$ inch (2.5 to 3 mm) long, grayish to black, slender, and mosquitolike with delicate long legs and one pair of clear wings. Fungus gnats reproduce in leaf litter and other decaying organic matter, and their larvae feed on decaying organic matter and living plant tissue, particularly root hairs and small feeder roots. The life cycle takes about a month, and reproduction can be continuous in the warmth of most homes. Adults live about 7 to 10 days.

To prevent fungus gnat infestations in house plants, always use sterile potting soil. Inspect plants carefully for signs of insect infestation before purchasing them, and inspect house plants that you have left outdoors during warm weather before bringing them back into the house. Overwatering, water leaks, and poor drainage may result in fungus gnat buildup. Allow soil to dry as much as possible between irrigations. Practice good sanitation by removing old plant material and debris. Electrocutor-light fly traps will attract and kill many adults at night. Insecticides are also available to kill adults and maggots. Read the label and follow safety precautions.

Pantry, Stored Product, and Fabric Pests

Pantry pests are insects and other organisms that commonly infest cereal products and other dried foodstuffs, such as cake mix, powdered milk, gelatin mix, dried fruits, dry pet food, and birdseed. Pantry pests eat and contaminate the food, making it unfit for human consumption.

Meal Moths and Flour Beetles

Meal moths (fig. 8.21) eat stored grain products and other foodstuffs (cereals, cake mix, dried pet food, powdered milk) in the household. They are often carried into the home in packaged groceries. Flour beetles (*Tribolium* spp., also known as bran bugs) (fig. 8.22) attack grain products such as flour and cereals. Both the flour beetle larvae and adults feed in the infested material. Every household is vulnerable to attack by these groups of pests. Proper sanitation and proper storage minimize infestations. Spilled food and foods in cracks and crevices attract these insects; foods not tightly sealed are susceptible to attack, as are foodstuffs stored in damp places. At the time of purchasing susceptible commodities, examine them for signs of pest infestation. Check packaging dates to establish freshness and avoid broken packages to reduce risk.

The meal moth (*Pyralis farinalis*), the Indianmeal moth (*Plodia interpunctella*), the brown house moth (*Hofmannophila pseudospretella*), and the Mediterranean flour moth (*Anagasta kuehniella*) are common examples of meal moths. Meal moth larvae are the feeding (pest) stage. The larvae spin webs and web together the stored products in which they feed and develop. Mature larvae may also leave the food source and crawl about the cupboard, walls, and ceilings. The brown house moth eats not only foodstuffs but also feeds on carpets, paper, furs, and insects. Adults may be found flying near the infestation site. Meal moths have several generations per year.

Other Cupboard and Pantry Pests

The drugstore beetle (*Stegobium paniceum*) and the cigarette beetle (*Lasioderma serricorne*) are aptly named. Drugstore beetle feeds on dried pet food, cereal products, most foodstuffs and spices, and also infests drugs, materials toxic to other insects, furniture fabric, and books. The drugstore beetle can feed on poisonous rodent baits containing strychnine. The cigarette beetle eats everything the drugstore beetle eats (it can feed on pyrethrum powder strong enough to kill cockroaches) and, in addition, it attacks tobacco products. Both species have C-shaped, grublike larvae and multiple generations per year, depending on the humidity and temperature. Both species fly. Bean weevils (*Acanthoscelides obtectus*) and pea weevils (*Bruchus pisorum*) attack dried beans and peas but do not infest cereals, cornmeal, flour, nuts, grains, pet food, or birdseed. Homegrown peas and beans are infested in the garden before harvest. To reduce damage, do not store peas and beans if their moisture content is greater than 12 percent. Larvae and adults of spider beetles (beetles with a spiderlike appearance) and sawtoothed grain beetles (*Oryzaephilus surinamensis*) infest stored food products, particularly cereals and flour. Spider beetles also feed on feces and dead insects.

Mites that feed in stored foods can attack flour, cereals, dried fruits, tobacco, sugar, dry pet food, paper, mold, and organic debris in bird nests. They prefer high humidity and high temperatures but can be prevalent in colder temperatures. They hide in crevices but may be visible in open shelving where they can resemble a pile of tan dust, which is actually composed of living and dead mites, shed mite skins, and feces. Contact with these mites can cause a skin irritation known as *grocer's itch*.

Figure 8.21

Indianmeal moth adult and larva.

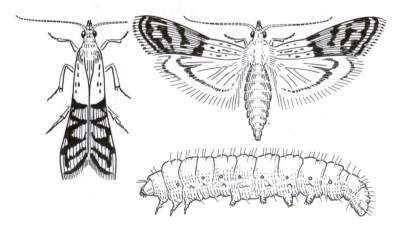

Figure 8.22

Cupboard and pantry beetles.

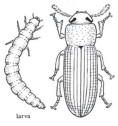

larva

Confused flour beetle

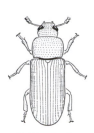

Red flour beetle

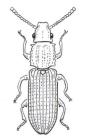

Sawtoothed grain beetle

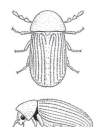

Drugstore beetle

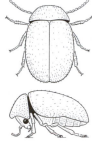

Cigarette beetle

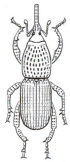

Granary weevil

Prevention and Control of Meal Moths, Flour Beetles, and Other Pantry Pests

Proper sanitation is the primary technique for avoiding stored product pests. Spilled and exposed foods attract and harbor these insects. Cookie crumbs, toaster crumbs, bits of dried pet food, and crumbs from food preparation that have fallen into cracks and corners in the kitchen and pantry attract these insects. Vacuum and scrub out-of-the-way locations to prevent infestations. Do not purchase quantities of flour, dried pet food, or cake mix that cannot be used in a reasonable amount of time, because products stored longer than 6 months are often sources of infestation. Over time, many of these pests can chew their way out of plastic storage bags and they can chew into cardboard packaging. Foodstuffs should be stored in containers with tight seals. Cool, dry storage is best. When cleaning storage areas, use a very hot detergent solution and allow the area to dry thoroughly before placing stored products on the shelves. Consider refrigerating infrequently used, important dry goods to prevent pest damage.

Mice can take dried pet foods and store them in wall voids and subfloor spaces. If insect pests locate the food stored by the mice, eradication of their food source will be more difficult.

When infestations do occur, locate the source and get rid of it immediately. Act promptly so that the infestation does not spread. Thoroughly examine unopened cardboard boxes for signs of infestation and dispose of them if necessary. Sanitize the area. Chemical controls (insecticides) are generally not recommended for controlling pests in food preparation areas. To supplement sanitation measures, sprays may be used only in cracks and crevices away from food where larvae are hiding. If a problem becomes widespread and severe, contact a licensed, reputable pest control operator who has the equipment, knowledge, insecticides, and experience to accomplish the needed pest control safely and efficiently.

If a suspected or infested material is worth saving, consider using temperature extremes as a nonchemical method of control. Heat can control stored-product pests. Insects infesting stored food products are killed if held at 120°F to 130°F (49°C to 54°C) for a minimum of 2 to 3 hours. Because the heat must reach all parts of the infested material, spread the product thinly and stir it to allow rapid penetration of the heat. If the particular item is degraded by heat, subjecting the item to low temperatures may be a better alternative. Insect activity usually ceases at temperatures below 50°F (10°C). Most insects that invade stored food products die or become inactivated when held at 40°F (4°C) for 2 to 3 days. Resistant insects will be killed if they are held in a freezer for 2 to 3 weeks.

Carpet Beetles

Carpet beetle larvae (fig. 8.23) are hairy, small pests that can be annoying throughout the house, feeding on dry foodstuffs (cereals and noodles), pet food, fertilizers (bonemeal), carpets, rugs, upholstery, woolens, furs, feathers, silks, other clothing, animal wall trophies, and lint. They consume animal proteins and survive effectively on soiled wool dresses or suits with perspiration stains. Carpet beetle larvae can be found in dresser drawers, closet corners, behind baseboards and moldings, and in cracks and crevices where lint and animal fibers, crumbs of food, or insect carcasses have accumulated. They can also be found under furniture, in ceiling lamp fixtures, and among

Figure 8.23

Carpet beetle adults and larvae.

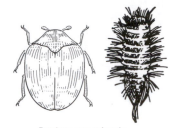
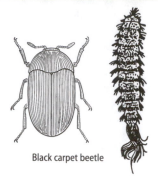
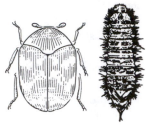

Varied carpet beetle   Furniture carpet beetle   Black carpet beetle

clothes and fabric samples that have been stored without proper protection.

Carpet beetles do not carry diseases or bite homeowners, nor are they a sign of poor housecleaning. They normally live outdoors and are found on dead animals, insect carcasses, and in bird or wasp nests. Adults can feed on pollen. They get into the household by flying in, or they can enter on flowers, purchased foodstuffs, and garage-sale items. They can also move in through cracks or wall sockets. They are attracted to lights.

Because it takes nearly a year for carpet beetles to complete their life cycle from egg to adult, they develop more slowly than some of the other pantry and fabric pests common in California. If you notice the larvae, try to locate the source of infestation by checking probable living spots and food preferences. Realize that even if you find several larvae, the larvae cannot multiply; only adults can lay eggs. Clean where you found the larvae (vacuum dark corners, baseboards, shelves). Clean infested clothing and bedding. Dry cleaning kills all stages of the carpet beetle. Discard infested cereals or pet food. Freeze-treat fur-covered toys. Store woolens with moth crystals according to label instructions. You may treat cracks and crevices with a household insecticide registered for use on carpet beetles in the home.

Clothes Moths

Clothes moths (*Tineola bisselliella, Tinea pellionella*) are small (about ½ inch [12 mm] long) bothersome pests of wool, fur, rugs, upholstery, and fabrics. Clothes stored in dark areas are particularly susceptible to infestation. Infestations can occur under heavy furniture that is moved infrequently as well as in wool garments, fabric remnants, and furs. Reduce the risk of attack by not permitting dust or lint to accumulate. Vacuum hard-to-reach places (behind radiators, baseboards, ducts, moldings). Do not store soiled garments, and use moth crystals according to label instructions. Store clothing in a cool, dry part of the household, if possible. Man-made fabrics, such as acetates, acrylics, nylon, and polyester are resistant to moths and other insects. Cotton, linen, rayon, and silk are resistant to moths and insects when clean. Soiled silks and certain finishes attract clothes moths. Wool, especially stained items, is very susceptible to clothes moths and carpet beetles.

To prevent infestations in rugs, vacuum regularly and clean soiled portions. Use vacuum cleaner brushes to keep cracks in floors and baseboards free of breeding spots. Sprays may be used along the edges of wall-to-wall carpeting, along baseboards and moldings, and in corners and cracks. Consider storing valuable rugs with professionals. If infestations are found in carpeting or upholstery, consider using professionals to manage and eliminate the problem.

Silverfish and Firebrats

Silverfish (*Lepisma saccharina*) and firebrats (*Thermobia domestica*) (fig. 8.24) feed on a variety of foodstuffs, such as cereals, dried meats, flour, and other household products, such as glue, wallpaper paste, bookbindings, paper, photographs, starch in clothing, cotton, linen, rayon, leather, and dead insects. They are often found in bathtubs and sinks. They hitchhike into the household on foodstuffs, furniture, old books, papers, and old starched clothing.

Silverfish are carrot-shaped wingless insects with two long, slender antennae on their heads and three long filamentous appendages at the rear. Silverfish and firebrats are active at night and hide during the day. Silverfish prefer damp, cool places, such as the basement, bathroom, and kitchen. A silverfish female may lay over 100 eggs during her lifetime. Adults can live 2 to 3 years. Firebrats can live in very hot (above 90°F [32°C]) places, such as around ovens, furnaces, fireplaces, and insulation around hot-water and heat pipes. They live in bookcases, around closet shelves, and behind baseboards. Firebrats are hardy and can survive without food for many months.

Sanitation is important, but not entirely effective in controlling silverfish and firebrat infestations because these insects hide between wall partitions, in insulation materials, in books and papers and book shelves. Remove old stacks of newspapers, magazines, papers,

books, and fabrics. Clean up spilled liquids and foodstuffs. Repair leaky plumbing fixtures and eliminate moisture around laundry areas. These measures can reduce populations by removing food sources. Dusts of boric acid and silica gel can be effective, but when infestations are persistent, a professional pest control operator may be needed.

Booklice

Booklice (*Liposcelis* spp.) are minute insects that feed on stored papers, books, wallpaper paste, mold, mildew, cereals, and flour, and prefer higher temperatures and humid conditions. They do not bite humans, spread disease, or damage household furnishings, but they can irritate the skin of susceptible individuals. Nymphs resemble adults. Depending on environmental conditions, the life cycle from egg to adult may take from 1 to 2 months.

To prevent booklice infestation, store cardboard boxes, books, and papers off the floor and repair plumbing leaks. Remove leaf litter, vines, and other debris from around the foundation of the home. Seal cracks. Mothball flakes are effective in infested file cabinets. Household products that control mold and mildew will reduce food sources for booklice. Severe infestations may require a licensed pest control operator.

Nuisance Pests

Some of the more common nuisance pests that invade the home are sowbugs, pillbugs and amphipods, earwigs, crickets, and filth-breeding flies, which include small fruit flies and house flies, among others. Three of the most important household nuisance pests with medical significance to children and adults are dust mites, molds, and grass pollens.

Sowbugs, Pillbugs, and Amphipods

Sowbugs and pillbugs (fig. 8.25) are found throughout California. They are insectlike creatures about ½ inch (12 mm) long with seven pairs of legs and sectioned shells, related to crayfish and other crustaceans. Some people call them "roly-polies" or "woodlice." The common name "pillbug" describes the ability of some species to roll up into a round, pill-like shape, which sowbugs do not have. Sowbugs and pillbugs usually live outdoors

Figure 8.24

Silverfish (left) and firebrat (right).

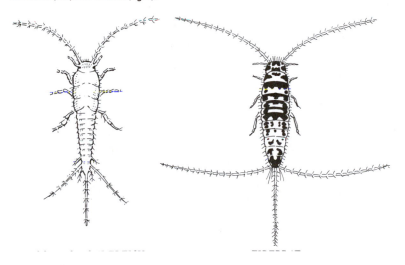

Figure 8.25

Pillbug.

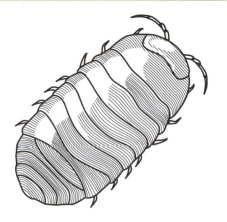

under flowerpots, under boards, and in damp organic matter and debris, feeding on mulches and grass clippings. When they enter the home, they are attracted to damp basements, bathrooms, garages, or interior areas where house plants are grown. Once they invade the home, they will die within a few days, unless they find a moist location. Sowbugs and pillbugs must live in damp places because they are unable to control water loss. They are most active at night when humidity and temperature are favorable for their survival.

Some people call the little orange amphipods along beaches "sand fleas" or "beach fleas." Although these creatures are arthropods, they are only distantly related to fleas and are not even insects (remember that all insects have six legs and amphipods always have more). They are also found around homes where high moisture conditions exist. Changes in outdoor conditions can lead amphipods to migrate indoors.

A number of insecticides are labeled for control of sowbugs and pillbugs. Unless you caulk access points (door thresholds, crawl spaces, windows) to make it more difficult for sowbugs, pillbugs and amphipods to enter the home, the problem may recur. Remove hiding places and organic matter from points adjoining the foundation. Keep the area around the foundation dry, and ventilate crawl spaces or damp basements. The family vacuum cleaner can also be an environmentally sound, effective control method.

Earwigs

The earwig (*Forficula auricularia*) is shiny, reddish-brown, fast-moving insects about ½ to ¾ inch (12 to 19 mm) long with a pair of

Figure 8.26

Earwig.

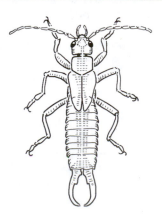

forceps (pincers) at the end of the abdomen (fig. 8.26). Pincers of males are more strongly curved than those of females. The name is derived from an unfounded superstition that earwigs invade the ears of humans, which is not true. Earwigs usually live outdoors in soil or debris and feed on a wide variety of plants, ornamental trees and shrubs, flower petals, garden vegetables, and dead organic matter. They can inflict significant foliar damage to bean, potato, beet, cabbage, cauliflower, pea, dahlia, zinnia, sweet william, fig, and orchard trees and berry bushes by chewing small, irregular holes in leaves. They are active at night and hide during the day. They seldom bite, but may try to pinch when disturbed.

Earwigs are transported easily from the garden into the house and can enter directly under doors or other improperly sealed areas. When they invade the home, they can be a nuisance because they hide in bedding, in laundry baskets, under dishes, or under papers. Indoors, earwigs can be killed mechanically or with insecticides registered for use on earwigs. Dust formulations are effective against earwigs in the home. Dust only infested areas or suspected hiding places. Before using an insecticide, read the label and follow the directions and safety precautions.

Crickets

Crickets can invade the home seeking moisture and can become a nuisance with their monotonous chirping, especially at night, when they can interfere with sleep. In the home, crickets can feed on clothing, fabrics, foods, and paper products. Cotton, linen, wool, rayon, nylon, silk, and furs are susceptible. Glue from bookbindings, sizing from wallpaper, fruit, vegetables, meat, and other materials can be attacked. An occasional cricket in the home does not present a serious problem, but they can bite if handled carelessly.

Crickets get their name from the high-pitched sound or "chirp" that males emit when they rub their front wings together to attract female crickets. Different types of crickets can be identified by listening to their songs. The house cricket (*Acheta domesticus*), field cricket (*Gryllus* spp.), ground cricket (*Gryllus* or *Nemobius* spp.), and tree cricket (*Oecanthus niveus*) resemble longhorned grasshoppers. They have long, tapering antennae, stridulating (singing) organs on the male's front wings and auditory organs on the front tibiae (fourth leg segment). Crickets are usually nocturnal (active at night), preferring to hide during the day. Many cricket species are attracted to lights.

House crickets are ¾ to ⅞ inch (19 to 22 mm) long, and are light yellowish brown with slender antennae much longer than the body. Females have a long ovipositor projecting from their abdomens for egg-laying. House crickets usually overwinter in the egg stage outdoors and live outdoors in warm weather, especially in garbage dumps, but they often seek shelter indoors when it gets colder. House crickets can also complete their entire life cycle indoors, where they lay eggs in cracks and crevices and behind baseboards. Each female cricket can lay more than 700 eggs. Nymphs reach adulthood in about 2 months. They are nocturnal insects and hide during the day. Adults are attracted to lights and can crawl, jump, or fly to second-story windows and roof skylights, where their chirping sounds can interfere with sleep.

Field crickets are usually black (sometimes brown) and range from ½ inch to 1¼ inches (1.3 to 3 cm). Most field crickets chirp and sing during the day and night. Field crickets overwinter as eggs or nymphs in moist soil. Each female lays 150 to 400 eggs. Nymphs reach adulthood in about 3 months. Field crickets are destructive agricultural pests that can become household pests in later summer and fall when they move out of fields to be indoors, but they cannot reproduce in buildings. Outbreaks can occur when rainfall follows a period of drought.

Ground crickets are smaller than the house and field cricket. Their song may sound like a soft, pulsating trill or buzz. Tree crickets occur in trees, shrubs, weeds, and high grass and are excellent singers. They chirp at a regular rate that varies with temperature. A good approximation of the temperature in degrees Fahrenheit is to add 40 to the number of chirps in 15 seconds. Tree crickets, which deliver loud trills, are the crickets commonly heard in the background noises of TV and movies. Tree crickets lay their eggs in the bark or stems of fruit and ornamental plants. Apple, peach, plum, prune, cherry trees and berries are food hosts.

Sanitation is the best method to remove crickets from the home. Keep all areas in and around buildings free of moisture, dense vegetation, and weeds (a 1-foot [30-cm] band next to the foundation). Mow lawns, cut weeds, and clean up garbage collection areas, because crickets are often found near dumpsters. Keep dumpsters as far from the house as possible. Do not store firewood next to the house foundation. Remove harborage sites, such as piles of bricks, stones, rotting wood, and other debris. Caulk and seal cracks and crevices. Make sure that windows and doors are tight-fitting and that they have proper screens. Because crickets are attracted to white, neon, and mercury vapor lights, avoid using them at entryways and switch to sodium-vapor yellow lights, which are less attractive to insects.

If only a few crickets are present, they can be killed with a fly swatter, collected by vacuum cleaner or broom and dustpan and discarded. Occasional invaders can be killed with an aerosol household insecticide spray. Large populations are difficult to control and usually require insecticide applications inside and outside the home. Indoors, apply insecticide to cracks, crevices, baseboards, in closets, under stairways, around fireplaces, in basements, and other hiding places. Outdoors, when populations are large, treat a 5- to 20-foot (1.5- to 6-m) swath around the house foundation. Read the label and follow directions and safety precautions before using insecticide.

Small Fruit Flies (Vinegar Flies)

Small fruit flies (*Drosophila* spp.) may become a nuisance in homes, fruit markets, restaurants, and other locations where fruit is overripe and in the process of decaying or rotting. Indoors, flies are often seen hovering around overripe fruits and vegetables, baked goods containing yeast, garbage cans, vinegar, and open beverages, such as fruit juices, cider, soft drinks, beer, and wine. Overripe and rotten bananas, potatoes, tomatoes, pineapples, and apples, dirty garbage receptacles, an unclean or sour dishcloth or mop, and empty tomato catsup bottles, can be associated with a heavy population of small fruit flies. Outdoors, they become numerous during the summer where fruits and vegetables are harvested, but they disappear in cold weather. Some species are attracted to human and animal excrement and also feed on fruits and uncooked foods, thereby serving as vectors of disease and causing human intestinal myiasis and diarrhea common among workers in grape vineyards. Wash all fruits and vegetables before eating them.

Adult fruit flies are about ⅛ inch (3 mm) long, brownish yellow to brownish-black with red eyes. Female flies lay about 500 eggs singly into moist, fermenting food, such as overripe fruit, rotten vegetables, dirty garbage containers, slime in drains, or waste materials. Eggs hatch in 24 to 30 hours into tiny larvae that feed near the surface of fermenting food masses, feeding primarily on the yeast in the fermenting fluids. Larvae pupate and adult flies emerge. The life cycle can be completed in 8 to 15 days, depending on the temperature.

Small fruit flies do not bite humans, but they are a nuisance. Prevent or eliminate the larval and breeding sites by practicing sanitation at home. Sometimes simply removing an overripe banana, jars of fermenting home-canned foods, cider, fruit juices, empty catsup containers, or dirty garbage cans will control this pest. Fruits and vegetables not consumed promptly should be refrigerated before fermentation begins. Replace mercury-vapor lamps with sodium-vapor lamps and use yellow lights not attractive to insects.

Small fruit flies can pass through ordinary house fly screening. Consider installing special screens, if necessary. Household insecticide sprays will effectively kill small fruit flies but repeated applications may be needed to kill newly emerging adults, because the life cycle is so short. Before using any insecticide, read the label and follow directions and safety precautions.

For light infestations, fruit fly traps are effective. The traps use fruit as bait, so they are a nonchemical method of control.

Moth Flies (Drain or Filter Flies)

Moth flies (Family Psychodidae) are very small flies, ⅟₁₆ to ⅛ inch (1.5 to 3 mm) long, which resemble small moths. They are commonly found in drainpipes in houses, primarily in kitchens and bathrooms. Adults are nocturnal and the larvae can withstand soap, caustic materials, hot water, and some insecticides. Plumbing cleaners available at the grocery store are normally effective in controlling these flies, but it is important to plug the sink tightly for several hours so that the fuming action of the chemical can get to the habitats of the fly. To provide long-term control, use a drain brush to remove the slime layer lining the pipe in which the larvae live.

House Flies

House flies (*Musca domestica*) are one of the most common insect pests worldwide. During the warmer months, house flies can produce a new generation in less than 2 weeks; thus, they have a tremendous breeding potential. In warm weather, two or more generations may be produced per month.

House fly eggs can be laid in almost any type of moist organic material. Animal manure, garbage can contents, and fermenting vegetation (grass clippings), are excellent breeding media. Eggs hatch within 24 hours into tiny larvae (maggots). In 4 to 6 days, the larvae pupate, and the pupal stage lasts about 3 days in warm weather. After the adult fly emerges, it crawls about rapidly, unfolds its wings, and its body dries and hardens. This process may take about an hour, and then mating occurs immediately. A house fly may go through its entire life cycle—egg, larva, pupa, adult—in 6 to 10 days, after which the adult fly may live about a month.

House flies are known as filth-breeding flies because of their filthy feeding habits. House flies spread many intestinal diseases, such as dysentery and diarrhea, because they feed on fecal material, invade homes, and then feed on human food. They use sponging mouth parts to soak up food that they have predigested with salivary secretions.

Control of House Flies, Fruit Flies, and Other Filth-Breeding Flies. Sanitation is the best method of controlling filth-breeding flies in and around the home. Flies seek breeding places where garbage, animal droppings, or vegetation residues are available. Clean thoroughly and dispose of dog, cat, or other animal excrement. Do not let garbage accumulate in the open and make sure that garbage cans have sound bottoms and tight-fitting lids. Screens on windows and doors should have a tight fit to bar flies from inside the house. Try to make all screen doors open outward. When flies do get inside the home, you can swat or kill them mechanically or use insecticides labeled for use on filth flies after reading the insecticide label and following directions and safety precautions.

Dust Mites

House dust is composed of living and non-living components. House dust includes dust mites (*Dermatophagoides pteronyssinus*), bacteria, fungi, insect debris, animal dander, pieces of human skin, and other environmental materials. Smaller than the size of a pinpoint, dust mites have eight legs, strong jaws, no eyes, and a tough, translucent shell. A typical mattress that is used for sleeping may have from 100,000 to 10 million dust mite inhabitants. (Never let it be said that you slept alone, because it's not an accurate statement!) Dust mites also live in pillows, carpets, upholstered furnishings, and draperies, but their prime habitat is mattresses.

A mite's life span is about 2 months; they transform from egg to adult in about a month and then live an additional month. Female mites can lay about 25 to 50 eggs, with a new generation produced about every 3 weeks. Mites prefer warm, humid surroundings and are most prevalent in coastal environments. Mites grow best at 75 to 80 percent relative humidity; they die when humidity is less than 50 percent. Steam cleaning can kill mites, and general cleaning (vacuuming, dusting with a damp cloth) can reduce mite populations.

One of dust mites' favorite foods is sloughed-off scales (flakes) from human skin, which is why mattresses are their preferred habitat. Mattresses provide adequate food, warmth, and humidity. Many people are allergic to proteins, which are digestive juices from the mites' guts, in dust mite droppings. These proteins and droppings can cause allergic symptoms even after the dust mite that produced them has died. Dust mites may be a factor not only in asthma and hay fever but also in eczema, conjunctivitis, and other allergic ailments. Dust mites can trigger allergic responses in the nose and chest of sensitive individuals, acting as both an allergen and irritant. (Allergens are distinguished from irritants in that allergens trigger an immunoglobulin-E [IgE] response and histamine release, whereas, irritants directly influence airways to constrict without triggering IgE antibodies).

Dust mites rank as one of the four most common causes of allergy, along with cat dander, cockroach droppings, and grass pollen. Reducing dust mite populations in the bedrooms of sensitive individuals is very important, because up to a third of the day is spent in the bedroom. Modifications of the bedroom can be made without disrupting the rest of the household. Some steps for controlling dust in the bedroom of sensitive individuals are listed in table 8.6.

Molds

Molds (mildew) can also be a problem pest in the household. Mold spores are present in the

---

Table 8.6

METHODS TO REDUCE DUST MITE POPULATIONS

- Avoid clutter in the bedroom. Ornate furnishings, knicknacks, and wall decorations collect dust.

- Individuals sensitive to dust mites should not have bookshelves in their bedrooms.

- Washable curtains or window shades that are wipeable are better than miniblinds or heavy draperies.

- The bedroom closet should be cleaned thoroughly and only the current season's clothing stored there.

- Hardwood, tile, or linoleum floors are preferable to carpeting, but since many people prefer carpeting in the bedroom, it is important to vacuum frequently.

- Use a high-quality vacuum cleaner with suitable dust collection bag and high efficiency filter so that it leaks very little allergen.

- Do not store anything under the bed.

- Enclose mattresses, pillows, and comforters in zippered allergy-proof casing. The casing functions as a barrier between the allergic person and the dust mites already in the mattress, pillows, or comforter.

- Use washable blankets and hypoallergenic pillows. To kill dust mites, wash all bedding (sheets, pillowcases, blankets, and mattress pad) in hot water at least 130°F (54°C) every 7 to 14 days.

- Limit stuffed toys in the bedrooms of dust-sensitive children. Choose machine washable stuffed toys that can be laundered in hot water with the bed linens.

- Do not allow pets in bedrooms of persons sensitive to dust or animal dander.

- Do not overhumidify in the winter because dust mites grow best at higher humidity. Try to keep relative humidity less than 50 percent.

- Replace upholstered furniture with a wipeable surface, such as leather, vinyl, wood, or plastic. Children enjoy vinyl-covered bean-bag chairs.

- The bedroom of the dust-allergic person should be cleaned weekly. Wipeable surfaces should be cleaned with a slightly damp cloth or a mop or cloth sprayed with an Endust-type product.

- Inspect filters (on air conditioner, heater, and vents) regularly and replace as needed. Consider using specialized filters, such as H.E.P.A. filters, that trap small, airborne allergens.

indoor and outdoor home environment year-round. Unlike pollens, molds are not limited to a particular season. Because molds flourish at high temperatures and high humidity, bathrooms are a popular habitat. Clean bathrooms thoroughly, using a fungicide (molds are fungi). Damp basements are also a problem area. Humidifiers, vaporizers, and air conditioners are potential sources of mold growth. Old pillows and mattresses can be problems. Foam pillows are a poor choice because perspiration can lead to mold growth. Dried flowers and plants often harbor molds. Repot plants outdoors to prevent bringing molds present in the soil into the house. Remove dead leaves and plant debris from potted plants because they can be a source of mold growth. Molds can grow outdoors in mulch because the shady, damp surroundings favor their growth.

Mold-sensitive individuals should avoid locations that typically harbor molds, such as basements, fallen leaves, cut grass, barns, and compost piles. Inside the home, prevent high levels of humidity. Excess humidity resulting from showering or cooking should be removed with an exhaust fan.

Pollen Grains

Pollen grains include the plant sperm that fertilizes the female eggs in seed-bearing flowering plants, such as fruit-bearing and ornamental landscape trees, shrubs, and grasses. Airborne pollen grains are one of the most frequent causes of allergy symptoms because they can come in contact with the nose, eyes, and lungs of sensitive individuals. The total pollen count is not the most significant information for allergy sufferers; rather, it is the specific type of airborne pollen to which that individual is sensitive that will determine the degree of symptoms. Once a person finds out which pollens are the cause of health problems, it is important to find out in which season those plants pollinate and, if possible, what time of day they tend to release pollen into the atmosphere. Keeping windows to the house shut during these times will help reduce the concentration of the offending pollen in the house. Do not operate the home air-conditioner on the ventilate mode because it takes in fresh, pollen-laden air from the outside and circulates it in the house.

Delusory Parasitosis

The caller says that she is being attacked by invisible mites. The attack has been going on for months, and she has visited half a dozen physicians, two of whom prescribed lotion but none of whom are able to help her. She has treated her skin with alcohol, vinegar, bleach, kerosene, and various home remedies. She boils her bed linens and clothing. She can describe the life cycle of the pest and has been able to extract specimens from some of the wounds. She offers to send you samples. She says the irritation is driving her crazy, and you're her last hope. How do you respond?

The sensation that insects are crawling on, biting, or burrowing in the skin, when no arthropod is involved, is termed *delusory parasitosis*. Typically the cause is not any insect or arthropod, but is instead some environmental, physiological, or psychological stimulus. Below are some of the conditions that typically manifest these symptoms.

Medical literature from the past 5 years shows over a hundred different causes of itching including infection with bacteria, fungi, viruses, nematodes, and various other pathogens and parasites. Itching is a side effect of over four dozen diseases and therapies.

Allergies are probably one of the most common causes of pruritus, erythema, and urticaria. Both food allergies and skin allergies may produce these symptoms. Some of the most common food allergies include those to milk, egg white, soybean, peanuts, chocolate, wheat, food additives, mangoes, oranges, nuts, and pineapple.

Atopic dermatitis can be caused by skin allergies to such materials as latex, textiles, soap, detergent, fabric softeners, shampoo, lotions, insect repellents, deodorants, and any other substance that contacts the skin. Most of these contain fragrances, colorants, stabilizers, emulsifiers, preservatives, and other components that may sensitize susceptible individuals.

Numerous medical conditions have itching or other skin irritations as symptoms, including uremia, diabetes, pregnancy, rheumatoid arthritis, autoimmune diseases, hyperthyroidism, hypothyroidism, depression, iron deficiency, hepatitis, cholestasis, neoplasia, and lymphoma. Nutritional deficiencies can produce itching, as can overdoses of many minerals and fat-soluble vitamins. Obvious causes such as parasitic diseases, fungal infections, and Lyme disease can produce similar symptoms.

Itching, urticaria, pruritus, hives, etc. are listed as potential side effects of the majority of both prescription and over-the-counter medications. Some common drugs with itching as a side effect are insulin, estrogen, arthritis medications, hypertension medications, etc. Incidence of these symptoms is accentuated by the interaction of two or more of these drugs. Recreational drugs such as cocaine and methamphetamines are particularly prone to produce the sensation of insects crawling on or burrowing in the skin. Itching, pruritus, urticaria, and paresthesia are also possible side effects of smoking, some insecticides, herbal and other "natural" health products, sun exposure, exposure to sea water, and myriad other causes.

Dry, sensitive skin is particularly susceptible to these sensations. Particles impinging on the skin because of static electricity may be perceived as "bites" or "stings." This is particularly true of materials with sharp projections such as paper fragments and fiberglass. Carpet fibers may also be attracted to lower portions of the body because of static electricity, and these, too, can feel like pinpricks.

Often, the fact that several people are experiencing the same sensation is used to demonstrate that it is not psychological. However, we are all familiar with the "crowd effect," or the power of suggestion. Everyone has noticed the infectious nature of yawns; one person in the room yawns and immediately everyone else does so as well. Similarly, scratching is subliminally picked up and repeated by members of the group.

It should always be determined whether, in fact, an arthropod is involved. Monitoring may include use of cellophane tape to entrap the culprit while it is attacking the skin, glueboards to survey the environment, or a hand-operated vacuum cleaner to sample the area in which attacks are occurring. Typical culprits include thrips brought in on flowers, bird or rodent mites from nests in or on the building, or cryptic pests such as bedbugs or swallow bugs. In all these cases, once the culprit has been identified, the source can be eliminated and the problem solved. Until an insect or mite can be identified as the culprit, no pesticidal applications should be made.

Monitoring and careful investigation of the situation may indicate that, while no arthropod is involved, there are physical causes such as insulation being blown through the air-handling system or nylon fragments from the newly installed carpet. Frequently such modifications as improved sanitation, installation of antistatic devices, and increased humidity will reduce the complaints.

If no physical cause can be identified, the individual should be referred to a physician and encouraged to pursue the possibility of one of the previously mentioned medical conditions serving as the basis of the symptomatology. Alternatively, an environmental hygienist might be brought in to assess alternative environmental effects.

Meanwhile, the individual should be encouraged to discontinue use of self-prescribed treatments. These materials, applied topically, are not good for the skin and are only likely to aggravate the problem. In particular, lindane shampoos and lotions should not be used any more than specifically stated on the label; this is a potent compound that will only increase the sensitivity of the skin when overused.

In summary, people experiencing delusory parasitosis are not crazy or mentally unbalanced. They are merely attributing to insects symptoms that are being caused by some other entity. Once the problem has been determined not to have an entomological basis, they can be directed to other avenues for help.

Bibliography

Africanized Bees in California. Website http://bees.ucr.edu/

Bee alert: Africanized honey bee facts. 1999. Oakland: University of California Division of Agriculture and Natural Resources Publication 21520.

Borror, D. J., and R. E. White. 1970. A field guide to the insects of America north of Mexico. Boston: Houghton Mifflin.

Borror, D. J., C. A. Triplehorn, and N. F. Johnson. 1989. An introduction to the study of insects. 6th ed. Philedelphia: Saunders College.

Ebeling, W. 1975. Urban entomology. Berkeley: University of California, Division of Agricultural Sciences.

Essig, E. O. 1958. Insects and mites of western North America. New York: Macmillan.

Furniss, R. L., and V. M. Carolin. 1977. Western forest insects. USDA Forest Service Misc. Publ. 1339.

Haney, P., P. A. Philips, and R. Wagner. A Key to ants of California. Oakland: University of California Division of Agriculture and Natural Resources Publication 21433.

Johnson, W. T., and H. H. Lyon. 1988. Insects that feed on trees and shrubs. 2nd ed. Ithaca, NY: Cornell University Press.

Klotz, J. n.d. Household ants and their control. Garden Information Series, n.n. Riverside: UC Cooperative Extension.

Lewis, V. R., and M. I. Haverty. 1996. Evaluation of six techniques for control of the western drywood termite (Isoptera: Kalotermitidae) in structures. Journal of Economic Entomology 89(4): 922–934.

Mallis, A. 1990. Handbook of pest control. 7th ed. Cleveland: Franzak and Foster.

Moore, W. S. 1988. Controlling household pests. San Ramon, CA: Chevron.

O'Connor-Marer, P. J. 1991. Residential, industrial and institutional pest control. Oakland: University of California Division of Agriculture and Natural Resources Publication 3334.

———. 2000. The safe and effective use of pesticides. 2nd ed. Oakland: University of California Division of Agriculture and Natural Resources Publication 3324.

Ohio State University Cooperative Extension Service. Home, Yard, and Garden Facts Publications. Available on the World Wide Web at http://ohioline.ag.ohio-state.edu/

Olkowski, W., S. Daar, and H. Olkowski. 1991. Common sense pest control. Newton, CT: Taunton Press.

Powell, J. A., and C. L. Hogue. 1979. California insects. Berkeley: University of California Press.

State of California Department of Health Services. 1986. Facts about Lyme disease. Sacramento: Department of Health Services.

U.S. Department of Health, Education, and Welfare. 1963. Houlsehold and stored food insects of public health importance and their control. Washington, DC: Public Health Service Publication 772.

UC IPM pest note series. B. L. P. Ohlendorf, ed. University of California Division of Agriculture and Natural Resources, Statewide Integrated Pest Management Program. Updated regularly. Available through UC Cooperative Extension county offices; also available on the World Wide Web at http://www.ipm.ucdavis.edu. Of special interest (titles with ANR publication numbers: Ants, 7411; Bed bugs, 7454; Bee and wasp stings, 7449; Brown recluse and other recluse spiders, 7468; Carpenter ants, 7416; Carpenter bees, 7417; Carpet beetles, 7436; Clothes moths, 7435; Cockroaches, 7467; Delusional parasitosis, 7443; Drywood termites, 7440; Fleas, 7419; Flies, 7457; Fungus gnats, shore flies, moth flies, and march flies, 7448; Head lice, 7446; Household ants, 7411; Lyme disease in California, 7485; Mosquitoes, 7450; Pantry pests, 7452; Silverfish and firebrats, 7471; Spiders, 7442; Termites, 7415; Wood wasps and horntails, 7407; Wood-boring beetles in homes,7418; Yellowjackets and other social wasps, 7450

Washington State University Cooperative Extension bulletins. Available on the World Wide Web at http://pubs.wsu.edu/

Western Wood Products Association. 1990. Insects in western wood. Portland, OR: Western Wood Products Association.

9

Weed Science

Richard H. Molinar

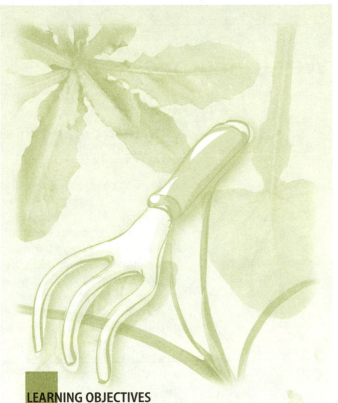

LEARNING OBJECTIVES

- Know the definition of a weed. Know the traits that make controlling weeds difficult.

- Develop an understanding of basic weed classification as a prerequisite to choosing effective weed-control strategies.

- Learn basic weed-control principles and methods. Learn about the four basic weed-management strategies. Develop a historical sense about the use of herbicides and other weed-control methods.

- Learn basic terminology associated with herbicides. Develop analytical skills for selecting the best herbicide. Develop basic understanding of herbicide formulations and application methods.

- Learn practical methods for controlling weeds in turf, ornamentals, and vegetable gardens.

  This chapter is intended to be used in conjunction with chapter 10, "Controlling Garden Pests Safely," in this handbook and with *Pests of the Garden and Small Farm* (Flint 1998); *Pests of Landscape Trees and Shrubs* (Dreistadt 1994); the *UC Guide to Solving Garden and Landscape Problems* CD-ROM (2000); and the *UC IPM Pest Notes* series (see the bibliography at the end of this chapter).

Weed Science

Definition and Function of Weeds

The simplest definition of a weed is "a plant growing where it is not wanted." From the point of view of the home gardener, many plant species can become weeds. Plants are called weeds when they interfere with the intended use of land and water resources. For example, a cantaloupe vine may be desirable in the garden, but in the front yard flower bed, it may be a weed. On the other hand, black mustard is a weed in the garden, but on a hillside prone to erosion, it is a desirable plant. In a vegetable garden, a dandelion may be a cultivated salad green, but in a lawn, it would be classified as a weed. In each gardening situation the intended use determines whether a plant would be considered a weed.

Scientists who specialize in studying weeds might take issue with the simple definition stated above. They would define weeds by specific characteristics that set them apart from other plants: competitiveness, persistence, and perniciousness. These traits make weeds an undesirable interference in home gardening and an economic hardship to agriculture when they are not controlled. Weed scientists would point out that weeds are particularly noteworthy for their seed dormancy, long-term survival of buried seeds, abundant seed production, rapid population establishment, capacity to occupy sites disturbed by human activities, and multiple adaptations for spread, often including vegetative reproductive structures.

Of the more than 250,000 plant species identified by scientists, only 250 plant species (0.1%) are major weed problems in world agriculture. Despite the limited number of species, weeds are extremely detrimental to crop production in California. Statewide, more dollars are spent to control weeds than to control other plant pests. Typically, losses caused by weeds exceed losses from any other category of agricultural pest. Some weeds are so difficult to control that California and other states have passed legislation identifying them as noxious weeds, providing for their intensive control or eradication by law.

The disadvantages of weeds are numerous.

- Weeds compete with crops for space, nutrients, water, and sunlight. Although some weeds, such as mistletoe, dodder, and witchweed, are parasites of crop plants, the majority of weeds are not parasitic. Most weeds exert their destructive influence by competing with crops for essential inputs: sunlight, carbon dioxide, water, space, and fertilizer. As a result of competition, crop plants may appear stunted and have reduced quality and yields. Without effective control measures, weeds would win the competition with cultivated crop species. Weed species have natural resistance to many of the pests that successfully attack crop plants; they often have high rates of seed production, hard seed coats, and protected underground structures, such as bulbs and rhizomes, which allow them to withstand environmental assaults and remain viable for years. Many weeds are more tolerant of heat, drought, and floods than domesticated crop plants. Some weeds have even evolved resistance to herbicides that were formerly effective in their control.

- Weeds can serve as hosts for insect pests and pathogens. Weeds increase the likelihood of disease because they serve as an overwintering host when the crop is not growing.

- Weeds provide cover or food for vertebrate pests, especially rodents.

- Weeds are allergens to many people. Weed pollen contributes to hay fever allergies, and weed foliage (poison oak) causes skin dermatitis in sensitive people.

Weeds do have some redeeming features, including

- reduction of dust and soil erosion

- cover and food for vertebrates such as birds

- nectar source for honeybees

- habitat for beneficial predator or parasite populations

- source of additional soil organic matter

- source of employment for people hired to control or remove them

- potential source of therapeutic pharmaceuticals

Because the detrimental effects of weeds outweigh their virtues, good horticultural practices promote conditions most favorable to crops and least favorable to weeds.

Weed Classification

Identification of a weed (its common name and/or genus and species) is very important for determining effective management strategies. Knowing the identity of a weed is the first step in learning about its life cycle, growth, and development. *The Grower's Weed Identification Handbook* (Fischer 1996) provides photographs that are useful for identifying weeds. Weeds can be classified by the plant family in which they are members, by their growth habit (annual, biennial, or perennial), and by how difficult they are to control. The majority of the worst weeds belong to a few plant families. General categories used to classify weeds are described briefly below.

Life Cycle

The majority of weeds are herbaceous species that live 1, 2, or more years, depending on the particular species.

Annuals complete their life cycle from seed to seed in one year or less. They grow, set seed, and die out completely, so that only new plants that germinated from seed appear the following year. There are two distinct kinds of annual weeds. Winter annuals germinate in the fall, live through winter, and produce seed during the winter and spring. Summer annuals germinate in the spring and produce seed in summer or autumn. Summer annuals, such as lambsquarters, spotted spurge, crabgrass, and pigweed, generally start to germinate about March 1 in Central California and continue growing throughout the summer. Knowing whether the weed germinates in the spring, winter, summer, or fall is critical for

effective timing of management techniques. Mallow, groundsel, and annual bluegrass are annual weeds that start to germinate about September 1 in Central California and continue germinating through the winter and spring.

Biennials complete their life cycle in 2 years. In the first year, they produce vegetative growth: leaves, stems, and a root system. The cold winter period that follows the first year's growth initiates flower development. In the spring and summer of the second year, biennial weeds flower, set seed, and die. Biennial weeds are not as serious a problem as annual weeds because gardeners generally remove them before they set seed. Bull thistle, oxtongue, mullein, and shepherd's purse are examples of biennial weeds.

Perennials live longer than 2 years and usually have a more extensive root system than annuals and biennials. Young perennials can be controlled with cultivation, but once established, they are difficult to eradicate. Simple perennials, such as dandelion, reproduce only by seed, whereas creeping perennials such as bermudagrass and woodsorrel (oxalis) can spread aggressively via vegetative structures (stolons, rhizomes, tubers, bulbs). Some perennials become dormant in the winter, only to send out new shoots in the spring. Nutsedge, dallisgrass, bindweed, oxalis, and poison oak are examples of perennial weeds.

Broadleafs and Grasses

Within the three life-cycle types, two taxonomic groups of weeds are recognized by plant biologists and weed scientists: broadleafs (dicots) and grasses (monocots). Weed specialists commonly classify weeds as annual or perennial broadleafs and annual or perennial grasses. The classifications in table 9.1 provide useful information for controlling weeds, particularly in the selection of a herbicide, a chemical designed to kill particular kinds of plants.

Other Classifications

Other classifications, less important to the home gardener, are the weed's uses (whether the weed is edible or poisonous to humans or livestock), and regulatory status (whether any laws have been passed regarding the weed's noxiousness).

Table 9.1

WEED TYPES

Type	Common name	Scientific name
annual broadleaf	cocklebur	*Xanthium strumarium*
	groundsel	*Senecio* spp.
	lambsquarters	*Chenopodium album*
	mallow	*Malva parviflora*
	pigweed	*Amaranthus* spp.
	purslane	*Portulaca oleracea*
	spotted spurge	*Chamaesyce maculata*
perennial broadleaf	dandelion	*Taraxacum officinale*
	field bindweed	*Convolvulus arvensis*
	horsenettle	*Solanum elaeagnifolium*
	oxalis	*Oxalis* spp.
	tolguacha	*Datura meteloides*
annual grass	annual bluegrass	*Poa annua*
	barnyardgrass	*Echinochola crus-galli*
	crabgrass	*Digitaria* spp.
	foxtail	*Setaria* spp.
	ryegrass	*Lolium* spp.
perennial grass or sedge	bermudagrass	*Cynodon dactylon*
	johnsongrass	*Sorghum halepense*
	nutsedge	*Cyperus* spp.
	quackgrass	*Agropyron repens*

Table 9.2

SEED PRODUCTION AND VIABILITY OF SELECTED WEEDS

Common name	Scientific name	Seed per plant	Percent viable after 38 years
mullein	*Verbascum thapsus*	223,200	48
redroot pigweed	*Amaranthus* spp.	117,400	—
johnsongrass	*Sorghum halepense*	80,000	—
lambsquarters	*Chenopodium album*	72,450	7
purslane	*Portulaca oleracea*	52,300	—
shepherd's purse	*Capsella bursa-pastoris*	38,500	—
curly dock	*Rumex crispus*	29,500	1
wild oats	*Avena fatua*	250	—

Sources: Adapted from California Weed Conference 1989, p. 31; Radosevich, Holt, and Ghersa 1997, p. 125; Ashton and Monaco 1991, p. 23.
Note: — = unknown.

Weed-Control Principles and Methods

Principles

Weed control is an easy concept in theory: simply remove the unwanted plants and prevent new ones from growing. In practice, weeds are difficult to control because they are so well adapted to the garden. Unlike crops that have been selected by plant breeders to germinate uniformly, weeds produce abundant numbers of seed that germinate unevenly. Dormant weed seeds do not germinate even when conditions are favorable, which complicates control. Because weed seed reservoirs may remain viable in the soil for many years, a basic principle of control is to overcome the weeds' survival mechanisms in the soil. For annuals, the objective is to prevent seed production and deplete seed reserves. For hardy perennials, the objective is to destroy underground vegetative reproductive organs. Although diligent application of this principle should, in theory, lead to weed eradication, it is seldom achieved in practice. Controlling weeds is a continuous part of production practice. Maintaining a crop in a superior competitive position requires the cultivator to modify some aspect of the environment or exploit key biological differences that favor the crop over the weed, minimizing the competitive advantage of weeds.

The goal in any weed-management program is to select the most effective practice that is least harmful to people and the environment, and to apply it at the proper time—which always means not waiting until after the weed has set its seed. As one weed scientist has warned, "A year of seeds means decades of weeds." Tables 9.2 and 9.3 show that weeds have the potential for reproducing in large quantities; some weeds can produce thousands of seed that can live for many years. Even a 1 percent viability presents the potential for a large number of weeds to grow from one single plant.

Methods of Weed Control

From the beginning of agriculture to the middle of the twentieth century, the plow and hoe were the primary methods of weed control. The modern era of weed control began in the 1940s, when the weed-controlling properties of the organic chemical 2,4-D were recognized. Burning, flooding, smothering weeds, and crop rotation have been employed for many years, but substantial progress in controlling weeds in production agriculture did not occur until the discovery of organic (carbon-containing) herbicides. For the home gardener, a number of alternatives to chemical weed-control methods are available, because the pressure of an economic return is not a critical issue. The primary weed-control methods to be used by the Master Gardener can be classified as cultural, mechanical and physical, and chemical. For other pests, breeding resistant crop varieties is a powerful control measure, but this is not the case with weeds.

Cultural. Cultural methods of weed control modify the immediate environment, improving the crop's competitive advantage and decreasing the weed's competitive edge. Cultural control methods include proper soil preparation, soil testing (pH, salts, fertility levels, etc.), irrigation management, correct crop plant selection, crop rotation, proper mowing heights, thatch control, and reduction of soil compaction. These practices are probably the most overlooked weed-control methods, which helps to explain why so many weed problems exist.

Good cultural control can account for up to 60 to 70 percent of the weed control in turf. Soil preparation prior to planting and selection of a well-adapted cultivar are two very important cultural practices in the initial stages. Consider laying sod instead of planting seed. Cool-season turf species such as fescue, bluegrass, and ryegrass do better and are more competitive in the coastal and northern regions of California. Bermudagrass and St. Augustinegrass do better in the interior valleys and deserts of California where summers are warmer.

Keeping turf in a healthy, vigorous state is important to the prevention of weed problems. Water deeply and infrequently to discourage weeds such as crabgrass. Dethatch the lawn if the thatch layer is more than 0.5 inch (1.25 cm) thick. Close mowing or scalping a lawn allows weeds to germinate and grow. Adjust mowing heights based on the turf species: hybrid bermudagrass, 0.5 to 0.75 inch (1.25 to 1.9 cm); tall fescue, 1.5 to 3.0 inch (4 to 7.5 cm). Never remove more than one-third of the leaf blade during a mowing. Fertilize with the recommended amount of fertilizer and at the appropriate times of the year. See chapter 12, "Lawns," for more detailed information on proper lawn care.

In landscape areas, select plants that fill in quickly and that are adapted to the region. Groundcovers differ in their rate of establishment, and some require frequent and tedious weeding during a long establishment phase (e.g., *Vinca* and *Hedera*). The use of bark or other mulches is very effective in controlling weeds.

Herbicides are not recommended in vegetable gardens because of the diversity of vegetables usually grown and the chemical registrations for different vegetables. Most gardeners should rely on cultural, mechanical, and physical controls for weeds. Cultivating should be shallow to avoid injuring vegetable roots and to avoid bringing additional weed seeds to the soil surface. Fast-growing vegetables can reduce weed problems through their shading. Vegetables such as squash, beans, pumpkins, cucumbers, tomatoes, potatoes, and melons provide good weed suppression as they grow. Other vegetables such as lettuce, carrots, peppers, greens, onions, broccoli, and radishes suppress weeds poorly if at all.

Table 9.3

VEGETATIVE REPRODUCTION OF SELECTED PERENNIAL WEEDS

Common name	Scientific name	Time	Vegetative production of single plant
cattail	*Typha latifolia*	6 mo	10 ft (3 m) in diameter
field bindweed	*Convolvulus arvensis*	1 yr	2.5 ft (75 cm) in diameter with roots 4 ft (1.2 m) deep
johnsongrass	*Sorghum halepense*	14 wk	85 ft (26 m) of rhizomes
yellow nutsedge	*Cyperus esculentus*	1 yr	1,918 plants

Source: Adapted from Aldrich 1984, p. 93.

Mechanical or Physical. Mechanical control methods, which are effective even against the most persistent weeds, include hoeing or cultivation, hand pulling, rototilling or discing, and mowing or chopping. Physical controls use a physical barrier or method to control weeds, including mulches and soil solarization. Mechanical and physical methods are some of the most common weed control methods used by home gardeners.

Mechanical controls work very well with annual weeds as long as they are cut at or below the soil line (crown) before they set seed. Perennial weeds will grow back, however, and therefore require repeat treatments. Eventually, the roots of perennial weeds will be starved for food and will die as a result of repeated mechanical control measures. Weed scientists refer to the success of this repeated attack as the process of carbohydrate starvation, which may require several or more years of diligent effort for perennial weeds. Mechanical methods of weed control are nonpolluting to the environment and do not require elaborate equipment or a special applicator's license. It is surprising that we have forgotten how easy it is to maintain an area weed-free with the hoe and a small investment of time on a weekly basis. Once most of the cool- or warm-season weeds have germinated in the top ½ inch (1.2 cm) of soil, and provided that weed seeds have not blown into the area, that area will remain relatively free from annual weeds as long as the soil is not disturbed.

"Sprinkle, sprout, spade, and spray" (or "water, wait, then cultivate") is an underused method of weed control that can eliminate up to 95 percent of a weed seed population for a particular season, allowing a planting to become established that is nearly weed-free. Prepare the area to the finished grade and then water to germinate weed seeds that will sprout at that time of year. After most have emerged, spray or spade them out and allow them to die. Then water a second time and repeat the process. This process eliminates most of the weed seeds in the top ½ inch (1.2 cm) of soil, where most of the germination occurs. Now is the time to plant. Disturb the soil as little as possible during planting, or a new crop of weed seeds will be brought to the top again.

Mulch. A mulch is simply a layer of opaque material over the soil surface. Mulches exclude light from weed seeds, eliminating photosynthesis. Mulches may be inorganic (synthetic), for example, plastic, or rock over plastic. Or, mulches may be organic, for example, ground bark, straw, hay, rice hulls, or compost. If the material is mixed into the soil, it is no longer a mulch.

Organic mulches can be very effective for controlling annual weeds. The coarser the material, the deeper the mulch needs to be. Organic mulches also cool the soil temperature (table 9.4) and should not be placed against the stem or trunk of plants, as this might cause disease. The mulch depth should be 1 to 3 inches (2.5 to 7.5 cm) for finer materials such as sawdust or grass clippings, and 3 to 6 inches (7.5 to 15 cm) for coarser materials such as bark, straw, or shredded plant matter.

Inorganic mulches include commercial weed blocks as well as polyethylene black plastic. Weed blocks are made of polyester, polypropylene, or a mixture of peat moss and cellulose. Their cost can range from $3.75 to $14.00 per 1,000 square feet (93 sq m).

Mulches work on two principles: blocking the sunlight required for germination of some weed seeds; and providing a thick layer that prevents weeds from reaching the sunlight and undergoing photosynthesis, which causes them to die of starvation. Use black plastic, not clear, for weed control in landscapes and gardens. The clear plastic used in the cultivation of strawberries and certain other agricultural crops influences soil temperature and keeps fruits from contacting the soil, but it does not provide weed control.

Besides providing effective weed control, mulches reduce water use significantly and can have favorable effects on soil temperature, (see table 9.4). If all other factors are equal, the

Table 9.4

CHARACTERISTICS OF MULCHES

Mulch	Soil temperature change		Comments
	°F	°C	
clear plastic	+10	+18	traps heat; no weed control
black plastic	+6	+10.8	transfers heat; good weed control
brown paper mulch	−8	−14.4	good weed control; biodegradable
organic mulches	−10	−18	good weed control if applied thick enough (3–6 in [7.5–15 cm])

Source: Adapted from *Gardening Shortcuts* 1974.

main criteria in choosing a mulch is its effect on soil temperature and aesthetics. A bark or straw mulch may be more aesthetically pleasing than black plastic.

When mulches are used, the soil stays moist longer, which means that irrigation schedules may need to be adjusted. The tendency to overwater may result in root rot development from *Phytophthora* or *Pythium* fungi.

Soil solarization. Developed in Israel, soil solarization uses a clear polyethylene plastic 1 to 4 mils in thickness with all of the edges securely weighted down or covered with soil. (The mil thickness is not critical, although the thinner mils seem to be a little more effective. Plastic treated with an ultraviolet light inhibitor is recommended.) The plastic must be left in place for 4 to 6 weeks during the warm summer months of June, July, August, and possibly into September. The soil should be loosened, moist, and finished to grade before placement. Solarization controls many (but not all) weeds and also effectively controls certain soilborne diseases such as Verticillium wilt and nematodes. For further information on soil solarization, see the UC ANR publication *Soil Solarization* (Elmore et al. 1997).

Weed species susceptible to solarization include *Poa annua* (annual bluegrass), annual sowthistle, barnyardgrass, Bermuda buttercup (*Oxalis pesacaprae*), cheeseweed, chickweed, henbit, lambsquarters, prickly lettuce, pigweed, and shepherd's purse. Partially susceptible are bermudagrass, creeping woodsorrel (*Oxalis corniculata*), bindweed, crabgrass, purslane, and wild oats. Solarization produces little to no control of sweet clover, bur clover, or filaree.

Biological. Biological control of weeds employs natural enemies such as insects and diseases that feed on weed plants and seeds to reduce the weed population below the level of economic injury. Although this control strategy has appeal and can be effective when combined with other control methods, the homeowner rarely uses this technique to control weeds. Master Gardeners should know, however, that there is ongoing research on biological control projects for such weeds as puncture vine and yellow starthistle.

Chemical: The Last Resort. Chemical weed-control methods include the use of *herbicides*, organic and inorganic chemicals that kill plants. No single herbicide will do the entire job of controlling all weeds. Herbicides are applied as foliar sprays, soil and water treatments, or stem applications. If used properly, herbicides can be safe and very effective, but they should be used by the home gardener only after the methods previously discussed have been considered. It is critical to investigate and diagnose the causes for weed problems before applying herbicides because herbicides often cover or hide the real reason for the weed problem. Do not adopt an "aspirin for the headache" philosophy with chemical treatments. Changing a cultural practice may increase the vigor of desired turfgrasses, vegetables, or ornamental plants, making them more competitive and reducing weed problems and the need for chemical herbicides.

In agricultural production today, herbicides account for about half of the pesticides used, but it is important to note that they were not the method of choice until the 1960s. Mechanical methods of weed control were the primary methods used then. The modern era of weed control began in the 1940s when scientists recognized for the first time that the chemical 2,4-D could be effective in small quantities, selectively killing weeds in the presence of crops and killing underground plant parts after being applied to the foliage. Production agriculture today usually combines mechanical and chemical methods of weed control to obtain the desired level of weed suppression or elimination.

A successful and safe chemical weed-control program is based on effective interactions among the herbicide used, the target weeds, and the surrounding environment. To select the best herbicide and method of application, one needs to know whether the crop and weed are annual, biennial, or perennial; the growth stage of each (germinating seed, seedling, or established plant); and the growth habit of each (deep or shallow root system, upright or horizontal leaves).

Just as the environment has profound effects on the interactions among crops and disease pathogens, it also influences the interaction among crops, weeds, and herbicides. Soil type, soil microflora, available water (rainfall or irrigation), temperature, and sunlight can determine whether a given herbicide application will have its desired effect. Because organic matter and clay in the soil can bind certain herbicides and prevent them from moving to the target weeds, some herbicide labels recommend higher application rates for soils with high organic matter or clay content. Herbicides are degraded by various environmental factors; environmental conditions favorable for the growth of soil microorganisms (warm temperatures and adequate moisture) accelerate herbicide decomposition. Rainfall shortly after a herbicide application may render it ineffective by removing it from leaf surfaces. Herbicides may leach into the groundwater, contaminating drinking water systems.

A discussion of herbicide terminology is necessary before herbicide usage can be described in more detail.

Preemergent versus postemergent. A herbicide application is preemergent if it is made before the weed seeds germinate. Preemergents are also referred to as *soil-residual herbicides* because they prevent germination of weed seeds or inhibit young seedling growth for a period of time. All preemergent herbicides are activated by mechanical incorporation or a sprinkling. The soil-residual effect may last from several weeks up to a number of years, depending on the particular chemical, rate used, and soil characteristics. Certain preemergents require activation within 24 hours (trifluralin, dichlobenil), whereas others can wait up to 7 days (napropamide, for professional use only) and still others, 21 days (oryzalin). The persistence of selected preemergent herbicides is given in table 9.5.

Postemergent applications are made to the weed foliage and require an overhead water-free period of 1 to 24 hours, depending on the chemical. These are not considered residual, nor are they effective on weed seeds. Postemergent herbicides include 2,4-D (Weed-B-Gon); diquat dibromide; fluazifop (Grass-B-Gon); glyphosate (Roundup); MCPP; MSMA (Crabgrass Killer); petroleum distillates (Scythe); and triclopyr (Brush-B-Gon, Turflon).

Contact versus systemic. Foliar-applied herbicides are of two types, *contact* or *systemic*. A chemical that kills only those parts of the plant it touches, usually the leaves, is a contact herbicide. If enough of the plant or the growing point is killed, the plant dies. Contact herbicides are effective on annuals, but perennials will generally grow back. Because contact herbicides do not move to untreated parts of the plant, regenerative rhizomes and stolons of perennial plants will recover. Diquat dibromide and petroleum distillates are examples of contact herbicides.

A *systemic herbicide* is absorbed into the plant and moves inside the plant's conductive tissues by *translocation*. The translocation pattern of a herbicide often determines whether it is applied to leaves, roots, or soil. Foliar-applied systemic herbicides move from the treated leaves to other plant parts and may have their greatest effect at these distant sites. Control of established perennial weeds requires a systemic herbicide, sometimes with repeat treatments. Established annual weeds can be controlled with contact herbicides, but better control is usually obtained with a systemic herbicide. Glyphosate and 2,4-D are examples of systemic herbicides.

Emerging weed seedlings can usually be controlled with an appropriate foliar-applied herbicide of either contact or systemic formulation.

Selective versus nonselective. *Nonselective* herbicides are used when all vegetation is to be killed. In general, contact herbicides are nonselective and are effective on a broad array of young annual weeds.

Systemic herbicides may be either nonselective or selective. A *selective* herbicide is used to control weeds in a crop or ornamental situation in which the weeds are killed but the desirable plants are not injured. The uninjured crop plants are said to be *tolerant* of the selective herbicide and the weed species is said to be *susceptible*. Unfortunately, not all weed

Table 9.5

PERSISTENCE OF SELECTED PREEMERGENT HERBICIDES

Chemical name	Trade name	Persistence (months)
benefin	Balan*	3–4
dichlobenil	Casoron	3–12
EPTC	Eptam*	1–3
oryzalin	Weed Stopper	6–10
oxadiazon	Ronstar	4–6
pendimethalin	Scotts Halts	3–8
trifluralin	Treflan*	3–12

Note:
* Professional product; not for homeowner use under this trade or common name.

species can be selectively controlled with herbicides. Selectivity is relative, not absolute. Extreme environmental conditions or excessive use of a selective herbicide can nullify the difference between tolerant and susceptible species. The mode of selectivity may be related to different growth patterns, rooting depths, locations of growing points, or physiological differences such as the ability or inability to degrade the herbicide into a nontoxic chemical.

Descriptive combinations. Combinations of the above terms are used to describe individual herbicides. The following are examples of herbicide descriptions:

- Roundup (glyphosate): postemergent, systemic, nonselective

- 2,4-D postemergent, systemic, selective

Fumigants. Fumigants are pesticides that nonselectively control many weeds, insects, and certain diseases. The fumigants metham (Vapam) and methyl bromide are no longer available to home gardeners and must be applied by licensed applicators to a prepared, moist soil, then watered in or sealed with a plastic tarp. No fumigants are available for homeowner use.

Selecting the Best Herbicide

Selecting the best herbicide is often more difficult than selecting insecticides or fungicides. Deciding which herbicide to use requires research and knowledge of certain characteristics of the herbicides under consideration, the environment (soil characteristics and climate), and the weed-crop complex, specifically, which weeds are to be controlled in which crop. Several questions must be considered.

- What weed species are to be controlled? What are their life cycles and growing seasons? Are they annuals, biennials, or perennials?

- Are the weeds present in a vegetable crop, turf, or ornamental species?

- What is the specific desired plant? Is it an annual, biennial, or perennial?

- What are the soil characteristics (sandy, loamy, clayey)?

- What are the surrounding environmental conditions (temperature, moisture, sunlight)?

- What type of herbicide application equipment is available?

- What is the desired duration of weed control?

- Will a preemergent or postemergent preparation be more effective given these parameters?

- If a preemergent herbicide has been selected, how and when will it be irrigated or incorporated into the soil?

- Given the complexity of these decisions, would it be easier to remove the weeds by hand?

Herbicide Formulations and Application Methods

Formulations

Almost all herbicides are combined with a liquid carrier such as water or a solid carrier such as vermiculite or perlite to facilitate uniform distribution during application. Other substances known as *adjuvants* or *surface-active agents* are added to enhance herbicide absorption by targeted plants. A herbicide formulation is comprised of the active ingredient (a.i.), the accompanying liquid or solid carrier, the surface-active agents, and other ingredients. Common types of herbicide formulations are spray concentrates, wettable powders (finely divided solids suspended in water), and granular materials.

Application Methods

Proper application methods are essential to successful herbicide treatments (see chapter 10, "Controlling Garden Pests Safely," for more details on pesticide use and safety). Herbicides must be applied uniformly and at the labeled rate over the area to be treated. Sprays can be applied to the soil surface or to plant foliage using push or hand-held spreaders, hand-operated compressed-air pumps (backpack sprayers), and power sprayers. An even travel speed (walking or driving), proper nozzles, correct spray height, and required nozzle spacing must be monitored and maintained to ensure uniform application. Backpack sprayers are most effective in small, scattered weed patches and in areas inaccessible to power sprayers. Poor application techniques may result in too little or too much herbicide, killing desirable plants, or ineffective weed control.

Spray equipment must be calibrated accurately if herbicides are to be used safely and effectively. Herbicide rates, especially for pre-emergents, are generally given in ounces or fluid ounces per 1,000 square feet in sufficient amounts of water to give uniform coverage. The rate essentially refers to spreading a specified amount of herbicide over a particular area. Water is often the liquid vehicle to help spread a preemergent herbicide evenly. Control might be achieved by using 2.25 gallons of water per 1,000 square feet (8.5 l per 93 sq m) or by using 1.13 gallons of water per 1,000 square feet (4.3 l per 93 sq m). For larger areas, this would be 100 or 50 gallons per acre, respectively (378.5 or 189.3 l per 4,047 sq m).

> Example: Oryzalin is a preemergent, selective herbicide with label rates of 1.5 to 3 fluid ounces per 1,000 square feet (44.3 to 88.7 ml per 93 sq m) in selected ornamentals. The lower rate is for short-term control (3 months) and the higher rate is for longer-term control (6 to 9 months). A $\frac{1}{2}$-inch (1.2 cm) rain or its equivalent in sprinkler irrigation is necessary to activate oryzalin. You want to cover 4,000 square feet (372 sq m) and you have a 4.5-gallon (17-l) backpack sprayer. How do you calibrate the herbicide application?
>
> Short-term rate: 1.5 fl oz oryzalin ÷ 1,000 sq ft × 4,000 sq ft = 6 fl oz oryzalin required (44.3 ml oryzalin ÷ 93 sq m × 372 sq m = 177.2 ml oryzalin required)
>
> Longer-term rate: 3 fl oz oryzalin ÷ 1,000 sq ft × 4,000 sq ft = 12 fl oz oryzalin required (88.7 ml oryzalin ÷ 93 sq m × 372 sq m = 354.8 ml oryzalin required)
>
> Since water is only a carrier, the amount used is not critical for a preemergent herbicide. Generally, 1.2 to 2.4 gallons (4.5 to 9 l) of water are used for each 1,000 square feet sprayed. Add 6 to 12 ounces (44.3 to 88.7 ml) of oryzalin to water in the contents of the 4.5-gallon (17-l) backpack sprayer. The 4.5 gallons of water should be adequate for the 4,000 square feet, based on 1.2 gallons

> of water per 1,000 square feet. If solution is left in the tank, simply go over the entire area again. If there was insufficient spray solution, you walked too slowly. It is recommended that you spray the area first with plain water to determine your walking speed.

Herbicides in granular form are applied to the soil by hand or with mechanical devices. Although typically more expensive than sprays, granules do have a few advantages. Premixed granular formulations eliminate calibration errors, application equipment is less complex, and water is not necessary. Granular herbicides are often prepackaged with fertilizers. Such formulations are not suitable for vegetables because of the risk of injury to the vegetables.

Weed Susceptibility to Herbicides

Herbicides are not a cure-all for every weed problem. Selective herbicides are selective not only for the crop but also for the weeds they control. For example, weeds such as spotted spurge, henbit, and burclover are controlled by only a few preemergent herbicides. Nonselective herbicides will not necessarily control all weeds in an area, either. For example, although it is nonselective, Roundup does not control weeds such as malva, filaree, and nettle.

It is therefore highly desirable to identify the weed species in question when recommending either chemical or cultural controls. Refer to the susceptibility charts in the *UC IPM Pest Notes* series for the specific weed when attempting to find a herbicide for a weed problem. For a current list of approved herbicides, see the Weed Research and Information Center's weed susceptibility chart at http://wric.ucdavis.edu or *UC IPM Pest Notes* for individual weeds at www.ipm.ucdavis.edu/PMG. The Pest Notes series is also avaialable from local UC Cooperative Extension county offices, and from ANR Publications (telephone 1-800-994-8849). Another useful resource is table 9.6, which gives the growth habits, descriptive characteristics, and recommended cultural and chemical controls for the most common problem weeds in California.

Table 9.6

COMMON GARDEN WEEDS IN CALIFORNIA

Common name (Scientific name)	Growth habit	Descriptive characteristics	Recommended controls
NARROWLEAF WEEDS			
annual bluegrass (*Poa annua* L.)	winter annual; bunchgrass	Tufted, light green, usually found in cool, frequently watered areas. Seed continue to form even if mowed as low as 1/4 in (0.6 cm).	Reduce soil compaction; improve water drainage. Water less frequently. Hoe or rogue plants and apply mulch. Apply preemergent herbicide in September.
bermudagrass (*Cynodon dactylon* L.)	perennial, prostrate; spreading	Has rhizomes and stolons; leaves have a conspicuous tuft of hair at base; does not grow well in shade; often used as a lawn.	Raise mowing height to greater than 1.5 in (4 cm) in cool-season turf.
crabgrass (*Digitaria* spp.)	summer annual; spreads and roots at nodes	Two main species, one hairy (large) and the other smooth. Both green to yellow-green; a problem especially in overwatered turf.	Water deeply and less frequently. Apply preemergent herbicide in February or March.
curly dock (*Rumex crispus* L.)	perennial	Grows from a large, thick taproot; wavy leaves grow from a rosette.	Remove taproot; apply postemergent herbicides.
dallisgrass (*Paspalum dilatatum*)	perennial, bunch-type growth from a spreading crown	Rhizomes are very closely jointed; seed heads are sparsely branched. Plant goes dormant in winter.	Remove established clumps with shovel or apply postemergent herbicide. Apply preemergent herbicide in February or March.
Italian ryegrass (*Lolium multiflorum*)	winter annual; bunchgrass	Glossy appearance; seed stalks are long with spikelets attached on alternate sides.	Hoe and mulch; apply preemergent herbicide in September.
kikuyugrass (*Pennisetum clandestinum*)	perennial; prostrate	Very thick rhizomes and stolens; similar to bermudagrass except coarser. Frequently mistaken for St. Augustinegrass.	Difficult to control, even with preemergent or postemergent herbicide.
spotted spurge (*Chamaesyce maculata*)	summer annual	Has milky sap in leaves with red spots in upper center of leaf.	Mulch; mow at recommended height. Apply preemergent and/or post-emergent herbicide.
wild barley (*Hordeum leporinum*)	winter annual; bunchgrass	Dull green, smooth leaves; a problem in newly seeded turf.	Mulch and hoe to prevent seed formation. Apply preemergent herbicide in September.
yellow foxtail (*Setaria glauca*)	summer annual; bunchgrass	Leaves are flat, some with a spiral twist; spikes are dense and erect; spikelets have 5 or more slender bristles.	Mulch and hoe. Apply preemergent herbicide after February.
yellow nutsedge (*Cyperus esculentus*)	perennial (dormant in winter)	Spreads by tubers; in sedge (not grass) family; leaves are stiff and upright; nutlets have almond taste. One plant can make 400 new tubers in 1 year.	Remove plants frequently to starve nutlets. Apply postemergent herbicide.

Table 9.6 cont.

Common name (Scientific name)	Growth habit	Descriptive characteristics	Recommended controls
BROADLEAF WEEDS			
birdseye speedwell (*Veronica persica* L.)	winter annual; stems 4–16 in (10–40 cm) long	Roundish leaves and small blue flowers with white centers; covered with hairs.	Mulch and hoe. Apply preemergent herbicide.
bristly oxtongue (*Picris echioides* L.)	biennial; mostly prostrate	Leaves 2–6 in (5–15 cm) long; rough and hairy on upper and lower surfaces; yellow flower heads.	Mulch and hoe. Difficult to control effecitvely with preemergent or postemergent herbicides.
cheeseweed (*Malva parviflora*)	winter annual or biennial	Leaves are large and rounded with red spots at base of the blade. Common in poorly managed turf.	Encourage healthy turf. Apply preemergent or postemergent herbicide.
chickweed (*Stellaria media* L.)	winter annual	Many-branched stems; opposite, pointed leaves.	Encourage healthy turf. Mow at proper height. Hand-pull or hoe plants.
creeping woodsorrel (*Oxalis corniculata* L.)	perennial with running rootstocks	Prefers shade. Leaves resemble those of clover; sour taste; seeds ejected 10–13 feet (3–4 m).	Encourage healthy turf; fertilize and water properly. Apply preemergent or postemergent herbicides.
dandelion (*Taraxacum officinale*)	perennial	Grows from a large, thick taproot.	Mow frequently. Apply postemergent herbicide. If pulling or hoeing, remove all pieces of taproot.
English daisy (*Bellis perennis* L.)	perennial	Low-growing, with oval basal leaves; white or pink flowers.	Apply postemergent herbidice; rogue or dig out plants.
field bindweed (*Convolvulus arvensis*)	perennial	Very deep rooted, 6–10 feet (1.8–3 m); twining stems; white or pink flowers are similar to morning glory.	Cultivate repeatedly to starve roots over 1 to 2 years. Apply postemergent herbicide.
knotweed (*Polygonum aviculare*)	summer annual	Forms a circular mat. Can grow in compacted, droughty soil.	Encourage healthy turf; fertilize and water properly.
plantain (*Plantago* spp.)	2 species, both perennial	Seed stalks of buckhorn are much longer than common broadleaf.	Hoe or pull plants; mulch; apply postemergent, selective herbicides in turf.
purslane (*Portulaca oleraceae*)	summer annual; prostrate	Very fleshy stems and leaves; pale yellow flowers; an edible plant.	Hoe or pull plants (turn plants upside down so they don't reroot).

Note: For a current list of approved preemergent and postemergent herbicides, see the Weed Research and Information Center's weed susceptibility chart at http://wric.ucdavis.edu or the IPM Pest Notes for individual weeds at www.ipm.ucdavis.edu/PMG. Apply herbicides at the labeled rate for labeled weeds; follow all label directions.

Turf Weed-Control Checklist

A healthy lawn will crowd out many weed problems. Weedy turf often results from a breakdown in the turf management program. A healthy lawn is encouraged by several factors.

- Proper irrigation management, including the amount, frequency, uniformity, and time of day of watering. Overwatering encourages seedlings of crabgrass and other annuals. Underwatering of cool-season grasses, such as perennial rye, stresses the turf, giving drought-tolerant broadleaf weeds such as clover or knotweed a competitive edge.

- Evaluation and correction of problems associated with soil pH, salt level, and infiltration rate.

- Proper application of selected fertilizers. Fertilizing at times or rates not conducive to the turf can encourage weeds.

- Thatch more than ½ inch (1.2 cm) thick interferes with water distribution and causes stress in the turf.

- Correct mowing height for a particular turf species. For example, Kentucky bluegrass mowed at ½ inch (1.2 cm) may contain twice as much *Poa annua* than if mowed at 1 inch (2.5 cm). Summer weeds tend to gain a competitive edge if cool-season turfgrasses are mowed too short (below 1–2 inches or 2.5–5 cm).

- Species of turfgrass selected. Turf-type tall fescues generally have fewer weed problems than bluegrass-ryegrass mixtures.

Determine the best herbicide if one is needed, using current weed susceptibility charts as guides (see also tables 9.5 and 9.6).

Ornamental Weed-Control Checklist

Many of the same considerations that apply to turf also apply to landscape ornamentals. Some additional considerations include:

When used properly, mulches are frequently very effective in controlling weeds. An organic or even a stone mulch on top of plastic collects weed seeds; with a little soil and water, seeds will germinate. Occasional pulling will control these weeds.

Several herbicides can be used in ornamentals that are not available for use in turf.

However, drift of herbicides onto adjacent susceptible ornamentals is a frequent cause of damage to the landscape. Always read and follow the label directions to avoid problems.

Certain ground-cover species such as *Gazania* and *Arctotheca* establish faster and have fewer weed problems. Ivy and *Vinca* establish slowly and require more weeding.

Vegetable Garden Weed Control

Herbicides are not generally recommended in vegetable gardens. A few herbicides are registered for use with certain vegetables, but because gardens usually contain a mixture of crop species, it is too difficult to make applications to only one species. Mechanical and cultural techniques, including mulches, hoeing, solarization, and "sprinkle-sprout-spray/spade" are practices recommended for managing weeds in vegetable gardens. See *UC IPM Pest Notes* for more information.

Bibliography

Aldrich, R. J. 1984. Weed-crop ecology. Brea, CA: Bretor Publishing.

Anderson, W. 1977. Weed science: Principles. New York: West.

California Weed Conference. 1989. Principles of weed control in California. Fresno: Thompson Publishing.

Dreistadt, S. H. 1994. Pests of landscape trees and shrubs: An integrated pest management guide. Oakland: University of California Division of Agriculture and Natural Resources Publication 3359.

Elmore, C. L., J. J. Stapleton, C. E. Bell, and J. E. DeVay. 1997. Soil solarization: A nonpesticidal method for controlling diseases, nematodes, and weeds. Revised. Oakland: University of California Division of Agriculture and Natural Resources Publication 21377.

Fischer, W. 1996. Grower's weed identification handbook. Oakland: University of California Division of Agriculture and Natural Resources Publication 4030.

Flint, M. L. 1998. Pests of the garden and small farm: A grower's guide to using less pesticide. 2nd ed. Oakland: University of California Division of Agriculture and Natural Resources Publication 3332.

Gardening shortcuts. 1974. San Francisco: Ortho Books.

Radosevich, S., J. Holt, and C. Ghersa. 1997. Weed ecology: Implications for vegetation management. 2nd ed. New York: Wiley.

UC IPM pest note series. B. L. P. Ohlendorf, ed. University of California Division of Agriculture and Natural Resources, Statewide Integrated Pest Management Program. Updated regularly. Available through UC Cooperative Extension county offices; also available on the World Wide Web at http://www.ipm.ucdavis.edu

10

Controlling Garden Pests Safely

Julie Newman

LEARNING OBJECTIVES

- Understand how to use pesticides safely.

- Recognize the nonchemical and biological pest control methods available to home gardeners.

- Understand what is meant by pesticide type, mode of action, and pesticide formulation.

- Recognize differences between home/garden and commercial-use pesticides.

- Learn how to read and understand the pesticide label.

- Learn how to avoid pesticide poisoning, how to recognize pesticide poisoning symptoms, and what to do when injury occurs.

- Become acquainted with legal issues associated with home gardeners' uses of pesticides.

- Learn about pesticide mixing, application equipment, calibration, and pesticide storage and disposal.

Controlling Garden Pests Safely

Principles of Integrated Pest Management*

Home gardeners can choose from an array of nonchemical and chemical methods (pesticides) to eliminate or reduce pest problems. Cultural practices, mechanical barriers, and the use of biological controls are safe and effective ways for people to manage pests in their gardens. Ideally, the use of pesticides should be considered only as a last resort to augment nonchemical pest management practices.

Integrated pest management (IPM) is the use of all suitable pest control methods in a compatible manner that minimizes adverse effects to the environment. A combination of several control methods is usually more effective in minimizing pest damage than any single control method. Control methods vary in their effectiveness, depending on differences in plant growth and productivity, pest damage, weather conditions, and cultural practices.

The University of California encourages gardeners to manage pests using an IPM strategy by selecting methods that provide long-term prevention or suppression of pest problems with minimum impact on human health, the environment, and nontarget organisms. In IPM programs, we prevent pest damage or keep pests at tolerable levels by using our knowledge about the pests and what encourages or discourages them in the garden.

Principal components of an IPM program are

- pest identification

- methods for detecting, monitoring, and predicting pest outbreaks

- knowledge of the biology of pests and their ecological interactions with hosts, natural enemies, and competitors

- ecologically sound management methods of preventing or controlling pests

Preferred management techniques in an IPM program include

- encouraging naturally occurring biological controls

- using alternative plant species or varieties that resist pests or stock that is certified pest-free

- selecting pesticides with lower toxicity to humans and nontarget organisms

- adopting cultivation, pruning, fertilization, and irrigation practices that reduce pest problems

- changing the habitat to make it incompatible with pest development

Concern over the use and misuse of pesticides has led increasing numbers of home gardeners to seek nonchemical pest control methods, and many are choosing not to use pesticides. Produce from the home garden does not have to live up to the near-perfect appearance of market standards. If the choice is between minor insect damage and a pesticide application, home gardeners may choose to accept the visible blemish.

Although some people do not have the time or knowledge to practice all available nonchemical methods for controlling pests, many cultural practices will help reduce losses. Proper soil preparation, careful plant selection, and good garden practices can be combined with biological and mechanical controls to reduce the need for pesticides.

Pesticides should be used only as a last resort when careful monitoring indicates they are needed, according to preestablished guidelines. When treatments are necessary, the least toxic and most target-specific pesticides should be chosen. Integrated pest management programs can be carried out in most gardens with almost no use of pesticides that are more toxic than soaps, horticultural oils, or microbials.

Effective control of specific insects and related species must begin with proper identification of the pests. Once a pest's identity is

*A contributor to this section was Mary Louise Flint, Pesticide Education Program, Statewide Integrated Pest Management Project, University of California, Davis.

known, its life cycle, seasonal cycle, and habits can be learned, and control measures can be implemented more effectively. Many of the specific examples given here focus on insect pests, but the principles and concepts apply to other garden pests as well.

The most important benefit of an IPM program is a more precise and effective pest management program. A better understanding of pests in the garden together with frequent monitoring allow gardeners to maximize their control efforts. Unnecessary pesticide sprays can be eliminated with the advantages of cost savings and reduced risk to health and the environment. Repeated application of pesticides frequently leads to the development of strains of pests resistant to the pesticides that once controlled them; minimizing pesticide use through an IPM program should limit the development of pesticide resistance.

An effective IPM program requires a well-trained and informed decision maker. See *Pests of the Garden and Small Farm* (Flint 1998), *Pests of Landscape Trees and Shrubs* (Driestadt 1994), and the *UC IPM Pest Note* series for general overviews of designing pest management programs and IPM programs for specific pest problems.

Cultural Control

Many cultural practices reduce pest damage to garden plants, including using resistant varieties, tilling and cultivating, crop rotation, using fertilizers properly, changing planting or harvesting times, and removing crop residues.

Using Resistant Varieties
Certain plant species that are resistant to or at least tolerant of pest activity can be effective in reducing pest problems. Pest resistance in plants is frequently interpreted as meaning "immune to pest damage." Actually, it refers to plant varieties that exhibit less pest damage compared to other varieties under similar growing and pest population conditions. Some varieties may be less desirable to pests or may possess certain physical or chemical properties that discourage pest feeding or reproduction. Others may be able to support large pest populations without suffering appreciable damage. Before buying seeds or plants, check seed catalogs for information on resistant varieties that grow well in your area. Some

varieties may be resistant to pest attack but may be subject to certain other restrictions such as soil pH, drainage, or temperature. Your experience with different varieties will indicate the ones best suited for your garden.

Digging, Tilling, and Cultivating
Mechanical controls such as digging, tilling, and cultivating a garden expose soil pests to adverse weather conditions as well as birds and other predators. In addition, deep digging buries some insects and prevents their emergence.

Crop Rotation
Rotating crops in the garden can be effective against pests that develop on a narrow range of food plants, especially if these pests have short migration ranges. Moving crops to different sites isolates such pests from their food sources. If an alternative site is not available, change the sequence of plants grown in the garden plot. Do not plant members of the same plant family in the same location in consecutive seasons; for example, do not follow melons with cucumbers or squash.

Proper Use of Fertilizers and Water
When properly used, fertilizers and water promote healthy plant growth and increase the capability of plants to tolerate pest damage. However, excessive amounts of compost or manure can encourage millipedes, pillbugs, white grubs, and certain other pests.

Changes in Planting or Harvesting Time
Planting and harvesting at specific times often reduces plant damage or keeps pests separated from susceptible stages of the host plant. Delaying planting until the soil is warm enough for corn and bean seeds to germinate quickly reduces seed maggot damage. Hot caps (milk cartons, paper sacks, or similar materials placed over plants) used during the early season not only preserve heat but also protect plants from damaging wind, hail, and insects. In some situations, a healthy transplant can overcome pest damage more easily than a seedling.

Sanitary Practices
Good sanitary practices, such as removing crop residues and disposing of weeds and

Figure 10.1

Paper tree protectors are mechanical devices that are used to exclude certain pests.

other volunteer plants, eliminates food and shelter for many pests, including cutworms, webworms, aphids, white grubs, millipedes, and spider mites. In addition, weeds and crop residues often serve as reservoirs for pathogens that may infect garden plants.

Companion Planting

An orderly mixing of crop plants (intercropping, or companion planting) is a cultural practice aimed at diversifying host plant populations. Numerous claims have been made about the ability of certain plants to protect certain other plants from pest damage. However, limited data are available from scientific studies to prove the value of companion plantings. Scientists are continuing to investigate these effects.

Mechanical Control

Mechanical controls reduce insects by using labor such as hand-picking, devices such as traps or barriers, and machinery. These methods include the following.

Preventive Mechanical Devices

Preventive mechanical devices often are easy to use, although their effectiveness varies. Such devices include

- paper collars around the stems of plants (fig. 10.1) to prevent damage from cutworm and other insects

- cheesecloth screens for hot beds and cold frames to prevent insect egg-laying

- mesh covers for small fruit trees, berry bushes, tomatoes, and other plants to keep out large insects and birds

- sticky barriers on the trunks of trees and woody shrubs to prevent damage by crawling insects

- reflective plastic mulches on the soil beneath rows of plants and the use of reflective mesh plant covers to repel aphids, insects related to aphids, and other insects (a number of companies package reflective plastic mulches, which also control weeds, specifically for home garden use).

Hand-Picking

Hand-picking of insects and insect egg masses ensures quick and effective control. This method is especially effective with foliage-feeding insects such as bean beetles, potato beetles, hornworms, and squash bugs, and with snails.

Washing

At times a fine stream of water under pressure can dislodge pests from plant stems and leaves. For example, spider mites can be physically controlled by washing them off leaves. This technique also increases humidity around leaves, which may help to bring spider mite infestations under control but can encourage foliar disease problems. To avoid plant damage, use water pressure only on sturdy plants.

Traps

Various types of traps are reportedly successful in reducing pest numbers:

- Earwigs can be trapped in rolled-up newspapers placed in the garden or other locations where these insects gather.

- Slugs and pillbugs can be trapped under boards placed on the ground.

- A small pan placed flush with the soil and filled with stale beer attracts and kill slugs and snails.

- A 2-quart (1.9-l) container half-filled with a 10-percent solution of molasses and water attracts and traps grasshoppers and certain beetles.

Environmental Control

Environmental (physical) control methods include using light and temperature and other environmental manipulation methods to control insects. Blacklight traps are effective tools for monitoring insect species but usually provide little control. Light traps attract both harmful and beneficial insects that ordinarily would not be found in the area. Insects may not be caught in the traps but may remain in the area, and the harmful ones may cause damage later. Some species (wingless insects and insects active only during the day) are not caught in the traps. Consequently, the value of blacklight traps in the home garden is questionable. Where blacklight traps are used, they should be placed 50 to 75 feet (15.2 to 22.9 m) away from the area to be protected. A physical control method that can be used effectively in home gardens is soaking flower bulbs in hot water (140° to 150°F, 60° to 65°C) to control certain pests. Composting is another heat treatment that is used to control soilborne pests.

Biological Control

Concepts and Terminology

Biological control can be defined broadly as any activity of one species that reduces the adverse effect of another. Species that provide biological control of pests are often called *beneficials* or *biological control agents* because they help to keep pest populations low enough to prevent significant economic damage (fig. 10.2). Naturally occurring biological control agents of pests include pathogens, parasites, predators, competitive species, and antagonistic organisms.

- *Pathogens* are microscopic organisms, such as bacteria, viruses, and fungi, that cause diseases in pest insects, mites, nematodes, or weeds. In a few cases, methods of introducing diseases to pest populations have been developed.

- *Parasites* attack pests and spend part or all of their life cycle associated with their host, the pest species. Parasites deposit one or more eggs in or on the host, and when the eggs of the parasite hatch, the larvae feed on or inside the host (see fig. 10.2).

Figure 10.2

Classical biological control involves locating the native home of a pest (usually outside the United States), finding and rearing one or more of its natural enemies, and releasing these natural enemies into the pest-infested area. This adult female *Trioxys pallidus* is laying an egg in a walnut aphid.

Eventually the host dies, and an adult parasite emerges from the host's body. The parasites of insect pests, such as aphids, scales, and whiteflies, are usually tiny wasps that sting their hosts but are too tiny to sting people. Look for pinhole-sized exit holes in scales and dried-out bodies of dead aphids (mummies). Other pests, such as cutworms, may be parasitized by wasps or flies.

- *Predators* are generally very mobile and, unlike parasites, are usually larger than their prey (the pest species). Predators include a wide range of beneficial insects (fig. 10.3), spiders, mites, and many other living organisms. A predator seizes, overpowers, or immobilizes its prey and then either consumes it entirely or sucks its body fluids. Larval stages and frequently adult stages feed on prey. General predators that feed on a wide variety of pest species are very important in gardens.

- *Competitors* can include cover crops in an orchard (such as grasses or legumes) or living mulches in a vegetable garden that have been selected and managed to outcompete weed pests but not to interfere with the crop species. Cover crops must be managed properly because they can be a source of pests as well as natural enemies.

- *Antagonists* are species that release toxins or otherwise change environmental conditions so that pest activities or populations are reduced.

Many beneficial organisms occur naturally around the garden and are at work controlling pest populations without any assistance from the gardener. According to Flint (1998 p. 28), the importance of biological control agents may not be appreciated until a broad-spectrum pesticide that kills certain natural enemies as well as targeted pests is applied and a new pest—suddenly released from biological control—becomes a serious problem. This type of phenomenon, known as *secondary pest outbreak*, occasionally occurs in gardens. One example might be the sudden outbreak of aphid, scale, mite, or whitefly populations throughout a garden soon after a large tree has been sprayed with a broad-spectrum insecticide such as carbaryl. Not only are the pest insects in the tree destroyed, but the insect parasites and other natural enemies in, beneath, and adjacent to the tree canopy are killed as well.

The relationships among the host, pest, and natural enemy make it impossible to have a pest-free environment and at the same time maintain sizable populations of beneficial species. Temperature, humidity, precipitation, and naturally occurring biological control agents all influence pest populations. In some years, pests may not be numerous enough to damage plants significantly. In other years, large populations may cause serious damage or completely destroy host plants.

Figure 10.3

Predators. Lacewing larvae (A) have strong mandibles (jaws) that they use to grasp their prey. They suck the fluids from soft-bodied insects and can be effective predators in home gardens. Lady beetles (B) are commonly available at retail nurseries for use in home gardens. However, their use is limited, as they tend to fly away, although naturally occurring populations may be more effective.

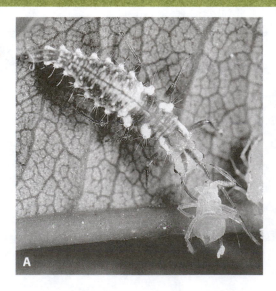

Biological Control Methods

Biological control methods fall into three categories:

- conserving beneficial organisms by the judicious use of pesticides and the maintenance of alternative host organisms, including plants, so parasites and predators can continue to develop

- enlarging existing populations of natural enemies by collecting, rearing, and releasing them back into the environment

- introducing natural enemies that are not native to the area, which then establish and perpetuate themselves

Pests of the Garden and Small Farm (Flint 1998) is an excellent resource for Master Gardeners to consult to increase their knowledge of biological control concepts and University of California–approved pest control alternatives, including biological control techniques appropriate in the home garden.

Conservation. Many beneficial organisms often occur naturally in home gardens, including pathogens; parasitic wasps, midges, and flies; and predators such as lacewing and flower (hover) fly larvae, lady beetles, spiders, and predatory mites. Conservation of beneficial species is an important biological control method. Listed below are some conservation tactics to help maintain beneficial species in your garden.

The most important thing you can do to encourage the activities of biological control agents is to avoid the use of pesticides whenever possible. Insecticides and some fungicides and soil fumigants can reduce the numbers of beneficials, upsetting the ecological balance between pests and their natural enemies. If chemical control is necessary, use the least disruptive materials such as soaps, oils, microbials, and botanicals. The following can also encourage the activities of beneficials and result in conservation.

- Keep food sources for beneficial species in the garden to enhance the activities of natural enemies. Pollen, nectar, and water are especially important for nonpredatory adult stages. Include varieties of flowering plants in the garden that bloom throughout the year.

- Tolerate small numbers of pests. Even though it is best to control pests early, it is also desirable to tolerate some pests to provide food for the beneficials. This can be done by "sacrificing" some plants in the garden or by making spot-treatment applications of pesticides rather than complete coverage. Spot treatments leave reservoirs of pests on which beneficials can survive. Then, if the pest numbers rise, the beneficials will still be present. If there is no food, the beneficials will leave or starve.

- Ants interfere with the ability of predators and parasites to control aphids or scales. Exclude ants from colonies of aphids and scales by applying sticky material such as Tanglefoot to the bases of infested plants (fig. 10.4).

Augmentation. Augmentation is the release of natural enemies to increase their population in an area. It can involve purchasing beneficials from commercial insectaries and releasing them into the environment. However, mass release of natural enemies is not the focus of biological control for home gardeners. More research is needed to determine the effectiveness of augmentation in home gardens. See *Pests of the Garden and*

Figure 10.4

A sticky paste works as a barrier to keep ants from entering an area or from reaching honeydew in plants infested with aphids or scale insects.

Small Farm (Flint 1998) for a more comprehensive discussion and a list of the biological control agents available for purchase in California. A list of some of the commercially available biological control agents that home gardeners may be interested in trying follows.

- **Predatory mites.** Mass releases of several predaceous mite species have been used successfully against mite pests. Their effectiveness depends on the pest species, the species of biological control agent released, and field conditions.

- **Parasitic nematodes (*Steinernema feltiae*).** Tiny parasitic worms have been used to attack soil-dwelling and burrowing insects, including weevils, scarabs, carpenterworms, navel orangeworms, and artichoke plume moths.

- **Mealybug destroyer (*Cryptolaemus montrouzieri*).** This species of lady beetle feeds on mealybugs, some small aphids, and scales. It has been used for controlling citrus mealybug and other mealybug species.

- *Trichogramma* **wasps.** These tiny parasitic wasps attack the eggs of many caterpillar species, including tomato fruitworms (corn earworms), loopers, and hornworms. Results have been mixed because of variable quality in the agents available and lack of reliable release procedures.

- **Green lacewings (*Chrysoperla* spp.).** Green lacewing larvae are general predators that feed on many small insects, including aphids, thrips, pear psylla, insect eggs, and mites. They are often called aphidlions because of their habit of feeding on aphids. Green lacewing eggs are laid on tall stalks.

- **Lady beetles.** Convergent lady beetles (*Hippodamia convergens*) are general predators that feed on small insects, especially aphids. Naturally occurring convergent lady beetles often provide effective control and work best in a small backyard situation. Releases may not provide reliable control because lady beetles generally disperse to other areas.

Chemical Control*

Pesticides are chemical substances that control pests. Home gardeners often use more pesticides per square foot than commercial farmers. The "if-a-little-is-good, more-will-be-better" attitude leads to serious misuse of pesticides. Overusing pesticides has a number of adverse effects. Food products may contain unsafe pesticide residues, and beneficial insects, earthworms, birds, and pets may be harmed or killed. Each time gardeners spray, they expose themselves to the possibility of inhaling or absorbing the toxicants. Careless use of pesticides near water may contaminate water supplies. Misuse of pesticides can lead to the development of chemical resistance in the target pest. Finally, the careless use of pesticides can cause previously minor pests to become serious problems.

Pesticides should be used only when nonchemical methods fail to provide adequate control of pests or when pest populations begin to cause unacceptable losses. If pesticides are applied early in an insect or mite infestation, pest populations are easier to control. The UC Statewide IPM Program generally (because of the diseases discussed below) does not recommend applying insecticides until pests are approaching damaging levels. Because this requires early detection of the insect or mite pests, inspect plant foliage on a regular basis. Pay particular attention to the undersides of leaves where damaging insects or mites and their eggs frequently occur.

Keep in mind that some home-use pesticides are sold in concentrated formulations, and they can be extremely hazardous if not used or handled properly. The label instructions must be read and followed explicitly each time any pesticide product is used (see "Pesticide Laws and Regulations," below).

When To Use a Pesticide

Pesticides are most effective when they are applied at the correct time. The pest must usually be present in the treated area and in a vulnerable life stage for the pesticide to have an impact. However, certain fungicides are

---

*Contributors to this section were Patrick O'Connor-Marer, Pesticide Training Coordinator, and Melanie Zavala, Farmworker Training Coordinator, Pesticide Education Program, Statewide Integrated Pest Management Project, University of California, Davis.

applied in anticipation of weather conditions that are favorable to plant diseases. For instance, fungicides are applied to peach trees in the fall or winter to control peach leaf curl, which appears in the spring.

Proper timing of any pesticide requires information about the pest's life cycle and about environmental conditions that favor the pest. Observations and monitoring should also be used to determine if beneficials are adequately controlling the pest. Never use pesticides until you are certain pests are present and actually causing damage.

With most pests, only certain life stages are susceptible to control by pesticides. For instance, if you are using a stomach poison insecticide to control a leaf-feeding moth, the pesticide works only when that insect is in a larval stage, since adults of moths do not feed on leaves. In addition, stomach poisons have no effect on insect eggs or pupae. Timing is also important with other types of pesticides. For example, some herbicides are only effective in controlling weeds when the plants are actively growing.

The location of the pest is also important when using pesticides because pesticides must, in some way, contact the pests. It is unlikely that a worm inside an apple will be controlled with a pesticide sprayed on the apple's surface. Pests that migrate into an area to feed and then move elsewhere, such as grasshoppers, will usually be controlled only if the application is made when they are in the area being treated.

Many types of pesticides lose their effectiveness or cause damage to treated plants during certain weather conditions. Extremes in temperatures, for instance, may render some pesticides ineffective. Fog, rainfall, or irrigation may wash pesticides off treated surfaces so they cannot function properly. High temperatures, wind, and lack of irrigation may cause treated plants to become stressed, and these plants may be damaged by the pesticides applied to them. This is especially true of the soaps and oils used to control insects and mites.

Proper timing may also contribute to the selectivity of certain pesticides. For example, dormant sprays with oils and insecticides help control overwintering insect and mite pests on deciduous trees without affecting natural enemies as they would if applied during spring or summer. Many herbicides have specific uses based on timing of applications as listed below.

- *Preplant:* use before planting by applying to the soil.

- *Preemergence:* use before weed seeds emerge from the soil.

- *Postemergence:* use after the weeds have germinated.

Types of Pesticides

Pesticides are classified in many different ways. One common classification is by the target pests they are intended to control. The names of these types of pesticides end in the suffix *-cide*. Examples of these pesticides are listed below.

- *Fungicides* control fungi.

- *Herbicides* control weeds.

- *Insecticides* control insects.

- *Miticides* control mites.

- *Molluscicides* control slugs, snails.

- *Nematicides* control nematodes.

- *Rodenticides* control rodents.

Some pesticide types are classified as pesticides even though they do not have the *-cide* suffix. Examples of these types are listed below.

- *Attractants* lure pests.

- *Desiccants* and *defoliants* remove or kill leaves and stems.

- *Plant growth regulators* alter (stop or speed up) normal growth processes.

- *Repellents* repel pests.

Pesticide Modes of Action

Although pesticides are usually grouped according to the pests they control, it is sometimes useful to know more about how a pest is killed by a pesticide and how it actually works. Terms used to describe the modes of action and levels of selectivity of various pesticides may make it easier to select the appropriate chemical. For example, systemics are carried in the blood of treated animals or tissues of treated plants to protect them from pests. Nonselective or broad-spectrum pesticides kill a wide range of plants or animals. They are not selective; the pest is poisoned by feeding on the treated plant or animal. To kill broadleaf weeds in a lawn, pick a *selective* herbicide that kills only broadleaf plants; to kill the whole lawn (weeds and grass), choose a *nonselective* herbicide. Some other pesticide modes of action are listed below.

Contact pesticides kill when the pesticide touches the target organism.

Stomach pesticides must be eaten by the pest.

Selective pesticides kill only certain kinds of plants or animals.

Translocated herbicides move from the point of initial application to circulate to other parts of the plants. For example, glyphosate (Roundup) applied to plant leaves is translocated to the roots, where it interferes with root functions, causing the plants to die.

Fumigants are gases that kill when they are inhaled or absorbed by pests.

Pesticide Formulations

A pesticide you purchase will be a mixture of the *active ingredients* and other materials (*inert ingredients*) combined into a *pesticide formulation*. The type of formulation (granule, aerosol, etc.) determines how the product will be applied and how it should be mixed before application. Only the active ingredients and highly toxic inert ingredients must be named and quantified on the label; the remainder of the formulation may be protected as a trade secret. The active ingredients are the ingredients that actually have pesticidal action. Certain inerts, like xylene, must be identified on the label because they present special health or environmental concerns. The more common pesticide formulations are described below.

Emulsifiable Concentrates (EC or E). The active ingredient is mixed with an oil base (often listed as petroleum derivatives), forming an emulsion that is diluted with water for application. ECs are common in the home-garden trade and are easy to mix and use. They can injure sensitive plants or plants stressed by heat, wind, or lack of moisture. They should be protected from freezing temperatures, which can break down the emulsifier. They are not soluble and require some agitation to keep them in suspension.

Solutions (S). Liquid pesticide formulations that dissolve in water are called *water-soluble concentrates* or *solutions*. Once dissolved, they require no further mixing or agitation. There are only a limited number of pesticides capable of dissolving in water and being formulated as a solution or water-soluble concentrate.

Flowables (F or L). A flowable, or liquid, can be mixed with water to form a suspension in a spray tank. They require constant agitation or they will settle out.

Aerosols (A). These are low-concentrate solutions, usually applied as a fine spray or mist directly from the container. They are generally sold in aerosol cans and are convenient but relatively expensive.

Wettable Powders (WP or W). Wettable powder formulations are made by combining the active ingredient with a fine powder. They look like dusts, but they are made to mix with water. The spray tank must be shaken frequently to maintain the suspension. Wettable powders are less likely to cause phytotoxicity damage to plants than emulsifiable concentrates.

Soluble Powders (SP). Soluble powder formulations dissolve when mixed with water. Constant agitation is not needed to keep them in solution.

Baits (B). A bait formulation is made by adding the active ingredient to an edible or attractive substance. Baits are often used to control slugs, snails, or small ground insects and rodents. They are applied directly from the package.

Granules (G). Granular formulations are made by adding the active ingredient to coarse particles (granules) of inert material such as fired clay particles. They are applied directly from the package without dilution.

Dusts (D). Some dust formulations are made by adding the active ingredients to a fine inert clay or talc. Others, such as some sulfur dusts, are pure active ingredient. Dusts are applied directly from the package. They should not be confused with wettable powder formulations, which are mixed with water and applied as a spray.

Adjuvants

Adjuvants are chemicals added to pesticide mixtures to enhance the active ingredients, improve coverage, or resist weathering after application. The addition of certain adjuvants is common practice in some commercial pesticide uses. Numerous adjuvants are on the market, but most are too expensive and are unnecessary for home gardeners. Pesticides sold for home-garden use may already contain certain adjuvants to make them easy to mix and apply. Home gardeners with special needs that require using adjuvants should consult *The Safe and Effective Use of Pesticides* (O'Connor-Marer 2000), which contains detailed information about different types of adjuvants.

Home-Garden Pesticides

Many types of pesticides are packaged specifically for home and home-garden use. These products are packaged in small containers and often in ready-to-use formulations. When these materials must be diluted before use, the dilution rates are often given in spoonfuls per gallon of water or ounces per 1,000 square feet (93 sq m) of treated area. Although this packaging is convenient, consumers pay a higher price for it.

Products packaged for commercial use may be less expensive, but they are not recommended for home gardeners. Commercial-use formulations are often more concentrated (have more active ingredient per unit of measure) than products sold for home-garden use and are recommended for larger areas. Because of the higher concentration of active ingredient in commercial pesticides, additional protective clothing may need to be worn during mixing and application than is required for noncommercial pesticides. The savings of buying larger quantities is usually not realized by home gardeners because they will probably never need that quantity of any single pesticide. These materials usually end up being stored on shelves and may create hazards to others if they are not kept in locked containers.

Certain pesticides are more suitable for use in the home garden than others. One reason for this is their safety. These are materials that often occur naturally, and they usually break down rapidly in the environment. Most have low toxicities to people and animals. These pesticides are packaged in small volumes and are readily available in garden-supply stores for home use. Some of these listed below.

***Bacillus thuringiensis* (Bt).** Microbial insecticides like Bt are commercially available formulations of microorganisms or their toxins that cause disease in specific groups of insects but have no effect on other organisms. The bacteria in the insecticide are harmless to warm-blooded animals and beneficial insects. The use of microbial insecticides is, in a sense, biological control. According to *Pests of the Garden and Small Farm* (Flint 1998), microbial insecticides are almost ideal insecticides with little impact on the environment or human health. At present, the only microbial insecticide registered for use on home gardens is Bt. Bt controls many species of lepidopteran larvae (butterflies and moths), coleopteran species, and mosquito larvae, depending on the variety of Bt used. Spray Bt as soon as you find eggs hatching, as it works best on newly emerged insects. Make sure all leaf surfaces are well coated with insecticide. Caterpillars infected by the bacteria stop eating, and their internal tissues disintegrate and liquefy. Multiple applications may be necessary.

Pyrethrums. Pyrethrums are botanical insecticides (plant derivatives) that are derived from the flowers of a *Chrysanthemum* species imported mainly from Kenya and Ecuador. The material causes rapid paralysis and controls a broad spectrum of insects, including mosquitoes, flies, aphids, beetles, moth larvae, thrips, and mealybugs. Pyrethrums are registered for use on most vegetables and fruits at any time during the growing season. Because pyrethrums break down quickly, they must be applied precisely when and where susceptible insects are located. Pests that migrate in after application will probably not be controlled. Multiple applications may be necessary.

Spray Oils. Horticultural spray oils have several advantages over conventional pesticides. Oils have a wide range of activity against most pests, yet are less harmful to beneficials than other pesticides with longer residual activity. No resistance to oils by target pests has been observed. Residual insecticides can kill natural enemies for long periods after a spray. By using oils instead, the more stationary and exposed pests, such as scales or aphids, are killed, but beneficials not located on treated surfaces at the time of the spray survive. In addition, oils are relatively nontoxic to people and are environmentally friendly. Spraying fruit trees with specially refined horticultural oils can kill overwintering eggs or pupae of leafrollers, certain moths, and other caterpillars on tree trunks. Oil sprays during the dormant season can be used to control aphids, scales, and mites.

Insecticidal Soap. Gardeners have been using soap to control insects since the early

1800s. Researchers have not yet determined exactly how soaps work. Some soaps dissolve the outer waxy coating of insect cuticle, destroying its watertight nature and causing desiccation. This is why soaps are most effective against soft-bodied insects. Insecticidal soaps control mites, aphids, whiteflies, and other plant-sucking arthropods. Soaps, like oils, kill only on contact, so repeated applications may be necessary. Compared to residual pesticides, soaps are less harmful to beneficials and are compatible with biological control. Soaps for home use are allowed on a wide range of fruits and vegetables. They are similar in toxicity to a solution of soapy dishwater, but certain plants can be sensitive. Check labels for hazards to plants.

Pesticide Laws and Regulations

The registration and use of pesticides are regulated by the federal Environmental Protection Agency (U.S. EPA) and the California Department of Pesticide Regulation (DPR). Locally, laws are inforced by the county agricultural commissioner.

The Pesticide Label

The safe and legal use of pesticides requires adherence to the printed information provided by the manufacturer or formulator of a pesticide. Pesticide labels include the label on the product container plus any brochures or flyers with additional use instructions or limitations. The label printed on or attached to a container of pesticide tells how to use the product correctly and what special safety measures need to be taken. Read this information carefully before using a pesticide. Pesticide labels are required to follow a specific format and usually must include each of the following sections. Use the sample pesticide label (fig. 10.5) to locate these sections. Sections on the sample label are numbered 1 through 10 to correspond to the numbers listed below.

1. **Brand name, chemical name, and common name.** A *brand name* is the name the manufacturer has given to the product. It is the name used for all advertising and promoting and is usually the largest and most conspicuous wording on the label. The *chemical name* describes the chemical

structure of a pesticide and is derived by chemists based on international rules for naming chemicals. Most pesticide chemicals have an official *common name* assigned to the active ingredient; this is a generic name, and it may be found on the label of many brands if each contains the same active ingredient. Common names and brand names are not the same, and not all labels list a common name for the pesticide.

2. **Formulation.** The formulation is the way the active ingredient is mixed with inert ingredients to make it ready for you to use.

3. **Ingredients.** All of the active ingredients in a pesticide formulation must be listed on the label. These are given as percentages by weight. The inert (nonpesticide) ingredients may not be listed by chemical name if the label shows what percentage of the total material in the formulation is inert ingredients.

4. **Contents.** The label tells you how much material is in the container.

5. **Manufacturer.** Each pesticide label must include the name and address of the company manufacturing and distributing the pesticide. The registrant may differ from the manufacturer.

6. **Registration and establishment numbers.** The U.S. EPA assigns registration numbers to each pesticide as it is registered. In addition, the EPA establishment number is a code that identifies the site of manufacture or repackaging.

7. **Statement of use classification.** The U.S. EPA categorizes every use of every pesticide as either *unclassified* or *restricted-use*. Unclassified pesticides are usually the least hazardous materials, and these will be the types available for home garden use. They offer little danger to people or the environment when used according to the label directions. *Restricted-use* pesticides are those that may be hazardous to the environment, the applicator, or other people, even when label directions are followed. Restricted-use pesticides may be used only by certified applicators or under the supervision of certified applicators. Home gardeners should avoid using restricted-use pesticides.

8. **Signal words and symbols.** Part of the registration process assigns each pesticide

Figure 10.5

Sample pesticide label.

PEST STOPPER
INSECT SPRAY EC ← ❷

❿

❶

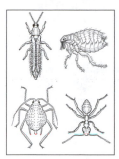

Use on Vegetables, Landscape Plants, Fruit Crops, and Lawns

This product must not be used on golf courses and sod forms.

← ❼

ACTIVE INGREDIENT: ← ❸
  Trithiogone: trihexo-1,3-diphospho-
  2H-thioate 9.6%
INERT INGREDIENTS 90.4%

NET CONTENTS
❹ → **1 QUART (946 ML)**

Keep out of reach of children
❽ → # WARNING
See side panel for additional precautionary statements

❺ → **Premier Chemicals and Fertilizer Co.**
  Anytown, USA
  EPA Est. 000 AT-0
❻ → EPA Reg No. 000-00000-00-0

PEST STOPPER INSECT SPRAY provides rapid kill and residual control of many insect pests on ornamental trees, vegetables, flowers, fruits, and lawns.

DIRECTIONS FOR USE: It is a violation of Federal law to use this product in a manner inconsistent with its labeling. For home garden or domestic use only.

GENERAL DIRECTIONS: SHAKE WELL BEORE USING. Use a clean tank or hose-end sprayer. Flush sprayer with clean water after each use. Carefully measure and mix the amount of PEST STOPPER insect spray and water as given in "Use Directions" chart. Use coarse drenching spray for lawns. Use medium-fine spray for trees, shrubs, flowers, and fruits. Obtain thorough coverage of plants. DO NOT USE on ferns, cactus, or succulents since injury may occur. The numbers in parenthesis next to each crop tell how many days to wait between spraying and harvest. Do not apply when honeybees are foraging in the garden.

USE DIRECTIONS—MAKES UP TO 64 GALLONS FINISHED SPRAY

WHERE TO USE	CONTROL THESE PESTS	AMOUNT TO USE
ROSES, FLOWERS, SHRUBS, TREES	Aphids, Scale Crawlers (Cottony-Cushion, Lecanium, San Jose, Pine Needle, Soft Brown Scale), Leafhoppers, Bagworms, Thrips, Holly Bud Moth, Whiteflies, European Pine Shoot Moths, Webworms, Spruce Aphid, Sawflies	1 tablespoon per gallon of water.

REMARKS: Be sure to wet undersides of leaves as well as the tops. Spray all leaves and branches to the dripping point. Repeat as necessary for insect control at 10- to 14-day intervals.

FRUITS, BERRIES

Apples (14), Peaches (20), Plums (10), Cherries, Grapes (10), Strawberries (5), Blackberries (7) Raspberries (7)	Aphids, Codling Moth, Cherry Fruit Fly, Strawberry Fruitworms	1 tablespoon per gallon of water.

REMARKS: Begin spraying after blooming and repeat full coverage sprays at 7 to 10 day intervals or as necessary.

CITRUS FRUIT (all 21)

Oranges, Lemons, Limes, Grapefruit, Tangerines, Kumquats	Aphids, Leafrollers, Thrips	1 tablespoon per gallon of water.

REMARKS: Apply first spray after bloom period (do not apply during bloom). Repeat as necessary.

VEGETABLES

Beans (7), Cabbage (7), Cucumbers (7), Lettuce (7), Melons (3), Squash Summer 7, Winter (3), Peas (0), Potatoes (35), Tomatoes (1).	Aphids, Beetles (Cucumber and Flea), Imported Cabbageworms, Loopers, Leafminers, Thrips, Diamondback Moths.	1 tablespoon per gallon of water.

REMARKS: Do not apply to seedlings until second true leaves appear. Be sure to wet undersides of leaves. Apply spray in early morning or in evening just before dark to avoid plant injury. Repeat as necessary for insect control at 7 to 10 day intervals.

LAWNS

Bluegrass, Bentgrass, Fescues, St. Augustine, Dichondra, Bermuda.	Sod Webworms, Chinch Bugs, Bermuda Mites, Clover Mites, Ants, Ticks, Billbugs, European Cranefly Larvae.	3 tablespoons per gallon of water to cover 125 sq. ft. of lawn (3/4 cup of water for 500 sq. ft.).

REMARKS: Thoroughly water lawn before treatment and avoid watering for 24 hours after treatment.

STORAGE AND DISPOSAL
Store this product in its original container and keep in a locked storage area out of reach of children and domestic animals. Store between 35°F and 95°F. Do not reuse container. Rinse thoroughly before discarding and securely wrap original container in several layers of newspaper and discard in trash.

---

❾ → **PRECAUTIONARY STATEMENTS—HAZARDS TO HUMANS AND DOMESTIC ANIMALS**
WARNING: May be fatal if swallowed. May be absorbed through skin. Do not breathe spray mist. Avoid contact with skin, eyes, and clothing. Wear shoes and protective clothing, including chemical-resistant gloves, when handling and spraying this product. Wash thoroughly after handling. Avoid contamination of feed and foodstuffs. Do not use on household pets or humans. Do not permit children or pets to go onto the sprayed area until the spray has completely dried. Keep out of reach of domestic animals.
STATEMENT OF PRACTICAL TREATMENT: If On Skin: Wash skin with soap and water. If In Eyes: Flush with plenty of water and get medical attention. If Swallowed: Call a physician immediately. Gastric lavage is indicated if material was taken internally. **DO NOT INDUCE** vomiting unless other treatment is not available. Vomiting may cause aspiration pneumonia. If it is necessary to induce vomiting, give victim one or two glasses of water and insert finger in back of throat. Repeat until vomit fluid is clear. Do not induce vomiting or give anything by mouth to an unconscious person. If inhaled: Remove victim to fresh air. Apply respiration if indicated. **NOTE TO PHYSICIAN:** Solvent may present aspiration hazard. Gastric lavage may be indicated if product was taken internally. This product contains a cholinesterase inhibitor. If symptoms of cholinesterase inhibition are present, atropine sulfate by injection is antidotal. 2-PAM is also antidotal and may be administered, but only in conjunction with atropine.
ENVIRONMENTAL HAZARDS: This product is toxic to fish, birds, and other wildlife. Birds feeding on treated areas may be killed. Do not apply directly to water. Do not contaminate water by cleaning of equipment or disposal of wastes. Do not apply when weather conditions favor drift from areas treated. Do not apply where runoff is likely to occur. This product is highly toxic to bees exposed to direct treatment or residues on crops. Do not apply when bees are actively visiting the crop, cover crop, or weeds blooming in the treatment area. Applications should be timed to provide the maximum possible interval between treatment and the next period of bee activity. **PHYSICAL OR CHEMICAL HAZARDS:** Do not use or store near heat or open flame.

NOTICE: Seller makes no warranty, expressed or implied, concerning the use of this product other than indicated on the label. Buyer assumes all risk of use and/or handling when such use and/or handling is contrary to label instructions.

to a toxicity category and prescribes which signal word must be used on the label. All products must bear the statement "Keep Out of Reach of Children." See table 10.1 for pesticide degrees of toxicity.

9. **Precautionary statements.** Precautionary Statements are used to describe the human and environmental hazards associated with a pesticide. *This is an extremely important section on a pesticide label* because it describes how to avoid exposure and provides information on the personal protective equipment that is required. This section includes first-aid instructions and often has information for physicians. It also tells you if the pesticide is corrosive, flammable, or explosive. Always read and follow the instructions and protective measures given in a Precautionary Statement.

10. **Directions for use.** This section of the label tells how to mix and apply the pesticide, how much to use, where to use the material, and may sometimes indicate when it should be applied. Also included is information on storage and disposal of the pesticide. This section lists target pests that the pesticide has been registered to control, plus the plant species, animals, or other sites where the pesticide may be used. The directions may also include special restrictions that must be observed, such as plant species that are sensitive to this material.

Always follow these "Directions for Use." It is a violation of law to use pesticides in a manner inconsistent with the label unless federal or state laws specify acceptable deviations from label instructions.

Under the amended Federal Insecticide, Fungicide, and Rodenticide Act (FIFRA), *it is illegal to use a pesticide on a site unless the site is listed on the label.* Therefore, if the pesticide label lists specific plants that the pesticide can be used on and your plant is not on the label, it is illegal to use that product on your plant. Sometimes, however, the label refers to broad categories of plants that the pesticide can be used on, such as *ornamentals.* It is illegal to exceed the rate of application given on the label. Using higher-than-label rates can result in dangerous residues on edible crops or cause injury to the plants being treated.

Liability

Home gardeners are liable for misuse of pesticides on their property. Misuse can result in injury to people, animals, desirable plants, and the environment.

The federal Clean Water Act of 1987 requires the elimination of discharge of pollutants, including pesticides, into surface waters to the maximum extent possible. See "Protecting the Environment from Pesticides," below, for ways to prevent pesticides from contaminating the environment, including bodies of water.

In addition to federal regulations, California has several state laws restricting the use of pesticides within the state. Proposition 65 (The Safe Drinking Water and Toxic Enforcement Act of 1986) mandated the creation of a panel of experts to review all pesticides registered for use in California to determine the carcinogenic and reproductive hazards of each chemical, and requires that warnings be given to people who might be exposed to the regulated chemicals.

Pesticide Safety

Preventing Pesticide Poisoning

Many pesticides are toxic, and if misused, some can cause severe illness or even death. The likelihood that injury will occur depends on the degree of toxicity of the active ingredient and the amount of exposure to the product

Table 10.1

DEGREES OF TOXICITY

Signal word	Toxicity	Approximate human lethal dosage	Category
Danger Poison*	highly toxic	a taste to 1 teaspoonful	I
Danger	highly hazardous	pesticide-specific (see label)	I
Warning	moderately toxic or hazardous	1 teaspoonful to 1 ounce (5–29.6 ml)	II
Caution	low toxicity	1 ounce (29.6 ml) or more; relatively nontoxic	III

Note: *When the word "poison" accompanies the signal word "danger," a skull and crossbones symbol appears on the pesticide label. Highly poisonous pesticides are in Category I. They are highly toxic when ingested, inhaled, or absorbed through the skin. Alternatively, these pesticides may pose a dangerous health or environmental hazard. Home gardeners should avoid using pesticides of this type.

during or after use. To avoid injury, it is important to understand several key points about pesticides and to follow the pesticide label directions carefully.

Overexposure to some pesticides can cause immediate, or *acute*, illnesses or injuries such as headaches, skin rashes, nausea, or muscle weakness. Some pesticides have been linked to certain long-term or chronic diseases such as cancer, reproductive disorders, birth defects, neurological disorders, or allergies. Chronic health problems may be difficult to associate with pesticide exposure because symptoms may not appear for months or years after the exposure incidents occurred.

To avoid illnesses or injuries of any type when using or handling pesticides, you must take precautions that protect yourself from exposure. Injuries can occur when pesticides contact the skin or eyes. Sometimes these injuries are limited to the areas of the body that received the exposure. However, pesticides can also be absorbed into the body through the skin and eyes, or through inhalation (breathing), or ingestion (swallowing). Pesticides that enter the body may cause serious illness or may damage internal organs. Wear protective clothing to help keep pesticides off your skin and out of your eyes and prevent these toxic chemicals from entering your body.

Keep other people and animals away from areas where you are applying pesticides. Do not let spray droplets or dust get onto people, animals, food, clothing, or anything other than the target plants or surfaces you are treating.

Children are the most frequent victims of pesticide poisoning in homes. Many have been injured, sometimes very seriously, because they drank from containers in which pesticides were stored (fig. 10.6). Keep pesticides in their original containers with the labels attached. Never put any pesticide in food or beverage containers. Store pesticides where children and other people cannot reach them, preferably in a locked cabinet.

Symptoms of Pesticide Poisoning

It is important to recognize general symptoms of pesticide poisoning so medical care can be obtained promptly. Unfortunately, all pesticide poisoning symptoms are not the same. The most common poisonings resemble the flu with symptoms such as nausea, headache, and malaise. A person may feel tired and ill, but not even realize that something as serious as pesticide poisoning has occurred.

Common symptoms of poisoning associated with some pesticides include

- **Mild exposure:** fatigue, headache, dizziness, blurred vision, excessive sweating and salivation, nausea and vomiting, stomach cramps, or diarrhea.

Figure 10.6

Children are the major group of nonagricultural pesticide poisoning victims. Improper storage of pesticides in the home is the prime reason for the problem.

- **Moderate exposure:** inability to walk, weakness, chest discomfort, muscle twitches, constriction of pupils of the eyes. Earlier symptoms (as described above in mild poisoning) become more severe.

- **Severe exposure:** unconsciousness, severe constriction of pupils of the eyes, muscle twitches, convulsions, secretions from mouth and nose, breathing difficulty, and death, if not treated. Illness may occur a few hours after exposure.

First-Aid Procedures for Pesticide Overexposure

Read and become familiar with the "Statement of Practical Treatment" on each label for pesticides you plan to use. Knowing how to perform the first-aid procedures described in these directions can save lives and prevent serious injuries.

The most common way to be exposed to a pesticide is through the skin. If a pesticide gets on your skin, remove the pesticide as quickly as possible by taking off contaminated clothes and washing with soap and plenty of running water. Prompt washing reduces the damage to the skin and lessens the amount of pesticide absorbed into the body.

If someone inhales pesticide vapors, get them into fresh air right away. Loosen all tight-fitting clothing. If needed, give artificial respiration immediately. Do not stop until the person is breathing regularly or medical help arrives.

If a pesticide is splashed into an eye, start rinsing the eye immediately with a steady, gentle stream of clean, cool water. Make sure the eye is open during rinsing (fig. 10.7). Do not add any eye drops or other medications to the eye. Continue rinsing for at least 15 minutes, then seek medical care.

If someone has swallowed a pesticide, get medical care immediately. Follow the first-aid instructions on the pesticide label. Some labels suggest making the person vomit, but others warn against this.

When a person shows signs of pesticide poisoning, immediately call an ambulance or transport the victim to the nearest medical facility. Provide the attending physician as much information about the pesticide as possible, including the common or generic name of the active ingredient, how the person was exposed (inhaled, splashed on skin or into eyes, or ingested), and, if known, how much exposure occurred. Try to provide the name of the manufacturer and the U.S. EPA registration

Figure 10.7

If pesticide gets into the eyes, they must be flushed immediately for 15 minutes with a gentle stream of clean water. Hold eyelids open while flushing. If irritation still persists, obtain medical treatment.

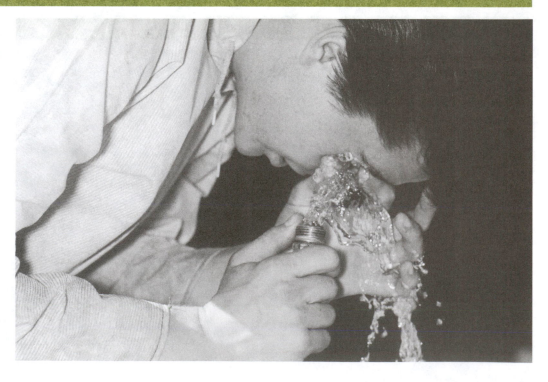

number. If the person has vomited and the identity of the pesticide is not known, collect some of the vomitus in a clear jar for analysis.

If for some reason you cannot take the victim to a medical facility immediately, contact a regional poison information center. These are located throughout the state and can be reached by telephone at any time. These centers provide quick, life-saving information on treatment for poisoning, but they should only be called in an actual emergency. Most telephone directories list the nearest center in the white pages, usually with other emergency numbers. Locate the number and post it in your pesticide storage area or near a telephone for quick access in an emergency. If you cannot locate the number in an emergency, dial 911.

Protective Equipment and Clothing

Pesticide labels provide information on the type of protective equipment and clothing to wear during mixing and application. Home gardeners should never apply pesticides while wearing clothes such as shorts or sandals. Minimal attire for applying pesticides is a long-sleeved shirt, long-legged pants, shoes, unlined rubber gloves, and safety glasses (fig. 10.8). Additional protection is provided by a wide-brimmed plastic hard hat that covers the back of the neck. Rubber gloves, a face shield, and a waterproof apron are particularly important when mixing or pouring concentrated pesticides.

Keep this protective equipment separate from all other clothing and use it only for pesticide applications. After each use, wash the clothing, gloves, safety glasses, hard hat, and apron in soap and water. If any of these items becomes seriously contaminated with a concentrated pesticide, throw them away.

Mixing Pesticides

Most serious injuries occur when mixing pesticides because mixing involves handling undiluted formulations. The mixing process can be avoided by purchasing ready-to-use formulations. The extra cost will be offset by the convenience and safety of not having to mix concentrated materials. If mixing is necessary, check the pesticide label for appropriate protective clothing and equipment. When mixing pesticides, avoid using metal measuring utensils. Take care that measuring equipment is not mistaken for kitchen utensils. Have a set of measuring cups and spoons especially for your pesticide dilutions, and label them as such with an indelible marker. If measuring outdoors, stand upwind to reduce

Figure 10.8

This person is wearing the minimal protective clothing for pesticide application. It consists of a long-sleeved shirt, long pants, shoes, and protective eyewear. The fabrics are tightly woven cotton materials. Consult pesticide label for additional protective clothing required during mixing and application.

chances of exposure. When measuring indoors, work in a well-lit and well-ventilated area. Reduce exposure hazards to your face and eyes by measuring and pouring below eye level and by wearing eye protection or a face shield. Open paper containers with a sharp knife or scissors rather than tearing the bags open.

Pesticide Application

When applying pesticides, wear the protective clothing and equipment the label recommends. To prevent leaks, always check application equipment for leaking hoses or connections and plugged, worn, or dripping nozzles before adding pesticide. Always have a bag of absorbent material, such as kitty litter or sand, on hand, in case you have a spill.

After application, thoroughly clean the inside of the spray equipment and rinse with water immediately. Don't forget to flush the hoses and nozzles. Do not dump the rinse water in a place where it will collect or puddle and become a pollutant. The rinsate should be sprayed onto a site listed on the label. Never pour pesticide-contaminated rinse water down the drain!

When washing protective equipment, leave gloves on to avoid hand contamination. After everything else has been cleaned, wash the outsides of your gloves with soap and water before taking them off, then wash your hands thoroughly. Shower as soon as possible using plenty of soap and water.

Some pesticides can damage and even kill the plants they are intended to protect. To avoid plant injury, do not apply pesticides to wilted plants or during the hottest parts of the day. Dusts should be applied only when the plants are dry. Apply pesticides only at recommended dosages; increased amounts can be dangerous, cause plant damage, and leave harmful residues without improving pest control.

Check the label for plants on which the pesticide may be used safely. All cultivars and varieties may not be listed, and there may be an important reason for this. If you are unsure of the effect of a pesticide, apply it to a small area first before treating the entire plant. Some types of pesticide formulations are more prone to injure plants. For example, emulsifiable concentrates are more likely to cause leaf burn than wettable powders. Be careful when combining two or more pesticides, as incompatibility problems may cause injury to some plants. Avoid using old pesticides because these may have been chemically altered from long periods of storage; these may cause plant injuries.

Do not use the same sprayer for weed and insect control. No matter how well a tank is rinsed after herbicide use, small amounts of residue can still remain in the tank, on gaskets, and in hoses. If the same tank is then used to apply an insecticide to plants, it is possible these residues may injure the plants. The wisest policy is to maintain two clearly labeled sprayers, one for herbicides and another for insecticides and fungicides.

Storage and Disposal

Store all pesticides in their original containers in a locked cabinet. Stored pesticides should be protected from temperature extremes, as some pesticides are damaged by freezing while others are altered by heat.

After you have completely emptied a container—except for an aerosol container—triple rinse it. Add the rinsate to the sprayer along with the last of the pesticide and apply to a label-approved site. Even after rinsing, some pesticide will remain in the container. Plastic and metal containers should be punctured so they cannot be reused. On the day of your street-side trash collection, you may dispose of most home-garden-use pesticide containers by wrapping empty, rinsed, and dried containers in several layers of newspaper. Never use empty pesticide containers for other purposes, and never allow children to play with empty containers.

Many communities provide household hazardous-waste collection services at periodic intervals. If your community has this service, use it to dispose of unwanted or old pesticides. For information on pesticide hazardous waste collection and disposal, contact your local county agricultural commissioner's office.

Pesticide Equipment and Calibration

Application Equipment

Pesticide application equipment is available in many shapes, sizes, types, and prices. Select durable equipment designed to do the job you want it to do (fig. 10.9). Make sure the sprayer is easy to fill, operate, and clean. It is best to keep a separate sprayer for herbicide applications. Examples of sprayers typically used in home gardens are shown in figure 10.10.

Calibrating Sprayers

Calibration involves adjusting the spray or dust output of the equipment to apply the desired rate of pesticide. Calibrate application equipment to ensure that each pesticide is being applied at the rate directed on the product label. Too much pesticide is dangerous; too little will not provide adequate pest control. Only by calibrating correctly can you ensure the best results with the product.

There are many ways to calibrate equipment. The preferred methods differ depending on the kind of equipment used. Consult directions on the equipment for proper calibration directions. The following is a basic method for calibrating compressed air or backpack sprayers.

Figure 10.9

Selection guide for nonpowered and hand-operated application equipment for liquid pesticides.

	Type	Uses	Suitable formulations	Comments
	Aerosol can	Insect control on house or patio plants, small areas, cracks and crevices, and confined spaces.	Liquids must dissolve in solvent; some dusts are available.	Very convenient. High cost per unit of active ingredient.
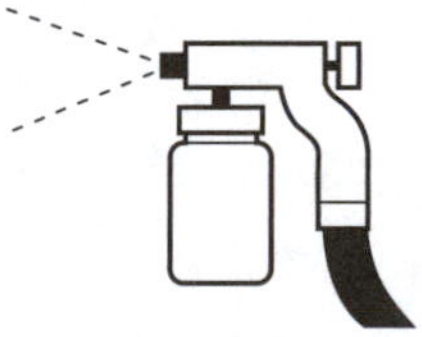	Hose-end sprayer	Home garden and small landscaped areas. Used for insect, weed, and pathogen control.	All formulations. Wettable powders and emulsifiable concentrates require frequent shaking.	Convenient low-cost way to apply pesticides to small outdoor areas. Cannot spray straight up.
	Trigger pump sprayer	Indoor plants, pets, and small home yard areas. Used for insect and pathogen control.	Liquid-soluble formulations best.	Low-cost and easy to use.
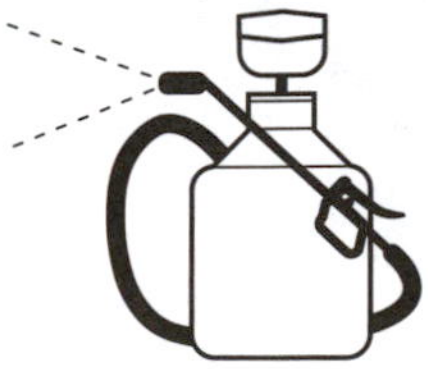	Compressed-air sprayers	Many commercial and homeowner applications. Can develop fairly high pressures. Used for insect and pathogen control. Often used indoors for household pest control.	All formulations. Wettable powders and emulsifiable concentrates require frequent shaking.	Good overall sprayer for many types of applications. Needs thorough cleaning and regular servicing to keep sprayer in good working condition and prevent corrosion of parts.
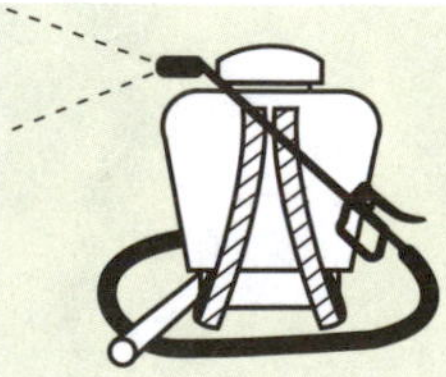	Backpack sprayers	Same uses as compressed-air sprayers.	All formulations. Wettable powders and emulsifiable concentrates require frequent shaking.	Durable and easy to use. Requires periodic maintenance.

- Fill the sprayer with water and fully pressurize. Determine delivery time by spraying water into a 1-pint (0.5-l) jar. Measure how much water is delivered into the jar in 30 seconds.

- Measure the square footage of the area to be treated. (Multiply length times width to determine the area of a rectangle or base times height divided by 2 to determine the area of a triangle.) If the area to be treated is large, divide it into sections equal to the capacity of the application equipment.

- Spray an area with water while operating at normal walking speed for 30 seconds. Measure the area sprayed. This tells how much area can be sprayed in 30 seconds and, therefore, the amount that is applied over that area (see the first step). For example, assume that 30 seconds of spraying delivers 8 fluid ounces (0.24 l) and

Figure 10.10

Sprayers commonly used in home gardens. (A) An aerosol container offers greater convenience without waste, although the cost is usually higher per unit of a.i.; it contains a low-concentration insecticide solution. (B) Hose-end sprayer. (C) A trigger pump sprayer can be used to apply small quantities of diluted pesticide to surfaces such as houseplants or pets, and for applying some types of pesticides to confined areas. It is relatively inexpensive and easy to use. (D) Backpack sprayer.

30 seconds of spraying covers 100 square feet (9.3 sq m), and the total area to be covered is 1,000 square feet (93 sq m). Treatment of the 1,000 square feet will require 80 fluid ounces (2.4 l) of diluted material (8 fluid ounces × 1,000 square feet ÷ 100 square feet, or 0.24 liter × 93 square meters ÷ 9.3 square meters).

If the pesticide label calls for 3 tablespoons of pesticide for 1,000 square feet (45 ml per 93 sq m), then 3 tablespoons (45 ml) of pesticide must be mixed with 80 ounces (2.4 l) of water to achieve proper spray coverage. Application rates for many chemicals are given in pints per 100 gallons of water. To convert rates to equivalents used by homeowners, consult table 10.2. This table gives approximate measurements that should be used as a guideline if the directions for mixing small quantities are not given elsewhere.

In general, the best spray pattern to cover an area of ground is one that gives uniform coverage with little spray overlap. The spray pattern used to apply the pesticide should be continuous and uninterrupted. However, in the case of applying an herbicide to control weeds that are spaced far apart, spot treatment should provide effective control.

The spray pattern should be directed so that the applicator does not walk in the spray while making the application. The spray pattern should form an arc no more than 3 to 4 feet (0.9 to 1.2 m) on either side of the operator. If good spray coverage is questionable (such as when using hose-end sprayers), cut the application rate in half and make two applications. First, apply the pesticide in an east-west direction, and then make a second application in a north-south direction.

Application rates are usually given in terms of amount of pesticide mixture per a given area, for example, 80 ounces per 1,000 square feet (2.4 l per 93 sq m). When the label gives no clear instructions about how much spray mixture to apply to individual plants, such as trees and shrubs, the usual practice is to spray to runoff. Make sure that spraying to runoff will not violate the label rate; you don't want to spray the amount recommended for 1,000 square feet (93 sq m) on a single tree!

Protecting the Environment from Pesticides

Misapplication of pesticides carries serious consequences. Pesticides can cause problems when they drift or otherwise move off target. For instance, fine mists of herbicides can drift to nearby areas and damage or kill landscape plants. Bees and other pollinators can be killed if they are in the garden while plants are treated with certain pesticides. Natural enemies of pests can also be killed by indiscriminate pesticide use. Life in streams or ponds can be wiped out by accidental spraying of ditches and waterways, runoff from sprayed areas, or careless container disposal.

There are steps you can take to reduce environmental impacts of using pesticides. If more than one pesticide is available to control a certain pest, choose the one that is the least

Table 10.2

PESTICIDE CONVERSION CHART

LIQUID MEASURE

If amount of chemical per 100 gallons is	Then amount of chemical per gallon is
4 oz	¹/₄ tsp
1 pt	1 tsp
1 qt	2 tsp
1 gal	2¹/₂ tsp
2 gal	5 tsp
4 gal	¹/₃ pt
11 gal	⁷/₈ pt

DRY WEIGHT

If amount of chemical per 100 gallons is (lb)	Then amount of chemical per gallon is (oz)
¹/₂	¹/₁₂
1	¹/₆
2	¹/₃
3	¹/₂
4	²/₃
16	2 ³/₅
20	3 ¹/₅

hazardous to the environment. To protect beneficial insects, avoid excessive use of insecticides and treat with pesticides only when there are no other effective control options.

The persistence of different pesticides in the environment varies primarily with the chemical characteristics of the active ingredient, the formulation, water pH, soil pH, and environmental conditions. Temperature, humidity, wind, and sunlight affect pesticide breakdown. Usually, the greater the extremes, the sooner the pesticides are detoxified. Not all pesticides break down in the environment the same way. In general, pesticides that break down quickly and remain in the environment a short time before being changed into harmless products are called *nonpersistent*. Pesticides that break down slowly and stay in the environment without change for a long time are called *persistent* pesticides. Some persistent pesticides, such as DDT, can build up in the bodies of animals, including people. These pesticides are said to *bioaccumulate*. (This is the reason DDT is no longer available.)

Prevent pesticides from harming the environment by following safety precautions and using common sense. The following are examples of recommended safety steps.

- Before buying a pesticide, identify the pest to be controlled. Find out which pesticides will control the pest. If there is a choice of several, choose one based on its ability to break down quickly, selectively control pests, have the lowest possible toxicity to nontarget animals and people, and be the least hazardous to the environment.

- To protect beneficial insects, use insecticides only when there are no other effective and practical control options.

- Before spraying, clear all people and pets from the area. Don't spray around animal feeding dishes, bird feeders, or drinking water.

- Volatilization (evaporation of an active ingredient) can occur during or after application. Volatilization can be reduced by making applications during cool periods such as the early morning or late evening. Choose pesticide formulations that do not evaporate easily. Some products are very volatile and can move for miles under favorable conditions. Do not apply highly volatile compounds when it is only slightly windy or when temperatures after application will be above 85°F (30°C). If moderate winds come up while you are working, stop immediately. Reduce drift by spraying at the lowest possible pressure and using the largest nozzle size that achieves adequate coverage. Herbicides should be applied when the wind is no more than 5 miles per hour (8 km/h) to avoid drift onto nontarget plants.

- Protect insect pollinators, such as honey bees. Do not use insecticides known to be highly toxic to bees. When bees are foraging in the garden, restrict your spraying to late evening or early morning when they are not active (fig. 10.11). Do not apply insecticides when temperatures are unusually low because residues will remain toxic to bees much longer.

- Before applying a pesticide, consider the chance of heavy rain or irrigation water washing it off treated surfaces. Beware of potential storm sewer and groundwater contamination.

- Read the pesticide label at purchase time to find out environmental precautions.

Figure 10.11

Honey bees may be poisoned if certain pesticides are applied while they are foraging for nectar or pollen. Avoid using materials toxic to bees when crops or weeds are in bloom. Use pesticides that have a low toxicity to bees, and apply sprays early in the morning, late in the afternoon, or at night to reduce chances of killing foraging bees.

Bibliography

Brenzel, K. N., ed. 2001. Sunset western garden book. Menlo Park: Sunset Publishing.

Dreistadt, S. H. 1994. Pests of landscape trees and shrubs: An integrated pest management guide. Oakland: University of California Division of Agriculture and Natural Resources Publication 3359.

Flint, M. L. 1998. Pests of the garden and small farm: A grower's guide to using less pesticide. 2nd ed. Oakland: University of California Division of Agriculture and Natural Resources Publication 3332.

O'Connor-Marer, P. J. 2000. The safe and effective use of pesticides. 2nd ed. Oakland: University of California Division of Agriculture and Natural Resources Publication 3324.

UC IPM pest note series. B. L. P. Ohlendorf, ed. University of California Division of Agriculture and Natural Resources, Statewide Integrated Pest Management Program. Updated regularly. Available through UC Cooperative Extension county offices; also available on the World Wide Web at http://www.ipm.ucdavis.edu

Welsh, D. F., and S. D. Cotner. 1989. The Texas master gardener handbook. College Station: Texas A & M University.

11

House Plants

Ralph C. Gay and Dennis R. Pittenger

LEARNING OBJECTIVES

- Understand the basic principles for growing house plants.

- Learn which varieties and cultivars of house plants are best suited to different interiorscape climates (temperature and sunlight exposure).

- Become acquainted with some of the major pests of house plants and learn basic information about how to control them.

House Plants

This chapter is designed to familiarize you with the basic principles of house plant care and provide information on the specific cultural requirements of many commonly grown interior foliage and flowering plants. Portions of the discussion in this chapter are based on information in Welsh 1989.

Homes, apartments, and offices are typically poorly suited to the needs of plants. At the nursery, house plants are grown under nearly ideal light intensity, temperature, and other conditions. The challenges for the house plant enthusiast are to select plants that can withstand the indoor conditions of a specific location and to acquire the knowledge necessary for maintaining the chosen plants' continued growth and good health.

Selecting an Interior Foliage Plant

Select plants that are sturdy, clean, well-rooted, shapely, and well-covered with leaves. Choose only foliage plants that appear to be free of insects and diseases. Inspect the undersides of the foliage, the axils of leaves, and the root system for signs of insects or disease. Avoid plants with spindly growth and those with yellow, spotted or chlorotic leaves, brown leaf margins, or wilted or water-soaked foliage. In addition, avoid plants with leaves that have mechanical damage. Plants that have good color and leaf buds along with young growth are usually of high quality.

It is easier and cheaper to select a plant that requires the environmental conditions in your residence or office than it is to alter the environment of your home or office to suit the plants.

Transporting House Plants

Extreme temperatures can damage plants. A temperature range of 50° to 85°F (10° to 30°C) is recommended to avoid damage to plants. In the summer, avoid placing plants in a closed car because the temperature will rise, destroying the plants in a short period of time.

If you must travel for any distance under these conditions, shade the plants from direct sunlight while they are in the car. Otherwise, the plants could be burned by the hot sun shining on them through the windows, even if you use an air conditioner and the temperature in the car is comfortable.

If temperatures are near freezing, wrap plants thoroughly before leaving the store. Even brief exposure to very low temperatures during transport from the store to the car can kill or severely damage tropical plants. If protective sleeves are not available, wrap plants thoroughly with newspaper or a bag, and place them in the front of the car with the heater on. The trunks of most cars are too cold to carry plants safely in severe cold.

On an extended trip, make arrangements so that plants will not be frozen or damaged by the cold. Many foliage plants suffer from chilling injury if temperatures drop below 50°F (10°C) for several consecutive hours, so maintain as warm a temperature as possible around these plants during transport.

Acclimatization

Because nurseries often grow tropical plants for production under high light intensity, these plants have so-called sun leaves that are structurally different from the leaves of plants grown in shade (shade leaves). The chloroplasts of sun leaves align deep in cells and concentrate in cells away from the leaf surface, whereas the chloroplasts of shade leaves line upper surfaces of cells at the leaf surface. Sun leaves are thicker, smaller in surface area, and photosynthetically less efficient than shade leaves. If these same plants are placed in low light, they usually drop their sun leaves and grow a new set of shade leaves, which are photosynthetically more efficient. To reduce the shock that occurs when a plant with sun leaves is placed in shade, gradually reduce the light levels to which it is exposed. This process is called *acclimatization*.

Before placing house plants outdoors in summer, acclimatize them by gradually increasing light intensities and then reversing the process before plants are brought indoors in the fall. Acclimatize newly purchased plants by initially locating them in a high-light (southern exposure) area of the home and gradually reducing their hours in that area over a 4- to 8-week period before moving them to a permanent, darker location.

Environmental Factors Affecting Plant Care

Light, water, temperature, relative humidity, ventilation, nutrition, and soil are the chief factors affecting plant growth. These factors are interrelated, so if one factor is limiting, it will prevent proper indoor plant growth. Table 11.1 provides general guidelines for light and water requirements of many indoor foliage and flowering plants.

Light

Light is probably the most essential factor for house plant growth and one of the most problematic. The sunniest location inside a home often provides less light than shady locations outside. Light is necessary for all plants because they use this energy source to photosynthesize their food. Three variables concerning light are important: intensity, duration, and quality. (See chapter 2, "Introduction to Horticulture," for additional information.)

Light Intensity. Light intensity (the brightness of the light) influences the synthesis of plant food, stem length, leaf color, and flowering. Plants grown in light that is too low in intensity tend to be spindly with light green leaves. Similar plants grown in very bright light would tend to be shorter, better branched, and have dark green leaves. The intensity of indoor light a plant receives depends on the nearness of the light source to the plant. Light intensity decreases rapidly as you move away from the light source.

The placement of the windows in your home affects the intensity of natural sunlight indoors. Southern exposures have the most intense light; eastern and western exposures receive about 60 percent of the intensity of southern exposures; and northern exposures receive 20 percent of a southern exposure. Other factors that can influence the intensity of light penetrating a window are the presence of draperies, trees outside the window, weather, seasons of the year, shade from other buildings, and the cleanliness of the window.

Reflective (light-colored) surfaces inside the home or office increase the intensity of light available to plants. Dark surfaces decrease light intensity.

House plants can be classified according to their general light requirements: very high, high, medium, and low. In general, low-light locations are more than 6 feet (1.8 m) from windows and receive no direct light. Medium-light locations are areas roughly 3 to 6 feet (0.9 to 1.8 m) from windows. High-light areas are within 3 feet (0.9 m) of south-, east-, or west-facing, brightly lit windows. Most house plants require medium or high light to remain aesthetically appealing (see table 11.1). Insufficient light is a major cause of house plant decline. On the other hand, light intensity that is too high can cause the foliage of many house plants to become pale, or the foliage can sunburn, turn brown, and die. Use a photo light meter to measure light intensity accurately.

Light Duration. Day length, or the duration of light received by plants during a 24-hour period, is also important, especially to flowering house plants that are photoperiodic (sensitive to light duration). Poinsettia, kalanchoe, and Christmas cactus initiate flowers only when day length is short (<11 hours of light). Most flowering and foliage house plants are indifferent to day length.

Compensate for low light intensity by increasing the duration of the plant exposure to the light, as long as the plant is not adversely sensitive to day length in its flowering response. Increased hours of low intensity light may allow the plant to make sufficient food to survive and/or grow.

Light Quality. Light quality refers to the color of the light, either sunlight or artificial light. Incandescent or fluorescent lights can provide supplemental lighting. Incandescent lights produce a great deal of heat and are not very efficient users of electricity.

If artificial lights are the only source of light for growing plants, light quality must be considered. For vegetative growth and photosynthesis, plants use blues and reds most efficiently. Incandescent lights produce mostly red, and some infrared light, but are very low in blue. Fluorescent lights vary according to the phosphorus coating used by the manufacturer. Cool-white lights produce mostly blue light and are low in red light. Foliage plants grow well under cool-white fluorescent lights,

Table 11.1

LIGHT AND WATER GUIDELINES FOR SELECTED FOLIAGE AND FLOWERING PLANTS

Scientific name	Common name	Light requirements*				Water requirements†		
		Low	Med	High	Very high	Dry	Moist	Wet
Abutilon spp.	flowering maple			■			■	
Acalypha hispida (A. wilkesiana)	chenille plant			■			■	
Achimenes spp.	magic flower			■			■	
Adiantum cuneatum	maidenhair fern		■					■
Aechmea fasciata	bromeliad		■				■	
Aeschynanthus pulcher	lipstick plant		■				■	
Agave americana	century plant		■			■		
Aglaonema modestum (A. commutatum, A. simplex)	Chinese evergreen	■					■	
Aglaonema × pseudo-bracteatum	golden aglaonema	■					■	
Aglaonema roebelenii	pewter plant	■					■	
Aloe variegata	aloe				■	■		
Alternanthera bettzickiana			■	■			■	
Ananas comosus	pineapple		■				■	
Anthurium andreanum	anthurium		■				■	
Aphelandra squarrosa	zebra plant			■			■	
Araucaria heterophylla (A. excelsa)	Norfolk Island pine			■			■	
Ardisia crispa	coral ardisia		■				■	
Asparagus plumosus (A. setaceus)	bride's bouquet fern			■			■	
Asparagus sprengeri (A. densiflora Sprenger)	asparagus fern							
Aspidistra elatior	cast-iron plant	■					■	
Asplenium nidus	bird's nest fern		■					■
Aucuba japonica	gold-dust plant		■			■		
Beaucarnea recurvata	pony tail palm		■			■		
Begonia rex	rex begonia			■			■	
Begonia 'Rieger'	Rieger begonia			■			■	
Begonia semperflorens	wax begonia			■			■	
Beloperone guttata	shrimp plant			■		■		
Billbergia zebrina	billbergia		■			■	■	
Bougainvillea glabra	bougainvillea				■	■		
Browallia speciosa	bush violet		■	■			■	
Caladium spp.	caladium			■			■	
Calathea makoyana	peacock plant		■				■	
Calceolaria herbeahybrida	pocketbook plant			■			■	
Campanula isophylla	star-of-Bethlehem			■			■	
Capsicum annuum	Christmas pepper			■			■	
Carissa grandiflora	Natal plum			■		■		
Cattleya hybrids	cattleya orchid		■				■	
Chamaedorea elegans (Neanthe bella)	parlor palm	■					■	
Chamaedorea erumpens	bamboo palm	■					■	
Chamaerops humilis	European fan palm			■			■	
Chlorophytum comosum	spider plant		■	■		■	■	
Chrysalidocarpus lutescens	areca palm		■				■	
Chrysanthemum morifolium	chrysanthemum				■		■	
Cissus antarctica	kangaroo vine			■			■	
Cissus discolor	rex begonia vine		■			■	■	

Scientific name	Common name	Light requirements*				Water requirements†		
		Low	Med	High	Very high	Dry	Moist	Wet
Cissus rhombifolia	grape ivy		■			■	■	
Cissus rotundifolia	Arabian wax cissus		■			■	■	
Citrus mitis	calemondin orange			■		■		
Clerodendrum thomsoniae	bleeding-heart vine		■	■			■	
Clivia miniata	Kaffir lily		■			■		
Clusia rosea	autograph tree		■			■	■	
Codiaeum variegatum	croton				■	■		
Coffea arabica	coffee tree		■				■	
Coleus blumei	coleus			■	■		■	
Columnea spp.	columnea		■				■	
Convallaria majalis	lily-of-the-valley			■			■	
Cordyline terminalis	Hawaiian ti plant		■				■	
Crassula spp.	succulents				■	■		
Crassula argentea	jade plant			■		■		
Crocus spp.	crocus			■			■	
Crossandra infundibuliformis	crossandra		■			■	■	
Cryptanthus spp.	dwarf bromeliad		■			■	■	
Cyanotis kewensis	teddy bear vine		■				■	
Cycas revoluta	king sago palm		■			■		
Cyclamen spp.	cyclamen			■			■	
Cymbidium hybrids	cymbidium orchid		■				■	
Cyperus alternifolius	umbrella plant		■					■
Cyrtomium falcatum	Japanese holly fern	■	■				■	
Dahlia pinnata	dahlia			■			■	
Davallia fejeensis	rabbit's foot fern	■					■	
Dichorisandra reginae	queen's spiderwort		■				■	
Dieffenbachia amoena	dumbcane		■			■		
Dieffenbachia 'Exotica'	dumbcane		■			■		
Dionaea muscipula	venus fly trap		■				■	■
Dizygotheca elegantissima	false aralia			■			■	
Dracaena deremensis	green dracaena		■				■	■
Dracaena deremensis 'Warneckii'	white-striped dracaena		■			■	■	
Dracaena fragrans massangeana	corn plant	■					■	■
Dracaena marginata	dragon tree		■				■	
Dracaena sanderiiana	ribbon plant		■				■	
Dracaena surculosa (*D. godseffiana*)	gold-dust dracaena		■				■	■
Echeveria spp.	hen-and-chicken		■			■		
Epiphyllum hybrids	orchid cactus			■			■	
Epipremnum aureum	pothos	■					■	
Episcia spp.	flame violet		■				■	
Eranthemum nervosum	blue sage		■				■	
Erica gracilis	heather			■			■	
Eriobotrya japonica	Japanese loquat			■			■	
Euphorbia lactea	candelabra cactus		■			■		
Euphorbia milii	crown-of-thorns			■		■		
Euphorbia pulcherrima	poinsettia				■	■	■	
Exacum affine	Persian violet, exacum		■				■	
Fatshedera lizei	botanical wonder		■				■	
Fatsia japonica (*Aralia japonica*)	Japanese aralia		■				■	
Ficus benjamina 'Exotica'	weeping java fig		■				■	
Ficus elastica 'Decora'	rubber plant		■				■	

Table 11.1 cont.

Scientific name	Common name	Light requirements*				Water requirements†		
		Low	Med	High	Very high	Dry	Moist	Wet
Ficus lyrata	fiddleleaf fig		■				■	
Ficus repens var. *pumila*	creeping fig	■	■				■	
Ficus retusa nitida	India laurel	■				■		
Ficus triangularis	triangleleaf fig		■				■	
Fittonia verschaffeltii	silver nerve plant		■				■	
Fuchsia spp.	fuchsia				■		■	
Gardenia jasminoides	gardenia				■		■	
Guzmania lingulata	scarlet star		■			■	■	
Gynura aurantiaca	velvet plant		■				■	
Haemanthus coccineus	blood lily				■		■	
Haworthia spp.	zebra haworthia, wart plant		■			■		
Hedera helix	English ivy	■	■				■	
Helxine soleirolii	baby's tears		■				■	
Hemigraphis exotica	waffle plant		■				■	
Hibiscus rosa-sinensis	Chinese hibiscus				■		■	
Hippeastrum vittatum	amaryllis			■			■	
Howea forsterana	kentia palm	■	■				■	
Hoya carnosa	wax plant, Hindu rope plant		■			■	■	
Hyacinthus orientalis	hyacinth			■			■	
Hydrangea macrophylla	hydrangea			■			■	
Hypocyrta nummularia (*Alloplectus nummularia*)	goldfish plant		■				■	
Hypoestes sanguinolenta	polka-dot plant		■				■	
Impatiens spp.	impatiens			■	■		■	
Kalanchoe spp.	kalanchoe			■		■	■	
Kalanchoe blossfeldiana	kalanchoe, panda plant		■	■		■	■	
Lantana camara	lantana, yellow sage			■		■	■	
Lantana montevidensis	trailing lantana			■		■	■	
Leea coccinea	leea		■				■	
Ligustrum lucidum	wax-leaf privet		■			■	■	
Lilium longiflorum	Easter lily			■			■	
Maranta leuconeura	prayer plant		■				■	
Mikania ternata	plush vine		■				■	
Mimosa pudica	sensitive plant			■			■	
Monstera spp.	swiss cheese plant, split-leaf philodendron	■	■				■	
Muscari spp.	grape hyacinth			■			■	
Narcissus pseudonarcissus	daffodil	■				■		
Nautilocalyx lunchii	coral plant		■				■	
Neoregelia carolinae tricolor	tricolor bromeliad		■			■	■	
N. spectabilis	fingernail plant		■				■	■
Nephrolepis exaltata bostoniensis	Boston fern		■				■	
Nerium oleander	oleander			■			■	
Nicotiana affinis	flowering tobacco			■		■		
Oxalis spp.	oxalis			■			■	
Pachystachys coccinea	lollipop plant		■				■	
Pandanus veitchii	screw pine		■			■	■	
Paphiopedilum hybrids	lady-slipper orchid		■				■	
Passiflora spp.	passion flower				■		■	

Scientific name	Common name	Light requirements*				Water requirements†		
		Low	Med	High	Very high	Dry	Moist	Wet
Pelargonium spp.	geranium				■	■	■	
Pellionia caperata	emerald ripple	■				■		
Pellionia daveauana	trailing watermelon vine		■				■	
Pellionia glabella 'Variegata'	variegated wax privet peperomia			■				■
Pellionia metallica	metallic peperomia		■				■	
Pellionia obtusifolia	oval leaf peperomia		■				■	
Pellionia pulchra	satin pellionia		■				■	
Pellionia scandens	philodendron peperomia		■				■	
Petunia hybrida	cascade petunia				■		■	
Phalaenopsis hybrids	phalaenopsis orchid		■				■	
Philodendron domesticum 'Hastatum'	elephant ear philodendron		■				■	
Philodendron micans	velvetleaf philodendron		■				■	
Philodendron oxycardium	common philodendron	■				■		
Philodendron panduriforme	fiddleleaf philodendron		■				■	
Philodendron selloum	selloum philodendron		■				■	
Phoenix roebelenii	dwarf date palm		■					■
Pilea cadierei	aluminum plant		■				■	
Pilea microphylla	artillery plant		■				■	
Pilea nummulariifolia	creeping charley		■				■	
Pisonia grandis 'Tricolor'	bird catcher tree			■			■	
Pittosporum tobira	mock orange			■		■		
Platycerium spp.	staghorn fern		■				■	■
Plectranthus australis	Swedish ivy		■				■	
Pleomele reflexa	green pleomele		■				■	■
Pleomele thalioides	lance dracaena		■				■	
Podocarpus macrophyllus	podocarpus			■			■	
Polyscias guilfoylei	parsley aralia		■				■	
Primula malacoides	fairy primrose			■			■	
Primula obconica	German primrose			■				
Pteris ensiformis	silver table fern		■				■	
Rhapis excelsa	lady palm		■					■
Rhipsalis spp.	mistletoe cactus			■		■	■	
Rhododendron spp.	azalea			■			■	
Rhoeo discolor	Moses-in-the-cradle		■				■	
Rosa chinensis v. *minima*	miniature rose				■		■	
Rosmarinus officinalis	rosemary			■			■	
Ruellia makoyana	ruellia		■				■	
Saintpaulia spp.	African violet			■	■		■	
Salvia splendens	scarlet sage			■			■	
Sansevieria trifasciata	snake plant	■				■		
Saxifraga sarmentosa	strawberry begonia, strawberry geranium				■	■	■	
Schefflera actinophylla (*Brassia actinophylla*)	schefflera		■				■	
Schlumbergera bridgesii (*Zygocactus truncatus*)	Christmas cactus			■			■	
Sedum morganianum	burro's tail		■		■			
Selaginella lepidophylla	resurrection plant	■	■			■		
Senecio cruentus	cineraria			■			■	
Senecio macroglossus 'Variegatum'	variegated wax ivy		■				■	
Senecio mikanioides	German ivy		■				■	

Table 11.1 cont.

Scientific name	Common name	Light requirements*				Water requirements†		
		Low	Med	High	Very high	Dry	Moist	Wet
Senecio rowleyanus	string of pearls		■			■		
Setcreasea purpurea	purple heart		■			■	■	
Sinningia spp.	gloxinia				■		■	■
Solanum pseudocapsicum	Jerusalem cherry			■		■	■	
Spathiphyllum 'Mauna Loa'	white flag		■			■	■	
Strelitzia reginae	bird of paradise		■	■			■	
Streptocarpus spp.	Cape primrose			■			■	
Strobilanthes dyerianus	Persian shield		■				■	
Syngonium podophyllum	arrowhead vine, nephthytis	■					■	
Tagetes spp.	marigold				■		■	
Thunbergia alata	black-eyed susan			■			■	
Thymus vulgaris	thyme			■			■	
Tolmiea menziesii	piggyback plant			■			■	
Tradescantia spp.	wandering Jew		■			■	■	
Tulipa spp.	tulip			■			■	
Verbena hortensis	verbena			■			■	
Vinca major 'Variegata'	periwinkle			■		■		
Viola tricolor	pansy, Johnny-jump-up			■			■	
Vriesea splendens	flaming sword		■				■	
Yucca spp.	yucca	■				■		
Zantedeschia spp.	calla lily			■			■	■
Zebrina spp.	wandering Jew		■				■	
Zinnia elegans	zinnia			■			■	

Source: Adapted from Poole and Pittenger 1980, pp. 16–19.

Notes:

*Light requirements: Light levels are for maintenance purposes only. They will not permit satisfactory growth. Light requirements are for 8 to 12 hours each day: low (25–50 foot-candles); medium (50–100 foot-candles); high (100–200 foot-candles); and very high (200–400 foot-candles).

which are cool enough to position quite close to plants. Extra infrared light required by flowering plants can be supplied by incandescent lights or special horticultural-type fluorescent lights that produce higher levels of blue and red.

Water

Overwatering and underwatering account for a large percentage of house plant losses. One of the most common question home gardeners ask is, "How often should I water my plants?" There is no simple answer. Differences in species, water-use rates, potting media, and environment influence water needs. Two important rules about proper watering techniques are: Never permit the soil medium to dry out completely between waterings; and never allow plants to stand in water for an extended time. Roots may die in both situa-

tions. In dry soil, roots can dry out and die. Conversely, soils that are too wet for too long encourage the growth of root pathogens and exclude air (oxygen), which is essential to keep roots alive. As a general rule, a plant needs water when the top 1 inch (2.5 cm) of soil is dry in pots less than 6 inches (15 cm) in diameter and the top 2 inches (5 cm) are dry in larger pots. Insert your index finger to the 1- or 2-inch (2.5- or 5-cm) depth and feel the soil to check for moisture. If the soil feels damp, do not water. Repeat the test until the soil is barely moist at the 1-inch (2.5-cm) or 2-inch (5-cm) depth.

Always water until a little water runs out of the bottom of the pot. This technique serves two purposes. First, it washes all the excess salts (fertilizer residue) from the soil. Second, it guarantees that the bottom two-thirds of the pot, which contains most of the roots, receives sufficient water. Do not let the pot stand more than several minutes in the water that has run out. Empty the saucer. After a thorough watering, wait until the soil dries at the 1- or 2-inch (2.5- or 5-cm) depth before watering again. See the discussion below on soluble salts to learn more about proper watering.

Water quality is not usually a problem when ordinary tap water is used on house plants. The chlorine and fluorine that are often added to potable water do not harm plants. However, water that is artificially softened should not be used regularly to water house plants. Water containing boron should not be used on house plants or any container-grown plants.

Table 11.1 provides watering guidelines. When testing, pay attention to the soil condition. If your index finger cannot penetrate 1 to 2 inches (2.5 to 5 cm) deep, you need a more porous soil mix, or the plant is becoming root-bound.

Temperature

Most house plants tolerate normal household temperature fluctuations. In general, foliage plants grow best between 70° and 80°F (21° and 27°C) during the day and between 60° and 68°F (16° and 20°C) at night. Most flowering house plants prefer the same daytime range but grow best at nighttime temperatures of 55° to 60°F (13° to 16°C). A cooler temperature at night is more desirable for plant growth. A good rule of thumb is to keep the night temperature 10 to 15 degrees lower than the day temperature. The lower night temperature induces physiological recovery from moisture loss, intensifies flower color, and prolongs flower life.

Excessively low or high temperatures may cause spindly appearance, foliage damage, leaf or flower drop, and general plant decline. Avoid putting plants in areas with widely fluctuating temperatures, such as on top of television sets. Move plants from window sills and doorways in cold winter months. A southern exposure is the warmest; eastern and western exposures are less warm; and a northern exposure is the coolest. Table 11.2 gives temperature requirements of selected house plants.

Relative Humidity

Atmospheric humidity is expressed as a percentage of the moisture saturation of air. Increase relative humidity in the vicinity of house plant containers by attaching a humidifier to the heating or ventilating system in the home or by placing gravel trays (in which an even moisture level is maintained) under the flower pots or containers. As the moisture around the pebbles evaporates, the relative humidity increases. Grouping plants close together also raises humidity somewhat. Spraying mist on the foliage of plants does not significantly affect relative humidity.

Ventilation

House plants, especially flowering varieties, are very sensitive to cold drafts or heat from registers. Do not place them directly in front of vents. Forced air dries plants rapidly, overtaxes their limited root systems, and may cause damage or plant death.

Fertilization

House plants need fertilizers containing three major plant nutrient elements: nitrogen (N), phosphorus (P), and potassium (K). These nutrients are available in many different combinations and under a multitude of brand names. The label on each product should indicate the percentage by weight of available elemental nitrogen, phosphate, and potash (potassium). Commercial fertilizers used for house plants are sold as liquids, granules, crystals, or tablets that are mixed with water for application, or as slow-release crystals and pellets that are placed on the soil surface or incorporated into the soil. Each should be used according to the instructions on the package label or diluted even more. Do not overfertilize because overfertilizing can kill house plants. See chapter 3, "Soil and Fertilizer Management," for more information.

The frequency of fertilizer application varies depending on the purpose of the plant and the formulation of fertilizer used. If the plant is a nonflowering foliage plant and the desire is to keep it healthy at a given size, fertilization may be necessary every 4 to 6 weeks. However, if the plant is a flowering one or if the desire is to have the plant grow vigorously, then fertilizer may be necessary every 2 to 4 weeks. Use of slow-release fertilizers extends the above intervals by a factor of 3 to 4. When applying liquid forms of fertilizer, make sure that some solution runs out of the bottom of the pot. This technique prevents the buildup of salts (excess fertilizer) and reduces the risk of injuring roots and foliage.

Table 11.2

TEMPERATURE REQUIREMENTS OF SELECTED HOUSE PLANTS

COOL-TEMPERATURE PLANTS
(grow best at 50° to 60°F [10° to 16°C] during the day and
45° to 55°F [7° to 13°C] at night)

Scientific name	Common name
Araucaria heterophylla (A. excelsa)	Norfolk Island pine
Aspidistra elatior	cast-iron plant[†]
Camellia spp.	camellia
Chrysanthemum morifolium	chrysanthemum
Citrus spp.	citrus (grapefruit, lemon, orange)
Euonymous japonica	spindle tree
Exacum affine	Persian violet
Fatsia japonica (*Aralia sieboldii, A. japonica*)	Japanese aralia
Ficus repens var. *pumila*	creeping fig
Hedera helix	ivy[†]
Hyacinthus orientalis	hyacinth
Hydrangea macrophylla	hydrangea
Jasminum spp.	jasmine
Lilium longiflorum	Easter lily[†]
Narcissus spp.	daffodil
Pittosporum tobira	mock orange[†]
Primula spp.	primrose
Rhododendron spp.	azalea
Rosa chinensis var. *mimia*	miniature rose[†]
Solanum pseudocapsicum	Jerusalem cherry
Tradescantia albiflora	wandering Jew[†]
Tulipa spp.	tulip
Various genera (during winter rest periods only)[*†]	cacti and succulents
Zantedeschia spp.	calla lily
Zebrina pendula	wandering Jew†

MEDIUM-TEMPERATURE PLANTS
(grow best at 60° to 65°F [16° to 18°C] during the day and
55° to 60°F [13° to 16°C] to at night)

Scientific name	Common name
Aechmea spp.	bromeliads[*]
Asparagus spp.	asparagus ferns
Aspidistra elatior	cast-iron plant[‡]
Asplenium nidus	bird's nest fern
Begonia spp.	begonia
Browallia spp.	bush violet
Cissus antartica	kangaroo vine[*]
Citrus spp.	citrus
Coleus hybridus	coleus

MEDIUM-TEMPERATURE PLANTS, cont.

Scientific name	Common name
Cryptanthus spp.	dwarf bromeliad[*]
Dracaena surculosa (*D. godseffiana*)	gold-dust plant
Euphorbia milii	crown-of-thorns[*]
Gynura aurantiaca	purple passion plant, purple velvet plant[*]
Hedera helix	English ivy[‡]
Hibiscus rosa-sinensis	hibiscus
Hippeastrum vittatum	amaryllis
Hoya carnosa	wax plant, Hindu rope plant
Kalanchoe tomentosa	panda plant
Lilium longiflorum	Easter lily‡
Oxalis spp.	shamrock plant
Peperomia spp.	peperomia
Persea spp.	avocado
Pilea cadierei	aluminum plant
Pilea microphylla	artillery plant
Pilea nummariifolia	creeping charley
Platycerium spp.	staghorn fern[*]
Podocarpus macrophillus	podocarpus
Sansevieria trifasciata	snake plant[*]
Saxifraga sarmentosa	strawberry geranium, strawberry begonia
Schefflera actinophylla (*Brassia actinophylla*)	schefflera
Schlumbergera bridgesii (*Zygocactus truncatus*)	Christmas cactus
Senecio mikanioides	German ivy
Soleirolia soleirolii	baby's tears
Tolmiea menziesii	piggyback plant
Trifolium repensminus	shamrock plant
Various genera	cacti and succulents[*‡]
Various genera	palms[*]

HIGH-TEMPERATURE PLANTS
(grow best at 70° to 80°F [21° to 27°C] during the day and
65° to 70°F [18° to 21°C] at night)

Scientific name	Common name
Acalypha hispida (*A. wilkesiana*)	chenille plant
Aechmea spp.	bromeliads
Aglaonema modestum (*A. commutatum, A. simplex*)	Chinese evergreen
Caladium spp.	caladium
Calathea makoyana	peacock plant
Cissus antartica	kangaroo vine [‡]

(grow best at 70° to 80°F [21° to 27°C] during the day and
65° to 70°F [18° to 21°C] at night)

Scientific name	Common name
Codiaeum variegatum	croton
Cordyline spp.	Cordyline, ti plant
Cryptanthus spp.	dwarf bromeliad ‡
Dizygotheca elegatissima	false aralia
Dracena spp.	dracaena †
Echeveria spp.	hen and chicks
Epipremnum aureum	pothos
Episcia spp.	flame violet
Euphorbia milii	crown-of-thorns ‡
Ficus spp.	ficus (tree types)
Gynura aurantiaca	velvet plant†
Impatiens spp.	impatiens

Scientific name	Common name
Maranta leuconeura	prayer plant
Mimosa pudica	sensitive plant
Monstera spp.	swiss cheese plant, split-leaf philodendron
Pandanus veitchii	screw pine
Pelargonium spp.	geranium
Philodendron spp.	philodendron
Platycerium spp.	staghorn fern ‡
Saintpaulia spp.	African violets
Sansevieria trifasciata	snake plant †
Various genera	cacti and succulents *‡
Various genera	palms†

Notes:
* Will also do well at high temperatures.
† Will also do well at medium temperatures.
‡ Will also do well at cool temperatures.

Soluble Salts

Soluble salts may accumulate on the top of the soil, forming a yellow or white crust. A ring of salt deposits may form around the pot at the soil line or around the drainage hole. Salts may also build up on the outside of clay pots. In house plants, signs of excess soluble salts include reduced growth, brown leaf tips, dropping of lower leaves, small new growth, dead root tips, and wilting.

Soluble salts are minerals dissolved in water. Fertilizer dissolved in water becomes a soluble salt. When water evaporates from the soil, the minerals or salts stay behind. As the salts in the soil become more and more concentrated, it becomes more difficult for plants to take up water. If salts build up to an extremely high level, water can be taken out of the root tips, causing them to die. High levels of soluble salts damage the roots directly, weakening the plant and making it more susceptible to attack from insects and diseases. One of the most common problems associated with high salt levels is root rot.

The best way to prevent soluble salt injury is to stop the salts from building up. When watering, allow some water to drain through the container and then empty the saucer. Do not allow the pot to sit in water. If the drained water is absorbed by the soil, the salts that were washed out are reabsorbed through the drainage hole or directly through a clay pot.

House plants should be leached at least every 4 to 6 months. To leach plants, pour excess water on the soil and let it drain completely. The amount of water used for leaching should equal twice the volume of the pot. Keep the water running through the soil to wash out the salts. If a layer of salts has formed a crust at the soil surface, remove the salt crust before leaching. Do not remove more than ¼ inch (6 mm) of soil. It is best not to add soil to the top of the pot. If the soluble salt level appears to be extremely high, repot the plant.

The level of salts that causes injury varies with the species of plant and how it is grown. A house plant may be injured by salts at a very low concentration, but the same plant growing in a greenhouse where watering is well managed may tolerate salts at high levels. Some nurseries and retail plant outlets leach plants to remove excess salts before the plant is sold. If you are not sure that a newly purchased plant has been leached, leach it the first time you water.

pH

The pH of commercially prepared potting soils is usually slightly to moderately acidic, which is acceptable to most house plants. Rarely is the pH too low (acidic) or too high (alkaline) to maintain house plants. If the pH of the medium may be inappropriate, wash the soil from the root system and repot the plant in new potting soil.

Growing Media

Potting soil or growing media for plants must be of good quality and meet certain performance criteria. The chemical and physical properties of a potting soil determine its performance. To sustain plant growth, the medium must hold large quantities of water in a limited volume and yet maintain a high volume of aeration. Because soil in a container does not behave the same as soil in the field, potting soils are typically formulated with a high percentage of bulky organic materials such as bark, wood chips, peat, or compost. These materials hold varying amounts of water and also create pockets of air in the medium. Media usually contain additional nonorganic materials such as sand, vermiculite, or perlite, which provide additional aeration and structure. Quality potting soils should be low in soluble salts, slightly acidic (pH of 5 to 6.5), and capable of holding essential nutrients for plant growth.

It is more practical to use a commercially prepared potting soil than to buy ingredients and formulate your own. However, potting soils sold though retail garden supply outlets vary widely in their performance as growing media. In California, manufacturers are required to label the product with the names of the ingredients in decreasing order of volume. Unfortunately, there are no consistent relationships between the physical and chemical properties of a potting soil and its ingredients list. The following recommendations help ensure successful potting.

Select mixes high in bark, forest materials, or sphagnum peat with vermiculite or perlite.

Thoroughly leach any potting soil before placing seed or plant material in the mix. Leaching will reduce soluble salts to acceptable levels in most mixes.

Fertilize with a soluble fertilizer according to the manufacturer's directions within 2 weeks after plants are growing in new potting soil to replace leached nutrients and those taken up by the plants.

Containers

A container should be large enough to provide room for soil and roots, have sufficient headroom for proper watering, provide good bottom drainage, and be an aesthetically pleasing shape and size in relation to the plant it holds. (Headroom is the amount of space between the soil level and the top of the pot that allows for watering a plant.) Containers may be made of ceramic, plastic, fiberglass, wood, aluminum, copper, brass, glass, or many other materials. Table 11.3 lists house plants suitable for many types of containers, including hanging baskets, tropical terraria, decorative tubs, and desert dish gardens.

Clay and Ceramic Containers

Unglazed and glazed porous clay pots with drainage holes are sometimes still used by commercial plant growers, although they are no longer the standard. Although easily broken, clay pots provide excellent aeration for plant roots and are considered by some to be the best type of container for a plant. Clay pots, unlike plastic ones, absorb and lose moisture through their walls. The greatest accumulation of roots in any container is frequently next to the walls of the pot.

Ceramic pots are sometimes glazed on both the outside and inside. Frequently, they are designed without adequate drainage holes. Use them only as a decorative sleeve to hide a well-drained but unattractive container. Avoid small novelty containers because they have little room for soil and roots and are largely ornamental.

If drainage holes are too large and the potting soil comes out of the holes, a few shards can be placed over drainage holes to prevent soil loss.

Plastic and Fiberglass Containers

Plastic and fiberglass containers are usually quite light and easy to handle. They have become the standard in recent years because they are relatively inexpensive and can be made quite attractive in shape and color. Plastic pots are easy to sterilize or clean for reuse, and because they are not as porous as clay pots, they need less frequent watering and tend to accumulate fewer salts.

PLANTS FOR SPECIFIC INDOOR GARDENING USES

PLANTS FOR LARGE-TUBBED DECORATIVE SPECIMENS

Scientific name	Common name
Acanthus mollis	artist's acanthus
Acanthus montanus	mountain acanthus
Alocasia spp.	giant caladium, elephant's ear
Alsophila australis	Australian tree fern
Codiaeum variegatum	croton
Dieffenbachia amoena	spotted dumbcane
Fatshedera lizei	botanical wonder
Fatsia japonica	Japanese aralia
Ficus eburnea	ivory fig
Ficus elastica 'Variegata'	variegated India rubber
Ficus lyrata	fiddleleaf fig
Monstera deliciosa	split-leaf philodendron
Pandanus veitchii	screw pine
Philodendron elongatum	philodendron
Philodendron giganteum	giant phildendron
Philodendron mandaianum	philodendron
Philodendron panduriforme	philodendron
Philodendron selloum	philodendron
Philodendron wendlandii	philodendron
Polyscias paniculata 'Variegata'	jagged-leaf aralia
Schefflera actinophylla (*Brassia actinophylla*)	schefflera
Strelitzia reginae	bird of paradise

LOW, CREEPING PLANTS FOR GROUND COVERS IN INTERIOR PLANTING BOXES

Scientific name	Common name
Episcia cupreata	flame violet
Ficus repens var. *pumila*	creeping fig
Ficus radicans	climbing fig
Fittonia verschaffeltii	silver nerve plant
Hedera helix	English ivy
Hemigraphis colorata	red ivy
Hemigraphis exotica	waffle plant
Pellionia daveauana	trailing watermelon vine
Pellionia pulchra	satin pellionia
Philodendron cordatum	heartleaf philodendron
Pilea nummulariifolia	creeping Charlie
Saxifraga sarmentosa	strawberry begonia, strawberry geranium
Scindapsus aureus (*S. pictus*)	devil's ivy
Tradescantia (all varieties)	wandering jew
Vinca major 'Variegata'	periwinkle

PLANTS THAT WITHSTAND DRY, WARM LOCATIONS

Scientific name	Common name
Bromeliads (all spp. and varieties)	bromeliads
Cacti (all spp. and varieties)	cactus

VINES AND TRAILING PLANTS FOR TOTEM POLES AND TRAINED PLANTS

Scientific name	Common name
Anthurium alemulum	climbing anthurium
Cissus antarctica	kangaroo vine
Cissus discolor	rex begonia vine
Cissus rhombifolia	grape ivy
Clerodendrum thomsoniae	bleeding-heart vine
Ficus repens var. *pumila*	creeping fig
Vanilla fragrans 'Marginata'	vanilla

PLANTS FOR HANGING BASKETS

Scientific name	Common name
Achimenes grandiflora	big purple achimenes
Aeschynanthus parasiticus	lobecup basketvine
Aeschynanthus parasiticus 'Black Pagoda'	black pagoda basketvine
Aeschynanthus radicans	Lobbs basketvine; lipstick plant
Aeschynanthus pulcher	lipstick plant, scarlet basketvine
Asarina erubescens	creeping gloxinia
Asparagus plumosus (*A. setaceus*)	bride's bouquet fern
Asparagus sprengeri (*A. densiflora* Sprenger)	asparagus fern
Begonia spp.	begonias
Callisia elegans	striped inch plant
Ceropegia woodii	string of hearts; rosary vine
Chlorophytum bichetii	St. Bernard's lily
Chlorophytum comosum 'Variegatum'	spider plant
Chrysanthemum morifolium 'Anna'	daisy cascade
Chrysanthemum morifolium 'Jane Harte'	daisy cascade
Cissus spp.	grape ivy, winged treevine, kangaroo treevine
Coleus rehneltianus 'Trailing Queen'	trailing coleus

Table 11.3 cont.

PLANTS FOR HANGING BASKETS cont.

Scientific name	Common name
Columnea × banksii	goldfish vine
Columnea microphylla	small-leaved goldfish vine
Commelina communis aurea-striata	variegated widow's tear
Cyanotis kewensis	teddy bear plant
Cyanotis somaliensis	pussy ears
Cymbalaria muralis	Kenilworth ivy
Davallia fejeensis (D. trichomanoides)	rabbit's foot fern
Epipremnum aureum	pothos
Episcia cupreata	ember lace episcia
Episcia cupreata 'Amazon'	Amazon flame violet
Episcia cupreata 'Chocolate Soldier'	carpet plant
Episcia cupreata 'Emerald Queen'	emerald queen episcia
Episcia cupreata 'Silver Sheen'	silver sheen episcia
Episcia dianthiflora	lace flower vine
Episcia 'Moss Agate'	Panama episcia
Euphorbia mammillaris	corncob plant
Fittonia verschaffeltii	silver nerve plant
Fittonia verschaffeltii var. Pearcei	snake skin plant
Fuchsia var. 'Jubilee'	jubilee fuchsia
Fuchsia var 'Swingtime'	swingtime fuchsia
Fuchsia triphylla 'Gartenmeister Bohnstedt'	honeysuckle fuchsia
Hatiora salicornioides	drunkard's dream
Hedera helix 'Hahn's Variegated'	variegated Hahn's English ivy
Hedera helix 'Ivalace'	Ivalace English ivy
Hedera helix 'Needlepoint'	needlepoint English ivy
Hemigraphis colorata	red ivy
Hemigraphis exotica	waffle plant
Hoya australis	porcelain flower
Hoya bella	miniature wax plant
Hoya carnosa 'Compacta'	compact wax plant
Hoya carnosa 'Exotica'	exotic wax plant
Hoya carnosa 'Krinkle Curl'	Hindu rope plant
Hoya carnosa 'Tri-color'	variegated wax plant
Hoya imperialis	honey plant
Hoya keysi	pubescent wax plant
Hoya longifolia shepherdii	shepherd's wax plant
Hoya motoskei	spotted wax plant
Hoya purpureo-fusca	silver pink wax plant
Hypocyrta nummularia (Alloplectus nummularia)	goldfish plant
Hylocereus undatus	night blooming cereus
Ipomoea batatas	sweet potato
Kalanchoe gastonis-bonnieri	life plant
Kalanchoe manginii	mangin kalanchoe
Kalanchoe pubescens	jinglebells kalanchoe

Scientific name	Common name
Kalanchoe uniflora	miniature kalanchoe
Mammillaria elongata	lace mammillaria, golden star cactus
Nephrolepis exaltata 'Bostoniensis'	Boston fern
Nephrolepis exaltata 'Fluffy Ruffles'	fluffy ruffles fern
Nephrolepis exaltata 'Rooseveltii'	tall featherfern
Pelargonium × fragrans	scented geranium
Pellionia acuminata	Mexico pepperface
Pellionia cubensis	Cuban pepperface
Pellionia daveauana	trailing watermelon vine
Pellionia glabella 'Variegata'	variegated wax privet peperomia
Pellionia pulchra	satin pellonia
Peristrophe hyssopifolia 'Aurea-Variegata'	marble-leaf
Philodendron micans	velvet leaf philodendron
Philodendron oxycardium	common philodendron
Pilea nummulariifolia	creeping charley
Platycerium alcicorne	staghorn fern
Plectranthus australis	Swedish ivy
Plectranthus coleoides 'Marginatus'	candle plant
Plectranthus oertendahlii	prostrate coleus
Plectranthus purpuratus	moth king
Plectranthus tomentosus	succulent coleus
Polypodium aureum	hare's foot fern
Portulacaria afra 'Variegata'	rainbow bush
Rhipsalis capilliformis	treechair rhipsalis
Rhipsalis cassutha	mistletoe rhipsalis
Rhipsalis houlletiana	snowdrop cactus
Rhipsalis paradoxa	China rhipsalis
Rhipsalis pentaptera	fivewing rhipsalis
Rhipsalis trigona	triangle rhipsalis
Ruellia makoyana	ruellia
Schlumbergera bridgesii (Zygocactus truncatus)	Christmas cactus
Schlumbergera gaertneri	Easter cactus
Scindapsus aureus (S. pictus)	devil's ivy
Sedum morganianum	burro's tail
Senecio jacobsenii	
Senecio rowleyanus	string of pearls
Setcreasea purpurea	purple heart
Stapelia gigantea	starfish flower, giant toadplant
Stenotaphrum secundatum variegatum	variegated St. Augustinegrass
Streptocarpus saxorum	false African violet
Tradescantia albiflora 'Albovittata'	giant white inch, wandering Jew
Tradescantia sillamontana	white velvet; white gossamer

PLANTS FOR TROPICAL TERRARIUMS

Scientific name	Common name
Aglaonema modestum (A. commutatum, A. simplex)	Chinese evergreen
Begonia boweri	miniature begonias
Chamaedorea elegans (Neanthe bella)	parlor palm
Cissus antarctica	kangaroo vine
Coffea arabica	Arabian coffee plant
Cordyline terminalis minima 'Baby Ti'	dwarf ti plant
Cryptanthus bivittatus minor	dwarf rose-stripe, earth star
Dizygotheca elegantissima	false aralia
Dracaena sanderana	ribbon plant
Dracaena surculosa (D. godseffiana)	gold-dust dracaena
Ficus diversifolia	mistletoe fig
Ficus repens var. pumila 'Minima'	dwarf creeping fig
Fittonia verschaffeltii	silver nerve plant
Maranta leuconeura	prayer plant
Nephrolepis exaltata cultivars	Boston fern
Peperomia sandersii	watermelon peperomia
Pilea cadierei 'Minima'	aluminum plant
Pilea depressa	miniature pilea
Pilea microphylla	artillary plant
Pilea nummulariifolia	creeping charley
Pteris spp.	brake or table ferns
Saintpaulia cultivars	miniature African violets
Selaginella kraussiana	creeping club moss
Selaginella emmeliana	sweat plant
Sinningia pusilla (and other miniature cvs)	miniature gloxinias
Syngonium podophyllum	arrowhead vine, nephthytis

PLANTS FOR DESERT DISH GARDENS

Scientific name	Common name
Adromischus spp.	calico hearts, leopard spots
Aloe spp.	medicine plant
Astrophytum myriostigma	bishop's cap
Cephalocereus nobilis	cylinder cactus
Cereus peruvianus 'Monstrosus'	curiosity plant
Crassula argentea	jade plant
Crassula lycopodioides	toy cypress, watch chain
Crassula rupestris	rosary vine
Echeveria spp.	—
Echinocactus grusonii	golden barrel cactus
Echinocactus pectinatus var. neomexicanus	rainbow cactus
Echinocactus reichenbachii	lace cactus
Echinocactus micromeris	button cactus
Euphorbia lactea cristata	crested euphorbia, frilled fan
Faucaria tigrina	tiger jaws
Gasteria liliputana	miniature gasteria/ ox tongue
Haworthia spp.	pearl plant, wart plant
Haworthia fasciata	zebra haworthia
Haworthia margaritifera	pearl plant
Lithops spp.	living stones
Mammillaria bocasana	powder-puff cactus
Mammillaria elongata	lace mammillaria, golden star cactus
Mammillaria fragilis	thimble cactus
Opuntia erectoclada	dominoes, pincushion cactus
Opuntia microdasys	bunny ears
Opuntia vilis	dwarf tree opuntia
Portulacaria afra	elephant bush
Portulacaria afra 'Variegata'	rainbow bush
Rebutia kupperiana	scarlet crown cactus
Rebutia minuscula	red crown cactus
Sedum spp.	stonecrop
Sedum acre	golden carpet, gold moss
Sedum adolphi	golden sedum
Sedum dasyphyllum	golden glow
Sedum lineare	carpet sedum
Sedum morganianum	burro's tail
Sedum multiceps	miniature Joshua tree
Sedum × rubrotinctum	Christmas cheer
Sedum stahlii	coral beads

Repotting

Actively growing house plants require occasional repotting. Slowly growing plants only rarely require repotting. Plants that grow more quickly require more frequent repotting. Foliage plants require repotting when their roots have filled the pot and are growing out of the bottom but before they start circling around the inside of the pot. Repot a plant as soon as it becomes necessary. The pot selected for repotting should have a diameter no more than about 2 inches (5 cm) larger than the pot in which the plant is currently growing. It should also have a minimum of one drainage hole and be clean. Wash soluble salts from clay pots with water and a scrub brush. Wash all pots in a solution of one part liquid bleach to nine parts water.

Before repotting begins, the medium should be moistened. Most plants can be removed easily from their pots if the lip of the container is knocked upside down against any solid object. Hold your hand over the soil, straddling the plant between the fore and middle fingers while knocking it out of its container. If the plant has become root-bound, cut any roots that encircle the plant; otherwise, the roots will never develop normally. If the soil surface has accumulated salts, remove them. Set the root ball in the middle of the new container and fill soil under the root ball and around the sides between the root ball and pot. Placing gravel or other coarse-textured material in the bottom of the pot does not improve drainage. In fact, it will usually impede drainage, which can result in root disease. Do not add soil above the original level on the root ball, unless the roots are exposed or some of the surface soil has been removed. Do not pack the soil. To firm or settle it, tap the pot against a table top or gently press the soil with your fingers.

After watering and settling, the soil level should be sufficiently below the level of the pot to leave headroom for watering. A guideline is to leave about 1 inch (2.5 cm) of headroom in a 6-inch (15-cm) pot and proportionately more or less for other pot sizes. A properly potted plant has enough headroom to allow water to drain through the soil and thoroughly moisten it.

Training and Grooming

Training and grooming refer to a number of activities, including pinching, pruning, and disbudding. Pinching is the removal of 1 inch (2.5 cm) or less of new stem and leaf growth just above the leaf node. This leaves the plant compact and stimulates new growth. It can be a one-time or continuous activity, depending on the plant's requirements and the appearance desired by the plant owner. Frequent pinching will make a plant compact but well filled out. Pinch growing tips of the tallest stems, removing them close to a node. New growth that forms just below the pinched tip makes the plant bushy.

Pruning is similar to pinching. It includes the removal of entire branches and shoots other than terminal shoot tips and is done sometimes for the sake of appearance, to improve a plant's structure, or to remove dead plant material.

Disbudding is another related care activity. Certain flower buds are removed either to obtain larger blooms from a few choice buds or to eliminate flowering of a very young plant or recently rooted cutting that should not bear the physical drain of flowering.

Keeping house plants clean and neat not only improves their appearance but reduces the incidence of insects and disease problems. Remove all spent flowers, dying leaves, and dead branches. Keep leaves dust-free by washing them with warm water and mild dish washing soap (cover the pot to prevent soap from entering the soil). If the tips of leaves become brown and dry, trim them neatly with sharp scissors.

Care of Potted Gift and Holiday Plants

When flowering holiday plants are brought into a home where the light and relative humidity are low and the temperatures are maintained for human comfort, many of these plants do not perform well for long periods. Do not expect to hold over a holiday plant from year to year. Enjoy them while they are attractive and in season and then discard them, or plant them outdoors if conditions permit.

Poinsettia. Poinsettias require bright light and should be kept away from drafts. A temperature between 65° and 70°F (18° and 21°C) is ideal. Avoid temperatures below 60° (16°C) and above 75°F (24°C). Keep plants well-watered but do not overwater. Some of the newer, long-lasting varieties can be kept attractive all winter.

Gardeners frequently ask whether they can carry their poinsettias over to bloom again next year. Satisfactory results can be obtained in mild climate zones of the state, where poinsettias can be planted outdoors. It is questionable whether the results are worth the effort in colder areas, as the quality of home-grown potted plants seldom equals that of commercially grown plants. For those who wish to try, the procedures outlined below can be followed.

After the bracts fade or fall, set poinsettia plants outdoors or place containers where they will receive indirect light and temperatures of 55° to 85°F (13° to 29°C). Water sparingly during this time, just enough to keep the stems from shriveling. Cut the plants back to within about 5 inches (12.5 cm) from the ground and repot in fresh soil. As soon as new growth begins, place in a well-lighted window. After danger of frost is over, place pots outdoors in a partially shaded spot. Pinch the new growth back to get a plant with several stems. Do not pinch after September 1. About Labor Day, or as soon as the nights are cool, bring plants indoors. Continue to grow them in a sunny room with a night temperature of about 65°F (18°C).

Poinsettias bloom only during short days. To initiate blooms, exclude artificial light, either by covering with a light-proof box each evening or placing in an unlighted room or closet for a minimum of 12 hours of darkness. Once short-day treatment is started, it must continue every night until plants develop the red color. Plants require full light in the daytime, so be sure to return them to a sunny window. Start the short-day treatment about mid-September to have blooms between December 1 and Christmas.

Azaleas. Azaleas require bright sunlight and constantly moist soil to remain healthy. Flowers can last up to 6 weeks in the home. A night temperature of 60°F (16°C) prolongs bloom. Azaleas drop leaves readily if kept in low light. Use an a fertilizer formulated especially for azaleas and, when repotting, use a mixture high in sphagnum moss. Azaleas can be planted in a shady spot in the garden during the summer months. Examine them frequently and keep them watered during dry periods. Greenhouse azaleas are not hardy and need to be brought indoors if long-term freezing weather is expected.

Gardenias. Gardenias grown indoors need special care. They require acid soil and should receive the same nutritional care as azaleas. The night temperature should be near 60°F (16°C), and the humidity around the plant should be kept high. High temperatures or low light intensity result in flower bud drop.

Amaryllis. The secret of growing amaryllis is to keep the plants actively growing after they finish blooming. Keep the plants in full sun, with a night temperature above 60°F (16°C). As soon as the danger of frost has passed, set the plants in the garden in a semi-shaded spot. In the fall, before the danger of frost, bring them in and store them in a cold, dark place to rest. They will be ready to force again about January 1. Bring them into a warm, lighted room and water moderately to begin new growth.

Christmas Cactus. At least three related species of Christmas cactus are sold, in addition to a number of cultivars. All have similar cultural requirements. The secret of good bloom is to control the temperature and photoperiod. Plants will develop buds and bloom if given bright light, short days, and night temperatures between 55° and 65°F (13° and 18°C) during bud formation. For Christmas bloom, the light and temperature treatment should be started in mid-September and continue for 8 weeks. Christmas cacti bloom best when somewhat pot-bound. Repotting is necessary only about once in 3 years. These plants grow naturally shaded by a canopy of leaves. Full sunlight is beneficial in midwinter, but bright sun during summer months can make plants look pale and yellow. Christmas cacti require less water from October to March than they do from April to September when growth is active. Care should be taken that soil never becomes waterlogged during the dark days of winter.

Cyclamen. Cyclamens require full sunlight and cool temperatures, with a night temperature between 50° and 60°F (10° and 16°C). They are heavy users of water and must be watered whenever the surface of the soil is dry. Flower buds will fail to develop if night temperature is too high or if light is poor. High light intensity and cool (70°F [21°C] or less) temperatures increase flower longevity. Cyclamens can be carried over, but, as with poinsettias, home-grown plants are seldom equal to those grown by a commercial grower. Let the plants die down after they finish flowering. Repot the fleshy corm in June, with the top of the corm above the soil line. Allow resting bulbs to dry, but they should not become shriveled.

Common House Plant Problems

Problems with house plants typically arise from improper care (too much or too little water and fertilizer), poor sanitation, adverse environmental conditions (low light intensity, low relative humidity), and insect or mite pests. Routinely check your house plants and treat problems promptly. When dusting and grooming plants, examine them for signs and symptoms of pest infestation or other types of damage and problems. A guide for diagnosing house plant problems is found in table 11.4. (For a broader discussion of diagnosing plant problems, see chapter 22.)

Before purchasing house plants, inspect them carefully for insect and mite pests and possible disease problems. Just because the plant has recently come from a commercial grower does not mean that it is pest-free. Reject any plants that have insect, mite, or disease infestations. After purchase, isolate plants for a few weeks from other plants in your home and check them again as an added precaution. A plant that appeared pest-free at purchase may have a microscopic mite infestation or may harbor insect eggs that could develop into pest problems.

Whenever you detect insect or mite pests on an established plant in your home or office, isolate the plant immediately to prevent pests from spreading to other plants. As an additional precaution, wash your hands after touching insect- or mite-infested plants. You can decide later how or whether to attempt to control the pests. Sometimes control is not practical or effective, and it is better to discard the plant and purchase a new one.

Environmental Problems and Improper Care

The majority of house plant problems are caused by improper care and by environmental factors in the home that are unfavorable to optimal plant growth. Get to know the growing requirements of each of your house plants (see tables 11.1–11.3).

The majority of problem symptoms can be caused by a number of factors:

- Brown leaf tips and burned leaf margins are usually caused by overfertilization (salt buildup) or excessively dry soil, but they may also result from too much sun or heat through a window, low relative humidity, or a drafty setting.

- Weak growth or light green to yellow leaves may be due to underfertilization (lack of nitrogen), root rot, exposure to too much or too little light, or sucking insects and mites.

- Small leaves with excessively long internodes (leggy growth) are usually caused by unfavorably low light levels.

- Yellowing and dropping leaves can be caused by low light intensity, chilling, overwatering, poor soil drainage, or soilborne insect or disease pests.

- Wilting is usually caused by underwatering or overwatering or light that is too intense, but it may also be due to root decay from soil pathogens. Inspect root systems whenever wilting occurs.

- A lack of flowers on a house plant that normally flowers may indicate that night temperatures are too high or that the duration or intensity of light is unfavorable.

- Soft stem bases usually are an indication of overwatering. Soggy soil can result from overwatering or improper drainage.

Controlling Insect Pests and Mites

Keeping your house plants clean and inspecting them regularly are the best defenses against insect pests and mites. The most common house plant insect and mite pests are aphids, spider mites, mealy bugs, scales, whiteflies, and thrips. The strategies against these pests depend on the pest and the plant. In some instances, control of the pest is impractical or nearly impossible once the pest is established. The best course of action in these situations is

Table 11.4

GUIDE FOR DIAGNOSING HOUSE PLANT PROBLEMS

Symptom	Possible causes
brown or scorched leaf tips	poor health from overwatering, excessive soil dryness (especially between waterings), excessive fertilizer or other soluble salts in the soil
	specific nutrient toxicities (such as fluoride, copper, or boron)
	low humidity
	pesticide or mechanical injury
leaf spots, blotches, blemishes, blisters, or scabby spots	intense light (sunburn) associated with a recent move of the plant
	chilling injury (below 50°F [10°C])
	chemical spray injury
	overwatering
	fungal or bacterial infections (rare unless plants have recently come from out-doors or greenhouses)
foliage yellow-green on older leaves	insufficient fertilizer, especially nitrogen
	poor root health from pot-bound growth, compacted soil, or poor drainage
	insufficient light
foliage yellow-green on newer leaves	soil pH imbalance
	trace element imbalance
foliage yellow-green generally throughout plant	too much light
	insufficient fertilization
	high temperatures, especially when associated with dryness
	insect infestation or root-rot disease
leaf drop; sudden wilting of foliage	poor root health from overwatering, excessive dryness, excessive fertilizer, or other soluble salts in the soil
	compacted soil or pot-bound roots
	sudden change in light, temperature, or relative humidity
	toxic chemical poured into soil
roots brown, soft, or rotted; roots with tissue that can easily be "slipped off," leaving behind the stringlike center tissues; associated with one or more of the symptoms noted above	poor root health from overwatering, excessive dryness, excessive fertilizer, or other soluble salts in the soil
	compacted soil or poorly drained container
yellowed leaves with tiny speckling; leaves later bronzed and drying; webbing may be noted near growing points	spider-mite infestation
leaves covered with a sticky substance; mold growing on leaves; small brown, white, or greenish objects seen on leaves or in crotches of branches; leaf drop or branch dieback; leaf or growing point distortion	scale, mealy bug, or aphid infestation

Source: Adapted from Powell and Lindquist 1983, p. 5.

to discard the plant and obtain a new one. Some soft-bodied insects and mites can be removed by forcefully washing the plant leaves and stems with plain or insecticidal soap solution (fig. 11.1). Others may require chemical controls, available as sprays or soil drenches. If a chemical control is chosen, use an insecticide or miticide that is recommended and labeled for use on house plants and follow all the label directions and safety precautions. If you use a formulation specifically for house plants, be certain that it is recommended for use on your particular plant. When applying sprays, wear protective gloves and spray stems, leaves, and leaf undersides thoroughly. Spray outdoors so that the spray residue will be dispersed outside and you will not have to worry about damaging furniture surfaces. Soil drenches can exterminate soilborne insects. The potting medium should be watered well before application. (See chapter 10 for more information on pesticide safety.)

Aphids. Aphids are small insects found on new growth or on the undersides of leaves. They suck plant juices and excrete a shiny, sticky sap, or honeydew, that attracts ants and sooty mold growth. Aphid infestations are often evident by the white cast skins that are shed and left behind when aphids molt. Aphids can attack almost all house plants, causing leaves to curl and become distorted. To eliminate aphids, spray leaves with insecticidal soap or use an insecticide labeled for house plants.

Scales. Scales are small, brown or grayish, stationary insects that have a shell-like covering (see fig. 11.2). A common pest of many house plants, they suck plant juices and excrete honeydew, initially giving leaves a shiny, sticky surface but later stunting plant growth and discoloring leaves. They sometimes are difficult to detect on fern fronds because they resemble spores. Scrape scales off plants, wash the plants with soapy water, and apply an insecticide. Scales may infest plant roots, which can become a source of chronic infestations of stems and leaves. In these cases, it may be necessary to repot the plant, removing much of the soil around the roots and drenching the soil.

Mealybugs. Mealybugs are small, oval-shaped, stationary insects that cover house plants with a cottony, powdery material along the veins of leaves or where the leafstalk joins stems (see fig. 11.3). Typical symptoms are stunted plant growth and leaf wilting. Mealybugs, like aphids, excrete honeydew and can be controlled using similar strategies. Mealybugs are common pests of palms and succulents and may infest plant roots.

Mites. Several mite species can attack indoor plants, often causing severe injury. The most common mite is the two-spotted spider mite. Spider mites have a wide host range, and very few indoor plants are immune to attack. Adult spider mites are about 1/50 inch (0.5 mm) long and are usually found on lower leaf surfaces. A 10× hand lens is useful in identifying these pests. Feeding injury on

Figure 11.1

Use soapy or plain water spray to control insect and mite pests.

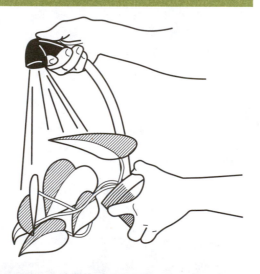

Figure 11.2

Brown soft scale.

many plant species usually involves lighter-colored, stippled areas of leaves. Webbing is also produced (fig. 11.4). Severe spider mite infestations cause leaves to dry and fall from the plants. At 75°F (24°C), mites develop from egg to adult in about 2 weeks.

Other mites, including the broad mite and cyclamen mite, can cause problems, too. These mites are very small (¹⁄₁₀₀ inch [0.25 mm] long) and almost impossible to see without a hand lens. Infestations are recognized by plant injury symptoms rather than by seeing the mites. Most feeding injury occurs on young foliage. Injury on these new leaves is characterized by thickened and brittle foliage with leaf margins cupped downward and stunted. Many of these symptoms are characteristic of injury by chemicals, so infestations can go unnoticed for long periods of time.

Some degree of mite control can be achieved by spraying plants with insecticidal soap sprays, miticides, special oils, or insecticides labeled for house plants.

Thrips. Thrips are small, slender, dark-colored insect pests less than ⅛ inch (3 mm) long that feed on plant leaves and flowers, distorting both. They are typically found on the undersides of leaves and often leave shiny black dots of fecal excrement. Leaves often turn yellow and drop, but heavy infestations result in leaves that have silvery gray areas. To control thirps, wash plants with a forceful stream of water and spray with insecticide. Remove flowers of infested plants because thrips often infest them.

Whiteflies. Both adult and juvenile whiteflies attack house plants. The juveniles attach to the undersides of leaves, suck plant juices, and excrete honeydew. The adults can be seen flying about the plants. Whiteflies infest poinsettias and many other plants, causing leaves to yellow and drop. To control them, dip or spray plants with insecticidal soap solution or spray with insecticide labeled for house plants.

Controlling House Plant Diseases

If a purchased plant is disease-free, infectious disease will rarely be an important role in the indoor life of the plant. The many foliar leaf spots and blights that can occur on plants outdoors or in the production greenhouse will not usually be a problem in the home or office because of the lack of damp air and splashing water. Of course, disease symptoms such as discolored stems and roots or leaf spots that are present on plants when they are purchased will not disappear. These plants should be rejected.

Recognizing infectious diseases on flower, leaf, and stem parts of plants is sometimes more difficult than recognizing insect or mite pests because the pathogens cannot be viewed directly. Most often, the pathogens will be fungi.

A fungus grows on a leaf similar to the way mold grows on bread or a rotted spot grows

Figure 11.3

Obscure mealybugs.

Figure 11.4

Spider mites and webbing.

on a fruit or vegetable. Circular lesions of growth sometimes overlap one another, giving a blotchy appearance. Concentric rings in the lesion give a "bullseye" appearance. Spores of these fungal pathogens appear on the surface of plant leaves as fluffy, moldy growth like that seen in powdery mildews. Look for black, pinpointlike pustules within the lesion. These pustules are actually fungal formations in which many spores are produced and pushed to the outside. Many different fungal pathogens can be found on foliage plants, and they produce different sizes, shapes, and colors of lesions.

Bacterial diseases sometimes appear as oily, greasy, or water-soaked spots on leaves. These are often visible by viewing the lesion from the underside of the leaf. Some bacterial diseases are systemic in nature and cause wilting and general yellowing of plants. Systemic diseases may occasionally cause rotting or cankering of the stem tissue. These cankers or rots will be soft and mushy in appearance an may have an unpleasant odor.

Infectious root rots can be diagnosed to some extent by direct observation of the root system. Off-color or brownish to blackish roots often indicate that root rot is present. Being able to pull off outer root tissue with your fingers (leaving the stringlike center of the root behind) is a good sign that root rot is present. To determine the health of a root system, you should know what a healthy root system looks like.

The following infectious diseases are commonly seen on indoor plants.

Systemic Bacterial Diseases. Many bacterial pathogens found on indoor plants can invade the vascular tissues of the plant and spread throughout its system. If conditions are favorable, these pathogens may begin to multiply in certain areas of the infected plants and cause stem rots, leaf blights, wilts and even root rots. They are spread by splashing water and contaminated hands and pruning tools.

Commonly encountered systemic bacterial diseases include soft stem rot of *Aglaonema, Dracaena, Kalanchoe,* and *Syngonium* (caused by *Erwinia carotovora*); and bacterial stem rot, leaf spot, and wilt of *Aglaonema, Dieffenbachia, Philodendron,* and *Syngonium* (caused by *E. chrysanthemi*).

Control tactics for these diseases depend on recognizing the systemic nature of the pathogen. Chemical sprays are not effective because the pathogens are throughout the plant and deep within its tissues. The organisms are most active under warm, damp conditions on soft tissues in heavily fertilized plants. Common systemic bacterial diseases can be managed reasonably in many cases in the interior environment through a combination of sparse watering and low fertilization. Cooler temperatures of many households are often the reason that the bacteria usually do not proliferate and cause a lot of yellowing and wilting of the affected plant. Splashing water must be avoided when trying to control bacterial diseases.

Localized Bacterial Diseases. Species of *Pseudomonas* and *Xanthomonas* bacteria cause leaf spots or leaf blights on many plants growing indoors. Common hosts of xanthomonads are *Dieffenbachia, Philodendron scandens oxycardium,* English ivy, *Pileas,* and *Pellionias.* Pseudomonads are found on *Aglaonema, Dracaena,* and *Monstera* spp., and pothos. The diseases are characterized by dark green, water-soaked spots that may turn tan, dark brown, or black with a yellow border. The spots can enlarge until the entire leaf blade is involved. Sometimes these lesions spread into the petioles and stems and may look almost exactly like the systemic bacterial diseases previously mentioned.

Control of these diseases generally involves prompt removal of infested plant parts. Clean hands with soap and water and disinfect pruning tools in 70 percent alcohol after such removal actions.

Powdery Mildews. Fungi that cause powdery mildew are host-specific. They are seen often on grape ivy, kalanchoe, begonias, or pileas. The white growth appearing on leaves, flowers, or stems is the fungus growing on the surface of the tissue. Powdery mildew usually will not kill a plant. The unsightly fungus lesions and partial defoliation that occur greatly reduce the quality of the plant, however.

Fortunately, environmental control of powdery mildew can be successful. Reduce the high humidity that often occurs at night by not watering late in the day. Use fans to circulate the air, but avoid drafts such as those caused by cold windows or doors.

Water Mold Rots. *Pythium* and *Phytophthora* are often called water molds because they have a spore stage that is adapted to spread by swimming in water. These organisms attack a wide variety of plants, causing root rots, stem rots, and cutting rots. Many times, *Pythium* will not kill a plant. These organisms will "prune" the root system, resulting in poor growth, yellowing, or stunting of the top portion of the plant.

Infectious root rot usually does not cause serious health problems indoors unless overwatering occurs. Of course, overwatering can occur as media ages, settles, and packs in the bottom of containers. An initially good root environment may become inhospitable as time progresses.

Correction of infectious root rot involves increasing the soil aeration, drainage, and adjusting the watering frequency of the plant. Root rot often may follow a high-salts episode. If soluble salt levels are maintained at low rates, root rot can be avoided easily.

Fungal Leaf Spots and Blights. These fungi are generally spread by splashing water containing spores that land on plants. Most notable among these fungi are *Cercospora, Colletotrichum, Curvularia, Fusarium, Coniothyrium, Helminthosporium, Leptosphaeria,* and *Alternaria* spp. *Botrytis,* which has a wide host range, produces spores and infects only if the relative humidity is high for several hours at a time. Many leaf-spotting fungi require water on leaf surfaces for several hours for infection to occur. Avoid splashing water, and water early in the day so the plants can dry as quickly as possible. The best control is to remove and discard infected leaves.

Bibliography

Barclay, L. W. and C. S. Koehler. 1980. Mealybugs on house plants and in the landscape. Oakland: University of California Division of Agriculture and Natural Resources Publication 21197.

Furuta, T. 1976. Plants indoors: Selections for various environmental conditions. Oakland: University of California Division of Agriculture and Natural Resources Publication 2898.

———. 1977 Plants indoors: Their care and feeding. Oakland: University of California Division of Agriculture and Natural Resources Publication 2941.

Poole, H. A., and D. R. Pittenger. 1980. Care of foliage and flowering plants for retail outlets. Ohio State University Cooperative Extension Service Bulletin 661.

Powell, C. C., and R. K. Lindquist. 1983. Pest and disease control on indoor plants. Ohio State University Cooperative Extension Bulletin 711.

U. S. Department of Agriculture. N.d. Home and Garden Bulletin 67.

Welsh, D. F. 1989. House plants. In D. F. Welsh, ed., The Texas Master Gardener Handbook. College Station: Texas A & M University Agricultural Extension Service.

12

Lawns

M. Ali Harivandi and Ralph C. Gay

LEARNING OBJECTIVES

- Understand the basic functions of turfgrass in California landscapes.

- Understand the procedures involved in lawn establishment and maintenance practices for commonly used lawn grasses in California.

- Learn the basic steps in renovating an old lawn.

- Become acquainted with the names and important characteristics of the recommended cool-season and warm-season turfgrasses for California lawns.

- Learn how to be an informed consumer when purchasing seed, stolons, and sod.

- Learn the basic concepts of routine turfgrass maintenance and management (mowing, fertilization, irrigation, and weed control).

- Become aware of the less frequent need for dethatching, aeration, and disease and insect control.

Lawns

A turfgrass lawn is no longer a simple or obvious choice in California. The days of plentiful water and relatively unrestricted use of pesticides are gone forever. Today, establishment and maintenance of turfgrass lawns can be regulated by local restrictions. At worst, homeowners may be cited for excesses in water or pesticide use; at best, home gardeners are constantly reminded by utility bills, the media, and neighbors that lawn maintenance consumes financial as well as community resources.

Is turfgrass, therefore, a vanishing component of California landscapes? The answer is no, for two indisputably good reasons: people truly enjoy turfgrass lawns, and no other material, either natural or man-made, functions as effectively as a playing surface for recreational activities and team sports or as a landscape surface for parks and cemeteries. Recent environmental concerns about water shortages and pesticide residues have focused attention on better planning and more efficient maintenance of lawns. The management program must meet the home gardener's needs for a beautiful lawn, and, at the same time, it must be environmentally acceptable. Without a sound management program, a high-quality lawn can deteriorate over a period of years.

Although the following discussion highlights some of the important aspects of lawn establishment and maintenance, not all aspects of lawn management are covered in detail. Table 12.1 provides a summary of establishment and maintenance practices for commonly used lawn grasses. UC publications also listed at the conclusion of this chapter contain more detailed information on specific topics.

Establishing a Lawn

A lawn may be established from seed or it may be established vegetatively from stolons or sod. The method chosen depends on the species of grass desired, the environmental situation, time limitations, and financial considerations (see the section "Seed verus Sod," below). The same fertilizer requirements and seedbed preparation apply for both seeding and vegetative establishment. Once a new lawn is established and growing well, a comprehensive maintenance program will keep it healthy and attractive.

Preplant Weed Control

Before planting, check the area to be planted for weeds. Grassy (monocot) weeds such as velvetgrass and dallisgrass are particularly troublesome in lawns; perennial grasses sometimes used for turf, such as bermudagrass, are weeds in lawns of other species and should be eliminated before planting. Almost all grassy weeds can be eliminated with a preplant application of glyphosate herbicide. Hard-to-kill grasses, such as bermudagrass, may require several applications.

Preplant Installation of Irrigation and Drainage

Install the irrigation system and drainage system (if necessary) before final grading. If considerable subsoil grading is necessary, stockpiling of topsoil for use in final grading is advisable.

Soil Preparation

Remove construction debris and other trash from the planned lawn area before grading. If these materials are buried before planting, they may cause mowing hazards, restrict root growth, and impede water movement. Slope the soil away from buildings and allow the lawn area to settle for 1 to 2 weeks before seeding or sodding. Several wetting and drying cycles will aid settling and help locate low spots that need filling. Minimum topsoil depth is 6 to 8 inches (15 to 20 cm). Avoid planting lawns on steep slopes or berms to reduce water waste from runoff. Generally, a 1- to 2- percent slope away from buildings is sufficient.

Fertilization

Apply a starter fertilizer before turf establishment and incorporate it to a depth of 2 to 4 inches (5 to 10 cm). Table 12.2 gives examples of appropriate fertilizers and application rates.

Seed versus Sod

Seeding a lawn is generally less expensive than sodding. Establishment is more difficult with seed, however, and if reseeding certain areas or even an entire lawn is necessary, the overall expense incurred may exceed that of sodding. In addition, during the time required for seed to germinate and to become rooted well, the area is vulnerable to erosion and sedimentation. Sodding also provides an immediately pleasing, quickly functional turf that can compete with viable weed seeds already in the soil. When using seed, a more intensive weed-control program may be required during the establishment period.

Seeding. A well-prepared seedbed is essential for the establishment of grasses. Till the seedbed to a depth of 6 to 8 inches (15 to 20 cm), with the starter fertilizer worked into the top 2 to 3 inches (5 to 7.5 cm) of soil before seeding. Prepare a smooth, firm seedbed of loose soil, then divide the seed in half and sow it in two directions perpendicular to each other. At low seeding rates, sawdust, sand, or other suitable material mixed with the seed aids in obtaining uniform coverage. Cover the seed to a depth of $^1/_{16}$ to $^1/_8$ inch (1.5 to 3 mm) by raking it in and lightly rolling or firming the soil. Avoid creating a smooth surface. The finished seedbed should have shallow uniform depressions (open rows) about $^1/_2$ inch (1.3 cm) deep and 1 to 2 inches (2.5 to 5 cm) apart (e.g., those made by a garden rake or a corrugated roller). Keep the soil moist during the germination period by applying frequent but light irrigations.

Germination of grass seed depends on temperature, moisture, and day-length conditions.

Table 12.1

COMMON CALIFORNIA LAWN GRASSES AND THEIR MAINTENANCE

Grass	Establishment Time	Rate of seed or stolons per 1,000 sq ft (100 sq m)	Mowing height (in)	Mowing height (cm)	Fertilizing weight N per yr*	Maintenance Root depth Water frequency†	Vertical mowing‡
WARM-SEASON GRASSES							
common bermudagrass (*Cynodon dactylon*)	late spring or early summer	1 lb seed (0.454 kg)	1.0	2.5	spring-summer-fall 2–4 lb (0.9–1.8 kg)	60 in. (150 cm) infrequent	yes
hybrid bermudagrass (*Cynodon* spp.)	late spring or early summer	4–6 bu stolons or sod	0.5–0.75	1.3–1.9	spring-summer-fall 4–6 lb (1.8–2.7 kg)	60 in. (150 cm) infrequent	yes
St. Augustinegrass (*Stenotaphrum secundatum*)	late spring or early summer	3–5 bu stolons or sod	0.5–1.5	1.3–3.8	spring-summer-fall 4 lb (1.8 kg)	12–24 in. (30–60 cm) frequent	no
zoysiagrass (*Zoysia* spp.)	late spring or early summer	4–6 bu stolons or sod	0.5–1.0	1.3–2.5	spring-summer-fall 2–4 lb (0.9–1.8 kg)	60 in. (150 cm) infrequent	yes
COOL-SEASON GRASSES							
Kentucky bluegrass (*Poa pratensis*)	fall or spring	2–3 lb seed (0.9–1.4 kg) or sod	1.5–2.0	3.8–5.0	fall-spring 4–6 lb (1.8–2.7 kg)	6–12 in. (15–30 cm) frequent	yes
perennial ryegrass (*Lolium perenne*)	fall or spring	6–9 lb seed (2.7 kg)	1.5–2.0	3.8–5.0	fall-spring 4 lb (1.8 kg)	6–12 in. (15–30 cm) frequent	no
tall fescue (*Festuca arundinacea*)	fall or spring	8–10 lb seed or sod (3.2–4.5 kg)	1.5–3.0	3.8–7.6	fall-spring 4 lb (1.8 kg)	18–30 in. (28–55 cm) frequent	no

Source: Adapted from an original prepared by Victor A. Gibeault, UC Cooperative Extension Environmental Horticulturist, UC Riverside, and John Van Dam, Turf Advisor, UC Cooperative Extension, San Bernardino County.

Notes:

* Suggested application seasons; amount given is total pounds actual N/1,000 square feet/year. Apply only 1 lb N per application.

† Frequent refers to irrigation every 1 to 3 days during summer; infrequent is irrigation every 7 days, approximately. See chapter 4, "Water Management," for more detailed information on irrigating turfgrass.

‡ Indiates need for periodic thatch removal.

Table 12.2

FERTILIZERS AND APPLICATION RATES

Fertilizer	Application rate	
	lb per 1,000 sq ft	kg per 100 sq m
5-10-5	20	9.6
16-20-0	6	2.9
10-20-10	10	4.8
5-20-10	20	9.6

Cool-season grasses, such as turf-type tall fescue, Kentucky bluegrass, and perennial ryegrass, are seeded best in September and October. The next-best time would be March through April. Warm-season grasses, such as common bermudagrass, are seeded most successfully from mid-April to mid-May.

Sodding. Soil preparation for sodding is similar to that for seeding, but one must take care not to make deep footprints or wheel tracks before planting. Such depressions restrict root development and give an uneven appearance to the installed sod. On hot summer days, the soil should be watered just before laying sod to avoid placing the turfgrass roots on a dry, hot surface.

Premium-quality sod is easier to transport and install than inferior grades. Good sod is light, does not tear easily, and quickly extends its root system into the prepared soil. The presence of mildew or a distinct yellowing of leaves are evidence of reduced turf vigor and poor-quality sod. Before ordering or obtaining sod, be prepared to install it quickly because sod is perishable and should not remain on the pallet or stack longer than 24 hours.

To install a sod lawn properly, establish a straight line lengthwise through the lawn area. Then lay the sod on either side of the line with ends staggered, similar to laying bricks. A sharpened masonry trowel is handy for cutting pieces, forcing the sod tight, and leveling small depressions. After the sod is laid, it should be rolled immediately and kept moist until well-rooted.

Sod may be laid any time of the year, but very hot or very cold weather should be avoided. Generally, it is best to lay sod when the turfgrass is actively growing. In California, this period corresponds to late spring and early fall.

Stolons and Plugs

Improved hybrid bermudagrasses, zoysiagrass, or St. Augustinegrass must be sodded or vegetatively established using either plugs or stolons. For plugging or stolonizing, the soil should be prepared as described for seeding. Stolons can either be broadcast over an area and covered lightly with soil by disking, or they can be planted in rows in 6- to 12-inch (15- to 30-cm) centers. In either case, nodes should be in contact with the soil. Stolons are usually sold by the bushel, with 1 bushel approximately equivalent to 1 square yard (0.9 sq m) of sod.

In most parts of the state, the best time to start a hybrid bermudagrass lawn from stolons is anytime from late April or early May into summer.

Postplant Irrigation

New seedlings and stolons require frequent but light irrigation to ensure successful establishment. Keep the soil moist, but not wet, for 30 days following planting. During hot periods, three or four light waterings each day may be required. If the soil dries out during germination, seedlings are likely to die. Sodded and plugged areas also require intensive irrigation management. With sod and plugs, heavy irrigation every second or third day is needed to ensure that the soil beneath the sod or plugs is moist to a 6-inch (15-cm) depth.

Renovating Old Lawns

A lawn that has a poor appearance but is in fair condition can be renovated. Renovation requires minimal soil preparation and involves less expense and mess than complete replacement. However, if a lawn is badly infested with weeds, if the soil has low fertility, or if the grade is very uneven, the lawn will require complete renovation. A list of basic steps in lawn renovation follows.

- Determine the cause of poor quality. Lawns usually require renovation for one or more of the following reasons: poor fertilization practices, inadequate drainage, excessive traffic, improper selection of grass species, weed invasion, drought, insect or disease damage, or excessive shade. Correct these problems during and after renovating the lawn.

- Remove weeds and undesirable grasses. If possible, plan a year ahead to control weeds so they will not compete with the new grass being established. If planning is not possible in advance, apply broadleaf weed killers 30 days before verticutting and seeding. If perennial weedy grasses are present, spot-treat with a nonselective herbicide such as glyphosate. Follow label directions closely when using any herbicide.

- Closely mow the remaining turf area and remove the clippings. Thorough raking and dethatching after close mowing is recommended to create a loosened surface for seeding or stolonizing.

- Dethatch and aerate. Thatch is a buildup of undecomposed organic matter. Because of its high cellulose content, roots and stems are slow to decay and form a semiwaterproof mat between the soil and grass leaves. Thatch should be removed with a mower that has vertical blades, known as a dethatcher or verticutter. After dethatching, lawns growing on heavy or compacted soils should be aerated. (This practice is also known as coring or plugging and is described in more detail later in this chapter.) In addition to relieving compaction, aeration loosens the soil and makes it suitable for seeding.

- Seed, fertilize, and irrigate. Broadcast seed throughout the lawn; broadcast it at a higher rate on bare areas. Starter fertilizer should be applied at the same time. Schedule frequent, light irrigations to keep the soil moist (not wet) until the grass is well established.

- Maintenance. To keep a newly renovated lawn healthy and attractive, begin a comprehensive lawn maintenance program immediately.

Recommended Turfgrasses for California

Turfgrasses fall into two basic categories: cool-season and warm-season. Cool-season grasses, such as Kentucky bluegrass, turf-type tall fescue, and perennial ryegrass, have a year-round growing season and provide attractive green winter color. Warm-season grasses, such as bermudagrass, buffalograss, kikuyugrass, paspalum, St. Augustinegrass, and zoysiagrass, go dormant in the late fall when soil temperatures drop to about 55°F (13°C). They stay brown throughout the winter months and into early spring. Although the brown winter color of warm-season grasses may make them less desirable, their maintenance costs are reduced because they require less water, fewer mowings, and a shorter growing season.

Cool-Season Grasses

Annual Ryegrass (*Lolium multiflorum*) (fig. 12.1). Annual ryegrass is annual and coarse. It is often sown at high rates to overseed dormant bermudagrass or to provide a temporary annual cover. Otherwise, it is not used for turf.

Perennial Ryegrass (*Lolium perenne*) (fig. 12.2). This grass performs well in coastal fog belts and performs adequately elsewhere. Where marginally adapted, perennial ryegrass

Figure 12.1

Annual ryegrass.

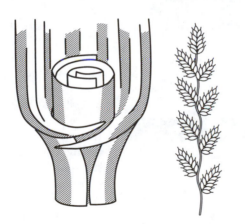

Figure 12.2

Perennial ryegrass.

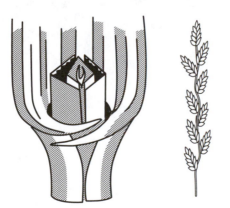

Figure 12.3

Kentucky bluegrass. (A) Strong rhizomes produce a dense turf. (B) The leaf tip is boat shaped. (C) A pale line parallels both sides of the midrib.

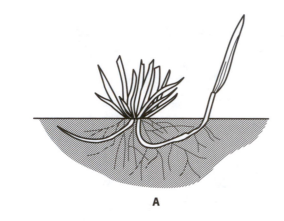

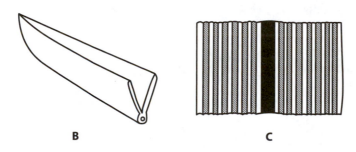

Figure 12.4

Tall fescue. (A) The top surface of the leaf blade is ribbed; (B) the underside is smooth and shiny.

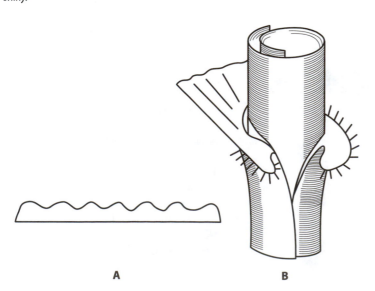

may form clumps and become difficult to mow in the summer. It has no rhizomes or stolons, so bare or worn areas should be reseeded. It is often used in seed mixtures with Kentucky bluegrass. It germinates quickly and provides a rapid turf cover. It is also used for overseeding winter-dormant bermudagrass lawns. Selected varieties include Palmer Brightstar, Secretariat, Calypso, Premier, Pennant, Monterey, Radiant, Line Drive, and Accent.

Kentucky Bluegrass (*Poa pratensis*) (fig. 12.3). In areas where it is well-adapted, Kentucky bluegrass is the standard of quality among turfgrasses. In areas of marginal adaptation, Kentucky bluegrass suffers from diseases, weed invasion, and hot weather. A lawn-seed mixture of Kentucky bluegrass and perennial ryegrass is more resistant to diseases than bluegrass alone. Each Kentucky bluegrass variety has virtues and faults; none is adapted to hot valley climates. Optimal results can usually be obtained by blending equal portions of seed of several varieties. Selected varieties include Midnight, Blacksburg, Ascot, Eclipse, Unique, Apex, Glade, Preakness, Alpine, and Princeton.

Tall Fescue (*Festuca arundinacea*) (fig. 12.4). When densely sown, a pure stand of tall fescue forms a moderately coarse-textured lawn that is trouble-free and uniform in appearance. Individual tall fescue plants in a mix with other cool-season grasses appear as coarse weeds. Tall fescue does not have runners, so bare or worn spots should be reseeded. New selections are finer in texture and shorter in stature than older ones and are known as turf-type tall fescues and dwarf turf-type tall fescues. They require the least maintenance of cool-season grasses in California. They are also very tolerant of drought and heat. Selected varieties include Crossfire, Masterpiece, Bonsai, Brandy, Aztec, Gazelle, Jaguar, Olympic Gold, Plantation, and Tulsa.

Red Fescue (*Festuca rubra*) (fig. 12.5). Two distinct growth habits have led to varietal or subspecies classification among red fescues. Creeping red fescue (*Festuca rubra rubra*) spreads slowly by very short rhizomes. Chewings fescue (*Festuca rubra commutata*) is a bunchgrass with an upright growth habit.

Red fescue is recognized by its fine texture. Except in shady, dry situations, it does not do well in hot climates. It does not tolerate close mowing or too much fertilizer. In areas where Kentucky bluegrass does well, red fescue forms an excellent companion grass for exposures with moderate shade or dry soil. Its color, texture, and growth habit are compatible with Kentucky bluegrass. Red fescue has moderate drought tolerance.

Red fescue and another fine-leaf fescue known as hard fescue (*Festuca longifolia*), which closely resembles red fescue, seldom exceed 8 inches (20 cm) in height, except when in flower. At cool mountain elevations, where they grow well, they are useful particularly for a neglected lawn, such as at a summer cabin, because a single mowing will remove the fruiting heads. Similarly, they are used for hillside erosion.

Selected Chewings fescue varieties include Victory, Longfellow, Banner, Enjoy, Shadow, Ivalo, Wilma, Magenta, Mary, Highlight, Jamestown, and Wintergreen. Selected creeping red varieties include Pennlawn, Ruby, Flyer, Pernille, Lovisa, Boreal, Robot, and

Commodore. Selected hard fescue varieties include Scaldis, SR3000, Tournament, and Spartan.

Bentgrasses (*Agrostis* spp.). Bentgrasses tolerate close mowing and can provide quality lawns. However, they require greater maintenance and extra disease control during the summer.

Colonial bentgrass (*Agrostis tenuis*) may spread very slowly by short rhizomes and also by short stolons, which are often lacking. The thatch layer extends above and below the soil line. Colonial bentgrass is adapted to the northern coastal climate. In other areas, it does not form a dense turf. Selected varieties include Astoria and Exeter.

Highland bentgrass (*Agrostis* spp. c.v. 'Highland') (fig. 12.6) is distinct from colonial bentgrass, but it is often classified improperly. Highland bentgrass is adapted to valley climates and will survive extensive droughts. It forms solid patches of grass that turn a frosty blue color from morning dew during cool seasons. It may form both short rhizomes and stolons.

Creeping bentgrass (*Agrostis palustris*) is used for specialized turf, such as golf, bowling, and tennis greens. The skill and expense required to maintain creeping bentgrass usually eliminate it as a lawn turf. Creeping bentgrass spreads by stolons to form a mat or thatch layer above the soil line. Selected varieties include SR1020, Pennlinks, Cobra, A-4, Putter, Providence, and Penncross.

Figure 12.5

Red fescue. (A) The leaves are fine or needlelike. (B) Mature leaves are folded.

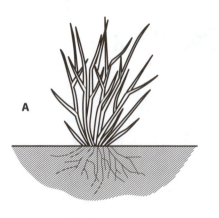
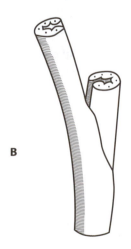

Figure 12.6

Highland bentgrass.

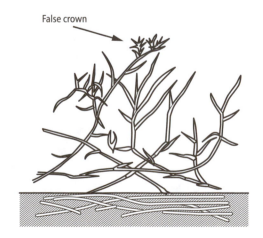

False crown

Figure 12.7

Bermudagrass. (A) Bermuda and other warm-season grasses have occasional opposite leaves. (B) The stolon is prominent.

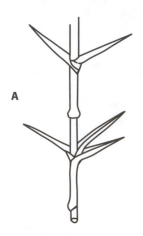

A

B

Figure 12.8

St. Augustinegrass. (A) A heavy stolon forms shoots at every node. (B) The collar is narrowed down to form a short stalk or petiole for the leaf blade.

A

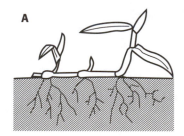

B

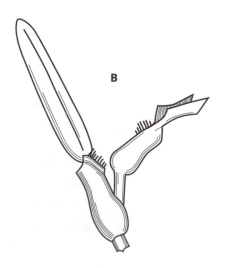

Warm-Season Grasses

Bermudagrass (*Cynodon dactylon* and hybrids) (fig. 12.7). Bermudagrass is adapted best to the warm regions of California. It spreads both by rhizomes and stolons and can be a troublesome invader of garden areas. Short mowing helps produce a neat, restrained turf. Bermudagrass does not tolerate shade and turns brown with continued low temperatures. Hybrid bermudagrasses are propagated vegetatively and require a high level of management. If ordinary management is available, common bermudagrass is preferable. Bermudagrasses are highly drought-tolerant. Selected hybrid varieties include Santa Ana, Tifdwarf, Tifgreen, Tifway, and Tifway II.

Seashore Paspalum (*Paspalum vaginatum*). Seashore paspalum does very well near the ocean where it is subjected to saltwater. It is hard to mow, subject to scalping, and slow to recover from mowing.

St. Augustinegrass (*Stenotaphrum secundatum*) (fig. 12.8). A subtropical grass of coarse texture, St. Augustinegrass has excellent shade tolerance. It is also drought- and salt-tolerant.

Kikuyugrass (*Pennisetum clandestinum*) (fig. 12.9). At present, kikuyugrass is considered a weedy grass in coastal and some inland areas of California. A native of high-altitude equatorial Africa, kikuyugrass thrives in climates with moderate, even temperatures. It is sometimes mistaken for St. Augustinegrass. Kikuyugrass forms vigorous stolons and has slightly flattened, hairy leaf sheaths and blades with files of hairs. It is tolerant of low fertility, drought, and frequent close mowing.

Zoysiagrass (*Zoysia* spp.). Zoysiagrass is well adapted to only the warmest areas of California. This high-quality, erect turf forms a dense carpet but may be difficult to mow evenly. Zoysia will tolerate moderate shade, although it is slow to become established, even in full sun. It turns off-color in cool weather.

Known as mascarengrass or Japanese temple grass, *Zoysia tenuifolia* is used in the nursery trade as a ground cover. It is a fine-leaved, dwarf plant that requires no mowing and slowly but strongly invades nearby plantings.

Known as Japanese lawn grass, *Zoysia japonica* is a very drought-tolerant grass. The Meyer variety resembles tall fescue in color and texture. El Toro is a University of California patented variety. It covers faster and is

Figure 12.9

Kikuyugrass.

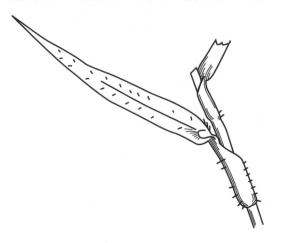

coarser than other zoysias. Selected zoysia varieties include El Toro, Emerald, and Meyer.

Purchasing Seed, Stolons, and Sod

Purchasing Quality Seed

A lawn is a long-term investment, and the seed you buy is an important element in its success. It is not possible to evaluate seed quality by looking at it. There are differences in lawn seed, and it pays to compare. Some of the information that will help you make a wise choice is printed on seed packages, which should be read carefully. The label must include certain information and will look something like the sample below. Definitions of label terms follow.

Sample Seed Label

LOT #TDC-89-07039, ID TRIPLE CROWN DWARF

Kind	% Purity	% Germ.
Monarch tall fescue	49.00	85
Emperor tall fescue	24.50	85
Wrangler tall fescue	24.50	85
% Crop seed	.80	
% Inert matter	1.10	
% Weed seed	.10	no noxious weeds

Origin or tested 6/00, sell by 9/01
John Doe Seed Company
Los Angeles, CA 90021
Limited warranty

% Purity. The percentage (by weight) that is actually seed of the crop specified (tall fescue in the sample) is called pure seed.

% Germination. This indicates the percentage of viable (live) seed. The germination percentage was determined on the test date listed, which should be within 12 months of sale or use.

% Crop seed. The percentage (by weight) of crop seeds other than the crop specified is called *crop seed.* For example, tall fescue may include orchardgrass and ryegrass seed.

% Inert matter. The percentage (by weight) of seed coats, dirt, trash, and anything else that is not seed is called *inert matter.*

% Weed seed. The percentage (by weight) of all weed seeds and the number of noxious weed seeds present. Avoid seed lots with noxious weeds.

Seed Blends and Mixtures. Grass seed is often sold as a blend of two or more varieties of the same species (as shown in the sample seed label) or as a mixture of two or more different species. The advantages of a blend are broader tolerance to pests and stress problems. Mixtures usually include sun-adapted and shade-tolerant species.

Cost Comparison of Seed Sources. The price of seed is only a small portion of the total cost of lawn establishment and maintenance. Because certified seed is guaranteed by the seller to be the kind and variety named on the label, buying it is a good practice. Seed quality should be the major factor when selecting among seed sources. Even if the seeds are of equal quality, costs may differ. When considering seed lots of similar quality, compare the amount of PURE LIVE SEED (PLS) in the package. You want to pay only for seed that will grow. To determine the percentage of PLS, multiply the germination percentage by the percentage of pure seed, then multiply the result by 100.

Example:
On the sample label,
germination = 85% and purity = 98%.
(Purity = 0.49 + 0.245 + 0.245 = 0.98, the kinds of tall fescue seed.)
$0.85 \times 0.98 = 0.833$
$0.833 \times 100 = 83.3\%$, the percentage of pure live seed (PLS).

To obtain the actual cost per pound of PLS, divide the price per pound (0.45 kg) of the packaged seed by PLS. If the seed in the example above costs $2.25 per pound, then divide $2.25 by 0.833 to obtain the actual cost per pound of PLS, in this case, $2.72.

Seeding and Stolonizing Rates

The amount of seed or stolons needed to establish a lawn varies according to the grass species used. Turfgrasses vary in their seed size, number of seed per pound, and growth habit. In general, a lawn will get a good start if seeded at the rate of 15 to 20 viable seed planted per square inch (6.45 per sq cm). The seeding rate increases as the seed size increases because there are fewer seed per pound. Excessively high seeding rates can cause problems such as weak, spindly seedlings that are susceptible to disease and slow to form a strong, mature sod. Consult table 12.3 to determine the quantity of seed or stolons to buy.

Purchasing Quality Sod

A number of turf species are available as sod in California, including Kentucky bluegrass, turf-type tall fescues, perennial rye, zoysia-grass, St. Augustinegrass, and hybrid bermudagrass. Because each of these sods is best suited for particular uses and geographic areas, it is important to select a high-quality, healthy sod that is adapted well to a specific site. Nurseries and sod growers can provide information about the desired sod. Warm-season grass sod usually consists of only one variety. Cool-season grass sod, however, often contains several varieties of the same species. Sod mixtures contain two or more species and usually include both shade-tolerant and sun-adapted grasses.

When buying sod, make sure it is moist but not too wet. It should have good green color with no yellowing areas. Sod thickness is important. The soil into which the sod is anchored should measure ¾ to 1 inch (1.9 to 2.5 cm) thick. Every effort should be made to lay sod within 24 hours after it is cut.

Table 12.3

TURFGRASS SEEDING AND STOLONIZING RATES

SEEDED GRASSES

Grass	Number of seed		Seeding rate	
	per lb	per kg	lb/1,000 sq ft	kg/100 sq m
Annual ryegrass	230,000	104,000	7–9	3.5–4.5
Bermudagrass (common)	1,750,000	795,000	1	0.5
Colonial bentgrass	8,000,000	3,630,000	0.5–1	0.3–0.5
Creeping bentgrass	7,000,000	3,180,000	0.5–1	0.3–0.5
Highland bentgrass	8,000,000	3,630,000	0.5–1	0.3–0.5
Kentucky bluegrass	2,200,000	999,000	2–3	1.0–1.5
Perennial ryegrass	230,000	104,000	6–9	3.0–4.5
Red fescue	615,000	279,000	3.5–4.5	1.8–2.3
Tall fescue	230,000	104,000	8–10	4.0–5.0

GRASSES GROWN FROM SOD OR STOLONS

Grass	Planted as	Stolon planting rate* bu/1,000 sq ft (bu/100 sq m)
Bermudagrass (hybrid)	sod or stolons	4–6
Seashore paspalum	sod or stolons	3–5
St. Augustinegrass	sod or stolons	3–5
Zoysiagrass	sod or stolons	4–6

Note:

*1 bu of stolons equals approximately 1 sq yd (9 sq ft) of sod.

Lawn Maintenance

The wide variety of microclimates and soil types across California make it difficult to formulate a general program for lawn maintenance. This section covers basic factors in maintaining a lawn. Practices may need modification to ensure success for a given location. Routine lawn maintenance includes mowing, fertilization, irrigation, and weed control. Additional cultural practices that may be necessary during some years are dethatching, aeration, and weed, disease, and insect control.

Mowing

The most obvious physical effect of mowing is a decrease in leaf surface area, which decreases a plant's ability to photosynthesize and to produce carbohydrates essential for root, shoot, rhizome, and stolon growth. Higher mowing heights maximize photosynthesis and reduce turf stress. They also increase drought survival through increased root development. Mowing frequency is determined by the species and its seasonal growth pattern. Mow often enough so that no more than one-third of the existing green foliage is removed with any one mowing. If more than one-third of the leaf area is removed during mowing, root growth is temporarily slowed by the plant's inability to produce sufficient carbohydrates. For example, when 50 percent of the existing Kentucky bluegrass foliage was removed by mowing, only 35 percent of the roots were growing 33 days later.

In cases of severe defoliation, the plant uses stored carbohydrates to produce new photosynthetic leaf surface. However, the carbohydrate reserves are limited and can be seriously depleted if plants are forced to recuperate frequently from mowing that is too severe. Wound hormones are produced every time grass is cut and are followed by the production of enzymes involved in wound healing. Production of these compounds occurs at the expense of food reserves. All mowing is a wounding process, but dull mowers inflict more severe wounds than sharp mowers. Improper mowing practices and equipment progressively weaken turf as the mowing season continues. As a result, the recuperative potential of the grass is reduced, and the turf is predisposed to weeds, diseases, insect pest problems, and drought injury. Recommended mowing heights for various turfgrasses is given in table 12.1.

Fertilization

Turfgrasses should be fertilized when they are actively growing. The timetable for fertilizing cool-season grasses is almost the reverse of that for warm-season grasses because warm-season species are dormant when cool-season grasses make their most effective use of fertilizer, and vice versa. Turfgrass nutritional needs also change from month to month because of temperature and moisture variations. Cool-season turfgrasses actively grow in the spring and fall and should receive most of their fertilizer in the spring and early fall. Warm-season grasses are fertilized for the first time when the lawn has fully greened up in the spring. The last application should be 6 to 8 weeks before the likely date of the first frost. Both zoysiagrass and bermudagrass retain better green color in cool weather if fertilized during the fall.

The numbers on a fertilizer bag (e.g., 10-10-10 or 46-0-0) indicate the percent of nitrogen (N), phosphate (P_2O_5), and potash (K_2O) in the fertilizer (fig. 12.10; see chapter 3 for more information on fertilizers). If low levels of phosphorus or potassium are present in the soil, a complete fertilizer (i.e., fertilizers with all three elements) should be used. If high levels of phosphorus and potassium are already present in the soil, supply nitrogen alone. For most established lawns, nitrogen is

Figure 12.10

Sample label of fertilizer bag.

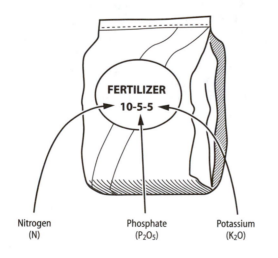

Nitrogen (N)   Phosphate (P_2O_5)   Potassium (K_2O)

Figure 12.11

Spread half the fertilizer quantity in each direction.

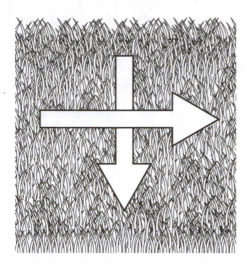

the only nutrient that needs to be supplied on a regular basis.

Excessive growth stimulated by nitrogen fertilizers can be more detrimental than no fertilization at all. The source of nitrogen in fertilizers determines whether nitrogen is quickly or slowly made available to plants. Quickly available materials are water soluble and immediately usable by the plant. Slow-release fertilizers make the nitrogen available over time and therefore can be applied less frequently and at higher rates than quickly available sources. In most areas, soluble fertilizers usually last about 4 weeks. A slow-release fertilizer may last 8 to 10 weeks. The portion of slow-release nitrogen is listed on the fertilizer bag as water-insoluble nitrogen (WIN). For example, a 20-10-10 fertilizer with 5 percent WIN actually has $\frac{5}{20}$ or ¼ of the nitrogen in the slow-release form. A 50-pound bag of this material would provide 10 pounds of total nitrogen (N), 2.5 pounds of which would be slowly available (WIN).

A fertilizer label provides the following information:

- guaranteed analysis
- total nitrogen (5.6% WIN)   16%
- available phosphoric acid (P_2O_5) 4%
- soluble potash   8%

To calculate the percent WIN, use the following formula:

(% WIN ÷ total N) ×100 = % of total N that is WIN (% slow-release N).

Using the guaranteed analysis in the sample label above, calculate the percentage of the total N that is WIN (slowly available as follows:

$$(5.6 \div 16) \times 100 = 35\%$$

If no WIN is listed on the fertilizer label, assume that all of the nitrogen is water-soluble or quickly available, unless the nitrogen includes sulfur-coated urea. Sulfur-coated urea fertilizers provide slow-release nitrogen, but the fertilizer label does not list it as WIN. If the fertilizer contains sulfur-coated urea, include that portion as part of WIN when determining the percentage of total N that is slowly available.

Because fertilizers vary in formula and type, application rates differ. Furthermore, different grass species require varying rates of nitrogen and other nutrients for optimal performance. In general, however, cool-season grasses perform well receiving 4 to 6 pounds (1.8 to 2.7 kg) of actual nitrogen per year. Warm-season grasses require 0.5 to 1 pound (0.22 to 0.45 kg) of actual nitrogen per growing month. To calculate the amount of material from any given fertilizer, divide the amount of actual nitrogen needed by the percentage of nitrogen specified on fertilizer bag. For example, to apply 1 pound (0.45 kg) of actual nitrogen to a lawn using a 16-8-8 fertilizer, divide 1 pound (0.45 kg) by 16 percent, which gives 6.25 pounds (2.8 kg) of actual nitrogen.

Fertilizer should be evenly distributed to avoid striping. It is best to spread half the fertilizer in one direction and the other half at right angles to the first (fig. 12.11).

Irrigation

Lawns can use 1½ inches (3.7 cm) or more of water per week in hot, dry weather. Because rainfall in California does not provide this much water, irrigation is necessary during the summer. A lawn should be watered when the soil begins to dry out but before the grass actually wilts. At the wilting stage, areas of the lawn begin to change color, displaying a blue-green or a smoky tinge. Loss of resilience can be observed when footprints on the lawn remain visible rather than bouncing right back. Ideally, the lawn should be watered before these signs of wilting are obvious. Consult chapter 4, "Water Management," for information on irrigation and guidance on watering turfgrass.

Cool-season grasses usually become semi-dormant in the hottest part of the summer, returning to full vigor in cooler fall weather. Regular deep watering is necessary to keep the lawn green through the summer.

Light sprinkling of the turf surface is harmful because it encourages root development near the soil surface. Shallow root systems require frequent watering to keep the surface wet, which creates an ideal environment for weeds and diseases. Therefore, water consistently and deeply. Encouraging deep root growth by infrequent heavy irrigation maximizes water-use efficiency and turfgrass quality. Avoid runoff and puddling as much as possible by cycling irrigations until the desired amount is applied.

The best time of day to water a lawn is early morning (2 A.M. to 8 A.M). Evaporation is minimal, making water-use efficiency optimal. Early evening or night watering is not recommended because during cool nights wet blades and thatch are highly susceptible to disease development.

Dethatching

In addition to the routine maintenance practices already discussed, it may be necessary to remove thatch in some years, depending on the turfgrass species (see table 12.1). Thatch is the tightly interwoven layer of living and dead stems, roots, stolons, rhizomes, and roots that exists between the green blades of grass and the soil surface (fig. 12.12). This layer of decomposing organic matter accumulates on the soil surface in an innocuous fashion. During the earliest stages of development, when it is less than ½ inch (1.2 cm) thick, thatch can actually be beneficial because it increases the wear tolerance of the turf by providing better dissipation of compaction forces; reduces weed populations by limiting germination conditions; reduces water evaporation by blocking sunlight and air exchange with the soil surface; and insulates crown tissue, protecting it from frost and traffic damage.

Thick thatch layers cause problems, however. The moist microclimate created by a thick thatch layer favors fungal growth and allows disease-causing microorganisms to live and sporulate. The probability of insect pests overwintering is increased by the insulating effect of thatch. Soilborne fungi and pest insects often escape chemical controls because of their inability to penetrate the thatch layer. The thatch layer also prevents adequate water infiltration, causing reduced root growth and increased potential for drought stress. When thatch layers are kept moist, roots tend to develop in this zone, and crown regions of the individual turfgrass plants tend to be elevated in the thatch. This elevation of the crown region away from the soil leads to increased exposure to temperature extremes and to a greater probability of stress damage. Interception of fertilizer by thatch layers produces erratic responses to fertilization. In some cases, microorganisms in the thatch tie up the applied nitrogen, making it unavailable to the turfgrass.

Thatch builds up when organic matter accumulates on the soil surface faster than it can decompose. Some of the many reasons for the imbalance between the rates of accumulation and decomposition are excess nitrogen fertilizer, grass species, excess irrigation, chemical use, and soil type. There is no simple method for controlling thatch development, but preventive programs for thatch reduction should be built into any maintenance program. Labor-intensive dethatching may be necessary at times. Preventive thatch management involves proper nutrition, aeration, mowing, and irrigation practices. Moderate use of nitrogen with more frequent, small

Figure 12.12

Thatch.

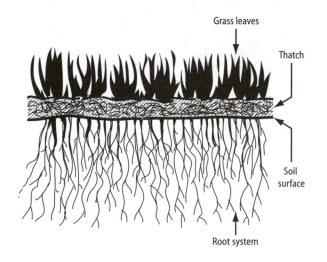

Grass leaves

Thatch

Soil surface

Root system

applications appears to decrease thatch buildup. Aeration and top-dressing of turfgrass speeds up thatch decomposition because aerobic microorganisms involved in thatch decomposition benefit from improved oxygen levels as much as turfgrass does. Light soil top-dressing can inoculate the thatch layer with microorganisms and improve moisture retention in the thatch layer, which increases microbial activity.

If the thatch layer in a lawn is more than ½ inch (1.2 cm) thick, dethatching will be beneficial. Vertical mowers or verticut machines can be rented for this purpose (fig. 12.13). Verticutting rakes the soil surface and leaves the thatch debris on top of the lawn.

This debris should be removed. If overseeding is planned, it should follow the verticutting or aerating process, because the grooves cut in the soil provide good soil contact for new seed. It is critical that dethatching be done when plants can recover quickly from the treatment. Kentucky bluegrass and other cool-season grass lawns should be dethatched in early fall or early spring.

Aeration

If the soil is heavy and compacted or if thatch buildup is a problem, aeration may be beneficial. Roots need oxygen as well as water and nutrients. Compacted soil restricts the absorption of water as well as the exchange and replenishment of oxygen from the atmosphere to the soil.

Aeration is done best by a machine that forces hollow metal tubes into the ground and brings up small cores of soil that are left lying on the surface (fig. 12.14). The soil should be moist (not too wet or too dry) when this is done. Simply punching holes with a spiked roller may improve water retention, but this practice also increases compaction in the soil. Aeration cores left on the surface will eventually break down, and small particles will move down into the thatch layer. Additions of soil and microbes into the thatch through the aeration process help create an environment conducive to faster thatch decomposition.

Figure 12.13

Vertical mower.

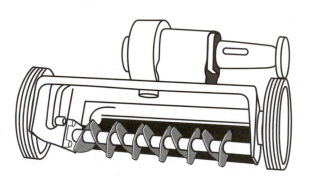

Figure 12.14

Coring aerifiers. (A) Roller-type aerifier. (B) Piston-driven aerifier.

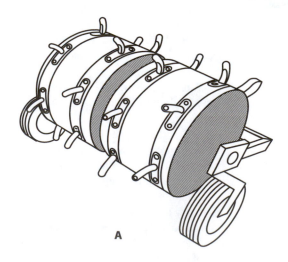

A

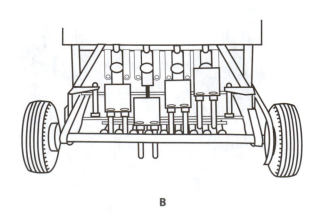

B

Weed Control

Weeds are minimized by good mowing, irrigation, and fertilization practices because these cultural practices increase the competitive advantage of the turfgrass in comparison to the weeds. If chemical weed control is necessary, it should be applied at the time of year and at the rates recommended on the herbicide label. Careless application of chemicals can result in damage to desirable grasses and to other ornamental plantings (see chapter 10, "Controlling Garden Pests Safely," for information on pesticide use).

As discussed in chapter 9, "Weed Science," two main groups of weeds are broadleaf weeds (such as dandelions, chickweed, clover, henbit, ground ivy, oxalis, plantain, and spurge) and weedy grasses (such as dallisgrass, crabgrass, sandbur, and goosegrass). Control for the two groups differs.

Good selective herbicides are available for broadleaf weed control. In general, broadleaf weeds respond best to weed killers when they are actively growing and are in the seedling stage, usually in late spring or early fall. When possible, fall applications are preferable because fewer ornamental and garden plants are actively growing, making them less susceptible to accidental injury from herbicides. Applying high rates of weed killer under hot, dry conditions may injure desirable grasses and ornamental plants.

Disease Control

Proper lawn management greatly reduces susceptibility to disease. Many disease problems can be traced to overwatering or selecting the wrong grass for a given climate. High use of nitrogen fertilizer is another cause of disease. The possible causes of disease damage may be difficult to identify because many symptoms of pathogens are similar to those caused by improper management practices or by environmental factors. Nearly all lawn diseases are caused by fungi. Fungicides are available to prevent and control them; however, their use on home lawns is often uneconomical and impractical.

Insect Control

Although many different types of insects are normally present in a lawn, most of them are not harmful to turfgrass. Insect control is not necessary unless an insect pest population causes visible damage. Close examination on your hands and knees is the best way to identify insect pests in a damaged lawn. You may be able to see the insect in action. To determine whether insects are a problem, both shoots and roots should be examined. Some turf insects, such as white grubs, are active only underground. Common insect pests in turfgrasses are lawn moth (sod webworms), cutworms, armyworms, skippers, leafhoppers, white grubs, and billbugs. Nematodes and rodents cause only occasional problems. See chapter 7, "Entomology," and chapter 10 for more information on insects and their management.

Bibliography

Ali, A. D., and C. L. Elmore. 1989. Turfgrass pests. Oakland: University of California Division of Agriculture and Natural Resources Publication 4053.

All about lawns. 1999. Des Moines, IA: Meredith/Ortho Books.

Gibeault, V., et al. 1973. Lawn aeration and thatch control. Oakland: University of California Division of Agriculture and Natural Resources Publication 2586.

———. 1991. Managing turfgrasses during drought. Oakland: University of California Division of Agriculture and Natural Resources Publication 21499.

Harivandi, A. 1983. Moss and algae control in lawns. Oakland: University of California Division of Agriculture and Natural Resources Publication 7145.

Harivandi, A., et al. 1984. Selecting the best turfgrass. Oakland: University of California Division of Agriculture and Natural Resources Publication 2589.

Harivandi, A., and V. Gibeault. 1996. Managing lawns in shade. Oakland: University of California Division of Agriculture and Natural Resources Publication 7214.

———. 1997. Managing lawns on heavy soils. Oakland: University of California Division of Agriculture and Natural Resources Publication 7227.

———. 1999. Mowing your lawn and "grasscycling." Oakland: University of California Division of Agriculture and Natural Resources Publication 8006.

Henry, J. 1997. Practical lawn fertilization. Oakland: University of California Division of Agriculture and Natural Resources Publication 21250.

Knoop, W. E. 1989. Lawns. In D. F. Welsh, ed. The Texas master gardener handbook. College Station: Texas A&M University.

Lawns and groundcovers. 1989. Menlo Park, CA: Sunset Publishing.

Madison, J. 1980. Know your turfgrasses. Oakland: University of California Division of Agriculture and Natural Resources Publication 2585.

Schwankl, L., et al. 1992. Evaluating turfgrass sprinkler irrigation systems. Oakland: University of California Division of Agriculture and Natural Resources Publication 21503.

Snyder, R. 1983. Watering lawns along California's South Coast. Oakland: University of California Division of Agriculture and Natural Resources Publication 21347.

———. 1988. Watering lawns along California's Central Coast. Oakland: University of California Division of Agriculture and Natural Resources Publication 21432.

———. 1991. Turfgrass evapotranspiration map: The Central Coast of California. Oakland: University of California Division of Agriculture and Natural Resources Publication 21491.

———. 1991. Turfgrass irrigation scheduling. Oakland: University of California Division of Agriculture and Natural Resources Publication 21492.

UC IPM pest management guidelines for turfgrass. Updated regularly. Oakland: University of California Division of Agriculture and Natural Resources Publication 3365-T.

UC IPM pest note series. B. L. P. Ohlendorf, ed. University of California Division of Agriculture and Natural Resources, Statewide Integrated Pest Management Program. Updated regularly. Available through UC Cooperative Extension county offices; also available on the World Wide Web at http://www.ipm.ucdavis.edu. Of special interest (title and ANR publication no.): Lawn insects, 7476; Crabgrass, 7456.

13

Woody Landscape Plants

Donald R. Hodel and Dennis R. Pittenger

LEARNING OBJECTIVES

- Learn how to select woody landscape plants.

- Learn how to plant woody landscape plants.

- Pruning: Learn how to make pruning cuts; train young trees; and prune mature broadleaf trees, conifers and other narrowleaf evergreens, hedges, broadleaf shrubs, ground covers, vines, and garden roses.

- Learn correct fertilizer techniques for woody plants.

- Learn how to design and maintain the landscape for fire protection.

Woody Landscape Plants

Plants in the urban landscape modify the environment, softening its harshness and making it more livable. Landscaping also adds significantly to the dollar value of commercial and residential property. However, in order to fully realize the potential amenities and benefits that landscaping can provide, one must select, install, and maintain plants with the utmost care.

Selection of Landscape Plants

Gardeners can minimize maintenance and future problems in the landscape by selecting the right plant for the right spot. Consider functional uses, growth habit, environmental tolerances, and site adaptation when selecting plants.

Functional Uses

Plants have many functions in the landscape that depend on the species and its inherent growth characteristics, including shape, size, color, texture, seasonality, and flowering and fruiting habits. Among these uses are environmental modification and energy conservation (by intercepting sunlight, screening reflecting and radiating surfaces, and enhancing summer temperature control and winter solar energy collection); wind protection and modification; noise reduction; air purification and dust collection; and water and erosion control. Plants can also be used to direct traffic, define space, develop a sense of privacy, screen unsightliness, provide security, serve as wildlife refuges, and enhance aesthetic and ornamental qualities.

Growth Habit and Size

The ultimate size and rate of growth are important considerations when selecting plants. Plants that become too large are a common problem in the landscape, and, as the typical residential lot continues to shrink, oversize plants will be increasingly troublesome. Oversize plants can block views, conflict with overhead utility lines, crowd out other plants, ruin designs, and damage hardscape as well as be hazardous, difficult to care for, and expensive to remove. Although homeowners often desire an instantly mature landscape, they should be aware that fast-growing plants, especially trees, are generally short-lived and often have invasive roots and inherently weak or brittle wood that is prone to breakage in wind. Patience is a gardener's best virtue, and the homeowner will be duly rewarded by selecting for permanence in the landscape and using species noted for their slow or moderate rate of growth and long life.

Plant growth characteristics such as seasonality of leaves, flowering and fruiting habit, presence of thorns, and branch and canopy structure are important considerations for placement in the landscape and future maintenance. A tree with excessive leaf, flower, and fruit litter could be annoying and hazardous in high-use areas like sidewalks, patios, and decks. The same tree placed away from high-use areas and with a ground cover beneath it to absorb litter is no problem at all, however. Remember that, because of branching habit and growth characteristics, some species require more frequent and intense levels of training and pruning to achieve the desired form.

Environmental and Pest Tolerances

The environmental adaptation of a species to a particular site is another important consideration. Simply because a local nursery stocks the plant does not signify that the plant is adapted to the climate and soils of the area. Consider wind, exposure (light), soil type, moisture, humidity, pests, fire, and extremes of temperature that your site offers in comparison to the needs and tolerances of the plant species being considered.

Susceptibility to common pests should also be considered when selecting plant species. Choose a pest-resistant or pest-tolerant cultivar or selection whenever possible; unfortunately, the availability of these cultivars or selections is limited. Lists of certain plants with known resistance or susceptibility to Armillaria root rot and Verticillium wilt, two serious soilborne fungal diseases, are found in tables 13.1 and 13.2.

General Tips

Some advance planning is necessary to integrate functional uses, growth characteristics, and environmental tolerances, and to attain an aesthetically pleasing but useful and purposeful landscape. Successful landscaping requires a knowledge of plant materials, careful assessment of the landscape site, and development of appropriate design solutions.

To become familiar with plant materials, especially how they will perform and look when mature, visit your local parks, botanical gardens and arboreta, street plantings, private gardens, and nurseries. Inquire and consult with people who live or work in or near these places. Although nurseries are good sources of information, remember that their stock is usually not full grown and the ultimate size and shape of the plants may not be represented accurately.

Consult the numerous references available in most libraries about selecting and caring for landscape plants. A good general guide for all of California is the *Sunset Western Garden Book*, and regional and local references are available for most parts of the state. Also, many UCCE county offices have prepared lists of trees recommended for local conditions.

Selecting Plants in the Nursery

The quality of the trees, shrubs, vines, and ground covers selected in a nursery can be just as important as species selection, site evaluation, planting, and maintenance in determining their success in the landscape. Carefully inspect plants from top to bottom before purchase to ensure that they meet crown, trunk, and root standards and are healthy, vigorous, and free from injury, disease, and pests.

Nurseries stock mostly container-grown plants. Container-grown plants can be transplanted successfully any time during the year in all areas of the state except those that experience extended periods of subfreezing weather. During the dormant winter season, however, a variety of deciduous, woody fruit, shade, and ornamental trees and vines are usually readily available bare-root. If handled and planted properly, bare-root plants are normally less expensive and grow just as well as container-grown ones, and their roots are easier to inspect.

Crown and Trunk Characteristics

The aboveground portions of plants are the easiest to inspect. Check the crown of leaves and shoots for health, turgidity, presence of disease or insects, and shape and structure. If the plant is staked, untie it and see if it bends over sharply at the soil line or if the trunk is loose in the soil, both of which indicate poor trunk and root development.

If trees were grown in the nursery with adequate space and without staking or severe pruning, they are usually capable of supporting themselves, even in wind. They should return to an upright position when bent down by the wind or hand if they have developed proper crown-to-trunk and crown-to-root ratios, trunk taper, and branch distribution. Proper development of these characteristics ensures even distribution of wind stress and less breakage and damage. Plants are often crowded in nurseries during production and may not attain these desirable characteristics.

The height and size of the crown should be in moderate proportion to the caliper of the trunk and size of root mass. If the tree has been grown in a series of containers for many years, the crown may be too large or too small in proportion to the roots. Trees in this condition require relatively high postplanting care. Judicious thinning or pruning will reduce the crown-to-root ratio and improve moisture and nutritional levels, lessening the need for continued high levels of care.

The trunk should be tapered, wider at the bottom and more slender near the top, bending only along a section near the ground when subjected to sufficient stress. Tapered trunks distribute wind loads evenly in their lower portions, thus minimizing the possibility of breakage or damage. Excessive crowding, staking, and severe pruning can produce trees without proper taper, leading to trunks that break easily or remain bent over even after the wind has stopped.

Branches along the trunk of a tree, especially a young one, will distribute wind stress evenly. The crown should have branches placed along the trunk so that about half of the foliage is on branches originating in the upper third of the trunk and the other half of the foliage is on branches originating in the lower two-thirds of the trunk. Lower branches

Table 13.1

RESISTANCE AND SUSCEPTIBILITY OF SELECTED ORNAMENTAL PLANTS TO ARMILLARIA ROOT ROT (*ARMILLARIA MELLEA*).

Scientific Name	Common Name	Scientific Name	Common Name
IMMUNE OR HIGHLY RESISTANT			
Abies concolor	Colorado or white fir	*Eucalyptus cinerea*	dollar-leaf eucalyptus, mealy stringbark
Abutilon vitifolium	Chinese lantern		
Acacia mearnsii	black wattle	*Eucalyptus grandis*	rose gum
Acacia longifolia	Sydney golden wattle, bush acacia	*Exochorda racemosa*	pearlbush
		Fabiana imbricata	fabiana
Acacia verticillata	whorl-leaved or star acacia	*Fraxinus oxycarpa*	Raywood or claret ash
Acer ginnala	ginnala maple, amur maple	*Fraxinus uhdei*	shamel ash, evergreen ash
Acer macrophyllum	bigleaf maple, Oregon maple	*Fraxinus velutina* var. *glabra* 'Modesto'	Modesto ash
Acer palmatum	Japanese maple		
Ailanthus altissima	tree-of-heaven	*Geijera parviflora*	Australian willow, wilga
Angophora costata	gum myrtle	*Ginko biloba*	maidenhair tree
Arbutus menziesii	madrone	*Gleditsia tricanthos* forma *mermis* 'Shademaster'	shademaster locust
Asimina triloba	pawpaw		
Berberis polyantha	barberry	*Gymnocladus dioica*	Kentucky coffee-tree
Betula pumila	swamp birch	*Hibiscus syriacus*	rose of Sharon
Brachychiton populneus	Kurrajong, bottle tree	*Hypericum patulum*	St. Johnswort (shrub form)
Broussonetia papyrifera	paper mulberry	*Ilex aquifolium*	English holly
Brugmansia suaveolens	angel's trumpet	*Ilex × aquipernyi*	San Jose or brilliant holly
Buxus sempervirens	common or English box	*Ilex cassine*	dahoon
Buxus sempervirens arborescens	common box (tree form)	*Ilex opaca*	American holly
Callicarpa japonica	beautyberry	*Jacaranda acutifolia*	jacaranda
Calocedrus decurrens	incense cedar	*Lagerstroemia × amabilis*	—
Calycanthus occidentalis	Western spice bush	*Ligustrum tschonskii*	privet
Carpenteria californica	bush anemone	*Liquidambar orientalis*	Oriental sweet gum
Catalpa bignonioides	common catalpa	*Liquidambar styraciflua*	American sweet gum, liquidambar
Catalpa hybrida var. *japonica*	—		
Catalpa ovata	Chinese catalpa	*Liriodendron tulipifera*	tulip tree
Celtis australis	European hackberry	*Lonicera nitidia*	box honeysuckle
Celtis occidentalis	hackberry	*Lyonia mariana*	stagger bush
Ceratonia siliqua	carob	*Maclura pomifera*	Osage orange
Cercis occidentalis	California redbud	*Magnolia grandiflora*	southern magnolia
Cercis siliquastrum	Judas tree	*Mahonia aquifolium*	holly mahonia, Oregon grape
Chaenomeles lagenaria	Japanese quince	*Mahonia nevinii*	Nevin mahonia
Chamaecyparis lawsoniana 'Ellwoodii'	Elwood cypress	*Malus floribunda*	Japanese flowering crabapple
		Malus ioensis	prairie crabapple
Clerodendron bungei	Kashmir bouquet	*Maytenus boaria*	mayten tree
Cotinus coggyrgia	smoke tree	*Melaleuca styphelioides*	prickly paperbark
Cryptomeria japonica	Japanese cryptomeria, Japanese cedar	*Metasequoia glyptostroboides*	dawn redwood
		Myrica pensylvanica	bayberry
Cupaniopsis anacardioides	carrotwood, tuckeroo	*Nandina domestica*	sacred bamboo
X *Cupressocyparis leylandii*	Leyland cypress	*Persea indica*	Indian avocado
Cupressus arizonica var. *glabra*	smooth Arizona cypress	*Phellodendron amurense*	Amur cork tree
Dais cotinifolia	pompon tree	*Phellodendron chinense*	Chinese cork tree
Elaeagnus angustifolia	oleaster, Russian olive	*Phlomis fruticosa*	Jerusalem sage
Erica arborea	tree heath	*Pinus canariensis*	Canary Island pine
Eucalyptus camaldulensis	red gum	*Pinus monticola*	western white pine
		Pinus nigra	Austrian pine

Scientific Name	Common Name
Pinus nigra ssp. *larico*	Corsican pine
Pinus patula	Mexican pine
Pinus radiata	Monterey pine
Pinus sylvestris	Scots pine
Pinus torreyana	Torrey pine
Pistacia chinensis	Chinese pistache
Pittosporum heterophyllum	—
Pittosporum rhombifolium	Queensland pittosporum
Prunus caroliniana	American cherry laurel
Prunus ilicifolia	holly-leaf cherry, California cherry
Prunus lyonii	Catalina cherry
Psidium cattleianum	strawberry guava
Quercus ilex	holly oak
Quercus lobata	valley oak, California white oak
Quillaja saponaria	soapbark tree
Rhus aromatica	fragrant sumac
Rhus copallina	shining sumac
Sambucus canadensis	American or sweet elderberry
Sapium sebiferum	Chinese tallow-tree
Sequoia sempervirens	coast redwood
Shepherdia argentea	buffaloberry
Sophora japonica	Japanese pagoda tree
Taxodium distichum	bald cypress
Ternstroemia sylvatica	Mexican ternstroemia
Ulmus parvifolia	evergreen Chinese elm
Vitex agnus-castus	blue chaste tree
Wisteria sinensis	Chinese wisteria

MODERATELY RESISTANT

Abelia × *grandiflora*	glossy abelia, white abelia
Acer negundo var. *californicum*	box elder
Albizia julibrissin	silk tree
Amorpha fruticosa	false indigo
Berberis darwinii	Darwin barberry
Berberis thunbergii	green Japanese barberry
Berberis wilsoniae	Wilson barberry
Cephalanthus occidentalis	buttonwillow
Chamaecyparis lawsoniana	Lawson cypress, Port Orford cedar
Chimonanthus praecox	wintersweet
Cladrastis lutea	yellow wood
Crataegus phaenopyrum	Washington thorn
Cytisus purpureus	purple broom
Dodonea viscosa	clammy hopseed bush
Elaeagnus commutata	silverberry
Eucalyptus polyanthemos	redbox gum
Eucalyptus pulchella	white peppermint
Euonymus japonica	evergreen euonymus, Japanese euonymus
Grevillea robusta	silk oak
Hebe × *andersonii*	Anderson speedwell

Scientific Name	Common Name
Hebe speciosa	showy or imperial speedwell
Hovenia dulcis	Japanese raisin-tree
Iochroma cyaneum	purple tobacco
Koelreuteria paniculata	goldenrain tree
Lagerstroemia indica	crape myrtle
Ligustrum japonicum	Japanese privet, wax-leaf privet
Melaleuca linariifolia	flaxleaf paperbark
Myrtus communis	myrtle
Nerium oleander	oleander
Picea abies	Norway spruce
Pinus eldarica	eldarica pine
Pinus jeffreyi	Jeffrey pine
Pittosporum tobira	Japanese pittosporum, tobira
Pseudotsuga menziesii	douglas-fir
Pyracantha coccinea	scarlet firethorn
Pyracantha coccinea 'Lalandei'	Lalande pyracantha
Pyracantha crenulata 'Kansuensis'	Kansu firethorn
Quercus chrysolepis	canyon life oak, golden cup oak
Sequoia giganteum	giant redwood
Spiraea prunifolia	bridal wreath, shoe-button spiraea
Wisteria macrostachya	wisteria
Zelkova serrata	Japanese zelkova

SUSCEPTIBLE

Acacia floribunda	Sydney acacia, Sydney wattle
Acer morrisonense	Formosan maple
Arbutus unedo	strawberry tree
Betula pendula	European white birch
Buddleia davidii	orange-eyed butterfly bush
Buddleia davidii var. *magnifica*	oxeye butterfly bush
Buddleia globosa	orange butterfly bush
Caesalpinia gilliesii	bird-of-paradise bush, poinciana
Callistemon viminalis	weeping bottlebrush
Carpinus betulus	European hornbeam
Caryopteris × *clandonensis*	blue mist
Cassia tomentosa	senna
Casuarina stricta	shea oak, beefwood
Ceanothus arboreus	Catalina mountain lilac, feltleaf ceanothus
Ceanothus thyrsiflorus	blue blossom
Cercidiphyllum japonicum	katsura tree
Cercis canadensis	eastern redbud
Choisya ternata	Mexican orange
Cinnamomum camphora	camphor tree
Cistus clusii	rockrose
Cistus × *cyprius*	hybrid rockrose
Cistus × *lusitanicus*	hybrid rockrose
Cistus palhinhae	St. Vincent rockrose
Cistus populifolius	rockrose

Table 13.1 cont.

Scientific Name	Common Name
Coprosma repens	coprosma, mirror shrub
Cotoneaster buxifolius var. vellaeus	boxleaf cotoneaster
Cotoneaster dielsianus	Diels cotoneaster
Cotoneaster franchetii	Franchet cotoneaster
Cotoneaster frigidus	Himalayan cotoneaster
Cotoneaster harrovianus	Harrow cotoneaster
Cotoneaster horizontalis	rock cotoneaster
Cotoneaster microphyllus	rockspray cotoneaster
Cotoneaster pannosus	silver-leaf cotoneaster
Cotoneaster salicifolius var. floccosus	hardy willowleaf cotoneaster
Cytisus × spachianus	Easter broom
Deutzia scabra	fuzzy deutzia
Erica herbacea	winter heath, Mediterranean heather
Erythrina crista-galli	cockspur coral tree, coral tree, cockspur
Escallonia × franciscana	rose or slippery-elm escallonia
Escallonia montevidensis	Montevideo escallonia
Escallonia pulverulenta	—
Escallonia rubra var. macrantha	red escallonia
Eucalyptus citriodora	lemon gum
Eucalyptus gracilis	yorrell, white mallee
Eucalyptus grossa	coarse-leaved mallee
Eucalyptus maculata	spotted gum
Eucalyptus pauciflora	cabbage gum
Eucalyptus pulverulenta	silver dollar tree
Eucalyptus rudis	desert gum, moitch eucalyptus
Eucalyptus sideroxylon	pink ironbark
Eucalyptus tessecoris	—
Euonymus japonica 'Aureo-marginata'	golden euonymus
Euphorbia pulcherrima	poinsettia
Fagus sylvatica	European beech
Fontanesia fortunei	—
Fraxinus holotricha	Kimberly blue ash
Fremontodendron mexicanum	Southern fremontia, Mexican fremontia
Hakea laurina	sea urchin tree
Hakea oleifolia	—
Hebe odora	boxleaf veronica
Heteromeles arbutifolia	toyon, Christmas berry, California holly
Hydrangea quercifolia	oakleaf hydrangea
Hypericum beanii	Henry St. Johnswort, goldflower

Scientific Name	Common Name
Hypericum prolificum	shrubby St. Johnswort, broombrush
Kerria japonica	Japanese rose, kerria, globe flower
Laburnum anagyroides	golden chain-tree
Laburnum × watereri	long cluster golden chain-tree
Leptospermum laevigatum	Australian tea tree
Ligustrum vulgare	'Aureum' yellowleaf European privet
Lithocarpus densiflorus	tanbark-oak
Malus hupehensis	tea crabapple
Malus × eleyi	eley crabapple
Malus sargentii	sargent crabapple
Malus toringoides	cutleaf crabapple
Melaleuca decora	—
Melaleuca hypericifolia	dotted melaleuca
Melaleuca leucadendron	cajeput tree or punk-tree
Melaleuca radula	—
Melaleuca styphelioides	prickly paperback
Myrtus communis 'Variegata'	variegated myrtle
Paulownia lilacina	—
Paulownia tomentosa	royal paulownia, empress tree
Picea pungens	Colorado blue spruce
Pinus monophylla	one-needled pinyon pine, pinyon pine
Prunus laurocerasus	cherry-laurel, English laurel
Prunus triloba	flowering almond
Pyracantha angustifolia	narrowleaf firethorn
Pyracantha crenato-serrata	Yunan firethorn
Pyracantha crenulata	Nepal firethorn
Pyracantha koidzumii	Formosa firethorn
Pyracantha rogersiana	Rogers firethorn
Quercus dumosa	California scrub oak
Quercus virginiana	southern live oak
Rhus ovata	sugar bush
Rhus trilobata	squawbush
Schinus polygamus	tree pepper
Schinus terebinthifolius	Brazilian pepper tree
Sesbania punicea	glory pea, scarlet wisteria tree
Severina buxifolia	Chinese box orange
Spartium junceum	Spanish broom
Sutherlandia frutescens	—
Syringa vulgaris	lilac
Thuja plicata	giant arborvitae, western red cedar
Ulex europaeus	gorse, furze
Viburnum tinus	laurustinus
Weigela florida	weigela

Source: Adapted from Raabe 1979, pp. 3–8.

Table 13.2

RESISTANCE AND SUSCEPTIBILITY OF SELECTED ORNAMENTAL PLANTS TO VERTICILLIUM WILT (*VERTICILLIUM DAHLIAE* OR *V. ALBO-ATRUM*).

Scientific Name	Common Name
RESISTANT OR IMMUNE FAMILIES	
Cactaceae	cactus family
Gramineae	cereal grains, corn, grasses, milo, sorghum, others
Gymnospermae	gymnosperms (cypress, fir, ginkgo, larch, juniper, pine, sequoia, spruce, others)
Monocotyledoneae	monocots (bamboo, banana, gladiolus, grasses, iris, lily, onion, orchids, palms, others)
Polypodiaceae	fern family (ferns)
RESISTANT OR IMMUNE TREES AND SHRUBS	
Arctostaphylos spp.	manzanita
Betula spp.	birch
Buxus spp.	box
Carpinus spp.	hornbeam
Ceanothus spp.	ceanothus
Cercidiphyllum japonicum	katsura tree
Cistus corbariensis	white rockrose
Cistus salviifolius	sageleaf rockrose
Cistus tauricus	rockrose
Citrus spp.	orange, lemon, grapefruit, others
Cornus spp.	dogwood
Crataegus spp.	hawthorn
Eucalyptus spp.	eucalyptus
Fagus spp.	beech
Ficus carica	fig
Gleditsia spp.	locust
Gleditsia triacanthos	honey locust
Hebe anonda	hebe
Hebe × *franciscana*	hebe
Hebe × *menziesii*	Menzies' hebe
Hebe salicifolia	willow leaved hebe
Ilex spp.	holly
Juglans spp.	walnut
Liquidambar styraciflua	liquidambar, sweet gum
Malus spp.	apple, flowering crabapples
Morus spp.	mulberry
Nerium oleander	oleander
Platanus racemosa	western sycamore, California sycamore
Platanus spp.	plane tree

Scientific Name	Common Name
Pyracantha spp.	pyracantha, firethorn
Pyrus spp.	pear
Quercus spp.	oak
Salix spp.	willow
Sorbus aucuparia	European mountain ash
Umbellularia californica	California laurel
Tilia spp.	linden
SUSCEPTIBLE TREES	
Acer spp.	maple
Acer negundo	box elder
Ailanthus altissima	tree-of-heaven
Carya illinoensis	pecan
Catalpa spp.	catalpa
Ceratonia siliqua	carob
Cercis canadensis	redbud
Cinnamomum camphora	camphor tree
Cladrastis lutea	yellow wood
Cupaniopsis anacardioides	carrot wood
Diospyros spp.	persimmon
Elaeagnus angustifolia	oleaster, Russian olive
Ficus benjamina	weeping fig
Ficus retusa	Indian laurel
Fraxinus spp.	ash
Koelreuteria paniculata	goldenrain tree
Liriodendron tulipifera	tulip tree
Magnolia grandiflora	southern magnolia
Nyssa sylvatica	black gum, pepperidge
Olea europaea	olive
Persea americana	avocado
Pistacia chinensis	Chinese pistache
Prunus spp.	almond, apricot, cherry, peach, plum, prune
Robinia pseudoacacia	black locust
Schinus molle	California pepper tree
Schinus terebinthifolius	Brazilian pepper tree
Ulmus spp.	elm
SUSCEPTIBLE GROUND COVERS, SHRUBS, AND VINES	
Berberis (*Mahonia*) spp.	barberry
Campsis radicans	trumpet creeper
Capsicum spp.	pepper
Carpobrotus edulis	ice plant
Cistus ladanifer	spotted rockrose
Cistus palhinhae	rockrose
Cistus × *purpureus*	orchid-spot rockrose
Cotinus coggygria	smoke tree
Dodonaea viscosa	clammy hopseed bush
Erica spp.	heather

Table 13.2 cont

Scientific Name	Common Name	Scientific Name	Common Name
Fremontodendron spp.	flannel bush	*Parthenium argentatum*	guayule
Fuchsia spp.	fuchsia	*Rhaphiolepis indica*	Indian hawthorn
Hebe bollonsii	hebe	*Rhaphiolepis umbellata*	yeddo hawthorn
Hebe × carnea 'Carnea'	hebe	*Rhus integrifolia*	lemonade berry
Hebe lewisii	hebe	*Rhus* spp.	sumac
Jasminum magnificum	angel-wing jasmine	*Rosa* spp.	rose
Jasminum mesnyi	primrose jasmine	*Rosmarinus officinalis* L.	rosemary
Lampranthus spectabilis	ice plant	*Syringa vulgaris*	lilac
Ligustrum spp.	privet	*Viburnum* spp.	viburnum, wayfaring-tree, others
Nandina domestica	sacred bamboo		

Source: Adapted from McCain et al. 1981, pp. 3–4, 7, 8.

on young trees not only help to distribute stress more evenly but also help the tree attain greater caliper and taper. Lower branches should be kept short in relation to higher, permanent, scaffold branches and can be removed altogether with time.

Future, main scaffold branches should be well-spaced both up and down the trunk as well as around it and should form wide angles at the point of attachment.

Roots

A healthy, well-developed root system is essential to establishing a plant successfully in the landscape. Carefully remove a plant from its container to inspect the roots. Plants in 1-gallon containers can be turned upside down and, while holding the stem between the fingers with the hand spread flatly against the soil surface, the rim of the pot tapped gently onto a solid object until the root ball slides out easily. Plants in 2- and 5-gallon containers can be carefully and slowly picked up at the base of the stem and, by tapping on the container rim, the container gently pushed down to expose the roots. If a plant this size begins to pull out of the soil ball, as it is being lifted, it is a poorly rooted specimen.

To inspect the roots of ground covers in flats, carefully place the flat nearly on edge and gently pull back on the plants in one corner to reveal the roots. Lift bare-root material and shake off the sawdust or other holding material to expose the roots.

When plants are removed from the container, the roots should be fibrous and of sufficient density to hold the soil and root mass together. Roots enclosing the outside of the root ball should be small- to medium-sized and not too densely entwined or matted. Main roots should be free of kinks and circles; all roots should be free of disease, insects, and nematodes.

Not all kinked and circling roots are necessarily harmful. Only main roots with more than a 90-degree turn and 80 percent of the root system below the kink and at the surface or center, or those that circle 80 percent or more of the root system by at least 360 degrees, generally cause problems. If necessary, remove or wash away some of the potting soil at the center around the trunk-surface area to examine the roots.

Circling roots on the outside of the root ball are fairly common, especially in container-grown plants, are usually not a problem and can be corrected at planting. The root system is probably not abnormally pot-bound if plant tops are healthy and vigorous.

Generally, healthy root tips are white or light-colored. Diseased or rotten roots are usually soft, dark, and mushy, and when pulled, the outer portion strips away easily, leaving a slender, threadlike core.

Although plants are generally sold by container size, there is not necessarily a relationship between the size of plants and their containers. If inspection of the root mass reveals few roots on the outside, one is probably paying for a larger plant than one receives.

Plant Health

Plant health is characterized by vigor (a measure of a plant's ability to do well once planted) and freedom from injury and pests. Indicators of vigor include green to dark green color, relatively large leaves and dense foliage, smooth bright bark, and adequate shoot growth. Evaluation of plant vigor is relatively subjective and requires a good knowledge of a species when making such assessments, because many of the indicators vary from species to species. Obviously, plants should be free in all their parts from injury, disease, and pests.

Planting

Once you have selected a healthy, vigorous, well-grown plant of the appropriate species for the right place in the landscape, the next step is to plant it properly. The performance of landscape plant material depends a great deal on how it is planted. The spring and fall months are usually the best times to transplant woody plants. Weather conditions are typically moderate, enabling plants to avoid heat or cold stress while they are establishing new root systems.

Figure 13.1

Planting a landscape tree from a container. *Source:* After Harris and Davis 1984, p.1.

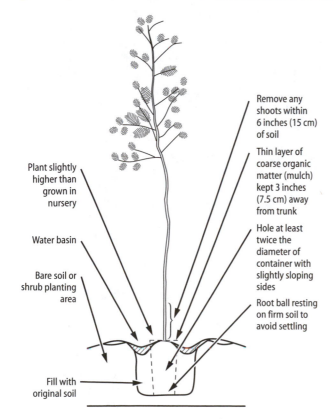

Plant slightly higher than grown in nursery

Water basin

Bare soil or shrub planting area

Fill with original soil

Remove any shoots within 6 inches (15 cm) of soil

Thin layer of coarse organic matter (mulch) kept 3 inches (7.5 cm) away from trunk

Hole at least twice the diameter of container with slightly sloping sides

Root ball resting on firm soil to avoid settling

Digging the Hole

Plant the tree, shrub, or vine "high" and not too deeply. Dig the hole to a depth about 2 inches (5 cm) less than that of the soil in the container or root ball. Planting more deeply or in loose soil that can settle with time, causing the plant to be deeper than intended, may lead to future problems such as crown rot.

The width of the hole should be a minimum of twice the diameter of the container or root ball. The wider the hole, the faster the roots will grow out of the root ball and into surrounding soil. For bare-root plants, spread the roots out evenly without bending or crowding them. If planting in compacted soils, it may be necessary to dig deeper to break up impervious zones or layers. If so, wait 2 to 4 weeks before planting to give the loosened soil the chance to settle. See figure 13.1 for an illustration of how to dig a hole for planting a landscape tree from a container.

Backfill

Place the plant's root ball so that it rests firmly on the undug bottom of the hole. Backfill around the root ball with unamended soil dug from the hole, being sure to water the soil thoroughly to remove air pockets. Recent studies have shown that nothing is gained by amending the backfill with organic matter, fertilizer, vitamin B_1, or other substances. In fact, the practice could be harmful. It is much better and more efficient to use organic matter as a mulch spread over the soil after planting to improve soil structure, conserve water, and discourage weeds.

Using the remaining soil dug from the hole, construct a water basin that is initially the same diameter as the root ball. Gradually widen the basin as the plant becomes established. Remove it completely after the first growing season.

Mulching and Irrigation

After planting, add a layer of coarse organic material as a mulch and irrigate thoroughly (flood the basin) to settle the soil. Keep the mulch 3 inches (7.5 cm) away from the trunk. Judicious water management is critical for newly planted landscape material. The original root ball must not be allowed to become completely dry for any extended period during the establishment of a woody plant. Remember that, although the new plant may be large, its root volume still occupies a rather limited area. Root balls of plants that were oversized in their container or slightly pot-bound can dry out more quickly than the surrounding back-filled soil. Until the roots grow out and become established in the parent soil, more frequent but lighter watering may be needed. As the plant becomes established, irrigations can become less frequent but deeper.

Plants in Lawns

If plants are installed in turf areas, keep the grass well away from the trunk of the new plant for 2 to 4 years to reduce competition from the grass for water and nutrients. Keeping the ground free of other plant growth at least 12 inches (30 cm) in all directions from the trunk also prevents damage from mowers, edgers, and weeders. Using plastic guards to

prevent this type of mechanical damage may be useful, because such damage can kill or severely dwarf young plants.

Staking

Trees should be staked for support, protection, or anchorage when needed. With few exceptions, there is little need to stake trees for trunk support if they were grown properly with adequate space in the nursery. Trees with large tops in proportion to their roots may need to be staked. Even these trees can often stand alone, however, without staking by simply thinning out about a third of the branches to lighten the crown and reduce its wind resistance.

If newly planted trees will not stand upright without support or if frequent, heavy winds are a problem, staking may be necessary. Staking to support a tree should be as low as possible on the trunk but still high enough that the tree will return to an upright position after being deflected. To determine the proper point at which to stake and tie a tree, hold the trunk in one hand, pull the top to one side, and release. Attach the ties at the height at which the trunk will return to upright when the top is released (see figs. 13.2 and 13.3).

Use two support stakes, one each on opposite sides of the trunk, positioning them so that a line drawn between them would be at right angles to the most troublesome wind direction. Make the stakes as short as possible but high enough to hold the tree upright under calm conditions. The tree should return to vertical after the wind has bent the top. Loosely tie the trunk to each stake at just one level, at the point near the top determined by the technique shown in figure 13.2. This technique allows the trunk below the tie to bend in the opposite direction from the top during a wind. Material used for ties should have a broad surface to minimize rubbing or girdling and have some elasticity to provide greater flexibility as well as support. Each tie should form a loose loop around the trunk, one right above the other one, and the two together should provide the necessary support at the right place (see figure 13.3).

Provide flexible movement at the tying point without allowing the tree to contact the stakes. Trees whose trunks and tops are allowed to flex, give, and move a little develop greater trunk caliper and taper, stronger wood, a larger root system, and less wind resistance, because the top is free to bend. They become

Figure 13.2

Stakes should be no higher than necessary to hold the tree upright, while allowing the top freedom to move in the wind. To find the correct height, grasp the trunk with one hand and bend the top (left). If the top returns to its upright position when released, tie the trunk to stakes at the height of the bend (right). *Source:* After Harris et al. 1978, p. 6.

self-supporting at an earlier age than trees that are rigidly staked.

As the tree grows and becomes better established, remove or lower ties and shorten the stakes so that they do not rub against the trunk and cause rubbing or girdling injury. Ties probably can be removed by the end of the second growing season. Use stakes for the shortest possible time.

To provide extra protection from lawnmowers and other mechanical damage, drive three stakes that are 2 inches by 2 inches (5 cm by 5 cm) thick and about 3 feet (0.9 m) long at equidistant positions around the root ball. Drive the stakes into the undisturbed soil until about 12 inches (30 cm) remains above ground level.

Even on newly planted trees whose trunks do not need support, trunk movement could break new roots growing out of the root ball into the parent soil if the root system is not well-anchored. Two or three short stakes placed as suggested above provide protection from mechanical damage and enough anchorage for the roots. Ties from each of the stakes to the trunk will usually be sufficient to keep the roots firmly in the ground. The top may need thinning to decrease wind resistance and weight. Ties can be removed after the first growing season and the stakes left for trunk protection.

Pruning

If the right plant species is selected for the right spot and purpose in the landscape, it is usually unnecessary to prune mature, well-established trees and shrubs. When done improperly, pruning can be one of the most destructive horticultural practices, destroying the shape and structure of a tree and predisposing it to severe future problems. Topping mature trees (heading back the main leader) is not usually recommended because it seriously injures trees and disfigures them. When proper techniques are used, however, judicious pruning of woody plants serves several useful functions. Pruning can be used to train young plants, groom for appearance, control shape and size, influence flowering and fruiting, invigorate stagnant growth, and remove damaged or pest-infested growth.

Types of Pruning Cuts

The two main types of pruning cuts are head, or heading back, and thin, or thinning out, and a woody plant responds differently to each type of cut. Heading back is cutting the plant back to a stub, lateral bud, or small lateral branch (fig. 13.4). Depending on the severity of pruning, heading back results in a flush of vigorous, upright, and dense new growth from just below the cut. New shoots formed on older, larger limbs are weakly attached and split out easily (figs. 13.5 and 13.6). Thinning (fig. 13.7) is removing a lateral branch at its origin or shortening a branch's length by cutting to a lateral large enough to assume the terminal role. A woody plant responds to thinning by becoming more open but retaining its natural growth habit and does not usually produce a flush of new vigorous growth from the cut. Foliage grows more deeply into the tree because more light can penetrate the canopy.

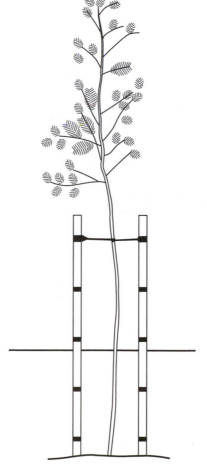

Figure 13.3

Tie tree to stakes at the correct height using flexible webbing material. *Source:* After Harris et al. 1978, p.9.

Making the Cut

Pruning shears (or loppers) are used for cutting small limbs, and saws are used for large ones. If diseased plants are pruned, disinfect pruning equipment after each cut to prevent spreading disease. Denatured alcohol or a chlorine bleach solution can be used to do this. When pruning trees and shrubs that have been grafted, remove new shoots that start below the graft union, but be careful not to remove all of the stems that start above the graft union. Small limbs, including suckers and water sprouts, should be cut close to the trunk or branch from which they arise. Cuts are made most easily with a single, upward cut of the blade. On most kinds of trees, new shoots will be less likely to grow from remaining latent buds if small limbs are cut closely.

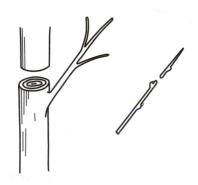

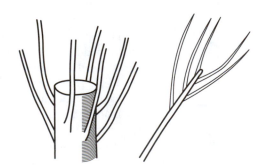

When heading back trees or shrubs, cut small stems back to about ¼ inch (0.6 cm) from a lateral bud or branch. Make the cut on a slight slant away from the bud or branch. New growth will usually grow in the direction the bud or branch points (figs. 13.8 and 13.9).

Large tree limbs must be cut with a saw. The recommended procedure is to remove a limb in two steps involving three cuts (fig. 13.10). Make the first cut on the underside of the branch 1 to 2 feet (30 to 60 cm) from the crotch and at least one-third of the diameter deep. Make the second cut, a downward one, 1 to 3 inches (2.5 to 7.5 cm) farther from the crotch than the first. The limb should then split cleanly between the two cuts without tearing the bark. The third cut to remove the remaining stub is made at the crotch, but its exact position is important to ensure rapid closure of the wound.

Most trees form ridges, called branch bark ridges (BBR) or shoulder rings, on the top and bottom of branches where they are attached to the trunk. The third cut should be made just outside the branch bark ridge (fig. 13.11). The cut will not be flush or parallel to the trunk but will be out from it slightly, with the lower edge of the cut farther away from the trunk than the top one. Such a cut will form a smaller wound than a flush cut and it will close more quickly.

Protecting pruning cuts with an asphalt emulsion or other coating material is of no value and could even be harmful to the tree. Coatings and coverings can trap moisture and increase the chances of decay and retard wound closure. The best practice is simply to let the wound dry in the air.

Painting water-based paint on the southwestern portions of the newly exposed trunk and branches after pruning may prevent bark injury from sunscald.

Pruning Trees at Planting

Landscape trees should not be pruned at planting time except to remove damaged branches or to correct those that show serious structural problems, such as branches with extremely narrow crotch angles and branches that cross or rub other branches. (Fruit trees are often treated differently. See chapters 17, 18, and 19.) In the past, it was commonly recommended to prune a portion of the shoots at planting. Recent research, however, has shown that the removal of terminal buds and leaf area

Figure 13.6

New shoots forced on older limbs are weakly attached and split out easily. *Source:* After Harris et al. 1981, p.4.

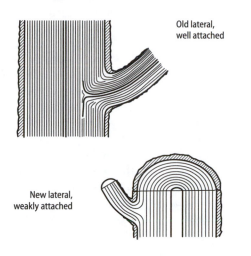

Old lateral, well attached

New lateral, weakly attached

Figure 13.7

Thinning removes a branch (A) or cuts to a larger one (B). *Source:* After Harris et al. 1981, p.4.

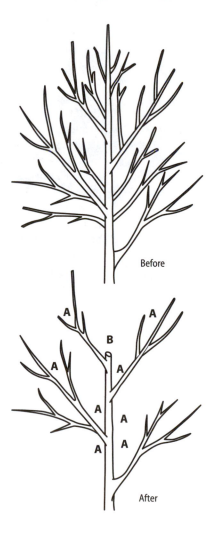

Before

After

can delay and reduce root system growth. Because the survival and establishment of a transplanted tree depend greatly on the growth and development of new roots, the practice of pruning at transplanting is no longer standard.

There is one exception, however. If irrigation is unavailable after planting, or if severe drought is anticipated after planting, limited thinning-type pruning may increase the chances of tree survival. Although this pruning may restrict root growth, thinning cuts remove foliage and thereby reduce transpiration and water loss.

Pruning To Train Young Trees

Directing the growth of young trees is important if the trees are to perform properly in the landscape when mature. The growth habit of a plant and its landscape use largely determine the extent to which a tree must be trained to obtain the desire form. Pruning is usually the most effective way to direct the growth habit of a plant. Young trees with a strong central leader, like conifers and liquidambar, may need little or no pruning. Other tree species, such as Chinese pistache and some flowering fruit trees, lack a strong central lead, have more irregular growth, and need a higher degree of training. Street trees should have higher scaffold branches than trees used for visual screening or windbreaks.

Prune a tree only enough to direct its growth effectively and correct any structural weaknesses. The height of the first permanent branch above the ground depends on the tree's intended landscape use. The lowest scaffolds on trees in lawn and garden areas are normally no higher than 6 to 8 feet (1.8 to 2.4 m) from the ground. Those on trees along streets and sidewalks should be 8 feet (2.4 m) above a sidewalk and 8 to 10 feet (2.4 to 3 m) above the street. The position of a limb on a trunk remains essentially the same throughout the life of the tree (fig. 13.12). Branches selected for permanent scaffolds should have wide angles of attachment, smaller in diameter than the trunk, and 18 to 24 inches (45 to 60 cm) apart vertically (fig. 13.13). Radial branch distribution should allow five to seven scaffolds to fill the circle of space around the trunk.

Many trees produce an abundance of lateral growth. Direct this growth during the growing season by heading back or thinning out shoots competing with the leader or interfering with those selected for scaffold branches. During the first and perhaps the second season, more shoots should be left unpruned than will finally be selected for scaffolds, allowing more choices later for selection of the best lateral branches. Often, on lightly or unpruned trees, the more vigorous branches will be naturally well-spaced, and other branches become rather weak.

If a tree seems reluctant to develop laterals for future scaffolds, pinch out (head back 1 to 2 inches [2.5 to 5 cm]) the tip during the growing season when the growing point reaches a height at which a lateral branch is desired (fig. 13.14). Select the most vigorously growing new shoot that developed from the buds below the pinch as the leader. Then choose as a lateral a second developing shoot growing in the desired direction by pinching the tips of the other shoots that were formed. Repeat this process as the leader develops until the desired number and spacing of laterals is obtained. A vigorously growing tree may permit forcing as many as three well-spaced laterals where they are wanted in one season.

Pinching during the growing season is much more effective, requires removing a much smaller quantity of shoot material, and results in less dwarfing effect of the plant than dormant pruning. A growing-season pinch of only 1 to 2 inches (2.5 to 5 cm) is just as effective and will make unnecessary the removal of a large branch later on during the dormant season. Without pinching during the growing season, the leader would require severe heading to the height at which the lowest lateral is desired during the dormant season.

Pruning Mature Trees

Once well-spaced scaffold branches and the main structure of a tree have been selected, usually by the third or fourth year, the tree will probably need little or no pruning for several years, especially if it is the right tree for the right place and purpose. Mature trees, however, may need to be pruned for health and appearance, size control, and flowering and fruiting response. Pruning the leader of a central-leader tree and wholesale topping (heading back) of mature trees are inappropriate. These practices destroy a tree's natural form, create large wounds, and force many vigorous upright shoots that are weakly attached (fig. 13.15).

Removal of dead, weak, diseased, and insect-infested limbs will improve tree health and appearance. Remove low, broken, and crossing limbs for appearance and safety. Open up the top of the tree to let in more light so that interior leaves and branches can remain healthy. Judicious pruning consisting of moderate thinning can open a tree to view and emphasize an attractive or picturesque feature to the viewer.

Although pruning for size control is a less preferred alternative to initial proper species selection, it may be necessary in some instances. If trees were planted too closely together or if the particular function or purpose for which a tree was originally selected has changed, size control through pruning could be the best alternative to removal or replanting.

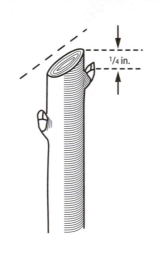

Figure 13.8

Make pruning cuts about ¼ inch (6 mm) above a bud and slightly angled away. *Source:* After Caldwell et al. 1972, p.10.

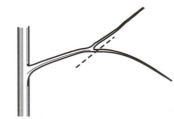

Figure 13.9

Prune back horizontal limbs to a more upright lateral or to an upward-growing bud. *Source:* After Harris et al. 1981, p.18.

Figure 13.10

To remove a large limb, make first cut at (A), second at (B), third at branch bark ridge (C). *Source:* After Harris et al. 1981, p. 5.

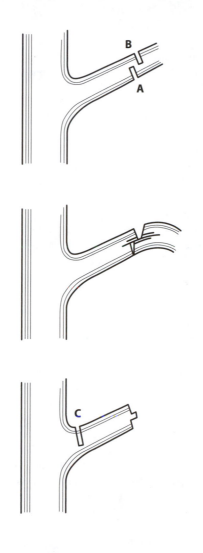

Figure 13.11

Pruning cuts should be made just outside the branch bark ridge (top of cut) and the collar (bottom of cut) so that the bottom of the cut is angled slightly outward. *Source:* After International Society of Arboriculture 1995, p. 3.

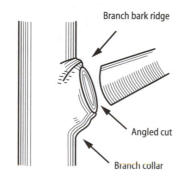

Branch bark ridge

Angled cut

Branch collar

Thinning, perhaps even the complete removal of some limbs, can be used to reduce the height and spread of a tree. A thinned tree retains its natural shape and is less prone to the formation of vigorous water sprouts than a headed tree (fig. 13.16). Pruning for size control, however, is most effective as soon as a tree reaches the desired size. Delaying pruning until the tree is larger makes pruning more difficult and less effective, leaves more noticeable scars, and encourages excessive growth. Heading and stubbing, while much more rapid and drastic in their effect, are in most cases much less desirable.

Severe pruning delays the onset of flowering in species that flower on 1-year-old growth, such as the flowering fruit trees. Once the tree has begun flowering, only a light annual thinning to remove 10 to 15 percent of the leaf area and to reduce crowding or weak branches is usually necessary. Perform such thinning at or near the end of the bloom period to encourage vigorous growth on which to bear next year's bloom.

On the other hand, trees flowering on current year's growth, such as crape myrtle, Japanese pagoda tree, and jacaranda, usually flower earlier and more profusely if pruned to stimulate and maintain vigorous growth. Plants with such flowering habits should be pruned more severely and during the winter before growth begins.

Pruning Conifers and Other Narrowleaf Evergreens

Although conifers usually require less pruning than broadleaf trees, the same basic principles apply for controlling size, creating special effects, and shaping. The crown configuration cannot be controlled as easily as with broadleaf trees. Dead, diseased, crowded, and structurally unsound branches should be removed first. Double leaders should be thinned to one unless the natural growth habit includes several main branches. Encourage branches with wide angles of attachment and smaller than the trunk from which they arise.

Pruning conifers differ from pruning broadleaf trees in several important ways. Conifers usually do not need pruning for spacing of laterals. Several branches arising at or near one level on the trunk seldom subdue the main leader of a conifer; thus, whorls of branches or those arising close together can remain, because it is unlikely they will crowd

Table 13.3

PRUNING GUIDELINES FOR CONIFERS

Plant	Branch pattern	Latent buds on old wood	Type of growth	Reduce size, direct growth	Slow growth Increase density	(Dwarf)	Comments
				Method of pruning for given response			
Abies spp.	whorled	no	All new growth from preformed buds.	Thin branch back to laterally growing shoot. Do not cut behind last remaining needles.	Remove apex of laterals only; do not pinch leader.	Root prune; prune late in summer.	Pruning not needed except to remove dead and diseased wood.
Juniperus spp.	random	some	Growth continues as long as conditions are favorable.	Thin branch back to laterally growing shoot.	Can be sheared or clipped, and some can be headed to old wood.	Root prune; prune late in summer.	
Picea spp.	whorled	no	All new growth from preformed buds.	Thin branch back to laterally growing shoot. Do not cut behind last remaining needles.	In spring, clip new shoots one-half their length when needles are one-half expanded.	Root prune; prune late in summer.	Pruning not needed except to remove dead and diseased wood.
Pinus spp. (most but not all)	whorled	no	All new growth from preformed buds	Thin branch back to laterally growing shoot. Do not cut behind last remaining needles.	Pinch candle when expanding in spring. Branching is induced between existing whorls by girdling trunk between whorls.	Root prune; prune late in summer.	
Pinus canariensis	whorled	yes	Often makes single flush of growth, but growth can continue under favorable conditions.	Thin branch back to laterally growing shoot.	Pinch candle when expanding in spring. Branching is induced between existing whorls by girdling trunk between whorls. Laterals can be headed to desired length.	Root prune; prune late in summer.	
Podocarpus spp.	random	no	Growth continues as long as conditions are favorable.	Thin branch back to laterally growing shoot. Do not cut behind last remaining needles.	Can be sheared, but form is retained by removing only apex of each shoot.	Prune late in summer.	
Pseudotsuga spp.	whorled	no	All new growth from preformed buds.	Thin branch back to laterally growing shoot. Do not cut behind last remaining needles.	In spring, clip new shoots one-half their length when needles are one-half expanded.	Prune late in summer.	
Sequoia spp.	random	yes	Growth continues as long as conditions are favorable.	Thin branch back to laterally growing shoot.	Can be sheared, but form is retained by removing only apex of each shoot. Can be headed back into old wood.		
Taxus spp.	random	yes	Growth continues as long as conditions are favorable.	Thin branch back to laterally growing shoot.	Can be sheared, but form is retained by removing only apex of each shoot. Can be headed back into old wood.	Prune late in summer.	Foliage of some is poisonous. Dispose of clippings safely.
Thuja, Chamaecyparis, Cupressus, Calocedrus spp.	random	no	Growth continues as long as conditions are favorable.	Thin branch back to laterally growing shoot. Do not cut below foliage.	Can be sheared or clipped.	Prune late in summer.	

Source: Adapted from Harris et al. 1981, p. 27.

Figure 13.12

Branches retain their position on the trunk but become slightly closer to the ground as they increase in diameter.
Source: After Harris et al. 1981, p. 11.

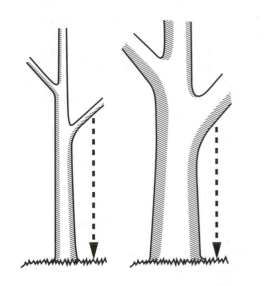

Figure 13.13

Well-spaced branches (left) are less likely to split or break than those close together (right).
Source: After Harris et al. 1981, p.12.

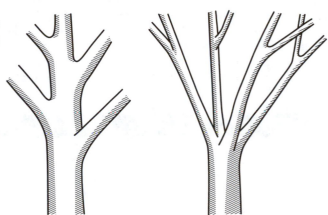

out the leader. Adequate vertical spacing between individual branches along the trunk occurs naturally in most conifers. The branches may be thinned to reduce wind resistance or to achieve aesthetic effects. For a strong, well-tapered trunk, branch whorls or laterals remain along the trunk.

Growth habit determines the severity of pruning. Conifers with a tall, straight trunk and central leaders are said to have *excurrent* growth. Almost all conifers are excurrent when young. Conifers are usually most attractive if the excurrent habit is preserved. Thus, the primary pruning removes or subdues any laterals

that challenge the leader. Other conifers, like many mature broadleaf trees, develop a wide-spreading crown after forming a short trunk and are said to have a diffuse, random branching habit. Some conifers may develop the diffuse branching habit if they have been propagated by cuttings from side branches. The diffuse branching pattern allows more latitude in pruning.

The distribution of latent buds or growing points often limits the severity of pruning conifers (table 13.3). In some conifers, all growth derives from buds formed in the previous growing season. When the preformed buds have expanded, growth ceases. These trees may have all their lateral buds in whorls just below the terminal bud (most pines), or lateral buds may be scattered along the shoot. Conifers with whorled buds should be pruned back only to active laterals or, in current season's growth, before the needles develop fully. If pruning is done early enough, new buds will develop near the cut for the following season's growth. In conifers with latent buds scattered along the younger shoots, prune back to a latent bud. These buds will become active and develop a new growing point.

Canary Island pine (*Pinus canariensis*) is a notable exception. Many latent buds survive just under the bark on large branches and even the trunk. Many of these buds grow when stimulated by heavy pruning into old wood or after a fire has killed the smaller branches.

If conditions are favorable, some conifers with preformed buds, including some pines, may have several growth flushes during a growing season. Young, expanding shoots may be pruned in any or all of these flushes. If there are no visible latent buds, pruning into old wood will usually result in a stub from which no new growth will arise.

Other conifer species have buds or dormant growing points (no bud scales formed) with shoots that continue to elongate. Such species usually have abundant latent buds that produce new growth even when severely pruned into old wood. Trees of these species usually have a spiral or random branching habit. Despite their tolerance of severe pruning, these species look most attractive when thinned. Conifers with an intermediate growth habit have a large number of latent buds randomly spaced along stems or retain active laterals or short shoots for many years on older wood. Growth continues as a series of flushes.

Pruning Spreading-Type Narrowleaf Evergreens. Plants such as junipers have a spreading growth habit. Prune junipers by cutting back enough growth to prevent leggy or uninhibited growth and to prevent needles from dropping off lower branches because of shading by upper branches. Cut back the longer branches that develop on top from a few inches to half the branch so the lower branches will be exposed to light, as illustrated in figure 13.17. Cut back some growth annually to prevent plants from getting out of bounds. Pfitzer juniper is an example of a vigorous, spreading narrowleaf evergreen that can produce 12 to 18 inches (30 to 45 cm) of growth annually. It may be necessary to cut back into the previous year's wood to maintain the desired size and shape of the plant.

Pruning Rounded-Type Narrowleaf Evergreens. Brown yew and globe arborvitae are good examples of rounded-type evergreens. They are normally globe-shaped and should not be sheared. Both can be maintained at whatever height and size desired, however. Because brown yew develops as a broad, rounded specimen, prune about one-fourth to one-half of the previous year's growth to keep it bushy and compact. Thinning individual branches, rather than shearing, yields a more attractive, natural-looking growth habit. Globe arborvitae requires little, if any, pruning because of its formal growth habit.

Pruning Hedges

Hedges should be pruned back to the point of the last cut. The tops of hedges should be slightly narrower than the bottoms to ensure that adequate light reaches lower leaves to maintain density (fig. 13.18).

Pruning Broadleaf Shrubs

Prune shrubs to keep their natural shape unless they are used as formal hedges. Shearing (heading cuts) should not be widely used; thinning of older, taller growth should be the primary type of pruning. Cut off the largest, oldest branches at or very near the ground and leave the younger, shorter stem (fig. 13.19). These may be headed back if they are very weak or very sparse. New shoots that develop can be thinned and headed as needed to reshape the plant. For extremely large, overgrown plants that need to be rejuvenated, it is best to cut out all old growth near the ground over a 2- to 3-year period so as not to destroy the plant's natural shape or flowering habit. Judicious thinning and selective heading of new shoots and young stems can then be used to shape and control growth until rejuvenation is required again. Rejuvenated plants may not

---

Figure 13.14

During the growing season, a nonbranching leader can be pinched to induce development of laterals. The two pinches induce branches to grow at the heights desired (leaves removed). *Source:* After Harris et al. 1981, p.14.

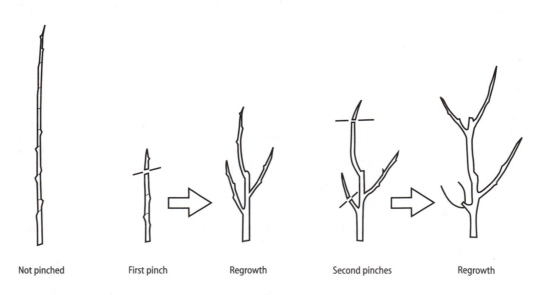

Not pinched   First pinch   Regrowth   Second pinches   Regrowth

bloom for one or more years depending on their growth rate and flowering habit.

Pruning Ground Covers

Pruning ground covers is usually necessary only to remove unhealthy tissue, awkward or straggling branches, or to keep a plant from becoming too invasive. Many ground covers are prone to decline as they age, however.

Figure 13.15

A headed tree will force many vigorous upright shoots, causing the tree to lose its natural form. *Source:* After Harris et al. 1981, p. 22.

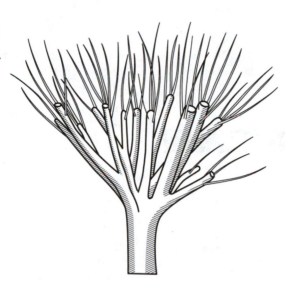

Figure 13.16

Thinning reduces height and opens up a mature tree (left), retaining the natural appearance and form of the tree (right). *Source:* After Harris et al. 1981, p. 22.

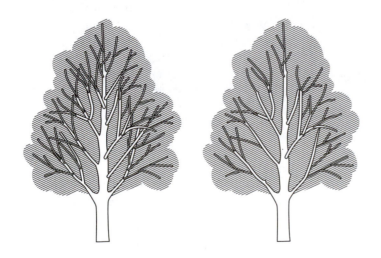

Others are so vigorous that controlling their growth is an ongoing maintenance task. Periodic mowing is one way you can keep ground covers vigorous, neat, and healthy with no significant loss of attractiveness. Mowing is a convenient way to check rampant growth, thin out excessive stem buildup and rejuvenate old, declining ground covers. Mowing also helps minimize problems with trash, vermin, fire, and sprinkler interference.

Suitable Ground Covers. Not all ground covers are suitable for mowing. Less vigorous varieties recover slowly, leaving an unsightly area prone to weed infestation for up to a year. Species with recovery times as long as 4 months still can gain in overall quality from mowing, however. Vigorous species, which usually recover within 1 or 2 months, respond well to mowing. Mowing can check their growth without harming visual appeal for an extended period. For example, in recent field studies at the University of California, mowing kept the growth of lantana in check yet had a negligible effect on overall quality. Other species, such as African daisy and coyote bush, responded similarly. Varieties with herbaceous or nonfibrous stems are also good candidates for mowing because it is easy to cut and bag their stems.

Timing of Mowing. Mowing ground covers at the correct time (table 13.4) is important to ensure quick recovery with little weed invasion or loss of aesthetic value. Mow spring-flowering species after they have finished blooming. Mowing too early reduces or delays flowering. Spring mowing is appropriate for varieties that flower in summer or fall. Avoid late-summer and fall mowing because the tender regrowth may be susceptible to early frost damage, and regrowth can be slow allowing weeds to invade the planting.

If ground covers develop heavy, succulent, or woody stems, they may become too difficult to mow. Mowing chops up the fleshy growth of succulent species, such as ice plant, making it impossible to collect and remove the cut debris. Large stems of woody species can clog or jam a mower. To achieve acceptable results, start mowing ground covers when they are young—just after establishment—and continue mowing regularly thereafter.

Mowing Techniques. Use an ordinary commercial rotary turf mower for ground covers with thin, nonfibrous stems and little thatch buildup, such as trailing lantana and garden verbena. Use a flail mower on ground covers with thick, woody stems or thatch buildup. Though flail mowers are relatively cumbersome, they may be necessary for the initial cut. A rotary mower should be adequate for subsequent mowings, if you perform them regularly.

Mow ground covers at or slightly above the branching points on stems—in most cases, 4 to 6 inches (10 to 15 cm) high. Although you usually cannot set mowers this high, a rotary turf mower tends to ride up on top of the ground cover as you mow. Thus, if you set the mower at its maximum cutting height, the cut should be acceptable. Mowing too low slows recovery, and mowing too high will not achieve the desired result. You may have to experiment to determine the best mowing height for a particular ground cover and condition.

Mow in the same pattern as an irregular turf area. Back-and-forth movement, keeping to the contours of the site, is best. Manually collect heavy clippings if the ground cover is so dense that the clippings remain on top as unsightly debris. Otherwise, let the clippings fall into the ground cover where they will decompose, or collect them in the mower bag as you would when mowing turf.

- For rapid recovery and to ensure good ground cover vigor, irrigate and fertilize with 1 to 2 pounds (0.45 to 0.9 kg) of nitrogen per 1,000 square feet (93 square meters) after mowing.

- Use a preemergence herbicide if recovery is slow and the ground cover is sparse. Check crop registrations and follow all label directions.

- Delay postbloom mowing if ground cover has a showy display of fruits.

- Consider an additional mowing to remove old, unsightly flowerheads or objectionable seeds or fruits. Set the mower height to remove seeds or fruit but not vegetative growth.

Pruning Vines

Vines usually need pruning to limit growth, to thin stems and branches, and to remove dead or damaged wood. Some vines, such as honeysuckle, grow so fast and become so thick that considerable pruning may be necessary, but other vines need little pruning. Prune most vines in the dormant season, including the summer-flowering clematis (Jackmani type). The Florida and Patens types, including *Clematis montana*, blossom on 1-year-old wood and should be pruned by thinning out in spring before growth. Prune dead, diseased, and damaged vines back to healthy wood. Interfering branches of woody vines, such as wisteria, should be cut back below the point of interference or all the way back to the junction with the main stem.

In general, prune out the top third of overgrown woody vines and prune by a third or more old, mature stems that are declining in vigor. Each year, prune stems of wisteria to promote new growth and flowers. Prune back plant tops to force out new branches. Pruning wisteria extensively during the dormant season may encourage rampant vegetative growth the

Table 13.4

MOWING TIMES FOR SELECTED GROUND COVERS

Scientific name	Common name	Mowing time
Achillea tomentosa	woolly yarrow	spring
Ajuga reptans	carpet bugle	summer
Baccharis pilularis	coyote bush	spring
Ceanothus gloriosus	Point Reyes ceanothus	summer
Ceanothus glorosus × 'Anchor Bay'	Anchor Bay ceanothus	summer
Cotoneaster dammeri	bearberry cotoneaster	spring
Drosanthemum hispidum	pink ice plant	summer
Euonymus fortunei 'Colorata'	purple-leaved winter creeper	spring
Hedera helix	English ivy	spring
Hypericum calycinum	Aaron's beard, St. Johnswort	spring
Juniperus spp.	juniper (prostrate forms)	spring
Lantana montevidensis	trailing lantana	spring/ summer
Lonicera japonica 'Halliana'	Hall's honeysuckle	spring
Mahonia repens	creeping mahonia	spring
Myoporum parvifolium	prostrate myoporum	summer
Osteospermum fruticosum	trailing African daisy	summer
Pachysandra terminalis	Japanese spurge	spring
Polygonum spp.	knotweed	spring
Potentilla tabernaemontanii	spring cinquefoil	spring
Rosa banksiae	Lady Banks' rose	spring
Rosa creeping varieties	alba meidiland, fairy	spring
Sedum spurium	stonecrop	spring
Trachelospermum jasminoides	star jasmine	summer
Vinca major	periwinkle	summer

next spring. Instead, prune out long, straggly growth in July, except branches needed for climbing. This technique is more likely to induce flowering. Shoots should be cut back to one-third to one-half of their length, which will induce production of short spurs on which next season's flower clusters will be borne.

Pruning Garden Roses

The proper time and technique for pruning roses are subjects of controversy. Certain fun-damental pruning practices pertain to all garden roses regardless of type:

- Remove any canes that have been broken or damaged by insects or disease.

- Remove one of two rubbing canes.

- Remove spindly canes or those smaller in diameter than the size of a lead pencil.

- Make clean cuts just above a bud or shoot that points toward the outside of the plant (see fig. 13.8).

When bare-root roses are planted, the tops should be cut back to 12 to 15 inches (30 to 37.5 cm). Remove any damaged or broken roots. For potted roses, these two pruning practices have probably already been performed before purchase. After pruning hybrid teas, floribundas, and grandiforas according to these general recommendations, cut them to a height of 18 to 24 inches (45 to 60 cm) or to a height in balance with other plants in the rose bed. Climbing roses are generally pruned according to the basic principles described above. In addition, cut out very old, heavy canes growing in the center of the plant that are not producing many leaves or flowers by pruning them completely to the ground. The newer canes will produce more growth and flowers. When the canes become quite long, prune them back to keep them in the desired area.

Timing for Pruning Trees

The time to prune depends on the kind of plant and the desired results. The following types of pruning can be done anytime: light pruning; pruning to remove unwanted growth when it is small; and removal of damaged, weak, or diseased branches. Rapid growth can be maintained by pruning before the period of most rapid growth, usually in the spring. Prune deciduous trees during the dormant period and evergreen trees just before growth resumes in the spring.

Conversely, to retard plant growth, prune when growth is nearly complete for that season. For many plants, this time for maximum dwarfing is late spring to middle summer. Directing the growth of young trees is done best during the growing season.

Generally, spring-flowering plants should be pruned as soon as the flowers fade and new growth begins. Their flower buds form on growth produced during the previous year, so

Figure 13.17

Spreading-type narrowleaf evergreens. Prune spreaders by cutting back longer upper branches as shown. Long branches should be cut back from a few inches to half the branch, as shown, to prevent shading of lower branches. *Source:* After Caldwell et al. 1972, p. 11.

Figure 13.18

Prune hedge so that the base is broader than the top. Regular pruning is needed. *Source:* After Caldwell et al. 1972, p. 13.

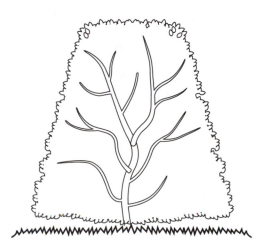

pruning these plants in the winter or just before they flower removes many of the flowers. Summer- and fall-flowering plants should be pruned in the winter or dormant season, because their flowers form on growth produced in the same growing season.

Fertilizing Woody Plants

Most mature woody trees and shrubs established in the landscape and growing in a healthy manner need little or no fertilization. In fact, fertilizing healthy trees can be detrimental by encouraging excessively vigorous growth that unnecessarily increases plant size and foliage density, produces succulent weak growth, and predisposes the plant to diseases, pests, and environmental stresses. In addition, excessive fertilizer is a significant contributor to groundwater contamination of aquifers. Do not fertilize plants unless they need it.

In most cases, trees and shrubs growing poorly in the landscape do not need extra fertilizer since the causes of their poor growth are usually not nutritionally related. Fertilizers may be helpful but only after the problem(s)

causing poor growth are corrected. Poorly growing plants may exhibit one or more of the following symptoms:

- light green or yellow leaves
- leaves with dead spots
- smaller leaves than normal
- fewer leaves or flowers than normal
- stunted twig growth or dieback
- wilting

Any number of problems may be responsible for these symptoms, including compaction, poor soil drainage or aeration, improper soil pH, diseases and pests, and adverse climatic conditions. Fertilizing will not remedy these problems.

In general, woody plants should not be fertilized at the time of planting, because fertilizer that is mixed with backfill or otherwise applied at this time may inadvertently injure roots. It is good insurance, however, to fertilize plants soon after planting. Fertilizing young, newly planted trees and other woody plants may promote more rapid growth so that the plants attain their optimal size more quickly. Fertilizing mature woody plants, vines, and ground covers is not routinely necessary unless plant vigor is low because of inadequate essential nutrients. As long as plants have good leaf color, leaf size, shoot growth, and canopy density, there is no need to fertilize them. In nearly all cases, however, if fertilizer is needed, only nitrogen is necessary, because other nutrients usually occur in adequate amounts in most soils. A notable exception are palm trees, which need potassium in nearly the same amounts as nitrogen. Potassium deficiencies often occur in palms growing on sandy, well-drained soils and those subject to frequent, heavy irrigation, such as occurs in turfgrass areas (see the discussion under "Fertilizing Palms," below).

The use of complete fertilizers (those containing nitrogen, phosphorus, and potassium) is usually not recommended for woody plants because soils are rarely deficient in all three elements. Even if such conditions did exist, it would be difficult to amend the soil satisfactorily with a complete fertilizer. For example, in a potassium-deficient soil, using a complete fertilizer to apply enough potassium would apply too much nitrogen.

Application to the soil surface is the easiest, quickest, and most effective method of apply-

Figure 13.19

Prune broadleaf shrubs to keep their natural shape by using mostly thinning cuts. Avoid making heading cuts or shearing the whole plant.

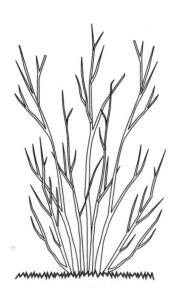
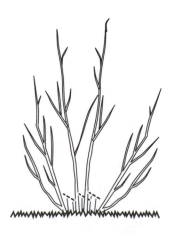

Table 13.5

NITROGEN FERTILIZATION RECOMMENDATIONS FOR NEWLY PLANTED TREES, SHRUBS, VINES, AND GROUND COVERS

Plant material	Nitrogen rate per application		Application frequency and timing
	lb/sq ft	kg/sq m	
newly planted tree, shrub, vine	0.2 lb N in 3 ft × 3 ft area around base of plant	0.09 kg N in 0.9 m × 0.9 m area around base of plant	Immediately after planting, 6–8 weeks after planting, and the following spring
newly planted ground cover	1–2 lb N per 1,000 sq ft	0.45–0.9 kg N per 93 sq m	Immediately after planting and again 6–8 weeks after planting

ing nitrogen to woody plants. Slow-release forms (organic or synthetic) are usually more expensive than other nitrogen sources, but their use may be justified when application is difficult or must be frequent, because they can be applied less frequently at higher rates. A less concentrated but more continuous supply of nitrogen is available with slow-release forms that have less likelihood of loss by leaching.

Newly planted, young (less than 2 years old) woody plants and ground covers in the landscape may be fertilized according to the recommendations in table 13.5. When established plantings of trees, shrubs, vines, or ground covers need fertilizer, evenly broadcast about 1 to 3 pounds (0.45 to 1.4 kg) of actual nitrogen per 1,000 square feet (93 sq m) of planted area (shrubs, ground covers, vines) or per 6 inches (15 cm) of trunk diameter (trees) when plants need it most, usually just before the period of most rapid growth in the spring. Double this rate for trees growing in turf areas, but split the total amount applied into two applications about 6 weeks apart. In either case, a second application about 2 months into the growing season may be beneficial. Wash any fertilizer off foliage and keep it away from the trunk or stems of plants. On slopes where fertilizers may be subject to erosion or rolling away, it is best to dibble the recommended amount of nitrogen into 10- to 12-inch (25- to 30-cm) deep holes 2 to 3 feet (60 to 90 cm) apart. Follow any fertilizer application with one or two thorough irrigations to move the nutrients into the root zone.

Micronutrients are usually present in the soil in sufficient quantities for adequate plant growth. High pH (above 7.0) and any situations that decrease root activity, such as low soil temperatures and damage from disease or poor aeration, may render these nutrients unavailable to plants, and deficiency symptoms may occur. For example, acid-loving (low-pH) plants such as gardenias and azaleas are susceptible to iron deficiency on heavy clay or alkaline soils, especially during cool winter months when soil temperatures are lower. Most plants will grow out of these symptoms with the advent of warmer weather and increased root activity.

Fertilizing Palms

Palms require large amounts of nitrogen, potassium, and magnesium and appear especially sensitive to certain micronutrient deficiencies. Macronutrient deficiencies usually occur as a result of insufficient nutrients in the soil. Nitrogen deficiency appears as a general yellowing of all leaves. Potassium and magnesium deficiency appear on the older leaves. Potassium deficiency shows as translucent orange or yellow flecking or speckling, and magnesium deficiency appears as a distinct orange-colored band around the outside of a leaf. Micronutrient deficiencies are on the newest leaves and are usually the result of environmental factors such as damaged roots or improper soil pH that affect the palm's ability to extract the nutrient from the soil. Iron deficiency shows as chlorosis, and manganese deficiency appears as chlorosis, stunting, and even frizzling. Deficiencies are more easily prevented than corrected by proper fertilization, good soil aeration, proper planting depth, root disease prevention, and proper soil pH. Palms respond best to a fertilizer with the N-P-K ratio of 3-1-3 or 3-1-2, all in slow-release form, and with magnesium and micronutrients.

Designing and Maintaining the Landscape for Fire Protection

As catastrophic events throughout California in recent years have graphically illustrated, the problem of brushfires and wildfires in the chaparral-covered hills surrounding urban areas is a serious concern. There is no such thing as a plant that will not burn; all plants will burn given enough heat and other conditions that favor combustion. Yet proper selection, planting, and maintenance of appropriate landscape materials around homes in fire-prone areas can significantly reduce the danger to life and property posed by brush fires.

Keys To Creating a Fire-Wise Landscape

There are several ways to reduce the hazard of brush fires.

- Plant turfgrass and low-growing, fire-resistant plants near buildings. Plant lawns, succulent ground covers, or other low-growing plants around structures, and water them regularly. Many California natives, especially chaparral plants, become highly flammable under drought conditions or in late summer and fall. If used in the landscape, native material should be well-spaced so that it will be less likely to carry fire. Dense plant material or chaparral, especially in a canyon below a house that has a chimney, is especially dangerous. Replace or modify these landscapes, using a low or discontinuous ground cover that produces less fuel.

- Irrigate landscape plantings adequately. Increase the effectiveness of fire-resistant plantings with an adequate sprinkler system. The ability to give one or two well-timed summer or fall irrigations to the landscape surrounding a home, even a drought-tolerant landscape, may determine whether the structure will be saved or not in a fire. Water-stressed plants burn readily. Large fires have shown that plants in well-watered and well-maintained landscapes do not burn at all or not as readily as dry plantings. Well-watered trees that are not too close to a house can form a barrier that prevents flying, burning material from reaching the house. Irrigated ground covers, such as ivy or iceplant, usually do not carry fire.

- Reduce or remove potential fuel to create defensible space around buildings. Keep the landscape clear of fuel by removing leaf litter, twigs, and fallen branches from under trees and shrubs and pruning deadwood. Remove dead and dried plant material, debris, and thatch buildup of ground covers and succulents. Thin or remove crowded woody plants to create space between trees and shrubs and to help prevent fire spread. Do not allow a continuous tree or brush canopy to develop close to buildings. State and local laws require brush clearance within a minimum distance (usually 30 feet [9 m]) of all structures. Ask your local fire department for regulations about the distance between structures and brush and grass. Recognize that buildings located on slopes require much more defensible space—often 100 to 400 feet (30 to 120 m) to ensure wildfire safety.

Bibliography

Brenzel, K. N., ed. 2001. Sunset western garden book. Menlo Park: Sunset Publishing.

Caldwell, J. L., E. M. Smith, and K. W. Reisch. 1972. Pruning landscape plants. Columbus: Ohio State University Cooperative Extension Bulletin 543.

Farnham, D. S. 1994. A property owner's guide to reducing the wildfire threat. Jackson, CA.: UC Cooperative Extension Amador County Leaflet.

Flint, M. F., and J. F. Karlik. 2000. Healthy roses: Environmentally friendly ways to manage pests and disorders in your garden and landscape. Oakland: University of California Division of Agriculture and Natural Resources Publication 21589.

Harris, R. W., J. R. Clark, and N. P. Matheny. 1999. Arboriculture: Integrated management of landscape trees, shrubs, and vines. 3rd ed. Upper Saddle River, NJ: Prentice Hall.

Harris, R. W., and W. B. Davis. 1984. Planting landscape trees. Oakland: University of California Division of Agriculture and Natural Resources Leaflet 2583.

Harris, R. W., A. T. Leiser, and W. B. Davis. 1978. Staking landscape trees. Oakland: University of California Division of Agriculture and Natural Resources Leaflet 2576.

Harris, R. W., J. L. Paul, and A. T. Leiser. 1979. Fertilizing woody plants. Oakland: University of California Division of Agriculture and Natural Resources Leaflet 2958.

Harris, R. W., W. D. Hamilton, W. B. Davis, and A. T. Leiser. 1981. Pruning landscape trees. Oakland: University of California Division of Agriculture and Natural Resources Leaflet 2574.

Hodel, D. R., and D. R. Pittenger. 1995. For healthy and attractive ground covers: Mow. Grounds Maintenance 30(5).

International Society of Arboriculture. 1995. Tree-pruning guidelines. Savoy, IL: International Society of Arboriculture.

Maire, R. G. 1979. Landscape for fire protection. Oakland: University of California Division of Agriculture and Natural Resources Leaflet 2401.

McCain, A. H., R. D. Raabe, and S. Wilhelm. 1981. Plants resistant or susceptible to Verticillium wilt. Oakland: University of California Division of Agriculture and Natural Resources Leaflet 2703.

Raabe, R. D. 1979. Resistance or susceptibility of certain plants to Armillaria root rot. Oakland: University of California Division of Agriculture and Natural Resources Leaflet 2591.

U. S. Department of Agriculture, Plant Genetics and Germplasm Institute, Agricultural Research Service. 1975. Pruning ornamental shrubs and vines. Washington: U.S. Government Printing Office.

14

Home Vegetable Gardening

Nancy Garrison and Dennis R. Pittenger

LEARNING OBJECTIVES

- Understand basic principles of successful home vegetable gardening.

- Learn how to plan and plant a vegetable garden.

- Know how to care for vegetable crops in the home garden.

- Know the basics of culinary herb cultivation in the home garden.

- Learn the basics of harvesting and storing home-grown vegetables and herbs.

- Become acquainted with the nutritional value of vegetables in the diet.

- Learn the basics of problem diagnosis for home-grown vegetables.

Home Vegetable Gardening

Vegetables can be grown in containers, home yards, community garden lots, or large ranch areas. To grow vegetables successfully, observe the following basic rules.

- Plant only as large a garden as you can maintain easily. Beginning gardeners often overplant and fail because their skills and time commitment are not great enough to accomplish the task. Gardening requires weed and pest control and irrigation when needed.

- Plan your garden on paper before you begin.

- Grow crops that produce the maximum amount of food in the space available.

- Plant during the correct season for the crop you plan to grow. Choose varieties recommended for your area.

- Select a site that receives at least 8 hours of full sun each day. It should be relatively level, well-drained, and close to a water source. Avoid shaded locations.

- Prepare the soil properly and amend and fertilize as needed.

- Harvest vegetables at their proper stage of maturity. Store them promptly if they are not to be used immediately.

Vegetable Classification

Most vegetables are classified as cool-season or warm-season crops.

Cool-Season Vegetable Crops

Cool-season vegetables grow best and produce the best-quality crops when average temperatures are 55° to 75°F (13° to 24°C), and they usually tolerate slight frost when mature. The food value of cool-season vegetables is usually higher per pound and per square foot than that of warm-season vegetables, because the edible parts of the plant are the vegetative parts—such as roots, stems, leaves, or immature flower parts—rather than the fruits. Examples include:

- **root:** beet, carrot, parsnip, radish, turnip
- **stem:** asparagus, white potato
- **leaf:** cabbage, celery (fleshy petioles), lettuce, onion, spinach
- **immature flower parts:** broccoli, cauliflower, globe artichoke

Warm-Season Vegetable Crops

Warm-season vegetables require long, hot days and warm soil to mature. They grow best and produce the best-quality crops when average temperatures are 65° to 95°F (18° to 35°C), and they are intolerant of prolonged freezing temperatures. The food value of warm-season vegetables is usually lower per pound and per square foot than that of cool-season crops because the fruit of the plant is eaten. Many warm-season vegetables are actually immature or mature fruits. In other words, vegetables such as tomatoes and squashes are fruits in the botanical sense, just as oranges are fruits. Examples include:

- **mature fruit:** cantaloupe, winter squash, tomato, watermelon
- **immature fruit:** sweet corn, snap and lima beans, summer squash

Planning Your Vegetable Garden

Location

When deciding where to plant your vegetable garden, choose the best available location by keeping the following factors in mind.

Good Soil. Although you may have little choice concerning the soil type available to you, you can use a simple test to find out whether your soil is in good condition for planting. Squeeze a handful of soil to test for moisture content. If the squeezed soil forms a clump, the soil is too wet to work. If you work soil that contains this much moisture, it might form into hard, cementlike clumps that can cause problems for the remainder of the year. If the soil crumbles easily when it is squeezed, it is in an ideal condition to work. Tilling or working the soil and incorporating organic soil amendments can improve poor soil and can increase yield, even in good soil.

Level Ground. Level ground is easier to prepare, plant, and irrigate than sloping ground. If you must plant on sloping ground, run rows across the slope, not up and down, to keep the soil from washing away during irrigation.

Water Supply. Locate your garden near an abundant supply of water easily reached with a garden hose.

Adequate Light. Vegetables need at least 8 hours of sunlight each day for best growth. Plant vegetables where they are not shaded by trees, shrubs, walls, or fences. Trees and shrubs also compete with vegetables for the water available in the soil.

Close to Home. Plant your garden near your home, if possible. You are more likely to spend time working in your garden if you can reach it easily. A nearby garden also means that you do not have to carry tools back and forth over a long distance. If your garden is large enough for you to use power tools, be sure you have easy access to a road or driveway wide enough for equipment movement.

Efficient Use of Space

The key to any successful garden is planning. Gardeners cannot waste time and space if they expect to produce large amounts of vegetables from a limited area. Gardeners should pay close attention to timing of planting and harvesting, selection of varieties, trellising, and other space-saving practices.

Timing. Timing refers to the maximum use of the available growing season. Depending on the location in California, there are three to four seasons when vegetables can be grown. Yet many gardeners grow only summer crops. By planting a spring crop, a summer crop, and a fall crop, a gardener can get three crops from the same space. This requires close rotation of crops, such as spring lettuce followed by summer green beans followed by fall spinach. The idea is to plant a cool-season crop, follow it with a warm-season crop, and then finish with another cool-season crop. Careful attention to days to maturity for each crop grown will establish the ideal rotation period (see table 14.1).

Trellising and Staking. Do not grow horizontally what you can grow vertically. Twining and vining crops, such as tomato, squash, cucumber, and pole beans, use a great deal of space when allowed to grow along the ground. Trellises, stakes, or other supports minimize the ground space used and increase garden productivity. Support materials can be wooden structures, extra stakes, twine, wire cages, or a nearby wire fence.

Spacing. Improved varieties may be the best way for the space-conscious gardener to achieve higher yields. Today, a gardener can select bush varieties of beans, cucumbers, melons, and squash that require much less space than standard varieties. *Determinant* tomatoes (which grow only to a certain height) can be trained more easily to a stake. Several bush-type tomato varieties are suited to container culture on patios or other small spaces. The cultivation guide for each vegetable in this chapter notes space-saving varieties.

Succession planting is sowing seed of a given crop at 1- to 2-week intervals to produce a continuous supply of vegetables. Beans, turnips, and beets are well suited to this practice.

Companion planting is planting two crops in the same place at the same time. Normally one crop matures and is harvested before the other. Radishes and carrots work well this way, because the radishes can be harvested long before the carrots are very large. The quick-growing radish seedlings also help to mark planted rows.

Intercropping involves planting early-maturing crops between the rows of late-maturing crops to increase production in a small area. For example, beans, radishes, green onions, spinach, or leaf lettuce may be planted between rows of tomatoes, peppers, cabbage, or corn. The quicker-maturing crops will be harvested before the others become very large.

Proper spacing between rows and within rows is extremely important (see table 14.2 for standard spacing for each crop). However, different spacings may be required in your garden. The use of power equipment requires that the distance between rows exceed the width of the equipment. Maximum production requires wider than standard rows or beds for planting. For instance, seeds of many crops, such as leaf lettuce or beets, can be broadcast in a bed 1 to 3 feet (30 to 90 cm) across and thinned to obtain proper spacing. Other crops, such as cabbage or broccoli, can be planted closely in wide rows so that their outer leaves will touch one another when the plants are about three-fourths mature. These methods

Figure 14.1

Sample garden plan with planting dates and bed widths.

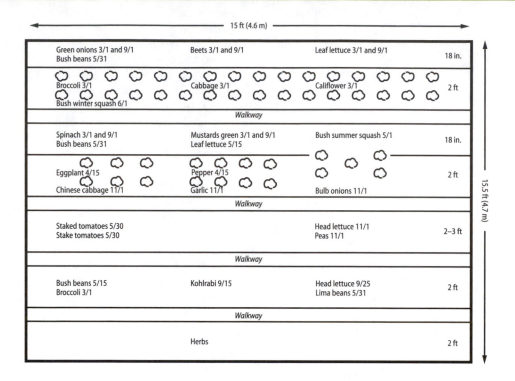

reduce space wasted as aisles and often provide such dense shade that weed growth is inhibited and evaporation of soil moisture is reduced.

Raised beds are often helpful in maximizing plant growing space in a garden. They provide the advantages noted above for wide beds, and they can be used to optimize soil otherwise poorly suited for vegetables. To raise beds, add large amounts of topsoil or organic soil amendments so that the bed is established above the previous soil level. Raised beds lend themselves well to the use of plastic mulch and improved drainage, if needed.

What To Plant

Plant enough of each vegetable crop to meet your family's needs for fresh, stored, and pre-served supplies (see table 14.2 for amounts to plant for a family of four). When choosing vegetable varieties, consider such factors as disease resistance, maturity date, compactness of plant, and the size, shape, and color of the vegetable desired. Keep in mind past experiences with a given variety and compare new varieties with your favorites. Information in this chapter and in seed catalogs may be helpful, or contact your local UC Cooperative Extension office for help in selecting varieties suited to your area.

Preparing a Garden Plan

Plan your garden on paper before planting. A well-planned garden can provide fresh or preserved vegetables for use year-round. The plan should contain crops and amounts to be planted, dates of planting and estimated harvest, planting location for each crop, specific spacing between rows, and trellising or support required (see fig. 14.1 and table 14.2 for planting dates in your area of the state). The plan will aid in buying supplies and serve as a handy guide in timing plantings during the season.

First, make a sketch of the garden area showing the dimensions of the garden. Prepare a list of vegetables you want to grow. Then arrange the crops in the garden according to the amounts you wish to grow, dates to be planted, and space available. Plant perennial crops such as rhubarb and asparagus to one side of the garden so they are not disturbed by preparations for future crops. Plant tall crops, such as corn and pole beans, on the north side of the garden so they will not shade low-growing crops.

Tools

Only a few good-quality tools are necessary for a small home garden.

- *Spade or spading fork.* Use to turn the ground, to turn under organic matter, and to break up large clumps of soil.

- *Rake.* Use to smooth out the soil after spading and after preparing the seedbed. It is also useful for clearing up rubbish and removing small weeds.

- *Hoe.* Use to remove tough weeds and to cover seeds after planting. Turned sideways, a hoe can be used to dig a V-shaped row for planting.

- *Yardstick, twine, and stakes.* Use to space rows evenly and lay out rows in straight lines.

- *Putty knife or spatula.* Handy for blocking out seedlings when transplanting and for cleaning tools.

- *Small hand sprayer and duster.* Use to keep insects and diseases under control.

- *Trowel.* One of the handiest garden gadgets, a trowel is useful for transplanting and for loosening soil around plants.

- *Dibble.* This short, round, pointed stick is used to make holes for transplanting seedlings and to firm the soil around the plant roots.

Care of Tools

Following these simple guidelines will keep your tools in good condition.

- Clean tools after each use. A putty knife is good for scraping off dirt. If tools get rusty, soak them in oil for a few hours, then use a wire brush or fine sand to scrub off the rust.

- Keep cutting tools sharp.

- Store tools where you can hang them up out of the way to prevent damage both to you and to them. Keep tools in a dry place to prevent rust.

Preparing for Planting

Seeds and Plants

You can grow many vegetables from seed, but you can also buy young plants from a nursery. Nursery plants are grown from seed under sheltered conditions and are started earlier than you could safely plant the seed outdoors. If you direct-seed vegetables, you must wait for the ground to warm up enough to germinate the seed. Vegetables produced by young plants are ready to harvest earlier than those grown from seed. The vegetables most commonly bought as young plants for transplanting are tomatoes, peppers, lettuce, broccoli, celery, cabbage, cauliflower, and eggplant. You can grow these vegetables ahead of the season indoors or in a hotbed or coldframe. For directions for making a hotbed or coldframe and information about seeding and transplanting, see "Growing Vegetable Plants for Early Production," below.

Buy seeds or plants from a reliable dealer or nursery. If a neighbor has been successful in growing garden vegetables, ask for advice on where and what to buy. Buy fresh seeds. Some seeds, such as onion, parsley, and parsnip, lose viability after about a year. Seeds of other vegetables are good for 3 years or more. Companies date their seed packets and may give germination percentages. If the seed is known to keep for several seasons, it may be more economical to buy it in larger amounts. Write the date of purchase on the seed packets and store any leftover seed in a cool, dry place. Do not use any seed for more than 2 or 3 years.

How To Store Seeds*

Seeds have their best germination potential at the moment they reach maturity on the plant. From that moment they decline in vigor until they can no longer germinate. However, they may continue to germinate well for years if they have been properly harvested and stored. Two factors shorten seed life: high seed moisture and high temperature. Note their importance: Each 1 percent decrease in seed moisture doubles the life of the seed.

Each 10°F (5°C) drop in storage temperature doubles the life of the seed.

A good illustration: Onion seed of 14-percent moisture content stored at 90°F (32°C) died in one week. However, some of that same seed was dried to 6-percent moisture and stored in a sealed container so it could not regain moisture. After 20 years, this seed germinated as well as did seed sown immediately after harvest. To get the maximum amount of storage life, you must first dry seed

---

*The author of this section is J. F. Harrington, Seed Physiologist, Department of Vegetable Crops, University of California, Davis.

to a safe level, then put it in a container that will keep it dry and store it in a cool place.

How should seed be dried? If the seed matures in summer or early fall, it is easy to dry it outdoors in most places in California because relative humidity is so low at that time. However, the seed should not be dried in direct sunlight. Spread the seed thinly on a screen or other flat surface off the ground and in shade and let dry for a week. Collect the seed in the late afternoon, place in a moisture-proof container, and store in as cool a place as possible. In late fall or during periods of humid weather, the seed may be similarly dried indoors where the temperature is above 70°F (21°C), and preferably in the 80s (27° to 32°C). A good place is in front of the heat outlet of your refrigerator.

An excellent moisture-proof container is a mason jar with a new lid. Heavy ziplock-type plastic bags are also good. A reasonably good seal can also be made by twisting the top of the bag and then tightly knotting it with a loop knot. Rigid plastic jars and cans and metal cans with tight-fitting gasketed lids are also good containers. Cloth and paper bags (even if plastic-coated) and thin plastic bags are not moisture-proof and should not be used for storage. Such bags can be used for keeping various lots of seed separate when placed in a moisture-proof container.

You may want to remove seed from your container from time to time. Let your container and seed warm up to room temperature in a dry room. Open it for only a minute or two to remove what you want and then tightly reseal it. This can be done numerous times without the remaining seed being harmed by gaining any appreciable moisture.

Storage temperature is not as important as thoroughly drying and sealing seed to keep it dry, but it is important. The seed should be stored at room temperature or cooler, below 75°F (24°C). Storage in a cool cellar is better than storage at room temperature. Still better is storage in a refrigerator (about 45°F [7°C]). For very long storage, a deep freeze is fine. The seed will not be harmed if it is properly dried before freezing. When removing seed from the freezer, handle it carefully and let it come to room temperature before using it because frozen seed is very fragile.

Insects may be a seed-storage problem, but at refrigerator or freezer temperature they are not active and therefore do no harm. If a nut-sized piece of dry ice is put in the jar or can before sealing and allowed to sublime, the air will mostly be replaced with carbon dioxide, which kills the insects without harming the dry seed. Seal the container to keep the carbon dioxide in.

Some seeds are obtained from wet fruits, such as tomatoes and muskmelons. Scoop out the seed or squeeze them into a glass container and let them ferment at room temperature for a day or two. Then wash the juice off through a sieve or screen and dry as described for dry harvest seeds. Do not exceed a 95°F (35°C) drying temperature.

Growing Vegetable Plants for Early Production

To get a head start on a vegetable garden, start seed in a hotbed or coldframe in order to transplant young plants early in the season. Use any extra space to produce early crops of small vegetables, such as radishes, spinach, and lettuce.

Making a Hotbed or Coldframe. One 3- by 6-foot (90- by 180-cm) hotbed or cold-frame sash is enough for the average home garden. Place the sash where there is:

- protection from strong, prevailing winds

- good natural drainage

- abundant sunlight

- available water supply

Make the sash frame out of wood, preferably redwood because it withstands weather well. The north end of the frame should be 16 inches (40 cm) deep and the opposite end 12 inches (30 cm) deep. This design allows water to drain off easily and the sun to heat the soil effectively. Place 4 to 6 inches (10 to 15 cm) of good soil in a pit the size of the sash. Add enough good soil so the surface is even with the soil surface at the bottom of the boards.

There are several methods of furnishing supplementary heat to a hotbed: Manure, hot air, hot water, steam, and electric heating cable all work well. Sometimes light bulbs are used as a source of heat in a small hotbed; they are not effective in heating the soil.

Lead-sheathed electric heating cable is inexpensive and is usually best for heating a garden hotbed. A 3- by 6-foot (90- by 180-cm) hotbed heated by electric cable commonly uses 1 kilowatt-hour of electricity per day. Use cable of the right length and correct type to deliver 150 to 200 watts to the hotbed. To provide this amount of heat to a 3- by 6-foot (90- by 180-cm) hotbed, use 60 feet (18 m) of number 19, lead-sheathed heating cable. Use a thermostat to control the temperature, because this type of cable can supply about 400 watts at 110 volts of AC current. Lay the cable about 3 to 4 inches (7.5 to 10 cm) below the soil surface. Accurately follow the manufacturer's recommendations for installing the cable. Be careful not to damage the cable when spading the soil in the hotbed (see fig. 14.2).

Of the several materials that can be used to cover a hotbed or coldframe, window glass is the best and the most expensive. More light passes through glass, which keeps the bed warmer than do other materials. Polyethylene plastic also serves as a good sash cover. It is cheaper than glass but must be replaced every year. On cold nights, however, place an additional cover, such as a blanket, canvas, or mats, over the glass or plastic to retain more heat in the bed. Be sure to remove the extra cover during the day.

Plant seeds in the hotbed in rows about 4 inches (10 cm) apart. Cover seeds with about ½ inch (1.2 cm) of soil. Seeds germinate best at temperatures of 65° to 75°F (18° to 24°C). You can lower the temperature through ventilation or raise it by using a transparent cover (plastic or glass). Seeds may also be planted in containers filled with soil mix that are placed in the hotbed. When the seedlings emerge, thin them so they are 2 inches (5 cm) apart in the row. Use a pencil or small dibble to thin and to make planting holes. Make sure the seedlings receive plenty of sun and good ventilation. Do not allow the temperature in the hotbed to become too warm; high temperatures cause plants to become weak, leggy, and subject to disease. On warm sunny days, provide ventilation by propping up the cover at one end of the bed or on the side away from the wind. When transplanting young plants to the garden, take up some soil with each plant as you remove it from the flat. Use a trowel for making planting holes. Lightly firm the soil around each plant and then water gently.

Hot Caps or Row Covers. Another method of promoting early plant growth and production is to cover seeds or young plants in the field with paper hot caps or polyethylene row covers. Either of these coverings keeps daytime air temperature higher but has little effect on soil or nighttime temperatures. If you use hot caps or row covers, you must harden the plants before completely removing the covering. When the plants start to fill the air space inside the covering, gradually harden the plants by opening the hot caps or row covers slightly on the north side. Gradually increase the amount of plant exposure over a week or two. You may take off the hot caps or open the row covers temporarily for thinning and weeding the seedlings.

Starting Vegetable Plants Indoors

Growing your own transplants indoors can extend your gardening season by several weeks, reduce your gardening costs, and allow you to grow transplants of some of the hard-to-find varieties of crops. In general, seeds should be sown from 6 to 8 weeks before the date that you wish to set the plants in the garden. Successful plant starting requires suitable soil mix; suitable containers; proper moisture, temperature, and aeration; adequate light; and conditioning plants to the outdoors. For details on starting plants from seed, see chapter 5, "Plant Propagation."

Figure 14.2

Diagram of an electric hotbed showing the placement of the heating cable, thermostat, and heat-sensitive bulb, which is used to measure soil temperature. Be sure to cover the heating cable with 3 to 4 inches (7.5 to 10 cm) of soil.

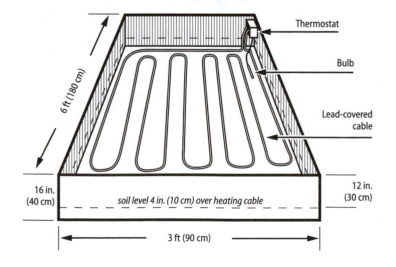

6 ft (180 cm)

Thermostat

Bulb

Lead-covered cable

16 in. (40 cm)

soil level 4 in. (10 cm) over heating cable

12 in. (30 cm)

3 ft (90 cm)

Soil Improvement and Preparation

The soil provides plants with air, water, and nutrients. Garden soils are of three general types.

- *Loam and sandy loam soils* are of medium texture, easy to irrigate, and usually drain well. These soils are easy to work.

- *Clay soil* is fine-textured and usually more fertile and productive than other soils. However, clay soil compacts easily, so it drains slowly. It must not be worked when very wet, and it crusts when dried out. If wet, it takes longer to warm up in the spring.

- *Sandy soil* is coarse-textured and has good drainage, but it retains very little water or nutrients. It is easy to work and irrigate.

Soil in good physical condition (good tilth) can hold and provide adequate quantities of nutrients, water, and air to plant roots. It will also drain well when large quantities of water are applied, and it will be easy to work without becoming sticky when wet and crusted when dry. If your garden soil has poor tilth, it can be improved by adding organic matter, such as compost, manure, sawdust, leaves, lawn clippings, or peat moss. Be careful to avoid excessive amounts of organic matter: for example, large quantities of manure can cause excessive salt buildup. Never use lawn clippings recently treated with pesticides. Additional nitrogen fertilizer may be needed when organic matter is used. Cover crops or green manures, such as rye, oats, wheat, etc., can also improve the condition of soil when they are tilled under in fall or spring. To produce these crop in time for fall or spring tilling, sow seeds in early fall. Additional information on amending garden soil can be found in chapter 3.

The first step in soil preparation is spading, rototilling, or plowing the garden. Do not till the soil if it is too wet, especially if it is clay. In some areas, it is possible to give the garden an early spading before winter rains or frosts occur. If it is not possible to work the soil before winter rains, prepare it as soon as it is dry enough to work easily without resulting in compaction. Work the soil to a depth of at least 6 inches (15 cm). Immediately after spading, break up large clods with a spading fork or rake to ensure that the soil is pulverized into pea-sized granules. Soil can be formed into beds if desired.

Fertilizers

Vegetables grown in most California soils often require some fertilizer for best growth. In general, the plants will need nitrogen; however, some soils are low in available phosphorus, and a few are deficient in potassium. You can use either organic forms (manures, composts) or inorganic forms (chemicals) to supply needed nutrients. Often, a combination of the two forms gives better results with vegetables than either used alone, particularly if phosphorus and potassium are required in addition to nitrogen. Tables 3.7 and 3.8 in chapter 3, "Soil and Fertilizer Management," provide analysis of several organic and inorganic fertilizers.

If you use manure, apply it several weeks or even months before planting and work it well into the soil. This usually allows adequate time for the manure to decompose and some of the manure salts to leach from the surface soil before seeding or transplanting. Adding 1 pound (0.45 kg) of dry steer or dairy manure per square foot of soil surface is usually sufficient. If you use poultry manure, which is more concentrated, apply it more sparingly (1 pound to 4 or 5 square feet [0.45 to 1.2 or 1.5 sq m]). If you use manure that contains litter (straw, shavings, sawdust, or similar materials), also apply nitrogen fertilizer to avoid tying up nitrogen already present in the soil as well as that being added as manure.

Commercial fertilizers are available in a wide variety of compounds and concentrations. If you use manure or other organic materials, the usual commercial fertilizer need is for nitrogen alone. Nitrogen fertilizers suitable for home garden use include alfalfa meal, cottonseed meal, ammonium nitrate, ammonium sulfate, calcium nitrate, and urea. Limit application of these materials to 0.5 to 1 pound (0.23 to 0.45 kg) per 100 square feet (30 sq m) whenever they are used.

If you do not apply manure or other organic matter, it is usually wise to apply fertilizer that contains both nitrogen and phosphorus before planting. Ammonium phosphate (16-20-0 or 11-48-0) is one such material. Other commonly used inorganic fertilizers, which contain potassium also, include 5-10-5, 5-10-10, 8-16-16, and 12-12-12. Apply 1 to 2 pounds (0.45 to 0.90 kg) per 100 square feet (30 sq m) whenever these materials are used. Chapter 3 includes some sample calculations for applying fertilizer.

You can apply fertilizer either by broadcasting it before preparing the seedbeds or in bands at seeding time. If you broadcast the fertilizer, work it into the soil fairly soon to prevent nitrogen losses through ammonia volatilization. Sometimes banding is a more efficient way to use fertilizer. To band a fertilizer, first determine where you are going to plant the seeds or plants. Then mark the row with a small furrow or a string tied from one end of the row to the other. Dig a shallow trench 2 to 4 inches (5 to 10 cm) to one side of the row and 2 to 4 inches (5 to 10 cm) below where the seed is to be placed. Place the fertilizer in the bottom of the trench and cover it with soil. To use furrow irrigation, place the fertilizer band between the seed or plant row and the irrigation furrow. To irrigate by sprinkler, band fertilizer on either side of the row. Use 1 to 2 pounds (0.45 to 0.90 kg) of fertilizer per 100 feet (30 m) of row.

After plants or transplants are well established and 3 to 4 inches (4 to 10 cm) high, it may be desirable to sidedress with nitrogen, particularly in sandy soils and where you have not applied any manure. Two or three sidedress applications will benefit crops grown for their leaves or other vegetative parts. Sidedress nitrogen at rates and in a manner similar to those described for banding fertilizer before planting. However, make the trench farther away from the plant row so the nitrogen is not placed close enough to burn plant roots.

It is also possible to apply fertilizer through a drip irrigation system. Follow the manufacturer's directions for this type of fertilizer application.

Time of Planting

Seasonal temperatures are very important in determining when to plant a crop. Seed of cool-season crops germinate better when soil temperatures are cool than do seed of warm-season crops. Average monthly temperatures for cool-season crops are 60° to 65°F (16° to 18°C) during the growing period; for warm-season crops, 65° to 80°F (18° to 27°C). (See chapter 5, "Plant Propagation"," for details on soil temperature conditions for seed germination of specific vegetable crops.)

Consult table 14.2 for recommended planting dates for the major regions of California. These dates are based on the average temperatures for each region; you may have to make some adjustment if your area varies widely from the average. Unless otherwise stated, the planting times given in the table are for seeds. In California, allow 6 to 8 weeks for seeds to produce plants large enough for transplanting.

Temperature is probably the most important climatic factor that affects the success of your garden. Carefully study table 14.2 for information about your area. It will repay you in the yield and quality of the vegetables you grow.

Other climatic factors that affect the growth and quality of vegetables are soil moisture and length of day from sunrise to sunset. For example, brussels sprouts and globe artichokes grow more successfully near the ocean where the humidity is high and temperatures are cool. Many annuals, such as radishes, lettuce, spinach, and Chinese cabbage, tend to produce flowers as the days grow longer in late spring.

Direct-Seeding and Transplanting Vegetables

The standard spacing for different vegetable crops is given in table 14.2. The distance between rows depends on the size of the plants when fully grown. Refer to the section "Efficient Use of Space" in this chapter before selecting spacing distance. The depth of planting, either in the garden or in a hotbed or coldframe, depends on the size of the seed. Plant small seed about $\frac{1}{4}$ to $\frac{1}{2}$ inch (0.6 to 1.2 cm) deep. Plant snap beans and sweet corn 1 to $1\frac{1}{2}$ inches (2.5 to 3.7 cm) deep.

A general rule for planting seed is to plant to a depth two to four times the average diameter of the seed. When setting transplants, plant them slightly deeper than they were growing in the hotbed or flat. Make planting holes large enough so that the roots are not crowded. Be sure to firm, but not pack, the soil around the roots. Water the plants well immediately. An application of 1 to 2 cups (235 to 475 ml) of diluted fertilizer solution may help each plant as a starter fertilizer.

Caring for Your Vegetable Crop

Irrigation

Gardens in most areas of California require regular irrigation to provide the soil with the moisture needed for maximum plant growth. During years of normal rainfall (12 inches

[30 cm] or more), winter rains in most areas usually wet the soil, by spring, to a depth of 6 feet (180 cm). If the soil is not wet to this depth, irrigate before seeding so that the soil is wet to a depth of several feet.

Chapters 3 and 4 include extensive information on soil water, the water-holding capacity of various soil types, and plant-available water and irrigation, including general methods to determine irrigation frequency and the amount of water to use at each irrigation in the home garden. Drought management techniques are also discussed at length. Irrigation as it applies to home vegetable gardens is presented here in a very brief format.

Vary the amount and frequency of irrigation according to each variety of vegetable you grow. In the home garden, it is usually best to adjust irrigation to meet the needs of shallow-rooted crops. If their needs are met, the medium- and deep-rooted crops automatically get enough water. This same rule applies where the topsoil is shallow—only 1 or 2 feet (30 or 60 cm) of soil is available for root growth. Shallow-rooted crops have main root systems in the top 1 to 2 feet (30 to 60 cm) of soil. Examples are cabbage, cauliflower, lettuce, celery, sweet corn, onion, white potato, and radish. Moderately deep-rooted crops are those with the main root system in the top 1 to 4 feet (30 or 120 cm) of soil. Examples are snap bean, carrot, cucumber, eggplant, peas, pepper, and summer squash. For deep-rooted crops, the main root system is in the top 1 to 6 feet (30 to 180 cm) of soil. Examples are asparagus, globe artichoke, cantaloupe, pumpkin, tomato, and watermelon. (The maximum rooting depths given here are the potential rooting depths under ideal soil conditions.)

Irrigate your vegetable garden about one or two times a week in summer. Wet the soil to a depth of at least 18 inches (45 cm) at each watering. If you only keep the surface of the soil moist, most of the water evaporates to the air.

Do not waste water. There are simple ways to measure how much water you give your garden. If you use a garden hose, turn it on to the force you commonly use and time it to find out how many minutes it takes to fill a 1-gallon (3.79 liters) can. This gives you the rate of water flow per minute. One gallon of water wets 1 square foot (0.093 sq m) of

ground to a depth of 1.6 inches (4 cm). If you use a sprinkler system, place some empty cans under the sprinkler spray at various spots. Keep track of the length of time the sprinklers are on and then measure the depth of the water in the cans when you turn off the water. Average the various depths to determine how much water is being applied to the garden at each sprinkling.

Furrow irrigation, unlike sprinklers, has the advantage of not wetting the leaves. Water on plant foliage sometimes increases the incidence of plant diseases. If you plan to use furrow irrigation, use raised beds that are 5 or 6 inches (15 cm) high and 32 to 40 inches (80 to 100 cm) apart from center to center. Rake the tops of the beds flat and make them 18 inches (45 cm) wide. Locate the seed rows about 3 inches (7.5 cm) from each edge of the flattened bed top. Raised beds are also good for winter crops because they allow excess rain water to drain off. Apply irrigation water in furrows placed between the beds. If you use the furrow irrigation method, you need to apply more water to wet the soil to the necessary depth of 2 feet (60 cm) than if you use sprinklers.

Drip irrigation is a relatively new method that offers several advantages to home gardeners: water is placed more accurately in the root zone; water is applied at a slow rate so there is little or no waste; the furrows are dry so you can work in the garden while irrigation is in process; less water is required; and little or no management is required while irrigating. The disadvantages are the added costs of the drip irrigation equipment and occasional problems of plugging of the tiny drip orifices. However, the advantages outweigh the disadvantages, and a drip irrigation system, when correctly installed and maintained, can be very helpful to the serious gardener.

Soaker hoses are a form of drip irrigation and can be used to advantage if rows are short (20 to 25 feet [6 to 7.5 m]) and the soil is level. For longer rows or on sloping soil, soaker hoses cannot be expected to provide as uniform an irrigation as that provided by a true drip system.

Weeding

Weeds adversely affect crop growth by competing with for nutrients, water, and sunlight. The key to successful weed control is to prevent weeds from getting well established. (See chapter 9, "Weed Science," for detailed information on weed management.)

The chief methods of weed control are cultivation, mulching, and hand weeding. Proper cultivation includes scraping the soil surface or very shallow penetration of the soil with a hoe or other suitable tool to cut off and remove small weeds. Deep cultivation can prune crop roots, which can cause loss of yield.

Mulching offers a potentially more efficient means of weed control, and it also serves to conserve soil moisture. Organic mulches, such as weathered sawdust, straw, lawn clippings, or other such materials, should be applied 2 to 4 inches (5 to 10 cm) deep on the soil. These mulches can be tilled under periodically to improve the condition of the soil. Some of these materials will require nitrogen during the decaying process, so apply about 2 pounds (0.90 kg) of fertilizer per 100 square feet (9.3 sq m) to assure that adequate nitrogen is available to the mulch and crops.

Weed-block fabric, newspapers, and other such materials can also serve as mulches. They serve the same functions as organic mulches, but they do not offer the soil conditioning potential of organic mulches. Black plastic can be placed on the soil and properly anchored against wind immediately after the soil is prepared for planting. Transplants can then be set through the plastic by cutting holes just large enough for the plant to fit through.

Thinning

Overcrowded plants cannot grow rapidly or reach a good size. Thin small root crops, salad crops, and those grown for greens early at the second or third true-leaf stage. Thin root crops, such as beets or carrots, so the plants are 2 inches (5 cm) apart in the row. Thin radishes so plants are 1 inch (2.5 cm) apart and head lettuce to 12 inches (30 cm) apart. Table 14.2 lists standard spacing for each crop. However, different spacings may be required in your garden.

Harvesting and Storing

To get the most out of your vegetables, harvest them when they are at the best stage for eating and store them under conditions that will keep them as close to garden fresh as possible. Vegetables will be crisper and cooler if harvested in the early morning. It is best to consume fresh vegetables soon after harvest or purchase. However, this is not always possible, and you may want to store fresh vegetables for a while before using them. It is usually not practical to store most fresh vegetables for long periods at home.

Store fresh vegetables at the right temperature and relative humidity to maintain quality and nutritive value. With few exceptions, fresh vegetables keep best in the refrigerator. Most home refrigerators maintain a temperature of about 40° to 45°F (4° to 7°C) in the main storage space and a slightly cooler temperature in the hydrator (crisper). The door storage areas are warmer.

To prepare vegetables for storage, discard any part that shows evidence of decay. Immediately use any bruised or soft vegetables. Most home-grown vegetables require cleaning before storage. Remove tops of root crops, such as carrots. Wash to remove dirt, then drain excess water thoroughly. If you store any vegetables in the refrigerator, but not in the crisper, place them in plastic bags or plastic containers.

Do not put ripe fruits together with vegetables in the crisper. Many ripe fruits produce ethylene gas, which causes yellowing of green vegetables, russet spotting on lettuce, toughening of asparagus, sprouting of potatoes, and a bitter taste in carrots. Cole crops (cabbage, broccoli, and others) give off strong odors that may be absorbed by other commodities; keep them only for a few days in the refrigerator. Root crops, such as radishes, may cause off-flavors in fruits and leafy vegetables; do not store them next to these commodities or store in plastic bags in the refrigerator. Do not store celery with onions or carrots.

Fresh vegetables are grouped in four groups according to storage requirements. Because it is not always possible to provide all these different conditions, make compromises if the storage time is short (a few days).

Group 1

Keep under cold, moist conditions (32° to 41°F [0° to 5°C] and 85 to 95% relative humidity). Store in the refrigerator crisper and maintain high humidity by keeping the crisper more than half full. Wash and drain vegetables well before storage.

- beet greens
- chard
- collards

- endive
- escarole
- green onions
- kale
- leeks
- lettuce
- mustard greens
- spinach
- turnip greens
- watercress

Store the following vegetables in a crisper separate from the above vegetables or in plastic bags or containers in the main compartment of the refrigerator.

- artichokes
- asparagus
- beets
- broccoli
- brussels sprouts
- cabbage
- carrots
- cauliflower
- celery
- lima beans
- mushrooms
- parsnips
- peas
- radishes
- rhubarb
- sweet corn (unhusked; keep close to freezer compartment)
- turnips

Group 2

Ideally, it is best to store these vegetables at 45° to 55°F (7° to 13°C) and 85 to 90 percent relative humidity because of sensitivity to chilling injury. Because this is not possible in most homes, store in the refrigerator for no longer than 5 days. Use soon after removing from the refrigerator.

- bell peppers
- chili peppers
- cucumbers
- ripe melons
- snap beans
- summer squash

Group 3

Store in a cool place (50° to 60°F [10° to 16°C]); lower temperatures cause chilling injury. Pantries, basements, or garages can provide a cool place during most of the year. However, noninsulated garages may be too

warm in summer and too cold in winter. If you do not have such a space available, store eggplant and okra as described for the vegetables in group 2; store ripe tomatoes, hard rind squashes and pumpkins, sweet potatoes, and potatoes as recommended for the vegetables in group 4.

- eggplant
- hard-rind squashes and pumpkins
- okra
- potatoes (protect from light to prevent greening)
- sweet potatoes

Group 4

Store these vegetables at room temperature (65° to 70°F [18° to 21°C]). Store them so they are away from direct sunlight.

- garlic, dry
- melons (unripe or partly ripe)
- onions, dry (in open-mesh container)
- tomatoes (mature green, partly ripe, and ripe)

A Guide for Vegetable and Herb Cultivation in California

The following notes and tips on selected vegetables and herbs provide an easy-to-use, alphabetical guide that summarizes a wide range of information concerning their culture, harvest, storage, common problems (pests and diseases), and their nutritional value. This guide is not intended to be a comprehensive reference source. You will need to consult other vegetable gardening materials to obtain detailed information, which is readily available to the interested home gardener. The guide includes the following features.

- **Table 14.1: Approximate days to maturity for selected vegetable crops.**

- **Table 14.2: Vegetable gardening at a glance: How to plant and store.** This table gives recommended planting dates for various locations in California, a summary of planting requirements, and advice about storage conditions. It also lists a suggested amount to raise for a family of four, the proper temperature for storage of harvested produce, recommendations on the length of time to store, and how to preserve. In addition to this table, UC Cooperative Extension publications on food preservation are also useful resources.

- **Table 14.3: Families of common vegetable crops.** This table lists the top ten families of vegetable crops grown in home gardens and their scientific names. Note that relatively few plant families are sources of the typical vegetables consumed. As you study the guide, note that similar pests and diseases attack plant families. For example, the cucurbit family (squash, cucumber, pumpkin, cantaloupe, and watermelon) and the cole family (cabbage, broccoli, cauliflower, brussels sprouts) are each attacked by similar pests and diseases.

- **Table 14.4: Approximate yield for selected vegetable crops.**

- **Table 14.5: General problem diagnosis for vegetables.** This table lists general problems and symptoms typical of many vegetables grown in home gardens in California.

- **Table 14.6: Disease resistance key.** This table lists the acronyms used in the guide for the pest, virus, or disease to which the recommended varieties are resistant.

- **Crop varieties.** For most vegetables, there are a number of varieties from which to choose. The crop varieties recommended in the guide possess attributes important to success in the home garden, including wide availability, adaptability to a range of microclimates, consistency of high-quality yields, and resistance to disease. Where several varieties are listed for a crop, you may want to grow more than one to determine which is best suited to your locality and your individual taste. If you are uncertain about which variety to plant, choose a variety designated "AAS." These All-America Selections perform well throughout most of the United States, and many are resistant to disease. Whether purchasing seeds or transplants, always note the specific crop variety. Avoid generic or unlabeled transplants, since characteristics can vary widely with different varieties of the same crop.

- **Culture and management.** For each crop there are general guidelines, cultural practices, and special tips for successful production.

- **Nutrition information.** Many vegetables are good sources of vitamins and minerals, especially vitamin C, vitamin A, folic acid, potassium, iron, and magnesium. In addition, they are very low in fat, sodium, and calories. Since vegetables are plant-based foods, they do not contain any cholesterol. The nutritional value of typical serving sizes for each vegetable is based on nutrient composition data extracted from *Food Values of Portions Commonly Used* (Pennington 1998).

Nutrition Labels, Percent (%) Daily Value, and RDAs. You probably have seen the "% Daily Value" nutrition labels on frozen vegetables at the grocery store. In response to the Nutrition Labeling and Education Act of 1990, the standard labeling on grocery products today, whether packaged or fresh, is the % Daily Value, which is based on a 2,000-calorie diet. Since a 2,000-calorie diet may or may not meet your caloric requirements (age, height, and weight are factors), the nutritional value of each vegetable featured in this chapter is presented in a different format, as % RDA (the percent of the Recommended Dietary Allowances of vitamins and minerals) for adult males (m) and females (f) contained in the serving size listed. The nutritional value information for potassium content is expressed as "% Minimum Requirement." To date, no RDA has been established for potassium. Retinol equivalents (RE) are listed with vitamin A when appropriate. The nutritional information provided is derived from Pennington 1998 and National Academy of Sciences 1989, 2001a, and 2001b. For background information on nutritional data, see appendix A.

- **Problem diagnosis.** For most vegetable crops, the guide offers crop-specific problem diagnosis information that includes a list of the most common diseases, insect pests, and cultural problems that home gardeners may experience. Also included, where appropriate, are more detailed comments about fruit-set problems in squash, melons, tomatoes, and cucumbers in home gardens; fruit drop problems, solar yellowing, and leaf roll disorder in tomatoes; premature heading in cauliflower and bitterness in cucumbers; and environmental factors that cause problems in cultivating radishes. In the few crops where there is no crop-specific pest and problem diagnosis information, there are seldom serious problems in growing these commodities. In these instances, consult table 14.5 and other UC references if pests or other problems are encountered.

Comprehensive information about managing vegetable pests, weeds, diseases, insects, mites, snails, slugs, and nematodes in California is available in *Pests of the Garden and Small Farm* (Flint 1998), which is recommended as an essential resource and reference book for Master Gardeners. Additional up-to-date informa-tion on many specific pests can be found in the UC IPM pest note series. See chapter 10, "Controlling Garden Pests Safely," for general information on pest management and pesticide safety. General information on diseases, insects, and weeds can be found in chapters 6, 7, and 9, respectively. For more specific advice about crop culture or pest and disease control, contact your UC Cooperative Extension advisor. In most cases, the guide in this handbook should provide enough know-how to get a crop from seed to harvest.

Table 14.1

APPROXIMATE DAYS TO MATURITY FOR SELECTED VEGETABLE CROPS

Vegetable	Days from planting to maturity under optimal growing conditions	Days from pollination to maturity under warm growing conditions
bean	48–60	7–10
beet	55–70	
broccoli	60–110	
cabbage	65–120	
carrot	120–150	
cauliflower	90–110	
celery (transplanted)	90	
corn, sweet	65–95	18–23 (from 50% silking)
cucumber (pickling)	50–60	4–5
cucumber (slicing)	60–75	15–18
eggplant (transplanted)	60–80	25–40 ($^2/_3$ max. size)
kohlrabi	50–60	
lettuce, head	70–90	
lettuce, leaf	40–50	
muskmelon	85–95	42–46
okra	50–60	4–6
onion, dry	90–150	
onion, green	50–60	
pepper (transplanted)	65–80	45–55 (green stage, about max. size); 60–70 (red stage)
potato	90–120	
pumpkin	100–120	65–90 (varies with variety)
radish	21–30	
spinach	40–50	
squash, summer	50–60	4–6
squash, winter	85–110	60–90 (varies with variety)
tomato (transplanted)	60–80	35–45 (mature green stage); 45–60 (red ripe stage)
turnip	45–75	
watermelon	85–95	42–45

Table 14.2

VEGETABLE GARDENING AT A GLANCE: HOW TO PLANT AND STORE

Vegetable	Recommended planting dates[a]				Crop type[b]	General planting requirements			Storage conditions		
	North and North Coast	South Coast	Interior Valleys	Desert Valleys		Amount to plant (4 persons)	Distance in inches[c] between plants in rows (cm)	Distance in inches[c] between rows (no beds) (m)	Best temp °F (°C)	Time length (weeks)	How to preserve[d]
artichoke[e]	Aug–Dec	May–Jul	Jul	Sep	C	3–4 plants	48 (122)	60 (1.5)	32 (0)	1–2	freeze whole, can, dry, or freeze hearts
asparagus[e]	Jan–Mar	Jan–Feb	Jan–Feb	Feb–Apr	C	30–40 plants	12 (31)	60 (1.5)	32 (0)	3–4	can, dry, or freeze
beans, lima[f]	May–Jun	May–Jun	May–Jun	—	W	15–25-ft row	6 (15) bush; (4.5–7.5-m row)	30 (0.8) bush; 24 (61) pole	40 (4)	1–3	can, dry, or freeze
beans, snap[f,g]	Jul; May–Jun	Mar–Aug	Apr–May; Jul–Aug	Jan–Mar; Aug	W	15–25-ft row (4.5–7.5-m row)	3 (7.5) bush; 24 (61) pole	30[h] (0.8)	45–55 (7–13)	1–2	can, dry, or freeze
beets[f,g]	Feb–Aug	Jan–Sep	Feb–Apr; Aug	Sep–Jan	C	10–15-ft row (3–4.5-m row)	2 (5)	18[h] (0.5)	32 (0)	3–10	can, dry, or freeze
broccoli[e,f,g]	Feb–Apr; Aug–Sep	Jun–Jul; Jan–Feb	Dec–Feb; Jul	Sep	C	6–10-ft row (2–3-m row)	12–18 (30–45)	36 (0.9)	32 (0)	1–2	dry or freeze
brussels sprouts[e]	Feb–May	Jun–Jul	—	—	C	15–20-ft row (4.5–6-m row)	24 (61)	36 (0.9)	32 (0)	3–4	dry or freeze
cabbage[e,f]	Jan–Apr; Jul–Sep	Aug–Feb	Jul; Feb	Sep–Nov	C	10–15 plants	24 (61)	36 (0.9)	32 (0)	12–16	dry or freeze
cabbage, Chinese[f]	Jul–Sep	Aug–Oct	Aug	Aug–Nov	C	10–15-ft row (3–4.5-m row)	6 (15)	30[h] (0.8)	32 (0)	2–3	dry or freeze
cantaloupes and other melons	May	Apr–May	Apr–Jun	Jan–Apr; Jul	W	5–10 hills	12 (30)	72 (1.8)	40–45 (4–7)	2–4	freeze
carrots[f,g]	Jan–May; Jul–Aug	Jan–Sep	Aug–Sep; Feb–Apr	Sep–Dec	C	10–25-ft row (3–7.5-m row)	2 (5)	24[h] (0.6)	32 (0)	16–20	can, dry, or freeze
cauliflower[e]	Jun–Jul;	Jul–Oct; Feb Jan–Feb	Jul–Aug	Aug–Sep	C	10–15 plants	24 (61)	36 (0.9)	32 (0)	2–3	pickle, dry, or freeze
celeriac	Mar–Jun	Mar–Aug	Jun–Aug	—	C	10–15-ft row	4 (10)	24[h] (0.6)	32 (0)	8–16	can, dry, or freeze
celery[e,f]	Mar–Jun	Apr–Aug	Jun–Aug	—	C	20–30-ft row (6–9-m row)	5 (13)	24[h] (0.6)	32 (0)	8–16	can, dry, or freeze
chard[f]	Feb–May; Aug	Feb–May	Feb; Aug	Sep–Oct	C	3–4 plants	12 (30)	30 (0.8)	32 (0)	1–2	freeze
chayote	—	Apr–May	May–Jun	—	W	1–2 plants	72 (183)	use trellis	—	—	use fresh
chives[f]	Apr	Feb–Apr	Feb–Mar	Sep–Feb	C	1 clump	—	—	—	—	use fresh
corn, sweet[g]	May–Jul	Mar–Jul	Mar–Jul; Aug	Feb–Mar	W	20–30-ft (6-9 m) in 4 rows	12 (30)	36 (0.9)	32 (0)	½–1	can, dry, or freeze
cucumbers	Apr–Jun	Apr–Jun	Apr–Jul	Feb–May; Aug	W	6 plants	24 (61)	48 (1.2)	45–55 (7–13)	1–2	freeze, pickle, or puree
eggplant[e,f]	May	Apr–May	Apr–May	Feb–Apr	W	4–6 plants	18 (46)	36 (0.9)	50–60 (10–16)	1–2	dry or freeze
endive[f]	Mar–Jul	Dec–Aug	Jan; Apr; Aug	Sep–Dec	C	10–15-ft row (3–4.5-m row)	10 (25)	24[h] (0.6)	32 (0)	2–3	use fresh
Florence fennel	Mar–Jul	Feb–Jul	Aug	Sep–Nov	C	10–15-ft row (3–4.5-m row)	4 (10)	30[h] (0.8)	32 (0)	2–3	can, dry, or freeze
garlic[f]	Oct–Dec	Oct–Dec	Oct–Dec	Sep–Nov	C	10–20-ft row (3–6-m row)	3 (7.5)	18[h] (0.5)	65–70 (18–21)	24–32	use fresh
kale	Feb–April	Aug–Oct	Aug–Sept	Sept–Nov	C	10 -ft row (3-m row)	18–24 (46–61)	24–30 (0.6–0.8)	32 (0)	2	use fresh
kohlrabi[f]	Jul–Aug	Jan; Aug–Sep	Aug	Oct–Nov	C	10–15-ft row (3–4.5-m row)	3 (7.5)	24 (0.6)	32 (0)	2–4	use fresh
leeks	Feb–Apr	Jan–Apr	Jan–Apr	—	C	10-ft row	2 (5)	24 (0.6)	32 (0)	4–12	use fresh
lettuce[f,g]	Feb–Aug	Aug–Apr	Aug; Nov–Mar	Sep–Dec	C	10–15-ft row or 5 ft (1.5m) each month	12 (30) head; (3–4.5-m row)	24 (0.6) 6 (0.15) leaf	32 (0)	2–3	use fresh

Table 14.2 cont.

Vegetable	Recommended planting dates[a]				General planting requirements				Storage conditions		
	North and North Coast	South Coast	Interior Valleys	Desert Valleys	Crop type[b]	Amount to plant (4 persons)	Distance in inches[c] between plants in rows (cm)	Distance in inches[c] between rows (no beds) (m)	Best temp °F (°C)	Time length (weeks)	How to preserve[d]
mustard	Apr; Jul–Aug	Aug–Feb	Aug; Apr	Oct–Dec	C	10-ft row (3-m row)	8 (20)	24[h] (0.6)	32 (0)	1–2	use fresh
okra	May	Apr–May	May	Mar	W	10–20-ft row	18 (46)	36 (0.9)	50–60 (10–16)	—	use fresh
onions, bulb[f]	Jan–Mar	Feb–Mar	Nov–Mar	Oct–Nov	C	30–40-ft row (9–12-m row)	3 (7.5)	18[h] (0.5)	32–36 (0–2)	12–32	can, dry, or freeze
onions, green[e,f,g]	Apr–Jul	All year	Aug–Dec	Sep–Jan	C				85–90 (30–32)		use fresh
parsley[f]	Dec–May	Dec–May	Dec–May	Sep–Oct	C	1–2 plants	8 (20)	24 (0.6)	32 (0)	1–2	dry or freeze
parsnips	May–Jun	Mar–Jul	May–Jul	Sep–Oct	C	10–15-ft row (3–4.5-m row)	3 (7.5)	24[h] (0.6)	32 (0)	8–16	freeze
peas[f,g]	Jan–Apr; Sep–Oct	Aug; Dec–Mar	Sep–Jan; Jan–Feb	Sep–Oct	C	30–40-ft row (9–12-m row)	2 (5)	36 (0.9) bush; 48 (1.2) vine	32 (0)	1–2	can, dry, or freeze
peppers[e,f]	May	Apr–May	May	Mar	W	5–10 plants	24 (61)	36 (0.9)	45–55 (7–13)	4–6	can, dry, or freeze
potatoes, sweet[e]	May	Apr–May	Apr–Jun	Feb–Jun	W	50–100-ft row 1 (15–30-m row)	2 (30)	36 (0.9)	55–60 (13–16)	8–24	can, dry, or freeze
potatoes, white	Early: Feb Late: Apr–May	Feb–May Jun–Aug	Feb–Mar; Aug	Dec–Feb	C	50–100-ft row (15–30-m row)	12 (30)	30 (0.8)	40–45 (4–7)	12–20	can, dry, or freeze
pumpkins	May	May–Jun	Apr–Jun	Mar–Jul	W	1–3 plants	48 (122)	72 (1.8)	55 (13)	8–24	can, dry, or freeze
radish[f,g]	All year	All year	Sep–Apr	Oct–Mar	C	4-ft row (1.2-m row)	1 (2.5)	6[h] (0.2)	32 (0)	—	use fresh
rhubarb[e]	Dec–Mar	Dec–Jan	Dec–Feb	—	C	2–3 plants	36 (91)	48 (1.2)	32 (0)	2–3	can or freeze
rutabaga	Jul; Mar–Apr	Jul–Sep; Aug–Mar	Aug	Oct–Dec	C	10–15-ft row (3–4.5-m row)	3 (7.5)	6[h] (0.2)	32 (0)	8–16	freeze
spinach[f]	Aug–Feb	Aug–Mar	Sep–Jan	Sep–Nov	C	10–20-ft row (3–6-m row)	3 (7.5)	18[h] (0.5)	32 (0)	1–2	dry or freeze
squash, summer[f]	May–Jul	Apr–Jun	Apr–Jul	Feb–Mar; Aug–Sep	W	2–4 plants	24 (61)	48 (1.2)	50–55 (10–13)	2–3	can, dry, or freeze
squash, winter[f]	May	Apr–Jun	Apr–Jun	Feb–Mar; Aug	W	2–4 plants	24–48 (61–122)	72 (1.8)	55 (13)	8–24	can, dry, or freeze
tomatoes[e,f]	May	Apr–Jul 15	Apr–May	Dec–Mar	W	6–10 plants	18–36 (46–91)	36–60 (0.9–1.5)	55–65 (13–18)	1–2	can, dry, or freeze
turnips[f]	Jan, Aug	Jan Aug–Oct	Feb; Aug	Oct–Feb	C	10–15-ft row (3–4.5-m row)	2 (2.5)	18[h] (0.5)	32 (0)	8–12	can
watermelons	May–Jun	Apr–Jun	Apr–Jun	Jan–Mar	W	6 plants	60 (152)	72 (1.8)	40 (4)	2–3	freeze

Notes:

[a] North and North Coast = Monterey County north; South Coast = San Luis Obispo County south; Interior Valleys = Sacramento, San Joaquin, and similar valleys; Desert Valleys = Imperial and Coachella Valleys. Because the areas shown here are large, planting dates are only approximate, as the climate may vary even in small sections of the state. Contact experienced gardeners in your community and experiment on your own to find more precise dates.

[b] C = cool season, W = warm season.

[c] Planting distances listed here are standards. Many crops can be spaced more closely for intensive production.

[d] Adapted from *Vegetable Gardening Illustrated* 1994.

[e] Transplants, shoots, or roots are used for field planting.

[f] This crop is suitable for a small garden if compact varieties are grown.

[g] In a suitable climate, these crops can be planted more than once per year for a continuous harvest.

[h] If grown in beds, plant two rows per bed. Space the beds about 32 to 40 inches (80 to 100 cm) apart and make the tops of the beds 18 inches (45 cm) wide.

Table 14.3

FAMILIES OF COMMON VEGETABLE CROPS

Family and common name	Scientific name
Amaryllidaceae	
chives	*Allium schoenoprasum*
garlic	*Allium sativum*
leek	*Allium ampeloprasum*
onion	*Allium cepa*
Chenopodiaceae	
beet	*Beta vulgaris*
chard	*Beta vulgaris* var. *cicla*
spinach	*Spinacia oleracea*
Cruciferae	
broccoli	*Brassica oleracea* var. *italica*
brussels sprouts	*Brassica oleracea* var. *gemmifera*
cabbage	*Brassica oleracea* var. *capitata*
cauliflower	*Brassica oleracea* var. *botrytis*
Chinese cabbage	*Brassica oleracea* var. *pekinensis*
kale	*Brassica oleracea* var. *acephala*
kohlrabi	*Brassica oleracea* var. *gongylodes*
mustard greens	*Brassica juncea*
radish	*Raphanus sativus*
rutabaga	*Brassica napus*
turnip	*Brassica rapa*
Compositae	
artichoke, globe	*Cynara scolymus*
endive	*Cichorium endivia*
lettuce	*Lactuca sativa*
Cucurbitaceae	
chayote	*Sechium edule*
cucumber (slicing and pickling)	*Cucumis sativus*
muskmelon (cantaloupe, honeydew)	*Cucumis melo*
pumpkin	*Cucurbita pepo*
squash, summer	*Cucurbita pepo* var. *melopepo*
squash, winter, acorn	*Cucurbita pepo*
squash, winter, butternut	*Cucurbita maxima*
watermelon	*Citrullus lanatus*
Gramineae (Poaceae)	
corn	*Zea mays*
Leguminosae	
bean, dry	*Phaseolus vulgaris*
bean, fava	*Vicia faba*
bean, lima	*Phaseolus limensis*
bean, snap	*Phaseolus vulgaris*
pea	*Pisum sativum*
Liliaceae	
asparagus	*Asparagus officinalis*
Malvaceae	
okra	*Abelmoschus esculentus*
Polygonaceae	
rhubarb	*Rheum rhabarbarum*
Solanaceae	
eggplant	*Solanum melongena*
pepper, bell or chili	*Capsicum annuum*
potato, white/sweet	*Solanum tuberosum*
tomato	*Lycopersicon esculentum*

Table 14.3 cont.

Family and common name	Scientific name
Umbelliferae	
carrot	*Daucus carota*
celeriac	*Apium graviolens* var. *rapaceum*
celery	*Apium graviolens* var. *dulce*
Florence fennel	*Foeniculum vulgare*
parsley	*Petroselinum crispum*
parsnip	*Pastinaca sativa*

Table 14.4

APPROXIMATE YIELD FOR SELECTED VEGETABLE CROPS

Crop	Pounds (or units) per 15-ft (4.5-m) row
asparagus	4.5
bean, lima (bush)	4
bean, snap (bush)	15
beets	41 (2 rows on raised bed)
broccoli	11
carrot	41 (2 rows on raised bed)
cabbage	22.5
cauliflower	15
chard	11
corn	18 ears
cucumber, slicing	41 (2 rows on raised bed)
cucumber, pickling	27
garlic	6
eggplant	15
kohlrabi	11 (2 rows on raised bed)
lettuce, head	15 heads (2 rows on raised bed)
lettuce, leaf	15 (2 rows on raised bed)
muskmelon	15 melons
mustard greens	22.5 (2 rows on raised bed)
okra	16
onion, bulb	34 (2 rows on raised bed)
pea	3
pepper, bell	20
potato, sweet	30
potato, white	36
spinach	20 (2 rows on raised bed)
squash, summer	52
squash, winter	45
tomato	42
turnip	27

Table 14.5

GENERAL PROBLEM DIAGNOSIS FOR VEGETABLES

What the problem looks like	Probable cause	Controls and comments
poor fruit yield; small fruit with poor taste	uneven moisture	Supply moisture during dry periods.
	poor soil fertility	Add compost or well-composted manure.
	improper temperature	Plant at right time of year.
plants grow slowly; light green leaves	insufficient light	Thin plants; do not plant in shade.
	cool weather	Provide hot caps, floating row cover.
	improper pH	Test for pH. If alkaline, add soil sulfur, aluminum sulfate peat moss.
	excess water	Do not overwater. Improve drainage by adding amendments and/or building raised beds.
seedlings do not emerge	insufficient soil moisture	Supply water.
	soil crusting	Apply light mulch to soil surface or water often enough to keep surface moist.
	damping-off (fungal problem)	Do not overwater; use treated seed.
	incorrect planting depth or seeds washed away	Use gentler watering technique.
	slow germination due to weather	In spring or fall, cover bed with clear plastic to increase soil temperature.
	root maggots	Use registered soil insecticide. Use floating row cover as exclusion method.
	old seed	Use current season seed.
seedlings wilt and fall over	dry soil	Supply water.
	damping off (fungal disease)	Do not overwater; treat with fungicide.
	cutworms	Destroy crop residues; keep garden weed-free. Use cardboard collars, floating row covers.
	root maggots	Use floating row cover as exclusion method; use soil insecticide.
	old seed	Use current season seed.
chewed seedlings, plants, fruit	birds, rodents, rabbits	Place fence around garden; cover with netting, floating row cover.
leaves stippled with tiny white spots	spider mites	Treat with registered miticide or insecticidal soap spray.
	air pollution (ozone)	Wash off foliage.
wilted plants	root rot (fungal disease)	Do not overwater. Remove old plant debris. Rotate crops.
	vascular wilt (fungal disease mainly affecting tomato, potato, eggplant, pepper)	Use resistant varieties. Use soil solarization techniques. Rotate crops.
	root knot nematodes	Use resistant varieties. Use soil solarization techniques. rotate crops.
	various root-feeding nematodes	Submit soil sample for nematode analysis. Use soil solarization or fumigation.
	waterlogged soil	Improve drainage.
general leaf yellowing; no wilting	nutrient or mineral deficiency	Test soil for deficiencies. Add complete fertilizer.
	insufficient light	Thin plants to reduce shading. Move to sunnier garden location.

What the problem looks like	Probable cause	Controls and comments
leaf margins turn brown and shrivel	dry soil	Supply water.
	salt damage	Do not place garden where de-icing salt may have been applied on nearby concrete. keep salty water off foliage. Leach with good-quality water.
	fertilizer burn	Do not overapply fertilizer. Flush soil with water. Test soil for soluble salts level.
	potassium deficiency	Test soil for defieiency. Apply potassium fertilizer, compost, or manure.
	cold injury	Protect from cold with hot caps, floating row cover.
discrete brown spots on leaves	chemical injury due to local application or drift	Do not apply chemicals that are not registered for use on the plant. Apply chemicals at registered rate.
white powdery growth on upper leaf surface	powdery mildew (fungal disease)	Choose resistant varieties. Use Safer's sulfur with surfactant.
leaves shredded or stripped from plant	rodents, deer, hail damage, slugs	Place fence around garden. Use slug bait.
leaves with yellow and green mosaic or mottle pattern; puckered leaves; stunted plants	virus disease	Use resistant varieties if possible. Remove infected plants. Remove old plant debris. Practice insect, weed control.
curled, puckered, or distorted leaves	herbicide injury	If you use lawn herbicides, apply after wind has died down. Do not apply herbicides in the heat of the day.
	virus disease	Use resistant varieties if possible. Remove infected plants. Remove old plant debris. Practice insect, weed control.
	aphids	Use soap-based spray, floating row cover.

Table 14.6

DISEASE RESISTANCE KEY

Abbreviation	Disease	Abbreviation	Disease
A	Alternaria diseases	LB	late blight
AAS	all-america selection (hardy in most areas, resists most diseases)	LMV	lettuce mosaic virus
		M	mosaic virus
		N	root knot nematode
ALS	angular leaf spot	PM	powdery mildew
AN	anthracnose	PVY	potato virus Y
B	bolting	R	rust
BR	black rot	S	scab
BS	black speck	SCLB	southern corn leaf blight
BSR	bacterial soft rot	SG	smog
BW	bacterial wilt	ST	smut
C	*Cercospora*-caused diseases	SW	stewart's wilt
CBM	common bean mosaic virus	TB	tipburn
CMV	cucumber mosaic virus	TMV	tobacco mosaic virus
DM	downy mildew	V	Verticillium diseases
F	Fusarium diseases	VR	other viruses
H	heat	?	disease reaction unknown
HS	hollow stem		

Artichoke, Globe
(*Cynara scolymus*)

Recommended Varieties

- Emerald
- Green Globe
- Imperial Star (spineless, for annual cropping)

Perennial Plantings

The globe artichoke is commonly a perennial, cool-season vegetable that yields and produces best when grown near or along the California coast where cool to mild climates prevail. Castroville, California, is known as the artichoke capital of the world. Perennial plantings are not recommended in areas where warm to hot temperatures are common. Shading and mist irrigation may help vegetative growth, but warm growing conditions tend to toughen bud scales, reduce palatability, and produce poor yields. Frosts damage outer portions of the buds; severe or frequent frosts damage or kill the plants. If correctly cared for, you can maintain production of plants for 5 years or more.

Use rooted offshoots or divisions from mature plants to propagate Green Globe. The other varieties may be obtained from seed or transplants. Plants become better established if you transplant shoots, root divisions, or transplants in the early fall so that the plants become well-rooted and of reasonable size before temperatures become cool during the winter. Production starts about a year after planting, although some buds usually develop the first spring after early fall plantings.

Once the plant is in normal cycle, bud production starts in the fall. A small number of buds develop during the winter, but cold temperatures limit plant growth. The edible parts are the immature, scaly flower buds, bracts (leaves), and heart. The buds are said to contain a chemical that makes food eaten after them taste sweet. Mature artichoke flowers are a brilliant sky blue color, but they are not edible.

To harvest, cut the bud together with 2 to 3 inches (5 to 7.5 cm) of stem. This length of stem is usually tender and edible. A mature plant produces 10 or more stems during a season; each stem can provide four to five buds.

A recommended cultural procedure is to cut the entire plant down to, or slightly below, soil level after the spring production peak. Then reduce or withhold irrigation for several weeks. This allows for a summer dormancy. Once you resume irrigation, it encourages rapid and vigorous regrowth of leaves and, shortly thereafter, new stems bearing new buds will develop for the fall production period.

Annual Plantings for Inland Valleys and Low Desert Regions

It is possible to grow high-quality artichokes in inland valleys and low desert regions of Southern California by handling the crop as a direct-seeded or transplanted annual crop. Until recently, it was believed that artichoke buds produced from seed-propagated plants were of inferior quality to those produced by vegetative propagation. Recent research at the University of California has shown that seed-initiated artichokes looked and tasted great. Moreover, annual cropping makes growing artichokes feasible in gardens with limited space because the crop does not require long-term space allocation. Quicker rotation with other vegetables is also possible.

To grow artichokes in warm inland climates, plant seeds or transplants of Imperial Star or Emerald in July for inland valley locations or in September for low deserts.

Nutritional Value of Artichoke Hearts

Serving size: ½ cup, boiled (84 g)

Calories	37
Fat	0.1 g
Calories from fat	2%
Sodium	55 mg
Protein	1.9 g
Carbohydrate	8.7g

Primary Nutrients		% RDA (m)	% RDA (f)	% Min. Requirement
Folic Acid	37 mcg	9.3	9.3	
Magnesium	33 mg	7.9	10.3	
Vitamin C	6.0 mg	6.7	8.0	
Iron	1 mg	12.5	5.6	
Cholesterol	0			
Potassium	221 mg			11

Problem	Probable cause
Holes, discoloration on bracts, stems, leaves. Caterpillars may be visible.	artichoke plume moth
Comments	
Cut plants down to ground level once per year. Chop and cover cuttings with 6 inches (15 cm) of soil. Remove thistle. Sprays of *Bacillus thuringiensis* and predaceous nematodes are effective.	
Sticky exudate on chokes. Black, sooty mold.	aphids
Comments	
Consult UC IPM Pest Note series or Flint 1998 for management options.	
Blackening of choke surfaces. Jagged holes in leaves, stems.	snails and slugs
Comments	
Consult UC IPM pest note series or Flint 1998 for management options.	
Curled leaves, dwarfed plant. Small, misshaped chokes. Reduced yield.	curly dwarf virus
Comments	
Remove and destroy infected plants immediately. Use noninfected stock for new plants. Remove milk thistle because it is an alternate host.	
Gray or brown fungus growth.	*Botrytis* fungus
Comments	
Common in rainy weather. Remove infected plant parts.	

Asparagus (*Asparagus officinalis*)

Recommended Varieties (Disease Resistance)

- 500W
- Mary Washington (R)
- UC72 (F)
- UC157 (F)

Asparagus is a very hardy, perennial, cool-season vegetable that can live 12 to 15 years or longer. It is one of the most valuable early vegetables and is well adapted to freezer storage. During the harvest period, spears develop daily from underground crowns. Asparagus does well where winters are cool and the soil occasionally freezes at least a few inches deep.

Start asparagus from seed or 1- to 2-year-old crowns. (The crowns are rhizomes—fleshy stems that store food for future plant growth—with roots attached on their undersurface and the buds of nascent spears sticking up.) For best results, buy crowns from a respectable nursery. Starting plants from seed requires an extra year before harvest. Seed may be started in peat pots; they are slow to germinate, so be patient. Seedlings may be transplanted in fall. Crowns are usually set out in winter or early spring. See table 14.2 to determine the best planting dates in your area of the state.

Choose a site with good drainage and full sun. The tall ferns of asparagus may shade other plants, so plan accordingly. Prepare the bed as early as possible and enrich it with additions of manure, compost, bone or blood meal, leaf mold, or wood ashes or a combination of several of these. In heavy soils, double-digging is recommended. To double-dig, remove the top 1 foot (30 cm) of soil from the planting area. Then, with a spading fork or spade, break up the subsoil by pushing the tool into the next 10 to 12 inches (25 to 30 cm) of soil and rocking it back and forth. Do this every 6 inches (15 cm) or so. Double-digging is ideal for the trench method of planting asparagus. The extra work of breaking up the subsoil will be well worth the effort, especially in heavy soil. The trench is dug 12 to 18 inches (30 to 45 cm) wide, with 4 to 5 feet (1.2 to 1.5 m) between trenches. The same method may be used in wide-bed plantings, with plants staggered in three rows. Mix the topsoil that has been removed with organic matter (ideally well-rotted manure) and spread about 2 inches (5 cm) of the mixture in the bottom of the trench or bed. Set the plants 12 inches (30 cm) apart, mounding the soil slightly under each plant so that the crown is slightly above the roots. Crowns should be a grayish-brown color, plump, and healthy-looking. Remove any rotten roots before planting. Spread the roots out over the mound of soil and cover the crown with 2 to 3 inches (5 to 7.5 cm) of soil. Firm well. As the plants grow, continue to pull soil over the crowns (about 2 inches [5 cm] every 2 weeks) until the trench is filled. Water if rainfall is inadequate.

Asparagus takes several years to mature. Asparagus shoots (spears) should not be harvested the first season after crowns are set. After spears shoot up, let them leaf out so that the foliage can nourish the growing roots and rhizome for future production. Harvest lightly

Problem Diagnosis for Asparagus

Problem	Probable cause
Pustules on stems and leaves are reddish-brown, orange, or black. Tops turn yellow, brown, and die back.	rust
Comments	
Caused by a fungus. Prevalent in humid areas. Use resistant varieties. Sulfur is helpful. Cut down diseased ferns at crown and destroy.	
Spears weaken, wilt, turn yellow and then brown; roots reddish.	Fusarium wilt
Comments	
Caused by soilborne fungus. Destroy infected plants. Use soil solarization methods. Disease can be introduced on transplants. Rotate planting area.	
	root rot fungi
Comments	
Rotate crops. Remove plant debris. Plant in well-drained area.	
Bent spears; drought-stricken and white or light green.	**Phytopthora crown and spear rot**
Comments	
Common in wet years.	
Chewed leaves; slime on leaves.	snails, slugs
Comments	
Use commercial snail bait. Put mushrooms in garden as attractant. Use flashlight; collect and kill any found. Apply copper banding as barrier around beds.	
Black stains on spears. Black eggs attached to spears.	**asparagus beetle**
Comments	
Adult is a blue-black beetle; larva is a dark green-gray grub about ³/₈ inch (9 mm) long. Promptly remove infected spears. Wash eggs, beetles, and larvae off with water. Use rotenone.	
Weak, spindly plants. Too few spears.	**too early or too heavy harvest; weed competition;**
frost injury; drought	
Comments	
Do not harvest too late in season; plants will not be able to store enough food for next season. Allow plants to recover. Mulch soil to prevent freezing.	
Fine whitish or yellowish stippling on shoots.	**spider mites**
Comments	
Sulfur is effective.	
Stunted, rosetted plants. Aphids on young ferns.	**European asparagus aphid**
Comments	
New pest that invaded California in the 1980s. Incorporate ferns into soil in fall to destroy eggs.	

for 3 to 4 weeks the second year. The fleshy root system still needs to develop and store food reserves to support perennial growth in future seasons. Plants harvested too heavily and too soon often become weak and spindly, and the crowns may never recover. An extra year is added to the above schedule for asparagus started from seed; that is, do not harvest at all the first two seasons, and harvest lightly the third. When the asparagus plants are in their fourth season, they may be harvested for 6 to 10 weeks per year.

Weed the bed each spring before the first shoots come up to avoid accidentally breaking off spears. During production, it is best to pull rather than hoe weeds, if possible.

Harvest spears daily during the harvest period, and use the asparagus or refrigerate it immediately in a plastic bag. The 6- to 8-inch (15- to 20-cm) spears are best and should be snapped or cut off just below the soil surface. If the asparagus is allowed to get much taller, the bases of the spears will be tough. Cutting too deeply can injure the crown buds that produce the next spears. Blanched asparagus is a gourmet item; to blanch (whiten) the spears, mound soil around them or otherwise exclude light from them so that chlorophyll is not formed in the stalks.

When harvest is over, allow the spears to grow and leaf out. Asparagus has an attractive, fernlike foliage that makes a nice garden border. Some gardeners prefer to support the growing foliage with stakes and strings to keep

---

Nutritional Value of Asparagus
Serving size: ¹/₂ cup, boiled (90 g)

Calories	22
Fat	0.3 g
Calories from fat	12%
Sodium	10 mg
Protein	2.3 g
Carbohydrate	3.8 g

Primary Nutrients		% RDA (m)	% RDA (f)	% Min. Requirement
Folic Acid	132 mcg	33.0	33.0	
Vitamin C	10 mg	11.1	13.3	
Thiamin	0.11 mg	9.2	10.0	
Vitamin B₆	0.11 mg	8.5	8.5	
Riboflavin	0.11 mg	8.5	10.0	
Iron	0.66 mg	8.3	3.7	
Vitamin A	48 RE	5.3	6.9	
Potassium	144 mg			7

them tidy. In high-wind areas, plant the rows parallel to the prevailing winds so that plants can support each other.

There are several ways to extend the harvest period of your asparagus planting. One method is to plant at different depths: 4 to 6 inches (10 to 15 cm), 6 to 8 inches (15 to 20 cm) and 8 to 10 inches (20 to 25 cm). The shallow plantings will come up first and can be harvested while the deeper plantings are just forming. This method results in a slightly longer harvest, but it may also cause some plants to be less vigorous than others.

A second technique for extending asparagus harvest has been the subject of university research and is highly recommended for home gardeners who have plenty of space. Plant double the amount of asparagus needed for your household. Harvest half of the plants as you normally would in early spring; then allow the foliage to grow for the rest of the season. During the early harvest period, allow the ferns to grow in the other half of the asparagus planting. Then, cut the ferns in this second half in July or August. This causes the crowns to send up new spears, which can be harvested until late in the season. If rainfall is short in summer, it helps to water the bed for good spear production. A light mulch helps keep the soil surface from becoming too hard for the shoots to break through easily. If using this method, harvest the spring bed only in spring and the fall bed only in fall. Otherwise, you risk weakening the crowns.

In all asparagus plantings, cut the foliage down to 2-inch (5-cm) stubs after freezing weather or when the foliage yellows. A 4- to 6-inch (10- to 15-cm) mulch of compost, manure, leaves, or other material added at this time will help control weeds and add organic matter and nutrients.

Beans
Phaseolus limensis (lima beans)
Phaseolus vulgaris (snap beans and dry beans)
Vicia faba (fava bean)

Recommended Varieties (Disease Resistance)

Bush yellow
- Goldencrop Wax (AAS, CBM, V)
- Resistant Cherokee Wax (CBM, V)

Lima
- Fordhook 242 Bush (AAS)
- Henderson's Bush (pole type)
- King of the Garden (bush butterbean type)
- Dixie Butterpea (butterbean type)
- Baby Fordhook Bush (butterbean type)

Snap-bush green
- Contender (CBM, PM)
- Harvester (CBM, V)
- Roman (CBM)
- Tendercrop (CBM, PM, V)

Snap-pole green
- Fortex
- Emerite
- Kentucky Wonder (R)
- Romano (Italian type)
- Scarlet Runner (attractive scarlet flowers)
- Kwintus

Beans are tender, annual, warm-season legumes that fix their own nitrogen once a good root system is established. Snap beans (also known as green or string beans) that are grown for their pods are the most common. Some beans, such as limas, soybeans, and dried beans, are grown primarily for the seed itself and not the pods. Bush snap beans are the most popular because they mature early and do not require trellising. Varieties include standard round and flat-podded green, yellow wax, and purple-pod types, giving gardeners a larger choice than is generally available in supermarkets. Although wax beans are yellow and waxy in appearance, their flavor is only subtly different from that of regular green snap beans. Purple-pod beans are different in appearance while growing, and the pods turn green when cooked. Flat-pod green snap beans are somewhat different in flavor and texture than the round-pod ones and are preferred by many gardeners. Many varieties are available in both bush and pole types.

First plantings of bush beans should be made after danger of frost is past in the spring and soil is warmed, because seed planted in

cold soils germinate slowly and are susceptible to rotting. Seedling growth also may be slow in cool temperatures. Plant two crops of bush beans 2 to 3 weeks apart for a longer harvest period. Snap beans should be kept picked to keep plants producing heavily. Harvest snap beans when the pods are full-sized. The pods will break easily with a snap when they are ready. The seed should not cause the pods to bulge.

Half-runner beans have a growth habit between that of bush and pole beans, producing beans usually used as snap beans. Though they have runners about 3 feet (90 cm) long, half-runners are generally grown like bush beans. Trellising, however, may increase production of these already heavy yielders.

Pole-type beans come in many varieties, generally bearing over a longer period than bush types and yielding more in the same amount of space because they require trellising. Pole beans are natural climbers but will not interweave themselves through horizontal wires. A tripod support can be made with three wooden poles or large branches that are lashed together at the top. Five to six seeds are planted in a circle 6 to 8 inches (15 to 20 cm) from each pole. Many types of homemade trellises work well as long as they provide the needed support. Trellises should be 6 to 8 feet (1.8 to 2.4 m) tall and sturdy enough to withstand strong winds and rain.

Nutritional Value of Snap Beans (green beans, includes Italian, green, and yellow varieties)

Serving size: 1/2 cup, boiled (62 g)

Calories	22
Fat	0.2 g
Calories from fat	8%
Cholesterol	0
Sodium	2 mg
Protein	1.2 g

Primary Nutrients		% RDA (m)	% RDA (f)	% Min. Requirement
Vitamin C	6 mg	6.7	8.0	
Iron	0.8 mg	10.0	4.4	
Folic Acid	21 mcg	5.3	5.3	
Carbohydrate	4.9 g			
Dietary fiber	1.1 g			
Potassium	185 mg			5

Nutritional Value of Lima Beans

Serving size: 1/2 cup, boiled (94 g)

Calories	109
Fat	0.35 g
Calories from fat	3%
Cholesterol	0
Sodium	2 mg
Protein	7.3 g
Carbohydrate	19.7 g
Dietary fiber	6.8 g

Primary Nutrients		% RDA (m)	% RDA (f)	% Min. Requirement
Folic Acid	78 mcg	19.5	19.5	
Iron	2.25 mg	28.1	12.5	
Thiamine	0.15 mg	12.5	14	
Magnesium	41 mg	9.8	12.8	
Zinc	0.9 mg	8.2	11.3	
Potassium	478 mg			24

Nutritional Value of Pinto Beans

Serving size: 1/2 cup, boiled (86 g)

Calories	117
Fat	0.4 g
Calories from fat	3%
Cholesterol	0
Sodium	2 mg
Protein	7.0 g
Carbohydrate	21.8 g
Dietary fiber	3.4 g

Primary Nutrients		% RDA (m)	% RDA (f)	% Min. Requirement
Folic Acid	147 mcg	36.8	36.8	
Iron	2.24 mg	28.0	12.4	
Thiamine	0.16 mg	13.3	15	
Magnesium	48 mg	11.4	15	
Vitamin B$_6$	0.14 mg	10.8	10.8	
Zinc	0.93 mg	8.5	11.6	
Calcium	41 mg	4.1	4.1	
Potassium	400 mg			20

Problem Diagnosis for Beans

Problem	Probable cause
Rotten seed, or seedlings collapse soon after they come up.	**damping-off fungi; seedcorn maggot**
Comments	
Fungi can rot seed or seedlings. Do not plant in cold, moist soils.	
Yellow leaves; weak, wilted dying plants; sunken, red oval spots at base of stem.	**Rhizoctonia root or stem rot**
Comments	
Favored by warm soil temperatures. Remove old plant debris. Rotate crops. Use registered fungicide.	
Wilted, stunted plants; yellow leaves.	**wet or dry soil; poor fertility**
Comments	
Provide good drainage. Do not overwater. Irrigate properly. Mulch in summer. Incorporate compost or manure before planting.	
Plants wilt, turn yellow. Roots and belowground stems have red spots that turn brown and decay.	**Fusarium root rot**
Comments	
Caused by soilborne fungus. Destroy infected plants. Use soil solarization methods. Disease can be introduced on transplants. Rotate planting area.	
Fine whitish or yellowish stippling on upper leaf surface. Fine grayish webbing on undersurface of leaves. Leaves look burned when heavily infested.	**spider mites**
Comments	
Irrigate adequately. Wash mites off leaves. Apply predatory mites or soap-based insecticide.	
Curled, deformed leaves. Black sooty mold. Leaves shiny from honeydew. Plants may be stunted.	**aphids**
Comments	
Use soap spray. Control ants with sticky barrier or insecticide.	
White stippling on upper surface of leaves with tip and margin burn. Undersurface of leaves shows small, white cast skins of insects.	**leafhoppers**
Comments	
Consult UC IPM pest note series or Flint 1998 for management options.	
Yellow leaves with black sooty mold; leaves shiny from honeydew. Clouds of tiny white insects fly when plant is disturbed.	**whiteflies**
Comments	
A nuisance that does not reduce yields.	
Stunted seedling plants with distorted leaves; yellowed leaves.	**thrips**
Comments	
Adults are tan to black and look like slivers of wood; young are yellow. Feed on plant growing points. Larger plants less affected than seedlings. Plants will outgrow and recover.	

Scarlet runner beans are a type of pole bean that is quite ornamental as well as productive and delicious. The vines grow rapidly, producing beautiful red flowers and beans, which may be harvested as snap beans when young and as green shell beans later. Beans are ready to pick in 75 to 85 days, and several pounds are produced per plant. The value of scarlet runner beans is mainly ornamental, although the lush 6- to 15-foot (180 to 450 cm) vines can be used to cover arbors, trellises, or fences. An added feature is that the flowers are attractive to hummingbirds. According to some catalogs, the scarlet runner bean grows best in cooler weather than standard beans prefer; in some very hot areas, the vines may not keep producing all summer, as they will in cooler regions. Keeping maturing beans picked off will prolong the life of the vines.

Lima beans are available in bush or pole types. Bush limas mature more slowly (65 to 75 days) than snap beans (50 to 60 days) but about 10 to 15 days earlier than pole limas. Pole-type limas have better yields and produce longer than bush forms. The soil temperature must be 65°F (18°C) for 5 days for lima beans to germinate well. Because the large seed store considerable amounts of carbohydrates, limas are quite susceptible to soil fungi and bacteria, which find these foods as nutritious as we do; the sooner the seedling starts using the stored food, the better. Seed treated with antifungal agents will help improve germination rates. Soil should be kept moist (but not soaking wet) until the seedlings come through the ground; do not allow a crust to form on the soil, because the seedlings will have trouble pushing through. Prevent crusting and conserve moisture by spreading a light mulch over the seeded row. A cold, wet spell can cause lima flowers to drop, as can excessively hot and dry periods, reducing yields. Baby limas or butter beans are less susceptible to blossom drop problems. Harvest lima beans when pods are bright green and the seeds are full-sized. The ends of the pod will be spongy.

Southern peas are not actually beans or peas, but are in a separate genus; however, they are used in the same ways. Three commonly grown types are black-eyed pea, cream pea, and crowder pea. Southern peas may be harvested in the green shell or in the dried pea stage. The yard-long or asparagus bean is related to black-eyed peas and has similar fla-

Problem Diagnosis for Beans cont.

Problem	Probable cause
Holes, skeletonized areas on leaves, flowers. Pollen eaten. Chewed leaves.	**cucumber beetles**
Comments	
Greenish, yellowish beetles ¼ inch (7 mm) long with black spots, black head.	
Buds and flowers drop off. Maturing beans pitted, blemished.	**lygus bugs**
Comments	
A few can be tolerated.	
Blossoms drop off.	**hot weather (>90ºF [>32ºC]); low soil moisture; smog during blossoming period**
Comments	
Plant early to avoid hot weather during flowering and fruiting period. Do not let soil dry out too much between irrigations.	
Poor yield; stunted plants. Roots appear to have knots or beads.	**nematodes**
Comments	
Most common in sandy soils Rotate crops. Soil solarization.	
Fluffy, white mycelium growing on leaves, stems, or pods. General rotting. Wilted, water-soaked leaves.	**white mold**
Comments	
Caused by a fungus. Increase spacing between plants to improve air circulation. Rotate crops. Remove old plant debris and broadleaf weeds.	
Brown spots without yellow halos on leaves and pods; withered leaves.	**fungal disease (any of several)**
Comments	
Submit sample for laboratory diagnosis.	
Small brown spots surrounded by yellow halos on leaves and pods; withered leaves.	**bacterial blight**
Comments	
Avoid overhead watering. Use registered copper bactericide.	
Mottled, distorted leaves; leaves may be thickened, brittle, easily broken from plant. Stunted plants. Poor yields.	**mosaic virus**
Comments	
Spread from plant to plant by aphids and leafhoppers. Remove diseased plants. Remove broadleaf weeds that serve as virus reservoir.	
Tiny white grubs inside seeds within pod. Circular exit holes may be visible in seed where adult weevils emerged.	**bean weevil**
Comments	
Field and storage pest. Remove and destroy bean plants immediately after harvest.	
Holes in pods; seed hollowed and eaten.	**lycaenid pod borers**
Comments	
Grublike caterpillars that become tiny butterflies as adults. Consult UC IPM pest note series or Flint 1998 for management options.	

vor, but the entire pod may be eaten. On trellised vines, pods may be produced which are 1½ to 2 feet (45 to 60 cm) long. ("Yard-long" is stretching it a bit!) Asparagus beans need warm temperatures and a long growing season to do well. Look for seed in novelty, gourmet, Oriental, or children's sections of seed catalogs.

Soybeans are increasing in popularity in home gardens because of their high nutritional value (protein content) and versatility. Catalogs often list them as edible soybeans; all soybeans are actually edible, but those in garden catalogs have been bred to do well under ordinary garden conditions, requiring a shorter season and not growing as tall as the field types. There is also a difference in flavor and texture, as there is between sweet and field corn. Soybeans are less sensitive to frost and may have fewer insect problems than standard beans. Soybeans are quite delicious when harvested as green shell beans but may also be allowed to dry on the vine. The pods of soybeans are quite difficult to open; cook for a few minutes to soften the pod before removing the beans.

Beans used primarily as dried beans are many and varied. Many can be used green but dry well for easy storage. In the small garden, growing dry beans is somewhat impractical, because the amount of space required to raise a large enough quantity for storage is great. Many types of dry beans may be purchased in supermarkets at a very low cost, so it may be more worthwhile to grow higher-value crops in the limited space. However, if you have a very large garden area and a desire to sit on the front porch rocking away and shelling beans in the fall, they are worth a try. Some varieties available to gardeners are either rare or completely unavailable in the supermarket.

The horticultural (October) bean is very widely grown in parts of the state. The colorful pods and beans of the horticultural bean make it an attractive addition to the garden and kitchen. The seeds of pinto beans look similar to those of the horticultural beans but are smaller. They are used widely as brown beans and as refried beans in Mexican dishes. Black beans or black turtle beans make an unusual, delicious black-colored soup. They are easy to grow if given plenty of air movement to prevent the disease problems to which they are susceptible. Kidney beans are the popular chili and baking bean, available in deep red or white types. Navy pea and Great Northern beans are used in soups and as baked beans.

Problem	Probable cause
Thin, white, powdery growth on leaves, pods, debris.	**powdery mildew**
Comments	
A fungal disease. Use resistant varieties. Spray leaves with strong spray of water. Prune off infected tissue. Rotate plants. Remove old plants. Use registered fungicide.	
Failure to set pods.	**excessive fertilizer or high temperatures; mature pods left on vines**
Comments	
Do not overfertilize. Plant earlier in season before it gets too hot. Pick pods regularly; mature pods cause seed production rather than pod set.	

Mung beans, native to India, have enjoyed a rise in popularity because of their use as sprouts in Oriental dishes and salads, and gardeners can now find seed available for home production. Mung beans require 90 days of warm weather for good yield in the garden. Garbanzos, or chickpeas, produce plants that do not look like other bean plants. Garbanzos are actually neither true beans nor peas, but are leguminous. Their fine-textured foliage is an attractive addition to the garden. Plant many seed; the meaty seed, like limas, tend to rot if they do not germinate and grow rapidly. Each pod also contains only one or two seed. These nutty-flavored beans of unusual texture are good roasted, in salads, and in soups. Garbanzos also require a warm climate and a long (100-day) growing season.

Fava beans, or broad beans, are quite hardy. In cool climates they are often substituted for limas. Favas are sown early in spring or late summer, as they do not grow well in warm weather. It should be noted that some people of Mediterranean origin have a genetic trait (enzyme deficiency) that causes a severe allergic reaction to fava beans. People of this descent should sample the beans in small quantities first.

Beet (*Beta vulgaris*)

Recommended Varieties (Disease Resistance)

- Ruby Queen (AAS)
- Detroit Dark Red
- Little Ball (gourmet baby beet)
- Early Wonder
- Burpee's Golden Beet (for greens and root)

Beets do best in a mild climate, but they grow adequately in warmer climates. However, if temperatures are high when the crop is maturing, some color loss and zoning (internal development of white circles) occur. Low temperatures—below 50°F (10°C)—for 2 to 3 weeks may cause seed stalks to develop before plant roots mature. In regions where the leafhopper that transmits the curly top virus is prevalent, early plantings allow the crop to mature before the virus develops.

In most sections of California, plant beets in January or February for harvest in the spring. Beets planted in August are ready for harvest by November or December. Thin when the plants are 4 inches (10 cm) high. At the end of the harvest period, leave roots in the ground and pull them up as desired. Plant roots of 2 inches (5 cm) or less in diameter produce the highest-quality beets.

Nutritional Value of Beets
Serving size: ½ cup slices, boiled (85 g)

Calories	26
Fat	0.09
Calories from fat	0%
Cholesterol	0
Sodium	42 mg
Protein	0.9 g
Carbohydrate	5.7 g

Primary Nutrients		% RDA (m)	% RDA (f)	% Min. Requirement
Dietary fiber	1.4 g			
Folic Acid	45 mcg	11.3	11.3	
Magnesium	31 mg	7.4	9.7	
Vitamin C	5 mg	5.6	6.7	
Iron	0.53 mg	6.7	2.9	
Potassium	266 mg			13

Problem Diagnosis for Beets

Problem	Probable cause
Small, circular spots with light centers and dark borders on leaves.	Cercospora leaf spot
Comments	
A fungal disease. Pick off and destroy affected leaves.	
Cracked roots and black areas on surface and inside roots. Stunted plants.	boron deficiency
Test soil. Maintain pH between 6 and 7. Apply micronutrients.	
Leaf margins rolled upward; brittle leaves puckered along veins. Stunted plants.	curly top virus
Comments	
Spread by beet leafhoppers. Control leafhoppers that spread the virus by practicing weed control.	
Misshapen roots.	overcrowding; lumpy, heavy clay soil
Comments	
Thin beets early.	
Cracked roots.	inadequate watering
Comments	
Maintain adequate soil moisture.	
Small holes on leaves.	flea beetle
Comments	
Use rotenone with insecticidal soap. Control weeds.	
Scarred or tunneled roots.	root maggot
Comments	
Destroy infected plants next year. Work in registered insecticide when preparing soil.	
Hard, woody beets.	overmaturity; drought
Comments	
Harvest at proper time. Water consistently.	
Tunnels in leaves.	leafminers
Comments	
Remove infested leaves. Spray insecticide.	
Leaves webbed together; eggs in rows on undersides of leaves.	beet webworms
Comments	
Clip off webbed leaves. Destroy caterpillars. Control weeds.	

Broccoli (*Brassica oleracea* var. *italica*)

Recommended Varieties (Disease Resistance)

- Green Comet (AAS, H)
- Premium Crop (AAS)
- Green Goliath
- Green Duke
- Green Valiant
- Emperor (BR, DM, HS)
- Packman

Broccoli matures in 60 to 110 days, depending on the time of year and the variety planted. Late-season varieties (those that overwinter) are not suitable for planting in the home garden. Broccoli grows in most of the cooler areas of the state throughout the year. In the warmer interior valleys, you can grow a fall crop and sometimes an early-spring crop. If temperatures get too high, broccoli will bolt into premature flower stalks that will bloom and go to seed.

The immature flower heads, parts of the attached small leaves, and a considerable portion of the stem—4 to 8 inches (10 to 20 cm)—are edible. Harvest before the flower buds open. One planting may produce for as

Nutritional Value of Broccoli

Serving size: ¹/₂ cup chopped, boiled (78 g)

Calories	22
Fat	0.3 g
Calories from fat	12%
Cholesterol	0
Sodium	20 mg
Protein	2.3 g
Carbohydrate	4.0 g
Dietary fiber	2.0 g

Primary Nutrients		% RDA (m)	% RDA (f)	% Min. Requirement
Vitamin C	58 mg	64.4	77.3	
Vitamin A	108 RE	12.0	15.4	
Folic Acid	39 mcg	9.8	9.8	
Vitamin B⁶	0.11 mg	8.5	8.5	
Riboflavin	0.09 mg	6.9	8.2	
Iron	0.65 mg	8.1	3.6	
Magnesium	19 mg	4.5	5.9	
Potassium	228 mg			11

Problem Diagnosis for Broccoli

Problem	Probable cause
Irregular holes in leaves; chewed leaves. Small seedling plants destroyed.	caterpillars (cabbage loopers, armyworms); snails, slugs
Comments	
Bacillus thuringiensis is very effective.	
Small holes in leaves; chewed growing points in young plants. Loose cocoons about ⅓ inch (0.8 cm) long on leaves.	diamondback moth caterpillar
Comments	
Bacillus thuringiensis is very effective. Older plants not damaged. Destroy weeds (mustard-type) before planting.	
Deformed, curled leaves. Colonies of gray-green insects on leaves. Sticky honeydew.	aphids
Comments	
Use insecticidal soap spray. Control ants with sticky barrier or insecticide. Encourage beneficials.	
Distorted leaves turning plant brown. Wilted plants.	harlequin bug
Comments	
Insects suck fluids from tissue. Handpick bugs and egg masses. Remove old, non-productive cole crops (wild radish, mustard) because they're alternate hosts.	
Tunnels through roots. Plants fail to grow; may wilt, die. Feeding tunnels in germinating seedlings, which fail to produce plants.	cabbage maggot
Comments	
Prevent infestation. No practical control when maggots occur on growing crop.	
Stunted, wilted plants. Yellowish leaves. Small, glistening white specks on roots.	cyst nematode
Comments	
Rotate crops. Do not plant cole crops on same site year after year.	
Wilted plants. Swollen, misshapen roots; roots rot. Plant dies in later stages.	clubroot
Comments	
Disease caused by a soilborne fungus. Common in acid soils. Add lime if pH is below 7.2. Rotate out of crucifer crops for at least 2 years.	
Irregular yellowish areas on upper leaf surface; grayish powder on undersides.	downy mildew
Comments	
Improve air circulation. Plant resistant varieties. Tolerate disease.	
Heads suddenly split.	improper watering
Comments	
Do not allow soil to get too dry. If it gets too dry, apply water slowly at first.	
Bolting.	physiological disorder
Comments	
Plant at right time.	
Heads soft and rotten.	bacterial soft rot
Comments	
Rotate crops. Plant in well-drained soil.	
Leaves riddled with shot holes.	flea beetles
Comments	
Control weeds. Use rotenone with insecticidal soap.	

long as 3 months in the late fall or winter because of production from axillary shoots that produce small heads after the main one is removed.

It is best not to plant *Brassica* family crops (cole crops such as cabbage, broccoli, cauliflower, brussels sprouts, turnips, collard and mustard greens) in the same spot year after year, because diseases and insect pests will build up. Rotate crops in your garden.

Brussels Sprouts (*Brassica oleracea* var. *gemmifera*)

Recommended Varieties (Disease Resistance)

- Jade Cross (AAS)
- Long Island Improved
- Prince Marvel

Brussels sprouts do much better along the coast where there is a long, cool growing season than they do in warmer areas. The plants require 80 to 100 days from transplanting until the first sprouts mature. Set out transplants when they are 7 to 8 weeks old. Sprouts form in the axis of each leaf and are clustered around the main erect stem. You can

Nutritional Value of Brussels Sprouts
Serving size: ½ cup, boiled (78 g)

Calories	30
Fat	0.4 g
Calories from fat	12%
Cholesterol	0
Sodium	17 mg
Protein	2.0 g
Carbohydrate	6.8 g
Dietary fiber	3.4 g

Primary Nutrients		% RDA (m)	% RDA (f)	% Min. Requirement
Vitamin C	48 mg	53.3	64.0	
Folic Acid	47 mcg	11.8	11.8	
Vitamin B$_6$	0.14 mg	10.8	10.8	
Iron	0.94 mg	11.8	5.2	
Thiamin	0.08 mg	6.7	7.2	
Vitamin A	56 RE	6.2	8.0	
Potassium	247 mg			12

harvest for a month or more, as the sprouts mature from the bottom of the plant upward. Pick the sprouts when they are green and hard, approximately 1 to 2 inches (2.5 to 5 cm) in diameter, and before the outer leaves have a slightly yellow appearance. Break away the leaf just below the sprout and snap off the sprout. Harvest upward along the stem to the point where the sprouts are too small. Allow these small sprouts to remain on the stem for further development.

It is best not to plant cabbage family crops (cole crops such as cabbage, broccoli, cauliflower, and brussels sprouts) in the same spot year after year, because diseases and insect pests will build up. Rotate crops within your garden.

Problem Diagnosis for Brussels Sprouts

See "Problem Diagnosis for Broccoli." Many of the cole crops (cabbage, broccoli, cauliflower, and brussels sprouts) suffer from the same diseases, insect pests, and cultural problems. Note for brussels sprouts: If brussels sprouts have loose tufts of leaves instead of firm heads, the sprouts probably developed during weather that was too hot.

Cabbage (*Brassica oleracea* var. *capitata*)

Recommended Varieties (Disease Resistance)

Early (<100 days from time of planting to harvest)

- Stonehead (AAS, F)
- Early Jersey Wakefield (F)
- Darkri, small heads
- Golden Acre (F)
- Copenhagen Market

Late, >100 days from time of planting to harvest

- Premium Flat Dutch
- Danish Roundhead

Red

- Ruby Ball Hybrid (AAS)
- Red Head (AAS, F)

Savoy

- Savoy Ace (AAS, F)
- Savoy King (AAS, BS)

Along the coast, cabbage grows year-round. Low temperatures may cause early bolting in young plants. Avoid this problem by planting slow-bolting types or delay planting until the weather warms up. In the interior valleys, cabbage does well when plants mature from late fall to early spring. Plants started in flats are ready for transplanting in about 8 weeks. Harvest when the heads are quite firm and well filled. Some cabbages can be kept reasonably well in the field during cool weather, and they

Nutritional Value of Cabbage (Red)
Serving size: ½ cup, shredded, boiled (75g)

Calories	16		
Fat	0.2 g		
Calories from fat	13%		
Cholesterol	0		
Sodium	6 mg		
Protein	0.8 g		
Carbohydrate	3.5 g		
Dietary fiber	1.8 g		

Primary Nutrients		% RDA (m)	% RDA (f)	% Min. Requirement
Vitamin C	26 mg	28.9	34.7	

Problem Diagnosis for Cabbage

Problem	Probable cause
Deformed, curled leaves; colonies of gray-green insects on leaves. Sticky honeydew.	aphids
Comments Use insecticidal soap spray. Control ants with sticky barrier or insecticide. Encourage beneficials.	
Irregular holes in leaves; chewed leaves. Small seedling plants destroyed.	caterpillars (cabbage loopers, armyworms); snails, slugs
Comments *Bacillus thuringiensis* is very effective.	
Tunnels through roots. Plants fail to grow, may wilt, die. Feeding tunnels in germinating seedlings, which fail to produce plants.	cabbage maggot
Comments Prevent infestation. Rotate crops. No practical control when maggots occur on growing crop. See fig. 14.3.	
Distorted leaves turning brown. Wilted plants.	harlequin bug
Comments Insects suck fluids from plant tissue. Hand-pick bugs and egg masses. Remove old, nonproductive cole crops (wild radish, mustard) because they're alternate hosts.	
Leaves riddled with shot holes.	flea beetles
Comments Control weeds. Use rotenone with insecticidal soap.	
Poor heading.	overcrowding; dry soil; root rot
Comments Thin plants early. Irrigate properly. Rotate crops; remove old plant debris.	
Stunted, yellowed plants.	poor fertility; dry soil; *Fusarium* fungus
Comments Test soil. Irrigate properly. Use resistent varieties.	
Small holes in leaves; loose cocoons about ⅓ inch (0.8 cm) long on leaves. Chewed growing points in young plants.	diamondback moth caterpillar
Comments *Bacillus thuringiensis* is very effective. Older plants not damaged. Destroy weeds (mustard-type) before planting.	
Stunted, wilted plants. Yellowish leaves. Small, glistening white specks on roots.	cyst nematode
Comments Rotate crops. Do not plant cole crops on same site year after year.	
Wilted plants. Swollen, misshapen roots; roots rot. Plant dies in later stages.	clubroot
Comments Disease caused by a soilborne fungus. Common in acid soils. Add lime if pH below 7.2. Rotate for at least 2 years.	

also store well after cutting. Overmature cabbage heads may burst.

It is best not to plant cabbage family crops (cole crops such as cabbage, broccoli, cauliflower, and brussels sprouts) in the same spot year after year, because diseases and insect pests will build up. Rotate crops within your garden.

Cabbage, Chinese (*Brassica pekinensis*)

Recommended Varieties (Disease Resistance)

- Chinese—Michili
- Jade Pagoda (B)
- Michili
- Chinese—Napa
- China Pride (BSR, DM, TB)
- Pak Choi or Mustard Cabbage
- Lei Choi
- Joi Choi

Chinese cabbage is extremely sensitive to climate. The crop matures in 80 to 90 days. Flower stalks develop under long-day summer conditions, which usually rule out spring planting unless your garden is located in a cool, coastal climate. Delay planting until mid or late summer so that plants mature in the fall. Plantings made later than summer may not head well because of too much cold weather. The plant grows rapidly and yields

Nutritional Value of Cabbage (Chinese)

Serving size: ½ cup, shredded, boiled (85 g)

Calories	10
Fat	0.1 g
Calories fromfat	9%
Cholesterol	0
Sodium	29 mg
Protein	1.3 g
Carbohydrate	1.5 g
Dietary fiber	1.4 g

Primary Nutrients		% RDA (m)	% RDA (f)	% Min. Requirement
Vitamin C	22 mg	24.4	29.3	
Vitamin A	218 RE	24.2	31.1	
Calcium	79 mg	7.9	7.9	
Iron	0.88 mg	11.0	4.9	
Potassium	315 mg			8

Problem	Probable cause
Head cracking.	**excess nitrogen fertilizer; excess water taken up by plant, may be overmature**
Comments Fertilize properly. Do not overwater. Harvest heads at maturity.	
Heads suddenly split.	**improper watering; drought; hot, dry weather followed by excessive water uptake**
Comments Do not allow soil to get too dry. If it gets too dry, apply water slowly at first. Prune roots to reduce water uptake and slow growth.	
Bolting.	**physiological disorder**
Comments Plant at right time of year.	
Heads soft and rotten.	**bacterial soft rot**
Comments Rotate crops; plant in well-drained soil.	

Problem Diagnosis for Chinese Cabbage

See "Problem Diagnosis for Cabbage."

well. Harvest when the cabbage is well-headed and firm.

Cantaloupe (Muskmelon) and Honeydew (*Cucumis melo*)

Recommended Varieties (Disease Resistance)
Orangeflesh

- Samson (AAS, F, PM)
- Ambrosia (DM, PM)
- Saticoy Hybrid (F, M, PM)
- Topmark (PM)
- Bush Star (AAS, F, PM)
- Honeybush (bush plant) (F)
- Crenshaw
- Casaba
- Galia
- Rocky Sweet

Honeydew

- Tam Dew, fruit slips when mature (DM, PM)
- Fruit Punch, distinctive flavor
- Limelight (F)

Melons require high temperatures during the growing season and therefore do best in warm interior valleys. Most varieties require 90 days to produce fruit.

Vines have separate male and female flowers, and bees are required for pollination. To prevent killing bees, use insecticides late in the evening, if at all. Male blooms form first and do not set fruit; thus, do not be concerned when male flowers fall off. A heavy rain when melons are ripening may cause some of the

Nutritional Value of Cantaloupe
Serving size: 1 cup cubes (160 g)

Calories	57
Fat	0.4 g
Calories from fat	6%
Cholesterol	0
Sodium	14 mg
Protein	1.4 g
Carbohydrate	13.4 g
Dietary fiber	1.3 g

Primary Nutrients		% RDA (m)	% RDA (f)	% Min. Requirement
Vitamin C	68 mg	75.6	90.7	
Vitamin A	516 RE	57.3	73.7	
Vitamin B$_6$	0.18 mg	13.8	13.8	
Folic Acid	27 mcg	6.8	6.8	
Niacin	0.9 mg	5.6	6.4	
Magnesium	17 mg	4.0	5.3	
Potassium	494 mg			25

Nutritional Value of Honeydew (green flesh)
Serving size: 1 cup cubes (160 g)

Calories	60
Fat	0.2 g
Calories from fat	3%
Cholesterol	0
Sodium	17 mg
Protein	0.8 g
Carbohydrate	15.6 g

Primary Nutrients		% RDA (m)	% RDA (f)	% Min. Requirement
Vitamin C	42 mg	46.7	56.0	
Potassium	461 mg			23

Problem Diagnosis for Cantaloupe

Problem	Probable cause
Deformed, curled leaves; small, soft-bodied insects on undersides of leaves. Sticky honeydew or black, sooty mold may be present.	aphids
Comments Use insecticidal soap.	
Fine stippling on leaves; yellow or brown leaves. Leaf undersides are silver-gray with fine webbing and yellow, orange, or red dots.	spider mites
Comments Use oil or soap spray.	
Leaves turn yellow. Honeydew or sooty mold present. Clouds of tiny white insects fly up when plant is disturbed.	whiteflies
Comments Remove infested plants as quickly as possible. Remove lower, infested leaves of plants not totally infested.	
Coarse, white stippling on upper surface of leaves; leaves may turn brown.	leafhoppers
Comments Consult UC IPM pest note series or Flint 1998 for management options.	
Blotches or tunnels on leaves.	leafminers
Comments Consult UC IPM pest note series or Flint 1998 for management options.	
Angular necrotic areas on leaves.	angular leafspot
Comments Caused by waterborne bacterium. Avoid wetting foliage with irrigation water.	
Swelling or beads on roots. Wilted plants. Poor yields.	nematodes
Comments Rotate crops. Use soil solarization.	
Holes chewed in leaves. Scarring of runners, young fruit, and crown. Wilting. Beetles are visible.	cucumber beetles
Comments Beetles are yellow-green with black stripes or spots. Use pyrethrins.	
Leaves have small specks that turn yellow, then brown. Vines wilt from point of attack to end of vine.	squash bug
Comments Trap adults beneath boards in spring. Turn over boards in morning and kill bugs. Pick off adults, young, egg masses.	
White, powdery spots on leaves and stems. Spots may enlarge and completely cover leaf. Defoliation may occur. Yields reduced.	powdery mildew
Comments Spores of powdery mildew fungus are spread by wind and air currents. Disease is less severe in hot, dry weather. Use resistant varieties. Dusting with sulfur can be effective. Remove old plant debris.	
Yellow spots on upper leaf surfaces. Grayish, fuzzy growth on undersides of spots.	downy mildew
Comments A fungal disease. Use resistant varieties. Remove old plant debris.	

fruit to split open. Fruit in contact with soil may develop rotten spots or be damaged by insects on the bottom. Place a board or a few inches of mulching material, such as sawdust or straw, beneath each fruit when it is nearly full-sized.

Harvest melons when the fruit is at "full slip," that is, when a slight crack completely circles the stem where it is attached to the fruit. If you harvest at the right time, you can pull off the stem, leaving a smooth cavity. However, the slip does not develop in crenshaw, casaba, or some honeydew varieties. Harvest these melons when the fruit softens at the blossom end and starts to turn yellow. Shade crenshaw fruit to protect from sunburn. Melons may only be stored for a short time, except casaba and honeydew, which store well for several weeks.

Melons are relatives of cucumbers, squash, pumpkin, and watermelon, all of which are known as the cucurbits. They suffer from similar pests and diseases. See "Fruit Set Problems in Squash, Melons and Cucumbers," in the squash section below.

Carrot (*Daucus carota*)

Recommended Varieties (Disease Resistance)

Baby or Gourmet, 3–5 inches [7.5–12.5 cm]; good in containers or garden

- Short 'n Sweet
- Little Finger
- Amstel
- Kundulus, round
- Lady Finger
- Amsterdam
- Minicor

Elevated Vitamin A

- A-Plus Hybrid, 8 inches (20 cm), tapered
- Vitasweet 500, 4–5 inches (10–12.5 cm), tapered
- Vitasweet 721, 9–10 inches (22.5–25 cm), slender
- Vitasweet 750, 5–8 inches (12.5–20 cm), blunt tip
- Vitasweet 771, 10 inches (25 cm) slender

Problem	Probable cause
Stunted plants. Small leaves with irregularly shaped light and dark spots (mottled). Yields reduced.	mosaic virus
Comments Transmitted by aphids. Remove infected plants as soon as detected. Control aphids. Control weeds. Aluminum foil is effective as soil mulch to reduce infection Deformed fruit is edible.	
Poor fruit set.	insufficient pollination; lack of bee pollinators
Comments Hand-pollinate using artist's paintbrush. Bee activity may be low because of cool weather or insecticides.	
Misshapen or bitter fruit.	inadequate pollination; dry soil or high temperatures; poor soil fertility
Comments See comments above. Supply water. Get soil tested.	
Poor flavor. Lack of sweetness.	poor soil fertility; low potassium, magnesium, or boron
Comments Get soil tested and adjust fertilizer.	
Plants wilt and die, beginning with older crown leaves. Light brown streaks occur inside lower stem, runners, and root. Visible when split lengthwise.	Verticillium wilt
Comments Caused by soilborne fungus. Rotate crops. Avoid soil previously planted in potatoes, peppers, eggplant, tomatoes, or cucurbits.	
Plants wilt suddenly. Roots rot.	sudden wilt
Comments Fungal disease. Avoid water stress after fruit set. Avoid wetting soil to the crown. Improve drainage. Plant on raised beds.	
Runners turn yellow and wilt. Entire plant collapses. One-sided brown lesion may form on affected runner for 1–2 feet (30–60 cm).	Fusarium wilt
Comments Caused by soilborne fungus. Plant resistant varieties. Rotate out of cantaloupe for 5 years.	
Water-soaked and sunken, brown or black spots on fruit not restricted to blossom end.	belly rot
Comments Rotate crops. Improve drainage. Stake or cage to keep fruit off ground.	
Watersoaked, sunken, brown or black spot at blossom end of fruit.	blossom end rot
Comments Water during dry periods; keep soil moisture even; remove affected fruit. mulch	
Excessive vegetative growth.	planting too close together
Comments Increase plant spacing.	

Long, Tapered (7–10 inches (17.5–25 cm); require deep soil)

- Gold Pak 28 (AAS, C)
- Imperator
- Danvers

Medium-long, 5–6 inches (12.5–15 cm); for shallower soils

- Nantes
- Chantenay (A, C)
- Danvers

Carrot seed germinate best under cool, moist conditions in the spring, but they may be started in slightly warmer weather if the soil is kept moist. Use or prepare soil that is deep and friable to avoid misshapen roots. Do not plant in areas where young plants may be subject to long periods of cold temperatures, which favors bolting. Thin so that plant roots are 1 to 2 inches (2.5 to 5 cm) apart in the row.

Carrots are ready to harvest about 90 days after seeding but continue to grow and enlarge thereafter. Harvest when the roots are of good size but still tender. Carrots may be stored in the ground during cool winter months unless freezes are expected. If frosts are predicted, dig up and store the carrots. If carrots are left too long in the soil or allowed to overmature, the roots become tough, woody, and may crack.

Nutritional Value of Carrot

Serving size: 1 carrot (2½ oz), raw (72 g)

Calories	31
Fat	0.1 g
Calories from fat	3%
Cholesterol	0
Sodium	25 mg
Protein	0.7 g
Carbohydrate	7.3 g
Dietary fiber	2.3 g

Primary Nutrients		% RDA (m)	% RDA (f)	% Min. Requirement
Vitamin A	2,025 RE	225.0	289.1	
Vitamin C	7 mg	7.8	9.3	
Vitamin B6	0.11 mg	8.5	8.5	
Potassium	233 mg			6

Problem Diagnosis for Carrot

Problem	Probable cause
Carrots fail to emerge.	**soil crusting; high soil temperatures; seedling pests**
Comments	
Maintain uniform soil moisture until seedlings emerge. Protect soil surface from rain or sprinklers. Do not plant too deeply.	
Thin, spindly growth.	**weed competition**
Comments	
Control weeds.	
White growth on leaves.	**powdery mildew**
Comments	
Use fungicide if extensive. Sulfur may help.	
Carrots twist around each other.	**plants too close together**
Comments	
Thin carrots to 1–2 inches (2.5–5 cm) apart when plants are small.	
Carrots rot or have enlarged white "eyes."	**overwatering**
Comments	
Water less often. Do not plant carrots in heavy soil.	
Rotten roots. White fungus growth on soil surface and clinging to roots. Small, oval honey-colored to brown sclerotia in fungal growth.	**Southern blight or white mold**
Comments	
Caused by a fungus. Avoid planting in infested soil. Nitrogen fertilizers may help.	
Roots have surface tunnels filled with rusty mush. Stiff, white maggots may be visible, but no aboveground symptoms.	**carrot rust fly**
Comments	
A small fly that lays its eggs in crowns of carrots. Control weed hosts. Peel off damaged area before using. Harvest carrots as soon as possible. Do not store carrots in ground through winter.	
Roots hairy, forked, misshapen.	**root knot nematode; over watering; roots in contact with fertilizer pellets or fresh manure; hard soil or rocks; overcrowding**
Comments	
Rotate crops. Use soil solarization. Remove rocks in soil. Thin carrots early.	
Yellowed, curled leaves. Stunted plants.	**leafhoppers**
Comments	
Use insecticidal soap.	
Brown spots on leaves or roots.	**leaf blight**
Comments	
Avoid planting in infested soil. Nitrogen fertilizer may help.	
Tiny holes on leaves.	**flea beetles**
Comments	
Control weeds. Use rotenone with insecticidal soap.	
Inner leaves yellowed; outer leaves reddish-purple. Roots stunted and bitter.	**aster yellows**
Comments	
A mycoplasma disease. Remove affected plants. Control weeds. Control leafhoppers with insecticide.	
Green root tops.	**roots exposed to sunlight**
Comments	
Cover exposed roots with soil or mulch.	

Cauliflower (*Brassica oleracea* var. *botrytis*)

Recommended Varieties (Disease Resistance)

- Snow King (AAS)
- Snowball 'Y'
- Snow Crown (AAS)

There are many Snow and Snowball cauliflower selections from which to choose; Snowball Y is usually the most successful. Snowball A is an early producer. Cauliflower grows best in cool, fairly moist climates. Plants are ready for transplanting 8 weeks after seeding, or the crop can be direct-seeded in the garden. Snowball may be grown as both a fall and spring crop and can produce good heads within 2 months after transplanting. Late varieties require 4 to 6 months and are not recommended for planting in most home gardens.

Avoid any condition that may check plant growth. Adequate moisture is essential. Good vegetative growth is very important for subsequent growth of the cauliflower head. Interference with rapid, uniform growth may cause premature development of the head. Such heads are smaller than usual. Cauliflower is the cole crop most sensitive to temperature. Stresses such as cold soil or air temperatures in the spring, lack of fertility, water stress, insect damage, disease, and using transplants with poor root growth or root-

Nutritional Value of Cauliflower

Serving size: ¹/₂ cup, raw (50 g)

Calories	12
Fat	0.1 g
Calories from fat	8%
Cholesterol	0
Sodium	7 mg
Protein	1.0 g
Carbohydrate	2.5 g
Dietary fiber	1.2 g

Primary Nutrients		% RDA (m)	% RDA (f)	% Min. Requirement
Vitamin C	36 mg	40.0	48.0	
Vitamin B⁶	0.12 mg	9.2	9.2	
Folic Acid	33 mcg	8.3	8.3	
Potassium	178 mg			9

Problem Diagnosis for Cauliflower

Problem	Probable cause
Irregular holes in leaves; chewed leaves. Small seedling plants destroyed.	**caterpillars (cabbage loopers, armyworms); snails, slugs**
Comments	
Bacillus thuringiensis is very effective.	
Small holes in leaves. Chewed growing points in young plants. Loose cocoons about ⅓ inch (8 mm) long on leaves.	**diamondback moth caterpillar**
Comments	
Bacillus thuringiensis is very effective. Older plants not damaged. Destroy weeds (mustard type) before planting.	
Deformed, curled leaves. Colonies of gray-green insects on leaves. Sticky honeydew.	**aphids**
Comments	
Use insecticidal soap spray. Control ants with sticky barrier or insecticide. Encourage beneficials.	
Distorted leaves turning brown. Wilted plants.	**harlequin bug**
Comments	
Insects suck fluids from plant tissue. Handpick bugs and egg masses. Remove old, nonproductive cole crops (wild radish, mustard) because they're alternate hosts.	
Tunnels through roots. Plants fail to grow, may wilt, die. Feeding tunnels in germinating seedlings, which fail to produce plants.	**cabbage maggot**
Comments	
Prevent infestation. No practical control when maggots occur on growing crop (see fig. 14.3).	
Leaves riddled with shot holes.	**flea beetles**
Comments	
Control weeds. Use rotenone with insecticidal soap.	
Stunted, wilted plants. Leaves yellowish-colored. Small, glistening white specks on roots.	**cyst nematode**
Comments	
Rotate crops. Do not plant cole crops on same site year after year.	
Wilted plants. Swollen, misshapen roots. Roots rot; plant dies in later stages.	**clubroot**
Comments	
Disease caused by a soilborne fungus. Common in acid soils. Add lime if pH below 7.2. Rotate for at least 2 years.	
Irregular, yellowish areas on upper leaf surface; grayish powder on undersides.	**downy mildew**
Comments	
Improve air circulation. Plant resistant varieties. Tolerate it.	
Poor heading.	**overcrowding; dry soil; root rot**
Comments	
Thin plants early. Irrigate properly. Rotate; remove old plant debris.	
Heads yellow or brown instead of white.	**sunburn**
Comments	
When head is 3 inches (7.5 cm) in diameter, tie outer leaves around head with twine. Harvest in 4 to 7 days.	

bound before transplanting can result in a condition known as buttoning. Varieties that mature a short time after transplanting are more susceptible to stress than varieties that require a longer period to mature. Properly grown transplants, adequate fertility, regular irrigation, and good insect and disease control help to ensure a successful crop. Premature heading in cauliflower is more frequent in home gardens than in commercial plantings.

As the heads enlarge, they may become exposed to the sun and discolor. Avoid this by folding the leaves over the heads or by tying the leaves together to protect the developing curd from the sun. Harvest when the heads are of good size, usually 5 to 6 inches (12.5 to 15 cm) in diameter and still compact. As the heads become overmature, they tend to segment or spread apart and the surface becomes fuzzy.

It is best not to plant cole crops (cabbage, broccoli, cauliflower, and brussels sprouts) in the same spot year after year, since diseases and insect pests will build up. Rotate crops within your garden.

Celeriac (*Apium graviolens* var. *rapaceum*)

Recommended Varieties

- Alabaster
- Marble Ball
- Large Smooth Prague

Celeriac is often called celery root because the enlarged, bulbous root is the edible part of the plant. It tastes like mild celery. Follow the

Nutritional Value of Celeriac
Serving size: 3½ oz, boiled (100 g)

Calories	25		
Fat	0.2 g		
Calories from fat	7%		
Cholesterol	0		
Sodium	61 mg		
Protein	1.0 g		
Carbohydrate	5.9 g		
Dietary fiber	0.8 g		

Primary Nutrients		% RDA (m)	% RDA (f)
Vitamin C	4 mg	4.4	5.3

Problem Diagnosis for Cauliflower cont.

Problem	Probable cause
Head cracking; leaves may grow through head.	excess nitrogen fertilizer; hot, dry weather, overmature
Comments Fertilize properly. Plant so crop develops in mild or cool weather. Do not let soil dry out.	
Heads suddenly split.	sudden, heavy watering after prolonged dry period
Comments Do not allow soil to get too dry. If it gets too dry, apply water slowly at first. Prune roots to reduce water uptake and slow growth.	
Bolting.	physiological disorder
Comments Plant at right time.	
Heads soft and rotten.	bacterial soft rot
Rotate crops; plant in well-drained soil.	

Problem Diagnosis for Celery

Problem	Probable cause
Poor growth; stunted plants.	crop not well adapted to many areas of California
Comments Time planting so that crop matures during cool season. Plant recommended variety.	
Tough, bitter stalks.	high temperatures; dry soil; poor fertility; overmaturity
Comments Plant at proper time. Celery requires lots of water and high nitrogen. Harvest when tender.	
Blotches or tunnels in leaves.	leafminers
Comments Use registered insecticide.	
Brown or gray spots on leaves and stalks.	fungal leaf spot
Comments Use registered insecticide.	
Bolting.	physiological disorder
Comments Plant recommended varieties. Plant at right time.	
Twisted, brittle stalks. Stunted, yellowed plants.	aster yellows
Comments A mycoplasma disease. Remove infected plants. Control weeds. Control leafhopper vectors with insecticide.	
Heart of plant may be black.	calcium deficiency; improper soil pH
Comments Test soil. Maintain pH between 6.5 and 8. Water during dry periods. Calcium deficiency can be due to uneven water supply.	
Wilted plants; soft, watery rot on leaves and stalks.	fungal crown rot
Comments Rotate crops. Remove old plant debris. Apply registered fungicide.	

same cultural procedures as for growing celery. The crop is usually direct-seeded; transplants often produce poorly shaped roots. Harvest when the roots are 3 to 5 inches (7.5 to 12.5 cm) in diameter. You can then peel the roots and use them raw or cooked in salads, soups, and stews.

Problem Diagnosis for Celeriac

See "Problem Diagnosis for Celery."

Celery (*Apium graviolens var. dulce*)

Recommended Varieties (Disease Resistance)

- Giant Pascal (BR)
- Tall Utah 52-70
- Golden Self-Blanching, waxy-yellow petioles
- Matador

Celery is usually produced from transplants. If you grow it from seed, place a shallow covering of soil over the seed and keep the soil quite moist. Do not seed when temperatures are high; heat induces seed dormancy, and the seed do not germinate. Use transplants that are 10 to 12 weeks old. Celery is a cool-season crop that grows best with temperatures at 60° to 65°F (16° to 18°C), and it requires ample water and nitrogen fertilizer.

The crop is ready to cut 90 to 120 days after transplanting. Harvest by cutting below the ground through the taproot. The edible

Nutritional Value of Celery

Serving size: 1 stalk (7.5" or 19 cm), raw

Calories	6
Fat	0.1 g
Calories from fat	15%
Cholesterol	0
Sodium	35 mg
Protein	0.3 g
Carbohydrate	1.5 g
Dietary fiber	0.6 g

Primary Nutrients		% RDA (m)	% RDA (f)	% Min. Requirement
Vitamin C	4 mg	4.4	5.3	
Folic Acid	17 mcg	4.3	4.3	
Potassium	115 mg			6

portion is the fleshy leaf petiole. If long periods of cool temperatures occur during growth, seed stalk development may occur. Overmature plants show cracking and pithiness of the petioles.

Chard (*Beta vulgaris* var. *cicla*)

Recommended Varieties

- Arsentata
- Fordhook Giant
- Lucullus
- Rhubarb Chard (red leaf, stems)
- Rainbow
- Bright Lights

Chard requires the same care as beets, one of its close relatives, although chard is grown for its succulent stalks and flavorful leaves. Plant in late winter or early spring to avoid severe damage from curly top virus. Plants bear heavily and produce greens for most of the year. The leaves can be cooked or used fresh in salads. Chard is easy to grow and ready for harvest in 50 to 60 days. Harvest by cutting or breaking away a few of the outer, fully expanded leaves from each plant near the base. New leaves develop in the center of the plants as the older ones are cut away. You can harvest from one plant numerous times. If you do not harvest the outer leaves, they become stringy and lose tenderness. Chard is often called Swiss chard in vegetable gardening books.

Problem Diagnosis for Chard

See table 14.5 for general techniques for recognizing and managing the common problems associated with chard. Because beets are one of chard's close relatives, also see "Problem Diagnosis for Beets." Common disease problems in chard include curly top virus and nematodes. Common insect pests that attack chard include aphids, cabbage worms, flea beetles, and leafminers.

Problem Diagnosis for Chayote

See table 14.5 for general techniques for recognizing and managing the common problems associated with chayote. Common pathogens that attack chayote include powdery mildew and nematodes. Common insect pests that attack chayote include aphids, cucumber beetles, mites, squash bug, and squash vine borer.

Nutritional Value of Chard

Serving size: ½ cup, chopped, boiled (88 g)

Calories	18
Fat	0.1 g
Calories from fat	4%
Cholesterol	0
Sodium	158 mg
Protein	1.7 g
Carbohydrate	3.6 g

Primary Nutrients		% RDA (m)	% RDA (f)	% Min. Requirement
Vitamin A	276 RE	30.7	39.4	
Vitamin C	16 mg	17.8	21.3	
Magnesium	76 mg	18.0	24.0	
Iron	2.0 mg	25.0	11.1	
Calcium	51 mg	5.1	5.1	
Potassium	483 mg			13

Chayote (*Sechium edule*)

Recommended Varieties

No named varieties are available.

The chayote, native to Central America, looks like a mango-shaped squash and tastes like a mild squash. Chayote is a perennial vine similar in growth habit to cucumber. It can be grown in warm, coastal areas for fall and early winter harvest. Plant whole fruits in warm soil in the spring. Place them, with the stem end up, on a slant in the soil. Train the vines on a trellis. The flowers appear in early fall, and the first fruit matures about 30 days later. Harvest as soon as the fruits are full-grown (4 to 6 inches [10 to 15 cm] long).

Nutritional Value of Chayote

Serving size: ½ cup of pieces, boiled (80 g)

Calories	19
Fat	0.4 g
Calories from fat	18%
Cholesterol	0
Sodium	1 mg
Protein	0.5 g
Carbohydrate	4.1 g

Primary Nutrients		% RDA (m)	% RDA (f)	% Min. Requirement
Vitamin C	6 mg	6.7	8.0	
Potassium	138 mg			7

Chives (*Allium schoenoprasum*)

Recommended Varieties

No named varieties are available.

Grow chives from seed or by dividing an already-established plant. Chives are extremely suitable for growing in small pots or other mini-gardens. A minimum of 4 to 6 inches (10–15 cm) of soil and a pot diameter of 6 to 8 inches (15–20 cm) are recommended. Chives give a mild onion flavor to salads and other dishes. They are relatives of onions, garlic, and leeks, which are all members of the *Allium* family.

Nutritional Value of Chives

Serving size: 1 tbs, chopped, raw (3 g)

Calories	1
Fat	0
Calories from fat	0
Cholesterol	0
Sodium	0
Protein	0.1 g
Carbohydrate	0.1 g

Primary Nutrients

None of the nutrients meet or exceed 5% of the RDA

Problem Diagnosis for Chives

See table 14.5 for general techniques for recognizing and managing common problems associated with chives. Because chives are relatives of onions and garlic, they suffer from similar pest insects, diseases, and cultural problems. Also see "Problem Diagnosis for Onion."

Corn, Specialty and Sweet (*Zea mays*)

Recommended Specialty Varieties

Baby (Harvest baby corn when silks first appear and ears are quite small.)

- Baby Asian and other white, sweet corns
- Candystick

Ornamental

- Rainbow
- Strawberry Popcorn
- Blue Tortilla
- Indian Fingers, small, multicolored ears, shiny kernels
- Papoose, small, multicolored ears
- Ornamental Indian Corn

Popcorn

- Golden Hybrid, yellow
- White Cloud, white
- Black Popcorn, black kernel with white interior
- Peppy Hybrid, white

Recommended Sweet Varieties (Disease Resistance)

Standard Sugary

- Golden Cross Bantam, yellow (BW)
- Jubilee, yellow (SG, ST)
- Butter and Sugar, bicolor (BW, SCLB)
- Silver Queen, white (BW, SW)

Sugary-enhanced

- How Sweet It Is, white (AAS)
- Breeder's Choice, light yellow
- Kandy Korn, yellow
- Concord, bicolor

Super Sweet

- Early Xtra Sweet, yellow (AAS)
- Ivory 'n Gold Bicolor, bicolor
- Butterfruit, yellow
- Sweetie, yellow
- Illini Gold, yellow
- Butterfruit Bi-color, bicolor
- Escalade, bicolor
- Supersweet Jubilee (yellow)
- Maxim, yellow

There are three types of sweet corn varieties: standard sugary, sugary enhanced, and supersweet. Standard sugary types are the older varieties in which sugar in the kernels converts rapidly to starch after harvest. Sugary enhanced and supersweet types possess genes that increase sweetness and, in supersweet types, slow the conversion of sugar to starch after harvest. Supersweet types do not lose sweetness after harvest as quickly as the other two types. Some supersweet types are less creamy than standard or sugary enhanced types, which may decrease their use for canning or freezing.

Problem Diagnosis for Corn

Problem	Probable cause
Young plants chewed off at ground level.	cutworms

Comments
Remove weeds. Destroy crop residues.

Distorted leaves or stalks. Stalks may be bent or leaves may fail to unfurl.	herbicide injury; cold weather; aphids

Comments
Use herbicides carefully. Plant at proper time. Use insecticidal soap.

Worms up to 1¾ inches (4.5 cm) long eat down through kernels. Before tasseling, worms found in whorl of plant feeding on developing tassel.	corn earworm

Comments
Worms range in color from green to black with lengthwise stripes of various colors. Apply mineral oil with medicine dropper to silk just inside the ear tip 3–7 days after silks first appear. Use 20 drops/ear. Break off wormy end of ear and discard. Insecticides will not control worms inside ear. Preventive treatment of silks (above) kills worms before they enter ears.

Holes in leaves.	armyworm; corn earworm; various beetles; grasshoppers

Comments
Ignore or hand-pick insects. Loss of small amount of leaf tissue will not reduce yields.

Sticky, shiny leaves. Stunted plants. Insects visible.	aphids

Comments
Use insecticidal soap. Consult UC IPM pest note series or Flint 1998 for management options.

Mottled leaves; leaves die along margins. Slow growth.	mosaic virus

Comments
No control; certain varieties are more resistant.

Ears, tassels, leaves have gray, gnarled growths (galls) that become powdery.	common smut

Comments
Caused by a fungus. Remove and destroy galls as soon as found. Keep black powder in galls from getting into soil. Plant resistant varieties. Plant early. Problem is more common in later harvests.

Brown spots (pustules) on leaves with powdery, rust-colored spores.	rust

Comments
Caused by a fungus. Plant resistant varieties. Fungicides are available if needed. Favored by cool temperatures, high humidity, overhead sprinklers.

Sweet corn varieties also differ significantly in time to maturity and may be yellow, white, or bicolor. Most varieties planted are hybrids that have been bred for greater vigor and higher yields in addition to sweetness. A continuous harvest can be planned by planting early-, mid-, and late-season varieties, or by making successive plantings of the same variety every 2 weeks or when the last planting has three to four leaves (corn sown in early spring will take longer because of cool temperatures). Use only the earliest varieties for late-summer or early-fall plantings to assure good fall crop. Fall-maturing sweet corn will almost always be the highest quality, because cool nights in fall increase sugar content. Sweet corn grows well in warm climates, but, if temperatures are too hot, ears may fail to fill out normally and quality is reduced.

Pollination is a very important consideration in planting sweet corn. Because corn is wind-pollinated, block plantings of at least three to four short rows will be pollinated more successfully than one or two long rows. Good pollination is essential for full kernel development. Most types of corn cross-pollinate readily. To maintain desirable characteristics and high quality, be certain that supersweet types are isolated from standard sugary and sugary enhanced types since cross-pollination results in supersweet ears with tough, starchy kernels. A distance of 400 yards (365 m) or planting so that maturity dates are

Nutritional Value of Corn

Serving size: ½ cup, about equal to the kernels from one ear, boiled (82 g)

Calories	89
Fat	1.1 g
Calories from fat	11%
Cholesterol	0
Sodium	14 mg
Protein	2.7 g
Carbohydrate	20.6 g
Dietary fiber	3.0 g

Primary Nutrients		% RDA (m)	% RDA (f)	% Min. Requirement
Thiamin	0.18 mg	15.0	16.0	
Folic acid	38 mcg	9.5	9.5	
Vitamin C	5 mg	5.6	6.7	
Niacin	1.3 mg	8.1	9.3	
Magnesium	26 mg	6.2	8.1	
Potassium	192 mg			5

Problem	Probable cause
Incomplete kernel development; shriveled kernels.	poor pollination
Comments	
Can be caused by not planting enough corn at one time. Plant at least 3–4 rows at least 8 feet (2.4 m) long.	
	insufficient soil moisture
Comments	
Supply enough water, especially from silking to harvest.	
	hot weather, high winds 2–3 weeks before harvest
	inadequate fertilizer
Comments	
Fertilize as directed. Check for potassium deficiency. Plant varieties adapted to your area.	
	birds
Comments	
Put paper bag over ear after pollination.	
Ears only partly filled. Shortened silks.	**earwigs**
Comments	
Earwigs feed on silks and prevent pollination, killing kernels. Use traps. Check daily for earwigs and destroy.	
Brown lesions on stalks near joints; stalks rotten inside. Kernels pink or moldy.	**stalk and ear rot**
Comments	
Caused by several fungi. Remove old plant debris. Maintain uniform soil moisture.	
Stunted plants with yellow-green stripe or mosaic pattern; older leaves pale yellow.	**maize dwarf mosaic virus**
Comments	
Control weeds, esp. johnsongrass. Control aphids. Destroy affected plants. Do not handle healthy plants after infected ones. Plant resistant varieties.	
Lodging (plants falling over).	**excess nitrogen fertilizer**
Comments	
Test soil. Adjust fertilization.	

harvest when silks first appear but ears are not filled out. Experimentation is the best way to determine when to harvest baby corn.

It is not necessary to remove suckers or side shoots that form on sweet corn. With adequate fertility, these suckers may increase yield, and removing them has been shown in some cases to actually decrease yield.

Mulching is a useful practice in growing corn because adequate moisture is required from pollination to harvest to guarantee that ears are well-filled. Mulching reduces evaporation of soil moisture and keeps the moisture content of the soil fairly constant. Most organic mulches are suitable; newspaper held down with a heavier material on top is an excellent moisture conserver in corn.

Normally, sweet corn is ready for harvest about 17 to 24 days after the first silk strands appear, more quickly in hot weather and more slowly in cool weather. Harvest corn when husks are still green, silks are dry-brown, and kernels are full-sized and yellow or white to the tip of the ear. Experienced gardeners can feel the outside of the husk and tell when the cob has filled out. Harvest corn at the "milk stage." Use your thumbnail to puncture a kernel. If the liquid is clear, the corn is immature; if the kernel is plump and the liquid is milky, it is ready to be picked; and if there is no sap, it is too late. Cover unharvested ears checked by this method with a paper bag to prevent insect or bird damage.

Pick corn that is to be stored for a day or two in the cool temperatures of early morning to prevent the ears from building up an excess of field heat, which causes more rapid conversion of sugars to starch. The best time to pick is just before eating the corn; country cooks say to have the pot of water coming to a boil as you are picking the corn, husking it on the way from the garden to the house! This is an exaggeration, but with standard varieties, sugar conversion to starch is rather rapid. Field heat can be removed from ears picked when temperatures are high by plunging the ears in cold water or putting them on ice for a short time. Harvested ears should be stored as cold as possible in the refrigerator until ready to use. Supersweet varieties will also benefit from this treatment, but they are not as finicky because they have a higher sugar content and they hold their sweetness longer.

1 month apart is necessary to ensure isolation. Sweet corn plantings must also be isolated from field corn, popcorn, and ornamental corn. White and yellow types also cross-pollinate, but the results are not as drastic.

Some gardeners are interested in growing baby corn, such as that found in salad bars and gourmet sections of grocery stores. Baby corn is immature corn, and many varieties are suitable, but Baby Asian and Candystick, with their small-diameter cob at maturity, are good to try. Harvesting at the right time is tricky;

Cucumber (*Cucumis sativus*)

Recommended Varieties (Disease Resistance)

Pickling

- Liberty Hybrid (AAS, ALS, DM, M, PM, S)
- Saladin (AAS, DM, CMV, PM)
- County Fair 83 (AN, DM, M, PM, S)
- Pickle Bush (compact, suitable for containers) (CMV, PM)
- Pot Luck (container only) (CMV)

Slicing

- Dasher II (CMV, DM, PM, S)
- Sweet Success (AAS, AN, ALS, CMV, DM, PM, S)
- Sweet Slice, burpless (AN, CMV, DM, S, PM)
- Burpee Hybrid (DM, M)
- Bush Champion, suitable for containers (M)
- Parks Bush Whopper, container
- Pot Luck, container only (CMV)
- Salad Bush (suitable for containers)
- Spacemaster (bush, suitable for containers) (M)
- Slice Nice (AN, DM, S)
- Slice Master Hybrid (ALS, AN, DM, M, PM, S)

Figure 14.3

Cucumber flowers.
Source: After Johnson 1981, p. 2.

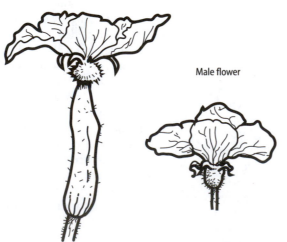

Female flower

Male flower

Varieties of cucumber include the slicing, or fresh salad, type; the pickling type (which can also be used fresh); and the standard, dwarf-vined, or bush varieties. On a normal cucumber plant, the first 10 to 20 flowers are male, and for every female flower, which will produce the fruit, 10 to 20 male flowers are produced. These facts indicated to plant breeders that production could be increased greatly if many more female flowers were produced. Some of the new varieties produce plants that have a greater proportion of female to male flowers, and others, called *gynoecious* types, have only female flowers. These plants tend to bear fruit earlier, with a more concentrated set and better yields overall.

In order for the flower to develop into a fruit, pollen must be carried by bees from male flowers on the same plant or on different plants to the female flower, the one with the tiny swollen pickle (see fig. 14.3). Gynoecious cucumber flowers are pollinated by male flowers from other plants, the seeds of which are usually included in the seed packet. Poor cucumber set is common during rainy weather when bees are inactive. (See "Fruit Set Problems in Squash, Melons, and Cucumbers" in the squash section, below.) If pesticides are needed, use them late in the afternoon to avoid harming the bee population.

Parthenocarpic cucumbers are all female and are seedless because the fruit is produced without being pollinated. This type is usually grown in greenhouses, but if it is planted near other varieties, pollination will occur and seed will form.

Burpless cucumbers are long and slender with a tender skin. Through plant breeding, the bitterness associated with the burp has been removed. Environmental causes of bitterness in cucumbers include temperature variation of more than 20 degrees, shaded conditions, and moisture stress. (See "Bitterness in Cucumbers," below.)

Most varieties of cucumber vines spread from row to row. Training on a cage, trellis, or fence along the edge of the garden will correct this and also lift the fruit off the soil. Trellising gets leaves up off the ground so that they dry off faster. Trellised vines are less likely to be stepped on or damaged during weeding. If trellising is not possible, many excellent bush varieties of cucumber are available. Most of them produce well for a limited amount of space and may be a desirable alternative in a

Problem Diagnosis for Cucumber

Problem	Probable cause
Deformed, curled leaves. Small, soft-bodied insects on undersides of leaves. Sticky honeydew or black, sooty mold may be present.	aphids
Comments Use insecticidal soap.	
Fine stippling on leaves; yellow or brown leaves; leaf undersides silver-gray with fine webbing and yellow, orange, or red dots.	spider mites
Comments Use oil or soap spray.	
Leaves turn yellow. Honeydew or sooty mold present. Clouds of tiny white insects fly up when plant is disturbed.	whiteflies
Comments Remove infested plants as quickly as possible. Remove lower, infested leaves of plants not totally infested.	
Coarse, white stippling on upper surface of leaves. Leaves may turn brown.	leafhoppers
Comments Consult UC IPM pest note series or Flint 1998 for management options.	
Blotches or tunnels on leaves.	leafminers
Comments Consult UC IPM pest note series or Flint 1998 for management options.	
Angular necrotic areas on leaves.	angular leafspot
Comments Caused by waterborne bacterium. Avoid wetting foliage with irrigation water.	
Swelling, beads on roots. Wilted plants. Poor yields.	nematodes
Comments Rotate crops. Use soil solarization.	
Holes chewed in leaves. Scarring of runners, young fruit. Wilting. Beetles visible.	cucumber beetles
Comments Beetles are yellow-green with black stripes or spots. Use pyrethrins.	
Leaves have small specks that turn yellow, then brown. Vines wilt from point of attack to end of vine.	squash bug
Comments Trap adults beneath boards in spring. Turn over boards in morning and kill bugs. Pick off adults, young, egg masses.	
White, powdery spots on leaves and stems. Spots may enlarge and completely cover leaf. Defoliation may occur. Yields reduced.	powdery mildew
Comments Spores of powdery mildew fungus are spread by wind and air currents. Disease is less severe in hot, dry weather. Plant resistant varieties. Dusting with sulfur can be effective. Remove old plant debris.	

small garden. If vines are not trellised, avoid destroying blossoms or kinking vines by gently rolling the vines away rather than lifting them when searching for harvestable fruit. In nontrellised plantings, organic mulches are useful to maintain soil moisture and keep the fruit clean.

Working in the vines when leaves are wet can spread disease. Wait until after morning dew or rain evaporates. There has been a significant increase in disease resistance in cucumber varieties in recent years. Select resistant varieties when possible.

Harvest cucumbers when they are about 2 inches (5 cm) long up to 8 to 10 inches (20 to 25 cm) long, but be sure to harvest before they begin to turn yellow. Remove fruits by turning cucumbers parallel to the vine and giving a quick snap to prevent vine damage and make a clean break.

Bitterness in Cucumbers

Each year, some home gardeners experience bitterness in cucumbers that they have grown for fresh use or pickling. Bitterness is due to the formation of two cucurbitacins (terpenoid compounds) that impart a bitter flavor to seedlings, roots, stems, leaves, and fruit (see Pittenger 1983). Two genes are involved in controlling bitterness in cucumber: a dominant gene produces extremely bitter fruit and a recessive gene inhibits the formation of curcurbitacin in foliage and fruit. An enzyme, elaterase, hydrolyzes cucurbitacins to nonbitter compounds. Elaterase activity is believed to be controlled independently of the genes controlling bitterness.

Nutritional Value of Cucumber
Serving size: ½ cucumber, raw (155 g)

Calories	21
Fat	0.3 g
Calories from fat	13%
Cholesterol	0
Sodium	3 mg
Protein	0.9 g
Carbohydrate	4.5 g
Dietary fiber	1.5 g

Primary Nutrients		% RDA (m)	% RDA (f)	% Min. Requirement
Vitamin C	6 mg	6.7	8.0	
Folic Acid	21 mcg	5.3	5.3	
Potassium	234 mg			12

Problem	Probable cause
Yellow spots on upper leaf surfaces. Grayish, fuzzy growth on undersides of spots.	**downy mildew**
Comments	
Caused by a fungus. Plant resistant varieties. Remove old plant debris.	
Stunted plants, small leaves with irregularly shaped light and dark spots (mottled). Yields reduced.	**mosaic virus**
Comments	
Transmitted by aphids. Remove infected plants as soon as detected. Control aphids. Control weeds. Aluminum foil is effective as soil mulch to reduce infection Deformed fruit is edible.	
Poor fruit set.	**insufficient pollination; lack of bee pollinators**
Comments	
Hand-pollinate using artist's paintbrush if bee pollinators are too few. Bee activity may be low due to cool weather or insecticides.	
Bitter fruit.	**cucurbitacin compounds**
Comments	
See text for discussion and recommendations.	
Plants wilt and die, beginning with older crown leaves. Light brown streaks occur inside lower stem, runners, and root. Visible when split lengthwise.	**Verticillium wilt**
Comments	
Caused by soilborne fungus. Rotate crops. Avoid soil previously planted in potatoes, peppers, eggplant, tomatoes, or cucurbits.	
Plants wilt suddenly. Roots rot.	**sudden wilt**
Comments	
Caused by fungus. Avoid water stress after fruit set. Avoid wetting soil to the crown. Improve drainage. Plant on raised beds.	
Water-soaked, sunken, brown or black spot on fruit not restricted to blossom end.	**belly rot**
Comments	
Rotate crops. Improve drainage. Stake or cage to keep fruit off ground.	
Excessive vegetative growth.	**planting too close together**
Comments	
Increase plant spacing.	

Note: Cucumbers (*Cucumis sativus*) are relatives of melons (*Cucumis melo*), including cantaloupe, honeydew, and crenshaw; winter and summer squash (*Cucurbita pepo* var. *melopepo*); pumpkin (*Cucurbita pepo* var. *pepo*); and watermelon (*Citrullus lanatus*). Known collectively as cucurbits, they suffer from similar pests and diseases, as evident from the problem diagnosis table.

Usually the bitter cucurbitacin does not accumulate very heavily in the fruit. When it does, it accumulates nonuniformly among fruits and within the fruit. Cucurbitacins are likely to concentrate at the stem end and in and just under the skin of the fruit.

The amount of bitterness in cucumbers appears to vary from year to year and from location to location. This may occur because elaterase production is stimulated or depressed under certain environmental conditions. Cool temperatures can enhance bitterness; fertilization, plant spacing, and irrigation frequency have exhibited little consistent effect on the number of bitter cucumbers produced. Also, varieties vary widely in their tendency to be bitter.

Avoid growing cucumbers in cool or shaded locations and provide uniform moisture and ample nutrients to ensure a good yield of quality fruit. Select the new hybrid varieties as they seem to have less of a tendency toward bitterness. If fruits express bitterness, it can usually be eliminated by peeling away the skin and outer flesh and removing the stem end. The direction of peeling does not have an effect on the spread of bitterness.

Eggplant (*Solanum melongena*)

Recommended Varieties (Disease Resistance)

- Black Beauty
- Epic (TMV)
- Early Bird (very early producer)
- Dusky (TMV)
- Imperial (TMV)
- Rosa Bianca

Oriental type

- Ichaban
- Tycoon

White

- Ghost

The standard eggplant produces egg-shaped, glossy, purple-black fruit 7 to 10 inches (17.5 to 25 cm) long when fully mature. Only a few plants are needed to meet the average family's needs. The long, slender oriental-type

Problem Diagnosis for Eggplant

Problem	Probable cause
Deformed, curled leaves. Plants stunted. Small, soft-bodied insects on undersides of leaves. Sticky honeydew or black sooty mold may be present.	aphids
Comments	
Use insecticidal soap.	
Small leaves with irregular mottle.	mosaic viruses
Comments	
Plant TMV-resistant varieties.	
Small holes in leaves; on lower leaves more than top ones.	flea beetle
Comments	
Tiny black beetles that jump. Consult UC IPM pest note series or Flint 1998 for management options.	
White, frothy foam on stems; insects visible beneath foam.	spittle bugs
Comments	
Green insects. Tolerate. Do not cause significant damage.	
Leaves wilt, turn yellow, then brown. Tiny white flies flutter when plant disturbed.	whiteflies
Comments	
Consult UC IPM pest note series or Flint 1998 for management options.	
Dark-colored dieback from growing tip. Fruit may have orange, yellow rings.	spotted wilt virus
Comments	
Spread by thrips. Control weeds that are host of virus and vector.	
Plants do not grow. Blossoms drop off. Fruit does not develop.	climate too cool; wrong variety
Comments	
Plant in warmer weather. Plant recommended varieties.	
Plants wilt and die. Brown streaks inside root and lower stem visible when stem is split lengthwise.	Verticillium wilt
Comments	
Caused by soilborne fungus. Avoid planting in soil previously planted to potato, tomato, or cucurbits.	
Leaves roll downward. No stunting; no yellowing of new leaves.	physiological leaf roll
Comments	
Not caused by pathogen; no action needed.	
Buds or fruits turn yellow; buds or young fruit may drop from plant. Fruit have holes, become misshapen, develop blotches.	pepper weevil
Comments	
Adults are dark beetles $1/8$ inch (0.3 cm) long. Larvae are white, legless, found inside fruit. Destroy plants as soon as harvest is over to reduce problem next year. Destroy nightshade plants, an alternate host.	

eggplants have a thinner skin and more delicate flavor. Both standard and miniature eggplants can be grown successfully in containers, but standard varieties yield a better crop. White ornamental varieties are available and edible but are of poor eating quality.

Plant and handle eggplant in the same way as tomatoes; eggplant is slightly more sensitive to cold than tomatoes. Warm to hot weather throughout the season is necessary for good production. Seed germinate quickly at 70° to 90°F (21° to 32°C), and plants should be grown for 8 to 9 weeks before setting them out. Cold temperatures will stop plant and root growth, reducing plant vigor and yields. Using hot caps or row covers protects plants from cold conditions.

Although eggplants do well in hot weather, they must have well-drained soil and do not thrive in very humid areas. Pick standard-type fruit when they are about 4 to 6 inches (10 to 15 cm) in diameter. Test for maturity by pressing with the thumb. If the flesh springs back, the fruit is green; if it does not and an indentation remains, the fruit is mature. Harvest when the fruit is about halfway between these stages. Mature fruit should not be left on the plant because they reduce overall productivity. Use a knife or pruning shears to cut the fruit from the plants.

Nutritional Value of Eggplant

Serving size: ½ cup, cubed, boiled (48 g)

Calories	13
Fat	0.1 g
Calories from fat	7%
Cholesterol	0
Sodium	2 mg
Protein	0.4 g
Carbohydrate	3.2 g

Primary Nutrients

None of the nutrients exceed 5% of the RDA

Problem	Probable cause
Normal-colored fruit, but small and flattened in shape. Few to no seed inside.	**poor or incomplete pollination**
Comments	
Plant in full sunlight. Tap flowers in midday to aid pollination.	
Large, sunken, watersoaked spot develops on blossom end of fruit; spot turns black and mold may develop.	**blossom end rot**
Comments	
Can be caused by uneven moisture supply. Give uniform irrigation. Supply water during dry periods. Mulch.	

Endive (*Cichorium endivia*)

Recommended Varieties

- Full Heart Batavian (smooth leaved escarole)
- Large Green Curled (deeply cut, curly leaves)

Plant and grow endive as you would lettuce, although it is hardier and may be produced as a winter crop in many locations where lettuce will not grow. Endive yields for a longer time than lettuce. The crop is ready for harvest 90 days after planting. When the plants reach 12 inches (30 cm) in diameter, tie the leaves together at the top to blanch the hearts. Do not tie the leaves when they are wet; this may cause decay.

Harvest when the hearts are well-blanched. Colder temperatures and blanching result in a milder taste. The crop can be used unblanched by harvesting the outer leaves (as with chard), rather than harvesting the entire plant. Endive can be used in salads as greens or as a garnish.

Problem Diagnosis for Endive

See table 14.5 for general techniques to recognize and manage common problems associated with endive. A common disease of endive is downy mildew. Common insect pests that attack endive include flea beetles, aphids, armyworms, leafhoppers, snails, and slugs.

Nutritional Value of Endive
Serving size: ½ cup, chopped, raw (25 g)

Calories	4
Fat	0.1 g
Calories from fat	22%
Cholesterol	0
Sodium	6 mg
Protein	0.3 g
Carbohydrate	0.8 g

Primary Nutrients		% RDA (m)	% RDA (f)
Folic Acid	36 mcg	9	9
Vitamin A	51 RE	5.7	7.3

Florence Fennel (*Foeniculum vulgare*)

Recommended Variety

- Florence

Florence fennel is often called Finocchio or sweet anise. The edible portions are the enlarged bases of the leaf petioles, which overlap each other to form a compact bulb. Fennel can be eaten cooked or raw, like celery, and, because of its licorice taste, is used in flavoring. It also stores well.

Nutritional Value of Florence Fennel
Serving size: 1 cup, sliced, raw (87 g)

Calories	27
Fat	0.2 g
Calories from fat	7%
Cholesterol	0
Sodium	45 mg
Protein	1.1 g
Carbohydrate	6.3 g

Primary Nutrients		% RDA (m)	% RDA (f)	% Min. Requirement
Vitamin C	11 mg	12.2	14.7	
Calcium	43 mg	4.3	4.3	
Potassium	360 mg			18

Problem Diagnosis for Florence Fennel

There are few serious problems in growing this crop. If problems occur, see table 14.5 for general techniques to recognize and manage possible problems and consult the UC IPM pest note

Garlic (*Allium sativum*)

Recommended Varieties

- California Late
- California Early

Garlic, if correctly handled, grows well in most parts of California. A few feet of row give an ample supply. Plant in fertile soil in late fall, winter, or early spring. Fall planting is best if winters are not severe. Give the crop the same care as described for onions. Harvest when the plant tops begin to die. Use a garden fork to lift bulbs out of the ground because pulling plants by hand could crack bulbs and reduce storage life. Let bulbs dry outdoors in the sun for about 3 weeks until the skins become papery. If you only grow a few plants, you can store the bulbs by braiding the tops and hanging the rope of garlic in a cool, dry place for use as needed.

Elephant garlic is a popular garden vegetable. It is similar to garlic, except that the bulb consists of one or two large cloves and numerous small cloves at the base of the bulb. Cultural requirements and culinary aspects are similar to those of garlic.

Garlic is related to onions, leeks, and chives (members of the *Allium* family) and suffers from similar pest, disease, and cultural problems.

Problem Diagnosis for Garlic

See "Problem Diagnosis for Onion."

Nutritional Value of Garlic
Serving size: 3 cloves, raw (9 g)

Calories	13
Fat	0.1
Calories from fat	7%
Cholesterol	0
Sodium	2 mg
Protein	0.6 g
Carbohydrate	3.0 g

Primary Nutrients
None of the nutrients meet or exceed 5% of the RDA

Kale (*Brassica oleracea* var. *acephala*)

Recommended Varieties

- Vates Dwarf Blue Curled (finely curled dwarf leaves)
- Salad Savoy (curled, colorful leaves—green on white)
- Winterbor (finely curled, blue-green)
- Ornamental (heavily fringed leaves—red on green or white on green; for containers or bedding plants)

Kale is a cool-season vegetable that can be used raw as salad greens, as a garnish, as an ornamental in the flower bed, or cooked. Plants produce rosettes of very decorative cut or curled leaves with colors rather than forming tight heads. Collards are a type of kale with larger, smoother leaves resembling cabbage. Kale greens have a healthy supply of vitamins and minerals and few calories. Slight frosts sweeten kale's flavor, whereas high temperatures and hot sun can lead to bitter leaves. Harvest leaves a few at a time starting with the outer leaves first.

Nutritional Value of Kale
Serving size: 1/2 cup chopped, boiled (65 g)

Calories	21
Fat	0.3 g
Calories from fat	13%
Cholesterol	0
Sodium	15 mg
Protein	1.2 g
Carbohydrate	3.7 g

Primary Nutrients		% RDA (m)	% RDA (f)	% Min. Requirement
Vitamin C	27 mg	30.0	36.0	
Iron	0.59 mg	7.4	3.3	
Vitamin A	481 RE	53.4	68.7	
Calcium	47 mg	4.7	4.7	
Potassium	148 mg			7

Problem Diagnosis for Kale

As a member of the Brassica family, kale is related to cabbage, cauliflower, turnips, kohlrabi, mustard greens, broccoli, and brussels sprouts. Kale suffers from similar pest insects, diseases, and cultural problems that plague its relatives. See "Problem Diagnosis for Cabbage."

Kohlrabi (*Brassica oleracea* var. *gongylodes*)

Recommended Varieties (Disease Resistance)

- Grand Duke (AAS)
- Early White Vienna
- Purple Vienna

In appearance, kohlrabi resembles an above-ground turnip with the leaves attached to the edible, enlarged, swollen, fleshy stem. The swollen stem enlarges to 4 inches (10 cm) in diameter. Harvest at about 2 inches (5 cm) in diameter when it is less vigorous and less stringy. Peel and eat kohlrabi raw in salads or cook by steaming. The flavor is similar to turnips and the texture resembles that of water chestnuts.

Nutritional Value of Kohlrabi

Serving size: ½ cup, slices, boiled (82 g)

Calories	24
Fat	0.1 g
Calories from fat	4%
Cholesterol	0
Sodium	17 mg
Protein	1.5 g
Carbohydrate	5.5 g

Primary Nutrients		% RDA (m)	% RDA (f)	% Min. Requirement
Vitamin C	44 mg	48.9	58.7	
Potassium	279 mg			14

Problem Diagnosis for Kohlrabi

As a member of the Brassica family, kohlrabi is related to cabbage, cauliflower, turnips, kale, mustard greens, broccoli, and brussels sprouts. Kohlrabi suffers from similar pest insects, diseases, and cultural problems that plague its relatives. See "Problem Diagnosis for Cabbage."

Leek (*Allium ampeloprasum*)

Recommended Varieties

- Large American Flag
- Electra
- Titan

The leek belongs to the onion family, but it has only a mild onion flavor. The plant does not form a bulb, but grows to about 1 to 1½ inches (2.5 to 3.7 cm) in diameter. Leeks are usually grown as a fall crop in most areas and may be left in the field for some time after maturity. When the plants are almost full size, hill the soil around them to a height of 6 to 8 inches (15 to 20 cm) to blanch the lower parts of the plants.

Nutritional Value of Leek

Serving size: ¼ cup chopped, raw (26 g)

Calories	16
Fat	0.2 g
Calories from fat	11%
Cholesterol	0
Sodium	6 mg
Protein	0.4 g
Carbohydrate	4.0 g

Primary Nutrients		%RDA (m)	%RDA (f)	% Min. Requirement
Iron	0.6 mg	7.5	3.3	
Folic acid	13 mg	3.3	3.3	

Problem Diagnosis for Leek

As a cousin of onions and garlic, leeks suffer from similar pest insects, diseases, and similar cultural problems. See "Problem Diagnosis for Onion."

Lettuce (*Lactuca sativa*)

Recommended Varieties (Disease Resistance)

Butterhead (Boston)

- Buttercrunch (AAS, B)

Batavian (French crisp)

- French
- Laura (B)
- Loma
- Nevada (DM)
- Sierra (red) (H,B)

Romaine (Cos)

- Parris Island (LMV, TB)
- Valmaine (DM)

Crisphead (Iceberg) (difficult to grow in home gardens)

- Great Lakes (AAS, TB)
- Vanguard (LMV)
- Calmar (TB)
- Empire (B, TB)

Loose Leaf

- Salad Bowl (AAS, B)
- Oak Leaf (B, H)
- Red Sails (deep red-bronze) (AAS), B)
- Ruby (red shading) (VAS, H)
- Royal Green

Lettuce, a cool-season vegetable, is extremely sensitive to high temperatures. If direct-seeded during high temperatures, seed dormancy may result. It is usually more successful to use transplants that are 3 to 4 weeks old. Time your planting of the crop so it matures during periods of cool temperatures. Several types of lettuce, described below, are commonly grown in home gardens.

Crisphead, also known as iceberg, is the lettuce most widely available as a fresh-market type. It has a tightly compacted head with crisp, light green leaves. Many home gardeners find this type difficult to grow because it requires a long, cool season and some of the most advertised varieties are not heat-resistant and tend to go to seed (bolt) as soon as temperatures go up. High temperatures during maturity of crisphead types (see below) may result in premature seed stalk development

and internal tip burn. For best results, select a slow-bolting variety and start seed indoors in late winter or late summer. Transplant in early spring or fall to take advantage of cool weather; mulch well to keep soil temperatures from fluctuating and to hold moisture in. Thin or space crisphead types so the plants are 10 to 12 inches (25 to 30 cm) apart. An organic mulch is more suitable than black plastic after soil warms up. Mulching also keeps soil off the leaves, reducing the chances of disease from soilborne organisms.

Butterhead, or bibb, lettuce, is a loose-heading type with dark green leaves that are somewhat thicker than those of iceberg lettuce. Butterheads develop a light yellow, buttery appearance and are very attractive in salads. They may be started indoors for an even longer season. Bibb lettuce will develop bitterness readily if temperatures get too high.

Romaine, also known as cos, is a fairly nutritious lettuce that deserves attention. It too is relatively easy to grow from transplants, forming upright heads with rather wavy, attractive leaves. Thin or space romaine types to 6 to 8 inches (15 to 20 cm) apart.

Most gardeners who grow lettuce raise the loose leaf type, either with green or reddish leaves. This type is a fast-growing, long-lasting lettuce used for salads, sandwiches, and in wilted lettuce salads. Thin or space leaf types to 4 to 6 inches (10 to 15 cm) apart.

Cultivate carefully because lettuce is shallow-rooted. Use frequent, light waterings and sidedress with nitrogen to encourage rapid growth; overwatering can encourage root and leaf diseases. Mulches are helpful in maintain-

Nutritional Value of Romaine Lettuce

Serving size: ½ cup, shredded, raw (28 g)

Calories	4
Fat	0.1 g
Calories from fat	22%
Cholesterol	0
Sodium	4 mg
Protein	0.5 g
Carbohydrate	0.7 g
Dietary fiber	0.5 g

Primary Nutrients		% RDA (m)	% RDA (f)	% Min. Requirement
Vitamin C	7 mg	7.8	9.3	
Folic acid	38 mcg	9.5	9.5	
Vitamin A	73 RE	8.1	10.4	

Problem Diagnosis for Lettuce

Problem	Probable cause
Seedling plants damaged by caterpillars feeding in crown. Plants may die.	**corn earworm; armyworms**
Curled, distorted leaves. Stunted plants. Green, pink, or black aphids on undersides of leaves, stems, or roots.	**aphids**
Comments Use insecticidal soap.	
Leaves have ragged holes. Holes bored into heads of lettuce. Leaves devoured.	**loopers**
Comments Use *Bacillus thurengiensis*.	
Leaves skeletonized or almost totally destroyed. Small holes in leaves or leaves heavily skeletonized	**armyworms; vegetable weevil**
Comments Attacks radish, carrot, turnip also. Damage is spotty. Adults do not fly.	
Inner leaves of head lettuce are black on edges.	**hot weather**
Comments Do not plant head lettuce for harvest in warmest months.	
Upper leaf surface has yellow to light green areas delineated by leaf veins. Undersurface has soft, downy white growth.	**downy mildew**
Comments Most prevalent under cool, moist conditions. Remove damaged outer leaves at harvest. Remove sources of disease (old lettuce plants and wild lettuce) before planting. Use resistant varieties.	
Lower leaves and whole plant wilt, get slimy. Hard, black sclerotia and white, cottony, moldy growth under lower leaves and plant crown.	**Sclerotinia drop (lettuce drop)**
Comments Caused by a fungus.	
Leaf veins lose green color and appear enlarged. Leaves appear puckered, ruffled.	**big vein**
Comments Viroid disease associated with fine-textured, poorly drained soil. Do not overwater. Plant tolerant varieties. Plant so that air temp. is >60ºF (>16ºC) to lessen severity of symptoms. Remove sick plants.	
Edges of internal leaves are brown and rotten. Not visible from outside of head.	**tipburn**
Comments Physiological disorder caused by calcium deficiency, aggravated by high soil fertility and high temps. Avoid excess potash. Keep nitrogen levels as low as possible. Avoid water stress. Keep calcium adequate.	
Leaves wilt temporarily, may turn dark green or gray-green. Smaller roots dead. Taproot in cross-section is yellow, red, or brown.	**ammonia injury**
Comments Common with urea fertilizer and chicken manure. Keep ammonium forms of nitrogen out of seed row. Cool, waterlogged soil is a problem.	

ing soil moisture and keeping lettuce leaves off the ground.

Lettuce planted in very early spring should be given full sun so that the soil will warm enough for rapid growth. For long-season lettuces, plant so that crops such as sweet corn, staked tomatoes, pole beans, or deciduous trees will shade the lettuce during the hottest part of the day. Interplanting—planting between rows or within the row of later-maturing crops like tomatoes, broccoli, and brussels sprouts—is a space-saving practice. Most lettuces are attractive in flower borders and in containers.

Lettuce is best planted in succession or by using different varieties that mature at different times. Thirty heads of romaine lettuce harvested at once can present a major storage problem! Leaf and bibb lettuces do well in hotbeds or greenhouses during the winter and in coldframes in spring and late fall.

Harvest heading types when they are firm but not hard. Hardening decreases flavor and other quality characteristics. Bibb lettuce is mature when the leaves begin to cup inward to form a loose head. The heads will never become compact. Romaine is ready to use when the leaves have elongated and over-lapped to form a fairly tight head about 4 inches (10 cm) wide at the base and 8 to 10 inches (20 to 25 cm) tall. Crisphead is mature when leaves overlap to form a head similar to those available in groceries; heads will be compact and firm.

Harvest looseleaf (nonheading) types when they reach full size. Use the older, outer leaves first. Correctly harvested and trimmed lettuce stores well in the refrigerator, where it should keep about 2 weeks. If lettuce is to be stored, harvest when dry but early in the day when water content of plants is high. Remove outer leaves but do not wash. Place in a plastic bag and store in the crisper drawer of the refrigerator.

Problem	Probable cause
Silvery leaves. Upper leaf surface separated from rest of leaf by water droplets.	frost injury
Comments	
Sudden temperature drop below freezing will injure Lettuce.	
Leaves faintly mottled. Yellowed, stunted plants.	viruses
Comments	
Plant virus-free seed, if available. After symptoms occur, there is no practical control. Aluminum foil mulches may help prevent infection by aphid and leafhopper-transmitted viruses. Plants showing symptoms near harvest are edible. Plants that show symptoms early may produce no or small heads. Remove infected plants. Control weeds and insects.	
Silvered areas on underside of leaves of head lettuce. Yellowed lower leaves have tiny brown spots.	smog
Comments	
Do not grow head lettuce in smoggy months.	
Plants begin to grow tall and send up flower stalks.	high temperatures
Comments	
Prolonged hot weather causes seed stalks to form. Grow lettuce only during cool months. Leafy types are more tolerant of heat. Plant in partial shade among corn in midsummer, or plant early or late to mature during cool weather.	
Bitter taste.	high temperatures
Comments	
See above.	
Torn areas on leaves.	birds
Comments	
Consult UC IPM pest note series or Flint 1998.	
Stem, lower leaves rotten. Dense, fuzzy gray mold on affected areas.	Botrytis gray mold
Comments	
Caused by a *Botrytis* fungus. Rotate crops; remove old plant debris. Plant in well- drained area.	
Sunken, water-soaked spots appear on lower leaves, which turn brown and slimy.	Rhizoctonia bottom rot
Comments	
Caused by a soilborne fungus. Rotate crops; remove old plant debris. Plant in well-drained area.	

Mustard (*Brassica juncea*)

Recommended Varieties

- Tendergreen
- Southern Giant Curled (curly deply cut leaves)
- Florida Broadleaf (large, smooth leaves)

Cultivated mustard varieties are more productive than wild mustard for use as spring greens. Grow and handle the crop as directed for spinach. Harvest by cutting or snapping off the outer leaves, allowing new inner leaves to increase in size. Do not allow the leaves to reach an excessive size, as the petioles become stringy. Small leaves are tender enough to use raw in salads; larger leaves are better when cooked.

Nutritional Value of Mustard

Serving size: ¹/₂ cup chopped, boiled (70 g)

Calories	11
Fat	0.2 g
Calories from fat	16%
Cholesterol	0
Sodium	11 mg
Protein	1.6 g
Carbohydrate	1.5 g

Primary Nutrients		%RDA (m)	%RDA (f)	% Min. Requirement
Vitamin C	18 mg	20.0	24.0	
Vitamin A	212 RE	23.6	30.3	
Calcium	52 mg	5.2	5.2	

Problem Diagnosis for Mustard

As a member of the Brassica family, mustard is related to cabbage, cauliflower, turnips, kale, kohlrabi, broccoli, and brussels sprouts. Mustard suffers from similar pest insects, diseases, and cultural problems that plague its relatives. See "Problem Diagnosis for Cabbage."

Okra (*Abelmoschus esculentus*)

Recommended Varieties (Disease Resistance)

- Clemson Spineless (AAS)
- Blondy (compact plants with whitish pods) (AAS)

Okra, sometimes called gumbo, is a summer and fall crop. Do not plant seed until the soil is warm. Soak seed in water for 24 hours before planting. Plant only those seed that are swollen. Plants grow to a height of 4 to 5 feet (1.2 to 1.5 m) and produce pods in about 60 days. Plants need to be staked. After the pods begin to form, pick them every 2 to 3 days. The plants stop bearing if you allow the pods to ripen on the stems.

Nutritional Value of Okra

Serving size: 1/2 cup slices, boiled (80 g)

Calories	25
Fat	0.1 g
Calories from fat	4%
Cholesterol	0
Sodium	4 mg
Protein	1.5 g
Carbohydrate	5.8 g

Primary Nutrients		% RDA (m)	% RDA (f)	% Min. Requirement
Calcium	50 mg	5.0	5.0	
Magnesium	46 mg	11.0	14.4	
Vitamin C	13 mg	14.4	17.3	
Vitamin B_6	0.15 mg	11.5	11.5	
Folic acid	37 mcg	9.3	9.3	
Thiamin	0.11 mg	9.2	10	
Potassium	257 mg			13

Problem Diagnosis for Okra

See table 14.5 for general techniques to recognize and manage the common problems associated with okra. Nematodes, aphids, corn earworm, and mites cause problems in okra.

Onion (*Allium cepa*)

Recommended Varieties

Early Bulb
- Grano (red or white)
- Granes (red or white)
- California Early Red

Green Bunching (scallions) (best quality obtained by growing seeds or transplants)
- Evergreen White
- Southport White
- White Sweet Spanish
- White Lisbon
- Tokyo Long White

Late Bulb
- Fiesta (Yellow Sweet Spanish type)
- Yellow Sweet Spanish
- White Sweet Spanish
- Southport White Globe
- Southport Red Globe
- Stockton Yellow Globe

Onions are often grouped according to taste. The two main types are strong flavored (American) and mild or sweet (sometimes called European). Each has three distinct colors: yellow, white, and red. Generally, the American onion produces bulbs of smaller size, denser texture, stronger flavor, and better keeping quality than European types. Globe varieties tend to keep longer in storage.

Onions vary in their pungency or hotness. In general, the softer varieties, such as Grano and Sweet Spanish, are milder than the harder varieties, such as Southport White Globe. The mild onions are preferred for fresh consumption, but the stronger flavored ones are better for cooking.

Onion varieties also have different requirements regarding the number of daylight hours (photoperiod) required to make a bulb. If the seed catalog lists the onion as long-day, it sets bulbs when it receives 15 to 16 hours of daylight. Short-day varieties set bulbs with about 12 hours of daylight.

The variety and the planting date are extremely important in the production of a good bulb crop. Before buying and planting, obtain advice from an experienced local gardener or your county UC Cooperative Extension farm advisor. If you live south of Bakersfield, use early varieties seeded or transplanted in October for June harvest. Sets and

late varieties are not recommended. If you live north of Bakersfield, seed or transplant early varieties from November through January for late-spring or summer harvest. Seed or transplant late varieties or sets from January through March for late summer or fall harvest.

You can grow onions from seed, sets, or transplants. Seed requires a longer growing period than onions grown by other methods, and the plants have to be thinned. However, it is the cheapest method and is the one most commonly used. Sets are small, immature onion bulbs that are planted the same way as seed. Sets are a good method for producing a quick crop of green onions. They are not recommended for the production of mature, dry bulbs because varieties used to produce sets are frequently not well adapted to California or they frequently result in bolting (going to seed) rather than bulbing.

Transplants are also an easy method for producing an early crop, but you may have to raise your own plants as they are rarely available from nurseries.

Dry onions are ready to harvest when the tops fall over (approximately 6 months after planting). Pull onions and let them dry for a few days on top of the ground. Cover the bulbs with the tops to prevent sunburn. When the tops and "necks" are dry, remove the tops and store the bulbs in a cool, dry place. Or, you can leave the tops on, braid them, and hang them in a cool, dry place. If onions are allowed to form seed stalks, the center of the bulb becomes woody, undesirable to eat, and unsuitable for long storage.

Plant green onions four to six times thicker than you would dry bulb onions. Harvest green onions when they are ¼ to ½ inch (0.6 to 1.2 cm) in diameter.

Problem Diagnosis for Onion

Problem	Probable cause
Seedlings are pale, thickened, deformed. Older plants are stunted, limp. Leaf tips dying back. Bulbs swollen at base.	**stem and bulb nematode**
Comments Use certified seed. Do not plant garlic or onions in areas where onions, garlic, leeks, or chives grew in previous years. Parsley and celery are also hosts. Remove and destroy infested culls.	
Leaves turn silvery; may also have white streaks, blotches.	**onion thrips**
Comments Most common during dry, warm weather. Use insecticidal soap.	
Tiny bulbs. Roots look white and normal.	**wrong variety; planted at wrong time; weed competition**
Comments Plant right variety at proper time. Garlic and onions do not compete well with weeds; control weeds.	
Seedstalks develop.	**cold weather after plants are 6–10 weeks old**
Comments Plant right variety at proper time. Do not overwinter.	
Roots rotten and pink. Yields drastically reduced.	**pink root**
Comments Caused by a soilborne fungus. Grow a pink root-resistant variety. Rotate crops to reduce disease severity.	
Tunnels and cavities in bulb and underground stem. Plant may die or become wilted and yellow. Tips may turn brown.	**onion maggot**
Comments Adults are small flies; larvae are off-white, legless. Preventive controls only. Nothing practical can be done once pest occurs on growing crop. Destroy culled garlic and onions after harvest.	
Yellow or white areas on leaves. Leaves and stalks bend, wilt, and die. Soft, white to purple spore (mold) growth during wet, humid weather.	**downy mildew**
Comments Fungus attacks plants only in the Allium (onion) family. Destroy old plant debris. Keep soil well-drained. Allow plants to dry out between irrigations. Keep air circulating. Plant resistant varieties.	
Plants collapse. Bulbs have soft, watery rot. Leaves or bulbs have white, fuzzy growth speckled with black bodies.	**white rot**
Comments Caused by fungi. Destroy diseased plants. To prevent spread in soil, do not compost. Rotate crops. Fungus survives in soil for years.	

Nutritional Value of Onion

Serving size: ½ cup chopped, boiled (105 g)

Calories	47
Fat	0.2 g
Calories from fat	4%
Cholesterol	0
Carbohydrate	10.7 g
Protein	1.4 g
Sodium	2 mg

Primary Nutrients		% RDA (m)	% RDA (f)	% Min. Requirement
Vitamin C	6 mg	6.7	8.0	

Parsley (*Petroselinum crispum*)

Recommended Varieties

- Extra Curled Dwarf
- Hamburg (forms edible white roots)
- Moss Curled
- Paramount (dark green, very curled)
- Plain or Single (smooth, leaf type)
- Italian Flat

Parsley seed germinates and emerges quite slowly. It is best to purchase transplants or start the seed indoors to produce transplants for planting in the spring. The plants will over-winter in mild climates, but they develop seed stalks as the days lengthen and the temperatures increase in the late spring. Harvest in the cool, early-morning hours to maintain maximum flavor and parsley odor. Pinch or cut off the mature outer stems to allow the inner leaves and stems to develop for later harvest.

Nutritional Value of Parsley

Serving size: ½ cup chopped, raw (30 g)

Calories	11			
Fat	0.2 g			
Calories from fat	8%			
Cholesterol	0			
Carbohydrate	1.9 g			
Protein	0.9 g			
Sodium	12 mg			

Primary Nutrients		% RDA (m)	% RDA (f)	% Min. Requirement
Vitamin C	40 mg	44.4	53.3	
Iron	1.86 mg	23.3	10.3	
Vitamin A	156 RE	17.3	22.3	
Folic acid	46 mcg	11.5	11.5	

Problem Diagnosis for Parsley

There are few serious problems in growing parsely aside from heat stress in hot summer periods of inland valleys and deserts. Spider mites occasionally damage plants, causing yellow or whitish deformed leaves. See table 14.5 for general techniques to recognize and manage other possible problems associated with parsley and consult the UC IPM pest note series or Flint 1998.

Parsnip (*Pastinaca sativa*)

Recommended Varieties

- All America
- Hollow Crown
- Harris Model

Grow parsnips by the same methods as described for carrots. Parships require a deep, well-worked seedbed for optimal root development and sizing. Some roots will exceed 12 inches (30 cm) in length. The seed germinates quite slowly, although presoaking it in water for a day before planting assists germination. The crop has a long growth period—up to and more than 4 months. Eating quality is improved by frost. You can store parsnips in the ground if frosts are not severe; otherwise store them in moist, cool conditions. Roots become tough if left in the soil too long or if seed stalks begin to develop.

Nutritional Value of Parsnip

Serving size: ½ cup slices, boiled (78 g)

Calories	63			
Fat	0.2 g			
Calories from fat	3%			
Cholesterol	0			
Carbohydrate	15.2 g			
Dietary fiber	2.1 g			
Protein	1.0 g			
Sodium	8 mg			

Primary Nutrients		% RDA (m)	% RDA (f)	% Min. Requirement
Magnesium	23 mg	5.5	7.2	
Vitamin C	10 mg	11.1	13.3	
Folic acid	45 mcg	11.3	11.3	
Potassium	287 mg			8

Problem Diagnosis for Parsnip

See table 14.5 for general techniques to recognize and manage common problems associated with parsnip. Nematodes, armyworms, cabbage root maggots, flea beetles, and leafhoppers cause problems in parsnip.

Problem Diagnosis for Pea

Problem	Probable cause
Leaves, stems covered with sticky honeydew, black sooty mold.	aphids
Comments Consult UC IPM pest note series or Flint 1998 for management options.	
Holes in leaves; black-spotted, greenish-yellow beetles present.	cucumber beetles
Comments Consult UC IPM pest note series or Flint 1998 for management options.	
Leaves skeletonized. Groups of tiny caterpillars feeding together.	armyworms
Comments Consult UC IPM pest note series or Flint 1998 for management options.	
Very fine, whitish to yellowish stippling on upper leaf surface; fine webbing on undersurface.	spider mites
Comments Consult UC IPM pest note series or Flint 1998 for management options.	
Deformed pods; surface scarring of pods.	thrips
Comments Control weeds.	
Winding white trails mined in leaves, stems, or pods.	leafminers
Comments Consult UC IPM pest note series or Flint 1998 for management options.	
Semicircular notches on leaf margins. Young plants may be chewed at ground level.	pea leaf weevil adults
Comments When plants have grown past the 6-leaf stage, treatment is not necessary.	
Leaves with white-purple cottony growth on underside only. Tops of leaves have yellow blotches. Dark spots on pods. Plants water-soaked.	downy mildew
Comments Caused by a soilborne or seedborne fungus.	
White powdery growth on top side of leaves. Leaves curled, dried out.	powdery mildew
Comments Caused by a fungus. Favored by warm, dry days and cool, damp nights. Remove plant debris to destroy overwintering fungus.	
New growth distorted, curled, mottled. Pods distorted. Plants may die.	viral disease
Comments Usually spread by aphids. Plant resistant varieties. Remove and destroy infested plants as soon as possible. Control weeds. Control insects.	
Yellowing of lower leaves. Stunted growth. Cross-section of lower part of stem may show reddish-orange discoloration.	Fusarium wilt
Comments Caused by soilborne fungus. Pull up and destroy infected plants. Do not replant peas in same soil for 5–10 years. Rotate crops.	

Pea (*Pisum sativum*) (green garden)

Pisum sativum var. *saccharatum* (China, snow, or sugar)

Pisum sativum var. *macrocarpum* (snap)

Recommended Varieties (Disease Resistance)

China, Snow, or Sugar
- Dwarf Gray Sugar (F)
- Mammoth Melting Sugar (F)

Cowpeas (Southern peas, blackeye peas)
- California Blackeye

Green Garden (dwarf vines)
- Little Marvel
- Progress No. 9 or Laxton's Progress (F)
- Greater Progress (F)

Green Garden (large vines requiring support)
- Freezonian (AAS, F)
- Green Arrow (DM, F, VR)
- Maestro (M, F, VR)

Snap (thick, edible pods)
- Sugar Ann (dwarf) (AAS, PM)
- Sweet Snap (semi-dwarf) (PM)
- Sugar Rae (dwarf) (PM)
- Sugar Daddy (stringless, dwarf) (PM)
- Sugar Snap (AAS)
- Super Sugar Mel

Bush peas have a shorter, earlier production period than the pole types. However, the pole types require extra work but yield more and produce for a longer time. Peas do best when grown during cool weather; warm weather shortens the harvest season. Bush types grow in most areas of California; vine types do best along the coast. It is essential to provide support for the climbing vine types. Do not use overhead irrigation; it increases the incidence of mildew.

Harvest peas when the seeds and pods are

Problem Diagnosis for Pea cont.

Problem	Probable cause
Plants stunted; vines off-color.	root rot complex
Comments	
Raised beds improve drainage.	
Roots rotten or absent. Occurs in patches along rows.	**poor soil drainage associated with low or wet spots**
Comments	
Rotate crops. Avoid wet soil or low areas where water collects.	
Small, chlorotic spots in spring.	**stink bugs**
Comments	
Trap adults under boards. Turn over in morning and hand-pick pest insects.	
Pods partially or entirely removed.	**birds**
Comments	
Consult UC IPM pest note series or Flint 1998.	
Plants stop producing peas, leaves turn yellow, then brown, and die.	**hot weather**
Comments	
Peas are cool-season vegetables. Plant early; plant heat-resistant varieties.	

well-developed but tender enough so they may be crushed between the fingers without separating into halves. Harvest edible pod types at the first sign of seed development. The sugar content of peas readily converts into starch; peas overmature quickly and starch conversion continues after picking. Therefore, cook or process (can or freeze) peas soon after shelling.

Nutritional Value of Pea
Serving size: ½ cup, boiled (80 g)

Calories	67
Fat	0.2 g
Calories from fat	2%
Cholesterol	0
Carbohydrate	12.5 g
Protein	4.3 g
Dietary fiber	2.2 g
Sodium	2 mg

Primary Nutrients		% RDA (m)	% RDA (f)	% Min. Requirement
Vitamin C	11 mg	12.2	14.7	
Thiamine	0.21 mg	17.5	19	
Vitamin B^6	0.17 mg	13.1	13.1	
Folic acid	51 mcg	12.8	12.8	
Iron	1.24 mg	15.5	6.9	
Niacin	1.6 mg	10.0	11.4	
Riboflavin	0.12 mg	9.2	10.9	
Magnesium	31 mg	7.4	9.7	
Potassium	217 mg			6

Pepper (*Capsicum annuum*)

Recommended Varieties (Disease Resistance)

Hot

- Tam Mild Jalapeño (mild heat with Jalapeño flavor) (PVY)
- Jalapeño Delicias
- Anaheim TMR 23 (chili pepper, moderately hot) (TMV)
- Anaheim (standard hot chili)
- Cayenne Long Red Slim (hot)
- Hungarian Yellow Wax (popular for canning, moderately hot)
- Serrano Chili Pepper (tabasco type)

Sweet Bell

- Bell Boy (AAS, TMV)
- California Wonder (TMV)
- Yolo Wonder (TMV)
- Keystone Resistant Giant (TMV)
- Jupiter (TMV)
- Golden Summer Hybrid (yellow when fully mature) (TMV)
- Golden Bell (yellow when fully mature)
- Early Pimento (used fresh or for canning) (AAS)

Sweet Yellow or Cubanelle

- Sweet Banana (AAS)
- Gypsy (AAS, TMV)
- Hy-Fry
- Cubanene
- Nardello
- Corni de Toro

There are two types of peppers: the large-fruited, mild-flavored bell types, preferred by most gardeners, and the hot varieties, which may be used green. The mild peppers include bell, banana, pimiento, and sweet cherry, while the hot peppers include cayenne, celestial, large cherry, serrano, tabasco, and jalapeño. Hot peppers are usually allowed to ripen fully and change colors (except for jalapeños) and have smaller, longer, thinner and more tapering fruits than sweet peppers. Yields are smaller for hot peppers.

Bell peppers, measuring 3 or more inches (7.5 cm) wide by 4 or more inches (10 cm)

Problem Diagnosis for Pepper

Problem	Probable cause
Deformed, curled leaves. Plants are stunted. Small, soft-bodied insects on undersides of leaves. Sticky honeydew or black sooty mold may be present.	aphids
Comments	
Use insecticidal soap. Buds or fruits turn yellow.	
Buds or young pods may drop from plant. Pods have holes, become misshapen, develop blotches.	pepper weevil
Comments	
Adults are dark beetles ⅛ inch (3 mm) long; larvae are white, legless, found inside fruit. Destroy plants as soon as harvest is over to reduce problem next year. Destroy nightshade plants, an alternate host.	
Small leaves with irregular mottle.	mosaic viruses
Comments	
Plant tobacco mosaic virus-(TMV)-resistant varieties. Dark-colored dieback from growing tip. Pods may have orange, yellow rings.	
	spotted wilt virus
Spread by thrips. Control weeds that are host of virus and vector.	
Plants do not grow. Blossoms drop off. Fruit do not develop.	climate too cool; wrong variety
Comments	
Plant in warmer weather. Plant recommended varieties.	
Plants wilt and die. Brown streaks inside root and lower stem, visible when stem is split lengthwise.	Verticillium wilt
Comments	
Caused by soilborne *Verticillium* fungus. Avoid planting in soil previously planted to potato, tomato, or cucurbits.	
Leaves roll downward. No stunting; no yellowing of new leaves.	physiological leaf roll
Comments	
Not caused by pathogen; no action needed.	
Small holes in leaves; on lower leaves more than top ones	flea beetle
Comments	
Tiny black beetles that jump. Consult UC IPM pest note series or Flint 1998 for management options.	
White, frothy foam on stems; insects visible beneath foam	spittle bugs
Comments	
Green insects. Tolerate. Not a cause of significant damage.	
Leaves wilt, turn yellow, then brown. Tiny white flies flutter when plant disturbed.	whiteflies
Comments	
Consult UC IPM pest note series or Flint 1998 for management options.	
Normal-colored fruit, but small, flattened. Few to no seed inside.	poor or incomplete in shape. pollination
Comments	
Plant in full sunlight. Tap flowers in midday to aid pollination.	

long, usually have three to four lobes and a blocky appearance. They are commonly harvested when green, yet turn red or yellow when fully ripe. About 200 varieties are available, including specialty colored varieties that are deep red, purple, and other colors.

Banana peppers are long and tapering and harvested when yellow, orange, or red. Another sweet pepper, pimiento, has conical, thick-walled fruit, 2 to 3 inches (5 to 7.5 cm) wide by 4 inches (10 cm) long. Most pimientos are used when red and fully ripe. Cherry peppers vary in size and flavor. They are harvested orange to deep red.

Slim, pointed, slightly twisted fruits characterize the hot cayenne pepper group. They can be harvested either when green or red and include varieties such as anaheim, cayenne, serrano, and jalapeño. Celestial peppers are cone-shaped, ¾ to 2 inches (1.9 to 5 cm) long, and very hot. They vary in color from yellow to red to purple, making them an attractive plant to grow. Slender, pointed tabasco peppers, 1 to 3 inches (2.5 to 7.5 cm), taste extremely hot and include such varieties as Chili Piquin and Small Red Chili.

The cultural and climatic requirements for both types of peppers are the same as those recommended for tomatoes. You can start peppers in a hotbed or coldframe for transplanting, or you can buy small plants from the nursery and set them out in the garden. Peppers generally need a long warm growing season but grow slowly during cool periods. When temperatures approach 100°F (38°C), pollination, fruit set, and yield are reduced. After the soil has thoroughly warmed in the spring, you can set out 6- to 8-week-old transplants to get a head start toward harvest. Practice good cultivation and provide adequate moisture. Mulching can help to conserve water and reduce weeds.

Harvest fruits of mild peppers when they are green or red-ripe. When allowed to mature on the plant, most varieties turn red and sweeter and increase in vitamin A and C content. Cut, instead of pulling, to avoid breaking branches. Hot peppers that you plan to dry should be allowed to ripen on the plant. Hot peppers turn red when ripe; they may then be cut with 1 inch (2.5 cm) of stem attached, strung on a thread, and hung in a sunny place until dry and brittle. Use a sharp knife for cutting, as the stems are tough.

Red bell peppers are similar to green bell peppers in calories, fat content, fiber, sodium,

Problem	Probable cause
Fruit have visible worms or holes where worms entered.	**corn earworm; omnivorous leafroller**
Comments	
Consult UC IPM pest note series or Flint 1998 for management options.	
Large, sunken, watersoaked spot develops on blossom end of fruit; spot turns black and mold may develop.	**blossom end rot**
Comments	
Can be caused by uneven moisture supply. Give uniform irrigation. Supply water during dry periods. Mulch.	

protein, and carbohydrate. However, red bell peppers have double the vitamin C content (95 mg, 158% RDA); in addition, a serving of ½ cup supplies about 30 percent of the RDA for vitamin A.

Nutritional Value of Green Bell Peppers (Sweet)

Serving size: ½ cup chopped, raw (50 g)

Calories	14
Fat	0.1 g
Calories from fat	6%
Cholesterol	0
Carbohydrate	3.2 g
Protein	0.4 g
Dietary fiber	0.8 g
Sodium	1 mg

Primary Nutrients		% RDA (m)	% RDA (f)	% Min. Requirement
Vitamin C	45 mg	5.0	6.0	
Vitamin B$_6$	0.12 mg	9.2	9.2	

Nutritional Value of Hot Chili Peppers

Serving size: 1 pepper, raw (45g)

Calories	18
Fat	0.1
Calories from fat	5
Cholesterol	0
Protein	0.9 g
Carbohydrate	4.3 g
Sodium	3 mg

Primary Nutrients		% RDA (m)	% RDA (f)	% Min. Requirement
Vitamin C	109 mg	121.1	145.3	
Potassium	153 mg			7.7

Potato, Sweet (*Ipomoea batatus*)

Recommended Varieties

Dry-fleshed (yellow)

- Jersey

Moist-fleshed (yams)

- Garnet (dark red)
- Jewel (deep orange)

Sweet potatoes grow best in light, sandy soils and are sensitive to temperatures below 50°F (10°C). For this reason, sweet potatoes do not grow well along the north coast or in the northern sections of the state.

Grow sweet potatoes from sprouts or slip produced by the following method: Place small sweet potatoes in a hotbed about March 1; cover with 3 to 4 inches (7.5 to 10 cm) of sand; keep the bed moist. Maintain a soil temperature of 70° to 75°F (24°C) in the hotbed. In about 6 weeks, sprouts about 8 inches (20 cm) long are ready for transplanting. Pull the sprouts and transplant them to raised beds. You may grow several crops of sprouts from the same planting. After setting out the sprouts, apply several light irrigations throughout the growing season.

Nutritional Value of Sweet Potato

Serving size: 4 oz, baked (114 g)

Calories	118
Fat	0.1 g
Calories from fat	0.8%
Cholesterol	0
Sodium	12 mg
Protein	2.0 g
Carbohydrate	27.7 g
Dietary fiber	3.4 g

Primary Nutrients		% RDA (m)	% RDA (f)	% Min. Requirement
Vitamin A	2,488 RE	276.4	355.4	
Vitamin C	28 mg	31.1	37.3	
Vitamin B$_6$	0.28 mg	21.5	21.5	
Riboflavin	0.15 mg	11.5	13.6	
Folic acid	26 mcg	6.5	6.5	
Magnesium	23 mg	5.5	7.2	
Thiamine	0.08 mg	6.7	7.0	
Iron	0.52 mg	6.5	2.9	
Potassium	397 mg			20

Problem Diagnosis for Sweet Potato

See table 14.5 for general techniques for recognizing and managing the common problems associated with sweet potato. Nematodes, aphids, flea beetles, leafhoppers, and wireworms cause problems in sweet potato plantings. See white potato, below, and consult the UC IPM pest note series or Flint 1998.

Problem Diagnosis for White Potato

Problem	Probable cause
Plants fail to emerge from ground after planting seed pieces.	**soil organisms; market potatoes used as seed**
Comments	
Soil organisms can rot seed pieces. Potatoes bought at the market are often treated to prevent sprouting. Plant only certified seed potatoes. Cut them when sprouts begin to form, and plant seed pieces immediately. Plant when soil temp. is >45°F (7°C).	
Tunneling in tubers, also visible in stalks, leaves. Pink tuber eyes from excrement. Shoots wilting and dying.	**potato tuberworm**
Comments	
Consult UC IPM pest note series or Flint 1998 for management options.	
Curled, distorted leaves. Stunted plants.	**aphids**
Comments	
Use insecticidal soap.	
Leaves curled upward; older leaves turn yellow, then brown; margins of young leaves may be purple. Nodes and petioles are enlarged, twisted. Foliage rosetted. Aerial tubers may be visible. Tubers small, produced in chains. Entire plant brown, stiff, upright.	**potato psyllid**
Comments	
Adults are size of aphids, winged, light gray to dark brown. Found on undersides of leaves. Immature forms are flat, disklike, yellowish with marginal fringe. Serious damage to young plants. Once tubers are formed, psyllids can be tolerated.	
White stippling on upper leaf surface; leaf margins, tips yellow or brown. Plants stunted.	**leafhoppers**
Comments	
Use insecticidal soap.	
Leaves full of small holes. Tubers with bumps and shallow winding trails on surface.	**flea beetles**
Comments	
Brown, black, or striped jumping beetles 1/16 inch (1.5 mm) long. Control usually not necessary. Peel away damage on tubers.	
Bumps or pimples on tubers; brown spots in outer part of tuber flesh. Swellings on roots.	**nematodes**
Comments	
Consult UC IPM pest note series or Flint 1998 for management options.	
Poor crop in spite of good growing practices. Leaves rough, crinkled.	**viruses**
Comments	
Plant certified seed potatoes	

You can harvest sweet potatoes when slightly immature if they are of suitable size; otherwise, leave them in the ground until the roots are full grown and the vines begin to turn yellow. However, if the leaves are killed by frost before they yellow, cut them off, dig up the roots, and store them at once in boxes in a warm, moist place. Do not bruise the roots when digging, as this increases the possibility of decay. Sweet potatoes improve during storage because a part of the starch content is converted into sugar.

Potato, White (Irish) (*Solanum tuberosum*)

Recommended Varieties (Disease Resistance)

- White Rose (LB)
- Kennebec
- Chieftain
- Norgold Russet
- Red Lasoda
- Yukon Gold

Many specialty varieties are also available.

Grow white potatoes from sections of tubers. Do not use grocery store potatoes or potatoes from your own garden as a source of seed. Buy seed potatoes from a nursery that displays a Certified Seed Potato tag. If the seed potatoes are not already cut, cut the tubers into 1½- to 2-ounce (42.5- to 56.7-g) pieces. Make sure each piece has at least one eye. Store the freshly cut pieces at room temperature for 1 to 3 days before planting. This allows the cut surfaces to dry and form a callus, which decreases rotting.

To plant, drop the seed pieces into furrows 3 inches (7.5 cm) deep with the pieces spaced 6 to 12 inches (15 to 30 cm) apart. Closer spacing gives more but smaller potatoes at harvest. Fill in the furrow to ground level. When the potato plants emerge, cover with 3 inches (7.5 cm) of soil, making furrows between the rows that are at least 6 inches (15 cm) deep. You can also plant the seed pieces in premade beds. Apply nitrogen fertilizer at planting time.

Potatoes are shallow-rooted and need light, frequent irrigations at least once a week during much of the growing season. Excessive irrigation, however, causes rotting. If soil

Problem	Probable cause
Leaves turn grayish brown with rings of gray-white downy spores when humidity is high. Leaves and stems die. Tubers have brown purple scars on surface and rot in storage.	late blight

Comments

Caused by a fungus that infects potatoes, tomatoes, and other potato family plants. Problem mainly in coastal areas and Bakersfield. Destroy, remove volunteer potatoes before planting. Use resistant varieties, such as Kennebec. Plant certified tubers. Keep tubers covered with soil hills. Bordeaux mixture is protectant. Cut vines 1 inch (2.5 cm) below soil surface and remove 10–14 days before harvest. Do not harvest under wet conditions. Eliminate all tubers and plants after harvest.

Problem	Probable cause
Plant leaves rolled, often with loss of dark green color and slowed growth. Brown speckling in stem end of tubers.	leafroll and other aphid-transmitted viruses

Comments

Use certified seed. Avoid saving seed potatoes from gardens. Use resistant varieties. Control insects. Control weeds.

Problem	Probable cause
Tubers knobby-shaped or with cavities.	alternate wet and dry conditions

Comments

Keep soil moisture uniform. Do not plant in heavy soils.

Problem	Probable cause
Vines progressively decline and die earlier than normal. Brown streaks inside lower stem visible when stem split lengthwise.	Verticillium wilt

Comments

Caused by a soilborne fungus. Rotate crops. Avoid ground planted to tomatoes, peppers, eggplant, or cucurbits.

Problem	Probable cause
Tubers have brown streaks and what appears to be a root inside.	nutsedge rhizomes

Comments

Keep potato plantings free of nutsedge.

Problem	Probable cause
Scabby spots or pits on surface of tubers.	scab

Comments

Caused by a soilborne bacterium. Disease is cosmetic. Affected tubers are edible. Plant resistant varieties. If scab occurs, change varieties next year. Disease is favored by neutral to basic soil. Sulfur may be worked into soil to make it slightly acid and reduce disease.

Problem	Probable cause
Green tubers.	exposure to sun

Comments

Do not eat green part of potato tuber because of toxin. Mound soil up around planting.

Problem	Probable cause
Tubers have slimy, smelly rot.	soft rot

Comments

Bacterial disease. Plant in well-drained soil. Store properly.

Problem	Probable cause
Tubers show irregular white or brown cavities when cut open.	hollow heart

Comments

Caused when plants grow too rapidly. Do not overfertilize or plant too far apart.

moisture conditions are alternately wet and dry, potatoes become rough and knobby. Potatoes do not grow well in soils containing moderate or large amounts of clay; sandy or loam soils are best.

When the plants are about 4 to 6 inches (10 to 15 cm) tall they should be "dirted," which means using a hoe or a similar tool to pull about 3 to 4 inches (7.5 to 10 cm) of soil up to the plants. The seed piece should ideally be about 6 inches (15 cm) beneath the surface of the soil after the dirting process. When the tops have grown too large to allow cultivation, a finishing cultivation, sometimes called "laying by" or "hilling up" is given. "Laying by" is throwing soil over the potatoes to prevent their exposure to sun, which can cause greening or scalding. A poisonous alkaloid makes green potatoes taste bitter and they should not be consumed.

Harvest early potatoes when large enough for table use. If you wish to store potatoes for later use, leave them in the ground until the plant tops are dead, or nearly so, and the skin on the tubers is firm, not flaky. Then dig them up and store in a cool, dark place.

Nutritional Value of White Potato

Serving size: 7 oz, baked with skin (200 g)

Calories	220
Fat	0.2 g
Calories from fat	0.8%
Cholesterol	0
Sodium	16 mg
Protein	4.7 g
Carbohydrate	51 g

Primary Nutrients		% RDA (m)	% RDA (f)	% Min. Requirement
Vitamin B$_6$	0.7 mg	53.8	53.8	
Vitamin C	26 mg	28.9	34.7	
Iron	2.75 mg	34.4	15.3	
Niacin	3.3 mg	20.6	23.6	
Thiamin	0.22 mg	18.3	20.0	
Magnesium	55 mg	13.1	17.2	
Folic acid	22 mcg	5.5	5.5	
Potassium	844 mg			42

Problem Diagnosis for Pumpkin

Problem	Probable cause
Deformed, curled leaves. Small, soft-bodied insects on underside of leaves. Sticky honeydew or black sooty mold may be present.	aphids
Comments Use insecticidal soap.	
Fine stippling on leaves; yellow or brown leaves; leaf underside silver-gray with fine webbing and yellow, orange, or red dots.	spider mites
Comments Use oil or soap spray.	
Leaves turn yellow. Honeydew or sooty mold present. Clouds of tiny white insects fly up when plant is disturbed.	whiteflies
Comments Remove infested plants as quickly as possible. Remove lower, infested leaves of plants that are not totally infested.	
Coarse, white stippling on upper surface of leaves. Leaves may turn brown.	leafhoppers
Comments Consult UC IPM pest note series or Flint 1998 for management options.	
Blotches or tunnels on leaves.	leafminers
Comments Consult UC IPM pest note series or Flint 1998 for management options.	
Angular necrotic areas on leaves.	angular leafspot
Comments Caused by a waterborne bacterium. Avoid wetting foliage with irrigation water.	
Swelling, beads on roots. Wilted plants. Poor yields.	nematodes
Comments Rotate crops. Use soil solarization.	
Holes chewed in leaves. Scarring of runners, young fruit. Wilting. Beetles visible.	cucumber beetles
Comments Beetles are yellow-green with black stripes or spots. Use pyrethrins.	
Leaves have small specks that turn yellow, then brown. Vines wilt from point of attack to end of vine.	squash bug
Comments Trap adults beneath boards in spring. Turn over boards in morning and kill bugs. Pick off adults, young, egg masses.	
White, powdery spots on leaves and stems. Spots may enlarge and completely cover leaf. Defoliation may occur. Yields reduced.	powdery mildew
Comments Spores of powdery mildew fungus are spread by wind and air currents. Disease is less severe in hot, dry weather. Plant resistant varieties. Dusting with sulfur can be effective. Remove old plant debris.	

Pumpkin (*Cucurbita pepo*)

Recommended Varieties (Disease Resistance)

- Spirit (semibush, multipurpose) (AAS)
- Autumn Gold (multipurpose, turns gold before maturity) (AAS)
- Jack O'Lantern (good for carving)
- Big Max (large fruit for showing)
- Bushkin (compact vine for large container or garden)
- Cinderella

Pumpkins can range in size from small jack-o'-lanterns to more than 100 pounds (45.4 kg) depending on the variety grown and the culture provided. Pumpkins need ample space. The bush types can spread to more than 20 feet (6 m). Check table 14.2 for the best planting dates in your area. Give pumpkins the same care and treatment as described for winter squash. Keep leaves dry to prevent foliar wilt diseases.

To monogram a jack-o'-lantern, scratch a name into the fruit before the shell is hardened (usually in late August or early September). The inscription will callus over and become more distinguishable as the pumpkin matures.

Nutritional Value of Pumpkin

Serving size: ½ cup, (can) (122 g)

Calories	41
Fat	0.3 g
Calories from fat	7%
Cholesterol	0
Sodium	6 mg
Protein	1.3 g
Carbohydrate	9.9 g

Primary Nutrients		% RDA (m)	% RDA (f)	% Min. Requirement
Vitamin A	2,691 RE	299.0	384.4	
Iron	1.7 mg	21.3	9.4	
Vitamin C	5 mg	5.6	6.7	
Magnesium	28 mg	6.7	8.8	
Potassium	251 mg			12.5

Problem	Probable cause
Yellow spots on upper leaf surfaces; grayish, fuzzy growth on undersides of spots.	**downy mildew**
Comments Fungal disease. Plant resistant varieties. Remove old plant debris.	
Stunted plants, small leaves with irregularly shaped light and dark spots (mottled). Yields reduced.	**mosaic virus**
Comments Transmitted by aphids. Remove infected plants as soon as detected. Control aphids. Control weeds. Aluminum foil is effective as soil mulch to reduce infection. Deformed fruit is edible.	
Poor fruit set.	**insufficient pollination lack of bee pollinators**
Comments Hand-pollinate using artist's paintbrush if bee pollinators are too few. Bee activity may be low because of cool weather or insecticides.	
Plants wilt and die, beginning with older crown leaves. Light brown streaks occur inside lower stem, runners, and root. Visible when split lengthwise.	**Verticillium wilt**
Comments Caused by soilborne fungus. Rotate crops. Avoid soil previously planted in potatoes, peppers, eggplant, tomatoes, or cucurbits.	
Plants wilt suddenly. Roots rot.	**sudden wilt**
Comments Caused by *Pythium* fungus. Avoid water stress after fruit set. Avoid wetting soil to the crown. Improve drainage. Plant on raised beds.	
Water-soaked, sunken, brown or black spot on fruit not restricted to blossom end.	**belly rot**
Comments Rotate crops. Improve drainage. Stake or cage to keep fruit off ground.	
Excessive vegetative growth.	**planting too close together**
Comments Increase plant spacing.	

Note: Pumpkin (*Cucurbita pepo* var. *pepo*) is a relative of melons (*Cucumis melo*), including cantaloupe, honeydew, and crenshaw; winter and summer squash (*Cucurbita pepo* var. *melopepo*); cucumbers (*Cucumis sativus*); and watermelon (*Citrullus lanatus*). Collectively known as the cucurbits, they suffer from similar pests and diseases, as is evident from the problem diagnosis table above.

Radish (*Raphanus sativus*)

Recommended Varieties (Disease Resistance)

Red
- Cherry Belle (AAS)
- Champion(AAS)
- Scarlet Knight (F)

Multicolored
- Easter Egg Hybrid

White
- April Cross Hybrid (long, pungent Oriental type)
- Icicle (tapered, mild)
- Snowbelle (round)

Radishes are easy to grow and, in cool areas, you can plant several successive crops during the season. The crop is ready for harvest 3 to 6 weeks after the seed is planted. Beware of overmaturity, which results in splits, cracks, hollowness, and pithy roots, as well as the development of a seed stalk.

Radish is classified as a cool-season crop. The best root shape and yield are produced at cool temperatures (50° to 70°F [10° to 20°C]) and relatively short days (10 to 12 hours). A number of environmental conditions can cause serious quality defects. One of the defects that often puzzles growers and gardeners is the lack of development of the edible part. The problem is known as thready root because the hypocotyl cells do not expand normally and everything below ground resembles a slender, often deformed tap root. Researchers have studied the problem and have determined that termperatures in the range of 70°F to 80°F (21° to 27°C) and long day lengths produce more deformed and thready roots. Bolting is

Nutritional Value of Radish

Serving size: ½ cup, slices, raw (50 g)

Calories	7
Fat	trace
Calories from fat	0
Cholesterol	0
Sodium	8 mg
Protein	0.6 g
Carbohydrate	1.3 g

Primary Nutrients		% RDA (m)	% RDA (f)	% Min. Requirement
Vitamin C	15 mg	16.7	20.0	

Problem Diagnosis for Radish

Problem	Probable cause
Roots fail to form.	crowded growing conditions
Comments	
Thin early to correct. Radishes "hot."	
	overmaturity; variety
Harvest at early stage.	
Some varieties are more pungent than others.	
Small holes in leaves.	flea beetles; cucumber beetles
Comments	
Flea beetles are small beetles, 1/16 inch (1.5 mm) long, that jump like fleas. Ignore problem if harvest is near. Otherwise, use insecticidal soap. Control weeds.	
Deformed foliage with whitish or yellowish spotting on leaves. Plants look wilted.	harlequin bug
Comments	
Bugs are black with bright red, yellow, or orange markings, suck fluids from plant tissue. Hand-pick bugs and egg masses. Eliminate old, nonproductive cole crops, wild radish, and mustard because they provide breeding sources.	
Small plants wilt and die. Grooves on surface of roots; winding tunnels through roots. Fleshy part may become streaked with brown from tunneling.	cabbage maggot; root maggot
Comments	
Prevent infestation. No practical control when maggots occur on growing crop (see fig. 14.4). Consult UC IPM pest note series or Flint 1998 for additional management options.	
Leaves with light green areas and a violet-colored downy growth on undersides. Roots with black network inside.	downy mildew
Comments	
Remove old plant debris. Rotate crops.	

also promoted by high temperatures and long day lengths.

Rhubarb (*Rheum rhabarbarum*)

Recommended Varieties

- Cherry (red stalks)
- Victoria (green stalks with red shading)

Rhubarb grows well along the coast and in cool sections of the Central Valley. Start plants in the winter or very early in the spring. It is common to grow rhubarb from pieces of an old plant (crown) or rootstock; be sure each piece has at least one good, strong bud. Fertilize the plants once a year just before the cutting season. The plants grow vigorously into early summer when they become dormant until the winter rains come. During the

Nutritional Value of Rhubarb

Serving size: 1 cup, diced, raw or frozen (137 g)

Calories	29
Fat	0.2 g
Calories from fat	6%
Cholesterol	0
Sodium	5 mg
Protein	0.8 g
Carbohydrate	7.0 g

Primary Nutrients		% RDA (m)	% RDA (f)	% Min. Requirement
Vitamin C	7 mg	7.8	9.3	
Calcium	266 mg	26.6	26.6	
Potassium	148 mg			7.4

Figure 14.4

Two preventive devices for protecting plants from cabbage maggot. The cone-shaped screen cover on the left is constructed from standard window screen fixed to a wooden frame. It can protect plants until they grow big enough to tolerate damage. The screen cone covers can be stacked and stored for future use. Another device (right) is a 3-inch- (7.5–cm)-diameter disk of tarred paper, foam rubber, or other sturdy material placed flat around the base of each plant as it is transplanted. Cut a hole in the center of each disk for the transplant's stem. The disk prevents adult flies from laying eggs near plant stems and may also encourage the aggregation of predatory beetles that eat cabbage maggot eggs and larvae. Both devices and other management strategies are described in detail in *Pests of the Garden and Small Farm* (Flint 1998).

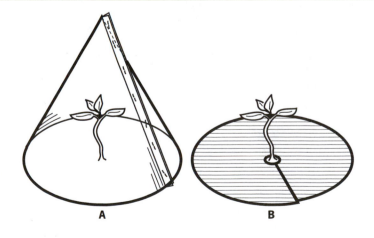

A   B

first growing season, few, if any, stalks will be ready for harvest. After that time, the plant can produce for many years. Divide the plants and replant the new rootstocks periodically.

Problem Diagnosis for Rhubarb

See table 14.5 for general techniques for recognizing and managing common problems associated with rhubarb, such as aphids, flea beetles, and leafhoppers.

Problem Diagnosis for Rutabaga

As a member of the *Brassica* family, rutabagas are related to turnips, cabbage, cauliflower, kohlrabi, mustard greens, broccoli, and brussels sprouts. Rutabagas suffer from similar pest insects, diseases, and cultural problems that plague its relatives. See "Problem Diagnosis for Cabbage." Cabbage root maggot is an important pest problem for rutabagas.

Problem Diagnosis for Spinach

Problem	Probable cause
Poor germination, emergence.	**high soil temperatures**
Comments	
Plant at correct time.	
Leaves partly or entirely consumed; light green caterpillars are visible.	**loopers**
Comments	
Hand-pick, or *Bacillus thuringiensis* is effective.	
Leaves become faded yellow.	**aphids**
Comments	
Wash aphids from leaves before eating.	
	inadequate nitrogen
Comments	
Sidedress with nitrogen fertilizer.	
Leaves have light green to yellow blotches. Pull back skin of blotch to find maggots in the mine.	**leafminers**
Comments	
Pick off and destroy infested leaves.	
Yellow to pale green areas on leaves; fluffy gray spores develop on undersurface of leaves after rain or heavy dew.	**downy mildew**
Comments	
Problem when weather is wet and humid or under frequent sprinkling. Plant resistant varieties. Remove old plant debris. Rotate crops.	
Plants begin to grow tall and send up flower stalks.	**bolting**
Comments	
Caused by long daylight periods from late spring to early fall. Plant spinach in fall or early spring. Choose varieties carefully.	

Rutabaga (*Brassica napus*)

Recommended Variety

- American Purple Top

Rutabagas can be grown in cooler areas of the state and require the same treatment as turnips. Prepare the soil as directed for carrots. Rutabagas require 90 to 100 days to grow until large yellow-fleshed roots, 3 to 6 inches (7.5 to 16 cm) in diameter, develop. The top half of the root usually grows above the ground and may have a purple pigmentation. Do not leave rutabagas in the soil if freezing conditions are likely to occur.

When rutabagas reach the desired size, dig up the roots and trim, wash, and dry them. Eating quality is improved by a short storage period. Rutabagas are sometimes waxed and stored under cool, humid conditions. Rutabaga greens are edible, but they are not as good a source of greens as turnips.

Nutritional Value of Rutabaga
Serving size: ½ cup cubes, boiled (85 g)

Calories	29
Fat	0.2 g
Calories from fat	6%
Cholesterol	0
Sodium	15 mg
Protein	0.9 g
Carbohydrate	6.6 g

Primary Nutrients		% RDA (m)	% RDA (f)	% Min. Requirement
Vitamin C	19 mg	24.1	25.3	
Magnesium	18 mg	4.3	5.6	
Potassium	244 mg			7

Spinach (*Spinacia oleracea*)

Recommended Varieties (Disease Resistance)

- Melody Hybrid (AAS, DM, V)
- America (AAS)

A cool climate is best for producing spinach. During periods of warm temperatures and long days, the leaves become tough and plants are likely to produce seed stalks before making desirable foliage growth. Spinach is fast-growing and short-lived and matures its leafy foliage in 7 weeks. It then quickly goes to seed, although it produces for a longer period in the cool, coastal areas before seed stalk

Nutritional Value of Spinach

Serving size: 1/2 cup, boiled (90 g)

Calories	21
Fat	0.2 g
Calories from fat	9%
Cholesterol	0
Sodium	63 mg
Protein	2.7 g
Carbohydrate	3.4 g
Dietary fiber	2.0 g

Primary Nutrients		% RDA (m)	% RDA (f)	% Min. Requirement
Vitamin A	737 RE	81.9	105.3	
Folic acid	131 mcg	32.8	32.8	
Iron	3.21 mg	40.1	17.8	
Magnesium	79 mg	18.8	24.7	
Riboflavin	0.21 mg	16.2	19.1	
Vitamin B$_6$	0.22 mg	16.9	16.9	
Vitamin C	9 mg	10.0	12.0	
Calcium	122 mg	12.2	12.2	
Potassium	419 mg			21

development occurs. When the plant is ready to harvest, either cut the entire plant or remove just the outer leaves. If you carefully cut the plant above the growing point, you can then obtain a second crop.

New Zealand and Malabar are not true spiniches. New Zealand spinach (*Tetragonia tetragonoides*), which forms short runners and resembles regular spinach in leaf shape, is frost-sensitive but tolerates warm weather much better than regular spinach. It is productive all season and can be cooked or used raw in salads, although the leaves are tougher than true spiniches.

Squash, Summer (*Cucurbita pepo*)

Recommended Varieties (Disease Resistance)

Scallop (patty pan)

- Peter Pan Hybrid (bush) (AAS)
- Sunburst (bright yellow) (AAS)
- Scallopini (bush) (AAS)
- Early White Bush (white)
- Trombocini or Zucchetta rampicante

Yellow

- Early Prolific Straightneck (AAS)
- Sundance (crookneck compact)
- Early Golden Summer Crookneck
- Dixie (crookneck compact)

Zucchini

- Aristocrat (AAS)
- Greyzini (compact) (AAS)
- Ambassador (compact) (PM)
- Gold Rush (golden fruit) (AAS)
- Burpee Fordhook (AAS)

Summer squash grows on nonvining bushes. Many varieties have different fruit shapes and colors. The three main types include the yellow straight neck or crooked neck; the white, saucer-shaped, scallop, or patty pan; and the oblong, green, gray, or gold zucchini.

Squash plants have extensive root systems, so soil containing plenty of well-rotted compost or manure is ideal, although good crops may be grown in average soils that have been fertilized adequately. For extra early fruit, plant seeds in peat pots or other containers indoors or in hotbeds and transplant about 3 weeks later after danger of frost is past. Older plants that have hardened off and stopped growing do not transplant well and should be discarded. Squashes are warm-season plants and do not do well until soil and air temperatures are above 60°F (16°C).

Squash plants have separate male and female flowers on the same plant. The male flowers do not produce fruit, but they do supply the pollen that fertilizes female flowers. Pollen must be transferred to the female flowers by bees for fruit to develop. If insecticides are necessary, use them late in the evening to avoid killing bees (see "Fruit Set Problems in Squash, Melons, and Cucumbers," below).

Seed or transplants can be planted through black plastic. Cover seed with 1 inch (2.5 cm) of soil. Under good growing conditions, summer squashes are ready for first harvest 50 to 65 days after seed are planted. Zucchini types should be harvested when immature, about 6 to 8 inches (15 to 20 cm) long and 1½ to 2 inches (3.7 to 7.5 cm) in diameter; patty-pan types, when 3 to 4 inches (7.5 to 10 cm) in

Figure 14.5

Squash flowers. *Source*:
After Johnson 1981, p. 1.

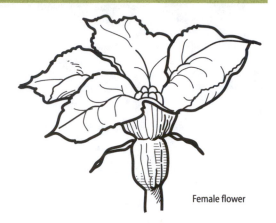

Female flower

Male flower

diameter; yellow crookneck, when 4 to 7 inches (10 to 17.5 cm) long. If the squash rind is too hard to be marked by a thumbnail, it is too old. Remove old fruit to allow new fruit to develop. Check plants daily once they begin to bear.

Fruit Set Problems in Squash, Melons, and Cucumbers*

Squash, melons, and cucumbers belong to the same family, often called cucurbits, and they have a flowering habit unique among vegetable crops. They bear two kinds of flowers, male and female, both on the same plant. In order for fruit set to occur, pollen from the male flower must be transferred to the female

flower. The pollen is sticky, so wind-blown pollination does not occur. Honeybees are the principal means by which pollen is transferred from the male to the female flower. Other insects cannot be depended on for pollination. Growers who produce these crops place hives of bees in their fields to ensure that pollination takes place. Wild honeybees are rare in some urban neighborhoods, and when bees are absent, fruit set on garden plants in the cucurbit family is very poor and often nonexistent. If only a few bees are present in the area, partial pollination may occur, resulting in misshapen fruit and low yield.

When no bees are present in the garden or the bee population is too low for good fruit set, the dedicated gardener can substitute for the bee by pollinating by hand. Hand-pollination is a tedious chore, but it is the only means of obtaining fruit set in the absence of bees. The pollen is yellow and is produced on the structure in the center of the male flower. You can use a small artist's paintbrush to transfer pollen, or you can break off a male flower, remove its petals to expose the pollen-bearing structure, and roll the pollen onto the stigma in the center of the female flower. When hand-pollinating, it is important to use only freshly opened flowers. Flowers open early in the morning and are receptive for only 1 day.

The female flower in cucurbits can be recognized easily by the presence of a miniature fruit (ovary) at the base of the flower (see fig.

Nutritional Value of Summer Squash (crookneck, zucchini, and all other types)

Serving size: ½ cup slices, boiled (90 g)

Calories	18
Fat	0.3 g
Calories from fat	15%
Sodium	1.0 mg
Cholesterol	0
Protein	0.8 g
Carbohydrate	3.9 g
Dietary fiber	1.3 g

Primary Nutrients		% RDA (m)	% RDA (f)	% Min. Requirement
Vitamin C	5 mg	5.6	6.7	
Magnesium	22 mg	5.2	6.9	
Potassium	173 mg			8.7

Problem Diagnosis for Summer Squash

Summer squash (*Cucurbita pepo*) is a relative of winter squash (*Cucurbita pepo*); pumpkin (*Cucurbita pepo*); melons (*Cucumis melo*), including cantaloupe, honeydew, and crenshaw; cucumbers (*Cucumis sativus*); and watermelon (*Citrullus lanatus*). The cucurbits suffer from similar pests and diseases. See "Problem Piagnosis for Cucumber" in this chapter to understand how to diagnose the most common insect pests and diseases that attack summer squash.

*The author of this section is Hunter Johnson Jr., retired UC Cooperative Extension Vegetable Specialist, Riverside Campus.

14.5). Female squash flowers are much larger than the female flowers on melon and cucumber plants. The male squash flower can be identified by its long, slender stem. The female squash flower is borne on a very short stem. In melons and cucumbers, male flowers have very short stems and are borne in clusters of three to five, whereas the female flowers are borne singly on somewhat longer stems.

Gardeners often become concerned when many flowers appear early but fruits fail to set. All of the early flowers are males. Female flowers develop somewhat later and can be identified by the miniature fruit at the flower base. In hybrid varieties of summer squash, however, the first flowers to appear are usually females, and these will fail to develop unless there are male squash flowers—and bees—nearby.

A common misconception is that squash, melons, and cucumbers will cross-pollinate. This is not true: the female flowers of each can be fertilized only by pollen from that same species. Varieties within each species, however, will cross-pollinate. For example, zucchini squash will cross with crookneck or acorn squash. This is also true among varieties of cucumber and among varieties of muskmelon. When more than one variety of a particular cucurbit is grown in the garden, they will readily cross-pollinate, and seed saved from these plants will produce fruit that will be different from either of the parents.

Squash, Winter

Cucurbita pepo (acorn) and *Cucurbita maxima* (butternut)

Recommended Varieties (Disease Resistance)

Acorn

- Table King (bush, strongly determinant) (AAS)

Problem Diagnosis for Winter Squash

Winter and summer squash (*Cucurbita pepo*) are relatives of pumpkin (*Cucurbita pepo*); melons (*Cucumis melo*), including cantaloupe, honeydew, and crenshaw; cucumbers (*Cucumis sativus*); and watermelon (*Citrullus lanatus*). The cucurbits suffer from similar pests and diseases. See "Problem Diagnosis for Cucumber" to understand how to diagnose the most common insect pests and diseases that attack winter squash.

- Table Ace (semibush)
- Jersey Golden (semibush) (AAS)
- Sweet Mama (AAS, F)

Butternut

- Waltham (AAS)
- Early Butternut (semibush) (AAS)
- Burpee Butterbush (bush)

Winter squash varieties differ widely in shape and color. Bush plants require less space than creepers but often produce fewer fruit. Plant groups of 3 or 4 seed 2 to 4 feet (1.2 m) apart in rows that are 6 feet (1.8 m) apart. Spacing for bush varieties can be reduced by one-third to one-half. Once the plants emerge, thin to one plant per group. Plant when the soil has warmed up in the spring.

The mature fruit has a hard outer shell. Use a sharp knife to cut stems of fruit to be stored. Leave a short piece of the stem attached to the fruit and avoid bruising. Store in a dry, fairly cool location.

Squash plants have separate male and female flowers on the same plant. The male flowers do not produce fruit but they do supply the pollen that fertilizes female flowers. Pollen must be transferred to the female flowers by bees for fruit to develop. If necessary, use insecticides late in the evening to prevent killing bees. (See "Fruit Set Problems in Squash, Melons, and Cucumbers" in the section on summer squash.)

Nutritional Value of Winter Squash (Acorn variety)

Serving size: ½ cup cubes, baked (102 g)

Calories	57
Fat	0.1 g
Calories from fat	2%
Cholesterol	0
Sodium	4 mg
Protein	1.1 g
Carbohydrate	14.9 g

Primary Nutrients		% RDA (m)	% RDA (f)	% Min. Requirement
Vitamin C	11 mg	12.2	14.7	
Vitamin B$_6$	0.2 mg	15.4	15.4	
Thiamin	0.17 mg	14.2	15.5	
Magnesium	43 mg	10.2	13.4	
Iron	.95 mg	11.9	5.3	
Folic acid	19 mcg	4.8	4.8	
Calcium	45 mg	4.5	4.5	
Potassium	446 mg			22

Tomatoes (*Lycopersicon esculentum*)

Recommended Varieties and Disease Resistance

Home-grown tomatoes are one of the most popular garden vegetables. (See below for cherry tomato varieties, container varieties, and standard-sized varieties, their adaptation to climatic zones in the state, and their resistance to diseases.) The varieties available to the home gardener are numerous, and the flavor and quality of home-grown, vine-ripened tomatoes are usually outstanding. Tomatoes require relatively little space for large production. Each tomato plant, properly cared for, yields 10 to 15 pounds (4.5 to 6.8 kg) or more of fruit. Choose varieties bred for disease resistance for best results. Fusarium (F) and Verticillium (V) wilt are common diseases that can destroy a whole tomato crop. Many varieties are resistant to these two diseases. Look for VF after the cultivar name, indicating resistance to the wilts. VFN means the plants are resistant to *Verticillium*, *Fusarium*, and nematodes; VFNT adds tobacco mosaic virus to the resistance list.

Tomato plants are described as determinate or indeterminate. These terms refer to plant growth habit. Determinate tomato plants grow like a bush to a certain size (about 3 to 5 feet [90 to 150 cm]), set fruit, and then gradually decline. Most of the early-ripening tomato varieties are of the determinate type. The vines of indeterminate plants continue to grow until frost or disease kills them. Many of the standard-sized, large-fruited tomatoes typical of the home garden are indeterminate types. Both types of plants require support of some kind for best results, to prevent the fruit from being in contact with the soil and thus being susceptible to rot. Supporting plants also saves garden space and makes it easier to harvest fruit.

The large number of tomato varieties available may seem overwhelming to a new gardener; ask gardening friends for the names of their favorites. Varieties differ in plant size and habit, disease resistance, and climatic requirements. Although tomatoes are a warm-season crop, they can be grown in the cooler areas of the state if you choose the right varieties.

Listed below are three climatic zones (A, B, and C) and the tomato varieties that are adapted to those zones. Look for your own climatic zone, and then select the varieties you want. A number of heirloom and specialty varieties are also available if you wish to experiment with them.

In addition to the usual round red tomato, home gardeners can choose to grow orange, yellow, pink, or striped tomato varieties that have little commercial appeal and are only available to the home market. Some of the yellow varieties, which are shaped like pears or plums, have a mild, sweet flavor with low acid content.

Climatic Zones for Tomato Varieties

Zone A

- coastal areas from Santa Barbara south
- coastal foothills and mountain ranges from San Diego through Marin Counties
- foothills surrounding the Central Valley
- Napa and Sonoma Valleys
- San Jose, Los Angeles, Santa Ana, and San Diego
- other areas where summer daytime temperatures are warm but usually below 95°F (35°C)

Zone B

- inland valleys, high and low deserts, and other inland areas where daytime temperatures regularly exceed 95°F during the summer growing season
- the Central, San Fernando, and San Gabriel valleys
- Pomona, Riverside, and El Cajon
- interior valleys of San Diego County

Zone C

- immediate central and north coastal areas
- cool coastal valleys from Santa Maria north to the Oregon border, the San Francisco Peninsula, and areas with direct exposure to San Francisco Bay
- northern coastal foothills
- most mountains and mountain valley regions
- Eureka, Oakland, and Monterey

Problem Diagnosis for Tomato

Problem	Probable cause
Seedlings or small transplants with small holes in leaves. In severe cases, entire plant may be destroyed.	flea beetles
Comments Rarely damaging except on seedlings. Tomatoes tolerate a lot of beetle damage if they are healthy.	
Leaves almost totally eaten off of young plants. Small, dark weevils on plants.	vegetable weevil
Comments Weevil attacks many vegetables but does not fly, so it spreads slowly through garden. Hand-picking adults off plants at night is effective if population is low. Rotenone is effective.	
Lower leaves, stems have bronze, oily brown color. Discoloration moves higher on plant. Dry lower leaves drop from plant or plant may lose leaves.	tomato russet mite
Comments Tiny mites not visible to naked eye; use 20X hand lens. Mites appear as slow-moving, whitish-yellow, pear-shaped bodies. Do not grow tomatoes near petunias or any solanaceous plant such as potato because they are alternate hosts. Sulfur is effective, but excessive rates may injure plant.	
Leaves yellowish, slightly curled. Some leaves and fruit with small shiny spots; others may appear blackened. Insects visible on undersides of leaves.	aphids
Comments Tiny, oval, yellowish to greenish scalelike insects. Not a problem unless honeydew or sooty mold becomes obvious. Can use insecticidal soap.	
Plants with poor vigor, reduced yields. Foliage yellows, turns brown from bottom up. May look wilted. Many beads or swellings on roots.	root knot nematode
Comments Nearly microscopic eelworms that attack feeder roots. Plant resistant varieties. Such varieties are labeled VFN (see text). Rotate crops. Remove old plant debris.	
Tiny, white, winged insects on undersides of leaves.	whiteflies
Comments Encourage beneficials.	
Trails, tunnels in leaves.	leafminers
Comments Use insecticides, natural enemies to control.	
Young plants cut off at ground.	cutworms
Comments Use cutworm collars or registered insecticide.	

- Other areas with cool to moderate summers with evening temperatures frequently in the 45°F to 55°F (7° to 13°C) range

Tomato Varieties

Cherry tomatoes
Cherry tomatoes have small, cherry-sized (or a little larger) fruit that are often used in salads. They grow in all three zones of the state. Plants of cherry tomatoes range from dwarf size to 7-footers (2.1 m) (Sweet 100). One standard cherry tomato plant is usually sufficient for a family, because they generally produce abundantly.

- Cherry Grande (VF)—F, V; medium, determinate plant, with large cherry fruit
- Sweet Cherry—F; large indeterminate plant, with medium to large cherry fruit
- Sweet 100—large, indeterminate plant with clusters of small cherry fruit
- Sungold—large, indeterminate plant with clustery, orange cherry fruit

Container varieties
Container varieties are adapted to all three zones of the state. Midget, patio, or dwarf tomato varieties have very compact vines and do best when grown in 5-gallon (19-l) or larger containers or large hanging baskets. Some produce large fruit, but the fruit are often of poorer quality than fruit from standard-sized plants. Container varieties are usually short-lived, producing their crop quickly over a short period.

- Patio—F; dwarf, determinate plant with small to medium fruit
- Better Bush—F, N, V; compact, determinate plant with small to medium fruit
- Small Fry—F, N, V; compact determinate plant with small cherry fruit
- Husky series (zones A, B, C)—F, N, V; red-pink, gold, medium-small fruit; compact yet indeterminate plants, may need some staking or caging

Standard varieties
Many standard-sized tomato varieties listed below are indeterminate or semideterminate plants that require some type of support. Beefsteak-type tomatoes are large-fruited types, producing a tomato slice that easily covers a sandwich. A single fruit may weigh 2 pounds (0.90 kg) or more. These usually vary in their yield and are late to ripen, so plant some other

Problem	Probable cause
Leaf veins turn purple and bronze. Leaves curl upward, feel thick, leathery, or brittle. Plant growth stops. Fruit ripen prematurely.	**curly top virus**

Comments
Spread by leafhoppers. After plants are infected, no practical control in the home garden. Purple leaves can also indicate phosphorus deficiency.

Leaves have irregular light and dark green pattern. May be wrinkled or frilly. Terminal growth may be spindly with narrow, wrinkled leaves.	**tobacco mosaic virus**

Comments
Plant resistant varieties (TMV). Do not handle plants more than necessary. Plant tomato seeds rather than transplants. Do not handle plants after smoking because TMV can be spread in tobacco. No cure for virus in infected plants. Infected plants produce edible fruit but yield, size, and quality are reduced.

Blossoms fall off.	**night temperatures too low (<55°F [<13°C]); day temperatures too high (>90°F [<32°C])**

Comments
Hormone sprays can improve fruit set during low temperatures but will not help in high temperatures. Keep soil moderately moist.

	smog during blossoming period

Comments
Tapping on blossom stems 3 times/week in midday when flowers are open may help set fruit.

	excess nitrogen fertilizer

Comments
Fertilize properly.

	too much shade from trees, house

Comments
Plant tomatoes in full sun.

	early blossoms

Comments
Early blossoms often fail to set fruit consistently. Do not plant too early.

	wrong variety

Comments
Plant varieties that are adapted to California's hot summers.

Lower leaves yellow with tiny brown specks. Leaves die. Blossoms drop. Poor growth.	**smog**

Comments
Some varieties more susceptible than others. Very difficult to diagnose accurately.

standard-sized tomatoes for an earlier and consistent harvest.

- Ace Hybrid (zones A, B)—F, N, V; medium, determinate plant grown with short stake or cage or as a large bush, with medium to large, attractive fruit
- Better Boy (zone A)—F, N, V; large, indeterminate plant grown with stake or cage
- Big Beef (zones A, B)—AAS, F, N, TMV, V; large, indeterminate plant grown with stake or cage, beefsteak-type fruit.
- Big Pick (zones A, B)—F, N, TMV, V; large, indeterminate plant grown with stake or cage
- Big Set (zones A, B)—F, N, V; medium, semideterminate plant grown with cage or as a bush
- Bingo (zones A, C)—F, TMV, V; medium, determinate plant with large fruit grown with short stake or cage or as a bush
- Carmelo (zone C)—F, N, TMV, V; medium, semideterminate plant grown with cage or as a bush
- Celebrity (zones A, B)—AAS, F, N, TMV, V; medium, semideterminate plant grown with stake or cage; widely adapted, with consistently large, firm fruit
- Champion (zones A, B, C)—F, N, TMV, V; large, indeterminate plant grown with stake or cage; large, attractive fruit; excellent for winter crop in inland valleys
- Early Bush 76 (zones A, B)—F, V; medium determinate plant grown with short stake or as large bush with concentrated production of large fruit; best determinate plant for zone A
- Early Girl (zone A)—V; large, indeterminate plant grown with stake or cage; continuous bearing of small to medium fruit
- Early Pick (zones A, B, C)—F, V; large, indeterminate plant grown with stake or cage; abundant medium to large attractive fruit
- Floramerica (zones A, B)—AAS, F, V; medium, determinate plant grown with short stake or cage with consistent yields of large fruit, some green shoulders
- Jackpot (zones A, B)—F, N, V; compact, determinate plant grown with short stake or as bush, with concentrated production of medium to large fruit
- Jet Star (zones A, B)—F, V; large, indeterminate plant grown with stake or cage; good quality medium to large fruit

Problem	Probable cause
Plants pale, turning yellowish with brown lesions on leaves. Brown stripes on some stems. Fruit poorly colored with circular light areas or distorted bumps. Plants eventually die.	spotted wilt virus

Comments
Spread by thrips from various crops, ornamentals, weeds. Remove and destroy infected plants. Control nearby weeds that can harbor virus or thrips vector.

Plants turn yellow, starting with one side or branch and gradually spreading. When cut off at base, main stem is dark reddish brown instead of normal ivory color. Plants wilt.	Fusarium wilt

Comments
Caused by a soil fungus that infects tomatoes only; favored by warm soil. Grow resistant varieties (F or VF). They are resistant to most (but not all) races of *Fusarium*.

Older leaves begin to yellow and eventually die. Yellowing begins between main veins of leaves. Internal stem is very slightly tan-colored, usually in small patches.	Verticillium wilt

Comments
Caused by a soil fungus that infects many plants favored by cool soil and air temperatures. Grow resistant varieties (V or VF). Avoid ground previously planted with tomatoes, potatoes, peppers, eggplant, or cucurbits. Symptoms most severe when plants are water-stressed in hot weather with fruit load.

Plants grow slowly and wilt. Roots have water-soaked areas that turn brown and dry up.	Phytopthora root rot

Comments
Caused by a soil fungus. Most common in heavier clay soils. Irrigate affected plants carefully to maintain them. Do not saturate soil for extended periods; water more frequently for short periods.

Plants wilt with white cottony growth on stem near soil line.	southern blight

Comments
Caused by a fungus. Rotate to corn or other nonhost crops for 2 to 3 years.

Fruit turns light brown, leathery on side exposed to the sun.	sunscald

Comments
Caused by overexposure to sun. Maintain plant vigor to produce adequate leaf cover.

Water-soaked brown areas on leaves and stems. Grayish white fungus grows on undersides of leaves, and they die. Fruit discolored but firm.	late blight

Comments
Caused by a fungus. Favored by high humidity and temperatures around 68°F (20°C). Avoid sprinkler irrigation. Destroy all tomato and potato debris after harvest.

- Quick Pick (zone A)—F, N, TMV, V; large, indeterminate plant grown with stake or cage; early, good quality small to medium fruit
- Marvel Stripe (zones A,B)—(?); yellow-red striped beefsteak-type fruit; indeterminate plant grown with stake.
- Royal Flush (Zones A, B)—F, N, V; compact, determinate plant grown with short stake or as a bush; concentrated production of large fruit
- Supersteak (zone A)—F, N, V; very large, indeterminate plant grown with stake or cage; large, high-quality fruit
- Valerie (zones A, C)—F, N, V; medium, determinate plant grown with short stake or as bush; early, medium fruit

Tomato Culture

Start tomato plants indoors from seed or purchase transplants. If starting your own plants, use a light soil mix and give the plants plenty of natural or artificial light. (See chapter 5, "Plant Propagation," for details on growing transplants.) The seeds should be sown 6 to 8 weeks before the last frost date in your area.

When you are ready to plant, select stocky transplants about 6 to 8 inches (15 to 20 cm) tall. Set tomato transplants in the ground covering the stems so that only two or three sets of true leaves are exposed. Horizontal planting of tomato plants is an effective way to use leggy plants and make them stronger. Roots will form along the buried portion of the stem, giving better growth and less chance of plant injury from a stem that is too weak. Do not remove the containers if they are peat or paper pots. If nonbiodegradable containers are used, knock the plants out of the pots before transplanting and loosen the roots somewhat. Press the soil firmly around the transplant so that a slight depression is formed for holding water. Pour approximately 1 pint (0.47 l) of starter solution or other dilute liquid fertilizer around each plant.

Keep the soil around new transplants moist for the first 3 to 4 weeks. Water established plants when the soil dries to about 2 to 3 inches (5 to 7.5 cm) deep. Apply enough water to wet the root zone thoroughly. Since weather and the depth of rooting vary, the right interval for applying water in the summer can vary from one to three times a week to once every 10 days or 2 weeks. Plants are

Problem	Probable cause
Irregular yellow blotches on leaves. Blotches turn brown and die but leaves usually do not drop unless disease is severe. No symptoms on stem or fruit.	powdery mildew

Comments

Caused by a fungus. Usually occurs late in summer or fall but does not cause significant loss unless very severe so no control normally needed. Avoid water stress. If young plants attacked, sulfur dust will control the disease.

Dark brown to black blotches surrounded by yellowing along edges of leaves. Superficial dark specks on green fruit.	bacterial speck

Comments

Develops only under wet, cool temperatures, usually in early spring. Daily mean temperatures >70°F (21°C) suppress it. If speck is a problem, consider delaying planting until temperatures are warm. Rotate crops. Avoid overhead watering.

Worms up to 1¾ inches (4.5 cm) long in immature or ripe tomatoes.	tomato fruitworm

Comments

Bacillus thuringiensis is somewhat effective. No control is needed unless infestation is severe.

Worms up to ⅜ inch (9.5 mm) long tunneling in fruit.	potato tuberworm

Comments

Do not plant tomatoes where potatoes were planted the year before. Destroy volunteer potato plants.

Worms never longer than ¼ inch (6 mm) tunnel in core and fleshy parts radiating from core. Leaves may be mined and folded together.	tomato pinworm

Comments

Pinworm is most common in Southern California and the central to southern end of the San Joaquin Valley. It occurs earlier in the season than fruitworm.

Leaves eaten, stems remain. Fruit with small to large gouged- out areas. Very large caterpillars may be present.	hornworms

Comments

Insects have distinctive horn on rear end. Hand-picking and *Bacillus thuringiensis* are effective controls.

Fruit surface eaten away or fruit hollowed out.	snails, slugs

Comments

Snails feed on surface of fruit. Slugs hollow out fruit. Stake tomatoes to get fruit off ground and away from slugs and snails.

Creamy to yellowish cloudy spots lacking definite margin on ripe tomatoes. Tissue beneath spots is spongy.	stink bugs

Comments

Green to gray shield-shaped bugs ¼ inch (6.5 mm) long. Stink bugs overwinter beneath boards in weedy areas, refuse piles. Remove debris from garden area. Hand-pick egg masses and bugs. Control weeds.

best irrigated by using soaker hoses, drip irrigation, or another means that applies water slowly without wetting the foliage.

Sidedress plants with nitrogen fertilizer when they set their first fruit and every 4 to 6 weeks thereafter. Always water well after applying fertilizer. If some form of manure was used at planting, reduce the fertilizer rate by one-half. Applying relatively high amounts of nitrogen, from organic or chemical sources, before plants begin setting fruit causes plants to grow lush, leafy growth and significantly delays flowering and fruit set. It usually takes 10 to 12 weeks from the time transplants are set in the garden to have the first ripe tomatoes.

Supporting tomato plants off the ground reduces fruit rots, makes pest management easier, provides easier harvesting, and allows more plants to be grown in the same space. There are three common methods of supporting tomatoes. One method is to drive sturdy wooden stakes, 6 feet (1.8 m) long by 1 to 1½ inches (2.5 to 3.8 cm) wide, into the ground about 1 foot (30 cm) deep and spaced 3 to 4 feet (90 to 120 cm) apart within the row. Twist and loop heavy twine tautly from stake to stake across plants at intervals of 10 to 12 inches (25 to 30 cm) up the stakes as plants grow. This creates a loose net that keeps plants upright in a solid row that is about 18 to 24 inches (46 to 60 cm) wide.

Another method is to tie plants individually to a fence or a wooden stake 5 to 6 feet (1.5 to 1.8 m) tall. As plants grow, pull the stems toward the fence or stake and loosely tie them at intervals of 10 or 12 inches (25 to 30 cm) using a flexible material, such as strips of cloth. Plants supported in this manner often require pruning or pinching out of some shoots or "suckers" from the main stem to keep the plants from becoming too heavy and large for their support.

Using a heavy-gauge metal cage is a third alternative, and one that requires the least amount of work. Cylindrical cages about 18 to 30 inches (46 to 76 cm) in diameter and 4 to 5 feet (1.2 to 1.5 cm) tall are set over each plant, and no tying or prining is needed. Use concrete reinforcing wire or similar heavy-duty material with at least 6-inch (15 cm) spacing between wires so that plant stems can easily grow through them and you can get your hand inside to harvest the tomatoes. Caged tomatoes develop a heavy foliage cover, reducing sunscald on fruits.

Harvest tomatoes when they are red ripe for best quality. Toward the end of the season, some whitish-green, full-sized tomatoes will probably still be on the vines. You can pick these tomatoes and store them at 70°F (21°C) to ripen. Picked tomatoes should be placed in the shade; light is not necessary for ripening immature tomatoes. Ripe tomatoes should be stored at 55° to 70°F (13° to 21°C) to maintain their fresh, ripe flavor. Lengthy refrigeration causes fruit to lose flavor.

Tomato Fruit Set Failure and Flower Drop*

Most people who raise backyard tomatoes have experienced the problem of poor fruit set. Under good environmental conditions, fruit set occurs normally; yet tomato plants may fail to set fruit for any one of several reasons. The most frequent problems are

- cold nights in the spring
- high temperatures in the summer
- low light intensity
- smog (ozone)

The tomato flower contains both male and female parts. In order for fruit set to occur, viable pollen from the anthers (male parts) must be transferred to the stigma (part of the female organs), germinate there, and send its tube down through the style to fertilize the ovules. When fertilized successfully, the developing ovules (young seed) produce a stimulus that results in fruit enlargement. Under adverse environmental conditions, one or more of these processes may fail to occur, and the flowers will fall from the plant. Occasionally fruit will enlarge without pollination or fertilization, but these are usually poorly formed and fail to develop to desirable size.

Prevention and Control of Fruit Drop

Cool nights. After several days of nighttime temperatures below 55°F (13°C), fruit set often fails in most varieties. Under these conditions, fruit set can be improved with the use of fruit-setting hormones available in most retail nurseries or agricultural supply houses. Research has shown that 4-CPA (parachlorophenoxyacetic adic) is more effective than BNOA (beta naphthoxyacetic acid).

Follow label directions carefully.

Hot days. Fruit set failure in tomato also often occurs when daytime temperatures consistently exceed 90°F (32°C). Some varieties are more tolerant of high temperatures and will continue to set fruit when others fail. Under these conditions, it is helpful to keep the plants in a healthy growing condition so that developing flowers will have a better chance to survive. Maintain a constant moisture supply, eliminate damaging insects, and control diseases. Fruit-setting hormones are not effective in hot weather.

Low light intensity. Tomato flowers may also fail to develop into fruit when sunlight is inadequate. This may occur when plants are growing under dense shade trees or along the north wall of a building. Avoid planting locations that do not allow at least several hours of direct sunlight. Best growth results where plants receive full sunlight throughout the day.

Smog. Research has shown that high concentrations of ozone, a principal air pollutant during summer months, significantly reduces fruit set in tomatoes. At present there is no solution for this problem.

Solar Yellowing in Tomatoes*

Yellow discoloration in tomatoes occurs in the late spring under greenhouse conditions, or from late spring through the summer in the open field in inland areas where daytime temperatures regularly exceed 85°F (30°C). An accurate term for this condition is "solar yellowing" because the source of the problem is the sun. The cause of the problem is not only heat, but also high light intensity. This was shown by Dr. Werner Lipton, who coined the term "solar yellowing" in research he conducted on the subject in 1970. His treatments involved shading or painting the fruit either black or white. Black-painted fruit were higher in temperature than exposed fruit, but discoloration was highest in the exposed fruit. His conclusion was that short-wave radiation was largely responsible for defective coloration.

The reason for the yellow or yellow-orange color, rather than the normal red, is that the red pigment (lycopene) fails to form above 86°F (30°C). This phenomenon was first described by researchers in 1952 and was later confirmed by others. When lycopene fails to form, only carotenes remain for fruit color. In

*The author of this section is Hunter Johnson Jr., retired UCCE vegetable specialist from the University of California, Riverside.

Problem	Probable cause
Fruits are brown-black on bottom (blossom) end. Affects both green and ripe fruit.	**blossom end rot**

Comments
A physiological disease (not caused by a microorganism) that involves calcium nutrition and water balance in plant. Aggravated by high soil salt content or low soil moisture. More common on sandier soils. Maintain even soil moisture.

| **Fruit with large cracks in concentric circles around stem.** | **rainfall or irrigation, especially after dry spell** |

Comments
Remove ripe fruit immediately after a rain to prevent cracking.

| **Fruit with large cracks radiating from stem.** | **high temperatures (>90ºF [<32ºC]); too much sunlight** |

Comments
Keep soil evenly moist. Maintain good leaf cover. In very hot regions, choose planting time to avoid fruit maturity when temperatures will consistently be above 90ºF (32ºC).

| **Fruit with black mold along growth cracks; develops on damaged, cracked tissue.** | **fruit rot** |

Comments
Prevent fruit cracking (see above). Handle fruit carefully.

| **Black, sunken spots on fruit.** | **Alternaria fruit rot** |

Comments
Use registered fungicide.

Nutritional Value of Tomato
Serving size: 1 (about 4 oz), raw (120 g)

Calories	26
Fat	0.4 g
Calories from fat	14%
Cholesterol	0
Dietary fiber	1.6 g
Protein	1.0 g
Sodium	11 mg
Carbohydrate	5.7 g

Primary Nutrients		%RDA (m)	%RDA (f)	% Min. Requirement
Vitamin C	24 mg	26.7	32.0	
Vitamin A	77 RE	8.6	11.0	
Iron	0.55 mg	6.9	3.1	
Folic acid	18 mcg	4.5	4.5	
Potassium	273 mg			13.7

the field, some red color forms when day temperatures rise above 85ºF (30ºC) because of fluctuation in noninhibiting temperatures _during other parts of the day or night. An orangey-red color results. In production areas where temperatures do not exceed 85ºF (30ºC), much redder color develops.

To develop a good uniform red color in tomatoes, protect fruit from high temperatures and from short-wave radiation in areas of high light intensity. Dr. Lipton showed that sprays of nonphytotoxic whitewash are helpful. In greenhouses, growers who intend to mature fruit in May and June should begin to alter their pruning practices in March by allowing two leaves to develop on axillary branches instead of following the standard practice of removing these branches.

Leaf Roll of Tomato
Leaf roll of tomato is a very common disorder in many varieties grown in California. Leaf roll does not develop markedly on plants until about the time of fruit setting of the first and second flower clusters. At this time, the older leaves begin to roll upward and inward rather suddenly. Affected leaves are stiff to the touch, brittle, and at times almost leathery. They are much thicker than normal leaves and shiny on both the upper and lower surfaces. In mild cases, leaves become trough-shaped. In severe cases, the leaves may form a very tight cylinder, with the leaf margins touching or overlapping. The severity of leaf roll varies with climatic conditions, cultural practices, and the particular variety grown. No pathogens have been identified as causal agents. When leaf roll is severe, three-fourths of the leaves on a plant may be involved, exposing fruit to full sunlight and resulting in the development of disorders such as yellow leaf discoloration and sun scald.

No control methods for leaf roll are recommended because it is not known to severely damage plants or fruit production and its actual cause is not fully understood. Susceptible varieties have been observed to express leaf roll most frequently when they are grown in staked culture and heavily pruned. Maintaining a high soil moisture content for prolonged periods of time is also believed to promote the disorder.

Observations of an experiment in Florida led to a hypothesis that leaf roll might be caused by an accumulation of excess amounts of carbohydrates (sugars and starch). This theory was tested in the Floradel variety by removing vegetative shoots, flowers, and developing fruits, which serve as sinks for photosynthates. These treatments resulted in rapid expression of leaf roll, completely to the tops of certain plants. A second test involved growing plants under 0 to 75 percent shade to inhibit photosynthate production. Under high shade conditions, the incidence of leaf roll was reduced to less than 50 percent. In the experiment leaves that originally were shaded and did not roll later developed leaf roll when exposed to full sunlight.

Although no definite conclusions can be drawn as to the cause-effect relationships of plant carbohydrate concentration to leaf roll, it does appear that leaf roll will be most severe when tomatoes are grown in staked culture under high light intensities and high soil moisture conditions.

Problem Diagnosis for Turnip

Problem	Probable cause
Distortion, stunting, wilting of plant. Soft-bodied insects in colonies on undersides of leaves.	**aphids**
Comments Consult UC IPM pest note series or Flint 1998 for management options.	
Holes in leaves. Chewing injury on buds or roots. Some plants may be cut off at soil level, much like cutworm damage.	**vegetable weevil**
Comments Damage is spotty. Adults do not fly, so infestation of new areas takes place slowly.	
Irregular holes in leaves. Small or seedling plants may be destroyed.	**caterpillars of cabbage looper; imported cabbage worm; armyworms**
Comments Hand-pick. Depending on the specific pest, *Bacillus thuringiensisis* somewhat to very effective.	
Deformed leaves with whitish or yellowish spotting. Plants may have wilted appearance.	**harlequin bug**
Comments Attractive, shield-shaped insects usually black with bright red, yellow, or orange markings. Injury is caused by bugs sucking fluids from tissues. Hand-pick the bugs and their egg masses. Eliminate old, nonproductive cole crops, wild radish, and mustard because they are breeding source.	
Feeding injury (engraving) on root surface or tunneling through roots of young plants or seedlings, which fail to grow properly. Plants may wilt or die.	**cabbage maggot (root maggot)**
Comments All control measures are preventative (see fig. 14.4). No practical control after maggots occur on the growing crop. Consult UC IPM pest note series or Flint 1998 for additional management options.	

Turnip (*Brassica rapa*)

Recommended Varieties (Disease Resistance)

- Purple Top White Globe (pure white root) (AAS)
- Tokyo Cross Hybrid (for greens only)
- Seven Top (for greens only, large smooth leaves)
- All Top Hybrid

Turnips are grown for the tops and also for the enlarged root. The crop may be produced within 60 days. Turnips grow best in a cool climate where both a spring and a fall crop are possible. The cultural practices for varieties used specifically for the production of greens are similar to those for growing table beets.

Nutritional Value of Turnip
Serving size: ½ cup cubes, boiled (78 g)

Calories	14
Fat	0.1 g
Calories from fat	6%
Cholesterol	0
Sodium	39 mg
Protein	0.6 g
Carbohydrate	3.8 g
Dietary fiber	1.6 g

Primary Nutrients		% RDA (m)	% RDA (f)	% Min. Requirement
Vitamin C	9 mg	10.0	12.0	

Watermelon (*Citrullus lanatus*)

Recommended Varieties (Disease Resistance)

Bush Vine

- Garden Baby (small round fruit)
- Bush Charleston Gray (small, oblong fruit) (F)
- Bush Jubilee (small, oblong fruit) (AN, F)
- Bush Sugar Baby (small, round fruit)

Large Vine

- Calsweet (large, oblong fruit) (F)
- Crimson Sweet (large, round fruit) (AN, F)
- Sugar Baby (small, round fruit)

- Sweet Baby (small, round fruit) (F)
- Charleston Gray (large, oblong fruit) (AN, F)
- Prince Charles (large, oblong fruit) (F)

Seedless
- Triple Sweet Hybrid
- Tri X-313 Hybrid
- Firecracker

Yellow-Fleshed Fruit
- Yellow Baby (small, round fruit) (AAS)
- Yellow Doll (small, round fruit; semi-compact vines)

You need a fairly large garden to grow watermelons successfully. The general methods of planting and handling are the same as those given for growing cantaloupes, their cucurbit relatives. The first fruit may be ready for harvest about 90 days after the seed are planted. In areas where winter rainfall is over 12 inches (30 cm) and the soil stores 9 inches (22.5 cm) of water, watermelons grow reasonably well with little irrigation, although irrigation increases yields. If you plan to provide limited irrigation, plant seed as early as possible in the spring and thin the plants to one plant per hill. If plants are stressed for water when they start to set fruit, melons will be small and yields reduced.

To test melons for ripeness, rap the side of the fruit with your knuckles. A light or metallic sound means that the fruit is still green; a dull sound means that it is ripe. This is most reliable in the early morning. During the heat of the day or after melons have been picked for some time, they all sound ripe. Fruits have a "ground spot" where they rest on the ground; this spot turns slightly yellow as the fruit matures. Watermelons tend to become rough as they mature. The tendrils closest to the fruit darken and dry up as the fruit ripens. Do not pull melons off the vine; cut the vines with a sharp knife.

For information on fruit set problem, see "Fruit Set Problems in Squash, Melons and Cucumbers" in the section on summer squash.

Problem Diagnosis for Watermelon

See "Problem Diagnosis for Cantaloupe." *Note*: Watermelon (*Citrullus lanatus*) is a relative of melons (*Cucumis melo*), including cantaloupe, honeydew, crenshaw; winter and summer squash (*Cucurbita pepo*); pumpkin (*Cucurbita pepo*); and cucumbers (*Cucumis sativus*). Collectively, known as the cucurbits, they suffer from similar pests and diseases, evident from the problem diagnosis table above.

Nutritional Value of Watermelon
Serving size: 1 cup cubes (160 g)

Calories	50
Fat	0.7 g
Calories from fat	13%
Cholesterol	0
Sodium	3 mg
Protein	1.0 g
Carbohydrate	11.5 g
Dietary fiber	0.6 g

Primary Nutrients		% RDA (m)	% RDA (f)	% Min. Requirement
Vitamin C	15 mg	16.7	20.0	
Vitamin B₆	0.23 mg	17.7	17.7	
Thaimin	0.13 mg	10.8	11.8	
Magnesium	17 mg	4.0	5.3	
Vitamin A	58 RE	6.4	8.3	
Potassium	186 mg			9

Herbs

Many culinary herbs—the herbs used to season food—are very easy to grow, and a bountiful harvest can be secured with a minimum of care. A few plants of each kind of herb add color and fragrance to the garden and provide an adequate supply for the average family.

Depending on the species, variety, and life cycle, herbs are divided into three groups. Annual herbs include such plants as anise, basil, coriander, and dill; biennial herbs include caraway and sage; and perennial herbs include chives, fennel, lovage, marjoram, mint, and thyme. In California's mild climate, some tender perennial herbs do quite well, whereas in colder climates, they grow as annuals. For both annuals and perennials, spring is the usual season to plant herbs.

Table 14.7 summarizes basic information about many common annual and perennial herbs grown in the home garden. When planning an herb garden, factor in the growth habit of the individual herbs. Perennial herbs are best planted around the edges of the garden or in the flower border, if they are also ornamental. Plant the taller herbs in the background, with lower ones in front, near walks and paths. A large number of herbs may be set either in beds or in rows for ease of irrigation and cultivation. Small-sized herbs, such as chives, basil, sweet marjoram, peppermint, rosemary, summer savory, and thyme, adapt to culture in pots or other containers that are 6 inches (1.5 cm) in diameter or larger.

In the garden, group herbs according to their light requirements (full sun or partial shade), and choose a soil that is well-drained and loamy for best results. Herbs prefer a soil pH about 6.0 to 7.0. Prepare the soil to a depth of 8 inches (20 cm) and incorporate an organic amendment if the soil is not loamy. Give perennial herbs an area that will not be disturbed by tilling. Herbs that spread by runners, such as the mints, should be given a large area or should be planted in containers to provide some control. Mints spread rapidly, and parsley and fennel seed themselves, so they can become nuisances in the garden.

Herbs may be propagated from seed, rooted cuttings, or division of a mother plant. Many common herbs are available as small transplants at nurseries and garden centers. Seeds may be started either indoors or outdoors. The easiest method is to sow them directly into peat pots or other small containers about 6 weeks before the last expected frost. (See chapter 5, "Plant Propagation," for details on starting seeds.)

Perennials may be started from seed, division, or cuttings. Root cuttings in flats or containers covered with plastic to maintain high humidity. A satisfactory rooting medium can be made from 4 to 5 inches (10 to 12.5 cm) of clean, coarse sand. Keep the sand moist, and keep plants out of direct sunlight when young. In 4 to 6 weeks or when cuttings are rooted, move them to pots or plant in the garden.

Transplant all herb plants after danger of severe frost. Control weeds during the growing season to prevent competition for water and nutrients. A light mulch conserves soil moisture and helps control weeds. Irrigation will be necessary for most herbs, although once established, many perennial herbs will tolerate some drought.

Harvesting

Herb leaves that are used fresh may be picked whenever the plant has enough foliage to maintain continued growth. Herbs for drying should be picked just before the flowers open,

when the leaves contain the highest content of aromatic volatile oils. The stems should be selected and cut individually about 6 inches (15 cm) below the flower buds. Remove dead or damaged leaves, and cleanse dirty leaves by rinsing them gently in cold water and drying them with paper towels. Plants may also be sprayed with a garden hose the day before harvesting. Discontinue harvesting leaves of perennials in late summer to allow the plants to store enough carbohydrates for overwintering and renewing growth next season.

You may save seeds for culinary uses or for starting plants the next year by allowing the plants to mature and flower. Harvest seeds when they change in color from green to brown or gray and allow them to dry thoroughly before storing.

Drying and Storage

Herbs may be dried by tying the cut stems in small bunches and hanging them in a well-ventilated, low-dust, darkened room. Each bunch should be labeled, because many dried herbs are very similar in appearance. The result will be obtained if leaves are dried rapidly without artificial heat or exposure to sunlight. However, in the case of plants with thick, succulent leaves, such as basil, rapid drying in an oven, dehydrator, or solar dryer may be the best method to retain color and maximum aromatic quality. If leaves are not too small, they may be removed from the stems and dried in a single layer on trays made of window screening or ¼-inch (0.6-cm) mesh hardware cloth. Label each herb. Stir the leaves gently once or twice a day to speed drying.

When drying is complete, remove the leaves from the stems or trays and place them in sealed glass jars in a warm place for a week. At the end of that time, examine the jars to determine whether any moisture has condensed on the inside of the glass. If there is condensation, remove the contents and spread out for further drying. If necessary, the final drying may be completed by spreading the leaves on a cookie sheet in an oven at 110°F (44°C) or less. Herb leaves are dry when they become brittle and will crumble into powder when rubbed between the hands. If you prefer to use herbs in powdered or ground form, crush the leaves with a rolling pin, pass them through a fine sieve, or grind them in a blender or with a mortar and pestle.

Table 14.7

USE AND CULTURE OF CULINARY HERBS

Common name (Scientific name)	Spacing in inches (cm) Height	Row	Plants	Propagation	Cultural hints	Uses
Annual Herbs						
anise (*Pimpinella anisum*)	24 (60)	18 (45)	10 (25)	seed	Plant in spring.	Leaves used for seasoning, garnish; dried seed used as flavoring in cakes, etc.
basil, sweet (*Ocimum basilicum, O. minimum*)	20–24 (50–60)	18 (45)	12 (30)	seed	Plant in spring. Pinch tips, flowers to favor leaves.	Seasoning for soups, stews, salads, sauces, omelets. Decorative when grown in containers.
borage (*Borago officinalis*)	24 (60)	18 (45)	12 (30)	seed	Best in dry, cool, sunny areas.	Young leaves used in salads. Leaf tips and flowers used in summer drinks. Flowers candied.
caraway* (*Carum carvi*)	12–24 (30–60)	18 (45)	10 (25)	seed	Biennial seed bearer.	Flavoring, especially in bakery items (bread, cake) and cheese; young leaves in salads, soups.
chervil (*Anethum graveolens*)	10 (25)	15 (37.5)	3–6 (7.5–15)	seed	Sow in early spring or fall. Partial shade best.	Aromatic leaves used in soups and salads and for garnish, like parsley. Tastes like mild anise.
coriander (cilantro) (*Coriandrun sativum*)	24 (60)	24 (60)	18 (45)	seed	Sow in early spring or fall.	Seed used in confections, curry; leaves in salad. Leaves, known as cilantro, used in Mexican, Asian, and Mediterranean dishes.
dill (*Anethum graveolens*)	24–36 (60–90)			seed	Sow in early spring.	Young leaves used in salads, seed in flavoring, especially for pickles.
fennel (Florence fennel) (*Foeniculum vulgare*) (*Finocchio foeniculum*)	60 (150)	18 (45)	18 (45)	seed	Sow in early spring.	Has aniselike flavor; seed used in soups, breads. Stalk eaten raw or braised; leaves for garnish.
parsley* (*Petroselinum crispum*)	5 (12.5)	18 (45)	6 (15)	seed	Slow to germinate. Needs some shade. Soak seed in water to improve germination.	Brings out flavor of other herbs. Leaves used for garnish and in salads. Fine base and seasoning. Popular, but only a few plants are needed in the home garden. Types include curly (French) and flat-leaved (Italian).
savory, summer (*Satureja hortensis*)	18 (45)	18 (45)	18 (45)	seed	Sow in spring.	Use leaves fresh or dry for salads, dressings, stews. Adds peppery flavor.
Perennial Herbs						
catnip (*Nepeta cataria*)	3–4 ft (90–120)	24 (60)	18 (45)	seed or division	Invasive.	Leaves for tea and seasoning.
chives (*Allium shoenosprasum*)	12 (30)	12 (30)	12 (30)	seed or division	Plant anytime but best in spring.	Favorite of chefs. Snip tops finely. Good indoor potted plant. Leaves used in omelets, salads, soups.
horehound (*Marrubium vulgare*)	24 (60)	18 (45)	15 (37.5)	seed, cuttings, division	Grow in light soil. Perennial.	Leaves used in candy or as seasoning.
hyssop (*Hyssopus officinalis*)	24 (60)	18 (45)	15 (37.5)	seed	Tolerates wide range of conditions.	A mint with highly aromatic, pungent leaves.

Common name (Scientific name)	Spacing in inches (cm)			Propagation	Cultural hints	Uses
	Height	Row	Plants			
Perennial Herbs cont.						
lavender (*Lavandula vera*)	24 (60)	18 (45)	18 (45)	cuttings, division	Grows in dry, rocky sunny locations. Divide in spring, take cuttings in spring or late summer.	Fresh in salads; use flowers dried for sachets, potpourri.
lovage (*Levisticum officinale*)	3–4 ft (90–120)	30 (75)	30 (75)	seed	Rich, moist soil. Plant in late summer.	Of the carrot family; culitvated in European gardens as a domestic remedy.
oregano (marjoram, wild marjoram) (*Origanum vulgare*)	24 (60)	18 (45)	9 (22.5)	seed, division	Cut back flowers. Good in containers.	Flavoring for tomato dishes, pasta, pizza. Leaves used in soups, roasts, stews, salad dressings.
peppermint (*Mentha piperata*)	36 (90)	24 (60)	18 (45)	seed, cuttings, division	Cut before it goes to seed.	Aromatic; multiple uses as flavoring. Oil used in products such as chewing gum, liqueurs, toilet water, soaps, candy.
rosemary (*Rosmarinus officinalis*)	3–6 ft (90–180)	18 (45)	12 (30)	cuttings, seed	Sow in spring.	Leaves flavor sauces, meats, soups, preserves, sweet pickles. One plant is enough for home garden. Can be grown indoors in containers.
saffron (*Crocus sativus*)	10 (25)			bulbs, division	Plant bulbs in early fall, 3–4 in. (7.5–10 cm) deep. Replant every few years.	Stigmas of flowers dried, used to color butter, cheese. Used to flavor creams, sauces, preserves.
sage (*Salvia officinalis*)	18 (45)	24 (60)	12 (30)	seed, cuttings	Grows slowly. Renew bed every 3–4 years.	Seasoning for meats, herb teas. Use fresh or dried.
savory, winter (*Satureja montana*)	24 (60)	15 (37.5)	18 (45)	seed, cuttings, division	Trim out dead wood.	Seasoning for stuffing, eggs, sausage; accents strong flavors; more pungent than summer savory.
spearmint (*Mentha spicata*)	18 (45)	24 (60)	18 (45)	cuttings, division	Invasive.	Aromatic; for flavoring, condiments, teas.
sweet marjoram (*Majorana hortensis*)	12 (30)	18 ft (540)	12 (30)	seed, cuttings	Overwinters as potted plant. Often grown as annual. Harvest before plant blooms.	Seasoning, fresh or dried. Fresh leaves used in salads. Dried leaves used to season meat, cheese, etc. Tastes like sweet oregano relative.
sweet woodruff (*Asperula adorata*)	8 (20)	18 (45)	12 (30)		Keep indoors in cold winter period.	Flavoring in drinks.
tarragon (*Artemisia dracunculus*)	24 (60)	24 (60)	24 (60)	division, root cuttings	Protect in cold winters.	European herb of aster family; aromatic seasoning. Leaves, tips used in dressings, tartar sauce, vinegar, preserves. Chopped leaves used in salads.
thyme (*Thymus vulgaris*)	8–12 (20–30)	18 (45)	12 (30)	seed, cuttings	Start new plants division, rooted tip cuttings every 3–4 years. Rooted tips in early spring are practical propagation method.	Aromatic foliage for seasoning meats, soups, dressings.

Note: *Biennal.

Store herbs in airtight bottles, preferably brown glass, and in a cool place out of direct sunlight. Using airtight containers allows the herbs to retain their essential oils and flavors.

Herbs as Potted House or Patio Plants

Most small-sized herb plants may be grown in 6-inch (15-cm) or larger pots. When given loving care in a sunny window, they will supply sprigs for culinary use throughout the year. If an enclosed porch or sunroom is available, larger herbs may be grown. Containerized herbs may be grown on a patio during the summer in all areas and year-round where mild winters are common. Some of the best to try are basil, sweet marjoram, oregano, rosemary, thyme, and bay laurel. Start potted plants from seed, cuttings, or divisions in midsummer, or, if available, purchase transplants. When making cuttings or divisions, be sure to hose off any insects or eggs that might be present.

Bibliography

Cotner, S. D. 1989. The vegetable garden. In D.F. Welsh, ed., Texas A&M Master Gardener's handbook. College Station: Texas A&M University.

Dietary reference intakes. 1998. Washington, DC: National Academy Press.

Flint, M. L. 1992. Integrated pest management for cole crops and lettuce. Oakland: University of California Division of Agriculture and Natural Resources Publication 3307.

———. 1998. Pests of the garden and small farm: A grower's guide to using less pesticide. 2nd ed. Oakland: University of California Division of Agriculture and Natural Resources Publication 3332.

Johnson, H. J., Jr. 1981. Fruit set problems in squash, melons, and cucumbers in the home garden. Oakland: University of California Division of Agriculture and Natural Resources Leaflet 21242.

Kader, A. A., J. Thompson, and K. Silva. 1999. Storing fresh fruits and vegetables for better taste. Oakland: University of california Division of Agriculture and Natural Resources Publication 21590. Poster.

National Academy of Sciences. 2001a. Dietary reference intakes (DRIs): Recommended intakes for individuals, elements. Washington, DC: National Academy of Sciences.

National Academy of Sciences. 2001b. Dietary reference intakes (DRIs): Recommended intakes for individuals, vitamins. Washington, DC: National Academy of Sciences.

National Academy of Sciences, Food and Nutrition Board. 1989. Recommended dietary allowances. 10th ed. Washington, DC: National Academy of Sciences.

Pennington, J. 1998. Bowe's and Church's food values of portions commonly used. 17th ed. Philadelphia: Lippincott.

Pittenger, D. R. 1983. Bitterness in cucumbers. Vegetable Briefs 223. UC Cooperative Extension Newsletter.

———. 1992. Home vegetable gardening. Oakland: University of California Division of Agriculture and Natural Resources Publication 21444.

Strand, L. L. 1992. Integrated pest management for potatoes. Oakland: University of California Division of Agriculture and Natural Resources Publication 3316.

———. 1998. Integrated pest management for tomatoes. 4th ed. Oakland: University of California Division of Agriculture and Natural Resources Publication 3274.

Tyler, K. B. 1981. Growing herbs for seasoning food. Oakland: University of California Division of Agriculture and Natural Resources Publication 2639.

UC guide to solving garden and landscape problems (CD-ROM). 2000. Oakland: University of California Division of Agriculture and Natural Resources Publication 3400.

UC IPM pest management guidelines. For many agricultural crops; updated regularly. Oakland: University of California Division of Agriculture and Natural Resources Publication 3339.

UC IPM pest note series. B. L. P. Ohlendorf, ed. University of California Division of Agriculture and Natural Resources, Statewide Integrated Pest Management Program. Updated regularly. Available through UC Cooperative Extension county offices; also available on the World Wide Web at http://www.ipm.ucdavis.edu

Vegetable gardening illustrated. 1994. Menlo Park, CA: Sunset Publishing.

Yates, A. A., Schlicker, S. A., and C. W. Suitor 1998. Dietary reference intakes: the new basis for recommendations for calcium and related nutrients, B vitamins, and choline. J. Am. Dietetic Assoc. 98(6): 699–706.

15

Grapes

Pamela M. Geisel, Delbert S. Farnham, and Paul M. Vossen

LEARNING OBJECTIVES

- Understand basic cultural practices for growing grapes in the home garden in California.

- Learn about which varieties and cultivars of grapes are suited best to different climates in California.

- Become acquainted with some of the major pests of grapes in the home garden and learn basic information about how to control them.

Grapes

Grapes have been cultivated since ancient times. The Mission padres introduced the Mission variety of grapes to California from Mexico, but this variety was not well adapted for producing raisins, quality wine, juice, jelly, or fresh fruit for eating. Many European grape varieties, brought to California in the 19th century, have provided the basis for today's thriving grape industry. Today home gardeners still grow some very old European varieties such as Muscat of Alexandria, Ladyfinger-type varieties, and Thompson Seedless. Plant breeders have also developed some outstanding new varieties such as Flame Seedless and Perlette.

Three types or species of grapes are available:

- American varieties (*Vitis labrusca*), such as Concord and Niagara

- European varieties (*V. vinifera*), which are the predominant wine, table, and raisin cultivars grown in California

- American hybrids, which are crosses of European and American species

Generally, American types are more cold-hardy than European types. The two types also differ in their fruit characteristics and growth habits. European varieties generally require a longer growing season to mature their fruit, although most grape varieties need some summer heat to produce good-quality fruit.

Soil Requirements

Grapes can grow on a wide range of well-drained California soils. Avoid soils with poor drainage or a high water table. Use raised beds to provide an adequate root zone if vines are to be grown on soils with hard pan, clay pan, or if shallow soil is located on top of impervious bedrock. Grapes will grow satisfactorily on poor, shallow soils as long as irrigation is available.

Spacing

Spacing between rows can be up to 12 feet (3.6 m), with 8 feet (2.4 m) between vines within the row. The wider spacings are appropriate for very vigorous varieties such as Thompson Seedless and Flame Seedless growing on deep, well-drained soils. Grow grapes in full sun to promote fruitfulness. Some form of trellising and training is necessary, as discussed later in this chapter.

Selecting Plants

Plant healthy 1-year-old vines available bare-root from retail nurseries. Cuttings may also be collected from healthy vines and planted directly where the vine is to grow permanently. Because bare-root vines and cuttings dry out very quickly, plant them immediately.

Rootstocks

Rootstocks are appropriate in areas where grapes cannot be grown on their own roots because of nematode and grape *Phylloxera* infestation, or in old vineyard areas that are being replanted. Several rootstocks are nematode-resistant and possess moderate *Phylloxera* resistance. The varieties used most frequently as rootstocks are Freedom and Harmony. In coastal areas one of the following *Phylloxera*-resistant rootstocks should be used: SO4, 5BB, 110R, 99R, or St. George.

Varieties for the Home Garden

A large number of grape varieties are available in California. Varieties are divided into table grapes and wine grapes according to their primary use. Some are suitable for multiple uses and may have secondary uses in making juices or jellies. American and American hybrids are typically grown for table grapes, raisins, juice, or jelly.

Figure 15.1

The earliest stages of grape flowers entering the bloom period. The calyptra (cap) covering the flower parts is beginning to open.

Figure 15.2

Three flowers, two with the calyptra almost off and one with the calyptra off, exposing the flower parts.

Figure 15.3

A grape flower in bloom after the calyptra has fallen off.

Figure 15.4

A flower cluster in about 85 percent bloom. Sprays of plant growth regulators (gibberellic acid) are applied commercially when about 50 to 70 percent of the calyptras have fallen off, producing big, lush grapes, but this is not common practice in the home garden.

Table grape and multiple-use type varieties are the ones most commonly grown by home gardeners. They are usually adapted to a range of local conditions and training systems. Numerous varieties are available, and suitable ones for various climate zones are listed in tables 15.1 and 15.2.

Wine grape varieties are suitable for many home gardens, but for optimal performance, the wine grape variety chosen should be suited to the climatic region and site. Table 15.3 provides variety information on wine grapes.

Growth Pattern and Growth Cycle

As with all fruits, the grape flowers must bloom first and be pollinated before the berries (fruit) begin to develop. Grape flower clusters begin their differentiation and development in dormant buds during the summer before the year that grapes are actually harvested. Flower differentiation is completed during the fall, by the time the vines lose their leaves. After dormancy and bud burst (see the next few sections on cultivation techniques), grape shoots begin to grow rapidly. When shoots reach 4 to 6 inches (10 to 15 cm) in length, grape flower clusters can be distinguished, and by 12 inches (30 cm), the flower clusters are well-separated on the growing shoot. The development of flower clusters on the emerging shoots usually starts in mid-March, and the flowers typically begin to bloom in May. Grape flowers have a protective cap, known as a *calyptra*, that covers the male and female sex organs until bloom, when it cracks open from the bottom and exposes the flower parts to pollination, which must occur before berries can develop. Because of their size and berrylike shape, flower clusters can be confused with developing berries before they bloom (see figs. 15.1–4).

After pollination, the male flower parts fall off (fig. 15.5), and the grape berries begin to grow and develop. Unpollinated flowers fall to the ground during the "shatter" stage. Pollinated flowers begin to form berries that continue to grow in size and increase in sugar content until harvest (fig. 15.6). The annual growth cycle of a typical grape vine is shown in figure 15.7. Note that the cycle has many facets, with several events, described above, occurring simultaneously.

Figure 15.5

A developing young berry. Following bloom and pollination, the male flower parts fall off and the berry begins to develop.

Figure 15.7 represents the annual growth and fruiting cycle of a grapevine duing the calendar year. For emphasis, the various events for the current and following year are shown separately. Actually, many of these events occur simultaneously in a mature grapevine.

Planting and Early Care

Planting

Set out plants in January or February. Trim off any broken or damaged roots just above the point of injury. Cut off all canes except the most vigorous one, and prune it back to two buds. Dig the planting hole large enough to accommodate the entire plant. Place the bare-root plant so the two buds left to grow are 4 inches (10 cm) above the soil surface. Irrigate the plants to settle the soil around the roots at planting. Additional irrigation should not be required until 6 to 12 inches (15 to 30 cm) of growth has developed in the spring.

Figure 15.6

A fruit cluster following the shatter stage when unpollinated flowers have fallen to the ground. Commercial producers begin using growth regulators at this stage, when berries are about 3/16 inch (0.48 cm) in diameter.

Protect the new shoots with a milk carton or plastic jug. Fertilize young vines in the early summer as shoots approach maturity.

Let all shoots grow the first season, since shoots and leaves produce a strong root system for future vine development. Protect the young vines from rodents, grasshoppers, and other pests. Insert a 6-foot (1.8-m) stake near the plant and train new growth to it by loosely tying it.

Weed Control

Practice clean cultivation the first year or use mulches. Herbicides should not be used until the vine trunk develops mature bark, which usually occurs at the end of the second or third growing season. For additional information on weed management options, see chapter 9.

Cluster Thinning

To ensure healthy vine development, pinch off all the clusters the first and second years as they appear. Also, pinch off all but one cluster per shoot in the third and fourth year. Allow full production after the fifth year.

Pruning at the End of the First Growing Season

Grapes can be pruned in the winter after the plants have dropped foliage and are dormant. However, it is usually best to wait until when growth just begins in the spring before pruning so that new growth will avoid damage from late-spring frosts. Remove all shoots except the most vigorous one. If first-season growth was relatively weak, prune the shoot back to two buds (a two-bud spur) and replace the vine protection (milk carton, etc.). Place a 6-foot (1.8-m) stake for training the vine if you did not do so at planting. Control weeds, gophers, snails, slugs, etc., as needed. If first-season growth was fairly vigorous, the single shoot can be tied to the stake or trellis without heading it back (see fig. 15.8A).

Training the Vine in Its Second Season

If plant growth was weak in the first season and was pruned back to a two-bud spur, select a single vigorous shoot to become the trunk and train it up the stake the second season. The shoot will need to be tied up every 1 to 2 weeks for adequate support as it grows. Use a vinyl tape that will stretch and not constrict

Table 15.1

CULTURAL INFORMATION FOR SELECTED TABLE GRAPE VARIETIES

Variety	Type of pruning	Typical no. of spurs or canes per vine	Typical no. of buds retained at pruning on each cane or spur	Requires shoot thinning	Climate zone(s)* period[†]	Average ripening	Color	Comments[‡]
Autumn Black	spur	12–16	2	—	3, 4	early Sep	purple-black	many small bunches
Autumn Seedless	cane or spur	4–6 canes or 12–14 spurs	canes 10–12 (canes mature poorly), 2 spurs	—	4	late Aug to Sep	yellow-green	seedless
Beauty Seedless	spur	12–14	2	yes	3, 4	mid Jul	black	seedless; E
Black Monukka	cane	4–6	12–14	no	2, 3, 4	late Aug	purple-black	seedless; E
Black Rose	spur	12–4	2	yes	2, 3, 4	mid to late Sep	purple to black	very delicate, will break down after rain; E
Blush Seedless	spur	12–14	2	yes	3, 4	late Aug to early Sep	red	seedless; E
Calmeria	cane and	2 short canes and 12–14 spurs	2 bud spurs and 12–14 bud canes	no	4	late Sep to early Oct	green to green-amber	poor eating quality
Cardinal	spur	12–14	1	yes	1, 2, 3, 4	late Jul	red	E
Catawba	cane or spur	4–6 12–14	12–14 4–6	—	2, 3	late Sep	coppery	large, round red berries; aromatic; A/E
Centennial Seedless	spur	12–14	2–3	no	3, 4	late Jul	white	seedless; E
Christmas Rose	spur	12–14	2–3	no	3, 4	mid Sep	red	crisp
Concord	cane spur	4–6 12–14	12–14 4–6	no	1, 2, 3, 4	Sep	green to blue black	uneven ripening, some green fruit; A/E
Dawn Seedless	spur	12–14	2–3	yes	3, 4	late Jul	white	seedless; E
Delight	spur	12–14	2	yes	1, 2, 3, 4	mid Jul	white	seedless
Emperor	spur	12 (24 on old vines)	2–3 (3 bud spurs on older, less productive vines)	—	4	late Sep to Oct	red-purple	E
Exotic	spur	12–14	2	yes	2, 3, 4	late Aug	black	E
Fiesta	cane	4–6	10–14	—	4	early Aug	white	seedless, may have hard seed coats; E
Flame Seedless	spur	12–14	2–3	yes	2, 3, 4	late Jul	red	seedless, very crisp berries; E
Golden Muscat	cane spur	4 12–14	10–14 4–6	—	1, 2	midseason	yellow-green	vigorous vines; A/E
Italia	spur	12–14	2	yes	3, 4	late Aug	white	slight muscat flavor, susceptible to flower thrip damage; E
Muscat of Alexandria	spur	12–14	2	no	3, 4	mid Sep	green to golden	strong muscat flavor, may require zinc treatments; E
Perlette	spur	12–14	2	yes	1, 2, 4	mid Jul	white	compact clusters require extensive prebloom flower thinning; seedless; E
Niabell	cane spur	4 12–14	10–14 4–6	—	2, 3	mid Jul	blue-black	large berries similar to Concord; excel. on arbors; vigorous, resisant to powdery mildew; A/E

Table 15.1 cont.

Variety	Type of pruning	Typical no. of spurs or canes per vine	Typical no. of buds retained at pruning on each cane or spur	Requires shoot thinning	Climate zone(s)* period[†]	Average ripening	Color	Comments[‡]
Niagara	cane spur	4 12–14	10–14 4–6	—	1, 2, 3	mid Aug to Sep	light green	vigorous, good on arbors, resistant to powdery mildew; A/E
Pierce	cane spur	4 12–14	10–14 4–6	—	1, 2	—	—	vigorous, good on arbors, resistant to powdery mildew; A/E
Queen	spur	12–14	2	no	3, 4	mid to late Aug	red-purple	
Red Globe	spur	12–14	2	yes	3, 4	mid Sep	pink-red	beautiful, large fruit, very appealing
Red Malaga	spur	12–14	2 (may add a cane to increase production)	yes	4	early Aug	red	poor home variety; E
Ribier	spur	12–14	1	yes	2, 4	late Aug	black	E
Ruby Seedless	spur	10–14	2	yes	2, 3, 4	mid Aug	purple	extremely susceptible to powdery mildew and bunch rot; seedless; E
Thompson Seedless	cane	4–6	10–14	no	3, 4	mid Aug to Sep	white	seedless; E
Tokay	spur	12–18	2 (bilateral or head train)	no	2, 3, 4	late Aug	white to pale pink	will not color well in hot climates, subject to sunburn; E

Notes:

* Climate zone key: 1 = South Coast; 2 = Central Coast; 3 = North Coast; 4 = inland valleys and other hot areas

[†] Ripening period key: Early = July to mid-August; Midseason = late August to mid-September; Late = late September through October

[‡] Comments key: A/E = American or American-European hybrid variety; E = European variety

Figure 15.7

Annual growth and fruiting cycle of a grapevine. *Source:* After Shaulis and Pratt 1965.

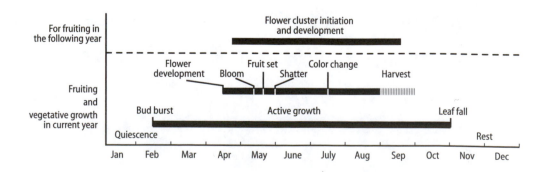

or girdle the shoot. Allow lateral shoots to develop but remove suckers from the base and lower lateral shoots. If growth was relatively vigorous and a single shoot was selected for training at the start of the second season, it should be trained to the trellis as described below (see fig. 15.8B).

Dormant Pruning at the End of the Second Year

Vines with Poor Vigor. If the shoot trained up the stake or post has not reached the trellis wire, prune the vine back to two buds and start the training process again as if it were the start of the second season.

Vines with Moderate Vigor. Shoots with moderate vigor either have made it to the trellis wire without extending out on the wires or have only very weak growth on the wire.

Prune the vine back to wood that is at least the diameter of a lead pencil. If vines are located in a frost-prone area, delay pruning until growth has started. Select and train shoots on the trellis the following spring.

Vigorous Vines. Vigorous vines should have well-developed trellis shoots and lateral shoots extending off the trellis wire. Thin the lateral shoots until they are 6 to 8 inches (15 to 20 cm) apart along the wire. Cut back the shoots to spurs of one or two buds. Shoots that develop from spurs will develop fruit and renewal wood for the following year. Watch for and remove all unwanted suckers and shoots early in the season when they are tender and can be rubbed off easily. In late spring, thin the fruit cluster to one cluster per shoot. Overcropping of young vines can set them back severely (see fig. 15.8C).

Figure 15.8

Several examples of early training of vines with different vigor, using cordon training. (A) Pruning the first winter after planting. (B) Training the vine in the second season. (C) Dormant pruning at the end of the second year. *Source:* After Jackson and Schuster 1981, pp. 80–81.

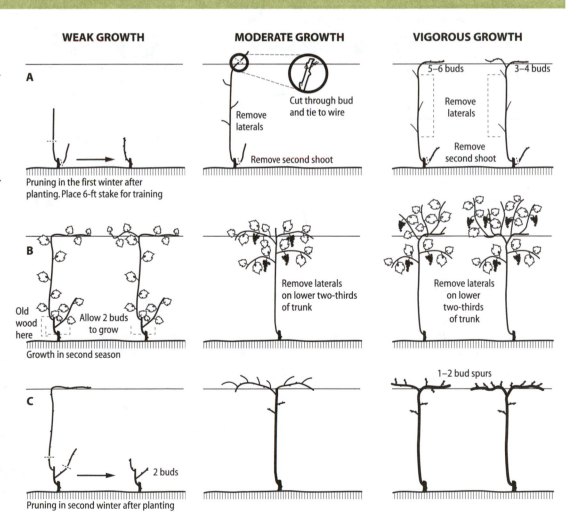

WEAK GROWTH

A
Pruning in the first winter after planting. Place 6-ft stake for training

Old wood here — Allow 2 buds to grow
Growth in second season

B

C
2 buds
Pruning in second winter after planting

MODERATE GROWTH

Cut through bud and tie to wire
Remove laterals
Remove second shoot

Remove laterals on lower two-thirds of trunk

VIGOROUS GROWTH

5–6 buds   3–4 buds
Remove laterals
Remove second shoot

Remove laterals on lower two-thirds of trunk

1–2 bud spurs

Table 15.2

CULTURAL INFORMATION FOR SELECTED AMERICAN AND AMERICAN-EUROPEAN HYBRID SEEDLESS TABLE GRAPE CULTIVARS

Cultivar	Ripening	Color	Flavor	Berry size	Cluster size	Cluster compactness	Vine vigor	Yield per vine	Winter hardiness
Canadice	early	red	good	medium	medium	tight	medium	high	high
Challenger	mid	red	good	large	medium	loose	medium	medium	medium
Glenora	mid	blue	good	medium	medium	compact	medium	low	low
Himrod	early	white	excellent	medium	medium	loose	medium	low	medium
Interlaken	very early	white	good	medium	medium	compact	medium	medium	low
Lakemont	mid	white	good	medium	large	compact	high	high	low
Mars	early	red	good	medium	small	compact	medium	medium	—
Reliance	early	red	good	medium	medium	loose	high	medium	high
Remaily	late mid	white	fair	large	large	compact	medium	high	low
Romulus	late	white	fair	small	large	compact	medium	medium	medium
Suffolk Red	mid	red	good	medium	medium	compact	medium	medium	high
Vanessa	mid	red	good	medium	medium	compact	medium	medium	high
Venus	very early	blue	good	large	large	tight	high	high	medium

Note: Many of these varieties are not adapted to hot inland climate areas.

Table 15.3

SELECTED WINE GRAPE VARIETIES

Variety	Type of pruning	Color	Comments
Cabernet Sauvignon	spur	red	best in cool climate; small, dark berries; vigorous vines
Chardonnay	cane	white	small berries, few seeds, tough skin; subject to spring frosts in cool areas
Chenin Blanc	spur	white	cool to warm climates; susceptible to bunch rot
French Columbard	spur	white	vigorous vines; good for warmer areas
Gewürztraminer	cane	red-brown	small berries, spicy flavor; picking at proper maturity critical; susceptible to spring frosts
Grenache	spur	light red	good for warm climates
Pinot Chardonnay	spur	white	good for cool climates
Ruby Cabernet	spur	red	very productive; good in warmer areas
White Riesling	spur	white	good for cool areas
Zinfandel	spur	red	cool to warm areas

Table 15.4

DRIP IRRIGATION SCHEDULE FOR GRAPES IN THE CENTRAL VALLEY

Week	Gallons (liters) of water per day per trellised vine under drip irrigation						
	Apr	May	Jun	Jul	Aug	Sep	Oct
1	0.5 (1.9)	5.0 (19.0)	8.0 (30.4)	8.0 (30.4)	10.0 (38.0)	6.5 (24.7)	5.0 (19.0)
2	1.0 (3.8)	5.0 (19.0)	8.0 (30.4)	8.0 (30.4)	6.0 (22.8)	6.5 (24.7)	5.0 (19.0)
3	2.0 (7.6)	7.0 (26.6)	8.0 (30.4)	10.0 (38.0)	6.5 (24.7)	5.0 (19.0)	3.0 (11.4)
4	3.5 (13.3)	8.0 (30.4)	8.0 (30.4)	10.0 (38.0)	6.5 (24.7)	5.0 (19.0)	3.0 (11.4)

Trellising and Training Vines

The type of trellis or support system to be used should be selected and built before second-season growth develops. Training vines to a trellis increases the amount of leaf area with full sun exposure, which leads to increased yields and better fruit quality. Grapevine trellises can be of many configurations. Wine grapes may be trellised at a 40-inch (100-cm) height, which is convenient for harvesting and pruning. A slightly higher height (5 ft [1.5 m]) is common in table grape production, but arbors or patio structures 7 feet (2.1 m) high or more may be used. Consider using horizontal cross arms that support canes and foliage for table grapes to spread the fruit and leaf area for better sunlight exposure and air circulation.

Training to the Trellis. There are two general systems for training vines to a trellis. In the "head-trained" system, a trunk is established and a few to several short main branches (arms or cordons) are developed that sustain renewal spurs and fruiting canes. The canes are placed on a trellis, arbor, or other support system. Cane pruning is typically practiced on head-trained vines in California, although spur pruning is possible if several main branches are developed (see figs. 15.9A and 15.10).

In the "cordon-trained" system, a trunk and two or more permanent horizontal arms, or cordons, are established and spur pruning is typically practiced (see fig. 15.9B). The cordons are trained on the trellis and serve as the base for several spurs that produce fruiting canes each year.

Train branches on the trellis wire as vigorous second-year vines develop. Vines or varieties with low vigor may take 1 or 2 additional years to develop. The branches are selected from buds that occur 6 to 12 inches (15 to 30 cm) below the trellis wire so that the shoots continue in an upward direction as they approach the wires. Allow the main upright shoot to grow approximately 1 foot (30 cm) above the trellis wire, then cut it back and tie it securely to the trellis. As a result of this procedure, the buds and shoots 1 foot below the trellis are mature enough to support and develop shoots that are trained out onto the trellis (see fig. 15.8C).

Training to the Trellis Wire. Shoots positioned to grow on the trellis wires should be allowed to grow 12 to 18 inches (30 to 45 cm) long before they are tied down to the wires (see fig. 15.11). Never tie the growing shoot tips to the wire because they will lose vigor and cease growing. Always leave at least 6 inches (15 cm) of shoot tip free beyond the last tie so it can grow in a vertical direction to maintain vigor.

With spur pruning, lateral shoots that form in the axil of leaves on the main shoot or cordon tied on the trellis wire are allowed to grow. They are spaced and thinned during the dormant pruning of the vine and form the fruiting spurs.

Pruning Established Vines

Proper pruning modifies the size and form of the vine, rendering it a better producer of high-quality, good-sized fruit. Pruning also aids in balancing vegetative growth and fruit production. Grapes are pruned while vines are dormant.

Spur Pruning

Most grape varieties are spur-pruned; that is, the dormant season shoots that grew the previous summer are selected and spaced along the vine's cordons (main permanent arms) at 6- to 8-inch (15- to 20-cm) intervals. Select shoots that grew upward in a well-lighted environment for fruitful spurs. Shoots that grew in the shade the previous summer often do not contain fruit buds. Cut each spaced shoot back to several buds and cut all extra shoots completely off the vine. Short spurs (2 to 3 buds) should be left on fruitful varieties such as Cardinal, Exotic, Ribier, and Muscat of Alexandria. Long spurs (4 to 6 buds) are sometimes used for moderately fruitful varieties such as Concord, Golden Muscat, Catawba, and Niagara. Keep a total of 20 to 40 buds on mature vines, depending on their vigor. (See the following discussion on matching crop and vine vigor.) The process is continued on an annual basis (see fig. 15.9).

Figure 15.9

Spur pruning on (A) a head-trained vine and (B) on a cordon-trained vine. *Source:* After Kasimatis et al. 1979.

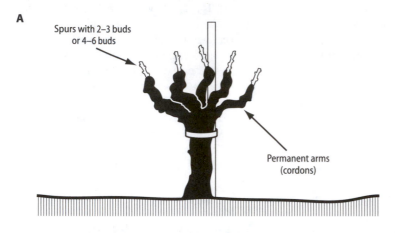

A

Spurs with 2–3 buds
or 4–6 buds

Permanent arms
(cordons)

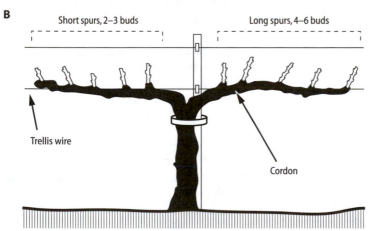

B

Short spurs, 2–3 buds

Long spurs, 4–6 buds

Trellis wire

Cordon

Cane Pruning

Thompson Seedless, Black Monukka, Fantasy Seedless, Concord, and Crimson Seedless are all cane-pruned because the basal buds that normally produce fruit on spur-pruned varieties often are not fruitful on these varieties. Retain well-matured round canes with a diameter in the range of ³⁄₈ to ⁵⁄₈ inch (0.9 to 1.5 cm). Choose canes that develop on top of the vine and were exposed to light during the growing season because the buds are more likely to be fruitful. The canes should have medium node spacing. After selecting the fruiting canes, chose an additional strong cane arising near the base of each fruiting cane and cut it off, leaving a spur with one or two buds. These are renewal spurs that will produce shoots to be selected as fruiting canes the next year (see fig. 15.10). When selecting fruiting canes and renewal spurs, avoid any flattened

canes, canes with excessively long internodes, or canes of poor maturity. Canes that arise from wood older than 1 year (sucker canes) tend to be vigorous and are often rejected; however, they should not be discriminated against on the basis of origin alone, because they can be as productive as canes that develop from the previous year's wood.

Prune to match the crop to the capacity of each vine. Weaker vines of low vigor should not be expected to carry the same crop load (number of canes) as stronger, more vigorous vines. One way to determine if a vine is pruned to the correct number of canes is to take an overall view of the cane development and maturity. Vines that develop mature canes of average diameter and internode spacing are the result of pruning to the proper number of canes. Any vine that develops weak canes of small diameter with very close internode spacing should be suspected of being overcropped, and the cane number should be reduced. Likewise, vines that produce excessively large-diameter canes with excessively long internodes and poor wood maturity might benefit from the addition of one or more canes. It is important to recognize that nitrogen fertilization, irrigation, and soil type are also important in vine vigor and cane development. As a general rule, leave 4 to 6 fruiting canes canes that have 10 to 14 buds along each cane. Cut the ends off these canes if necessary to attain the desired number of buds (see fig. 15.10).

Producing Quality Wine Grapes

For many years, California winemakers have associated high-quality grapes and wines with low-producing vines that have moderately vigorous shoots. Recent studies by viticulturists at the University of California, Davis, and in the Napa Valley have shown that vigorous vines can produce high-quality grapes and wines if they are trained to permit light to reach the fruit clusters and if enough fruiting spurs and shoots are left at the end of the growing season. Encouraging a larger number of relatively short shoots allows light to reach the fruit. The light also reaches the buds that will be saved to produce grapes the following year. Leaf removal from the base of the shoots and opposite the fruit clusters at flowering will also

Figure 15.10

A head-trained vine with cane pruning. *Source:* After Kasimatis et al. 1979.

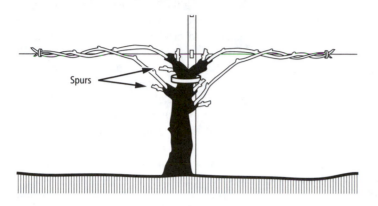

Spurs

improve lighting conditions and air circulation around the fruit. The leaves that are removed often contain most of the overwintering leafhoppers. This pest can be controlled by raking them away from the vine row. They are in the nymphal stage and will die when exposed to sunlight. The leaves can then be added to the compost pile. The improved air circulation also reduces powdery mildew and bunch rot problems.

Producing Quality Table Grapes

Many home grape growers are frustrated that their berries do not look as big and lush as the ones in the market. One of the reasons for these results is that most home gardeners fail to thin the fruit clusters enough or they do not girdle the vines, nor do they use any of the commercial techniques such as plant growth

Figure 15.11

Tying a cane on a wire. *Source:* After Jackson and Schuster 1981, p. 76.

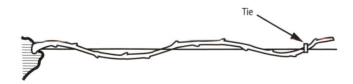

Tie

regulators. For detailed information on the use of plant growth regulators, thinning techniques, or girdling methods, see the UC Cooperative Extension Fresno County publication *Growing Quality Table Grapes in the Home Garden* (Andris, Jensen, and Elam 1985).

Irrigation

Irrigation is essential for good vine growth and production. Grapes will adapt to low water conditions, but fruit production will be reduced. Applying water deeply and thoroughly filling the root zone with water is an ideal way to furrow-irrigate. Irrigation frequency will depend on the soil type, the rooting depth of the vines, the depth of the soil, and the weather. Irrigating every 2 to 3 weeks is usually adequate under good soil conditions and a moderate climate. Grapes may require more frequent irrigations in hot climates in inland valleys. Drip irrigation is also an excellent method, although the frequency of irrigation should be increased.

Generally, a fully trellised vine on a warm day in the Central Valley requires about 8 to 10 gallons (30.3 to 37.9 l) of water per vine per day. Vines that are less vigorous or untrellised require 6 to 8 gallons (22.7 to 30.3 l) of water per vine per day. Table 15.4 is a drip irrigation schedule for an average trellised vine. These figures are for the Central Valley and should be used only as a guide. In areas along the coast and in northern parts of the state, the rates will be lower. Requirements in the southern part of the state should be similar to the Central Valley irrigation schedule. Check the soil profile to be sure that the plants are getting adequate water but not too much (see chapter 4, "Water Management," for details on soil water-holding properties and irrigation).

Timing of irrigations is a critical factor for producing the best quality grapes. Avoid water stress from the bloom period to berry softening, which occurs when berries give in to finger pressure. Usually, color begins to appear on colored varieties at the same time. Fruit on the vines may succumb to cracking if the vines are allowed to dry and then wetted again. Maintain an even level of soil moisture to avoid cracking. Also avoid excessive irrigation to prevent having more vine than fruit.

Grape Nutrition

Given good drainage, grapes are well adapted to a wide range of soils and generally have few nutritional needs, with the exception of nitrogen, zinc, and potassium. Applying these nutrients at the right time and in the proper amounts contributes significantly to a successful crop. Overfertilizing with nitrogen can be a problem, whether the nitrogen source is a fertilizer or a leguminous cover crop that fixes nitrogen. Nitrogen fertilizer should be used sparingly on grapes unless a specific deficiency has been diagnosed. Fertilizing with high levels of nitrogen can contribute to excess vegetative vigor in the vines and may reduce fruit set, fruit quality, or both. Table 15.5 is a simple guide to fertilizer management for grapes.

Pest Management

Grape pests can be difficult to manage. The key to good pest control is knowing which pests are going to be a problem and planning accordingly. Some of the most common pests include leafrollers, leaffolders, western grapeleaf skeletonizer, thrips, spider mites, and leafhoppers. Leafhoppers have several generations during the growing season. Beneficial wasps can control leafhoppers if provided with a suitable overwintering site, such as blackberries or prune or plum trees. Planting blackberries or a prune plum tree near your grapes can encourage parasitic wasps, which parasitize the leafhopper eggs and control the pest. Removal of basal leaves and leaves opposite fruit clusters eliminates leafhoppers in the young crawler stage and open berries to sunlight, which improves color and reduces disease.

Spider mites cause grape foliage to turn a strawlike color. In severe cases, the leaves may dry up and the fruit will not mature. Pest mites live on the underside of grape leaves. Thorough washing of all leaf surfaces, repeated every 10 days, may help to remove pest mites off the leaves. Spider mites can be controlled by sulfur-tolerant beneficial predaceous mites that feed on the pest mites. Be sure to purchase the sulfur-tolerant beneficials; otherwise, they will be eliminated by the sulfur that is used to control powdery mildew. Avoid dust

Table 15.5

GRAPE FERTILIZATION

Element needed	Fertilizer	Amount per vine	When to apply	Comments
nitrogen	ammonium sulfate	½ lb (227 g)	Berry set stage or following bloom.	Berry set occurs when berries reach ¼ inch (6.5 mm) diameter.
	ammonium nitrate	⅜ lb (170 g)		
	urea	¼ lb (113 g)		
	mixed fertilizers	follow label		
	poultry or rabbit manure	5–10 lb (2.3–4.5 kg)	Jan or Feb	Poultry manure may cause zinc deficiency in light, sandy soils.
	steer or cow manure	5–20 lb (6.8–9 kg)	Jan. or Feb	
zinc	basic or neutral zinc sulfate (52% Zn)	0.1 lb/gal (11.9 g/l)	Apply 2 weeks prior to bloom or at full bloom sprayed on foliage.	Apply before bloom to reduce "shot" berries.
potassium (applied in a deficiency situation)	potassium sulfate (44% K)	severe def.: 5–6 lb/vine (2.3–2.7 kg/vine)	When deficient, apply to soil 6 inches (15 cm) deep, 18 inches (46 cm) from trunk. Concentrate at vine.	Irrigate after application.
		moderate def.: 4 lb/vine (1.8 kg/vine)		
		mild def.:3 lb/vine (1.4 kg/vine)		

as it favors mites. Be aware that many pesticides used to control other grape pests may stimulate mite populations.

The diseases of most concern to home gardeners are powdery mildew and bunch rots. Powdery mildew causes grapes to shrivel and fail to mature. The canes and fruit become covered with a white, powdery fungus. To treat for powdery mildew, dust with sulfur beginning at 4 to 6 inches (10 to 15 cm) of shoot growth and every 10 to 14 days thereafter unless temperatures exceed 100°F (38°C). Once temperatures drop, continue sulfur applications. Continue applications up to harvest for table grapes. Other fungicides are registered for powdery mildew control. Treatments with these materials should begin when the shoots are 4 to 6 inches (10 to 15 cm) long. Bunch rots generally can be reduced by thinning out four or five basal leaves of the shoots. An application of an appropriate fungicide between bloom and pea-sized berries will also help.

For specific pest control procedures, see the UC Cooperative Extension publications *Grape Pest Management* (Flaherty 1992) and *Pests of the Garden and Small Farm: A Grower's Guide to Using Less Pesticide* (Flint 1998).

Bibliography

Andris, H., F. Jensen, and P. Elam. 1985. Growing quality table grapes in the home garden. UC Cooperative Extension Fresno County Publication.

Flaherty, D. L., ed. 1992. Grape pest management. Oakland: University of California Division of Agriculture and Natural Resources Publication 3343.

Flint, M. L. 1998. Pests of the garden and small farm: A grower's guide to using less pesticide. 2nd ed. Oakland: University of California Division of Agriculture and Natural Resources Publication 3332.

Jackson, D., and D. Schuster. 1981. The production of grapes and wine in cool climates. Melbourne, Australia: Nelson Publishers.

Kasimatis, A. N., B. E. Bearden, and K. Bowers. 1979. Wine grape varieties in the North Coast counties of California. Oakland: University of California Division of Agriculture and Natural Resources Publication 4069.

Shaulis, N. J., and C. Pratt. 1965. Grapes: Their growth and development. J. Farm Res. 30:10–11.

16

Berries

Paul M. Vossen

LEARNING OBJECTIVES

- Understand basic cultural practices for growing berries (blackberries, raspberries, blueberries, strawberries, currants, and gooseberries) in the home garden in California.

- Learn about which cultivars of berries are best suited to different climates in California.

- Become acquainted with some of the major pests of berries in the home garden and learn basic information about how to control them.

Berries

Blackberries

Of all the berries, blackberries are the most adapted to California, primarily because of their heat tolerance. Although blackberries do well in a variety of soil types, they perform much better in very deep, well-drained, alluvial soils. In all locations, blackberries require frequent irrigations so that they are always moist. They do very well on the coast because cool temperatures bring out and maintain excellent flavor qualities.

Cultivars

The two basic types of blackberries are erect and trailing. Erect blackberries have stiff, arching canes that are somewhat self-supporting. Trailing blackberries have canes that are not self-supporting. On the East Coast, trailing blackberries are also known as dewberries. Blackberry plants live for many years; however, the canes grow one season (primocanes), produce fruit the second season (floricanes), and then die. Berries are borne on short lateral shoots produced on the floricanes. Listed below are important erect and trailing blackberry cultivars in California and their fruiting characteristics.

Erect Blackberries

- **Black Satin.** Midseason; berries large, shiny black fruit, tart flavor; thornless, hardy, vigorous; good for processing.

- **Cherokee.** Midseason; berries medium large, black, firm; vigorous; thorny, tolerates heat.

- **Cheyenne.** Early; berries very large, firm, attractive; vigorous, moderately thorny, hardy, tolerates heat.

- **Chester.** Late; berries large, round, deep black, tart flavor; canes thornless, very vigorous and productive. Good processing berry.

- **Darrow.** Vigorous, hardy, productive.

- **Hull Thornless.** Midseason to late; berries large, firm, good sweet flavor; thornless, vigorous, productive.

- **Shawnee.** Midseason; long fruiting season; berries very large, shiny black, medium firm; vigorous, thorny, very productive, tolerates heat.

Trailing Blackberries

- **Boysen.** Midseason; berries very large, deep maroon, soft, excellent distinct flavor; thorny but thornless types available; tolerates heat.

- **Kotata.** Midseason; berries large, glossy black, firm, good flavor; thorny, vigorous, productive.

- **Logan.** Early; berries medium, long, dark red, soft, excellent, unique flavor; thornless type available.

- **Marion.** Midseason; berries large, bright black, firm, excellent flavor; thorny, productive.

- **Ollalie.** Midseason; berries medium to large, bright black, firm, good flavor; vigorous, productive.

- **Silvan.** Early to midseason; berries large, black; medium firm, excellent flavor; thorny, very productive.

Figure 16.1

Approximate dimensions of cane and bush berry raised beds.

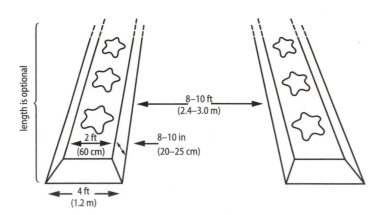

length is optional

8–10 ft
(2.4–3.0 m)

2 ft
(60 cm)

8–10 in
(20–25 cm)

4 ft
(1.2 m)

Figure 16.2

Three-wire trellis for trailing blackberries during the growing season (leaves not shown for clarity). (A) Canes that have just borne fruit and will die. (B) New growth that will bear fruit the following year. *Source:* After Strik 1993, p. 5.

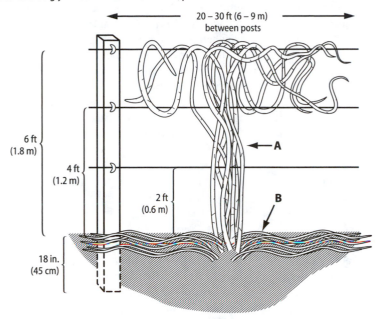

- **Tayberry**. Early; berries large, medium red, soft, flavor distinctive; thorny.

- **Thornless Evergreen.** Late; berries medium, dark black, firm, mild flavor; very productive, suckers from roots may be thorny.

- **Waldo.** Midseason; berries medium, glossy black, firm, mild flavor; thornless, productive.

- **Young.** Midseason; berries very large, maroon, sweet, excellent flavor.

It is best to purchase certified disease-free plants from a nursery. Although propagating your own berry plants is very easy to do, plants derived from a neighbor's canes could introduce unwanted root-rot organisms or viruses into your garden.

Soil Requirements

Blackberries do best in well-drained sandy or loamy soils with a pH of 5.5 to 6.5. A good supply of organic matter in the soil improves aeration and drainage and increases water-holding capacity. You may apply organic matter during the summer or fall before you plant. Incorporate about 1 pound per square foot (4.8 kg/sq m) of fully decomposed

organic matter such as compost into the soil before making raised beds. Raw organic matter sources such as manure, straw, or peat moss can also be used but should be allowed to decompose in the soil for several months prior to planting. Do not incorporate raw, high-carbon forms of organic matter such as sawdust, wood chips, or rice hulls. These materials should be used only as surface mulches to avoid tying up nitrogen during their decomposition.

Raised Beds

Raised beds improve the drainage and growth of blackberries considerably by decreasing the negative effects of heavy soils, heavy winter rains, or excessive summer irrigation. Raised beds are constructed by shoveling soil from the aisles (the area between the rows) to form beds 2 feet (60 cm) wide at the top that widen to 4 feet (120 cm) at the base. Beds are generally 8 to 10 inches (20 to 25 cm) high and can be as long as you desire. See figure 16.1 for the approximate dimensions of cane and bush berry raised beds.

Planting Requirements

Plant berries in the fall, winter, or as early as you can work the soil in the spring. Dig a shallow hole just large enough to accommodate the roots, prune off any damaged root parts, spread the root mass, and set the plant at about the same depth it was in the nursery. Cover the roots with soil and press firmly to remove air pockets. Water the plants to settle the soil. Cut the canes on newly set plants to 6 inches (15 cm) at planting time. For best sun exposure, plant rows in a north-south direction, if possible.

Spacing

Space all cultivars 2 to 4 feet (0.6 to 1.2 m) apart in the row, leaving 8 to 10 feet (2.4 to 3 m) between rows. Blackberries tend to produce few root suckers, but new canes emerge every year from the crown area.

Trellis Systems

Trailing blackberries require a trellis system to support the fruiting canes the second year. Erect blackberries grow without support, but trellises will keep the planting neater and make harvest easier. Therefore, it is advisable to trellis all blackberries (fig. 16.2). Set heavy posts at least 2 feet (60 cm) into the ground at each end of the row. Set lighter posts about 20 to 30 feet (6 to 9 m) apart in the row. After setting, the posts should be about 6 feet (1.8 m) tall. A two-wire trellis system is generally adequate, with the top wire at approximately 5 feet (1.5 m) from the ground and the bottom wire at approximately 3½ feet (1.1 m). Some gardeners use a three-wire system, spacing the wires at 6 feet (1.8 m), 4 feet (1.2 m), and 2 feet (0.6 m).

Fertilization

If you use manure, compost, or another source of organic fertilizer, apply it in the late fall or early winter. Apply approximately 50 pounds (22.7 kg) of an organic-type fertilizer per 100 feet (30 m) of row. Inorganic fertilizers should be spread over the surface of the soil in the row in early spring just when growth is starting. Apply 5 to 6 pounds (2.3 to 2.7 kg) of 20-20-20 fertilizer per 100 feet (30 m) of row. If plants lack vigor, apply an additional 1 pound (454 g) of ammonium nitrate per 100 feet (30 m) of row at bloom or midsummer, just prior to an irrigation.

Irrigation

Blackberry plants require approximately 1 to 2 inches (2.5 to 5 cm) of water per week from mid-May through October. It is best to keep the plants moist at all times without soaking and rotting the roots. Generally, irrigate twice a week; however, during the fruiting stage or during windy and hot conditions, greater amounts and more frequent quantities of water should be applied. When using drip irrigation, blackberries should be watered every day for 1 to 2 hours, longer in hot weather or when fruit is ripening (see chapter 4 for more information on water management).

Pruning

Little to no pruning is required during the first year after planting.

Erect Cultivars. Erect types produce stiff, upright new canes (primocanes) from the crown that arch over after they grow about 5 to 6 feet (1.5 to 1.8 m) long. During the summer of the second growing season, when the primocanes are approximately 3 feet (90 cm) tall, pinch off the top 1 to 2 inches (2.5 to 5 cm). These canes will branch and produce fruit the next year. Alternatively, the canes can be left unheaded and wrapped around the wires for fruiting next year. Immediately after

harvest until midwinter, remove the floricanes. These canes will eventually die anyway. Thin primocanes to three or four of the strongest canes per plant.

Trailing Cultivars. In the spring, trailing cultivars produce primocanes that grow along the ground. Keep these trained in a narrow row beneath the bearing canes to prevent injury. After harvest, remove the floricanes. Thin the primocanes, leaving 6 to 12 of the sturdiest canes on each plant to bear next season. Wrap the primocanes around the trellis right after harvest and subsequent removal of floricanes. Wrap one or two canes at a time in a spiral around the wires of the trellis, working each way from the plant. Top the primocanes of trailing berries if they grow beyond 10 feet (3 m) long.

Pests

The UC Cooperative Extension publications *Insect and Disease Management for Home Berry Plantings* (Barclay and Koehler 1982) and *Pests of the Garden and Small Farm: A Grower's Guide to Using Less Pesticide* (Flint 1998) provide information about pests of blackberries. Several key points are summarized below.

Weeds. Blackberries require a weed-free site in to perform well. Before developing the site, control all perennial weeds with herbicides or diligent cultivation. Once the plants are in the ground, the best method of weed control is a heavy mulch. Apply mulch materials, such as bark chips, sawdust, peat moss, shredded bark, etc., to a depth of approximately 3 to 4 inches (7.5 to 10 cm) extending 2 feet (0.6 m) on each side of the row. Maintain the mulch throughout the life of the planting. If cultivation is necessary, do not dig very deeply because blackberry roots grow very near the surface of the soil.

Insect and Mite Pests. *Red berry mite.* Small mite that causes berries to ripen abnormally. Parts or all of the berry remain red and hard at harvest. To control, apply approximately 8 ounces (237 ml) of liquid lime sulphur per gallon (3.8 l) of water during the spring when leaf buds are ½ to 1 inch (1.2 to 2.5 cm) long. Be sure to achieve thorough coverage.

Spider mites. Extremely small mites that cause stippled yellow leaves that eventually become totally yellow. Leaves turn dry and brown. Plant vigor and fruit production are noticeably reduced. To control, prevent mite buildup by reducing dust in the planting area and never allowing plants to become drought-stressed. Apply a registered miticide or insecticidal soap.

Raspberry horntail. S-shaped, segmented worm (larval stage), up to 1 inch (2.5 cm) long, with white body and dark-brown head. It has three pairs of legs near the head end and short spines on the tail end. Horntail feeding causes tips of young shoots to wilt during the spring. Cutting open the affected portion of the cane reveals the worm and its tunnel, containing brownish granular frass. To control, remove and destroy infested canes. If the insect continues to be a problem, apply a registered insecticide immediately after bloom.

Crown borers. Worms (larval stage) up to 1 inch (2.5 cm) long with whitish body and brown head. Plants lack vigor, portions become stunted and weakened, lateral growth wilts in spring, and the entire cane may die. Cutting open lower canes or the crown area reveals worms tunneling through plant tissue. To control, keep plants irrigated properly and growing vigorously, since borers are attracted to stressed plants. Prune out and destroy infested shoots and canes.

Diseases. *Verticillium wilt.* Fungus survives and builds up in the soil on other host plants and then is transmitted to blackberry canes. It primarily affects floricanes, but rarely primocanes. Floricane leaves turn yellow, wither, and fall, beginning at the base of the cane and progressing upward. They take on a bluish-black cast and die during the summer as fruit are maturing. Small groups of plants may be affected here and there. There is no cure for Verticillium wilt. Remove and destroy infected plants; avoid planting blackberries in soils formerly planted with other hosts of the fungus. Plant resistant cultivars such as Logan, Chehalem, and Ollalie.

Armillaria root rot. Fungus survives in the soil for many years and attacks blackberry canes. The entire plant becomes weakened and can be killed quite rapidly once the first symptoms appear. White fungal growth between the bark and wood near the ground level is evidence of the fungus. There is no cure for Armillaria root rot. Remove diseased plants as soon as possible; do not replant berries in the affected area for at least 2 years.

Phytophthora root rot. Fungus infects weakened roots as a result of excess soil moisture. In the spring, plants fail to leaf out fully; small leaves turn yellow and the entire plant dies. Interior wood on canes in the root-crown area turns brown and rots. To control, plant berries on raised beds in deep, well-drained soils. Do not stress plants for water, but be careful not to overwater plants in the summer.

Leaf and cane spot. Fungus survives on infected canes and leaves. Spores are dispersed by splashing water. Infection appears as small red-bordered spots with whitish centers on leaves and canes. Plants have reduced vigor and may lose some leaves prematurely, leading to sunburn of canes. To control, avoid overhead irrigation. After harvest and before fall rains, prune out and destroy old wood and apply fixed copper fungicides labeled for use on berries. A second application in January may be necessary in rainy locations.

Yellow rust. Fungus overwinters on fruiting canes. Spores released from infected canes are spread by wind during spring and summer. Small yellow blisterlike pustules appear in the spring, first on fruiting canes and then on new leaves. Canes dry out and crack, preventing proper ripening of fruit. To control, avoid overhead irrigation. Prune out and destroy diseased canes before fall rains. Apply a fixed copper fungicide in spring when new laterals are leafing out and again when flowers begin to open.

Orange rust. Fungus is systemic and remains in the host plant. Orange blisterlike pustules cover the undersides of leaves in spring. Spores are released from the pustules and are spread by wind in the spring. Diseased shoots seem to recover by midsummer, but developing canes are smaller than normal and bear no fruit the following year. To date, no fungicides on the market are effective against this fungus. Remove and destroy infected plants, including roots.

Crown gall. Bacterium survives in the soil and is spread by splashing water, pruning, and cultivation tools. Wartlike growths appear on the roots and crown area of canes. Severely affected plants become stunted. To control, cut out infected canes during hot, dry weather, and disinfect pruning tools before using on healthy plants. Do not purchase any plants that show evidence of crown gall symptoms.

Dwarf virus. Transmitted by aphids after feeding on infected plants. Symptoms include weak, spindly canes and leaves that cup downward and redden prematurely in fall.

Plants become unproductive in 2 to 3 years, and berries crumble. There is no cure for dwarf virus. Remove infected plants immediately. Obtain virus-free plants from nursery.

Dieback. Physiological disorder. Canes and laterals leaf out after a delay, then wilt and die back at tips in early spring as first leaves are unfolding. This disorder may be associated with freezing injury, winter drought, or insufficient chilling. To control, maintain late-fall and winter irrigations so that plants do not become drought stressed.

Raspberries

Raspberries are best adapted to the cool coastal climates of California, with one exception: the Bababerry cultivar seems to tolerate the heat of the southern and central valleys of California. Raspberries generally require deep, well-drained soils and adequate summer irrigations to produce consistent crops. Raspberry cultivars can be divided into four groups, based on their fruit color: red, golden-yellow, black, and purple. Red cultivars are by far the most common. Raspberries are closely related to blackberries. The fruit can be distinguished at harvest: in raspberries, the recepticle stays on the plant and the fruit drupelets form a thimble-shaped fruit.

Cultivars

Red Raspberries. Red raspberries can be divided into two types. Summer-bearing cultivars are the most common. These produce biennial canes (primocanes) that grow one year and develop into floricanes and then bear fruit the next. Fall-bearing cultivars produce canes that bear fruit on the top portion of the current season's growth in late summer and fall. If these canes are left to overwinter, they bear fruit in the spring on the lower portions that did not fruit the previous fall. The characteristics of several important raspberry cultivars are given below.

Summer-bearing red raspberries

- **Canby.** Berries medium to large, bright red, firm; susceptible to root rot.

- **Chilcotin.** Berries large, bright red, fairly firm, harvested over a long season; very productive, susceptible to root rot.

- **Chilliwack.** Berries large, bright red, firm, resistant to fruit rot, excellent flavor; vigorous, spine-free, hardy, some root-rot resistance.

- **Comox.** Berries large, medium red, firm, resistant to fruit rot, fair flavor; productive but highly susceptible to root rot.

- **Haida.** Berries medium-sized, medium red, firm, good flavor; some root-rot resistance.

- **Meeker.** Berries medium to large, medium to dark red, firm, good flavor.

- **Newburgh.** Berries large, light red, medium firm, resistant to root rot.

- **Nootka.** Berries medium-sized, medium red, firm; very productive, susceptible to root rot.

- **Skeena.** Berries medium to large, bright red, firm, good flavor, long harvest season; highly susceptible to root rot; nearly spine-free.

- **Sumner.** Berries medium-sized, medium red, firm, sweet, excellent flavor; most tolerant cultivar for heavy, poorly drained soils.

- **Tulameen.** Berries very large, firm, late, good flavor; high-yielding.

- **Willamette.** Berries large, dark red, fairly firm, mild flavor; susceptible to root rot; primocanes produce a late-fall crop.

Fall-bearing red raspberries

- **Amity.** Berries medium-sized, medium dark red, very firm, good flavor; susceptible to root rot, almost spine-free.

- **August Red.** Early maturing; berries medium-sized, bright red, soft, good flavor; self-supporting plants.

- **Autumn Bliss.** Early ripening; berries very large, excellent flavor.

- **Bababerry.** Berries very large, red, soft; good producer, tolerates summer heat.

- **Fall Red.** Berries small, red, fairly firm, good flavor; vigorous and productive but require support.

- **Heritage.** Large fall crop ripens in August; berries medium, red, very firm, attractive, mild flavor.

- **Indian Summer.** Berries red, very aromatic, crumbles frequently, good flavor; productive and vigorous.

- **Redwing.** Ripens 2 weeks earlier than Heritage; berries medium-sized, red, firm, good flavor.

- **September.** Berries medium-sized, bright red, firm, attractive, good quality.

- **Summit.** Matures about 10 days earlier than Heritage; berries similar in size and firmness, but slightly darker.

Golden-Yellow Raspberries. These raspberries are simply mutants of red raspberries. Except for fruit color, they have all the characteristics of the red raspberry.

- **Fall Gold.** Ripens 10 days before Heritage; berries yellow, moderately firm, very good flavor; moderate to poor production; often virus-infested.

- **Golden Harvest.** Berries similar to Heritage in size, season, and sweetness.

- **Honey Queen.** Summer-bearing; berries medium-sized, sweet; good-yielding.

Black Raspberries (Black Caps). Black cap raspberries produce fruit on arched or trailing canes. New canes are not produced from old roots; instead, they develop from the base of old canes.

- **Bristol.** Berries medium-sized, firm, good flavor.

- **Cumberland.** Berries small, firm, good flavor.

- **Munger.** Ripens in July; Berries small, blue-black, firm, good flavor; intolerant of wet soils.

Purple Raspberries. Purple raspberries are hybrids of red and black raspberries. Their growth habit is similar to that of blackberries. The berries are excellent for pies because of their distinctive flavor.

- **Royalty.** Summer-bearing; highly productive; berries very large, soft, and sweet when fully ripe; suckers produced from roots like red raspberries.

- **Brandywine.** Summer-bearing; berries large, round, reddish-purple, very tart

flavor; plant habit similar to black caps, but more vigorous; no root suckers formed; one of the best cultivars for pies or processing.

- **Amethyst.** Summer-bearing; Berries large, oval, firm, purple, shiny skin; no root suckers; very productive; excellent for desserts.

Propagation

Most raspberries develop a proliferation of shoot suckers from the root system, which can be broken off easily to propagate plants. It is best, however, to purchase certified disease-free raspberry plants from a nursery. Plants from a neighbor's yard could introduce root-rot organisms or viruses into the garden.

Soil Requirements

Raspberries grow best when the soil pH is between 5.5 and 6.5. A good supply of organic matter in the soil improves aeration and drainage and increases water-holding capacity. Incorporate about 1 pound per square foot (4.8 kg/sq m) of fully decomposed organic matter such as compost into the soil before making raised beds. Raw organic matter sources such as manure, straw, or peat moss can also be used but should be allowed to decompose in the soil for several months prior to planting. Do not incorporate raw, high-carbon forms of organic matter such as sawdust, wood chips, or rice hulls. These materials should be used only as surface mulches to avoid tying up nitrogen during their decomposition. All raspberries should be grown on raised beds. Raised beds can be prepared by shoveling soil into a berm and flattening it off to whatever length desired. These berms should be approximately 2 feet (60 cm) wide and 8 to 10 inches (20 to 25 cm) high. Raised beds help prevent problems caused by poor drainage associated with heavy winter rains, heavy soils, or too much summer irrigation (see fig. 16.1).

Planting Requirements and Systems

It is important to plant raspberries at the proper depth. The primary roots of red raspberries, which grow mainly in a horizontal direction, are the ones that give rise to the shoots of primocanes. If the primary roots are planted much more than 2 inches (5 cm)

Figure 16.3

Four-wire trellis for raspberries. Upper crossarm is optional and may be replaced with a single wire attached to the posts.

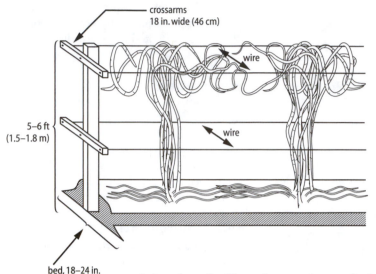

crossarms
18 in. wide (46 cm)

wire

wire

5–6 ft
(1.5–1.8 m)

bed, 18–24 in.
(46–61 cm)

the outside edges of the rows at the ends of crossarms on large posts placed about 20 feet (6 m) apart. The posts should be 6 to 7 feet (1.8 to 2.1 m) tall. A three- or four-wire system is usually easiest to manage (fig. 16.3). The two lower wires used in either system are approximately 30 inches (75 cm) above the ground on crossarms about 18 inches (45 cm) wide at the edge of the row. If large posts with crossarms are not used, wires can be supported with smaller wooden or steel posts every 6 to 8 feet (1.8 to 2.4 m) down the row. These wires prevent the canes from flopping over into the aisle. In the three-wire system, an additional wire is placed about 5 to 6 feet (1.5 to 1.8 m) above the ground. In the four-wire system, a crossarm 18 inches (45 cm) wide is placed 5 to 6 feet (1.5 to 1.8 m) above the ground with wires attached to each arm.

Fertilization

Apply manures, composts, or other organic fertilizers in the late fall or early winter at a rate of approximately 50 pounds per 100 feet (22.7 kg per 30 m) of row. Apply inorganic fertilizers in early spring when new growth starts at a rate of 4 to 6 pounds (1.8 to 2.7 kg) of 20-20-20 per 100 feet (30 m) of row. Fall-bearing raspberries require an additional fertilizer application before fruiting. When new canes start to bloom, spread 1 to 2 pounds (0.45 to 0.9 kg) of ammonium nitrate or 3 to 6 pounds (1.4 to 2.7 kg) of blood meal, fish meal, or feather meal per 100 feet (30 m) of row.

Irrigation

Raspberries require 1 to 2 inches (2.5 to 5 cm) of water per week from June through September and about half that amount when the weather is cooler in early spring and fall. Extremely warm and windy conditions increase water requirements. Raspberries should be kept moist at all times without saturating the soil and causing the roots to rot. If raspberries are fruiting during warm weather, daily irrigation may be required. Generally, however, irrigations are applied twice per week. Overhead irrigation is not recommended for raspberries because it promotes fruit rot and leaf rust diseases. The best irrigation systems are mini-sprinklers or double drip lines that have numerous emitters (spaced 6 to 12 inches [15 to 30 cm] apart) that wet an entire band underneath the foliage. With

below the soil surface, the roots frequently do not have enough energy to push shoots up through the ground.

Plant raspberries from late fall through early spring. Dig a shallow hole large enough to accommodate the roots. Prune off any damaged root parts. Spread the root mass and set the plant so that the highest point of root attachment to the cane is 1 to 2 inches (2.5 to 5 cm) below ground level. Cover the roots with soil and press firmly to remove air pockets. Water the plants to settle the soil. Cut the canes on newly set plants to 6 inches (15 cm) long.

If a hedgerow system is desired, space red raspberry plants 1 to 2 feet (30 to 60 cm) apart in the row with 8 to 10 feet (2.4 to 3 m) between rows. If possible, run the rows in a north-south direction to get equal sun exposure on both sides. Allow the primocanes (new growth from roots) to develop and spread along the row. Prevent them from spreading wider than 12 to 15 inches (30 to 37.5 cm) by removing suckers that develop outside the rows in the aisles.

Black and purple raspberries typically need more space than red raspberries. Set plants 2 to 4 feet (0.6 to 1.2 m) apart in the row, with 8 to 10 feet (3 m) between rows. Some purple raspberries produce root suckers; these should not be allowed to grow.

In most cases, raspberries need a supporting structure to hold the canes upright. In the hedgerow system, wires are supported along drip irrigation, raspberries should be watered daily for 1 to 2 hours, especially during fruiting or hot weather. See chapter 4 for more information on managing water.

Pruning

Summer-Bearing Red Raspberries. After harvest, remove all floricanes on which fruit was borne. These canes will die soon anyway. Do not tip or pinch the primocanes. In the dormant season, remove all weak, broken, and disease- and insect-damaged canes. In the hill system, leave 10 to 12 of the strongest canes in each hill; in the hedgerow system, narrow the row to 15 inches (37.5 cm) wide and thin to about four to five strong canes per foot (30 cm) of row. Again, in the dormant season, shorten the remaining canes in both planting systems to about 6 feet (1.8 m). Tie the canes to the trellis system, if necessary.

Fall-Bearing Cultivars. You can grow fall-bearing raspberries for a fall crop only. For this method, cut all canes to ground level when plants are dormant, usually in the early spring before growth begins. When the new primocanes emerge, maintain a row width of 12 to 15 inches (30 to 37.5 cm) by removing suckers that grow outside of the row. These canes will develop a crop in the fall on the tips of the primocanes. If you would like to have an early summer crop from those same canes, they can be left to overwinter and will fruit the following spring on the lower portion of the canes that did not fruit the previous year. In the dormant season, remove weak or damaged canes and the tips that fruited last fall. Again, thin them to 4 to 5 strong canes evenly spaced per foot (30 cm) of row.

Black and Purple Raspberries. Tip the primocanes by removing 3 to 4 inches (7.5 to 10 cm) of new growth during the late spring or early summer. Top black caps to a height of 2 feet (60 cm) and purples to 2½ feet (75 cm). Topping usually needs to be done two or three times during the summer. Primocanes produce many laterals. During the dormant season, remove all damaged canes and those less than ½ inch (1.2 cm) in diameter. Lateral branches also should be shortened during the dormant season to approximately 8 to 10 inches (20 to 25 cm) for black caps and 12 to 14 inches (30 to 35 cm) for purple cultivars. Cut unbranched canes to 2½ to 3 feet (75 to 90 cm). After harvest the following summer, cut all floricanes down to the ground.

Pests

The UC Cooperative Extension publications *Insect and Disease Management for Home Berry Plantings* (Barclay and Koehler 1982) and *Pests of the Garden and Small Farm* (Flint 1998) provide information about pests of raspberries. Several key problems are summarized below.

Weeds. In the year before you plant, eliminate all perennial weeds and do not permit weeds to go to seed. Use a combination of herbicides or very diligent cultivation. After planting, the best method for controlling weeds in raspberries is to apply a heavy layer of mulch approximately 2 to 4 inches (5 to 10 cm) deep surrounding the plants. Maintain this mulch throughout the life of the planting. Good materials to use include sawdust, shredded bark, bark or wood chips, newspaper, grass clippings, or compost. Raspberries must be maintained completely weed-free to grow and fruit properly.

Insects and Mites. *Spider mites.* Extremely small mites that cause leaves to turn stippled or yellow, eventually becoming totally yellow, then dry and brown, reducing plant vigor and fruiting capabilities. To control, eliminate dust that accumulates around plant leaves, which favors development of mite colonies. Apply insecticidal soaps or miticides registered for home use. Spraying water on the foliage will remove some mites and dust, but it may exacerbate foliar disease problems.

Raspberry horntail. S-shaped segmented worm up to 1 inch (2.5 cm) long with a white body and dark brown head. It has three pairs of legs near the head end and a short spine on the tail end. Its feeding causes tips of young shoots to wilt during the spring; canes may die back by summer. Cutting open the affected portion of the cane reveals a thick white worm or a tunnel containing brownish granular material. There is one generation per year; adults emerge through a hole cut in the side of old canes in April or May and lay eggs inside new canes, causing pronounced swelling. To control, remove and destroy infested canes. If this insect has been a problem in past years, apply carbaryl immediately after bloom.

Crown borers. Worm (larvae) up to 1 inch (2.5 cm) long with whitish body and brown head. Plants lack vigor, portions become stunted and weakened, lateral growth wilts in the spring, and the entire cane may die later. Cutting open lower canes or the crown area reveals worms tunneling through plant tissue. Raspberry crown borer requires 2 years to complete one generation. Adults emerge from the crown area in late summer and lay eggs on leaves and stems. Larvae penetrate the bark and remain there through winter. Feeding occurs inside canes in the crown area during the next two growing seasons. To control, keep plants properly irrigated and growing vigorously because borers are attracted to stressed plants. Prune out and destroy infested shoots and canes.

Raspberry saw fly. Worm up to ⅔ inch (16 mm) long with smooth, pale-green body and dark brown stripes down its back. Small holes appear in leaves and increase in size in May and June until only the veins remain. Leaves become skeletonized. One generation per year. Adults emerge from the soil in April or May and insert eggs in leaf tissue. Larvae feed until June, then drop to the ground and pupate in the soil. No control is necessary unless plants become completely defoliated. If control is needed, apply carbaryl.

Raspberry aphid. Small, green, pear-shaped insect up to ¹⁄₁₆ inch (1.5 mm) long that may or may not have wings. They sometimes cluster on new growth or along the stem. Damage is not serious unless the entire plant becomes covered with insects. To control, apply a strong spray of water or insecticidal soap mix.

Rose leafhopper. Small, narrow, whitish insect up to ⅛ inch (3 mm) long that flutters and may be confused with whiteflies but look more like tiny grasshoppers. Tiny white spots appear on leaves in the spring through fall. Numerous spots may coalesce, resulting in bleached-looking foliage. Undersides of leaves are inhabited by these insects that crawl forward and jump quickly. Damage is rarely serious enough to justify treatment.

Diseases. *Verticillium wilt.* Fungus survives in the soil, building up on other hosts. Leaves turn yellow, wither, and fall, beginning at the base of canes and progressing upward. Fruiting canes may take on a blue-black cast and die during the summer as fruits are maturing. Small groups of plants may be affected. There is no cure for Verticillium wilt. Remove and destroy infected plants. Avoid planting cane fruits in soils formerly planted with other *Verticillium* hosts. Do not move affected plants to other parts of the garden.

Armillaria root rot. Fungus survives for many years in diseased roots in the ground.

Entire plant is weakened and may die suddenly. Often a group of plants is affected. There is no cure for Armillaria root rot. Remove diseased plants and those adjacent to them. Remove and destroy as many roots as possible. Do not replant in affected areas.

Phytophthora root rot. Fungus that infects roots weakened by excess soil moisture. Plants in the spring fail to leaf out fully; small leaves turn yellow and the entire plant dies. To control, plant on raised beds in deep, well-drained soils and do not allow plants to become stressed.

Cane and leaf spot. Only a minor problem on raspberries.

Crown gall. Bacterium that survives in the soil. Spread by splashing water and pruning or cultivating tools. Wartlike growths appear on the roots and the crown area of canes. Severely affected plants may become stunted. To control, cut off and dig out infected canes during hot, dry weather and destroy plants. Do not plant plants with crown gall symptoms.

Yellow rust. See discussion under blackberry diseases.

Viral diseases. Viruses are transmitted mostly by aphids when they feed. Weak, spindly canes develop; leaves cup downward, redden prematurely in fall; plants become unproductive in 2 to 3 years; berries crumble. There is no cure for viral diseases. Remove infected plants immediately. Purchase only virus-free plants from the nursery.

Spring dieback. Physiological disorder associated with delayed leafing-out. Canes and laterals wilt and die back at the tips in early spring as first leaves unfold. The cause is not yet determined, but it may be associated with freezing injury, winter drought, or insufficient chilling. To control, maintain adequate irrigation for plants until winter rains take over.

Blueberries

Of the three species of blueberries grown in the United States, the most important is *Vaccinium corymbosum* (high-bush blueberry). The plants are vigorous, upright, and grow best in moist, well-drained acid soils. The plants reach a size of approximately 4 feet (1.2 m) wide by 6 to 8 feet (1.8 to 2.4 m) tall. The fruit are large and have a very intense flavor, especially when grown in cool climates. Rabbit-eye blueberries (*V. ashie*) are very vigorous, productive high-bush cultivars that are drought-tolerant but not winter-hardy. Rabbit-eyes are primarily grown in the Southeast. Low-bush blueberries (*V. angustifolium*) spread by underground stems and seldom grow more than 18 inches (45 cm) tall. This species is native to the northeastern United States and Canada and is grown there as a very cold-hardy fruit.

In California, very limited amounts of high-bush blueberries (*V. corymbosum*) are grown, mostly on the coast in cool climates where soils are moist and have a low pH. Low-bush blueberries perform poorly in California, where they receive inadequate chilling. The rabbit-eye cultivars have not been adequately tested in California. In the last few years, significant success has been achieved with several new cultivars of Southern Highbush blueberries in the Central Valley and Southern California. These varieties require less winter chilling are more tolerant of higher pH soils and hot climates.

Cultivars

Blueberry cultivars are listed in order of ripening, not alphabetically. Ripening begins in approximately mid-May, but this depends on the warmth of the growing area.

- **Early Blue.** Berries medium-sized, loose clustered, light blue, firm, resistant to cracking, good sweet flavor; vigorous, erect, productive; resistant to powdery mildew but very susceptible to root rot.

- **Duke.** Berries medium-sized, light blue, firm, good flavor; vigorous, erect, open, productive.

- **Reka.** Berries mild-flavored; rapid growing, higly productive.

- **Spartan.** Berries very large, light blue, firm, excellent flavor; vigorous, erect, open, productive.

- **Patriot.** Berries very large, slightly flat, medium blue, excellent flavor; vigorous, moderately erect, open, very productive; tolerates heavier, wetter soils.

- **Collins.** Berries large, light blue, firm, excellent flavor; medium-sized, slightly spreading, productive.

- **Oneal.** Berries large with excellent color and flavor. Spreading bush with low chilling requirement.

- **Misty.** Berries medium large, excellent quality. Evergreen foliage, very low chilling requirement.

- **Bladen.** Berries medium sized, light blue, vigorous upright growth, low chilling requirement.

- **Blue Ray.** Berries very large, light blue, firm, excellent flavor; vigorous, erect, open, productive.

- **Chandler.** Berries extremely large, excellent flavor; moderate vigor.

- **Blue Crop.** Berries very large, light blue, firm, good flavor; vigorous, erect, open, very productive (tends to overproduce); one of the main commercial cultivars.

- **Berkeley.** Berries very large, light blue, firm, mild flavor and mild acidity; vigorous, open, spreading, very productive.

- **Nelson.** Berries very large, excellent flavor; vigorous, high yielding.

- **Darrow.** Berries medium-sized, light blue, firm, excellent flavored; vigorous, erect, consistently productive.

- **Late Blue.** Berries large, firm, good flavor; vigorous, erect, productive.

- **Elliott.** Berries medium-sized, mild flavor, tart; vigorous, erect, consistently productive.

Soil Requirements

Blueberries require a sunny location and have done best in cool climates with sandy soils that are well-drained and moist throughout the growing season. The pH should be in the range of 4.5 to 5.5. Peat and muck soils are suitable, but contrary to popular belief, blueberries do not do well in wet soils or shade.

Soil conditions are often modified in blueberry plantings to adjust pH and to improve drainage with the addition of organic matter. If the soil pH is below 4, incorporate finely ground dolomitic limestone following recommended rates. If the pH is above 5.5, which is more likely, acidify the soil by adding one of the following amendments 1 year before planting:

- elemental sulfur at a rate of approximately 1 to 2 pounds per 100 square feet (0.45 to 0.9 kg per 9.3 sq m) to lower the pH one unit (e.g., from 6 to 5)

- aluminum sulfate at a rate of 6 to 12 pounds per 100 square feet (2.7 to 5.4 kg per 9.3 sq m) to lower the pH one unit (e.g., from 6 to 5)

It is highly recommended to plant blueberries on raised beds that are 8 to 18 inches (20 to 45 cm) high and 3 to 4 feet (90 to 120 cm) wide to provide additional drainage and aeration (see fig. 16.1).

Planting

Plant healthy, 2- to 3-year-old plants from fall through winter and into early spring. Purchase bare-root or container-grown plants from a reputable nursery. Plants should be spaced approximately 8 to 10 feet (2.4 m to 3.0 m). Set plants shallow, spreading the roots in all directions and covering them with 1 to 2 inches (2.5 to 5 cm) of soil. Firm the soil around the plants. Water thoroughly after planting, but do not fertilize at planting.

Strip off all flower buds or blossoms that appear the year the plants are set so that no crop is produced. If possible, set up blueberry rows to run north and south to take advantage of better sun exposure. After planting, apply a surface mulch of old sawdust, wood chips, or some other suitable organic material, which helps to keep the soil cool, conserves moisture, adds organic matter, and controls weeds. Blueberry bushes are free-standing and require no trellis.

Fertilization

Four weeks after planting, apply 10-10-10 fertilizer at the rate of about 1 ounce (1½ tbsp or 237 ml) per plant. Sprinkle it evenly within 12 to 18 inches (30 to 45 cm) of each plant, but not directly on the crown or stems. If possible, use mixes in which the potassium is supplied as potassium sulfate rather than potassium chloride. One of the best nitrogen sources is ammonium sulfate, which helps acidify the soil. As the plants reach mature size, apply the above fertilizers at a rate of ½ cup (0.24 l) per plant 3 to 4 times per year, starting in the early spring when growth starts and at 2-month intervals. Organic-based fertilizers can also be used. Apply 1 pound (454 g) of feather meal, blood meal, or fish meal per plant.

Irrigation

Blueberries have a shallow, fibrous root system, so they are very susceptible to drought injury. A uniform and adequate water supply is essential for optimal growth. Plants require approximately 1 to 2 inches (2.5 to 5 cm) of water per week from May through September. The greatest demand for moisture occurs from berry swell through early harvest and when fruit buds are being formed, usually mid-July through August. Generally, two irrigations per week are adequate to maintain the proper moisture. Avoid overwatering blueberry plants because the roots are very susceptible to root rot. Blueberries prefer minisprinkler irrigation instead of drip irrigation since the minisprinklers wet more of the root system. Drip can be used but two lines should be run, one on each side of the plants. Minisprinklers are normally run 2 to 3 times per week; drip is run every day during the hot months of summer for 1 to 2 hours. See chapter 4 for more information on managing water.

Pruning

At planting time, prune all branches back by about 30 percent to encourage vigorous new growth. Young plants require little pruning for the first 2 to 3 years. Remove only dead or dying parts of branches and less vigorous, spindly growth around the plant base to encourage vigorous, upright growth. To encourage good vegetative growth the first 3 years, blueberries are normally thinned of all fruit by removing the blossoms during bloom. After the third year, blueberries should be pruned annually. Fruit is produced on 1-year-old wood. If you prune too little, plants become twiggy with small, spindly growth that produces small fruit on weak wood. Excessive pruning leads to fewer, larger berries, more new wood, but a poor crop. Pruning is most effective in the dormant season when there are no leaves so you can see what you are doing.

First, cut out any dead, damaged, or diseased wood. Keep the bush open by removing basal shoots that tend to crowd the inside of the plant or shoots that are smaller in diameter than a lead pencil. Leave larger shoots to develop into next year's fruiting wood. Cut out older wood (4 or 5 years old) with small, weak lateral branches and few fruit buds. Cut these canes back to the ground or to a strong new side shoot. Limit the number of canes to one for each year of age of the plant, or a maximum of six to eight canes for old bushes.

If you remove one or two canes yearly and one or two new canes are produced, no canes will be over 4 to 6 years old. Remove small sucker shoots growing from the base of the plant and weak, twiggy wood, especially from the top of the plant. to allow light to reach the center. If plants overbear, remove some of the weakest 1-year-old wood and, if necessary, tip back some of the remaining 1-year-old wood. Then cut off about one-third of the flower buds, which can be distinguished from vegetative buds by their fatter, less pointed appearance. Flower buds appear at the tip of last year's growth.

Pests

Weeds. Because mulches are essential ingredients in good blueberry production, weeds are rarely a problem. Maintain a constant mulch around the base of the plants by adding at least 1 inch (2.5 cm) per year to a total depth of approximately 3 to 4 inches (7.5 to 10 cm).

Insects. Fortunately, blueberries have very few problems with insect pests. Aphids can be present and will occasionally leave a sticky film on the berries. Orange tortrix occasionally feeds on leaves but does very little damage. Root weevils, such as the black vine weevil, can sometimes feed on roots and stunt plants. Thrips occasionally feed on the developing fruit at the blossom stage and scar the fruit.

Diseases. *Botrytis twig and blossom blight.* This gray mold fungus can be a problem in prolonged rainy springs. Copper fungicides can be applied at the beginning of petal fall and repeated at 10-day intervals during wet weather.

Phytophthora Root Rot. This root rot causes problems in poorly drained or over irrigated plantings. It can be prevented by planting on raised beds in very well-drained soil and being careful not to overwater plants during the summer.

Birds. Many species of birds feed on blueberries. The principal species are starlings, robins, and bluebirds. The most effective method of control is to exclude them with bird netting.

Strawberries

Strawberries are grown in backyards throughout California. Very specific planting dates combined with proper cultivar selection and planting location have led to an extremely successful commercial industry in California.

Backyard production can be enhanced considerably with better understanding of the horticultural characteristics of the strawberry plant. There are basically two types of strawberries: short-day cultivars and day-neutral cultivars. Short-day cultivars produce when days are short in late fall, winter, and early spring. Day-neutral cultivars do not respond to day length and continue to produce flowers and fruit all year long, including in the summer, as long as temperatures do not get too high. Ever-bearers are generally considered synonymous with day neutrals; however, other locations outside California list specific cultivars as ever-bearers, many of which are not available in California.

If short-day plants are manipulated into receiving less than their required chilling (less than the number of hours of cold temperatures to ensure good fruiting), they will continue to flower and fruit over a very long time, as long as temperatures remain below about 75°F (24°C). This explains why you see major strawberry production in the cool coastal regions of California.

Planting systems

Two planting systems—summer and winter—are used in California strawberries.

Winter Planting. In Southern California, plantings are made from late October through December using the current season's plants shortly after they are harvested from high-elevation nurseries. Because winters are mild, plants begin to grow immediately and fruit quite soon after planting.

Summer Planting. Summer plantings are made in the Central Valley and the northern coastal regions of California. Here, plants are planted from August in inland areas to October through spring on the coast, using plants dug from the previous winter that were stored at 28°F (−2°C). These plants develop during the fall, winter, or spring and then begin fruiting heavily in the spring or summer.

If short-day cultivars are planted in the spring (the beginning of long days), they will not flower and fruit adequately. All the plant's energy goes into producing runners, and the plant does not produce fruit. In cool areas, day-neutral cultivars can be planted in spring for a summer crop if runners are removed early.

Cultivars

Experiment with various strawberry cultivars by planting several different ones on different dates to see which work best at your location.

Short-Day Strawberries

- **Douglas.** Early producer; berries very large, good color, good flavor, conical; typically a winter-planted cultivar, planted the first 2 weeks of October.

- **Pajaro.** Berries dark red, large, conical, good flavor; principally a summer-planted cultivar used in northern California, planted in August and September.

- **Chandler.** Berries exceptional in flavor, color, and size; typically a winter-planted cultivar.

- **Camarosa.** Berries large, excellent flavor; for winter planting.

- **Sequoia.** Berries large, soft, excellent flavor; resistant to Verticillium wilt.

Day-Neutral Strawberries

- **Selva.** Berries exceptionally firm, mild flavor, must be fully red before harvesting; high-yielding; should not be planted before September 10 for optimal performance.

- **Muir.** Berries conical, better flavor than Selva and lighter in color.

- **Irvine.** Berries conical, medium-sized, excellent flavor; winter-planted.

- **Fern.** Berries medium-sized, excellent quality; strongly day-neutral; excellent potential for home gardens because it produces all season long (July-November); plant in the spring as soon as the ground is workable.

- **Hecker.** Berries abundant, small to medium-sized, mild flavor, deep red; produces throughout the year; plant in late fall to spring.

Soil Requirements

Strawberries perform best in sandy, well-drained soils on beds 6 to 8 inches (15 to 20 cm) high and 12 to 18 inches (30 to 45 cm) wide. Liberal amounts of well-decomposed organic matter applied at approximately 1 pound per square foot (4.8 kg/sq m), worked into the ground before planting, helps prolong the life of the plants and improves water-holding capacity. Strawberries require a soil pH in the range of 5.5 to 7.5.

Planting

After raking smooth and preirrigating beds, use a trowel to open a V-shaped hole about 6 to 7 inches (15 to 17.5 cm) deep. Place 1 level teaspoon (4.8 ml) of slow-release fertilizer, ammonium sulfate, or a concentrated organic fertilizer such as fish, feather, or blood meal in the bottom of each hole and cover with about 1 inch (2.5 cm) of soil to prevent root burn. Spread the roots out in a fan shape in the hole and cover with soil, firming it around the roots. Set plants at the exact level that they were growing in the nursery. Plants set too high will be weak, and plants set too deep will rot. Evenly space plants from 8 to 15 inches (20 to 37.5 cm) apart in the bed. Keep cultivation to a minimum because strawberry root systems are shallow. Mulch the planting with compost, sawdust, straw, or wood chips, or grass clippings to control weeds.

Irrigation

Strawberry plants' shallow roots require consistent moisture throughout the growing season. Newly planted strawberry plants are generally overhead-irrigated to get good initial vegetative growth and then switched to drip irrigation as the season progresses. Drip irrigation keeps moisture away from the fruit and prevents fruit rot. Overhead irrigation can be used during the growing season but should be monitored carefully to minimize the period that the plants and fruit are actually wet.

Strawberries require 1 to 2 inches (2.5 to 5 cm) of water per week during the growing and fruiting season. If drip-irrigated, strawberries should be watered every day for 1 to 2 hours. See chapter 4 for more information on managing water.

Fertilization

Provide additional nitrogen fertilizer 6 weeks after planting if plant growth is weak and leaves are light green. Broadcast ammonium nitrate, or a similar nitrate fertilizer, or a concentrated organic fertilizer such as fish, feather, or bone meal at a rate of approximately ½ pound per 100 square feet (230 g per 9.3 sq m) of row. Irrigate immediately after fertilization to move the nutrient material down into the root zone. Strawberries may need to be fertilized several times during the growing season, depending on the reaction of the plants. Poor vigor and light green leaves indicate a need for fertilization. Slow-release fertilizers work very well in strawberry plantings because they release their nutrients slowly over the entire season.

Before planting, strawberries can be fertilized organically by incorporating a legume cover crop or organic matter (compost or manure) at a rate of up to 500 pounds per 100 square feet (227 kg per 9.3 sq m) of row. A large amount of these materials is needed because they have a low concentration of plant-essential nutrients (see chapter 3 for detailed analysis some organic materials). After planting, the various organic fertilizers should be broadcast under the plant twice per season and irrigated in. If the strawberry plants are drip-irrigated, certain water-soluable fertilizers can be injected directly into the irrigation water lines.

Pruning

Trim off all runners as they develop. The runners weaken the mother plant and reduce fruit size. They essentially become weeds in the planting. For spring-planted day-neutral cultivars, remove the first flowers that appear after planting to keep them from setting fruit and weakening the plant. Subsequent flowers can be left on for fruiting.

Pests

Weeds. Traditionally, strawberries were mulched with straw, but they can be mulched with another organic or inorganic material placed around the plants to an adequate depth to control weeds. Most modern and commercial plantings use clear plastic polyethylene mulches. Mulches offer the advantages of controlling weeds, keeping the roots cool and moist, and preventing direct contact of the fruit with soil organisms that can soften and rot the fruit before and after harvest. Plastic mulches are generally laid down in late winter over the plant tops and secured on the sides; then a hole is cut for each plant to grow through. Excessive cultivation may disturb strawberry plants because their root systems are shallow.

Insects and Mites. *Weevils.* Several weevils attack strawberries above and below the ground. Most insecticides are ineffective against them. Abandoning the planting and moving to a pest-free area is recommended.

Spider mites. Spider mites produce webbing and stippling of the foliage, which stunts strawberry plants, reducing yields and fruit quality. Dusty conditions contribute to spider mite populations. Overhead watering, especially when combined with an insecticidal soap, is effective in controlling most mites because it washes them off the plants and destroys their habitat.

Aphids. Aphids can stunt plants and cause damage to foliage and fruit during the early, cool part of the season. Generally, insecticidal soap applied at weekly intervals provides adequate control.

Leafrolling caterpillars. The salt marsh caterpillar and cutworm feed on strawberry plants. They can be controlled effectively with *Bacillus thuringiensis* (Bt) and registered insecticides.

Slugs and snails. Feed on foliage and fruit and can be controlled with repeated applications of metaldehyde, iron phosphate, or by hand-picking.

Diseases. *Verticillium wilt.* Caused by a soilborne fungus that can cause strawberry plantings to die. Avoid land that has previously been planted in susceptible crops, such as tomatoes, potatoes, cucumbers, peppers, and areas infested by nightshade weeds. Plant resistant cultivars, such as Hecker.

Root rot. Caused by several fungi, but mainly by *Phytophthora* spp., which attack the crowns and roots, particularly in poorly drained or overirrigated plantings. There is no control for affected plants. Prevent root rot by planting on raised beds.

Botrytis fruit rot. A very serious rot of strawberry fruit, also known as gray mold. It is most serious during cool, wet weather. One of the best controls is to use plastic mulch that separates the fruit from direct contact with the ground. Fungicides are essentially ineffective.

Additional information on pest management in strawberries can be found in Barclay and Koehler 1982, Flint 1998, and Strand 1994.

Currants and Gooseberries

Currants and gooseberries are generally not grown in California, primarily because they need cold winters with adequate chilling. However, parts of the North Coast and Sierra Foothills have excellent climates for these fruits.

Cultivars

Red Currants

- **Red Lake.** Clusters well-filled; long stems, large red berries.

- **Cherry**. Clusters long, well-filled, easy to pick; performs equally as well if not better than Red Lake in many areas.

- **Wilder.** Consistently high yields, great resistance to leaf spot; widely planted commercially.

Black Currants

- **Consort.** Productive, self-fruitful, mid-season.

- **Crandall.** Fruit dark red to black, attractive yellow flowers; American native.

White Currants

- **White Imperial.** Fruit white with a pink blush, sweet, rich flavor.

- **White Grape.** Fruit large, white, good flavor; productive.

Green Gooseberries

- **Invicta.** Spiny, high-yielding, disease-resistant.

- **Pixwell.** Generally distributed by nurseries; very productive.

Red Gooseberries

- **Poorman.** Fruit large, excellent flavor; very productive; recommended cultivar.

- **Fredonia.** Fruit medium-sized, red-pink; very productive.

Propagation

Currants and gooseberries are propagated by hardwood cuttings made in the fall after leaves have dropped. Medium-sized cuttings 8 to 10 inches (20 to 25 cm) in length from 1-year-old wood are preferred. Plant cuttings directly in the nursery or store them in moist sawdust until spring. Some cultivars are very slow to root and may require greenhouse mist and bottom heat, along with rooting hormones (see chapter 5, "Plant Propagation," for more information). Most nurseries supply one or two cultivars of currants or gooseberries.

Soil Requirements

A fertile, well-drained loam soil with adequate organic matter is best for currants and gooseberries. These plants do not tolerate wet growing conditions; the roots will rot. Avoid light, sandy soil because of droughty conditions and high soil temperatures. Plant on raised beds as for cane berries or blueberries.

Planting

Space plants from 2 to 4 feet (60 to 120 cm) apart within rows and 8 to 9 feet (240 to 270 cm) between rows. Currants and gooseberries are self-fruitful and do not require interplanting or cross-pollination. Place a heavy mulch around the base of the plants soon after the plants are in the ground. The mulch will keep the soil cool and moist and prevent weed growth.

Fertilization

For most soil types, 1½ pounds (680 g) of actual nitrogen applied per 100 square feet (9.3 sq m) per year is adequate. It should be divided into at least two, possibly three, applications, beginning early in the spring when growth starts. Avoid using muriate of potash, which is injurious to currants and gooseberries. Apply organic fertilizers and soil amendments at a rate of about 1 pound per square foot (4.8 kg/sq m) several months before planting.

Irrigation

Contrary to popular belief, currants and gooseberries are not drought-tolerant and perform much better when the soil is kept uniformly moist throughout the growing season. Generally 1 inch (2.5 cm) of water split into two applications per week from May through September is necessary for good berry production. See chapter 4, "Water Management," for more information on managing water.

Pruning

Gooseberries and currants are upright bushes that tend to have crowded branches. Pruning to thin out branches keeps the plant more open. Begin pruning the third year after planting and aim to have nine main branches on each plant. Three of the branches should be new; three should be 1 year old; and three should be 2 years old. Take out the oldest canes and leave three new ones to replace them each year.

Pests

Mites. Mites are a common problem on currants and gooseberries in the warm climate of California. Keep plants moist (not stressed) and apply overhead water to wash mites off.

Anthracnose. A fungus that attacks leaves in wet spring weather. Keep the bush open so that good air circulation can dry the leaves quickly.

Bibliography

Barclay, L. W., and C. S. Koehler. 1982. Insect and disease management for home berry plantings. Oakland: University of California Division of Agriculture and Natural Resources Publication 21320.

Flint, M. L. 1998. Pests of the garden and small farm: A grower's guide to using less pesticide. 2nd ed. Oakland: University of California Division of Agriculture and Natural Resources Publication 3332.

Pritts, M. P., and D. Handley. 1989. Bramble production guide. Ithaca, NY: Northeast Regional Agricultural Engineering Service Publication 35.

Pritts, M. P., J. F. Hancock, and B. C. Strik. 1992. Highbush blueberry production guide. Ithaca, NY: Northeast Regional Agricultural Engineering Service Publication 55.

Strand, L. L. 1994. Integrated pest management for strawberries. Oakland: University of California Division of Agriculture and Natural Resources Publication 3351.

Strik, B. C. 1989. Growing blueberries in your home garden. Corvallis: Oregon State University Extension Service Publication ED 1304.

———. 1989. Growing raspberries in your home garden. Corvallis: Oregon State University Extension Service Publication ED 1306.

———. 1993. Growing blackberries in your home garden. Corvallis: Oregon State University Extension Service Publication EC 1303.

17

Temperate Tree Fruit and Nut Crops

Paul M. Vossen and Deborah Silva

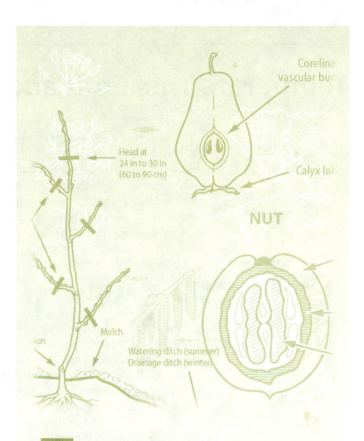

LEARNING OBJECTIVES

- Learn the basic principles about the growth and development of temperate tree fruits and nuts.

- Become familiar with varieties of selected temperate tree fruits and nuts that perform well in the home garden in various climate zones in California.

- Learn the basic cultural requirements of temperate tree fruits and nuts.

- Learn the basic principles of pest and disease management of selected temperate tree fruits and nuts grown in California.

- Learn about the nutritional value of selected deciduous fruits and nuts.

Temperate Tree Fruit and Nut Crops

California is the most important state in the United States for production of temperate tree fruit and nut crops. Our state leads the nation in production of apricots, peaches, nectarines, olives, plums, prunes, pears, almonds, walnuts, pistachios, figs, persimmons, pomegranates, grapes, strawberries, and kiwifruit; annual production statewide exceeds 10 million metric tons. Many of these fruits and nuts can also be enjoyed from backyard trees throughout the state.

This chapter introduces you to *selected* temperate fruits and nuts that can be grown in the home garden in California. Basic physiological principles of temperate fruit and nut tree growth and development are discussed, and selected varieties for planting in the home garden are described. The chapter presents some basic information on planting, tree care, and fertilization practices. Environmental stresses, insect pests, and diseases that can attack trees, fruits, and nuts are discussed. The nutritional value of many of these crops is also highlighted.

Types of Temperate Fruit and Nut Trees

Pomology is the technical term for the science and art of fruit culture. Scientists who study fruit and nut crops are known as pomologists. Scientists who study citrus and avocados, two subtropical evergreen tree fruit crops, are also pomologists, but they are said to specialize in *subtropical* horticulture. This handbook features three chapters on fruit trees: one on citrus (chapter 18), one on avocados (chapter 19), and this one on temperate tree fruits and nuts.

The diverse fruit and nut crops featured in this chapter are temperate zone trees native to climates with distinct summer-winter patterns. The majority are deciduous woody perennials, which means that the trees lose their leaves and go into dormancy (quiescence) in autumn and must receive a specific number of winter chilling hours below 45°F (7°C) during winter to resume growth, flower normally, and set fruit in the spring. Since many locations in Southern California lack sufficient winter chill, home gardeners in that part of the state must be careful to select "low chill" varieties adapted to the subtropical climate of these regions. Varieties adapted to all regions of the state are discussed in this chapter.

Temperate tree fruits and nuts grow best in latitudes between 30° and 50° worldwide, which encompasses most of the United States. Nonetheless, most domestic production is confined to California and a few regions in about 11 other states (the Pacific Northwest, the eastern shores of the Great Lakes, a narrow belt along the Appalachian Mountains, the Northeast, and the Southeastern states). Successful production can be extended to lower latitudes if the site is sufficiently high in elevation to provide adequate chilling. Olives are the exception; they are evergreen and will not tolerate temperatures below 22°F (−5°C), yet they require some cold temperature in the winter to develop good bloom and fruit set.

Temperate tree fruit and nut crops grown in California and featured in this chapter include the following fruit types.

Pome Fruits
Apple (*Malus domestica*), pear (*Pyrus communis*) and Asian pear (*P. serotina, P. pyrifolia*), pomegranate (*Punica granatum*), and quince (*Cydonia oblonga*) are grouped together by botanists because their fruit type is a *pome* (fig. 17.1A). The flowers of pome fruits arise conjointly above the ovary, and the fruits are derived from the fusion of the ovaries, calyx cup (sepals), and floral tube. The fleshy part of the pome fruit that is consumed is nonovarian calyx (sepal) and receptacle tissue. Less-widely planted pome fruits grown in California such as the evergreen loquat (*Eriobotrya japonica*) are discussed in some of the resources listed in the bibliography at the end of this chapter. Pome fruits and the stone fruits (listed below) are members of the Rosaceae family.

Stone Fruits
Apricot (*Prunus armeniaca*), sweet and sour cherry (*Prunus avium* and *Prunus cerasus*, respectively), nectarine and peach (*Prunus per-*

Figure 17.1

Sections of selected fruits and nuts: (A) pome (pear); (B) drupe or stone (peach); (C) nut (walnut); (D) berry; (kiwi); (E) multiple fruit (fig). *Source:* After Westwood 1993 p. 71 and Hasey et al. 1994, p. 88.

A

POME

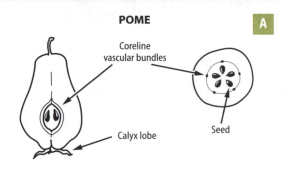

Coreline
vascular bundles

Calyx lobe

Seed

B

DRUPE

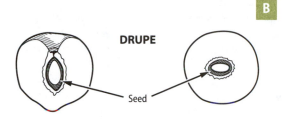

Seed

C

NUT

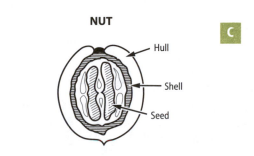

Hull

Shell

Seed

D

BERRY (Kiwi)

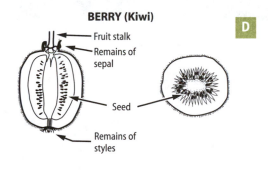

Fruit stalk

Remains of sepal

Seed

Remains of styles

E

MULTIPLE FRUIT

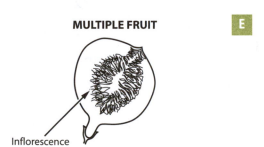

Inflorescence

sica), European plum and prune (dried European plums, *Prunus domestica*) and Japanese plum (*Prunus salicina*), like all stone fruits, belong to the genus *Prunus*, as do almonds (*Prunus dulcis*, formerly *P. amygdalus*). Their fruit is botanically known as a *drupe* (fig. 17.1B), a one-seeded fruit derived entirely from an ovary with a "stony" endocarp containing the seed. Botanists group almonds with the stone fruits rather than with the nut crops. This distinction is similar to the fact that many fruits—tomatoes, green peppers, cucumbers, zucchini, corn, and squash—are classified as fruits by botanists but are consumed as vegetables and are not thought of as fruits by most consumers. This chapter includes almonds with the nut crops because they are consumed as nuts.

Nut Crops

Almond (*Prunus dulcis*), chestnut (*Castanaea* spp.), filbert (also known as hazelnut, *Corylus* spp.), pecan (*Carya illinoensis*), pistachio (*Pistacia vera*), and walnut (*Juglans regia* [English or Persian walnut] and *J. hindsii* [black walnut]) are, with the exception of almonds, hard, woody, usually one-seeded fruits derived from the fusion of ovary and perianth (petals and sepals). Chestnuts are also different in that the edible portion is a high carbohydrate, low oil content fruit/nut, unlike the other nuts (fig. 17.1C).

Vines

Kiwifruit (*Actinidia deliciosa* and *A. chinensis*) is classified as a berry, a multiseeded fruit derived from a single ovary (fig. 17.1D). Other vine fruits, such as grapes, berries, and strawberries (cranberries, blueberries, currants, gooseberries, raspberries, blackberries), are discussed in chapters 15, "Grapes," and 16, "Berries."

Miscellaneous Fruits

Fig (*Ficus carica*), olive (*Olea europaea*), and persimmon (*Diospyros kaki*) do not fit into the above categories, yet they are important trees in the home garden. The fig, a *multiple fruit* (fig. 17.1E), is derived from the fusion of ovaries and receptacles (the part of the flower stalk that bears the floral organs) of many flowers. The olive fruit is a drupe.

Growth and Development

Planning to grow temperate fruit and nut trees in the home garden requires more careful attention and research than planning a vegetable garden. Temperate fruit and nut trees can make beautiful, practical additions to the home garden and landscape due to their striking flowers, edible harvest, and ability to double as shade trees, but they are considerably more expensive to grow than annual vegetable crops. Since fruit and nut trees are perennials, the varieties chosen and their location in the home landscape are long-term decisions requiring careful planning and knowledge of the trees' growth and development habits.

Even though temperate zone fruit and nut trees are diverse in individual character, their similarities in growth, development, and cultural practices allow their presentation together in this chapter.

Scions and Rootstocks

Temperate fruit and nut trees available for purchase at a nursery usually consist of a scion/rootstock combination (fig 17.2A) in which the rootstock provides the lower few inches of the trunk and the tree's roots, and the scion includes the major portion of the trunk, all branches, leaves, and, most impor-

tant, the fruit variety. Nursery-grown fruit trees are usually 1 to 2 years old when sold to the public. The scion is cut from mature wood of the desired fruiting variety during the dormant season. Usually, scion varieties are grafted or budded onto rootstocks that have been selected for improved disease and nematode resistance, tolerance to adverse soil conditions, nutrient uptake, cold hardiness, and their favorable influence on the performance of the scion variety, including tree size (dwarfing effects), fruit quality (sugar-to-acid ratio, flavor, texture, size), and productivity (yield efficiency). (For recommended rootstock and scion varieties for the tree fruit and nut crops discussed in this chapter, as well as the effects of various rootstocks on scion varieties, see table 17.4.)

By grafting or budding mature fruiting wood onto a selected rootstock, the tree begins fruiting sooner compared to vigorous juvenile wood from a young ungrafted seedling. Seedling trees must pass through a lengthy juvenile phase of growth before they become mature enough (*competent*) to flower and for the flowers to set and bear fruit (fig. 17.2B). Some trees, such as olives, are simply grown from cuttings without any rootstock.

Size Control in Fruit and Nut Crops

Home gardeners in California have the option of growing varieties as various sizes of trees:

Figure 17.2

Grafted and ungrafted fruit trees. (A) Grafted tree is composed of a scion and rootstock. It is all mature wood above the bud union. (B) Seedling tree has juvenile wood from the base up into the crown, a transition zone midway up trunk, and mature wood in the top and branch ends. *Source*: After Westwood 1993, p. 218.

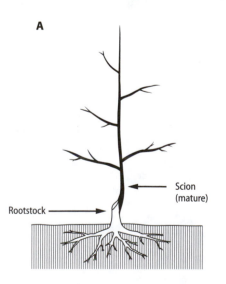

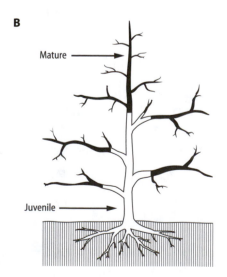

Figure 17.3

Size control in temperate fruit trees. (A) Standard variety with no size control; (B) and (C) standard variety on semidwarfing rootstock or semidwarf variety; (D) standard variety on dwarfing rootstock or genetic dwarf variety.

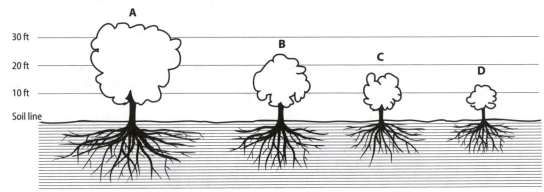

- standard-sized trees grow to the typical size of the variety, about 15 to 35 feet (4.5 to 10 m) tall (fig. 17.3A)

- semidwarf trees grow to about 12 to 20 feet (3.5 to 6 m) tall, about two-thirds of standard size (fig. 17.3B–C)

- dwarf trees attain about half of the standard size, approximately 8 to 12 feet (2.5 to 3.5 m) tall (fig. 17.3D)

While rootstocks can have a size-reducing effect on tree growth, they usually have little or no effect on fruit size. Although dwarf trees do not have smaller fruit, they may set more fruit per given area if the shoots have shorter internodes and compressed fruit buds. Because fruit set can far exceed the reduced canopy's capacity to size the fruit, the home gardener must be careful to thin dwarf trees properly (see the section later in this chapter on fruit thinning).

Temperate fruit trees that are dwarf in size are typically one of three types:

- *Genetic dwarfs*: In peaches and nectarines, some fruiting varieties have been bred to include a dwarfing gene, producing a naturally small-growing tree. In apples, mutations of standard varieties that have compressed growth and produce an abundance of fruiting spurs are sometimes discovered in orchards. These mutations are called "spur" type trees. Genetic dwarf and spur-type trees are usually grafted onto a standard rootstock.

- *Dwarfing rootstock*: Normal-growing varieties can be grafted onto rootstocks that have dwarfing effects on overall tree size.

- *Interstem*: Normal-growing varieties can be grafted onto standard or semidwarf rootstocks with interstems grafted between the scion and rootstock, producing dwarfing effects on overall tree size.

Doubling of the dwarfing effect by using genetic dwarf or spur-type varieties grafted onto dwarfing rootstocks or interstems produces extreme dwarfing in trees. These combinations are generally not viable because the trees are too small and lack sufficient vigor.

There are only a few species of fruit trees with reliable dwarfing rootstocks: apples (E. Malling Series and MM Series from England; EMLA Series, virus-free plants also from England; P Series from Poland; V Series from Vineland Canada; Bud Series from Russia; and the MAC Series from Michigan), and a few varieties of pears (quince rootstock). Recently, the University of California and private nurseries have been actively testing and evaluating dwarfing rootstocks for cherry, peach, and nectarine. A recent relese of Giesla Series rootstocks for cherry and Citation for peach and nectarine has made dwarfing available in those species for home orchardists. The Citation rootstock produces only a slight dwarfing effect on apricot, plumcot, and plum. No effective dwarfing rootstocks are available for almond, apricot, plum, Asian pear, olive, persimmon, fig, pomegranate, walnut, pecan, or chestnut.

The number of years from planting a grafted nursery tree to the time that it bears fruit depends on many factors, including the scion variety, the size of the tree (whether it is standard size, semidwarf, or dwarf) and how the tree is pruned. In very general terms, standard-sized peach and nectarine trees bear fruit earlier than cherry, pear, apple, apricot, and plum trees because of the bearing habit of the species. Typically, dwarf trees begin to bear 1 to 3 years earlier than standard-sized trees.

Standard-sized trees of the taller temperate species, such as walnut, pecan, chestnut, almond, olive, apple, pear, and sweet cherry, can double as shade trees if space is available, but a ladder will be needed for pruning and harvest. On the other hand, dwarf varieties permit growing a wider variety of fruits in limited space. Also, pruning, thinning, and harvesting them can be done without ladders and should take less time per tree. Unfortunately, there is a limited selection of high-quality fruits available on dwarfing rootstocks.

Some dwarfing rootstocks are shallow-rooted and inadequately anchored compared to other rootstocks and may require staking. Dwarfing of fruit trees by rootstocks is usually a physiological response as the limited vigor of the rootstock is transferred to the scion. In some cases, dwarfing is also caused by a slight incompatibility between the scion and rootstock.

The lower-vigor dwarf trees require more care, such as frequent irrigations, careful pruning, and better fertility, than standard rootstock trees with greater size and vigor. Standard-sized trees are much more able to survive adverse conditions and neglect. Neglected dwarf and semidwarf trees often become stunted and full of fruiting spurs without any new vegetative growth. For the first couple of years, this is not a problem, but the fruit eventually becomes smaller on old wood, and the tree becomes less fruitful without adequate new growth.

Dormancy and Winter Chill

The growth of deciduous fruit and nut trees follows an annual pattern that changes with the seasonal transitions in the surrounding environment. Typically, temperate fruit and nut trees grow rapidly during the spring and first half of the summer. Later in the season, the growth rate declines. In the fall, the growth of deciduous fruit and nut trees stops as day length and temperatures decrease and the trees drop their leaves. In a reaction to day length and temperature, growth inhibitors (hormones) are produced in the tree that prevent it from growing. In the winter months, the tree's internal processes are in a state of rest, known as *dormancy*, due to the presence of these growth inhibitors. During dormancy, growth will not occur even under ideal temperature conditions. This prevents the trees from beginning to grow during atypical periods of warm weather only to become damaged by freezing temperatures later in the winter or early spring.

Dormancy is broken when sufficient cold temperature breaks down the growth inhibitors within the tree. This cold period is called *chilling*, *winter chill*, or sometimes *vernalization* (see chapter 1 for more on vernalization). A specific number of cumulative hours of chilling (temperatures lower than 45°F, or 7°C) is required to break dormancy; the number of hours differs from variety to variety. Once the variety has accumulated the appropriate number of hours of chilling, active growth resumes in the spring, but only after trees are exposed to temperatures warm enough for natural growth processes to begin. Most of Northern California receives between 800 and 1,500 hours of chilling each winter. Southern California may only receive 100 to 400 hours.

Temperate trees and shrubs grow best in climates in which the winters are warm enough that plant tissue is not killed from extreme low temperatures but not so warm that buds receive inadequate chilling to break dormancy. Flower and shoot buds of deciduous fruit trees and olives grow normally in the spring only after exposure to sufficient winter cold. After winters with inadequate chilling, the plants leaf out late in the season (delayed foliation), blossoming is prolonged, buds may deteriorate or drop, and few, if any, flowers are produced. Without flowers, there will be no fruit to harvest.

Winter Chilling Index. *The number of hours below 45°F (7°C) is a fair index of the adequacy of winter chilling. Both the absolute number and distribution of the hours below 45°F must be considered.* The chilling requirements of selected temperate tree fruits and nuts expressed as the number of hours less than 45°F needed to break dormancy are given in table 17.1. December and January are usually the most critical months. If each of these months has approximately 400 hours of temperatures below 45°F, and if these hours are distributed fairly evenly, then troubles related to mild winters are less likely. Regular accumulation of chilling weather is essential for many varieties to perform optimally. Periods of a few days to a week or more of mild weather may offset or reduce the effectiveness of accompanying periods of good chilling weather. Greater seasonal totals are usually necessary in those years or districts with interrupted periods of adequate low temperatures and warm, sunny days. Cloudy or foggy weather that maintains temperatures below 45°F is often necessary in parts of California to achieve adequate chilling hours.

Low-Chill Varieties. Over the years, plant scientists and breeders around the world have been selecting and developing varieties that require less chilling: many require 300 hours or less of temperatures below 45°F. The development of these "low-chill" varieties has extended the range of climates and latitudes in which temperate tree fruits and nuts can be produced. Certain varieties of apple, pear, apricot, nectarine, peach, Japanese and hybrid plums, and kiwifruit are reported to have low chilling requirements (see table 17.4).

In general terms, the relatively low chilling requirements of quince, fig, persimmon, almond, olive, chestnut, and pecan have enabled many varieties of these fruits and nuts to thrive in low latitudes. On the other hand, sweet and sour cherries and filbert (hazelnut) are not suitable for the low latitudes of Southern California because of the lack of low-chill varieties.

Bud Development and Classification

During the growing season, some buds (potential growing points) and branches are actively growing, but most of the buds are at rest (latent). In most cases, latent buds are controlled by an inhibiting hormone called *auxin* produced by the apical bud (terminal growing point). Auxins are strongly influenced by gravity. They travel down the shoot and prevent the lower buds from growing. Buds within vertical (upright) shoots are more strongly affected by gravity because of the orientation of the shoots; therefore, those shoots tend to grow strongly from one apical bud and become dominant.

Pruning off the apical bud (a heading cut) can temporarily release the lower lateral buds from inhibition by the auxin, causing the growth of multiple lateral shoots (the "bush" effect). These shoots are typically less vigorous because more buds grow than just the bud at the apex of the branch. The lower vigor of these lateral shoots results in the development of more flower buds and increased fruitfulness. Home orchardists influence the development of branches and flowers through careful pruning techniques and by bending upright branches into more horizontal positions.

Buds are classified by their activity level (active or latent), their function (vegetative or flowering or both), and by position or origin on the stem (terminal, lateral, or adventitious). Active buds produce the current season's shoots as terminal growth or as short lateral shoots known as spurs. Active buds may also develop into flowers. Buds that do not become active are latent and can be induced to grow

Table 17.1

CHILLING REQUIREMENTS OF TEMPERATE TREE FRUITS AND NUTS

Type of fruit	Approx. hours at <45°F (7°C) needed to break dormancy	Equiv. time in days if continuously exposed to 45°F (7°C) or below
almond	250–500	10–20
apple*	500–1,000	20–40
apple (low-chill)	400–600	16–24
apricot*	300–800	12–32
cherry, sour	1,200	48
cherry, sweet	700–800	28–32
chestnut	400–500	16–20
fig	100	4
filbert (hazelnut)	800	32
kiwifruit*	300–800	12–32
olive	200–300	8–12
peach/nectarine*	500–800	20–32
pear*	700–800	28–32
pear (Asian)	350–450	14–18
pecan	250	10
persimmon	100–200	4–8
pistachio	800	32
plum, American*	3,000	120
plum, European*	600–800	24–32
plum, Japanese	250–700	10–28
plumcot	400–600	16–24
pomegranate	100–150	4–6
quince	300	12
walnut, Persian	500–700	20–28

Note: *See table 17.4 for low-chill varieties of these fruits, which have been reported to require <300 hours of temperatures <45°F (7°C) to break dormancy.

by pruning. Buds that give rise to shoots are known as vegetative buds. Buds that give rise to flowers are called flower buds. Buds that give rise to both flowers and leaves are called mixed buds. Shoots arising from mixed buds can bear their flowers terminally or laterally. New growing points arising from positions where buds are not normally found are called adventitious buds. Suckers, strong vertical shoots arising from the roots, and water sprouts, strong upright shoots arising from older branches, are the most common examples of growth from adventitioius buds. When large branches are topped, the new shoots that grow from callus tissue formed at the wound also come from adventitious buds.

Flower Bud Formation

Even though the grafted or budded nursery tree is adult tissue (see fig. 17.2A), trees may not flower immediately after planting. They usually go through a vegetative phase called juvenility. The transition to becoming a mature flowering tree is controlled by complex hormones and is influenced by carbohydrate accumulation, light exposure, age, and nitrogen nutrition. Once a tree does begin flower

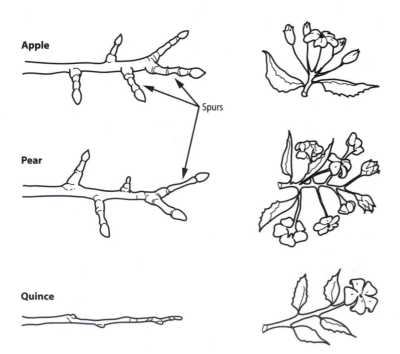

Figure 17.4

Pome fruit flowering habits. *Source*: After Westwood 1993, p. 220.

Apple

Spurs

Pear

Quince

development, cultural practices (pruning, fruit thinning, and fertilizing) and environmental conditions can influence additional flower bud formation during a particular season.

In most cases, it is desirable for trees to grow vigorously without fruit formation for the first 2 to 3 years so that they can fill their allotted space in the garden or orchard. Trees grow more slowly after they begin bearing fruit because they are putting their energy into fruit production. This is a simple energy displacement: Fruit is a demanding sink for carbohydrates (sugars) produced by the leaves. The flow of most of the energy source to the fruit reduces that available for shoot growth. Once they begin to fruit, it may be difficult to get trees to grow significantly and fill their space, especially with dwarf trees. In most cases, neglected trees become stunted and never reach their full growth or fruit-bearing potential. These trees should be replaced, and the new tree should be encouraged to grow vigorously for the first few years through adequate water, fertilization, and weed control.

During the early stages of tree development, minimal pruning favors flower bud formation and earlier fruit set because more lower-vigor shoots are produced. Over time, however, unpruned trees develop thick canopies, which limits light penetration into the tree and results in poor flower bud formation and poor fruit set in all but the uppermost portions of the tree. Young buds that are exposed to full sunlight produce flowers with greater longevity and larger fruit. Unpruned trees do not develop as much sun-exposed renewal (new) wood for future flower and fruit development. Pruning is discussed more fully in its own section later in this chapter.

Excessive nitrogen (N) fertilization creates excessive vegetative growth in fruit trees, which reduces light penetration into the canopy and results in less flower bud formation and lower fruit yield. It is therefore important to avoid oversupplying nitrogen, not only because it reduces fruit and nut yield but also because it can pollute groundwater resources if leached. Nitrogen fertilization is discussed more fully in the section on fertilization later in this chapter.

Alternate Bearing

Alternate (biennial) bearing, the term used to describe fruit trees that produce a heavy crop one year and a light crop the next, is caused

Figure 17.5

Stone fruit flowering habits. Note that flowers are always borne on 1-year-old shoots. *Source:* After Westwood 1993, pp. 220–221.

Peach

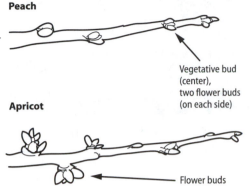

Vegetative bud (center), two flower buds (on each side)

Apricot

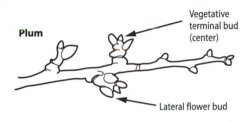

Flower buds

Plum

Vegetative terminal bud (center)

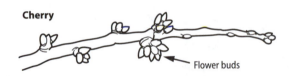

Lateral flower bud

Cherry

Flower buds

by alternate blooming. In years with heavy bloom, excessive fruit may be set. During the time between the full bloom stage and the small fruit stage, most fruit trees are also producing flowers in the buds for next year. In most tree crops, a large crop on the tree produces hormones that send a chemical message to the developing buds not to initiate flowers the following year. Consequently, next year's bloom is light, fewer fruit have an opportunity to set, and the yield is much smaller. During the light cropping year, many flowers are initiated in the buds, which leads to heavy flowering the following year, more fruit set, and an alternate bearing cycle.

The most effective way to reduce alternate bearing and increase final fruit size is to hand-thin the tiny fruit within 30 to 45 days after full bloom, when the fruit reach ⅜ to 1 inch (1.0 to 2.5 cm) in diameter. The advantage of early thinning is that the fruit removal occurs

during or prior to flower initiation and therefore has a positive influence on blooming the next year. Early thinning also provides the maximum benefit for fruit size on the remaining fruit in the current year. Early thinning reduces the number of fruit acting as sinks for a longer time, making more food from photosynthesis available for the remaining fruit.

Pruning can also have an impact on alternate bearing. In peaches and nectarines, removal of almost half of last year's growth effectively thins the canopy and leads to more even cropping. In olives, pruning is done during bloom every other year in the season that is expected to have a large crop. Trees with heavy bloom are pruned more than trees with a light bloom to even out the crop from year to year.

Flowering and Fruiting Habits

It is useful to understand the flowering habits of deciduous fruit and nut trees because flowers are essential to fruit production (tables 17.2 and 17.3). This information can also influence fruit thinning, pruning, fertilization, and other cultural practices.

Pome Fruits. On apple, flower buds are usually borne terminally on shoots or short spurs 2 years old and older, but they may also be borne on lateral buds of 1-year-old shoots (see table 17.2 and fig. 17.4). Flowers are initiated in early summer for next year's crop. Apple blossom clusters are determinate cymes that contain 5 flowers. Pear inflorescences contain 7 or 8 flowers, and they are indeterminate (lateral blossoms open first and the terminal bloom opens last); flowers are borne on shoot terminals and on short spurs 2 years old and older. Most European pears are not alternate bearing and require little or no fruit thinning. Unlike apples and pears, the quince flower bud contains only one flower. Anatomically, pome flowers are perfect, containing both male and female parts, but most require pollen from another variety (cross-pollination) in order to set fruit (see the section on pollination requirements, below; see also table 17.3).

Stone Fruits. Almond, peach, cherry, and plum flower buds (see table 17.2 and fig. 17.5) are quite different than the flowers of pome fruits. The solitary flowers are always in a lateral (not terminal) position and are borne on 1-year-old shoots (last year's growth). Each node usually contains 3 buds (2 flower buds on each side of a vegetative bud). The fruit forms above the petals, whereas in pome fruits the fruit forms below the petals. Floral initiation begins in summer for the following year's crop. After a heavy crop year, peaches tend to bloom lighter the next year. Peaches and nectarines can bloom and bear fruit the second or third year after planting. Apricot flowers are solitary. They are initiated in late summer on lateral buds on 1-year-old shoots and short spurs. On plums and prunes, flowers are borne in lateral buds on 2-year-old and older spurs and on 1-year-old wood. Initiation occurs in the summer for next year's crop. Each bud produces 1 to 3 flowers; terminal

Table 17.2

TIME OF FLOWER INITIATION AND FULL BLOOM IN SELECTED TREE FRUIT AND NUT CROPS

Flower type	Beginning of induction/ initiation	Flowers borne on	Season of full bloom relative to season of initiation
POME FRUITS			
apple	mid-Apr–mid-June	terminal buds, 2-yr spurs or lateral buds, 1-yr shoots	next spring
pear	early June–early July	terminal buds, 2-yr spurs	next spring
quince	early spring–June	terminal shoots, current growth	same spring
STONE FRUITS			
almond	mid-Aug–mid-Sep	lateral buds, 1-yr shoots	next spring
apricot	early Aug	lateral buds, 1-yr shoots and 2-yr spurs	next spring
cherry, sour	mid-July	lateral buds, 2-yr spurs	next spring
cherry, sweet	early July	lateral buds, 2-yr spurs	next spring
peach and nectarine	late June–late July	lateral buds, 1-yr shoots	next spring
plum, Japanese	mid-July–early Aug	lateral buds, 1-yr shoots and 2-yr spurs	next spring
prune	late June–mid-Aug	lateral buds, 1-yr shoots and 2-yr spurs	next spring
NUTS			
almond	*see Stone Fruits, above*		
filbert, female	July–Sep	lateral buds, 1-yr shoots	next winter
filbert, male	May	lateral buds, 1-yr shoots	next winter
pecan, female	early spring	terminals of current shoots	same season
pecan, male	early summer	lateral buds, 1-yr shoots	next spring
pistachio	late Apr	lateral buds, 1-yr shoots	next spring
walnut, female	late summer	terminals of current shoots	next spring
walnut, male	early summer	lateral buds, 1-yr shoots	next spring
VINES			
kiwifruit	late summer	lateral buds, 1-yr canes	next spring
MISCELLANEOUS FRUITS			
fig (crop 1)	late summer	lateral buds, 1-yr shoots	next spring
fig (crop 2)	early summer	lateral buds, current growth	same season
olive	late winter	lateral buds, 1-yr shoots	next spring
persimmon	July	lateral buds, 1-yr shoots	next spring

buds are vegetative. Sweet and sour cherry flowers are borne in clusters of 2 to 4 buds borne laterally on 2-year-old wood. The flowers of stone fruits contain both male and female parts, but most cultivars of plum, plumcot, cherry, and almond require cross-pollination (see table 17.3). Peach, nectarine, and apricot do not require cross-pollination.

Nut Crops. Chestnut, filbert (hazelnut), pecan, and walnut are monoecious, which means that they have separate male and female flowers on the same tree (table 17.2 and fig. 17.6). Walnuts and pecans are similar in that the male catkins are borne in lateral buds on 1-year-old wood (last year's growth), and female flowers are borne terminally on the current season's growth. The female flowers have no petals and consist of a large, reflexed stigma attached to an ovary. Walnut, pecan, pistachio, chestnut, and filbert are pollinated by wind.

In filbert, the male catkins and female flowers are borne on lateral buds of 1-year-old wood. Female flowers have no petals; in the winter, they look like small red tufts (stigmas) protruding from the bud. In chestnut, male and female flowers are borne on the current season's shoots. Male flowers are borne on lateral buds along the lower portion of the shoot; three female flowers are usually located at the base of male catkins.

Pistachios differ from the other nuts discussed in this chapter in that they are usually dioecious, which means that they have separate male and female trees. Both female and male flowers are borne laterally on 1-year-old wood. Female flowers lack petals. Pistachios tend to bear biennially. For the development of flowers and fruits in almonds, see the section on stone fruits above and figure 17.6.

Table 17.3

GROWTH AND DEVELOPMENT OF SELECTED POME AND STONE FRUIT TREES

Fruit type and rootstock	Pollination requirements*	Mature height† (ft)	(m)	Mature spread† (ft)	(m)	Years to bear after planting	Yield per tree per season (bu)	(l)	Bearing period
almond (standard)	SS	25–35	7.6–10.7	20–25	6.1–7.6	3–5	1–2	50–100	Aug–Sep
apple									
dwarf	SS or PSF	6–10	1.8–3	8–10	2.4–3	2–3	3–5	106–176	Jun–Nov
semidwarf	SS or PSF	10–14	3–4.3	14–18	4.3–5.5	4–5	5–10	176–352	Jun–Nov
standard	SS or PSF	15–30	4.6–9.1	20–25	6.1–7.6	5–7	10–25	352–881	Jun–Nov
apricot	PSF or SF	20–25	6.1–7.6	18–20	5.5–6.1	4–5	2–4	70–141	May–Jul
cherry, sweet									
semidwarf	SS	14–20	4.3–6.1	14–18	4.3–5.5	4–6	20–40 qt	19–38	May–Jun
standard	SS	25–35	7.6–10.7	20–25	6.1–7.6	4–6	30–60 qt	28–57	May–Jun
peach and nectarine									
genetic dwarf	SF	3–6	0.9–1.8	5–8	1.5–2.4	3	1–1.5	35–53	Apr–Oct
standard	SF	8–18	2.4–5.5	18–20	5.5–6.1	4	3–5	106–176	Apr–Oct
pear (Asian)									
standard	SS	8–16	2.4–4.9	12–16	3.7–4.9	3–4	5–6	176–211	Aug–Oct
pear (European)									
dwarf	SS	10–15	3–4.6	10–12	3–3.7	3–4	1–3	35–106	Aug–Oct
standard	SS	25–40	7.6–12.2	20–25	6.1–7.6	5–7	4–6	141–211	Aug–Oct
plum (standard)									
European	PSF	18–22	5.5–6.7						Jun–Oct
Japanese	SS								Jun–Oct
American	SF or PSF								Jun–Oct

Notes:

*PSF = partially self-fertile, which means that a heavier fruit crop is set when two or more varieties are planted nearby; SF = self-fertile, which means that one variety is needed for pollination; SS = self sterile, which means that two varieties are needed for pollination. Exceptions to these general statements about specific fruit types will occur with some varieties.

†Summer and winter pruning influence tree height and spread.

Figure 17.6

Flowering habits of selected nut crops. *Source:* After Westwood 1993, pp. 224–225.

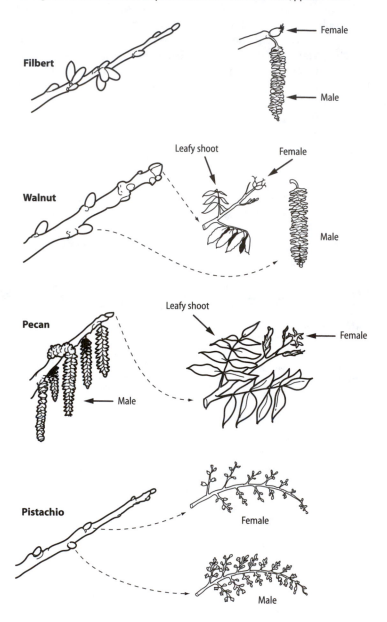

Filbert

Female

Male

Walnut

Leafy shoot

Female

Male

Pecan

Leafy shoot

Female

Male

Pistachio

Female

Male

Vines. Kiwifruit are functionally dioecious because the female flowers, although appearing to be perfect, produce nonviable pollen. Male plants rarely produce fruit. Flowers are initiated in late summer, developing from buds in the axils of leaves formed on the current season's shoots (table 17.2 and fig. 17.7).

Miscellaneous Fruits. Figs often have two crops per season. The flowers of the first crop are initiated on lateral buds in late summer and fall. They overwinter and produce next season's first crop in the spring. Second-crop flowers are initiated in early summer and bear

figs in the fall of the same season (table 17.2 and fig. 17.8). Olive flowers are borne laterally in the axils of leaves on last year's shoot growth and, less often, from dormant buds 1 to 2 years old. Olives bear perfect and staminate (male) flowers. Persimmons are dioecious. Both male and female flowers are borne at leaf axils on new growth (table 17.2 and fig. 17.9).

Pollination

Growing high-quality temperate fruits and nuts with efficient yields in the home garden requires an understanding of pollination. In almond and particularly in multiseeded fruits, such as kiwi, apple, and pear, good pollination, fertilization, and seed development are important to the production of large, attractive fruits. Most nuts (walnut, pistachio, chestnut, pecan, and filbert) and olive are wind-pollinated; many of the temperate fruits are insect-pollinated, primarily by bees, whose presence is absolutely necessary for good fruit set. Some fruit and nut trees have separate male and female flowers, but their bloom times do not always overlap; others have perfect flowers, but the pollen is not compatible for self-fertilization. Thus, cross-pollination is essential to good fruit set in these trees. It may be necessary to have more than one tree of a particular fruit or nut and to plant more than one variety to set a good crop. On the other hand, a few deciduous fruit trees are self-fertile, eliminating the need for more than one tree.

For tree fruits with good blooming habits, only a small percentage of the blossoms need pollination to set a full crop of fruit. For nuts, because a higher percentage of the flowers become nuts, the trees require more extensive pollination. Under adverse weather conditions or if bloom is sparse, gardeners can ensure an adequate set by planting pollenizer trees to provide pollen through synchronized bloom. Except for the wind-pollinated species, honey bees or other pollenizing insects are necessary to make sure pollen is transferred between blossoms. Erring on the side of setting too many fruit and then hand-thinning excess fruit is preferable to not setting enough fruit. For the wind-pollinated nut crops and olives, some dry weather is needed during the flowering period to get good set. The nut crops are not thinned.

For pollination requirements for most of these crops, see table 17.3. Some general pollination problems are noted below.

Figure 17.7

Kiwifruit flowering habit. *Source:* After Hasey et al. 1994, p. 53.

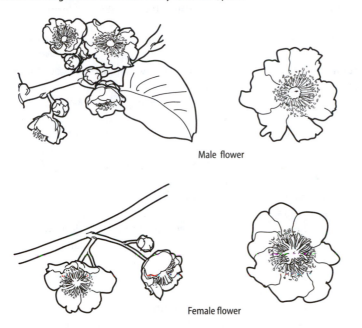

Male flower

Female flower

Figure 17.8

Flowering habit of fig. *Source:* After Westwood 1993, p. 222.

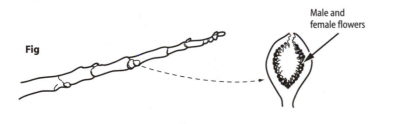

Male and female flowers

Fig

Figure 17.9

Flowering habit of persimmon. *Source:* After Westwood 1993, p. 223.

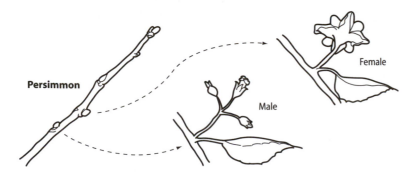

Persimmon

Male

Female

Pome and Stone Fruit Trees. Flowers of many pome and stone fruit trees are perfect; they have both male and female organs, *but not all varieties are self-fertile* (SF) (see table 17.3). Those varieties that are self-fertile (apricot, peach, nectarine, quince) set a good fruit crop when pollinated by flowers on the same tree, which means that only one specimen tree is needed in the garden. 'Golden Delicious' apples are a self-fertile variety. *Partially self-fertile* (PSF) species and varieties set some fruit when pollinated by other flowers on the same tree, but they set better crops if pollinated by a different variety, which means that gardeners may consider planting two varieties in the garden, depending on the yield desired. Olives are considered to be partially self-fertile. *Self-sterile* (abbreviated SS, but also known as self-infertile or self-incompatible) varieties require a second variety nearby to set fruit because pollen of flowers on the same tree or of the same variety does not lead to fertilization and fruit development due to numerous factors. Some varieties, such as 'Gravenstein' apple, have sterile pollen. Other causes include self-incompatibilities between stigmas and pollen grains, resulting in abortion of developing pollen tubes of the same variety as they attempt to carry sperm to egg-laden ovules in the ovary. Such self-incompatible varieties can be cross-pollinated effectively by a second variety planted in close proximity, if bloom times overlap. When choosing varieties for cross-pollination, be sure that their bloom times overlap. A very early bloomer may be almost finished before a late bloomer begins, which could frustrate your efforts for good fruit set in a self-incompatible variety.

Nut Trees. In walnut, the pollination problems stem primarily from *dichogamy*—the time when the stigma is receptive on female flowers does not coincide with the time when the pollen is shed from male flowers—rather than from incompatibility. Dichogamy tends to be more pronounced in young trees, but prevailing temperatures, humidity, and overall climate also influence this trait. In general, it is best to plant a protogynous walnut variety (female flowers are receptive before male flowers shed pollen) and a protandrous variety (male flowers shed pollen before female flowers are receptive) so that the male bloom of each type overlaps the female bloom of the other type, thereby facilitating effective pollination. Almonds (see table 17.3) require cross-pollination by another variety because they are self-sterile.

Causes of Reduced or Failed Fruit Set

Pollination Problems. As discussed above, many cultivated fruit and nut trees are completely or partially self-unfruitful, have dichogamy problems, or depend on an adequate supply of bees for pollen transfer from one flower to another. In many cases, the home gardener should review the tree's blooming habits and determine if they have been adequately met. In some cases this means having two different varieties flowering at the same time. Rain during bloom reduces pollen transfer of wind-pollinated species because the wet pollen grains stick together and become too heavy for wind dissemination. Strong winds, rain, and cold temperatures also greatly reduce or prevent adequate bee activity.

Natural Abscission of Buds, Flowers, and Fruits. Even when pollination is successful and the trees are in good health, not all pollinated flowers lead to effective fertilization of ovaries that later become edible fruits. A number of environmental and endogenous factors contribute to reduced fruit set due to abscission (separation) of buds, flowers, and fruits. Large-fruited trees, such as apple, may shed 90 percent or more of their pollinated flowers and young fruits. However, since a mature apple tree may have more than 100,000 flowers at full bloom, it is a benefit that not all flowers set fruit. Small-fruited species shed a lower percentage of flowers. On many fruit and nut trees, flower buds, flowers, and immature fruit abscise from the trees at distinct times during the year, particularly during "June drop" (which occurs in May in California). The fruit that remain on the tree are said to have "set."

Weather. Flower buds can fail to develop and can drop off the tree when exposed to freezing spring temperatures. The open blossoms of practically all fruit trees may be killed if the temperature drops below 27°F (−3°C). Even when buds or young fruits appear normal after a severe frost, if the internal female organs have been killed, the trees bear few fruit. Lack of winter chill may also lead to flower bud abscission, particularly during bud swell prior to bloom, resulting in reduced fruit yield. Varieties that need a higher number of hours below 45°F (7°C) (see table 17.1) shed

more buds after a relatively warm winter season than low-chill varieties. Cold temperatures above freezing (33° to 45°F, or 1° to 7°C) during bloom can also reduce fruit set because pollen tube growth is temperature-sensitive. Most flowers are only viable for 1 to 2 weeks during which the fertilization process can occur. Under low temperature conditions, the pollen tube grows too slowly to reach the ovary while the eggs are still viable. Hot, dry winds during bloom can dessicate blossoms. An extremely hot summer with temperatures above 104°F (40°C) for several days may also lead to abscission of flower and vegetative buds. Some varieties of cherries set both ovaries or portions of both ovaries, causing double fruit, when temperatures are high during flower initiation the previous year.

Competition. In some plants, during the juvenile phase of plant growth, flowers develop but do not set. When competition for nutrients and carbohydrates between the developing fruit and the simultaneous vegetative growth is quite high, inflorescence (flower) buds can abscise. Flower abscission also occurs in walnut female flowers that are over-pollinated, causing too many pollen tubes to grow down the style.

Disease and Insect Pests. Soilborne diseases, foliar diseases, and damage caused by insect pests, nematodes, and physiological disorders (see table 17.7) can cause reduced fruit yield because they weaken the tree's health and directly affect the flower or fruit.

Biennial (Alternate) Bearing. The tendency of some varieties to bear in alternate years also limits fruit set in the "off" year. Since the flower buds were actually formed the previous summer (see table 17.2), an especially heavy crop during bud formation may prevent adequate flower buds from forming or cause them to abscise. Heavy thinning or pruning during a year when the tree is producing a large yield can induce a more consistent bearing in some species.

Shade. Adequate sunlight is important for flower differentiation and fruit yield. Fruit trees do best in full sun; do not plant them where shade from a house or other trees will limit light exposure and fruit set.

Improper Pruning. Severe dormant pruning can remove most of the flower buds that were formed the previous year or lead to excessive vegetative vigor and very poor fruit set.

Factors Affecting Fruit Growth and Size

After pollination and fruit set, the developing fruit are quite small. Many factors influence their growth rate and final size, including cultural practices, fruit physiology, and the environment.

Cultural Practices. The home fruit gardener can have a significant effect on the ultimate size of the fruit harvested. The cultural practices that most influence size are *thinning* and *pruning* (removing excess fruit on the tree) and *irrigation* (allowing little or no water stress). Fruit size is influenced by the *leaf-to-fruit ratio* on the tree. Many fruit trees must be thinned early in the season because they set too many fruit in comparison to the number of leaves on the tree. With insufficient leaf area, each fruit would be tiny if allowed to continue growing. Water stress on fruit and nut trees limits cell enlargement of the fruit. It also causes the leaf stomates to close down in order to prevent water loss, which reduces gas exchange (CO_2 absorption and O_2 release) in the leaves. Less gas exchange results in less photosynthesis and less growth. Thinning and irrigation are discussed later in this chapter.

Fruit Physiology. The number of cells per fruit and their growth potential determine final fruit size. Physiological (internal) and environmental factors influence the duration of the cell division period in a particular fruit type and the extent of cell enlargement. For plums, peaches, and apples, the period of cell division may last about 1 month. For pears, cell division may last about 2 months. During the cell division period, cell enlargement also begins. Most fruit growth follows a sigmoidal, or S-shaped, curve in which growth is slow initially, then increases, and ultimately slows again (fig. 17.10).

The *reserve food supply* that supports growth is located in storage cells of branches, roots, and the trunk. Once leaves reach a certain size, they begin exporting their photosynthates to supply food needs throughout the tree. If fruit set too heavily when reserve and current food supplies are limited, the cell division period in those fruit is cut short, limiting fruit size. Competition between the developing small fruit and simultaneous vegetative growth is stronger in early-ripening cultivars (late spring to early summer), which must maintain a higher leaf-to-fruit ratio to yield fruit of high quality and adequate size.

Environment. Excessively high temperatures, cold spells, water stress, high winds, and improper exposure to sunlight also affect fruit growth and size during the summer. High winds and high temperatures increase the transpiration rate in leaves and the respiration rate in fruits, which can reduce fruit size. Heat stress also causes water core in apples, pit-burning in apricots, side-cracking in prunes, and blackening in peaches (see table 17.7).

California Climate Zones for Growing Temperate Tree Fruits and Nuts

University of California scientists divide the state into six main agricultural districts for the production of temperate fruit and nuts (fig. 17.11):

(1) San Joaquin Valley
(2) Sacramento Valley
(3) Central Coast
(4) North Coast
(5) Sierra Nevada Foothills
(6) Southern California

The six regions and their important climatic characteristics with respect to growth of temperate fruit and nut crops are described below.

San Joaquin Valley (Zone 1 on fig. 17.11). In this region, the maximum temperature during the hottest months of the year (June through August) may exceed 104°F (40°C). Average temperatures in July and

Figure 17.10

Typical sigmoidal fruit growth curves for pome and stone fruits. *Source*: After Westwood 1993, p. 255.

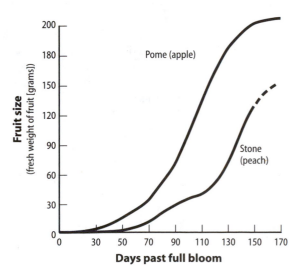

January in Stockton in the northern part of the valley are 75°F (24°C) and 45°F (7°C), respectively, whereas average temperatures in July and January in Bakersfield in the southern part of the valley are 84°F (28°C) and 47°F (8°C), respectively. More than 80 percent of the area's precipitation occurs in the winter, with an average 5.7 inches (14.5 cm) per year at Bakersfield and 14.3 inches (36.3 cm) at Stockton. Dense fogs lasting a week or more are common in the winter. This region is relatively flat due to alluvial deposits from several California rivers (Stanislaus, Tuolumne, Merced, Fresno, San Joaquin, Kings, Kern, and Kawaeah). Temperate tree fruit and nut crops grown here commercially include almond, apple, cherry, chestnut, fig, kiwifruit, nectarine, olive, peach, pear, pecan, persimmon, pistachio, plum, pomegranate, prune, quince, chestnut, and English and black walnut. The San Joaquin Valley is also the most important area in the state for production of citrus fruits and grapes.

Figure 17.11

Major temperate fruit and nut producing zones in California. *Source:* After Ogawa and English 1991, p. 3.

Zone 1	San Joaquin Valley
Zone 2	Sacramento Valley
Zone 3	Central Coast
Zone 4	North Coast
Zone 5	Sierra Nevada Foothills
Zone 6	Southern California

Sacramento Valley (Zone 2 on fig. 17.11). In this region, the winters are cool and moist with fogs that may last a week or more; summers are clear, hot, and dry. Average temperatures in July and January in Sacramento are 75°F (24°C) and 45°F (7°C), respectively. Annual precipitation in Sacramento averages 17.2 inches (43.5 cm), whereas annual precipitation in Redding in the northern part of the Sacramento Valley averages 40.9 inches (103.9 cm). Like the San Joaquin Valley, this region is relatively flat. It is drained by the south-flowing Sacramento River, which is joined by several rivers from the Sierra Nevada. The main temperate fruit and nut crops grown commercially in the Sacramento Valley are almond, apple, apricot, kiwifruit, olive, peach, pear, pecan, pistachio, plum, prune, chestnut, and English and black walnut. Some wine grapes and cold-hardy citrus are also grown.

Central Coast (Zone 3 on fig. 17.11). The climate in the Central Coast is influenced by the Pacific Ocean. Salinas, which is about 10 miles (16 km) from the ocean in Monterey County, has an average January temperature of 50°F (10°C) and an average temperature of 74°F (23°C) in September. Annual precipitation in Salinas averages 13.7 inches (34.8 cm). The region generally has a mild climate with cool summers on the coast, where fog is common, and warm summers in the interior, but not as warm as the Central Valley. Although frosts are infrequent in the winters near San Francisco, low-lying areas in the interior of this region can have temperatures below freezing. Winter protection and site selection can be critical factors in some locations in this region. The main temperate fruit and nut crops grown commercially in this area are almond, apple, apricot, cherry, pear, plum, prune, olive, and English and black walnut. It is also a major wine grape and berry production area.

North Coast (Zone 4 on fig. 17.11). The North Coast is the wettest region of the state. Annual precipitation averages 25 to 80 inches (63.5 to 203 cm), which causes some disease problems in the spring during bloom and root rot problems due to excess soil moisture. The North Coast has a rugged terrain with coastal plains and a few small valleys. The main temperate tree fruit and nut crops grown commercially in this region are apple, pear, prune, olive, chestnut, and English and black walnut.

It is also the primary premium wine-grape-growing region of the state.

Sierra Nevada Foothills (Zone 5 on fig. 17.11). This region is a narrow, hilly area on the east side of the Central Valley. Although commercial production has declined in this region due to competition from higher-yielding orchards in the Central Valley, home gardeners can grow many temperate fruit and nut crops in this region at elevations ranging from 500 to 3,000 feet (150 to 915 m). In many locations in this region, soils are shallow and rocky, but a few narrow valleys have alluvial, valley bottom, and terrace soils. Annual precipitation ranges from 20 to 40 inches (51 to 102 cm). Spring frosts, especially at the higher altitudes, can cause production problems. The main temperate fruit and nut crops grown commercially in this region are apple, cherry, peach, pear, pistachio, quince, persimmon, plum, prune, olive, chestnut, and English walnut.

Southern California (Zone 6 on fig. 17.11). The Southern California coast is influenced by the Pacific Ocean and has a mild climate due to the marine air. Summers are moderate in temperature and coastal fog is common. Hot, dry winds known as Santa Anas can be damaging on the coast and in the inland areas of Southern California. The interior is more subject to hot, dry desert air than the coast and is considerably warmer. Higher-elevation areas in Southern California have a climate more similar to the mountain foothills. Annual rainfall along the coast can be as high as 16 inches (40.5 cm) in Santa Barbara and as low as 9 inches (23 cm) in San Diego.

Droughts are not uncommon, and all crops are irrigated. The main temperate fruit and nut crops grown commercially in this region are apple, macadamia, olive, peach, persimmon, and English walnut. Since winters along the Southern California coast and interior are usually mild and often frost-free, temperate tree fruit varieties with low winter chill requirements are usually chosen because the low latitudes in this region receive a more limited number of total hours at 45°F (7°C). (See table 17.4 for varieties of apple, pear, peach, nectarine, apricot, Japanese and hybrid plums, and kiwifruit reported to have low winter chilling requirements that can be grown successfully in this region by home gardeners.)

Varieties

The climate zone (see fig. 17.11) determines which varieties of temperate tree fruit and nut crops perform best in the home garden, when fruits and nuts are harvested, and which pest and disease problems are more common. Table 17.4 describes *selected* varieties of the major and minor temperate fruit and nut crops that are suitable for home gardeners in California. The table could easily be doubled or tripled in size if all heirloom varieties and newer varieties available at nurseries or through mail order were included. Grapes, berries, and other tree crops are discussed in two separate chapters in this book. Refer to these chapters for variety information.

Certain varieties are superb eaten fresh; other varieties tend to be used more often for cooking, canning, and freezing. Experts do not always agree about which varieties are best suited for various uses because individual tastes differ. The comments in table 17.4 regarding these issues are offered as points of interest only, not as official advice endorsed by the University of California.

Table 17.4

SELECTED TEMPERATE TREE FRUIT AND NUT VARIETIES FOR PLANTING IN THE HOME GARDEN AND LANDSCAPE

POME FRUITS

APPLE (*Malus domestica*)

Apples are adapted to many areas of California. A cool climate is needed for coloration in most red varieties. Winter chilling requirements for most varieties are 500 to 1,000 hr below 45°F (7°C); low-chill varieties need about 400 to 600 hr below 45°F. Foggy days and dews can cause heavy cosmetic russetting on fruit. There are hundreds of apple varieties, and some varieties have several strains, each with its own characteristics. Spur-type (short shoot growth and abundant spur production) varieties do poorly on dwarfing rootstocks; they are best grown on seedling rootstock. Several rootstocks are available that impart dwarfing and pest resistance. Apple varieties exhibit considerable genetic diversity. Some require as few as 70 days to mature; others take 180 days or more. Some varieties are very cold-hardy; others are tender. Apples require cross-pollination from another variety that blooms at the same time and produces abundant, viable pollen. Many varieties are self-unfruitful and have sterile pollen; others are partially self-fruitful (not all of their pollen is viable); a few are self-fruitful. It is best to plant apple trees from January to March.

Rootstock	Comments
M7a	Semidwarf rootstock. Usually produces a tree about 60% the size of the same tree on seedling rootstock. Performs well in irrigated replant situations but tends to sucker. Spacing is same as M106.
M9	Dwarfing rootstock. Usually produces a very small tree less than 30% the size of the same tree on seedling rootstock. Commercially, the most frequently planted rootstock worldwide. However, a poor performer if not adequately managed. Poorly anchored, has brittle root system. Must be trellised, irrigated frequently, and without weed competition.
M26	Semidwarf to dwarfing rootstock. Usually produces a tree 30 to 50% the size of the same tree on seedling rootstock. Performs poorly in most California locations. May need a support system and is highly susceptible to fire blight disease.
M106	Semidwarf rootstock. Usually produces a tree about 65 to 75% the size of the same tree on seedling rootstock. Provides good anchorage. Imparts early bearing to fruit and is easily propagated. Reportedly resistant to woolly apple aphid. Requires irrigation. Tree spacing ranges from 10 x 18 ft to 6 x 12 ft (3.0 x 5.5 m to 1.8 x 3.6 m).
M111	Semidwarf rootstock. Usually produces a tree 80% the size of the same tree on seedling rootstock. Tolerates many soil conditions. Reportedly resistant to woolly apple aphid. Imparts earlier bearing than seedling, but not as early as more dwarfing stocks. Requires irrigation. Vigor is difficult to control.
Mark	Dwarfing rootstock. Similar in size to M9. Very precocious. Poor performer in all apple-growing regions of California.
Seedling	Used for nonirrigated sites, low-vigor sites, and weaker or spur-type varieties. Very vigorous; produces large, full-sized trees that come into bearing late (7 to 10 yr). Susceptible to woolly apple aphid. Trees can fill a 30 x 30 ft (9 x 9 m) space and grow 30 ft (9.1 m) tall.

Standard Apple Varieties

	Harvest*					
Scion variety	San Joaquin Valley	Sacramento Valley	Central Coast	North Coast	Sierra Nevada Foothills	Southern California
Fuji	Oct–Nov	late Oct–Nov	Nov	Nov	late Oct–Nov	NA[†]
Round to flat apple with very sweet yellow-orange flesh. Skin is red if given enough sunlight and cool temperatures. One of the best sweet eating apples. Stores well.						
Gala	late Jun	late Jun	early Jul	late Jul	early Jul	late Jun
Small to medium-sized, conic-shaped red apple with excellent flavor and keeping qualities. The best variety for the early season. Will not cross-pollinate Golden Delicious.						
Gravenstein	late Jun	late Jun	early Jul	late Jul	early Jul	NA
Medium-large fruit with short, fat stem. Skin is greenish yellow overlaid with red stripes. Excellent flavor when fully ripe. Crisp, subacid, and aromatic. A good sauce and pie apple. Stores and ships poorly. High percentage of windfalls. Sterile pollen.						

	Harvest*					
Scion variety	San Joaquin Valley	Sacramento Valley	Central Coast	North Coast	Sierra Nevada Foothills	Southern California
Golden Delicious	late Aug	late Aug	Sep	late Aug–Sep	Sep	NA

Conic-shaped apple with a long stem, yellow to green skin, yellow flesh, and russet dots. Sweet, juicy, fine-textured. Number one on the North Coast for fresh-eating quality and processing. Stores well but susceptible to bitter pit, bruising, russeting. Erratic in self-fruitfulness.

Granny Smith	Oct–Nov	late Oct–Nov	Nov	Nov	late Oct–Nov	NA

Round, green to yellow-skinned apple that is quite firm. Keeps very well. Crisp flesh. If harvested early, it is green and tart. Late-harvested fruit are yellow and sweet.

Jonathan	Aug	Aug	late Aug–Sep	mid-Aug–Sep	mid-Aug	NA

Round, red apple with pure white flesh. Crisp, juicy, and slightly subacid. Excellent for eating fresh, sauce, and juice. Highly susceptible to mildew, fire blight, and Jonathan spot.

Red Delicious	late Aug	late Aug	Sep	late Aug–Sep	Sep	NA

Conic-shaped apple with tapered base and five distinct lobes. Skin color varies from solid red to a mixture of red and green stripes. Crisp, sweet, mild-flavored yellow flesh. Many strains. Used fresh. Stores well.

Rome Beauty	Oct–Nov	late Oct–Nov	Nov	Nov	late Oct–Nov	NA

Round fruit with a deep cavity, no lobes, and little russet. Several strains, including the old standard and several new, solid-red-skinned strains, such as Taylor and Law. Stores moderately well. Tree leafs out late, flowers late, and produces flowers and fruit on long spur growth that requires modification in pruning. Good for baking.

Spur-Type Apple Varieties
Strains (mutations) of the original varieties that have shorter internodes and are naturally dwarfing. Best on seedling rootstock: **Golden Delicious Spur (Nugget Spur, Goldspur, Yelo Spur, and Starkspur), Red Delicious Spur (Silverspur, Crimson Spur, Skyspur, Bisbee Spur, Spured Royal, Oregon Spur, Wellspur, Scarletspur, Cascade Spur), Starkspur, Spur McIntosh, Granny Smith Spur (Greenspur and Granspur), Rome Beauty Spur (Law Spur and Spuree), Winesap Spur, Arkansas Black Spur.**

Low-Chill Apple Varieties
These varieties are adapted to the low latitudes of Southern California because they have low winter chilling requirements (<300 hr): **Anna, Beverly Hills, Dorsett Golden, Einshemer, Gordon, Tropical Beauty.**

Antique Apple Varieties
These varieties do well in much of California if there is adequate chilling and summer heat is not too intense. They are hard to find because they lack commercial value. Many have excellent flavor and perform well in home gardens: **Arkansas Black, Baldwin, Black Twig, Cox's Orange Pippin, E. Spitzenburg, McIntosh, Newtown Pippin, Northern Spy, Red Golden, Rhode Island Greening, Sierra Beauty, Smith Cider, Staymen Winesap, Wagner, Winesap, Winter Banana.**

Early-Summer Apple Varieties
These varieties do not have the high-quality characteristics of standard varieties but ripen early when no other fresh apples are available. They are good for eating fresh and cooking:
Akane (similar to Jonathan but earlier, good solid red color, white flesh, good for eating fresh and juice); **Jerseymac** (large, good red color, excellent flavor, firmer than McIntosh, stores 4 to 8 wk); **Jonamac** (similar to McIntosh but has better color, firmness, and storage life); **Paulared** (high quality, white flesh, stores fairly well, tree requires thinning); **Vista Bell** (terminal bearing habit, white-fleshed fruit, stores well).

Disease-Resistant Apple Varieties
Several scab-resistant apple varieties have been developed in breeding programs for the eastern United States where this disease is quite severe due to summer humidity and rain. Some have received limited testing under California growing conditions. In growing districts with extended spring rains, organic growers should experiment with these varieties to see how they perform:
Enterprise: A large-fruited, late-maturing, dense, crisp variety that has good keeping qualities. The skin is dark red over a yellow-green background. One of the best of the scab-resistant varieties. **Florina:** A promising scab-resistant selection from France, with large, round-oblong, purple-red colored fruit; ripens late and has a mixed sweet tart flavor. **Freedom:** A late-season variety with large fruit and mild flavor; not completely immune to scab. **Goldrush:** A scab-immune selection with Golden Delicious parentage; late-maturing, large, firm-textured and tart with an excellent flavor; stores well. **Jonafree:** A midseason apple that compares with Jonathan, with soft flesh and uneven coloring. **Liberty:** One of the best-quality apples of the disease-resistant varieties; is very productive and requires heavy

Table 17.4 cont.

early thinning to achieve good size; ripens in midseason, has an attractive red color with some striping, and a good sweet flavor. **Prima:** An early-season, uneven-ripening, moderate quality variety. **Priscilla:** A late-season variety with small fruit, soft flesh, and mild flavor. **Pristine:** Moderate to large, tart, yellow apple immune to scab and resistant to fire blight and mildew. **Red Free:** Matures in early July, heat-sensitive, small-fruited; susceptible to water core, sunburn, and russet. **Williams Pride:** Early-maturing, scab-immune; also resistant to fire blight and mildew; medium to large fruit with a round-oblique shape; attractive red color.

PEAR (*Pyrus* spp.)

Of all the deciduous fruit tree species, pears are the most tolerant of wet soil conditions, but they perform best on deep, well-drained sites. Pears are the most pest-ridden of all fruit trees, and they require the most sprays to produce quality fruit. Without dwarfing rootstock or summer pruning, pear trees get very large, requiring a spacing of 18 x 18 ft (5.5 x 5.5 m). Pear trees have a tendency to grow very upright and must be trained to develop a spreading growth habit. Most pear varieties are self-sterile and require cross-pollination by another variety to get a good crop set. One exception is in the Sacramento River delta region, where Bartlett is self-fruitful, setting crops of parthenocarpic fruits. Fire blight (a bacterial disease) is a serious problem in pears. Bartlett, which makes up 75% of the world's production and acreage, has a chilling requirement of about 800 hr. Days from full bloom to harvest range from about 115 to 165 for European and Asian pears.

Rootstock	Comments
Betulaefolia	Best rootstock for most Asian pears. An oriental seedling. The most vigorous, producing the largest tree on the poorest site. Best tolerance of wet and drought conditions. Resistant to decline, blight, root aphid, and root rot. Poor stock for D'Anjou.
Calleryana	Moderately vigorous rootstock. Resistant to "wet feet" (*Phytophthora*), fire blight, root aphid, and most nematodes. Not the best stock for Asian varieties. Produces a tree a bit larger than French Seedling.
French Seedling	Seed from Bartlett or Winter Nellis are used for this rootstock, which withstands both "wet feet" and dry conditions. Resistant to oak root fungus but is very susceptible to fire blight. Good for general use.
Old Home × Farmingdale	A *Pyrus communis* rootstock propagated by cuttings or layering. Somewhat dwarfing. Compatible with most varieties. Resistant to fire blight.
Quince (several strains)	Semidwarfing rootstock. Resistant to decline, root aphid, root rot, and most nematodes. Trees are 50% of standard size and are very productive. Compatible with Anjou, Comice, Flemish Beauty, and Swiss Bartlett. Graft incompatible with Bartlett, Bosc, Clapp, and Seckel; requires an interstem of Old Home. On poor sites trees tend to be runty. Fruit quality is lower than on other stocks. Several different species are used for pear rootstocks, but they vary only slightly in their tolerance to "wet feet" and size control. Quince is the only dwarfing stock available, and it is incompatible with some varieties. Trees on quince should be spaced about 8 to 12 feet (2.5 to 3.7 m) apart.

European Pear Varieties (*Pyrus communis* L.)

These varieties mostly have the traditional pear shape and are harvested green when they begin to drop off the tree. They are then stored at 33°F to 45°F (1° to 7°) for several weeks. As the fruit is brought up to room temperature, it softens and turns buttery. If allowed to ripen on the tree, "stone" cells develop within the fruit and make the fruit gritty.

	Harvest*					
Scion variety	San Joaquin Valley	Sacramento Valley	Central Coast	North Coast	Sierra Nevada Foothills	Southern California
Bartlett	Aug	Aug	late Aug	late Aug	Aug	NA
The best-quality pear fruit. Bell-shaped with white flesh and excellent flavor. Tree is susceptible to fire blight. Fruit keep relatively well, up to 2 months after maturing in August. Sensation is a red Bartlett.						
Bosc	Oct	Oct	Oct	Oct	Oct	NA
Late variety that bears heavy crops regularly. Fruit are long, tapering, with a long neck and stem. Skin is golden russet brown.						
Comice	Oct	Oct	Oct	Oct	Oct	NA
Inconsistent bearer. Excellent-quality fruit, green color with red blush. Delicate skin, chubby shape. Very vigorous tree, does best on Quince rootstock. Late maturing.						

	Harvest*					
Scion variety	San Joaquin Valley	Sacramento Valley	Central Coast	North Coast	Sierra Nevada Foothills	Southern California
D'Anjou	Sep	Sep	Sep	Sep	Sep	NA
Good-quality pear with excellent keeping qualities. A large, vigorous tree. Egg-shaped fruit with a small shoulder. Light green to yellow-green color with a white flesh. French origin. There is a red strain called Red Anjou.						
Seckel	Sep	Sep	late Sep	late Sep	Sep	NA
Small fruit is reddish green with very dense, sweet, and flavorful flesh. Excellent quality for the home orchard. Resistant to fire blight and pear scab.						
Winter Nellis	Oct	Oct	Oct	Oct	Oct	NA
Medium-small, almost round fruit with light russeting over a green skin. Resistant to blight. Large tree. Regular producer. Late-maturing.						

Low-Chill Pear Varieties

These pear varieties are adapted to the low latitudes of Southern California because they have low winter chilling requirements (<300 hr): **Baldwin, Carnes, Fan Stil, Florida Home, Garber, Hengsan, Hood, Kieffer, Orient, Pineapple, Seleta, Spadona.**

Asian Pear Varieties (*Pyrus serotina* L.)

Asian pears are round fruit that remain very firm, crisp, and juicy when eaten ripe. Also known as salad pears or pear apples. The best rootstock for these varieties is Betulaefolia. Generally require cross-pollination. Fruit must be heavily thinned in May or June to size properly; the largest fruit are produced if flowers are thinned during bloom. Harvest by taste and pick exposed fruit first. Unlike European pears, Asian pears ripen on the tree.

	Harvest*					
Scion variety	San Joaquin Valley	Sacramento Valley	Central Coast	North Coast	Sierra Nevada Foothills	Southern California
Chojuro	late July	late July	Aug	early Aug	early Aug	Aug
Greenish-brown to brown russet skin. Coarse, tasty flesh.						
Hosui	late Aug	late Aug	Sep	early Sep	late Sep	early Sep
Brown skin, juicy white flesh with a sweet aromatic flavor.						
Kikusui	Aug	Aug	late Aug	mid-Sep	late Aug	NA
Yellow-green skin. White flesh, excellent flavor. Fruit drop from tree when ripe.						
Niitaka	late Sep	late Sep	mid-Oct	Oct	Oct	late Sep
Very large, juicy fruit with an aromatic flavor.						
Nijisseiki	Aug	Aug	late Aug	mid-Sep	late Aug	NA
Also known as **Twentieth Century.** Excellent quality. Very popular variety, with yellow-green skin.						
Shinko	late Sep	late Sep	mid-Oct	Oct	Oct	late Sep
Brown russet skin; firm, crisp flesh; very aromatic flavor.						
Shinseiki	Aug	Aug	late Aug	mid-Sep	late Aug	NA
Amber yellow skin. White flesh that is crisp but softens rapidly; less flavor than other varieties.						
Tsu Li	late Sep	late Sep	mid-Oct	Oct	Oct	late Sep
Blooms early. Use Ya Li (see below) as pollenizer. Chinese type (pear shape). Light green color, crisp tasty flesh.						
Ya Li	late Sep	late Sep	mid-Oct	Oct	Oct	late Sep
Blooms early. Use Tsu Li (see above) as pollenizer. Chinese type (pear shape). Light, shiny yellow color, crisp, tasty flesh.						

Table 17.4 cont.

POMEGRANATE (*Punica granatum* L.)

Pomegranates are exotic fruit that grow on a small tree or shrub 15 to 20 ft (4.6 to 6.1 m) tall that has shiny foliage and a long flowering season. The tree is very long-lived. It is sensitive to frost in fall and spring and does not mature well in cool climates. The tree tolerates wet, heavy soils but performs better in deep, well-drained loams. Fruit crack with first fall rains. Propagated from cuttings. Requires only a short chilling period. Resistant to oak root fungus (*Armillaria mellea*); not attacked by codling moth or twig borers. Unharvested ripe fruit attract ants and fruit flies.

Scion variety	Harvest*					
	San Joaquin Valley	Sacramento Valley	Central Coast	North Coast	Sierra Nevada Foothills	Southern California
Ambrosia	Sep	Sep	Oct	Oct–Nov	Sep	Sep
Huge fruit, pale pink skin; similar to Wonderful.						
Eversweeet	Aug	early Sep	Oct	Oct	early Sep	early Sep
Very sweet, almost seedless fruit. Red skin, clear juice. Good for coastal areas.						
Granada	Aug	early Sep	Oct	Oct–Nov	early Sep	early Sep
Deep crimson fruit color. Matures early but needs heat.						
Ruby Red	Sep	Sep	Oct	Oct–Nov	Sep	Sep
Matures late (with Wonderful) but not as sweet or colorful as Wonderful. All fruit matures at once.						
Wonderful	Sep	Sep	Oct	Oct–Nov	Sep	Sep
Large, deep red fruit. Large, juicy, red kernels. Small seed. Matures late. Juice is made into grenadine syrup.						

QUINCE (*Cydonia oblonga* Mill.)

Quince fruits grow on a small tree or shrub (8 to 12 ft [2.4 to 3.6 m] tall) with twisted, bumpy branches. Grown as a flowering ornamental or for fruit processing. Adapted to many climates. Tolerates "wet feet" better than most other deciduous fruit trees. Quince trees bloom late, which means that they avoid spring frosts. Quinces have many of the same pest problems as apple and pear. Varieties are self-fruitful; used as a dwarfing rootstock for pear.

Scion variety	Harvest*					
	San Joaquin Valley	Sacramento Valley	Central Coast	North Coast	Sierra Nevada Foothills	Southern California
Champion	early Oct	early Oct	Oct	Oct	Oct	early Oct
Green-yellow flesh. Pear-shaped fruit.						
Orange	early Sep	early Sep	Sep	Sep	Sep	early Sep
Orange-yellow flesh. Golden skin. Rich flavor. Low-chill variety.						
Pineapple	early Oct	early Oct	Oct	Oct	Oct	early Oct
The preferred variety. Pineapple flavor. White flesh. Golden skin. Low-chill fruit.						
Smyrna	early Oct	early Oct	Oct	Oct	Oct	early Oct
Large fruit with brown pubescence. Light, tender flesh. Yellow skin. Low-chill fruit.						
Van Deman	early Sep	early Sep	Sep	Sep	Sep	early Sep
Pale yellow, coarse flesh. Orange skin turns red when cooked.						

ALMOND *(Prunus dulcis)*
Almonds are stone fruits but consumed as nuts. Please see "Nut Crops," below.

APRICOT *(Prunus armeniaca* L.)
Apricots bloom in February and early March. In some areas of the state, such as the North Coast counties, this usually coincides with cold and rain; consistent crops are unlikely in these areas. Apricots perform best in climates with dry spring weather. They are susceptible to late-spring frosts. Bacterial canker is a common disease of young trees in California. Plant trees at a spacing of about 14 to 20 ft (4.3 to 6.1 m). Apricots are mostly self-fruitful and ripen in late June to July (100 to 120 days from full bloom). The hot weather in areas of the Central Valley often cause the fruit to "pit burn" (soften and turn brown around the pit), which lowers quality.

Rootstock	Comments
Citation	One of the best rootstocks for apricots. Slightly dwarfing. Less susceptible to bacterial canker; tolerant of "wet feet."
Lovell Peach	Imparts some resistance to bacterial canker. Susceptible to oak root fungus. Not as tolerant of wet soils as other apricot rootstocks.
Marianna 2624	Somewhat resistant to oak root fungus. Tolerates "wet feet" much better than apricot or peach root.
Prunus besseyi	Semidwarfing rootstock. Short-lived. Suckers profusely. Produces inferior fruit in the scion variety.

Standard Apricot Varieties

	Harvest*					
Scion variety	San Joaquin Valley	Sacramento Valley	Central Coast	North Coast	Sierra Nevada Foothills	Southern California
Autumn Royal	late Jun	late Jun	Jul	Jul	early Jul	Jun
Blenheim sport (mutation). Ripens in late summer to fall.						
Moorpark	Jun	Jun	early Jul	late Jun	late Jun	Jun
Excellent flavor, ripens unevenly, highly colored.						
Royal (Blenheim)	Jun	Jun	early Jul	late Jun	late Jun	Jun
Large, very flavorful, used for eating fresh and drying.						
Tilton	early Jul	Jul	late Jul	late Jul	Jul	Jul
Large fruit, heavy producer. Mild flavor. Used for canning.						

Low-Chill Apricot Varieties
These apricot varieties are adapted to the low latitudes of Southern California because they have low winter chilling requirements (<300 hr):
Early Golden, Goldkist, Newcastle.

Other Apricot Varieties to Consider
These varieties are newer and should be evaluated for your climate zone and site before being selected:
Castlebright, Golden Amber, Goldrich, Improved Flaming Gold, King, Pomo, Riland, Rosa, Royalty, Sun Glo.

CHERRY *(Prunus avium* L., *P. cerasus* L.)
Two types of cherries can be planted: **sweet,** for fresh eating, and **sour,** for pies and preserves. Generally, cherries are the most difficult fruit trees to keep alive. They do not tolerate "wet feet" and are very susceptible to brown rot, bacterial canker, cytospora canker, root and crown rots, and several viruses. Trees must be planted 14 to 20 ft (4.3 to 6.1 m) apart in well-drained soil and up on a small mound or berm. Sweet cherries require cross-pollination (many varieties are self-sterile and intrasterile, as noted below). Sour cherries are self-fertile and do not require pollenizers. Both types require less than 100 days to mature.

Rootstock	Comments
Colt	Somewhat dwarfing rootstock. The leading rootstock in California.
Giesla series	These dwarfing rootstocks are relatively new and in most cases produce smaller trees (8 to 10 ft [2.4 to 3 m]). They also tend to impart early bearing. The smaller trees are easier to cover with netting to discourage birds.

Table 17.4 cont.

Mahaleb	Very susceptible to root and crown rots. Some resistance to buckskin virus, bacterial canker, and root lesion nematode.
Mazzard	Good rootstock for cherries in coastal California. Produces a large, vigorous tree that is delayed in coming into bearing. Less susceptible to root rots and gophers than Mahaleb but more susceptible to bacterial canker than Mahaleb.
Stockton Morello	Somewhat dwarfing rootstock. Not readily available. Makes an overgrowth at the bud union. Propagated from a cutting. As tolerant as Mazzard to "wet feet." Somewhat resistant to gophers; less susceptible to bacterial canker. Generally a very good rootstock

Sweet Cherry Varieties

	Harvest*					
Scion variety	San Joaquin Valley	Sacramento Valley	Central Coast	North Coast	Sierra Nevada Foothills	Southern California
Bing	Jun	Jun	late Jun	late Jun	Jun	NA
Industry standard. Deep mahogany red fruit. Produces very heavily. Very susceptible to bacterial canker. Pollenized by Van, Black Tartarian, or Sam. Bing, Lambert, and Royal-Ann will not pollinate each other (they are intrasterile).						
Black Tartarian	Jun	Jun	late Jun	late Jun	Jun	NA
Small, black fruit. A good pollenizer for Bing and most other varieties.						
Brooks	mid-Jun	mid-Jun	Jun	Jun	Jun	NA
A large, dark red fruit with good flavor. Produces few doubles even in hot climates						
Early Burlat	early Jun	early Jun	Jun	Jun	Jun	NA
Moderate-sized fruit. Ripens 2 weeks before Bing. Soft flesh. Pollenized by Bing and Tartarian.						
Early Ruby	early Jun	early Jun	Jun	Jun	Jun	NA
Early season. Large, dark red fruit. Prolific. Fruit hold on tree.						
Lambert	late Jun	late Jun	Jul	Jul	Jul	NA
Dark, large, firm fruit. Pollenized by Van. Late season. Lambert, Bing, and Royal-Ann do not pollinate each other.						
Rainier	Jun	Jun	late Jun	late Jun	Jun	NA
Yellow-red blush. Large, crack-resistant fruit.						
Royal-Ann	early Jun	early Jun	Jun	Jun	Jun	NA
Yellow fruit with a red blush. Pollenized by Van. Late season. Royal-Ann, Lambert, and Bing will not pollinate each other.						
Stella	late Jun	late Jun	Jul	Jul	Jul	NA
Dark-fleshed fruit. Matures just after Bing. Self-fruitful.						
Van	Jun	Jun	late Jun	late Jun	Jun	NA
Large, dark fruit. Pollenized by Bing or Lambert.						

Low-Chill Sweet Cherry Varieties
None available.

Sour "Pie" Cherry Varieties

	Harvest*					
Scion variety	San Joaquin Valley	Sacramento Valley	Central Coast	North Coast	Sierra Nevada Foothills	Southern California
Early Richmond	early Jun	early Jun	Jun	Jun	Jun	NA
Very early ripening. Bright red fruit.						
Meteor	Jun	early Jun	Jun	Jun	Jun	NA
Semidwarf. early						
Montmorency	early Jun	early Jun	Jun	Jun	Jun	NA
The leading sour variety. Medium-sized, dark red fruit.						
North Star	early Jun	early Jun	Jun	Jun	Jun	NA
Semidwarf. Self-fruitful.						

Low-Chill Sour Cherry Varieties
None available.

NECTARINE (*Prunus persica*)

Nectarines are fuzzless peaches. They do well in most of California if given the proper growing conditions. Nectarines require very well-drained soils, abundant nitrogen fertility, plenty of summer water, fruit thinning, and sprays to prevent peach leaf curl and brown rot. New variety developments have greatly improved this fruit as a tree for backyard and commercial use. Trees can bear the second year. Nectarines (like peaches) are self-fruitful and do not require a pollenizer tree. Tree spacing should be about 8 to 12 ft (2.4 to 3.6 m) apart.

Rootstock	Comments
Citation	A new peach-plum hybrid that provides some dwarfing to most varieties. Tolerates wet winter conditions. Produces trees that are smaller in trunk diameter without any height reduction in some varieties.
Lovell Peach	The best choice for coastal California. A seedling that tolerates wet winter soils better than any other peach rootstock. Produces a full-sized tree that is managed easily.
Nemaguard Peach	The best choice for the Central Valley. A nematode-resistant rootstock best adapted to sandy, dry sites that don't get too wet.
Prunus besseyi	Semidwarfing rootstock. Suckers profusely. Produces inferior fruit on the scion variety. Has not performed well. Somewhat incompatible with most nectarine varieties.

Standard Nectarine Varieties

Scion variety	Harvest* San Joaquin Valley	Sacramento Valley	Central Coast	North Coast	Sierra Nevada Foothills	Southern California
Arctic Glo Small, fantastic flavor. White flesh. Early.	mid-Jun	mid-Jun	early Jul	Jun	Jun	NA
Fantasia Large, brightly-colored yellow freestone. Late.	late Jul	Aug	late Aug	mid-Aug	Aug	Aug
Flamekist Excellent quality. Large, firm, yellow, clingstone.	late Aug	early Sep	Sep	Sep	Sep	Sep
Flavortop Large, excellent flavor. Yellow, freestone. Midseason.	mid-Jul	late Jul	Aug	Aug	Aug	late Jul
Goldmine Large, great flavor. White flesh. Freestone.	Aug	late Aug	Sep	Sep	Sep	Sep
Heavenly White Large, excellent flavor. White flesh. Fruit tends to crack.	late Jul	late Jul	mid-Aug	early Aug	early Aug	NA
May Grand Large, yellow-fruited, freestone. Early.	early Jun	mid-Jun	late Jun	late Jun	Jun	Jun
Panamint Medium-sized fruit. Red skin, golden flesh. Freestone, low-chill variety.	late Jul	early Aug	Aug	Aug	Aug	Aug
Red Gold Large, excellent flavor. Stores well. Late.	late Aug	early Sep	Sep	Sep	Sep	Sep
Rose Old favorite white freestone with excellent flavor and low-chilling requirement.	mid-Jul	late Jul	Aug	Aug	Aug	late Jul
September Red Large, yellow. Very late.	late Aug	early Sep	Sep	Sep	Sep	Sep
Snow Queen Early-season white freestone, juicy and tasty.	late Jun	Jul	late Jul	late Jul	late Jul	Jul
Summer Grand One of the best. Large, yellow, freestone.	mid-Jul	late Jul	Aug	Aug	Aug	late Jul

Low-Chill Nectarine Varieties

These nectarine varieties are adapted to the low latitudes of Southern California because they have low winter chilling requirements:
Desert Dawn, Desert Delight, Panamint, Pioneer, Rose, Silver Lode.

Table 17.4 cont.

PEACH (*Prunus persica*)

Peaches are very popular fruit trees that can be grown successfully in many parts of California. They require adequate summer watering, deep and well-drained soils, high nitrogen fertility, fruit thinning, and sprays to prevent peach leaf curl and brown rot. Peach trees are short-lived (15 to 20 yr). Peaches (like nectarines) are self-fruitful (self-compatible), which means that they do not require a pollenizer tree. Plant trees 10 to 16 ft (3.0 to 4.9 m) apart.

Rootstock	Comments
Citation	A new peach-plum hybrid that provides some dwarfing to most varieties. Tolerates wet winter conditions. Produces trees that are smaller in diameter without any height reduction in some varieties.
Lovell Peach	The best choice for coastal California. A seedling that tolerates wet winter soils better than any other peach rootstock, but still requires good drainage. Produces a full-sized, small tree that is managed easily.
Nemaguard Peach	The best choice for the Central Valley. A nematode-resistant rootstock best adapted to sandy, well-drained sites. Full-sized tree.
Prunus besseyi	Semidwarfing rootstock. Suckers profusely. Produces inferior fruit on the scion variety. Has not performed well. Somewhat incompatible with most peach varieties.

Standard Peach Varieties

Thousands of peach varieties have been developed worldwide. Some perform better in warmer areas; others have better fruit quality when grown in cooler climates along the coast of California. Three listed below (La Feliciana, Loring, and Veteran) are somewhat more disease-resistant than the others.

Scion variety	Harvest*					
	San Joaquin Valley	Sacramento Valley	Central Coast	North Coast	Sierra Nevada Foothills	Southern California
Autumn Gold	Sep	Sep	Oct	Oct	Oct	NA
Medium-large fruit. Yellow flesh. Keeps well.						
Babcock	late Jun	Jul	Jul	late Jul	Jul	late Jun
Medium-sized. White flesh. Freestone, low-chill variety.						
Earligrande	May	late May	Jun	Jun	Jun	May
Excellent flavor. Yellow-red blush. Semi-freestone, low-chill variety.						
Fairtime	Sep	Sep	Oct	Oct	Oct	NA
Large fruit. Yellow, firm flesh. Excellent flavor.						
Fay Elberta	late Jul	late Jul	mid-Aug	early Aug	Aug	NA
Large fruit. Yellow flesh. Freestone.						
Forty-Niner	late Jul	late Jul	mid-Aug	early Aug	Aug	NA
Large fruit. Yellow flesh. Freestone.						
Indian Blood	late Aug	late Aug	Sep	Sep	Sep	NA
Cling. Red skin and flesh. Tart. Prolific.						
La Feliciana	mid-Jul	late Jul	Aug	Aug	late Jul	NA
Medium-sized. Firm, red. Excellent flavor.						
Loring	late Jul	Aug	late Aug	late Aug	Aug	NA
Very large fruit. Red skin. Yellow flesh. Freestone.						
Nectar	late Jul	late Jul	mid-Aug	early Aug	Aug	NA
White flesh. Pink skin. Excellent flavor.						
O'Henry	late Jul	late Jul	mid-Aug	early Aug	Aug	NA
One of the best. Large fruit. Yellow flesh. Freestone.						
Redhaven	early Jul	Jul	late Jul	late Jul	Jul	NA
Yellow. Semi-freestone. Needs heavy thinning.						
Rio Oso Gem	Aug late	Aug	Sep	Sep	Sep	NA
Very large fruit. Yellow flesh. Freestone.						

Scion variety	Harvest*					
	San Joaquin Valley	Sacramento Valley	Central Coast	North Coast	Sierra Nevada Foothills	Southern California
Springcrest	early Jun	mid-Jun	late Jun	late Jun	late Jun	NA
Medium-sized. Yellow flesh. Semi-freestone. Excellent flavor.						
Suncrest	early Jul	Jul	late Jul	late Jul	Jul	NA
Large fruit. Yellow flesh. Freestone. Midseason. Excellent flavor.						
Veteran	late Jul	Aug	late Aug	late Aug	Aug	NA
Red blush. Elberta-type. Freestone. Dependable, heavy producer, excellent flavor.						

Low-Chill Peach Varieties

These peach varieties are adapted to the low latitudes of Southern California because they have low winter chilling requirements:
August Pride, Babcock, Bonita, Desertgold, Early Amber, Earligrande, FlordaGrand, FloridaPrince, Midpride, Tropic-Berta, Topic Sweet.

PLUM and PRUNE (*Prunus domestica, Prunus salicina*)

Plum trees are one of the best-adapted fruit trees for almost anywhere in California. They are easy to grow. Available rootstocks are very tolerant of wet winter soils; they bloom late enough to avoid most spring frosts; and they have few pest problems. Plum trees get relatively large and require spacing of 12 to 18 ft (3.6 to 5.5 m). Most plums, but not all, require cross-pollination to set adequate crops; plan to plant two different varieties. There are two different kinds of plums: Japanese (*Prunus salicina*) and European (*Prunus domestica*). European types are either very sweet fresh plums or plums used for drying (prunes). Most Japanese plums bloom earlier and mature earlier than European plums, and they typically require less chilling. Both types of plums require about 140 to 170 days to mature.

Rootstock	Comments
Citation	A new peach-plum hybrid that produces a full-sized tree. Tolerates wet soils.
Lovell Peach	Less susceptible to bacterial canker, but the most intolerant plum rootstock of heavy soils, "wet feet," oak root fungus, and root rots. Produces a moderately large tree that fruits earlier and sets more consistent crops. Compatible with most plum or prune varieties.
Marianna 2624	The overall best choice. Resistant to oak root fungus, root rots, root knot nematodes, and crown gall, but susceptible to bacterial canker and root lesion nematode. A cutting that is shallow-rooted and produces a smaller tree. It is the best for poor, wet soil conditions, but tends to sucker.
Myrobalan 29C	A cutting selection immune to root knot nematodes. Susceptible to oak root fungus, root rot, and root lesion nematode. Produces a tree with just a little less vigor than the Myrobalan seedling.
Myrobalan Seedling	The largest and most vigorous of the plum or prune rootstocks. Hardy, long-lived, adapted to most soils. Tolerates wet winter soil conditions. Susceptible to oak root fungus and nematodes, but somewhat resistant to root and crown rots.
Prunus besseyi	Semidwarfing rootstock. Suckers profusely. Produces inferior fruit quality on the scion variety. Partially incompatible with plum varieties.

Standard Plum Varieties

Scion variety	Harvest*					
	San Joaquin Valley	Sacramento Valley	Central Coast	North Coast	Sierra Nevada Foothills	Southern California
Autumn Rosa	late Aug	late Aug	Sep	Sep	Sep	NA
Large. Purple skin. Self-fertile. Japanese plum.						
Beauty	Jun	Jun	Jul	Jul	Jun	Jun
Green skin, amber flesh, heart-shaped. Poor keeper. Japanese plum.						
Burgundy	early Aug	early Aug	late Aug	late Aug	Aug	Aug
Red skin and flesh. Self-fertile. Holds well.						
El Dorado	early Jul	mid-Jul	Aug	Jul	Jul	Jul
Purple skin. Amber flesh. Large, oblong.						
Elephant Heart	early Aug	early Aug	late Aug	late Aug	Aug	NA
Purple skin. Large, heart-shaped. Japanese plum						

Table 17.4 cont.

Scion variety	Harvest*					
	San Joaquin Valley	Sacramento Valley	Central Coast	North Coast	Sierra Nevada Foothills	Southern California
Friar	mid-Aug	mid-Aug	late Aug	late Aug	Aug	NA
Black skin. Amber flesh. Mild-flavored, old variety. Japanese plum.						
Golden Nectar	late Aug	late Aug	Sep	Sep	Sep	NA
Large. Yellow flesh. Tender skin. Great flavor. Japanese plum.						
Howard Wonder	early Aug	early Aug	late Aug	late Aug	Aug	NA
Large, pink skin. Yellow flesh. Japanese plum.						
Kelsey	early Aug	early Aug	late Aug	late Aug	Aug	Aug
Green-yellow skin and flesh. Japanese plum.						
Laroda	mid-Aug	mid-Aug	late Aug	late Aug	Aug	NA
Red-purple skin. Yellow flesh.						
Mariposa	Aug	Aug	late Aug	late Aug	Aug	Aug
Green-yellow skin. Red flesh. Large, heart-shaped. Japanese plum.						
Nubiana	early Aug	early Aug	late Aug	late Aug	Aug	NA
Purple-black skin. Yellow flesh. Oblong. Japanese plum.						
President	late Aug	late Aug	Sep	Sep	Sep	NA
Large. Blue skin. Yellow flesh. European plum. Could be dried into a large prune.						
Red Beaut	early Jun	early Jun	Jun	mid-Jun	Jun	NA
Red skin, yellow flesh, excellent flavor.						
Roysum	Sep	Sep	Oct	Oct	Oct	NA
Light purple skin. Yellow flesh.						
Santa Rosa	early Jul	early Jul	late Jul	mid-Jul	Jul	Jul
Purple skin. Amber flesh. Excellent flavor. Japanese plum.						
Satsuma	early Aug	early Aug	late Aug	late Aug	Aug	Jul
Red skin and flesh. Small, round. Japanese plum.						
Shiro	early Jul	early Jul	late Jul	mid-Jul	Jul	NA
Light green-yellow skin. Yellow flesh.						
Simka	early Aug	early Aug	late Aug	late Aug	Aug	NA
Dark black skin. Yellow flesh. Oblong.						
Sprite Cherry Plum	early Aug	early Aug	late Aug	late Aug	Aug	late Jul
Black, sweet skin. Exotic flavor. Small.						
Wickson	Jul	Jul	Aug	Aug late	Jul	NA
Green-yellow skin. Yellow flesh. Large, heart-shaped. Japanese plum.						

Low-Chill Plum Varieties

These plum varieties are adapted to the low latitudes of Southern California because they have low winter chilling requirements:
Beauty Burgundy, Delight, El Dorado, Howard Wonder, Kelsey, Mariposa, Meredith, Methley, Santa Rosa, Satsuma, Sprite.

Standard Prune Varieties

Scion variety	Harvest*					
	San Joaquin Valley	Sacramento Valley	Central Coast	North Coast	Sierra Nevada Foothills	Southern California
French	Aug	Aug	late Aug	late Aug	Aug	NA
Medium-sized purple fruit. Self-fertile. late maturing. European plum. Used for fresh eating or drying.						
Green Gage	Aug	Aug	late Aug	late Aug	Aug	NA
Greenish-yellow skin. Amber flesh. Old, European plum.						

	Harvest*					
Scion variety	San Joaquin Valley	Sacramento Valley	Central Coast	North Coast	Sierra Nevada Foothills	Southern California
Imperial	Aug	Aug	late Aug	late Aug	Aug	NA
Large fruit. Requires cross-pollination. Late maturing. European plum.						
Italian	Aug	Aug	late Aug	late Aug	Aug	NA
Large fruit. Purple skin. Yellow flesh. European plum.						

NUT CROPS

ALMOND (*Prunus dulcis*, formerly *Prunus amygdalus*)

Almonds are stone fruits that are consumed as nuts. All almonds produced commercially in the U.S. are grown in California. The earliest to bloom of stone fruits (February); generally do poorly in North Coast counties, where they bloom when weather is cold and rainy. Very susceptible to spring frosts. Almonds do not tolerate wet soils. The Central Valley and drier regions of the southern coast are very favorable for almonds. Trees are very susceptible to bacterial canker. Cross-pollination is required; all varieties are self-sterile, and some are cross-unfruitful due to incompatibilities. Almonds are harvested by shaking trees when hulls begin to split. Almonds need 180 to 240 days to mature the nuts. After harvest, the nuts (embryo and shell) are dried to preserve freshness.

Rootstock	Comments
Almond Seedling	Long-lived, deep-rooted; needs well-drained soil. Not used much due to disease susceptibility.
Lovell Peach	Produces a smaller tree than almond rootstock; susceptible to many diseases.
Mariana 2624	Marginally compatible with most almond varieties.
Almond-Peach hybrids	New stocks that are nematode-resistant and vigorous.
Nemaguard Peach	Nematode-resistant; good for sandy soils.

Standard Almond Varieties

	Harvest*					
Scion variety	San Joaquin Valley	Sacramento Valley	Central Coast	North Coast	Sierra Nevada Foothills	Southern California
Carmel	Aug	Aug	Sep	Sep	Aug	Aug
Excellent quality. Nut well sealed in the shell. Excellent pollinizer for Nonpareil.						
Mission	Aug	Aug	Sep	Sep	Aug	Aug
Late-blooming, productive tree. Hard shell, short kernel.						
Neplus Ultra	Aug	Aug	Sep	Sep	Aug	Aug
Large, soft-shelled nut. Long, flat kernel. Good pollinizer for Nonpareil.						
Nonpareil	Aug	Aug	Sep	Sep	Aug	Aug
The most popular paper-shelled variety. Interfruitful with Price, Mission, Carmel.						
Price	Aug	Aug	Sep	Sep	Aug	Aug
Very similar to Nonpareil. A good pollinizer, except that it tends to alternate bloom.						

Table 17.4 cont.

CHESTNUT (*Castanaea* spp.)

Little research has been done on the chestnut in California. Thus, we know little about its specific adaptability or productive capacity. Chestnuts are monoecious (separate female and male flowers are borne on one plant, like walnuts) and some cultivars are self-unfruitful; thus, two different varieties should be grown for cross-pollination to produce consistent crops. Trees reach a height of 80 ft (24 m) and spread to 60 ft (18 m) under ideal conditions. Chestnuts are excellent and fruitful shade trees if grown in very well drained soil. Chestnuts are almost pest-free in California. Seedling is the only known rootstock. Edible chestnuts should not be confused with the poisonous horse chestnut (*Aesculus californica*). Fresh chestnuts contain about 50% moisture. Unlike other nuts, chestnuts have low oil content (8%).

Standard Chestnut Varieties

Scion variety	San Joaquin Valley	Sacramento Valley	Central Coast	North Coast	Sierra Nevada Foothills	Southern California
			Harvest*			
Colossal	early Oct	early Oct	late Oct	late Oct	mid-Oct	early Oct
The industry standard and the overall best choice. Large-fruited. Excellent quality.						
Dunstan	early Oct	early Oct	late Oct	late Oct	mid-Oct	early Oct
A cross of American and Chinese varieties. Medium-small nuts. Sweet and blight-resistant. Late flowering.						
Eurobella	early Oct	early Oct	late Oct	late Oct	mid-Oct	early Oct
Large nut. Good pollinizer for Colossal.						
Seedling	early Oct	early Oct	late Oct	late Oct	mid-Oct	early Oct
Not a "named" variety. Each tree is genetically different. Unknown fruit quality. Unknown tree shape and fruit size. Only known rootstock						
Silverleaf	early Oct	early Oct	late Oct	late Oct	mid-Oct	early Oct
Medium-sized nut. Good pollinizer for Colossal, but shell splits are a problem.						

Other Varieties for Trial:

Castel del Rio, Fowler, Marrone di Maradi, Montesol.

FILBERT (HAZELNUT) (*Corylus* spp.)

The nut-bearing filbert plants grow naturally as suckering shrubs but can be trained as trees by continually removing the suckers. They reach a height of 15 to 20 ft (4.6 to 6.1 m) with an even greater spread. Filberts are monoecious (separate male and female flowers on the same plant, like walnuts) but are self-unfruitful; cross-pollination is required to set fruit, so two different varieties must be planted. Crop production is not consistent in California, which may be due to summer heat that causes catkins (male flowers) to fall off prematurely. Filberts are grown on their own roots. They need a 180-day growing season.

Standard Filbert Varieties

Scion variety	San Joaquin Valley	Sacramento Valley	Central Coast	North Coast	Sierra Nevada Foothills	Southern California
			Harvest*			
Barcelona	Sep	Sep	Oct	late Sep	late Sep	NA
The old industry standard. Use Davianna or Du Chilly as pollinizer.						
Brixnut	Sep	Sep	Oct	late Sep	late Sep	NA
A secondary main production nut. Use Davianna or Du Chilly as a pollinizer.						
Butler	Sep	Sep	Oct	late Sep	late Sep	NA
Pollenizer for Ennis.						
Davianna	Sep	Sep	Oct	late Sep	late Sep	NA
Use Barcelona or Du Chilly as a pollinizer.						
Du Chilly	Sep	Sep	Oct	late Sep	late Sep	NA
Use Barcelona or Davianna as a pollinizer.						
Ennis	Sep	Sep	Oct	late Sep	late Sep	NA
A new variety that has better quality than Barcelona. Use Butler as a pollinizer.						
White Aveline	Sep	Sep	Oct	late Sep	late Sep	NA
General pollinizer.						

PECAN (*Carya illoensis*)

Pecans are not a good choice for Northern California. They require a deep, well-drained soil, a hot climate to mature the nuts properly, and adequate soil moisture. At least two different varieties must be planted for good pollination, because even though pecans are largely self-fertile, the flowers are dichogamous, which means that there is little overlap between pollen shedding and stigma receptivity. Most varieties require at least 180 days for nuts to mature. Commercial production in California is limited to the southern San Joaquin Valley. Pecans are native to the United States and grow well in the south-central states. Their native range extends into the Midwest; varieties grown there tolerate cold winters and short growing seasons. The varieties listed here require a very long growing season and freedom from frost. They can be tried in the warmest regions of the state. The trees get as large as walnut trees. Pecans are grown on seedling rootstocks.

Standard Pecan Varieties

| | Harvest* | | | | | |
Scion variety	San Joaquin Valley	Sacramento Valley	Central Coast	North Coast	Sierra Nevada Foothills	Southern California
Apache Late pollen shed. Early receptivity.	Oct	late Oct	NA	NA	late Oct	late Oct
Barton Early pollen shed and receptivity.	Oct	late Oct	NA	NA	late Oct	late Oct
Bradley Excellent pollenizer for Western Schley.	Oct	late Oct	NA	NA	late Oct	late Oct
Choctaw Late pollen shed. Early receptivity.	Oct	late Oct	NA	NA	late Oct	late Oct
Comanche Late pollen shed. Early receptivity.	Oct	late Oct	NA	NA	late Oct	late Oct
Shawnee Early pollen shed. Midseason receptivity.	Oct	late Oct	NA	NA	late Oct	late Oct
Sioux Early pollen shed and receptivity.	Oct	late Oct	NA	NA	late Oct	late Oct
Western Schley Early pollen shed and receptivity.	Oct	late Oct	NA	NA	late Oct	late Oct
Wichita Late pollen shed. Early receptivity.	Oct	late Oct	NA	NA	late Oct	late Oct

PISTACHIO (*Pistacia vera*)

Pistachio trees require long, hot, dry summers and mild winters. April frosts kill flowers, and cool summers do not promote good kernel development. Adequate winter chilling and good weather during bloom (pistachio is wind-pollinated) are required. Pistachio trees are dioecious (male and female trees); male trees must be planted near female trees to get a good crop set. Trees become large and should be planted about 20 ft (6.1 m) apart. Although the warmest regions in the state are adapted for pistachio production in the backyard, pistachios are a poor choice for coastal California.

Rootstock	Comments
Pistacia atlantica	Resistant to many nematodes, but susceptible to cold (below 15° to 20°F [–9° to –6°C]) and Verticillium wilt.
P. integerrima	Resistant to *Verticillium*. Very susceptible to cold damage.
P. terebinthus	The best rootstock. Most tolerant of cold. Resistant to nematodes. Susceptible to Verticillium wilt.

Table 17.4 cont.

Standard Pistachio Varieties

	Harvest*					
Scion variety	San Joaquin Valley	Sacramento Valley	Central Coast	North Coast	Sierra Nevada Foothills	Southern California
Kerman	Oct	late Oct	NA	NA	late Oct	late Oct
Female. Best nut-producing variety.						
Peters	Oct	late Oct	NA	NA	late Oct	late Oct
Male. Good for pollination.						
Joley	Oct	late Oct	NA	NA	late Oct	late Oct
Female. Smaller nuts. Fewer blanks. More splits.						
Sfax	Oct	late Oct	NA	NA	late Oct	late Oct
Smaller, good-quality nuts.						

WALNUT (*Juglans regia, J. hindsii*)

Walnuts need a deep, well-drained soil (at least 5 ft [1.5 m]). Shoots, particularly blossoms, do not tolerate frosts. Once growth begins in the spring, rainy weather can cause severe losses due to walnut blight. Trees range in size from very large (80 ft [24 m] tall) to medium height (40 to 50 ft [12 to 15 m] tall). They require a 30 to 60 ft (9 to 18 m) spacing. Walnut culture has changed drastically in the last few years due to the introduction of new varieties. Production in coastal climates should be limited to the late-leafing varieties. Walnuts are monoecious (separate male and female flowers on one tree) and dichogamous (pollen is shed when female flowers are not receptive); two different varieties must be planted to ensure overlapping bloom periods, fertilization, and fruit set.

Rootstock	Comments
Black Walnut	This has been the standard rootstock in California, known as Northern California Black Walnut. It is resistant to oak root fungus but susceptible to crown rot, root rot, root lesion nematode, and blackline virus.
English Walnut	This rootstock is seedlings of English walnut. It is very susceptible to oak root fungus but less susceptible to blackline virus. It is the least tolerant of wet soils.
Paradox	The best rootstock choice, in general. A hybrid between Black and English Walnuts. Very vigorous. Tolerates poorer soil conditions than the others. Less susceptible to crown and root rot. Susceptible to crown gall and blackline virus.

Standard Walnut Varieties

	Harvest*					
Scion variety	San Joaquin Valley	Sacramento Valley	Central Coast	North Coast	Sierra Nevada Foothills	Southern California
Chandler	Oct	late Oct	late Oct	late Oct	late Oct	NA
Best choice for coastal California. New variety. 80% fruitful lateral buds. Produces a smaller tree that requires careful pruning and training. Blooms late. Leafs out late.						
Hartley	Oct	late Oct	late Oct	late Oct	late Oct	NA
The main variety grown in California. Excellent-quality nuts. Huge tree that requires little pruning. 5% fruitful lateral buds. Leafs out late, blooms late.						
Howard	Oct	late Oct	late Oct	late Oct	late Oct	NA
New variety. 80% fruitful lateral buds. Produces a smaller tree that requires careful pruning and training. Blooms late. Leafs out late.						
Mayette	Oct	late Oct	late Oct	late Oct	late Oct	NA
Old-time variety. Plant as a pollenizer for late-blooming varieties. Poor producer. Leafs out late. Blooms late. Large tree.						
S. Franquette	Oct	late Oct	late Oct	late Oct	late Oct	NA
Old-time variety. Should be planted as a pollenizer for the late-blooming varieties. Poor producer. Leafs out late. Blooms late. Large tree that requires little pruning.						

Scion variety	San Joaquin Valley	Sacramento Valley	Central Coast	North Coast Coast	Sierra Nevada Foothills	Southern California
			Harvest*			
Tehama	Oct	late Oct	late Oct	late Oct	late Oct	NA

Good choice. New variety. 80% fruitful lateral buds. Produces a smaller tree that requires careful pruning and training. Blooms late. Leafs out late.

Black Walnut Varieties

Scion variety	San Joaquin Valley	Sacramento Valley	Central Coast	North Coast Coast	Sierra Nevada Foothills	Southern California
			Harvest*			
Seedling	Oct	late Oct	late Oct	late Oct	late Oct	NA

Not a true variety. Seedlings of Northern California Black Walnut trees.

Eastern Black Walnut Varieties

Scion variety	San Joaquin Valley	Sacramento Valley	Central Coast	North Coast Coast	Sierra Nevada Foothills	Southern California
			Harvest*			
Thomas, Ohio,	Oct	late Oct	late Oct	late Oct	late Oct	NA

and **Meyers** are three named varieties that may be worthy of consideration.

VINES

KIWIFRUIT (*Actinidia deliciosa,* formerly *A. chinensis*)

Kiwifruit is a large, frost-sensitive, temperate-zone vine that requires plenty of heat to mature the fruit properly. Kiwifruit do well when grown in warm sites on a trellis or arbor protected from the wind. Soil must be well drained but kept moist at all times. Kiwifruit can tolerate temperatures as low as 10°F (–12°C) in January but only if fall temperatures gradually decrease over several days. Late-spring frosts and early-fall frosts can kill vines. Overhead frost protection is desirable. As noted below, fuzzy varieties are not as cold hardy as smooth-skin varieties. Plant kiwifruit about 15 to 20 ft (4.6 to 6.1 m) apart. The plants are functionally dioecious. Successful fruit production requires a female cultivar and a male with viable pollen when the female is receptive. Vines leaf out in March, bloom occurs in May, and fruits are harvested in late September, October, and November.

Rootstock	Comments
Cutting	Own-rooted. From ½-inch (13-mm)-diameter midsummer wood or dormant wood. Grows back after frost damage.
Seedling	Extracted seed from ripe kiwifruit.

Fuzzy Kiwifruit Varieties

Scion variety	San Joaquin Valley	Sacramento Valley	Central Coast	North Coast	Sierra Nevada Foothills	Southern California
			Harvest*			
Chico	Oct	late Oct	late Nov	early Nov	Nov	NA

Male vine used to pollinate Hayward, 8:1 female-male ratio.

Hayward	Oct	late Oct	late Nov	early Nov	Nov	NA

The commercial female variety grown in California. Large fruit. Excellent flavor. Will ripen on the vine but can be picked when still hard, placed in cold storage (32°F [0°C]), and removed to room temperature for final ripening. Will keep for up to 6 months.

Matua	Oct	late Oct	late Nov	early Nov	Nov	NA

Male vine used to pollinate Hayward, 8:1 female-male ratio.

Tamori	Oct	late Oct	late Nov	early Nov	Nov	NA

Male vine used to pollinate Hayward, 8:1 female-male ratio.

Table 17.4 cont.

Smoothskin Kiwifruit Varieties

Scion variety	Harvest*					
	San Joaquin Valley	Sacramento Valley	Central Coast	North Coast	Sierra Nevada Foothills	Southern California
Anna	late Sep	late Sep	early Oct	Oct	Oct	NA
Nickel-sized fruit. Unique flavor. Very productive.						
Issai	late Sep	late Sep	Oct	early Oct	Oct	NA
Dime-sized fruit that requires no cross-pollination.						
Ken's Red	late Sep	late Sep	Oct	early Oct	Oct	NA
Dime-sized fruit. Red flesh and skin. Excellent flavor.						

Low-Chill Varieties

These kiwi varieties are adapted to the low latitudes of Southern California because they have low winter chilling requirements (50 to 250 hr):

Abbott, Allison, Blake, Bruno, Elmwood, Tewi, Vincent.

MISCELLANEOUS TEMPERATE FRUITS

FIG (*Ficus carica* L.)

Figs can be grown easily, but they require a protected location in the cooler parts of the state because they require heat to mature the fruit properly. Fig trees do best in well-drained soils but will tolerate wet soils better than most other fruit trees. Gophers must be controlled. Figs are grown on their own roots from cuttings. Trees reach a height of 20 to 30 ft (6.1 to 9.1 m) with an equal spread but can be pruned to a smaller size. Most varieties require no cross-pollination. Several varieties set fruit parthenocarpically, and several varieties have two crops per year (shown below as "Jun/Sep"). The "breba" crop (first crop) matures in midsummer in 100 to 120 days, and the second crop matures in late summer or fall. Figs require very little winter chilling and are considered a "borderline" temperate zone species by many pomologists. The Smyrna types require caprification (pollination by caprifigs nearby).

Standard Fig Varieties

Scion variety	Harvest*					
	San Joaquin Valley	Sacramento Valley	Central Coast	North Coast	Sierra Nevada Foothills	Southern California
Adriatic	Jun/Sep	Jun/Sep	Oct	Oct	Jun/Sep	Jun/Sep
Good fresh but especially good for drying. Yellow skin and amber flesh. Good for cooler locations.						
Black Mission	Jun/Sep	Jun/Sep	Nov	Nov	Jun/Sep	Jun/Sep
The most dependable variety for the home orchard. Purple-black skin with red flesh.						
Brown Turkey	Jun/Sep	Jun/Sep	Nov	Nov	Jun/Sep	Jun/Sep
Large fruit. Excellent quality. Purple-green skin. Red flesh.						
Italian Everbearing	Jun/Sep	Jun/Sep	Nov	Nov	Jun/Sep	Jun/Sep
Brown. Turkey-type. Very prolific.						
Kadota	Jun/Sep	Jun/Sep	Nov	Nov	Jun/Sep	Jun/Sep
Requires high temperatures and a long growing season to perform well. Yellow-green fruit with amber flesh. Produces both breba and a second crop with moderate pruning.						
Osborn	Jun/Sep	Jun/Sep	Oct	Oct	Jun/Sep	Jun/Sep
Performs well only in cool coastal areas. Purple-bronze fruit with amber flesh. Very prolific.						
Smyrna-type	Jun/Sep	Jun/Sep	Nov	Nov	Jun/Sep	Jun/Sep
Requires cross-pollination by the caprifig female wasp to produce a crop. caprifigs containing female wasps may be difficult to locate for backyard fruit tree producers.						
White Genoa	Jun/Sep	Jun/Sep	Oct	Oct	Jun/Sep	Jun/Sep
Good for coastal locations. Large fruit. Yellow-green, thin skin. Strawberry flesh. Ripens when others won't.						

OLIVE (*Olea europaea* L.)

The olive tree is an evergreen tree that performs best in hot, dry areas of California; it does not tolerate wet winter soils. It is an attractive ornamental and produces table fruit and oil. Crop production is irregular under cool coastal conditions. Rooted cuttings are used without specific rootstocks. Space trees 16 to 20 ft (4.9 to 6.1 m) apart. Olives for canning and pickling are usually harvested in September and October in California. Commercially, heavy crops of small fruit unsuited for canning are left on the trees until December, January, or February and harvested for their oil. Some new varieties grown specifically for oil have recently been imported into California from the Mediterranean countries. Only a few of the thousands of varieties are listed here.

Table Olive Varieties

| Scion variety | Harvest* | | | | | |
	San Joaquin Valley	Sacramento Valley	Central Coast	North Coast	Sierra Nevada Foothills	Southern California
Ascolano	late Sep	early Oct	mid-Oct	mid-Oct	mid-Oct	Oct
Large-fruited variety, the most cold hardy of all table varieties in California. Large fruit. Oil is very aromatic.						
Manzanillo	late Sep	early Oct	mid-Oct	mid-Oct	mid-Oct	Oct
The main variety used for the black "California"-style olive. Low, spreading, medium-sized tree, early-maturing fruit with a medium oil content. Trees are susceptible to cold injury, peacock spot, and olive knot. Oil is very fruity.						
Mission	late Sep	early Oct	mid-Oct	mid-Oct	mid-Oct	Oct
Medium-sized fruit, high oil content, hardy. A good blending oil.						
Sevillano	late Sep	early Oct	mid-Oct	mid-Oct	mid-Oct	Oct
Largest fruit. Many minor problems. Oil is very aromatic.						

Oil Olive Varieties

| Scion variety | Harvest* | | | | | |
	San Joaquin Valley	Sacramento Valley	Central Coast	North Coast	Sierra Nevada Foothills	Southern California
Arbequina	mid-Nov	late Nov	Dec	early Dec	late Nov	late Nov
A variety from northern Spain that produces a very high-quality fruity oil. Fruit is small. Very fruitful.						
Frantoio	mid-Nov	late Nov	Dec	early Dec	late Nov	late Nov
Italian variety used as one of the main ingredients in gourmet olive oil production. Very high oil content and excellent flavor.						
Leccino	mid-Nov	late Nov	Dec	early Dec	late Nov	late Nov
Italian variety used in olive oil blends with Frantoio. Ripens a little earlier than other varieties.						
Maurino	mid-Nov	late Nov	Dec	early Dec	late Nov	late Nov
Italian variety used in olive oil blends. Very flavorful, spicy oil.						
Mission	late Sep	early Oct	mid-Oct	mid-Oct	mid-Oct	Oct
Medium-sized fruit. High oil content. Late maturing. Trees are very cold tolerant and grow quite tall. Can be used for table fruit or oil.						
Pendolino	mid-Nov	late Nov	Dec	early Dec	late Nov	late Nov
Italian variety used in olive oil blends. Also used as a pollenizer.						

PERSIMMON (*Diospyros kaki*)

Persimmons are a very good fruit tree for home planting. They bloom late, avoiding spring frosts, and they do not require much winter chilling. They perform well throughout the state except in very cool coastal areas, where they ripen late and crack from rain. Persimmon trees do not need ideal soil. They will tolerate "wet feet" in winter and dry conditions in the summer. The fruits are almost pest free. Cross-pollination is not usually necessary. Cross-pollinated fruit will have seeds; whereas, fruit from a lone tree probably will not.

Rootstock	Comments
Diospyros kaki	An adequate rootstock. Produces a long taproot and small, branching, fibrous roots.
D. lotus	Most widely used seedling rootstock. Best choice. Compatible with most varieties. Tolerates wet soil.
D. virginiana	This native species produces a very good, fibrous root system, tolerates drought and excess moisture fairly well, but may sucker profusely and may produce trees of variable size.

Table 17.4 cont.

Standard Persimmon Varieties

| Scion variety | Harvest* | | | | | |
	San Joaquin Valley	Sacramento Valley	Central Coast	North Coast	Sierra Nevada Foothills	Southern California
Baru	Oct	late Oct	Nov	Nov	late Oct	late Oct
Round, orange skin. Sweet brown flesh.						
Diospyros virginiana	Oct	late Oct	Nov	Nov	late Oct	late Oct
Native species, not a variety. Very small, very flavorful fruits. Must be eaten when soft.						
Fuyu	Oct	late Oct	Nov	Nov	late Oct	late Oct
Large, flat, orange-red color. Flesh is firm like an apple. Fruit loses astringency at maturity while still firm and crunchy. Cross-pollination is not required, but when present, fruit will have seeds. Trees are small, requiring 14 to 16 ft (4.3 to 4.9 m) .						
Hachiya	Oct	late Oct	Nov	Nov	late Oct	late Oct
Large, deep orange-red, acorn-shaped fruit. Flesh turns brown around the seeds and must be very soft to eat. Does not need cross-pollination. Trees get large and require 20 ft (6.1 m). Fruit is astringent until very ripe and soft.						
Hyakume	Oct	late Oct	Nov	Nov	late Oct	late Oct
Cinnamon-chocolate-colored flesh.						

For further information, see: chilling requirements, table 17.1; flower initiation and bloom, table 17.2; pollination requirements and tree height, table 17.3; water management, table 17.5; calendar of operations, table 17.6; problem diagnosis, table 17.7; nutritional value, table 17.8.
Notes:
*Harvest periods may vary slightly from year to year and can be influenced by microclimates. The harvest periods listed should not be interpreted as absolutely precise. In a given climate zone, home gardeners typically harvest later in the season than commercial growers do.
†NA = not applicable due to chilling requirements.

Planting and Care

Site Selection

When planning to grow deciduous fruits and nuts in the garden, consider the climate, soil, drainage, light intensity, and the diurnal temperature pattern at the proposed site. Fruit trees need to be grown in full sun; even small amounts of shade reduce flower bud formation and fruit set. Fruit quality is influenced by temperature and light during the growing season, as well as by the gardener's cultural practices and the genetic potential of the variety. Planting sites near a large body of water can moderate temperature; those in mountain sites at high elevations usually experience extremes of hot and cold, which is the most difficult condition for fruit trees. North-facing sites are colder and tend to retard bud development in the spring; hotter south-facing sites accelerate development. The delay of bloom typical of north-facing sites can be an advantage in avoiding frost injury. Since flowers and young fruit are more tender than mature fruit, spring frosts are much more damaging than early fall frosts. If frosts or cold, rainy spring weather are common, early-blooming crops such as apricots and almonds become very difficult to grow. Peaches, plums, and cherries bloom later, but still 15 to 20 days before apples and pears. The fruit tree species and variety should be selected to reduce the risk of early-spring frosts and late-spring rains at the site.

If a soil nutrition problem is suspected at the planting site, the soil should be tested for pH and analyzed for phosphorus (P), potassium (K), calcium (Ca), magnesium (Mg), and sodium (Na). Necessary amendments should be applied prior to planting to adjust nutrient levels and to achieve a pH of approximately 6 to 7 (see chapter 3 for details on adjusting pH). Phosphorous deficiency is very rare in California, but low potassium is more common. The calcium-to-magnesium ratio for temperate fruits should be at least 1:1 and up to 5:1 in favor of calcium. Soils with extremely high magnesium are rare but make it very difficult to grow fruit trees. Nitrogen (N) is not usually tested for in soil because this element is so mobile and will almost always need to be added annually. Micronutrient levels such as zinc (Zn), boron (B), manganese (Mn), iron (Fe), and copper (Cu) are determined by analyzing specific portions of the plant tissue and by observing color changes in the leaves. Micronutrient testing for deficiencies or excesses is usually done only if a specific problem is common in the area or is suspected to be causing a problem in tree performance. Soil and plant tissue testing are most accurately done by a certified laboratory.

For good tree growth, the soil should be very well drained and about 3 to 5 feet (0.9 to 1.5 m) deep. Shallow, poorly drained sites produce smaller, weaker trees with lower yields. Such trees have more pest problems and require special water management practices. Soil compaction should be corrected by deep digging prior to planting. In areas with heavy winter rainfall or very heavy clay soils that drain poorly, drainage can be improved by planting the trees on raised mounds. Home gardeners can also modify the planting site by installing planter boxes, raised beds, and drainage systems to improve tree performance. If good soil is added to a planting site, it should always be mixed in so that there is a gradual change from one soil to the next without layering (see chapter 3 for more on amending soil).

Planting Bareroot Trees

Temperate fruit and nut crops are usually purchased and planted as bareroot trees. These trees benefit from mound or raised bed planting (fig. 17.12). Mound planting is especially helpful for improving growth and reducing root and crown rots for apple, walnut, fig, cherry, apricot, almond, and peach rootstocks. Bareroot trees should never be planted in saturated or wet soil. Work the ground in the fall and cover it if necessary to keep it dry. Bareroot trees can then be planted anytime, but because they do best when they develop new roots and shoots during cool spring weather, they are usually planted in the winter. Roots of bareroot trees should never be allowed to dry out. Keep them in moist organic matter or dig a shallow trench and bury the roots temporarily before planting.

The most fragile part of a tree is the crown, the transitional section at or just below the soil surface where the trunk joins the roots (see fig. 17.13). When planting the tree, plant it high, keeping the crown area above the original soil line (see bud union noted on fig. 17.12). The crown should be kept as dry as possible, especially in the spring when the tree is leafing out. Raised planting prevents puddling near the trunk and crown areas. Do not plant the trees in a basin. If the planting area is too dry, it should be thoroughly watered a few days prior to planting, and the trees should be watered right after planting. After the tree is planted, apply compost, wood chips, grass clippings, or other mulch material 3 to 4 inches (7.5 to 10 cm) deep in a radius 2 to 3 feet (0.6 to 0.9 m) from the trunk for weed control and nutrient enhancement. Do not dig a large hole and fill it with amended soil containing organic materials, sand, or additives like perlite, vermiculite, peat, or lava rock. This creates a pot-like situation where roots tend to remain in the more favorable root growing conditions of the amended soil instead of growing out into the native soil.

Follow these step-by-step instructions for mound planting (see fig. 17.12).

1. Prepare the soil by working an area about 16 sqare feet (4 ft × 4 ft) (1.5 sq m, or 1.2 m × 1.2 m). Dig just deep enough to remove any compacted layers.

Figure 17.12

Mound planting of temperate fruit and nut trees.

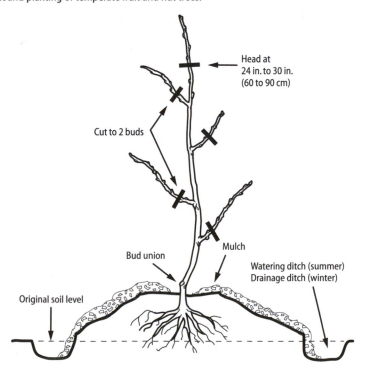

Head at
24 in. to 30 in.
(60 to 90 cm)

Cut to 2 buds

Bud union

Mulch

Watering ditch (summer)
Drainage ditch (winter)

Original soil level

Figure 17.13

Fruit tree framework terms. *Source: After Westwood 1993, p. 204.*

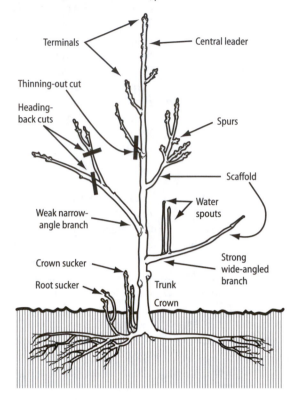

2. Clip off broken, twisted, or girdling roots. Do not plant trees with rotted roots or warty growths on the roots (possibly due to crown gall caused by bacterial infection—see table 17.7). Return trees with these problems to the nursery for a refund. Do not over-prune roots.

3. Place the tree on top of the ground and shovel soil from the surrounding area around the roots, forming a mound. The ditch created can be used to water the tree the next spring and summer and will aid in winter drainage.

4. Head the tree at 20 to 24 inches (51 to 61 cm) from the top of the mound to encourage low branching and balance the scion and root growth (see the section on pruning later in this chapter).

5. Cut back to 2 buds any lateral branches below 24 inches (51 cm) from the ground.

6. Paint the lower two-thirds of the tree trunk with a mixture of one-half water and one-half interior white latex paint to reduce sunburn and prevent attack by Pacific flat-

head borers (see table 17.7). Leaving the upper 6 to 8 inches (15 to 20.5 cm) unpainted increases budbreak and reduces the chance of damaging the buds during painting.

Most homeowners and commercial growers want trees that do not get too tall and that bear fruit close to the ground for easy thinning and picking. The only way to get low branching on fruit trees, that is, branch formation originating on the main trunk below 2 feet (0.6 m) from the ground, is to cut the top of the tree (*heading* or *topping*) at planting at 20 to 24 inches (51 to 61 cm) from the ground. New, vigorous growth occurs only within 6 to 8 inches (15 to 20 cm) of where the heading cut is made. Heading has little to no influence on the development of branches lower than that in the tree. Since the most vigorous growth occurs nearest the heading cut, heading trees too high at planting creates main branch development and most fruit production higher in the tree.

Training and Pruning Temperate Fruit and Nut Trees

The five main reasons to prune a fruit tree are to train the tree for easy management (thinning, harvest, spraying); influence fruit size (grow larger fruit); regulate annual bearing; allow light into the lower portion of the tree; and improve vigor (renews the fruit-bearing wood). Over time, unpruned trees develop thicker canopies, which limits light penetration into the tree and results in poor flower bud formation, poor fruit set, and poor fruit color.

Training Young Trees. There are two primary training systems: the central leader system and the open center system. Which system to use depends upon the natural growth habit and structural form of the tree.

The *central leader* system (fig 17.14A) employs an upright vertical trunk with 3 to 10 primary scaffold limbs. These primary scaffold limbs should have wide crotch angles that are evenly distributed about the trunk and that are separated vertically from each other in two to three tiers. The lower primary scaffold limbs arise from the trunk at 45° angles and are longer than the upper primary limbs, which are at 60° to 90° angles to the trunk. Since the shorter upper branches are attached at wider angles, their vigor is reduced, giving the tree a pyramid shape. The number of tiers

Figure 17.14

Central-leader and open-center training systems.

Central leader
A

Open center
B

Figure 17.15

Growth of lateral branch with strong, wide-angled attachment. Note that the point of branch attachment remains large and strong. *Source*: After Westwood 1993, p. 169.

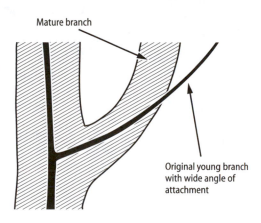

Mature branch

Original young branch with wide angle of attachment

depends on the ultimate tree height desired. This shape is good for light penetration since the top does not shade the lower limbs. The narrower crotch angles of the four to five lower branches helps them maintain vigor while producing 90 percent of the fruit.

To create the central leader system in most trees, the young scaffold branches need to be held in place at the appropriate angle for several months until they stiffen. Most scaffold limbs tend to grow excessively upright and must be propped outward with spreaders, weighted down with weights, or bent and tied down with string or tape. A combination of pruning and branch spreading is often needed to maintain a tree's shape. The central leader system works well for apple, pear, persimmon, and pecan.

The *open center or vase* training system (see fig. 17.14B) is based on development of 3 to 4 scaffold branches that emerge at wide crotch angles from a main trunk starting about 12 inches (30 cm) from the ground. Ideally, the branches have vertical spacing of about 6 inches (15 cm) between branches and are evenly spaced around the trunk. The primary scaffold branches originating at 45° to 60° angles from the trunk create an open tree center. This system creates an upside-down pyramid. To prevent the top from shading the lower limbs, the center must be open. This is the most common form used for peach, nectarine, pear, olive, plum, apricot, and cherry.

As a tree ages, the trunk grows over and around wide-angled branches, which makes their attachment very strong (fig. 17.15). A weak tree framework has narrow crotch angles and may have three or more scaffold branches arising from the same junction. This type of weak structure does not allow for the dominant trunk to grow around lateral branches since all branches are about the same size. The narrow crotch angle usually develops a bark inclusion between the branches and is a spot for debris and wood-rotting organisms to collect (fig. 17.16). As the weight of fruit increases during the year, limbs with narrow crotch angles often break or split open.

Minimal pruning favors flower bud formation during the early stages of tree development; consequently, young trees should be pruned only to develop a specific tree form. This is especially true for the olive, an evergreen tree that holds its energy in the leaves. Over-pruning olive trees during the first

Figure 17.16

Weak, narrow-angled branch attachment.

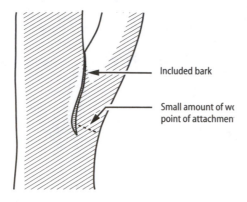

Included bark

Small amount of w(
point of attachmen

4 years reduces total tree size and delays fruiting by at least 2 years. Although not as sensitive as olive, severe pruning of deciduous trees must also be avoided to prevent delays in fruiting. Make cuts carefully to achieve the desired shape. Avoid cuts that reduce tree size unnecessarily. For deciduous species, dormant pruning invigorates the buds that remain on the tree and can be very beneficial for developing a few strong scaffold branches in young trees.

Bending Branches and Shaping Trees. The apical bud on fruit tree branches is typically the most dominant. Its dominance is based on its production of growth-regulating hormones that flow downward by gravity and retard the growth of the buds and flowers below. By changing the angle of the branch from vertical to horizontal, the influence of gravity on the flow of growth-inhibiting hormones is moderated or stopped. The greater the angle, the greater the influence, even to the point of branches drooping at an angle greater than 90°. Vertical branches tend to grow vigorous vegetation; horizontal and drooping branches are less vigorous and grow more flower buds. Branches with angles from 45° to 60° are well balanced in both fruitfulness and vegetative vigor. Different species and varieties respond differently to branch bending, and the rootstock and cultural practices also influence fruitfulness and vegetative vigor.

It is often difficult to direct branch angles, yet most fruit trees will not develop their maximum productive potential with pruning alone. Various devices can be used to hold branches at their desired angle until they become stiff enough to stay there by themselves. Gardeners use small weights, clothespins, props, spreader sticks, electrical tape, and string to bind vertical branches to their desired angle.

Pruning Mature Bearing Trees. Pruning objectives change as the tree changes from a young, nonbearing tree to a mature tree that has attained full size. In general terms, the pruner must shape the tree so that there is good sun exposure throughout the tree, permitting optimal photosynthesis that supports high-quality fruit and nut growth. The basic anatomy of a mature tree, including terms used in pruning, is given in figure 17.13.

Prior to pruning any tree, the tree should be evaluated for its vigor. Evaluate the quantity of new wood. The best fruit comes from new wood less than 5 years old; in some species, fruit comes only from wood that is 1 year old. If the tree lacks vigor, it should be heavily pruned in the dormant period to encourage more vegetative vigor. If a tree is overly vigorous, it should probably not be pruned while it is dormant, because dormant pruning tends to invigorate the buds that remain on the tree, causing even more growth. Instead, bend its branches to wider crotch angles to reduce vigor or prune the tree in the summer to reduce leaf area and slow growth. Most nut trees and olives are not pruned to modify vigor; it is difficult to reduce their size without severely affecting fruit or nut production.

Ideally, maintenance pruning preserves the tree form established in the training process and creates a balance between the growth of renewal wood and fruiting wood, and also improves light exposure in the lower portion of the tree. Appropriate tree vigor depends on the fruit tree type, but in general there should be about 12 to 18 inches (30 to 45 cm) of new wood on vigorous new shoots. Prune to remove excess growth that threatens to shade lower areas. For species bearing on 1-year-old wood (e.g., peach, nectarine, and kiwi), remove some or most of the old wood that bore the previous year's fruit, since its fruitfulness is less than the newer growth. In low-vigor trees with spurs (e.g., apples, pears, plums), the spurs may need to be shortened for renewal and stiffened to support fruit without bending severely. Leave some weak, short, lateral branches unheaded so that they can develop into spurs for the future. Approximately 20 percent of the older spur wood should be renewed annually in order to maintain quality fruit production. New spur wood produces fruit for about 5 years.

Proper pruning can help reduce alternate bearing in some tree species (e.g., olive, apple, plum, kiwi). During a heavy bearing ("on") year, trees proceed into dormancy with fewer flower buds due to hormonal signals and competition for nutrients. The smaller crop produced in the "off" year allows for less competition, greater growth, and more flower bud differentiation for the next "on" year. To help reduce alternate bearing, prune the trees more heavily prior to the "on" year. This heavy dormant pruning reduces the number of flower buds produced in the "on" year, which decreases competition, providing the nutrients needed for increased flower bud differentiation in the following "off" year.

Types of Pruning Cuts. There are two types of pruning cuts: *heading* and *thinning*. A heading cut is essentially topping a branch at a point one-third to one-half or more of the distance from the tip to the point of attachment. Heading cuts are made to shorten branches (reduce tree size), invigorate growth, and force lateral branching. A thinning cut is made at the base of a branch located in an undesirable position to remove the branch and reduce crowding. Thinning cuts are made to improve light penetration to fruiting wood, maintain tree vigor (less invigorating than heading cuts), and reduce the tree's fruiting potential (excess fruiting). As trees mature, thinning cuts are made more often than heading cuts.

The correct location for thinning cuts is just *outside* the branch collar (fig. 17.17). A cut at this point develops callus tissue that fills in the cut surface and leads to rapid wound healing. Thinning cuts should not leave short stubs because stubs can die back to the base and become entry points for wood-rotting organisms, or they can allow unwanted shoots to grow from dormant buds located at the base of the stub. The cut should not be made flush with the branch because it leaves a larger wound.

Long, heavy branches should be removed in three stages to prevent tearing of the bark (see fig. 17.17). First, cut the underside of the branch about one-third of the way into the branch diameter. This cut should be about 20 inches (50 cm) away from where the final cut will be, and the cut should not be too deep. Second, cut the upper side of the branch about 8 inches (20 cm) farther out on the branch from the first cut. The weight of the branch will split the underside of the branch from the second cut to the first. Then, cut the stub that remains at the branch collar, near the base. Research has shown that healing of large wounds is not hastened by covering with tree sealants. The best defense against disease and insect attack is to avoid stubs and not to remove the branch collar. Large wounds can be covered with grafting wax for cosmetic purposes or a fungicide to temporarily prevent the introduction of disease organisms.

Dormant Pruning versus Summer Pruning. The time of year when pruning occurs has a strong impact on shoot growth and fruit development. *Dormant pruning* is the removal during the winter months of branches that grew during the previous season; *summer pruning* is the removal of shoots during mid- to late spring or early summer. Both forms of pruning reduce the total bearing capacity of the tree but have distinctly different effects on future tree development.

Dormant pruning is the most invigorating pruning period. Buds that remain have a greater proportion of the reserve carbohydrates stored in the tree and thus grow at a faster rate. This is very beneficial for the development of young trees, where a few strong scaffold branches and rapid growth is desired. It is also important for the development of new wood in mature trees needed for continued fruit production. Dormant pruning can be done from the beginning of leaf fall up to bloom.

Figure 17.17

Pruning cuts should be made just outside the branch bark ridge (top of cut) and the collar (bottom of cut) so that the bottom of the cut is angled slightly outward. *Source:* After International Society of Arboriculture 1995, p. 3.

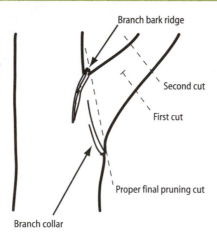

Branch bark ridge
Second cut
First cut
Proper final pruning cut
Branch collar

Summer pruning is useful to selectively promote the growth of primary and secondary scaffold branches and to remove undesirable competing branches in young trees. This can be done several times throughout the growing season. To eliminate unwanted shoots without affecting tree vigor, remove them before they reach 6 inches (15 cm) in length, usually before May. Summer pruning is also done on mature trees for size control and to reduce their vigor. It is a devigorating practice because it removes leaf area, reducing the production of food. Summer pruning (a combination of thinning and heading cuts) is best done between May and July.

Effects of Fruit and Nut Tree Bearing Habit Classification on Pruning. The bearing habit of a fruit or nut tree influences pruning practices. Some species (such as apples) bear primarily on long-lived spurs that continue to bear no matter what happens with the new shoot growth. The spurs need to be renewed periodically by topping them back when they get too long, usually after 5 to 10 years. The spurs must also have adequate sun exposure to produce large, fully colored fruit. Maintaining adequate sunlight in the lower portion of the canopy often requires thinning of shoots and branches in the upper canopy.

The other extreme is species that bear laterally on 1-year-old growth (such as peaches). These species require a lot of shoot growth in order to fruit well the following year. Since shoot growth and fruit production occur at the same time, they are in competition for carbohydrates produced by the leaves. An excess of fruit or lack of pruning leads to poor shoot growth and less crop the following year. Shoot-bearing species are winter-pruned more heavily than spur-bearing species to ensure adequate shoot growth along with fruit production.

Some species (such as plums) bear on both spurs and 1-year-old wood. They are treated more like spur-bearing species to maintain production on the spurs while having the bonus of some crop on last year's shoot growth. Fruit and nut trees are classified according to their predominant bearing habit as on spurs or shoots or both:

- spur: apple, pear, cherry, European plum
- 1-year-old wood: peach, nectarine, fig, persimmon, quince, pecan, olive, kiwi, and walnut

- shoot and spur: almond, some apples, apricot, and Japanese plum

Spur-bearing species. Spurs arise during the second growing season primarily from lateral shoots. On species that bear terminally on long-lived spurs (apple, apricot, pear), most of the shoots that grew the previous season can be removed during dormant pruning, especially those strong, vigorous shoots that grow vertically within the tree and shade the lower spur-bearing branches. Some species, such as Asian pear, produce excess spurs. The spurs can be thinned to reduce the crop load, reduce the need for excessive hand-thinning, and to instigate more lateral shoot growth to renew old spurs.

One-year-old-wood bearing species. On peach and nectarine trees, which bear their fruit laterally on last season's growth, all old, weak wood and at least 50 percent of last year's growth should be removed. Pruning in this manner leaves the moderately vigorous lateral shoots to bear and provides shoot growth for the following season. Even with this level of pruning, fruit thinning may still be necessary (fig. 17.18). Downward-growing branches should be thinned, not headed. On olive, peach, nectarine, pecan, and walnut, it is important to assure sufficient shoot growth each year to get a good crop the next year.

Summary of Basic Pruning Tips

1. Initial pruning should be done immediately after planting a new bareroot fruit tree, as shown in figure 17.12 and discussed above in steps 4, 5, and 6 in the "Planting Bareroot Trees" section, above. Trees should be topped at 20 to 24 inches (50 to 60 cm) in order to balance the top with the root system that was cut off at the nursery and to encourage low branching.

2. Most temperate fruit trees should be pruned during the dormant season when the leaves are off the tree. It is easier to see what you are doing, and removal of dormant buds (growing points) invigorates the remaining buds. Summer pruning, which is usually done from May to July, is used to manage overly vigorous trees or trees that are too large. During summer pruning, the leaf area used to manufacture photosynthates (food) is reduced, which may slow fruit ripening and expose some fruit to sunburn.

3. For the first years, young trees should be very lightly pruned to encourage structural strength and rapid growth until the trees fill their allotted space. Leave most of the small, horizontal branches untouched for later fruiting. Place spreaders or weights in the tree to encourage proper tree form. For vase-trained trees, the main scaffolds should be attached at angles of about 45° to 60° to the trunk and evenly spaced around the trunk. For central leader trees, the lower branches should be attached at angles of about 45° to 60° to the trunk. Higher branches should be attached at angles of 60° to 90°.

4. Evaluate the vegetative vigor of the tree to be pruned. If excessive, prune very lightly in the winter or do not prune at all; consider summer pruning to reduce vigor. If vigor is lacking, prune the tree heavily to stimulate growth in the remaining buds. Balanced trees should have about 12 to 18 inches (30 to 45 cm) of shoot growth throughout the tree.

5. When deciding which branch to cut and where to cut it, remember that topping a vertical branch encourages vegetative growth, branching, and excessive shading of lower branches. Thinning cuts that remove entire branches open the tree to more sunlight. Heading horizontal branches is done to renew fruiting wood and to thin excessive fruit. Horizontal shoots left uncut bear earlier and heavier crops.

6. In general, upright branches remain vegetative and vigorous, whereas horizontal branches are more fruitful. A good combination of the two is necessary for fruiting now and in future years. Remove suckers, water sprouts, and most competing branches growing straight up into the tree (see fig. 17.13). Downward-bending branches bear fruit early but eventually lose vigor; cut off the part hanging down.

7. Make clean cuts within ¼ inch (6.5 mm) of a bud. Do not leave stubs. The response to pruning is localized: new growth is stimulated only within 6 to 8 inches (15 to 20 cm) of the cut. The more buds that are cut off, the more vigorous the new shoots will be.

8. Do most of the pruning in the top of the tree so that the lower branches are exposed to sunlight. Sun-exposed wood remains fruitful and produces the best fruit. Excessive shade in the lower portion of the canopy results in loss of fruitwood, requiring several heading cuts to stimulate new growth.

9. Use spreaders or other means to get create angles of 45° to 60° on branches of upright, vigorous trees. Bending should occur before the branches become large in diameter to prevent breaking (usually up to the second year).

10. Adjust the pruning level to tree vigor. Weak trees require heavier dormant pruning to renew vigor. For peach, nectarine, and kiwi trees, remove about 50 percent of last year's growth. For apple, pear, plum, apricot, olive, walnut, pecan, chestnut, persimmon, pomegranate, and fig trees, remove about 20 percent of last year's growth.

Fruit Thinning

Removal of flowers or immature fruit early in the spring can lead to increases in fruit size by limiting the number of fruit that continue growing. Thinning increases the leaf-to-fruit ratio and removes smaller fruit that would not reach optimal size or quality. Apple, European and Asian pear, apricot, peach, plum, kiwifruit, table olives, and persimmon are almost always thinned until the leaf-to-fruit ratio is favorable for supporting the growth of adequately sized fruit (see fig. 17.18). Nut crops and cherries are typically not thinned.

Large fruit grow from flower buds that developed in full sunlight on trees that have a favorable leaf-to-fruit ratio (not too many fruit per branch). Proper dormant pruning followed by hand-thinning creates fruit that attain a good size and encourages a good number of flower buds for the next year. Fruit on trees that are not thinned are edible but are usually smaller. Excess fruit can also break branches.

The earlier that fruit are thinned and the leaf-to-fruit ratio is increased, the larger the fruit will be at harvest and the greater the effect on next year's bloom. The home fruit gardener should use judgment regarding spacing of the fruit and removing small and damaged fruit. Spacing fruit every 4 inches (10 cm) evenly along a branch or leaving only one fruit per spur is a good practice, but it is more important to leave the largest fruit, even

Figure 17.18

Fruit thinning in peach. Same branch before (left) and after (right) thinning. *Source:* After LaRue and Johnson 1989, pp. 58, 59.

if the spacing is slightly irregular. Adjust the number of fruit to branch vigor, leaving fewer fruit on smaller limbs. Most home fruit producers do not thin enough fruit; it usually takes 2 to 3 years of harvesting small fruit from inadequate thinning to learn to thin the fruit properly.

Blossom thinning can be used to increase the leaf-to-fruit ratio since competition between potential fruit and elongating shoots and roots is relieved early; however, there is the risk of over-thinning if bad weather during or after bloom reduces fruit set even more.

Standard apple and peach cultivars require leaf-to-fruit ratios between 40:1 and 75:1 (40 to 75 leaves per fruit) to reach a good size at harvest. Early varieties need a larger ratio. Spur-type apple varieties require a smaller leaf-to-fruit ratio of 25:1. This seems to be related to the fact that photosynthates and stored food reserves are distributed more to fruit growth than vegetative growth in spur-type trees. Nut crops are not thinned because kernel size is not an important factor.

Watering Fruit and Nut Trees

Fruit and nut trees grow best if irrigated regularly. Drought stress reduces fruit size and shoot growth, especially in young trees. One of the first things that happens when fruit trees are water-stressed is that the leaf pores (stomates) close to conserve internal water. In so doing, the exchange of gases is reduced, which limits the supply of carbon dioxide (CO_2) for photosynthesis. If the tree is severely water-stressed, the leaves wilt, curl, and sunburn; the fruit also grow smaller, lose water, shrivel, and sunburn. Good irrigation practices supply water at sufficient intervals to prevent plant stress. This ensures maximum plant growth, fruit size, and yield. In some circumstances, however, a slight water stress induced at specific growth stages can improve fruit flavor, enhance sugar or oil content, and limit vegetative growth. This is known as regulated deficit irrigation (RDI).

Water quality may be an issue in parts of California that have excess salt or mineral content in irrigation water. If a problem is expected, irrigation water should be tested for its mineral content to avoid toxicity to trees.

The amount of water evaporating from the soil surface plus the water used (transpired) by the tree is called crop evapotranspiration (ET). The amount of water a fruit tree uses depends primarily on how big it is and how hot the day is. Several other factors also influence water use, such as relative humidity and wind, but they are less important. Table 17.5 is a water management guide for temperate fruit trees based on evapotranspiration rates and tree size. Since the summer days in the main fruit-growing regions of California are predictably sunny and warm, this chart can be used to determine the water use requirements for fruit trees. In the spring and fall when the days are shorter and cooler, the trees need less water. (For a broader discussion of ET, irrigation concepts, and conserving water in home orchards see chapter 4, "Water Management.")

Water use by fruit trees is very similar between species. The greatest difference in water use is due to tree size. For example, table 17.5 shows that a tree that occupies 36 square feet (6 ft by 6 ft) uses 5.6 gallons of water per day; a tree that is about three times as large, 100 square feet (10 ft by 10 ft), uses almost three times as much water (15.6 gallons per day). This is based on a typical hot midsummer day using 0.25 inches of water per day.

Water use for a medium-sized semidwarf fruit tree is about 16 gallons of water per day (0.25 in/day) on a hot summer day on the coast of California without any fog influence.

That same tree in the Central Valley would use about 19 gallons of water per day (0.3 in/day). A tree in the Central Valley equipped with two 1-gallon-per-hour drip emitters would have to be irrigated about 9 to 10 hours every day to supply the needed water. The tree on the coast would be irrigated for 7 to 8 hours every day.

Drip Irrigation. Unlike basin or sprinkler irrigation, drip irrigation does not use the soil as a reservoir for water; it supplies the tree's water requirements as needed on a daily basis. Drip irrigation wets only a small area, limiting weed growth, and it is easily adapted to many landscape situations. Although a small area is wetted under drip emitters, the root density increases in this zone to ensure adequate water uptake. Soil type or depth has very little influence on drip-irrigated trees since the water use rate is determined by weather and tree size. Soil water-holding capacity is also unimportant due to daily irrigations. Drip irrigation should begin in early spring before much soil moisture has been used because this stored water may be needed later in case the drip system is accidentally shut down. Only 10 to 20 percent of the rooting area needs to be wetted for good tree performance. Below are two examples that show how long to drip-irrigate trees in various conditions.

Example 1: A young semidwarf fruit tree, 2 years old, occupies a space of 10 square feet. It has two 1 gal/hr emitters, and on a warm spring day the water use rate is about 0.20 in/day.

How much to water: Table 17.5 shows that the tree requires 1.25 gal/day.

How often to water: 1.25 gal/day ÷ 2 emitters = 37.5 min/day, or 75 min (1 hr 15 min) every other day.

Example 2: A mature, large, standard-sized fruit tree occupying an area of 300 square feet has four 1 gal/hr emitters. On a hot summer day the water use rate is about 0.25 in/day.

How much to water: Table 17.5 shows that the tree requires 46.8 gal/day.

How often to water: 46.8 gal/day ÷ 4 emitters = 11.7 hr/day, or 23.4 hr every other day.

Sprinkler Irrigation. Sprinkler-irrigated trees use the same amount of water as drip-irrigated trees plus an additional 20 percent for loss due to evaporation and the nonuniformity of application. Sprinklers apply more water at once, and some water is stored in the soil before the next irrigation. A larger area is also watered compared to drip irrigation, and weed growth also covers a greater area.

Another important difference between drip- and sprinkler-irrigated trees is that the soil rooting depth and the soil water-holding capacity, which is based on soil type (sand, clay, or loam), are important since water must be stored in the soil. The capacity for the soil to hold water is based on the size of the mineral and organic matter particles in the soil. Most soils hold about 2 inches (5 cm) of available water per foot of rooting depth:

- sandy soil: 1–1.5 in/ft (2.5 cm to 3.8 cm per 30.5 cm)

- loamy soil: 1.5–2.5 in/ft (3.8 cm to 6.4 cm per 30.5 cm)

- clay soil: 2.5–3.5 in/ft (6.4 cm to 8.9 cm per 30.5 cm)

Because sprinkler-irrigated trees are irrigated only periodically, the trees deplete the water stored in the soil over a period of several days. Eventually the trees can become water-stressed as the water in the soil is used up. To prevent significant water stress, the amount of

Table 17.5

WATER MANAGEMENT GUIDE FOR TEMPERATE FRUIT TREES

Tree age/size	Daily water use (gal/day)			
	Cool, early spring or late fall, foggy 0.10 in/day	Warm, spring or fall, some fog 0.20 in/day	Hot, midsummer, windy, no fog 0.25 in/day	Very hot (100°F, 38°C), midsummer 0.30 in/day
1 sq ft	0.062	0.125	0.156	0.187
1 yr old (4 sq ft)	0.25	0.50	0.62	0.75
2 yr old (10 sq ft)	0.62	1.25	1.56	1.87
3 yr old (36 sq ft)	2.25	4.5	5.61	6.73
4 yr old (100 sq ft), semidwarf, mature	6.20	12.5	15.6	18.7
large standard mature tree (300 sq ft)	18.6	37.5	46.8	56.1
1 acre solid cover (43,560 sq ft)	2,715	5,431	6,788	8,146

stored water should never be allowed to become completely depleted. Most fruit tree growers use a figure of 50 to 75 percent allowable depletion before irrigating to prevent water stress to the trees.

Both overirrigation and underirrigation have a negative effect on tree performance. If trees are overirrigated, the water that sinks below the root zone is wasted; overirrigation can also encourage weeds, pests, and diseases. Underirrigation, which is caused by too long an interval between watering or an insufficient quantity of water per irrigation, can lead to water stress. Care should be taken to apply the proper amount of water at the proper time (see the example below).

Example: A mature, large, standard-sized fruit tree occupies an area of 300 square feet. The rooting depth is 3 feet in loam, and the daily water use (ET) is 0.25 in/day in July.

How much to water: The water-holding capacity of loam is about 2 inch/foot. 3 foot rooting depth × 2 inches water = 6 inches of available water. 6 inches water × 75% allowable depletion = 4.5 inches, + 20% efficiency loss = 5.4 inches.

How long to water: Set open containers under the sprinklers and measure how long it takes to apply 1 inch of water. Multiply the duration times 5.4 inches of water to get the total amount of time needed. If a sprinkler applies 0.3 inch of water per hour, it would take 18 hours to apply 5.4 inches of water.

How often to water: 5.4 inches water ÷ 0.25 inches water use/day = about once every 21 days.

Sprinklers irrigate various areas and patterns. Large areas may require impact sprinklers, which have high application rates. Plastic minisprinklers, small sprinklers attached to drip tubing, are usually sufficient in the home garden. Their water application rates are also easily accommodated by city water systems. Each minisprinkler usually delivers about 10 to 20 gallons per hour, or 10 times the average drip emitter. The minisprinkler system is typically run 2 to 3 times per week, with some water held in the soil in storage. Run times can be calculated from the daily water use table (see table 17.5), multiplied by number of days between irrigation intervals. Care must be taken to investigate the depth that the irrigation water is reaching for minisprinklers.

Some emit fine streams that wet an area up to 15 feet (4.5 m) in diameter; they require an excessive amount of time to wet soil to a depth of 24 inches.

Most fruit tree roots are located from 6 to 36 inches (15 to 90 cm) deep in the soil. This topsoil area contains most of the nutrients and oxygen. Irrigation should focus on maintaining adequate moisture in this zone. Contrary to belief, roots do not seek moisture but grow where moisture is present. Home orchard trees that are on deep soils can get by with less intensive irrigation because the tree roots are deeper, providing a buffering capacity for drought stress. Shallow soils need to be managed much more intensively, with lighter, frequent irrigations. It is very difficult to determine how much water fruit trees are getting if they are watered by hand with a garden hose. The soil moisture should be checked with a small trowel or shovel down to a depth of at least 1 foot (0.3 m) a day after watering to determine if the soil moisture is going deep enough. For more information on soil water, see chapter 3, "Soil and Fertilizer Management."

Fertilizing Temperate Tree Fruit and Nut Crops at Home

Successful fruit production requires that trees have an adequate supply of essential nutrients. The primary nutrient that home gardeners need to supply on a regular basis is nitrogen (N). Zinc (Zn) is the second-most-common deficiency in tree crops; potassium (K) is often required because many of the soils of California are somewhat deficient. Phosphorus (P) deficiency is very rare in tree fruits and nuts. In some instances, magnesium (Mg), iron (Fe), manganese (Mg), copper (Cu), calcium (Ca), boron (B), or molybdenum (Mo) may be deficient or in excess. The symptoms of many of these micronutrient problems are very difficult to identify properly. One solution to suspected deficiencies is to apply compost, since it contains small quantities of most of the nutrients. As the organic material decomposes, it slowly releases these basic minerals into the soil for the trees to take up. This is often less complicated than trying to find the exact micronutrient missing, but the release of nutrients is slow and may take a long time to correct a deficiency.

There are many conditions that may limit a fruit or nut tree's ability to take up the proper quantity of nutrients even when an adequate

Table 17.6

CALENDAR OF HOME GARDENING OPERATIONS FOR SELECTED TEMPERATE FRUIT AND NUT TREES

Fruit or nut	Winter Dormant season	Spring Bloom season	Summer Growing season	Fall Harvest season
almond	Prune trees in Dec/Jan to allow more light into tree and promote growth of new fruiting wood. Remove dead, diseased, drooping branches and suckers in center of tree. Remove and destroy all old nuts on trees and on ground to reduce overwintering navel orangeworms. Spray trees with dormant oil to kill peach twig borer, San Jose scale, and mite eggs.	Just prior to first irrigation, fertilize mature trees with 2 lb urea or 50 lb of compost and water in. Young trees: use small, frequent doses of N throughout the growing season. Drip-irrigate daily to meet tree needs. Sprinkler-irrigate every 1–3 wk starting 2–3 wk after winter rains stop. Apply 2–3 in of water per irrigation. Trees growing in shallow or sandy soils need more frequent watering.	Continue irrigating as during spring bloom season. Fertilize trees again at same rate as in spring, just prior to last irrigation before harvest. Water in.	Nuts are ready for harvest after hulls split and shell is dry and brown. Separate hulls from nut and discard. Nuts can be in shell or out. Freeze in-shell nuts for 1–2 wk to kill resident worms. Store in plastic bags to prevent reinfestation. Spray trees with fixed copper during or after leaf fall but before onset of winter rains to reduce damage from shot hole fungus the following spring.
apple	Spray trees with dormant oil to control San Jose scale, aphid eggs, mite eggs. Prune 15–20% of last year's growth to let light in. Remove diseased or broken limbs.	Spray trees with a fungicide to control apple scab and powdery mildew at green tip stage, pink bud stage, and at 10-day intervals thereafter until rain stops. Thin apples by hand within 30–69 days after full bloom to about 1 apple per 6 inches of shoot growth. Fertilize prior to first irrigation. Mature trees, use 2 lb urea or 50 lb compost spread on the surface.	Fertilize young irrigated trees monthly (through August). Use 1 oz urea or 20 lb compost/tree. Water in. Do not exceed 1 oz urea/emitter/appl. Spray (May 1–Sep 1) to control codling moth worms; time sprays to visual ID of worm holes in fruit. Control aphids if damage exceeds 50% of leaves crinkled and aphids present. Control mites if damage is severe. Drip-irrigate daily or sprinkler-irrigate every 2–3 weeks.	Continue irrigating; fertilize mature trees after harvest. Repeat rates from summer. At leaf fall, remove and destroy or compost leaves to prevent the spread of apple scab. Control weeds throughout the season with an organic mulch. Harvest from July–Nov, depending on fruit taste.
apricot	Spray trees with dormant oil to control San Jose scale, aphid eggs, mite eggs, and peach twig borer. Do not use sulfur on apricots; use fixed copper.	Spray to control brown rot and shot hole fungus as blooms start to open. Sprays may be required at 10–14 day intervals if weather is rainy. Drip-irrigate daily or sprinkler-irrigate every 2–3 weeks. Fertilize before first irrigation with 1–2 lb of urea or 30–50 lb of compost. Water in. Thin fruits to about 4–6 inches apart when $1/2$–$5/8$ inch in diameter. Paint trunks with 50-50 mix of white interior latex paint and water to prevent sunburn and borer infestation.	Continue same irrigation schedule as in spring. Fertilize young trees monthly (through August) at one-quarter spring rates to encourage vigorous growth.	Harvest when fruit begin to turn soft. Prune trees before onset of winter rains to prevent *Eutypa* fungus infection of pruning wounds. Remove about 20% of last year's growth to let light into tree. Prune to remove old, broken, or diseased branches. Spray trees during or after leaf fall but before onset of winter rains to control shot hole fungus. Do not use sulfur on apricots; use fixed copper.

Table 17.6 cont.

Fruit or nut	Winter Dormant season	Spring Bloom season	Summer Growing season	Fall Harvest season
cherry	Spray with dormant oil to control San Jose scale. Prune 10% of last year's growth on mature trees to let light in. Remove broken or diseased branches. Cherries may do better against bacterial canker (gummosis) if treated with fixed copper spray.	Apply fungicide to control brown rot at popcorn and full bloom stages. Fertilize nonirrigated mature trees just before or during a rain with about 2 lb urea or 50 lb compost. Fertilize irrigated trees just before an irrigation.	Cover trees with bird netting to control birds. Drip-irrigate daily with amount equal to size of tree (see table 17.5). Sprinkler-irrigate about every 2–3 wk with 3–5 inches water per irrigation, depending on soil depth and water use. After harvest, fertilize mature trees with 2 lb urea or 50 lb compost and water in immediately.	Irrigate to maintain good tree vigor through summer heat and into fall until winter rain takes over. Drip-irrigate daily to match daily use. Sprinkler-irrigate every 3–4 wk to wet all soil in root zone but stop Sep 1 to prevent root rot. Harvest when fruit is soft and sweet.
olive	Spray with fixed copper to prevent peacock spot, especially in wet years. For oil varieties apply just after harvest.	Prune trees during the bloom period. To reduce alternate bearing, remove more shoots from trees with heavy bloom and skip trees with light bloom. Fertilize mature trees with 2 lb of urea or 50 lb of compost. Begin irrigating trees so there is no water stress during bloom.	Control weeds with organic mulch or cultivation, especially on young trees. Fertilize young trees with 1 oz of urea under each drip emitter every month (May–Sep.) and irrigate in. For sprinkler-irrigatation, fertilize once with 1/2 lb (227 g) of urea just prior to an irrigation. Apply drip irrigation every day according to water use requirements.	For table fruit, harvest when fruit is still green, just before the straw-yellow stage. For oil, harvest when the fruit has turned black on the outside, but the flesh is still green/yellow. Continue irrigation right up to harvest if weather is dry; do not allow fruit to shrivel. Apply fixed copper to prevent peacock spot before first major fall rains. Wash copper off fruit prior to processing or apply after harvest.
peach and nectarine	Spray trees with dormant oil to control San Jose scale. Spray fixed copper to control peach leaf curl Dec 1 and Feb 1. Prune 50% of last year's wood to thin the crop and ensure good shoot growth and fruiting potential for future years.	Apply fungicide during bloom to prevent brown rot, which may require 1–3 sprays, depending on weather. Rainy periods require more spray. Fertilize young trees monthly with high-N fertilizer beginning Mar 1. Use 0.5 lb urea or 25 lb compost/tree per application. Mature trees need 50% more. Water fertilizer in. For drip irrigation, use 1 oz (28 g) of material applied under emitters every month. Do not exceed 1 oz urea/emitter/month. Thin fruits to about 8 inches apart when marble-sized. Thinning reduces number of fruit, increases size, and prevents limb breakage.	Fertilize young trees monthly (through August). Use 0.5 lb urea or 25 lb manure/tree per application. Mature trees need 50% more. Water fertilizer in. Do not exceed 1 oz urea/emitter/month. Drip-irrigate daily or sprinkler-irrigate about every 3 weeks. Maintain a weed-free area around the base of the trees within 3 ft of the trunk with an organic mulch 3-4 inches deep.	Spray fixed copper for shot hole fungus in late Nov. before first heavy rain. Harvest as fruits turn soft but before they fall from the tree. Fertilize and irrigate just after harvest. Remove mummies from tree.

Fruit or nut	Winter Dormant season	Spring Bloom season	Summer Growing season	Fall Harvest season
pear	Spray trees with dormant oil to control San Jose scale, aphid eggs, mite eggs, and overwintering adult pear psylla. Prune 20% of last year's growth to let light in. Remove diseased (fire blighted) and broken limbs.	Spray trees with a fungicide to control pear scab at green tip stage, full bloom, and at 10-day intervals until rain stops. Thin pears to 6 inches apart if crop is heavy. Fertilize prior to first irrigation. Apply 1.5 lb urea or 40 lb compost/tree.	Fertilize young trees monthly (through Aug.) using $1/2$ oz. urea/emitter each time. Spray monthly (May 1–Aug.1) to control codling moth worms. Time sprays to visual ID of worm holes in fruit. Control aphids if damage exceeds 50% of leaves crinkled and aphids present. Drip-irrigate daily or sprinkler-irrigate every 2–3 weeks.	Using spring rates, fertilize and irrigate mature trees right after harvest. Clean up fallen fruit to reduce codling moth. Harvest as fruit soften and by flavor. At leaf fall, remove and destroy or compost leaves to prevent the spread of apple scab.
plum and prune	Spray trees with dormant oil to control San Jose scale, aphid eggs, mite eggs. Prune 20% of last year's growth to let light in. Remove diseased or broken limbs.	Spray trees with a fungicide to control brown rot as blossoms appear. 2–3 sprays may be needed if weather is rainy, cloudy. Fertilize mature trees with 1–2 lb urea or 30–50 lb compost/tree. Irrigate about every 2–3 weeks or drip-irrigate every day. Fertilize trees just prior to irrigation. Use lower rates for vigorous trees. Thin fruit to about 4–6 inches apart. If larger fruit is desired, leave fewer fruit. Control aphids if severe damage (50% of leaves curled and aphids present).	Fertilize young trees monthly (through August). Use 1 oz urea or 10 lb compost per application. Water in. Do not exceed 1 oz urea/emitter per application. Drip-irrigate daily or sprinkler-irrigate about every 2–3 weeks. Use organic mulch to maintain a weed-free area within 3 ft of the tree.	Fertilize and irrigate mature trees just after harvest with 1–2 lb urea or 20–40 lb compost/mature tree. At leaf fall or before major rains, spray fixed copper to prevent shot hole fungus.
walnut	Prune trees by thinning out crowded areas to let light into tree. Remove broken or dead branches. Spray trees with dormant oil to control scale insects, if needed.	Spray for blossom blight when female flowers appear (tiny nuts with feathery pistil) and at 7-day intervals until rainy weather stops. Blight appears as black blossom ends of nuts in June and later as black hollow nuts. Remove all weeds from tree base to reduce competition and pest problems. Fertilize mature trees with 5–7 lb urea or 90–150 lb compost.	Keep tree base dry to reduce crown rot problems. Irrigate trees at the dripline but away from trunks. Sprinkler-irrigate with about 3 inches water every 3–4 wk or drip-irrigate daily during May-Oct. Young, small trees need 4–12 gal water/day; large trees about 20–40 gal/day. Spray for walnut husk fly about Aug 1 and Aug 15. Damage is cosmetic, control is optional. Spray to control codling moth worms or tolerate damage.	Harvest nuts by shaking or poling the tree when green hulls begin to break away from the shell. Nuts are fully mature at this stage. If left on the tree or allowed to fall on their own, the hulls will rot and stick to the shell. Hull nuts, then freeze in-shell nuts to kill resident worms. Store in plastic.

quantity of the nutrients is present in the soil. Cold or wet soils can limit root growth and activity to the point that some nutrient deficiency symptoms become visible; extremely dry soils may cause a similar situation. These are usually temporary conditions that are corrected when the soil warms up or is properly irrigated. In severe cases, tree roots or crown areas become partially rotted and unable to pick up soil nutrients. Adding additional fertilizers to control the visual symptoms of nutrient deficiency when the roots are rotted is useless. Also, some plant viruses, herbicides, or other pesticides can cause symptoms that can be confused with nutritional problems. It is therefore important to properly identify the cause of the problem, if possible.

The bibliography at the end of this chapter lists several comprehensive University of California publications about the fruits and nuts discussed in this chapter. These publications include color photographs of deficiency symptoms and extensive discussions about fertilization practices. While many of these publications are written for commercial growers, the fertilization principles, photographs, and issues discussed are valuable for the home gardener as well. To properly identify a specific plant nutrient deficiency, UC farm advisors use both visual symptoms and laboratory analysis of tissue samples from the tree in question.

Fertilization in the Prebearing Years. In the prebearing years, fruit and nut trees should be fertilized to encourage maximum early growth. Neither commercial fertilizer nor manure should be put in the planting hole when planting temperate fruit and nut trees because either may burn the roots. Zinc and nitrogen deficiency are fairly common in the early growing years. For most soils, fertilizer is needed during the first growing season, but the fertilizer should not be applied until early summer, when there is 6 to 8 inches (15 to 20 cm) of new growth. Then apply about 2 ounces (56 g) of a nitrogen-containing fertilizer such as ammonium sulfate (21-0-0) or 16-16-16, or 1 ounce (28 g) of urea (46-0-0), or 2 pounds (0.9 kg) of compost once a month until leaf fall. To add zinc, apply 1 to 2 ounces (28 to 56 g) of zinc sulfate per tree to the soil once per year. Either scatter the fertilizer on the soil under the tree, keeping it at least 1 foot (30 cm) from the trunk, and then water it in, or place it directly under drip emitters if drip irrigation is used. If nitrogen

fertilizers lie on the soil surface without being watered into the soil, some of the nitrogen value can be lost into the air by volitalization. The same is true for compost, but to a lesser degree because it releases its nutrients more slowly.

The second year, apply approximately twice the first-year rate. In subsequent years the rate should increase proportionately with the size of the trees. Keep the trees well fertilized, especially with nitrogen, so that they grow rapidly to fill their allotted space. Once the trees enter the flowering and bearing years, the fertilizer rates should be reduced (see below).

Fertilization of Mature, Bearing Trees. Nitrogen status can have a profound effect on the vigor of fruit and nut trees. It is one of the ways to manage shoot growth and influence fruit set and bearing. Lower nitrogen levels lead to less vigor and shorter shoot growth, which may be perfect for apples or pears but not enough for peaches or walnuts. Limiting nitrogen often enhances fruit set, improves fruit color, and advances the fruit maturity date. It also reduces shoot growth, which leads to better light penetration and less need for pruning, and may also help limit the size of overgrown trees. Fully bearing, average-size mature trees in the home orchard should be fertilized at the rates and times stated in table 17.6.

Nitrogen (N). Nitrogen deficiency appears as a general light-green color or yellowing of the leaves; in peaches and nectarines, the leaves also appear reddish on the margins. Trees with very low nitrogen have stunted growth, poor fruit set, and smaller fruit size than trees with higher levels of nitrogen.

There is no "blanket" rate of nitrogen fertilization recommended for all tree types listed in table 17.6; the rates vary from 1 to 2 pounds (0.45 to 0.9 kg) of *actual* nitrogen per tree per year (N/tree/year), depending on the tree type. Often, the nitrogen fertilizer program recommended for mature trees is divided into two applications, the first in the spring just prior to bud break and the second in late summer while trees can actively take it up. To determine how to calculate the amount of a given fertilizer product needed to deliver the recommended rates, see the discussion of fertilizers in chapter 3.

When selecting a fertilizer, take into consideration extremes in soil pH. Soils with low acidity (high pH, above 7.5) should be fertilized with a fertilizer that will gradually reduce the soil pH, such as ammonium sulfate, ammonium nitrate, or urea. For soils with high acidity (low pH, below 5.5), use a neutral fertilizer such as calcium nitrate. Check the list of ingredients on fertilizer bags for the original source of the form of nitrogen. The source of the nitrogen makes very little difference to the tree. Most plants take up nitrogen primarily in the form of nitrate (NO_3), and some take it up in the form of ammonium (NH_4). The ammonium forms of fertilizers are gradually broken down into nitrate in the soil. Even organic fertilizers made up of nitrogen-containing proteins and amino acids eventually break down into the nitrate form for plant uptake.

When considering how much nitrogen to use, more is not necessarily better. Excessive nitrogen fertilization overinvigorates vegetative growth on bearing trees, which reduces light penetration into the canopy and results in reduced flower bud formation and reduced fruit yield. Provide enough nitrogen to maintain healthy nutritional status, but to not oversupply nitrogen. Excess application is a waste that may stimulate weed growth and pollute surface water and groundwater resources.

Phosphorous (P). Phosphorous deficiency in fruit or nut trees in California has never been documented. There is apparently enough phosphorous in the soil, and it is readily available to the trees. In some cases where there has been land excavation or very poor soils, a preplant application of phosphorous in the soil might be necessary, and phosphorous could also be applied in a complete fertilizer on a regular basis. In most cases, however, applying phosphorous is a waste of money and resources.

Potassium (K). Potassium deficiencies are sometimes found in peach, plum, nectarine, and kiwifruit in the San Joaquin and Sacramento Valleys, and elsewhere on sandy soils. When potassium is deficient, leaves turn pale greenish-yellow and tend to curl inward (boating) and burn along the margins and tips. Poor fruit size is commonly associated with low potassium. Because potassium is required in large amounts by fruit and nut trees, deficiency symptoms may be induced when there are other problems in the root zone, such as root diseases, drought, or excess water. If potassium deficiency does occur, one treatment usually corrects the problem for several years. A fall application of potassium sulfate at a rate of 5 to 10 pounds (2.2 to 4.5 kg) per tree in sandy soils and 15 pounds (6.8 kg) per tree in finer-textured soils should be sufficient to correct deficiency symptoms for 3 to 5 years. Compost contains potassium and if used on a regular basis should prevent any deficiency except in very sandy soils.

Magnesium (Mg). Magnesium deficiency appears as marginal chlorosis on the leaves in an inverted V-shaped pattern. It mostly affects basal leaves of the shoot; terminal leaves are not affected. It usually occurs in soils with very high potassium and with young trees. To correct this problem the trees can be sprayed or ground-treated with small quantities of Epsom salt (magnesium sulfate).

Zinc (Zn). Zinc deficiency is the second-most-common nutrient deficiency in tree crops in California. Zinc deficiency causes "mottleleaf"—small terminal leaves with yellow mottling between the large leaf veins. Leaves near the growing tips are small, narrow, and bunched together. In the spring, shoots take on a yellowish cast and mottleleaf is quite evident. Dieback of twigs may occur in severe zinc deficiency. Zinc-deficient trees may have poor and/or delayed bloom and small fruit of low quality.

Foliar sprays and chelated formulations are available to combat zinc deficiency. Application timing depends on the fruit or nut tree in question. An early- to mid-November application of zinc sulfate is recommended for almond, apple, apricot, cherry, pear, plum, and prune. Leaf burn and defoliation may occur as a result of this spray, but it is not detrimental at this time of year. The dormant zinc spray should not be made at the same time as a dormant oil spray. Use 1 to 2 ounces (28 to 56 g) of zinc sulfate (36% metallic Zn) in 1 gallon (3.8 l) of water. To correct for zinc deficiency in peach and nectarine in the home orchard, an application in April of ⅔ ounce basic zinc sulfate (52% metallic Zn) is recommended; on walnut, a spring application is recommended. During the growing season, basic (neutral) zinc, or chelated zinc, sprays can be applied without leaf burn. Liberal applications of compost applied to the soil surface under the trees will eventually correct the problem, but depending of the severity of the deficiency, this may take several years. Fertilizers high in phosphorous such as poultry manure bind zinc and render it less available to the tree.

Iron (Fe). Iron-deficient leaves are quite striking. Bleached yellow to white leaves with green veins are the symptoms most often seen. Leaf size is usually normal. The fruit tend to ripen early and the fruit quality is normal. If the tree is severely deficient, causing shoot dieback and poor growth, production and fruit quality are reduced. Iron deficiency is usually caused by alkaline soil (high pH, above 8.0) or very wet soils. Iron deficiency, or chlorosis, can be caused by overwatering: the lack of oxygen that results from the excess water inhibits root function and iron absorption by plants. Iron chlorosis may also be caused by high lime content in the soil (lime-induced chlorosis).

Adding only iron to soil seldom corrects iron deficiency symptoms. Correcting or adjusting the soil pH is the most important thing to do. This is best accomplished by adding sulfur to the soil around the tree. In most cases only a small portion of the soil profile under the tree needs to be modified in order to get a response in the tree. Usually, filling a few 2-inch-diameter (5-cm) holes or a narrow trench around the tree with soil sulfur is effective.

In some cases, symptoms of iron deficiency can be corrected by adjustments in irrigation. Several foliar sprays containing iron may be used to partially combat iron chlorosis. Wetting agents should be added to the spray to promote good coverage, and several sprays of dilute solution may be preferable to one spray at full concentration. If deficiency symptoms occur on pears, add ½ pound (227 g) of iron chelate to the soil during nitrogen fertilization in the spring. While the chelated iron may correct many cases of leaf yellowing related to iron deficiency, chelated iron is very acidic and should be used with caution because it can cause leaf burn. Soil-applied iron slurries are longer-lasting than foliar chelate sprays.

Boron (B). Excess boron can be a problem on the western side of the San Joaquin Valley and in isolated geothermal areas. Peach and nectarine, two of the most sensitive crops to boron toxicity, exhibit small necrotic spots on the underside of the midrib; cankers along the midrib, on petioles, and on young twigs; leaf yellowing, defoliation, twig dieback, and gumming in severe cases; and distorted fruit. This condition is corrected by leaching the boron out of the root zone. If you suspect boron toxicity, test the irrigation water; the boron level in it should not be above 2 to 5 ppm. Applying

additional nitrogen fertilizer as calcium nitrate may help alleviate boron toxicity.

Boron deficiency can occur in some soils in California and may be related to low boron levels in water. Deficiency symptoms include shoot tip dieback, blossom blast, and misshapen fruit. Boron deficiency is corrected by a single application of ¼ to ½ pound (114 to 227 g) boric acid (H_3BO_3) or borax ($Na_2B_4O_7 \cdot 10H_2O$) per tree.

Manganese (Mn). Deficiency of manganese appears as interveinal chlorosis with a herringbone pattern affecting only basal leaves; terminal leaves are not affected. It is usually associated with high-pH soils. Reducing soil pH and foliar treatments with chelated manganese corrects this problem for several seasons.

Weed Control

Weeds can have a dramatic effect on tree growth by competing for soil moisture, physical space, and nutrients, and some weeds may have an antagonistic or allelopathic effect on trees. Experiments comparing various weed control methods have demonstrated that the growth of young trees can be reduced by one-third to one-half in the first few years if weeds are allowed to compete with trees.

One of the best ways to maintain a weed-free area under home orchard trees is with an organic mulch. The mulch keeps the soil moist and reduces evaporation, and as it breaks down, it releases nutrients to the tree. Mulch must be at least 3 inches (7.5 cm) deep to adequately control weeds and must be reapplied periodically to maintain that depth. Other alternatives to organic mulches, such as heavy-duty weed cloth, eliminate the need for frequent reapplication. The best weed cloth blocks all the light, controls weed growth, allows water to pass through, and lasts 5 to 10 years. Another advantage is that it can be easily cleaned of fallen leaves and fruit to prevent the spread of diseases. Mechanical cultivation with a tiller or hand hoe also suppresses most weeds; the important thing is to keep the area free of weeds from the beginning of growth in the spring until leaf fall.

In the dormant period, it is not critical to maintain a weed-free area under the trees: cover crops or ornamentals can be grown to improve the soil or for the sake of appearance. Mature trees can tolerate more weeds, turf, or cover crops growing within their dripline since they already have an established root system, are full sized, and don't need to grow as much. Do not allow lawns to grow within 2 feet (0.6 m) of the tree trunk. This prevents crown rot and trunk damage from mowing or edging tools, especially weed trimmers, which often girdle the trunk.

Harvesting and Storage

Optimal Harvesting Dates

Determining the optimal harvesting date for fruit and nut crops is as much an art as a science. Expect the harvesting date to vary a little from year to year because the maturation and ripening processes in temperate fruits and nuts depend on many factors. The exact number of days from full bloom to maturity cannot be fixed because tree vigor, age, water stress, heat unit accumulation, and heat stress vary each year due to the weather, cultural practices, and other factors in the environment.

Fruits. Horticulturists distinguish between the terms *mature* and *ripe*. Ripe fruits are ready to eat. Mature fruits have attained a physiological developmental stage such that they are able to ripen after harvest. The maturation process involves a number of physical, physiological, and biochemical changes, such as a decrease in skin chlorophyll; an increase in carotenes, anthocyanins, and xanthophyll pigments; a decrease in organic acid content; an increase in sugars, soluble solids, and soluble pectins; and changes in respiratory activity.

The best criterion for determining fruit maturity and ripeness is taste. In addition, several other criteria can be used to evaluate the maturity of the fruit crop and help decide when to harvest: number of days from full bloom, flesh firmness (pressure test), skin color and changes in skin color, flesh color, seed color, and starch or sugar content testing. The starch test and sugar tests (soluble solids or brix) are used commercially on apples to determine whether the fruit meets minimum harvest standards. One primary reason for growing fruit trees at home is to let fruits ripen fully, beyond the minimum of maturity and ripeness.

Whether fruits should be harvested when fully ripe or physiologically mature often depends on the intended usage—fresh eating, canning, freezing, or drying. In the home orchard, fruits intended to be eaten right away are harvested when they are fully ripe. Pears, winter apples, fresh plums, apricots, and peaches can also be harvested when they are "firm mature" (physiologically mature) but unripe and then allowed to ripen off the tree for fresh eating later. Prunes used for drying should be harvested more mature than those used for canning. European pears are usually harvested when they are green and firm, stored at least 1 week at cold temperatures (32°F or 0°C) and then transferred to room temperature and 85 percent relative humidity to ripen.

Nuts. Nuts should be harvested when they are ripe. Hazelnut (filbert) maturity occurs when filberts are shed from the husk in September, October, or November. When they drop, they are fully mature, but they must be "cured" and dried to 8 to 10 percent moisture content. (Since it is difficult to test nuts for moisture content, taste them and compare them to commercially dried nuts.) Walnuts are mature 1 to 4 weeks before hull cracking (dehiscence). They can be dried to 5 percent moisture (on a kernel basis) immediately after harvest. Almonds are mature and ready for harvest when they are loose enough to be knocked from the tree and hulled. Mature pecans do not fall from the tree all at once; they reach maturity when the husks open from around the nuts. Pistachios reach maturity when their skin changes from translucent to opaque and the hull shrivels and separates easily from the shell. Chestnuts mature over a period of weeks from September into November, depending on the climate. When mature, they fall easily from the tree and separate easily from the burr. Chestnuts are not like other nuts; for fresh eating, they should be stored like apples at 32°F (0°C) and high relative humidity. They can also be peeled and dried for later rehydration or grinding into chestnut flour.

Harvesting Technique

Harvest most fruits by twisting and lifting the fruit up, not by pulling straight down from the spur or branch. Be careful to minimize bruising and injury. Place fruits gently in your harvesting container; do not just drop them in. Softer fruits require careful handling to avoid bruises, and firmer fruits require careful handling to avoid skin punctures. Prevention of bruises and skin damage greatly increases the storage life of fruits.

Pests, Diseases, and Environmental Stresses

A number of pests, diseases, and environmental stresses attack temperate tree fruit and nut crops in California. Certain crops and varieties are more susceptible to pests and diseases, but healthy trees that are irrigated and fertilized properly and that receive the kinds of preventive care described in table 17.6 should have little pest damage. If the home gardener is willing to overlook an occasional chewed leaf or fruit blemish and instead focus on the more serious enemies that compromise the overall health of the trees, the pest control program will be efficient and rewarding.

Table 17.7 describes some of the more common insect and mite pests, diseases, and environmental stresses that attack tree fruit and nut crops, what the symptoms look like, the probable causal agent, which parts of the plant are attacked, and what can be done to control the problem. Two important University of California publications on this subject are *Pests of the Garden and Small Farm* (Flint 1998), which has many pages of easy-to-use information and excellent color photographs of pests, diseases, and environmental stresses, and *Diseases of Temperate Zone Tree Fruit and Nut Crops* (Ogawa and English 1991), a more technical publication that presents a thorough coverage of the biotic and abiotic diseases of these crops. Table 17.7 was adapted from these two UC publications and from other UC references listed in the bibliography at the end of the chapter. Consult the bibliography for further information on pest problems in temperate tree fruits and nuts.

Since this chapter discusses numerous crops attacked by many of the same pests and diseases, table 17.7 is organized so that each pest or disease is presented once with useful information about the temperate tree fruit and nut crops attacked. Thus, unlike other tables in this chapter that are structured with separate categories for the pome fruits, stone fruits, nuts, vines, and miscellaneous temperate fruits, this table is organized by the type of pest (fungi, bacteria, and nematodes) because many pests and diseases have wide host ranges. Some pests and diseases attack practically all deciduous tree fruit and nut crops, whereas, others, as noted in the table, have a limited host range or can be much more damaging to the pome fruits than the stone fruits, for example. Sometimes, the name of the disease changes depending on the crop or plant part attacked. The "Comments" section of table 17.7 notes in boldface type which crops are hosts for each pest or disease described.

For comprehensive information about postharvest diseases or other disease information organized by specific crop or crop group (pome fruits, stone fruits, nut crops, vines), refer to *Diseases of Temperate Zone Tree Fruit and Nut Crops* (Ogawa and English 1991) Postharvest and storage diseases (Alternaria rots, Botrytis and other molds, *Aspergillus* and mycotoxins, etc.) are not covered in table 17.7, which focuses on the preharvest enemies of your home fruit and nut trees.

Temperate tree fruit and nut crops are susceptible to attack from many fungal, viral, and bacterial pathogens. However, pest and disease problems should be few if trees are healthy when purchased and have tolerant rootstocks (see table 17.4), and if preventive measures are taken to reduce or eliminate conditions favoring these organisms. The damage potential of many temperate tree fruit and nut crop diseases and pests depends on the rootstock and scion combination, soil conditions, site selection, and fertilizer and water management practices.

Fungi that infect the trunk and roots, especially feeder roots that have critical roles in water and nutrient uptake, are important in California. Due to the state's semiarid climate, fungi that attack fruits are less damaging here than in other regions where temperate tree fruits and nuts are grown. Many diseases are described according to the plant part(s) they damage. For example, *Phytophthora* fungi cause a number of diseases with different names depending on the part of the tree affected—roots (Phytophthora root rot), trunk (crown rot or collar rot), or fruit (brown rot of citrus).

In addition to Phytophthora root rot, one other root disease commonly affects temperate fruit tree roots in California: oak root fungus (Armillaria root rot), which attacks many crops, including almond, apple, apricot, pear, plum, prune, and walnut. *Phytophthora* destroys feeder roots and no mycelia are visible; *Armillaria* also moves into the wood (xylem) of the root and crown, and fan-shaped mycelia are visible (see table 17.7).

Prevention is the most important and economical method of controlling diseases. Preventive measures can include use of tolerant rootstocks (see table 17.4), preplant soil preparation, good drainage, judicious irrigation management and sanitation, and adequate fertilization. Reputable nurserymen and your local UC Cooperative Extension farm advisor are familiar with the most important diseases in your area and know which scion/rootstock combinations are most tolerant and vigorous.

Environmental stresses such as nutrient deficiencies or adverse weather and soil conditions (excessive or too little irrigation water, poor drainage) may cause symptoms described as *abiotic disorders* (see chapter 6, "Plant Pathology"). Symptoms associated with several environmental stresses and physiological disorders and a few comments on managing them are included in table 17.7.

Control Measures

Whenever possible, combat pests with mechanical control methods (remove diseased limbs, clean up debris, dislodge pests with strong blasts of water or with soap or oil sprays) and biological control methods (release natural enemies). Use chemical pesticides as a last resort. Unlike commercial growers, home gardeners are not faced with the same economic demands for fruit appearance, so they can tolerate more damage. Chemical controls kill the target pests but may also kill the biological enemies naturally present or introduced into the garden. See chapter 10, "Controlling Garden Pests Safely," to obtain additional information on these subjects. For the most recent pesticide recommendations, consult UC publications listed in the bibliography and your UC Cooperative Extension county office.

Mechanical Control of Insect and Mite Pests

Mechanical methods are nonpolluting, nonpersistent pest control techniques that are effective against a number of insect and mite pests. For example, strong blasts of water usually dislodge aphids, and hand-picking snails and slugs is effective in small gardens. Sanitation, the removal of diseased or insect-infested leaves and fruit, is an excellent mechanical means of reducing pest problems.

Organic Materials and Biological Agents

The definition of organic materials was developed by various certification groups and officially adopted by the state and federal governments. "Organic" materials are usually natural products that have not been significantly modified by people. They include various mineral products (copper and sulfur for disease control) and soaps and oil sprays (mostly for control of soft-bodied insects and mites). To avoid damage to your trees, use soaps, oils, and sulfur sprays only when the trees have been well irrigated and when the temperature is cooler than 90°F (32°C).

Soaps are moderately effective on contact against soft-bodied insects and mites. They penetrate pest cell membranes and kill without harming trees or fruit. Apply soaps in the early morning or late afternoon. Insecticidal soaps can be purchased or made at home by using 2 tablespoons of liquid dishwashing soap per gallon (4 ml/l) of water, but be aware that some soaps are phytotoxic. Repeated applications may be necessary; be willing to accept some injury to trees or fruit.

Horticultural oils smother and kill soft-bodied insects and mites. "Summer" oils list the words *supreme*, *superior*, or *narrow-range* on the label. Horticultural oils were originally applied to deciduous plants during the dormant season (dormant oil), and even though they now may list application rates for use during the growing season, they are formulated differently from true summer oils. Do not apply oil mixed with sulfur within 2 weeks of an application of sulfur onto nondormant trees. Do not apply oil to dry trees; wait for a good rain or irrigate dry soil prior to application.

Sulfur is a very effective natural mineral that controls eriophyid mites, powdery mildew, apple and pear scab, and peach leaf curl. Unfortunately it kills some beneficials. It comes in several forms: dust, wettable powder, micronized wettable powder, and mixed with lime in a liquid form called lime sulfur. Do not apply a mixture of oil and sulfur onto green leaves, blossoms, or fruit. Lime sulfur and oil can be applied to dormant trees. Sulfur is an irritant; wear protective clothing during application and protect the skin and eyes.

Copper is another naturally occurring mineral that is extensively used in organic

Table 17.7

PROBLEM DIAGNOSIS IN TEMPERATE TREE FRUIT AND NUT CROPS

What the problem looks like	Probable cause

SELECTED CATERPILLARS

Small hole in the fruit skin with brown granular material that looks like sawdust coming out. At the core, fruit turns brown and has a worm in it. Fruit may drop off prematurely.	codling moth (*Cydia pomonella*)

Comments

White to pink caterpillars with a mottled brown head; not too distinctive. The most serious caterpillar pest of apples, pears, and walnuts. Larvae penetrate fruit and bore into the core or cause more shallow blemishes on the fruit surface. One of the few caterpillars found inside apples and pears. Eggs, which are difficult to find in the field, are laid on fruit or nearby leaves. Codling moth is very difficult to control organically in the home garden. Practice good sanitation. Clean up fallen fruit in spring daily and spray the trees with summer oil or conventional insecticide timed when symptoms first appear. Spray 2–3 times in the growing season. See *Pests of the Garden and Small Farm* (Flint 1998), UC IPM Pest Note 13, *Codling Moth*, and UC IPM publications on apples and pears listed in the bibliography. Codling moth is a less serious pest on plums and other stone fruit than on apples and pears. The caterpillars occasionally bore into stone fruits all the way to the pit.

Green walnuts drop off or dry up on tree. Little webbing in nut. Older nuts are worm-infested. Hull with masses of brown fecal material protruding from entry holes. Most caterpillars leave nuts before harvest.	codling moth (*Cydia pomonella*)

Comments

White to pink caterpillars with a mottled brown head; not too distinctive. The most serious caterpillar pest of walnuts. Larvae feed on nut kernels. Early-season varieties are most susceptible, with damaged nuts dropping off trees. Later in the season, damaged nuts remain on trees but kernels are inedible. One of few caterpillars found inside walnuts. Eggs are laid on nuts or nearby leaves. Practice good sanitation. Clean up fallen nuts in spring daily for maximum effectiveness. See *Pests of the Garden and Small Farm* (Flint 1998) and *Integrated Pest Management for Walnuts* (Flint and Kobbe 1993) for additional control methods.

Leaves eaten in spring. Small gouges in newly set or young fruit. Damaged areas later scab over. Rarely attacks older fruit.	western tussock moth (*Orgyia vetusta*)

Comments

Long hairs make the caterpillar easy to identify. Young larvae are black with long bristles. Older larvae have numerous red and yellow spots, four white tufts of hair, and many more groups of bristles. Look for light brown pupal cases in the dormant season. This caterpillar attacks apples, cherries, plums, prunes, and walnuts. It can defoliate deciduous fruit and nut trees in spring or take bites out of young fruit. Check for eggs in winter and larvae in spring. Most damage occurs in mid-March and mid-May. Removing egg masses and newly hatched caterpillars should provide sufficient control in backyard trees. Oil spray in winter kills egg masses on deciduous trees. Bt is an effective control on most crops.

New leaves have holes and are webbed and rolled together. Caterpillars also feed on buds and developing fruit, often rolling and webbing fruit and leaves together. Deeply gouged young fruit may fall to the ground. Less severely damaged fruit reach maturity badly misshapen or with deep bronze-colored scars and rough surfaces. All leafrollers wriggle and drop on a spun thread when disturbed.	fruittree leafroller (*Archips argyrospilus*) omnivorous leafroller (*Platynota stultana*) green fruitworms (various spp.) orange tortrix (*Argyrotaenia citrana*)

Comments

Attack apples, pears, almonds, and other stone fruits. Fruittree leafroller caterpillars are green with a shiny black head feeds on young leaves, buds, and developing fruit, webbing leaves and fruit together. Damage to fruit may expose it to decay organisms. Most damage occurs in spring and early summer. One generation per year. Hand-pick damaged tissue and destroy. Omnivorous leafroller attacks kiwi and most fruit trees. Has many generations per year. Caterpillars are so translucent their main blood vessel is visible down their backs. General sanitation and natural parasites are effective controls. Green fruitworms include at least 10 species of caterpillars. They attack apples, pears, apricots, cherries, plums, and prunes. One generation per year. Damage occurs in spring on very young fruit. Bt is a control. Orange tortrix attacks stone fruits, kiwifruit, and apples mostly in coastal areas and interior valleys of coastal areas. It is greenish orange, feeds in web; when disturbed, it hisses and drops on a silken thread. Prefers a tree's top half to the bottom half. Control can be achieved by hand picking on small trees or by applying Bt in an early spring spray. Thinning apples to 1–2 fruit per cluster reduces damage. *Pests of the Garden and Small Farm* (Flint 1998) has excellent photographs of leafroller pests and more detailed information.

What the problem looks like	Probable cause
Caterpillars enter nuts after hulls or husks split, feed directly on nutmeats, and contaminate nuts with large quantities of excrement and webbing. Large quantities of webbing and excrement in the nut are tell-tale signs that identify this pest as the causal agent.	navel orangeworm (*Amyelois transitella*)

Comments

Milky white to pink worm with reddish-brown head. Pair of crescent-shaped marks on 2nd segment behind head distinguishes it from codling moth, oriental fruit moth, and other larvae found in nuts. Attacks almonds, pistachios, and walnuts. In spring, eggs are laid singly on damaged or mummy nuts that remained on trees after harvest and through the winter. Later generations lay eggs on hulls of newly forming or ripening nuts. In winter, check trees for unharvested mummy nuts. Remove and destroy them by Feb 1. Crack open mummy nuts to gauge the extent of infestation. Insecticide sprays should be unnecessary if sanitation is practiced and nuts are harvested as soon as hullsplit occurs in almonds and as early as possible in walnuts. Store nuts in sealed containers as soon as they are dry. Parasitic wasps and nematodes that attack navel orangeworms have been used to control this pest.

What the problem looks like	Probable cause
Caterpillars bore into the growing shoots of twigs and ripening fruit or nuts. Shoots and leaves wilt and die back 1 to several inches from the growing tips of twigs in spring. Small worm with dark brown bands may be found inside each affected shoot. Ripening fleshy fruits (peaches, nectarines) infested with worms near stem end, apricot fruit near seams. Almond kernels have superficial scarring, no webbing. More superficial feeding on green and ripening fruit than oriental fruit moth.	peach twig borer (*Anarsia lineatella*)

Comments

Black head, chocolate-colored body with white segments in between, giving a banded appearance. Max. length is about ½ inch (12.5 mm). Attacks almond, apricot, nectarine, peach, plum, and prune. Monitor by looking for overwintering "cells" in the fall, winter, and early spring. The "cells" look like minute, chimney-like reddish piles of excrement and sawdust on the bark surface of 1- to 4-year-old wood. During the growing season, check trees for wilting or wormy shoot tips and wormy fruit. Pheromone traps may be used to monitor adult males. Natural enemies, although there are many, do not provide reliable control. The most reliable control is a dormant oil and organophosphate insecticide spray applied in winter to kill overwintering caterpillars on tree branches. Good coverage will reduce populations more than 95%. Dormant oil alone will not kill peach twig borer. Once fruit and twigs are infested in the spring, control is much more difficult. Sprays during the growing season must be applied to control hatching larvae before they enter twigs or fruit.

What the problem looks like	Probable cause
Damage to twigs similar to peach twig borer, but caterpillars bore right into the center to feed around the pit unlike peach twig borer, which feeds superficially. No webbing, which distinguishes it from the navel orangeworm in almonds.	oriental fruit moth (*Grapholita molesta*)

Comments

White or pink with brown head; ⅝ inch (16 mm) long. Attacks almond, apricot, nectarine, peach, plum, and prune. Tiny disk-shaped eggs are laid on leaves, twigs, and fruit. Look for caterpillars in wilted shoots and fruits. Prefers to feed in tops of trees. Sample fruits in tree tops to monitor for presence. Dormant oil sprays do not control this pest nor do naturally occurring biological controls.

APHIDS AND ASSOCIATED SOOTY MOLD FUNGI

What the problem looks like	Probable cause
Black film on leaf surfaces.	sooty mold fungus

Comments

Most active in cool, moist conditions. This fungus feeds on honeydew excreted by aphids, mealybugs, scale insects, and whiteflies. Sooty mold should be washed off leaves because it can reduce photosynthesis and tree productivity if prolonged. Wash off fruit. Cosmetically unappealing, but usually no serious harm. Apply control measures for the causal pest and sooty mold will disappear.

What the problem looks like	Probable cause
Distorted, curled leaves, stunting of shoots, sticky honeydew exudates on leaves, which leads to growth of sooty mold fungus. Ants are often associated with aphids on tree crops. If you see ants climbing the tree trunks, check for aphids on the limbs and leaves above.	aphids

Table 17.7 cont.

What the problem looks like	Probable cause

Comments

Small, soft-bodied insects. Dozens of species in California. Green, yellow, brown, red, or black, depending on species and food source. Pair of protruding cornicles (exhaust pipes) at back end of body. Aphids attack many fruit and nut trees in California. Usually feed in dense groups on stems or leaves. Many generations per year. Can produce asexually without mating or laying eggs. Many species can develop from newborn nymph to reproducing adult in less than 2 wk. Each adult can produce up to 100 offspring per wk, so populations can increase rapidly if not controlled. Small numbers of aphids do not cause much damage and can be tolerated. Check garden and orchard for aphids twice weekly when plants are growing rapidly. Curled, distorted leaves protect aphids from natural enemies or pesticides. Check undersides of leaves where aphids prefer. Control needed only for heavy infestation on young trees. Dislodge with jet streams of water or use soap or oil sprays. Oil treatments on dormant trees kill overwintering aphid eggs if applied as eggs begin to hatch in early spring. Oil treatments are effective against woolly apple aphid, green apple aphid, rosy apple aphid, mealy plum aphid, and black cherry aphid. Insects suck sap from tender, new growth. Honeydew provides a medium for growth of sooty mold fungus.

White, cottony masses on woody parts of trees, often near pruning wounds. Warty growths on limbs and roots. Clear, sticky honeydew and black sooty mold on foliage and fruit. Tree declines if root infestation heavy for many years.	woolly apple aphid

Comments

Reddish insect <1/8 inch (3 mm) long covered with white, cottony material. Very sluggish movements. Aphids spend winter on roots and branches of apple tree. Little visible cottony material. In summer and fall, successive generations migrate from roots to branches and vice versa. Bands of sticky substances around trunks and branches can help prevent migration. Dormant oil sprays kill colonies on branches. Not easily washed off with soapy water solution. No chemical control for root colonies. Tiny parasitic wasps are important natural control agents. Aphids can become numerous when these wasps are killed by insecticides.

New leaves severely distorted and curled; shoots get twisted. Large amounts of clear, sticky honeydew drip onto foliage and fruit. Many young apples become puckered and fail to grow. Clusters of small, sedentary purplish insects in curled leaves and on fruit stems.	rosy apple aphid

Comments

Pear-shaped insect <1/8 inch (3 mm) long with 2 tiny "pipes" protruding from back end. Young are dark green. Mature are reddish to purplish and covered with powdery bloom. Winged are brownish green. Spring pest only. Overwinters as egg on bark of apple tree. Young appear with first new leaves. Migrates to plantain and ribgrass in June. New growth will cover up damage by summer. Dormant oil kills overwintering eggs. See *Pests of the Garden and Small Farm* (Flint 1998) for other control measures and UC IPM Pest Note 5, *Aphid Control*.

New growth stunted; large amounts of clear sticky honeydew and black sooty mold on foliage and fruit. Colonies of small, sedentary yellowish-green insects on new shoots.	green apple aphid

Comments

Pear-shaped insect <1/8 inch long with 2 tiny "pipes" protruding from back end. Young are dark green. Mature are bright yellowish green. Winged are yellowish brown. On apple all year. Most serious where climate remains cool and moist. Overwinters as egg on bark of tree. Young aphids appear at bud burst. Dormant oil sprays kill overwintering eggs. However, infestations can still be severe due to movements of winged aphids from other trees. Shoot damage is primarily a concern on young trees. See *Pests of the Garden and Small Farm* (Flint 1998) for other control measures.

In spring, foliage infested with pale green, slow-moving insects that produce white, mealy substance. Leaves, fruit covered with clear sticky honeydew that turns black because of sooty mold fungus growth. Fruit may split.	mealy plum aphid

Comments

Pear-shaped insect <1/8 inch long with 2 tiny "pipes" protruding from back end. Pale green. Attacks apricots, plums, and prunes. Overwinters as egg on tree. Leaves tree for weeds in July; returns in early winter to lay eggs. Dormant oil spray kills overwintering eggs. Often, only one or two limbs affected. Control measures seldom necessary. New growth will cover up damage by summer. Japanese hybrid plums unaffected.

What the problem looks like	Probable cause

In spring, leaves severely curled by clusters of small, sedentary, shiny black insects. **black cherry aphid**

Comments

Pear-shaped insect <$1/8$ inch (3 mm) long with 2 tiny "pipes" protruding from back end. Black, shiny. Some winged, others wingless. Attacks cherries. Overwinters as egg on bark of cherry tree. Leaves tree for weeds in midsummer; returns in autumn to lay eggs. Dormant oil spray reduces spring population. Spring pest only. New growth will cover damage by summer. See *Pests of the Garden and Small Farm* (Flint 1998) for other control measures.

Leaves become curled, covered with tiny, sedentary greenish insects. **green peach aphid**

Comments

Green, pear-shaped aphid. Attacks peaches and nectarines. Chemical control usually not necessary.

Leaves distorted, new foliage stunted. Maturing fruit looks russeted. Clusters of sedentary, greenish insects on new shoots. **various aphids**

Comments

Attack pears. Minor problem in home orchards. Distorted leaves soon covered up by normal foliage.

Leaves, nuts covered with clear, sticky honeydew. Turns black due to sooty mold growth. Leaf drop may occur. Nuts become sunburned. Size, quality of nuts reduced. Tiny, yellow insects along veins on leaf undersides. **walnut aphid**

Comments

Tiny insect, $1/16$ inch (1.5mm) long, oval to pear-shaped. May have two dark bands across back in fall. Moves sluggishly. Attacks walnuts. Many generations per year. Overwinters as egg in rough places on twigs. Not much of a problem because an introduced parasitic wasp usually controls this pest. See *Pests of the Garden and Small Farm* (Flint 1998).

SELECTED BORING INSECTS THAT DAMAGE TRUNKS AND MAJOR LIMBS

Larvae bore in the crown area of many fruit tree species. Small piles of reddish-brown frass visible at base of tree trunk. Tree looks weak. **peachtree borer (*Synanthedon exitiosa*)**

Comments

Larvae are light brown or pink with darker head. Attacks almond, apricot, nectarine, peach, plum, prune (stone fruits). Occurs primarily in the Santa Clara Valley and Contra Costa County. Eggs are laid on on bark at the base of tree trunks in summer. Hatching larvae tunnel into the tree at or below ground level. Larvae feed in the crown area and burrow into tree, leave reddish-brown frass at based of tree trunk. Pupate in spring near their burrows or in soil. Adult moths emerge about a month later. One generation per year. Monitor your trees in the fall for frass and sap exuding from tunnels. Use good sanitations methods. Home gardeners can use the instructions in *Pests of the Garden and Small Farm* (Flint 1998) and kill them with a small knife. Major problems are on newly planted trees or trees weakened by attack from other pests, poor cultural practices, or sunburn.

Larvae bore into aboveground areas on trunk previously injured by sunburn. Bark may die or girdle. No frass. Young larvae feed under bark in rapidly growing wood. May kill young tree. **pacific flathead borer (*Chrysobothris malis*)**

Comments

Light-colored larvae with distinctive flattened enlargement just behind the head. Attacks almond, apricot, nectarine, peach, plum, prune (stone fruits), apples, other pome fruits, and walnuts. Occurs throughout the state. Attacks aboveground portions of trunk previously damaged by sunburn or other causes. Larvae excavate tunnels below the bark; sap will seep out. No frass. Pupate in spring within trunk. Wrapping or painting the trunks of newly planted trees from 1 inch (2.5 cm) below the soil line to 24 inches (60 cm) above the ground with white indoor latex paint or whitewash protects the trunk from sunburn and borer invasion. Spraying for this insect is not recommended.

Sap leaking from many small holes on trunks or scaffolds. Tiny black beetles visible under bark. May girdle or kill young tree. **shothole borer (*Scolytus rugulosus*)**

Comments

Tiny black beetles, $1/10$ inch (2.5 mm) long. Attacks almond, other stone fruits, apples, and pears. A pest of trees already weakened by root diseases, insufficient irrigation, sunburned limbs, other borers. Females bore small holes, which look like shot holes, in the bark and lay eggs in a gallery 1 to 2 inches (2.5 to 5 cm) long running lengthwise down the cambium layer of the tree. Hatching larvae feed and

Table 17.7 cont.

What the problem looks like	Probable cause

excavate secondary galleries at right angles to the egg gallery. Two to three generations per year. Larvae spend the winter in their galleries beneath the bark. Prevent by keeping trees healthy with sufficient irrigation and fertilizer and use good sanitation and cultural practices. The presence of shothole borers usually indicates that there was serious plant stress. Prune out infested area and burn the wood before growing season starts. Spraying for this insect pest is not recommended.

SELECTED SCALE INSECTS

Armored scales: Water stress, yellow leaves. Twigs, limbs may die. Bark cracks, gums. Blemishes, halos on fruit. Trees may die. Soft scales: Reduced tree vigor but tree not commonly killed. Honeydew, sooty black mold, and ants. Ants are good indicator of soft scale infestation. Most soft scales infest leaves and twigs but do not attack fruit directly.	scale insects

Comments

Attack all types of fruit and nut trees and kiwifruit. Unusual-looking pest; many people do not recognize scales as insects. Adult females and many immature forms do not move and are hidden under a disklike waxy covering. Adult males have wings. Scales have long piercing mouthparts used to suck juices out of plants. May occur on twigs, leaves, branches, or fruit. Severe infestations can cause overall decline and death of trees. Most scales have many natural enemies that control them. Others are well controlled with oil sprays in the dormant season. Two groups of scales, armored scales and soft scales, are important fruit tree pests. Armored scales have a hard cover that is separate from their body and lose their legs a day or two after hatching from eggs. Soft scales have smooth or cottony covers attached to their bodies. Some soft scales retain their legs for life and can move around. Like aphids, soft scales excrete copious amounts of honeydew, attracting ants and causing growth of sooty mold fungus. Armored scales have many generations per year; soft scales, one generation per year. See UC IPM Pest Note 9, *Scales*.

See general comments above for armored scales. Twigs and branches heavily infested with this scale retain their leaves during winter and are easy to spot.	San Jose scale (*Quadraspidiotus perniciosus*)

Comments

Armored scale. Adult females are round, $^1/_{10}$ inch (2.5 mm) in diameter, with gray-brown to black cover. If cover is removed scale beneath is bright yellow. Attacks most deciduous fruit and nut trees. Specially refined horticultural oils called *supreme* or *superior-type* oils are effective against San Jose scale. When applied as a delayed dormant spray just before budswell, oil treatment can also kill a some of overwintering mite, aphid, or caterpillar eggs on woody portions of tree. Make treatments before budswell and when trees are not water-stressed. Apply right *after* a rain or foggy weather. Monitor by examining trees, especially during dormant season. Check prunings for scale infestation. Natural enemies provide some control; oils do not harm natural enemies. San Jose scale is encouraged by spraying conventional insecticides for control of other pests which in turn kills the natural enemies that usually control the scale.

See general comments above for armored scales and for San Jose scale.	walnut scale (*Quadraspidiotus juglansregiae*)

Comments

Armored scale. Adult females are yellow underneath cover. More indented than San Jose scale. Attacks walnuts. See comments for San Jose scale.

Not found on leaves or fruit. Feeds on bark, sometimes causing leaves to yellow and dry up. Usually only a few limbs affected at first.	oystershell scale (*Lepidosaphes ulmi*)

Comments

Armored scale. Resembles a mussel shell in shape. Attacks most deciduous fruit and nut trees, especially apples, pears, and walnuts. Survey trees regularly, examining bark below yellowing or dried up leaves. Prune out infested limbs. Sprays are effective in late May or early June when crawlers are present. Oils applied during the dormant season are not effective because susceptible stages are not present at that time.

What the problem looks like	Probable cause

Round, red-brown scales on fruit, leaves and twigs. Leaves may yellow and drop and twig dieback may occur. Damage most visible in late summer and early fall. Reduced tree vigor.

California red scale
(*Aonidiella aurantii*)

Comments
Armored scale. Adult males are tiny yellow-winged insects almost identical to adult male San Jose scales. Can be distinguished from yellow scale (*Aonidiella citrina*) under a microscope. Attacks olives. Natural enemies (parasitic wasps of *Aphytis* and *Encarsia* spp.) can provide good control in many parts of California. If needed, oil spray should be applied between July and Sep. See general comments for armored scales.

Fruit and leaves covered with honeydew, sooty mold, ants. Tree vigor reduced. Scales on leaves, twigs, rarely on fruit.

citricola scale
(*Coccus pseudomagnoliarum*)

Comments
Soft scale. Resembles brown soft scales except that immatures are mottled dark brown and matures are gray. Attacks walnut, pomegranate. One generation per year. Look for adults in spring and early summer on twigs. In summer and fall check undersides of leaves for immature scales. Natural enemies and oil sprays are effective controls. Keep ants out of trees because they protect scales from natural enemies. Citricola is more serious in the San Joaquin Valley than in Southern California. *Metaphycus* spp. parasitic wasps provide some control in Southern California. Late summer or fall is best time to control.

See general comments for soft scales.

European fruit lecanium
(*Parthenolecanium corni*)
calico scale
(*Eulecanium caerasorum*)

Comments
European fruit lecanium is also known as brown apricot scale. Domed shell is shiny brown, about $^3/_8$ inch (9.5 mm) in diameter with several ridges on the back. Attack most deciduous fruit and nut trees. Calico scale adult has mottled white/brown calico pattern. *Metaphycus* spp. parasites are effective control for both types. Dormant oils must be applied by mid-Jan.

See general comments for soft scales.

frosted scale
(*Parthenolecanium pruinosum*)

Comments
Attacks walnuts and pistachios. Frosted scale has a frosted, waxy coating in spring from early March to mid-April. Later, wax erodes and scale looks shiny dark brown. See comments for calico scale for control measures.

MEALYBUGS

Fruit and leaves covered with honeydew and sooty mold. Mealybugs feeding in dense colonies. Fruit drop can occur if mealybugs feed along a stem. (Pears: whitish, cottony masses in calyx end of fruit, at bases of twigs, and fruit clusters.)

mealybugs (*Pseudococcus, Planococcus* spp.)

Comments
Soft, oval, distinctly segmented insects covered with mealy white wax. Adults about $^1/_8$–$^1/_4$ inch (3–6.5 mm) long. Sluggish movements. Attacks apples, pears, and apricots. Overwinters in loose bark as nymphs or eggs. Adults have waxy protective coat. Natural enemies usually control. Eliminate ants because they feed on honeydew produced by mealybugs and protect them from natural enemies. Mealybug populations can decrease in summer due to their heat sensitivity. Control by hand-picking them, hosing them off with water, or applying soap or oil sprays. Mealybugs extract plant sap from stems, leaves, and shoots, reducing tree vigor.

Table 17.7 cont.

What the problem looks like	Probable cause

ANTS

| Ants feeding on twigs, bark, leaves, and honeydew excreted by other insect pests. Argentine worker ants travel in distinct trails. | Argentine ant (*Iridomyrmex humilis*) Southern fire ant (*Solenopsis xyloni*) |

Comments

Ants feed on honeydew excreted by soft scales, mealybugs, and aphids. Ants can interrupt biological control of these pests. Control ants by denying access to the canopy. Apply a band of sticky material to base of trunk that mechanically impedes ants. Prune the canopy up (above 30 inches or 0.75 m) off the ground so that ants can't get into the tree without climbing the trunk.

SNAILS

| Holes in leaves and fruit; slimy trails. | brown garden snail (*Helix aspersa*) gray garden slug (*Agriolimax reticulatus*) |

Comments

Brown garden snail is about 1 inch (2.5 cm) in diameter; brown snail with distinct color pattern; gray garden slug is a snail relative that lacks a shell. Most active at night and early morning when it's damp. Manage by skirt pruning and trunk treatment. Release predatory decollate snails (*Rumina decollata*) in counties where it is legal. Use wooden boards with cleats for monitoring. Remove collected snails and slugs daily. Crush to destroy or use a 50-50 solution of household ammonia and water in a spray bottle. Keep ammonia solution off leaf surfaces since it can damage plants. Copper barriers, such as trunk banding can be effective. Apply organic or conventional bait.

MITE PESTS

| Leaves have pale yellow stippling on upper leaf surfaces. No webbing. Bright red globular eggs laid on bark or leaves. Adults found mostly on young leaves. | red mites (*Panonychus* spp.) |

Comments

A barely visible red mite (use hand lens). Long bristles protrude from adult's back. Attacks almost all fruit and nut trees. Overwinters in egg stage on bark of deciduous trees. New generation every 2 wk in spring. Natural enemies often are sufficient control in unsprayed home orchards. If not, a supreme or superior-type delayed dormant oil spray just as eggs are about to hatch should keep mites below damaging levels.

| Leaves, twigs, fruit covered with webbing; stippling on leaves. Mites visible with hand lens on bark or leaves. | webspinning spider mites (*Tetranychus* spp.) |

Comments

Barely visible (use 10x hand lens); looks like tiny moving dots to naked eye; $<\frac{1}{20}$ inch (1.3 mm) long. Arachnid, not an insect. Attacks almost all fruit and nut trees. Spider mites live in colonies on lower leaf surfaces. Webbing distinguishes them from mite species. Overwinter on deciduous trees as red or orange females under rough bark scales, in ground litter, and trash. Eggs laid in spring. Numbers increase in June-Sep. One generation per wk in hot weather. Mites cause damage by sucking cell contents from leaves. Damage compounded by water stress. Provide adequate irrigation. Dusty conditions favor spider mites. Many natural enemies limit their numbers, but spraying for insect pests can lead to outbreak of mites because mite enemies are killed by the insecticide, and because some insecticides can increase nitrogen levels in leaves, favoring mite reproduction. Forceful sprays of water and insecticidal soaps help to control. See UC IPM Pest Note 6, *Spider Mites*.

| Stippling of whitish gray spots on young leaves. No webbing. Leaves do not drop. | brown mite (*Bryobia rubrioculus*) |

Comments

Larger than most other mites; produces no webbing; causes leaf stippling. Attacks stone fruits, almonds, apples, and pears. Largest of common pest mites in California but rarely causes enough damage to warrant treatment in backyard orchards. Many natural enemies. Found on leaves, twigs, wood.

What the problem looks like	Probable cause
Rust mites and silver mites feeding on leaf or fruit surfaces. Blister mites feeding in protected areas in buds or blisters. Damage is noticed long before these microscopic mites are detected. *Rust mites:* Fruit becomes rough, brown, and russeted, especially at stem and flower ends. Foliage looks dry, rusty. *Blister mites:* Leaves and flower buds develop reddish blisters that later turn brown or black. Fruits develop sunken, brown, russeted areas and may become deformed.	Eriophyid mites: peach silver mite (*Aculus cornutus*) pearleaf blister mite (*Phytoptus pyri*) pear rust mite (*Epitrimerus pyri*)

Comments

Attacks peach, pear, pomegranate, and apple, among others. Includes the blister, rust, bud, and gall mites. These mites have only 4 legs instead of the typical 8 legs of arachnids. Their legs appear to be coming out of their heads. These mites are much smaller than the spider mites and red mites; you need a 15× to 20× hand lens to see them. They have many generations per year. Overwinter as nonfeeding adults behind leaf bud scales or any other protected 1- to 2-year-old wood. Rust mites feed until no more new foliage develops. Control measures seldom necessary for them. Damage is mostly cosmetic, affecting fruit appearance. For rust mites and blister mites, an oil spray with lime sulfur in Oct or Nov decreases population for the following season and prevents blister mites from moving deeper into buds. Sulfur dust is an effective control as long as summer temperatures are below 90°F (32°C).

SELECTED MISCELLANEOUS INSECTS

Leaves have brownish patches from top layer being eaten. Later, leaf tissue eaten completely through, leaving fine network of veins.	pearslug (*Caliroa cerasi*)

Comments

Olive-green to blackish slimy insect up to ½ inch (12.5 mm) long with head end widest part of body. The adult is a sawfly. Attacks cherries, pears, plums, prunes. Two generations per year. Adults emerge in early spring and lay eggs in leaf tissue. Mature larvae enter soil to pupate. Second generation that appears in summer does the most damage. Pick pearslugs off by hand and dislodge from foliage with strong stream of water. Insecticidal soap may be effective. Road dust applied to foliage can kill them but should be washed off after several days to discourage spider mites.

Fruit and foliage sticky, becoming black with sooty mold. Stunted vegetative growth or tree defoliated. Beads of clear, sticky honeydew enclose tiny, yellowish insects on leaves.	pear psylla (*Cacopsylla pyricola*)

Comments

Tiny insect up to 1/10 inch (2.5 mm) long. Yellow in immature stages, reddish brown as adult. Dark spot on back. Clear wings held rooflike over body. Attacks pears. About five generations per year. Adult overwinters in sheltered places in bark or underground. Eggs laid on or near new foliage. Dormant oil spray kills many overwintering adults. Eggs and mature young (nymphs) are resistant to insecticides but adults and smaller nymphs can be controlled during growing season with 2–3 oil sprays applied weekly. Pear decline disease is transmitted by this insect.

Small black spots on husk become large, blackened areas that remain soft, unsunken and smooth. Areas damaged by walnut blight dry up. Hull difficult to remove from shell. Shell darkly stained. Nut meat not affected. Infested nuts tend to remain on tree.	walnut husk fly (*Rhagoletis completa*)

Comments

White to yellowish maggots up to 3/8 inch (9.5 mm) long. Adult fly is small, brown, has yellow spot on back, three dark bands on each wing. Attacks walnuts. Maggots are found in blackened areas of hull, never inside shell. One generation per year. Eggs laid in hull from late July to early Aug. Larvae pupates in ground. Adult flies emerge following summer. Most home orchardists ignore this pest because nutmeats are unaffected. For control measures, see *Pests of the Garden and Small Farm* (Flint 1998).

Table 17.7 cont.

What the problem looks like	Probable cause

NEMATODES

Fruits decreased in size, yellowed leaves, twig dieback, general loss of vigor. General stress symptoms; premature autumn leaf loss.	root knot nematode (*Meloidogyne* spp.) root lesion nematode (*Pratylenchus* spp.) citrus nematode (*Tylenchulus semipenetrans*)

Comments

Nematodes, microscopic wormlike pests, are tiny eel-like soil-dwelling roundworms that feed on roots. By feeding on roots, nematodes cause general tree decline. Root knot nematodes cause distinct swellings (galls) on roots of infested trees. Root lesion nematodes reduce growth of young feeder roots and produce lesions on root surfaces of many, but not all, damaged trees. One of the simplest management strategies is to plant scions on nematode-resistant or nematode-tolerant rootstocks (Nemaguard or Nemared). See *Pests of the Garden and Small Farm* (Flint 1998) for other control methods.

SELECTED DISEASES CAUSED BY FUNGI

Most deciduous fruit and nut trees worldwide are affected by diseases known as crown rot, root rot, collar rot, and trunk rot caused by *Phytophthora* spp. fungi. In California, root and crown rots caused by *Phytophthora* spp., discussed below, kill more almond, apple, cherry, nectarine, and peach trees than perhaps any other disease. All species of stone fruit, pome fruit, kiwifruit, chestnut, and walnut are more or less affected.

Leaves turn yellow, red, or purple, and drop. Tree looks drought stressed. Beads of sap ooze from trunk lesions. Gumming may be visible in spring. Inner bark is brown, slimy, and/or gummy, but the discoloration does not extend into the wood. Bark can dry, harden, and crack. Decline of tree due to disruption of water and nutrient transport may be rapid.	Phytophthora crown rot (*Phytophthora cactorum* and at least 15 other *Phytophthora* spp. that infect the tree trunk and crown)

Comments

Attacks all deciduous fruit and nut trees. Prevent this disease with good water management. Keep trunk dry. Do not allow sprinkler water to hit the trunk. Scrape away all diseased bark and include a buffer strip (about 1 inch or 2.5 cm) of healthy light brown to greenish bark around margins. Allow to dry. Repeat if infection recurs. Keep mounded soil and water away from trunk. Improve ventilation by removing branches that touch the ground. Avoid injuring bark with lawnmowers, weed whackers (the worst) and pruning tools, since wounds give fungus an easy entry to cause disease.

Trunk cankers at the base of older trees, originating at or below ground level. Canker appears as a dark region with a red, resinous exudate that dries to a white, crystalline deposit. Underneath the superficial canker is an orange-tan to brown lesion, instead of the normal white or cream-colored tissue. Lesion has a fruity odor when exposed. Decline may be sudden and tree death can occur.	Phytophthora canker (many *Phytophthora* spp.)

Comments

Attacks phloem tissue of lower trunks of deciduous fruit and nut trees. As with all *Phytophthora* spp., disease is favored by excess soil moisture, such as occurs with overirrigation or poor drainage. Fungus can be spread on contaminated nursery stock, irrigation water, and cultivation equipment. Use sanitation measures. Do not allow the lower trunks of trees to stay wet because the high humidity favors infection. Drip emitters should be placed away from tree trunks and minisprinklers should be aimed to avoid wetting tree trunks. Also, avoid wounding the trunks during pruning. If cankers are detected at an early stage, they can sometimes be controlled by cutting out the infected tissue. Cankers can also be caused by bacteria, as discussed in this table.

Leaves turn yellow, red, or purple, and drop. Trees look drought stressed. Roots are destroyed. Bark of infected roots slides off easily when pinched. Symptoms appear similar to lesions or cankers, but may be difficult to distinguish from nematode, salt, or flood damage.	Phytophthora root rot (many *Phytophthora* spp.)

Comments

Caused by the same fungi (*Phytophthora* spp.) that cause crown rots, but they infect roots in causing this disease. Attacks deciduous fruit and nut trees. Called "wet feet" in the trade. Can occur when water is in direct contact with the base of the trunk and trunk is allowed to stay wet. Shorter, less frequent irrigations may help if damage is not severe. Avoid waterlogging soil. Use rootstocks tolerant of "wet feet." Do not plant fruit and nut trees in the lawn where watering is too frequent. If damage is severe, remove tree. Fumigate if replanting. Fungi can survive in soil for years. No fungus mycelia are visible, distinguishing this disease from Armillaria root rot.

Poor growth, loss of tree vigor. Small, yellowing leaves; premature leaf drop; wilting, collapse. In winter, Armillaria often forms clusters of mushrooms at base of infected trees a few days after a rain. White, fan-shaped fungus mycelia grow between bark and wood in crown region. Decayed bark has mushroom odor.	Armillaria root rot (*Armillaria mellea*)

Comments

Also known as oak root fungus and shoestring root rot. Attacks apple, cherry, almond, olive, peach, prune, plum, apricot, and kiwifruit, all of which are highly susceptible. Pear, fig, persimmon, and black walnut are comparatively resistant. Visible symptoms may not appear until fungus is well established. Normally kills the lower trunk cambium layer, girdling the tree, and can destroy entire root system. Once symptoms appear, it is very difficult to save a tree, and disease may have spread to roots of adjacent trees. After aerial parts of infected trees are gone, the fungus remains alive in the roots, ready to infect any replanted susceptible trees, such as citrus, avocado, or any of the susceptible deciduous fruit and nut trees listed above. Use resistant rootstocks, if available; for example, Marianna 2624 and certain selections of myrobalan plum exhibit resistance. Let soil dry out between irrigations. Once established, this disease is difficult to eradicate. It may survive for many years in the soil.

Dark, olive-green to black spots on foliage blossoms and fruits. Fruit spots later become scablike. Twisted, puckered leaves have black, circular, scabby spots on upper surfaces. Spots velvety on leaf undersides. Infected fruits become distorted and crack, allowing entry of secondary organisms. Young fruit may drop.	apple scab (*Venturia inaequalis*) pear scab (*Venturia pirina*)

Comments

Attacks apples, pears, and other pome fruits. The most serious disease of apples in California. Causes loss or severe surface fruit blemishing. Occurrence is most severe in northern and coastal areas of California, where spring weather is cool and moist. Fungus overwinters in dead leaves on the ground. Spores are released during spring rains, landing on and infecting leaves, flowers, and fruits. New spores produced on infected leaf or fruit surfaces 10–20 days later, spreading disease. Infection occurs most rapidly from 55° to 75°F (13° to 24°C); leaves must remain wet continuously for several hours for infection to occur. Manage disease in the backyard by removing leaves beneath trees in winter. Fall foliar fertilizer (urea) applications hasten leaf fall and decomposition and help reduce spore numbers in following spring. Operate sprinklers between sundown and noon to allow adequate leaf drying before significant infection can occur. Synthetic fungicides and wettable sulfur are also effective treatments. See UC IPM Pest Note 14, *Apple Scab*.

Sudden limb death during summer heat. Rough, dark cankers at pruning wounds. Gum may ooze from edge of cankers. Fungus gains entry via pruning wounds.	Eutypa dieback of apricot (*Eutypa lata*, formerly *Cytosporina* spp.)

Comments

Attacks apricots. Cankers can spread 6 inches (15 cm) per year. Fungus may reach trunk if affected branches not removed. Summer-prune trees when risk of rain is minimal (July through September). Remove infected limbs, cutting at least 6 inches below discolored area. Paint fresh, large wounds with benomyl solution, ⅕ tbs per gallon water (0.75 ml/l).

Distorted, reddened leaves visible in spring; later fall off. Leaves thickened, puckered, causing them to curl. Fruit production is reduced if disease is severe.	leaf curl (*Taphrina deformans*)

Comments

Attacks leaves, shoots, and fruit of nectarines and peaches. Common problem for backyard gardeners. Fungus overwinters underneath bud scales and other protected spots as conidia (resting fungal spores). In the spring, conidia are moved by splashing water to newly developing leaves where infection occurs. A preventive fungicide treatment is necessary every autumn after leaves have fallen to prevent leaf curl. If timed properly, a single fall treatment of copper-based fungicide can prevent leaf curl and shot hole disease. If trees have shown symptoms in the spring, be sure to treat the following fall to prevent more serious losses the next year. In areas of high rainfall, a second treatment in the late winter when buds begin to swell but before any green color appears may be advisable. Although symptoms of leaf curl will be seen primarily as new leaves develop, the disease is difficult to control at this time.

Table 17.7 cont.

What the problem looks like	Probable cause
Small, round, purplish spots on leaves and fruits enlarge to about ¼ inch. Centers of leaf spots turn brown. Dark specks at centers of brown spots (fungus spores) visible only with hand lens. Centers of brown spots fall out, so leaves have "shot holes." Affected fruits become scabby.	shothole disease (*Stigmina carpophila*) (*Coryneum beijerinckii*)

Comments

Also known as coryneum blight. Attacks almonds, apricots, peaches, nectarines, and cherries. Rare on peaches and nectarines. Does not cause holes in leaves, but gumming of small twigs. Fungus survives winter on infected buds, twigs. Rain or overhead irrigation spreads fungus spores to young leaves, twigs, buds, and blossoms where they can cause infection if given 24 hours continuous wetness. Wind carries water-splashed spores. Buds and twigs affected in peaches, nectarines, and almonds. Leaves and fruits affected in apricots. Practice good sanitation. Remove and destroy infected twigs, buds, blossoms, and fruit when symptoms appear. Protectant copper-based fungicides in the fall, pink bud stage, and full bloom may be needed if disease incidence has been high.

Leaves suddenly wilt on one part of tree or on the entire tree and then turn brown and die but do not drop off for months. Brown to gray-brown streaks are visible in wood of branches or roots (plugged-up xylem tissues).	Verticillium wilt (*Verticillium* spp.)

Comments

Also known as vascular wilt. Attacks many deciduous fruit and nut trees, including almond, olive, pistachio, stone fruits, pome fruits, walnut, and persimmon. Many stone fruits used as rootstocks are susceptible. A soil fungus that enters the roots and moves upward, attacking and plugging up the water-conducting tissues (xylem). May kill the entire tree or only part of it, with the remainder having complete recovery. Do not plant fruit and nut trees on soil previously used for other susceptible crops. If disease is severe or recurs, removal of soil and all roots is the only solution.

Light-colored powdery spore growth on shoots, both sides of leaves, and sometimes flowers. Fruits may develop weblike, russeted scars. New growth is dwarfed, distorted, and covered with white powdery substance.	powdery mildew

Comments

Attacks many deciduous fruit and nut trees. Fungus species depends on crop attacked: *Podosphaera leucotricha* on apple, quince, pear, almond; *Podosphaera oxycanthae* on leaves/shoots of cherry, peach, plum; *Sphaerotheca pannosa* on leaves/fruit of apricot, peach, plum, rose. Powdery mildew survives from one season to the next in infected buds or as fruiting bodies on the bark of stems and trunks. Fungus spores (in chains) can be seen with a hand lens. Does not require high humidity, unlike most other fungi. Moderate temperatures and shady conditions are generally the most favorable for powdery mildew. In most cases, planting resistant varieties and following good cultural practices will control powdery mildew. Plant in full sun, provide adequate irrigation, and avoid excess fertilizer. Fungicide applications are often needed on highly susceptible crops, such as apples. Wettable sulfur works well. Monitor the orchard and prune out infected tissues. See UC IPM Pest Note 7, *Powdery Mildew*.

Browning and withering of blossoms; blossoms, associated twigs, and leaves shrivel and die. Gummy ooze at base of dead flower. In humid weather, shriveled petals bear tiny grayish-brown masses (fungus spores), which spread disease. Cankers (sunken brown areas) may develop around twigs at base of infected flowers, causing leaves at tips of twigs to shrivel up. After harvest, ripe fruit can also develop brown rot fruit rot on the tree or in storage. The rot spreads rapidly with the initial brown or tan spots developing gray to tan tufts of spores within a day or so.	brown rot of stone fruits (*Monilinia* spp.)

Comments

Attacks almond, apricot, peach, plum, cherry, nectarine, and quince. One of the most common and serious blossom and fruit diseases. Causes withering of flowers and girdling of twigs. Fungus survives the winter on diseased twigs and mummies (old, rotted fruits) on the ground or in the tree. In spring, spores are spread by air currents, rain splash, and insects. Spores infect flowers of the new year's crop. Prompt removal and destruction of diseased plant parts prevents the buildup of brown rot inoculum in isolated trees or small orchards and may be sufficient to keep brown rot below damaging levels. Prune trees from the time they are planted to allow good ventilation in the canopy. Avoid wetting blossoms, foliage, and fruit during irrigation. When possible, plant varieties less susceptible to brown rot. After leaves drop but before the first fall rains, remove all fruit and nut mummies and prune out branches with diseased twigs. Destroy mummies and prunings by burning, burying, or bagging. During the bloom period and as fruits begin to ripen, check trees for brown rot

What the problem looks like	Probable cause

symptoms. Remove and destroy all diseased tissue. After harvest, remove all fruit and nuts left on trees and destroy them because they are potential overwintering sites for brown rot and other pests. If inoculum builds up, a protectant fungicide application may be needed to prevent serious loss. Sprays must be applied before each spring rain to be effective.

Bark and wood develop localized dead areas near pruning wounds or other injuries. Branches become girdled; leaves wither.	Phomopsis canker of fig (*Phomopsis cinerascens*)

Comments

Attacks fig. Kadota and Calimyrna varieties most susceptible. Mission rarely attacked. Prune late in dormant season. Remove diseased branches from orchard and burn them. Fungus survives in cankers in trees or dead wood in surrounding areas.

SELECTED DISEASES CAUSED BY BACTERIA AND MYCOPLASMALIKE ORGANISMS (MLO)

Young blossoms, shoots, and fruit wilt and collapse, turning brown to black. Sticky brown ooze appears on diseased shoots during humid weather. Cankers appear on limbs and secrete dark ooze in spring. Entire branches or tree can die in one season.	fire blight of pome fruits (*Erwinia amylovora*)

Comments

Attacks pear, apple, and quince. Blossoms and succulent shoots are most susceptible. Bacterium survives in cankers; spread by splashing rain and insects. Favored by warm, humid weather during bloom. Cut diseased branches back about 12 inches (30 cm) into healthy wood, removing all diseased tissue. Avoid planting susceptible rootstocks such as M-26. Sterilize pruning tools in household disinfectants before making each cut. Apply diluted copper fungicides during bloom period as preventive sprays. See UC IPM Pest Note 15, *Fire Blight*.

Bacterial canker: Irregularly-shaped brown water-soaked or gum-soaked areas develop in bark and outer sapwood of spurs, branches, and sometimes trunk. Small cankers can develop on twigs at base of infected buds. When trees begin active growth in spring, amber-colored gum may exude from canker margins. Cankers are darker than healthy bark. Underlying diseased tissue is reddish brown, moist, and sour-smelling. *Bacterial blast:* Blossoms "blasted" (blighted), turn brown, shrivel, cling to trees. Dark brown or black spots on leaves, fruit. Leaves drop. Symptoms on apple and pear similar to fire blight, but blast does not extend as far down the shoot from the tip, and blast does not produce ooze. Bark of infected twigs is tan and papery.	bacterial canker, bacterial blast (*Pseudomonas syringae*)

Comments

Also known as gummosis. Attacks almond, cherry, peach, nectarine, apricot, plum, apple, pear, and kiwifruit. *Bacterial cankers* develop during the dormant season and early spring and occur primarily on stone fruit trees. *Bacterial blast* or blight of buds, blossoms, leaves, green shoots, and green fruit can occur on pome and stone fruits in wet, cold spring weather. Under favorable conditions, bacteria enter via buds, leaf scars, wounds, and natural openings (leaf or branch pores). Infections occur in fall, winter, and early spring. Canker growth ceases in summer, may resume in fall. Damage from bacterial canker and blast can be minimized by cultural practices. Losses can be reduced by selecting resistant rootstocks, avoiding planting on shallow soil, providing adequate nutrition (particularly nitrogen), and protecting trees from freezing temperature during bloom or early fruit growth by covering them or providing protective shelters. In California, feeding by high populations of ring nematodes is thought to be the most important factor making almonds and stone fruit trees susceptible to bacterial canker. Select planting site carefully. Trees receiving adequate N fertilizer recover better from bacterial canker infection. If trees are damaged, remove entire affected branches in the summer, being sure to eliminate entire canker and a few inches below.

Table 17.7 cont.

What the problem looks like	Probable cause
Walnut hull has rough, sunken, hard, blackened areas. If young nuts affected, they drop prematurely. Older nut kernels turn black and shrivel. Infected florets first appear water-soaked and wilted, later turn black.	blight of English walnut (*Xanthomonas campestris*)

Comments

Attacks English walnuts. Bacteria overwinter in buds, twig lesions, and old nuts. They infect catkins, fruit, green shoots, leaves, and buds. Bacteria are spread by rain splash. Disease is worse in early-leafing varieties. Black walnut species seldom affected. On susceptible varieties, avoid wetting foliage with sprinklers. Avoid irrigation during bloom. Prune trees for better air circulation. Fruit may become infected at any time after formation until harvest. This long susceptibility period is one of the chief obstacles to disease control. Specific fertilization or cultivation practices offer little control for walnut blight. Planting late-blooming varieties can be beneficial. One to three fixed copper spray treatments are the most effective control. The first application should be made no later than the first appearance of the pistillate bloom.

Cherries fail to ripen, are conical, tasteless, and tan-colored. Leaves in midsummer are yellow. One or a few limbs may be affected. On peach, leaves turn yellow; tree declines; small shoots die.	X-disease of cherry

Comments

Also known as buckskin disease. Attacks sweet and sour cherry. Caused by a myoplasma-like organism. Leafhoppers transmit the pathogen. Trees on Mahaleb rootstock may die within weeks as if girdled. Remove infected limbs or trees. Practice good sanitation.

Crown galls, (rough, warty tumors caused by this soil-dwelling bacterium) first appear as smooth swellings.	crown gall (*Agrobacterium tumefaciens*)

Comments

Attacks pome fruits, stone fruits (including almonds), and walnuts. Most damaging to young trees and vines. Obtain good quality material from a reputable nursery and use careful planting and pruning techniques. Can survive in soil for at least 2 yr without host tissue. Established trees and vines are infected only through fresh wounds such as those caused by growth cracks, pruning, cultivation equipment, or freezing injury. Seedlings may be infected during germination. Bacteria are released into soil when galls are wet or when older gall tissue disintegrates. On trees, galls develop on large roots at the crown. Larger trees and vines can usually tolerate galls. Younger trees affected. Treat by applying bactericide in dormant season, spring or early summer. Rinse soil away from galls and allow to dry thoroughly before treating.

SELECTED DISEASE CAUSED BY VIRUS

Poor terminal growth; yellowing; premature defoliation; tree stunted, eventually dies. Small holes, cracks in bark at graft union.	blackline virus

Comments

Also known as cherry leafroll virus. Attacks walnut. No known cure. Remove affected trees to protect adjacent healthy trees. Virus transmitted by grafting and infected pollen. When bark is removed, horizontal black line is visible at the graft union. All English walnut on black walnut rootstocks are believed to be susceptible.

SELECTED PHYSIOLOGICAL (ABIOTIC) DISORDERS

Pit-burning of apricot. Inner mesocarp of ripe apricots becomes brown, gelatinous.	air temperatures of 104°F (40°C) for a few days

Comments

Green, immature apricots do not show this symptom when exposed to these same high temperatures for an equivalent period of time. Disorder is attributed to lack of oxygen in inner mesocarp resulting from high respiration rates due to heat stress. Select varieties that do not pit burn easily.

Blackening of peach. Portions of flesh of ripening peaches becomes grayish black. air temperatures of 102°F (39°C) for a few days
Comments
Discoloration is easier to detect in white-fleshed cultivars. Darkening is worse near the pit, suggesting that oxygen supply is insufficient there. Oxygen used by heat-stressed fruit cells for respiration cannot be replenished fast enough.

Internal browning of prune. Flesh turns brown or black instead of amber. high temperatures
Comments
Discoloration is worse near the pit and is related to lack of oxygen there.

Premature shriveling of prune. Prunes turn blue and shrivel. hot, dry winds
Comments
High winds cause an increase in the transpiration rate, and tree cannot supply fruit with sufficient water. Disorder is attributed to both heat and water stress.

Water core of apple and pear. Core zones have glazed, water-soaked appearance. temperature stress, including temperature gradient; overmaturity

Comments
A temperature-gradient related disorder. Asian pears are more susceptible than European pears. Highly pigmented red apple varieties are more susceptible than yellow- or green-skinned varieties because darker skin absorbs more heat. Fruit keeps poorly.

Pink calyx of pear. Calyx of Bartlett pear turns pink. low temperature of 68°F (20°C) 4–6 wk before harvest

Comments
These fruits soften rapidly after harvest.

Black kernel of walnut. Kernel shrivels, darkens, becomes worthless. sunburn
Comments
Nuts are at risk from sunburn because they are borne terminally on spurs. Heat from sunburn is transmitted to the kernel. Spraying whitewash does not lower fruit temperature enough to prevent sunburn.

Bud failure of almond. Vegetative buds abscise; buds that remain go dormant or grow vigorously. Sparse growth on some parts of tree; vigorous growth on other parts. Called "crazy top" or "witches' broom" due to appearance. high summer temperatures
Comments
All varieties are susceptible. Appears sporadically in the whole tree or parts of a tree after exposure to extremely high summer temperatures. Symptoms get worse after each heat spell.

Cracking of sweet cherry. Fruits are cracked. rain
Comments
Droplets of water left on ripe fruits cause them to split because water penetrates mesocarp faster than the epidermal cells can expand.

End-cracking of prune. Bottom end of fruits crack in June. Cracking of apple skin. Skin cracks on fruits, particularly on side of tree that gets most sun. water stress followed by irrigation
Comments
Prunes: Appears on trees irrigated after water stress. Mesocarp separates from endocarp when fruit regains turgidity due to water uptake. Apples: Apple skin loses elasticity from heat stress due to sun; subsequent uptake of water by fruit cells after irrigation leads to cracking. Irrigate when soil is still somewhat moist. Prune and fertilize to maintain full canopy.

Side-cracking of prune. Sides of fruits crack in July. excess water uptake
Comments
Appears on fruits exposed to direct sunlight and cool night temperatures such that dew forms. Mesocarp cells take up water, become turgid; epicarp and mesocarp crack. Mesocarp cells of immature prunes can become meristematic, forming ugly callus tissue. When ripe prunes crack, sugars and gums are exuded that can support mold growth. Some molds can produce carcinogenic aflatoxins.

Table 17.7 cont.

What the problem looks like	Probable cause
Russeting of apple and pear. Brown corky layers on epidermis due to moisture condensation or "frost rings."	moisture condensation, frost, or pesticide sprays

Comments

Fog, dew, and spray droplets that do not dry rapidly lead to this problem, especially in coastal California. Cover fruit with bags to avoid condensation on fruit skin in areas of morning fog. Young apple and pear fruits can develop "frost rings," a type of russeting. Cortical tissue growth is inhibited.

Splitting of the endocarp. Split pits on peaches, nectarines, almonds, plums, sweet cherries, olives.	growth-related disorder (stress between mesocarp and endocarp)

Comments

Prevalent in early-ripening peach and nectarine cultivars. Do not thin crop just prior to the pit-hardening growth phase. Do not irrigate immediately after thinning. Cultural operations that favor fruit growth during pit hardening causes a sudden surge of water and/or carbohydrates into mesocarp cells, increasing their turgor pressure.

Gumming. Leaves, fruits of stone fruits exude gums, mucilages onto epidermis. Ugly gum pockets on skin.	growth disorder

Comments

Gums and mucilages are complex carbohydrates synthesized by the leaves and fruits of stone fruits. They create internal pressure in mesocarp cells and diffuse to fruit surface. Fruits may abscise early or become culls at harvest.

Bitter pit of apple. Necrotic spots appear on fruits before or after harvest.	leaf-to-fruit ratio too large; poor pollination; frost damage during bloom

Comments

When crop is light, shoot growth outcompetes fruit for calcium. This large transpiring area draws calcium into foliage rather than into fruits. Fruits are calcium-deficient. As a result, they respire more rapidly and have shorter shelf life. Summer pruning reduces incidence of bitter pit by regulating the leaf-to-fruit ratio, which means that less calcium is diverted to leaves. Control is achieved by spraying the trees with a calcium-containing fertilizer such as calcium nitrate with 2 to 4 applications starting when fruit are very small.

Wilting and shriveling of fruits.	premature harvest

Comments

Even if fruits are put into refrigerated storage at the proper relative humidity, if they are harvested when still immature, they will shrivel and wilt because their soluble solids content is too low and they are less capable of preventing water loss than mature fruits.

agriculture. The primary form, copper sulfate ($CuSO_4$), or fixed copper, is mixed with hydrated lime in order to fix the copper and form copper hydroxide. It is used for the prevention of root and crown rot, apple and pear scab, peach leaf curl, shothole fungus, brown rot, fire blight, bacterial canker, and walnut blight with varying degrees of success depending on the disease, timing, and rates applied. As with all pesticides, wear protective clothing during the application.

Biological control agents such as predatory and parasitic insects and antagonistic disease organisms used to control pests do not usually control problems as quickly as conventional pesticides do. With many of these methods, home gardeners will need to be patient and must expect long-term results with some immediate damage. Biological control of insect and mite pests is generally more effective in coastal regions than in the Central Valley or the southern desert valleys because the cooler temperatures help prolong the life of most organisms. UC scientists are actively engaged in detecting and importing biocontrol agents of major pests of crops important in California agriculture. A number of biological control agents effective against pests of temperate fruit and nut trees are native to California. When native California parasites and predators are not available, UC entomologists travel to the areas of the world where many pest species are believed to have originated to search for the pests' natural predators and parasites. If a particular parasite or predator looks promising, UC scientists bring it back to California with the appropriate permits and place it into UC quarantine facilities to undergo intensive research. UC entomologists release the imported biological control agents into the environment only after research results document their effectiveness and safety.

Conventional Pesticides

Pesticides used to kill or prevent damage from pests are commonly used on fruit trees; in some cases there is no other effective or practical control method. Great care must be taken when using conventional pesticides since they are toxic substances that can harm nontarget beneficial organisms or pollute the environment if not used properly. In most cases, they should be used only as a last resort. Misuse is the most common reason for problems associ-

ated with pesticides. Read the label carefully prior to use and follow all labeled instructions and restrictions. For more information on using pesticides safely and effectively in the home garden see chapter 10, "Controlling Garden Pests Safely."

Nutritional Values

Temperate fruits, their juices, and nuts are good sources of several important vitamins and minerals. Table 17.8 summarizes the nutritional value of a typical serving size of the fruits and nuts discussed in this chapter, as well as fruit juices and nut oils. Table 17.8 is divided into two sections: fruits and fruit juices, and nuts and nut oils. Crops are presented in alphabetical order within each section.

Since temperate fruits, juices, and nuts are plant-based foods, they do not contain any cholesterol. Temperate fruits are low in fat, sodium, and calories, and as an added benefit,

Table 17.8

NUTRITIONAL VALUE OF SELECTED TEMPERATE FRUITS, JUICES, AND NUTS

FRUITS AND JUICES

Apple (with skin)

Serving size:	1 med., raw (5 oz)	Primary Nutrients		% RDA (m)	% RDA (f)	% Min. Requirement
Calories	81	Vitamin C	8.0 mg	8.9	10.7	
Fat	0.5 g	Vitamin E	0.81 mg α TE	5.4	5.4	
Calories from fat	5.5%	Potassium	159 mg			8.0
Sodium	1 mg					
Protein	0.3 g					
Carbohydrate	21.1 g					
Water	115.8 g					
Cholesterol	0					
Dietary Fiber	3.0 g					

Unsweetened Applesauce

Serving size:	1 cup	Primary Nutrients		% RDA (m)	% RDA (f)	% Min. Requirement
Calories	106	Vitamin C	4.0 mg	4.4	5.3	
Fat	0.2 g	Potassium	182 mg			9.0
Calories from fat	1.8%					
Sodium	4 mg					
Protein	0.4 g					
Carbohydrate	27.6 g					
Water	215.6 g					
Cholesterol	0					
Dietary Fiber	3.6 g					

Table 17.8 cont.

Apple Juice, Unsweetened

Serving size:	1 cup (8 fl oz)	Primary Nutrients		% RDA (m)	% RDA (f)	% Min. Requirement
Calories	116	Iron 0.9 mg	9.0	11.2	5.0	
Fat	0.3 g	Potassium 296 mg				14.8
Calories from fat	2.3%					
Sodium	7 mg					
Protein	0.2 g					
Carbohydrate	29.0 g					
Water	218.1 g					
Cholesterol	0					
Dietary Fiber	–					

Apricots, Fresh

Serving size:	3 raw (about 4 oz)	Primary Nutrients		% RDA (m)	% RDA (f)	% Min. Requirement
Calories	51	Vitamin A	277 RE	30.8	39.6	
Fat	0.4 g	Vitamin C	11 mg	12.2	14.7	
Calories from fat	7%	Iron	0.58 mg	7.3	3.2	
Sodium	1 mg	Potassium 313 mg				15.7
Protein	1.5 g					
Carbohydrate	11.8 g					
Water	91.5 g					
Cholesterol	0					
Dietary Fiber	1.4 g					

Apricots, Dried

Serving size:	10 halves (1.25 oz)	Primary Nutrients		% RDA (m)	% RDA (f)	% Min. Requirement
Calories	83	Vitamin A	253 RE	28.1	36.1	
Fat	0.2 g	Iron	1.65 mg	20.6	9.2	
Calories from fat	2%	Niacin	1.0 mg	6.3	7.1	
Sodium	3 mg	Potassium	482 mg			24.1
Protein	1.3 g					
Carbohydrate	21.6 g					
Water	0					
Cholesterol	0					
Dietary Fiber	2.7 g					

Apricot Nectar

Serving size:	8 fl oz	Primary Nutrients		%RDA(m)	%RDA(f)	% Min. Requirement
Calories	141	Vitamin A	330 RE	33	41.3	
Fat	0.2 g	Iron	0.96 mg	12	5.3	
Calories from fat	1.3%	Potassium	286 mg			14.3
Sodium	9 mg					
Protein	0.9 g					
Carbohydrate	36.1 g					
Water	213.0 g					
Cholesterol	0					
Dietary Fiber	0.8 g					

Sour Cherries (canned, water pack)

Serving size:	1 cup (w/o pits)	Primary Nutrients		% RDA (m)	% RDA (f)	% Min. Requirement
Calories	86	Vitamin A	184 RE	20.4	26.3	
Fat	0.2 g	Vitamin C	6 mg	6.7	8.0	
Calories from fat	2%	Folate	20 mcg	5.0	5.0	
Sodium	18 mg	Potassium	240 mg			12
Protein	1.8 g					
Carbohydrate	21.8 g					
Water	219.4 g					
Cholesterol	0					
Dietary Fiber	—					

Sweet Cherries, Fresh

Serving size:	10 raw	Primary Nutrients		%RDA(m)	%RDA(f)	% Min. Requirement
Calories	49	Vitamin C	5 mg	5.5	6.7	
Fat	0.7 g	Potassium	152 mg			7.6
Calories from fat	12.9%					
Sodium	0 mg					
Protein	0.8 g					
Carbohydrate	11.3 g					
Water	54.9 g					
Cholesterol	0					
Dietary Fiber	1.1 g					

Figs, Raw

Serving size:	3 med. (about 5 oz)	Primary Nutrients		% RDA (m)	% RDA (f)	% Min. Requirement
Calories	111	Vitamin B$_6$	0.18 mg	13.8	13.8	
Fat	0.6 g	Thiamin	0.09 mg	7.5	8.2	
Calories from fat	4.9%	Iron	0.54 mg	6.8	3.0	
Sodium	3 mg	Riboflavin	0.09 mg	6.9	8.2	
Protein	1.2 g	Magnesium	24 mg	5.7	7.5	
Carbohydrate	28.8 g	Calcium	54 mg	5.4	5.4	
Water	118.8 g	Potassium	348 mg			17.4
Cholesterol	0					
Dietary Fiber	—					

Figs, Dried

Serving size:	3 med. (about 5 oz)	Primary Nutrients		% RDA (m)	% RDA (f)	% Min. Requirement
Calories	111	Iron	1.27 mg	15.9	7.1	
Fat	0.6 g	Vitamin B$_6$	0.18 mg	13.8	13.8	
Calories from fat	4.9%	Calcium	81.5 mg	8.2	8.2	
Sodium	3 mg	Magnesium	33.6 mg	8.0	0.5	
Protein	1.2 g	Potassium	404 mg			20.2
Carbohydrate	28.8 g					
Water	118.8 g					
Cholesterol	0					
Dietary Fiber	—					

Table 17.8 cont.

Kiwifruit

Serving size:	1 med., raw (2.5 oz)	Primary Nutrients		% RDA (m)	% RDA (f)	% Min. Requirement
Calories	46	Vitamin C	75 mg	83.3	100.0	
Fat	0.3 g	Magnesium	23 mg	5.5	7.2	
Calories from fat	5.9%	Potassium	252 mg			12.6
Sodium	4 mg					
Protein	0.8 g					
Carbohydrate	11.3 g					
Water	63.1 g					
Cholesterol	0					
Dietary Fiber	2.6 g					

Nectarines

Serving size:	1 med., raw (5 oz)	Primary Nutrients		% RDA (m)	% RDA (f)	% Min. Requirement
Calories	67	Vitamin A	100 RE	11.1	14.3	
Fat	0.6 g	Vitamin C	7 mg	7.8	10.0	
Calories from fat	8.1%	Niacin	1.3 mg	8.1	9.3	
Sodium	0 mg	Potassium	288 mg			14.4
Protein	1.3 g					
Carbohydrate	16.0 g					
Water	117.3 g					
Cholesterol	0					
Dietary Fiber	2.2 g					

Olives, Black

Serving size:	5 large	Primary Nutrients		% RDA (m)	% RDA (f)
Calories	25	Iron	0.8 mg	10.0	4.4
Fat	2.4 g				
Calories from fat	84%				
Sodium	192 mg				
Protein	0.2 g				
Carbohydrate	1.4 g				
Water	0				
Cholesterol	0				
Dietary Fiber	0.7 g				

Olives, Green

Serving size:	5 large	Primary Nutrients	% RDA (m)	% RDA (f)
Calories	27	None of the nutrients meet or exceed 5% of the RDA.		
Fat	2.9 g			
Calories from fat	99%			
Sodium	552 mg			
Protein	0.3 g			
Carbohydrate	0.3 g			
Water	0			
Cholesterol	0			
Dietary Fiber	0.6 g			

Olive Oil

Serving size:	1 tbs	Primary Nutrients		% RDA (m)	% RDA (f)
Calories	119	Vitamin E	1.67 mg α TE	11.1	11.1
Fat	13.5 g				
Calories from fat	100%				
Sodium	0 mg				
Protein	0 g				
Carbohydrate	0 g				
Water	0				
Cholesterol	0				
Dietary Fiber	0 g				

Peaches, Fresh

Serving size:	1 med., raw (3 oz)	Primary Nutrients		% RDA (m)	% RDA (f)	% Min. Requirement
Calories	37	Vitamin C	6 mg	6.7	8.0	
Fat	0.1 g	Potassium	171 mg			8.6
Calories from fat	2.4%					
Sodium	0 mg					
Protein	0.6 g					
Carbohydrate	9.7 g					
Water	76.3 g					
Cholesterol	0					
Dietary Fiber	1.4 g					

Peaches, Dried

Serving size:	5 halves (2.25 oz)	Primary Nutrients		% RDA (m)	% RDA (f)	% Min. Requirement
Calories	155	Iron	2.64 mg	33.0	14.7	
Fat	0.5 g	Niacin	2.85 mg	17.8	20.4	
Calories from fat	2.9%	Vitamin A	141 RE	15.7	20.1	
Sodium	4.5 mg	Riboflavin	14 mg	10.8	12.7	
Protein	2.4 g	Magnesium	27 mg	6.4	8.4	
Carbohydrate	39.9 g	Potassium	647.5 mg			32.4
Water	20.7 g					
Cholesterol	0					
Dietary Fiber	5.4 g					

Peach Nectar (canned)

Serving size:	8 fl oz	Primary Nutrients		% RDA (m)	% RDA (f)	% Min. Requirement
Calories	134	Vitamin C	13 mg	14.4	17.3	
Fat	0.1 g	Vitamin A	64 RE	7.1	9.1	
Calories from fat	0.4%	Potassium	101 mg			5.1
Sodium	17 mg					
Protein	0.7 g					
Carbohydrate	34.7 g					
Water	213.2 g					
Cholesterol	0					
Dietary Fiber	0.4 g					

Pears, Fresh

Serving size:	1 med., raw (6 oz)	Primary Nutrients		% RDA (m)	% RDA (f)	% Min. Requirement
Calories	98	Vitamin C	7.0 mg	7.8	9.3	
Fat	0.7 g	Potassium	208 mg			10.4
Calories from fat	6.4%					
Sodium	1 mg					
Protein	0.7 g					
Carbohydrate	25.1 g					
Water	139.1 g					
Cholesterol	0					
Dietary Fiber	4.3 g					

Table 17.8 cont.

Pears, Dried

		Primary Nutrients		% RDA (m)	% RDA (f)	% Min. Requirement
Serving size:	5 halves (3 oz)					
Calories	230	Iron	1.84 mg	23.0	10.2	
Fat	0.6 g	Riboflavin	0.13 mg	10.0	11.8	
Calories from fat	2.3%	Niacin	1.2 mg	7.5	8.6	
Sodium	5.0 mg	Magnesium	29 mg	6.9	9.1	
Protein	1.7 g	Vitamin C	6 mg	10.0	10.0	
Carbohydrate	61.0 g	Potassium	466 mg			23.3
Water	0.05 g					
Cholesterol	0					
Dietary Fiber	—					

Pear Nectar (canned)

		Primary Nutrients	% RDA (m)	% RDA (f)
Serving size:	8 fl oz			
Calories	149	None of the nutrients meet or exceed 5% of the RDA.		
Fat	0 g			
Calories from fat	0			
Sodium	9 mg			
Protein	0.3 g			
Carbohydrate	39.4 g			
Water	210.0 g			
Cholesterol	0			
Dietary Fiber	1.6 g			

Pears, Asian

		Primary Nutrients	% RDA (m)	% RDA (f)	% Min. Requirement
Serving size:	1 med., raw (4.4 oz)				
Calories	51	None of the nutrients meet or exceed 5% of the RDA.			
Fat	0.3 g	Potassium 148 mg			7.4
Calories from fat	5.3%				
Sodium	0 mg				
Protein	0.6 g				
Carbohydrate	13.0 g				
Water	107.7 g				
Cholesterol	0				
Dietary Fiber	—				

Persimmons

		Primary Nutrients		% RDA (m)	% RDA (f)	% Min. Requirement
Serving size:	1 med., raw (6 oz)					
Calories	118	Vitamin A	364 RE	40.4	52.0	
Fat	0.3 g	Vitamin C	13 mg	14.4	17.3	
Calories from fat	2.3%	Potassium	270 mg			13.5
Sodium	3 mg					
Protein	1.0 g					
Carbohydrate 3	1.2 g					
Water	134.9 g					
Cholesterol	0					
Dietary Fiber	—					

Plums

Serving size:	2 med., raw (4.75 oz)	Primary Nutrients		% RDA (m)	% RDA (f)	% Min. Requirement
Calories	72	Vitamin C	12 mg	13.3	16.0	
Fat	0.8 g	Riboflavin	0.12 mg	9.2	10.9	
Calories from fat	10%	Vitamin B$_6$	0.1 mg	7.7	7.7	
Sodium	0 mg	Potassium	226 mg			11.3
Protein	1.0 g					
Carbohydrate	17.2 g					
Water	112.4 g					
Cholesterol	0					
Dietary Fiber	—					

Pomegranate

Serving size:	1 med., raw (5.5 oz)	Primary Nutrients		% RDA (m)	% RDA (f)	% Min. Requirement
Calories	104	Vitamin C	9 mg	10.0	12.0	
Fat	0.5 g	Potassium	399 mg			20.0
Calories from fat	4.3%					
Sodium	5 mg					
Protein	1.5 g					
Carbohydrate	26.4 g					
Water	124.7 g					
Cholesterol	0					
Dietary Fiber	—					

Prune Juice

Serving size:	8 fl oz	Primary Nutrients		% RDA (m)	% RDA (f)	% Min. Requirement
Calories	181	Iron	3.03 mg	37.9	16.8	
Fat	0.1 g	Riboflavin	0.18 mg	13.8	16.4	
Calories from fat	0.5%	Niacin	2.0 mg	12.5	14.3	
Sodium	11 mg	Vitamin C	11 mg	12.2	14.7	
Protein	1.6 g	Magnesium	36.0 mg	8.6	11.3	
Carbohydrate	44.7 g	Potassium	706 mg			35.3
Water	208.0 g					
Cholesterol	0					
Dietary Fiber	—					

Quince

Serving size:	1 med., raw (3 oz)	Primary Nutrients		% RDA (m)	% RDA (f)	% Min. Requirement
Calories	53	Vitamin C	14 mg	15.6	18.7	
Fat	0.1 g	Iron	0.64 mg	8.0	3.6	
Calories from fat	1.7%	Potassium	181 mg			9.1
Sodium	4 mg					
Protein	0.4 g					
Carbohydrate	14.1 g					
Water	77.1 g					
Cholesterol	0					
Dietary Fiber	—					

Table 17.8 cont.

NUTS AND THEIR OILS

Almonds, Dried, Unblanched

Serving size:	1 oz	Primary Nutrients		% RDA (m)	% RDA (f)	% Min. Requirement
Calories	167	Magnesium	84.1 mg	20.0	26.3	
Fat	14.8 g	Riboflavin	0.2 mg	15.4	18.3	
Calories from fat	80%	Iron	1.0 mg	12.5	5.6	
Sodium	3 mg	Calcium	75.5 mg	7.5	7.5	
Protein	5.7 g	Zinc	0.8 mg	7.3	10.0	
Carbohydrate	5.8 g	Potassium	207.9 mg			10.4
Water	—					
Cholesterol	0					
Dietary Fiber	1.9 g					

Almond Oil

Serving size:	1 tbs	Primary Nutrients	% RDA (m)	% RDA (f)
Calories	120	Vitamin E 5.3 mg α TE	53.3	35.3
Fat	13.6 g			
Calories from fat	100%			
Sodium	0 mg			
Protein	0 g			
Carbohydrate	0 g			
Water	—			
Cholesterol	0			
Dietary Fiber	—			

Chestnuts

Serving size:	1 oz	Primary Nutrients		% RDA (m)	% RDA (f)
Calories	70	Vitamin C	7.4 mg	8.2	9.9
Fat	0.6 g	Vitamin B$_6$	0.1 mg	7.7	7.7
Calories from fat	8%	Folate	19.9 mcg	5.0	5.0
Sodium	1 mg				
Protein	0.9 g				
Carbohydrate	15.0 g				
Water	—				
Cholesterol	0				
Dietary Fiber	3.7 g				

Filberts (Hazelnuts), Dried, Unblanched

Serving size:	1 oz	Primary Nutrients		% RDA (m)	% RDA (f)
Calories	179	Magnesium	80.9 mg	19.3	25.3
Fat	17.8 g	Vitamin B$_6$	0.2 mg	15.4	15.4
Calories from fat	89%	Iron	0.9 mg	11.3	5.0
Sodium	1 mg	Thiamin	0.1 mg	8.3	9.1
Protein	3.7 g	Calcium	53.4 mg	5.3	5.3
Carbohydrate	4.4 g	Folate	20.4 mcg	5.1	5.1
Water	—				
Cholesterol	0				
Dietary Fiber	1.8 g				

Hazelnut (Filbert) Oil

Serving size:	1 tbs	Primary Nutrients		% RDA (m)	% RDA (f)
Calories	120	Vitamin E	6.4 mg α TE	42.7	42.7
Fat	13.6 g				
Calories from fat	100%				
Sodium	0 mg				
Protein	0 g				
Carbohydrate	0 g				
Water	—				
Cholesterol	0				
Dietary Fiber	0				

Pecans, Dried

Serving size:	1 oz	Primary Nutrients		% RDA (m)	% RDA (f)
Calories	189	Thiamin	0.2 mg	16.7	18.2
Fat	19.2 g	Zinc	1.6 mg	10.7	13.3
Calories from fat	91%	Magnesium	36.4 mg	8.7	11.4
Sodium	0.3 mg	Iron	0.6 mg	7.5	3.3
Protein	2.2 g	Vitamin E	0.87 mg α TE	5.8	5.8
Carbohydrate	5.2 g				
Water					
Cholesterol	0				
Dietary Fiber	1.9 g				

Pistachios, Dried

Serving size:	1 oz	Primary Nutrients		% RDA (m)	% RDA (f)	% Min. Requirement
Calories	164	Iron	1.9 mg	23.8	10.6	
Fat	13.7 g	Thiamin	0.2 mg	16.7	18.2	
Calories from fat	75%	Magnesium	44.9 mg	10.7	14.0	
Sodium	2 mg	Vitamin E	1.46 mg α TE	9.7	9.7	
Protein	5.8 g	Potassium	310.4 mg			
Carbohydrate	7.1 g					15.5
Water	—					
Cholesterol	0					
Dietary Fiber	3.1 g					

Walnuts, Black, Dried

Serving size:	1 oz	Primary Nutrients		% RDA (m)	% RDA (f)
Calories	172	Magnesium	57.4 mg	13.7	17.9
Fat	16.1 g	Vitamin B$_6$	0.2 mg	15.4	15.4
Calories from fat	84%	Iron	0.9 mg	11.3	5.0
Sodium	0.3 mg	Zinc	1.0 mg	9.1	12.5
Protein	6.9 g	Vitamin E	0.73 mg a TE	4.9	4.9
Carbohydrate	3.4 g				
Water	—				
Cholesterol	0				
Dietary Fiber	1.4 g				

Table 17.8 cont.

Walnut Oil

Serving size:	1 tbs	Primary Nutrients	% RDA (m)	% RDA (f)
Calories	120	None of the nutrients meet or exceed 5% of the RDA.		
Fat	13.6 g			
Calories from fat	100%			
Sodium	0 mg			
Protein	0 g			
Carbohydrate	0 g			
Water	—			
Cholesterol	—			
Dietary Fiber	0			

Sources: Adapted from Pennington 1998; National Academy of Sciences 2001a,b.

many are high in vitamin C, vitamin A, potassium, and other nutrients. With the exception of chestnuts, nuts are high-fat (60 to 95% fat), high-calorie foods, but they are recognized as a good source of monounsaturated fat in the diet, which can help to control serum cholesterol if eaten in moderation. With the exception of chestnuts, the nuts discussed in this chapter are far too high in calories for routine snacking. However, many of the nuts discussed in this chapter contain significant quantities of vitamin E, iron, magnesium, folic acid, and potassium. Their oils, with the exception of walnut oil, have notable quantities of vitamin E, an important antioxidant vitamin.

The nutritional information provided is derived from Pennington 1998 and National Academy of Sciences 1989, 2001a, and 2001b. The nutritional value information for potassium content is expressed as "% Minimum Requirement." To date, no RDA has been established for potassium. Retinol equivalents (RE) are listed with vitamin A when appropriate.

To put the data in table 17.8 in perspective, some additional background information is required: see appendix A, "Background Information on Nutritional Data."

Bibliography

Commercial apple growing in California. 1976. Oakland: University of California Division of Agriculture and Natural Resources Leaflet 2456.

Commercial plum growing in California. 1976. Oakland: University of California Division of Agriculture and Natural Resources Leaflet 2458.

Crane, J. C., and J. Maranto. 1988. Pistachio production. Oakland: University of California Division of Agriculture and Natural Resources Publication 2279.

Flint, M. L. 1998. Pests of the garden and small farm: A grower's guide to using less pesticide. 2nd ed. Oakland: University of California Division of Agriculture and Natural Resources Publication 3332.

———. 1993. Integrated pest management for walnuts. 2nd ed. Oakland: University of California Division of Agriculture and Natural Resources Publication 3270.

Hasey, J. K., R. S. Johnson, J. A. Grant, and W. O. Reil, eds. 1994. Kiwifruit growing and handling. Oakland: University of California Division of Agriculture and Natural Resources Publication 3344.

International Society of Arboriculture. 1995. Tree-pruning guidelines. Savoy, IL: International Society of Arboriculture.

Kader, A. A., ed. 2002. Postharvest technology of horticultural crops. 3rd ed. Oakland: University of California Division of Agriculture and Natural Resources Publication 3311.

LaRue, J. H., and R. S. Johnson, eds. 1989. Peaches, plums, and nectarines: Growing and handling for fresh market. Oakland: University of California Division of Agriculture and Natural Resources Publication 3331.

Micke, W. C., ed. 1996. Almond production manual. Oakland: University of California Division of Agriculture and Natural Resources Publication 3364.

National Academy of Sciences. 2001a. Dietary reference intakes (DRIs): Recommended intakes for individuals, elements. Washington, DC: National Academy of Sciences.

National Academy of Sciences. 2001b. Dietary reference intakes (DRIs): Recommended intakes for individuals, vitamins. Washington, DC: National Academy of Sciences.

National Academy of Sciences, Food and Nutrition Board. 1989. Recommended dietary allowances. 10th ed. Washington, DC: National Academy of Sciences.

National Gardening Association. 1985. Gardening: The complete guide to growing America's favorite fruits and vegetables. Reading, MA: Addison-Wesley.

Ogawa, J. M., and H. English. 1991. Diseases of temperate zone tree fruit and nut crops. Oakland: University of California Division of Agriculture and Natural Resources Publication 3345.

Ohlendorf, B. L. P. 1999. Integrated pest management for apples and pears. 2nd ed. Oakland: University of California Division of Agriculture and Natural Resources Publication 3340.

Pennington, J. A. T. 1998. Bowes & Church's food values of portions commonly used. 17th ed. Philadelphia: Lippincott.

Ramos, D., ed. 1998. Walnut production manual. Oakland: University of California Division of Agriculture and Natural Resources Publication 3373.

Ryugo, K. 1988. Fruit culture: Its science and art. New York: Wiley.

Strand, L. L. 1999. Integrated pest management for stone fruits. Oakland: University of California Division of Agriculture and Natural Resources Publication 3389.

Swezey, S. L., ed. 2000. Organic apple production manual. Oakland: University of california Division of Agriculture and Natural Resources Publication 3403.

UC IPM pest note series. B. L. P. Ohlendorf, ed. University of California Division of Agriculture and Natural Resources, Statewide Integrated Pest Management Program. Updated regularly. Available through UC Cooperative Extension county offices; also available on the World Wide Web at http://www.ipm.ucdavis.edu

Westwood, M. N. 1993. Temperate-zone pomology: Physiology and culture. Portland, OR: Timber Press.

18

Citrus

*Deborah Silva, Carol Lovatt,
and Mary Lu Arpaia*

Terminal
flower bud

Flower buds

LEARNING OBJECTIVES

- Become familiar with citrus varieties that do well in the home garden in various climate zones in California.

- Learn the basic cultural requirements of citrus trees.

- Learn some basic principles of pest and disease management of citrus.

- Become acquainted with the relationship between the citrus industry and research at the University of California (past and present).

- Learn about the nutritional value of citrus fruits.

Citus

Citrus is one of the crops that was an essential part of the development of California agriculture and the horticultural research programs at the University of California. Worldwide, more fruit is produced by citrus trees than by all the deciduous fruit trees (e.g., apples, peaches, pears) combined. Home gardeners in California can grow edible or ornamental citrus varieties as standard-sized trees (trees that grow to the size typical of the variety), as semidwarfs (trees that attain about two-thirds of standard size), or as dwarfs (trees that attain about half the standard height). Fruit on all tree types reach full size; dwarf trees do not have smaller fruit. Home gardeners can plant citrus trees in the yard, in pots on the patio, or as espaliers along a fence or wall. They can choose commercially successful varieties or varieties that lack commercial interest but have appeal to the home garden trade.

Citrus trees available today, whether dwarf, semidwarf, or standard size, are the products of considerable scientific research. They usually consist of a scion/rootstock combination in which the rootstock provides the lower few inches of the trunk and the tree's roots, and the scion provides the major portion of the trunk, all branches, leaves, and fruit (fig. 18.1). Scion varieties are usually grafted onto rootstocks selected for improved disease resistance, cold hardiness, productivity (yield), favorable effects on fruit quality, and other desirable traits, such as dwarfing characteristics. By grafting mature fruiting wood onto a selected rootstock, the tree begins fruiting in a few years, rather than in the 10 to 15 years that would be required for a tree grown from a seed. Seedling trees must pass through a lengthy juvenile phase of growth before they become mature enough (*competent*) to flower and bear fruit.

History of Citrus in California

Citrus has a rich heritage in California. Believed to be a native of China, citrus, over the centuries, has traveled the routes of conquerors and missionaries. None of the citrus species grown in California is indigenous to the New World. Citrus was introduced into California in 1769 when the Spanish missionary and Franciscan priest Father Junipero Serra planted it at Mission San Diego. In 1841, William Wolfskill planted the first commercial citrus grove in Los Angeles. In 1856, Judge Joseph Jewis planted the first citrus trees in Northern California. The "Mother Orange" in Oroville, one of the judge's original trees, is the oldest citrus tree in the state. By 1867, the United States Department of Agriculture (USDA) reported that 17,000 orange trees and 3,700 lemon trees were growing in California, primarily in the Los Angeles area.

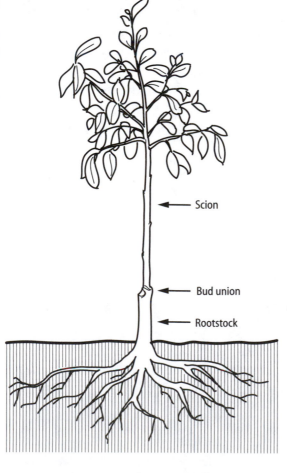

Figure 18.1

A cultivated citrus tree is two joined parts that originated as two separate trees. The top portion, known as the scion, is the fruiting variety, which is grafted onto a rootstock. The bud union is the point at which the scion joins the rootstock. *Source: After Citrus* (1996), p. 31.

Scion

Bud union

Rootstock

In 1869, a serious citrus pest, the cottony-cushion scale (*Icerya purchasi*) was imported into the state, and within 15 years it threatened to destroy all of the citrus plantings in California. In the late 1880s, an entomologist affiliated with the USDA, Albert Koebele, conquered the cottony-cushion scale with a natural predator of the pest imported from Australia, the Vedalia beetle (*Rodolia cardinalis*), more commonly known as the ladybug or lady bird beetle. It was the first spectacular biological-control success story.

Navel Oranges

Navel oranges, which were to become famous as California "eating oranges," were planted in Riverside by Eliza and Luther Tibbets in 1873. The Tibbetses had been given two branches of a new, untested orange variety from Brazil that was fresh out of quarantine in Washington, D.C. The orange was named the Washington navel in honor of its domestic source, Washington, D.C., and in recognition of its "belly button" base.

The trees that the USDA shipped to Riverside started bearing fruit in 1878, and their quality as eating oranges was superior to any variety previously grown in California. (The navel orange is distinct from the juice orange because the former does not have seed and comes apart in neat sections, making it a superior "eating orange." In addition, its thicker, easily peeled skin not only protects the delectable fruit sections but also allows for shipping to distant markets.

Riverside has an ideal climate for growing navels, and "citrus culture" (usually shortened to "citriculture") literally changed Southern California's landscape as groves spread across Riverside, San Bernardino, Orange, Los Angeles, and Ventura Counties. Today, one of the two original trees planted by the Tibbetses, known as the "Parent Navel Orange" tree, still grows and bears fruit in Riverside.

Commercial Expansion

Transcontinental railroads opened up the rest of the country to California's commercial citrus harvest in the 1870s and 1880s. In 1887, the first cold-storage shipment of Riverside navels was sold on the floor of a Boston exchange. During this period, northern groves were also bearing fruit in Porterville, Sacramento, and Marysville.

In the 1890s, cooperative citrus exchanges were established to promote and cooperatively market the increasing production. The Southern California Fruit Exchange, established in 1893, was incorporated in 1905 as the California Fruit Growers Exchange to recognize the inclusion of northern growers. The California Fruit Growers Exchange advertised fresh California citrus aggressively to midwesterners and easterners, calling it a "warm ray of California sunshine." The California Fruit Growers Exchange pioneered packing and shipping technologies and advertising techniques critical to the growth and development of the California citrus industry. Today it is known as Sunkist Growers, Inc., and represents California and Arizona citrus growers.

University of California Experiment Station

The University of California (UC) established the Citrus Experiment Station at Riverside on February 14, 1907, preceding the UC campus at Riverside by about half a century. (The institution is now known as the Citrus Research Center and Agricultural Experiment Station.) The selection of Riverside was preceded and followed by bitter battles among the competing Southern California citrus interests that desperately wanted the coveted UC facility in their city.

In less than a decade, the Riverside facility achieved recognition as the world's outstanding research institution on citrus and subtropical horticulture. By June 1917, numerous experimental plots were established at the Citrus Experiment Station, including studies in cultivation and fertilization and a Citrus Variety Collection containing 500 types of citrus from all over the world. Much of the original research on citrus varieties, cultivation techniques, insect pests, and diseases began at Riverside. New fruiting varieties of mandarins (Kinnow, Gold Nugget), oranges (Trovita), and grapefruits (Melogold, Oroblanco) have been released over the years. Many citrus pests and diseases are held in check by the management strategies developed by UC entomologists, plant pathologists, and nematologists. Pioneering studies on irrigation management, breeding, fertilization, mineral nutrition, cultivation practices, and pruning techniques have influenced practices in citrus orchards.

Disease and Innovation

UCR's Citrus Research Center and Agricultural Experiment Station, notably its Citrus Variety Collection, rescued the California citrus industry in the 1940s from the *Tristeza* virus, also known as quick decline. Experiment Station scientists identified the disease, determined how it was transmitted, and discovered that the trees died because the rootstock of choice was susceptible to the disease. Due to the *Tristeza* outbreak and research at UCR, citrus growers regrew their orchards on a new, *Tristeza*-resistant rootstock (Troyer citrange) tested and developed by UCR scientists.

Dwarf Citrus. Nurseryman Floyd Dillon decided in 1946 that the home gardener needed a citrus version of the dwarf apple and pear.

Dillon was motivated to develop an 8-foot (2.4-m) tree capable of producing full-sized fruit 2 years after planting. Working with a scientist at the UC Riverside Citrus Experiment Station who specialized in citrus rootstocks, and with other researchers, Dillon was successful. In 1949, dwarf citrus trees were sold for the first time.

Dwarf citrus are particularly beneficial to space-limited home gardeners. Dwarf citrus trees are available at many nurseries and via mail-order catalogs. Dwarf trees may consist of a scion grafted onto a dwarfing rootstock (look for the bud union and bark that may appear to have two different colors), or they may be dwarf trees growing on their own roots.

Disease-Free Citrus. In the 1970s, using citrus trees as a model, a horticulturist at the UC Riverside Experiment Station developed the first tissue culture technique to exclude viruses from fruit tree crops. The propagation technique is still in use today by UC's Citrus Clonal Protection Program (CCPP), which provides certified, disease-free citrus budwood to nurseries for reproduction. Historically, the Citrus Variety Collection at Riverside was used as a resource for genetic material for the CCPP. Today, the CCPP operates its own germplasm collection at the UC's Lindcove Research and Extension Center at Exeter in Tulare County in the San Joaquin Valley. It is the primary source of budwood for the California citrus industry today and contains more than 1,000 trees of about 200 different scion and rootstock varieties of commercial importance. All citrus trees for commercial sale in California must be certified by the California Department of Food and Agriculture (CDFA) as having met certain requirements. The regulations of the CDFA and UC's CCPP have resulted in California having the lowest disease incidence and the highest fruit quality of all citrus-producing areas in the world.

Citrus Research Facilities in California

In 1987, UCR's research facilities in California became the site of the nation's only citrus clonal germplasm repository funded by the USDA's Agricultural Research Service (ARS), known as the USDA-ARS National Clonal Germplasm Repository for Citrus and Dates. UCR's repository is one of several clonal fruit and nut repositories nationwide, a living defense system against devastating diseases and insect pests.

The USDA repository is adjacent to UC's internationally renowned Citrus Variety Collection at Riverside, which has become a living museum of more than 1,700 trees representing 860 different kinds of citrus and its near relatives. Recently, scientists have used the collection to conduct research on citrus limonoids as anticancer agents and to map the citrus genome.

UC scientists have pioneered the application of plant growth regulators (hormones) to citrus, such as the use of gibberellic acid (GA_3) on navel oranges to reduce preharvest rind degeneration and on lemons to delay fruit maturity.

In the early 1990s, the California State Parks opened the California Citrus State Historic Park in Riverside that has two goals: to preserve a vanishing cultural landscape and to tell the story of the citrus industry's role in the history of California by recreating, during a future phase of the park's development, an old-time citrus producing community as it looked earlier last century.

The locations of some of California's major citrus production areas have shifted because of the pressures of urbanization, high cost of land, and disease problems, but citrus research at UC and fruit productivity are thriving. Today, California and Arizona are the major producers of fresh citrus fruits, and Florida is the major producer of juice and processed products. California produces 80 percent of the nation's lemons. The farm-gate value of California fresh oranges was $611 million in 1998; the total annual value of California citus often establishes it among the top 10 crops in the state.

The experiment station at Riverside continues to be one of the world's leading research institutions in its studies of citrus and other commodities important to California agriculture. UC continues to develop new varieties of citrus from which the home gardener can choose varieties for home-grown fruit and for their ornamental value to the landscape.

For more information on the history of citrus in California, see *The Citrus Industry* (5 vols.; Reuther, Batchelor, and Webber 1967–1989); *Citrus: How to Select, Grow, and Enjoy* (Ray and Walheim 1980); and *Citrus Genetic Resources Task Force Report* (Kahn 2000).

Citrus Growth and Development

Unlike annual vegetable crops in which the focus is a single season's harvest, fruit trees such as citrus are perennials. The gardener's attention must be on the current season's harvest as well as on long-term care to maintain tree health and vigor for many years. Citrus trees are evergreen and drop their leaves throughout the year, a few at a time, not all at once in the fall as is typical of deciduous fruit trees such as apple and pear. Although both evergreen and deciduous fruit tree types are nonbearing (fruit production is absent or light) the first 3 or 4 years after planting, and both types have seasonal cycles during the year, evergreen fruit tree growth and development

are different from that of deciduous fruit trees, and the care they require is different. (One important exception is trifoliate orange, a deciduous citrus tree. Because trifoliate orange is used only as a rootstock in the citrus belt, its deciduous growth habit does not affect the home gardener.)

Roots

The first year that a citrus tree is in the ground is the most important for root development. Stresses caused by diseases, nematodes, weed competition, insufficient watering, or overwatering can hinder root development and scion development. Citrus roots can extend up to twice as far as the *drip line*, that imaginary circle below the canopy edge. Gardeners should consider these facts when irrigating and fertilizing citrus.

Leaves

Citrus trees have thick, leathery leaves whose function is more complex than that of deciduous fruit tree leaves. In both fruit tree types, leaves engage in photosynthesis, but in citrus the evergreen leaves—along with twigs, branches, and roots—are also involved in storing excess photosynthate (food) through the winter. In citrus leaves, the maximum amount of food stored is in late February or early March, just before the spring bloom and growth flush; thus, pruning should not be done at this time of year because leaf loss would reduce subsequent fruit yield.

Leaves are arranged spirally on the stem and typically remain on the tree for 1 to 2 years. An axillary bud occurs in the axil of each citrus leaf. During the spring flowering period of most citrus types, leaf drop can be pronounced and new leaf growth is most vigorous. Environmental factors, such as high temperatures, wind, low soil moisture, low relative humidity, nutrient deficiencies, and high soil salinity, can cause premature leaf drop. Other causes are disease or pest problems and rootstock-scion incompatibility.

The leaves of some citrus species contain essential oils that are important ingredients in pharmaceutical products, perfumes, and condiments used in cooking.

Flowers and Fruits

Citrus flowers, which are white to purplish, are known for their alluring fragrance. Oils from the flowers of the sour orange (*Citrus*

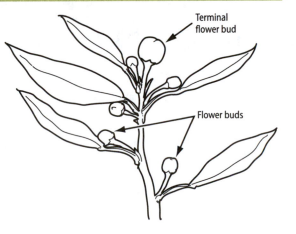

Figure 18.2

Citrus flower buds form on new vegetative growth arising from older leafy stems. *Source:* After Reuther et al., vol 2, 1968, p. 25.

Terminal flower bud

Flower buds

aurentiam) Bouquet de Fleurs are used in perfumes, as are the oils of Bergamot citrus (*Citrus bergamia*), which is grown in southern Europe. Nectar from citrus flowers is a favorite food of bees and is the raw ingredient of citrus-based honey.

After winter or drought dormancy, flowers form on new vegetative growth that arises from dormant buds on older leafy stems, and the vegetative apical meristem is transformed into a terminal flower bud (fig. 18.2). Citrus flowers usually bloom abundantly, but most flowers and young fruit are shed without setting fruit that survive to maturity. Citrus flowers are perfect, complete with male and female structures. Most citrus types are self-compatible, which means that they can be fertilized by their own pollen (self-pollinated) and can produce a crop even if a single tree is planted in isolation from other citrus trees. Unlike most citrus, Clementine mandarins, some grapefruit hybrids, and pummelos are self-incompatible, which means that they cannot be fertilized by their own pollen. To set a large crop of fruit, some Clementine mandarin varieties must be pollinated by another mandarin or tangelo planted nearby.

Citrus fruits are a type of berry known as a *hesperidium*. Scientists identify the parts of the fruit using precise terminology (fig. 18.3). Citrus fruits usually attain edible quality 8 to 16 months after bloom and have a variable harvest season of about 2 to 6 months, depending on climate. (Varieties that store well

on the tree and details about the nutritional value of citrus fruits are noted later in the chapter.) It is interesting to note that only about one-fourth of the ascorbic acid (vitamin C) in citrus fruits is found in the juice. The remainder is in the peel, concentrated primarily in the flavedo, the outer colored portion (see fig. 18.3).

When a citrus fruit is of sexual origin, the sperm cell in the pollen grain (of which there are many) fertilizes the egg cell in the ovule, which then develops into a seed, and the surrounding ovary develops and matures into the fruit (see fig. 18.3), as described in chapter 2, "Introduction to Horticulture." However, the sex life of citrus and the development of its fruit often are more complex than many other crops in the home garden, as will be discussed below in the section on nucellar embryony and parthenocarpy.

Annual Growth

During the first 3 or 4 years after planting a citrus tree, fruit production is light, and this period is known as the *nonbearing years*. Major root growth occurs during this period, and the framework of the tree is developing for fruit production. *Bearing trees* have a seasonal cycle that begins in the spring with the enlargement of flower buds that produce the current season's crop (see fig. 18.2). Early-opening inflorescences tend to be totally floral. The predominance of this type of inflorescence is referred to as a popcorn bloom. Flowers opening late in the bloom period tend to be on leafy floral shoots and produce more fruit that survive to harvest. Any weather conditions, pests, or diseases that lead to blossom injury will adversely affect the season's fruit production. Faster-growing ovaries tend to set fruit better and survive to harvest, whereas slower-growing fruit are more likely to drop at an early stage of development.

In California's subtropical climate, citrus trees usually have several growth flushes: in spring, summer, and fall. Each growth flush can produce flowers and set fruit, but in most varieties, the spring flush is the most productive. After pollination and fertilization of flowers that bloomed during the spring growth flush, the citrus tree typically yields a single crop of fruit as early as fall or as late as the following summer, depending on variety. Citrus types that are everbearing in California, such as lemons and citrons, can bloom and set fruit

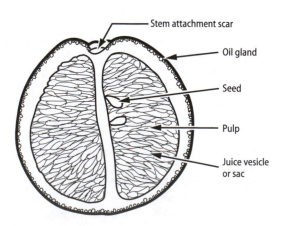

Figure 18.3

Schematic of a section through a mature citrus fruit. The rind consists of the thin, pigmented flavedo, and the thicker white albedo.

Stem attachment scar

Oil gland

Seed

Pulp

Juice vesicle or sac

throughout the year, but they tend to bloom most abundantly in the spring.

Citrus trees grow best between 70° and 90°F (21°C and 32°C). For this reason, the citrus belt lies between 35°N and 35°S latitude. The maximum northern latitude at which citrus is grown is in Spain at 44°N because of the modifying effects of the Canary current. The maximum northern latitude at which citrus is commercially grown in California is 39°N because of the modifying effect of the Japanese current. When temperatures reach 100°F (38°C) or drop to 55°F (13°C), citrus trees may appear to stop growing, but they actually reduce their growth rate. Reduced growth in response to cold winter temperatures approaches dormancy, but citrus trees do not go dormant the way deciduous fruit trees do. During this period of reduced growth, trees maintain a basal rate of water transport and starch consumption.

Mature Tree Size

Mature tree size depends primarily on the fruiting variety (scion) and rootstock but is also affected by growing conditions and cultural practices. Mature, standard-sized orange and grapefruit trees are 20 feet and 30 feet (6.1 and 9.1 m) tall, respectively. The only true genetic dwarf rootstock currently available is Flying Dragon trifoliate orange. On Flying Dragon rootstock, mature trees grow to less than half of standard size. Other rootstocks may have a dwarfing effect on mature tree size in certain fruiting varieties; such trees may be labeled *semidwarfs* and can grow to about two-thirds the standard size. Because the nursery industry is not regulated in using the term *dwarf*, deal with a reputable firm when purchasing citrus because some trees labeled as dwarfs may attain standard size at maturity. Some scion trees on their own roots may be sold as dwarfs; therefore, attempt to find out which rootstock you are purchasing with the fruiting variety chosen.

Citrus Botany and the Importance of Nucellar Embryony

Not all scientists agree on the number of citrus species, but scientists do concur that their botany is complicated. In many kinds of plants, species within a genus will not interbreed, and if they do, the offspring (the hybrid cross) are sterile. But in citrus, interfertility is usual and common. Thus, sweet oranges (*Cit-*

rus sinensis) have crossed successfully with mandarin oranges (*Citrus reticulata*) to yield tangors, and mandarin oranges have crossed with grapefruits (*Citrus paradisi*) to yield tangelos. Some botanists believe that the grapefruit itself is a hybrid cross between a pummelo (*Citrus grandis*) and a sweet orange, and some also believe that the sweet orange originated with a cross between a mandarin orange and a pummelo. However, the ease of hybridization does not tell the complicated story of the citrus fruit botany. Not only do recognized citrus species hybridize, but the offspring of these matings are able, after pollination but *without fertilization*, to produce seed that give rise to plants that are duplicates (clones) of the parent tree. Thus, not all citrus seeds and trees are of sexual origin.

Many of the citrus varieties you can grow in the garden produce two types of embryos in the same seed, a condition known as *polyembryony*: a sexual embryo develops after fertilization, and one or more asexual embryos arise from female nucellar tissue within the same ovule. The extra, asexual embryos that derive from cells of the nucellus (from the mother only) are known as *nucellar embryos*. Nucellar embryos are common in varieties of *Citrus* (oranges, grapefruits, lemons, mandarins), *Fortunella* (kumquat), and *Poncirus* (trifoliate orange). The stimulation of pollination is required for the nucellar embryos to develop. Nucellar embryos often crowd out the sexual embryo. Because nucellar embryos develop asexually from tissues of the female parent without any input from a male parent, they are genetically identical to (are clones of) the female parent, which is of practical importance in citrus breeding, particularly in producing clonal propagating material, such as clonal rootstocks. Nucellar-derived rootstocks are clones of the female parent, whose traits are known and selected by breeders, and they have predictable effects on fruit quality and yield and predictable resistance or tolerance to diseases and pests.

Polyembryony can be observed by germinating citrus seeds. If more than one seedling develops from one seed (fig. 18.4), one of the embryos (usually the weakest one) is of sexual origin, and the others are nucellar in origin. Reproduction primarily by nucellar embryony is an important trait of clonal citrus rootstocks in use today such as *Poncirus trifoliata*. Its seed are about 90 percent nucellar. The highly

Figure 18.4

Polyembryony in a citrus seed indicated by multiple seedlings. Usually the weakest seeding is sexual and the others, nucellar.

nucellar polyembryony of citrus rootstocks allows propagators in the citrus industry to rely on seedling rootstock production.

Seedlessness and Parthenocarpy

Navel oranges and Satsuma mandarins do not produce viable pollen or fertile eggs; they set fruit without flowers ever being pollinated or fertilized, and therefore the fruits are seedless. Such fruits are known as *parthenocarpic* fruits. Parthenocarpic fruits may develop without pollination, fertilization, and seed development, as occurs in some citrus types, or without fertilization and seed development (as occurs in orchids).

Alternate Bearing

Scientists have studied the problem of alternate bearing (the tendency for some citrus' such as Valencia oranges and some mandarins, to bear a heavy crop one year and a sparse crop the next) but they have not been successful to date in overcoming this problem. You can balance the yields by removing some of the fruit when they are still tiny and green during the heavy-bearing year and by harvesting a significant portion of the crop as soon as it matures.

June Drop

Considerable numbers of young, immature, and very small citrus fruits (less than 1 inch [2.5 cm] in diameter) may drop from trees in May, June, and July. Fruit drop is a natural phenomenon, a self-regulating thinning process that protects citrus trees from bearing too large of a crop. It is known as "June drop" and should be expected. Usually, less than 5 percent of citrus blossoms produce mature fruit. Flowers on shoots with few or no leaves rarely set fruit. An overwhelming number of flowers drop during and right after bloom. Dropping of immature fruit follows. When citrus fruits reach about 1 inch (2.5 cm) in diameter, they tend to stay on the tree. Excessive fruit drop, as opposed to June drop, is not a self-regulatory thinning mechanism and can be due to nitrogen deficiency, excessive nitrogen fertilization, sudden high temperatures, lack of water, heavy pruning, infestations of thrips or mites, or the occurrence of Santa Ana wind conditions. Keeping trees in good health minimizes fruit drop to expected levels.

Fruit Color and Regreening of Fruits

Fruit coloration in citrus (a change from green to orange or yellow) is associated with a loss of cholorophyll (green pigment) and an increase in carotenoids (yellow, orange, and red pigments) and occurs naturally as fruit matures. However, loss of green color and an increase in orange or yellow color in the fruit rind may not be correlated with fruit edibility. For example, in the fall, when temperatures are decreasing, chlorophyll loss occurs naturally in the fruit rind and carotenoids increase, but the color change, which is related to temperature, is not a good indicator of eating quality. Despite the mature-looking color of the fruit rind, chilling may be required to increase sugar content or to decrease acidity in the juice vesicles before eating quality becomes acceptable.

Rinds of ripe Valencia oranges that remain on the tree during hot weather may revert from orange to green, but the fruit flavor does not change. The chromoplasts in the rind, which contain orange and yellow carotenoid pigments, can revert to chloroplasts, which reflect the color green. In addition to high heat, high nitrogen fertilization may also contribute to regreening.

Sports

Sports are genetic mutations that affect only part of the tree, perhaps a branch or two. Typically, these mutations are not desirable, but if they are favorable, citrus breeders may choose to develop a sport into a new variety. The varieties (cultivars) of the eating oranges Skaggs Bonanza and Robertson navel, among others, began as sports of the Washington navel. Washington navel was likely a sport of Bahia navel from Brazil. Sports have foliage and fruit that are different from the rest of the tree. Pink Lemonade, which has pink flesh and variegated foliage, began as a sport of Eureka lemon. Development of sports is common in navel orange and grapefruit varieties.

Fruit Quality and Production of Inferior Fruit

As a home gardener, your taste buds will be the judge of fruit quality. Commercially, oranges are graded according to size, sugar-acid ratio, weight, freedom from blemishes, color, juice content, and other fruit qualities. Each citrus-producing state has its own grading system. Many citrus types yield bland fruit for the first few years of production, but quality improves as trees mature. *Off-bloom fruit* of sweet orange, grapefruit, and tangelo (fruit that develop from flowers that bloom in the off-season) are often inferior. Disease, rainfall, or a dry spell followed by irrigation can trigger irregular or off bloom. The inferior fruit that result tend to be thick-skinned and puffy.

Citrus Varieties

Where you live (which climate zone of the state) affects which citrus varieties will perform best in your home garden or landscape, when fruits are harvested, and what pest and disease problems are more common. Table 18.1, although not exhaustive, describes many varieties of major and minor citrus crops grown by home gardeners. Home gardeners may grow nearly all the citrus types listed in table 18.1, if varieties are selected prudently for adaptation to the climate in a particular region. If varieties are selected that ripen at different times, fresh fruit can be harvested almost year-round. Selecting early ripening varieties in freeze-prone areas can facilitate harvesting before the danger of frost. In California commercial citrus production, navel oranges predominate in the San Joaquin Valley, Valencia (juice) oranges in the coastal and inland regions, lemons in the coastal regions, and grapefruit in the desert.

The primary sweet oranges consumed in California and worldwide are navels for eating as fresh fruit and Valencias for juice. Navel orange varieties include the Washington navel and varieties that began as sports of Washington, such as Robertson and Skaggs Bonanza. Some pomologists divide the sweet orange category listed in table 18.1 into two subcategories, navel oranges and common oranges, a catch-all group of navel-less sweet orange varieties that are juiced (Valencia) or eaten fresh and juiced (Trovita, Shamouti).

Climate Zones for Growing Citrus

The harvesting (ripening) dates given in table 18.1 are approximate and broad, based on dividing the state into five citrus-growing regions: Southern California Coast, Inland Southern California, California Desert Valleys, Central Valleys (San Joaquin and Sacramento Valleys), and Northern California Coast. The most important factor that determines when fruits ripen and are ready for harvest is total heat. Ripening periods may vary from year to year and are influenced by microclimates. Citrus fruits grown in the desert are usually the first to ripen, followed by citrus in the inland valleys. Citrus grown in coastal areas ripens last. Fruits grown in the coastal zones can hang on the tree longer after maturity without deteriorating. Important attributes of the five zones are described below.

Southern California Coast. This regions extends from San Diego to San Luis Obispo and includes Santa Barbara, Ventura, western portions of Los Angeles County and Orange County, and San Diego. The entire region is influenced by the Pacific Ocean, and the marine air produces a mild climate. Summers are moderate in temperature, and coastal fog is common. Winter temperatures here are not usually a threat to citrus. Because many areas are frost-free, more tender varieties (limes and citrons) can be grown. Hot, dry winds known as Santa Anas can be damaging here. This zone (Ventura County) is the most important commercial lemon production area in the United States. In this region, the Eureka lemon bears almost year-round. Valencia and Washington navel oranges do well in the more inland areas that have some protection from winds. Compared to other citrus growing regions in the state, fruit grown here ripen last.

Table 18.1

SELECTED CITRUS VARIETIES FOR PLANTING IN THE HOME GARDEN AND LANDSCAPE

Scion variety	Harvest period*				
	Southern California Coast	Southern California Inland	California Desert	Central Valley	Northern California Coastal Valleys
SWEET ORANGES (*Citrus sinensis*)					

The most important citrus crop worldwide, with a taste different from sour and blood oranges. Believed to be natives of China, sweet oranges were first introduced into California by missionaries in 1769. The Washington navel was first planted in the state in 1873 in Riverside. Sweet oranges have had an important role in the development of California and continue to be a major player in the state's agricultural economy. Some references divide the sweet oranges into navels and "common" oranges.

Lane Late	Feb–Jul	Feb–Jun	NR†	Jan–May	NR

Late navel. Matures 4 to 6 weeks after Washington. Adapted to warm inland and coastal valleys.

Robertson Navel	Jan–May	Nov–Apr	Nov–Jan	Nov–Apr	Dec–Apr

Fruit smaller and earlier than Washington navel by about 2 to 3 weeks. Fruit borne in clusters near outside of tree. Grown on dwarf rootstock in home gardens. Dwarf trees are highly productive. More heat resistant than Washington navel. Slow-growing but bears at young age. Seedless, large fruit.

Shamouti	NR	Jan–Apr	Dec–Mar	Jan–Apr	NR

Midseason, nearly seedless eating orange developed in Israel. Has generated interest in some parts of California. Dense foliage, large leaves, and large fruit with excellent flavor. Grown on dwarf rootstock in home gardens. Highly productive. Popular in Europe and Israel. Also known as Jaffa.

Skaggs Bonanza	Jan–May	Nov–Apr	Nov–Jan	Nov–Apr	Dec–Apr

Bud sport of Washington navel. Ripens about 2 weeks earlier than Washington. Trees bear fruit at earlier age than Washington. Can be picked earlier than Washington navel—a good choice where frost is concern but fruit do not hold on the tree as long. Heavy bearer. Performs well on coast.

Trovita	Feb–Jun	Feb–Apr	Jan–Feb	Feb–Apr	Feb–Jun

A navel-less sport of Washington navel developed at UC. A seedless, mid-season eating and juice orange. Fruits well in desert conditions (unlike the navel), in moderate climates, and near the coast. Prized in San Francisco Bay Area because it develops excellent flavor without requiring high temperatures. Smaller fruit than Washington but juicier. Ripens later than Washington. Bears heavily in alternate years. One of the Arizona Sweets, a group of non-navel oranges (including Hamlin, Marrs, and Pineapple) favored in Arizona because they tend to ripen before hard frosts.

Valencia	Apr–Oct	Mar–Aug	Feb–May	Feb–Aug	Apr–Oct

Often called "juice oranges." Thin skinned, smaller fruit than navels, with highly juicy pulp. Few seed. Ripens later than Washington navel: midwinter (hottest areas) to summer (coolest areas). Fruit store well on tree, improving in flavor, but may regreen in summer. Vigorous, productive tree available as dwarf or standard. Some newer varieties are sold as "improved" Valencias, which ripen earlier, set fruit inside the canopy (more protected), and boast bigger fruit. Three sold under separate names are Delta, Midknight, and Rhode Red. Valencia is still the most important orange variety worldwide.

Washington Navel	Jan–May	Jan–Apr	NR	Nov–Apr	Dec–May

Large, seedless fruit eaten fresh, typically not juiced commercially. For the home gardener, the navel is excellent for fresh-squeezed juice if consumed immediately. Storage results in the accumulation of a compound in the juice that results in a bitter taste. Navels are suited to cooler production areas. Ripens early; fruit can usually be picked before damaging cold weather begins. Easy to peel and separate. Primary commercial navel variety and the original one from which other navels have been developed. Does not do well in desert climates. Fruit splitting in Jan, Feb and Sep is a common problem. Fruit stores on tree 3–4 months. Standard tree is 20 to 25 ft (6.1 to 7.6 m). On dwarf rootstock, it is about 8 ft (2.4 m).

	Harvest period*				
Scion variety	Southern California Coast	Southern California Inland	California Desert	Central Valley	Northern California Coastal Valleys

BLOOD ORANGES (*Citrus sinensis*)

Important commercially in Mediterranean, but not in the United States. Many varieties popular worldwide. Red blush on rind may not indicate internal flesh color, which is deepest in hot, interior regions. A gourmet's citrus, having rich orange flavor with raspberry overtones.

Moro	Feb–May	Jan–Mar	Nov–Feb	Dec–Apr	Feb–Apr

Fruit is deep red, almost seedless. Juice is almost burgundy. Vigorous, spreading, productive, medium-sized tree. Fruit borne in clusters near outside of tree, making it an attractive ornamental. Early-ripening Italian variety. Best rind color (red blush) occurs in hot interior regions of state. The only blood orange with good color and flavor in coastal Northern California. Very thorny.

Sanguinelli	Apr–Jun	Mar–May	Feb–Apr	Mar–May	Apr–Jun

Rosy-skinned fruit makes plant decorative. The most popular blood orange in Spain. Sweet-tart juice vesicles are streaked with burgundy. Adapted best to warm inland and desert valleys.

Tarocco	Mar–May	Jan–Mar	NR	Jan–Mar	Mar–May

Less productive than Moro, but deep red fruit are larger, with good flavor. Little rind blush. Few seed. Juice is almost burgundy. Vigorous, spreading, medium-sized tree. For reliable color and sweetest flavor, adapted best to inland valleys. Color is not reliable in other locations. Fruit do not hold well on tree. Italian variety.

SOUR ORANGES (*Citrus aurantium*)

Sour oranges include many unique citrus varieties used as landscape ornamentals, for making the liqueurs Curacao and Cointreau, as an ingredient in perfumes, and for manufacturing marmalade, candies, and rind oils. Fruit is very sour, almost bitter, and too strong for many people. Flowers are very aromatic and the aroma of leaves and rind oils is distinctive. Sour oranges have darker green foliage and more flattened fruit that tend to be deeper orange than other orange types. Smaller sour orange trees are useful as hedges. The larger Seville is a common street tree in Southern California and Arizona. Fruit can be held on the tree for 9 to 10 months.

Bouquet	Jan–Mar	Dec–Jan	Nov–Dec	Dec–Jan	Feb–Mar

Prized ornamental with deep orange fruit set among unique, round, deep green, densely clustered foliage. Has the most aromatic of all citrus flowers; set in massive clusters; used by perfume makers. A good hedge or container plant for the patio. Tree is small, 8 to 10 ft (2.4 to 3 m), spreading. The dwarf variety can be used as an ornamental shrub wherever pittosporum would be effective in the . landscape Also known as Bouquet de Fleurs.

Chinotto	Jan–Mar	Dec–Feb	Nov–Dec	Dec–Feb	Jan–Mar

Sometimes called myrtle-leaf orange. Small, symmetrical tree (7 ft [2.1 m]) with dense, compact growth habit. Fruit set in clusters. Prized in Italy for making candy, and fruit are also used for jellies and preserves. Fruit hold on the tree almost year-round. Attractive ornamental tree in the yard or as a container plant. Can also be trimmed as a hedge.

Seville	Jan–Mar	Dec–Feb	Nov–Dec	Dec–Feb	Jan–Mar

Upright, thorny, large tree (20 to 30 ft [6 to 9 m]). Its seedy fruit make excellent marmalade. Excellent as an ornamental for the home landscape. Traditionally used in courtyards.

Table 18.1 cont.

	Harvest period*				
Scion variety	Southern California Coast	Southern California Inland	California Desert	Central Valley	Northern California Coastal Valleys

LEMONS (*Citrus limon*)

Lemons are a sour-fruited citrus. Acid content is highest just prior to fruit maturity. Pick when fully ripe. Left on the tree, lemons become pithy and lose flavor. Lemons are more frost-sensitive than other citrus types but do not need high heat to ripen since they are not sweet. Most commercial lemons are grown in the coastal regions of California, particularly in Ventura County. Lisbon and Eureka are the true "supermarket" lemons. Unlike many other citrus types, some lemon varieties should be pruned.

Eureka	Feb–Sep	Feb–Jul	Sep–Jan	Feb–Jul	year-round

Depending on location, Eureka may be everbearing or harvested 3 to 4 times per year. Tree is medium–sized (20 ft [6.1 m]), nearly thornless. Fruit and flowers are in highly visible clusters. Attractive as container tree. Frost-sensitive. Flowers and new growth tinged with purple. Productive, high-quality fruit, but relatively short-lived tree. A major commercial variety. Needs periodic pruning. Good for espalier.

Lisbon	Jan–Aug	Dec–Jul	Sep–Jan	Dec–Jul	year-round

Depending on location, may be everbearing. Vigorous, tall (30 ft [9.1 m]), thorny tree. Most productive, cold-hardy, and heat tolerant of true lemons. Flowers tinged with purple. Highly acid, juicy fruit. Pick when ripe. A major commercial variety. Fruit is similar to Eureka, but tree is thornier and more frost-tolerant. The best lemons for the desert; fruit is borne inside the canopy. Needs pruning once per year to keep within bounds and shapely.

Improved Meyer	year-round	Nov–Mar	Nov–Mar	Nov–Mar	year-round

Fruit is round, thin-skinned, and almost orange when ripe. Hybrid between a lemon and a sweet orange or mandarin. Very juicy fruit with less acid than other lemons. Some seed. Imported from China; the most popular citrus in the home garden. Usually grown as a rooted cutting. Often bears fruit the first year. Ornamental, hardy, spreading, small tree (<15 ft [4.6 m]). Ideal for containers. Also makes an excellent hedge. Few thorns. Needs no pruning. More cold-hardy than a true lemon.

Variegated Pink	Feb–Sep	Feb–Jul	Sep–Jan	Feb–Jul	year-round

Sport of Eureka with green and white leaves and green stripes on immature fruit. Light pink flesh. Grows to about 8 ft (2.4 m). Frost-sensitive. Good as container plant. Also known as Pink Lemonade.

GRAPEFRUIT (*Citrus paradisi*)

Grapefruit trees are among the largest citrus types. Standard trees grow to about 30 ft (9.1 m). On dwarf rootstock they are about 8 ft (2.4 m) tall. Grapefruit are borne in grapelike clusters toward the outside of the tree, which, with its fruit and large, glossy, green leaves, is very ornamental. Grapefruit requires high heat to develop the best sweet-tart flavor. Excellent grapefruit grow in Texas and Florida where humidity is above 60 percent, summers are hot with warm nights, and winters are sunny with cool nights. Good grapefruit can be grown in California, but ripening time will vary from 6 months to more than a year, depending on climate, because of the total heat required. Allow fruit to hang on the tree to sweeten up. The grapefruit × pummelo hybrids developed at UC Riverside (Melogold and Oroblanco) do not require as much heat to ripen. Nonetheless, all grapefruits should be planted in the warmest location (a southern exposure or in front of a wall that will reflect the heat of the sun). Grapefruits have pale yellow or rosy flesh.

Duncan	NR	NR	Nov–May	NR	NR

Oldest grapefruit variety in Florida. Variety from which all others in the United States developed. Better flavor than modern seedless types but very seedy white flesh. Great for juice. Adapted to the California Desert, but not recommended in cool coastal areas.

	Harvest period*				
Scion variety	Southern California Coast	Southern California Inland	California Desert	Central Valley	Northern California Coastal Valleys
Marsh **Redblush**	May–Nov	Feb–Aug	Jan–May	Jan–Jun	Apr–Nov

Marsh is the standard, commercial white-fleshed grapefruit. Seedless. Originated in Florida as a seedling of Duncan. A parent of Redblush, which is rosy-fleshed if it receives enough heat. Redblush is also known as Ruby and Ruby-Red. Marsh and Redblush are almost identical trees. Desert conditions are best for peak quality due to the high heat requirement. In other climates, fruit ripen later and are less sweet.

Oroblanco **Melogold**	Jan–Apr	Nov–Jan	Nov–Jan	Nov–Jan	Jan–Apr

Both are grapefruit ✕ pummelo hybrids adapted to warm inland valleys and coastal regions. Both were developed at UC Riverside. Sweet and low in acid. Seedless, white flesh. Needs less heat than true grapefruit. Oroblanco is sweeter than Melogold and is more frost-tolerant.

Other varieties	NR	Feb–Aug	NR	Jan–Jun	NR

Star-Ruby is well-suited to western Riverside, San Bernardino, and San Diego Counties but is not recommended for desert climates or the coasts. Frost-sensitive, erratic bearer, but reddest color of flesh. Rio-Red may be more dependable than Star-Ruby and is also recommended for desert valleys.

LIMES (*Citrus aurantifolia*)
Like lemons, limes are an acid-fruited citrus. They are one of the least cold-hardy citrus types and must be grown in frost-protected locations. Limes are divided into large and small-fruited types. Left on the tree, limes turn yellow. Ripeness is a function of juiciness, not rind color. The Rangpur "lime" is actually a sour-acid mandarin and is included in that category in this table.

Bearss	Aug–May	Aug–Mar	Aug–Jan	Aug–Mar	Aug–Mar

Also known as the Persian or Tahitian lime in Florida and Texas. A large-fruited, seedless lime sold in grocery stores. A Tahitian variety that was introduced into the state at Porterville. Like the lemon and unlike the Mexican lime, Bearss does not require much heat to ripen. Attractive, ornamental, medium-sized, vigorous tree. Fruit are pale yellow when ripe but can be used when green. The most valuable lime for western gardeners because there is a better chance of success with it than with the Mexican variety.

Mexican	Jul–Dec	Jul–Dec	Jul–Oct	Jul–Nov	Aug–Dec

The bartender's lime. In Florida, known as the Key lime. A small-fruited lime more adapted to tropical climates in Florida and Mexico rather than California. High heat demand and almost no tolerance to frost. Planting a dwarf in a sheltered location, in a container, or in front of a south-facing wall may help. Highly aromatic. Twiggy, thorny, small tree usually grown on its own roots. Also known as the West Indian lime.

Other Varieties:	—	—	—	—	—

Keiffer limes are popular in Thai and Cambodian cooking. Fruit, leaves, and rind are used. Also known as the Indonesian lime.

SOUR-ACID MANDARINS
Most mandarins are sweet and eaten fresh, but a few mandarins (Rangpur and Calamondin) are distinctly acidic. Both can be used as ornamentals. Dwarfs of Rangpur and rooted cuttings of Calamondin make excellent house plants, fruiting reliably indoors. Both Rangpur and Calamondin are everbearing in mild climates and are cold-hardy.

Calamondin	—	—	—	—	—

Mandarin ✕ kumquat hybrid, popular in Asia, particularly the Philippines. Its easy-to-peel rind is sweet and edible (due to its kumquat parentage), and the fruit is acidic and tangy. It looks like a small orange. In the United States, calamondins are used primarily as ornamentals. The variegated form of Calamondin is especially ornamental.

Rangpur	—	—	—	—	—

Native to India. It is used as a rootstock for other citrus varieties. Its acidic juice can be substituted for lime juice, but it is not a lime, even though it is sometimes referred to as the Rangpur lime. Its reddish-orange fruit look and peel like mandarins and can hang on the tree all year.

Table 18.1 cont.

Scion variety	Harvest period*				
	Southern California Coast	Southern California Inland	California Desert	Central Valley	Northern California Coastal Valleys

MANDARINS
(*Citrus reticulata; C. unshiu; C. deliciosa; C. nobilis*)
The mandarins are the largest, most varied group of edible citrus. They are described as "zipper-skinned" because they are easy to peel and separate into segments. In the United States, mandarins are often called "tangerines." Fruit are smaller and often sweeter than sweet oranges. Many varieties mature in winter and do not have a high heat requirement to yield a good crop. Other varieties yield a sweeter, juicier crop if heat is high during the latter part of the ripening period. Harvest fruit when ripe; early-season varieties do not store well on the tree, but mid- and late-season varieties store better. The rind will get puffy and the flesh will lose its flavor if fruit are left on the tree too long. Many are alternate bearers. Removing some of the crop during the heavy-bearing year can even out the harvests a little. There is probably a mandarin variety for every climate in the citrus belt. Foliage is more cold-tolerant than the fruit. Grow early-ripening varieties in frost-prone areas. Mandarin trees are small to medium-size (10 to 20 ft [3 to 6.1 m]) with few thorns.

Scion variety	SCC	SCI	CD	CV	NCCV
Clementine (*C. reticulata*)	Jan–Apr	Nov–Jan	Nov–Dec	Nov–Jan	Jan–Apr

Major commercial variety in California. Excellent flavor, early-season fruit. Introduced from North Africa and Spain. Fruit holds on tree, making it an excellent ornamental, but fruit quality is reduced. Yields best fruit in the interior but produces well in cooler climates. There are many selections. Those that require a pollinizer for good production have seedy fruit. Dancy and Kinnow mandarins, Orlando tangelo, and Valencia orange are commonly used as pollinizers. If you have room for only one tree, choose a variety that does not require a pollinizer. Clementine has produced many hybrids, such as Page, Fairchild, Ambersweet, Lee, Nova, Robinson.

Dancy	Feb–Apr	Jan–Mar	Dec–Jan	Jan–Mar	Feb–Apr

Seedy. Better suited to Florida than California. Needs high heat to yield sweet fruit. Introduced into Florida from Morocco. Smaller than most mandarins. Heavy bearer in alternate years. Sunburn can be a problem in the desert.

Nour	—	—	—	—	—

High-quality, later-maturing Clementine selection originating in Morocco. Has distinctive shape. Field experience with this variety in California is limited. Harvest periods in California unknown.

Satsuma (*C. unshiu*)	Dec–Apr	Nov–Jan	NR	Nov–Jan	Dec–Apr

The most cold-hardy citrus and the earliest bearer. Can be grown in areas normally too cold for citrus. Ripens before dangerous frosts occur, and the foliage survives temperatures to about 22°F to 18°F (–6° to –8°C). Popular in the Sacramento Valley and Sierra foothills as well as other areas in the state. Easy-to-peel seedless fruit with mild, sweet flavor. Dobashi Beni, Okitsu Wase, and Owari are Satsuma selections that thrive in cooler regions. None are suited to low deserts. Dobashi Beni and Okitsu Wase both have mature fruit at the end of October. Owari is a month later. Do not leave fruit on the tree; it becomes puffy and insipid. Owari can degenerate into a poor tree due to Satsuma's ability to sport.

MANDARIN HYBRIDS

Encore	May–Jul	Apr–Jul	Mar–Jun	Apr–Jul	May–Aug

Developed at UC Riverside. Late-maturing variety. Sweet, juicy, seedy, easy-to-peel, medium-sized, speckled fruit. Medium-sized tree. Alternate bearer. Hybrid of King × Mediterranean mandarins (*C. nobilis* × *C. deliciosa*).

Fairchild	NR	Nov–Jan	Nov–Dec	Nov–Jan	NR

Early ripening Clementine mandarin × Orlando tangelo hybrid adapted to the desert and inland valleys but not to the coasts. The most widely grown commercial mandarin in California. Rich-flavored, medium-sized, juicy fruit hold fairly well on tree. Tree has few thorns.

Gold Nugget	Mar–Jun	Feb–May	Dec–Jan	Mar–May	unknown

Seedless, late-maturing, with a rich sweet flavor. Fruit store exceptionally well, up to 6 months. Rind is paler and coarser than other mandarins. Parentage is complex; a hybrid of Wilking × Kincy (King × Dancy) mandarins.

	Harvest period*				
Scion variety	Southern California Coast	Southern California Inland	California Desert	Central Valley	Northern California Coastal Valleys
Honey	Feb–Apr	Jan–Mar	Dec–Feb	Jan–Apr	Feb–Apr

Mid-season variety. Very sweet, juicy, seedy, fruit. Hybrid of King × Mediterranean mandarins (*C. nobilis* × *C. deliciosa*). Superior flavor. Very easy to peel. Small fruits. Alternate bearer. Medium to large tree. Do not confuse with the "Honey tangerine" sold in grocery stores, which is Florida's Murcott tangor.

Kinnow	Apr–May	Feb–Apr	Dec–Feb	Feb–Apr	Apr–May

Developed at UC Riverside. Very sweet, juicy, seedy, medium-size, easy-to-peel fruit. Aromatic. Large, willow-like, ornamental tree. Alternate bearer. Hybrid of Mediterranean × King mandarins (*C. deliciosa* × *C. nobilis*).

W. Murcott, aka Delite	Mar–Apr	Feb–Mar	NR	Feb–Mar	Mar–May

A new Murcott tangor × Clementine mandarin hybrid released by UC's Citrus Clonal Protection Program (CCPP) at UC Riverside under the W. Murcott name, but marketed as Delite. High-yielding, alternate bearer of medium-sized fruit with excellent, rich flavor. Available to the home gardener from nurseries or budwood purchased from the CCPP. Best on Carrizo citrange or trifoliate rootstocks. A late-maturing mandarin. Known as Afourer in Morocco, where it originated. Parentage is unknown.

Page	Feb–May	Dec–Feb	NR	Dec–Feb	Feb–May

Result of a cross between a Clementine mandarin and a Minneola tangelo. Small- to medium-sized, usually seedless fruit whose rich flavor is considered by some to be the finest among the mandarins. Easy to peel. Attractive tree with few thorns.

Pixie	Apr–Jun	Mar–Jun	NR	Apr–Jul	Apr–Jul

Late-maturing variety adapted to coastal regions and inland valleys. Seedless, mild, sweet fruit. Alternate bearer. Easy to peel. Small to medium-sized fruit. Bumpy rind.

TANGELO (*Citrus tangelo*)

Tangelos are hybrids between a mandarin and a grapefruit. The "tang" portion of the name is a shortened version of "tangerine," a popular name for mandarins. The "elo" comes from pummelo, a term the citrus industry was promoting instead of grapefruit. Tangelos are adapted best to hot climates. Their yields are higher and seedier if a mandarin or tangor is nearby for cross-pollination. At the grocery store, tangelos are sometimes incorrectly called oranges, mandarins, or tangerines.

Minneola	Feb–Apr	Jan–Mar	Jan–Feb	Jan–Mar	Mar–May

The most important commercial tangelo in California and the best for home gardens. Bright orange-red fruit with conspicuous neck. Minneola is a cross between a Dancy mandarin and a Duncan grapefruit. The fruit has good color and is borne toward the outside of the tree, making it a good ornamental. A cross-pollinator (Dancy, Clementine, or Temple tangor) increases production. Seedy, juicy fruit. Peels well. Rich, tart, unique flavor. Best in hot climates.

Orlando	NR	Dec–Feb	Nov–Dec	Dec–Feb	NR

Same parentage as Minneola. Fruit ripen a month earlier than Minneola and are more orange-like in shape and color. Very juicy, seedy, mildly sweet. Tastes more like a mandarin than Minneola. Slightly hardier than Minneola. Adapted well to hot desert regions. Not recommended for coastal areas. Tree is similar, except for cupped leaves. For best results, requires a cross-pollinator. Peels poorly.

TANGOR (*Citrus nobilis*)

Tangors are hybrids between a mandarin and a sweet orange. In the grocery store, they are often mislabeled as oranges. They are adapted best to Florida's climate but can be grown in the California desert or hot inland valleys, depending on the variety

Murcott	NR	—	NR	—	NR

So sweet it is marketed under the name Honey tangerine. Its fruit are yellowish-orange and seedy. Can be grown in hot inland valleys, but is not recommended for the California coasts or desert. Ripens late. Easy to peel. Holds well on tree.

Table 18.1 cont.

Scion variety	Harvest period*				
	Southern California Coast	Southern California Inland	California Desert	Central Valley	Northern California Coastal Valleys
Temple	NR	NR	—	NR	NR

Often called Temple orange. Is adapted only to the California desert. It needs high heat and is not recommended in the coastal valleys, the inland valleys, or the Central Valley. Tart, seedy fruit ripen in winter. Trees are more sensitive to cold than mandarins and oranges.

KUMQUAT (*Fortunella* spp.)

Kumquats are oval to round-shaped citrus fruits that look like very small oranges, except that their rinds are edible, spongy, and sweet. The pulp is tangy and moderately acidic. Whole, unpeeled fruits are edible—rind and all—which makes kumquats unique citrus fruits. Dwarf trees grow to about 3 to 6 ft (0.9 to 1.8 m) tall. Standard trees are about twice that size and have multiple uses in the landscape. Trees are very ornamental and symmetrically shaped with dark green leaves, richly perfumed white blossoms, and showy orange-colored fruit. Dwarf varieties make excellent hedges or container plants for patios. Kumquats require high heat to bloom and set fruit. They are the most cold-hardy citrus. Scientists have hybridized them with other citrus types (limes, mandarins), seeking cold-tolerant hybrids. Kumquats are named after the botanist Robert Fortune (*Fortunella*), rather than grouped with the fruits in the *Citrus* genus. Kumquats grow actively only in high heat, but nighttime chill is essential for good color and flavor development. Kumquats bloom later than other citrus types and stop growing earlier; thus, they are adapted to the coolest limits of the citrus belt.

Meiwa (*Fortunella crassifolia*)	Jan–Apr	Dec–Mar	Dec–Mar	Dec–Mar	Jan–Apr

A popular variety in China and Japan. The best variety for eating fresh fruit and for cooler climates. Sweet flesh, spicy, thick rind. In Asia, it is also used for making candies and preserves. Excellent ornamental. Few to no thorns. Does well in warm, sunny locations. Fruit can store on the tree for up to a year. Sweeter, juicier, and less seedy than Nagami. Very cold hardy.

Nagami (*Fortunella margarita*)	Jan–Apr	Dec–Mar	Dec–Jan	Dec–Mar	Jan–Apr

The most popular commercial variety in the United States. Slightly seedy. Good container plant. Easy to espalier; thornless. Fruit can store on tree for up to a year. Sweet rind, tart flesh.

LIMEQUAT

Tavares **Eustis**	Dec–Jul	Nov–Jul	Nov–Jul	Nov–Jul	Dec–Jul

Limequats are hybrids of a Mexican lime, which is very cold-sensitive, and a kumquat, which is very cold-hardy. The USDA, which sponsored the breeding program, was attempting to capitalize on the cold-hardiness of kumquats and extend that trait to other citrus types. Limequats are an excellent lime substitute and are much more cold-hardy than the lime parent. Fruit have flavor and aroma that approximate a lime with an edible, sweet rind from the kumquat parentage. Limequats require less heat than their lime parents. Fruit are yellow when ripe. Not a commercial success but worthy of consideration by home gardeners. On dwarf rootstock, they are 3 to 6 ft (0.9 to 1.8 m) tall. Highly ornamental and easy to espalier, they bear abundant fruit. Adapted to all citrus-growing zones in California.

ORANGEQUAT

The USDA sponsored the plant breeding program that led to the development of the orangequat, which is a cross of a Meiwa kumquat and a Satsuma mandarin.

Nippon	Dec–Sep	Dec–Jul	Nov–Mar	Nov–Aug	Dec–Sep

Fruit are deep orange in color, a little larger than a kumquat, and can be eaten rind and all. The spongy rind is sweet and the pulp is juicy and slightly acidic. The overall flavor is sweeter than a kumquat. Fruit require less heat to ripen than kumquats. They have few seed and are adapted to all citrus regions in California. Compact, handsome plant excellent for espalier or containers. Fruit stores on the tree for months before losing flavor. Use fresh or for marmalade or candied fruit. Especially prolific during the Christmas season. Very cold-hardy.

	Harvest period*				
Scion variety	Southern California Coast	Southern California Inland	California Desert	Central Valley	Northern California Coastal Valleys

PUMMELO (*Citrus grandis*)

Pummelos are the largest citrus fruit. They have firm flesh but thicker rinds and lower juice content than grapefruit. Pummelos are not eaten in the same manner as grapefruit; they are peeled, segmented, and the juice vesicles are shelled out of their membranes. The shelled segments are eaten with or without sugar. Pummelos vary in flavor from very sour to high sugar/low acid to nonacid. The color of juice vesicles ranges from buff to pink to deep red. Some are seedy and others are seedless. Trees vary in size, shape, and growth habit. Pummelos need less heat to ripen than grapefruit. Fruit can hold on the tree for several months.

Chandler	Apr–Jun	Dec–Apr	Dec–Feb	Dec–Apr	Apr–Jun

Developed at the UC Riverside Experiment Station. Good sugar-acid pummelo flavor. Large, woody flowers. Yellow rind with pink flesh. A hybrid between two pummelos (Siamese Pink × Siamese Sweet). Many seed unless grown in isolation from other citrus. Open growth habit suitable for espalier.

Reinking	Apr–Jun	Dec–Apr	Dec–Feb	Dec–Apr	Apr–Jun

Developed at the USDA Citrus and Date Experiment Station in Indio. Not as sweet as Chandler. Rind is yellow with pale yellow flesh. Many seed unless isolated from other citrus.

Other varieties	NR	—	—	—	NR

Tahitian (white-fleshed) and Hirado Buntan (pink-fleshed), adapted to inland valleys and desert.

CITRON (*Citrus medica*)

Like the lemon and lime, the citron is a sour fruit, but unlike the lemon and lime, the flesh of the citron is lacking in juice. The fruit are large and oblong and the yellow rind is very thick. Since the rind oils are very aromatic, historically it was used as a room deodorizer and moth repellent. Today, its most typical uses are in religious ceremonies and in fruitcakes. The citron rind is candied and used to make fruitcake "fruit."

Buddha's Hand	ever-bearing	ever-bearing	ever-bearing	ever-bearing	ever-bearing

Sometimes referred to as a "fingered" citron, since it is divided into finger-like sections at one end. Others have referred to the fact that it looks like a citrus octopus or a bunch of gnarled bananas. The fruit consist entirely of rind, no pulp. In Buddhism, this fruit is a symbol of happiness. Grown in the United States as a novelty, it is used as a perfumant and as an ornamental in Asia. Very cold-sensitive.

Etrog	ever-bearing	ever-bearing	ever-bearing	ever-bearing	ever-bearing

The fruit used by Jews to celebrate the Feast of Tabernacles. Shaped like an oversized lemon but has ridges along the rind. Very dry, acidic pulp with little practical use other than for candying. Very cold-sensitive.

Sources: Ray and Walheim 1980; Brenzel 2001; Walheim 1996.

Notes: *Harvest periods are broad and general for a particular climate zone. Harvest periods (ripening dates) may vary slightly from year to year and can be influenced by microclimates. The harvest periods listed should not be interpreted as absolutely precise. These harvest periods are tailored to the home gardener who can wait for fruit to fully ripen before harvesting. In a given climate zone, home gardeners typically harvest later in the season than commercial growers.

†NR = Not recommended.

Inland Southern California. This region includes Riverside, San Bernardino, Pasadena, Glendale, Burbank, the San Fernando Valley, Ojai Valley, and Santa Paula. This region is hotter and drier in summer and colder in winter than the Southern California Coast and is more subject to hot, dry desert air. Santa Ana winds can damage fruits. In the past, this region was one of the state's most important commercial citrus areas. Today, sizeable acreage remains, but urbanization has encroached significantly. Home gardeners in this area can grow almost any citrus variety. Summer heat needed to sweeten fruits is plentiful, and if the site is chosen prudently, trees and fruits can be protected from damaging winter cold.

California Desert Valleys. This region includes Palm Springs, Indio, and El Centro—the Coachella and Imperial Valleys. Summers are hot, long, and harsh. Daytime and nighttime temperatures fluctuate widely, and humidity is low year-round. Citrus varieties that have high heat requirements, such as grapefruit and Valencia oranges, thrive in this region, yielding sweet, high-quality fruit. Lemons (Eureka and Lisbon), mandarins (Fairchild and Royal) and tangelos are also grown in the desert valleys. Citrus grown here ripens early. Sunburned fruits, especially on the south side of the tree, can be a problem. Wind and extreme heat may adversely affect some citrus; some varieties are not recommended for this region, such as Washington navels and Satsuma mandarins (see table 18.1). In the winter, frost protection may be needed. Citrus grown in the desert generally has less juice and a tougher rind than the same varieties grown in milder climates.

Central Valleys. This region includes the San Joaquin and Sacramento Valleys of central California and extends from Bakersfield to Redding. The San Joaquin Valley (Bakersfield, Visalia, Fresno) has hot, dry, sunny summers and cold, wet winters. Winter temperatures are influenced by elevation and land slope. The tule fog in this region favors citrus because it acts as a thermal blanket. Today, the San Joaquin Valley is the most important citrus-producing area in the state. The Sacramento Valley includes the cities of Sacramento, Marysville, Oroville, Paradise, and Chico and surrounding areas. Summers are warm, and winters are cold and often dominated by tule fog. The slope and exposure of the planting site influence the varieties that will perform well. Early, hardy citrus varieties, such as Washington navels and Satsuma mandarins, do best, but others can do well with protection.

Northern California Coastal Valleys. This region contains several climates influenced by the Pacific Ocean: the San Francisco Bay Area, Santa Cruz, San Jose, Monterey, Santa Rosa, Vacaville, Cloverdale, Napa, and Crescent City. In the summer, the weather can be cool, windy, and foggy near the coast but warm in inland areas, although usually not as warm as the Sacramento Valley. Varieties with lower heat requirements do best near the coast. Although frosts are infrequent in the winters near San Francisco and in the thermal belts of many valleys in this region, low-lying inland areas can have temperatures below freezing. Site selection and winter protection are important factors in many locations in this region.

Cold-Hardiness of Citrus Varieties

Different citrus types have different tolerance to cold temperatures. Citron and lime trees are the most tender types and cannot tolerate freezing weather; sweet orange and grapefruit varieties are intermediate; and Satsuma mandarins and kumquats are the most cold-hardy. Such cold-hardiness comparisons refer to the trees, not the fruit. In general, the most tender to most hardy species are

- citron
- Mexican lime
- lemon
- grapefruit = pummelo
- tangelo = tangor = sweet orange
- sour orange
- Satsuma mandarin = Meyer lemon
- kumquat

Mexican lime trees are damaged at temperatures below freezing (32°F or 0°C), whereas kumquats are cold-hardy to 18° to 20°F (–8° to –7°C). Larger fruits such as grapefruit that are protected by leafy branches can endure temperatures of 24°F (–4°C). The duration of the cold temperatures, the fruit's position on the tree, the tree's location, its age, and the cold tolerance of the rootstock are important factors that affect cold-hardiness. Foliage can act to protect fruit from the cold. Avoid planting citrus in low spots in the garden where cold air accumulates. Young, succulent growth and blossoms are the most susceptible to cold; thus, late spring frosts can be the most damaging.

As a home gardener, you have the alternative of growing citrus in containers and sheltering your plants in the winter by bringing them indoors if the outdoor winter temperatures exceed the plants' cold-hardiness range. To succeed in growing citrus, you must do everything you can to avoid subjecting your plants to temperatures beyond their cold-hardiness range.

Heat Requirement of Citrus Varieties

The more acid citrus varieties, which do not need to sweeten up, such as lemons and limes, do not have high heat requirements. They perform well in cooler locations along the coast, which permit several harvests year-round. Lemons can also be grown in hotter regions, but the heat limits harvest dates. In the desert, lemons ripen mainly in late fall and winter. Unlike lemons, grapefruit has a high heat requirement and is of the highest quality when grown in desert locations. When homeowners grow grapefruit near the coast, they should leave them on the tree to increase gradually in sweetness.

In areas of the state that are too cool for high-quality grapefruit, home gardeners can choose the grapefruit × pummelo hybrids Melogold and Oroblanco, which require less heat to sweeten (see table 18.1). Grapefruit grown in pots can be brought indoors to avoid exposure to freezing temperatures.

Rootstock Varieties

Unless you do your own bud grafting, when you purchase a citrus tree at a nursery, you will be buying a scion variety listed in table 18.1 grafted onto a rootstock variety selected by the nursery. Labeling laws in California do not require the nursery to state the rootstock variety used. Knowledgeable nursery personnel may be able to inform you. Because the rootstock variety provides the lower portion of the trunk and the roots of the tree, it influences fruit productivity, size, and quality, overall tree vigor, resistance to soilborne fungal diseases, nematodes, viruses, viroids,

environmental stresses, and cold-hardiness (table 18.2). Thus, it is useful to know which rootstock variety you have purchased. Because rootstocks have a major influence on tree performance and fruit quality (table 18.3) and are important to the California citrus industry, UC conducts long-term research projects on rootstock varieties. This brief discussion of citrus rootstocks has been adapted from *Integrated Pest Management for Citrus*, 2nd ed. (Kobbe and Dreistadt 1991) and *California Citrus Rootstocks* (Ferguson, Sakovich, and Roose 1990). See those resources for more detailed information.

The UC's Citrus Clonal Protection Program should eliminate the possibility of viral and viroid bud-transmissible infections in the scion, such as *Tristeza*, *Exocortis*, and *Psorosis*. However, to avoid any future problems, it is best to select a rootstock resistant to these infections in the scion. Proper preplant assessment and preparation of the soil should eliminate or control the soilborne pests and diseases that can attack citrus. But if parasitic nematodes and *Phytophthora* fungi are endemic in the area where you live, you should choose a resistant or tolerant rootstock (see table 18.2).

Four Dominant Rootstock Varieties

Troyer and Carrizo Citranges (sweet orange × trifoliate orange hybrids). In the citrus industry today, Troyer and Carrizo citranges, which are hybrids of *Citrus* and *Poncirus*, are the most common rootstocks used with scions of sweet oranges, mandarins, grapefruit, and some lemons. In climates outside the citrus belt, citranges are grown as landscape or fruit trees. They are hardy to 5° to 10°F (−15° to −12°C).

Until the late 1940s, sour orange, rough lemon, sweet orange, and Cleopatra mandarin were the major California rootstocks, but today, Troyer and Carrizo citranges have largely replaced these older rootstocks because the citranges are more resistant to some serious diseases in California, particularly *Tristeza* (see table 18.2). Approximately 65 percent of the rootstocks produced between 1950 and 1970 were Troyer. It has become the standard by which all other California rootstocks are judged. Recently, Carrizo and C-35 (see below) have also been widely planted. Both Carrizo and Troyer are prone to zinc and manganese deficiencies.

Table 18.2

PEST AND DISEASE SUSCEPTIBILITY AND STRESS RESPONSES OF SELECTED ROOTSTOCKS USED IN CALIFORNIA CITRUS

Condition*	Trifoliate orange	Troyer citrange	Carrizo citrange	Alemow	C-32/C-35 citranges	Swingle	Rough lemon	Sour orange	Sweet orange
Tristeza virus	T	T	T	S	T	T	T	S	T
Phytophthora root rot	T	I	I	T	T	T	S	I	S
Phytophthora gummosis†	T	T	T	T	T	T	S	T	S
Armillaria root rot	—	S	S	S	—	—	S	S	—
Exocortis (viroid)	S	T	T	T	—	T	CD	T	T
citrus nematode (*Tylenchulus semipenetrans*)	T	S	S	S	T (C-35) S (C-32)	T	S	S	S
cold hardiness	G	A	A	P	—	G	P	G	A
poor drainage	A	U	U	CD	—	—	U	A	U
salinity	P	U	U	A	—	A	A	A	—
calcareous soils	P	U	U	A	U	U	A	A	P
scion used	oranges mandarins	oranges mandarins Lisbonlemon grapefruit	oranges mandarins Lisbonlemon grapefruit	lemons (only)	oranges mandarins Lisbonlemon grapefruit	oranges mandarin Lisbonlemon grapefruit	lemon grapefruit oranges kumquat	oranges grapefruit	oranges mandarins grapefruit

Sources: Kobbe and Dreistadt 1991, pp. 16–17; Ferguson, Sakovich, and Roose 1990, pp. 16–17.

Notes: *A = acceptable; CD = conflicting data; I = intermediate; G = good; P = poor; S = susceptible; T = tolerant; U = unsatisfactory; — = no data.

†Phytophthora gummosis is a synonym for Phytophthora crown/foot rot.

Trifoliate Orange (*Poncirus trifoliata*) (Rubidoux and Pomeroy). As noted in table 18.2, both the citranges and trifoliate orange are tolerant to *Tristeza* virus and Phytophthora root rot and resistant to Phytophthora crown (foot) rot but susceptible to Armillaria root rot. Trifoliate orange is resistant to citrus nematode but susceptible to *Exocortis*. (These diseases and pests of citrus are discussed in table 18.4 and later in this chapter.)

Trifoliate orange is cold-hardy to about –15°F (–26°C), which is its major advantage. Because it is the most cold-hardy rootstock, trifoliate orange has been used extensively in plantings in the San Joaquin and Sacramento Valleys. It is a common rootstock used with scions of sweet oranges and mandarins. Outside or inside the citrus belt, trifoliate orange can be grown as an ornamental. It is a spiny, deciduous shrub or small tree that produces large, fragrant blossoms in spring followed by leaves consisting of three leaflets. Its fruit are inedible but hang on the tree until the following winter, making it a decorative landscape plant. Although fruit quality is good with trifoliate orange as the rootstock, fruit rinds may crease and split. It is sensitive to *Exocortis*, alkaline soils, and zinc deficiency. Trees on trifoliate orange develop a bench at the bud union because the rootstock is larger than the scion.

Flying Dragon Trifoliate Orange. A natural dwarf that grows to about 6 feet (2 m) tall, Flying Dragon has a dwarfing effect on fruiting varieties grafted onto it, which typically grow to about half the standard size.

Alemow (*Citrus macrophylla*). Alemow is the most popular rootstock for lemons grown along the coast. It is susceptible to *Tristeza*, cold temperatures, and citrus nematode, but resistant to Phytophthora root rot, *Exocortis*, and salinity.

Older Rootstock Varieties Not Currently Favored

Sour Orange (*Citrus aurantium*). Sour orange is very susceptible to *Tristeza*. Until the *Tristeza* outbreak in the 1940s, sour orange

Table 18.3

EFFECTS OF ROOTSTOCKS ON HORTICULTURAL TRAITS

Trait	Trifoliate orange	Troyer citrange	Carrizo citrange	Alemow	C-32/C-35 citranges	Swingle	Rough lemon	Sour orange	Sweet orange
tree vigor	low	medium	medium	high	low (C-35) high (C-32)	low	high	medium	medium
tree size	variable*	medium	medium	medium	small (C-35)* large (C-32)	medium	medium	medium	large
drought tolerance	low	medium	medium	—	—	high	high	high	low
total soluble solids in fruit†	high	high	high	low	high	high‡	low	high	high
fruit acidity	high	high§	high	low	high	high‡	low	high	high
fruit juice %	high	high	high	low	high	high	low	high	high
fruit size	small/ medium	medium	medium	large	medium	medium	large	medium	medium small
fruit yield	medium	medium	medium	high	medium (C-35) high (C-32)	medium‡	high	medium	medium high
fruit peel	smooth/thin	medium//	medium//	coarse/thick	medium	medium//	coarse/thick	smooth/thin	—

Source: Adapted from Ferguson, Sakovich, and Roose 1990.

Notes: *Varies with scion.

†Abbreviated TSS; a measure of the sugar content of citrus fruits.

‡In arid climates, produces better yields and higher quality of Redblush grapefruit and Orlando tangelo than most rootstocks, including sour orange.

§Can produce acid fruit in cool areas.

//Exacerbates creasing with a sweet orange scion.

was the rootstock of choice for sweet oranges in California because of the rootstock's resistance to gummosis (Phytophthora root rot), which had devastated the California citrus industry earlier this century. Today, 15 to 20 percent of California citrus acreage is planted on sour orange rootstock. Sour orange is still the most common rootstock for sweet orange in Texas, because, unlike California, Texas has not had a problem with *Tristeza* virus.

Rough Lemon (*Citrus jambhiri*). Rough lemon is not cold hardy and is susceptible to Phytophthora root rot, but it can be used as a rootstock for lemon and grapefruit in desert regions.

Rootstock Varieties Recently Released by UC

C-32 Citrange (sweet orange × trifoliate orange hybrid). C-32 citrange, an unpatented UC release in the early 1990s, produces a large, vigorous tree with good yields of excellent quality. It is equal to Troyer citrange in *Phytophthora* and nematode tolerance. It

appears to have the best potential as a San Joaquin Valley rootstock for navel and Valencia oranges.

C-35 Citrange (sweet orange × trifoliate orange hybrid). C-35 citrange produces a smaller tree with all scion varieties. Fruit quality is good and yields are good, except with navels. C-35 is very tolerant of nematodes and is generally more tolerant of *Phytophthora* than C-32 or Troyer. This rootstock was an unpatented UC release in the early 1990s. Since 1995, it has been used for many trees sold to home gardeners.

Swingle Citrumelo (grapefruit × trifoliate orange hybrid). The major advantages of swingle citrumelo are resistance to Phytophthora foot (crown) rot, drought and cold tolerance, nematode resistance, and *Tristeza* tolerance. *Exocortis* usually causes no obvious symptoms, although some stunting has been reported. This rootstock produces high yields of good-quality fruit and internal quality equal to Troyer/Carrizo citrange. It is more salt-tolerant than trifoliate. Disadvantages include sensitivity to high water tables and calcareous soils, evidence of scion overgrowth in both oranges and grapefruits, and a tendency for the fruit to exhibit the rind disorder known as creasing.

Schaub Rough Lemon. Schaub rough lemon has not been tested extensively but so far has more *Phytophthora* resistance than rough lemon.

Volkameriana (*Citrus volkameriana*). The major advantage of Volkameriana is its cold tolerance, which is superior to that of rough lemon or Alemow. It also produces better-quality fruit than rough lemon or Alemow, but is otherwise similar to rough lemon.

Rootstock Incompatibilities with Scions

True incompatibilities between a scion and a rootstock are rare. Most less-than-effective scion/rootstock combinations are eliminated in the research stage because of poor productivity, poor tree performance, and poor fruit quality and size. For example, Eureka lemon is incompatible with trifoliate orange and most citranges. However, some incompatibilities, such as some bud union disorders, do not manifest until 10, 15, or 20 years later. One example is bud union crease, a fold formed at the bud union, which, with increasing overgrowth, compresses the conducting elements and girdles the tree. The one- to two-decade delay before this problem is evident confirms how essential the long-term UC research on citrus rootstocks and scions is to the California citrus industry and the home gardener. The most susceptible combinations are Frost nucellar navel on trifoliate orange, followed by Satsuma mandarin on Troyer citrange (bud union creasing occurs at 15 to 20 years) and certain scion lines on sour orange. Frost nucellar navels on trifoliate rootstocks have shown decline at 10 to 20 years because of bud union disturbance.

Future Development of California Citrus Rootstocks

Currently, there are no pressures on the California citrus rootstock industry equal to that of *Tristeza* virus in the 1940s. However, new rootstock varieties need to be developed because of continuing disease and pest problems, the continuing shift northward of the commercial citrus industry, and the current lack of optimal rootstocks for nearly 30 percent of the state's citrus production, which consists of grapefruit, lemons, limes, tangelos, tangors, and mandarins. *Tristeza*, *Phytophthora parasitica*, *P. citrophthora*, and citrus nematode continue to be major problems among widely used rootstocks. Only trifoliate orange and Swingle citrumelo tolerate all four well.

A Consumer Guide to Identification of Citrus Rootstocks*

Citrus trees are sold on many different rootstocks. The characteristics summarized in this chapter show that rootstocks can alter many aspects of tree behavior; thus, the consumer may wish to know what rootstock is used for a tree. There are two situations when rootstock identification may be important: when purchasing a tree at the nursery and when an older tree has problems that may relate to its rootstock.

Identifying the Rootstock on a New Purchase. When the tree is purchased, it may be labeled with the rootstock, but this is relatively rare. Sometimes trees are labeled by painting colored rings onto the trunk, but different codes are used by different nurseries, so this is not very helpful to the buyer. Generally, the only clue to the rootstock is given by the expected tree size (dwarf, semidwarf, standard), as shown below:

Labeled size	Rootstocks used
dwarf	Flying Dragon, occasionally others
semidwarf	C-35, trifoliate, Swingle
standard	Carrizo, Troyer, rough lemon, sweet orange, sour orange

Trees on the dwarfing rootstock Flying Dragon trifoliate are the easiest to identify. Even young trees will have a characteristic bud union with the scion being smaller than the rootstock. This bench will become quite pronounced by the time the trees are several years old. If the tree is not labeled and does not have this characteristic bud union, it is rather difficult to determine the rootstock.

Identifying the Rootstock on an Older Tree. For older trees that are already planted in the ground, an educated guess can often be

---

*The author of this section is Mikeal Roose, Professor of Genetics, UC Riverside.

made about the rootstock using the guidelines listed below.

Identifying characteristics bud union	Possible rootstock
almost undetectable	sweet orange
smooth but detectable	sour orange
lumpy bulge; lemon scion	Alemow
slight bulge, many suckers from rootstock	rough lemon
moderate bench	Troyer, Carrizo, C-32, C-35
pronounced bench	Trifoliate, Swingle
severe bench; dwarf tree	Flying Dragon

As indicated above, if the rootstock and scion are similar in size but there is a bulge just at the union, the rootstock is probably Alemow (for lemon scions) or rough lemon. If shoots arise from below the bud union, their leaf type can be helpful in identifying the rootstock. Sweet orange, sour orange, Alemow, and rough lemon have unifoliate leaves, whereas the other rootstocks have trifoliate leaves.

Selecting, Budding, and Buying Citrus Trees

Purchase plants from a reputable nursery or mail-order supplier and be certain that the label identifies the scion precisely. Find out which rootstock has been used. Mail-order citrus is available bare-root or potted. Citrus at the nursery or garden center is available in containers of 5, 7, or 15 gallons (18.9, 26.5, or 56.7 l) and sometimes in cans of 1 or 2 gallons (3.8 or 7.6 l). Younger specimens that have not begun to bear usually transplant more easily and are less expensive than the larger trees. Inspect carefully before you buy. Choose a healthy-looking plant that has foliage with strong green, uniform color, no blemishes or nicks on the bark, a smooth bud union, fairly symmetrical branching, and no obvious pest damage (chewed leaves or signs of insects). Inspect the undersides of leaves, the shoots, the bark, the soil surface, and the bud union. Make sure that the bud union is located far enough above the soil level to prevent rot disease problems. A straight, strong trunk is preferred because it may not require staking. Plants that have roots protruding from the container have been in the container too long and should not be purchased.

Budding a Citrus Tree

To bud or graft a citrus tree, refer to the section on budding in chapter 5, "Plant Propagation." Note especially the T-budding technique, which is commonly used with citrus. You will need budwood (a twig of the scion variety with buds along its length) and a rootstock.

You may be able to purchase budwood from a local nursery or from the UC's certified disease-free budwood program, the Citrus Clonal Protection Program (CCPP), Plant Pathology Department, UC Riverside, Riverside, CA 92521 (e-mail: dgumpf@citrus.ucr.edu or fax 909-686-5612). The program focuses on protecting citrus varieties from bud-transmissible diseases and testing new varieties for the state's commercial industry. Budwood can be sold to home gardeners, although minimum orders are required. The average cost is about $1.50 per bud plus shipping and handling. A minimum of 12 buds is required. Budwood is cut three times per year (September, January, and June) and a printed list of available varieties can be requested. Because the UC's CCPP facilities are a quarantine facility, budwood can be sold throughout the state, but it is illegal for home growers to move budwood from county to county or to move trees and propagating materials without permits from the local county agricultural commissioner or the California Department of Food and Agriculture.

Before budding your tree, be certain that the scion/rootstock combination is compatible and that the rootstock is adapted to your area. Bud when the rootstock is actively growing and the bark is "slipping" (loose enough to peel back when you make the T-cut), which occurs in California from April through August. Bud far enough above the soil line to avoid rot problems. In commercial citrus propagation in California, buds are inserted at a height of about 12 to 18 inches (30 to 46 cm). Note that the citrus tree scion is genetically identical to its parent tissue, and the rootstock is genetically identical to its parent tissue. The process of budding the scion to the rootstock is known as clonal propagation.

Multiple-Variety Citrus Trees

You might consider creating a multiple-variety citrus tree. Such trees are sometimes referred to as "fruit cocktails" and may be a useful alternative if space is limited. Because each variety grows at a different rate, the multiple-variety tree may not be as attractive or aesthetically balanced as the single fruiting variety, but it may serve a useful purpose in your garden. You can bud additional varieties onto an existing citrus tree in your yard or create your unique tree at the outset. Follow the basic T-budding instructions in chapter 5. Sweet orange, mandarin, tangelo, grapefruit, and kumquat can all be used interchangeably as budwood on several compatible rootstock varieties. Eureka and Lisbon lemons do not work well in multiple-variety formats; they are best as single trees. If you are not interested in doing the budding yourself, multiple-variety citrus trees can be purchased.

Planting

To grow citrus successfully in your garden, select a site wisely, choose appropriate scions and rootstocks adapted to your area, and employ cultural management practices that yield high-quality, abundant fruit.

When To Plant

Although citrus can be planted any time of year, the best timetable depends on the climate in your area. Your goal in selecting when to plant is to give the tree's roots the longest possible time to become established before they are subjected to environmental stresses. In freeze-prone regions, early spring is usually best because it gives the tree many months of growth to become acclimated before cold weather and danger of frost occur. In areas that have very hot summers, such as the desert, fall planting is good because the tree will have time to get acclimated before scorching heat occurs. Autumn planting is also a good option in frost-free regions along the coast.

Site Location: Where To Plant

Citrus can be planted indoors or outdoors, in containers, or directly into the ground. Soil pH should be between 6.0 and 7.5, and soil depth must be at least 1½ feet (45 cm). Soil textures ranging from sandy to clay loams are best. A wind-free location that has full sun and heat, preferably a south-facing exposure, is ideal. Other locations are workable if you take advantage of their slope and exposure to radiant energy (the sun) and avoid cold air pockets. If you plant in a location where citrus or avocado trees have previously died, you may need to consider whether a fungicide treatment of the soil is needed to eradicate root rot fungi that could interfere with tree establishment.

A Garden's Microclimates. Every garden has microclimates—smaller areas in the garden that differ from the general climate, such as the cool shade under a large tree on a hot summer day or areas where increased light and heat are reflected from a wall. You can take advantage of these microclimates in selecting the site for growing citrus. The south-facing side of a house typically gets the most consistent sun all day. It is the warmest location, especially in the winter. Citrus grown on the south side, unless it is shaded by tall trees, will receive the most sun and warmth. Heat-demanding varieties, such as grapefruit, will probably do best in the hottest microclimate in your garden. Night temperatures against a south-facing wall that releases heat absorbed during the day may be several degrees higher than in an open area.

The west side is warm and sunny in the afternoon and is the second warmest area of the yard. The east side is usually the first to warm up in the morning but is less warm than the west side. The north side tends to have more shade and is the coldest microclimate. North-facing slopes are cooler and moister than south-facing slopes, which are usually warmer and drier.

Planting in raised beds and espaliering against a south wall (see "Maximizing the Planting Area" later in this chapter) are two methods to increase available heat to citrus. Screens can reflect heat onto trees and deflect damaging winds. Because cold air moves toward the lowest altitude and can cause frost damage to citrus if temperatures are low enough, it is important to provide cold air drainage in your home garden and to plant on the slope rather than at its base where cold air accumulates. A fence at the base of a slope can trap cold air. Wind can increase heat loss, resulting in additional fruit damage. Judicious

Figure 18.5

Planting a citrus tree. (A) Hole should be twice the width of root ball and the depth adjusted so that the upper surface of the tree ball is about 1 inch (2.5 cm) above the surrounding ground. (B) Slice container and remove from root ball, then backfill with native soil and gently tamp.

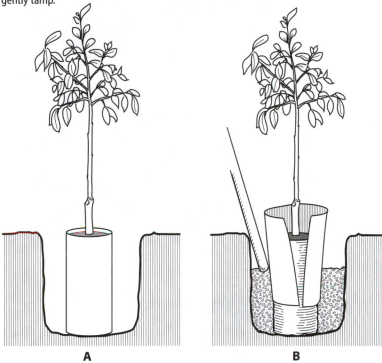

A   B

use of wind screens or buffers can direct cold or dessicating winds away from trees, while at the same time reflecting more heat onto trees.

Sizing Up the Site. Allow enough space for the tree to grow to its mature size. Over the years, a standard-sized citrus tree may grow up to 20 to 30 feet (6.1 to 9.1 m) tall and be equally wide. Its roots will extend well beyond the canopy. As discussed above in the section on roots, citrus roots may extend twice as far as the drip line, that imaginary circle below the canopy edge. Space should be available for a root system of this size, and water and fertilizer applications should include the area beyond the drip line. Do not plant citrus trees near plants with aggressive root systems that will compete for water and nutrients.

Dwarf trees need much less space than a standard-sized tree, but the caveats about allowing enough space to overcome competition for nutrients and water still apply because their roots extend beyond the canopy edge. If space is very limited, consider espaliering the citrus trees—training them to grow flat against a wall or supporting structure as discussed later in this chapter (see fig. 18.9).

Planting a citrus tree in a lawn is not recommended. If the lawn is the only space available, then remove the turf in a 3- to 5-foot (90- to 150-cm) circle, depending on the mature tree size, to reduce competition from turf roots for water and nutrients. Removing the turf also eliminates the risk of a lawnmower nicking the tree's trunk, which would allow a portal for entry by pathogens. Citrus trees should not be irrigated on the same schedule as the turf because the risk of root rot increases.

How To Plant a Citrus Tree

A fully leaved subtropical evergreen tree, such as a citrus, must be treated differently from a typical bareroot, deciduous temperate fruit tree. The following discussion of planting a citrus tree is adapted from *Care of Citrus and Avocado Trees* (Brokaw n.d.).

Citrus is planted in the spring or fall as discussed in "When to Plant." Special allowance must be made for citrus' high transpiration rate. Citrus trees have tender, succulent roots, so their earthen balls may not be as physically stable as those of other plants. Never lift or carry them by grasping the trunk or stake. Be sure the tree is lowered and correctly set in the planting hole before you slit the poly container.

- Dig a hole much wider than the ball of your tree. In general, the hole should be about as deep as the root ball and about twice its diameter (fig. 18.5). For a tree in a 3.5-gallon (13-l) sleeve, an ideal hole is about 16 to 18 inches (41 to 46 cm) wide and about 20 inches (51 cm) deep. Save the soil for backfill. If the soil in your yard is not too light (sand) or heavy (clay), you do not need to add soil amendments to the hole. UC Farm Advisors recommend that you do not use soil amendments at planting time unless extreme conditions exist, such as adobe clay soils.

- Adjust the hole's depth so that the upper surface of the tree ball is about 1 inch (2.5 cm) above the surrounding ground when the tree is lowered into it. Moist soil against the trunk above the original soil line increases the risk of disease.

- Lower the tree into the hole. Then slice the container open vertically on one side. Next, backfill with 6 to 8 inches (15 to 20 cm) of loose soil (which should fill the hole about one-third full) to stabilize the

Figure 18.6

Basin irrigation. *Source:* After *Citrus* (1996), p. 38.

tree before removing the slit container. It is important not to move the root ball after the container is slit.

- Take the plastic tube container out of the hole and place it away from the tree to be discarded. The poly container is recyclable but not degradable. This procedure will leave the roots exposed on the surface of the ball. Note that many of the roots are concentrated at the outside of the vertical surface.

- Gently tamp the loose soil around the ball immediately. Promptly fill the rest of the hole with loose soil, gently tamping as you fill. Fill it to the top, but leave the upper surface of the original ball exposed.

- The soil used to backfill the hole should be free of large clods because they can cause large air spaces that prevent fine roots from contacting the soil and are detrimental to water movement through the backfill.

- The upper surface of the ball is left exposed so that you may add water directly to the ball, even after the tree is planted. It is best to leave the upper surface exposed because the soil in the ball may have been specially formulated with nutrients and designed so the ball will readily absorb

water to its upper surface. If you cover this surface with anything, do not use soil; use sand, loose sawdust, coarse gravel, or anything through which water will pass very rapidly.

- Because citrus trees can have many shallow roots, the soil around them should not be disturbed by cultivation. Control weeds with frequent mowing, hand-weeding, or mulches. Mulches have several advantages, as noted later in this chapter. Herbicides should be used only as a last resort and must be applied carefully so as not to harm the tree. Use only herbicides labeled for use on citrus and follow label directions.

- It is very important to water the tree immediately after planting and to keep the root ball moist until roots grow out into the surrounding soil. The surface roots concentrated at the outside of the ball will die if they dry out.

Watering

Timely irrigation is essential for proper citrus tree growth, development, and fruiting. Never allow the root system to completely dry out, as trees may become stunted, have reduced yields, and die from drought stress. Yet more citrus trees die from excess water, which can be due to overirrigation or poor soil drainage, than die from drought. Because citrus trees are evergreen, they need water year-round. Demand for water is high when trees are growing actively, which usually occurs from late winter or early spring through the summer. Demand is highest when evapotranspiration (ET) is highest, usually in the summer months. (For a discussion of ET and irrigation concepts, see chapter 4, "Water Management.")

The most critical period for irrigation is from the year's initial growth flush until the young fruit are at least 1 inch (2.5 cm) in diameter. Trees cannot perform well if denied a quality water supply. Irrigation water should be relatively free of salt and toxic ions. Irrigation water should not come into contact with the base of the tree trunk because such water may encourage fungal diseases such as Phytophthora root rot and Phytophthora foot (crown) rot (also known as gummosis), which can kill the tree. The trunk and the bud union should stay dry.

It is very important to water newly planted trees immediately after planting, because the surface roots concentrated at the outside of the ball will not be able to function properly unless they are kept moist. The tree's active, working leaves must be supplied with water at all times to ensure proper functioning. Three excellent irrigation methods for citrus trees are basin flooding, sprinkler irrigation, and drip irrigation.

Basin-Flooding Young Trees. Build a basin with a 3-foot (91-cm) diameter around the newly planted tree (fig. 18.6). During the first year, fill the basin with water until the water penetrates just below the bottom of the original root ball. Eventually, the water will need to penetrate 2 to 3 feet (0.6 to 0.9 m). If the soil or rootball have settled, re-form the bottom of the basin. Once the basin has stabilized, the bottom can be covered with straw, sawdust, or some other mulching medium. Basin irrigation can be used for up to a full year, but the basin should be broken down during the wet season if water has any tendency to stand in it. Avoid allowing water to pond around the trunk.

Sprinkler Irrigation. If sprinkler irrigation is used for citrus trees, enough water must be applied during an irrigation to wet most of the root system. Supplemental irrigation using a hose may be needed to keep the root ball of newly planted trees thoroughly moist. Construction of a basin, as in flood irrigation, is useful with sprinkler irrigation during the first year after planting because it aids in holding irrigation water over the rootball and facilitates the hand-watering that may be needed.

If your citrus tree is located in the lawn, which is not recommended, it is important to recognize that sprinkler irrigation is not ideal for citrus. Lawn sprinklers are effective for watering the turf, which has roots that may extend several inches deep, but they are not particularly effective in providing moisture to citrus tree roots, which are located to a depth of about 2 feet (0.6 m). In general, the top roots of the tree are overwatered when it is located in the lawn.

Drip Irrigation. Drip irrigation systems dispense water slowly, in gallons per hour, rather than in the gallons per minute typical of lawn sprinklers. If you use drip irrigation, be sure that the emitter is fastened to the exposed ball of a newly planted tree with a U-shaped piece of wire or hook because it prevents the

dripper from creeping away from the root ball as the hose expands and contracts. Check your emitters frequently to be sure that each tree is getting watered. Clogged emitters are a common problem.

Originally, the emitter is placed over the root ball. In the second year, it is best to use two emitters, one on each side of the trunk about 8 inches (20 cm) away. As the tree grows, more emitters can be added. A mature tree about 8 to 10 years old may have 6 to 8 emitters. In orchards, two parallel lines of emitters are sometimes used. The majority of citrus roots are in the top 2 feet (0.6 m) of soil, with the heaviest concentration in the top foot. Most feeder roots are usually in the top 6 to 12 inches (15 to 30 cm).

Irrigation Frequency

Irrigation frequency is influenced by climate; thus, the irrigation schedule must be changed as seasons change through the year. Some of the water applied is absorbed by the roots; some is lost from leaf surfaces by transpiration; and some evaporates from the soil surface. Evapotranspiration losses increase during hot, dry, windy conditions, and consequently the demand for water increases. Soil type also influences irrigation frequency because of its effects on water-holding capacity. Disregard the dryness of the top inch of soil, which dries out rather quickly even though the underlying soil may still be moist. As a rule of thumb, water when the top few inches of soil are dry but the rest of the root zone still feels slightly moist. Young trees are usually watered every 5 to 10 days for a period of 6 to 10 weeks in June through September, but pay attention to the weather in case adjustments are needed. Hot, windy weather will necessitate more frequent irrigation. Younger trees require more frequent irrigations than older ones because their root masses dry out more quickly. A young tree may need water more often than once a week in warm weather. Cool, overcast days place little demand on the water supply, and irrigation is required less frequently.

Irrigation Amount. In general, for a newly planted tree, 2 to 5 gallons (7.6 to 19 l) of water per irrigation per tree is sufficient to keep the root ball moist. Once the tree has begun to establish a root system, keep the soil damp, but do not allow the soil to remain soggy (saturated). Saturated soil lacks air in pore spaces, creating an anaerobic environment that favors disease. Alternate wetting and drying allows oxygen to enter the soil, which is necessary for root growth.

Table 4.2 in chapter 4 lists average daily evapotranspiration (ET) rates for a 4-inch-high (10-cm) cool-season turfgrass when unlimited water is available, which is the reference planting that scientists refer to in comparing water use among plant species. Mature citrus trees use about 0.7 times the figures in the table. Younger trees use less and newly planted trees use the least, about 0.02 times the reference ET rates.

Water deeply since citrus root systems are usually several inches to 2 feet (0.6 m) deep. A mature tree with an extensive root system requires more water to wet the root zone than does a young tree with a smaller root mass, but the young tree's roots dry out faster. On newly planted trees, you can use a soil core probe slanted toward the side of the rootball so that it penetrates the ball about 12 inches (30 cm) below the soil surface in order to determine soil moisture content, and apply water according to the needs of the tree (fig. 18.7).

Drought Stress and Dried-Out Fruit. When a citrus tree is water-stressed, it will extract water from developing and mature fruit, causing them to dry out. Developing and mature fruit serve as a source of water for the tree when the tree is experiencing drought. Keep trees adequately watered while fruit are developing to prevent this problem.

Protecting Citrus Trees

Citrus trees and fruits are at risk from freezes. Temperatures in the middle 20°F (−4°C) range result in fruit losses; low 20°F (−7°C) and high teens (−8°C) are thresholds for leaf and twig damage; and lower temperatures extensively kill large branches and limbs. Choice growing sites take advantage of slope and exposure to obtain energy from the sun and avoid cold-air pockets. If you live in a frost-prone area, a number of short-term protection measures and long-term precautions can increase your overall preparedness.

Immediate and Long-Term Frost Protection

Young citrus trees, particularly the foliage, are very vulnerable to prolonged frost conditions, but immediate precautions can protect the trunk and foliage and will often save a tree when a frost is predicted.

Short-Term Response to Prediction of Frost. *Protecting the trunk: Thermal wraps.* Wrap the trunk of a new tree with an insulating material, such as heavy corrugated cardboard, several layers of newspapers, corn stalks, or special thermal wraps. Wrap to a point above the bud union (fig. 18.8). Even if the exposed parts of your tree are killed, it is likely that you will have a budded tree when winter is over. At the onset of spring, you will be able to unwrap the damaged tree and select a shoot or shoots above the bud union to renew the tree. Do not remove dead tree parts until new shoots are growing well.

Protecting the trunk: Sawdust-filled collar. A more effective insulation alternative to preserve the bud union is a collar 5 or 6 inches (12.5 or 15 cm) in diameter filled with sawdust to about 6 to 12 inches (15 to 30 cm) above the union. It is almost impossible to freeze tissue within this mass of sawdust.

Protecting the foliage: Use canopies, not plastic. A suspended canvas and wood canopy above the tree will help to protect foliage. Wrapping around and through foliage with straw can also provide insulation. Some home growers

Figure 18.7

Use a soil core probe to detect soil moisture content. *Source:* After Brokaw n.d., p. 1.

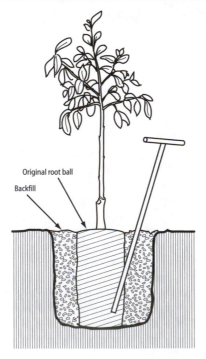

Original root ball

Backfill

Figure 18.8

Wrapping the trunk of citrus in an insulating material to protect it from freezing temperatures. *Source*: After *Citrus* (1996), p. 16.

have used lighted electric bulbs inside tents in extreme conditions. Trees do not survive well in darkness; they must be allowed sunlight during the day. Do not use polyethylene or other non-breathing plastic. A completely enclosed covering of these materials is often worse than nothing, especially when it touches the tree. Foliage touching the cover will be damaged by the cold.

Irrigation practices when a frost is predicted. Water the soil a day or two before the freeze and again after it hits. Moist soil holds more heat than dry soil. The irrigation water will release heat as it cools and freezes. Do not sprinkle the tree because ice forming on branches can break them.

Long-Term Frost Precautions. *Variety selection: Cold-hardiness and early ripening.* Choose cold-tolerant scion varieties and rootstocks. Review the information about cold-hardiness of different citrus types in tables 18.1 and 18.2 before making your selection. Choose early-ripening varieties, such as Satsuma mandarins and Washington navels, which will allow you to harvest before the threat of frost occurs.

Site selection. Take advantage of your garden's warmest microclimate.

Fertilization practices. To prevent stimulating new growth during the coldest time of year,

start fertilizing after the last spring frost and stop in late summer.

Irrigation practices. Because stressed plants are more susceptible to freeze damage, keep citrus trees well irrigated in frost-prone areas. Frost-injured fruit will dry out on the tree.

Pruning practices. Do not prune in fall or winter because pruning can stimulate tender new growth.

Container planting. If freezes are frequent and severe, plant citrus in containers that can be sheltered during the harshest times of year.

Sunburn Protection

The trunk and large limbs should be protected from sunburn. Lemon trees are particularly sensitive to sunburn. Wrap the trunk of the newly planted tree with newspapers or tree wraps, and tie loosely. The trunks and exposed branches of older trees can be painted with white, water-based latex paint (diluted 1:1 with water) or with a Bordeaux powder to which water has been added (make it a thick paint) to protect them from sunburn.

Fertilizing

Successful fruit production requires an adequate supply of essential nutrients to trees. Deficiencies reduce yields and adversely affect size, color, sweetness, and peel texture of fruit. Professional growers use leaf tissue analysis information as guidelines for their yield production. The primary nutrient that home gardeners need to supply is nitrogen (N); phosphorus and potassium do not need replenishment as often. In certain areas of the state and in some soils, magnesium, iron, zinc, manganese, copper, boron, and molybdenum may be deficient. In other soils, boron may be in excess.

Nitrogen Fertilization and the Nonbearing Years

Young citrus trees in the nonbearing years (the first 2 to 3 years) have different nitrogen requirements than mature, fully bearing trees. In the nonbearing years, citrus trees should be fertilized adequately to encourage maximum early growth.

Home gardeners may sprinkle a tablespoon of nitrogen-bearing fertilizer (ammonium nitrate or urea, for example) every 3 or 4 weeks over the root area of nonbearing trees and water it in thoroughly. Several UC farm advisors recommend that home gardeners spread 2 tablespoons (30 ml) of nitrogen fertilizer three to four times per year under young citrus trees before irrigation. On a quantitative basis, both of these fertilization rates approximate to $1/10$ pound (45 g) nitrogen fertilizer per year for a tree that is 1 to 2 years old. For a 3-year-old tree, the rate can be more than doubled ($1/4$ pound [110 g] nitrogen fertilizer/year). Increase the dosage to $1/2$ pound (225 g) nitrogen per year for a 4-year-old tree. Apply fertilizer around the drip line or in the path of irrigation water, being careful not to concentrate the fertilizer application in one area.

Fertilization of Fully Bearing Citrus Trees

Research at UC has contributed to the use of leaf analysis as a guide to planning fertilizer programs for commercial growers. Effective application methods and sophisticated models for determining when to fertilize have been developed for nitrogen, potassium, magnesium, and micronutrients. However, the home gardener does not use sophisticated analytical tools to determine which fertilizer to use, at what rate, and when to apply. The recommendations stated here should be interpreted as guidelines only because quantitative, scientific leaf analysis of your trees does not underlie the recommendations.

Nitrogen (N). Fully bearing, average-sized mature orange, lemon, and grapefruit trees (15 to 20 feet [4.6 to 6.1 m] foliage diameter) in the home garden and landscape should be fertilized at a rate of about 1 pound (0.45 kg) of *actual* nitrogen per tree per year. Because ammonium nitrate (33-0-0) is 33 percent actual nitrogen, a mature tree needs 3 pounds (1.4 kg) of ammonium nitrate, or 5 pounds (2.3 kg) of ammonium sulfate (20-0-0), or 2 pounds (0.9 kg) of urea (46-0-0). (See the general discussion about fertilizers in chapter 3, "Soils and Fertilizer Management.") To determine the pounds of nitrogen in a given weight of fertilizer, multiply the weight in pounds by the percentage of total nitrogen stated on the label.) Ammonium sulfate is less advisable than other fertilizer types as a nitrogen source on soils with pH below 6.0. For smaller or dwarf trees, fertilizer dosages should be reduced proportionally, according to the area of the tree canopy.

Because adequate levels of nitrogen are required during flowering and fruit setting, late-winter or early-spring broadcast fertilizer applications to the soil can provide the required nitrogen supply. Some references recommend dividing the nitrogen fertilization requirement into thirds, giving a total of three doses per year (early spring, summer, and fall) to equal the total needed, but UC Cooperative Extension specialists point out that high levels of nitrogen fertilizer are to be avoided for oranges and grapefruit during the summer and fall, as they contribute to thicker rind, lower juice content, and regreening of Valencia oranges. On the other hand, lemons give a beneficial yield response to high nitrogen levels during the summer.

Water-soluble formulations of nitrogen fertilizer need to be reapplied more frequently than slow-release types, which break down more gradually, releasing nutrients over many months. Thus, a single recommendation about when to apply may not be appropriate for all citrus types, all fertilizer types, or all climates. UC farm advisors who specialize in citrus have noted that whether a homeowner fertilizes in late winter alone (in time to have nitrogen available for spring bloom) or splits the dosage or skips an entire year will not make a lot of difference for a mature tree. With regard to technique, the nitrogen fertilizer should be scattered over the root area of the tree, which means under the tree and at least 1 to 2 feet (30 to 60 cm) outside the drip line. The fertilizer should be washed into the soil with a good soaking of about 1 inch (2.5 cm) of water.

Citrus trees in a lawn area will not receive adequate nitrogen when the lawn is fertilized. The area under the tree should be fertilized more often than the lawn to ensure adequate nutrition for the tree. The grass will take most of the nitrogen applied. When tree leaves show a slight yellowing (pale green color), they can be sprayed with 1 ounce (2 heaping tsp or about 9 g) of urea (46-0-0) in 1 gallon (3.8 l) of water. Foliar applications of urea are effective sources of nitrogen during spring growth and fruit-setting periods. Exceeding the concentration recommended can burn foliage. Apply very early in the morning or at sunset. Do not spray urea during hot weather.

If manure is used, it should be applied cautiously in the fall (September to October) because its potentially high salt concentration can burn citrus trees. Foliage may turn yellow and shoot tips may die from salt toxicity when the salts in the manure are carried into the root zone with irrigation water. For these reasons, steer and chicken manure should be used sparingly.

Zinc (Zn). Zinc deficiency causes mottle-leaf (small terminal leaves with yellow mottling between the large leaf veins). Dieback of twigs may occur in severe zinc deficiency. Foliar sprays and chelated formulations are available to combat the problem. Late winter or early spring is the best time to use them. Use approximately 1 heaping teaspoon (4.5 g) of zinc sulfate (36% metallic Zn) in 1 gallon (3.8 l) of water or approximately 4 teaspoons (13.6 g) of zinc sulfate mixed with approximately 3 teaspoons (11.3 g) of hydrated lime in 1 gallon (3.8 l) of water. Treat for zinc deficiency at least 6 weeks before or after phosphate fertilizer application. Zinc and phosphate cannot be absorbed by plants at the same time. Read and carefully follow label directions.

Iron (Fe). Iron deficiency manifests as a yellowing of leaf tissues between the veins (iron chlorosis), but the veins usually stay green. When the deficiency becomes severe, new leaves are completely yellow or yellow-white, and twig dieback may occur. Iron chlorosis is not a soil deficiency symptom but indicates that the roots are not absorbing iron or making it available. It can be caused by overwatering, which leads to iron deficiency symptoms. The lack of oxygen that results from the excess water inhibits root function and iron absorption by plants. In addition to overwatering, iron chlorosis may be caused by high lime content in the soil.

Foliar sprays containing iron may be used to combat iron chlorosis. Wetting agents are added to the spray to promote good coverage. Several sprays of dilute solution may be preferable to one spray at full concentration. Although chelated iron may correct many cases of leaf yellowing related to iron deficiency, chelated iron is very acidic and should be used on citrus with caution because it can cause leaf burn. Soil-applied iron slurries are longer-lasting than foliar chelate sprays. Micronutrient sprays are available that contain iron, zinc, and manganese. Since zinc and manganese deficiencies are more common than iron deficiency (one deficiency may actually mask others), a prudent course of action for fertilizing backyard citrus, which does not have the benefit of scientific leaf analysis, is to treat for several micronutrient deficiencies with a combination foliar spray. Follow label directions.

Magnesium (Mg) and Manganese (Mn). When magnesium is deficient, older leaves turn yellow between the veins and drop. It is most noticeable in late summer and fall and in rainy climates. Application of magnesium sulfate (epsom salts) can correct magnesium deficiency. When manganese is deficient, young leaves turn light green between the veins. It is often more noticeable on a tree's north side. Manganese deficiency may occur in conjunction with zinc and iron deficiencies.

Phosphorus (P) and Potassium (K). Citrus fruit trees require little added phosphorous. Apply about 1 pound (0.5 kg) of phosphate to the top 1 inch (2.5 cm) of soil around the tree's root system every 3 to 4 years. Potassium fertilizer sources include chloride, sulfate, and nitrate forms. Chloride salts may injure citrus. If potassium appears deficient, soil applications of 2.5 to 5 pounds (1.1 to 2.3 kg) per mature tree per year for 2 years are advisable. Response may be delayed by 2 to 3 years.

Boron (B). Excess boron can cause leaf tips and margins to turn yellow and subsequently become necrotic. Lemons and grapefruits are more sensitive than oranges. If you suspect boron toxicity, check your irrigation water. If the level of boron is greater than 5 ppm, your water source may be the problem. Additional nitrogen fertilizer as calcium nitrate may alleviate boron toxicity. Boron deficiency can occur when citrus is grown in low-boron soils and irrigated with low-boron water. Boron deficiency symptoms are most frequent when maturing trees are not irrigated sufficiently, which may occur, for example, when additional drip emitters are not added soon enough. Boron deficiency is easily corrected in drip irrigation by adjusting the number of emitters and by making a single application of ¼ to ½ pound (110 to 220 g) boric acid (H_3BO_3) or borax ($Na_2B_4O_7 \cdot 10H_2O$).

Fertilization of Container-Grown Citrus

The more frequent irrigation required in container-grown trees washes nutrients away from the root zone; thus, container-grown citrus trees require more frequent fertilization than citrus grown in the ground. To compensate, use a complete, slow-release fertilizer rather than a sole nitrogen source, and follow the manufacturer's instructions. Micronutrients may also be deficient in container-grown citrus. Yellowing of foliage may not be due to nitrogen deficiency alone: iron deficiency is common in potted plants, and iron, zinc, or manganese deficiencies may cause chlorosis. Some complete fertilizers include chelated forms of these nutrients. Foliar sprays are most effective if applied in the spring when leaves are approaching their full size. Container-grown citrus is also susceptible to boron deficiency because of constant leaching.

Pruning

Citrus needs little pruning compared to many ornamental trees in the home landscape and deciduous fruit trees, which are pruned routinely every year (see McCarty et al. 1982). The location of food storage tissues in citrus, which differs from that of deciduous fruit trees, and the fact that citrus is evergreen are critical factors in pruning. During the summer, the majority of excess food manufactured by deciduous trees is stored in the root system; thus, pruning deciduous trees during the dormant season does not appreciably reduce the supply of stored food, which remains available for the spring growth flush. In citrus trees, on the other hand, carbohydrates (excess food) are stored in the leaves, twigs, and branches of the scion; a lesser amount goes to the root system. In citrus, the maximum amount of stored food is reached in February to early March just before spring growth activity. The canopy of a citrus tree serves as an important food storage area. Besides removing foliage, pruning removes flowering buds, which are often referred to as fruiting points. Because citrus trees bloom and bear fruit on new growth flushes, lopping off branch tips reduces the number of flower buds and also reduces yield at harvest. Therefore, pruning should be done judiciously. Pruning of mature citrus trees is often limited to removing dead, diseased, or broken branches. Removal of unproductive stems is prudent because it allows more light and air through the branches, which encourages healthy, new growth. Pruning can also be used to bring a balance between fruiting and vegetative growth to increase fruit size.

Most home garden citrus trees need no pruning for 2 or 3 years after planting. Pruning young, nonbearing trees may delay fruiting and should be limited to removing suckers, which are shoots of the rootstock variety that originate below the bud union on the trunk or from underground. Remove watersprouts (vigorous upright scion shoots that grow in undesirable places, such as in branch crotches, or along the trunk above the bud union). You may decide to prune lower branches off the ground for aesthetic reasons, or you may choose to leave these lower branches because they shade the ground, preventing weed growth, and they bear fruit that are easy to reach.

Selecting Scaffold Branches

Selection of permanent scaffold branches during the first 2 years and limited pruning to establish good tree form are worth the sacrifice of some fruit. Additional pruning will be required because, as the tree grows older and increases in size, the center usually fills with closely spaced and crossing branches, whose growth pattern can benefit from light pruning. When the tree is about 3 or 4 years old (depending on size and growth rate), light, selective thinning may be done to remove branches that are too closely spaced, crossed, or entangled. Pruning should be just sufficient to reestablish a scaffold framework.

Small irregularities in the canopies of young trees should be ignored. Left alone, citrus trees normally develop a relatively even, spherical shape as they mature. Lopsided trees caused by a dominant, fast-growing limb are the exception. Although pruning may be used to force a lopsided tree into a more normal growth habit, the condition will usually correct itself if left unpruned, and the tree will assume a normal shape.

Pruning during the next 5 to 6 years should be limited to removal of occasional branches that interfere with the growth of a sturdy framework of scaffold limbs. Undesirable shoots that sprout following pruning should be removed when they are a few inches long and are still tender enough to be removed with a gloved hand. Allowed to grow, they deplete the tree of food reserves and necessitate more severe pruning later.

It is best to remove unwanted limbs where they originate or cut them back to a lateral. This reduces the sprouting of new buds in the area around the cut. Heading of a wanted limb may be done when needed to induce branching or to strengthen its growth if it is weak or willowy. Pruning cuts should be made as close to the vertical plane as possible, because the nearer to horizontal the cut, the greater the sprouting of new buds.

Lemon trees tend to need more pruning than oranges or grapefruit because lemon trees produce long, spindly shoots that are mechanically weak and easily broken. It is often necessary to remove some of these by thinning or to shorten others back to laterals to strengthen them. Lemon trees also send out strong laterals through the center of the tree. Without pruning, the interior of the tree fills with crossing limbs. A good framework of scaffold branches helps prevent limb breakage. Branches at a wide angle to the central axis of the tree should be retained as scaffold branches. Those with a narrow angle should be removed. If early selective pruning of lemon trees is neglected, heavy cutting will be needed later, which delays and reduces yield. Lisbon lemon, especially, needs pruning, or it will become unmanageable.

Pruning the Mature Citrus Tree

Bearing orange and grapefruit trees require little pruning. Most of the experimental work with citrus indicates that yield from healthy trees is reduced in proportion to the severity of pruning. Light thinning in the top of the tree to promote the growth of inside fruitwood may be helpful. For better pest control and ease of harvesting, limiting tree height may have merit, but, if pruning is excessive, its advantages are outweighed by the loss of flowering and fruiting points on the tree. As a tree ages, the top branches are usually the first to decline in production and fruit quality. Light thinning of the top promotes the growth of new fruitwood, but pruning should not open a tree so much that exposed branches are sunburned. If a limb is exposed to sunburn, it should be protected by a coating of whitewash. When thinning the tree top, do not cut back branches to leave stubs. Instead, cut the limb should back to another branch or lateral. Most deadwood and weak, nonproductive wood should be removed from the center of the tree, but vigorous shoots, should, where possible, be retained and bent over to fill thinly foliated areas with fruitwood.

The skirt, or lower portion, of the tree bears a large portion of the fruit, and pruning there should be slight until the productive wood begins to decline. Nonproductive skirt branches should be removed by cutting from beneath, leaving the upper and newer foliage to replace what is removed. Known as undercutting, this helps ensure the bearing efficiency of the skirt. Pruning to hold trees to a given size requires judicious hand pruning and results in some loss in yield.

The growth habit of mature lemon trees is more open and irregular than other citrus varieties; unpruned, they usually produce abundantly but grow into a tangle of weak and interlaced branches. Such trees are difficult to harvest, and efficient pest control is a problem. Crowding also makes other cultural operations more difficult. Not pruning hastens the development of sieve-tube necrosis in certain lemon varieties. Dysfunction of sieve tubes in the phloem can be reduced, if not eliminated, by proper pruning. A systematic pruning program, begun when lemon trees are small, should be continued into maturity. Light, frequent pruning is advisable. Periodic thinning of unwanted branches and shortening of others to laterals result in the development of a low-spreading tree with fruit that are easy to harvest.

Time of Pruning

Because time of pruning is not highly critical with citrus, trees are often pruned when other cultural operations are at a low ebb. Experiments have shown that the best results, from the physiological standpoint of the tree, can be expected if pruning takes place early in the spring after the danger of frost has passed and before the start of a new growth cycle. The rate of foliage regeneration is most rapid on spring-pruned trees and least rapid when trees are pruned late in the fall. Fall pruning also stimulates a late flush that is tender and more susceptible to frost injury during the winter. Winter pruning under temperature conditions that are not conducive to growth does not produce a vegetative flush. If pruning is done under temperature conditions conducive to growth, a vegetative flush will result.

Time of pruning may be restricted by the presence of mature fruit on the tree. Little problem is presented with navel oranges and winter grapefruit, when the crop is harvested before spring. With Valencia orange and summer grapefruit trees, both young and mature fruits are on the tree at the same time, and late-summer pruning after harvest may be preferred when fruits are scarcest. In coastal areas, lemons are usually pruned after the last main summer harvest so that fewer nearly mature fruit are lost. To avoid losing fruit, it may be desirable to take advantage of the alternate-bearing tendency of some citrus species by pruning during the light-crop year. During the heavy crop year, removing some of the fruitlets can help to even out production and increase fruit size.

Pruning Injured Trees

Trees injured by frost, severe windburn, or rodents require special pruning. Periodic freezes of moderate to severe intensity occasionally occur in all of the major citrus-growing areas of the state. (See the section "Treating Freeze-Damaged Citrus Trees" for information about pruning freeze-damaged trees.)

Windburn. Hot, dry winds occasionally injure trees. Many of the defoliated limbs will recover; however, recovery is usually slower than from frost injury. Branches that do not recover should be pruned from the tree carefully so that a minimum of healthy foliage is lost. Breakage from strong winds sometimes occurs. Young, vigorously growing lemons are most susceptible. Where a crop is on the tree, and the limb is still attached enough to allow the fruit to mature, pruning can be put off until after harvest. A follow-up pruning will be needed to thin excessive regrowth.

Gopher Injury. Trees damaged by gophers are usually healthy enough to recover unless they are badly girdled. When root damage is so extensive that remaining roots cannot supply water for the scion, the scion-root balance should be restored by pruning the canopy.

Rejuvenation Pruning

In older orange trees, reduced tree vigor can result in small fruit and low yields. Loss of vigor is usually accompanied by dieback of twigs and small branches. Decline may be caused by a number of factors either separately or in various combination, such as tree age, low rainfall, faulty irrigation, salt accumulation in the soil, air pollution, and virus and pest problems. Rejuvenation pruning forces the tree to produce new fruitwood and ranges from a moderate thinning of the canopy to complete skeletonization of the tree. The latter removes all foliage and wood smaller than 1 inch (2.5 cm) in diameter, leaving only the main scaffold and adjoining branches. When older and weaker parts of the tree are removed, new buds sprout, and new fruitwood is formed. However, unless the cause of the decline has been corrected, the effects of pruning are temporary and the tree soon declines again.

Care of Pruning Wounds

In California's dry climate, decay-producing organisms rarely enter through pruning wounds. Research has shown that healing of large wounds is not hastened by covering with tree sealants or wound dressings. Bark on limbs grown in the shade is susceptible to sunburn after pruning; a few hours of exposure may cause injury. The exposed portion of limbs should be treated with whitewash. Treatment of branches other than those exposed to the sun is unnecessary and may even be detrimental, since whitewash provides an excellent habitat for the development of red spider mites.

Care of Pruning Tools

When pruning citrus, protect yourself by using heavy gloves and goggles (many citrus varieties have sharp thorns) and by using proper pruning tools. You need a good pair of hand pruners to remove stems with small diameters and a pruning saw to remove larger wood. If you have several citrus trees, equipment should be disinfested and sanitized by using a bleach solution (1:9) of household bleach with water before moving to the next tree. To counteract the corrosive action of the disinfectant, pruning tools should be cleaned after use in a mixture of 2 teaspoons (10 ml) of emulsifiable oil in ½ cup (118 ml) of vinegar diluted with water to a total volume of 2 cups (472 ml). This mixture should be shaken vigorously just before use.

Treating Freeze-Damaged Citrus Trees

Damaging freezes tend to occur in California citrus districts about once a decade. Certain techniques have been found to hasten tree recovery and to maximize desirable growth responses in cold-injured citrus trees. The discussion of freeze damage in this section is adapted from *Treatment of Freeze-Damaged Citrus and Avocado Trees* (Platt and Opitz 1974); see that source for more information.

Determine the Extent of Damage

Shoot and foliage injury usually becomes visible in a few days. Twigs and small limbs may show little or no signs of cold damage for 2 to 4 weeks. The rate at which freeze damage becomes apparent depends on the prevailing temperatures and humidity and on the condition of growth before and after the freeze period. Except when trees are killed outright, it may be impossible to determine the extent of severe injury for several months or even for an entire year following a freeze.

Delay Pruning

Corrective pruning should be postponed until the full extent of damage can be determined clearly. Deadwood removed while dieback is in progress frequently contributes to further dieback through wound cuts. If pruning is not postponed, some limbs that would have recovered might be removed unnecessarily, and a second pruning to rid the tree of undesirable brush and limb stubs is then necessary. Experience at UC has shown that early-pruned trees recover more slowly than trees pruned later.

Remove Frozen Fruit

If the fruit has no value, remove it as soon as possible. The longer fruit remains on the tree, the greater it decreases yield in the succeeding crop.

Trunk and Limb Treatment

The degree of injury provides a guide to the type of treatment required.

Light Damage. No treatment is necessary when only foliage and small twigs are injured. No pruning except "dead brushing" should be done the ensuing season. All foliage should be retained to nourish the root system and support the developing crop.

Medium Damage. When a considerable part of the scion is killed but the trunk and crown limbs appear sound, the extent of damage can be determined only after several months. Do not prune until the full extent of the damage is visible. Save as much of the tree's framework as possible. Old limbs must be cut back below all serious bark injuries. Cut back to good, strong shoots. The distribution of new framework branches can be controlled to some degree by selection and light pruning during the summer. After injured branches have been cut back to new leaders, further pruning consists of gradually thinning excessive sprouts over several years. These shoots (suckers) crowd and interfere with growth and branching of the leaders forming the tree's new framework.

Severe Damage. When most of the scion and crown limbs are killed, but the trunk shows little injury as when medium damage has been sustained, no pruning should be done until the full extent of the damage is visible, usually after midsummer. At that time, the entire top of the tree should be removed by cutting below all large areas of injured bark. By this time, numerous sprouts from different locations on the trunk will have made considerable growth. From these, the new head of the tree must be formed. Select the uppermost good sprout and cut the old trunk off just above this sprout, sloping the cut downward away from the sprout. Then choose two or three other sprouts properly spaced to form a new head and favor their growth by pinching back sprouts that crowd them. All sprouts should be left until a balance between root and top is established. Unnecessary sprouts should then be removed gradually.

Very Severe Damage. When the scion is killed and the injury extends well down the trunk but is followed by the appearance of strong sprouts above the bud union, a new trunk and head must be developed. They can be produced from one or more strong shoots originating from above the bud union. With young trees, it is usually best to favor one strong shoot. The top of the tree may then be removed, leaving the old trunk as a support to which this special shoot may be tied. The shoot chosen for development should be favored and forced into growth by pinching back all others.

When the new scion growth has reached the size of a healthy 2-year-old orchard tree, the old trunk should be removed carefully by a cut starting just above the base of the new trunk and sloping downward. The surface of the cut should be allowed to dry. No wound dressing is necessary (see related discussion under "Pruning," above).

With large trees, recovery will be more rapid if several shoots are used to form the new head. There is no objection to trees with multiple trunks. When several shoots are used, it is best to remove the old trunk as soon as the extent of the freeze damage can be determined. Otherwise, new shoots may be damaged excessively by the saw. Treat the cut surface as described above. During the year following the freeze and until the new head is well-formed, all sprouts should be allowed to grow. The growth of temporary shoots must be controlled by pinching back.

Extreme Damage. In most cases, trees killed to the bud union should be removed and replaced by new trees. When it is necessary to retain such trees, the suggestion for very severely damaged trees should be followed, but shoots selected for forming the new tree must be budded to the desired variety as soon as they are large enough to take a bud, about ¼ to ⅜ inch (6 to 9 mm) in diameter. It is best to place the buds at a height of 18 inches to 2 feet (46 to 61 cm) because it allows shoots to grow around the base of the tree without shading the buds and interfering with their development.

Treatment of Damaged Bark
Bark on the trunk of injured young trees may crack and curl. On injured trees of various ages, scattered patches of dead bark may appear on large limbs or on trunks even where no splitting occurs. When the extent of these injuries becomes clearly visible 2 or 3 months after a freeze, the dead areas of bark should be cut out smoothly and the exposed wood disinfected and painted.

Protection from Sunburn after a Freeze
Protection of the trunk and large limbs from sunburn is advisable in warmer areas if regrowth has not occurred before hot weather arrives. It is necessary to whitewash only the parts of the trunk and large limbs that face south and southwest. Lemons are particularly susceptible to sunburning, and the tops of large horizontal limbs should be protected.

Irrigation after a Frost
Irrigate cautiously after a freeze. When leaves are damaged or destroyed by a freeze, the tree uses less water than under normal conditions until a new crop of leaves has developed because water removed from the soil by the tree is lost through its leaves by evapotranspiration. Irrigate only when soil conditions indicate a need. Determine soil moisture content by examining the soil or use tensiometers (see chapter 3). Irrigations should be less frequent, and smaller amounts of water should be applied until trees have regained their ability to use normal amounts of water. In the case of severely damaged trees, this reduced irrigation requirement may last the entire growing season.

Fertilization after a Frost
The amount of fertilizer applied will depend largely on the extent of damage. It is best to withhold fertilizers until the extent of damage is determined. Freeze-damaged trees do not respond better if heavily fertilized. In fact, more harm than good may occur. Slightly injured trees will recover most rapidly and will usually set crops in the spring following the freeze. Such trees require normal fertilization.

Severely damaged trees usually put forth a good deal of sucker or shoot growth that, through selection, will be used to rebuild the tree. Until the tree regains its full top, an imbalance exists between the root system and the top. Trees that have received regular fertilization or are growing on fertile soils have ample nutrients to satisfy their needs the first year following freeze damage. Fertilizer applied before the top has been reestablished may force additional sucker growth, which will be difficult and costly to control. For severely damaged trees, reduce or omit fertilization during the first season.

The imbalance between the root system and the top, together with vigorous sucker growth following a freeze, often results in micronutrient deficiencies that can retard recovery. Zinc is the element most likely to be deficient in citrus, but manganese and copper may also be at deficient levels. Zinc, manganese, and copper should be applied as foliar sprays when symptoms occur. With the rapid growth of new shoots, two or three applications may be necessary during the first season. Regular micronutrient foliar sprays containing the needed elements may be used. Use copper only if a deficiency is known to exist. Symptoms of iron deficiency sometimes appear. These symptoms are often the result of excessive soil moisture and can be corrected by reducing irrigation.

Benefits of Mulching

Mulches have numerous benefits in the cultivation of citrus trees, particularly the reduction of urban waste disposal problems, the improvement in citrus tree root health, the suppression of nematodes and *Phytophthora* spp., and the improvement of soil physical properties due to the soil's increased organic matter content. Mulching was a common practice in citrus production until the 1940s, when cheap, easy-to-apply chemical fertilizers became readily available. Scientists in the past have shown that bean, barley, and alfalfa straw (green manures) increased navel orange production by up to 25 percent and conserved water use at the same time. Citrus trees treated with green manures have been shown to be superior in terms of tree size, yield, and fruit size compared to trees treated with animal manures. Recent research at UC Riverside has shown that yard waste (wood chips, grass clippings, and leaves) makes an excellent citrus mulch. Several of the benefits of mulching citrus trees are discussed briefly below.

Reduction of Weed Problems

If mulches are at least 2 inches (5 cm) thick, they can reduce weed problems by preventing germination of weed seeds. Citrus trees, like other commodities, are more productive if they do not have to compete with weeds for water and essential nutrients. When weeds do grow, they should be hand-pulled because cultivation equipment can damage the tree's surface roots.

Conservation of Water

Mulches conserve water by reducing evaporation from the soil, reducing runoff and erosion, increasing the permeability of the soil surface, and increasing the water-holding capacity of the soil. At field capacity, mulched soils with a high organic matter content have more water available to trees.

Improvement in Soil Physical Properties

Organic mulches can improve soil physical properties (soil structure and porosity) by increasing the soil's organic matter content, which results in aggregation of soil particles, increased pore size distribution, and better gas exchange (O_2 and CO_2), facilitating better utilization of the top 12 inches (30 cm) of soil, the area where citrus tree roots are most active.

Improvement in Nitrogen Fertility

Organic mulches can eliminate or reduce nitrate contamination of groundwater by providing a continuous, slow release of nitrogen, reducing the need for nitrogen applied as chemical fertilizer. Typically, citrus groves in California have less than 1 percent organic matter in the soil. Maintaining high levels of organic matter in the soil is a primary factor in improving soil fertility. Increasing the organic matter content of the soil with mulches increases the soil's cation exchange capacity, which increases the availability of many nutrient elements to plant roots. Alfalfa straw has been shown to be one of the most valuable mulches for citrus because it supplies nitrogen and conditions the soil.

Mulches with a high carbon-to-nitrogen ratio may cause a short-term initial nitrogen depletion, necessitating increased nitrogen fertilization, because of the increased populations of microorganisms produced during the decomposition process. However, the long-term benefit of decomposed mulch is an increased, slow release of nitrogen to the soil. Legume mulches or leafy plant material supply nitrogen and several other essential plant nutrient elements.

Control of Root-Rot Diseases

Thick mulches applied to the soil surface can create conditions deleterious to pathogenic soil organisms, such as nematodes and *Phytophthora* fungi, which cause root rot diseases in both citrus and avocado. Mulches are especially effective in suppressing *Phytophthora* when the mulches are combined with applications of gypsum ($CaSO_4$).

Research has indicated that when the soil's organic matter content is kept in the range of 7 percent with organic mulches, the soil becomes suppressive to *Phytophthora*. Several mechanisms have been proposed to explain why mulches can reduce *Phytophthora* root rot in citrus and avocado:

- Mulching increases the population of soil microbes that compete with or inhibit fungal pathogens.

- Soils amended with alfalfa meal or other decaying organic matter are known to have higher concentrations of gases such as ammonia, which can inhibit *Phytophthora*.

■ Mulches create a natural litter layer favoring the proliferation of tree roots and disfavoring *Phytophthora* infection. The interface of the soil surface and mulch is a natural microenvironment where roots grow well but where *Phytophthora* cannot survive. The fungus needs saturated soil conditions to release its zoospores, which must then swim to tree roots to cause new infections. Water drains so quickly from the mulch layer that saturated conditions may not last long enough for zoospores to be released and to swim to tree roots.

■ Chemicals produced during the decomposition of organic matter in mulched soil, such as ammonium (NH_4^+), saponins, and nitrite, are toxic at low concentrations. They prevent propagule germination in *Phytophthora parasitica* and retard disease development.

■ Organic matter can entrap fungal zoospores, preventing them from swimming to plant roots.

■ Soil gases and compounds released during organic matter decomposition in the mulch can increase the level of host (citrus) resistance in the roots to *Phytophthora*.

Yard Waste as a Citrus Mulch

One of the most compelling reasons to use yard waste as a citrus mulch is that it contributes to solving the problem of urban waste disposal. About 20 percent of solid waste dumped in landfills is estimated to be yard (green) waste. California's Integrated Waste Management Act mandates a significant reduction in the amount of waste that each county and city sends to landfills, with 1990 serving as the base year. Use of yard waste as a bio-enhanced mulch on citrus trees in the home garden and landscape is also beneficial to citrus tree growth, particularly the health of tree roots.

Yard waste consisting of wood chips, grass clippings, and leaves was one of several mulches that UC Riverside scientists have shown to be beneficial to citrus culture, particularly the health of citrus roots. This is caused in part because the yard waste enhanced growth of two biological control agents, *Trichoderma harzianum* (a beneficial fungus) and *Pseudomonas fluorescens* (a beneficial bacterium), which are effective in suppressing Phytophthora root rot in citrus when they are present in the native soil.

The results of the research at UCR, which was conducted on six 12-month-old Troyer citrange seedlings grown in the greenhouse, showed that the percentage of healthy citrus roots growing in the mulch treatments was positively correlated with the cation exchange capacity of the mulches and the populations of *Pseudomonas fluorescens* supported by the mulches. An important benefit of the yard waste tested at UCR was that the high carbon (C) to nitrogen (N) composition of the wood chips was offset by the high nitrogen concentration of the grass clippings, which reduced any temporary nitrogen shortage. The proportion of yard waste components with either high or low nitrogen content can be adjusted to optimize mulch efficiency.

For more information on yard waste as a citrus mulch, see *Urban and Agricultural Wastes for Use as Mulches on Avocado and Citrus and for Delivery of Microbial Biocontrol Agents* (Casale et al. 1995).

Improvement in Soil Temperature

Mulches can reduce wide fluctuations in soil temperature by reducing the soil's absorption of heat, which is beneficial to root growth, especially in young trees and in areas where summer temperatures are very high. Lower soil temperatures are also less favorable to *Phytophthora*. When frosts are predicted, remove mulch, if possible, because bare soil can absorb more radiant energy than most mulches.

As discussed, you can use yard waste (wood chips, grass clippings, and leaves), straw (grain or bean), wood shavings, alfalfa meal, or any inexpensive source of inert organic material. If you use straw, beware of potential damage from field mice and rats; these rodents often make nests in the straw. Do not use mushroom compost or animal manure until the trees are at least 3 years old because these materials may contain excessive amounts of nitrogen (ammonia) or soluble salts that can be leached into the root zone and injure the trees' roots or cause tip burn of the leaves. Excessive amounts of ammonia released during decomposition of animal manures have also been shown to be detrimental to the growth of soil microbes that serve as biological control agents against disease-causing organisms.

For more information on mulching, see *Mulching To Control Root Disease in Avocado and Citrus* (Turney and Menge 1994).

Harvesting and Storage

Unlike fruits that continue to ripen after harvest, citrus ripens only on the tree. Judging ripeness may not be easy without sampling a few fruit. Rind color is not a reliable indicator. The rinds of oranges may have green pigmentation and yet be ripe in hot weather if temperatures do not cool in the evening. Lemons and limes are ripe when they are juicy; rind color may be green or yellow, although yellow fruit are more juicy. Sampling fruit is a reliable method to determine ripeness, according to your individual palette. Some prefer their fruit sweeter. Others prefer a more acidic taste. Included in table 18.1 are harvesting periods for each variety in the different citrus-growing regions in the state and comments about whether the fruits hold well on the tree. The timing and length of the harvest period depend on the variety and the climate in your area. Most citrus tends to hold on the tree longer in cooler climates than in warmer regions where night temperatures remain high.

Harvest most fruits by giving them a quick twist or by using hand pruners. You should use hand pruners for loose-skinned mandarins because pulling the fruit may cause the rind to tear off around the stem.

Although the best place to store fresh fruit is on the tree, once it has been harvested it should be refrigerated, where it can last from 2 to 6 weeks. Before juicing citrus, fruit should be brought to room temperature because at room temperature it will yield slightly more juice. If you roll the fruit on a hard surface before juicing, you will be able to extract more juice. Use fresh citrus juice promptly: Juices from navel and blood oranges develop off-flavors within a few hours. Juices from other varieties can be refrigerated for up to 36 hours before a significant loss in quality will occur. The juice of lemons, limes, and Valencia oranges can be frozen for up to 3 or 4 months. It may be convenient to store lemon and lime juice in ice cube trays to facilitate future use of small quantities in cooking.

Maximizing the Planting Area

Growing Dwarf Citrus Trees

Many dwarf trees grow to a height and width of about 8 feet (2.4 m) and are usually globular in shape. The tree's environment—water quality, nutrition, planting density, soil texture, temperature—influences its performance and size. True dwarfs are typically less than half the size of standard trees of the same variety. Thus, dwarfs of kumquats are considerably smaller than dwarfs of Valencia oranges, the former being 3 to 6 feet (9.1 to 1.8 m) and the latter about 8 feet (2.4 m).

Dwarf trees yield full-sized fruit. Under good cultural conditions, they yield about 50 to 60 percent as much fruit as a standard-sized tree but in one-fourth of the space, which is beneficial to many home gardeners whose space is limited. Four dwarf varieties can grow in the space of one full-size tree.

The only true genetic dwarf rootstock is Flying Dragon, a mutation of trifoliate orange rootstock. Scion varieties grafted onto Flying Dragon rootstock grow to less than half the size of standard trees of the same variety. Other rootstocks have a dwarfing effect on certain fruiting varieties; the resulting trees, known as semidwarfs, are about two-thirds of the standard size. Although not dwarfed, the growth rate is somewhat reduced. Almost all citrus varieties sold in California are available dwarfed to some extent, with the exception of Eureka and Lisbon lemons, which are too vigorous for dwarfing. Eureka lemon scions are incompatible with Flying Dragon rootstocks. Some citrus varieties are natural dwarfs, such as Improved Meyer lemon.

Citrus Espaliers

By selective pruning, the branches of citrus trees can be espaliered, that is, trained to grow flat against a wall or a framework, allowing you to grow fruit in a confined space such as a narrow bed or side yard. Standard and dwarf citrus trees can be espaliered; trees with an open growth habit and vining branches are the best candidates. According to the Sunset book *Citrus* (1996), some of the best choices for espalier are Eureka lemon, Nagami kumquat, Eustis limequat, Tarocco blood orange, and Chandler pummelo. Start with a young tree because it will be easier to train. You can design an informal espalier in which you plant the tree directly in front of a structure, allow it to branch naturally, and prune any branches that stick out too far, or you can design a formal espalier, in which you train the tree into a precise geometric pattern (fig. 18.9). For the novice, an informal design is easiest. In a climate at the edge of the citrus belt, citrus espalier may have a distinct advantage. Training a citrus tree against a sunny, south-facing wall may supply enough heat that fruit ripening and winter survival will be more likely.

Pests, Diseases, and Environmental Stresses

In comparison to other fruit trees grown in the home garden, such as apples and peaches, citrus trees have relatively few pest and disease problems if they receive good care. Certain varieties are more susceptible to pests and diseases, but healthy trees that are irrigated and fertilized properly should have little pest damage. Since lemon trees set fruit throughout the year in many climate zones, fruit are at various stages of development year-round, which can present some special pest management problems. But if you are willing to overlook an occasional chewed leaf or rind blemish and

focus on the more serious enemies that can compromise the overall health of your trees, your pest control program at home will be efficient.

Table 18.4 lists the most common citrus insect and mite pests, diseases, and environmental stresses and gives information about what the symptoms look like, the probable causal agent, and some comments about control. A comprehensive reference on this subject is UC's *Integrated Pest Management for Citrus*, 2nd edition (Kobbe and Dreistadt 1991). UC's *Pests of the Garden and Small Farm* (Flint 1998) also has excellent information and color photographs of pests, diseases, and environmental stresses on citrus and other commodities.

A more technical UC reference on citrus pests and their management is the *UC IPM Pest Management Guidelines: Citrus*, which is updated frequently and intended to be used in conjunction with *Integrated Pest Management for Citrus*. Please see the references at the end of the chapter for the availability of the guidelines. For each citrus pest, the guideline lists the scientific name of the pest and provides a user-friendly but semitechnical discussion describing the pest and its life cycle, damage caused, cultural control measures, biological control measures, selectivity, organically acceptable control methods, monitoring techniques, and when to treat, along with specific pesticide treatments, their recommended rates, and minimum days to treat before harvest.

Citrus is susceptible to fungal, viral, and bacterial diseases, but if you purchase healthy trees with rootstocks tolerant to the major offenders (see tables 18.2 and 18.3) and employ preventive measures to reduce or eliminate conditions favoring these organisms, you should not expect to have many problems. The damage potential of many citrus diseases depends on the rootstock and scion, soil conditions, and water management practices of the gardener.

One bacterium, several viruses, and a few fungi cause the major infectious diseases in California citrus (see table 18.4). Fungal and bacterial diseases of citrus cause more losses in the Central Valley because of the long, wet winters in comparison to other climate zones in the state.

Fungi that infect the trunk and roots, especially feeder roots that have critical roles in water and nutrient uptake, are most important in California. Because the state's climate is

Figure 18.9

Two examples of espalier designs for citrus. *Source:* After *Citrus* (1996), pp. 26–27.

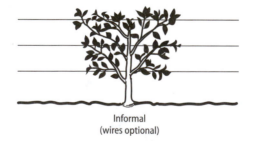

Informal
(wires optional)

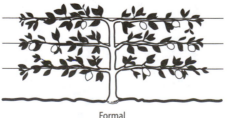

Formal
(Attach and train branches to wires)

Table 18.4

PROBLEM DIAGNOSIS FOR CITRUS

What the problem looks like	Probable cause
Round, red-brown scales on fruit, leaves, and twigs. Leaves may yellow and drop and twig dieback may occur. Damage most visible in late summer and early fall. Reduces tree vigor.	**California red scale** (*Aonidiella aurantii*)

Comments
An armored scale. Armored scales suck plant tissue and can overwinter on citrus. Related to yellow scale (*A. citrina*). Can be distinguished from yellow scale under a microscope. One of the most important pests in California citrus. Widely distributed. Lemon is the most susceptible, followed by grapefruit, Valencia, navel, and mandarin oranges. Unlike soft scales, does not secrete honeydew. Natural enemies (parasitic wasps—*Aphytis* and *Encarsia* spp.) can provide good control in many parts of California. Chemical treatment may be needed in San Joaquin Valley.

Black film on leaf surfaces.	**sooty mold fungus**

Comments
Most active in cool, moist conditions. Feeds on honeydew excreted by aphids, mealybugs, scale insects, and whiteflies. Sooty mold should be washed off leaves because it can reduce photosynthesis and tree productivity if prolonged. Cosmetically unappealing on fruit; usually no serious harm, but wash it off.

Fruit and leaves covered with honeydew and sooty mold. Scales on leaves and twigs, rarely on fruit. Tree vigor may be reduced.	**various soft scales:** **citricola scale (*Coccus pseudomagnoliarum*)** **brown soft scale (*C. hesperidum*)** **black scale (*Saissetia oleae*)**

Comments
Soft scales suck plant juices from leaves and twigs. Citricola is more serious in San Joaquin Valley than in Southern California. Natural enemies and oil sprays are effective controls. Keep ants out of trees because they protect scales from natural enemies. *Metaphycus* parasites can be purchased and released for additional control. Time treatments to target new brood right after hatching.

Distorted, curled leaves, honeydew, and sooty mold.	**aphids:** **spirea aphid (*Aphis citricola*)** **cotton or melon aphid (*A. gossypii*)**

Comments
Insects suck sap from tender, new growth. Honeydew provides a medium for growth of sooty mold fungus. Control needed only for heavy infestation on young trees. Dislodge with jet streams of water or use soap or oil sprays. See comments for sooty mold fungus, above.

Fruit and leaves covered with honeydew and sooty mold. Tiny whiteflies fly out when branches are disturbed. Immature insects look like transparent spots on leaves.	**whiteflies:** **woolly whitefly (*Aleurothrixus floccosus*)** **citrus whitefly (*Dialeurodes citri*)** **ash whitefly (*Siphoninus phyillyreae*)**

Comments
Whiteflies excrete honeydew, which attracts ants and promotes growth of sooty mold. Whiteflies also suck phloem sap from leaves, causing leaves to wilt and drop. Adults have mealy, white wax on their wings and bodies. Natural enemy parasites usually provide control. Eliminate ants and control dust; they interfere with natural enemies. Chemical controls not effective.

Fruit and leaves covered with honeydew and sooty mold. Cottony secretion on scales and twigs. Scales extract plant sap from leaves, twigs, and branches, reducing tree vigor.	**cottony cushion scale (*Icerya purchasi*)**

Comments
Newly hatched nymphs are red and found on leaves and twigs. Older scales are on twigs and covered with a cottony secretion. Eggs are in a fluted white egg sac about $1/2$ inch (1.3 cm) long. Becomes a pest only when its natural enemies (Vedalia beetle and a parasitic fly) are destroyed by insecticides. Reestablish natural enemies and avoid use of insecticides. In the 1880s, this pest threatened the entire citrus industry in Southern California, but success with natural enemies brought it under control. Today, light infestations occur every summer in the San Joaquin Valley because of temporary destruction of the pest's natural enemies. Occurs on a wide variety of fruit trees, nut trees, and ornamentals.

Table 18.4 cont.

What the problem looks like	Probable cause
Fruit and leaves covered with honeydew and sooty mold. Mealybugs present.	**mealybugs (*Pseudococcus* or *Planococcus* spp.)**

Comments

Soft, oval, distinctly segmented insects covered with a mealy white wax. Adults about ⅛ to ¼ inch (3 to 6 mm) long. Mealybugs extract plant sap, reducing tree vigor. If a cluster of mealybugs feeds along a fruit stem, fruit drop can occur. Natural enemies usually control. Eliminate ants. At home, you can hand-pick them, hose them off with water, or apply soap or oil sprays. A predator, the mealybug destroyer, is available commercially for release.

A ring or partial ring of scarred tissue on fruit rind near stem end. Young leaves may be deformed and scarred.	**citrus thrips (*Scirtothrips citri*)**

Comments

A tiny yellow insect about ¹⁄₂₅ inch (1 mm) long. Very active. Damage is primarily aesthetic, cosmetic. Ignore in home gardens. Botanical pesticides are used in commercial orchards. Irrigate adequately, because they prefer dry plants. When monitoring, you must be able to distinguish this pest from flower thrips, which feed on flower parts but do not damage citrus (see Kobbe and Dreistadt 1991).

Surface feeding or holes in blossoms, leaves, or young, developing fruit. Chewed leaves.	**orangeworms**

Comments

"Orangeworm" is a collective term for all moths and butterflies that are pests of citrus in the larval (caterpillar) stage. Trees can tolerate some foliage damage and loss of blossoms. Orangeworms can cause substantial damage by feeding on fruits. Examples of orangeworms are the citrus cutworm and leafrollers (see below), the western tussock moth, citrus looper, and orange tortrix. Larvae of the major orangeworms are difficult to distinguish. All produce webbing except the citrus cutworm.

Surface feeding or holes in blossoms, leaves, or young, developing fruit. Chewed leaves.	**citrus cutworm (*Xylomyges curialis*)**

Comments

Brown to green, smooth-skinned caterpillar with a prominent white stripe on each side. Curls up when disturbed. Develops into moth. A problem primarily in the San Joaquin Valley. Damage occurs in spring. Natural enemies (parasitic wasps) are often effective. *Bacillus thuringiensis* is also effective. Not a problem in desert or coastal areas. Citrus cutworm is a citrus orangeworm (see above).

New leaves have holes and are webbed and rolled together. Caterpillars also feed on buds and developing fruit, often rolling and webbing fruit and leaves together.	**leafrollers:** **fruittree leafroller (*Archips argyrospilus*)** **omnivorous leafroller (*Platynota stultana*)** **orange tortrix (*Argyrotaenia citrana*)**

Comments

Fruittree leafroller attacks citrus, apples, almonds, pears, stonefruit. It has the same geographical distribution as the citrus cutworm, and the two species often occur together. Damage to fruit may expose it to decay organisms. Most damage occurs in spring and early summer. One generation per year. Omnivorous leafroller has many generations per year and damage can occur throughout the growing season. Translucent caterpillars. General sanitation and natural parasites are effective controls.

Holes in leaves and fruit; slimy trails.	**brown garden snail (*Helix aspera*)** **gray garden slug (*Agriolimax reticulatus*)**

Comments

Brown garden snail is about 1 inch (2.5 cm) diam. with distinct color pattern; gray garden slug is a snail relative, lacks shell. Most active at night and early morning when it's damp. Manage by skirt pruning and trunk treatment. Release predatory decollate snails (*Rumina decollata*) in counties where it is legal. Use wooden boards with cleats for monitoring. Remove collected snails and slugs daily. You can crush to destroy or use a 1:1 solution of household ammonia and water in a spray bottle. Keep ammonia solution off leaf surfaces because it can damage plants. Copper barriers, such as trunkbanding of citrus trees, can be effective.

Ants feeding on twigs, bark, leaves, and honeydew excreted by other insect pests. Argentine worker ants travel in distinct trails.	**Argentine ant (*Iridomyrmex humilis*)** **Southern fire ant (*Solenopsis xyloni*)**

Comments

Ants feed on honeydew excreted by soft scales, mealybugs, aphids, cottony cushion scales, and whiteflies. Ants can interrupt biological control of these pests. Control ants by denying access to the canopy. Apply a band of sticky material to base of trunk that mechanically impedes ants. Prune the canopy up (above 30 inches [76 cm] off the ground) so that ants cannot get into the tree without climbing the trunk.

What the problem looks like	Probable cause

Leaves and green fruit have a pale yellow stippling. No webbing. Bright red globular eggs laid on bark or leaves.

citrus red mite (*Panonychus citri*)

Comments
A barely visible red mite (use hand lens) found mostly on young leaves. Can be a problem on patio trees and indoor house plants. Oil sprays between August and September will control problems in most areas. Natural controls should be sufficient in unsprayed backyard trees. Weekly washings with soapy water are an effective control, but they will not eliminate the problem.

Oddly misshapen and distorted flowers, fruits, and leaves. Primarily a problem on lemons in coastal areas.

citrus bud mite (*Eriophyes sheldoni*)

Comments
Very small, barely visible, elongated, yellow mite with only four legs that appear to be coming out of their heads. Smaller than red mites. Petroleum oil sprays during May and June or September through November can control. Natural predators are also effective. To detect bud mites before damage occurs, check buds on green angular twigs from midspring to fall.

Destroyed rind cells, causing russeting on mature oranges and silvering of rind tissue on lemons.

citrus rust mite (*Phyllocoptruta oleivora*)

Comments
Very small, barely visible mite, deeper yellow than bud mite but about the same size. A sporadic pest in coastal citrus plantings. Called silver mite on lemons and rust mite on oranges. Most damage occurs from late spring to late summer. No effective natural enemies are known. Monitor by looking for rust mites on foliage in early spring using a 10x to 14x hand lens. On lemons, check fruits for scarred rind tissue. If treatment is required, check the latest UC pest management guideline for citrus.

Maggots inside fruit pulp.

fruit flies:
Oriental fruit fly (*Dacus dorsalis*)
Mediterranean fruit fly (*Ceratitis capitata*)
Mexican fruit fly (*Anastrepha ludens*)

Comments
Female fruit flies lay eggs in the fruit rind. Importation of these pests from Mexico and Hawaii is a constant threat. They attack citrus, other subtropical fruits, and deciduous fruits. Maggots develop inside the fruit pulp, destroying what were once edible juice vesicles. Infestations have occurred several times in Southern California in recent years. Contact your local Ag. Commissioner's office if you suspect fruit fly infestation.

Leaves turn pale green to yellow, especially in winter and spring. No mites present.

nitrogen deficiency

Comments
Symptoms may appear in spring when soil temperatures are cold and trees are not able to take up nutrients despite adequate amounts in the soil. Check to see that fertilizer requirements are met. Can apply foliar nitrogen as urea to increase bloom set and yield.

Leaves turn yellow and drop. No mites present. Abnormal number of blossoms.

overwatering

Comments
Decrease irrigation frequency. Avoid planting ferns, annual flowers, or plants that need lots of water near citrus trees.

Leaves turn yellow and drop. Beads of sap ooze from trunk lesions. Gumming is more pronounced in spring. Inner bark is brown and gummy, but the discoloration does not extend into the wood. Bark can dry, harden, and crack. Overall decline of tree due to disruption of transport of water and nutrients.

Phytophthora gummosis
(*Phytophthora parasitica* or *P. citrophthora*)

Comments
When infection is just above the bud union, it is often called foot rot; when infection is higher up on the trunk, it is often called gummosis. When it spreads down into the crown, it is referred to as foot rot. Fungus infects the tree trunk and may spread to crown and woody roots. Keep trunk dry. Do not allow sprinkler water to hit the trunk. Scrape away all diseased bark and include a buffer strip (about 1 inch [2.5 cm]) of healthy light brown to greenish bark around margins. Allow to dry. Repeat if infection recurs. Keep mounded soil and water away from trunk. Improve ventilation by removing branches that touch the ground. Avoid injuring bark with lawn mowers, weed whackers (the worst), and pruning tools, since wounds give fungus an easy entry.

Table 18.4 cont.

What the problem looks like	Probable cause
Leaves turn yellow and drop. Root bark of infected roots slides off easily when pinched. Feeder roots destroyed. Symptoms may be difficult to distinguish from nematode, salt, or flood damage.	**Phytophthora root rot (*P. citrophthora*)**

Comments

Caused by the same fungus that causes gummosis, but it infects the root system in this disease. Survives in soil a long time. Disease can occur when water is in direct contact with the base of the trunk and the trunk is allowed to stay wet. Shorter, less frequent irrigations may help if damage is not severe. Avoid waterlogging. If damage is severe, remove tree. Fumigate if replanting. Use tolerant rootstock. Trifoliate orange, Troyer/Carrizo citrange and C-32/C-35 citrange rootstocks are tolerant (tables 18.2, 18.3). Do not plant citrus in the lawn where it will be watered too frequently.

| **Ripe fruit turns light brown and becomes soft. Water-soaked spots on rind become soft and turn brown. Pungent odor.** | **brown rot (*P. citrophthora*)** |

Comments

Caused by the same fungus that causes gummosis, but it infects fruit in this disease. Occurs primarily on fruit borne near ground during wet weather. Fungus spores on the ground get splashed onto fruit on lower branches by rain or irrigation water. Remove diseased fruit. A preventive Bordeaux treatment ($Cu(SO_4)_2$) before first fall rains can be applied to tree skirts up to 4 ft (1.2 m) and to the ground beneath trees.

| **Fruit decreased in size, yellowed leaves, twig dieback, general loss of vigor.** | **citrus nematode (*Tylenchulus semipenetrans*)** |

Comments

Microscopic, wormlike pest. Nematodes feed on citrus roots. Belowground symptoms include poor growth of feeder roots. May occur in conjunction with Phytophthora root rot. Plant trees with resistant rootstocks (see table 18.2).

| **Poor growth, dieback of shoots. Small, yellowing leaves and premature leaf drop. In winter, mushrooms may be at base of infected trees a few days after a rain.** | **Armillaria root rot (*Armillaria mellea*)** |

Comments

Also known as oak root fungus. Symptoms may not appear until fungus is well established. Once symptoms appear the disease has probably already spread to roots of surrounding trees. Pathogen invades roots and crown and can destroy entire root system. Rarely a problem in desert areas because fungus requires cool, moist soil for development and spread. Management relies on preventing infection in new trees. Once infection is apparent, it is very difficult to save a tree. If your planting site may be infested, fumigate it before planting. Remove and burn infected trees and neighboring healthy trees. Note: Not all mushroom growth indicates presence of *Armillaria*.

| **Internal black rot in navel orange fruit. Rot starts at stem end, extends into core. Can occur on lemons in storage.** | **Alternaria rot (*Alternaria citri*)** |

Comments

A fungus disease. Also known as black rot on navels. More of a problem when the navel is split. Preventing stress reduces susceptibility. No chemical control.

| **Tan to reddish-brown spots on Valencia orange, lemons, grapefruit.** | **Septoria spot (*Septoria* spp.)** |

Comments

Occurs primarily in the San Joaquin Valley and interior districts of Southern California during cool, moist weather. Spores are spread in dew or rainwater. *Anthracnose* or *Alternaria* spp. can occur as secondary infections on lesions caused by *Septoria*. Home growers do not need to spray.

| **Whitish mycelium on fruit; blue and/or green spores appear on fruit.** | **blue mold (*Penicillium digitatum*) green mold (*Penicillium italicum*)** |

Comments

May occur on injured fruit in the field but more often is a storage, postharvest disease. Early infections are almost impossible to detect. Easily recognizable when whitish mycelium and blue or green spores appear. Both types may occur together. To reduce infection, do not pick wet fruit and handle fruit carefully during picking. Immediately discard infected fruit and wash all stored fruit nearby in soapy water.

Small, lopsided fruit; stunted growth. Small leaves held upright, not flat. Inferior, off-bloom fruit.

stubborn disease (*Spiroplasma citri*)

Comments

Viruslike disease. Afflicts primarily sweet orange, grapefruit, and tangelo trees in hot inland areas of Southern California and the desert. No control available. Infected young trees yield small harvests. See chapter 6, "Plant Pathology."

Small, lopsided fruit; stunted growth. Small leaves held upright, not flat. Inferior off-bloom fruit. Small harvest from infected trees.

Tristeza virus

Comments

Use resistant rootstocks when planting new trees. Widespread on old trees, but rootstocks used today (table 18.2) are tolerant. No control available. Remove infected trees; sanitize area. Use certified, virus-free budwood from the UC's CCPP.

Scaling, flaking of bark on scion cultivar. Patches of bark on trunk, scaffold branches show small pimples or bubbles that later enlarge and become loose scales.

Psorosis virus

Comments

Graft-transmissible disease, presumably a virus found in old citrus plantings. Infected trees, mostly orange and grapefruit, slowly decline. Gumming can occur around lesions. Disease-free budwood from the UC's CCPP prevents damage.

Excessive fruit drop, especially on young trees.

sudden temperature change (heat wave at fruit set)
too much or too little moisture
nutrient deficiency

Comments

Nutrient deficiencies can be identified by the pattern of leaf yellowing (chlorosis) and by noting whether it occurs on new or old foliage. When problem is identified, adjust fertilization program to add needed nutrient in form that roots can extract (chelated) or as foliar spray. Nutrient deficiencies can also result from too little water. Add a second or additional drip emitter as citrus tree matures if lack of water is a problem. *Nitrogen deficiency:* Starts with older leaves near bottom of tree and foliage turns a uniform yellow. *Zinc deficiency:* Young leaves are abnormally small with yellow blotches between the veins. Symptoms are most obvious on the south side of the tree. Use foliar spray. *Iron deficiency:* Young leaves turn yellow between the veins. Veins stay green. Common in alkaline, poorly drained, overwatered soils. Add chelated iron, not foliar sprays. *Manganese deficiency:* Young leaves turn a lighter green between the veins. Often more noticeable on tree's north side. May occur with iron and zinc deficiencies. *Magnesium deficiency:* Older leaves turn yellow between veins and drop. Most noticeable in late summer–fall and in rainy climates.

Bark dries, cracks, and may lift in thin strips. Droplets of gum also appear under loose bark. "Shelling."

Exocortis (*Exocortis* viroid)

Comments

Of minor importance in California today because of strict regulations on budwood sources. Widespread in older plantings. A mild disease that causes moderate stunting and some loss of productivity. Spreads on infected budwood and contaminated propagation tools. The UC's CCPP provides viroid-free budwood to nurseries, which can be grafted onto susceptible rootstocks, such as trifoliate orange. Heat does not kill the viroid. Remove infected trees because pruning clippers can transmit disease unless disinfested with a bleach solution.

Brittle wood peels off in patches. Fruit rind develops tough, brownish spots and fruit may dry out.

sunburn

Comments

A problem in hot, sunny areas. For newly planted trees, wrap the trunk in white cardboard or use whitewash or flat latex paint in white or a light brown color that blends with tree trunk.

Random fruit scarring. Scarring does not form a ring around the stem end as with damage from thrips.

wind abrasion

Comments

Minor problem. Create a windbreak or plant trees in a nonwindy area. High winds can also cause premature leaf drop.

Table 18.4 cont.

What the problem looks like	Probable cause
Leaves, twigs look watersoaked, then wither, darken. Leaves may drop quickly or persist on tree. When fruit freezes, flesh dries out and brownish pits (ice marks) may form on the rind. Branches die back and bark splits in severe cases.	**frost damage**

Comments

Wait before treating frost damage. Allow the tree time to recover before removing frost-killed wood. After new growth appears in early spring, wait for any dieback, then cut back to live wood (identified by a green layer just under the bark). Pruning cuts will heal naturally, so there's no need to paint them.

Navel oranges crack and split. Small percentage of fruit affected.	**late growth spurt**

Comments

Cause unknown. Problem may occur in the fall when the rind does not expand as fast as the underlying flesh during a late growth spurt, causing splits.

Yellow leaves.	**various**

Comments

Excessive watering, nitrogen deficiency, girdling of trunk by rodents, root diseases, sunburn, and high lime content of soil, causing iron deficiency, may result in leaf yellowing. Some grapefruit tree leaves develop a yellow color in winter months. This is genetic, particularly in young Rio Red trees, and not a symptom of a problem.

Source: Adapted from Flint 1998, pp. 246–247; Kobbe and Dreistadt 1991.

semiarid, fungi that attack fruits are less important here. The distribution of citrus blast, the one bacterium that causes citrus disease in the state, is limited by climate to Northern California, where there are long wet periods in winter and spring.

Exocortis is of minor importance today in California because of strict regulations on budwood sources. Until very recently, the *Tristeza* virus was limited to old citrus-growing areas of Southern California because of UC research that led to the identification of the disease and the propagation of trees for new citrus planting made from *Tristeza*-free budwood. However, the San Joaquin Valley is no longer free of *Tristeza*, despite restrictions on the movement of propagating material, the clonal protection programs that have eliminated viruses from budwood, and the programs to detect and eradicate diseased trees.

Many citrus diseases are described according to the plant part or parts that they damage. For example, *Phytophthora* fungi cause a number of citrus diseases with different names depending on the part of the tree affected—roots (Phytophthora root rot), trunk (gummosis or foot rot), crown (foot rot), or fruit (brown rot) (see table 18.4).

In addition to Phytophthora root rot, two other diseases commonly affect citrus roots in California: dry root rot and Armillaria root rot.

The first visible symptoms are usually yellowing of leaves and a slow decline of the scion. Phytophthora root rot destroys feeder roots, whereas the other two diseases also move into the wood (xylem) of the root and crown (see table 18.4).

Prevention is the most economical method of controlling citrus diseases. Preventive measures can include use of tolerant rootstocks (see table 18.2) and virus-free budwood, preplant soil preparation, good drainage, judicious irrigation management and sanitation, adequate fertilization, and control of other pests. Buy trees with a high bud union, and when planting them, maintain the same soil level as in the nursery to prevent disease problems. Reputable nurserymen and your local UC Cooperative Extension farm advisor will be familiar with the most important citrus diseases in your area and will know which scion/rootstock combinations are most tolerant and vigorous in your area.

Environmental stresses, such as nutrient deficiencies or adverse weather and soil conditions (excessive or too little irrigation water, poor drainage), may cause symptoms described as "abiotic diseases" or as "abiotic disorders" (see chapter 6, "Plant Pathology"). Root damage from biotic diseases can predispose citrus and other commodities to environmental stresses, and vice versa. Symptoms associated with several environmental stresses and a few comments on managing them are included in table 18.4.

Mineral deficiencies or excesses, which may be toxic, usually show up first in leaf tissue, but they eventually affect fruit size, quality, and yield. In California citrus, a few nutrient deficiencies can be problematic. The most common deficiencies are nitrogen and zinc, followed by manganese and magnesium. Iron deficiency is less common. (For a description of common mineral deficiency symptoms, see table 18.4.) Mineral toxicities are less common than deficiencies, but boron can cause toxic symptoms if irrigation waters or soils contain excess concentrations. If you suspect boron toxicity, the irrigation water should be checked.

Foliar sprays can correct zinc, iron, and manganese deficiencies. Chelated formulations applied to the soil near the tree are also effective. A general recommendation is given earlier in this chapter in the section "Fertilization of Fully Bearing Citrus Trees," but you may also consult with your local UC Cooperative Extension farm advisor about the most effective methods in your area.

Control Measures

Whenever possible, use mechanical control methods (remove diseased limbs, clean up debris, dislodge pests with strong blasts of water or with soap or oil sprays) and biological control methods (release natural enemies) to combat pests. Use chemical pesticides as a last resort. Chemical controls not only kill the target pests but they also accelerate development of pesticide resistance. Chemicals may also kill beneficials, the biological enemies naturally present or introduced into the garden. For the most recent pesticide recommendations, consult the *UC IPM Pest Management Guidelines: Citrus* 1996. For additional information on general pest management and pesticide use, see chapter 10, "Controlling Garden Pests Safely."

Mechanical Control of Insect and Mite Pests. Mechanical methods are nonpolluting, nonpersistent pest control techniques that are effective against a number of insect and mite pests. Strong blasts of water usually dislodge aphids. Soaps and oil sprays are effective against a number of soft-bodied insects and mites. Use soaps and oils only when your trees have been well irrigated and

when conditions are not windy and not too hot (<90°F [<32°C]).

Soaps are effective against soft-bodied insects and mites on contact. They penetrate pest cell membranes and kill without harming trees or fruit. Apply soaps in the early morning or late afternoon. You can purchase insecticidal soaps or make your own by using 2 tablespoons (30 ml) of liquid dishwashing soap per gallon (3.8 l) of water, but be aware that some soaps are phytotoxic.

Horticultural oils smother and kill soft-bodied insects and mites. Summer oils that can be applied to evergreen trees such as citrus are available. Summer oils list the words "supreme," "superior," or "narrow-range" on the label. The original formulations of horticultural oils were applied to deciduous plants during the dormant season, and even though they may list application rates for use during the growing season, they are formulated differently from true summer oils. Avoid spraying horticultural oils in foggy or humid weather because the oil will dissipate so slowly that it can injure trees.

Biological Control of Insect and Mite Pests. Biological control of insect and mite pests is generally more effective in coastal regions than in the San Joaquin Valley or desert valleys. UC scientists are actively engaged in detecting and importing biocontrols of major citrus pests. A number of biological control agents that are effective against citrus pests are native to California, but UC entomologists travel to the areas of the world where citrus is believed to have originated to search for natural predators and parasites of citrus pests when indigenous parasites and predators are not available. When a particular parasitic wasp or predator looks promising, UC scientists bring them back to California with the appropriate permits and place them into UC quarantine facilities to undergo intensive research. UC entomologists release the imported biological controls into the environment only when research results document their effectiveness and safety.

Nutritional Value

It is common knowledge that orange juice is a good source of vitamin C, but the other vitamins and minerals contained in citrus fruits are less well-known. In addition to vitamin C, oranges have notable quantities of folic acid, thiamin, and potassium. Citrus fruits are low in fat, sodium, and calories. Because citrus fruits are plant-based foods, they contain no cholesterol. Table 18.5 summarizes the nutritional value of a typical serving size of several citrus fruits discussed in the chapter. Included in table 18.5 are percentages of the recommended dietary allowance (% RDA) for adult males (m) and females (f) contained in single servings of selected citrus fruits and juices. The nutritional value information for potassium content is expressed as "% Minimum Requirement." To date, no RDA has been established for potassium. Retinol equivalents (RE) are listed with vitamin A when appropriate. For background information on nutritional data, see appendix A.

Table 18.5

NUTRITIONAL VALUE OF SELECTED CITRUS FRUITS

Navel Oranges*

Serving size: 1 medium, raw (140 g)

Calories	65
Fat	0.1 g
Calories from fat	1.4%
Sodium	1 mg
Protein	1.4 g
Carbohydrate	16.3 g
Water	121.5 g
Cholesterol	0

Primary Nutrients		% RDA (m)	% RDA (f)	% Min. Requirement
Vitamin C	80 mg	88.9	107	
Folic acid	47 mcg	12.0	12.0	
Thiamin	0.12 mg	10.0	11.0	
Calcium	56 mg	5.6	5.6	
Vitamin A	26 RE	2.9	3.7	
Potassium	250 mg			12.5

Valencia Orange*

Serving size: 1 medium, raw (121 g)

Calories	59
Fat	0.4 g
Calories from fat	6.1%
Sodium	0
Protein	1.3 g
Carbohydrate	14.4 g
Water	104.5 g
Cholesterol	0

Primary Nutrients		% RDA (m)	% RDA (f)	% Min. Requirement
Vitamin C	59 mg	65.6	78.7	
Folic acid	47 mcg	12.0	12.0	
Thiamin	0.11 mg	9.2	10.0	
Calcium	48 mg	4.8	4.8	
Vitamin A	28 RE	3.1	4.0	
Potassium	217 mg			11

*The medium-sized Valencia orange that was analyzed is smaller than the medium-size navel and has correspondingly fewer calories and less vitamin C.

Fresh-Squeezed Orange Juice

Serving size: 8 fluid oz (248 g)

Calories	111
Fat	0.5 g
Calories from fat	4.1%
Sodium	2 mg
Protein	1.7 g
Carbohydrate	25.8 g
Water	219.0 g
Cholesterol	0

Primary Nutrients		% RDA (m)	% RDA (f)	% Min. Requirement
Vitamin C	124 mg	138.0	165.0	
Folic acid	109 mcg	27.0	27.0	
Thiamin	0.22 mg	18.0	20.0	
Magnesium	27 mg	6.4	8.4	
Vitamin A	50 RE	5.6	7.1	
Calcium	27 mg	2.7	2.7	
Potassium	496 mg			25

Pink or Red Grapefruit*

Serving size: 1/2 medium, raw (123 g)

Calories	37
Fat	0.1 g
Calories from fat	2.4%
Sodium	0 mg
Protein	0.7 g
Carbohydrate	9.5 g
Water	112.4 g
Cholesterol	0

Primary Nutrients		% RDA (m)	% RDA (f)	% Min. Requirement
Vitamin C	47 mg	52.0	63.0	
Folic acid	15 mcg	3.8	3.8	
Thiamin	0.04 mg	3.3	3.6	
Vitamin A	32 RE	3.6	4.6	
Calcium	13 mg	1.3	1.3	
Potassium	158 mg			7.9

*White grapefruit has just slightly less vitamin C than pink or red grapefruit and less vitamin A.

Table 18.5 cont.

Fresh, Unsweetened Grapefruit Juice

Serving size: 8 fluid oz (247 g)

Calories | 96
Fat | 0.3 g
Calories from fat | 2.8%
Sodium | 2 mg
Protein | 1.2 g
Carbohydrate | 22.7 g
Water | 222.3 g
Cholesterol | 0

Primary Nutrients		% RDA (m)	% RDA (f)	% Min. Requirement
Vitamin C	94 mg	104.0	125.0	
Folic acid	not given			
Thiamin	0.10 mg	8.3	9.1	
Calcium	22 mg	2.2	2.2	
Vitamin A	not given			
Potassium	400 mg			20

Lemon

Serving size: 1 medium, raw (58 g)

Calories | 17
Fat | 0.2 g
Calories from fat | 10.5%
Sodium | 1 mg
Protein | 0.6 g
Carbohydrate | 5.4 g
Water | 51.6 g
Cholesterol | 0

Primary Nutrients		% RDA (m)	% RDA (f)	% Min. Requirement
Vitamin C	31 mg	34.0	41.0	
Thiamin	0.02 mg	1.7	1.8	
Calcium	15 mg	1.5	1.5	
Folic acid	6 mcg	1.5	1.5	
Vitamin A	2 RE	0.2	0.29	
Potassium	80 mg			4

Fresh-Squeezed Lemon Juice (Unsweetened)

Serving size: 8 fluid oz(244 g)

Calories | 60
Fat | 0
Calories from fat | 0
Sodium | 2 mg
Protein | 0.9 g
Carbohydrate | 21.1 g
Water | 221.4 g
Cholesterol | 0

Primary Nutrients		% RDA (m)	% RDA (f)	% Min. Requirement
Vitamin C	112 mg	124.0	149.0	
Folic acid	32 mcg	8.0	8.0	
Thiamin	0.07 mg	5.8	6.4	
Calcium	18 mg	1.8	1.8	
Vitamin A	5 RE	0.56	0.71	
Potassium	303 mg			15

Lime

Serving size: 1 medium, raw (67 g)

Calories | 20
Fat | 0.1 g
Calories from fat | 4.5%
Sodium | 1 mg
Protein | 0.5 g
Carbohydrate | 7.1 g
Water | 59.1 g
Cholesterol | 0

Primary Nutrients		% RDA (m)	% RDA (f)	% Min. Requirement
Vitamin C	20 mg	22.2	26.7	
Calcium	22 mg	2.2	2.2	
Thiamin	0.02 mg	1.7	1.8	
Folic acid	6 mcg	1.5	1.5	
Vitamin A	1 RE	0.11	0.14	
Potassium	68 mg			3.4

Tangerine (Mandarin)

Serving size: 1 medium, raw (84 g)

Calories | 37
Fat | 0.2 g
Calories from fat | 4.9%
Sodium | 1 mg
Protein | 0.5 g
Carbohydrate | 9.4 g
Water | 73.6 g
Cholesterol | 0

Primary Nutrients		% RDA (m)	% RDA (f)	% Min. Requirement
Vitamin C	26 mg	29.0	35.0	
Calcium	12 mg	1.2	1.2	
Thiamin	0.09 mg	7.5	8.1	
Folic acid	17 mcg	4.3	4.3	
Vitamin A	77 RE	8.6	11.0	
Potassium	132 mg			6.6

Sources: Pennington 1998; National Academy of Sciences 1989, 2001a, 2001b.

Bibliography

Brenzel, K. N., ed. 2001. Sunset western garden book. Menlo Park, CA: Sunset Publishing.

Brokaw, W. H. n.d. Care of citrus and avocado trees. Saticoy, CA: Brokaw Nursery.

Casale, W. L., V. Minassian, J. A. Menge, C. J. Lovatt, E. Pond, E. Johnson, and F. Guillemet. 1995. Urban and agricultural wastes for use as mulches on avocado and citrus and for delivery of microbial biocontrol agents. J. Hortic. Sci. 70(2): 315-332.

Citrus. 1996. Menlo Park, CA: Sunset Publishing.

Esau, K. 1977. Anatomy of seed plants. New York: Wiley.

FDA Consumer Memo. 1981. Nutrition labels and U.S. R.D.A. 81-2146.

Ferguson, L., N. Sakovich, and M. Roose. 1990. California citrus rootstocks. Oakland: University of California Division of Agriculture and Natural Resources Publication 21477.

Flint, M. L. 1998. Pests of the garden and small farm: A grower's guide to using less pesticide. 2nd ed. Oakland: University of California Division of Agriculture and Natural Resources Publication 3332.

Hamill, P. V. V., T. A. Drizd, C. L. Johnson, R. B. Reed, A. F. Roche, and W. M. Moore. 1979. Physical growth: National Center for Statistics percentiles. American Journal of Clinical Nutrition 32:607–629.

Kader, A. A., ed. In press. Postharvest technology of horticultural crops. 3rd ed. Oakland: University of California Division of Agriculture and Natural Resources Publication 3311.

Kahn, T. 2000. Citrus genetic resources task force report. Riverside: University of California, Riverside.

Kobbe, B., and S. H. Dreistadt. 1991. Integrated pest management for citrus. 2nd ed. Oakland: University of California Division of Agriculture and Natural Resources Publication 3303.

McCarty, C. D., S. B. Boswell, and R. M. Burns, et al. 1982. Pruning citrus trees. Oakland: University of California Division of Agriculture and Natural Resources Publication 2449.

National Academy of Sciences. 2001a. Dietary reference intakes (DRIs): Recommended intakes for individuals, elements. Washington, DC: National Academy of Sciences.

National Academy of Sciences. 2001b. Dietary reference intakes (DRIs): Recommended intakes for individuals, vitamins. Washington, DC: National Academy of Sciences.

National Academy of Sciences, Food and Nutrition Board. 1989. Recommended dietary allowances. 10th ed. Washington, DC: National Academy of Sciences.

Ohr, D. H., and J. W. Eckert. 1985. Postharvest diseases of citrus fruits in California. Oakland: University of California Division of Agriculture and Natural Resources Publication 21407.

Pehrson, J. n.d. Citrus production—Best management practices. University of California Lindcove Field Station.

Pennington, J. A. T. 1998. Bowes & Church's food values of portions commonly used. 17th ed. Philadelphia: Lippincott.

Pittenger, D. R. 1992. Home vegetable gardening. Oakland: University of California Division of Agriculture and Natural Resources Publication 21444.

Platt, R. G. 1981. Micronutrient deficiencies of citrus. Oakland: University of California Division of Agriculture and Natural Resources Publication 2115.

Platt, R. G., and K. W. Opitz. 1974. Treatment of freeze-damaged citrus and avocado trees. Oakland: University of California Division of Agriculture and Natural Resources Leaflet 214.

Ray, R., and L. Walheim. 1980. Citrus: How to select, grow, and enjoy. Tucson, AZ: Horticultural Publishing.

Reuther, W., L. D. Batchelor, and H. J. Webber eds. 1967–1989. The citrus industry. Vols. 1–5. Berkeley and Oakland: University of California Division of Agriculture and Natural Resources. (Vols. 1-5 are available in libraries; vol. 4 [UC ANR Publication 4088] and vol. 5 [UC ANR Publication 3326] are also sold by UC ANR.

Turney, J., and J. Menge. Dec 1994. Root health: Mulching to control root disease in avocado and citrus. Circular CAS-94/2. Saticoy, CA: California Avocado Society, California Avocado Commission, and Citrus Research Board.

UC IPM pest management guidelines: Citrus. Updated regularly. In ANR Publication 3339. Oakland: Division of Agriculture and Natural Resources. Also available at UCCE county offices, or on the World Wide Web at http://www.ipm.ucdavis.edu.

Walheim, L. 1996. Citrus: Complete guide to selecting and growing more than 100 varieties for California, Arizona, Texas, the Gulf Coast, and Florida. Tucson, AZ: Ironwood Press.

19

Avocados

Deborah Silva, Carol Lovatt,
and Berthold O. Bergh

LEARNING OBJECTIVES

- Become familiar with avocado varieties that do well in the home garden in various climate zones in California.

- Learn the basic cultural requirements of avocado trees.

- Learn some basic principles of pest and disease management of avocados.

- Become acquainted with the relationship between the avocado industry and research at the University of California.

- Learn about the nutritional value of avocados.

Avocados

This chapter introduces you to avocados, one of California's important subtropical tree crops. Avocados are gaining in popularity nationwide. The avocado (*Persea americana* Mill.) is unique among tree fruits. It is neither sweet nor acidic, with a mild, anise-like, nutty flavor. It has significant nutritional benefits due to its high (in comparison to other fruits) mineral, vitamin, and protein content and high monounsaturated fat content, which helps to lower "bad" cholesterol (low-density lipoprotein). In South Africa, the avocado is considered the perfect food for toddlers and young children because of its high nutritional value and digestibility.

Worldwide, avocados are often eaten alone or with salt, lemon juice, or lime juice, or as part of a salad. In Mexico, you can enjoy avocado ice cream. In Brazil, the flesh of some avocado varieties is commonly sweetened and eaten as a dessert. In many countries, the avocado is a main ingredient in shampoos, soaps, and cosmetics, including skin creams.

The flavor and texture of avocados are such that many adults encountering avocados for the first time need to acquire a taste for them. The usual progression of impressions is from varying degrees of aversion at first taste, through steadily increasing acceptance to the point that avocados are prized as a distinctive delicacy. Guacamole dip, which uses mashed avocado as its base, is increasing in popularity throughout the United States. In the early 1970s, it was estimated that people in the United States averaged about one avocado per person per year (0.85 lb/person [385 g/person]). Today, that figure has almost doubled (1.63 lb/person [738 g/person]), according to the California Avocado Commission's evaluation of trends in per capita consumption.

This chapter provides a brief introduction to past and present research on avocados at the University of California; discusses basic physiological principles of avocado tree growth and development, particularly the unique behavior of avocado flowers; describes and recommends varieties for planting in the home garden; presents some basic information on planting, tree care, fertilization, environmental stresses, diseases, and insect pests; and highlights the nutritional value of avocados.

Wild avocados can be found in regions of Mexico and neighboring Central American countries; the crop originated in this general area. There are historic sites in Guatemala and Michoacan, Mexico, that mark the origins of the avocado.

Mexico is the world's leading producer of avocados, where they are referred to as "the butter of the poor," but in terms of monetary value, U.S. production ranks first worldwide. California is the major domestic producer of avocados. About 59,000 acres (23,900 ha) are planted with avocados in California, yielding a market value of about $339 million in 1999/2000, placing avocados among the state's top 20 crops. Florida has some commercial production, and Hawaii has a more limited crop.

In addition to the United States and Mexico, avocados are also grown in Central America, the West Indies, South America, Africa, Spain, Israel, the Philippines, Indonesia, New Zealand, and Australia. Central American production is largest in El Salvador, Costa Rica, and Guatemala. In South America, Brazil is the major producer, with modest industries in Venezuela, Colombia, and Chile. In the West Indies, the Dominican Republic is the major producer, with sizeable production also in Haiti. Africa grows avocados in Cameroon, Zaire, and countries in Southern Africa, which export much of their crop to Europe, as does the large Israeli avocado industry.

While avocados are an expensive luxury food in much of the world, they have been a staple in the diet of Central America since pre-Columbian times. In fact, the English word *avocado* is a corruption of the Spanish word *aguacate* that dates back to the seventeenth century as a shortened version of *ahuacaquahuitl* in the language of the Aztecs. Since the time of the Spanish conquest, *aguacate* has been the common name for avocado fruit in Mexico, Central America, and the Caribbean.

Avocados are members of the aromatic laurel family (Lauraceae). *Persea*, the avocado genus, is one of about 50 genera in the Lauraceae. Nearly all of the 1,000 or more laurel species are tropical, but a few are subtropical, and there are even a few temperate species, such as the classic laurel (sweet bay) of the Mediterranean area and sassafras of the eastern United States. In addition to *Persea*, the only laurel genus cultivated appreciably is *Cinnamomum* from which commercial cinnamon and camphor are derived.

Types of Avocados and Horticultural Races

Scientists refer to avocados as having three distinct horticultural races, known as botanical varieties (as opposed to cultivated varieties), that were named for their presumed centers of origin: Mexican, Guatemalan, and West Indian. The three races are designated respectively as *Persea americana* var. *drymifolia*, *P. americana* var. *guatemalensis*, and *P. americana* var. *americana*. A summary comparison of the three horticultural races is provided below.

- *Mexican race*. The leaves of this variety are anise-scented. It blooms earliest in the season (fall to spring in California) and takes about 6 months from flowering to fruit maturity. The Mexican fruit are small, pear-shaped or round, and have a very thin, waxy, dark-colored skin rarely more than $1/32$ inch (0.75 mm) thick. Seed are relatively large to very large and often loose. Fruit pulp is commonly rich to strong in flavor, sometimes with an anise aroma and often fibrous. Mexican fruit have the highest oil content of the three races. It is the most cold-hardy and the most resistant to heat and low humidity but the least tolerant of soil salinity. It rarely does well in a coastal environment. The Mexican avocado is a semitropical tree that would not be expected to flower or set fruit in a tropical climate, but it is the most likely to survive winter frost. In Mexico, Mexican-race trees are reported to mature fruit almost continuously throughout the year at varying elevations.

- *Guatemalan race*. The leaves of this variety do not have an anise scent. Young foliage is often reddish. Of the three races, the Guatemalan avocado blooms latest in the season, and fruit may require a year or more (up to 18 months) to achieve maturity in California but may require just 9 to 12 months in Florida. Fruit are small to large and more often rounded than pear-shaped. Fruit skin is rough, leathery, sometimes woody, and always thick, often more than $1/4$ inch (6 mm) thick. Fruit are green or black, but not as dark as the Mexican race. Seed are relatively small and almost never loose. In adaptation and tolerance to soil and climate, the Guatemalan race is intermediate between the Mexican race and the West Indian race. It is a subtropical tree and would not be expected to thrive in a tropical climate or to survive hard frost.

- *West Indian race*. The leaves of this variety do not have an anise scent. Its foliage is pale in color. Fruit are small to large, with about 6 months from flowering to fruit maturity. Fruit skin is shiny and leathery, but seldom more than $1/16$ inch (1.5 mm) thick, and it is green or reddish in color. The seed are relatively large and slightly loose. The pulp is mild to watery in flavor. This variety has a lower oil content than the other two races. It is the least cold-hardy of the three races and the least tolerant of low humidity. The West Indian avocado is not adapted to grow anywhere in California. It is a tropical tree that would set little or no fruit in California's climate and would not be expected to survive a winter frost. It does perform well in the semitropical climate of Florida. It is the most tolerant to soil salinity, either as rootstock or scion. Despite the established name of this race, evidence now points to the Pacific coast of Central America as the place of origin of the West Indian race.

There are no known fertility barriers among the three botanical races. Hybridization occurs readily wherever trees of different races are growing in proximity, which has resulted in cultivated varieties improved by scientific plant breeding techniques. The cultivar (cultivated variety) that led California production for many years, Fuerte, is a pear-shaped natural Mexican × Guatemalan hybrid that is green at maturity. The Hass cultivar, which currently leads California production, is generally regarded as straight Guatemalan, but breeding studies at UC Riverside have indicated that Hass is perhaps one-quarter Mexican. Hass has a rounder fruit shape than Fuerte, and Hass is black at maturity. The leading cultivars in Florida are Guatemalan ×

West Indian hybrids, which have a different flavor from their California cousins.

The Remarkable Avocado Flower

Avocado flower behavior is noteworthy—nothing quite like it is known in any other plant. The avocado flower has both female and male organs, which means it is structurally "perfect," or "bisexual," which is not unusual. What is unusual is that the avocado male and female organs within one flower do not function at the same time. Each avocado flower is functionally unisexual. Each flower is female when it first opens. That is, its stigma will receive pollen from other avocado flowers, but its stamens do not shed pollen at this first opening.

The female-stage avocado flower has a receptive stigma but also nonfunctional male parts (fig. 19.1). The female stage flower opens first, but for only 2 or 3 hours. The flower then closes and remains closed the rest of the day and that night. The following day, the flower opens again. But now the stigma will ordinarily no longer receive pollen. Instead, the flower now sheds pollen, and is known as a male-stage flower. After remaining open

for several hours on the second day, the male-stage flower closes again, this time permanently. Thus, each avocado flower is female at its first opening and male at its second opening.

In California, honey bees transfer pollen from male-stage flowers to stigmas of female-stage flowers. Once pollen has been successfully transferred to the stigmas, a process known as *pollination*, the pollen germinates, producing a pollen tube that advances through the style and ovary tissues to the ovule, which contains the egg (fig. 19.2). Depending on temperature, the pollen tube requires only about 2 to 4 hours to reach the ovule. Once the pollen tube delivers the sperm to the egg inside the ovule, the sperm and egg must fuse, a process known as *fertilization*, which results in formation of the embryo. The process of fertilization initiates the development of the ovary into a mature avocado fruit, and the ovule into the seed, inside of which is the embryo. This embryo can then develop into the young seedling avocado tree of the next generation. The seed provides plant growth regulators necessary for fruit set and fruit development.

Nature has provided for avocado cross-pollination by creating two kinds of botanical varieties. The A type flower is functionally female in the morning of the first day and functionally male in the afternoon of the second day, if the weather is warm. The B type flower is functionally female in the afternoon of the first day and functionally male in the morning of the second day, as diagrammed below.

	First day		Second day	
	Morning	Afternoon	Morning	Afternoon
A type	Female (stigmata receptive)			Male (sheds pollen)
B type		Female	Male	

Since different flowers open on different days, the two types of avocado cultivars complement each other with their diurnal synchrony. Both are functionally female on their first day and functionally male on their second day, but they differ in the time of day that they are male and female. A variety of one type provides pollen (functionally male) when a variety of the other type is receptive (functionally

Figure 19.1

Schematic view of the avocado flower. *Source:* After Bergh 1975.

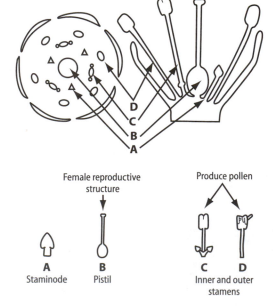

Female reproductive structure

Produce pollen

A Staminode **B** Pistil **C D** Inner and outer stamens

Figure 19.2

Avocado pollination and fertilization. *Source:* After Lovatt 1990.

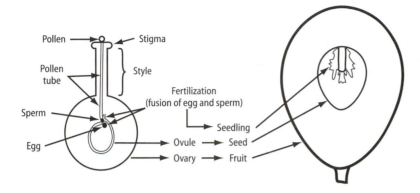

female). Therefore, the pollination and fertilization necessary for fruit set can occur.

On trees of an A-type cultivar, flowers open for the first time in early or midmorning, remain open and pistil-receptive until about noon, then close and remain closed until about noon of the second day, when they reopen and begin shedding pollen with the pistil no longer receptive. Finally, they close permanently that night. On a single tree, there may be thousands of flowers that open for the first time the same morning and then follow the same behavior pattern synchronously hour after hour for their 2-day existence. The total opening cycle on an A-type tree covers about 36 hours. Flowers on trees of a B-type cultivar function analogously but with transposed timing. The opening cycle on a B-type tree spans about 24 hours. The difference in cycle time reflects the relative length of the closed period between openings.

The two flowering types behave with clock-like exactness only when the average temperature (night minimum and day maximum) is above about 70°F (21°C). As the temperature falls, the daily openings for the functionally male and female flowers become delayed and irregular such that a single tree may have flowers in both the female and male stages at the same time, which explains how large blocks of just one cultivar set heavy crops via self-pollination. With colder temperatures, the second (male) opening may be delayed 1 or more days, and other abnormalities in flower behavior may occur. Either opening may continue through the night and

into the next day. Below about 60°F (16°C), however, there may be zero fruit set.

Recent research at UC Riverside has shown a weak positive correlation between cross-pollination and yield in some Hass avocado orchards, but the total data suggested that self-fertilization was responsible for a substantial portion of fruit set in California groves. However, in earlier studies, when an A-type and a B-type variety grew with their branches overlapping or at least close together, fruit set increased by 40 to 150 percent. Many commercial growers plant B-type cultivars to provide a complimentary source of pollen for the Hass avocado, an A-type, and place beehives in their orchards. Since home gardeners are not concerned about yield and bottom-line profit like a commercial grower, they do not need to make provision for cross-pollination. Nevertheless, it is useful to understand the factors that can influence fruit set and that can be used to increase fruit set, if desired.

A sampling of cultivated varieties classified as A types or B types are listed below.

- A-type cultivars: Hass, Gwen, Pinkerton, Reed, Anaheim, Lamb Hass

- B-type cultivars: Fuerte, Zutano, Bacon, Whitsell, SirPrize

Under typical California weather conditions, which are subtropical, both the A- and B-type cultivars bloom continuously for about 2 months, and it is rare for the earliest cultivar to finish blooming before the latest begins. Whereas summer flush vegetative shoots of the Hass avocado in California transition to reproductive shoots and initiate inflorescences sometime from the end of July through August, individual avocado flower buds are initiated at most about 2 months before the tree is in full bloom. The seasonal cycles of flowering, fruit set, and fruit development for the Hass avocado in San Diego–Riverside environmental conditions are shown in figure 19.3.

Avocados produce two types of floral shoots: determinate floral shoots, in which the apical bud is a flower, and indeterminate floral shoots, in which the apical bud remains vegetative and produces a vegetative shoot. Determinate floral shoots occur along the branch, and indeterminate floral shoots are formed at the end of a shoot (branch) (fig. 19.4). The number of flowers per inflorescence of the Hass avocado is approximately 150.

Figure 19.3

Flowering, fruit set, and fruit development of the Haas avocado in California. *Source:* After Lovatt 1999.

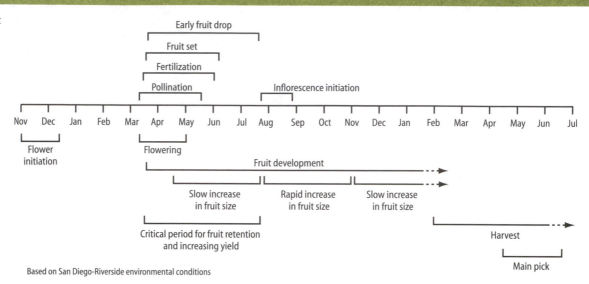

Hass avocado trees in California produce approximately 90 percent indeterminate floral shoots. This type of floral shoot sets less fruit than a determinate floral shoot. However, fruit set should not be a concern since a single tree will likely have a million flowers in bloom during a single spring bloom period. Despite the fact that less than 0.1 percent of this total results in fruit that hold to maturity, good yields are obtained. A yield of 200 8-ounce (229-g) fruit, or about 100 pounds (45 kg) per tree, results from approximately 0.02 percent fruit set.

Avocado trees have a strong tendency to alternate or biennial bearing, alternating moderate to heavy crops one year with light crops (low yields) the next year. This condition can be initiated by climatic or cultural conditions that result in excessive fruit drop and poor yield or by optimal conditions for fruit set that result in a bumper crop. Spring flush vegetative shoots arising from indeterminate floral shoots that set fruit do not produce inflorescences the following spring. Thus, when trees are carrying a heavy crop, the number of shoots that can produce inflorescences the next spring is significantly reduced. This is the cause of the low fruit set and yield that occur in the year following the heavy crop.

Avocado Breeding Objectives

Like many tree fruits, avocado trees sold today are not grown on their own roots. Avocado trees at the retail nursery consist of a scion/rootstock combination in which the rootstock provides the lower few inches of the trunk and the tree's roots. The scion includes the major portion of the trunk, all branches, leaves, and fruit (fig. 19.5). Thus, it is necessary to bud or graft scions of desirable and high-yielding fruiting cultivars (see table 19.1) to rootstocks preferably with superior disease-tolerant traits. Scientists and nurseries have

Figure 19.4

Floral shoots of a Hass avocado are either determinant or indeterminant.

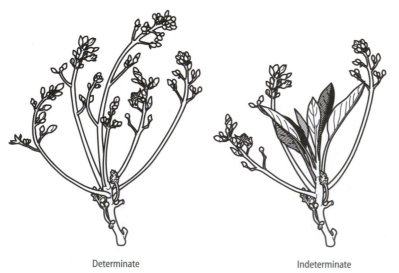

Determinate   Indeterminate

Figure 19.5

Typical container-grown nursery avocado tree showing scion grafted to rootstock.

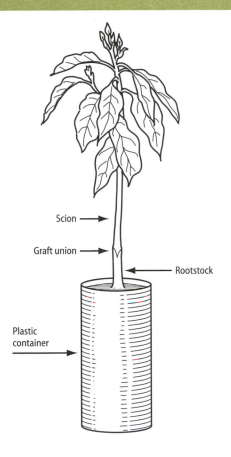

Scion →

Graft union →

← Rootstock

Plastic container →

breeding programs, such as the one at the University of California, are being planted commercially and in the backyard.

Fruit-Bearing Scions

Unlike citrus, the avocado produces only sexual seed, never seed of nucellar origin that are clones of the mother. In addition, the flowering habit in avocados, known as *dichogamy*, largely ensures cross pollination because the female and male flower parts mature at different times. Consequently, seedlings produced by a single tree (or cultivar) are extremely variable, providing an abundance of genetic variability among their offspring from which to select.

With respect to horticultural traits, breeders have selected for trees with

- cold-hardiness
- good fruit set (high yield)
- consistent and early production
- high-quality fruit that have superior, rich flavor and a long storage life on the tree
- fruit that weigh about 10 ounces (300 g) (not too large) with relatively small seed and a uniform shape and size
- skin that peels easily but that is thick enough to protect the flesh in transit to markets yet not so thick that it adds unnecessary waste material or prevents the consumer from determining ripeness by gentle palm pressure
- acceptable fruit color when ripe

The desired fruit color depends on consumers' past experiences and expectations. Today, a dark skin color is preferred in most domestic markets, where Hass has become the standard. Color is unimportant in a few markets, and green is preferred where Fuerte has been established as the standard of quality.

Although breeders have developed controlled hybridization techniques, these methods have not led to major success in developing a new commercial variety of avocado. Breeders have hand picked male-stage flowers with their clumped pollen and have hand-pollinated the stigmas of female-stage flowers by daubing them with the pollen grains of the selected male flowers to ensure that the resulting fruit have seed that bear the hybrid progeny of selected male and female

specific breeding and propagating objectives for the fruiting variety (scion) and rootstock.

Until the 1980s, every avocado cultivar grown on a large scale worldwide originated as a chance seedling; none of importance was derived from breeding programs. Fuerte was a chance seedling on a tree in Atlixco, Mexico, imported into California in 1911. Hass, Bacon, and Zutano were once chance California seedlings that became three commercially successful cultivars. Their seed parents are unknown, which is typical of privately produced chance seedlings. Hass was one of about 300 seedlings of miscellaneous origin grown by a letter carrier, Rudolph Hass, in La Habra, California, in the late 1920s. The original Hass tree was really a mistake—a lucky chance seedling—now known as the "Hass Mother" tree. It was the children who first brought the tree to their father's attention. They preferred the fruit. Since fruit quality was high, and the tree bore well, Hass patented it in 1935. Today, Hass is the leading commercial variety in California. Newer varieties that have been developed by avocado parents. But since breeders have no way of knowing which avocado flowers will set fruit any more than the average layperson (less than 0.1 percent of the million-plus flowers on a tree will set fruit, and the ones that do look no different from the ones that do not), this technique has produced very little benefit for the time and energy expended on it. No commercial cultivar has resulted from this labor-intensive method of breeding. To produce larger numbers of seedlings of known parentage, breeders have used bee-proof cages to select specific parents for hybridization or self-pollination, and they have also grown selected trees in isolation.

At present, newer avocado cultivars are being developed and tested via systematic selection, rather than originating as chance seedlings, but none is the result of a known, specific hybrid cross in which the male and female parents are known precisely. Thus, the term *breeding* in this context refers to selection.

Selection of Avocado Fruiting Varieties at the University of California. The avocado breeding program at UC Riverside has been recognized for decades as a world leader. Berthold O. (Bob) Bergh headed the program for 35 years until his retirement in the early 1990s. Bergh's Riverside laboratory had a steady stream of visiting scientists from avocado-producing countries around the globe, who would work with him for a month to a year. In 1984, Bergh and the University of California Regents patented three avocado varieties: Gwen, Whitsell, and Esther. The latter two have since revealed fatal flaws. The Gwen fruit, compared to the Hass standard, remain green-skinned when ripe, are a little rounder, have similarly superior flavor, and retain their superior flavor later in the season, but they may shrivel when picked at the beginning of the Hass harvest season. Gwen is more precocious, and, under favorable conditions (which in some cases appears to involve a nearby cross-pollinator), Gwen can produce twice as much fruit as Hass per acre on semi-dwarf trees with lower picking costs and easier spraying, if needed. These features reduce production costs per pound and increase competitiveness and profitability for commercial growers. Gwen's commercial expansion in California has been limited by its green-skinned fruit in a market where Hass dominance has made a black-skinned fruit highly preferred, by mediocre production in some locations, and by its susceptibility to persea mite. For backyard purposes, however, skin color is usually unimportant, and the smaller, narrower Gwen tree has several advantages.

The UC Riverside avocado breeding program has produced two recent patents for Lamb Hass and SirPrize. Lamb Hass apparently matches Gwen's high productivity on a somewhat more vigorous tree with a fruit that ripens black but has eating quality a little below the Hass and Gwen ideal. SirPrize is a high-quality, early-season black fruit (earlier than Hass) on a tree that should not grow as tall as the Bacon or Zutano early-season standards. It has a tendency to be a shy-bearer, meaning that it is not especially prolific in setting fruit. Its B-type flower is promising as a pollinator for major A-type cultivars.

Many selections in the University of California avocado breeding program are Gwen offspring, and they may prove to be the chief commercial contribution of Gwen. Because many of Gwen's seedlings inherit its greater precocity and smaller tree size, they permit closer spacing of trees and more rapid turnover, thereby increasing the efficiency of the breeding program's evaluation process.

Figure 19.6

Eight climate zones for growing avocados in California. *Source:* California Avocado Society 1976.

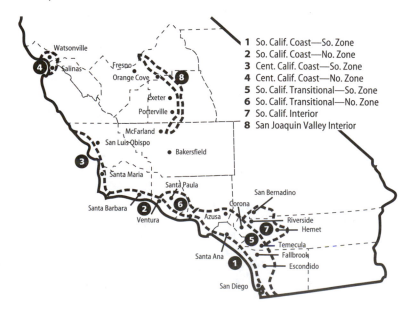

1 So. Calif. Coast—So. Zone
2 So. Calif. Coast—No. Zone
3 Cent. Calif. Coast—So. Zone
4 Cent. Calif. Coast—No. Zone
5 So. Calif. Transitional—So. Zone
6 So. Calif. Transitional—No. Zone
7 So. Calif. Interior
8 San Joaquin Valley Interior

Avocado Rootstocks

Avocado breeders have important objectives with respect to rootstocks as well as fruit-bearing scions. The most sought-after rootstock objective is resistance to *Phytophthora cinnamomi*, a soilborne fungus that causes root rot, the most serious avocado disease in California and other avocado-producing regions of the world. (The disease is discussed later in the chapter in the section "Avocado Diseases, Insect Pests, and Environmental Stresses.") Other soilborne fungi to which rootstock resistance has been sought are collar rot, caused by *Phytophthora citricola;* wilt, caused by *Verticillium albo-atrum;* and canker, caused by *Dothiorella gregaria.* Avocado rootstocks are not known to have significant effects on fruit quality, although they do affect tree vigor and productivity. Fuerte and Hass scion tops grow up to twice as rapidly on Guatemalan rootstocks when compared with Mexican rootstocks, and fruit set is about proportional to tree size.

George A. Zentmyer, plant pathologist emeritus at UC Riverside and member of the National Academy of Sciences, searched widely in California and throughout Mexico and Central America for sources of resistance to the *Phytophthora cinnamomi* fungus. Of his several tested rootstock selections, the Duke 7 performed best and has considerable commercial usage in California and other avocado-growing countries. The avocado rootstock program at UC Riverside is now under the direction of plant pathologist John A. Menge, who is making large-scale field tests of newer selections resistant to root rot, mostly from hybridizations of Zentmyer's introductions, in isolation plots established by Bob Bergh. About a dozen of Menge's selections are now approaching prepatent disclosure, and several appear highly promising.

In avocados, asexual propagation of rootstocks is used to produce *clonal* rootstocks. Clonal rootstocks are preferred over seedling rootstocks because root rot–resistant traits of the parent tree from which the clone derives are preserved; whereas, in a seedling rootstock, the parent's root rot–resistant traits are usually lost due to cross-pollination and reorganization of genes. Until about 1977, practically all of California's commercial avocado trees grew on sexually produced seedling rootstocks; only the scions (fruiting tops, such as Hass or Fuerte) were asexually produced (cloned).

The original method for producing clonal avocado rootstocks was invented at the University of California at Los Angeles by E. F. (Ted) Frolich and was adapted to commercial avocado rootstock production by Brokaw Nursery, Inc. in Saticoy, California. To create a clonally propagated rootstock with the root rot–resistant traits of the parent avocado tree using the Brokaw clonal rootstock method, the nursery grafts budwood from a rootstock tree with proven root rot resistance to a nurse seedling. Shortly after budding, a constriction ring is placed around the stem of the nurse seedling. The young rootstock is allowed to grow for a few weeks; then, it is placed in the dark in order to form elongated growth with softened bark. This process is known as *etiolation.* After 4 to 6 weeks in the dark, the etiolated rootstock shoot still on the nurse seedling is placed back on the greenhouse bench, and potting soil with rooting hormone is placed around the graft union of the rootstock to the nurse seedling. As the young rootstock grows and forms roots, the nurse seedling is gradually killed by the constriction ring. After several months, the rootstock has its own roots and is now the free-living clonal rootstock. A bud of the desired fruit-bearing cultivar that serves as the scion, such as Hass or Gwen, is then grafted to the clonal rootstock.

Dr. Menge's laboratory screens more than 8,000 avocado seedlings a year for improved resistance to Phytophthora root rot. In addition, sometimes a particular grower has an orchard that has been decimated by Phytophthora root rot but has one or more trees that seem to have tolerated the disease—these are known as *escape trees.* Dr. Menge's lab uses techniques to force shoots from below the graft union on the escape tree in order to recover a clone from the older rootstock that appeared tolerant to Phytophthora root rot under field conditions. In the early 1990s, the University of California was recommending the clonal rootstock Thomas as the rootstock of choice because of its superior resistance to root rot. It performed better than G755, Duke 7, and G6 clonal rootstocks, but its effects on fruit productivity and fruit quality in the scion varieties grafted onto it need continual, long-term evaluation. Today, the clonal Toro

Canyon rootstock competes well with Thomas for root rot resistance. Both rootstocks were recovered from escape trees.

The University of California operates a quarantine facility and receives avocado germplasm from overseas for evaluation of root rot resistance. Scientists at the UC Kearney Agricultural Center in Parlier are evaluating new rootstocks for increased tolerance to salinity, hoping to expand the locations where avocados can be grown in California and making the crop less exacting of irrigation water quality.

In addition to selecting new rootstocks, Menge's lab is also selecting beneficial soil fungi and bacteria for their proficiency in competing with Phytophthora root rot in the rhizosphere (that portion of the soil where the majority of the avocado tree roots grow) or for their penchant for attacking the *Phytophthora* spores and eating them as a source of food. In some of their experiments, Menge and his staff irrigate avocado trees in soil infested with root rot with a solution of water and beneficial fungi or beneficial bacteria and study how effectively the beneficial microbes attack the disease-causing *Phytophthora*.

Avocado Cultivars for Planting in the Home Garden

The climate zone you live in determines which avocado cultivars perform best, when fruit are harvested, and what pest and disease problems are more common. Table 19.1, although not exhaustive, describes the major attributes of 14 avocado cultivars available to the home grower. Particular climatic requirements and home-growing conditions are noted in table 19.1 and in the section "California Climate Zones for Growing Avocados" below.

Several of the cultivars listed in table 19.1 are not recommended for commercial growers because their productivity or quality is less than Hass, the current industry standard. Two of the older commercial cultivars, Bacon and Zutano, are listed in table 19.1 because they are widely grown. Niether cultivar is recommended for the home grower because both grow quite tall, which makes harvesting difficult, and because newer cultivars are good replacements with higher-quality fruit.

Harvesting periods given in table 19.1 are approximate and broad. The timing of maturation of the fruit of a particular cultivar may vary slightly from year to year, and microclimates in the home orchard affect time to maturity as well; thus, the periods given in table 19.1 should not be interpreted as absolutely precise.

California Climate Zones for Growing Avocados

In California, avocados grow where temperatures do not fall much below freezing—usually in areas having coastal climates or in thermal belts surrounding some of the interior valleys. Avocado trees grow well under a variety of conditions, but good fruit production depends upon favorable weather, especially during bloom. Chilling breezes may reduce or cause complete failure of fruit set for some varieties, and sudden hot spells often cause young fruit to drop. In general, the two major dangers for avocado trees growing in California are freezing injury, especially for the tender, higher-quality cultivars, and above-freezing chilling injury, which prevents proper tree growth and independently limits fruit set on healthy trees. Hard Santa Ana winds in fall and winter blow leaves and fruit off the tree and can break brittle avocado limbs. The risk from wind varies from year to year and from region to region, but it is appreciable from Oxnard south.

Figure 19.6 depicts eight climate zones where avocados can be grown in California. This diagrammatic scheme is based on proven commercial success, but a backyard grower can certainly produce avocado fruit in much more of California than the zones depicted in figure 19.6. In the markedly colder areas of the state, backyard growers will be limited to the cold-hardy, short-season cultivars, such as Duke or Mexicola, with Jim, Stewart, and Sir-Prize worth trying, as noted in table 19.1. It should also be taken into account that zones 3 and 4 include quite diverse climates with very different avocado possibilities. Home gardeners are encouraged to consult the most recent edition of the *Sunset Western Garden Book* for much more detailed climatic zoning and useful climate analysis. In the discussion below of important climate zone attributes, reference is made to both figure 19.6 and to *Sunset* zones. Two additional valuable sources of information are local UC Cooperative Extension farm advisors in your county who have expertise in subtropical horticulture and your own observations of avocado trees already growing in the area of interest.

Some important attributes of climatic regions for growing avocados in California are described below.

Southern California Coast (Zones 1 and 2 in figure 19.6; *Sunset* Zone 24). This coastal region extends from the Mexican border through San Diego, Orange, Los Angeles, and Ventura Counties to about Point Conception, west of the city of Santa Barbara. This coastal strip varies from a few yards to a few miles wide, depending on the location of cliffs or hills that obstruct ocean air flow. Note that *Sunset* treats this region as one climate zone (24), whereas commercial avocado interests consider that it has separate southern and northern sections. There is little climatic difference of significance between these two sections, the chief variability being the winter cold from the mouths of canyons at certain points in both sections. The influence of the Pacific Ocean in this coastal zone means that some places here have not recorded a frost for decades, and nearly all of this region is considered functionally frost-free. In this zone, climatic limitations for growing avocados derive from chilling injury. Avocado trees exposed directly to constant, on-shore cool summer breezes may be so stunted that they never bloom; therefore, some natural or artificial barrier is needed. Most Mexican-race varieties are expected to have inferior yields in this zone, and among Guatemalans, B types may also yield poorly, which is believed to be related to chilling at bloom time. Soils immediately adjacent to the Pacific Ocean may be high in salinity due to spray and mist. Saline soils are inappropriate for avocado production.

Central California Coast (Zones 3 and 4 in figure 19.6; *Sunset* Zones 17 [portion] and 16). Here, the southern and northern zones are indeed distinct climate zones. The southern zone of the Central California coast is comprised of the coastal strip north of zone 2 in figure 19.6 to the town of San Simeon. This region averages cooler temperatures than the Southern California coast; thus, the chilling danger is greater and limits suitable avocado growing sites. The northern zone of the Central California coast along the Monterey Bay shares with southern Spain the distinction of being the most northerly commercial avocado region on earth. However, the

portion of *Sunset* zone 17 extending northward from San Simeon is too cold for avocado production; slightly more inland, *Sunset* zone 16 is sufficiently warmer, with low frost risk, and in limited inland places around the Monterey Bay avocados are commercially successful.

Southern California Transitional (Zones 5 and 6 in figure 19.6; *Sunset* Zones 21 and 23). These are much broader regions, inland from and adjoining the Southern California coastal region. The southern zone (5) is especially large, including the Escondido-Fallbrook avocado heartland and a wide northwest sweep past Los Angeles. Note that figure 19.6 may be misleading in suggesting that the entire area enclosed is commercial avocado country. As shown in the *Sunset Western Garden Book,* some regions here are colder in winter than others. But the areas defined in the *Sunset Western Garden Book* as zones 21 and 23 can probably grow successfully any of the avocado cultivars listed in table 19.1. Preference would ordinarily be for the longer-season, higher-quality cultivars adapted to this relatively mild climate. The northern zone of this Southern California transitional region (zone 6) has a smaller but also very favorable region for avocados, including the Santa Paula–Fillmore Valley and extending southwest past Moorpark, Somis, and Camarillo to the northern tip of the Southern California coast. Again, some parts of zone 6 are too cold for growing choice avocados without suffering freeze damage in some years.

Southern California Interior (Zone 7 in figure 19.6; *Sunset* Zone 19). This region generally includes Riverside, San Bernardino, and Hemet, which are hotter and drier in summer and colder in winter than the Southern California Coast. A number of specific, cautionary comments are essential. In this region, figure 19.6 could be misleading in that a large part of zone 7 in figure 19.6 is the colder zone 18 in the *Sunset Western Garden Book*. Both zones 18 and 19, as defined in *Sunset*, are irregularly intermixed. The Inland Empire cities of Riverside, Hemet, Perris, and Elsinore are actually in *Sunset* zone 18. That is, the cities are centered in valley bottoms where cold air settles, draining away from the hillsides that are therefore warmer and identified in zone 19. But temperature varies inversely with altitude, so higher elevations become progressively colder again. Any barrier that

Table 19.1

RECOMMENDED AVOCADO CULTIVARS FOR PLANTING IN THE HOME GARDEN

Cultivar	Parentage*	Fruit skin Ripe color	Fruit skin Texture	Fruit skin Thickness	Fruit quality	Fruit flavor	Seed size	Bearing habit†	Flower type	Cold limit‡	Mature season§
Bacon	Mexican	green	smooth	thin	good	sweet, mild	large	consistent	B	24ºF −4.4ºC	Nov–Mar

Upright tree growth can make harvesting difficult. Peel deteriorates if fruit left on tree too long.

Duke	Mexican	green	smooth	very thin	good	spicy	large	consistent	A	20ºF −6.7ºC	Sep–Oct

Not a commercial cultivar due to short season, loose seed, skin too thin for shipping. Valuable to the backyard grower for its agreeable flavor, good fruit size, wind and heat tolerance, and especially its maximum cold tolerance. Mostly used as rootstock.

Fuerte	Guatemalan × Mexican	green	leathery	thin	excellent	mild	medium	alternate	B	27ºF −2.8ºC	Nov–Mar

Fuerte blooms Feb–Apr. Was California's leading commercial cultivar due to its excellent fruit, long season, and some cold hardiness. Now largely replaced by the better-bearing Hass but may be worth a try where there is plenty of space for this very large tree.

Gwen	mostly Guatemalan	green	small pebbly	medium	excellent	rich nutty	medium	fairly consistent	A	30ºF −1.1ºC	Apr–late summer

Patented in 1984 by UC Riverside. Small, upright tree takes little backyard space and usually bears early and heavily. Not productive everywhere. May need a pollinator. Very susceptible to persea mite. Very susceptible to wind, heat, cold, and dryness. Commercial season is delayed until April because of skin shriveling when ripened earlier.

Hass	mostly Guatemalan	black	pebbly	medium	excellent	rich nutty	small-medium	alternate	A	30ºF −1.1ºC	Jan–Jul or year-round

Most common commercial variety. Comprises more than 80% of California acreage. Wide adaptability, except in cold, interior regions. High quality and long season appeal to backyard growers, if enough space is available for its large tree. Where summers are not too hot, fruit that stay on tree beyond July may develop undesirably strong flavor late in season. Susceptible to persea mite.

Jim	mostly Mexican	green	smooth	thin	very good	mild spicy	medium	fairly consistent	B	24ºF −4.4ºC	Nov–Feb

Green, thin-skinned avocados are fading commercially. Jim has advantages over the two old-time standards Bacon and Zutano. Jim has a longer season and better fruit quality than Zutano, better fruit set (in some places) than Bacon, and shorter trees than either of them. Jim may be useful where considerable cold-hardiness or a B-type flower pollinator is needed.

Lamb Hass	mostly Guatemalan	black	pebbly	medium	very good	fairly rich	medium	somewhat alternating	A	unknown (estimated at 30ºF [−1.1ºC])	May–Nov

Patented in 1996 by UC Riverside. Production higher than Hass on smaller, compact trees. Has done well but additional testing is needed. Superior to Hass in tolerance to wind, heat, and persea mite. Consumer taste tests rate fruit highly, but to connoisseurs, it is below Hass or Gwen excellence. Its cold hardiness is unknown, but better than 30ºF is not expected.

Mexicola	Mexican	purple	very smooth	very thin	good	anise-like	large	consistent	A	20ºF 6.7ºC	Aug–Sep

Extremely cold hardy like Duke but noncommercial because of thin skin, short season, too small a fruit. Mexicola's flavor preferred by some over that of the best commercial Guatemalans, such as Hass.

Cultivar	Parentage*	Ripe color	Texture	Thickness	Fruit quality	Fruit flavor	Seed size	Bearing habit†	Flower type	Cold limit‡	Mature season§
Pinkerton	mostly Guatemalan	green	pebbly	medium	excellent	rich	small	usually consistent	A	30°F −1.1°C	Dec–Apr

With cross-pollination (and sometimes without it), Pinkerton is a superior producer of superior fruit. Where the ocean moderates summer heat, fruit can hang on the tree well past April without flavor deterioration, as in Hass. Wide adaptation, but not northerly (Zones 4 and 8, fig. 19.6). Low persea mite tolerance. Its often large fruit become quite necked inland. The smallest seed of California commercial varieties.

Cultivar	Parentage*	Ripe color	Texture	Thickness	Fruit quality	Fruit flavor	Seed size	Bearing habit†	Flower type	Cold limit‡	Mature season§
Reed	Guatemalan	green	fairly smooth	thick	excellent	rich	medium	very consistent	A	30°F −1.1°C	May–Nov

A heavy producer of round fruit that become larger than commercially desirable. Large size encourages early picking, but in May flavor is usually bland. Rich flavor develops considerably later in its long season. Dubious for zones 3, 4, 7, and 8 (fig. 19.6). Moderately tolerant to persea mites.

Cultivar	Parentage*	Ripe color	Texture	Thickness	Fruit quality	Fruit flavor	Seed size	Bearing habit†	Flower type	Cold limit‡	Mature season§
SirPrize	Mexican × Guatemalan	black	leathery	thin	excellent	nutty rich	small	somewhat alternating	B		Nov–Mar

Patented 1996 by UC Riverside. Fruit are like large, black, rough Fuerte. Earlier than Hass. Better eating quality and longer season than other early-maturers, except the alternate-bearing Fuerte. Both traits are desirable for home gardeners. Black skin is commercially advantageous. Mature fruit easily identifiable. Tends to be a light producer. Young fruit have distinct ridge. So far, moderate tolerance to wind and persea mites. Cold hardiness is hoped for. Needs additional testing.

Cultivar	Parentage*	Ripe color	Texture	Thickness	Fruit quality	Fruit flavor	Seed size	Bearing habit†	Flower type	Cold limit‡	Mature season§
Stewart	mostly Mexican	purple	leathery	thin	excellent	flavorful	medium	variable	A	25°F −3.9°C	Oct–Dec

Of the cultivars suited to colder regions, only Stewart receives top rating for total fruit quality: medium size, very attractive appearance, small seed for its season, flesh neither nutty nor spicy, yet delicious, and superior peeling in spite of thin skin. Production is good in some locations and inferior in others.

Cultivar	Parentage*	Ripe color	Texture	Thickness	Fruit quality	Fruit flavor	Seed size	Bearing habit†	Flower type	Cold limit‡	Mature season§
Wurtz	Guatemalan	green	pebbly	medium	good	mild	large	alternating	A	31°F −0.6°C	May–Aug

Small tree (8–10 ft) ideal for small gardens or large containers. May also be sold as Dwarf, Littlecado, or Minicado. Only real virtue is unique, weeping-umbrella short tree.

Cultivar	Parentage*	Ripe color	Texture	Thickness	Fruit quality	Fruit flavor	Seed size	Bearing habit†	Flower type	Cold limit‡	Mature season§
Zutano	Mexican	green	smooth	thin	mediocre	watery	large	consistent	B	24°F −4.4°C	Oct–Feb

Upright tree growth can make harvesting difficult. Mediocre flavor. Pear-shaped fruit. Newer cultivars are better.

Source: Adapted from Bender 1996; information based in large part on observations by Bob Glein and Gray Martin.

Notes:

*Guatemalan or Mexican, the two avocado races adapted to California.

†The majority of avocado trees are alternate bearing, meaning that they bear a heavy crop one year and a sparse crop the next; however, there are varietal differences. For the home gardener with only one tree giving fruit in a given season, alternation is undesirable. All cultivars listed in this table bear fruit in approximately 3 years.

‡The approximate tolerance of established trees 3 years or older to cold temperatures. Tolerance varies with crop size, degree of hardening off before the freeze, any cultural weaknesses, length of time at that temperature, and other factors.

§Mature season can vary with factors affecting time of bloom and with seasonal weather, especially mean temperature. Usually the earlier the maturation, the shorter the time until the fruit drops or breaks down, but this depends partly on mean temperature also. Flavor improves as fruit remains on the tree after it has reached palatable maturity; however, eventually, as noted for Hass, flavor may deteriorate.

impedes air movement may increase frost damage by trapping cold air in the slope above it and reducing air drainage below it. Conversely, by choosing close proximity to the south side of a tall wall or even dense trees, the backyard avocado grower may trap enough heat to make a crucial difference. Frost risk increases a bit with each step from *Sunset* zones 24 to 23 and from zones 21 to 19, but the varieties in table 19.1 that are most frost-sensitive, as well as highest in fruit quality, are well worth trying here also, especially in favored locations.

The progression from *Sunset* zone 24 to 23 and from zone 21 to 19 is a progression of increasing summer heat and dryness. Avocados thrive on heat, but the lower humidity means increased irrigation needs. Note that zone 19 extends irregularly from zone 7 in figure 19.6 south to the Mexican border and west to San Fernando and Chatsworth.

San Joaquin Valley Interior (Zone 8 in figure 19.6; *Sunset* Zone 9). This region includes a narrow strip of the San Joaquin Valley from northern Kern through Tulare and Fresno Counties. It gets more winter rain than zone 7, which is beneficial not only in reducing water costs but also in better leaching of soil salts, to which the avocado is especially sensitive. Like *Sunset* zone 19, zone 9 is favorable for commercial avocados because it is elevated above neighboring land for good cold air drainage. But it is much farther north and inland; the more rigorous climate rules out the industry standard Hass variety in spite of its exceptionally wide adaptability. Of the standard, hardy cultivars, Bacon bears poorly in this region. There is interest in testing the new SirPrize in this region.

Influence of Microclimate on Backyard Avocado Growing

This general discussion of climate, particularly in the Southern California interior, points to the great importance of local microclimates to any avocado grower. These microclimates are quite obscured by the broad outlines in figure 19.6 and even by the much greater detail of the *Sunset Western Garden Book*. The microclimate issue is of special significance to the backyard grower in choosing tree location. The *Sunset* zoning can lead to the misconception of too great precision: not only do the zones shade imperceptibly into each other, but the approximate boundary line can shift back and

forth many miles with unusual weather conditions. Finally, the grower needs to be prepared, at least mentally, for erratically occurring severe freezes that cause devastation, even into parts of the Southern California Coast (*Sunset* zone 24). The backyard grower is, of course, not limited to the cultivars and regions that constrain the commercial farmer selling for profit. Avocados can be produced successfully in many other parts of California if one is willing to settle for the shorter picking season of the hardier avocado cultivars (see table 19.1).

In California, Mexican-race trees usually do better inland whereas Guatemalan types generally do better in the coastal avocado growing areas. Hass has an exceptionally wide adaptability, except for cold sensitivity (see table 19.1). But even in the best Hass locations, Lamb Hass may be superior. The most cold-hardy cultivars (noted in table 19.1), Duke, Mexicola, and to a lesser degree, Jim and Stewart, are recommended not only for frostier locations but also for other adverse climate conditions such as high heat, wind, and other stresses. Fuerte bears well only in very limited locations.

Through its Variety Committee, the California Avocado Society has given excellent guidance on choosing commercial varieties for specific climate zones. The home gardener can use this information as a starting point, while recognizing that he or she has a much wider choice because profitability and keeping a business afloat are not primary factors in the decision-making process.

Fruit Maturity

Unlike many fruits, avocados are not edible on the tree. That is, maturity is not synonymous with ripeness. Only after its stem is severed will an avocado fruit begin ripening—the ethylene-mediated physiological processes that induce softening of internal fruit tissues so that the fruit can be eaten. The fact that avocados do not ripen on the tree is a major advantage. Because the fruit of the better avocado cultivars can be stored on the tree for months after reaching palatable maturity (see table 19.1), the backyard grower can pick a few when ripe fruit are needed a few days later.

Cultivars vary widely in their time of achieving maturity and length of tree storage before fruit drop or deteriorate. Table 19.1 gives approximate months of fruit maturity for the zone 5 (see fig. 19.6) commercial heartland. At least four factors will influence time of maturation:

- Elevation. Maturity is delayed about 1 month for each increase of 325 yards (297 m).

- Latitude. Maturity is steadily delayed as one moves northward.

- Local temperature differences. Air currents and sun exposure affect maturity.

- Location. Southwest-facing slopes can speed up maturity due to light and heat.

All four factors reflect the correlation between temperature and a plant's internal physiological activity. For any climate zone, weather will vary from year to year; differences especially in mean temperature can advance or retard maturation of avocado fruit by a couple of weeks or more and can have an even more pronounced effect on the length of time fruit can be stored on the tree. Thus, predicting precise timing of fruit maturity is as complicated as predicting the weather.

Usually, the quicker a variety matures fruit, the shorter its season. Hence, Mexican-race types have a much shorter season than Guatemalans (see table 19.1). But varieties do differ. The Fuerte and the new SirPrize have remarkably long picking seasons, considering their early maturity. The Hass and Gwen have such good on-tree storage that, from a single tree, edible (if not very palatable) fruit can be picked year-round. Maturity variability on a given tree often results from differing time of fruit set. For example, the Pinkerton cultivar blooms over a very long period. A few, early-set, nearly round fruit can mature a month or two before the much glossier and slimmer late-set fruit, with the end of the season differing accordingly.

Palatability usually increases with time past minimum maturity, but late in maturity, the seed inside an avocado fruit may germinate and the root of the new plant can grow into the flesh of the fruit and even out through the skin, obviously not desirable for eating.

Selecting and Buying Avocado Trees

Producing a clonal avocado rootstock requires special facilities and expertise; thus, it is more practical for home gardeners to buy, from a reliable retail nursery, professionally produced trees consisting of a rootstock grafted with the desired fruiting cultivar (see table 19.1). The numerous retail nurseries throughout the state are supplied by a few wholesale nurseries that specialize in grafting avocado trees. Most retail avocados are on ordinary seedling rootstocks (not clonal rootstock), but the knowledgeable home gardener can have his or her local retail nursery order a special clonal-rootstock tree, recognizing that the cost will be considerably higher. In addition, because most of the fruiting varieties in table 19.1 are noncommercial cultivars, obtaining the desired fruiting variety may require a special order, even if the scion is not grafted onto a clonal rootstock.

Before making a purchase, check with the nursery to verify that the fruiting cultivar will produce well in your climate zone and in the microclimate in your home garden or orchard. Decide on the number of trees you will need and order them well in advance of your intended planting date. It takes time to propagate avocado trees, and the nursery may need 9 to 12 months' advance notice to meet your planting date, depending on the quantity you intend to purchase and especially on the cultivar you choose.

Inspect a tree before purchasing it. Make sure that the bud union (the point where the scion and rootstock join) is smooth and well-healed. Avoid trees that have weak and ragged bud unions. Do not accept stunted trees or trees with off-type foliage, off-colored or sparse foliage, or a wilted appearance because they may be signs of disease such as avocado root rot. The likelihood of buying diseased trees from a reputable retail nursery is slim, but if a tree lacks vigor and has some of the visible symptoms described above, reject it. Even at a reduced price, a "bargain" tree may be no bargain.

Two types of avocado trees are available to the home gardener: field-grown and greenhouse-grown. Field-grown trees are grown outdoors in nursery rows or in plastic containers. They may be standard-budded or tip-grafted. Some nurseries prefer to use a combination method, growing the seedlings and grafting in the greenhouse and then moving the young, grafted seedlings outside in containers to complete their development. Greenhouse-grown trees are grown in containers in the greenhouse and are propagated by tip grafting only. When both types of trees are sold to home growers at the retail nursery, field-grown trees are older (12 to 18 months old), larger, and have been hardened to outdoor conditions. Greenhouse-grown trees are sold at a younger age (8 to 12 months). They are smaller, have a more delicate root system, and require more careful attention after planting, particularly during the first year. They are less expensive than field-grown trees. Usually, greenhouse-grown trees have a lighter-textured leaf and more tender growth overall, but it may not be obvious that a particular tree is greenhouse-grown rather than field-grown, so make your preference known to the nursery when you order your tree(s).

Two voluntary programs of the California Department of Food and Agriculture (CDFA) allow wholesale avocado nurseries to register and certify trees sold to avocado growers if they are produced under specific conditions. Certified trees are grown under conditions that minimize root rot. These conditions include heat treating the seed, fumigating the potting soil, fencing the nursery site, isolating the nursery from known root rot infection, and other phytosanitary precautions. Registered trees are grown on clonal rootstocks tolerant to root rot and are also propagated from trees free of sunblotch viroid. Registered avocado trees sold to growers actually have three registrations: the nurse seed that starts the process, the rootstock, and the scion variety.

Planting

Before planting an avocado tree(s), it is advisable to know about the history of the soil at the site you have selected. This is because if it has been infested with *Phytophthora cinnamomi,* the fungus that causes avocado root rot, you might consider a different location or a different tree crop. At the very least, you will be apprised of the obstacles to be overcome and will have a realistic understanding of the likelihood of success. The clonal rootstocks that UC has developed are somewhat tolerant of root

rot, but they are not totally resistant. While their increased benefits are available to the commercial grower, the home gardener may not have access to them because retail nurseries typically do not sell these clonal rootstocks absent a special request. Thus, if you determine that the soil has been infested with *Phytophthora cinnamomi* and you do not have another site, you might consider hiring a registered, professional pest control operator to treat the soil before planting. Additionally, you should consider purchasing a more expensive clonal tree by special request, due to its known higher tolerance to root rot.

If you cannot plant your tree(s) immediately after delivery, store field-grown trees in full sun. Greenhouse-grown trees should be placed where they will get morning sun but will be shaded in the hotter part of the day. Keep the soil moist until you can plant.

The optimal time to plant avocado trees is March, but April, May, or June may be suitable, especially near the coast. If your site is in a cold location, plant the tree(s) as soon as possible after the danger of frost has passed to take advantage of the longer growing season. The earlier the spring planting date, the greater the tree growth the first year. Trees planted after June are smaller and less tolerant of adverse weather during the first winter than trees planted earlier in the year. Where summers are hot, trees planted earlier are less likely to be heat-injured.

How To Plant an Avocado Tree

A fully-leaved subtropical evergreen tree, such as an avocado, must be treated differently from a typical bareroot, deciduous temperate fruit tree. The following discussion of planting an avocado tree is summarized from *Care of Citrus and Avocado Trees* (Brokaw n.d.).

In most locations, avocado trees are often planted later in the spring than temperate fruit trees to take advantage of warmer soil. Special allowance must be made for an avocado's high transpiration rate. Avocado trees have tender, succulent roots, so their earthen balls may not be as physically stable as those of other plants. Therefore, do not lift or carry avocado trees by grasping the trunk because doing so often results in part of the root ball and soil breaking off. Be sure the tree is lowered into and correctly set in the planting hole before you slit the poly container.

Figure 19.7

Planting an avocado tree. (A) Hole should be twice the width of root ball and the depth adjusted so that the upper surface of the tree ball is about 1 inch (2.5 cm) above the surrounding ground. (B) Slice container and remove from root ball, then backfill with native soil and gently tamp.

A   B

- Dig a hole much wider than the ball of your tree. In general, the hole should be about as deep as the root ball and about twice its diameter (fig. 19.7A). For a tree in a 3.5-gallon (13-l) sleeve, an ideal hole is about 16 to 18 inches (41 to 46 cm) wide and about 20 inches (51 cm) deep. Save the soil for backfill. If the soil in your yard is not too light (sand) or heavy (clay), you do not need to add soil amendments to the hole. UC Farm Advisors recommend that you do not use soil amendments at planting time unless extreme conditions exist, such as adobe clay soils.

- Adjust the hole's depth so that the upper surface of the tree ball is about 1 inch (2.5 cm) above the surrounding ground when the tree is lowered into it. Moist soil against the trunk above the original soil line increases the risk of disease.

- Lower the tree into the hole. Then slice the container open vertically on one side. Next, backfill with 6 to 8 inches (15 to 20 cm) of loose soil (which should fill the hole about one-third full) to stabilize the

tree before removing the slit container (fig. 19.7B). It is important not to move the root ball after the container is slit.

- Take the plastic tube container out of the hole and place it away from the tree to be discarded. The poly container is recyclable but not degradable. This procedure will leave the roots exposed on the surface of the ball. Note that many of the roots are concentrated at the outside of the vertical surface.

- Gently tamp the loose soil around the ball immediately. Promptly fill the rest of the hole with loose soil, gently tamping as you fill. Fill it to the top, but leave the upper surface of the original ball exposed.

- The soil used to backfill the hole should be free of large clods because they can cause large air spaces that prevent fine roots from contacting the soil and are detrimental to water movement through the backfill.

- The upper surface of the ball is left exposed so that you may add water directly to the ball, even after the tree is planted.

It is best to leave the upper surface exposed because the soil in the ball may have been specially formulated with nutrients and designed so the ball will readily absorb water applied to its upper surface. If you cover this surface with anything, do not use soil; use sand, loose sawdust, coarse gravel, or anything through which water will pass very rapidly.

- At the time of field planting, protect any exposed parts of the stem from sunburn with a coat of whitewash or white latex (water-base) paint diluted 1:1 with water; nonlatex bases will kill tender plant tissue. Stake the tree for a year, longer in windy areas (see chapter 13 for tree staking technique).

- Because avocado trees have shallow roots, the soil around them should not be disturbed by cultivation. Control weeds with frequent mowing, hand-weeding, or mulches. Mulches have several advantages, as noted later in this chapter. Herbicides should be used only as a last resort and must be applied carefully so as not to harm the tree. Use only herbicides labeled for use on avocados and follow label directions.

- It is very important to water the tree immediately after planting and to keep the root ball moist until roots grow out into the surrounding soil. The surface roots concentrated at the outside of the ball will die if they dry out.

Protecting Avocado Trees

Sunburn and Wind Protection

Both greenhouse-grown trees and field-grown trees require protection from extremes in climate and from rodents. To protect greenhouse-grown trees, place cardboard cylinders 10 to 12 inches (25 to 30 cm) in diameter and 12 to 15 inches (30 to 38 cm) in height around the tree. Small trees may be completely enclosed by the cylinder. In time, the tree will grow out of the cylinder. On hot days, the air temperature inside the cylinder may become hot enough to damage tender stems and leaves. To provide air circulation, punch several holes in all sides of the cylinder or attach the cylinder to a stake and drive the stake into the soil beside the tree until the bottom of the cylinder is 3 inches (7 cm) from the soil level. This will allow air to flow freely through the cylinder (fig. 19.8).

To protect field-grown trees, use a small, waxed, cardboard protector stapled or tied around the lower portion of the tree. If you use binder twine to hold the protector in place, be sure the twine is loose enough to allow the tree to grow without constriction. Later, when tree growth causes the tie to become tight, loosen or remove the twine. Do not use black building paper; it absorbs too much heat, which can be harmful to a tender trunk. Never use wire, paper-covered wire, or heavy plastic bands for ties; they can cause severe damage due to girdling if not loosened or removed as the tree grows. Place the protective cover so it reaches from near soil level to at least 6 or 8 inches (15 or 20 cm) above the bud union.

Tree protectors provide protection from sun, wind, and rodents; they do not protect trees from frost unless they are made of insulated materials and wrapped snugly around tree trunks. If it is likely that strong winds may damage trees, tie the trees to 2-by-2-inch (5-by-5-cm) stakes for protection. If you use plant stakes, you can attach the protective cylinders to them.

Figure 19.8

Sunburn protection.

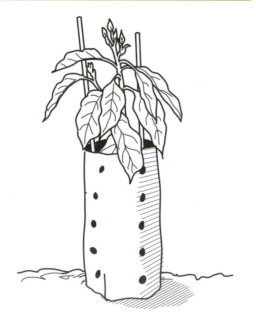

Frost Protection

If your only option is to plant avocado trees in a cold location, consider planting only those varieties known to be tolerant to frost (see table 19.1). Cold damage varies and depends on the duration of the cold, the season in which it occurs, the stage of tree growth, tree health, and similar factors. Fruit and stems may be damaged if temperatures remain below 28°F (−2°C) for any length of time. If your planting site is located where temperatures frequently fall below freezing, provide some form of frost protection. Tree wraps, if made of insulated material, provide some degree of stem protection. During the first winter, corn stalks or palm fronds placed firmly around the tree trunk and held securely in place can also be effective for protecting the stem and some of the foliage. For only one or a very few trees, it may be practical to erect a tent. Four posts with a plastic tarp (or other solid material) placed over them should be constructed so that nothing touches any part of the tree and so that heat is prevented from escaping. (For additional information on frost protection, see the related discussion in chapter 18, "Citrus.")

When damaging freezes do occur, UC has developed techniques that will maximize desirable growth responses. See the section "Treatment of Freeze-Damaged Avocado Trees," below.

Figure 19.9

Basin irrigation.
Source: After Brokaw n.d., p.1.

Watering

Timely irrigation is essential for proper avocado tree growth, development, and fruiting. In the backyard, more trees become stunted and die due to drought stress than any other cause. Never allow the ball to dry out. Avocado trees are extremely sensitive to excess water, which can be caused by overirrigation or poor soil drainage. The root fungus *Phytophthora cinnamoni* thrives in saturated soil. Since avocado trees are evergreen, they need water year-round. Demand for water is high when trees are growing actively, which usually occurs from late winter or early spring through the summer. Demand is highest when evapotranspiration (ET) is highest, usually in the summer months. The most critical period for irrigation is from the year's initial growth flush until the young fruit are at least 1 inch (2.5 cm) in diameter. (For a discussion of ET concepts, see chapter 4, "Water Management.")

Trees cannot perform well if denied a quality water supply. Irrigation water should be relatively free of salt and toxic ions such as sodium and chloride. Irrigation water should not come into contact with the base of the tree trunk because such water may encourage fungal diseases such as Phytophthora root rot and Phytophthora trunk canker, which can kill the tree. The trunk and the bud union should stay dry.

It is very important to water the tree immediately after planting, because the surface roots concentrated at the outside of the ball will not be able to function properly unless they are kept moist. The tree's active, working leaves must be supplied with water at all times to ensure proper functioning. Irrigate young trees with about 8 to 10 gallons (30 to 37 l) of water each week. Three excellent irrigation methods for avocado trees are basin flooding, sprinkler irrigation, and drip irrigation, described below.

Basin-Flooding Young Trees. Build a basin with a 3-foot (91-cm) diameter around the tree (fig. 19.9). The basin should have a capacity of about 5 gallons (19 l). Fill the basin with water once. If it drains rapidly, fill it again. If it requires 2 minutes or more to drain, do not refill. During the first year, fill the basin with water until the water penetrates just below the bottom of the original plant container. Eventually, the water will need to penetrate 2 to 3 feet (0.6 to 0.9 m). If the soil or root ball has settled, re-form the bottom of the basin, but be sure the top of the ball is still exposed. Once the basin has stabilized, the bottom can be covered with straw, sawdust, or some other mulching medium. Basin irrigation can be used for up to 2 years, but the basin should be broken down during the wet season if water has any tendency to stand in it.

Sprinkler Irrigation. If sprinkler irrigation is used for avocado trees, enough water must be applied during an irrigation to wet most of the root system. Supplemental irrigation using a hose may be needed to keep the root ball of newly planted trees thoroughly moist. Construction of a basin, as in flood irrigation, is useful with sprinkler irrigation during the first year after planting because it aids in holding irrigation water over the root ball and facilitates the hand-watering that may be needed. Be sure sprinklers give a good distribution pattern and discharge water at a rate the soil will absorb without runoff.

As with citrus, avocado trees commonly fail to thrive if planted in the lawn because of differing irrigation needs of tree roots and turf. A lawn often gets frequent watering that may

soak down only about 6 inches (15 cm) (the depth of many turf roots); deeper avocado roots will be too dry, while the upper avocado roots will be kept too wet and suffer from insufficient oxygen. Avocado trees can coexist with a deeper-rooted drought-tolerant grass such as hybrid bermuda, so that irrigation can occur much longer and less frequently, depending on soil and weather. The tree may need some extra irrigations from a hose in the summer to aid in water supply and to leach out salts.

Drip Irrigation. Drip irrigation systems dispense water slowly, in gallons per hour rather than in the gallons per minute typical of lawn sprinklers. If you use drip irrigation, be sure that the emitter is fastened to the exposed ball of a newly planted tree with a U-shaped piece of wire or hook because it prevents the dripper from creeping away from the root ball as the hose expands and contracts. Check emitters frequently to be sure that each tree is getting watered. Clogged emitters are a common problem.

Initally, the emitter is placed over the root ball. Once the tree is established and the roots start reaching out into the surrounding soil (usually about 1 to 2 months after planting),

Table 19.2

AVOCADO IRRIGATION GUIDE

Canopy diameter (ft)	Mature avocado tree irrigation water requirements gal/day (l/day)											
	Jan	Feb	Mar	Apr	May	Jun	Jul	Aug	Sep	Oct	Nov	Dec
20	7 (27)	13 (49)	20 (76)	29 (110)	40 (152)	47 (179)	53 (201)	47 (179)	36 (137)	20 (76)	9 (34)	7 (27)
18	7 (27)	12 (46)	19 (72)	28 (106)	37 (141)	44 (167)	51 (194)	44 (167)	35 (133)	19 (72)	9 (34)	7 (27)
16	5 (19)	11 (42)	17 (65)	25 (95)	33 (125)	39 (148)	45 (171)	39 (148)	31 (118)	17 (65)	8 (30)	5 (19)
14	5 (19)	9 (34)	15 (57)	23 (87)	29 (110)	35 (133)	40 (152)	35 (133)	28 (106)	15 (57)	8 (30)	5 (19)
12	4 (15)	9 (34)	13 (49)	20 (76)	27 (103)	31 (118)	35 (133)	31 (118)	24 (91)	13 (49)	7 (27)	4 (15)
10	4 (15)	7 (27)	11 (42)	14 (53)	21 (80)	25 (95)	29 (110)	25 (95)	20 (76)	11 (42)	5 (19)	4 (15)
8	3 (11)	5 (19)	8 (30)	13 (49)	17 (65)	20 (76)	23 (87)	20 (76)	16 (61)	8 (30)	4 (15)	3 (11)

Source: Adapted from Bender 1999.

Note: Spacing for trees is 20 ft × 20 ft (6.1 m × 6.1 m). The water requirements of an avocado tree with this spacing approximate the water needs of a single, free-standing mature tree in the home garden.

Figure 19.10

Using a soil probe to check soil moisture content near a newly planted tree.

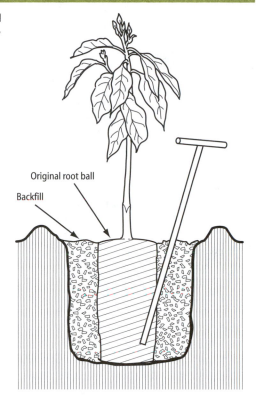

Original root ball

Backfill

the emitter should be moved away from the top of the root ball to a distance of about 6 to 8 inches (15 to 20 cm). In the second year, it is best to use two emitters, one on each side of the trunk about 8 inches (20 cm) away. As the tree grows, more emitters can be added. A mature avocado tree (about 6 years old) may have 4 to 5 or more emitters spaced in a ring around the tree near the drip line (the imaginary line below the canopy edge).

Drip irrigation systems are quite flexible. You can adjust the amount of water applied, not only by changing the interval between irrigations or the length of each irrigation, as with other methods, but also by selecting emitter number and emitter discharge rate. You can also place the emitter(s) precisely where wanted.

Irrigation Frequency

Irrigation frequency is influenced by climate; thus, a set schedule will not work under all conditions year-round. Evapotranspiration losses increase during hot, dry, windy conditions, and with longer days, and consequently the demand for water increases. The more leaves on a tree, the larger the total leaf surface area and the greater the transpiration water use. A densely foliated tree will use more water than a sparsely foliated one, and larger trees use more water than smaller ones. Soil type also influences irrigation frequency because of its effects on water-holding capacity (see chapter 3 for more information). Disregard the dryness of the top inch of soil, which dries out rather quickly even though the underlying soil may still be moist. Since 80 percent of the feeder roots of mature avocado trees are in the top 6 inches (15 cm) of the soil, it is imperative not to let this soil dry out before irrigating. However, do not irrigate wet soil, because this can damage the tree's roots.

Because of variable weather factors (relative humidity, day length, temperature, wind speed, etc.) and variable soil factors, it is impossible to give specific instructions for timing irrigations. In general, the older and larger the tree, the more total water it needs, but it needs watering less frequently. A mature avocado tree with an extensive root system requires more water to wet the root zone than a young tree with a smaller root mass, but the young tree's roots dry out faster. A newly planted tree still has its roots in the restricted container ball, which is not large enough to hold much water, even for the little tree above it. If the weather turns hot, dry, and windy soon after planting, such a tree might need daily watering. Even after the young tree has sent roots into the surrounding soil, it still has a small root-water supply and is also susceptible to foliar and stem injury from drying. Gradually, the amount of irrigation water is increased and the frequency is decreased, encouraging downward root growth in the soil. The sooner that the ground surface can be allowed to dry out between irrigations the better. Keeping avocado soil soggy is a recipe for disaster. Saturated soil lacks air in pore spaces and favors root rot disease.

Irrigation Amount

For information on average daily evapotranspiration (ET) standardized rates, see chapter 4, "Water Management." The reference plant material that scientists refer to in comparing water use among plant species is a 4- to 6-inch-high (10- to 15-cm-high), cool-season turfgrass when unlimited water is available. A mature avocado tree uses about 70 percent of the water listed in tables 4.2 and 4.3 in chapter 4, which can exceed 50 gallons (189 l) per day in hot, dry weather.

In general, for a newly planted tree, 2 to 4 gallons (7 to 15 l) of water per irrigation should suffice if the water is directed into the ball. Basin irrigate as described above, and do not let the root ball dry out. Water enough to encourage deeper rooting. A soil core probe slanted in to reach the ball at 12 to 14 inches (30 to 35 cm) below the soil surface can be illuminating because it provides information about soil water content in the middle of the root ball (fig. 19.10).

For a mature tree, water should be applied at each irrigation to a depth of about 2 feet (60 cm). During the summer, if leaf tip burn indicates salt accumulation in the soil, a heavier irrigation is needed to leach the salts below the root zone. Table 19.2 provides an avocado irrigation guide that factors in tree spacing, canopy diameter, and climate variation during the year.

The water requirements in table 19.2 assume a mature avocado tree is planted in a well-drained soil, that the irrigation system delivers water to the edge of the canopy, and that the tree is watered about every 3 to 4 days, unless adjustment factors are used. To deliver the amount of water recommended in table 19.2, you need to know the discharge rate of your irrigation system. Water requirements may be higher during hot and windy periods. The suggested irrigation requirements in table 19.2 are based on the average ET rates from the Escondido CIMIS (California Irrigation Management Information System) station representing a southern California interior valley climate in San Diego County. Avocado trees growing closer to the coast use less water. Trees growing in hotter or windier locations use more water (see table 4.2 and 4.3 in chapter 4 to compare ET rates). If the soil has a heavy texture, it should be irrigated with less water than is stated in table 19.2 because the soil will retain more water.

Maintaining leaf litter or an organic mulch on the soil surface reduces ET, helps maintain adequate soil moisture where needed, and reduces soil temperature. Therefore, do not remove the natural leaf litter (mulch) from your avocado tree. Take advantage of it.

Drought can cause serious fruit drop, especially of small fruit. Older fruit may still hang on the tree but will shrivel. When an avocado tree is water-stressed, it will extract water from mature fruit, causing them to dry out and shrivel. Fruit serve as a water source for the tree when the tree is experiencing drought. Overwatering also causes problems for avocado trees due to increased disease, particularly from Phytophthora root rot, which flourishes in waterlogged soils.

Fertilizing

Avocado trees have comparatively few mineral deficiencies in California. Only nitrogen and zinc need to be applied extensively; iron chlorosis occurs occasionally. Fertilizer applications of these three nutrients are discussed below. New research on potassium is also mentioned. Other nutrient deficiencies are rare in California avocados, even in areas where phosphorus, potassium, manganese, and magnesium deficiencies have been found on other subtropical fruit crops. Thus, additions of these nutrients are not recommended. Needless phosphorus applications may induce or aggravate a zinc deficiency.

Nitrogen

Nitrogen (N) is the most widely used fertilizer in California avocado production. For optimal yields, avocado trees need annual nitrogen fertilization. Young trees need only a few ounces of nitrogen per tree annually. Recently planted trees should be fertilized very cautiously until roots are well established. After roots are established, a small amount of nitrogen should be used several months apart and eventually, as the tree grows larger, a larger nitrogen concentration should be used once per year in the spring. Excessive amounts on a tree of any size applied at any one time can cause root damage, leaf burn, and defoliation. In severe cases, trees may be killed. Symptoms of nitrogen starvation include lack of vegetative growth; pale green, small leaves; lower yields; premature defoliation; and leaves with yellow veins.

Nitrogen needs vary with the avocado cultivar. Commercial avocado growers use laboratory analysis of spring flush leaves from nonfruiting shoots collected in August through October to determine nitrogen nutrition in their trees and to guide fertilization practices. Where leaf analysis is not used, annual applications of ½ to 1 pound (227 to 454 g) of elemental (actual) nitrogen per tree is suggested for mature trees.

Young Trees. Fertilize with nitrogen sparingly to prevent harm, yet sufficiently to ensure maximum growth. The following program of soil-applied nitrogen fertilizer is suggested per tree for average conditions. If nitrogen is applied in a drip irrigation system, suggested amounts are given in table 19.3. In all cases below, the fertilizer should be broadcast evenly above the root system just before a rain is expected or irrigation is applied.

- First year: Apply ¹⁄₁₀ pound (45 g) actual nitrogen annually, divided into equal monthly portions during the irrigation season (normally 8 months).

- Second year: Apply ¹⁄₅ pound (90 g) actual nitrogen annually, divided into four equal portions during the irrigation season.

- Third year: Broadcast a total of ¹⁄₃ pound (151 g) of actual nitrogen during March through October.

- Fourth year: Broadcast a total of ½ pound (227 g) of actual nitrogen during March through October.

Nitrogen Sources. Continuous use of ammonium sulfate for many years may make the soil too acidic, depending on the original pH of the soil. Continuous use of ammonium nitrate, anhydrous ammonia, or urea will also acidify the soil, but less rapidly than ammonium sulfate. Alkaline irrigation waters tend to offset this effect. You may consider supplying part of the nitrogen in fall in the form of a bulky organic matter such as a manure that is cultivated into the soil. If soil is or becomes too acidic (pH below 5.5), calcium nitrate should be used as a nitrogen source. (See chapter 3 for more discussion on fertilizers.)

Timing of Application for Mature Trees. The nitrogen requirement is greatest during the period of flowering and fruit setting. If adequate nitrogen is supplied for this period, there will usually be enough left in the soil to take care of the tree until the following spring. Chemical forms of nitrogen applied over the area occupied by the roots will be moved into the root zone by rain or irrigation water.

Zinc

Zinc deficiency, commonly called *mottle leaf*, occurs in many avocado-growing areas in Southern California. The avocado tree may decline and even die without a small, but essential, amount of zinc. The earliest symptoms of zinc deficiency are mottled leaves developing on a few of the terminals. The areas between the veins are light green to pale yellow. As the deficiency progresses, the yellow areas get larger, and the new leaves produced are smaller. In advanced stages, a marginal burn develops on these stunted leaves; twig dieback occurs; and the distance between the leaves on the stem is shortened, giving a crowded "feather duster" appearance. Yield is reduced, and some of the fruit may be more round than is normal for the variety.

Zinc deficiency can be controlled by applying zinc as a spray to the foliage or by applying it to the soil in some situations. Foliar applications require wetting the foliage with conventional pest control equipment. UC Cooperative Extension farm advisors

Table 19.3

NITROGEN APPLICATIONS VIA DRIP IRRIGATION

Tree age	Amount per tree per month, lb (g)		
	Urea (46% N)	Ammonium nitrate (33% N)	Calcium nitrate (15.5% N)
first year	0.03 (13.4)	0.04 (17.9)	0.08 (35.8)
second year	0.05 (22.4)	0.08 (35.8)	0.16 (71.7)
third year	0.09 (40.3)	0.13 (58.2)	0.27 (121.0)
fourth year	0.14 (62.7)	0.19 (85.1)	0.40 (179.2)
fifth year (and older)	0.14 (62.7)–0.27 (121.0)	0.19 (85.1)–0.38 (170.2)	0.40 (179.2)–0.81 (362.9)

Note: Pounds of fertilizer material per tree per month during a typical 8-month irrigation season (March to October), which equates to rates of actual nitrogen (¹⁄₁₀ lb, year 1; ¹⁄₅ lb, year 2; ¹⁄₃ lb, year 3; ½ lb, year 4; ½ lb, year 5) given in the text.

recommend 1 pound (454 g) of zinc sulfate in 100 gallons (378 l) of water for commercial orchards, which can be reduced for the home orchard to 1 ounce (29 ml) per 6 gallons (23 l) of water. Timing is normally not critical, but applications are most effective in June and July when spring-cycle leaves are two-thirds fully expanded but not hardened. Because zinc does not translocate readily from sprayed leaves to young growth occurring after spraying, severely affected trees may require respraying several months later. However, there is recent evidence that zinc may not be as well absorbed by avocado leaves as once thought, making soil applications more attractive.

Soil applications of zinc have been successful on acid soils in San Diego and Santa Barbara Counties. Responses to soil applications have lasted up to 5 years, whereas foliar sprays must be repeated annually. The effectiveness of zinc applications depends on the soil type, the amount used, and the method of application. In commercial settings, the dosage per tree must be determined for each orchard. For home growers, no absolutely precise recommendation can be given. Suggested amounts of zinc sulfate (36% metallic zinc) are given in table 19.4. Material may be applied as a surface band or in holes augered into the soil about 6 inches (15 cm) deep around the dripline of the tree. Applications should be repeated every 3 to 5 years if trees continue to show deficiency symptoms.

Chelated forms of zinc may also be used, but they do not appear to have any advantages over zinc sulfate, and they are more expensive. On trees more than 10 years old, the total zinc sulfate recommended should be divided into two or three applications about 1 month apart. Foliar applications provide zinc to deficient trees immediately. Soil applications of provide zinc slowly and continuously to the tree over the months and years ahead.

Iron

Iron deficiency is difficult to correct, but fortunately, it is not common in California avocado orchards. In mild forms of iron deficiency, leaves show a network of green veins and veinlets against a lighter green background. As the deficiency increases, the interveinal area becomes yellowish white, and the veins lose their green color. In severe cases, leaves are smaller, completely chlorotic (yellow), and show tip and marginal burn accompanied by defoliation and twig dieback. Iron chlorosis may occur on individual limbs or affect the entire tree, and yield may be reduced.

Iron deficiency usually occurs in high-pH soils containing lime (calcium carbonate), which limits the utilization of iron by the tree. The deficiency is accentuated by excess soil moisture and low oxygen content in the soil. The use of Mexican race rootstocks rather than rootstocks of the Guatemalan race has minimized iron chlorosis. The most effective application methods are to inject iron chelates in solution into the root zone or to rake back the leaves, broadcast the material, and work it into the surface soil, pushing the leaves back and irrigating immediately. Often, just reducing irrigation frequency or amount will rectify the problem and save water as well.

Potassium

Guy Whitney, research coordinator for the California Avocado Commission, recently reported that potassium deficiency can cause leaf edge necrosis, resembling tip burn, and brown spots between leaf veins. Excess potassium degrades avocado fruit quality. Avocado trees have more than 60 enzymes that need potsssium to operate properly in photosynthesis and other metabolic functions. The most cost-effective fertilizer source is potassium sulfate. Potassium chloride is the most common form but will add too much chloride the the soil. Potassium is often applied after bloom and fruit set but research on optimal timing is incomplete.

Table 19.4

SUGGESTED AMOUNTS OF ZINC SULFATE FOR SOIL APPLICATIONS

Tree age (yr)	Dosage per tree (lb)			
	Surface band		Inserted in holes	
	(lb)	(kg)	(lb)	(kg)
2	0.7	0.3	—	—
5	2.0	0.9	0.7	0.3
7	2.6	1.2	1.3	0.6
10	3.3	1.5	2.0	0.9
15	5.2	2.4	2.6	1.2
20	6.5	3.0	3.3	1.5

Pruning

Most avocado trees require little or no pruning. Whenever possible, allow trees to develop naturally, and you will avoid disturbing the balance between foliage and fruiting wood, which is essential for high yields. Prune avocado trees cautiously. An abundance of foliage, which manufactures food (photosynthate) for the tree, keeps fruiting vigorous. If this food supply is reduced by severe pruning, fruit yield will suffer.

Pruning avocado trees may

- control the height of tall varieties
- correct poor growth habits
- prevent wind damage
- regulate severe alternate bearing

But it may also

- stunt full tree growth
- reduce yield
- stimulate foliage growth at expense of fruiting
- make trees susceptible to frost injury

Avocados grow irregularly, and most trees will develop a better structure if they are not pruned at all. Nevertheless, the height of some varieties can make harvesting difficult. An avocado tree may grow too tall for a backyard, with most of the fruiting in the top of the tree. If you determine that pruning is necessary, follow these four simple rules:

1. Prune sparingly. Remove as little green wood and as few green leaves as possible. Prune only after the tree has developed sufficient upper foliage to prevent sunburning.

2. Avoid pruning in late summer and early fall. Pruning at these times stimulates vegetative growth and may make trees susceptible to frost injury.

3. Make pruning cuts as close to a lateral branch as possible. The greatest growth stimulation is nearest the cut. Removing large branches stimulates vegetative growth over the entire tree. Please refer to chapters 13, "Woody Landscape Plants," and 5, "Plant Propagation" for general information about pruning cuts.

4. Let pruning wounds dry out naturally. Research has shown that healing of pruning wounds is not hastened by covering with tree sealants or wound dressings. Dry pruning wounds close naturally and are less susceptible to wood rot.

The more erect types of trees may be tipped repeatedly (pinch back the terminal bud and repeat after each growth flush) to develop a bushier, more compact tree. Pruning of low-hanging branches may keep fruit off the ground or make irrigation management easier, but keep pruning to a minimum. Heavy cuts on low branches force growth upward. Removing deadwood is not essential, but it may make picking and pest control easier. In coastal regions, removing deadwood may help prevent Dothiorella rot, which causes avocado fruit to decay when softening.

Since avocado trees grow irregularly, and different varieties have individual growing habits, it is difficult to give general pruning directions that apply to all trees. You may have to experiment to develop the pruning methods best suited to your trees. The variety of trees, their vigor, and soil and climate conditions should influence your pruning practices. In some instances, no pruning is needed at all. Fruit thinning is typically not needed on avocado trees unless too much fruit is set on one or more branches and could cause breakage. Even then, bracing the branch is usually a better solution. On young trees, thinning is sometimes practical because very heavy crops can reduce the vitality of the tree. However, leaving fruit on the tree will slow the growth of trees and keep them from becoming too large too quickly.

Mulching

Mulches have numerous benefits in the cultivation of avocado trees, including suppression of *Phytophthora cinnamomi,* the cause of avocado root rot, the most serious avocado disease worldwide. Yard waste (wood chips, grass clippings, and leaves), straw (grain or bean), wood shavings, alfalfa meal, or any inexpensive organic material can be used for mulching. If straw is used, beware of potential damage from field mice and rats since they often make nests in straw. Do not use mushroom compost or animal manure until trees are at least 3 years old because these materials may contain excess nitrogen (ammonia) or soluble salts that can be leached into the root zone and injure roots or cause tip burn of the leaves. (Methods for calculating the nitrogen available in manures are provided in chapter 3, "Soil and Fertilizer Management.") Several benefits of mulching avocado trees are discussed briefly below. This discussion of mulching is adapted from Turney and Menge 1994.

Control of Avocado Root Rot Disease

Thick mulches applied to the soil surface can create conditions harmful to pathogenic soil organisms, such as nematodes and the fungus *Phytophthora cinnamomi*. Alfalfa meal mixed with soil at rates of 1 to 5 percent and alfalfa straw have often provided good control of Phytophthora root rot in avocado. In Australia, intensive mulching combined with applications of gypsum (CaSO$_4$) have controlled Phytophthora root rot in avocado. Research has indicated that when the soil's organic matter content is kept in the range of 7 percent with the use of organic mulches, the soil becomes suppressive to *P. cinnamomi*. Several mechanisms have been proposed to explain why mulches can reduce Phytophthora root rot in avocado:

- Mulching increases the population of soil microbes that can compete with or inhibit fungal pathogens.

- Soils amended with alfalfa meal or other decaying organic matter are known to have higher concentrations of gases, such as ammonia, which can inhibit *Phytophthora*.

- Mulches create a natural litter layer favoring the proliferation of tree roots and disfavoring *Phytophthora* infection. The interface of soil surface and mulch is a natural microenvironment where roots grow well but where *Phytophthora* cannot survive. The fungus needs saturated soil conditions to release its zoospores, which must then swim to tree roots to cause new infections. But water drains so quickly from the mulch layer that saturated conditions may not last long enough for zoospores to be released and to swim to tree roots.

- Chemicals produced during the decomposition of organic matter in mulched soil, such as ammonium (NH$_4$+), saponins, and nitrite, are toxic at low concentrations and prevent propagule germination in *P. cinnamomi*, thus retarding disease development.

- Organic matter can entrap fungal zoospores, preventing them from swimming to plant roots.

- Soil gases and compounds released during organic matter decomposition in the mulch can increase the level of host (avocado) resistance in the roots to *Phytophthora*.

- The incorporation of calcium into mulch in the form of gypsum (CaSO$_4$) appears to have a critical role in reducing avocado root rot. Scientists have shown that entrapment of fungal zoospores and host resistance are enhanced with additions of calcium in mulch. Soils with poor infiltration and high expendable sodium have the highest incidence of avocado root rot. Organic mulches combined with applications of gypsum increase soil drainage and remove excess sodium from the upper soil profile, which renders the soil less conducive to root rot caused by *Phytophthora*.

Reduction of Weed Problems

If mulches are at least 2 inches (5 cm) thick, they can reduce weed problems by preventing germination of weed seeds. Avocado trees are more productive if they do not have to compete with weeds for water and essential nutrients. When weeds do grow, it is best to hand-pull them because cultivation equipment can damage the tree's surface roots. However, if you do use a weed whacker around the tree, be careful not to cut the bark of the tree.

Conservation of Water

Mulches can conserve water by reducing evaporation from the soil, reducing runoff and erosion, increasing the permeability of the soil surface, and increasing the water-holding capacity of the soil. At field capacity, mulched soils with a high organic matter content will have more water available to trees.

Improvement in Soil Physical Properties

Organic mulches can improve soil physical properties by increasing the soil's organic matter content, which results in aggregation of soil particles and increased pore size distribution, improved water infiltration, and better gas exchange (CO_2 and O_2). This facilitates the utilization of the top 12 inches (30 cm) of soil where avocado roots are most active.

Improvement in Nitrogen Fertility

Mulches can eliminate or reduce nitrate contamination of groundwater by providing a continuous, slow release of nitrogen, thereby reducing the need for nitrogen applied as chemical fertilizer. Mulches with a high carbon-to-nitrogen ratio may cause a short-term, initial nitrogen depletion that would necessitate increased nitrogen fertilization due to the increased populations of microorganisms produced during the decomposition process. However, the long-term benefit of decomposed mulch is the slow and increased release of nitrogen to the soil. Organic mulches also supply several other essential plant nutrient elements, in part because they increase the soil's cation exchange capacity, which increases the availability of many nutrient elements to plant roots.

Improvement in Soil Temperature

Mulches can reduce wide fluctuations in soil temperature by reducing the soil's absorption of heat. This is beneficial to root growth, especially in young trees and in areas where summer temperatures are very high. Lower soil temperatures are also less favorable to *Phytophthora*. However, when frosts are predicted, remove mulch, if possible, because bare soil can absorb more radiant energy than most mulches.

Harvesting and Storage

Unlike citrus, avocados do not become edible on the tree. They mature on the tree but must be severed from their stems and held for several days to ripen, that is, to soften for edibility. Harvest by cutting the stem with hand clippers as close to the fruit as possible without injury. Protruding stems may injure other maturing fruit, and pulling fruit from the stems can leave wounds that invite rot.

Table 19.1 gives a basic guide to the maturity seasons of the different scion cultivars, but the precise maturity season can vary, depending on the climate zone, the weather in a particular growing season, and other factors. As expected maturity approaches, pick a couple of the more mature-looking fruit and allow them to ripen to test palatability. Fruit size is not a good maturity indicator. Purple or black varieties are usually mature when the fruit begins to turn from green to dark. Varieties whose skin stays green at maturity and during ripening change from a bright green to a duller, yellower, or grayer green, often with small corky areas (rusty brown specks) on the skin. The number of days from harvest to ripeness varies with the variety and decreases with a higher level of maturity and temperature. Room temperature is about optimum. Mature fruit ripen in a reasonable time to good consistency without appreciable shriveling or creasing, which means that the flesh is soft without staying rubbery or having hard areas and without a bitter or "green-bark" immature flavor.

To determine when an avocado is soft enough to eat (ripe), hold the fruit in your palm and gently squeeze with your whole hand; a uniform, slight softness without a rubbery feel indicates ripeness. The thumb is usually the most sensitive tester, but be careful not to press so hard as to leave a discoloring bruise in the ripe or near-ripe fruit. These ripeness-testing techniques soon become second nature. Feel, not color, is the final authority on ripeness. Color indicates maturity rather than ripeness; however, some fruit of a black variety will turn from green to black only as they ripen.

Once you have determined that your avocado fruit are palatably mature, you can pick them as needed, harvesting the number of fruit wanted with a lead time in days corresponding to the estimated ripening time. In practice, this usually means being a ripe avocado or two ahead, stored in the refrigerator. For successful postharvest storage of ripe avocado fruit, UC researchers recommend temperatures of 41° to 46°F (5° to 8°C) (refrigeration) for no longer than 1 to 2 weeks. Fresh-picked, mature fruit that are refrigerated before ripening may never soften properly. But fruit that are half-ripe can be stored in the refrigerator for up to 3 weeks or so and then should ripen just fine. Avocados ripen in 2 to

5 days when placed in a paper bag with a banana or an apple. This sort of flexibility, combined with long on-tree storage of mature fruit in the better avocado cultivars, means that the backyard grower can eat avocados off his or her tree daily for 6 months or more. In addition to certain availability, the backyard grower can be even more certain of high fruit quality.

Avocado Diseases, Insect Pests, and Environmental Stresses

Compared to other deciduous fruit tree crops grown in the home garden, such as apples and peaches, avocado trees have relatively few pest and disease problems if they receive good care. Healthy trees that are irrigated and fertilized properly should have little pest damage. Many avocado trees in California produce for decades or a lifetime without any disease treatment whatsoever. This is especially true for the home gardener for whom maximum fruit production and absence of commercial culls are not important issues.

Table 19.5 lists the most common avocado diseases, insect and mite pests, and environmental stresses and also describes what the symptoms look like, indicates the probable causal agent and plant part(s) affected, and comments on control measures. Although table 19.5 is long, it should not be discouraging because proper irrigation, fertilization, and cultural practices can prevent the majority of the problems listed. The information in table 19.5 has three purposes. First, it stresses prevention; for the major avocado diseases, the best control measure is to avoid the problem in the first place. Second, it provides guidance when problems do appear, helping the backyard grower decide when to seek advice from the local UC Cooperative Extension farm advisor, apply treatment, live with the problem, or, as a last resort, remove the tree(s). Finally, for the gardener who is seriously interested in avocados, table 19.5 provides a deeper understanding of the crop and its reactions to environmental influences. *Avocado Diseases* (Ohr, Faber, and Grech 1994) is a comprehensive reference on avocado diseases with excellent color photographs and text by UC plant pathologists. *Pests of the Garden and Small*

Farm (Flint 1998) also has information and color photographs of avocado pests and diseases. Before finalizing any treatment plans, check the most recent UC recommendations and references.

An important point that cannot be overemphasized is that many of the problems noted in table 19.5 are more likely to occur in trees under stress. By providing good care, especially irrigation and fertilization as needed, the backyard grower can do much to minimize the chances of an occurrence of the problems in table 19.5. For example, deficient water can injure the whole tree and make it more susceptible to several pests. Conversely, excess water (from overwatering or from failure to provide surface drainage for heavy winter rains) can open the door to Phytophthora root rot or asphyxiate roots, injuring the tree and making it more susceptible to pests and other disorders.

Control Measures

Mechanical Control. Mechanical methods are nonpolluting, nonpersistent pest control techniques, such as removing diseased fruit and branches, cleaning up debris, dislodging pests such as whiteflies and mites with strong blasts of water from a garden hose, hand-picking and disposal of snails and slugs, washing off dust to facilitate better biological control of avocado pests, and setting up mechanical ant barriers. Soaps and oil sprays are two types of mechanical control that are effective against a number of soft-bodied insects and mites.

Soaps. Soaps are safe to use even on edible plant parts. Soaps are effective against soft-bodied insects and mites on contact. They penetrate their cell membranes and kill them without harming trees or fruit. You can purchase insecticidal soaps at most nurseries. Soaps are best applied in the early morning or late afternoon. Use soaps only when your trees have been well irrigated and when conditions are not windy and not too hot (<90°F [32°C]).

Summer oils. Special horticultural oils have long been used on dormant deciduous trees. For evergreens like the avocado, still more refined oils, labeled "supreme," "superior," or "narrow-range," can be applied to smother mites (and their eggs), whiteflies, scales, and mealybugs. Avoid spraying horticultural oils in foggy and humid weather because the oil will dissipate so slowly that leaf and stem injury can occur.

Table 19.5

PROBLEM DIAGNOSIS FOR AVOCADO

MICROSCOPIC DISEASE-CAUSING ORGANISMS (PRIMARILY FUNGI)

What the problem looks like	Probable cause

Small, pale green, wilted leaves. Sparse foliage. New growth absent or if it occurs, new leaves small with poor color. Small branches die back at top of tree, allowing other branches to become sunburned due to lack of foliage. Small, fibrous feeder roots absent or, if present, blackened, brittle, dead.

avocado root rot (*Phytophthora cinnamomi*)

Comments

A fungus with more than 1,000 hosts. Attacks small feeder roots. The most serious avocado disease in California. Fungus thrives in excess soil moisture (overirrigation and poor drainage). Attacks trees of any size or age. Absence of feeder roots prevents moisture uptake so the soil under diseased trees stays wet even though tree appears wilted. Roots of pencil-size or larger seldom attacked by fungus. Diseased trees may set a heavy crop of small fruit but will decline and die, either rapidly or slowly. Fungus can spread by contaminated nursery stock, water in contact with infested soil, shoes, and cultivation equipment. Control measures: Use an integrated approach of prevention, culture, treatment. Prevention: Plant on soil with good internal drainage; avoid overwatering; use clean nursery stock, preferably certified disease-free; use resistant rootstocks; prevent soil or water movement from infested areas.

Disease treatment:

- Fumigate small spots of disease. If detected early, cut off the tree at ground level and fumigate soil. Check with your local UC Cooperative Extenstion farm advisor or a licensed pest control advisor for current availability and use of soil fumigants.
- Fungicides. Use as part of an integrated control program.
- Replant infested soil with immune plants.
  Even though *Phytophthora cinnamomi* has a wide host range, there are many garden plants that are not susceptible, including all varieties of *Citrus,* cherimoya, all types of vegetables, most annual flower crops, and many deciduous fruit trees and berries.

Poor growth, loss of tree vigor. Small, yellowing leaves; premature leaf drop; wilting, collapse. In winter, clusters of mushrooms form at base of infected trees a few days after a rain. White, fan-shaped fungus mycelium grows under bark of diseased roots.

Armillaria root rot (*Armillaria mellea*)

Comments

Also known as oak root fungus. Attacks roots. Visible symptoms may not appear until fungus is well established in the roots. Can destroy entire root system and kill tree. Once symptoms appear, it is very difficult to save a tree, and disease may have spread to roots of adjacent trees. After aerial parts of infected trees are dead, the fungus remains alive in the roots to infect any replanted, susceptible trees, such as citrus, peach, or avocado. Fumigate before replanting. Let soil dry out between irrigations.

Poor growth, loss of tree vigor. Chlorotic (yellowing) foliage. Poor fruit production. Cankers on trunk and branches. Leaf blotching, wilting. Rapid death of some new growth. Often death of entire tree eventually.

avocado black streak (ABS)

Comments

Causal organism unknown. Attacks trunk and branches. Present in California for more than 60 years but observed only on Guatemalan varieties, such as Hass and Reed, and only after prolonged stress. Since many symptoms are similar to those attributable to other causes, cankers on trunk and branches are diagnostic of ABS. Cankers vary in size and have a dry, powdery, water-soluble sugar that exudes through tiny cracks in the bark. Shallow, red-brown lesions under cankers are revealed when bark is removed. Management of ABS consists of maintaining tree health with good fertilizer and irrigation practices. Remove unhealthy trees; it is safest to fumigate the soil if replanting to avocado.

Leaves suddenly wilt on one part of tree or on the entire tree and then turn brown and die but do not drop off for months. Brown to gray-brown streaks are visible in wood of branches or roots (plugged xylem tissues).

Verticillium wilt (*Verticillium albo-atrum*)

Comments

Attacks xylem tissue. Enters roots and moves upward. May kill all or part of tree, with the remainder having complete recovery. If disease is severe and recurring, contact a UC Cooperative Extension farm advisor or a pest control adviser about soil fumigation. Mexican rootstocks are more resistant than Guatemalan. Do not plant on soil that has been used for other crops susceptible to Verticillium wilt, such as tomato, eggplant, pepper, many berries, apricot, potato, and several flower crops. Do not plant any of these near an avocado tree.

Table 19.5 cont.

MICROSCOPIC DISEASE-CAUSING ORGANISMS (PRIMARILY FUNGI)

What the problem looks like	Probable cause
Bark cankers exude white powder. Outer bark cracks and sheds easily. Diseased trees die back and may look unthrifty but rarely die.	Dothiorella canker (*Dothiorella gregaria*)

Comments

Attacks trunk and branches. A minor fungal problem favored by moisture. Keep irrigation water off tree base. Guatemalan rootstocks or scion tops are much more susceptible than Mexican. Control not usually needed. Scraping off outer bark removes some infection and encourages regeneration of vigorous bark.

Trunk cankers at base of older trees, originating at or below ground level. Canker appears as a dark region with a red, resinous exudate that dries to a white, crystalline deposit. Underneath the superficial canker is an orange-tan to brown lesion instead of the normal white or cream-colored tissue. Lesion has a fruity odor when exposed. Gradual decline over years or sudden tree death.	Phytophthora canker (collar rot) (*Phytophthora citricola*)

Comments

Attacks phloem tissue, lower tree trunk. Collar rot is now widespread in California, second only to avocado root rot in severity. Disease is favored by excess soil moisture, such as from overirrigation or poor drainage. Spreads by contaminated nursery stock, irrigation water, and cultivation equipment. Use sanitation measures noted for other *Phytophthora* species. Seedling rootstocks are generally more sensitive than clonal stocks, such as Duke 7 and Toro Canyon. Since *P. citricola* is found increasingly together with *P. cinnamomi*, an integrated approach to control both. Do not allow the lower trunks of trees to stay wet. Place drip emitters away from tree trunks. Aim minisprinklers to avoid wetting tree trunks. Avoid wounding trunks. If cankers are detected at an early stage, they can sometimes be controlled by cutting out the infected tissue. No chemicals are currently registered for use on this disease.

Fruit hanging near the ground has a distinct, rounded black area, usually at the end toward the soil. Rot soon extends internally, sometimes to the seed.	Phytophthora fruit rot (*Phytophthora citricola*)

Comments

Attacks fruit. Limited to prolonged wet weather in a dry climate like California. Probably caused by disease organisms splashing up from the soil, so a mulch or leaf layer should help. Removing fruit that touches the ground will remove a likely source of disease inoculation since this soil fungus can sporulate easily.

Unlike Phytophthora fruit rot (above), symptoms develop after fruit is picked and starts to soften. Purple-brown spots appear on fruit surface. Spots can enlarge until they cover entire fruit. Fruit flesh becomes discolored and has an unpleasant odor.	Dothiorella fruit rot (*Dothiorella gregaria*)

Comments

Attacks fruit. Like Phytophthora fruit rot, this disease is rarely important in our dry climate. When it does develop, it is usually on dead branches, leaves, and leaf margins. If needed, remove dead material. Do not let dead debris accumulate. Minimize leaf tip burn; avoid saline conditions because the fungus can live on the dead portions of leaves. See excess salts for more information. After picking, move fruit to a minimum of 41°F (5°C) as quickly as possible. Ripen under 60°F (16°C) (cooler than room temperature) to minimize rot.

Brown, scattered, dead areas on leaves. If extensive, causes severe leaf drop. Infected fruit develops small, dark spots at lenticels. Like Dothiorella fruit rot, major fruit rot develops upon ripening, after harvest; unlike Dothiorella, the flesh rots are many and smaller.	Anthracnose (*Colletotrichum gloeosporioides*)

Comments

Attacks leaves and fruit. Becomes serious in California only with wet, mild winters. As with Dothiorella fruit rot, important to cool fruits quickly after picking and to ripen them at below room temperature, if possible. Removing dead material and pruning to open the tree canopy for better aeration are helpful, if needed. Spores germinate and penetrate the fruit before harvest, causing brown to black spots, but the disease does not develop further until after harvest. Resumes growth during ripening.

Active lesions on bark are dark, slightly sunken areas with watery, necrotic pockets under the surface. Bark splits on one side of canker and watery fluid oozes out and dries, leaving a white, powdery residue at the lesion. Cankers range in diameter from 1 to 4 in (2.5 to 10 cm). Usually appear first at the base of the tree and often spread upward on one side of the trunk or branch.	bacterial canker (*Xanthomonas campestris*)

MICROSCOPIC DISEASE-CAUSING ORGANISMS (PRIMARILY FUNGI)

What the problem looks like	Probable cause

Comments

Attacks trunk and branches. Widespread disease but relatively unimportant in California. Most groves have a few infected trees without noticeable harm. Affected trees often have leaf symptoms with boron deficiency. If the disease is severe, affecting yield, the tree should be removed. Mild infections seem to have little effect and are too common and spread too little to justify tree removal.

Twigs have narrow, yellow, red, or necrotic shallow indentations that occur lengthwise. Rectangular Fruit with white, yellow, or reddish blotches or streaks that may be depressed. cracking of bark on trunk and larger branches, known as "alligator bark." Tree is stunted.	**sunblotch (avocado sunblotch viroid, ASBVD)**

Comments

Small, single-stranded, circular RNA molecule. Attacks all parts of tree. Formerly caused devastation in California. Discovery in the 1970s that disease is result of a viroid (a smaller, "naked" virus) led to effective control. Purchase registered trees for which scion top and rootstock are indexed as viroid-free. Established infected tree can contaminate nearby healthy avocados by unseen root-to-root grafting and by human-mediated wound-to-wound cutting tools. Removal is recommended in such cases. Occasional symptomless trees can cause infection directly or through symptomless seedlings used in rootstocks. Sterilize pruning tools and harvesting clippers between trees.

MITES, INSECTS, AND GARDEN SNAILS AND SLUGS

Light green or yellow areas on upper leaf surfaces along the midrib, later extending to the smaller veins and entire leaf. Areas of severe feeding later turn brown (bronzing of leaves) and leaves may drop.	**avocado brown mite (*Oligonychus punicae*)**

Comments

Tiny, brown-colored mite about the size of a period, the same size as the persea mite and the avocado mite. Attacks upper leaf surface. Trees injured in proportion to the amount of green leaf area lost. See persea mite for further details.

Light green or yellow areas on underside of leaves along the midrib and larger veins. Heavy infestations can cause leaf drop.	**avocado mite**

Comments

Tiny, yellow to pale green mite about size of period; a pest of avocados primarily in coastal areas. Attacks underside of leaves. Formerly known as six-spotted mite. See persea mite for more details.

Small necrotic spots on the underside of leaves along the midrib and main veins. As population increases, new necrotic spots appear between the veins. Each spot is covered with fine webbing that shines silvery in sunlight. Necrotic spots can coalesce and block transport of carbohydrates from leaf cells to veins. At this point leaves drop, and if extensive, fruit drop follows.	**persea mite (*Oligonychus perseae*)**

Comments

Attacks underside of leaves. A yellowish mite about the size of a printed period. This new mite pest, a native to Mexico, was first detected in California in 1990. It spreads rapidly since its webbing protects it and its eggs from the predacious mite *Amblyseius hibisci*, a common biological control agent in California. In severe infestations, mite population can reach 1000 mites per leaf. Its numbers peak with dry summer heat and decline rapidly in the fall, but enough winter survival occurs (eggs overwinter) to repeat the cycle, allowing buildup of adult populations in spring. Gwen is a favorite host, then Hass, Reed, and other varieties. Certain new UC Riverside experimental selections are comparatively resistant (see table 19.1). Other hosts include citrus fruits (not leaves), deciduous fruits (apricot, peach, nectarine, plum, persimmon), grapes, sumac and liquidambar trees, roses, and acacias.

To confirm the identity of persea mite, hold a white sheet of paper horizontally under symptomatic foliage and rap the stem sharply; the mites will be evident on the paper as moving specks. With a hand lens, the 8 distinguishing mite legs will be visible, and yellow color should be definitive. The persea mite is gradually coming under good biological control because the population of a predacious mite native to California, *Galendromus annectens*, which can penetrate the persea mite webbing, is increasing. Another predacious mite imported to California by UC scientists for the purpose of controlling persea mite, *Galendromus helveolus*, also holds promise. In the meantime, small and few trees can be helped by water-jet washing, which is more effective if insecticidal soap is added. To minimize initial infection, avoid drought and other stress. Contact your local UC Cooperative Extension farm advisor or a pest control adviser for up-to-date recommendations for control methods approved for home growers.

Table 19.5 cont.

MITES, INSECTS, AND GARDEN SNAILS AND SLUGS
What the problem looks like | Probable cause

Scarring on young fruit that starts near the stem end and spreads over entire surface. Feeding on fruit stems causes fruit drop. Pest also feeds on leaves, but defoliation is not primary problem. Darkened, leathery patches on upper leaf surface and random feeding lines on leaf underside. Unlike mites, thrips leave small black fecal pellets.
avocado thrips
(*Scirtothrips perseae*)

Comments
Similar to citrus trips *(Scirtothrips citri)*; a very active, oval, yellow insect about ¹⁄₂₅ inch (1 mm) long. Attacks leaves and fruit. New exotic avocado pest first noticed in July 1996 in Ventura County. Has spread to many avocado groves statewide. Believed native to Central America. Scarring can be severe, leading to "alligator skin." Damage is usually cosmetic. Sanitary precautions recommended, not spraying, because insecticides disrupt beneficial insects. Thrips can fly but are also spread by wind, contaminated clothing, and equipment. UC entomologists are working on introducing new biocontrols.

Fruit and leaves covered with honeydew and sooty mold. Mealybugs present.
mealybugs (*Pseudococcus* or *Planococcus* spp.)

Comments
Attack leaves and fruit. Soft, oval, segmented insects, usually whitish, under ¹⁄₄ inch (6 mm) long, covered with a mealy wax. They suck plant juices, leading to stunting and, rarely, death. Natural enemies usually control mealybugs, but ants protect them from their natural enemies. If ants are controlled, natural predators such as ladybird beetles will control mealybugs. Hand pick small mealybug infestations or daub with rubbing alcohol. For larger infestations, hose off with water or apply soap or oil sprays.

Ants present. Ants do not feed on avocado trees but drive away the natural enemies of insect pests of avocados. Argentine worker ants travel in distinct, narrow trails.
Argentine ant
(*Iridomyrmex humilis*)
Southern fire ant
(*Solenopsis xyloni*)

Comments
Ants feed on honeydew excreted by scales, mealybugs, and other insect pests and can interrupt biological control of pests. Control ants by denying access to the tree. Apply a band of sticky material around the base of the trunk of mature trees that mechanically blocks ants; prune trees about 2 feet (0.6 m) above the ground so ants cannot get into trees without climbing the trunk. Any ant activity is a danger sign. Insecticide or poison baits can reduce ant numbers.

Holes in leaves and fruit. Slimy trails. Diameter of the brown garden snail is about 1 inch (2.5 cm). Gray garden slug is a snail relative that lacks shell.
brown garden snail
(*Helix aspersa*)
gray garden slug
(*Agriolimax reticulatus*)

Comments
Attack leaves and fruit. Most active at night and early morning when ground is damp. Home gardener can hand-pick; best hunting is after 10 p.m. Or place short, wide boards with cleats at either end to keep the boards about 1 inch (2.5 cm) off the ground; these will be daytime hiding places. Pests can then be squashed or killed with a solution of 1 part household ammonia and 1 part water in a spray bottle. Keep ammonia off leaves since it damages plants. Other methods include chemical baits; predatory decollate snails; drowning snails in fermented liquid, such as beer; and copper barriers around trunk. Keep snails out of trees by pruning branches up off the ground.

New leaves have holes and are webbed and rolled together. Caterpillars also feed on developing fruit, scarring it and often rolling and webbing it together with leaves. Caterpillars make shelters by webbing two leaves or a leaf and a fruit. Caterpillar pupates inside fruit. Adult, night-flying, brownish moth emerges. Leaf damage on terminal shoot growth is especially evident for omnivorous looper.
avocadoworms (leafrollers):
amorbia moth
(*Amorbia essigana*)
omnivorous looper
(*Sabulodes aegrotata*)
orange tortrix
(*Argyrotaenia citrana*)

Comments
Attack leaves and fruit. Different leafroller pests are often called avocadoworms. Omnivorous looper eats holes in leaves, skeletonizing them so that only the midrib and larger veins remain. Feeds on fruit and causes scarring. Crawls with a looping motion. Usually found

What the problem looks like	Probable cause

near damaged leaves. Can spin a silken thread and hang suspended from it when disturbed. May vary in color from pale green to pink or yellow with stripes or other markings. Grows to 1½ to 2 inches (4 to 5 cm) long. Amorbia moth caterpillars are yellow-green, about 1 inch (2.5 cm) long. Orange tortrix caterpillars are greenish to bright yellow or pale straw-colored and prefer the top half of trees. Small parasitic wasps and flies usually keep the avocadoworm population low. Certain fungi and viruses are also natural biological controls. The home gardener can destroy avocadoworms by picking them out of their shelters or squashing them in place. Rare, severe outbreaks can be sprayed with *Bacillus thuringiensis* or a chemical insecticide as a last resort.

OTHER PATHOLOGICAL CONDITIONS

Excess chloride: tip and marginal burn of older leaves, premature defoliation, and sometimes a progressive mottled yellowing behind the burn. Excess sodium: interveinal leaf burn and twig dieback. Other elements rarely in harmful excess.	**excess salts (chloride and sodium)**

Comments

Affects leaves. Salt accumulations are often confused with nutritional deficiencies. Avocados are particularly sensitive to salts, accumulating chlorides and sodium more readily than most other tree crops. Rapid burn at the base or leaf tip followed by defoliation suggests either an excessive fertilizer application or inadequate irrigation. Extra root-zone leaching during the summer is indicated.

Pale green to yellow, small leaves with yellow veins; lack of vegetative growth; lower yields; premature defoliation.	**nitrogen deficiency**

Comments

Affects leaves and fruit yield. Apply N during the first irrigation of each month from Mar–Oct. Young trees need N applications at different rates than older, mature trees. See "Fertilizing" section in this chapter.

Light yellow (chlorotic) areas between veins, starting at leaf margins, extending to midrib and base. Small, narrow leaves. Pear-shaped fruit become oval to round, smaller than normal. Terminal growth looks like feather duster. Twig dieback. Defoliation. Reduced yields.	**zinc deficiency**

Comments

Affects leaves, twigs, fruit yield. Can be controlled by applying zinc as a spray to foliage or to the soil. Foliar applications most effective in June and July. Methods of soil application vary and effectiveness can last longer than foliar sprays. See "Fertilizing" section in this chapter.

Interveinal yellowing on leaves. Tip and marginal leaf burn. Defoliation. Twig dieback. Reduced yields.	**iron deficiency**

Comments

Affects leaves and fruit yield. Can occur in high-pH soils containing lime (calcium carbonate) but not common in California. Deficiency accentuated by excess soil moisture. Mexican race rootstocks are less sensitive. See "Fertilizing" section in this chapter.

Leaves, twigs look watersoaked, then wither, darken. Branches die back, and bark splits in severe cases. Leaves may drop quickly or persist on tree. When fruit freezes, flesh dries out and brownish pits called "ice marks" may form on skin. Xylem (water-conducting elements) in the fruit turn black.	**frost damage**

Comments

Attacks leaves and fruits first; attacks progressively larger wood after harder frosts. Allow tree to recover before removing frost-killed wood. After new growth appears in early spring, wait for any dieback, then cut back to live wood (identified by a green layer just under the bark). Pruning cuts heal naturally, so no need to paint them. See discussion in "Treatment of Freeze-Damaged Avocado Trees" in this chapter.

Large and small branches blacken, die. Wood peels off in patches. Fruit skin develops tough, brownish spots, and fruit may dry out.	**sunburn**

Comments

Affects trunk, branches, fruit. A problem in hot, sunny areas. Wrap the trunk in white cardboard or use whitewash or flat white latex paint. Maintain adequate nitrogen and water for good foliage. See "Sunburn and Wind Protection" section in this chapter.

Sources: Adapted from Ohr et al. 1994; Flint 1998.

Biological Control. Biological control is generally more effective in coastal regions than in the San Joaquin Valley or desert areas. University of California scientists are actively engaged in detecting, testing, and importing predators and parasites of major avocado pests. A number of effective biological control agents are native to California, but if indigenous ones are not available, University of California entomologists and plant pathologists travel to the areas of the world where avocados or their pests are believed to have originated to search for natural predators and parasites. When a particular natural enemy looks promising, specimens are brought back to California with the appropriate permits and placed into quarantine facilities to undergo intensive research. The entomologists and plant pathologists release the imported biological controls into the environment only when research results document their effectiveness and safety.

Chemical Control. Pesticides should be used as a last resort. Chemical controls not only kill the target pests but they also accelerate development of pesticide resistance. Chemical pesticides may also kill beneficials, the biological enemies naturally present or introduced into the garden. Chemical pesticides also raise questions of environmental pollution and health risks. For additional information on general pest management and pesticide use, see chapter 10, "Controlling Garden Pests Safely."

Treatment of Freeze-Damaged Avocado Trees

Damaging freezes tend to occur in California avocado districts erratically, averaging about one a decade. Certain techniques hasten tree recovery and maximize desirable growth responses in cold-injured avocados; for more information, see *Treatment of Freeze Damaged Citrus and Avocado Trees* (Platt and Opitz 1974).

Determine the Extent of Damage. Shoot and foliage injury usually becomes visible in a few days. Twigs and small limbs may show little or no signs of cold damage for 2 to 4 weeks. The rate at which freeze damage becomes apparent depends upon the prevailing temperatures and humidity and on the condition of growth before and after the freeze period. Except when trees are killed outright, it may be impossible to determine the extent of severe injury for several months or, rarely,

even for an entire year following a freeze.

Delay Pruning. Corrective pruning should be postponed until the full extent of damage can be determined clearly. Dead wood removed while dying-back is in progress frequently contributes to further dieback through wound cuts. If pruning is not postponed, some limbs that would have recovered might be removed unnecessarily, and a second pruning to rid the tree of undesirable brush and limb stubs is then necessary. Experience at the University of California has shown that early-pruned trees recover more slowly than trees pruned later.

Remove Frozen Fruit. If the fruit has no value, remove it as soon as possible. The longer fruit remains on the tree, the greater it decreases yield in the succeeding crop.

Treat the Trunk and Limbs. The degree of injury provides a guide to the type of treatment required.

Light damage. No treatment is necessary when only foliage and small twigs are injured. No pruning except "dead brushing" should be done the ensuing season. All live foliage should be retained to nourish the root system and support the developing crop.

Medium damage. When a considerable part of the scion is killed, but the trunk and crown limbs appear sound, the true extent of damage can be determined only after several months. Do not prune until the full extent of the damage is visible. Save as much of the tree's framework as possible. Old limbs must be cut back below all serious bark injuries. Cut back to good, strong shoots. Distribution of new framework branches can be controlled to some degree by selection and light pruning during the summer. After injured branches have been cut back to new leaders, further pruning consists of gradually thinning excessive sprouts over several years. These shoots (suckers) crowd and interfere with growth and branching of the leaders forming the tree's new framework.

Severe damage. When most of the top and crown limbs are killed, but the trunk shows little injury, no pruning should be done until the full extent of the damage is visible, which will usually become apparent after mid-summer. Then, the entire top of the tree should be removed, cutting below all large areas of injured bark. By this time, numerous sprouts from different locations on the trunk will have made considerable growth. From these, the new head of the tree must be formed. Select the uppermost good sprout and cut the old trunk off just above this sprout, sloping the cut downward away from the sprout. Then choose two or three other sprouts properly spaced to form a new head and favor their growth by pinching back sprouts that crowd them. All sprouts should be left until a balance between root and top is established. Unnecessary sprouts should then be removed gradually.

Very severe damage. When the top is killed and the injury extends well down the trunk but is followed by the appearance of strong sprouts above the bud union, a new trunk and head must be developed. They can be produced from one or more strong shoots originating from above the bud union. With young trees, it is usually best to favor one strong shoot. The top of the tree may then be removed, leaving the old trunk as a support to which this special shoot may be tied. The shoot chosen for development should be favored and forced into growth by pinching back all others.

When the new head has developed to the size of a good 2-year-old orchard tree, the old trunk should be removed carefully by a cut starting just above the base of the new trunk and sloping downward. The surface of the cut should be allowed to dry. No wound dressing is necessary (see related discussion under "Pruning").

With large trees, recovery is more rapid if several shoots are used to form the new head. There is no objection to trees with multiple trunks. When several shoots are used, it is best to remove the old trunk as soon as the extent of the freeze damage can be determined. Otherwise, new shoots may be damaged excessively by the saw. Treat the cut surface as described above. During the year following the freeze and until the new head is well-formed, all sprouts should be allowed to grow. But, as indicated above, growth of temporary shoots must be controlled by pinching back.

Extreme damage. Usually, trees killed to the bud union should be removed and replaced by new trees. If you must retain such trees, the suggestions for very severely damaged trees should be followed, but shoots selected for forming the new tree must be budded to the desired variety as soon as they are large enough to take a bud (about 1/4- to 3/8-inch

[6 to 9.5 mm] in diameter). It is best to place the buds at a height of 18 to 24 inches (46 to 61 cm) because it allows shoots to grow around the tree base without shading the buds or interfering with their development.

Treatment of Damaged Bark. Bark on the trunk of injured young trees may crack and curl. On injured trees of various ages, patches of dead bark may show up here and there on large limbs or on trunks even where no splitting occurs. When the extent of these injuries becomes clearly visible 2 or 3 months after a freeze, the dead areas of bark should be cut out smoothly and the exposed wood disinfected and painted.

Protection from Sunburn After a Freeze. Protection of the trunk and large limbs from sunburn is advisable in warmer areas if regrowth has not occurred before hot weather arrives. It is only necessary to cover that part of the trunk and large limbs that "see" south and southwest with whitewash or inexpensive white latex paint.

Irrigation and Fertilization After a Frost

Irrigation. Irrigate cautiously after a freeze. When leaves are damaged or destroyed by a freeze, the tree uses less water than under normal conditions until a new crop of leaves has developed. Most water removed from the soil by the tree is lost through its leaves by evapotranspiration. Irrigate only when soil conditions indicate a need. Determine soil moisture content by examining the soil (for detailed discussions on soil moisture monitoring and irrigation, see chapters 3 and 4.) Irrigations should be less frequent, and smaller amounts of water should be applied until trees have regained their ability to use normal amounts of water. In the case of severely damaged trees, this reduced irrigation requirement may last the entire growing season.

Fertilization. The amount of fertilizer applied will depend largely upon the extent of damage. It is best to withhold fertilizers until the extent of damage is determined. Freeze-damaged trees do not respond better if heavily fertilized. In fact, more harm than good may occur. Slightly injured trees will recover most rapidly and will usually set crops in the spring following the freeze. Such trees require normal fertilization.

Severely damaged trees usually put forth a good deal of sucker or shoot growth which, through selection, will be used to rebuild the tree. Until the tree regains its full top, an imbalance exists between the root system and top. Trees that have received regular fertilization or are growing on fertile soils have ample nutrients to satisfy their needs the first year following freeze damage. Fertilizer applied before the top has been reestablished may force additional sucker growth that will be difficult and costly to control. Reduce or omit

fertilization during the first season on severely damaged trees.

The imbalance between the root system and top, together with vigorous sucker growth following a freeze, often results in micronutrient deficiencies that can retard recovery. Zinc is the element most likely to be deficient in avocados. Zinc deficiency may be corrected by foliar sprays, although recent evidence suggests that foliar applications are less effective than previously thought. Sometimes iron is also deficient after a freeze. As in citrus, iron deficiency is often the result of excessive soil moisture and can be corrected by reducing irrigation.

Table 19.6

AVOCADO NUTRITION FACTS IN TERMS OF PERCENT DAILY VALUE

Serving Size: ⅕ of 1 medium-sized avocado, uncooked (30 g, or 1.1 oz)

Amount Per Serving
Calories 55
Calories from fat 45

	% Daily Value*
Total Fat 5 g	8%
Saturated 1 g	
Polyunsaturated 1 g	
Monounsaturated 3 g	
Cholesterol 0m g	0%
Sodium 0 mg	0%
Potassium 170 mg	5%
Total Carbohydrate 3 g	1%
Dietary Fiber 3 g	12%
Sugars 0 g	
Protein 1 g	

Vitamin A	0%	Vitamin C	4%
Calcium	0%	Iron	0%
Vitamin E	4%	Riboflavin	2%
Niacin	2%	Vitamin B6	4%
Folate	6%	Pantothenic	2%
Magnesium	2%	Acid	

	Calories:	2,000	2,500
Total Fat	Less than	65 g	80 g
Saturated Fat	Less than	20 g	25 g
Cholesterol	Less than	300 mg	300 mg
Sodium	Less than	2,400 mg	2,400 mg
Potassium		3,500 mg	3,500 mg
Total Carbohydrate		300 g	375 g
Dietary Fiber		25 g	30 g

Source: California Avocado Commission.

*Percent Daily Values are based on a 2,000 calorie diet. Your daily values may be higher or lower depending on your caloric needs.

Nutritional Value

Since avocados are high in fat—more than 85 percent of the calories in an avocado derive from fat—weight watchers often mistakenly think they must eliminate avocados from their diets. Before writing off avocados, read the following summary of the avocado's health benefits. More information on this topic can be found in Bergh 1992.

Health Benefits of the Avocado

The edible portion of the avocado fruit is the mesocarp, a highly nutritious oily pulp rich in protein, several B vitamins, vitamin C, potassium, and other minerals. Some consumers are aware that avocados are an excellent source of monounsaturated fatty acids, the type of fat that has a significant role in lowering "bad" cholesterol, but most consumers do not realize that ounce for ounce, avocados are a richer source of potassium than bananas; nor do they know that avocados have the highest protein concentration of any commercially produced deciduous, subtropical, or tropical fruit. California's Hass avocado averages 2.4 grams of protein per 100 grams fresh weight. Avocados routinely exceed 2.3 percent protein per unit fresh weight, making them an unusually rich source of fruit-based protein. Moreover, avocados contain all essential amino acids, which means they are a source of balanced protein nutrition.

Avocados and Your Heart. Avocado fat is predominantly monounsaturated oleic acid, which has been shown to reduce blood levels of low density lipoprotein (LDL), known as "bad" cholesterol. Cardiologists have noted that diets high in monounsaturated fats have lower incidence of heart disease. For California's dominant Hass cultivar, the results of average fat analyses of 700 avocado fruit yielded 82 percent monounsaturated fat, 8 percent polyunsaturated fat, and 10 percent saturated fat, which means the Hass avocado is superior to olives in oleic acid content. As a refined cooking oil, avocado oil is milder and more delicate in flavor than many olive oils, and it has a higher "smoke point" (about 490°F [254°C]) than olive oil.

The avocado is also a good source of the antioxidant vitamins A, C, and E, which have important roles in reducing heart disease by reducing blood LDL oxidation. LDL oxidation can lead to plaque deposits in arteries. The avocado has a high content of soluble fiber, which has been shown to benefit the heart. Water-soluble fiber, such as pectin, has been shown to decrease serum cholesterol. Avocados have four times as much soluble fiber as apples.

Avocados and Stroke. Less than half an avocado supplies more than 400 milligrams of potassium. A daily increase in potassium intake has been associated with reduced risk of stroke. Ounce-per-ounce, an avocado has more than 1.5 times the potassium of a banana.

Avocados and Your Skin. Compared with almond, corn, olive, and soybean oils, avocado oil has the highest skin penetration. Synthetic sunscreen chemicals such as PABA, while highly effective, are skin irritants to some people. When compared with seven other plant oils, avocado oil was shown to be the most effective sunscreen. Avocado oil can be used as a natural skin moisturizer, cleansing cream, makeup base, sunscreen, lipstick, bath oil, and hair conditioner.

Avocado Nutrition Data

Table 19.6 lists the official Percent Daily Value from the California Avocado Commission of one-fifth of a medium avocado, which is an individual serving size weighing about 30 grams (1 oz). Since it may be difficult to slice an avocado into fifths and since a 2,000-calorie diet may or may not meet your caloric requirements (age, height, and weight are factors), the nutritional value of one whole, medium-sized avocado (6 oz [173 g]) is presented in a different format in table 19.7. For background information on nutritional data, see appendix A.

Table 19.7

NUTRITIONAL VALUE OF AVOCADOS IN TERMS OF RECOMMENDED DIETARY ALLOWANCES (RDA)

Serving size: 1 medium avocado, uncooked (173 g)

		Primary nutrients		% RDA (m)*	% RDA (f)*
Calories	306	vitamin B6	0.48 mg	37	37
Fat	30 g	folic acid	113 mcg	28	28
Percent calories from fat	88	vitamin E	2.32 mg	15	15
Sodium	21 mg	vitamin C	14 mg	16	19
Protein	3.6 g	niacin	3.3 mg	21	24
Carbohydrate	12.0 g	iron	2.04 mg	25	11
Saturated FA†	4.5 g	magnesium	70 mg	17	22
Mono-unsaturated FA	19.4 g	riboflavin	0.21 mg	16	19
Polyunsaturated FA	3.5 g	thiamin	0.19 mg	16	17
Cholesterol	0	vitamin A	106 RE‡	12	15
Water	125.5 g		—	—	—
Dietary Fiber	4.7 g	potassium	1,097 mg	55§	55§

Sources: Pennington 1998; National Academy of Sciences 1989, 2001a, 2001b.

Notes:

* RDA percentage for adult males (m) and females (f).

† FA = fatty acid

‡ RE = Retinol Equivalents. See notes to table A.1 in appendix A.

§ % Min. Requirement. The nutritional value information for potassium content is expressed as % Min. Requirement. To date, no RDA has been established for potassium, but a minimum requirement for healthy persons is based on age (see appendix A).

Bibliography

Anonymous. 1998. Nutrient requirements get a makeover: The evolution of the recommended dietary allowances. Food Insight, September/October.

Bender, G. S. 1999. Avocado irrigation guide for trees spaced 20 ft. by 20 ft (6.1 m by 6.1 m). San Diego: UC Cooperative Extension San Diego County Publication CP-509.

Bergh, B. O. 1969. Avocado (*Persea americana* Miller). In F. P. Ferwerda and F. Witt, eds., Outlines of perennial crop breeding in the tropics. Wageningen, Netherlands: University of Agriculture, Wageningen.

———. 1974. The remarkable avocado flower. In California avocado society yearbook, 1973–74. Saticoy, CA: California Avocado Society.

———. 1975. Avocados. In J. Janick and J. N. Moore, eds., Advances in fruit breeding. West Lafayette, IN: Purdu Univ. Press. 541–567.

Bergh, B. O., and E. Lahav. 1992. The avocado and human nutrition. In C. J. Lovatt, ed., Proceedings of the second world avocado congress. Vol. 1. Riverside: University of California and California Avocado Society.

———. 1996. Avocados. In J. Janick and J. N. Moore, eds., Fruit breeding. Vol. 1: Tree and tropical fruits. New York: Wiley.

Brenzel, K. N., ed. 2001. Sunset western garden book. Menlo Park: Sunset Publishing.

Brokaw, W. H. Care of citrus and avocado trees. Saticoy, CA: Brokaw Nursery.

California Avocado Society. 1976. Avocado varieties for commercial planting in California. Saticoy, CA: California Avocado Society.

Flint, M. L. 1998. Pests of the garden and small farm: A grower's guide to using less pesticide. 2nd ed. Oakland: University of California Division of Agriculture and Natural Resources Publication 3332.

Lovatt, C. J. 1990. Factors affecting fruit set/early fruit drop in avocado. In J. S. Shephaer, ed., California Avocado Society 1990 yearbook. Saticoy, CA: California Avocado Society.

———. 1999. Timing citrus and avocado foliar nutrient applications to increase fruit set and size. HortTechnology 9:607–612.

National Academy of Sciences. 2001a. Dietary reference intakes (DRIs): Recommended dietary intakes for individuals, vitamins. Washington, DC: National Academy of Sciences.

———. 2001b. Dietary reference intakes (DRIs): Recommended dietary intakes for individuals, elements. Washington, DC: National Academy of Sciences.

National Academy of Sciences, Food and Nutrition Board. 1989. Recommended dietary allowances. 10th ed. Washington, DC: National Academy of Sciences.

Ohr, H. D., B. Faber, and N. Grech. 1994. Avocado diseases. Saticoy, CA: California Avocado Society and California Avocado Commission, Circular No. CAS-94/1.

Pennington, J. 1998. Bowes & Church's food values of portions commonly used. 17th ed. Philadelphia: Lippincott.

Platt, R. G., and K. W. Opitz, 1974. Treatment of freeze damaged citrus and avocado trees. Oakland: University of California Division of Agriculture and Natural Resources Leaflet 214.

Salazar-Garcia, S., E. M. Lord, and C. J. Lovatt. 1998. Inflorescence and flower development of the 'Hass' avocado (*Persea americana* Mill.) during "on" and "off" crop years. Journal of the American Society of Horticultural Science 123 (4): 537–544.

Turney, J., and J. Menge. 1994. Root health: Mulching to control root disease in avocado and citrus. Saticoy, CA: California Avocado Society, California Avocado Commission, and Citrus Research Board, Circular No. CAS-94/2.

UC IPM pest note series. B. L. P. Ohlendorf, ed. University of California Division of Agriculture and Natural Resources, Statewide Integrated Pest Management Program. Updated regularly. Available through UC Cooperative Extension county offices; also available on the World Wide Web at http://www.ipm.ucdavis.edu

Whitsell, R. H., G. E. Martin, B. O. Bergh, A. V. Lypps, and W. H. Brokaw. 1989. Propagating avocados: Principles and techniques of nursery and field grafting. Oakland: University of California Division of Agriculture and Natural Resources Publication 21461.

20

Landscape and Garden Design

John F. Karlik

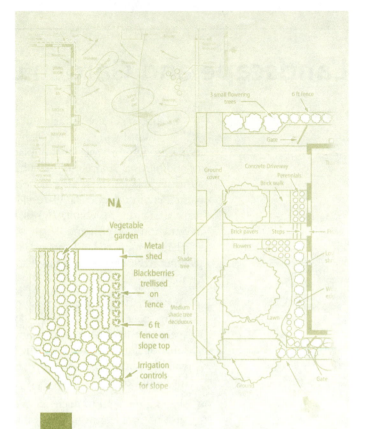

LEARNING OBJECTIVES

- Understand basic principles of landscape design.

- Understand xeriscape concepts.

- Develop the knowledge to visualize plants (trees, shrubs, turf, and ground covers) as key elements in a comprehensive landscape design plan.

- Understand how to design a landscape plan step by step.

Landscape and Garden Design

Landscape design is the art of organizing and improving outdoor living space through the placement of plant materials and hardscape structures in a functional, attractive relationship that enhances the natural environment. The discussion of landscape design in this chapter is based on information in Welsh and Welch 1989.

There is more to landscaping than merely planting trees, shrubs, and turf. Landscaping means

- creating a design plan to make outdoor living space an extension of indoor living space (the landscape design should be functional and attractive for the family that will be using the space and paying the bills for its upkeep)

- shaping the land to make the most of the site's natural features and advantages

- assessing the site's drawbacks and minimizing them

- building fences, walls, decks, or patios

- installing an efficient, water-conserving irrigation system (for most of California)

- selecting and growing plants, trees, and shrubs that best fit the design

- adding accent lighting, if appropriate

The final design should define uses for specific areas in the landscape and identify circulation patterns.

The smaller the house, grounds, and budget, the greater the need for effective and complete planning, because every square foot of space and every dollar must produce maximum results. No landscape is maintenance-free. If a family is more interested in family outings than in being weekend slaves to maintaining an attractive landscape, then planning for the best use of the site will include learning which plants resist local diseases and pests, which plants are most effective for the various usages defined, and which plants require minimal care but still provide a pleasant appearance in terms of the overall color scheme, texture, and form.

A well-designed and maintained landscape not only increases curb appeal and resale value of a home, it also increases the home's utility, privacy, aesthetics, and recreational value. Although it is not necessary to develop the landscape for a new lot or to renovate an existing landscape all at once, an overall plan to the design will ensure that work will be in harmony with the house and the rest of the landscaping. In other words, plan in advance for complete development or renovation. Do not allow a spade of earth to be turned until a grading schedule has been prepared from a well-studied plan for the house and lot. Doing otherwise may sacrifice valuable trees and soil.

Factors Influencing Landscape Design

The fundamental principle of landscape design is that each project should be based on a plan that takes into account the following.

- Family needs: The cultural needs, allergies to plants, individual desires, and expectations from outdoor living space of the people who will use the landscape.

- Climate: The overall climate as well as microclimates on the site, and how they influence the choices of suitable planting materials, the design of the irrigation system, and hardscape features.

- Site analysis: The nature of the site, its immediate surroundings, topographic and ecological conditions, and all natural and human-made objects now existing on the site or planned for the future.

- Materials: Available materials, methods of fabrication, and individual preferences.

- Budget: Available resources of money and time.

The designer should ask the family that will use the landscape what they want and what they plan to do outdoors. The designer should understand the client's desires and needs, and determine what space, climate, materials, methods of fabrication, and budget are available to accommodate these well-defined goals. A questionnaire is helpful. Analyze family activities and routines, and consider outdoor living, relaxing, entertaining, playing, gardening, and household servicing. Small children need open lawn for playing; gardeners need space for growing vegetables and flowers. Make allowances for future changes in the landscape. The original plan for a young family could include open areas in which children and pets can play. As the family reaches its middle years, more extensive and expensive plantings could be put in, and the children's play area could be converted to a lily pond or swimming pool.

Because site analysis, climate, and budgetary constraints (both time and money) are such critical factors in landscape design, they are discussed in detail below.

Site Analysis

In developing a design, preserve all the best natural resources on the site, such as mature trees, brooks, ponds, rock outcroppings, good soil, turf, and interesting variations in the terrain. These natural elements affect the ease of construction and landscape possibilities. Make a careful survey to determine whether site conditions will be a deterrent or whether they can be incorporated into a design plan. If wildfires are likely to occur around the site, see "Designing and Maintaining the Landscape for Fire Prevention" in Chapter 13. Microenvironmental problems on a site—such as low places with cold air drainage or small areas with poor soil and water drainage—may require consideration.

Changes in elevation can add interest and variety to the home landscape. The character of the land and its hills, slope, and trees should determine the basic landscape pattern. A hilly, wooded lot lends itself to an informal or natural design, with large areas left in their natural state. In such a setting, large trees can be retained.

Although slopes can be an asset because they provide variation and an opportunity to incorporate focal points and unique views, avoid creating too many artificial slopes. Berms need to have gradual slopes to look natural and to facilitate irrigation and mowing. Grading of terraces or construction of retaining walls may be necessary to control water drainage. Design terraces and walls to complement the natural setting of the lot.

In planning the home grounds, give careful consideration to foot traffic patterns, permit-ting easy access from one area to another. Traffic may be served by walkways, terraces, or open stretches of lawn. In areas of heavy use, paved surfacing materials are best.

The design of the walkway to the front door often depends on the location of the front door, where guests' cars will be parked, and the topography of the land. The entry should be clearly identified as an outcome of the design. If guest parking is at the edge of the street, a relatively straight walk is probably best, if the grade is suitable. If guest parking is on the property, the walk might lead more logically from the guest parking area to the front door. Foot traffic can use the driveway and its aprons in many situations.

Sometimes the topography of the land or the shape of the lot make it desirable to have the entrance walk start at the edge of the property and curve to the front door to take advantage of a gradual grade. However, avoid curved walks that have no apparent reason for curving. Generally, the walk to the front door parallels the house and joins the driveway. This design, used sometimes if the driveway entrance grade at the street is less steep than the area directly in front of the door, might eliminate the need for stairs. In running the walk parallel to the house, be sure sufficient space is left for plant material.

Keep good views open and screen out undesirable ones. Often a shrub or two will provide the necessary screening. Plantings, fences or walls can serve as noise barriers. The principal rooms of the house should look onto the lawn or the garden and view specially designed landscape elements or areas.

Climate

Climate refers to the average sunlight, precipitation, wind, and temperature. Climate can affect the placement of a house on a lot, land use, and the plant materials selected. In planning the landscape, do not fight the climate; capitalize on its advantages. In warm regions, enlarge the outdoor living area. In cold regions, plant so that the winter scene can be enjoyed from inside. Evergreens and hedges are picturesque covered with snow. Because people respond differently to sun and shade, it is important to study the amount and location of each on the lot. Just as the angle and location of the sun at sunrise and sunset vary seasonally, sunlight and shade patterns in the landscape change seasonally, vary throughout the day, and can be controlled by the location of structures, fences, and trees. Allow for shade from trees and houses on neighboring lots.

Plan shade from tree plantings with great care in order to keep sunny areas for garden plants and summer shade for the house and terrace. Deciduous trees (those that shed their leaves) shade the house in summer and admit sunlight in winter. Place trees off the corners rather than the sides of the house, where they will accent the house and not block views or air circulation from windows. Overplanting trees tends to shut out sun and air.

Cost-Effective, Low-Maintenance Landscape Design

Determine the budget—the maintenance standards and costs—acceptable to the family's needs. A low-maintenance plan, which is the goal of most homeowners, may be achieved to a large extent in the planning stage by careful attention to the layout of the site and the selection of plant species. A low-maintenance, cost-effective landscape may be achieved by adopting one or more of the following design elements.

- Use turf effectively for function rather than appearance only. Consider substituting ground covers or natural mulches.

- Use paving in heavily traveled areas to facilitate circulation.

- Use brick, concrete, or redwood mow strips for flower beds and shrub borders.

- Use fences or walls instead of clipped formal hedges for screening.

- Design raised flower and vegetable beds for easy access and weed control.

- Install a permanent, automated irrigation system in areas of low rainfall.

- Limit the area of annual flower beds, which require recurring expense and work because of their growth habit. Use containerized plants and flowering trees and shrubs for color accents.

- Be selective when choosing plant materials. Choose plants that require less work and are resistant to pests and diseases. Among the desired plants, some will require much less pruning, spraying, and watering than others but will be equally effective in pro-

viding color, shade, texture, privacy, or in meeting other design objectives.

- Keep the design simple, unified in theme, and functional.

Definition of Landscape Use Areas and Design Considerations

One approach to landscape design divides available space into use areas. A commonly used division is the private area, the service/storage/work area, and the public area. The outdoor living room or private area is for the family and may contain a patio, deck, or porch for outdoor sitting, entertaining, or dining. A play area may be incorporated, depending on the family's interest and the presence and ages of children. The service, storage, and work area should provide a place for composting, garden tools, and storage that is convenient for use but screened from the other areas. Also included in this area may be a bed for cut flowers or a vegetable garden. The public area is the section of the landscape seen by passersby. It is generally in front of the house and should present an attractive public view. Because small tract lots exist in much of California, these use areas may overlap or be combined. Fruit trees may be used as ornamentals, for example, and front entry areas can be converted into a family patio.

Private or Outdoor Living Area

The private living area or outdoor living room has become an important part of the California home. No yard is too small to have a private outdoor sitting area where family and guests can gather. Access from the house to the outdoor area should be unrestricted. The ideal arrangement is to have the living room or family room open onto a porch or terrace and have the kitchen near the outdoor dining area. The outdoor living room can be as simple as an open grassy area. A more elaborate outdoor plan can include a patio and series of gardens or garden features. Consider the following guidelines when planning private areas.

Year-Round Interest. If the private area is visible from the house, the outdoor living area should be planned so that the plant material selected offers a variety of interest (color and texture) throughout the year. For winter interest, select shrubs and trees with a winter flowering habit, colorful bark, evergreen foliage, or colorful fruit. The rest of the year, use an assortment of flowers, shrubs, and trees to create interest. Pools, stone steps, paving, walls, bird-feeding stands, and other architectural features that do not change with the seasons will add interesting dimensions to the garden throughout the year.

Climate Control. Control of weather in the outdoor living area helps to extend its period of usefulness. Shade trees screen the area from the hot sun. Windbreaks reduce wind velocity. An awning or trellis-type roof can protect against inclement weather. A garden pool or fountain can convey a cooling effect during the hot summer season, as can the use of cool colors, such as blue and violet flowers.

Terrace or Sitting Area. The center of activity for a living area is often a space arranged with garden or patio furniture. It may be a porch, deck, or terrace next to the house, or a special section of the outdoor living area that might be under the shade of a large tree or in a shady corner. Flagstone, brick, concrete blocks, or concrete with redwood dividers are hardscape materials commonly used for surfacing an outdoor sitting area, but turf can also be used. Wooden decks are appropriate when slopes or other grade changes occur in the area. The landscape can repeat colors, textures, and materials used in the dwelling.

The size of the paved terrace depends on its expected use, the type and amount of furniture desired, and the budget. An area 10 feet by 10 feet (3 m by 3 m) is about the minimum size for accommodating four people comfortably. Increase the size if more people need to be accommodated regularly or if outdoor cooking and grilling are planned.

Play Area. The play area can be a part of the outdoor living area or separate from it. For very young children, a small fenced area near the kitchen or living area is desirable. This area can have a swing, sand box, or other play equipment. Yards with a good deal of open lawn space have room for croquet, badminton, or a portable wading pool. A large tree in the back yard may be ideal for a tree house. A paved driveway or parking area is suitable for skateboarding or basketball for older children, as well as tricycling or roller skating for younger ones. Because the ages of children in a family are always changing, the design must adjust to meet changing recreational needs.

Enclosed Front Yard as a Private Area. The landscape area in front of the home has traditionally been the public area, left more or less open so passersby can view the home. However, front-yard plantings such as hedges or a screen of trees and shrubs along the street can render the public area private. Privacy in the front yard may be desirable on small lots, if a picture window faces the street, or if the front yard is used for outdoor sitting. East and north sides can be especially desirable for afternoon shade. Where space is limited, a tall, attractive fence may provide privacy and be an effective background for shrubs and smaller plants. Check local ordinances before planting or building close to the street. A design that could probably be used much more in California is partially enclosing the front entry space. By adding a low wall or fence and screen plantings, the area close to the front door becomes more private and usable. However, care must be taken to ensure that the security of the entry is not compromised by completely screening it from view.

Service, Storage, and Work Area

Space often needs to be provided for permanent clothes lines, garbage cans, air-conditioner units, tool storage, wood storage, vegetable gardens, compost, a cut-flower garden, propagating structures, small greenhouses, or a kennel. Service facilities should not be visible from the outdoor living area or from the street. An exception might be an attractive greenhouse or tool storage building designed and constructed so that it blends well into the overall setting, with an interesting composition of plant material around it. Wood or wire fences, brick or masonry walls, and plants alone or in combination are the materials most commonly used to hide or partially screen service areas. To provide unity, consider using the same materials, colors, and textures that are used on the walls of the house.

Public Area

Traditionally, the public area is the front yard area facing the street. The landscape in this area creates "first impressions" about your home and should give the illusion of spaciousness. Keep the lawn open; keep shrubs to the side and in foundation plantings. When selecting a planting scheme to define the front entry, consider texture, color, size, and shape so the plants will enhance the total effect of welcoming guests. Tall trees in the backyard and medium-sized trees on the sides and in front help accomplish this effect. The house is to be the focal point of the public view. On small lots, the family may prefer to modify this type of plan and choose to enclose the front yard, making it a private area, as discussed above.

Driveways should be safe, functional, and pleasing in appearance. Parking areas and turnabouts should be provided when practical. If possible, the driveway should be hard-surfaced because it is neater and requires less maintenance than an unpaved drive. Specialized paver blocks that allow ground cover or turf in the interior are available. Do not plant tall shrubbery at a driveway entrance or allow vegetation to grow so tall that it obstructs the view of the street or highway in either direction.

The front walkway should be at least 32 inches (0.8 m) wide, but ideally it should be 4 feet (1.2 m) wide. Use materials that provide a sure footing in all types of weather. Avoid using materials that are extremely rough or raised, because it is possible to trip over or catch one's heel on such materials. Design steps so they will be safe, especially in wet or icy weather. Make the treads wider and the risers shorter than the treads and risers used indoors. Install handrails where needed. Avoid right-angle turns; curves are much friendlier.

City Ordinances and Zoning. Many communities have setback ordinances that specify fence heights, the permissible height of plants and trees at various distances from the curb, and distances from the lot line or curb that must be maintained when adding structures or features. Corner lots may carry restrictions so that views of drivers are unimpaired. Fences, decks, lattice work, and other structures may require a building permit. If irrigation is being installed, a backflow preventer is usually mandated. Local ordinances vary greatly, so consult your city or county planning department.

Elements and Principles of Landscape Design

There are no hard and fast rules for landscaping, because each design is a unique creation.

Like all art forms, landscaping is based on certain elements and principles of design.

Scale

Scale refers to the proportion between two sets of dimensions. Knowing the eventual or mature size of a plant is critical when locating it near a building such as a house. Plants that grow too large will overwhelm a building. Small plantings around a large building can be similarly inappropriate. It is essential, therefore, to know the final size of a particular plant before using it in a landscape. Both the mature height and spread of a plant should be considered.

Balance

Balance in landscaping refers to creating equal visual weight on either side of a focal point of interest via an aesthetically pleasing integration of elements. Balance gives a sense that two parts have equal visual weight or mass. There are two types of balance: symmetrical and asymmetrical. Symmetrical balance is a formal balance. It has an axis with everything on one side duplicated or mirrored on the other side, as in formal gardens. Asymmetrical balance is an equilibrium or balance achieved by using different objects. For example, if a very large object is on one side of a seesaw, it can be counterbalanced by many smaller objects on the other side. The concept of asymmetrical balance applies to landscaping when there is a large existing tree or shrub. To achieve visual equilibrium, a grouping or cluster of smaller plants is used to counterbalance the large existing tree or shrub. Balance may also be achieved through the use of color and texture.

Perspective

Because many California lots are small, perspective is very important. Certain techniques can make spaces seem larger, whereas others can shrink the same area. Usually the goal is to make an area seem larger. A strong accent in the center of a space draws the eye, making the space seem larger. Obstructing the view with overhead tree canopies or structures will close in a space. Similarly, many backyards have turf surrounded by a border of shrubs, which brings the eye to a terminus and confines the space. Overuse of dividers relegates the space to small boxes and becomes claustrophobic.

Effective use of color can expand space. Because distant objects appear fine-textured and gray to the eye, use gray, fine-textured plants across a yard to expand the apparent distance between the viewer and the plant material. Strong colors and coarse textures at the front of a border also expand the area. To contract space, reverse these concepts and use strong colors and coarse texture to the rear, tapering to softer tones and finer textures at the front. To create perspective with flowers, try rotating a bed 90 degrees, making the eye follow outward. At the perimeter, darkness and shadow can appear to increase space. Darkness limits the view but carries an implication of more space beyond. Shadows can be used similarly. Create a dramatic illusion by making a façade with stepping stones leading behind it. Tapering walkways or plantings toward a vanishing point creates the illusion of distance.

Unity

To achieve unity, group or arrange different parts of the design to appear as a single unit. Strong, observable lines and the repetition of geometric shapes contribute significantly to the unity of a landscape design, which should provide a pleasant picture from every angle. Turfgrass and ground covers act as unifying elements. The colors white and gray can be used as unifiers in a flower bed of mixed colors. A landscape with too many ideas expressed in a limited area lacks unity. Too many showy plants, plant varieties, lawn accessories, or accent plants with contrasting textures, form, or color violate the principle of unity. The landscape would claim more attention than the house itself, which is not the objective.

Rhythm

Rhythm refers to the repetition of design elements which directs the eye through the design. Rhythm results only when the elements appear in regular measures and in a definite direction. Rhythm can be expressed in color as well as form.

Simplicity

Application of the design concept "less is more" depends greatly on the design. Perennial borders and garden areas may be very diverse by nature. Unless you are creating an arboretum, limit the number of shrub and tree plant species used, because it is more effective to use fewer species in groupings than to install a few of many kinds.

Every square foot of landscape does not have to have something in it. Objects such as bird baths, statuary, and other ornaments may be overused in the landscape. Strive to create spaces, not fill them up. Create simple curves and lines that add interest rather than multiple odd-shaped lines that detract from the design and become difficult to irrigate and maintain.

Repetition

Do not confuse repetition in the landscape with monotony. Like a theme repeated in music, repetition is not only more subtle than monotony but it contributes to unity and simplicity. For example, consider the use of curves in the landscape design. Curves may begin in bed lines in the front yard, continue in the side yard, and be picked up once more in the backyard. Alternatively, the repeated use of right angles on a grid design can be used successfully to achieve unity in the landscape. The right angles may begin in the front yard, perhaps on the sidewalk, then be used in the bed lines which go around the property, and be picked up again in the backyard. By subtly repeating such design elements as bed lines in the yard, one can achieve a continuity or flow to the entire landscape.

Harmony

Harmony is achieved through a pleasing arrangement of parts. Where more than one plant community or style is used, transitions should be defined.

Accent

Accent—also referred to as dominance, focalization, or climax—is important in the total picture. Without accent, a design may be dull or static. Various parts, if skillfully organized, lead the eye toward the focal point. Accent can be used to increase the feeling of space. Accents may be a garden accessory, plant specimen, plant composition, or a water feature. Emphasis may also be obtained through the use of contrasting textures, color, or form or by highlighting portions of a plant composition with garden lights. Boulders are often used as accents, but they should not be overused. To look natural, boulders should be partly buried. Note also that water does not spring from the highest point of land in nature, so recirculating streams should have their source below the grade of other landscape features.

Space Dividers, Accents, and Transitions

Space dividers, accents, and transitions are three elements present in all successful landscape compositions. They provide an easy method of combining plant and architectural characteristics.

Space dividers such as fences, walls, plants as hedges, or plants as borders define or give privacy to spaces, create the background for outdoor living activities, and create dominance. Overuse of dividers makes space seem smaller because the view is blocked. Accents should be minority elements of the composition and should create interest via contrasting characteristics. Like sculpture, they may be displayed in two ways: hidden in niches within the space dividers or standing free within the area created by the space dividers. Container plants on a patio may fulfill this role.

Transitions form the connecting link between space dividers, accents, or horizontal and vertical surfaces, such as those between the house and the land. For example, if a foundation planting is used, it is most effective 3 to 4 feet (0.9 to 1.2 m) from the upright wall.

Dominance and Contrast

In any composition, a majority of dominant or repeated characteristics are accented by a minority of contrasting characteristics. The magnitude of contrast refers to the degree of change between visual characteristics, such as plant type, height, form, color, and texture.

An example of a plant composition containing a strong contrast of space dividers, transitions, and accents is described as follows: A space divider is formed by a grouping of redwoods and eldarica pines (all narrow-leaf evergreen trees), an accent by a massing of crape myrtles (flowering deciduous trees), and a transition by a massing of blue fescue. Four elements create the contrast between the space dividers and the accents:

Tree types: Needle evergreen and deciduous.

- Form: Evergreens are strongly upright compared to the rounded crape myrtles.

- Height: The evergreens grow to at least 30 feet (9 m), whereas the crape myrtles grow to about 15 feet (4.5 m).

- Color. Crape myrtles have bright, almost fluorescent summer flowers and the needle evergreens form a fine-textured green backdrop.

Irrigation Design

Irrigation is a vital part of most California landscapes. It can seem very complicated, but it need not be for residential installation. Components are commonly available and easy to install. For a detailed discussion of irrigation, see chapter 4, "Water Management."

What Is "Xeriscape"?

A registered trademark of the National Xeriscape Council, the term *xeriscape* may be defined as horticulture that emphasizes water conservation. Derived from the Greek word *xeros,* which means dry, xeriscape uses specific landscape design elements and management practices to achieve the goal of water conservation. Xeriscape may also encompass other goals, such as creating habitat, using native plants, responding to the local environment, and using inspiration and materials from the regional landscape. Xeriscape does not preclude using high-water-use plant materials as design elements, but it limits their use in concert with the water conservation objective and stresses their relationship to the overall design. Xeriscape makes good economic and ecological sense, considering California's limited water supply. About 25 to 30 percent of the water consumed in urban areas of the state is used for landscape irrigation. A properly designed and installed xeriscape can reduce net energy consumption by providing shade in summer and allowing the sun to warm dwellings in winter. If properly executed, xeriscapes can be less costly but just as beautiful as traditional landscapes.

Xeriscapes follow ten common principles.

- Group plants according to their requirements for sun and water, for example, ferns with baby's tears and rockrose with rosemary.

- Zone irrigation systems to match plant requirements. For example, shrubs may need water only once per week. Flowers may require water once per day. Separate irrigation lines can be programmed to meet differences in frequency and duration.

- Adjust irrigation frequency and/or duration at least four times a year. Water-use rates in the landscape vary greatly from season to season. During winter months, no irrigation may be needed. Many landscape areas are overirrigated, which encourages weed and disease problems, in addition to wasting water.

- Design irrigation systems to emphasize uniformity, especially on turf areas. The delivery system is appropriate for the type of plant material being irrigated, with drip irrigation a practical alternative in many situations.

- Use turf for function more than appearance. Other plant materials can substitute for turf where frequent foot traffic or play does not occur. If properly selected and managed, turf can be a water-thrifty plant material. Warm-season grasses are preferred in warmer areas of the state because they offer as much as 50 percent water savings during the growing season over cool-season grasses. However, many homeowners in Southern California still choose cool-season grasses because they remain green year-round.

- Use islands of intensely managed and irrigated plantings for accent. A tasteful grouping of plants can make a strong statement with much less water than rambling shrubs or turf.

- Use plants in climatic conditions to which they are well adapted. Mediterranean-climate plants are suited to much of California. California natives may be used, but not all of them are drought-tolerant. Xeriscape is not limited to natives, and plants requiring high moisture or humidity can be used in suitable microenvironments.

- Include hardscape design elements, such as patios and decks, in the landscape design. They enhance the outdoor environment, require no water, and can provide additional color through the use of container plants.

- A good xeriscape is economical. Monthly water bills reflect the water savings that can result when water use is reduced. Appropriate xeriscape plant materials are available in the trade at no greater cost than plants that demand more water. Fewer pest problems may occur when plants adapted to the site are grown. Precise application of water limits weed growth and plant diseases.

- A good xeriscape combines function and beauty. Crushed gravel from the street to the front door is not California xeriscape. Variations in plant and landscape color, texture, and form are part of a professional xeriscape design.

Drawing a Landscape Plan

Drawing a landscape plan on paper is highly recommended, even if it is not detailed, because it provides a road map to follow as the project is completed. A written plan facilitates moving forward in an orderly fashion without wasting resources. An easy way to develop ideas is to prepare a map of existing features and then sketch on tracing paper overlays. Computer software packages are also available to assist in this process. The following section provides the information necessary to draw a landscape plan that embodies the elements of good design. Completing these steps enables you to develop a final plan that can be implemented over several years as time and money permit.

Step 1: Prepare the Baseline Map
When analyzing the site, prepare a map to scale of the home grounds (fig. 20.1). Use graph paper and let one square equal a given number of feet or draw to scale using a ruler or an architect's scale. The map should include the following elements:

- property lines
- undesirable features of home grounds or adjoining property
- north point
- views (point arrows in the direction of each good view)
- house, garage, other buildings
- existing trees, rock outcroppings
- existing walks and driveways
- contour of the land (use an arrow to show the direction of surface water flow)

Figure 20.1

Figure 20.1. A sample baseline map. This map is a scale drawing showing the exact location and orientation of every major plant, structural feature, sun and wind patterns, views, slopes, and drainage characteristics, plus other essential data. This base map becomes the foundation on which the final landscape plan is built. *Source:* After *Sunset Landscaping Illustrated* 1985, p. 35.

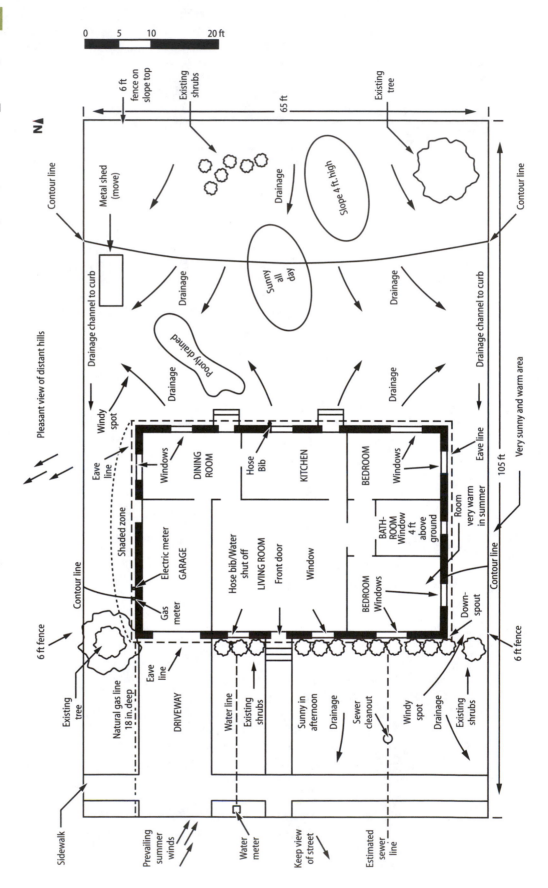

- scale used
- location of septic tank or sewer lines
- location of utility lines and easements

Although accidentally cutting through a gas line with a shovel may be exciting, it is less thrilling to pay the repair cost. If you do not know where underground utilities are located, call the utility company and ask for the locator service. Just because you see where gas, telephone, and electric lines enter a building is no guarantee those utilities run in a straight line to the street. They may circle the house. In older neighborhoods, lines may not be in a common trench.

Step 2: Decide Usage Options for the Landscape

Listed below are usage options most often included in the final development. Make a list that suits your individual needs.

- front lawn area or public area
- outdoor living room or private area
- laundry, service, and storage area
- children's play area
- vegetable garden
- small fruits (berries, grapes, etc.)
- cooking and eating area
- driveway
- garden pools
- guest parking
- walks
- turnabouts
- flower beds
- garage
- spa
- swimming pool
- fruit trees
- other items particular to your needs

Step 3: Place Use Areas on the Map

Place the use areas on the map (fig. 20.2). You may use tracing paper over the base map to sketch ideas. Fit them together with two considerations: traffic flow and use. How will people move from one area to another or from the house to an outside area? Will movement be comfortable? Will the outdoor area be functional in relation to the house? Will it make use of existing features, such as views or

changes in the terrain? Try different combinations in relation to rooms of the house, surrounding areas, and potential views.

Step 4: Develop the Landscape Plan

Design driveways, parking areas, walks, and other paved areas. Indicate where plant masses are needed for separating areas, screening undesirable views, providing shade, windbreaks, and beauty (see fig. 20.2). Do not attempt at this point to name the trees and shrubs, but think in terms of how plant masses will serve a purpose and help tie the various areas together into a unified plan. Consider the design elements discussed previously and then consider the mature height, width, and function of the plant.

In preparing the plan, use landscape symbols to indicate trees and shrub masses. Draw symbols to scale to represent the actual amount of space that will be involved. For example, a Japanese black pine tree at maturity will have a spread of approximately 15 feet (4.5 m); make the scale diameter of the symbol in this case 15 feet (4.5 m). Indicate on the map where paving, plants, and structures will be. Check to see if the proposed scheme is practical and if you can answer the following questions satisfactorily.

- Is the driveway design safe, useful, and pleasing? Have a safe entrance, turnabout, and guest parking been provided for? Will guests use the front door? Will the proposed drive be too steep?

- Are the walks convenient?

- Will the view be attractive from the living room, French doors, patio, or dining room?

- Has a private, outdoor living area been provided, and is it screened from neighbors, the service area, and other buildings?

- Is the clothes line close to the laundry?

- Do all the parts fit together into a unified plan?

- Have a good setting, background, and privacy been provided?

- Have local ordinances been checked?

Figure 20.2

Figure 20.2. A sample final plan. Shown is one possible design developed from the base map in figure 20.1. *Source:* After *Sunset Landscaping Illustrated* 1985, p. 43

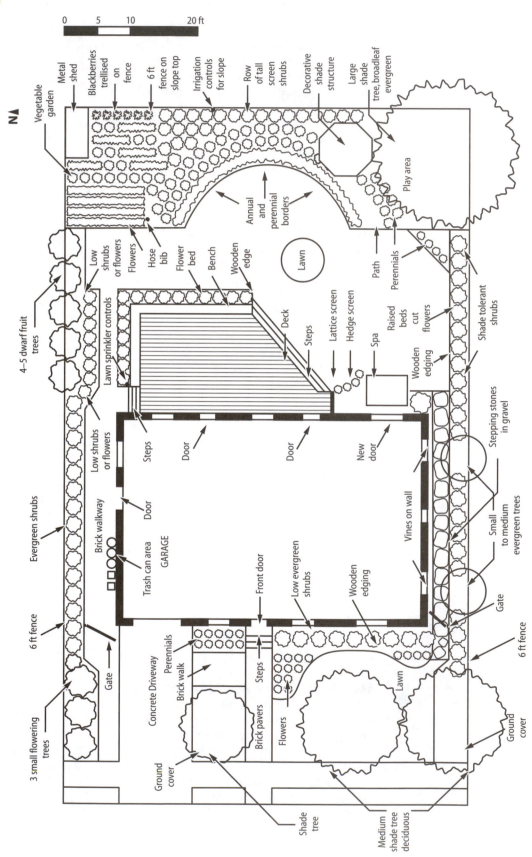

0 5 10 20 ft

N

Metal shed

Vegetable garden

Blackberries trellised on fence

6 ft fence on slope top

Irrigation controls for slope

Row of tall screen shrubs

Decorative shade structure

Large shade tree

Large broadleaf evergreen

Play area

Annual and perennial borders

Low shrubs or flowers

Flowers

Hose bib

Flower bed

Bench

Wooden edge

Lawn

Path

Perennials

Perennials

Shade tolerant shrubs

4–5 dwarf fruit trees

Lawn sprinkler controls

Deck

Steps

Lattice screen

Hedge screen

Spa

Raised beds cut flowers

Wooden edging

Low shrubs or flowers

Steps

Door

Door

New door

Stepping stones in gravel

Evergreen shrubs

Brick walkway

Door

Trash can area

GARAGE

Front door

Low evergreen shrubs

Vines on wall

Wooden edging

Small to medium evergreen trees

Gate

6 ft fence

Gate

6 ft fence

Concrete Driveway

Perennials

Brick walk

Ground cover

Brick pavers

Steps

Flowers

Lawn

Ground cover

3 small flowering trees

Shade tree

Medium shade tree deciduous

- Have underground obstacles, such as septic tanks, or overhead obstacles, such as utility lines, been taken into account? Are trees placed accordingly?

Step 5: Create General and Specific Planting Plans

On the map developed in step 4, designate specific plantings. For each tree or shrub mass on the plan, make a set of specifications, which include the following:

- Height: low, medium, tall

- Form: spreading, upright, arching, globe

- Purpose: shade, background, hedge, screen, accent, mass

- Seasonal interest: fruit, flowers, foliage

- Type: evergreen, broadleaf evergreen, deciduous

- Maintenance: subject to insects or plant diseases

- Cultural needs: shade, sunlight, moisture requirements

Then, select a plant or group of plants to meet the specifications. Reviewing the information in the next section of this chapter may help. In addition, consult garden books, nursery catalogs, or visit a local nursery. Become familiar with plant material and discuss your planned needs with nursery staff.

Selection of Plant Materials in Landscape Design

Well-chosen plants are necessary to achieve the desired landscape effect, and hundreds of varieties of trees, shrubs, vines, and perennials are available. Plants are not merely ornamental accessories. They make up masses and define space in the yard and, consequently, create the silhouettes that produce the garden design. When selecting plants, consider their form, color, texture, seasonality, and overall aesthetic value.

Cultural Considerations in Selecting Plants

Adaptation refers to a plant's suitability for use in a particular climate, ability to grow during local winter and summer seasons, longevity or permanence, likely pest problems, and need for extra maintenance. If you cannot grow the plant species desired, consider creating an appropriate microclimate that will allow its use. Soil and moisture conditions are important components of the plant's environment. Some respond unfavorably when a change occurs in this environment. For example, some plants can tolerate extremely dry or wet conditions, while others cannot. The intensity of sun or degree of shade within a site will dictate where certain species can be located in the landscape. Some plants cannot tolerate full sun, while others require full sun for best display.

Maintenance. In selecting plant materials, consider how much maintenance the plant will require. Choose trees and shrubs that tend to be resistant to diseases and pests. The mature size of a plant should also be considered. A common mistake is selecting plants that soon become too large for their location.

Aesthetics. The aesthetic value of a plant includes its texture, color or foliage, flowers, fruit, and bark. Select colors compatible with the house interior or exterior, especially if the plant is used close to the house. Strongly contrasting textures can create interesting effects. The texture of plant materials depends on the size and disposition of the foliage. Plants with large stems or large leaves that are widely spaced have coarse texture; plants with visible small twigs or small closely spaced leaves have fine texture. Texture can vary on a seasonal basis, depending on whether the plant is deciduous or evergreen.

Color. Green is the basic color of most plant materials in the landscape. Desirable variety may be secured by using plants with lighter or darker foliage tones. Accents may be introduced by the selection of plants with colored foliage, attractive flowers, or colorful, persistent fruit. Many California landscapes are much brighter than their eastern counterparts because the plant species available offer vibrant colors, such as pink ice plant or flaming bougainvillea. Color may have seasonal variation, depending on the plants chosen. Good designers create landscapes with attractive color year-round.

Color is especially important when planning flower gardens. Mixed colors tend to keep people moving. Massed single colors attract attention and act as focal points or accents. White and gray tend to act as unifiers by tying other colors together. Gray can be used for softening or for accent. Color has significant effect on space perception and perspective, as discussed earlier in the chapter.

Shrubs and Trees. Planting several shrubs of one species or color, rather than a hodge-podge of the many shrubs you like, will unify the landscape theme. Trees and shrubs used in landscaping develop many distinct forms. The more common forms are: prostrate or spreading, round or oval, vase, pyramidal, and columnar. The form of mature shrubs and trees usually is more open and spreading than that of young plants. For example, the head of a young oak tree may be pyramidal in shape; during middle age the head is an irregular oval; and during old age a large, massive oak may have a spreading vase form. Listed below are examples of some common shrub forms.

- Low-spreading: prostrate rosemary
- Round or upright: the majority of shrubs, including pittosporum and nandina
- Vase: *Spiraea vanhouttei*
- Pyramidal: arborvitae
- Columnar: junipers

Trees are long-lived and relatively inexpensive in initial cost and maintenance compared to lawns, flower beds, and many other features of the design. In the past, many builders have committed costly errors by destroying trees in establishing new residential subdivisions. Most real estate developers now appreciate the value of trees and attempt to save them when land is graded prior to the construction of houses. Regardless of your affection for trees, it must be understood that they do not live forever. Old and improperly located trees should be removed and new more suitable specimens should be planted.

Large shade trees should be planted first, since they are such striking landscape design elements. Smaller understory trees should be planted next. Trees typically grow from 15 to 60 feet (4.5 to 18 m) tall, depending on the species, and commonly have only one main stem or trunk, although some species are available and attractive with multiple trunks

(e.g., birch, orchid tree, some palms). The canopy of the tree develops a typical form:

- Round or oval: most common trees, including maple, oak, and Aleppo pine
- Vase: American elm
- Pendulous or weeping: willow, birch, bottlebrush
- Pyramidal: spruce, fir
- Columnar: Italian cypress

Turf and Ground Covers. Ground covers such as turf, low-spreading shrubs, creeping plants, and prostrate vines are essential materials in landscaping. The principal use of turf is for the lawn area. Other ground cover plants are commonly used as transitions or in lieu of turf on slopes too rough or steep to mow or under trees where grass will not grow satisfactorily. Ground cover areas may require high maintenance.

For more specific details on landscape plant selection, see chapter 12, "Lawns," and chapter 13, "Woody Landscape Plants," and consult references in the bibliography.

Resources

A number of professionals are available to help you with landscape design, if you think you would prefer to work with someone in executing your plans. *Landscape architects* are licensed professionals trained to design commercial and residential landscapes. Although many homeowners may not be able to afford their professional services, Master Gardeners should contact local landscape architects for advice and support. They can be found by looking under landscape architects in telephone yellow pages or by contacting the local chapter of the American Society of Landscape Architects (ASLA). *Landscape contractors* are licensed and trained to install landscapes, plantings, paving, and irrigation systems. They are also trained to interpret and implement the plans of a landscape architect. Some landscape contractors offer design services in the total price for materials and installation. Persons who call themselves *landscape designers* are usually unlicensed and vary in educational background. Some retail nurseries offer design services as part of the incentive to purchase plant materials from them. Before hiring a person who claims to be a licensed professional, verify that the license is current with the appropriate state agency and check that other consumers have not filed complaints. Get competing bids and ask to see a landscaping project in your area that the licensed professional has recently completed.

Additional resources include local public gardens and arboreta, which offer garden design ideas, such as demonstration gardens; nurseries that offer design services; and schools of landscape architecture, whose students often provide design consultation. Universities and colleges in California with landscape architecture programs include UC Davis, UC Berkeley, Cal Poly Pomona, and Cal Poly San Luis Obispo.

Excellent publications listed in the bibliography along with computer software programs are available to supplement the concepts you have learned in this chapter.

Bibliography

Brenzel, K. N., ed. 2001. Sunset western garden book. Menlo Park: Sunset Publishing.

Brookes, J. 1991. The book of garden design. New York: Macmillan.

Clouston, B., ed. 1979. Landscape design with plants. New York: Van Nostrand Reinhold.

Francis, M., and R. T. Hester Jr., eds. 1990. The meaning of gardens: Idea, place, and action. Cambridge, MA: MIT Press.

Hayes, J., ed. 1972. Landscape for living; The 1972 yearbook of agriculture. Washington, D.C.: U.S. Department of Agriculture.

Motloch, J. 1991. Introduction to landscape design. New York: Van Nostrand Reinhold.

Roth, S.A. 1991. The weekend garden guide: Work-saving ways to a beautiful backyard. Emmaus, PA: Rodale Press.

Smith, K. 1978. Western home landscaping. Los Angeles: HP Books.

Sunset landscaping illustrated. 1985. Menlo Park, CA: Sunset Publishing.

Welsh, D. F., and W. C. Welch. 1989. Landscape

21

Poisonous Plants

Allison M. Beale

LEARNING OBJECTIVES

- Develop a general understanding of how to prevent poisoning from common toxin-containing plants in the home and garden.

- Learn the importance of identifying the plants in the home and garden that contain toxins. Learn how to compile a plant identification file. Learn that common trees, shrubs, vegetables, weeds, flowers, and holiday plants may contain toxins in various plant parts.

- Learn about health symptoms associated with plants that contain toxins.

- Learn basic information about the common types of skin injury that plants can cause (mechanical, primary contact dermatitis, allergic contact dermatitis, and photosensitization dermatitis).

Poisonous Plants

Although many plants contain significant amounts of natural toxins to some extent, this does not mean that plants should be eliminated from the home and garden. It just means that homeowners should be prepared to identify any plant on their property and have some knowledge of adverse symptoms associated with poisonous plants. Some of the most beautiful trees, shrubs, vegetables, and vines are poisonous. They may provide shade, colorful flowers, or food, but parts of the plant (sap, leaves, seeds, flowers, stems) may also cause skin rashes, serious illness, or death. More than 500 species of poisonous plants grow in the United States. Skin rashes are the most common health complaints that arise from handling poisonous plants, but fatalities can occur when toxin-containing plants or plant parts are ingested. Children are usually more susceptible to the effects of plant poison than adults. Thus, it is critical to watch them when they are playing if there are any poisonous plants in the home or garden, and it is critical to teach children that certain plants are beautiful but dangerous and should not be eaten. Children should be told not to eat seeds, berries, or leaves from any plant. Do not assume a plant is nontoxic because birds or wildlife can consume it without harmful effects. Do not use twigs as sticks for roasting hot dogs. The twigs may contain toxins that cooking will not destroy.

This chapter describes typical adverse symptoms and health effects that selected common poisonous plants and plant parts can cause. The chapter also includes tables of poisonous plants commonly found around the home and garden and explains how to compile a plant identification file. The tables in this chapter are categorized by plant type (e.g., tree, vegetable, weed) and, for most plants, include toxicity information: the name of the toxin, which part of the plant contains the toxin, and which part(s) of the body is (are) affected by the toxin. Pay close attention to the plants listed in the tables in this chapter whose toxins adversely affect the heart. Plants associated with poisonings and other health problems that are frequently reported to the Poison Control Center in Sacramento, California, which is linked with the UC Davis Medical Center, are listed. Plant species that can cause dermatitis (an inflammation or swelling of the skin) or some form of poisoning, as reported by other reliable sources, are also included. Sources used in compiling this information include Poison Control Center data, textbooks, scientific journal articles, field guides, and personal communications with specialists in the areas of toxicology and botany. A short bibliography at the end of the chapter provides reference materials.

Plant poisoning can be prevented. If you spend some time studying the plants in your house and garden and develop the plant identification file described below, you will know which plants are poisonous. If you employ practical precautionary measures, such as storing bulbs and seeds where children cannot reach them and teaching children about poisonous plants, you can prevent problems.

Be prepared for an emergency by keeping an ounce or more of syrup of ipecac on hand. The signs of poisoning may not appear for as long as 6 to 15 hours after tasting, chewing, or swallowing poisonous plant parts. If you suspect that someone has been poisoned by a plant, telephone your doctor immediately or, if the doctor is not available, call the local Poison Control Center. The information you provide about the plant that was consumed will help a health professional determine the proper treatment. If you are advised to go to the hospital, take a sample of the poisonous plant with you, if possible.

Some of the most poisonous plants also can be sources of valuable pharmaceuticals. For example, digitalis, which is derived from the leaves and seeds of foxglove (*Digitalis purpurea*), can strengthen the heartbeat of an ill person, but unless a doctor prescribes the proper dosage, consumption can be fatal. Children have been poisoned by swallowing foxglove seeds and sucking on foxglove flowers, which contain toxins known as cardiac glycosides.

Keeping Plant Identification Records

Plant poisonings account for the bulk of the emergency telephone calls to the Regional Poison Control Center at the UC Davis Medical Center in Sacramento. The majority of the victims are under six years of age. If you have small children or pets, you should keep a list of the plants you have in and around your home. When you have compiled your plant identification records, you will be better prepared if a poisoning emergency occurs.

- Create a file called "Plants: Identification." Keep it with your important papers or as part of your home maintenance files or store it in your computer. Enter the telephone number of your nearest Poison Control Center in your file and in the front cover of your telephone book. Check your local telephone directory for the location and telephone number of the Poison Control Center nearest you. Keep it updated.

- Keep identification tags from the plants you buy, and put them directly into your plant identification file.

- To identify plants already in your home or garden, consult resources, such as the *Sunset Western Garden Book* (Brenzel 2001) or *Poisonous plants of California* (Fuller and McClintock 1986). Contact a California Certified Nurseryman (CCNPro) or contact your local UC Cooperative Extension county office for help in identifying your plants. Specimens may be useful.

- Once the plants have been identified, take pictures or slides of them. Use a flash both indoors and out to fill in shadows. The best outdoor light for taking identification photographs and slides occurs early in the morning, late in the afternoon, or on cloudy days. Use an indelible marker to write the names of the plants on the back of the photos or on the cardboard frame of the slides. Assemble the photos or slides in your plant identification file. Make sure to let baby sitters or pet sitters know about the file and its location.

Plants That Injure the Skin

The most common injury following an exposure to a toxic plant is dermatitis, an inflammation or swelling of the skin accompanied by redness, itching, and tenderness to touch. In addition to several types of dermatitis, there are several other kinds of injury to the skin that contact with plants can cause. The following paragraphs describe these types of dermatitis and injuries and the common plants that cause them.

Mechanical Injury

When thorns, needles, spines or other bits of plant material become embedded in the skin, chronic irritation may result if the material is not removed promptly. A simple way to remove the hairlike thorns common on cacti is to apply a thin layer of white (Elmer's) glue over the thorns. Allow the glue to dry, and then apply a piece of masking or electrician's tape over the glue. Remove the thorns by quickly peeling off the tape-glue plaster.

Thorns that embed deeply in the skin near joints may cause painful, inflamed joints similar to chronic arthritis. If they embed near bones, they may cause a granulation reaction in which the body walls off the thorn in solid, tough tissue that may resemble a tumor (bulla). The granulation reaction may also occur even if the thorn is not near bone, but it is less common.

Plants commonly associated with mechanical injury include:

- agave
- blackberry (*Rubus* spp.)
- cacti
- citrus
- some *Melaleauca* spp.
- some palms
- roses (*Rosa* spp.)
- sweet hakea (*Hakea sauveolens*)

Primary Irritant or Contact Dermatitis

Irritant dermatitis is caused by caustic or irritating substances produced by plants that come in contact with or injure the skin, resulting in nonallergic, inflammatory skin reactions or rash. Not everyone will develop an allergy, but no one is safe from an irritant. If enough of the material contacts the skin, a rash will develop.

Irritant dermatitis is a very common complaint with plants in the *Arum* family, which includes such common house plants as dieffenbachia, philodendron, and pothos. All of these plants have special cells that contain oxalic acid crystals. The cells contract when mechanically stimulated (when a leaf is brushed, grabbed, broken, or bent) and eject the crystals. The force is sufficient to embed the crystals in the skin or whatever surface is in contact with the plant. Oxalic acid is extremely irritating. Small children and pets who taste these house plants may end up with severe swelling of the tongue, lips, and throat. Injury may extend to the stomach and bowel if enough of the plant is consumed.

Plants commonly associated with irritant dermatitis include:

- arum family (dieffenbachias, philodendrons, pothos, caladium)
- many bulbs (tulips, daffodils, hyacinths, buttercups, narcissus)
- carrot
- castor beans
- celery
- century plant (*Agave parryi*)
- cowslip
- cucumber
- *Ficus* spp. (fig, rubber tree)
- foxglove
- milkweed
- mushrooms
- parsley
- parsnip
- pencil tree (*Euphorbia tirucalli*)
- poinsettia (*Euphorbia pulcherrima*)
- tomato
- turnip

Allergic Contact Dermatitis (ACD)

Allergic contact dermatitis differs from irritant contact dermatitis in that only sensitized individuals (allergic individuals) will respond to contact with the plant material, which is known as the allergen. It is very rare for allergic individuals to respond the first time they are exposed to an allergen. The first encounter sensitizes the allergic individual, resulting in the production of white blood cells that recognize the allergen. Usually, the second and subsequent encounters with the allergen stimulate the allergic response. In the skin, allergic contact dermatitis (ACD) usually results in redness, itching, and the development of small blisters (vesicles), but may become so severe that large fluid-filled bullae form. As with irritant dermatitis, injury is localized, limited to the skin area exposed to the chemical or plant material.

Often, people exposed to plant allergens will use topical anesthetics (containing benzocaine, dicucaine, or other chemicals ending in the "-caine" suffix) and will develop an ACD reaction to the medication in addition to the primary ACD reaction. Sensitive persons may experience allergic reactions to topical antibiotics (neomycin and streptomycin), topical antihistamines (diphenhydramine and promethazine), and topical mercury compounds (mercurochrome and merthiolate) (Zamula 1990). Nickel is the most common metallic sensitizer; it causes more ACD problems than all other metals combined (Zamula 1990).

Plants commonly associated with allergic contact dermatitis include:

- asters
- birch (Birch pollen can cross-sensitize people to apples, carrots, and celery.)
- bulbs (tulip, narcissus)
- carrots
- castor beans
- cedar trees
- celery
- chrysanthemums
- English ivy
- garlic
- geraniums
- ginger
- ginkgo (female trees only; fruit of *Ginkgo biloba*)
- lichens
- liverwort
- magnolias
- oleanders
- onions
- philodendrons

- pine trees
- primrose
- *Rhus* spp. (poison oak, ivy, sumac)
- sawdust from various trees, includine tulip tree (*Liriodendron tulipifera*), Grecian laurel (*Laurus nobilis*), Brazilian pepper (*Schinus terebinthifolius*), and silk oak (*Grevillea robusta*).
- smoke tree (*Cotinus coggygrra*)

Photosensitization Dermatitis. Two types of photosensitization dermatitis occur. Both forms are special cases of ACD in which sunlight is required to cause injury. The first type of photosensitization dermatitis occurs primarily in livestock animals and results from their grazing on forages that produce chemicals capable of injuring the skin when activated by sunlight. The second type of photosensitization dermatitis is more common in humans. After recovery from photosensitization dermatitis, the skin will be darkened permanently as a result of hyperpigmentation caused by derivatives of the toxins (furocoumarins) produced by these plants. Furocoumarins are used in medicine to treat people who have abnormally light pigmentation in their skin (hypopigmentation).

Plants associated with livestock photosensitization dermatitis reactions include:

- blue-green algae
- kochia (*Scoparia trichophylla*) (burning bush, Mexican fire bush)
- *Lantana* spp.
- lecheguilla
- *Tetradymia* spp. (horsebrush) eaten with *Artemesia* (sagebrush)
- *Tribulus terrestris* (goatshead)

Plants associated with human photosensitization dermatitis reactions include:

- buttercup
- carrots
- celery (with pink rot)
- dill
- figs
- Klamath weed
- lime (and other citrus rinds)
- mustard
- parsley

Flowers and Holiday Plants That Contain Toxins

Numerous poisonous flowering plants occur worldwide, and some are found in California homes and gardens (table 21.1). Some of these plants, such as foxglove, have been used for centuries in both medicine and mayhem. Most of these very toxic plants also taste very bitter, reducing the risk of poisoning. Even so, the best prevention for plant poisonings is to teach children not to touch these plants, put any of the plant parts (seeds, leaves, sap, stems, flowers, etc.) in their mouths, or make a tea from them. If you can, limit their access to these plants. The toxicity of these plants should be taken seriously.

A number of plants could have been listed in table 21.1 that are included instead in table 21.2. Azaleas (*Rhododendron* spp.), yellow jessamine (*Carolina jessamine*), and mornin glories are listed as poisonous shrubs and vines. Hydrangeas and lantana appear on both lists, but the overlap could have been much broader.

Common Flowers That Contain Toxins

Lily-of-the-Valley (*Convallaria majalis*)
Fragrant, spring-blooming perennial herb with bell-shaped white flowers. Good ground cover in partial shade. Fruit is a red-orange berry. Leaves, flowers, berries, and rootstocks are well-known for containing the toxic cardiac glycosides convallarin and convallamarin. Signs of poisoning include an irregular heartbeat and irregular pulse accompanied by digestive upset. Consumption of large amounts of the toxin lead to mental confusion, weakness, depression, collapse of circulation, and death. Reaction is similar to that of digitalis in foxglove.

Foxglove (*Digitalis purpurea*)
Biennial garden herb that grows 2 to 5 feet (0.6 to 1.5 m) tall. Tubular purple or white-lavender flowers. Rosettelike leaves are one of the sources of the drug digitalis, a cardiac gly-

Table 21.1

FLOWERS AND HOLIDAY PLANTS THAT CONTAIN TOXINS

Common name	Scientific name	Toxic part*	Toxin†	Effect‡
amaryllis	*Hippeastrum* spp.	UP	—	GI
anemones (pasque flower)	*Anemone tuberosa* (*A. patens*)	WP, FL	—	GI, SK
autumn crocus (meadow saffron, naked ladies)	*Colchicum autumnale*	WP	COL	GI
azaleas	*Rhododendeon* spp.	WP	CT, R	CV, GI
belladonna lily (naked lady, pink lady, resurrection lily)	*Amaryllis belladonna*	UP	A	NS, RP
bleeding heart	*Dicentra* spp.	LF, UP	A	NS
blue weed	*Echium vulgare*	LF, ST	—	SK
buttercup	*Ranunculus* spp.	WP	G	GI, SK
caladium	*Caladium bicolor*	WP	OX	GI, SK
calla lily	*Zantedeschia* spp.	WP	OX	GI, SK
carnation	*Dianthus* spp.	AG	—	GI, SK
chrysanthemum	*Chrysanthemum* spp.	AG	PN	SK
clematis (virgin's bower)	*Clematis* spp.	WP	G, O	GI, SK
climbing lily	*Gloriosa* spp.	WP	A	NS
crynum lily	*Crinum asisticum*	UP	A	GI
cyclamen	*Cyclamen purpurascens*	WP	G	GI
daffodil	*Narcissus pseudonarcissus*	UP	OX	mild GI
delphinium (larkspur)	*Delphinium* spp.	WP, SC	A, CT	GI, NS
euphorbia (snow-on-the-mountain, crown of thorns)	*Euphorbia* spp.	SP	—	SK
flaming flower	*Anthurium* spp.	WP	OX	GI, SK
four-o'-clock (marvel of Peru)	*Mirabilis jalapa*	SD	weak A	GI
foxglove	*Digitalis purpurea*	WP	CARD	severe CV
hellbore (Christmas rose)	*Helleborus* spp.	WP	G	GI, SK
hyacinth	*Hyacinthus orientalis*	UP	OX	GI, SK
hydrangeas	*Hydrangea* spp.	WP	CG	ETS, GI
impatiens	*Impatiens* spp.	WP	—	
iris	*Iris* spp.	LF, UP	CG	ETS
jack-in-the-pulpit	*Arisaema triphyllum*	WP	OX	GI, SK
lady's slipper orchid	*Cypripedium* spp.	LF, ST	—	SK
lantana	*Lantana camara*	WP	—	GI, CV
lily-of-the-valley	*Convallaria majalis*	WP	CARD	severe CV
lobelia	*Lobelia* spp.	WP	—	SK
lords and ladies	*Arum maculatum*	WP	OX	GI, SK
mistletoe	*Phoradendron* spp., *Viscum album*	WP	P	CV, GI
moonflower	*Ipomea alba*	SD	—	—
narcissus	*Narcissus tazetta*	UP	—	GI, NS, SK
nicotiana	*Nicotiana* spp.	WP	A	NS
pheasant's eye	*Adonis* spp.	LF, ST	G	GI
poinsettia	*Euphorbia pulcherrima*	SP	PH	SK, GI
poppy	*Eschscholtzia mexicana; Papaver somniferum* (opium poppy)	FR	NAR	NS, GI
primrose	*Primula* spp.	WP	—	SK
spider lily	*Hymenocallis aviaricana*	—	—	—
star-of-bethlehem	*Ornithogalum* spp.	WP	CARD, strong CT	CV, GI
sweet pea	*Lathyrus odoratus* spp.	WP	P	NS
tulip	*Tulipa* spp.	UP	OX	GI, SK
zephyr lily	*Zephyranthes* spp.	LF, UP	OX	GI

Notes:

—: Information on the toxic part, toxin, or effect could not be found or is unknown.

*Toxic parts: AG = aboveground parts; FL = flower; FR = fruit; LF = leaf; SD = seed; SP = sap; ST = stem; UP = underground parts; WP = whole plant.

†Toxins: A = alkaloid; CARD = cardiac glycoside; CG = cyanogenic glycoside; COL = colchicine; CT = cardiotoxin; G = glycoside; NAR = narcotic; O = oil; OX = oxalate; P = proteins or amino acids; PH = phorbol; R = resin.

‡Effect (organ system[s] affected): CAR = carcinogen; CV = cardiovascular; ETS = cell respiration, electron transport system; GI = gastrointestinal; NS = nervous system; RP = respiratory paralysis; SK = skin.

coside, which is used to stimulate a weakened heart. Eating fresh or dried leaves and swallowing seeds can cause poisoning and death. Children have been poisoned by sucking on foxglove flowers and swallowing the seeds. Signs of poisoning include digestive upset, bloody diarrhea, severe headache, mental confusion, blurred vision, trembling, lack of appetite. After ingesting large amounts, symptoms include irregular heartbeat and pulse, convulsions, and death.

Lantana (*Lantana* spp.)

Both the foliage and ripe berries of lantana contain toxins. Unripe, green berries contain the highest concentration of toxin. Symptoms of poisoning appear within a day of consuming poisonous plant parts. Symptoms include severe stomach and intestinal upset, rapid heartbeat, sensitivity to sunlight, and difficulty in breathing. Kidneys are affected. If vessels carrying blood to the heart collapse, death follows quickly.

Lady's Slipper Orchid (*Cypripedium* spp.)

This beautiful orchid has blooms in shades of white, yellow, crimson-pink, or purplish-brown. Flowers have pouchlike lip. Toxin contained in the stems and leaves frequently causes contact dermatitis. Depending on the susceptibility of the individual, the skin irritation may be minor or it may be a painful inflammation with blisters that lasts for days or weeks.

Hydrangea (*Hydrangea macrophylla*)

Deciduous shrub or vine with bold pink, white, or blue dense, globe-shaped flower clusters. Very poisonous, because of cyanide compounds in leaves and branches (stems). Buds also contain cyanide. Hydrangea buds added to a salad are said to have poisoned a family in Florida. Signs of poisoning include severe digestive upset and bloody diarrhea, rapid heartbeat, nervous excitement, staggering, convulsions, and death. There are numerous cultivated varieties and wild species.

Weeds, Wildflowers, and Miscellaneous Plants That Contain Toxins

Of all plant catagories covered in this chapter, weeds are responsible for most of the deaths resulting from poisonous plant ingestion, especially among livestock. Most weeds have a variety of defense mechanisms, including very poisonous natural toxins, many of which are alkaloids (see table 21.2). Alkaloids can be excreted in milk. Poisonings have occurred when livestock owners have consumed milk from livestock that have grazed on weeds containing alkaloids, such as lupine.

Jimsonweed (*Datura* spp.)

Believed to be of North American origin, this weed is found in foothills, dry pastures, and vacant city lots all over the country. Grows to 5 feet (1.5 m) high and has trumpetlike white or pale violet flowers with coarsely toothed leaves. Egg-shaped fruits are covered with spines. Both seeds and leaves contain narcotics used in medicine. Even the plant's strong, offensive odor is said to cause drowsiness. Contact with the leaves and flowers can cause dermatitis. Consuming large amounts can be fatal. Powerful alkaloids (hyoscyamine) throughout the whole plant make its juice poisonous. Sucking nectar from the flowers has poisoned children. Native California Indians knew that eating boiled plants led to altered behavior. They prepared potions from the plants for their children to encourage visions, especially at puberty, but expert shamans are said to have regulated the dosage. Signs of poisoning include abnormal thirst, distorted sight and dilated pupils, irrational behavior, delirium, convulsions, circulatory collapse, and death.

Larkspur (*Delphinium* spp.)

More than 250 species of annual larkspurs and perennial delphiniums exist worldwide. Leaves are deeply lobed, and flowers are borne on long terminal stalks. Many species are weedy, but others are cultivated. Leaves and seeds may cause contact dermatitis. If planted in the garden, larkspur should be out of the reach of small children because all species contain toxic alkaloids. Toxicity decreases as the plants age. Eating young leaves before the flowers appear can cause poisoning. Seeds are poisonous, a source of concentrated alkaloids. Signs of poisoning include upset stomach, abdominal cramps, bloating, twitching, paralysis, and death.

Monkshood (*Aconitum* spp.)

Found along creeks, in woods, and on mountain slopes, monkshood has showy wildflowers. *Aconitum napellus* is the source of the drug aconitine, used as a heart sedative. Flow-

Table 21.2

WEEDS AND MISCELLANEOUS PLANTS THAT CONTAIN TOXINS

Common name	Scientific name	Toxic part*	Toxin†	Effect‡
bittersweet	*Solanum dulcamara*	LF, FR	A	NS
bracken fern	*Pteridium aquilinum*	WP	CG	BL, CAR
castor bean	*Ricinus communis*	young LF, SD	RS	CV, severe GI, RP, SK, seed very toxic
common ragwort	*Senecio jacobaea*	WP	A	—
common tansy	*Tanacetum vulgare*	LF	—	—
cow cockle	*Saponaria vaccaria*	SD	G	GI
desert marigold	*Baileya multiradiata*	WP	—	—
dock	*Rumex* spp.	LF	OX	GI, SK
false hellebore (skunk cabbage)	*Veratrum californicum*	WP	A	NS, RP
jimsonweed	*Datura stramonium*§	WP	A	severe NS
lamb's quarters (goosefoot)	*Chenopodium album*	WP	N, OX	BL, GI, SK
larkspur	*Delphinium virescens*	WP	A, CT	GI, NS
lupine	*Lupinus* spp.	WP	A	severe NS, RP
milkweed	*Asclepias* spp.//	WP	A, G, R	severe NS
monkshood (aconite)	*Aconitum columbianum*, *Aconitum* spp	WP (UP, SD)	A, CT	GI, severe NS
morning glory	*Ipomoea tricolor*	SD	NAR	NS
mustard	*Brassica nigra*	UP, SD	—	SK
nightshade///	*Solanum nigrum*	LF, FR	A	NS
oxalis (bermuda buttercup)	*Oxalis* spp.	WP	OX	GI, SK
poison hemlock	*Conium maculatum*	WP	A	NS, RP
poison ivy	*Toxicodendron rydbergii*	WP	O	severe SK
poison oak	*Toxicodendron diversilobum*, *Rhus diversiloba*	WP	O	severe SK
sneezeweed	*Helenium* spp.	WP	G	GI
spurge (ground, spotted, thyme-leaved)	*Euphorbia* spp.	SP	PH	SK
white snakeroot	*Eupatorium regosum*	LF, ST	—	—

Notes:

—: Information on the toxic part, toxin, or effect could not be found or is unknown.

*Toxic parts: AG = aboveground parts; FL = flower; FR = fruit; LF = leaf; SD = seed; SP = sap; ST = stem; UP = underground parts; WP = whole plant.

†Toxins: A = alkaloid; CARD = cardiac glycoside; CG = cyanogenic glycoside; COL = colchicine; CT = cardiotoxin; G = glycoside; N = nitrate; O = oil; OX = oxalate; PH = phorbol; R = resin; RS = risin.

‡Effect [organ system(s) affected]: BL = blood; CAR = carcinogen; GI = gastrointestinal; NS = nervous system; SK = skin.

§*Datura* spp. in general are toxic.

//All *Asclepias* spp. should be considered poisonous, even those cultivated as ornamentals.

///All ornamental and wild *Solanum* spp. should be considered poisonous.

ers are blue, purple, white, or yellow; leaves are deeply lobed. The plant's tuberous root has been mistaken for a wild horseradish, sometimes with fatal results. Warn children that the toxic juice in the flowers, leaves, stems, and black seed are poisonous. Poisoning symptoms include burning followed by numbness of lips and tongue, ringing in the ears, dizziness, vomiting, weak heartbeat, chest pains, convulsions, and death. Ingesting only a small amount of the juice can be fatal within hours.

Nightshade (*Solanum nigrum*)

An introduced weed naturalized in waste places, cultivated fields, and around homes, nightshade has white flowers with large yellow anthers. Fruit are dull black when fully ripe. The whole plant contains toxic solanum alkaloids (solanine). Juice from wilted leaves is especially toxic. *Solanum americanum* is a related native weed that is common along roadsides. The fruit is glossy black, and the entire plant is equally poisonous. Signs of poisoning include gastrointestinal upset, rapid heartbeat and pulse, trembling, depression, drowsiness, unconsciousness, and death.

Vegetables That Contain Natural Toxins

Common vegetables can produce natural toxins that cause skin rashes, upset stomachs, and death (table 21.3). Two very strong toxins are produced by diseased celery and potatoes. When potatoes are stressed, either by injury, disease, or excess sunlight, they produce an alkaloid that can damage the liver. Potatoes can become toxic if they have a green color under the skin. Do not eat potatoes with cuts, bruises, or sprouted eyes. Instead of eating them, cut them up and use them as seed pieces. Diseased celery produces a toxin activated by sunlight that can cause a severe skin rash known as celery picker's disease.

Asparagus (*Asparagus officinalis*)

Asparagus is a perennial vegetable. Eating raw, green, young shoots can cause dermatitis. Red berries that form on feathery branches are poisonous. Signs of poisoning vary from mildly reddened skin to painful swelling accompanied by blisters and itching. Severity depends on the amount consumed and individual sensitivity.

Potato (*Solanum tuberosum*)

Potato tubers are very nourishing, but eating potato leaves, sprouts, and vines, and sun-greened potatoes—all of which contain alkaloids—has caused fatalities. Remove green spots and sprouts before cooking potatoes because heat does not destroy the poisonous alkaloids. Signs of poisoning include digestive upset, cold perspiration, lowered temperature, mental confusion, weakness, numbness, dilated pupils, paralysis, circulatory disturbances, and death.

Tomato (*Lycopersicon esculentum*)

The annual garden tomato is closely related to the deadly nightshade. For centuries tomato fruit were thought to be poisonous, and the plant was cultivated only as an ornamental. We now know that fresh tomatoes are harmless, but the leaves and vines (stems) do contain alkaloid poisons (solanine). Livestock have died from eating the foliage and vines. Children have been poisoned from making a

Table 21.3

VEGETABLES THAT CONTAIN NATURAL TOXINS

Common name	Scientific name	Toxic part*	Toxin†	Effect‡
asparagus	*A. officinalis* (garden asparagus)	AG	—	SK
carrot	*Daucus carota*	SP	FU	SK
cassava	*Manihot esculenta*	UP (uncooked)	CG	
celery§	*Apium graveolens*	AG, SP	FU	severe SK
potato	*Solanum tuberosum*	G	A	LV
rhubarb//	*Rheum rhabarbarum*	LF	OX	GI, SK
tomato	*Lycopersicum esculentum*	LF, ST, green FR	A, S	GI

Notes:

—: Information on the toxic part, toxin, or effect could not be found or is unknown.

*Toxic parts: AG = aboveground parts; FR = fruit; G = green parts; LF = leaf; ST = stem; SP = sap; UP = underground parts.

†Toxins: A = alkaloid; CG = cyanogenic glycoside; FU = furocoumarin; OX = oxlate; S = saponin.

‡Effect [organ system(s) affected]: ETS = cell respiration, electron transport system; GI = gastrointestinal; LV = liver; SK = skin.

§Toxins are produced almost solely by celery infected by pink rot fungi.

//Because of the lethal amounts of oxalic acids concentrated in its leaf blade, rhubarb is considered one of the most dangerous of all plants in a garden.

tea from the leaves. Signs of poisoning include nausea, vomiting, bloody diarrhea or constipation, abnormal flow of saliva, trembling, paralysis, and death, if poisonous parts are eaten in large quantities.

House Plants That Contain Toxins

Numerous house plants belonging to the Araceae (arum) family contain various forms of oxalic acid, usually as sharp, needlelike oxalate crystals held in a special delivery device in the plant tissues (table 21.4). Touching, crushing, or breaking the plant may cause the release or "firing" of these devices. The crystals are extremely irritating. You may have noticed your fingers or arms itching after handling one of these plants. If a child or pet bites into a

leaf, the irritation in and around the mouth and throat may be severe enough to require medical attention. Common house plants that contain oxalates and some that do not are listed below. Different parts of different house plants have varying degrees of toxicity. Factors affecting the toxicity of a given plant include health (stressed plants tend to be more toxic) and age (the effects of age are unpredictable).

Philodendron (*Philodendron* spp.)
Philodendron spp. and *Monstera deliciosa* (split-leaf philodendron) are among the most popular house plants. They are cultivated in containers and large tubs for their attractive, deep-green glossy foliage. Leaves are oval, heart-shaped, or deeply cut. Leaves and stems are very poisonous because they have toxic calcium oxalate crystals. Ingesting one leaf can be fatal to a child, depending on the size of both. The calcium oxalate crystals can penetrate into mucus membranes, causing intense burning and irritation very destructive to the kidneys. Signs of poisoning include burning lips, mouth, and tongue immediately after swallowing poisonous plant parts. Swelling makes breathing difficult. Kidney failure and death are final results.

Caladium (*Caladium* spp.)
Cultivated for their beautiful leaves, caladiums are used extensively as house plants or as summer bedding plants outdoors. Leaves are colored with bands and blotches of white, silver, red, pink, rose, and green. A tuberous rooted perennial with white flowers, all caladiums have a bitter, poisonous juice containing toxic oxalate crystals. Signs of poisoning after ingesting a small amount of the leaves include a burning swelling mouth with intense burning in the throat. After the tongue and throat swell, blocked air passages can lead to death.

Dumbcane (*Dieffenbachia* spp.)
These evergreen foliage plants are favorite interiorscape ornamentals for homes, apartments, restaurants, and businesses. They have striking leaves with variegations in white or pale cream. Colors vary from dark green to yellow-green. The commonly cultivated species, *Dieffenbachia picta* and *D. seguine*, are called dumbcane because chewing on the leaves may paralyze the vocal chords and lead to temporary speechlessness. Leaves and stems are poisonous because they contain calcium

Table 21.4

HOUSE PLANTS THAT CONTAIN TOXINS

Common name	Scientific name	Toxic part*	Toxin†	Effect‡
asparagus fern	*A. densiflorus* 'Myers' and 'Sprengeri'; *A. setaceus*; (fern asparagus)	AG	—	SK
caladium caladium	*Caladium bicolor*	WP	OX	GI, SK
chinese evergreen	*Aglaonema* spp.	AG	OX	GI, SK
dumbcane	*Dieffenbachia* spp.	WP	OX	GI, SK
elephant's ear	*Colocasia antiquorum*	WP	OX	GI, SK
monstera (split-leaf philodendron)	*Monstera delicosa*	FR, LF	OX	GI, SK
philodendron	*Philodendron* spp.	WP	OX	GI, SK
pothos	*Epipremnum aureum*	LF	OX	GI, SK
schefflera	*Schefflera* spp.	AG	OX	GI, SK
German ivy	*Senecio mikanioides*	LF, ST	—	—
crown of thorns	*Euphorbia milii*	WP	PH	GI, SK
weeping fig	*Ficus benjamina*	AG	OX	GI, SK
Jerusalem cherry (winter or Christmas cherry)	*Solanum pseudocapsicum*	WP	strong CARD	CV

Notes:

—: Information on the toxic part, toxin, or effect could not be found or is unknown.

*Toxic parts: AG = aboveground parts; FL = flower; FR = fruit; LF = leaf; ST = stem; WP = whole plant.

†Toxins: CARD = cardiac glycoside; OX = oxalate; PH = phorbol.

‡Effect [organ system(s) affected]: CV = cardiovascular; GI = gastrointestinal; SK = skin.

oxalate needlelike crystals. Signs of poisoning include intense burning and irritation of lips, mouth, and tongue after biting or chewing the stem or leaves. Swelling may interfere with breathing and cause choking. Death can occur if the swelling of the tongue blocks the air passage to the throat.

Shrubs and Vines That Contain Toxins

In general, shrubs cause very few of the cases of accidental poisoning reported to the UC Medical Center's Poison Control Center, but the category contains two very notable exceptions: oleander and rhododendrons. Candelabra cactus, holly, and privet are the next most common shrubs that contain toxins (table 21.5).

Yellow Jessamine (*Gelsemium sempervirens*)
Yellow jessamine, used to cover porches and trellises, has fragrant, tubular, bright yellow flowers. The entire plant contains several alkaloids (gelsemine) related to strychnine. The greatest concentration of toxin is in the rootstock and flower nectar. Children have died from sucking the nectar from the blossoms. The nectar can poison bees, and honey made from the nectar is toxic. Flowers, leaves, and roots can also cause dermatitis. Poisoning symptoms include heavy perspiration, abdominal cramps, shallow breathing, paralysis, convulsions, and death from respiratory failure, unless emergency measures are taken.

Holly (*Ilex* spp.)
An evergreen shrub with sharply toothed leaves and red berries, holly is widely planted in California. Often used for Christmas decorations. Berries are harmless to birds but poisonous to humans. This shrub is considered especially dangerous to children because they may eat the berries in large quantities. Signs of poisoning include nausea, vomiting, diarrhea, and nervous system depression. Eating holly may be fatal.

Oleander (*Nerium oleander*)
Oleander is an evergreen shrub with showy, long-lasting blooms in white, pink, crimson, or dark red. It is cultivated as an outdoor ornamental and used to adorn freeways. The entire plant, including dried leaves, contain deadly glycosides (oleandrin) that stimulate the heart. Children can become gravely ill from eating a single oleander leaf or from sucking nectar from oleander flowers. Nectar collected by bees yields a poisonous honey. Smoke from burning oleander affects sensitive people, and people have been poisoned by meat roasted over oleander branches or with oleander branches as skewers. Oleander leaves and branches may cause dermatitis. Poisoning symptoms can include digestive upset, bloody diarrhea, irregular pulse and heartbeat, blurred vision, coma, lung paralysis, and death.

Azalea/Rhododendron (*Rhododendron* spp.)
Azaleas have tubular, funnel-shaped flowers that bloom in crowded heads. Colors can vary from white, pink, and crimson red to lilac-purple and rose-purple. Evergreen and deciduous varieties are cultivated. The entire plant contains toxic resins (andromedotoxins), but they are more concentrated in the foliage. Eating a few leaves or sucking the flowers can lead to poisoning. Symptoms can be delayed, depending on the amount consumed. Typical signs of poisoning are acute digestive upset, salivation, and increased tear formation. In more severe cases, paralysis, stupor, and heart depression have occurred. Fatalities have been reported. The poison also contaminates honey made by bees that have visited azaleas.

Pittosporum (*Pittosporum* spp.)
More than 100 species of *Pittosporum* have been identified. These evergreen tress and shrubs are planted widely in California. The leaves, stems, and reddish fruits are poisonous.

English Ivy (*Hedera helix*)
English ivy is a well-known woody evergreen vine cultivated throughout the United States for ground cover or for climbing on walls, fences, and trellises. Leaves are generally lobed but squarish and without lobes on flowering branches of mature plants. Fruits are black berries. Both foliage and berries contain toxins (saponins). Leaves may cause allergic contact dermatitis. Signs of poisoning include severe stomach cramps and diarrhea. If poisonous parts are consumed in quantity, coma and death can occur.

Table 21.5

SHRUBS AND VINES THAT CONTAIN TOXINS

Common name	Scientific name	Toxic part*	Toxin†	Effect‡
azaleas	*Rhododendron* spp.	WP	CT, R	CV, GI
bamboo palm	*Chamaedorea erumpens*	FR	SK	—
bird-of-paradise	*Caesalpinia gilliesii*	SD	UNK	GI
boxwood	*Buxus microphylla, B. sempervirens*	FL, ST (WP)	A, R, O	GI
buckthorn (coffeeberry, pigeonberry)	*Rhamnus* spp.	LF, ST, FR, SP	—	SK, GI (laxative)
bushman's poison	*Acokanthera* spp.	WP	—	very toxic
buttonbush	*Cephalanthus occidentalis*	LF	G	—
canary bird bush	*Crotalaria* spp.	WP	A	—
candelabra cactus	*Euphorbia lactea, E. grandicornis*	FL, ST, SP	PH	GI, SK
castor bean	*Ricinus communis*	young LF, SD	RS	CV, severe GI, RP, SK; seed very toxic
century plant	*Agave americana*	LF, SP	O, OX	GI, SK
cestrum (night-blooming jessamine)	*Cestrum* spp.	LF, ST	—	—
clematis	*Clematis* spp.	WP	G, O	GI, SK
culvers root	*Veronica virginica*	UP	—	—
cup-of-gold-vine	*Solandra* spp.	LF, FL	—	—
daphne	*Daphne* spp.	ST	—	very toxic
elderberry	*Sambucus* spp.	FR (raw)	A, CG	GI
English holly	*Ilex aquifolium*	FR	GI, NS	—
English ivy	*Hedera helix*	FR, LF	G	GI, NS, SK
euonymus, European burning bush	*Euonymus europaea, E.* spp.	LF, FR	—	—
firethorn	*Pyracantha* spp.	FR	—	severe SK
flax	*Linum usitatissimum*	WP	N, cyanide	RP
golden dewdrop	*Duranta repens*	FR, LF	G	GI
holly	*Ilex* spp.	FR	EM	GI, NS
hydrangea	*Hydrangea* spp.	WP	CG	ETS, GI
Japanese privet	*Ligustrum japonicum, L. vulgare*	FR, LF	A, G	GI, NS
kara nut; laurel	*Corynocarpus laevigata*	SD	—	—
lantana	*Lantana* spp.	WP	—	GI, CV
morning glory	*Ipomea tricolor*	SD	NAR	NS
mountain laurel	*Kalmia latifolia*	LF	—	—
ngaio (myoporum)	*Myoporum laetum*	LF	—	very toxic
nightshade	*Solanum* spp.	WP, especially FR	CARD	CV
oleander	*Nerium oleander*	WP	CARD	CV, GI
pittosporum	*Pittosporum* spp.	LF, ST, FR	—	very toxic
privet	*Ligustrum* spp.	LF, FR	—	—
rattlebox	*Daubentonia punicea, Sesbania punicea*	SD	—	—
rhododendron	*Rhododendron* spp.	WP	CT, R	CV, GI
St. John's wort	*Hypericum perforatum*§	WP	—	SK
toyon, Christmas berry	*Heteromeles arbutifolia*	LF	—	—
traveler's joy	*Clematis vitalba*	LF	G, O	GI, SK
Virginia creeper (American ivy)	*Parthenocissus quinquefolia*	FR, LF	OX	GI, SK
wisteria	*Wisteria* spp.	SD	G	strong GI
yellow jessamine	*Gelsemium sempervirens*	WP	A	GI, SK, RP
yellow oleander	*Thevetia peruviana*	WP	—	—
yew	*Taxus* spp.	WP (SD)	strong A	NS, GI

Notes:
—: Information on the toxic part, toxin, or effect could not be found or is unknown.
*Toxic parts: AG = aboveground parts; FL = flower; FR = fruit; LF = leaf; SD = seed; SP = sap; ST = stem; UP = underground parts; WP = whole plant.
†Toxins: A = alkaloid; CARD = cardiac glycoside; CG = cyanogenic glycoside; COL = colchicine; CT = cardiotoxin; G = glycoside; NAR = narcotic; N = nitrate; O = oil; OX = oxalate; PH = phorbol; R = resin; RS = risin; UNK = unknown.
‡Effect [organ system(s) affected]: CV = cardiovascular; ETS = cell respiration, electron transport system; GI = gastrointestinal; NS = nervous system; RP = respiratory paralysis; SK = skin.
§This is not the commonly used species in California, which is *H. calycinum*

Flax (*Linum usitatissimum*)

Since prehistoric times, flax has been cultivated for its linen fibers and seed oil (linseed oil). Flax fruit are dry capsules, each containing 10 glossy brown seed. The whole plant is poisonous, but ingesting the seed, which have high concentrations of nitrates and cyanide, can be fatal.

Trees That Contain Toxins

Trees are not the most common cause of accidental poisonings around the home, but a few species may present a hazard (table 21.6).

Apple (*Malus domestica*)

Several hundred named varieties of apples are grown in orchards and gardens throughout the United States. All varieties of apples contain cyanide, but the black seed inside the fruit core have the highest concentration of this toxin. Fatalities have occurred from eating large quantities of apple seed. Do not eat apple seed. Symptoms of apple seed poisoning include vomiting, dizziness, staggering, difficulty breathing, spasms, coma, and death.

Buckeye or Horsechestnut (*Aesculus* spp.)

Many species of *Aesculus* are planted as shade trees and ornamental shrubs. Leaves, flowers, young sprouts, and seed have high concentrations of the glycoside aesculin. Roots and branches have smaller concentrations. Children have been poisoned by consuming a tea made from the leaves and have died from eating the seed. Honey made from the California buckeye is toxic. Signs of poisoning include vomiting, diarrhea, twitching muscles, depression or elation, dilated pupils, and stupor. Consumption of large quantities may cause paralysis and death.

Chinaberry (*Melia azedarach*)

The chinaberry, a deciduous tree adapted to a wide area in California, makes a good shade tree. The tree has clusters of fragrant lilac flowers in spring or early summer followed by yellow, hard, berrylike fruit, which are not poisonous to birds, although the berries and leaves contain the highest concentration of toxic resins. Children have been poisoned from making a tea from the leaves. Signs of poisoning include nausea, vomiting, constipa-

tion or diarrhea, elation or depression, irregular breathing, mental confusion, stupor, and coma. Fatalities have been reported.

Fig (*Ficus* spp.)

Figs are borne on deciduous trees grown in home orchards or for commercial production. There are also several *Ficus* species grown as ornamental shade trees. Skin irritants that can cause dermatitis are present in the milky sap in stems, leaves, and in immature, unripe fruit. Sap is released when stems are cut, leaves are broken, or unripe fruit is picked. The irritants in the milky sap may cause itching, burning, redness, or blistering on contact. Symptoms can occur around the mouth if raw, unpeeled fruit is eaten. Ripe fruit has little to no milky sap.

Oak (*Quercus* spp.)

About 80 species of oak trees grow in the United States. In the spring, oak pollen can cause allergies. In addition, all species contain high concentrations of tannins in their leaves and unleached acorns. Children should be told not to chew on acorns, but large quantities of unleached acorns must be consumed before the kidneys are adversely affected. Consumption of oak leaves and buds has killed livestock within 24 hours. In humans, signs of oak poisoning appear after several days or weeks. Symptoms include abdominal pains, constipation, excessive thirst, and frequent urination. In severe cases, symptoms include bloody diarrhea, rapid but weak pulse, liver and kidney damage, and death.

Peach (*Prunus persica*)

Hundreds of named varieties of peaches are grown in home orchards and commercially throughout the United States. The familiar, fleshy fruit surrounds a hard, furrowed peach kernel or stone. All parts of the tree contain cyanide-producing compounds that are released when peach kernels, bark, or leaves are eaten. The kernels have poisoned adults, and children have died from eating the kernels, chewing on peach twigs, or making tea from peach leaves. If lethal amounts of toxin have been ingested, poisoning occurs rapidly, causing death within less than an hour. Common symptoms that appear within minutes are breathing changes, such as gasping, overstimulation, and prostration.

Table 21.6

TREES THAT CONTAIN TOXINS

Common name	Scientific name	Toxic part*	Toxin†	Effect‡
almond	*Prunus dulcis amara*	FR	CG	ETS
apple	*Malus sylvestris*	SD, LF	CG	ETS
apricot	*Prunus armeniaca*	SD, LF	CG	ETS
bird-of-paradise bush (poinciana)	*Caesalpinia gilliesii*	SD, FR	UNK	GI
black locust	*Robinia pseudoacacia*	ST, LF, SD	G	GI, BL
buckeye	*Aesculus arguta*	SD, FL, LF	G	GI, NS
cherry	*Prunus* spp.	SD, LF, ST	CG	ETS
chinaberry (chinatree, chinabell tree, umbrella tree)	*Melia azedarach*	WP (FR)	complex	NS
elderberry	*Sambucus* spp.	WP	A, CG	GI
figs	*Ficus* spp.	SP	PS	SK
ginkgo (maidenhair tree)	*Ginkgo biloba*	FR (female trees only)	—	SK
golden chain	*Laburnum anagyoides*	LF, SD	—	very toxic
horsechestnut, buckeye	*Aesculus* spp.	LF, FR	—	—
loquat	*Eriobotrya japonica*	LF, SD	CG	ETS
mulberry	*Morus* spp.	FR, SP	—	SK, NS
oak	*Quercus* spp.	FR, LF	tannin	mild GI
osage orange	*Maclura pomifera*	SP	—	SK
peach (edible and onamental)	*Prunus persica*	WP	CG	ETS
pittosporum	*Pittosporum* spp.	LF, ST, FR	—	very toxic
plum	*Prunus domestica*	SD LF	CG	ETS
Queensland nut	*Macadamia ternifolia*	LF	—	—
tree of heaven	*Ailanthus altissima*	LF, FL	—	SK
walnut	*Juglans* spp.	SP	—	SK
yew	*Taxus* spp.	WP (SD)	strong A	NS, GI

Notes:

—: Information on the toxic part, toxin, or effect could not be found or is unknown.

*Toxic parts: AG = aboveground parts; FL = flower; FR = fruit; LF = leaf; SD = seed; SP = sap; ST = stem; WP = whole plant.

†Toxins: A = alkaloid; CG = cyanogenic glycoside; G = glycoside; PS = psoralin; UNK = unknown.

‡Effect [organ system(s) affected]: BL = blood; ETS = cell respiration, electron transport system; GI = gastrointestinal; NS = nervous system; SK = skin.

Bibliography

Brenzel, K. N. 2001. Sunset western garden book. Menlo Park, CA: Sunset.

Connor, H. E., and N. M. Adams. 1951. The poisonous plants of New Zealand. Wellington: New Zealand Department of Scientific and Industrial Research Bulletin 99.

Enari, L. 1972. Poisonous plants of Southern California. Arcadia, CA: County of Los Angeles Department of Arboreta and Botanic Gardens.

Fernald, M. L., A. C. Kinsey, and R. C. Rollins. 1958. Edible wild plants of eastern North America. New York: Harper.

Frohne, D., and H. J. Pfander. 1984. Colour atlas of poisonous plants. London: Wolfe Science Books.

Fuller, T., and E. McClintock. 1986. Poisonous plants of California. Berkeley: University of California Press.

Hardin, J. W., and J. M. Arena. 1974. Human poisoning from native and cultivated plants. Durham, NC: Duke University Press.

Hurst, E. 1942. The poisonous plants of New South Wales. Sydney, Australia: Poison Plants Committee of New South Wales.

James, W. R. 1973. Know your poisonous plants. Healdsburg, CA: Naturegraph Publishers.

Kingsbury, J. M. 1964. Poisonous plants of the United States and Canada. Englewood Cliffs, NJ: Prentice-Hall.

Lampe, K. F., and R. Fagerstrom. 1968. Plant toxicity and dermatitis. Baltimore: Williams and Wilkins Co.

Mitchell, P. J. 1984. Poisonous plants. Sweetwater: Oklahoma State University Department of Horticulture.

Muenscher, W. C. 1951. Poisonous plants of the United States. New York: Macmillan.

Stephans, H. A. 1980. Poisonous plants of the central United States. Lawrence: Regents Press of Kansas.

Stone, E., and A. King. 1997. Know your plants: Safe or poisonous. Half Moon Bay, CA: UC Cooperative Extension San Mateo–San Francisco Counties.

Tucker, J. M., and M. H. Kimball. 1978. Poisonous plants in the garden. Berkeley: University of California Division of Agriculture and Natural Resources Leaflet 2561.

West, E. 1957. Poisonous plants around the home. Gainesville: University of Florida Agricultural Experiment Station Bulletin S-100.

Wyman, D. 1986. Wyman's gardening encyclopedia. New York: Macmillan.

Zamula, E. 1990. Contact dermatitis: Solutions to rash mysteries. FDA Consumer 24(4): 28–31.

22

Diagnosing Plant Problems

Dennis R. Pittenger

LEARNING OBJECTIVES

- Learn how to approach a plant problem and how to deal with clientele.

- Understand how to gather information and formulate a diagnosis.

Diagnosing Plant Problems

Learning how to diagnose plant problems involves much more than memorizing a large number of photographs depicting symptoms of specific plant problems. In fact, memorizing symptoms can be dangerous because a given problem may not always produce the same symptoms, and many plant problems express a variety of symptoms that are not always consistent in appearance. It is difficult to teach and learn diagnostics; experience is necessary to become skilled. Successful diagnosticians are good detectives who develop a systematic approach to problem solving, ask many questions, keep an open mind, and draw on their knowledge of plant growth and development along with available facts or references before they offer a diagnosis. In many instances, it is possible only to narrow the causes of a plant problem to two or three possibilities or to offer a tentative diagnosis.

A primary function of a Master Gardener is to help people via education. Thus, a Master Gardener should use the process of diagnosing clients' plant problems as an opportunity to teach basic concepts of plant growth, development, and culture as well as help them to solve a problem. Understanding what went wrong is important to prevent the problem from recurring or to save remaining plants.

Knowledge Needed To Diagnose Plant Problems

Diagnosing plant problems requires a basic level of knowledge in horticultural science, entomology, plant pathology, and soil and irrigation management. These topics are addressed in detail in specific chapters in this book. Although a few general concepts are provided here, a thorough review of those chapters is recommended before actively diagnosing plant problems.

Basic Horticultural Science Concepts

The primary plant processes (photosynthesis, respiration, transpiration, translocation) are affected greatly by the environmental factors of light, temperature, water availability, and soil conditions. Suboptimal environmental conditions as well as pest activities, improper cultural practices, or human activity can disrupt or limit these primary plant processes or injure plant tissues, resulting in a sick or abnormal plant that expresses symptoms (fig. 22.1). Healthy plants are typically less susceptible to serious insect, disease, or abiotic problems.

Every plant has certain genetic capabilities and limitations that dictate what the normal plant should look like, what its expected life span will be, and what its mature size will be under a given set of environmental and growing conditions. One must know what normal is to determine whether a plant's condition or

Figure 22.1

Pathogens, insects, other pests, or environmental factors can disrupt plant processes or injure plant tissues. When they do, a plant often responds by producing symptoms. *Source*: After Hasey 1985, p.4.

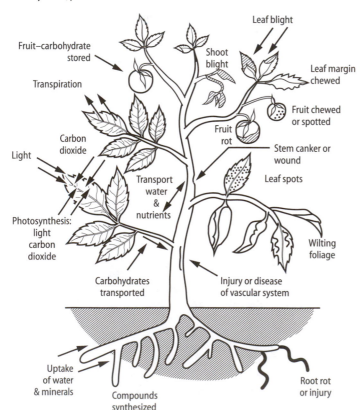

appearance is abnormal. When a plant's size, color, flowering, growth rate, or other features are noticeably abnormal, there is reason to investigate to determine possible causes. It is important to understand how environmental conditions may affect a given plant's vegetative and flowering (reproductive) growth phases.

Knowledge of the basic cultural practices needed by plant species is essential to diagnosing problems. Planting and establishment procedures, fertilizer needs, irrigation needs, and other requirements must be known.

In diagnosis, identification of the affected plant is the first step. Thus, good plant identification skills and knowledge of plant identification references can facilitate faster, more accurate problem diagnosis and instill confidence in the client. Most references on plant pests and problems are organized by plant species, so knowing the plant's scientific name is usually essential for using them.

Plant Insect, Mite, and Disease Concepts

When a plant dies, looks somewhat abnormal, or is growing poorly, many average gardeners automatically assume that an insect or disease is the cause. This is especially true if there are active insects on or near the plant or if foliage is distorted in some fashion. The mere presence of an insect does not correlate with its being a pest, however. In many instances, improper cultural practices or some other nonpest issue is the cause of the problem. Factors that may predispose a plant to pest infestations (e.g., drought, overfertilizing, improper planting techniques) must always be considered. Basic knowledge about insects, mites, and will enable a diagnostician to more accurately and rapidly reach an accurate diagnosis of the problem or determine whether the plant is actually growing normally.

It may be difficult to become familiar with all of the different insects and mites that damage plants, but it is possible to learn to recognize the various types of damage caused by different types of insects and mites. If you recognize the type of damage and you know the identity of the host plant, you can sometimes diagnose the pest involved using reference books, including this handbook and other University of California publications. Not all insects found on a sick plant are the cause. Some may be beneficial insects, or they may simply be there by chance.

A good diagnostician must gain a working knowledge of the symptoms and signs of common plant diseases. A disease symptom is a change in the appearance or growth of the plant. Wilting, galls, leaf spots, blights, and root rots are all disease symptoms. However, other nonpest factors may also cause these symptoms. A disease sign is the actual disease-causing pathogen or its parts. The mildew seen on a plant affected by the disease powdery mildew is a sign of the disease because the white mildew is made of visible fungal structures. If you can recognize the symptoms and identify the host plant, you can use various reference materials to make, or at least, narrow down a diagnosis. When examining a plant sample, note all symptoms and signs.

Other Animal Pests

Sometimes animals other than insects and mites affect plants. Deer eat the bark off trees, pull up tulips, and prune shrubs; mice feed on plant roots, causing wilt; gophers, ground squirrels, and moles sever the roots; birds peck holes in trees or eat vegetable seedlings; dogs and cats mark their territory by spraying urine on objects, turf, and landscape plants, causing blighted shrubs, grass, and flowers.

Diagnosing Plant Problems

A diagnosis is the process of gathering information about a plant problem and determining the cause. Solutions or recommended treatment options can be suggested once the diagnosis has been completed. Diagnosing problems usually involves a great deal of detective work and investigation to obtain adequate information and clues. It is important to remember that real problems are always caused by something. A logical explanation or solution can usually be found, and if you are serving a client, your job is to try to identify it. However, always be conservative and admit that you do not know why or that you can only narrow the causes to a few possibilities when the evidence or information available is incomplete or inconclusive. As a last resort, it is acceptable to make an educated guess as long as the client understands that is what is being offered.

Table 22.1

CHECKLIST FOR PLANT DIAGNOSIS

Plant Information

A. Species and cultivar

_____

B. Source of plants

_____

C. Plant age or date planted

_____

D. Location of affected plants
1. Shade or sun _____
2. Outdoor or indoor _____
3. Exposure (N, S, E, or W) _____
4. Near building _____
5. Container, or planted in the ground _____
6. Wind exposure _____
7. Proximity to utilities (lines, trenches, leaks)

_____

8. Root disturbance (excavations) _____
9. Proximity to hardscape, bodies of water, other landscaped ares (i.e., near or in turf area, next to driveway) _____

Problem description

A. Description of symptoms
1. Plant parts affected _____
2. Chlorosis _____
3. Wilts _____
4. Leaf spots _____
5. Leaf distortion _____
6. Rots (soft, firm, stem, or root) _____
7. Other (specify) _____

B. Degree of symptom expression
1. Whole plant _____
2. In isolated section of plant _____
3. A few leaves or shoots _____
4. A few roots _____

C. Are symptoms on the entire planting or isolated on a few plants?

_____

D. How many plants with symptoms
1. 1–2 plants _____
2. 10% _____
3. 25% _____
4. 50% _____
5. 75% _____
6. 100% _____

E. Length of time symptoms observed (days, weeks, months)

_____

Soil information

A. Texture
1. Light (sandy) _____
2. Medium (loam) _____
3. Heavy (clay) _____
4. Other (specify) _____

B. Drainage

_____

C. Grade changes or other disturbances

_____

D. Has soil been amended?

_____

E. Compaction evident?

_____

F. Water infiltration and percolation

_____

Fertilization

A. Rates

_____

B. Application method

_____

C. Frequency or timing of applications

_____

Pesticides or other materials used

A. Type (insecticide, herbicide, fungicide, other)

_____

B. Product name

_____

C. Rate, concentration

_____

D. Application date and frequency

_____

Watering

A. Method(s)

_____

B. Frequency

_____

Recent weather conditions

A. Day and night temperature patterns

_____

B. High winds

_____

C. Rain or hail

_____

Plant or soil testing

A. Prior diagnosis provided?
1. Who provided it _____
2. Results _____
B. Sample collection procedure

_____

Figure 22.2

Patterns of plant symptoms. Symptoms in turfgrass areas may produce regular patterns (A) or irregular patterns (B). In woody plants, determine whether whole areas of the plant (C) or selected portions or a few leaves (D) are showing symptom patterns.

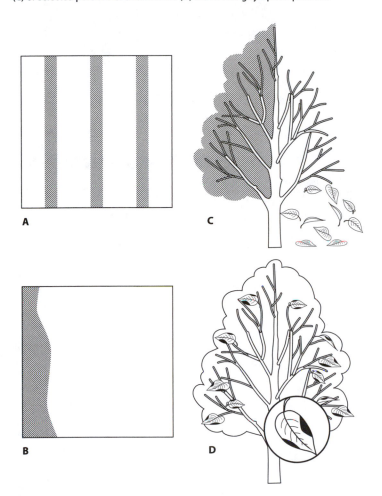

The majority of plant problems found in California home gardens are caused by improper plant selection or cultural practices as opposed to diseases, insects, or the chemical properties of the soil. Improper planting, irrigating, and fertilizing are the most commonly misapplied cultural practices.

Steps in Diagnosing Plant Problems

There are five general steps in reaching a diagnosis. Each Master Gardener needs to develop a method of questioning and information gathering based on the five steps outlined below. It requires considerable experience to diagnose effectively. Always be courteous to clients, focus on helping them identify practi-

cal solutions to their problems, and educate them to prevent the problem from recurring. Be prepared to say, "I don't know, but I will investigate further." Table 22.1 is a sample checklist for plant diagnosis that may be helpful.

Identify the Plant. Determine the common and scientific name of the plant. Failure to do this can make an accurate diagnosis difficult.

Define the Problem. Examine the plant carefully, including the roots if at all possible (especially for container plants). Note symptoms or signs of pests and determine what, if anything, is abnormal about the plant. Are many or few plants affected? Which plant parts are affected? Are symptoms on one or several species? Keep an open mind and avoid snap conclusions as to the problem's cause.

Collect Information. Ask questions and make observations about the soil and site conditions, the cultural practices that were followed, approximate age of the plant, past and present weather conditions, and other relevant information. You may have to proceed with incomplete information regarding cultural practices. Eliminate any obvious or very common causes first. Look beyond the immediate symptoms for clues.

Look for Patterns. If more than one plant or a large area is affected, look for patterns in the distribution of the problem or symptoms among plants in the area (fig. 22.2). Check for patterns on individual plants, too, by observing the range of plant tissues affected and the severity of the problem on and among plant parts—compare old and new growth, leaf margins and whole leaves, and so on. Try to compare a normal plant (or part of a plant) with one that shows mild symptoms and one that shows severe symptoms. Attempt to observe the root system, if possible. There may be more than one problem, and one can be causing the other. Also, consider past weather conditions and compare them to the affected plant's environmental requirements and those of its common insect, mite, or disease pests. Base the diagnosis on the evidence and information collected, along with your knowledge of the plant and its needs and common problems.

Formulate a Tentative Diagnosis. A tentative diagnosis often means that the cause of the problem can be narrowed to two or three possible answers. Keep in mind that the problem may be new or unique, and you may not be able to make a diagnosis. Attempt to confirm a tentative diagnosis or narrow the possible causes by focusing on further examination of the plant, collecting more detailed information, consulting references or colleagues, and, if feasible, using laboratory services for soil and pest analysis.

Asking Effective Questions

In order to help and teach clients, a diagnostician must develop effective communication skills in asking questions. The diagnostician should take control of the conversation by following a logical line of questions that provides the information needed to solve the problem. Allowing the client to do most of the talking is best. Asking effective questions takes some experience and a great deal of thought, especially when attempting to diagnose a problem by a telephone conversation. Questions must be phrased in such a way that the diagnostician gets a clear picture of the plant's symptoms, size, and age, along with the cultural practices followed. Comparing this information to general knowledge and understanding of how the species in question should grow and develop makes it possible to assess what is abnormal and how the problem might be solved.

Equipment and Tools Helpful in Diagnosis

Many items can be useful, even essential, in making a diagnosis. Some of the most widely used tools are the following:

- sharp knife
- hand lens
- soil probe
- shovel
- hand pick
- pruning shears
- plastic bags and ties (for collecting plant, pest, or soil samples)
- small vials with lids (for insect samples)
- permanent marker and labels
- notebook and pencil
- portable plant press (for making reference specimens)
- camera (to record site and observations)
- binoculars (for viewing upper portions of tall trees)

- styrofoam cooler (to keep samples cool and fresh in warm weather)

Because horticultural science and plant problem solving include a large knowledge base, good diagnosticians also know where to search for more information regarding plants, their specific needs, and their potential problems. It is essential for a diagnostician to become familiar with reference books, keys, and other materials that can be consulted and used in conjunction with personal experience in plant problem solving.

Working with Clients and Assisting Gardeners

When you are diagnosing someone's plant problem, they view you as the expert and usually expect a quick, succinct identification of the problem and a single cure for it. Occasionally, clients are only trying to get you to agree with or to confirm their own suspicions or inaccurate diagnoses. Also recognize that sometimes a client is embarrassed that they may have done something to cause the problem and they may not tell the whole truth about the practices they have followed. Always maintain a good bedside manner. Be courteous, personable, and sincere in helping clients identify practical solutions to their problems. Focus on teaching clients so that they can grow plants with minimal future problems. Use your knowledge and remain confident in your abilities to find answers. Explain to the person you are assisting that diagnosis is often difficult because many problems are the result of complex interactions of plants, pests, and the environment. Respectfully disagree with a client's perceptions or conclusions about the problem if appropriate, but be certain to explain to the client why he or she is wrong, based on your knowledge of horticultural science and related disciplines covered in this book and the reference materials you consulted.

Involving clients in diagnosing a problem and identifying solutions to it provides an excellent opportunity to educate gardeners about their plants' cultural requirements and common pest problems. Sharing your expertise during this process may give clients enough knowledge to allow them to solve their own problems in the future. In these circumstances, your role is that of an educator/facilitator and not a doer.

In today's high-technology world where communications occur rapidly and diagnosis of human health problems is usually executed quickly and precisely, gardeners typically expect diagnosis of plant health problems to be completed just as rapidly and precisely. However, diagnosing plant problems can be more difficult and less precise than diagnosing human ailments because the affected plant(s) cannot communicate to the diagnostician. In addition, the plant diagnostician deals with thousands of host species, each with a number of unique potential pests, problems, and symptoms, whereas the medical professional knows one species and its pests, problems, and symptoms. Finally, the technology for solving plant problems is often much more limited. If a gardener is disappointed with the speed or precision of a plant problem diagnosis, it may be necessary to relate these concepts to him or her so that the frame of reference and expectations are based on realistic perceptions of the factors involved in diagnosis.

Recognize that not all plant problems can be treated, either because a treatment does not exist or because it is not practical. Clients often do not like to hear this, and the diagnostician must educate them more fully about the problem and how to avoid it in the future.

Prescribing Solutions and Recommendations

Once you have correctly diagnosed the problem, effective solutions are available from a variety of reference materials from the University of California, personal knowledge, or other reliable and unbiased sources. If the diagnosis consists of two or more likely but unconfirmed causes, offer potential solutions for each possible cause. Not every plant problem can be overcome. Clients also sometimes fail to recognize or become concerned with a troubled plant until it is too severely damaged to be treated effectively.

It is important to give the client the entire range of possible treatments or solutions. In the case of a specific insect or disease pest, for example, discuss and provide information about cultural practices, pesticides, and other possible alternatives that could manage the pest and reduce its damage. Give the strengths and weaknesses of each option, if known, along with indicators of improvement or success expected to result from choosing a particular option. When plant symptoms appear to be the result of improper pH, salinity or nutrient levels, it is often inexpensive, effective, and practical for the home horticulturist to apply a treatment for the suspected problem and then observe whether the plant improves. Also explain the likely consequences of doing nothing about the problem if they are not obvious. Clients must decide on their own which solution(s) best match their interests.

Certified UC Master Gardeners must follow specific statewide and local policies on making recommendations. A copy of the policies is available at UC Cooperative Extension offices.

Sample Collection and Laboratory Testing

In certain cases, a sample of the affected plant or suspected pest is very helpful in reaching or confirming a diagnosis. Samples can be especially useful if the affected plants cannot be viewed in person by the diagnostician or if further, detailed study of the plant tissue is needed. Before taking a sample, the diagnostician must first consider how the sample will help in reaching a diagnosis. If the need is questionable, obtaining a sample may not be warranted.

Samples of soil surrounding the affected plant can also be useful in reaching or confirming a diagnosis. Soil can be analyzed for important chemical properties (pH, salinity, and levels of essential plant nutrients or toxic elements) and physical properties (texture and bulk density) if one or more of these components is seriously suspected as the cause. Testing soil for disease organisms is possible but is usually not practical for diagnosing home garden problems because the laboratory tests are relatively expensive. Soil analysis can reveal the level of nutrients contained in the soil. Soil analysis and plant tissue analysis for nutrient content are both needed to determine whether the plant is taking up enough nutrients.

Following proper techniques and procedures when gathering plant, soil, or other samples maximizes their usefulness in reaching or confirming a diagnosis. Place samples of plants and soil in plastic bags, if possible, to maintain freshness and make them easier to handle. Refrigerate plant samples to keep them fresh, too.

Plant samples should include as much of the affected plant as is practical. Attempt to get a whole branch or several small stems of a tree rather than just one or two leaves, for example. Larger portions of plant tissue often allow the evaluation of general plant health. Always seek to get samples of both healthy and unhealthy plants or plant parts so that they can be compared. Samples of the root system are often helpful when soil-related causes are suspected. For turfgrass problems, a minimum of 1 square foot (930 sq cm) of turf is usually

necessary, the most useful sample includes turfgrass that is healthy, unhealthy, and of intermediate condition.

Typically, about a pint of soil is needed to conduct soil tests. The sample submitted should be a subsample from a mixture of small samples taken at various depths and locations from the area where affected plants are growing.

Insect samples should be placed (dead or alive) into small vials, boxes, or other containers that will protect them and keep them intact. The containers from 35-mm photographic film containers are often useful for this purpose.

The University of California does not operate plant, soil, or pest diagnostic laboratories for the public. Clients can obtain plant and soil analysis from commercial laboratories around the state. In some counties, the county agricultural commissioner's office will provide free insect and plant disease identification services. Before submitting any type of samples to a laboratory, contact them for information on prices and sample requirements. Master Gardeners do not submit samples for laboratory analysis on behalf of home gardening clients, but they can provide advice on sampling and shipping procedures.

Diagnosing Problems in Various Types of Plants

California gardeners grow a wide variety of plant materials, including tropical, subtropical, and temperate landscape plants; vegetable and fruit crops; and indoor plants. The following tips address general problem solving and problem solving for particular groups of plant materials. In addition, the other chapters in this handbook that address specific crops include useful information on pests and problems associated with the respective crops.

General Tips

Whenever an entire plant shows wilting, or general decline and poor vigor, first evaluate the root system and main stem or trunk for evidence of injury or other disorder. When individual branches or shoots express these symptoms, examine the base of the branch or shoot.

Wilting, leaf scorch (brown margins), and general yellowing of all foliage are often symp-

Figure 22.3

Growth structures of a woody plant stem

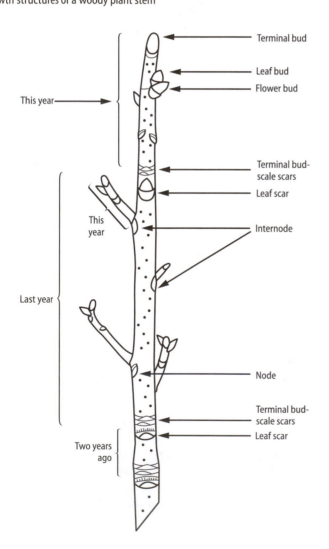

- Terminal bud
- Leaf bud
- Flower bud

This year

- Terminal bud-scale scars
- Leaf scar

This year

- Internode

Last year

- Node

- Terminal bud-scale scars
- Leaf scar

Two years ago

toms of soil problems or of a disorder in the vascular system or root system. Evaluate soil moisture content, irrigation management, and fertilizer practices and root and stem tissues first to eliminate them as causes before looking further.

Woody Plants

When diagnosing problems in woody plants, it is important to know the size of the plant, its vigor, and the general site conditions surrounding the plants. Remember that there is sometimes a delay between the time a problem occurs and the appearance of symptoms or recognition by the client that something is wrong with the plant. Plant vigor, both past and present, can usually be evaluated by measuring the distance between the terminal bud-scale scars. Each growing season, many woody plants, especially deciduous and broadleaf evergreens, form terminal buds at the ends of shoots and branches (fig. 22.3). When new shoot growth emerges from these buds, a scar (small noticeable ridges or rings) remains on the stem where the bud scales were. The distance between any two bud-scale scars or the existing shoot tip and last year's bud-scale scar can be measured to judge the amount of growth the plant has made. A tree that is dying or is "suddenly" dead will often show small amounts of growth over the past few years, which means the plant has been in decline for some time. Site and cultural history are useful in narrowing the causes of the decline to such common factors as poor irrigation management, root disorder, compacted soil, grade changes, poor planting technique, or a combination of these factors. Declining plants are also vulnerable to attacks by insect and disease pests that do not usually infest vigorous plants. In some cases, insect and disease problems that would not damage a healthy plant will kill a declining one.

When woody plants decline or die, it is important to assess the root system's health. Some sort of root injury or disorder should be suspected first when an entire plant declines or dies. Digging out or around newly planted woody plants makes it possible to evaluate their root systems. For older established plants, root health can be evaluated by digging small holes or slices, or by inserting a soil probe in several locations at various distances from the base of the plant. It is usually necessary to explore about one to two feet deep since most of the root system will be present in this zone. Look for numerous fine roots (0.1 inch [2.5 mm] diameter) that are firm and entirely white or white inside with a dark outer cover. If very few fine roots are found or if they are soft, rotten, and brown, then the root system may not be vigorous and healthy enough to support the plant.

Herbaceous Plants and Vegetables

Plants in this group are typically planted in masses and their root systems are more accessible. Look closely for patterns of symptoms and incidence of the problem among plants wherever possible. Carefully check their root systems for signs of soil-related problems or damage to the root system from pests or other injuries. It may be feasible to remove entire plants for evaluation without destroying the whole planting. These plants are often easy to replant and reestablish if a serious, difficult-to-treat problem is present or if the diagnosis cannot pinpoint the exact cause of the problem.

Indoor Plants

Indoor plants are largely dependent on the grower for their needs, and obtaining detailed information from clients about the care given to the plants will usually guide you to a diagnosis. Always evaluate the root system of these plants by removing them from the container (where possible). Assess light levels provided and determine if any sudden changes have occurred in light levels. Weak, spindly growth is a key symptom that light is inadequate.

Proper soil moisture and aeration levels are critical to maintain healthy container-grown plants. Attempt to determine whether proper watering and fertility practices are being followed. General decline, yellow foliage, scorched leaves and stunted growth are symptoms that these factors are not optimal.

Lawns

Many lawn problems are described as "brown patches in my turf," which can be caused by any number of things. Lawn pests often occur in only certain seasons or during certain weather conditions and only on certain species of turfgrass. Knowledge of these components aids in narrowing the potential causes. Improper irrigation (too much, too little, too frequent) often contributes to pest problems and is sometimes the sole cause of a brown turf problem. Look for patterns of symptoms, carefully evaluate the root system, and assess the thatch development when turf problems occur. Damage to turfgrass can often be repaired easily, but it is beneficial to teach the client proper turf management practices so that future problems are minimized.

Bibliography

Brenzel, K. N., ed. 2001. Sunset western garden book. Menlo Park: Sunset Publishing.

Chupp, C., and A. F. Sherf. 1960. Vegetable diseases and their control. New York: Wiley.

Dreistadt, S. H. 1994. Pests of landscape trees and shrubs: An integrated pest management guide. Oakland: University of California Division of Agriculture and Natural Resources Publication 3359.

Flint, M. L., 1998. Pests of the garden and small farm: A grower's guide to using less pesticide. 2nd ed. Oakland: University of California Division of Agriculture and Natural Resources Publication 3332.

Forsberg, J. L. 1975. Diseases of ornamental plants. Urbana: University of Illinois Press.

Harris, R. W., J. R. Clark, and N. P. Matheney. 1999. Arboriculture: Integrated pest management of landscape trees, shrubs, and vines. Upper Saddle River, NJ: Prentice Hall.

Hasey, J. 1985. Plant disease diagnosis. Yuba City, CA: UC Cooperative Extension Sutter-Yuba Counties.

Metcalf, C. L., and W. P. Flint. 1962. Destructive and useful insects. New York: McGraw-Hill.

Smith, M. D., ed. 1989. Ortho problem solver. San Ramon, CA: Ortho Information Services.

Stewart, B. 1993. Diagnosing plant problems. In D. D. Sharp, ed., Maryland Master Gardener handbook. College Park: University of Maryland Cooperative Extension.

Tattar, T. A. 1989. Diseases of shade trees. San Diego: Academic Press.

UC guide to solving garden and landscape problems (CD-ROM). 2000. Oakland: University of California Division of Agriculture and Natural Resources Publication 3400.

UC IPM pest management guidelines for turfgrass. Oakland: University of California Division of Agriculture and Natural Resources Publication 3365-T.

UC IPM pest note series. B. L. P. Ohlendorf, ed. University of California Division of Agriculture and Natural Resources, Statewide Integrated Pest Management Program. Updated regularly. Available through UC Cooperative Extension county offices; also available on the World Wide Web at http://www.ipm.ucdavis.edu

Westcott, C. Plant disease handbook. 5th ed. R. K. Horst, ed. New York: Van Norstrand Reinhold.

Appendix A

Background Information on Nutritional Data

Nutrition Labels, Percent Daily Value, Recommended Dietary Allowances, and Dietary Reference Intakes

Deborah Silva

The Recommended Dietary Allowances (RDAs) are based on the recommendations of the Food and Nutrition Board of the National Academy of Sciences (NAS). For more than 50 years, the RDAs have set the standard as the most authoritative reference in assessing the nutritional value of foods for groups of people. The relationship of the RDAs to the nutritional labels on grocery items, which state the % Daily Value, is noteworthy. The % Daily Value has as its nutrition reference the RDAs that were published by the NAS in 1968, more than 35 years ago. Nutrition labels on grocery products are governed by the U.S. Food and Drug Administration (FDA), not the NAS. It is unclear why the FDA chose the older, 1968 RDAs as its reference for current nutrition labeling on grocery products, rather than a more recent edition of the RDAs. The percentages listed in nutritional value tables in this handbook are based on recent RDAs.

It is important to understand that the vitamin and mineral contents of the crops listed in the tables of this book are averages. The exact amounts vary depending on the crop variety, the soil in which it was grown, geography, season, crop maturity at harvest, storage conditions and duration, preparation or processing for consumption (raw, canned, cooked, roasted), sampling techniques, and the method of nutrient analysis. The home gardener may have more control regarding nutrient losses than the average consumer. Vitamin C content is usually reduced as storage time increases due to oxidation. Many B vitamins are water-soluable and can be lost when excessive amounts of cooking water are used.

The RDAs: 1941 to 1993

RDAs have been prepared by the Food and Nutrition Board of the NAS since 1941 when the objective was to prevent diseases caused by nutrient deficiencies and to maintain good nutrition for healthy persons in the United States, including the nation's military serving in World War II. Since their debut, the RDAs have been updated ten times. The NAS published the 10th edition of *Recommended Dietary Allowances* in 1989. The introductory information in the 1989 edition provides some insight into the purpose and meaning of the RDAs during this period, particularly the emphasis on groups of people:

> …RDAs are intended to reflect the best scientific judgment on nutrient allowances for the maintenance of good health and to serve as the basis for *evaluating the adequacy of diets of groups of people.* [emphasis added] (p. 1)

> …the RDAs provide a safety factor appropriate to each nutrient and exceed the actual requirements of most individuals. The RDA for energy [caloric needs], however, reflects the mean population requirement for each group, since consumption of energy at a level intended to cover the variation in energy needs among individuals could lead to obesity in most persons. (p. 2)

> For many nutrients, digestion, absorption, or both are incomplete and recommendations for dietary intake must make allowance for the portion of the ingested nutrient that is not absorbed … the degree to which the RDA, a *dietary* allowance, exceeds the *physiological* requirement also varies among nutrients. (p. 13)

The Makeover of the RDAs in the Late 1990s: A New Paradigm

Now, for the first time since the RDAs were developed, the NAS is expanding their definition to include individual dietary goals. As of the writing of this *Master Gardener Handbook*, the NAS is introducing a new paradigm for the public and the nutrition community called Dietary Reference Intakes (DRIs), which include RDAs and focus on individual dietary goals as well as the needs of populations. The new RDAs still prevent nutrient deficiencies, but they are now set with the additional purpose of reducing the risk of diet-related chronic conditions in individuals, such as heart disease, diabetes, hypertension, and osteoporosis. The NAS has modified the RDA definition slightly, as discussed below, and has also introduced three new values: Estimated Average Requirements (EARs), Adequate Intakes (AIs), and Tolerable Upper Intake Levels (ULs). Collectively, the four reference values—the RDAs, EARs, AIs, and ULs—are called Dietary Reference Intakes (DRIs). The DRIs expand on the old RDAs.

The RDAs are now defined as "the average daily dietary intake level that is sufficient to meet the nutrient requirements of nearly all (97 to 98%) healthy individuals in a group" (Yates et al. 1998, p. 699). In the DRI framework, the only use of the RDA is "serving as a goal for individuals," (Yates et al. 1998, p. 699) as is indicated in the heading and notes of tables A.1 and A.2.

The process for setting the RDA for a nutrient now depends upon being able to set an EAR. An EAR is "the amount of a nutrient that is estimated to meet the nutrient requirements of half the healthy individuals in a life stage and gender group" (Yates et al. 1998, p. 700). The RDA is set to exceed the EAR by two standard deviations if the requirement for the nutrient is symmetrically distributed. If an EAR cannot be established for a particular nutrient, then an RDA cannot be set because RDAs are based on EARs in the new DRI paradigm. In such cases when an EAR cannot be established due to insufficient scientific evidence, an adequate intake (AI) is determined instead of an RDA. According to the NAS, "the AI thus serves to underscore the need for more research on requirements for that nutrient" (Yates et al. 1998, p. 700). Note that tables A.1 and A.2 include AIs and RDAs. Both may be used as goals for individual intake, as stated in the table notes. Table A.3 reports minimum requirements for sodium, chloride, and potassium.

The fourth dietary reference intake category in the new DRI paradigm is the tolerable upper intake level (UL), which is the highest level of daily nutrient intake that is likely to pose no risk of adverse health effects to almost all individuals in the general population. The NAS says, "ULs are useful because of the increased interest in and availability of fortified foods and the increased use of dietary supplements" (Yates et al. 1998, p. 700). ULs have been set for vitamins and elements (tables A.4 and A.5).

Retinol Activity Equivalents (RAE).

Not all forms of vitamin A are equal with respect to how the human body processes them. Some forms of vitamin A are not absorbed very efficiently by the human body; the vitamin A contained in a particular food may not be bioavailable even though it was consumed. Retinol is a fat-soluble form of vitamin A that is required for new cell growth and prevention of night blindness. Beta-carotene (β-carotene) is a vitamin A precursor that the body converts to vitamin A. Although consumers are usually more familiar with the term "beta-carotene" when describing vitamin A, nutritionists often describe the vitamin A activity in foods in terms of micrograms (μg) retinol activity equivalents (RAE), as stated in the notes to table A.1.

How To Use the Nutritional Value Tables in This Handbook

As stated in the chapters of this handbook, the nutritional value tables provided are based on nutrient composition data adapted from *Bowes and Church's Food Values of Portions Commonly Used*, 17th ed. (Pennington 1998). In the future, when the NAS updates the daily requirements for specific vitamins and elements, you have the tools in this handbook to compute updated nutritional value percentages for the crops featured. The fundamental nutrient composition data for crops in this book are not affected by the new DRI nutrition paradigm from the NAS.

Bibliography

Anonymous. 1998. Nutrient requirements get a makeover: The evolution of the Recommended Dietary Allowances. Food Insight, September/October.

National Academy of Sciences. 2001a. Dietary reference intakes (DRIs): Recommended intakes for individuals, elements. Washington, DC: National Academy of Sciences.

National Academy of Sciences. 2001b. Dietary reference intakes (DRIs): Recommended intakes for individuals, vitamins. Washington, DC: National Academy of Sciences.

National Academy of Sciences. 2001c. Dietary reference intakes (DRIs): Tolerable upper intake levels, elements. Washington, DC: National Academy of Sciences.

National Academy of Sciences. 2001d. Dietary reference intakes (DRIs): Tolerable upper intake levels, vitamins. Washington, DC: National Academy of Sciences.

National Academy of Sciences, Food and Nutrition Board. 1989. Recommended dietary allowances. 10th ed. Washington, DC: National Academy of Sciences.

National Academy Press. 2001. Website www.nap.edu. Accessed May 23, 2001.

Otten, J. 1999. Personal communication. Communications Specialist, Food and Nutrition Board, Institute of Medicine, National Academy of Sciences.

Pennington, J. 1998. Bowes and Church's food values of portions commonly used. 17th ed. Philadelphia: Lippincott.

Yates, A. A., S. A. Schlicker, and C. W. Suitor. 1998. Dietary reference intakes: The new basis for recommendations for calcium and related nutrients, B vitamins, and choline. J. Am. Diet. Assoc. 98: 699–706.

DIETARY REFERENCE INTAKES (DRIs): RECOMMENDED INTAKES FOR INDIVIDUALS, VITAMINS

Life Stage Group	Vitamin A (μg/d)[a]	Vitamin C (mg/d)	Vitamin D (μg/d)[b,c]	Vitamin E (mg/d)[d]	Vitamin K (μg/d)	Thiamin (mg/d)	Riboflavin (mg/d)	Niacin (mg/d)[e]	Vitamin B$_6$ (mg/d)	Folate (μg/d)[f]	Vitamin B$_{12}$ (μg/d)	Pantothenic Acid (mg/d)	Biotin (μg/d)	Choline[g] (mg/d)
Infants														
0–6 mo	400*	40*	5*	4*	2.0*	0.2*	0.3*	2*	0.1*	65*	0.4*	1.7*	5*	125*
7–12 mo	500*	50*	5*	5*	2.5*	0.3*	0.4*	4*	0.3*	80*	0.5*	1.8*	6*	150*
Children														
1–3 y	**300**	**15**	5*	**6**	30*	**0.5**	**0.5**	**6**	**0.5**	**150**	**0.9**	2*	8*	200*
4–8 y	**400**	**25**	5*	**7**	55*	**0.6**	**0.6**	**8**	**0.6**	**200**	**1.2**	3*	12*	250*
Males														
9–13 y	**600**	**45**	5*	**11**	60*	**0.9**	**0.9**	**12**	**1.0**	**300**	**1.8**	4*	20*	375*
14–18 y	**900**	**75**	5*	**15**	75*	**1.2**	**1.3**	**16**	**1.3**	**400**	**2.4**	5*	25*	550*
19–30 y	**900**	**90**	5*	**15**	120*	**1.2**	**1.3**	**16**	**1.3**	**400**	**2.4**	5*	30*	550*
31–50 y	**900**	**90**	5*	**15**	120*	**1.2**	**1.3**	**16**	**1.3**	**400**	**2.4**	5*	30*	550*
51–70 y	**900**	**90**	10*	**15**	120*	**1.2**	**1.3**	**16**	**1.7**	**400**	**2.4**[h]	5*	30*	550*
> 70 y	**900**	**90**	15*	**15**	120*	**1.2**	**1.3**	**16**	**1.7**	**400**	**2.4**[h]	5*	30*	550*
Females														
9–13 y	**600**	**45**	5*	**11**	60*	**0.9**	**0.9**	**12**	**1.0**	**300**	**1.8**	4*	20*	375*
14–18 y	**700**	**65**	5*	**15**	75*	**1.0**	**1.0**	**14**	**1.2**	**400**[i]	**2.4**	5*	25*	400*
19–30 y	**700**	**75**	5*	**15**	90*	**1.1**	**1.1**	**14**	**1.3**	**400**[i]	**2.4**	5*	30*	425*
31–50 y	**700**	**75**	5*	**15**	90*	**1.1**	**1.1**	**14**	**1.3**	**400**[i]	**2.4**	5*	30*	425*
51–70 y	**700**	**75**	10*	**15**	90*	**1.1**	**1.1**	**14**	**1.5**	**400**	**2.4**[h]	5*	30*	425*
> 70 y	**700**	**75**	15*	**15**	90*	**1.1**	**1.1**	**14**	**1.5**	**400**	**2.4**[h]	5*	30*	425*
Pregnancy														
≤ 18 y	**750**	**80**	5*	**15**	75*	**1.4**	**1.4**	**18**	**1.9**	**600**[j]	**2.6**	6*	30*	450*
19–30 y	**770**	**85**	5*	**15**	90*	**1.4**	**1.4**	**18**	**1.9**	**600**[j]	**2.6**	6*	30*	450*
31–50 y	**770**	**85**	5*	**15**	90*	**1.4**	**1.4**	**18**	**1.9**	**600**[j]	**2.6**	6*	30*	450*
Lactation														
≤ 18 y	**1,200**	**115**	5*	**19**	75*	**1.4**	**1.6**	**17**	**2.0**	**500**	**2.8**	7*	35*	550*
19–30 y	**1,300**	**120**	5*	**19**	90*	**1.4**	**1.6**	**17**	**2.0**	**500**	**2.8**	7*	35*	550*
31–50 y	**1,300**	**120**	5*	**19**	90*	**1.4**	**1.6**	**17**	**2.0**	**500**	**2.8**	7*	35*	550*

Source: National Academy of Sciences 2001b.

Note: This table (taken from the DRI reports, see www.nap.edu) presents Recommended Dietary Allowances (RDAs) in **bold type** and Adequate Intakes (AIs) in ordinary type followed by an asterisk (*). RDAs and AIs may both be used as goals for individual intake. RDAs are set to meet the needs of almost all (97 to 98 percent) individuals in a group. For healthy breastfed infants, the AI is the mean intake. The AI for other life stage and gender groups is believed to cover needs of all individuals in the group, but lack of data or uncertainty in the data prevent being able to specify with confidence the percentage of individuals covered by this intake.

[a] As retinol activity equivalents (RAEs). 1 RAE = 1 μg retinol, 12 μg β-carotene, 24 μg α-carotene, or 24 μg β-cryptoxanthin. The RAE for dietary provitamin A carotenoids is two-fold greater than retinol equivalents (RE), whereas the RAE for preformed vitamin A is the same as RE.

[b] cholecalciferol. 1 μg cholecalciferol = 40 IU vitamin D.

[c] In the absence of adequate exposure to sunlight.

[d] As α-tocopherol. α-Tocopherol includes *RRR*-α-tocopherol, the only form of α-tocopherol that occurs naturally in foods, and the *2R*-stereoisomeric forms of α-tocopherol (*RRR*-, *RSR*-, *RRS*-, and *RSS*-α-tocopherol) that occur in fortified foods and supplements. It does not include the *2S*-stereoisomeric forms of α-tocopherol (*SRR*-, *SSR*-, *SRS*-, and *SSS*-α-tocopherol), also found in fortified foods and supplements.

[e] As niacin equivalents (NE). 1 mg of niacin = 60 mg of tryptophan; 0–6 months = preformed niacin (not NE).

[f] As dietary folate equivalents (DFE). 1 DFE = 1 μg food folate = 0.6 μg of folic acid from fortified food or as a supplement consumed with food = 0.5 μg of a supplement taken on an empty stomach.

[g] Although AIs have been set for choline, there are few data to assess whether a dietary supply of choline is needed at all stages of the life cycle, and it may be that the choline requirement can be met by endogenous synthesis at some of these stages.

[h] Because 10 to 30 percent of older people may malabsorb food-bound B$_{12}$, it is advisable for those older than 50 years to meet their RDA mainly by consuming foods fortified with B$_{12}$ or a supplement containing B$_{12}$.

[i] In view of evidence linking folate intake with neural tube defects in the fetus, it is recommended that all women capable of becoming pregnant consume 400 μg from supplements or fortified foods in addition to intake of food folate from a varied diet.

[j] It is assumed that women will continue consuming 400 μg from supplements or fortified food until their pregnancy is confirmed and they enter prenatal care, which ordinarily occurs after the end of the periconceptional period—the critical time for formation of the neural tube.

Table A.2

DIETARY REFERENCE INTAKES (DRIs): RECOMMENDED INTAKES FOR INDIVIDUALS, ELEMENTS

Life Stage Group	Calcium (mg/d)	Chromium (µg/d)	Copper (µg/d)	Fluoride (mg/d)	Iodine (µg/d)	Iron (mg/d)	Magnesium (mg/d)	Manganese (mg/d)	Molybdenum (µg/d)	Phosphorus (mg/d)	Selenium (µg/d)	Zinc (mg/d)
Infants												
0–6 mo	210*	0.2*	200*	0.01*	110*	0.27*	30*	0.003*	2*	100*	15*	2*
7–12 mo	270*	5.5*	220*	0.5*	130*	11*	75*	0.6*	3*	275*	20*	**3**
Children												
1–3 y	500*	11*	**340**	0.7*	**90**	**7**	**80**	1.2*	**17**	**460**	**20**	**3**
4–8 y	800*	15*	**440**	1*	**90**	**10**	**130**	1.5*	**22**	**500**	**30**	**5**
Males												
9–13 y	1,300*	25*	**700**	2*	**120**	**8**	**240**	1.9*	**34**	**1,250**	**40**	**8**
14–18 y	1,300*	35*	**890**	3*	**150**	**11**	**410**	2.2*	**43**	**1,250**	**55**	**11**
19–30 y	1,000*	35*	**900**	4*	**150**	**8**	**400**	2.3*	**45**	**700**	**55**	**11**
31–50 y	1,000*	35*	**900**	4*	**150**	**8**	**420**	2.3*	**45**	**700**	**55**	**11**
51–70 y	1,200*	30*	**900**	4*	**150**	**8**	**420**	2.3*	**45**	**700**	**55**	**11**
> 70 y	1,200*	30*	**900**	4*	**150**	**8**	**420**	2.3*	**45**	**700**	**55**	**11**
Females												
9–13 y	1,300*	21*	**700**	2*	**120**	**8**	**240**	1.6*	**34**	**1,250**	**40**	**8**
14–18 y	1,300*	24*	**890**	3*	**150**	**15**	**360**	1.6*	**43**	**1,250**	**55**	**9**
19–30 y	1,000*	25*	**900**	3*	**150**	**18**	**310**	1.8*	**45**	**700**	**55**	**8**
31–50 y	1,000*	25*	**900**	3*	**150**	**18**	**320**	1.8*	**45**	**700**	**55**	**8**
51–70 y	1,200*	20*	**900**	3*	**150**	**8**	**320**	1.8*	**45**	**700**	**55**	**8**
> 70 y	1,200*	20*	**900**	3*	**150**	**8**	**320**	1.8*	**45**	**700**	**55**	**8**
Pregnancy												
≤ 18 y	1,300*	29*	**1,000**	3*	**220**	**27**	**400**	2.0*	**50**	**1,250**	**60**	**13**
19–30 y	1,000*	30*	**1,000**	3*	**220**	**27**	**350**	2.0*	**50**	**700**	**60**	**11**
31–50 y	1,000*	30*	**1,000**	3*	**220**	**27**	**360**	2.0*	**50**	**700**	**60**	**11**
Lactation												
≤ 18 y	1,300*	44*	**1,300**	3*	**290**	**10**	**360**	2.6*	**50**	**1,250**	**70**	**14**
19–30 y	1,000*	45*	**1,300**	3*	**290**	**9**	**310**	2.6*	**50**	**700**	**70**	**12**
31–50 y	1,000*	45*	**1,300**	3*	**290**	**9**	**320**	2.6*	**50**	**700**	**70**	**12**

Source: National Academy of Sciences 2001a.

Note: This table presents Recommended Dietary Allowances (RDAs) in **bold type** and Adequate Intakes (AIs) in ordinary type followed by an asterisk (*). RDAs and AIs may both be used as goals for individual intake. RDAs are set to meet the needs of almost all (97 to 98 percent) individuals in a group. For healthy breastfed infants, the AI is the mean intake. The AI for other life stage and gender groups is believed to cover needs of all individuals in the group, but lack of data or uncertainty in the data prevent being able to specify with confidence the percentage of individuals covered by this intake.

Table A.3

ESTIMATED SODIUM, CHLORIDE, AND POTASSIUM MINIMUM REQUIREMENTS OF HEALTHY PERSONS

Age	Weight (kg)[a]	Sodium (mg)[a,b]	Chloride (mg)[a,b]	Potassium (mg)[c]
Months				
0–5	4.5	120	180	500
6–11	8.9	200	300	700
Years				
1	11.0	225	350	1,000
2–5	16.0	300	500	1,400
6–9	25.0	400	600	1,600
10–18	50.0	500	750	2,000
>18[d]	70.0	500	750	2,000

Source: National Academy of Sciences, Food and Nutrition Board 1989, p. 253.

[a] No allowance has been included for large, prolonged losses from the skin through perspiration.

[b] There is no evidence that higher intakes confer any health benefit.

[c] Desirable intakes of potassium may considerably exceed these values (~3,500 mg for adults).

[d] No allowance included for growth. Values for people under 18 assume a growth rate at the 50th percentile reported by the National Center for Health Statistics and averaged for males and females.

DIETARY REFERENCE INTAKES (DRIs): TOLERABLE UPPER INTAKE LEVELS (ULs) , VITAMINS

Life Stage Group	Vitamin A (µg/d)[b]	Vitamin C (mg/d)	Vitamin D (µg/d)	Vitamin E (mg/d)[c,d]	Vitamin K	Thiamin	Ribo-flavin	Niacin (mg/d)[d]	Vitamin B$_6$ (mg/d)	Folate (µg/d)[d]	Vitamin B$_{12}$	Pantothenic Acid	Biotin	Choline (g/d)	Carot-enoids[e]
Infants															
0–6 mo	600	ND[f]	25	ND	ND	ND	ND	ND	ND	ND	ND	ND	ND	ND	ND
7–12 mo	600	ND	25	ND	ND	ND	ND	ND	ND	ND	ND	ND	ND	ND	ND
Children															
1–3 y	600	400	50	200	ND	ND	ND	10	30	300	ND	ND	ND	1.0	ND
4–8 y	900	650	50	300	ND	ND	ND	15	40	400	ND	ND	ND	1.0	ND
Males, Females															
9–13 y	1,700	1,200	50	600	ND	ND	ND	20	60	600	ND	ND	ND	2.0	ND
14–18 y	2,800	1,800	50	800	ND	ND	ND	30	80	800	ND	ND	ND	3.0	ND
19–70 y	3,000	2,000	50	1,000	ND	ND	ND	35	100	1,000	ND	ND	ND	3.5	ND
> 70 y	3,000	2,000	50	1,000	ND	ND	ND	35	100	1,000	ND	ND	ND	3.5	ND
Pregnancy															
≤ 18 y	2,800	1,800	50	800	ND	ND	ND	30	80	800	ND	ND	ND	3.0	ND
19–50 y	3,000	2,000	50	1,000	ND	ND	ND	35	100	1,000	ND	ND	ND	3.5	ND
Lactation															
≤ 18 y	2,800	1,800	50	800	ND	ND	ND	30	80	800	ND	ND	ND	3.0	ND
19–50 y	3,000	2,000	50	1,000	ND	ND	ND	35	100	1,000	ND	ND	ND	3.5	ND

Source: National Academy of Sciences 2001d.

Notes:

[a] UL = The maximum level of daily nutrient intake that is likely to pose no risk of adverse effects. Unless otherwise specified, the UL represents total intake from food, water, and supplements. Due to lack of suitable data, ULs could not be established for vitamin K, thiamin, riboflavin, vitamin B$_{12}$, pantothenic acid, biotin, or carotenoids. In the absence of ULs, extra caution may be warranted in consuming levels above recommended intakes.

[b] As preformed vitamin A only.

[c] As α-tocopherol; applies to any form of supplemental α-tocopherol.

[d] The ULs for vitamin E, niacin, and folate apply to synthetic forms obtained from supplements, fortified foods, or a combination of the two.

[e] β-Carotene supplements are advised only to serve as a provitamin A source for individuals at risk of vitamin A deficiency.

[f] ND = Not determinable due to lack of data of adverse effects in this age group and concern with regard to lack of ability to handle excess amounts. Source of intake should be from food only to prevent high levels of intake.

Table A.5

DIETARY REFERENCE INTAKES (DRIs): TOLERABLE UPPER INTAKE LEVELS (ULs), ELEMENTS

Life stage group	Arsenic[b]	Boron (mg/d)	Calcium (g/d)	Chromium	Copper (μg/d)	Fluoride (mg/d)	Iodine (μg/d)	Iron (mg/d)	Magnesium (mg/d)[c]	Manganese (mg/d)	Molybdenum (μg/d)	Nickel (mg/d)	Phosphorus (g/d)	Selenium (μg/d)	Silicon[d]	Vanadium (mg/d)[e]	Zinc (mg/d)
Infants																	
0–6 mo	ND[f]	ND	ND	ND	ND	0.7	ND	40	ND	ND	ND	ND	ND	45	ND	ND	4
7–12 mo	ND	ND	ND	ND	ND	0.9	ND	40	ND	ND	ND	ND	ND	60	ND	ND	5
Children																	
1–3 y	ND	3	2.5	ND	1,000	1.3	200	40	65	2	300	0.2	3	90	ND	ND	7
4–8 y	ND	6	2.5	ND	3,000	2.2	300	40	110	3	600	0.3	3	150	ND	ND	12
Males, Females																	
9–13 y	ND	11	2.5	ND	5,000	10	600	40	350	6	1,100	0.6	4	280	ND	ND	23
14–18 y	ND	17	2.5	ND	8,000	10	900	45	350	9	1,700	1.0	4	400	ND	ND	34
19–70 y	ND	20	2.5	ND	10,000	10	1,100	45	350	11	2,000	1.0	4	400	ND	1.8	40
> 70 y	ND	20	2.5	ND	10,000	10	1,100	45	350	11	2,000	1.0	3	400	ND	1.8	40
Pregnancy																	
≤ 18 y	ND	17	2.5	ND	8,000	10	900	45	350	9	1,700	1.0	3.5	400	ND	ND	34
19–50 y	ND	20	2.5	ND	10,000	10	1,100	45	350	11	2,000	1.0	3.5	400	ND	ND	40
Lactation																	
≤ 18 y	ND	17	2.5	ND	8,000	10	900	45	350	9	1,700	1.0	4	400	ND	ND	34
19–50 y	ND	20	2.5	ND	10,000	10	1,100	45	350	11	2,000	1.0	4	400	ND	ND	40

Source: National Academy of Sciences 2001c.

[a] UL = The maximum level of daily nutrient intake that is likely to pose no risk of adverse effects. Unless otherwise specified, the UL represents total intake from food, water, and supplements. Due to lack of suitable data, ULs could not be established for arsenic, chromium, and silicon. In the absence of ULs, extra caution may be warranted in consuming levels above recommended intakes.

[b] Although the UL was not determined for arsenic, there is no justification for adding arsenic to food or supplements.

[c] The ULs for magnesium represent intake from a pharmacological agent only and do not include intake from food and water.

[d] Although silicon has not been shown to cause adverse effects in humans, there is no justification for adding silicon to supplements.

[e] Although vanadium in food has not been shown to cause adverse effects in humans, there is no justification for adding vanadium to food and vanadium supplements should be used with caution. The UL is based on adverse effects in laboratory animals and this data could be used to set a UL for adults but not children and adolescents.

[f] ND = Not determinable due to lack of data of adverse effects in this age group and concern with regard to lack of ability to handle excess amounts. Source of intake should be from food only to prevent high levels of intake.

Appendix B

Useful Conversions

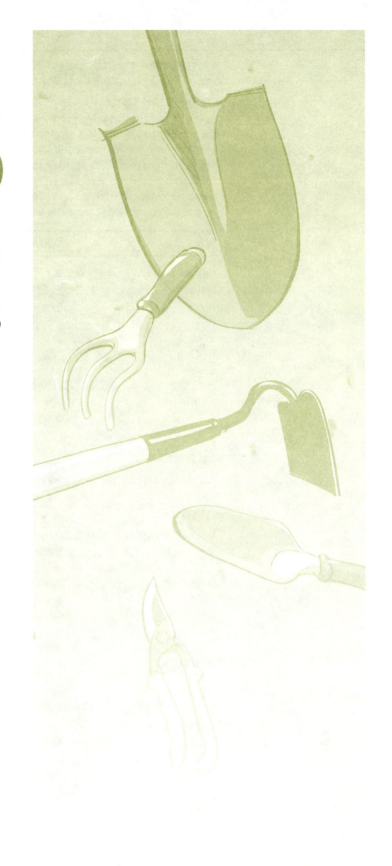

CONVERSION TABLE

To use this conversion table, find the measure in column A or B for the known value (English measures are grouped together first in each category). If the value you know is in column A, multiply the number by the value in the column to the left (A to B). If the known value is in column B, multiply it by the number to the right (B to A) to get the converted number.

Example: How many miles is 10 kilometers? Kilometers are in column A, miles in column B. The conversion factor for A to B is 0.621. So 10 km × 0.621 = 6.21 mi. To find how many kilometers 10 miles is, look to the conversion value under B to A (1.609). So 10 miles × 1.609 = 16.09 kilometers.

A to B	COLUMN A	COLUMN B	B to A
LINEAR AND AREA MEASURES			
0.083	inch	foot	12
0.333	foot	yard	3
0.000189	foot	mile	5,280
0.000568	yard	mile	1,760
0.02296	1,000 sq ft	acre	43.56
640	square mile	acre	0.00156
0.000579	cubic inch	cubic foot	1,728
43,560	acre	square feet	0.00002
0.394	centimeter	inch	2.54
3.281	meter	foot	0.305
1.094	meter	yard	0.914
0.621	kilometer	mile	1.609
0.0247	are	acre	40.5
2.47	hectare	acre	0.405
0.386	square kilometer	square mile	2.59
VOLUME MEASURES OR LIQUID MEASURES			
0.333	level teaspoon	level tablespoon	3
2	fluid ounce	level tablespoon	0.5
0.125	fluid ounce	cup	8
0.0625	fluid ounce	pint	16
0.5	cup	pint	2
0.5	pint	quart	2
4	gallon	quart	0.25
28.875	pint	cubic inch	0.0346
57.75	quart	cubic inch	0.0173
231	gallon	cubic inch	0.00433
1.057	liter	quart	0.946
0.265	liter	gallon	3.79
1,000	liter	milliliter	0.001
0.03378	milliliter	fluid ounce	29.6
2.11	liter	pint	0.473
1.0	milliliter	cubic centimeter	1.0
DRY WEIGHTS			
16	pound	ounce	0.0625
0.0005	pound	ton (short)	2,000
0.0353	gram	ounce	28.35
0.0022	gram	pound	453.6
0.001	gram	kilogram	1,000
2.205	kilogram	pound	0.454
1.102	ton (metric)	ton (short)	0.907

A to B	COLUMN A	COLUMN B	B to A
VOLUME OR WEIGHT PER AREA			
0.02296	pound/acre	pound/1,000 sq ft	43.56
0.02296	gallon/acre	gallon/1,000 sq ft	43.56
2.938	gallon/acre	ounce/1,000 sq ft	0.3403
0.893	kilogram/hectare	pound/acre	1.12
0.0205	kilogram/hectare	pound/1,000 sq ft	48.79
0.107	liter/hectare	gallon/acre	9.35
CONCENTRATIONS			
0.0001	ppm	percent	10,000
0.013	ppm	oz by weight in 100 gallons	76.9
0.781	oz by weight per gallon	percent	1.28
0.125	lb per 100 gallons	percent	8
0.1	gram/liter	percent	10
0.1	gram/kilogram	percent	10
1,000	gram/liter	parts per million	0.001
WATER MEASUREMENTS			
7.48	cubic foot	gallons	0.134
62.4	cubic foot	pounds of water	0.016
8.34	gallon	pounds of water	0.120
0.000023	cubic foot	acre-foot	43,560
0.0000031	gallon	acre-foot	325,829
0.0000368	gallon	acre-inch	27,152
TEMPERATURE			
(°C + 17.98) × 1.8	Centigrade	Fahrenheit	(°F − 32) × 0.5555
DRY VOLUME			
7.48	cubic foot	gallon	0.1337
27.0	cubic yard	cubic foot	0.037
PLANT NUTRIENTS			
2.29	P	P_2O_5	0.437
1.20	K	K_2O	0.830
1.39	Ca	CaO	0.715
1.66	Mg	MgO	0.602
MISCELLANEOUS			
0.000145	pascal	pound/in^2 (psi)	6,900
9.90	megapascal	atmosphere	0.101
10	megapascal	bar	0.1
10	siemen/meter	millimho/cm	0.1
METRIC SYSTEM			
0.001	milli-		1,000
0.01	centi-		100
0.1	deci-	Base: 1 gram,	10
10	deka-	1 liter, 1 meter,	0.1
100	hect(o)-	1 are, etc.	0.01
1,000	kilo-		0.001

COMMON WEIGHT AND MEASURE EQUIVALENTS FOR THE HOME GARDENER

WEIGHTS	
Pounds per acre	Equivalent quanity per 100 sq ft
100	3 $\frac{1}{2}$ oz
200	7 $\frac{1}{2}$ oz
300	11 oz
400	14 $\frac{3}{4}$ oz
500	1 lb 2 $\frac{1}{2}$ oz
600	1 lb 6 oz
700	1 lb 10 oz
800	1 lb 13 oz
900	2 lb 1 oz
1,000	2 lb 5 oz
2,000	4 lb 10 oz

MEASURES (APPROXIMATE)	
1 level tsp	$\frac{1}{6}$ oz
1 level tbsp	$\frac{1}{2}$ oz
1 level c	8 oz
1 pt	1 lb
1 qt	2 lb
1 gal	8 lb

Glossary

abscission. The dropping off of a leaf, fruit, or flower.

acid. *See* **pH**.

adventitious. Plant structures or organs, such as buds, shoots, or roots, produced in an abnormal position or that arise from other plant tissues.

aeration (soil). The process in which air in the spaces around soil particles is renewed.

aerobic. Occurring only in the presence of oxygen, or requiring oxygen.

aggregates (soil). Clusters of soil particles variable in shape, size, and degree of association, such as granules, clods, or prisms, that give a soil its structure.

agronomy. The science of the production of crops grown on large acreages, such as grains and forages.

air layering. A propagation technique in which plant parts are rooted while they remain attached to the parent plant.

alkaline. *See* **pH**.

alternate bearing. The bearing of heavier and then lighter crops of fruits in successive years.

alternate bud and leaves. The arrangement of buds or leaves singly at a node, usually on either side of the stem.

anaerobic. Occurring in the absence of oxygen or not requiring oxygen.

angiosperms. Flowering plants that produce their seeds within a fruit (ovary); the most advanced class of plants.

anion. A negatively charged ion. *See* **ion**.

annual. A plant in which the entire life cycle is normally completed in a single growing season.

anther. The upper portion of the stamen that produces pollen grains.

apical. Located at or pertaining to the apex or tip.

apical dominance. The influence of a terminal bud (apical bud) in suppressing the growth of lateral buds.

apical meristem. The tissues at the tip of roots and shoots where cells divide, giving rise to new growth.

apomictic seed. A seed developed from an unfertilized egg.

arthropods. Invertebrate organisms of the animal kingdom that include insects, spiders, and Crustacea; organisms characterized by an external skeleton and legs with movable segments or joints.

asexual (or vegetative) propagation. Production of a new plant by using a part of a parent plant, as opposed to sexual union; reproduction of a plant by any means other than seed.

assimilation. The conversion of food into cell walls and cell contents.

auxin. A generic term for a group of plant hormones that are active at low concentrations and that regulate plant growth and development, particularly cell division, cell elongation, adventitious root initiation, and bud dormancy.

available moisture. The amount of water in a soil that roots can absorb.

axil. The angle formed between a leaf and the stem on which it is attached.

bacteria. Microscopic, one-celled organisms that lack chlorophyll and may be parasites on plants or animals, causing disease; most are beneficial agents of fermentation and decay of organic matter.

banding. The placement of fertilizer in the soil close to a row of seed.

bare-root transplanting. A method of transplanting in which plants are dug from the ground with little or no soil left on the roots.

bark. The outermost tissue of a woody stem that usually includes portions of the phloem.

bark grafting. A technique in which the scion is inserted between the bark and the xylem of the stock.

basal. Pertaining to the base or lower part of an organ or plant part.

basal plate. The short, flattened stem at the base of a bulb.

biennial. A plant that normally requires two growing seasons to complete its life cycle. Only vegetative growth occurs the first year; flowering and fruiting occur the second year.

binomial system of nomenclature. The system in which the scientific name for any plant or other organism is composed of two Latin terms that designate genus and specific epithet; together, the genus and specific epithet create a species name.

biological pest control (biocontrol). The action of parasites, predators, pathogens, or competitors in reducing another organism's population density.

biotic. Pertaining to life or living.

bipinnate. Twice pinnate, as in a leaf blade.

blade. The usually broad, flattened part of a leaf.

blanching. To whiten (etiolate) a vegetable as it is growing by wrapping the stalk and leaves with paper or outer leaves, or by mounding soil around the portion to be whitened, such as celery.

blight. A disease causing sudden, severe leaf damage and/or general killing of stems or flowers.

blossom-end rot. A disorder of tomato fruit in which a sunken dry rot develops on the bottom; associated with calcium deficiency and water stress.

bolting. Premature flower and seedstalk formation, usually in biennial crops during their first year of growth.

botany. The scientific study of all facets of plant structure and behavior.

bract. A modified leaflike structure closely associated with a flower, sometimes petal-like.

bramble. Any plant of the genus *Rubus*, such as the blackberry and raspberry.

branch collar. The distinct enlarged portion of woody tissue formed at the base of a branch where it attaches to the trunk.

broadleaf. Plants possessing leaves that are thin, wide, and flattened.

bud. A protuberance on a plant stem containing an embryonic leafy or flowering shoot, or both.

budding. Grafting by inserting a single bud (scion) under the bark of the rootstock.

bulb. An underground storage structure composed of a short stem and overlapping, fleshy leaf bases surrounding a bud, as in onions and tulips.

bulk density (soil). The weight per unit of volume of nondisturbed soil that has been completely dried, commonly expressed as grams per cubic centimeter (g/cc); a means of characterizing the amount of macropores and compaction in soil.

calcareous (soil). A soil containing relatively high amounts of calcium carbonate, usually alkaline.

callus. Nonspecific tissue that forms a protective covering over a wounded plant surface.

calyx. The outer or lowest of the series of floral parts composed of the sepals. Usually green and leaflike, but may be colored like the petals.

cambium. A very thin zone or cylinder of meristematic cells, lateral in position, that gives rise to xylem and phloem; the tissue responsible for increases in stem and root diameter.

cane. The woody stem of small fruits such as grape or raspberry; sometimes applied to the stems of roses.

cane pruning. A system of pruning grapes in which all canes that previously fruited are removed, then a few 1-year-old canes are headed back and usually placed on a trellis.

canker. A localized area of diseased tissue on a stem, often sunken or swollen, surrounded by healthy tissue.

capillary forces. The absorptive force between a liquid (water) and the surrounding material (soil particles), coupled with the cohesive force in the liquid's surface (surface tension); forces that enable water to rise or be held in small spaces against the force of gravity.

capillary moisture. The water that is held by the soil against the force of gravity and that is available for plant absorption; the amount of water a soil will hold between wilting point and field capacity.

carbohydrate. An organic molecule composed of carbon, hydrogen, and oxygen, such as sugar, starch, or cellulose.

carbohydrate-nitrogen balance. The relative proportion of accumulated carbohydrates and nitrogen in stems and leaves of plants; important because it influences flower bud initiation and fruit set.

cation. A positively charged ion.

cation exchange. The interchange between a cation in solution and another cation on the surface of a colloidal or other surface-active material such as a particle of clay or organic matter in the soil.

cation exchange capacity. A measure of soil's ability to retain fertility (cationic forms of plant-essential elements); the sum of exchangeable cations absorbed by a soil, expressed in milliequivalents per 100 g of soil equivalent to the milligrams of H^+ that will combine with 100 g of dry soil.

cell. The structural unit composing the bodies of plants and animals; an organized unit of protoplasm, in plants usually surrounded by a cell wall.

cell membrane. The structure inside the cell wall that appears to have the function of regulating the flow of nutrients and other materials into and out of the cell.

cell wall. The membranous covering of a cell secreted by the cytoplasm in growing plants; consists largely of cellulose.

cellulose. A complex carbohydrate; the chief component of the cell wall in most plants.

central leader system. A system of tree training in which the trunk is encouraged to form a central axis with branches distributed laterally around it.

chelate. A metal ion bonded to an organic molecule from which it can be readily released, such as iron chelate or sequestrene 138 Fe.

chilling requirement. The cumulative hours of temperature below 45°F (7°C) required by many temperate woody plants in order to overcome bud dormancy and to retain vigor.

chlorophyll. The green plant pigment that absorbs light energy necessary to the process of photosynthesis.

chloroplast. A specialized body in the cell cytoplasm that contains chlorophyll.

chlorosis. Interveinal yellowing of foliage that results from a loss or deficiency of chlorophyll.

clay. 1. Soil particles less than 0.002 mm in diameter. 2. A textural class of soil.

clone. A group of genetically identical plants produced by asexual propagation from a single plant.

cold frame. A bottomless box with a removable clear top used to protect, propagate, or harden plants. No heating device is used.

cole crop. Any plant of the genus *Brassica*, of the crucifer family (e.g., cabbage, cauliflower, broccoli).

coleoptile. Sheathlike pointed structure covering the shoot of grass seedlings; commonly interpreted as the first leaf of the plant above the cotyledon.

companion planting. A form of intercropping in which specific kinds of plants are reported to mutually benefit from close association in the garden.

complete fertilizer. A fertilizer containing nitrogen, phosphorus, and potassium.

complete flower. Flower having all of the floral parts (stamens, pistil, petals, and sepals).

compound leaf. A leaf divided into two or more parts, or leaflets, all attached to the stem by a single petiole.

conifers. Plants that bear cone fruits, such as pines, cedars, spruces, and firs.

contact pesticide. A substance that kills a pest primarily by contacting its tissue rather than by internal absorption.

cool-season crop. Crop that thrives best or produces highest-quality crops in cool weather.

cordon. The main upper woody portion of a grape vine that is trained to a trellis and from which fruiting canes develop; also, a main branch of an espaliered fruit tree.

core. 1. The innermost part of pome and certain other fruits that contains the seed. 2. Receptacle tissue in certain plants, as in the raspberry.

corm. A short, thickened underground storage organ formed usually by enlargement of the base of the main plant stem.

corolla. The petals of a flower, collectively.

cortex. Unspecified outer tissues of the stem or root.

cotyledon. A seed leaf that is distinct from the characteristic leaves of a plant.

cross-pollination. The transfer of pollen from the anther of one plant to the stigma of another plant.

crown. 1. The upper part of a tree or shrub, or the aboveground portion of a plant consisting of branches and leaves. 2. The area where the stem and root join.

cucurbit. Any plant of the family Cucurbitaceae (e.g., cucumber, squash, watermelon).

cultivar (cultivated variety). A taxonomic group of plants, originally developed and now maintained under cultivation, that are significant in agriculture (horticulture) and are clearly distinguished by a characteristic that is retained when plants are propagated. In common horticultural usage, *cultivar* is synonymous with *variety*. Cultivars can be classified as those which are sexually reproduced and those which are asexually reproduced. In this *Handbook*, cultivar names are enclosed in quotation marks only when used as part of the scientific (Latin) name.

cuticle. A thin waxy or varnished-like layer that covers the epidermis of aboveground plant parts.

cutting. Any part that can be severed from a plant and used to regenerate a whole new plant, most commonly stem, root, leaf or bud cuttings.

cytoplasm. The living material in a cell (protoplasm), excluding the nucleus.

damping-off. Rotting of seedlings and cuttings caused by any of several fungi; a fungal attack near the soil line that causes cuttings or emerged seedlings to fall over and die.

day-neutral plant. A plant in which the flowering period or some other process is not influenced by length of daylight.

deciduous. Trees or shrubs that drop their leaves at the end of each growing season; contrasted with evergreen plants.

determinant. A growth habit in which the main plant stem(s) (axis) terminate(s) in the development of a flower as in corn and some varieties of tomato.

dicot (dicotyledon). A flowering plant having two seed leaves, characteristic net-veined leaves, vascular tissues arranged in concentric rings, and flower parts in multiples of fours or fives.

difusion. The dispersal of molecules from an area of greater concentration to an area of less concentration until the molecules are uniformly distributed.

dioecious. Literally, "two houses"; plants bearing staminate and pistillate flowers (or pollen and seed cones of conifers) on different individuals of the same species; species that produce separate male and female plants.

division (propagation). The technique of dividing a plant into two or more parts in which each part is a whole plant; often used with perennials.

dormancy. A period of inactivity or physiological rest, especially in bulbs, buds, seeds, and spores.

drip line. The imaginary verticle line extended from the outermost branch tips of a tree to the soil directly below.

drupe. A simple fleshy fruit in which the inner part of the ovary wall develops into a hard stony or woody endocarp, as in the peach.

dwarf. A plant that is much smaller when mature than others of its species, often achieved by grafting.

efficacious. Capable of producing the desired effect; effective.

element. A substance in its simplest form that cannot be broken down further (e.g., carbon, oxygen, nitrogen).

embryo. A rudimentary plant formed within a seed.

endosperm. The tissue in seeds that serves as a food reserve used by the embryo at germination; a large part of a mature seed may be endosperm tissue.

entomology. The scientific study of insects, including their anatomy, physiology, and behavior.

epidermis. The outermost layer of cells of the leaf and of young stems and roots.

espalier system. A method of tree training in which the tree is usually planted against a wall and the main branches trained in a plane parallel to the wall in a geometric design.

ethylene. A plant hormone that regulates ripening and flowering; ripening fruit and damaged plant tissues give off large quantities; used artificially for many purposes, including ripening and coloring certain fruit.

etiolate. To cause stems to become elongated, weak, and pale green in color, usually due to insufficient light.

evapotranspiration (ET). The loss of water from soil by evaporation from the soil surface and plant transpiration.

evergreen. Plants that retain leaves or needles longer than one growing season so that some leaves are present throughout the year.

exocarp. Outermost layer of the fruit wall; often the skin of the fruit.

fasciation. Flattening and enlargement of a branch as if several stems were fused, often accompanied by curving. Believed to be caused by injury to the cells of the bud or by multiple terminal buds arranged in a single plane.

fastigiate. A narrow, upright growth habit.

fertilizer. A substance added to soil to provide plants with essential nutrient ions.

fertilization (botanical). The union of two gametes to form a zygote, as when a pollen grain germinates and unites with an ovule to form an embryo.

fertilizer analysis. A statement, usually on the label of a fertilizer container, of the percentages by weights of nitrogen, phosphoric acid, and potash contained in the material.

fertilizer formula. The quantity and grade of crude stock materials used in making a fertilizer mixture.

fibrous rooted. A root system in which the roots branch near the crown and become finely divided.

field capacity. The amount of water a soil can hold against gravity. *See* **capillary moisture**.

filament. The stalk of the stamen supporting the anther.

flocculate. To aggregate individual particles into small clusters; the aggregation of soil particles into variously shaped small groups (crumbs, plates, clods, prisms) that create structure.

floret. An individual flower that is a part of a flower head.

floricane. In raspberries, the two-year old stems (canes) that produce flowers and fruit.

flower. The reproductive structure of the angiosperms.

foot-candle. The density of light striking the inner surface of a sphere with all the surface area being 1 foot away from a 1-candle-power source.

frass. The solid fecal material produced by insect larvae.

fruit. 1. (botanical) The matured ovary of a flowering plant containing seed.
2. (horticultural) A fleshy, ripened ovary of a plant eaten for its dessert quality.

fruit set. The inhibition of a fruit to drop after a flower is pollinated.

full-slip. In harvesting of melons, the point of maturity when there is easy separation of the fruit from the vine.

fungi. A lower order of plant organisms, excluding bacteria, that have no chlorophyll or vascular system. Their vegetative body consists of threadlike hyphae, and they often develop spore-producing structures. Some cause diseases of horticultural crops; others (mushrooms) are grown as food; most are beneficial saprophytes.

fungicide. A substance that kills or inhibits fungi.

furrow. A depression in the ground surface dug along a prescribed line for planting seed, irrigating, controlling surface water, or reducing soil loss.

gamete. A reproductive body capable of fusion with another; the sperm from the pollen grain and the egg from the ovule.

gametophyte. Typically a haploid, gamete-producing plant derived from a spore, as in ferns; in higher plants, the sperm and egg and the haploid cells from which they develop.

gene. A unit of inheritance, located on chromosomes, composed of DNA.

genus. A group of closely related plants that is clearly differentiated from other groups.

germination. The beginning or resumption of growth of a seed, embryo, or spore, including pollen grain on a stigma; the sprouting of a seed.

germ plasm (germplasm). Hereditary materials (chromosomes, genes, and any other self-propagating particles); the total genetic resources available in the entire population of a crop or species.

gibberellins (gibberellic acid, GA). A group of plant hormones regulating stem elongation, seed germination, and other growth.

girdling. Constricting or removing the outer tissues around a stem as deep or deeper than the cambium, which disrupts the flow of carbohydrates through the phloem.

grafting. The process of inserting a part of one plant into or onto another in a way that the two will unite and continue growth as a single unit.

granule (soil). Rounded or subangular, relatively small, dense soil aggregate.

gravitational water. Water that moves through soil under the force of gravity.

green manure. A crop plowed under when green for its beneficial effect on soil structure and fertility.

gray water. Water discharged after household use, including water used for clothes washing, dish washing, and bathing, but excluding water from toilets.

guard cells. Specialized crescent-shaped epidermal cells that surround a stomate and control its aperture.

gymnosperms. Seed-producing, nonflowering plants having ovules borne on open cones or scales rather than an enclosed ovary, such as the needle evergreens, pine, fir, and cedar.

half-slip. In harvesting of melons, a stage of maturity in which, as the fruit is pulled from the vine, only a portion of the stem separates easily from the base of the fruit.

haploid. Having the gametic number of chromosomes, or half the number characteristic of somatic (nonreproductive) cells.

hardening. Treating plants to make them more resistant to adverse environmental conditions, usually by exposing them gradually to increased light, temperature changes, and drought.

hardening-off. *See* **hardening**.

hardpan. A subsurface layer of compacted or cemented soil.

hardscape. The portions of a landscape or garden area that are paved.

hardwood stem cutting. A mature shoot of the last season's growth that is removed from the plant after the leaves have fallen to be used in propagating new plants.

heading back. Pruning the end of a branch or stem by cutting it back to a bud or side branch.

heartwood. Nonliving, often darker-colored wood toward the center of a tree trunk that is surrounded by sapwood.

hedgerow. A widened row sometimes used for bramble fruits in which new canes are permitted to grow between the original plants in the row.

herbaceous. A plant or portion of a plant that lacks pronounced woody structure or tissue.

herbicide. A substance that kills plants.

horizon (soil). A distinctive soil layer that has well-defined characteristics.

hormone. An organic substance that, in minute quantities, is usually produced in one part of an organism and transported to another, where it affects or regulates growth and development of tissues.

horticulture. The art and science of cultivating high-value, often highly perishable crops (sometimes called "garden crops"), including fruits, vegetables, flowers, and landscape trees and shrubs.

hotbed. Small enclosed garden bed, having a transparent covering, in which the soil is heated.

humus. Organic matter in a highly decayed state, rich in plant nutrient ions, and very retentive of water when added to soil.

hybrid. Progeny of a cross between two individuals differing in one or more genes (characteristics).

hypha (pl., hyphae). A threadlike structure composed of one or more tubular cells that make(s) up the body of a fungus.

hypocotyl. Part of the stem of an embryo or seedling below the cotyledons and above the radicle or embryonic root.

imperfect flower. Flower containing either stamens or pistil but not both.

incomplete flower. Flower lacking one or more of the floral organs (sepals, petals, stamens, or pistil).

indeterminant. A growth habit in which the main plant stem(s) (axis) remain(s) vegetative and in which flowers form on axillary buds; growth and flowering can continue indefinitely through the plant's life cycle as in cucumber and some tomato varieties.

infection. The establishment of the pathogen in the host.

inflorescence. The arrangement of a flower or flowers on an axis; a flower cluster.

inoculum. A pathogen or its parts (spores, mycelium, etc.) that can incite infection.

inorganic. 1. Not composed of or derived from plant or animal materials. 2. A compound that does not contain carbon.

insecticide. A substance that kills insects.

instar. The period between molts in the larvae of insects.

integrated pest management (IPM). A strategy that centers on long-term prevention or suppression of pest problems through a combination of techniques such as resistant varieties, biological control, cultural practices, habitat modification, and the use of pesticides when careful field monitoring indicates they are needed according to treatment thresholds.

intercropping. Growing two or more crops in the same planting area simultaneously, as in planting squash in between rows of corn.

internode. The portion of the stem between any two nodes.

ion. An atom or group of atoms that carries a negative (anion) or positive (cation) charge, formed by the breakup (disassociation) of molecules as happens when certain molecules or compounds are dissolved in water.

IPM. *See* **integrated pest management**.

iron chlorosis. A yellowing or loss of green color in leaf tissue, commonly between the veins, due to an insufficient concentration of iron in the plant.

June drop. The dropping of immature tree fruits during the early summer; believed to be caused most frequently by embryo abortion or an extremely large crop load.

juvenility. The early period in a plant's life cycle characterized by vigorous vegetative growth, sometimes distinctive in form from mature growth, and no flower production.

lateral bud. A bud attached to the side of a stem.

layering. A method of vegetatively propagating woody plants by covering portions of their stems or branches with moist soil or sphagnum moss so that adventitious root will form. The branch is then removed from the parent plant. *See* **air layering**.

leaching. 1. Removing salts, ions, or other soluble substances from soil by abundant irrigation combined with drainage.
2. Movement of soluble materials downward with percolating water.

leaf. A plant organ typically attached to a stem, varying in size and shape but usually flattened or needlelike and green in color that is concerned primarily with the manufacture of carbohydrates by photosynthesis.

leaflet. A segment of a compound leaf.

legume. A plant of the family Leguminosae, such as peas and beans; characterized by a fruit pod that opens along two sutures when ripe.

lenticel. Opening through the bark or outer covering of fruits and stems (and sometimes other organs), that permits exchange of gases from the inner tissues with the surrounding air.

lignification. The process in which plant cells become woody by conversion of certain constituents of the cell wall into lignin; generally considered to include the hardening, strengthening, and cementing of the cell walls in the formation of wood.

loam. A soil that contains 7 to 27 percent clay, 28 to 50 percent silt, and less than 52 percent sand, which has an ideal structure for cultivation and plant growth.

long-day plant. A plant in which the flowering period or other process is regulated by daily exposure to light longer than a certain minimum number of hours, usually more than 12 hours.

macronutrient. Plant-essential elements required in relatively large amounts by plants.

macropores. The relatively large spaces among soil aggregates from which water readily drains and in which air resides.

massive structure (soil). A type of soil structure in which no aggregates naturally form, and when disturbed by digging, large clods are created, as in heavy clay, and compacted soils or soil particles remain totally separate, as in beach sand; a soil without structure.

meristem. A region in which new cells and tissue arise, resulting in growth.

metabolism. The total of the chemical processes in a plant or other organism.

microclimate. Local variations from the general or regional climate resulting from slight differences in elevation, direction of slope exposure, soil, density of vegetation, etc.

micronutrient. Plant-essential element required by plants in very small amounts.

micropores. The relatively small spaces among soil aggregates that hold plant-available water by capillary force.

mineralization. The conversion of an element from an organic compound, in which it is unavailable to plants, to an ionic form in which it is available to plants.

miticide. A substance that kills mites.

mixed bud. A bud that produces both leaves and flowers.

modified central leader system. A training system extensively used with apples and pears in which the central leader is headed back slightly but not completely removed.

monocot (monocotyledon). A flowering plant having one seed leaf, parallel-veined characteristic leaves, scattered vascular bundles, and flower parts in multiples of threes.

monoecious. Bearing both staminate (male) and pistillate (female) flowers (or pollen and seed cones of conifers) at different locations on the same plant; common in plants of the Araceae and Cucurbitaceae families.

mulch. Any materials placed on the soil to conserve soil moisture, moderate soil temperature, prevent soil erosion, or prevent weed growth.

mycelium. A mass of hyphae of a fungus.

necrosis. The death of a cell, tissue, or organ while the remainder of the plant is still living.

nematocide. A substance that kills nematodes.

nematode. Any of the round, cylindrical, unsegmented worms of the phylum Nematoda; some cause plant diseases.

node. A point on the stem where leaves are attached and buds arise in the axils of the leaves.

nucleus. A specialized body within a cell that contains genetic information and is associated with the control of essential processes within the cell.

obligate. An organism that can develop and survive in only one type of environment; as in *obligate parasite*, which is any parasite that cannot exist independently of its living host.

offset. A short, prostrate offshoot or branch growing from the crown of a plant and having a fleshy, scaly bud or a rosette of leaves located terminally. Offsets often form roots and are used to vegetatively propagate some plants.

offshoot. A lateral shoot that rises from the main stem of a plant; often used for vegetative propagation of some plants, e.g., date palms.

open center system. *See* **vase system**.

opposite buds and leaves. Arrangement in which buds and leaves occur in pairs at a node, directly across the stem from each other.

organic. 1. Composed of or derived from plant or animal material. 2. A compound that contains carbon.

ovary. The swollen basal portion of a pistil; the flower part containing the ovule(s) or seed.

ovule. Part of the ovary containing one female gametophyte (egg). Following fertilization, the ovule develops into the seed.

palisade layer. A layer of tightly spaced, elongated cells lying under the upper epidermis of leaves. Photosynthesis is most active in these cells.

palmate. Having the general shape of human hand with the fingers extended.

parthenocarpic fruit. Fruit produced without fertilization.

ped. An individual, natural soil aggregate such as crumb, prism, or granule.

perennial. A woody or herbaceous plant that lives from year to year and does not die after flowering once.

perfect flower. A flower containing both stamens and pistil; a bisexual flower.

perlite. White and very porous volcanic mineral that is sometimes used as a medium for rooting cuttings or as a soil amendment.

petiole. The thin stalk that attaches a leaf to the stem.

pH. The negative logarithm of the hydrogen-ion concentration of a solution; a notation to express the alkalinity or acidity of a solution, as in the solution formed when water is present in soil, on a scale from 0.0 to 14.0. A pH of 7.0 is neutral, values less than 7.0 are acid, and values greater than 7.0 are alkaline.

pheremone. A substance that is produced and discharged by one organism and that induces a physiological response in another, such as the sexual attractants of insects.

phloem. Vascular tissue that conducts synthesized carbohydrates in vascular plants.

photoperiod. The length of light in a 24-hour day.

photoperiodism. The response of some plants to the relative lengths of day and night, expressed as formation of flowers, tubers, etc.

photosynthesis. The production of carbohydrate (sugar) from carbon dioxide and water in the presence of chlorophyll, using light energy and releasing oxygen.

phytotoxic. Harmful or poisonous to a plant or portions of a plant; substances that are poisonous to all or certain plants.

pinnate. The pattern of arrangement of dicot leaf veins, leaflets of compound leaves, lobes, etc., that resembles the structure of a feather in that they are arranged along the sides of a central axis (e.g., a major leaf vein, major petiole, etc.).

pistil. The central and female part of a flower consisting of the stigma, style, and ovary, and having one or more compartments (carpels) that bear the ovule(s).

plumule. The bud of an embryonic plant.

pollen (grain). Tiny, grainlike structures in the anther of a stamen containing sperm nuclei that represent the male gamete in seed plants.

pollen tube. The tube formed in the style following germination of the pollen grain.

pollination. Transfer of pollen from the anther to the stigma of the same or another flower.

pome. A fleshy fruit with a leathery core as produced by apple, pear, and quince.

porosity (soil). The degree to which a soil is permeated with open spaces, cavities, or pores; expressed as a percentage of the total volume of a quantity of undisturbed soil.

postemergent herbicide. An herbicide that is applied before weed seeds emerge or geminate.

pot herb. Greens; any plant yielding foliage that is edible when cooked, such as spinach, kale, chard, mustard.

predator. Any animal, including insects, that preys upon and devours other animals. Distinguished from a parasite, which lives on only one host at a time and usually does not destroy the host.

preemergent herbicide. An herbicide that is applied before weed seeds emerge or germinate.

primocanes. One-year old (or less) stems in blackberries and raspberries that do not bear fruit.

prismatic (soil structure). A type of soil structure in which the aggregates that naturally form are relatively large and angular, resembling a prism.

propagate. To generate or to multiply by sexual or asexual means.

propagule. A newly propagated plant.

protoplasm. The living material of and in a cell.

pupa. In insects with complete metamorphosis, the inactive stage between the larva and adult, usually enclosed in a protective structure.

quiescent. Dormant or inactive.

radicle. The basal end of an embryonic stem that grows into the primary root.

receptacle. A part of the axis of a flower stalk that supports or surrounds the floral parts.

reproductive. Growth, tissues, or processes concerned with the growth and development of flowers and fruits as opposed to leaves stems, and roots; sexual.

respiration. The controlled process in cells in which carbohydrate is biologically broken down (oxidized) and energy is released.

rhizome. A specialized stem, usually horizontal in position at or just below the soil surface, distinguished from a root by the presence of nodes and internodes and sometimes buds.

root ball. In container-grown and dug plants, the mass of roots attached to the plant.

root cap. The protective, thimble-shaped mass of cells over the root rip.

rootstock. In grafted plants, the rooted plant or plant part to which a scion is attached.

runner. A thin, specialized stem that grows along the soil surface and produces adventitious roots and shoots.

russeting. Brownish, roughened areas on the skins of fruits, tubers of potatoes, etc., resulting from abnormal production of cork tissue. May be caused by disease, insects, or injury, or may be a natural varietal characteristic.

saline soil. A soil containing sufficient soluble salts to impair plant growth and development.

sand. A group of textural classes of soil in which the particles are finer than gravel but coarser than silt, ranging in size from 2.00 to 0.5 mm in diameter. Any soil class that contains 85 percent or more sand and not more than 10 percent clay.

sap. The liquid contents of a cell or the liquid flowing through xylem or phloem.

saprophyte. An organism that obtains its food from the remains of dead plants or animals.

sapwood. The outer wood of a stem or tree trunk, usually light in color and physiologically very active.

scaffold (branches). The main branch(es) of a tree.

scarification. The abrasion, scratching, or modification of a seed's surface to increase water absorption and break dormancy.

scion. A branch, bud, or shoot removed from one plant and grafted onto another plant (the stock or rootstock).

scoring. A type of phloem disruption that consists of running a knife blade around the stem to make a narrow cut through the phloem.

seed. Structure that is formed by seed plants following fertilization and that contains an embryonic plant and usually a food supply and protective covering; a fertilized ovule.

seed coat. The outer covering of a seed.

self-compatible (self-fruitful). Able to produce normal fruit and seed with self-pollination; sets and matures fruit without pollen from another cultivar.

self-incompatible (self-unfruitful). Unable to produce fruit and seed when self-pollinated; requires cross-pollination from another cultivar.

self-pollination. Transfer of pollen from the anther to the stigma of the same flower or of another flower on the same plant or within a cultivar.

senescence. The stage in the life of a plant or plant part when its rate of metabolic activity declines prior to death.

sepal. One segment of the calyx.

set. A small propagative part (bulb, shoot, tuber, etc.) suitable for setting out or planting.

sexual propagation (seed propagation). Propagation that uses the fusion of male and female gametes to develop a new individual plant.

sexual reproduction. *See* **sexual propagation**.

shoot. The upper part of a plant consisting of stems and leaves; a young growing branch or twig.

short-day plant. A plant in which the flowering period or some other process is regulated by daily exposure to light shorter than a certain maximum number of hours, usually less than 12 hours.

sidedressing. Applying fertilizer to the soil at the side of a plant row, usually after the crop has started to grow.

silt. 1. Small, mineral soil particles ranging from 0.05 to 0.002 mm in diameter. 2. Textural class of soils that contains 80 percent or more silt and less than 12 percent clay.

slip. A cutting from a plant, usually softwood or herbaceous, used for propagation or grafting.

slip (melon harvesting). *See* **full-slip** and **half-slip**.

STM. *See* **soil moisture tension**.

sodic soil. A soil that contains sufficient sodium to adversely affect its physical properties and water infiltration; a soil with an exchangeable sodium percentage greater than or equal to 15 percent.

soil. The natural medium on the surface of the earth composed of minerals, organic matter, water, air, and various organisms, in which plants typically grow.

soil amendment. A substance added to soil to alter one or more of its physical or chemical properties.

soil horizon (profile). A layer of soil with well-defined physical and chemical characteristics produced through the soil-formation processes.

soil moisture tension (SMT). The amount of force under which a given quantity of water is held by a soil.

soil structure. The degree that soil particles (sand, silt, clay) naturally arrange into aggregates that vary in form and size, such as granular, platy, massive, and single-grained.

soil texture. The relative proportions of sand, silt, and clay in a soil expressed as a percent by weight; the coarseness or fineness of a soil.

species. A group of closely related individuals that are self-perpetuating and usually intercross; the basic unit of the binomial system of naming organisms, as in *Liquidambar styraciflua* (American sweetgum), which consists of a genus name and its specific epithet. Abbreviated sp. (sing.) or spp. (pl.).

specific epithet. In the botanical or binomial system of identifying organisms, the descriptive term that modifies the genus in a specific name, often mistakenly called species; e.g. *Liquidambar styraciflua* is the species name, *Liquidambar* is the genus and *styraciflua* is the specific epithet.

sperm. A mature male germ cell.

spore. A minute reproductive body or cell produced by lower plants.

spur. A short, stubby shoot primarily bearing flowers, as in some fruit trees.

spur pruning. A system of pruning grapes in which dormant canes are headed back to create short stubs bearing two or three buds.

spur-type tree. A fruit tree (primarily apple and cherry) that has shortened internodes and a greater number of spurs; about two-thirds the height of standard non-spur-type trees.

stamen. The male part of the flower producing the pollen, usually composed of anther and filament.

staminate. A flower that has stamens but no pistil and hence is imperfect; a plant bearing only male flowers.

stem. An axis of a plant usually bearing leaves with buds in the axils. It may be above or below ground, and the leaves may be functional or specialized.

stem cutting. Any part of a stem used for plant propagation by severing it from the parent plant.

stigma. The apex of the pistil that receives pollen.

stock. *See* **rootstock**.

stolon. A horizontal or trailing stem that gives rise to new shoots; a runner.

stomate (stoma) (pl., stomata). The opening or pore, mainly in leaves, through which gases are exchanged and water vapor is lost; controlled by guard cells.

stratification. A method of storing seeds or other reproductive structures at a temperature from 35° to 45°F (2° to 7°C) in alternate layers with (or mixed in with) moist sand, peat moss, or other medium, as a means of overcoming dormancy.

style. The part of the pistil that connects the ovary and stigma, through which the pollen tube grows to the ovule.

subspecies. A group of individuals within a species, distinguished by certain common geographical or varietal characters. Abbreviated ssp. (pl.).

subtropical crop. A crop that will survive very short periods of freezing temperatures but will not survive in areas with a cold winter climate.

succession planting. Growing two or more crops, one after the other, on the same land in one growing season.

sucker. A rapidly-growing, upright secondary vegetative shoot that develops from the root, crown, or stem of a plant.

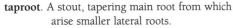

taproot. A stout, tapering main root from which arise smaller lateral roots.

temperate zone crop. A crop able to adapt so that it survives temperatures considerably below the freezing point.

terminal bud. A bud that develops at the end of a stem or shoot.

thatch. The layer of dry, dead plant material and organic matter at the soil surface, common in turfgrass.

thinning out. Removal of an entire shoot or branch.

tilth. The physical condition of the soil in relation to its ability to support plant growth.

tissue. A group of organized plant cells that perform a specific function.

topdressing. A material, such as sand or fine-textured organic matter, applied thinly to the soil or crop surface as a fertilizer, soil conditioner, or to reduce thatch.

topping. The cutting off of the main leader of a tree.

training. Directing the growth of a plant to a desired shape by pruning while young or fastening the stem and branches to a support.

translocation. The movement of a substance such as water, carbohydrates, or a pesticide from one part of a plant to another.

transpiration. The loss of water from plant tissues in the form of vapor, mainly through stomata.

tropical crop. A crop that originated in tropical areas and is usually subject to cold injury at temperatures near the freezing point.

tuber. An enlarged, fleshy, underground stem bearing buds; usually a storage organ.

tuberous root. An enlarged root that tapers toward both ends, as in dahlia and sweet potato; usually a storage organ.

unavailable water. Water held by the soil at and below the wilting point; water held by soil so tightly that plants cannot absorb it.

vascular tissue. The tissue consisting of xylem and/or phloem that is responsible for transporting water, carbohydrates, and/or the associated soluble materials through higher plants.

vacuole. The large cavity within the protoplasm of a cell containing a solution of sugars, salts, etc.

variety. In the botanical or binomial system of identifying organisms, a naturally occurring population of individuals constituting a subdivision of a species. Although technically different, *variety* and *cultivar* are commonly synonymous.

vascular bundle. A strandlike portion of the vascular tissue of a plant, composed of xylem and phloem, typical in monocots.

vascular cambium. *See* **cambium**.

vase (open-center) system. A system of training in which the central leader is cut off 18 to 30 inches (45 to 75 cm) from the ground, and three to five side branches become the scaffolds and spread to form the framework of the tree.

vector. An organism, usually an animal, that can transmit a pathogen.

vegetative. Growth, tissues, or processes concerned with the growth and maintenance of the plant body; asexual; concerned with leaves, stems, roots as opposed to flowers and fruits.

vegetative propagation. *See* **asexual propagation**.

vein. The vascular bundle forming a part of the framework of the conducting and supporting tissue of a leaf or other plant organ.

vernalization. The inducement or promotion of flowering by exposure to low temperature, as in some bulbs and biennial plants.

virulence. A strong capacity to produce disease.

volatilization. Evaporation of a substance under normal temperature and pressure ranges.

warm-season crop. A crop, usually of tropical origin, that goes dormant or is injured as soon as temperatures drop slightly below freezing; crops that grow best or produce highest quality produce during the warmest season(s).

water sprout. *See* **sucker**.

weed. Any plant growing out of place; a plant growing where it is unwanted or interferes with more desirable plants.

whorl. A pattern of arrangement with three or more buds, leaves, or branches, usually at a single node, each on a different plane.

wilted. Lacking turgidity; drooping or shriveling of plant tissue usually due to a deficiency of water.

wilting point. The stage in soil moisture depletion where a plant is unable to take additional moisture from the soil and, as a consequence, becomes wilted.

WIN (water insoluble nitrogen). In fertilizer, a source of nitrogen that is not readily soluble in water and not subject to immediate leaching.

xylem. Vascular tissue primarily responsible for transporting water and mineral nutrients from the roots to the shoots; the primary component of wood in trees.

zygote. A single cell resulting from the fertilization of an egg by a sperm and capable of developing into an embryo.

Index

Page references followed by *t* indicate tables. Page references in *italic type* indicate photographs or illustrations.

curly dock, 243
currants and gooseberries, 446–447
cuticle, defined, 12
cuttings
    canelike stems, 101
    defined, 99
    disease transmission, 135
    environmental control, 98, 101, 103,
        103
    hardening off, 103–104
    hardwood stem, 101
    house plants, 108–111t
    leaf, 101–102, 102
    perennials, 104–107t
    root, 102–103
    roots of, 9
    semi-hardwood, 101
    softwood, 100, 100–101
cutworm, 572
cycads, 16
cyclamen, 287–288
cypress tip miner, 163
cytokinins, 20, 21
cytoplasm, 6

d-limonene toxicosis, 217
Daily Value %, 349
daisy, English, 244
dallisgrass, 243
damping-off, 130, 138
damsel bugs, 157
damselflies, 160
dandelion, 244
Danger (pesticide warning), defined, 260
Danger Poison (pesticide warning),
        defined, 260
day length. See photoperiod
day-neutral plants, 24, 25t
deciduous plants, 14, 25, 100–101
decline, symptoms, 130
decomposition, soil organic matter,
        39–43, 40, 41, 61–63, 129, 152
DEET, 190
deflocculate, defined, 36
defoliants, 255
delusory parasitosis, 230–231
Dermaptera (earwigs), 156, 156, 173, 226,
        226, 251
dermatitis
    allergic contact, 638–639
    atopic, 230–231
    defined, 636
    flea allergy, 214, 215, 218–219
    irritant, 637–638
    photosensitization, 639
desiccants, 206, 207, 255

determinant growth, 339
diagnosing diseases and disorders,
        139–141, 163, 653, 658
    See also specific plants, diseases, and dis-
        orders
diagnosing insect and mite problems,
        163–164, 166, 248–249, 653, 658
    See also specific plants, insect and mite
        pests
diagnostic skills
    checklist, 654
    equipment and tools, 656
    horticultural science concepts,
        652–653
    recognizing symptoms, 653
    steps in diagnosis, 655–656
    tips, 658–659
    working with clients, 656
diagnostic test kits, 124
dichogamous flowering habit, 461, 587
dicots, 10, 16, 17
dieback
    of berries, 436, 440
    Eutypa, 513
    symptoms, 130
Dietary Reference Intakes, 662–663,
        664–665t
diffusion, water and nutrient uptake, 19,
        49
dioecious, defined, 13
diplopods (millipedes), 152, 152
Diptera (flies, mosquitoes, gnats, midges),
        156–157, 173
disbudding, 286
disease cycles, 125–127, 132–133
    anthracnose, 126, 127
    fire blight, 132
    Lyme disease, 192
    nematodes, 135–136
disease pyramid, 128
disease triangle, 127–128, 137, 138
diseases, human
    bacterial, 131
    cockroaches and, 178–179
    fleas and, 161
    lice and, 193
    phytoplasmas, 133
    ticks and, 191–192
    viruses, 134
    See also specific diseases
diseases, plant
    abbreviation key, 355t
    in compost, 46
    of container-grown plants, 312
    crop-loss statistics, 123
    defined, 124–125
    diagnosing, 140–141, 163
    environmental factors, 122
    epidemics, 123, 128

and fruit set problems, 462
management strategies, 3, 123–124,
        128, 137, 141–146
and nitrogen levels, 28
noninfectious (see abiotic disorders)
postharvest (see postharvest diseases)
predisposition to, 124, 125, 135–136,
        137–140
and propagation methods, 92
pruning and, 322, 324
quarantine laws, 123
resistance to, 312
and saturated soils, 79, 137–138, 568,
        599, 601–602
signs, 128, 129, 653
symptoms, 126, 128, 652, 653
    See also specific plants and diseases
dividing plants
    defined, 99, 113
    house plants, 108–111t
    perennials, 104–107t
DNA, 7, 134
dodder, 135, 137
dormancy
    buds, 11, 20, 26
    citrus, 537
    fruit and nut trees, 454
    function, 94
    pruning, 324, 330–331, 489–491
    seeds, 94–96, 20–21
    triggers, 21, 26, 28
dormant sprays, 257
Dothiorella canker, 589, 610
double digging, 66
downy mildew, 130
dragonflies, 160, 160
drainage
    and disease management, 128,
        137–138, 550
    for fruit and nut trees, 485
    infiltration, 49
    and irrigation systems, 70–71
    for lawns, 296, 307
    and soil structure, 34, 61–65
driveways, role in garden design, 624
drought/drought stress
    as abiotic disorder, 137–138
    and air in soil pores, 30
    avocado, 601, 602
    citrus, 556, 558
    and dormancy, 21, 27
    and fire danger, 334
    frequently asked questions, 85–86
    fruit and nut trees, 492
    house plants, 278
    plant responses to, 19, 27
    symptoms, 78, 82, 88
drought-tolerant plants, 19–20, 72–73,
        81, 85, 115, 627

See also biological control; *specific beneficial insects*
integrated pest management (IPM)
  of diseases, 144
  of insect pests, 164–165, 213, 219
  and pesticide use, 254–255
  principles, 248–249
intensive management, 6
intercropping, 250, 339
International Soil Science Society, 32–33
internodes, defined, 9
interstem grafting, 453
iron
  absorption, 52
  for avocado, 604
  for citrus, 561
  deficiency, 39, 52–54, 60, 139, 333,
    613
  for fruit and nut trees, 494, 500
  function, 52
  toxicity, 52
irrigation
  amount, 71, 346
  assessing soil moisture, 78–80, 79t
  defined, 49
  depth, 71
  excessive (*see* overwatering)
  and fire danger, 334
  and freezing damage, 559, 566
  and fruit development, 463
  general principles, 79–80
  germinating seeds, 22, 93, 97–98
  large v. small plants, 72
  mulching and, 83–84, 238–239, 567,
    606
  and nutrient disorders, 53–54
  pathogen dissemination, *126*, 132
  as pest management tool, 79, 249
  and pesticide use, 268
  and *Phytophthora*, 599, 601, 602
  role in garden design, 626
  runoff, 49, 71, 80–81, 84, 87, 296
  on slopes, 84–85
  xeriscapes, 626–627
  See also specific plants
irrigation systems
  basin, *556*, *557*, *599*, 599–600
  chemigation, 60
  drip, 80–81, 84, 345–346, 493, 557,
    600–601
  fertilizer application, 345
  furrow, 80, 346
  for lawns, 73, 296
  maintaining, 77, 82
  misting, 98
  soaker hoses, 346
  sprinklers, 77–78, 80, *80*, 493–494,
    557, 600
  subirrigation, 98

and water infiltration, 70–71
irritants, 229
isopods (sowbugs and pillbugs), 152, *152*
Isoptera. *See* termites
ivy, English, as toxic, 645

kale, 383
kikuyugrass, 243, 302, *303*
killer bees. *See* honey bees, Africanized
kitchen waste, in compost, 66
kiwifruit, 458t, 460, *461*, 481–482t, 522t
knotweed, 244
kohlrabi, 384
kumquat, 546t, 548

Japanese lawn grass (zoysiagrass), 297,
  302
jessamine, yellow, 645
jimsonweed, 641
June drop, 23, 538
juniper twig girdler, 155, 166
juvenility, 22, 28, 456
juvenoid growth regulators, 218, 219

labels
  citrus plants, 549, 552–553
  fertilizers, 55, 57, *305*, 305–306
  herbicides, 240
  nutrients in foods, 661
  pesticides, 167, 258–260, 262–265,
    267–268
  seeds, 92, 303, 341
laboratories, diagnostic, 129, 657–658
lacewings, 160, *160*, *252*, 254
lacustrine soils, 32
landscape design
  defined, 620
  factors influencing, 620–622
  principles of, 624–626
landscape plans, 627–631, *628*, *630*
landscape professionals, 632–633
lantana, as toxic, 641
larkspur, as toxic, 641, 643
latent infections, 126
lateral meristems, 7, 21, 455
lawns
  aerating, 299, 308, *308*
  clippings as mulch, 344
  cool-season, 73, 297t, 299–301, 304,
    307
  design role, 625, 632
  diagnosing problems, *655*, 659–660
  diseases, 307, 309

fertilizing, 60, 237, 245, 296, 298t,
  305–308
  insect pests, 307, 309
  mowing, 7, 237, 245, 304
  pesticides, 296
  removing, 82, 85
  renovating, 298–299
  restrictions, legal, 296
  seeding, 297–298, 303–304, 304t
  sodding, 298
  soil preparation, 296–298
  stolons and plugs, 298
  thatch, 237, 245, 299, 307–308
  turfgrass meristems, 7
  warm-season, 73, 297t, 302–303
  weed control, 237, 245, 296, 309
  woody plants in, 84, 320, 321, 560,
    600
lawns, irrigating, 306–307
  climate zones, 73, 74–76t
  frequency, 73, 77
  postplant, 298
  on slopes, 84
  systems, 73, 77–78, 296, 627
  water conservation, 83, 85–86
layering plants, 99, 107, *107*, 111,
  111–112, *112*
leaching, 31, 49, 54, 64, 278, 282
leaching component, 55
lead contamination, 65
leaf curl, 130, 513
leaf cuttings, 101–102, *102*, 108–111t
leaf drop, 25, 26
leaf scorch disease, 134
leaf spot, fungal, 130, 293, 435, 440
leaf-to-fruit ratio, 491–492
leafhoppers, 133–135, 158, 427–428, 440
leafrollers, 445, 572, 612
leaves
  arrangement on stem, *11*
  function, 24
  structure, 12, *12*
  types, 11, *11*, *12*, 272
  venation patterns, *12*, 16, *17*
leek, 384
legumes, and nitrogen-fixing bacteria, 41,
  50n
Leguminosae, 353
lemon, 542t, 548, 563, 579
Lepidoptera (butterflies and moths), 159,
  160, 166, 173, 257
lettuce, 385–387
lice, human, 173, 193, *193*
light
  artificial, 25, 26, 98, 273, 278
  blacklight traps, 251
  for cuttings, 103
  for flowers and fruits, 23, 456, 462
  for house plants, 273, 274–278t

pest control professionals, 195, 199, 201, 206, 217–219, 225
pest control recommendations, 3, 164, 657
Pest Notes series, UC IPM, 242
pesticide safety
    environmental contamination, 267–268, 519, 201, 240, 260
    first-aid procedures, 262–263, *263*
    poisoning prevention, 260–262
    storing pesticides, 261
    toxicity, degrees, 260*t*
pesticides
    and beneficial insects, 151, 252, 253, 267–268, 503
    bioaccumulation, 268
    defined, 254
    formulations, 167–168, 254, 256–257, 268
    fumigants, 199–201, 241, 256
    home v. commercial, 254, 257
    labels, 167, 258–260, *259*, 262–265, 267–268
    liability for misuse, 260
    modes of action, 20, 255–256
    residue, tolerance, 167
    resistance to, 249, 254
    when to use, 248, 254–255
    See also fungicides; herbicides; insecticides; miticides; nematicides
pesticides, applying
    adjuvants, 256–257
    application rates, 267
    calibrating sprayers, 265–267
    climate and, 254–255
    conversion charts, 267*t*
    drift, 267
    with fertilizers, 61
    spray equipment, 241–242, 265, *266*
    spray patterns, 267
    timing, 254–255
    volatilization, 268
petals, 13
petiole, leaf, 11
pets, insect pests of, 213–221
philodendron, 22, 644
phloem, 9, 20
Pholcidae (cellar spiders), 185, *186*
Phomopsis canker, 515
phosphorus
    absorption, 51
    applying, 61
    for citrus, 561
    deficiency, 51, 60
    in fertilizers, 55, 56, 59
    for fruit and nut trees, 494, 499
    function, 51
    in gray water, 86

mobility, 60, 61
and mycorrhizae, 41
and soilborne lead, 65
toxicity, 51
photoperiod, 23–26, 273
photoperiod-temperature interactions, 27
photosynthesis
    chemical equation, 17
    chloroplasts and, 7
    drought and, 27
    photoperiod and, 25
    and respiration, *18*, 18–19
    temperature and, *19*
Phylloxera, of grapes, 418
phytohormones. *See* hormones, plant
phytopathology, 121–147
Phytophthora
    of avocado, 589–590, 596, 599, 601–602, 605–606, 609–610
    of berries, 440, 445
    biological control, 590
    of citrus, 549–552, 558, 573–574, 576
    of fruit and nut trees, 502, 512
    gummosis, 131, 573
    of house plants, 292–293
    late blight of potato, 123
    mulching to control, 567–568
    root rots, 129, 131, 443
    saturated soils and, 137–138, 568, 601–602
phytoplasmas, 133
Pierce's disease, 134
pillbugs, 152, *152*, 225, 225–226, 251
pinching plants, 286, 324, *328*
pine
    Canary Island, 327
    See also conifers
pinnate leaves, 12
pistachio, *460*, 479–480*t*, 527*t*
pistillate flowers, 13
pistils, 13
pittosporum, as toxic, 645
plant growth regulators, 255, 534
plant pathology, 121–147
Plantae, classification, 16
plantain, 244
planting
    amending soil, 63–65, 319
    depth, 345
    in droughts, 85
    fertilizing at time of, 333
    pregerminated seeds, 97
    pruning at time of, 322–323, 331, 420
    space-saving techniques, 339
    transplanting seedlings, 97–100, 119
    vegetable gardens, 339, 345, 351–352*t*

woody plants, *319*, 319–320
    See also specific plants
planting dates
    as disease-management tool, 128, 249
    vegetables, 339, 345, 351–352*t*
planting media
    for cuttings, 101, 102
    for house plants, 282
    for layered plants, 111
    for seed germination, 96
    for seedlings, 98
    sterilizing, 96
    for tissue culture, 118
plastids, 7
platy soils, 37–38
play areas, designing, 621, 623
plugs, for lawns, 298
plum, *457*, 475–476*t*, 497*t*, 525*t*
Poaceae (Gramineae), 353
poinsettia, as house plant, 287
Poison Control Center, 636
poison oak, 234
poisonous plants
    about, 636
    in compost, 43, 64
    dermatitis, 637–639
    flowers, 639–641, 640*t*
    holiday plants, 639
    house plants, 644–645, 644*t*
    identification records, 637
    mechanical injury, 637
    shrubs and vines, 645–647, 646*t*
    trees, 647, 648*t*
    vegetables, 643–644, 643*t*
    weeds and wildflowers, 641–643, 642*t*
pollen, 13, 230
pollination
    about, 92
    cross-pollination, 23–24, 584–585, 587–588
    and disease transmission, 135
    and fruit development, 23, 402–403
    grafting to ensure, 115
    by insects, 150, 158–159, 180–181, 184–185, 206
    See also specific plants
polyembryony, 537–538, *538*
Polygonaceae, 353
polymerase chain reaction (PCR), 133
polymers, 85
pome fruits, 450, *451*
    flowering habits, *456*, 457, 458*t*
    growth and development, 459*t*, *463*
    pollination, 461
    varieties, 466–470*t*
pomegranate, 470*t*, 525*t*
pomology, defined, 450
popcorn bloom, 536

lead contamination, 65
nutrient-storage capacity, 34–35
profiles, *31*, 31–32, 38, 62–63
reservoirs, 81
saline (*see* salts in soils)
saturated (*see* overwatering)
structure, 36–38, *38*, 47–48, 57,
  61–63, 338–339
tilth, 33, 61–62, 344
for vegetable gardens, 338–339
water-holding capacity, 34–35, 47–48,
  48, 81–82, 493
water infiltration, 34, 36, 38, 57,
  62–63
See also planting media
soil amendments, 57, 59, 62*t*, 63–64, 64*t*
soil moisture
  availability to plants, 46–48
  and disease triangle, 127
  and dormancy, 21
  excessive (*see* overwatering)
  and flower induction, 23
  and fruit development, 23
  lack of (*see* drought)
  measuring, 47, 78–79, 79*t*, 81–82,
    558, 601
  and photosynthesis, 18–19
  plant responses to, 27
  and seed germination, 22, 38
  soil structure and, 36–38, 61–63
  soil texture and, 70–71, *71*, 71*t*
  and transpiration, 19
soil moisture meters, 78
soil moisture tension, 47
soil organisms, beneficial, 30–31, 39–41,
  55, 61–63
soil pH
  adjusting, 54–55, 64
  and fertilizers, 55–57, 498–499
  for house plants, 281
  and lead, 65
  and nutrient uptake, *54*, 54–55, 333
soil porosity, 30, 38, *38*
  and bulk density, 36
  and drainage, 34
  and organic matter, 41
  and water infiltration, 46–48, 61–63
soil solarization, 143, 152, 239
soil temperature
  mulches and, 238–239, 568–569, 607
  seed germination and, 22, 95*t*
  soil color and, 39
soil testing, 53, 60, 484, 657
soil texture, *38*
  assessing, 33–34, *34*
  classes, *33*
  defined, 33
  mulching to improve, 567, 607

and nutrient-storage capacity, 34–35
and soil-management practices, 38,
  61–63, 344
and soil temperature, 34
for vegetable gardens, 338–339, 344
and water-holding capacity, 34–35,
  47–48, *48*, 48*t*, 493
and water infiltration, 71, 71*t*
and weed control, 241
soilless mixes, 96, 98
Solanaceae, 353
solar yellowing, of tomatoes, 410
soluble powders, 256
solution formulations, 256
sooty mold, 130, 158, 163, 505, 571
sowbugs, 152, 225–226
soybean meal, 59
soybeans, 362
specific epithets, 16
speedwell, birdseye, 244
spider plant, 113
spiders, 151–152
  anatomy and reproduction, 185
  bites, treating, 188, 189
  black widow, *151*, 151–152, *187*,
    187–188
  cellar, 185, *186*
  cobweb, 185, *186*
  controlling, 187
  crab, *186*, 187
  grass, 187
  house, *151*, 152, 185, *186*
  jumping, 185, *186*, 187
  as natural enemies, 151
  orb weaver, *186*, 187
  recluse, 151–152, 188–189
  tarantulas, 189
  venom, 185
  wolf, *186*, 187
spinach, 400–401
spirochetes, 191–192
spiroplasmas, 133–134
spores
  fern, 99
  fungal, 129, 138, 229–230
sports, of citrus, 538–539
spray equipment
  calibrating, 265–267
  for herbicides, 241–242
  selecting, 265, *266*
spray oils, horticultural, 257, 503, 577,
  608
spur pruning, 425, *426*
spurge, spotted, 243
spurs, fruiting, 455, 490
squash bugs, 157
squashes, 401–403
St. Augustinegrass, 297, 302, *302*

staking
  container-grown plants, 313
  roots, 321
  trees, *320*, 320–321, *321*
  in vegetable gardens, 339
stamens, 13
staminate flowers, 13
stems and shoots
  bending and stretching, 25–26
  function and structure, 9–11
  meristems, 7, *9*
  modifications, *8*, 11
sticky barriers, 250, *253*
stink bugs, 157, *157*
stolons, *8*, 112, 298
stomata, 12, 17, 19–20, 25, 140
stone fruits, 450–451, *451*, 471–477*t*
  flowering habits, *457*, 457–458, 458*t*
  growth and development, 459*t*
  pollination, 461
  storage conditions, 18, 27–28, 347–348,
    351–352*t*
  See also specific plants
straight-cut cuttings, 101, *102*
strains, of viruses, 129
stratification, defined, 26
strawberries, *8*, 27, 113, 443–446
Streptomyces, 132
Structural Pest Control Board, 195
stubborn disease, of citrus, 575
stunting, virus diseases, 134
stylets, 135, 154
subsoil, 31
subtropical plants, defined, 14
succession planting, 339
suckers, 456
sucking insects, 154
sulfur
  to adjust pH, 54–55, 64
  deficiency, 53, 60
  as fungicide, 428–429, 503, 518
sulfur dioxide pollution, 139
summer oils, 257, 503, 577, 608
sunburn (sunscald)
  of avocado, 598, *598*, 613, 614–615
  of citrus, 559, 566, 575
  high temperatures and, 138
  light intensity and, 26
surfactive agents, 241, 256–257
sweet potato, *8*
symptoms
  air pollution, 139–140, 139*t*
  bacterial pathogens, 132–134
  delusory parasitosis, 230–231
  as diagnostic tool, 140–141, 652, *652*
  drought stress, 78, 88
  fungal pathogens, 129, 130*t*
  insect pests, 154, 163, 199

Umbelliferae, 353
undercutting, defined, 563
USDA-ARS National Clonal Germplasm
    Repository for Citrus and Dates,
    534
USDA, soil classification system, 32–33

vacuoles, 7
variants, fungi, 129
variegated plants, 102
varieties, defined, 16
vascular systems, 9, *10*, 16, *17*
vascular wilts, 130–131, 133, 312
    See also Fusarium wilts; Verticillium
        wilts
vegetable gardens
    diagnosing problems, 354–355*t*, 659
    fertilizing, 344–345
    irrigating, 71, 339, 345–346
    light requirements, 339
    pesticides, 257
    plans, 340, *340*
    planting, 338–339, 341, 345,
        351–352*t*
    propagating plants, 95*t*, 342–343
    soil texture, 338–339, 344
    staking, 339
    thinning, 347
    tools and equipment, 341, 343
    weed control, 237, 242, 245,
        346–347
vegetables
    buying seeds or plants, 341
    cool-season, 338, 339, 345
    days to maturity, 350*t*
    distinguished from fruits, 13, 15
    families, 353*t*
    harvesting, 347
    selecting, 340
    storing, 347–348, 351–352*t*
    toxic, 643–644, 643*t*
    warm-season, 338, 339
    yields, 353*t*
    See also specific vegetables
vegetative development, 20, 25, 28
veins, leaf, 12, *12*, 16, *17*
ventilation, for house plants, 279
vermiculture, 66
vernalization, 27, 95–96, 454
Verticillium wilts, 131
    of avocado, 589, 609
    of blackberry, 435
    and crop rotation, 165
    of fruit and nut trees, 514
    and nematodes, 136
    of raspberry, 440

resistance, 312, 317–318*t*
    of strawberries, 445
vinegar flies, 227–228
vines
    defined, 14
    fertilizing, 61, 332
    indoor, 283*t*
    natural layering, 107
    pruning, 330
    toxic, 645–647, 646*t*
    See also specific types of vines
viroids, 135, 611
virulence, of pathogens, 127
viruliferous, defined, 134
viruses, 134–135
    blackline, 516
    classification, 129
    control, 145–146
    dwarf, 435–436
    insect-transmitted, 154
    nematode-transmitted, 135, 136
    Psorosis, of citrus, 575
    of raspberry, 440
    ring spot, 134
    Tristeza, of citrus, 123, 534, 575, 576
virusoids, 135
volatilization, of pesticides, 268

walnut, *460*, 480–481*t*, 497*t*, 527–528*t*
warm-season crops, 15
Warning (pesticide), defined, 260
wasps, 158
    paper, *180*, 183–184
    predatory, 158, 166, 254, 428
    treating stings, 184
    wood, *207*, 207–208
water
    availability and uptake, 19, 46–48
    function in plant, 6–7, 70
    gravitational, 47
    gray, 85, 86–87
    household usage, 82–83
    molecules, properties, 70
    pathogen dissemination, *126*
    quality, 260
    to remove insect pests, 251, 290, *290*
    soil (*see* soil moisture)
    from swimming pools, 85
    and transpiration rate, 19–20
    See also drought/drought stress; irriga-
        tion
water balance, 48–49
water budgets, 78–79
water conservation
    frequently asked questions, 85–86
    guidelines, 81–83
    in home orchards, 87–88

and landscape design, 622
    lawns, 83, 85–86
    mulching and, 83–84, 88, 567, 606
    preventing runoff, 49, 71, 87, 296
    and sprinkler maintenance, 77–78
    and tree health, 84
    water restrictions, 83, 85, 88
    xeriscapes, 626–627
water cycling in plants, 70, *70*
water infiltration rate. *See* drainage
water-insoluble nitrogen (WIN), 56, 306
water management. *See* irrigation
water mold rots
    house plants, 292–293
    Pythium, 138, 292–293
    See also Phytophthora; root rots
water potential, defined, 70
water quality, 279, 492, 599
water-storage capacity, 81–82
water supply, for vegetable gardens, 339
waterbugs, 174, *175*, 176
watermelon, 411–412
weed-block fabrics, 238, 500
weed control
    around trees, 84
    biological, 239
    to control diseases, 143
    cultural, 237
    history, 236–237
    mechanical, 63, 238, 347
    mulches, 237–239, 245, 347, 500,
        567, 606
    in organic gardens, 66
    principles, 236, 245
    soil solarization, 239
    sprinkle, sprout, spade, spray, 238,
        245
    See also herbicides; *specific plants*
Weed Research and Information Center,
    242
weeds
    as allergens, 234
    annual, 235–236, 236*t*, 240
    biennial, 235–236, 236*t*
    broadleaf, 235–236, 236*t*, 309
    of California, 243–244*t*
    classification, 235
    economic importance, 123, 234
    function, 234–235
    identifying, 241, 242
    perennial, 235–238, 236*t*, 237*t*, 240
    as pest and disease reservoirs, 133,
        135, 234, 249–250
    redeeming features, 234–235
    seeds, 45–46, 56–57, 234, 236, 236*t*
    as toxic, 641–643, 642*t*
    See also specific weeds
weevils, 156, *156*, 222, 223
wettable powders, 168, 256

white rot wood decay, 203
whiteflies, 135, 158, 291, 571
wildflowers, as toxic, 641–643, 642*t*
wind
    as abiotic disorder, 138, 564, 575,
      590, 598
    and insect dissemination, 162
    role in garden design, 623
    and tree staking, 320
winter chilling, 450, 454–455, 455*t*, 538
wisteria, pruning, 330–331
witches' brooms, 130
wood ashes, 45, 59
wood-destroying pests
    carpenter ants, 205–206
    carpenter bees, 206–207
    termites, 195–203
    wood-boring beetles, 204–205
    wood-decay fungi and dry rot, 203
    wood wasps, 207–208
woodsorrel, creeping, 244
woody plants
    anatomy, 7, 7–12, *9*, *10*, 313, 318
    Armillaria susceptibility, 312,
      314–316*t*
    classification, 14

    diagnosing problems, *655*, 659
    fertilizing, 332–333
    fire protection, 334
    grafting, 114
    growth and development, 21, 23, 312
    irrigating, 72–73, 81–82, 319
    in lawns, 84, 320, 321, 560, 600
    mulching, 319
    planting, *319*, 319–320
    pruning, 321–332
    role in landscape, 312
    selecting, 313, 318–319
    staking, 313, *320*, 320–321, *321*
    Verticillium susceptibility, 312,
      317–318*t*
    See also specific woody plants

X-disease, of cherry, 515
Xanthomonas, 132, 292
xeriscapes, 626–627
Xylella, 132
xylem, 9–10, 19–20

yellowjackets, *180*, 183–184

zinc
    for avocado, 603–604, 604*t*, 616
    for citrus, 561
    deficiency, 52, 60, 613
    for fruit and nut trees, 494, 499
    function, 52
    toxicity, 52
zoysiagrass, 297, 302